All the luck in
the world to your newest
undertaking & I don't mean
a funeral!

Phyllis

Jan 30-47

THE MODERN LIBRARY
of the World's Best Books

THE POEMS AND PLAYS
OF
ALFRED LORD TENNYSON

>>

The publishers will be pleased to send, upon request, an illustrated folder setting forth the purpose and scope of THE MODERN LIBRARY, *and listing each volume in the series. Every reader of books will find titles he has been looking for, handsomely printed, in unabridged editions, and at an unusually low price.*

>>>

THE POEMS AND PLAYS
OF
ALFRED LORD TENNYSON

THE MODERN LIBRARY

NEW YORK

THE MODERN LIBRARY

IS PUBLISHED BY

RANDOM HOUSE, INC.

BENNETT A. CERF · DONALD S. KLOPFER · ROBERT K. HAAS

Manufactured in the United States of America
Printed by Parkway Printing Company   *Bound by H. Wolff*

CONTENTS

CONTENTS

INTRODUCTION

The latter half of the nineteenth century in England saw the flowering to maturity of two of the great poetic figures of English literature—Tennyson and Browning. They were born within three years of one another, early in the century, and died within three years of one another, after living on through the pomp of imperialistic days, down to the end of the Victorian era. With them died something of the greatness of English poetry, for no man since has risen to claim a seat beside either of them.

This may be the result of England's political, economic, and sociological woes during the last forty or fifty years. Certainly her sweetest singers are found to exist during periods of national exaltation. Chaucer saw the renascence of Anglo-Saxon self-consciousness, which had been held in abeyance by the Normans, but which, during his lifetime, flowered more finely than before as a result of the fusing of the two bloods. Little need be said of the heady national spirit which intoxicated the lyric writers and dramatists of the Elizabethan period. Milton's day signalized the release of the nation from the corruption of a dissolute court. The Romantic Poets found their inspiration in a surge of democracy and hope for mankind which was international in scope. Browning and Tennyson wrote at a time when England's wealth and power made her the equal of the Roman Empire in Virgil's day. Since then English poetry has languished, as has England's prestige.

Alfred Tennyson was born in the country village of Somersby in Lincolnshire on the sixth of August, 1809. He was the fourth in a family of twelve children. His father, the Rev. George Clayton Tennyson, came of a much respected family of Lincolnshire landed gentry, but had been disinherited by his father, and at the time of Alfred's birth was settled comfortably, but none too opulently, as the rector of Somersby Parish. All the children inherited from him a strong and morbid strain of melancholy, which was particularly pronounced in Alfred, and had a powerful effect on his later career.

The first six years of Tennyson's life were spent at home in close contact with the rich and lovely Lincolnshire countryside. His sensitivity to nature was almost immediately apparent in his devotion to plants, fields, sky and running water. He had a way with animals, and once on a summer evening he succeeded in calling an owl to the window of his bedroom and taming it. The family into which he was born, in spite of its inherited melancholy strain, was an unusually happy and closely knit one. It was also an ideal one for the future poet. His brothers and sisters were talented and attractive, depending for their amusement on intellectual rather than on physical pastimes. Conversation was stimulating. There was much reading and story-telling, and a good deal of writing on the part of the children, who were encouraged in these pursuits by the scholarly bent and excellent library of their father.

When Alfred was six he went to Louth to grammar school, where he stayed for five years. Here he displayed a taste for poetic composition, and followed in the steps of his brothers, Frederick and Charles, who were inveterate verse-writers already. In point of volume, however, he soon out-stripped them, and by the time he was thirteen or fourteen he had composed an epic of 6,000 lines, a long play in blank verse, and a quantity of shorter pieces. On his return from Louth his education was continued at home by his father. He was not an exceptional student, but he had an enduring love for the classics, and when the time came for his matriculation at Cambridge he was able to recite from memory the entire Odes of Horace.

His first venture into print was made in 1827 when he and his brother Charles published anonymously a joint collection of short verses called *Poems by Two Brothers*. They were scholarly, but of no exceptional merit, and in common with the youthful effusions of most poets, they are not generally included in Tennyson's collected works. The next year the boys entered Cambridge together. Here they lived a quiet and secluded life for a time, both being extremely shy, but gradually they made friends, and were finally received into a group known as "The Apostles." Among them were Monkton Milnes, Richard Trench, James Spedding, Arthur Hallam, Edward Fitzgerald, W. H. Thompson, W. H. Brookfield, J. M. Noble, and others, most of whom became distinguished in later life. This group was one of the best that could have been imagined for developing the talents and personality of such a man as Tennyson. His response to its literary and intellectual atmosphere was immediate. He continued to write poetry, won the Chancellor's Prize medal with a poem "Timbuctoo," and showed continually greater promise in his lyrics. He was looked on with much respect, and was generally regarded by his friends and preceptors as a man marked for greater things. He was grave and reserved, and apt to be moody, but the warming glow of the Apostles, particularly Hallam, made his college life a happy one, and gave him enough courage to publish in 1830 his first signed volume, *Poems, Chiefly Lyrical*. This book revealed him as a poet of extraordinary promise, with an exceptionally delicate and resourceful ear for words. However, it also showed him as having not yet achieved proper control over verse forms or over his soaring imagination. It was partly praised, partly criticized. The criticism Tennyson could not stomach, and he struck out violently at it, a trait which he exhibited until the end of his life.

His friendship with Hallam deepened until the two men were almost inseparable. Hallam spent much of his time visiting at Somersby, and in 1831 he became engaged to Tennyson's sister Emily. This year and the next were two of the best in Tennyson's life. In spite of the death of his father in February, he was in continually high spirits. His health was excellent and he was almost never melancholy. During this time he wrote much of the superb verse which appeared at the end of 1832 under the title, *Poems*.

As the work of a young man of twenty-three, *Poems* represents one of the most remarkable early flowerings of mature genius in the history of English literature. The full force of his magnificent control of words was poured out for the first time. Gone was the over-sweetness and immaturity of the earlier volume, the shaky craftsmanship and riotousness of the verse forms for which Coleridge had rightly criticized him two years earlier. If there had been any doubt before as to Tennyson's rank, there was now none in the minds of those who had read and appreciated "Oenone," "The Lady of Shalott," "Mariana in the South," "The Lotos-Eaters," "The Miller's Daughter," "The Dream of Fair Women," and many others. He was hailed as a new standard bearer by advanced and discerning critics. But in spite of the volume's exceptional merits, there was again a good deal of adverse criticism, and again the author writhed and groaned under it.

In 1833 Arthur Hallam died in Vienna of a ruptured blood vessel in his brain. This plunged Tennyson into a profound state of gloom which lasted for the better part of ten years. Hypochondria and melancholy descended on him with an overpowering weight. He sat about at Somersby, doing little or nothing for months at a time beyond brooding and smoking his pipe. His health was bad and there was some family alarm at it. But for a man of his talents, this could not go on forever. Gradually he began doing a little writing and considerable studying. He commenced work on two ambitious and later successful undertakings, the *Idylls of the King* and *In Memoriam*. Finally, in 1842, he published a two-volume edition of his poems, containing much new material. He was still inclined to be a solitary, brooding man, but he was occasionally seen in the houses of his friends in London, and by degrees his life became more nearly what it had been before.

Since the death of their father, the Tennysons had been living in fairly straitened circumstances. This had never bothered Alfred much, until he was induced by a speculator to put all his savings and entire small inheritance into a scheme for carving wood into patterns by machinery. This collapsed, leaving him penniless and in such a state of complete physical and nervous prostration that his life was feared for and he was placed in a sanitarium. His health and spirits gradually improved until he was able to leave, but his financial condition remained acute. The future looked black, so black that his friends took it upon themselves to do something about his utter poverty, and prevailed upon the government to give him a pension of £200 a year. This was a life-saver. It rallied him at a time when he most sorely needed it; it enabled him to devote his attention to an important work, *The Princess*, on which he was engaged at the time; and it helped pay for treatment during another siege of hypochondria and melancholy in 1847, an aftermath of the first.

He still had his critical difficulties. The publication of *The Princess*, which contains some of the loveliest lyrics in the English language, resulted in a sad shaking of heads over him by Carlyle and Fitzgerald, both of whom he had come to know, and whose opinions were of great current weight.

These years were ones of gradually strengthening reputation. He made a number of literary friends, and was quite often seen in their circles. Among them were Thackeray, and Robert Browning, with whom he developed a long and lasting friendship. This was also a period of gathering of his literary forces, which had been more or less scattered during the past few years. He had many projects in mind. *In Memoriam*, on which he had worked spasmodically ever since the death of Hallam, was published in 1850 anonymously. It is a great poem, and a great tribute to his dearest college friend. There was a good deal of discussion and speculation about its authorship, and some criticism. Its structural weaknesses (the result of the haphazard way the poem had been composed), obvious even today in the blinding light of Tennyson's fame, were pounced upon. One reviewer expressed the opinion that the poem was probably the outpourings from the "full heart of the widow of a military man." However, the public reaction to his work was more and more favorable. His life was more secure and stable than it had been since his college days. He was earning more money, and he took advantage of this to marry Miss Emily Sarah Sellwood, to whom he had been engaged for ten years.

It has been said by Tennyson, and affirmed over and over again by his friends, that his marriage was the greatest blessing of his life, and a very important contribution to his success as a poet. By all accounts an intelligent and noble woman, his wife provided a cheerful and stabilizing domestic atmosphere, made her husband more generally happy than at any time in his early life, and bore him two children, of whom he was exceedingly fond. She was well educated and possessed of more than average talents, yet she always remained in the background, content to occupy herself with the provision of a home and family for her husband.

With his marriage the tone of Tennyson's life changed, and the honors began to roll in, elevating him to a position in the world of English letters that has been held by no other poet during his own lifetime. He twice refused a baronetcy, but later in life accepted a peerage. He became a friend of Gladstone and also of Queen Victoria, to whom he was first presented in

1862. The wave of fame and success was started by his being appointed to the poet laureateship, which had been left vacant by the death of Wordsworth. He took his duties as laureate very seriously, although this and subsequent honors made him uncomfortable, and two famous poems, "Ode on the Death of the Duke of Wellington" and "The Charge of the Light Brigade," were among the immediate results of his official tenure.

In 1865 he published *Maud*, a poem on which he had perhaps worked harder than on any other, and into which he had poured more passion and violent emotion. It is a masterpiece, and its author may well be excused for his wrath when it was received with little grace by a public which had come to expect a calmer and more directly appealing kind of verse from him. He had stormed before at criticism, but this was his heaviest burden, and his sensibilities were seriously wounded by it. He became brooding and remote, particularly as his increasing fame began to interfere with his privacy, and he made himself more and more inaccessible until he became the object of tremendous general speculation and curiosity. He traveled with his wife now, visiting Norway and Portugal, working all the time at a series of Arthurian legends which developed finally into the complete *Idylls of the King*. These were published at intervals from 1859 to 1872, with the exception of "Balin and Balan" which was added in 1885. The *Idylls* were more enthusiastically received by an adoring public than it is possible to imagine. With their publication he found himself for the first time universally recognized as a great poet.

In 1862 *Enoch Arden* was published and 60,000 copies were sold rapidly. This marked the height of his popularity. The period from then on to his death was signalized by a very gradual decline from this pinnacle. There are various reasons for this. One is that the best of his work had been done, another that he spent the latter years of his life vainly trying to establish himself as a dramatist, and another that few men, however gifted, can support extravagant praise indefinitely. This latter reaction was particularly to be expected in Tennyson's case because of the extent of the rhapsodies he had evoked; and it continued on into the 1920's. Since then his work has tended to seek a more fitting level. Another contribution to his temporary eclipse, and a significant one, is found in the waxing strength and reputations of other poets, particularly Browning, Swinburne, and the Pre-Raphaelites, who tended to take the spotlight away from him who had been enjoying it alone for so many years.

Tennyson's preoccupation with the theater began with the publication in 1875 of *Queen Mary*. He had in his mind the construction of a panorama of England's history by a series of sweeping tragedies, and to this end he bent his energies with a determination which is not quite understandable in view of the general apathy with which his efforts were persistently met. It is possible that he regarded indifference and condemnation only as further manifestations of the criticism he had found so hard to swallow in his youth, and which was later proved to be unfounded. At any rate, he continued to pour out plays, starting with *Harold* in 1876, and following it with *The Falcon* in 1879, *The Cup* in 1881, *The Promise of May* in 1882, and *Becket* in 1884. *Becket* was the last of his dramatic efforts (until he wrote *The Foresters* just before his death in 1892) and after its completion he seemed to realize that success in this direction was not to be his, although he did not become resigned to it.

Taken as a whole, these plays are no mean achievement. They are epic in scope, dignified and poetic in content, but they are not particularly dramatic, and never seem to have come alive on the stage. *Harold* is perhaps the one best suited for production, but ironically enough, it has not been staged.

With the waning of the dramatic fever came an increased activity in Tennyson's poetic output. He was now nearly eighty but he continued to write with great vigor. *Tiresias and Other Poems* was published in 1885, and *Locksley Hall 60 Years After* in 1886. These were followed in 1889 with *Demeter and Other Poems*, and the three volumes are an astonishing tribute to the strong frame and mind of their ageing author. Those who knew him at this time have remembered best the calm patriarchal power which seemed a part of him, and which apparently would carry him on indefinitely. But soon after the publication of *Demeter* he suffered a severe shock in the death of his old and dear friend Robert Browning. He was now alone. All his friends and most of the literary titans of the century were gone, and for about a year he seems to have felt keenly that he had long outlived his time. However, even this failed to daunt him entirely. He rallied strongly and in a year or two was in good health and spirits, working hard at a series of poems which comprise the body of the posthumous volume, *The Death of Oenone*.

In August, 1892, he was eighty-four years old, and his strength had suddenly begun to wane alarmingly. Even so, his faculties were crystal-clear up to the day of his death, so that on the afternoon of October 6th he was able to derive great pleasure from reading *Cymbeline*. He died that night, slipping from life with a peacefulness and calm which was reflected in the beauty of the moonlight countryside he loved so much. He was buried next to Browning in the Poets' Corner in Westminster Abbey.

August, 1938.   MAITLAND EDEY

TO THE QUEEN

Revered, beloved—O you that hold
  A nobler office upon earth
  Than arms, or power of brain, or birth
Could give the warrior kings of old,

Victoria,—since your Royal grace
  To one of less desert allows
  This laurel greener from the brows
Of him that utter'd nothing base;

And should your greatness, and the care
  That yokes with empire, yield you time
  To make demand of modern rhyme
If aught of ancient worth be there;

Then—while a sweeter music wakes,
  And thro' wild March the throstle calls,
  Where all about your palace-walls
The sun-lit almond-blossom shakes—

Take, Madam, this poor book of song;
  For tho' the faults were thick as dust
  In vacant chambers, I could trust
Your kindness. May you rule us long,

And leave us rulers of your blood
  As noble till the latest day!
  May children of our children say,
'She wrought her people lasting good;

'Her court was pure; her life serene;
  God gave her peace; her land reposed;
  A thousand claims to reverence closed
In her as Mother, Wife, and Queen:

'And statesmen at her council met
  Who knew the seasons when to take
  Occasion by the hand, and make
The bounds of freedom wider yet

'By shaping some august decree
Which kept her throne unshaken still,
Broad-based upon her people's will,
And compass'd by the inviolate sea.'

March, 1851.

CLARIBEL

A MELODY

WHERE Claribel low-lieth
  The breezes pause and die,
    Letting the rose-leaves fall;
But the solemn oak-tree sigheth,
    Thick-leaved, ambrosial,
    With an ancient melody
    Of an inward agony,
Where Claribel low-lieth.

At eve the beetle boometh
  Athwart the thicket lone;
At noon the wild bee hummeth
  About the moss'd headstone;
At midnight the moon cometh,
  And looketh down alone.
Her song the lintwhite swelleth,
The clear-voiced mavis dwelleth,
  The callow throstle lispeth,
The slumbrous wave outwelleth,
  The babbling runnel crispeth,
The hollow grot replieth
  Where Claribel low-lieth.

NOTHING WILL DIE

WHEN will the stream be aweary of flowing
  Under my eye?
When will the wind be aweary of blowing
  Over the sky?
When will the clouds be aweary of fleeting?
When will the heart be aweary of beating?
  And nature die?
Never, O, never, nothing will die;
  The stream flows,
  The wind blows,

3

The cloud fleets,
The heart beats,
 Nothing will die.

Nothing will die;
All things will change
Thro' eternity.
'T is the world's winter;
Autumn and summer
 Are gone long ago;
Earth is dry to the centre,
But spring, a new comer,
A spring rich and strange,
Shall make the winds blow
Round and round,
Thro' and thro',
 Here and there,
 Till the air
And the ground
 Shall be fill'd with life anew.

The world was never made;
It will change, but it will not fade.
 So let the wind range;
For even and morn
 Ever will be
 Thro' eternity.
Nothing was born;
Nothing will die;
All things will change.

ALL THINGS WILL DIE

CLEARLY the blue river chimes in its flowing
 Under my eye;
Warmly and broadly the south winds are blowing
 Over the sky.
One after another the white clouds are fleeting;
Every heart this May morning in joyance is beating
 Full merrily;
 Yet all things must die.
 The stream will cease to flow;
 The wind will cease to blow;
 The clouds will cease to fleet;
 The heart will cease to beat;
 For all things must die.
 All things must die.

Spring will come never more.
O, vanity!
Death waits at the door.
See! our friends are all forsaking
The wine and the merrymaking.
We are call'd—we must go.
Laid low, very low,
In the dark we must lie.
The merry glees are still;
The voice of the birds
Shall no more be heard,
Nor the wind on the hill.
O, misery!
Hark! death is calling
While I speak to ye,
The jaw is falling,
The red cheek paling,
The strong limbs failing;
Ice with the warm blood mixing;
The eyeballs fixing.
Nine times goes the passing bell:
Ye merry souls, farewell.
The old earth
Had a birth,
As all men know,
Long ago.
And the old earth must die.
So let the warm winds range,
And the blue wave beat the shore;
For even and morn
Ye will never see
Thro' eternity.
All things were born.
Ye will come never more,
For all things must die.

LEONINE ELEGIACS

Low-FLOWING breezes are roaming the broad valley dimm'd in the gloam-
    ing;
Thoro' the black-stemm'd pines only the far river shines.
Creeping thro' blossomy rushes and bowers of rose-blowing bushes,
Down by the poplar tall rivulets babble and fall.
Barketh the shepherd-dog cheerly; the grasshopper carolleth clearly;
Deeply the wood-dove coos; shrilly the owlet halloos;
Winds creep, dews fall chilly: in her first sleep earth breathes stilly:
Over the pools in the burn water-gnats murmur and mourn.

Sadly the far kine loweth; the glimmering water outfloweth;
Twin peaks shadow'd with pine slope to the dark hyaline.
Low-throned Hesper is stayed between the two peaks; but the Naiad
Throbbing in mild unrest holds him beneath in her breast.
The ancient poetess singeth that Hesperus all things bringeth,
Smoothing the wearied mind: bring me my love, Rosalind.
Thou comest morning or even; she cometh not morning or even.
False-eyed Hesper, unkind, where is my sweet Rosalind?

SUPPOSED CONFESSIONS

OF A SECOND-RATE SENSITIVE MIND

O GOD! my God! have mercy now.
I faint, I fall. Men say that Thou
Didst die for me, for such as *me*,
Patient of ill, and death, and scorn,
And that my sin was as a thorn
Among the thorns that girt Thy brow,
Wounding Thy soul.—That even now,
In this extremest misery
Of ignorance, I should require
A sign! and if a bolt of fire   10
Would rive the slumbrous summer noon
While I do pray to Thee alone,
Think my belief would stronger grow!
Is not my human pride brought low?
The boastings of my spirit still?
The joy I had in my free-will
All cold, and dead, and corpse-like grown?
And what is left to me but Thou,
And faith in Thee? Men pass me by;
Christians with happy countenances—   20
And children all seem full of Thee!
And women smile with saint-like glances
Like Thine own mother's when she bow'd
Above Thee, on that happy morn
When angels spake to men aloud,
And Thou and peace to earth were born.
Good-will to me as well as all—
I one of them; my brothers they;
Brothers in Christ—a world of peace
And confidence, day after day;   30
And trust and hope till things should cease,
And then one Heaven receive us all.

How sweet to have a common faith!
To hold a common scorn of death!
And at a burial to hear
The creaking cords which wound and eat
Into my human heart, whene'er
Earth goes to earth, with grief, not fear,
With hopeful grief, were passing sweet!

Thrice happy state again to be   40
The trustful infant on the knee,
Who lets his rosy fingers play
About his mother's neck, and knows
Nothing beyond his mother's eyes!
They comfort him by night and day;
They light his little life alway;
He hath no thought of coming woes;
He hath no care of life or death;
Scarce outward signs of joy arise,
Because the Spirit of happiness   50
And perfect rest so inward is;
And loveth so his innocent heart,
Her temple and her place of birth,
Where she would ever wish to dwell,
Life of the fountain there, beneath
Its salient springs, and far apart,
Hating to wander out on earth,
Or breathe into the hollow air,
Whose chillness would make visible
Her subtil, warm, and golden breath,   60
Which mixing with the infant's blood,
Fulfils him with beatitude.
O, sure it is a special care
Of God, to fortify from doubt,
To arm in proof, and guard about
With triple-mailed trust, and clear
Delight, the infant's dawning year.

Would that my gloomed fancy were
As thine, my mother, when with brows
Propt on thy knees, my hands upheld   70
In thine, I listen'd to thy vows,
For me outpour'd in holiest prayer—
For me unworthy!—and beheld
Thy mild deep eyes upraised, that knew
The beauty and repose of faith,
And the clear spirit shining thro'.
O, wherefore do we grow awry
From roots which strike so deep? why dare

Paths in the desert? Could not I
Bow myself down, where thou hast knelt,   80
To the earth—until the ice would melt
Here, and I feel as thou hast felt?
What devil had the heart to scathe
Flowers thou hadst rear'd—to brush the dew
From thine own lily, when thy grave
Was deep, my mother, in the clay?
Myself? Is it thus? Myself? Had I
So little love for thee? But why
Prevail'd not thy pure prayers? Why pray
To one who heeds not, who can save   90
But will not? Great in faith, and strong
Against the grief of circumstance
Wert thou, and yet unheard. What if
Thou pleadest still, and seest me drive
Thro' utter dark a full-sail'd skiff,
Unpiloted i' the echoing dance
Of reboant whirlwinds, stooping low
Unto the death, not sunk! I know
At matins and at evensong,
That thou, if thou wert yet alive,   100
In deep and daily prayers wouldst strive
To reconcile me with thy God.
Albeit, my hope is gray, and cold
At heart, thou wouldest murmur still—
'Bring this lamb back into Thy fold,
My Lord, if so it be Thy will.'
Wouldst tell me I must brook the rod
And chastisement of human pride;
That pride, the sin of devils, stood
Betwixt me and the light of God;   110
That hitherto I had defied
And had rejected God—that grace
Would drop from His o'er-brimming love,
As manna on my wilderness,
If I would pray—that God would move
And strike the hard, hard rock, and thence,
Sweet in their utmost bitterness,
Would issue tears of penitence
Which would keep green hope's life. Alas!
I think that pride hath now no place   120
Nor sojourn in me. I am void,
Dark, formless, utterly destroyed.

Why not believe them? Why not yet
Anchor thy frailty there, where man
Hath moor'd and rested? Ask the sea

At midnight, when the crisp slope waves
After a tempest rib and fret
The broad-imbased beach, why he
Slumbers not like a mountain tarn?
Wherefore his ridges are not curls   130
And ripples of an inland mere?
Wherefore he moaneth thus, nor can
Draw down into his vexed pools
All that blue heaven which hues and paves
The other? I am too forlorn,
Too shaken: my own weakness fools
My judgment, and my spirit whirls,
Moved from beneath with doubt and fear.

'Yet,' said I, in my morn of youth,
The unsunn'd freshness of my strength,   140
When I went forth in quest of truth,
'It is man's privilege to doubt,
If so be that from doubt at length
Truth may stand forth unmoved of change,
An image with profulgent brows
And perfect limbs, as from the storm
Of running fires and fluid range
Of lawless airs, at last stood out
This excellence and solid form
Of constant beauty. For the ox   150
Feeds in the herb, and sleeps, or fills
The horned valleys all about,
And hollows of the fringed hills
In summer heats, with placid lows
Unfearing, till his own blood flows
About his hoof. And in the flocks
The lamb rejoiceth in the year,
And raceth freely with his fere,
And answers to his mother's calls
From the flower'd furrow. In a time   160
Of which he wots not, run short pains
Thro' his warm heart; and then, from whence
He knows not, on his light there falls
A shadow; and his native slope,
Where he was wont to leap and climb,
Floats from his sick and filmed eyes,
And something in the darkness draws
His forehead earthward, and he dies.
Shall man live thus, in joy and hope
As a young lamb, who cannot dream,   170
Living, but that he shall live on?
Shall we not look into the laws

Of life and death, and things that seem,
And things that be, and analyze
Our double nature, and compare
All creeds till we have found the one,
If one there be?' Ay me! I fear
All may not doubt, but everywhere
Some must clasp idols. Yet, my God,
Whom call I idol? Let Thy dove   180
Shadow me over, and my sins
Be unremember'd, and Thy love
Enlighten me. O, teach me yet
Somewhat before the heavy clod
Weighs on me, and the busy fret
Of that sharp-headed worm begins
In the gross blackness underneath.

O weary life! O weary death!
O spirit and heart made desolate!
O damned vacillating state!   190

THE KRAKEN

BELOW the thunders of the upper deep,
Far, far beneath in the abysmal sea,
His ancient, dreamless, uninvaded sleep
The Kraken sleepeth: faintest sunlights flee
About his shadowy sides; above him swell
Huge sponges of millennial growth and height;
And far away into the sickly light,
From many a wondrous grot and secret cell
Unnumber'd and enormous polypi
Winnow with giant arms the slumbering green.
There hath he lain for ages, and will lie
Battening upon huge sea-worms in his sleep,
Until the latter fire shall heat the deep;
Then once by man and angels to be seen,
In roaring he shall rise and on the surface die.

SONG

THE winds, as at their hour of birth,
Leaning upon the ridged sea,
Breathed low around the rolling earth
With mellow preludes, 'We are free.'

The streams, through many a lilied row
  Down-carolling to the crisped sea,
Low-tinkled with a bell-like flow
  Atween the blossoms, 'We are free.'

LILIAN

I

Airy, fairy Lilian,
  Flitting, fairy Lilian,
When I ask her if she love me,
Clasps her tiny hands above me,
  Laughing all she can;
She'll not tell me if she love me,
  Cruel little Lilian.

II

When my passion seeks
  Pleasance in love-sighs,
She, looking thro' and thro' me
Thoroughly to undo me,
  Smiling, never speaks:
So innocent-arch, so cunning-simple,
From beneath her gathered wimple
  Glancing with black-beaded eyes,
Till the lightning laughters dimple
  The baby-roses in her cheeks;
    Then away she flies.

III

Prythee weep, May Lilian!
  Gaiety without eclipse
Wearieth me, May Lilian;
Thro' my very heart it thrilleth
  When from crimson-threaded lips
Silver-treble laughter trilleth:
  Prythee weep, May Lilian!

IV

Praying all I can,
  If prayers will not hush thee,
    Airy Lilian,
Like a rose-leaf I will crush thee,
    Fairy Lilian.

ISABEL

Eyes not down-dropt nor over-bright, but fed
  With the clear-pointed flame of chastity,
    Clear, without heat, undying, tended by
      Pure vestal thoughts in the translucent fane
Of her still spirit; locks not wide-dispread,
Madonna-wise on either side her head;
      Sweet lips whereon perpetually did reign
    The summer calm of golden charity,
Were fixed shadows of thy fixed mood,
    Revered Isabel, the crown and head,
The stately flower of female fortitude,
    Of perfect wifehood and pure lowlihead.

The intuitive decision of a bright
  And thorough-edged intellect to part
    Error from crime; a prudence to withhold;
    The laws of marriage character'd in gold
Upon the blanched tablets of her heart;
A love still burning upward, giving light
To read those laws; an accent very low
In blandishment, but a most silver flow
    Of subtle-paced counsel in distress,
Right to the heart and brain, tho' undescried,
    Winning its way with extreme gentleness
Thro' all the outworks of suspicious pride;
A courage to endure and to obey;
A hate of gossip parlance, and of sway,
Crown'd Isabel, thro' all her placid life,
The queen of marriage, a most perfect wife.

The mellow'd reflex of a winter moon;
A clear stream flowing with a muddy one,
  Till in its onward current it absorbs
    With swifter movement and in purer light
    The vexed eddies of its wayward brother;
    A leaning and upbearing parasite,
    Clothing the stem, which else had fallen quite
  With cluster'd flower-bells and ambrosial orbs
    Of rich fruit-bunches leaning on each other—
    Shadow forth thee:—the world hath not another
(Tho' all her fairest forms are types of thee,
And thou of God in thy great charity)
Of such a finish'd chasten'd purity.

MARIANA

'Mariana in the moated grange.'
Measure for Measure

WITH blackest moss the flower-pots
    Were thickly crusted, one and all;
The rusted nails fell from the knots
    That held the pear to the gable-wall.
The broken sheds look'd sad and strange:
    Unlifted was the clinking latch;
    Weeded and worn the ancient thatch
Upon the lonely moated grange.
      She only said, 'My life is dreary,
        He cometh not,' she said;   **10**
      She said, 'I am aweary, aweary,
        I would that I were dead!'

Her tears fell with the dews at even;
    Her tears fell ere the dews were dried;
She could not look on the sweet heaven,
    Either at morn or eventide.
After the flitting of the bats,
    When thickest dark did trance the sky,
    She drew her casement-curtain by,
And glanced athwart the glooming flats.   **20**
      She only said, 'The night is dreary,
        He cometh not,' she said;
      She said, 'I am aweary, aweary,
        I would that I were dead!'

Upon the middle of the night,
    Waking she heard the night-fowl crow;
The cock sung out an hour ere light;
    From the dark fen the oxen's low
Came to her; without hope of change,
    In sleep she seem'd to walk forlorn,   **30**
    Till cold winds woke the gray-eyed morn
About the lonely moated grange.
      She only said, 'The day is dreary,
        He cometh not,' she said;
      She said, 'I am aweary, aweary,
        I would that I were dead!'
About a stone-cast from the wall
    A sluice with blacken'd waters slept,
And o'er it many, round and small,
    The cluster'd marish-mosses crept.   **40**

Hard by a poplar shook alway,
   All silver-green with gnarled bark:
   For leagues no other tree did mark
The level waste, the rounding gray.
      She only said, 'My life is dreary,
         He cometh not,' she said;
      She said, 'I am aweary, aweary,
         I would that I were dead!'

And ever when the moon was low,
   And the shrill winds were up and away,   50
In the white curtain, to and fro,
   She saw the gusty shadow sway.
But when the moon was very low,
   And wild winds bound within their cell,
   The shadow of the poplar fell
Upon her bed, across her brow.
      She only said, 'The night is dreary,
         He cometh not,' she said;
      She said, 'I am aweary, aweary,
         I would that I were dead!'   60

All day within the dreamy house,
   The doors upon their hinges creak'd;
The blue fly sung in the pane; the mouse
   Behind the mouldering wainscot shriek'd,
Or from the crevice peer'd about.
   Old faces glimmer'd thro' the doors,
   Old footsteps trod the upper floors,
Old voices called her from without.
      She only said, 'My life is dreary,
         He cometh not,' she said;   70
      She said, 'I am aweary, aweary,
         I would that I were dead!'

The sparrow's chirrup on the roof,
   The slow clock ticking, and the sound
Which to the wooing wind aloof
   The poplar made, did all confound
Her sense; but most she loathed the hour
   When the thick-moted sunbeam lay
   Athwart the chambers, and the day
Was sloping toward his western bower.   80
      Then said she, 'I am very dreary,
         He will not come,' she said;
      She wept, 'I am aweary, aweary,
         O God, that I were dead!'

TO ——

I

CLEAR-HEADED friend, whose joyful scorn,
  Edged with sharp laughter, cuts atwain
    The knots that tangle human creeds,
    The wounding cords that bind and strain
    The heart until it bleeds,
Ray-fringed eyelids of the morn
    Roof not a glance so keen as thine;
    If aught of prophecy be mine,
Thou wilt not live in vain.

II

Low-cowering shall the Sophist sit;
  Falsehood shall bare her plaited brow;
  Fair-fronted Truth shall droop not now
With shrilling shafts of subtle wit.
Nor martyr-flames, nor trenchant swords
  Can do away that ancient lie;
  A gentler death shall Falsehood die,
Shot thro' and thro' with cunning words.

III

Weak Truth a-leaning on her crutch,
  Wan, wasted Truth in her utmost need,
  Thy kingly intellect shall feed,
Until she be an athlete bold.
And weary with a finger's touch
  Those writhed limbs of lightning speed;
Like that strange angel which of old,
  Until the breaking of the light,
Wrestled with wandering Israel,
  Past Yabbok brook the livelong night,
And heaven's mazed signs stood still
In the dim tract of Penuel.

MADELINE

I

THOU art not steep'd in golden languors,
  No tranced summer calm is thine,

Ever varying Madeline.
Thro' light and shadow thou dost range,
Sudden glances, sweet and strange,
Delicious spites and darling angers,
And airy forms of flitting change.

II

Smiling, frowning, evermore,
Thou art perfect in love-lore.
Revealings deep and clear are thine
Of wealthy smiles; but who may know
Whether smile or frown be fleeter?
Whether smile or frown be sweeter,
Who may know?
Frowns perfect-sweet along the brow
Light-glooming over eyes divine,
Like little clouds sun-fringed, are thine,
Ever varying Madeline.
Thy smile and frown are not aloof
From one another,
Each to each is dearest brother;
Hues of the silken sheeny woof
Momently shot into each other.
All the mystery is thine;
Smiling, frowning, evermore,
Thou art perfect in love-lore,
Ever varying Madeline.

III

A subtle, sudden flame,
By veering passion fann'd,
About thee breaks and dances:
When I would kiss thy hand,
The flush of anger'd shame
O'erflows thy calmer glances,
And o'er black brows drops down
A sudden-curved frown:
But when I turn away,
Thou, willing me to stay,
Wooest not, nor vainly wranglest,
But, looking fixedly the while,
All my bounding heart entanglest
In a golden-netted smile;
Then in madness and in bliss,
If my lips should dare to kiss
Thy taper fingers amorously,

Again thou blushest angrily;
And o'er black brows drops down
A sudden-curved frown.

SONG—THE OWL

I

WHEN cats run home and light is come,
    And dew is cold upon the ground,
        And the far-off stream is dumb,
    And the whirring sail goes round,
    And the whirring sail goes round;
        Alone and warming his five wits,
        The white owl in the belfry sits.

II

When merry milkmaids click the latch,
    And rarely smells the new-mown hay,
And the cock hath sung beneath the thatch
    Twice or thrice his roundelay,
    Twice or thrice his roundelay;
        Alone and warming his five wits,
        The white owl in the belfry sits.

SECOND SONG

TO THE SAME

I

THY tuwhits are lull'd, I wot,
    Thy tuwhoos of yesternight,
Which upon the dark afloat,
    So took echo with delight,
    So took echo with delight,
        That her voice, untuneful grown,
        Wears all day a fainter tone.

II

I would mock thy chaunt anew;
    But I cannot mimic it;
Not a whit of thy tuwhoo,
    Thee to woo to thy tuwhit,

Thee to woo to thy tuwhit,
  With a lengthen'd loud halloo,
    Tuwhoo, tuwhit, tuwhit, tuwhoo-o-o!

RECOLLECTIONS OF THE ARABIAN NIGHTS

WHEN the breeze of a joyful dawn blew free
In the silken sail of infancy,
The tide of time flow'd back with me,
  The forward-flowing tide of time;
And many a sheeny summer-morn,
Adown the Tigris I was borne,
By Bagdat's shrines of fretted gold,
High-walled gardens green and old;
True Mussulman was I and sworn,
  For it was in the golden prime   10
    Of good Haroun Alraschid.

Anight my shallop, rustling thro'
The low and bloomed foliage, drove
The fragrant, glistening deeps, and clove
The citron-shadows in the blue;
By garden porches on the brim,
The costly doors flung open wide,
Gold glittering thro' lamplight dim,
And broider'd sofas on each side.
  In sooth it was a goodly time,   20
  For it was in the golden prime
    Of good Haroun Alraschid.

Often, where clear-stemm'd platans guard
The outlet, did I turn away
The boat-head down a broad canal
From the main river sluiced, where all
The sloping of the moonlit sward
Was damask-work, and deep inlay
Of braided blooms unmown, which crept
Adown to where the water slept.   30
  A goodly place, a goodly time,
  For it was in the golden prime
    Of good Haroun Alraschid.

A motion from the river won
Ridged the smooth level, bearing on
My shallop thro' the star-strown calm,
Until another night in night
I enter'd, from the clearer light,

Imbower'd vaults of pillar'd palm,
Imprisoning sweets, which, as they clomb
Heavenward, were stay'd beneath the dome
 Of hollow boughs. A goodly time,
 For it was in the golden prime
 Of good Haroun Alraschid.

Still onward; and the clear canal
Is rounded to as clear a lake.
From the green rivage many a fall
Of diamond rillets musical,
Thro' little crystal arches low
Down from the central fountain's flow
Fallen silver-chiming, seemed to shake
The sparkling flints beneath the prow.
 A goodly place, a goodly time,
 For it was in the golden prime
 Of good Haroun Alraschid.

Above thro' many a bowery turn
A walk with vari-colored shells
Wander'd engrain'd. On either side
All round about the fragrant marge
From fluted vase, and brazen urn
In order, eastern flowers large,
Some dropping low their crimson bells
Half-closed, and others studded wide
 With disks and tiars, fed the time
 With odor in the golden prime
 Of good Haroun Alraschid.

Far off, and where the lemon grove
In closest coverture upsprung,
The living airs of middle night
Died round the bulbul as he sung;
Not he, but something which possess'd
The darkness of the world, delight,
Life, anguish, death, immortal love,
Ceasing not, mingled, unrepress'd,
 Apart from place, withholding time,
 But flattering the golden prime
 Of good Haroun Alraschid.

Black the garden-bowers and grots
Slumber'd; the solemn palms were ranged
Above, unwoo'd of summer wind;
A sudden splendor from behind
Flush'd all the leaves with rich gold-green,

40
50
60
70
80

And, flowing rapidly between
Their interspaces, counterchanged
The level lake with diamond-plots
   Of dark and bright. A lovely time,
   For it was in the golden prime
     Of good Haroun Alraschid.
Dark-blue the deep sphere overhead,
Distinct with vivid stars inlaid,   90
Grew darker from that under-flame;
So, leaping lightly from the boat,
With silver anchor left afloat,
In marvel whence that glory came
Upon me, as in sleep I sank
In cool soft turf upon the bank,
   Entranced with that place and time,
   So worthy of the golden prime
     Of good Haroun Alraschid.

Thence thro' the garden I was drawn—   100
A realm of pleasance, many a mound,
And many a shadow-chequer'd lawn
Full of the city's stilly sound,
And deep myrrh-thickets blowing round
The stately cedar, tamarisks,
Thick rosaries of scented thorn,
Tall orient shrubs, and obelisks
   Graven with emblems of the time,
   In honor of the golden prime
     Of good Haroun Alraschid.   110

With dazed vision unawares
From the long alley's latticed shade
Emerged, I came upon the great
Pavilion of the Caliphat.
Right to the carven cedarn doors,
Flung inward over spangled floors,
Broad-based flights of marble stairs
Ran up with golden balustrade,
   After the fashion of the time,
   And humor of the golden prime   120
     Of good Haroun Alraschid.

The fourscore windows all alight
As with the quintessence of flame,
A million tapers flaring bright
From twisted silvers look'd to shame
The hollow-vaulted dark, and stream'd
Upon the mooned domes aloof

In inmost Bagdat, till there seem'd
Hundreds of crescents on the roof
 Of night new-risen, that marvellous time   130
 To celebrate the golden prime
  Of good Haroun Alraschid.

Then stole I up, and trancedly
Gazed on the Persian girl alone,
Serene with argent-lidded eyes
Amorous, and lashes like to rays
Of darkness, and a brow of pearl
Tressed with redolent ebony,
In many a dark delicious curl,
Flowing beneath her rose-hued zone; · 140
 The sweetest lady of the time,
 Well worthy of the golden prime
  Of good Haroun Alraschid.

Six columns, three on either side,
Pure silver, underpropt a rich
Throne of the massive ore, from which
Down-droop'd, in many a floating fold,
Engarlanded and diaper'd
With inwrought flowers, a cloth of gold.
Thereon, his deep eye laughter-stirr'd 150
With merriment of kingly pride,
 Sole star of all that place and time,
 I saw him—in his golden prime,
  THE GOOD HAROUN ALRASCHID.

ODE TO MEMORY

ADDRESSED TO ——

I

THOU who stealest fire,
From the fountains of the past,
To glorify the present, O, haste,
 Visit my low desire!
Strengthen me, enlighten me!
I faint in this obscurity,
Thou dewy dawn of memory.

II

Come not as thou camest of late,
Flinging the gloom of yesternight

On the white day, but robed in soften'd light   10
      Of orient state.
Whilome thou camest with the morning mist,
    Even as a maid, whose stately brow
The dew-impearled winds of dawn have kiss'd,
      When she, as thou,
Stays on her floating locks the lovely freight
Of overflowing blooms, and earliest shoots
Of orient green, giving safe pledge of fruits,
    Which in wintertide shall star
    The black earth with brilliance rare.   20

III

Whilome thou camest with the morning mist,
    And with the evening cloud,
Showering thy gleaned wealth into my open breast;
Those peerless flowers which in the rudest wind
      Never grow sere,
When rooted in the garden of the mind,
    Because they are the earliest of the year.
      Nor was the night thy shroud.
In sweet dreams softer than unbroken rest
Thou leddest by the hand thine infant Hope.   30
The eddying of her garments caught from thee
The light of thy great presence; and the cope
    Of the half-attain'd futurity,
    Tho' deep not fathomless,
Was cloven with the million stars which tremble
O'er the deep mind of dauntless infancy.
Small thought was there of life's distress;
For sure she deem'd no mist of earth could dull
Those spirit-thrilling eyes so keen and beautiful;
Sure she was nigher to heaven's spheres,   40
Listening the lordly music flowing from
      The illimitable years.
    O, strengthen me, enlighten me!
    I faint in this obscurity,
    Thou dewy dawn of memory.

IV

Come forth, I charge thee, arise,
Thou of the many tongues, the myriad eyes!
Thou comest not with shows of flaunting vines
      Unto mine inner eye,
      Divinest Memory!   50
    Thou wert not nursed by the waterfall

Which ever sounds and shines
   A pillar of white light upon the wall
Of purple cliffs, aloof descried:
Come from the woods that belt the gray hillside,
The seven elms, the poplars four
That stand beside my father's door,
And chiefly from the brook that loves
To purl o'er matted cress and ribbed sand,
Or dimple in the dark of rushy coves,   60
Drawing into his narrow earthen urn,
    In every elbow and turn,
The filter'd tribute of the rough woodland;
    O, hither lead thy feet!
Pour round mine ears the livelong bleat
Of the thick-fleeced sheep from wattled folds,
    Upon the ridged wolds,
When the first matin-song hath waken'd loud
Over the dark dewy earth forlorn,
What time the amber morn   70
Forth gushes from beneath a low-hung cloud.

V

Large dowries doth the raptured eye
   To the young spirit present
     When first she is wed,
      And like a bride of old
    In triumph led,
      With music and sweet showers
       Of festal flowers,
   Unto the dwelling she must sway.
Well hast thou done, great artist Memory,   80
   In setting round thy first experiment
    With royal framework of wrought gold;
Needs must thou dearly love thy first essay,
And foremost in thy various gallery
   Place it, where sweetest sunlight falls
   Upon the storied walls;
     For the discovery

And newness of thine art so pleased thee
That all which thou hast drawn of fairest
Or boldest since but lightly weighs   90
With thee unto the love thou bearest
The first-born of thy genius. Artist-like,
Ever retiring thou dost gaze
On the prime labor of thine early days,
No matter what the sketch might be:

Whether the high field on the bushless pike,
Or even a sand-built ridge
Of heaped hills that mound the sea,
Overblown with murmurs harsh,
Or even a lowly cottage whence we see   100
Stretch'd wide and wild the waste enormous marsh,
Where from the frequent bridge,
Like emblems of infinity,
The trenched waters run from sky to sky;
Or a garden bower'd close
With plaited alleys of the trailing rose,
Long alleys falling down to twilight grots,
Or opening upon level plots
Of crowned lilies, standing near
Purple-spiked lavender: 110
Whither in after life retired
From brawling storms,
From weary wind,
With youthful fancy re-inspired,
We may hold converse with all forms
Of the many-sided mind,
And those whom passion hath not blinded,
Subtle-thoughted, myriad-minded.

My friend, with you to live alone
Were how much better than to own   120
A crown, a sceptre, and a throne!

O, strengthen me, enlighten me!
I faint in this obscurity,
Thou dewy dawn of memory.

SONG

I

A spirit haunts the year's last hours
Dwelling amid these yellowing bowers.
          To himself he talks;
For at eventide, listening earnestly,
At his work you may hear him sob and sigh
          In the walks;
     Earthward he boweth the heavy stalks
Of the mouldering flowers.
          Heavily hangs the broad sunflower
               Over its grave i' the earth so chilly;

Heavily hangs the hollyhock,
Heavily hangs the tiger-lily.

II

The air is damp, and hush'd, and close,
As a sick man's room when he taketh repose
      An hour before death;
My very heart faints and my whole soul grieves
At the moist rich smell of the rotting leaves,
      And the breath
Of the fading edges of box beneath,
And the year's last rose.
      Heavily hangs the broad sunflower
      Over its grave i' the earth so chilly;
      Heavily hangs the hollyhock,
      Heavily hangs the tiger-lily.

A CHARACTER

WITH a half-glance upon the sky
At night he said, 'The wanderings
Of this most intricate Universe
Teach me the nothingness of things;'
Yet could not all creation pierce
Beyond the bottom of his eye.

He spake of beauty: that the dull
Saw no divinity in grass,
Life in dead stones, or spirit in air;
Then looking as 't were in a glass,
He smooth'd his chin and sleek'd his hair,
And said the earth was beautiful.

He spake of virtue: not the gods
More purely when they wished to charm
Pallas and Juno sitting by;
And with a sweeping of the arm,
And a lack-lustre dead-blue eye,
Devolved his rounded periods.

Most delicately hour by hour
He canvass'd human mysteries,
And trod on silk, as if the winds
Blew his own praises in his eyes,
And stood aloof from other minds
In impotence of fancied power.

With lips depress'd as he were meek,
    Himself unto himself he sold:
Upon himself himself did feed;
    Quiet, dispassionate, and cold,
And other than his form of creed,
    With chisell'd features clear and sleek.

THE POET

THE poet in a golden clime was born,
    With golden stars above;
Dower'd with the hate of hate, the scorn of scorn,
    The love of love.

He saw thro' life and death, thro' good and ill,
    He saw thro' his own soul.
The marvel of the everlasting will,
    An open scroll,

Before him lay; with echoing feet he threaded
    The secretest walks of fame:
The viewless arrows of his thoughts were headed
    And wing'd with flame,

Like Indian reeds blown from his silver tongue,
    And of so fierce a flight,
From Calpe unto Caucasus they sung,
    Filling with light

And vagrant melodies the winds which bore
    Them earthward till they lit;
Then, like the arrow-seeds of the field flower,
    The fruitful wit

Cleaving took root, and springing forth anew
    Where'er they fell, behold,
Like to the mother plant in semblance, grew
    A flower all gold,

And bravely furnish'd all abroad to fling
    The winged shafts of truth,
To throng with stately blooms the breathing spring
    Of Hope and Youth.

So many minds did gird their orbs with beams,
    Tho' one did fling the fire;

Heaven flow'd upon the soul in many dreams
    Of high desire.

Thus truth was multiplied on truth, the world
    Like one great garden show'd,
And thro' the wreaths of floating dark upcurl'd,
    Rare sunrise flow'd.

And Freedom rear'd in that august sunrise
    Her beautiful bold brow,
When rites and forms before his burning eyes
    Melted like snow.

There was no blood upon her maiden robes
    Sunn'd by those orient skies;
But round about the circles of the globes
    Of her keen eyes

And in her raiment's hem was traced in flame
    WISDOM, a name to shake
All evil dreams of power—a sacred name.
    And when she spake,

Her words did gather thunder as they ran,
    And as the lightning to the thunder
Which follows it, riving the spirit of man,
    Making earth wonder,

So was their meaning to her words. No sword
    Of wrath her right arm whirl'd,
But one poor poet's scroll, and with *his* word
    She shook the world.

THE POET'S MIND

VEX not thou the poet's mind
    With thy shallow wit;
Vex not thou the poet's mind,
    For thou canst not fathom it.
Clear and bright it should be ever,
    Flowing like a crystal river,
Bright as light, and clear as wind.

II

Dark-brow'd sophist, come not anear;
    All the place is holy ground;

Hollow smile and frozen sneer
        Come not here.
    Holy water will I pour
    Into every spicy flower
Of the laurel-shrubs that hedge it around.
The flowers would faint at your cruel cheer.
        In your eye there is death,
        There is frost in your breath
        Which would blight the plants.
    Where you stand you cannot hear
            From the groves within
            The wild-bird's din.
In the heart of the garden the merry bird chants.
It would fall to the ground if you came in.
        In the middle leaps a fountain
            Like sheet lightning,
            Ever brightening
    With a low melodious thunder;
All day and all night it is ever drawn
        From the brain of the purple mountain
        Which stands in the distance yonder.
It springs on a level of bowery lawn,
And the mountain draws it from heaven above,
And it sings a song of undying love;
And yet, tho' its voice be so clear and full,
You never would hear it, your ears are so dull;
So keep where you are; you are foul with sin;
It would shrink to the earth if you came in.

THE SEA-FAIRIES

SLOW sail'd the weary mariners and saw,
Betwixt the green brink and the running foam,
Sweet faces, rounded arms, and bosoms prest
To little harps of gold; and while they mused,
Whispering to each other half in fear,
Shrill music reach'd them on the middle sea.

Whither away, whither away, whither away? fly no more.
Whither away from the high green field, and the happy blossoming shore?
Day and night to the billow the fountain calls;
Down shower the gambolling waterfalls
From wandering over the lea;
Out of the live-green heart of the dells
They freshen the silvery-crimson shells,
And thick with white bells the clover-hill swells
High over the full-toned sea.

10

O, hither, come hither and furl your sails,
Come hither to me and to me;
Hither, come hither and frolic and play;
Here it is only the mew that wails;
We will sing to you all the day.   20
Mariner, mariner, furl your sails,
For here are the blissful downs and dales,
And merrily, merrily carol the gales,
And the spangle dances in bight and bay,
And the rainbow forms and flies on the land
Over the islands free;
And the rainbow lives in the curve of the sand;
Hither, come hither and see;
And the rainbow hangs on the poising wave,
And sweet is the color of cove and cave,   30
And sweet shall your welcome be.
O hither, come hither, and be our lords,
For merry brides are we.
We will kiss sweet kisses, and speak sweet words;
O, listen, listen, your eyes shall glisten
With pleasure and love and jubilee.
O, listen, listen, your eyes shall glisten
When the sharp clear twang of the golden chords
Runs up the ridged sea.
Who can light on as happy a shore   40
All the world o'er, all the world o'er?
Whither away? listen and stay; mariner, mariner, fly no more.

THE DESERTED HOUSE

I

LIFE and Thought have gone away
        Side by side,
        Leaving door and windows wide;
Careless tenants they!

II

All within is dark as night:
In the windows is no light;
And no murmur at the door,
So frequent on its hinge before.

III

Close the door, the shutters close,
        Or thro' the windows we shall see

The nakedness and vacancy
Of the dark deserted house.

IV

Come away; no more of mirth
    Is here or merry-making sound.
The house was builded of the earth,
    And shall fall again to ground.

V

Come away; for Life and Thought
    Here no longer dwell,
But in a city glorious—
A great and distant city—have bought
    A mansion incorruptible.
Would they could have stayed with us!

THE DYING SWAN

I

THE plain was grassy, wild and bare,
Wide, wild, and open to the air,
Which had built up everywhere
    An under-roof of doleful gray.
With an inner voice the river ran,
Adown it floated a dying swan,
    And loudly did lament.
It was the middle of the day.
Ever the weary wind went on,
    And took the reed-tops as it went.   10

II

Some blue peaks in the distance rose,
And white against the cold-white sky
Shone out their crowning snows.
    One willow over the river wept,
And shook the wave as the wind did sigh;
Above in the wind was the swallow,
    Chasing itself at its own wild will,
    And far thro' the marish green and still
    The tangled water-courses slept,
Shot over with purple, and green, and yellow.   20

III

The wild swan's death-hymn took the soul
Of that waste place with joy
Hidden in sorrow. At first to the ear
The warble was low, and full and clear;
  And floating about the under-sky,
  Prevailing in weakness, the coronach stole
  Sometimes afar, and sometimes anear;
  But anon her awful jubilant voice,
  With a music strange and manifold,
Flow'd forth on a carol free and bold;
As when a mighty people rejoice
With shawms, and with cymbals, and harps of gold,
And the tumult of their acclaim is roll'd
Thro' the open gates of the city afar,
To the shepherd who watcheth the evening star.
And the creeping mosses and clambering weeds,
And the willow-branches hoar and dank,
And the wavy swell of the soughing reeds,
And the wave-worn horns of the echoing bank,
And the silvery marish-flowers that throng
The desolate creeks and pools among,
Were flooded over with eddying song.

      40

A DIRGE

I

Now is done thy long day's work;
Fold thy palms across thy breast,
Fold thine arms, turn to thy rest.
    Let them rave.
Shadows of the silver birk
Sweep the green that folds thy grave.
    Let them rave.

II

Thee nor carketh care nor slander;
Nothing but the small cold worm
Fretteth thine enshrouded form.
    Let them rave.
Light and shadow ever wander
O'er the green that folds thy grave.
    Let them rave.

III

Thou wilt not turn upon thy bed;
Chaunteth not the brooding bee
Sweeter tones than calumny?
  Let them rave.
Thou wilt never raise thine head
From the green that folds thy grave.
  Let them rave.

IV

Crocodiles wept tears for thee;
The woodbine and eglatere
Drip sweeter dews than traitor's tear.
  Let them rave.
Rain makes music in the tree
O'er the green that folds thy grave.
  Let them rave.

V

Round thee blow, self-pleached deep,
Bramble roses, faint and pale,
And long purples of the dale.
  Let them rave.
These in every shower creep
Thro' the green that folds thy grave.
  Let them rave.

VI

The gold-eyed kingcups fine,
The frail bluebell peereth over
Rare broidery of the purple clover.
  Let them rave.
Kings have no such couch as thine,
As the green that folds thy grave.
  Let them rave.

VII

Wild words wander here and there;
God's great gift of speech abused
Makes thy memory confused;
  But let them rave.
The balm-cricket carols clear

> In the green that folds thy grave.
>   Let them rave.

LOVE AND DEATH

WHAT time the mighty moon was gathering light
Love paced the thymy plots of Paradise,
And all about him roll'd his lustrous eyes;
When, turning round a cassia, full in view,
Death, walking all alone beneath a yew,
And talking to himself, first met his sight.
'You must begone,' said Death, 'these walks are mine.'
Love wept and spread his sheeny vans for flight;
Yet ere he parted said, 'This hour is thine;
Thou art the shadow of life, and as the tree
Stands in the sun and shadows all beneath,
So in the light of great eternity
Life eminent creates the shade of death.
The shadow passeth when the tree shall fall,
But I shall reign for ever over all.'

THE BALLAD OF ORIANA

> My heart is wasted with my woe,
>   Oriana.
> There is no rest for me below,
>   Oriana.
> When the long dun wolds are ribb'd with snow,
> And loud the Norland whirlwinds blow,
>   Oriana,
> Alone I wander to and fro,
>   Oriana.

> Ere the light on dark was growing,
>   Oriana,
> At midnight the cock was crowing,
>   Oriana;
> Winds were blowing, waters flowing,
> We heard the steeds to battle going,
>   Oriana,
> Aloud the hollow bugle blowing,
>   Oriana.

> In the yew-wood black as night,
>   Oriana,

10

20

Ere I rode into the fight,
　　Oriana,
While blissful tears blinded my sight
By star-shine and by moonlight,
　　Oriana,
I to thee my troth did plight,
　　Oriana.

She stood upon the castle wall,
　　Oriana;
She watch'd my crest among them all,   30
　　Oriana;
She saw me fight, she heard me call,
When forth there stept a foeman tall,
　　Oriana,
Atween me and the castle wall,
　　Oriana.

The bitter arrow went aside,
　　Oriana;
The false, false arrow went aside,
　　Oriana;   40
The damned arrow glanced aside,
And pierced thy heart, my love, my bride,
　　Oriana!
Thy heart, my life, my love, my bride,
　　Oriana!

O, narrow, narrow was the space,
　　Oriana!
Loud, loud rung out the bugle's brays,
　　Oriana.
O, deathful stabs were dealt apace,   50
The battle deepen'd in its place,
　　Oriana;
But I was down upon my face,
　　Oriana.

They should have stabb'd me where I lay,
　　Oriana!
How could I rise and come away,
　　Oriana?
How could I look upon the day?
They should have stabb'd me where I lay,   60
　　Oriana—
They should have trod me into clay,
　　Oriana.

O breaking heart that will not break,
  Oriana!
O pale, pale face so sweet and meek,
  Oriana!
Thou smilest, but thou dost not speak,
And then the tears run down my cheek,
  Oriana.   70
What wantest thou? whom dost thou seek,
  Oriana?

I cry aloud; none hear my cries,
  Oriana.
Thou comest atween me and the skies,
  Oriana.
I feel the tears of blood arise
Up from my heart unto my eyes,
  Oriana.
Within thy heart my arrow lies,   80
  Oriana.

O cursed hand! O cursed blow!
  Oriana!
O happy thou that liest low,
  Oriana!
All night the silence seems to flow
Beside me in my utter woe,
  Oriana.
A weary, weary way I go,   90
  Oriana!

When Norland winds pipe down the sea,
  Oriana,
I walk, I dare not think of thee,
  Oriana.
Thou liest beneath the greenwood tree,
I dare not die and come to thee,
  Oriana.
I hear the roaring of the sea,
  Oriana.

CIRCUMSTANCE

Two children in two neighbor villages
Playing mad pranks along the heathy leas;
Two strangers meeting at a festival;
Two lovers whispering by an orchard wall;
Two lives bound fast in one with golden ease;

Two graves grass-green beside a gray church-tower,
Wash'd with still rains and daisy-blossomed;
Two children in one hamlet born and bred:
So runs the round of life from hour to hour.

THE MERMAN

I

Who would be
A merman bold,
Sitting alone,
Singing alone
Under the sea,
With a crown of gold,
On a throne?

II

I would be a merman bold,
I would sit and sing the whole of the day;
I would fill the sea-halls with a voice of power;
But at night I would roam abroad and play
With the mermaids in and out of the rocks,
Dressing their hair with the white sea-flower;
And holding them back by their flowing locks
I would kiss them often under the sea,
And kiss them again till they kiss'd me
    Laughingly, laughingly;
And then we would wander away, away,
To the pale-green sea-groves straight and high,
    Chasing each other merrily.

III

There would be neither moon nor star;
But the wave would make music above us afar—
Low thunder and light in the magic night—
    Neither moon nor star.
We would call aloud in the dreamy dells,
Call to each other and whoop and cry
    All night, merrily, merrily.
They would pelt me with starry spangles and shells,
Laughing and clapping their hands between,
    All night, merrily, merrily,
But I would throw to them back in mine
Turkis and agate and almondine;

Then leaping out upon them unseen
I would kiss them often under the sea,
And kiss them again till they kiss'd me
    Laughingly, laughingly.
O, what a happy life were mine
Under the hollow-hung ocean green!
Soft are the moss-beds under the sea;
We would live merrily, merrily.

THE MERMAID

I

Who would be
A mermaid fair,
Singing alone,
Combing her hair
Under the sea,
In a golden curl
With a comb of pearl,
On a throne?

II

I would be a mermaid fair;
I would sing to myself the whole of the day;
With a comb of pearl I would comb my hair;
And still as I comb'd I would sing and say,
'Who is it loves me? who loves not me?'
I would comb my hair till my ringlets would fall
    Low adown, low adown,
From under my starry sea-bud crown
    Low adown and around,
And I should look like a fountain of gold
    Springing alone
With a shrill inner sound,
    Over the throne
In the midst of the hall;
Till that great sea-snake under the sea
From his coiled sleeps in the central deeps
Would slowly trail himself sevenfold
Round the hall where I sate, and look in at the gate
With his large calm eyes for the love of me.
And all the mermen under the sea
Would feel their immortality
Die in their hearts for the love of me.

III

But at night I would wander away, away,
   I would fling on each side my low-flowing locks,
And lightly vault from the throne and play
   With the mermen in and out of the rocks;
We would run to and fro, and hide and seek,
   On the broad sea-wolds in the crimson shells,
Whose silvery spikes are nighest the sea.
But if any came near I would call, and shriek,
And adown the steep like a wave I would leap
   From the diamond-ledges that jut from the dells;
For I would not be kiss'd by all who would list
Of the bold merry mermen under the sea.
They would sue me, and woo me, and flatter me,
In the purple twilights under the sea;
But the king of them all would carry me,
Woo me, and win me, and marry me,
In the branching jaspers under the sea.
Then all the dry-pied things that be
In the hueless mosses under the sea
Would curl round my silver feet silently,
All looking up for the love of me.
And if I should carol aloud, from aloft
All things that are forked, and horned, and soft
Would lean out from the hollow sphere of the sea,
All looking down for the love of me.

ADELINE

I

MYSTERY of mysteries,
   Faintly smiling Adeline,
   Scarce of earth nor all divine,
Nor unhappy, nor at rest,
   But beyond expression fair
   With thy floating flaxen hair;
Thy rose-lips and full blue eyes
   Take the heart from out my breast.
   Wherefore those dim looks of thine,
   Shadowy, dreaming Adeline?

II

Whence that aery bloom of thine,
　　Like a lily which the sun
Looks thro' in his sad decline,
　　And a rose-bush leans upon,
Thou that faintly smilest still,
　　As a Naiad in a well,
　　Looking at the set of day,
Or a phantom two hours old
　　Of a maiden past away,
Ere the placid lips be cold?
Wherefore those faint smiles of thine,
　　Spiritual Adeline?

III

What hope or fear or joy is thine?
Who talketh with thee, Adeline?
　　For sure thou art not all alone.
　　　Do beating hearts of salient springs
　　Keep measure with thine own?
　　　Hast thou heard the butterflies
　　　What they say betwixt their wings?
　　　Or in stillest evenings
With what voice the violet woos
To his heart the silver dews?
　　　Or when little airs arise,
　　How the merry bluebell rings
　　To the mosses underneath?
　　Hast thou look'd upon the breath
　　　Of the lilies at sunrise?
Wherefore that faint smile of thine,
Shadowy, dreaming Adeline?

IV

Some honey-converse feeds thy mind,
　　Some spirit of a crimson rose
　　In love with thee forgets to close
　　His curtains, wasting odorous sighs
All night long on darkness blind.
What aileth thee? whom waitest thou
With thy soften'd, shadow'd brow,
　　　And those dew-lit eyes of thine,
　　　Thou faint smiler, Adeline?

V

Lovest thou the doleful wind
    When thou gazest at the skies?
Doth the low-tongued Orient
    Wander from the side of the morn,
    Dripping with Sabæan spice
On thy pillow, lowly bent
    With melodious airs lovelorn,
Breathing Light against thy face,
While his locks a-drooping twined
Round thy neck in subtle ring
Make a carcanet of rays,
    And ye talk together still,
In the language wherewith Spring
    Letters cowslips on the hill?
Hence that look and smile of thine,
    Spiritual Adeline.

MARGARET

I

O sweet pale Margaret,
O rare pale Margaret,
What lit your eyes with tearful power,
Like moonlight on a falling shower?
Who lent you, love, your mortal dower
    Of pensive thought and aspect pale,
    Your melancholy sweet and frail
As perfume of the cuckoo flower?
From the westward-winding flood,
From the evening-lighted wood,
    From all things outward you have won
A tearful grace, as tho' you stood
    Between the rainbow and the sun.
The very smile before you speak,
That dimples your transparent cheek,
    Encircles all the heart, and feedeth
The senses with a still delight
    Of dainty sorrow without sound,
    Like the tender amber round
    Which the moon about her spreadeth,
Moving thro' a fleecy night.

II

You love, remaining peacefully,
    To hear the murmur of the strife,
    But enter not the toil of life.
Your spirit is the calmed sea,
    Laid by the tumult of the fight.
You are the evening star, alway
    Remaining betwixt dark and bright;
Lull'd echoes of laborious day
    Come to you, gleams of mellow light
    Float by you on the verge of night.

III

What can it matter, Margaret,
    What songs below the waning stars
The lion-heart, Plantagenet,
    Sang looking thro' his prison bars?
Exquisite Margaret, who can tell
The last wild thought of Chatelet,
    Just ere the falling axe did part
    The burning brain from the true heart,
Even in her sight he loved so well?

IV

A fairy shield your Genius made
    And gave you on your natal day.
Your sorrow, only sorrow's shade,
    Keeps real sorrow far away.
You move not in such solitudes,
    You are not less divine,
But more human in your moods,
    Than your twin-sister, Adeline.
Your hair is darker, and your eyes
    Touch'd with a somewhat darker hue,
    And less aerially blue,
    But ever trembling thro' the dew
Of dainty-woeful sympathies.

V

O sweet pale Margaret,
O rare pale Margaret,
Come down, come down, and hear me speak.
Tie up the ringlets on your cheek.

The sun is just about to set,
The arching limes are tall and shady,
And faint, rainy lights are seen,
Moving in the leavy beech.
Rise from the feast of sorrow, lady,
Where all day long you sit between
Joy and woe, and whisper each.
Or only look across the lawn,
Look out below your bower-eaves,
Look down, and let your blue eyes dawn
Upon me thro' the jasmine-leaves.

ROSALIND

I

My Rosalind, my Rosalind,
My frolic falcon, with bright eyes,
Whose free delight, from any height of rapid flight,
Stoops at all game that wing the skies,
My Rosalind, my Rosalind,
My bright-eyed, wild-eyed falcon, whither,
Careless both of wind and weather,
Whither fly ye, what game spy ye,
Up or down the streaming wind?

II

The quick lark's closest-caroll'd strains,
The shadow rushing up the sea,
The lightning flash atween the rains,
The sunlight driving down the lea,
The leaping stream, the very wind,
That will not stay, upon his way,
To stoop the cowslip to the plains,
Is not so clear and bold and free
As you, my falcon Rosalind.
You care not for another's pains,
Because you are the soul of joy,
Bright metal all without alloy.
Life shoots and glances thro' your veins,
And flashes off a thousand ways,
Thro' lips and eyes in subtle rays,
Your hawk-eyes are keen and bright,
Keen with triumph, watching still
To pierce me thro' with pointed light;
But oftentimes they flash and glitter

Like sunshine on a dancing rill,
And your words are seeming-bitter,
Sharp and few, but seeming-bitter
From excess of swift delight.

III

Come down, come home, my Rosalind,
My gay young hawk, my Rosalind.
Too long you keep the upper skies;
Too long you roam and wheel at will;
But we must hood your random eyes,
That care not whom they kill,
And your cheek, whose brilliant hue
Is so sparkling-fresh to view,
Some red heath-flower in the dew,
Touch'd with sunrise. We must bind
And keep you fast, my Rosalind,
Fast, fast, my wild-eyed Rosalind,
And clip your wings, and make you love.
When we have lured you from above,
And that delight of frolic flight, by day or night,
From North to South,
We'll bind you fast in silken cords,
And kiss away the bitter words
From off your rosy mouth.

ELEÄNORE

I

THY dark eyes open'd not,
    Nor first reveal'd themselves to English air,
    For there is nothing here
Which, from the outward to the inward brought,
Moulded thy baby thought.
Far off from human neighborhood
    Thou wert born, on a summer morn,
A mile beneath the cedar-wood.
Thy bounteous forehead was not fann'd
    With breezes from our oaken glades,
But thou wert nursed in some delicious land   10
    Of lavish lights, and floating shades;
And flattering thy childish thought
The oriental fairy brought,
    At the moment of thy birth,
From old well-heads of haunted rills,

And the hearts of purple hills,
And shadow'd coves on a sunny shore,
    The choicest wealth of all the earth,
Jewel or shell, or starry ore,   20
To deck thy cradle, Eleänore.

II

Or the yellow-banded bees,
Thro' half-open lattices
Coming in the scented breeze,
Fed thee, a child, lying alone,
   With whitest honey in fairy gardens cull'd—
A glorious child, dreaming alone,
In silk-soft folds, upon yielding down,
With the hum of swarming bees
    Into dreamful slumber lull'd.   30

III

Who may minister to thee?
Summer herself should minister
To thee, with fruitage golden-rinded
On golden salvers, or it may be,
Youngest Autumn, in a bower
Grape-thicken'd from the light, and blinded
With many a deep-hued bell-like flower
Of fragrant trailers, when the air
Sleepeth over all the heaven,
And the crag that fronts the even,   40
    All along the shadowing shore,
Crimsons over an inland mere,
            Eleänore!

IV

How may full-sail'd verse express,
    How may measured words adore
The full-flowing harmony
Of thy swan-like stateliness,
        Eleänore?
The luxuriant symmetry
Of thy floating gracefulness,   50
        Eleänore?
Every turn and glance of thine,
Every lineament divine,
        Eleänore,
    And the steady sunset glow

That stays upon thee? For in thee
Is nothing sudden, nothing single;
Like two streams of incense free
From one censer in one shrine,
Thought and motion mingle, 60
Mingle ever. Motions flow
To one another, even as tho'
They were modulated so
To an unheard melody,
Which lives about thee, and a sweep
Of richest pauses, evermore
Drawn from each other mellow-deep;
Who may express thee, Eleänore?

V

I stand before thee, Eleänore;
I see thy beauty gradually unfold, 70
Daily and hourly, more and more.
I muse, as in a trance, the while
Slowly, as from a cloud of gold,
Comes out thy deep ambrosial smile.
I muse, as in a trance, whene'er
The languors of thy love-deep eyes
Float on to me. I would I were
So tranced, so rapt in ecstasies,
To stand apart, and to adore,
Gazing on thee for evermore, 80
Serene, imperial Eleänore!

VI

Sometimes, with most intensity
Gazing, I seem to see
Thought folded over thought, smiling asleep,
Slowly awaken'd, grow so full and deep
In thy large eyes that, overpower'd quite,
I cannot veil or droop my sight,
But am as nothing in its light.
As tho' a star, in inmost heaven set,
Even while we gaze on it, 90
Should slowly round his orb, and slowly grow
To a full face, there like a sun remain
Fix'd—then as slowly fade again,
And draw itself to what it was before;
So full, so deep, so slow,
Thought seems to come and go
In thy large eyes, imperial Eleänore.

VII

As thunder-clouds that, hung on high,
Roof'd the world with doubt and fear,
Floating thro' an evening atmosphere,   100
Grow golden all about the sky;
In thee all passion becomes passionless,
Touch'd by thy spirit's mellowness,
Losing his fire and active might
    In a silent meditation,
Falling into a still delight,
    And luxury of contemplation.
As waves that up a quiet cove
    Rolling slide, and lying still
    Shadow forth the banks at will,   110
Or sometimes they swell and move,
  Pressing up against the land
  With motions of the outer sea;
And the self-same influence
Controlleth all the soul and sense
  Of Passion gazing upon thee.
His bow-string slacken'd, languid Love,
  Leaning his cheek upon his hand,
  Droops both his wings, regarding thee,
And so would languish evermore,   120
Serene, imperial Eleänore.

VIII

But when I see thee roam, with tresses unconfined,
While the amorous odorous wind
Breathes low between the sunset and the moon;
Or, in a shadowy saloon,
On silken cushions half reclined;
    I watch thy grace, and in its place
My heart a charmed slumber keeps,
    While I muse upon thy face;
And a languid fire creeps   130
    Thro' my veins to all my frame,
Dissolvingly and slowly. Soon
    From thy rose-red lips MY name
Floweth; and then, as in a swoon,
With dinning sound my ears are rife,
    My tremulous tongue faltereth,
    I lose my color, I lose my breath,
    I drink the cup of a costly death,
Brimm'd with delirious draughts of warmest life.

I die with my delight before
    I hear what I would hear from thee;
    Yet tell my name again to me,
I *would* be dying evermore,
So dying ever, Eleänore.

KATE

I KNOW her by her angry air,
Her bright black eyes, her bright black hair,
    Her rapid laughters wild and shrill,
As laughters of the woodpecker
    From the bosom of a hill.
    'T is Kate—she sayeth what she will,
For Kate hath an unbridled tongue,
    Clear as the twanging of a harp.
    Her heart is like a throbbing star.
Kate hath a spirit ever strung
    Like a new bow, and bright and sharp
    As edges of the scimitar.
Whence shall she take a fitting mate?
    For Kate no common love will feel;
My woman-soldier, gallant Kate,
    As pure and true as blades of steel.

Kate saith 'the world is void of might.'
Kate saith 'the men are gilded flies.'
    Kate snaps her fingers at my vows;
Kate will not hear of lovers' sighs.
I would I were an armed knight,
Far-famed for well-won enterprise,
    And wearing on my swarthy brows
The garland of new-wreathed emprise;
    For in a moment I would pierce
The blackest files of clanging fight,
And strongly strike to left and right,
    In dreaming of my lady's eyes.
    O, Kate loves well the bold and fierce;
But none are bold enough for Kate,
She cannot find a fitting mate.

'MY LIFE IS FULL OF WEARY DAYS'

I

My life is full of weary days,
   But good things have not kept aloof,
Nor wander'd into other ways;
   I have not lack'd thy mild reproof,
Nor golden largess of thy praise.

And now shake hands across the brink
   Of that deep grave to which I go,
Shake hands once more; I cannot sink
   So far—far down, but I shall know
   Thy voice, and answer from below.

II

When in the darkness over me
   The four-handed mole shall scrape,
Plant thou no dusky cypress-tree,
   Nor wreathe thy cap with doleful crape,
   But pledge me in the flowing grape.

And when the sappy field and wood
   Grow green beneath the showery gray,
And rugged barks begin to bud,
   And thro' damp holts new-flush'd with may,
   Ring sudden scritches of the jay,

Then let wise Nature work her will,
   And on my clay her darnel grow;
Come only, when the days are still,
   And at my headstone whisper low,
   And tell me if the woodbines blow.

EARLY SONNETS

I

TO ——

As when with downcast eyes we muse and brood,
And ebb into a former life, or seem
To lapse far back in some confused dream
To states of mystical similitude,

If one but speaks or hems or stirs his chair,
Ever the wonder waxeth more and more,
So that we say, 'All this hath been before,
All this hath been, I know not when or where;'
So, friend, when first I look'd upon your face,
Our thought gave answer each to each, so true—
Opposed mirrors each reflecting each—
That, tho' I knew not in what time or place,
Methought that I had often met with you,
And either lived in either's heart and speech.

II

TO J. M. K.

MY hope and heart is with thee—thou wilt be
A latter Luther, and a soldier-priest
To scare church-harpies from the master's feast;
Our dusted velvets have much need of thee:
Thou art no Sabbath-drawler of old saws,
Distill'd from some worm-canker'd homily;
But spurr'd at heart with fieriest energy
To embattail and to wall about thy cause
With iron-worded proof, hating to hark
The humming of the drowsy pulpit-drone
Half God's good Sabbath, while the wornout clerk
Brow-beats his desk below. Thou from a throne
Mounted in heaven wilt shoot into the dark
Arrows of lightnings. I will stand and mark.

III

MINE be the strength of spirit, full and free,
Like some broad river rushing down alone,
With the selfsame impulse wherewith he was thrown
From his loud fount upon the echoing lea;—
Which with increasing might doth forward flee
By town, and tower, and hill, and cape, and isle,
And in the middle of the green salt sea
Keeps his blue waters fresh for many a mile.
Mine be the power which ever to its sway
Will win the wise at once, and by degrees
May into uncongenial spirits flow;
Even as the warm gulf-stream of Florida
Floats far away into the Northern seas
The lavish growths of southern Mexico.

IV

ALEXANDER

Warrior of God, whose strong right arm debased
The throne of Persia, when her Satrap bled
At Issus by the Syrian gates, or fled
Beyond the Memmian naphtha-pits, disgraced
For ever—thee (thy pathway sand-erased)
Gliding with equal crowns two serpents led
Joyful to that palm-planted fountain-fed
Ammonian Oasis in the waste.
There in a silent shade of laurel brown
Apart the Chamian Oracle divine
Shelter'd his unapproached mysteries:
High things were spoken there, unhanded down;
Only they saw thee from the secret shrine
Returning with hot cheek and kindled eyes.

V

BUONAPARTE

He thought to quell the stubborn hearts of oak,
Madman!—to chain with chains, and bind with bands
That island queen who sways the floods and lands
From Ind to Ind, but in fair daylight woke,
When from her wooden walls,—lit by sure hands,—
With thunders, and with lightnings, and with smoke,—
Peal after peal, the British battle broke,
Lulling the brine against the Coptic sands.
We taught him lowlier moods, when Elsinore
Heard the war moan along the distant sea,
Rocking with shatter'd spars, with sudden fires
Flamed over; at Trafalgar yet once more
We taught him; late he learned humility
Perforce, like those whom Gideon school'd with briers.

VI

POLAND

How long, O God, shall men be ridden down,
And trampled under by the last and least
Of men? The heart of Poland hath not ceased
To quiver, tho' her sacred blood doth drown
The fields and out of every smouldering town

Cries to Thee, lest brute Power be increased,
Till that o'ergrown Barbarian in the East
Transgress his ample bound to some new crown,—
Cries to Thee, 'Lord, how long shall these things be?
How long this icy-hearted Muscovite
Oppress the region?' Us, O Just and Good,
Forgive, who smiled when she was torn in three;
Us, who stand now, when we should aid the right—
A matter to be wept with tears of blood!

VII

CARESS'D or chidden by the slender hand,
And singing airy trifles this or that,
Light Hope at Beauty's call would perch and stand,
And run thro' every change of sharp and flat;
And Fancy came and at her pillow sat,
When Sleep had bound her in his rosy band,
And chased away the still-recurring gnat,
And woke her with a lay from fairy land.
But now they live with Beauty less and less,
For Hope is other Hope and wanders far,
Nor cares to lisp in love's delicious creeds;
And Fancy watches in the wilderness,
Poor Fancy sadder than a single star,
That sets at twilight in a land of reeds.

VIII

THE form, the form alone is eloquent!
A nobler yearning never broke her rest
Than but to dance and sing, be gaily drest,
And win all eyes with all accomplishment;
Yet in the whirling dances as we went,
My fancy made me for a moment blest
To find my heart so near the beauteous breast
That once had power to rob it of content.
A moment came the tenderness of tears,
The phantom of a wish that once could move,
A ghost of passion that no smiles restore—
For ah! the slight coquette, she cannot love,
And if you kiss'd her feet a thousand years,
She still would take the praise, and care no more.

IX

WAN Sculptor, weepest thou to take the cast
Of those dead lineaments that near thee lie?

O, sorrowest thou, pale Painter, for the past,
In painting some dead friend from memory?
Weep on; beyond his object Love can last.
His object lives; more cause to weep have I:
My tears, no tears of love, are flowing fast,
No tears of Love, but tears that Love can die.
I pledge her not in any cheerful cup,
Nor care to sit beside her where she sits—
Ah! pity—hint it not in human tones,
But breathe it into earth and close it up
With secret death for ever, in the pits
Which some green Christmas crams with weary bones.

X

If I were loved, as I desire to be,
What is there in the great sphere of the earth,
And range of evil between death and birth,
That I should fear,—if I were loved by thee?
All the inner, all the outer world of pain
Clear Love would pierce and cleave, if thou wert mine,
As I have heard that, somewhere in the main,
Fresh-water springs come up through bitter brine.
'T were joy, not fear, claspt hand-in-hand with thee,
To wait for death—mute—careless of all ills,
Apart upon a mountain, tho' the surge
Of some new deluge from a thousand hills
Flung leagues of roaring foam into the gorge
Below us, as far on as eye could see.

XI

THE BRIDESMAID

O BRIDESMAID, ere the happy knot was tied,
Thine eyes so wept that they could hardly see;
Thy sister smiled and said, 'No tears for me!
A happy bridesmaid makes a happy bride.'
And then, the couple standing side by side,
Love lighted down between them full of glee,
And over his left shoulder laugh'd at thee,
'O happy bridesmaid, make a happy bride.'
And all at once a pleasant truth I learn'd,
For while the tender service made thee weep,
I loved thee for the tear thou couldst not hide,
And prest thy hand, and knew the press return'd,
And thought, 'My life is sick of single sleep:
O happy bridesmaid, make a happy bride!'

THE LADY OF SHALOTT
AND OTHER POEMS

THE LADY OF SHALOTT

PART I

On either side the river lie
Long fields of barley and of rye,
That clothe the wold and meet the sky;
And thro' the field the road runs by
     To many-tower'd Camelot;
And up and down the people go,
Gazing where the lilies blow
Round an island there below,
     The island of Shalott.

Willows whiten, aspens quiver,
Little breezes dusk and shiver
Thro' the wave that runs for ever
By the island in the river
     Flowing down to Camelot.
Four gray walls, and four gray towers,
Overlook a space of flowers,
And the silent isle imbowers
     The Lady of Shalott.

By the margin, willow-veil'd,
Slide the heavy barges trail'd
By slow horses; and unhail'd
The shallop flitteth silken-sail'd
     Skimming down to Camelot:
But who hath seen her wave her hand?
Or at the casement seen her stand?
Or is she known in all the land,
     The Lady of Shalott?

Only reapers, reaping early
In among the bearded barley,
Hear a song that echoes cheerly

From the river winding clearly,
        Down to tower'd Camelot;
And by the moon the reaper weary,
Piling sheaves in uplands airy,
Listening, whispers ' 'Tis the fairy
        Lady of Shalott.

PART II

There she weaves by night and day
A magic web with colors gay.
She has heard a whisper say,
A curse is on her if she stay   40
        To look down to Camelot.
She knows not what the curse may be,
And so she weaveth steadily,
And little other care hath she,
        The Lady of Shalott.

And moving thro' a mirror clear
That hangs before her all the year,
Shadows of the world appear.
There she sees the highway near
        Winding down to Camelot;   50
There the river eddy whirls,
And there the surly village-churls,
And the red cloaks of market girls,
        Pass onward from Shalott.

Sometimes a troop of damsels glad,
An abbot on an ambling pad,
Sometimes a curly shepherd-lad,
Or long-hair'd page in crimson clad,
        Goes by to tower'd Camelot;
And sometimes thro' the mirror blue   60
The knights come riding two and two:
She hath no loyal knight and true,
        The Lady of Shalott.

But in her web she still delights
To weave the mirror's magic sights,
For often thro' the silent nights
A funeral, with plumes and lights
        And music, went to Camelot;
Or when the moon was overhead,
Came two young lovers lately wed: 70
'I am half sick of shadows,' said
        The Lady of Shalott.

PART III

A bow-shot from her bower-eaves,
He rode between the barley-sheaves,
The sun came dazzling thro' the leaves,
And flamed upon the brazen greaves
     Of bold Sir Lancelot.
A red-cross knight for ever kneel'd
To a lady in his shield,
That sparkled on the yellow field,   80
     Beside remote Shalott.

The gemmy bridle glitter'd free,
Like to some branch of stars we see
Hung in the golden Galaxy.
The bridle bells rang merrily
     As he rode down to Camelot;
And from his blazon'd baldric slung
A mighty silver bugle hung,
And as he rode his armor rung,
     Beside remote Shalott.   90

All in the blue unclouded weather
Thick-jewell'd shone the saddle-leather,
The helmet and the helmet-feather
Burn'd like one burning flame together,
     As he rode down to Camelot;
As often thro' the purple night,
Below the starry clusters bright,
Some bearded meteor, trailing light,
     Moves over still Shalott.

His broad clear brow in sunlight glow'd;   100
On burnish'd hooves his war-horse trode;
From underneath his helmet flow'd
His coal-black curls as on he rode,
     As he rode down to Camelot.
From the bank and from the river
He flash'd into the crystal mirror,
'Tirra lirra,' by the river
     Sang Sir Lancelot.

She left the web, she left the loom,
She made three paces thro' the room,   110
She saw the water-lily bloom,
She saw the helmet and the plume,
     She look'd down to Camelot.

Out flew the web and floated wide;
The mirror crack'd from side to side;
'The curse is come upon me,' cried
  The Lady of Shalott.

PART IV

In the stormy east-wind straining,
The pale yellow woods were waning,
The broad stream in his banks complaining,   120
Heavily the low sky raining
  Over tower'd Camelot;
Down she came and found a boat
Beneath a willow left afloat,
And round about the prow she wrote
  The Lady of Shalott.

And down the river's dim expanse
Like some bold seër in a trance,
Seeing all his own mischance—
With a glassy countenance   130
  Did she look to Camelot.
And at the closing of the day
She loosed the chain, and down she lay;
The broad stream bore her far away,
  The Lady of Shalott.

Lying, robed in snowy white
That loosely flew to left and right—
The leaves upon her falling light—
Thro' the noises of the night
  She floated down to Camelot;   140
And as the boat-head wound along
The willowy hills and fields among,
They heard her singing her last song,
  The Lady of Shalott.

Heard a carol, mournful, holy,
Chanted loudly, chanted lowly,
Till her blood was frozen slowly,
And her eyes were darken'd wholly,
  Turn'd to tower'd Camelot.
For ere she reach'd upon the tide   150
The first house by the water-side,
Singing in her song she died,
  The Lady of Shalott.

Under tower and balcony,
By garden-wall and gallery,
A gleaming shape she floated by,
Dead-pale between the houses high,
    Silent into Camelot.
Out upon the wharfs they came,
Knight and burgher, lord and dame,   160
And round the prow they read her name,
    The Lady of Shalott.

Who is this? and what is here?
And in the lighted palace near
Died the sound of royal cheer;
And they cross'd themselves for fear,
    All the knights at Camelot:
But Lancelot mused a little space;
He said, 'She has a lovely face;
God in his mercy lend her grace,   170
    The Lady of Shalott.'

MARIANA IN THE SOUTH

WITH one black shadow at its feet,
    The house thro' all the level shines,
Close-latticed to the brooding heat,
    And silent in its dusty vines;
A faint-blue ridge upon the right,
    An empty river-bed before,
    And shallows on a distant shore,
In glaring sand and inlets bright.
      But 'Ave Mary,' made she moan,
        And 'Ave Mary,' night and morn,   10
      And 'Ah,' she sang, 'to be all alone,
        To live forgotten, and love forlorn.'

She, as her carol sadder grew,
    From brow and bosom slowly down
Thro' rosy taper fingers drew
    Her streaming curls of deepest brown
To left and right, and made appear
    Still-lighted in a secret shrine
    Her melancholy eyes divine,
The home of woe without a tear.   20
      And 'Ave Mary,' was her moan,
        'Madonna, sad is night and morn,'
      And 'Ah,' she sang, 'to be all alone,
        To live forgotten, and love forlorn.'

Till all the crimson changed, and past
  Into deep orange o'er the sea,
Low on her knees herself she cast,
  Before Our Lady murmur'd she;
Complaining, 'Mother, give me grace
  To help me of my weary load.'   **30**
And on the liquid mirror glow'd
The clear perfection of her face.
    'Is this the form,' she made her moan,
      'That won his praises night and morn?'
    And 'Ah,' she said, 'but I wake alone,
      I sleep forgotten, I wake forlorn.'

Nor bird would sing, nor lamb would bleat,
  Nor any cloud would cross the vault,
But day increased from heat to heat,
  On stony drought and steaming salt;   **40**
Till now at noon she slept again,
  And seem'd knee-deep in mountain grass,
  And heard her native breezes pass,
And runlets babbling down the glen.
    She breathed in sleep a lower moan,
      And murmuring, as at night and morn,
    She thought, 'My spirit is here alone,
      Walks forgotten, and is forlorn.'

Dreaming, she knew it was a dream;
  She felt he was and was not there.   **50**
She woke; the babble of the stream
  Fell, and, without, the steady glare
Shrank one sick willow sere and small.
  The river-bed was dusty-white;
  And all the furnace of the light
Struck up against the blinding wall.
    She whisper'd, with a stifled moan
      More inward than at night or morn,
    'Sweet Mother, let me not here alone
      Live forgotten and die forlorn.'   **60**

And, rising, from her bosom drew
  Old letters, breathing of her worth,
For 'Love,' they said, 'must needs be true,
  To what is loveliest upon earth.'
An image seem'd to pass the door,
  To look at her with slight, and say
  'But now thy beauty flows away,
So be alone for evermore.'
    'O cruel heart,' she changed her tone,

'And cruel love, whose end is scorn,
Is this the end, to be left alone,
To live forgotten, and die forlorn?'

But sometimes in the falling day
An image seem'd to pass the door,
To look into her eyes and say,
'But thou shalt be alone no more.'
And flaming downward over all
From heat to heat the day decreased,
And slowly rounded to the east
The one black shadow from the wall.
'The day to night,' she made her moan,
'The day to night, the night to morn,
And day and night I am left alone
To live forgotten, and love forlorn.'

At eve a dry cicala sung,
There came a sound as of the sea;
Backward the lattice-blind she flung,
And lean'd upon the balcony.
There all in spaces rosy-bright
Large Hesper glitter'd on her tears,
And deepening thro' the silent spheres
Heaven over heaven rose the night.
And weeping then she made her moan,
'The night comes on that knows not morn,
When I shall cease to be all alone,
To live forgotten, and love forlorn.'

THE TWO VOICES

A STILL small voice spake unto me,
'Thou art so full of misery,
Were it not better not to be?'

Then to the still small voice I said:
'Let me not cast in endless shade
What is so wonderfully made.'

To which the voice did urge reply:
'To-day I saw the dragon-fly
Come from the wells where he did lie.

'An inner impulse rent the veil
Of his old husk; from head to tail
Came out clear plates of sapphire mail.

'He dried his wings: like gauze they grew;
Thro' crofts and pastures wet with dew
A living flash of light he flew.'

I said: 'When first the world began,
Young Nature thro' five cycles ran,
And in the sixth she moulded man.

'She gave him mind, the lordliest
Proportion, and, above the rest,
Dominion in the head and breast.'   20

Thereto the silent voice replied:
'Self-blinded are you by your pride;
Look up thro' night; the world is wide.

'This truth within thy mind rehearse,
That in a boundless universe
Is boundless better, boundless worse.

'Think you this mould of hopes and fears
Could find no statelier than his peers
In yonder hundred million spheres?'   30

It spake, moreover, in my mind:
'Tho' thou wert scatter'd to the wind,
Yet is there plenty of the kind.'

Then did my response clearer fall:
'No compound of this earthly ball
Is like another, all in all.'

To which he answer'd scoffingly:
'Good soul! suppose I grant it thee,
Who'll weep for thy deficiency?

'Or will one beam be less intense,   40
When thy peculiar difference
Is cancell'd in the world of sense?'

I would have said, 'Thou canst not know,'
But my full heart, that work'd below,
Rain'd thro' my sight its overflow.

Again the voice spake unto me:
'Thou art so steep'd in misery,
Surely 't were better not to be.

'Thine anguish will not let thee sleep,
Nor any train of reason keep;
Thou canst not think, but thou wilt weep.'

I said: 'The years with change advance;
If I make dark my countenance,
I shut my life from happier chance.

'Some turn this sickness yet might take,
Even yet.' But he: 'What drug can make
A wither'd palsy cease to shake?'

I wept: 'Tho' I should die, I know
That all about the thorn will blow
In tufts of rosy-tinted snow;

'And men, thro' novel spheres of thought
Still moving after truth long sought,
Will learn new things when I am not.'

'Yet,' said the secret voice, 'some time,
Sooner or later, will gray prime
Make thy grass hoar with early rime.

'Not less swift souls that yearn for light,
Rapt after heaven's starry flight,
Would sweep the tracts of day and night.

'Not less the bee would range her cells,
The furzy prickle fire the dells,
The foxglove cluster dappled bells.'

I said that 'all the years invent;
Each month is various to present
The world with some development.

'Were this not well, to bide mine hour,
Tho' watching from a ruin'd tower
How grows the day of human power?'

'The highest-mounted mind,' he said,
'Still sees the sacred morning spread
The silent summit overhead.

'Will thirty seasons render plain
Those lonely lights that still remain,
Just breaking over land and main?

'Or make that morn, from his cold crown
And crystal silence creeping down,
Flood with full daylight glebe and town?

'Forerun thy peers, thy time, and let
Thy feet, millenniums hence, be set
In midst of knowledge, dream'd not yet.   90

'Thou hast not gain'd a real height,
Nor art thou nearer to the light,
Because the scale is infinite.

' 'T were better not to breathe or speak,
Than cry for strength, remaining weak,
And seem to find, but still to seek.

'Moreover, but to seem to find
Asks what thou lackest, thought resign'd,
A healthy frame, a quiet mind.'

I said: 'When I am gone away,   100
"He dared not tarry," men will say,
Doing dishonor to my clay.'

'This is more vile,' he made reply,
'To breathe and loathe, to live and sigh,
Than once from dread of pain to die.

'Sick art thou—a divided will
Still heaping on the fear of ill
The fear of men, a coward still.

'Do men love thee? Art thou so bound
To men that how thy name may sound   110
Will vex thee lying underground?

'The memory of the wither'd leaf
In endless time is scarce more brief
Than of the garner'd autumn-sheaf.

'Go, vexed spirit, sleep in trust;
The right ear that is fill'd with dust
Hears little of the false or just.'

'Hard task, to pluck resolve,' I cried,
'From emptiness and the waste wide
Of that abyss, or scornful pride!   120

'Nay—rather yet that I could raise
One hope that warm'd me in the days
While still I yearn'd for human praise.

'When, wide in soul and bold of tongue,
Among the tents I paused and sung,
The distant battle flash'd and rung.

'I sung the joyful Pæan clear,
And, sitting, burnish'd without fear
The brand, the buckler, and the spear—

'Waiting to strive a happy strife,   130
To war with falsehood to the knife,
And not to lose the good of life—

'Some hidden principle to move,
To put together, part and prove,
And mete the bounds of hate and love—

'As far as might be, to carve out
Free space for every human doubt,
That the whole mind might orb about—

'To search thro' all I felt or saw,
The springs of life, the depths of awe,   140
And reach the law within the law;

'At least, not rotting like a weed,
But, having sown some generous seed,
Fruitful of further thought and deed,

'To pass, when Life her light withdraws,
Not void of righteous self-applause,
Nor in a merely selfish cause—

'In some good cause, not in mine own,
To perish, wept for, honor'd, known,
And like a warrior overthrown;   150

'Whose eyes are dim with glorious tears,
When, soil'd with noble dust, he hears
His country's war-song thrill his ears:

'Then dying of a mortal stroke,
What time the foeman's line is broke,
And all the war is roll'd in smoke.'

'Yea!' said the voice, 'thy dream was good,
While thou abodest in the bud.
It was the stirring of the blood.

'If Nature put not forth her power   160
About the opening of the flower,
Who is it that could live an hour?

'Then comes the check, the change, the fall,
Pain rises up, old pleasures pall.
There is one remedy for all.

'Yet hadst thou, thro' enduring pain,
Link'd month to month with such a chain
Of knitted purport, all were vain.

'Thou hadst not between death and birth
Dissolved the riddle of the earth.   170
So were thy labor little worth.

'That men with knowledge merely play'd,
I told thee—hardly nigher made,
Tho' scaling slow from grade to grade;

'Much less this dreamer, deaf and blind,
Named man, may hope some truth to find,
That bears relation to the mind.

'For every worm beneath the moon
Draws different threads, and late and soon
Spins, toiling out his own cocoon.   180

'Cry, faint not: either Truth is born
Beyond the polar gleam forlorn,
Or in the gateways of the morn.

'Cry, faint not, climb: the summits slope
Beyond the furthest flights of hope,
Wrapt in dense cloud from base to cope.

'Sometimes a little corner shines,
As over rainy mist inclines
A gleaming crag with belts of pines.

'I will go forward, sayest thou,   190
I shall not fail to find her now.
Look up, the fold is on her brow.

'If straight thy track, or if oblique,
Thou know'st not. Shadows thou dost strike,
Embracing cloud, Ixion-like;

'And owning but a little more
Than beasts, abidest lame and poor,
Calling thyself a little lower

'Than angels. Cease to wail and brawl!
Why inch by inch to darkness crawl?   200
There is one remedy for all.'

'O dull, one-sided voice,' said I,
'Wilt thou make everything a lie,
To flatter me that I may die?

'I know that age to age succeeds,
Blowing a noise of tongues and deeds,
A dust of systems and of creeds.

'I cannot hide that some have striven,
Achieving calm, to whom was given   210
The joy that mixes man with Heaven;

'Who, rowing hard against the stream,
Saw distant gates of Eden gleam,
And did not dream it was a dream;

'But heard, by secret transport led,
Even in the charnels of the dead,
The murmur of the fountain-head—

'Which did accomplish their desire,
Bore and forebore, and did not tire,
Like Stephen, an unquenched fire.

'He heeded not reviling tones,   220
Nor sold his heart to idle moans,
Tho' cursed and scorn'd, and bruised with stones;

'But looking upward, full of grace,
He pray'd, and from a happy place
God's glory smote him on the face.'

The sullen answer slid betwixt:
'Not that the grounds of hope were fix'd,
The elements were kindlier mix'd.'

I said: 'I toil beneath the curse,
But, knowing not the universe,   230
I fear to slide from bad to worse;

'And that, in seeking to undo
One riddle, and to find the true,
I knit a hundred others new;

'Or that this anguish fleeting hence,
Unmanacled from bonds of sense,
Be fix'd and frozen to permanence:

'For I go, weak from suffering here;
Naked I go, and void of cheer:
What is it that I may not fear?'   240

'Consider well,' the voice replied,
'His face, that two hours since hath died;
Wilt thou find passion, pain or pride?

'Will he obey when one commands?
Or answer should one press his hands?
He answers not, nor understands.

'His palms are folded on his breast;
There is no other thing express'd
But long disquiet merged in rest.

'His lips are very mild and meek;   250
Tho' one should smite him on the cheek,
And on the mouth, he will not speak.

'His little daughter, whose sweet face
He kiss'd, taking his last embrace,
Becomes dishonor to her race—

'His sons grow up that bear his name,
Some grow to honor, some to shame,—
But he is chill to praise or blame.

'He will not hear the north-wind rave,
Nor, moaning, household shelter crave   260
From winter rains that beat his grave.

'High up the vapors fold and swim;
About him broods the twilight dim;
The place he knew forgetteth him.'

'If all be dark, vague voice,' I said,
'These things are wrapt in doubt and dread,
Nor canst thou show the dead are dead.

'The sap dries up: the plant declines.
A deeper tale my heart divines.
Know I not death? the outward signs?   270

'I found him when my years were few;
A shadow on the graves I knew,
And darkness in the village yew.

'From grave to grave the shadow crept;
In her still place the morning wept;
Touch'd by his feet the daisy slept.

'The simple senses crown'd his head:
"Omega! thou art Lord," they said,
"We find no motion in the dead!"

'Why, if man rot in dreamless ease,   280
Should that plain fact, as taught by these,
Not make him sure that he shall cease?

'Who forged that other influence,
That heat of inward evidence,
By which he doubts against the sense?

'He owns the fatal gift of eyes,
That read his spirit blindly wise,
Not simple as a thing that dies.

'Here sits he shaping wings to fly;
His heart forebodes a mystery;   290
He names the name Eternity.

'That type of Perfect in his mind
In Nature can he nowhere find.
He sows himself on every wind.

'He seems to hear a Heavenly Friend,
And thro' thick veils to apprehend
A labor working to an end.

'The end and the beginning vex
His reason: many things perplex,
With motions, checks, and counterchecks.   300

'He knows a baseness in his blood,
At such strange war with something good,
He may not do the thing he would.

'Heaven opens inward, chasms yawn,
Vast images in glimmering dawn,
Half shown, are broken and withdrawn.

'Ah! sure within him and without,
Could his dark wisdom find it out,
There must be answer to his doubt,

'But thou canst answer not again.   310
With thine own weapon art thou slain,
Or thou wilt answer but in vain.

'The doubt would rest, I dare not solve.
In the same circle we revolve.
Assurance only breeds resolve.'

As when a billow, blown against,
Falls back, the voice with which I fenced
A little ceased, but recommenced:

'Where wert thou when thy father play'd
In his free field, and pastime made,   320
A merry boy in sun and shade?

'A merry boy they call'd him then,
He sat upon the knees of men
In days that never come again;

'Before the little ducts began
To feed thy bones with lime, and ran
Their course, till thou wert also man;

'Who took a wife, who rear'd his race,
Whose wrinkles gather'd on his face,
Whose troubles number with his days;   330

'A life of nothings, nothing worth,
From that first nothing ere his birth
To that last nothing under earth!'

'These words,' I said, 'are like the rest;
No certain clearness, but at best
A vague suspicion of the breast:

'But if I grant, thou mightst defend
The thesis which thy words intend—
That to begin implies to end;

'Yet how should I for certain hold,   340
Because my memory is so cold,
That I first was in human mould?

'I cannot make this matter plain,
But I would shoot, howe'er in vain,
A random arrow from the brain.

'It may be that no life is found,
Which only to one engine bound
Falls off, but cycles always round.

'As old mythologies relate,
Some draught of Lethe might await   350
The slipping thro' from state to state;

'As here we find in trances, men
Forget the dream that happens then,
Until they fall in trance again;

'So might we, if our state were such
As one before, remember much,
For those two likes might meet and touch.

'But, if I lapsed from nobler place,
Some legend of a fallen race
Alone might hint of my disgrace;   360

'Some vague emotion of delight
In gazing up an Alpine height,
Some yearning toward the lamps of night;

'Or if thro' lower lives I came—
Tho' all experience past became
Consolidate in mind and frame—

'I might forget my weaker lot;
For is not our first year forgot?
The haunts of memory echo not.

'And men, whose reason long was blind,   370
From cells of madness unconfined,
Oft lose whole years of darker mind.

'Much more, if first I floated free,
As naked essence, must I be
Incompetent of memory;

'For memory dealing but with time,
And he with matter, could she climb
Beyond her own material prime?

'Moreover, something is or seems,
That touches me with mystic gleams,
Like glimpses of forgotten dreams—   380

'Of something felt, like something here;
Of something done, I know not where;
Such as no language may declare.'

The still voice laugh'd. 'I talk,' said he,
'Not with thy dreams. Suffice it thee
Thy pain is a reality.'

'But thou,' said I, 'hast missed thy mark,
Who sought'st to wreck my mortal ark,
By making all the horizon dark.   390

'Why not set forth, if I should do
This rashness, that which might ensue
With this old soul in organs new?

'Whatever crazy sorrow saith,
No life that breathes with human breath
Has ever truly long'd for death.

' 'T is life, whereof our nerves are scant,
O, life, not death, for which we pant;
More life, and fuller, that I want.'

I ceased, and sat as one forlorn.   400
Then said the voice, in quiet scorn,
'Behold, it is the Sabbath morn.'

And I arose, and I released
The casement, and the light increased
With freshness in the dawning east.

Like soften'd airs that blowing steal,
When meres begin to uncongeal,
The sweet church bells began to peal.

On to God's house the people prest;
Passing the place where each must rest,   410
Each enter'd like a welcome guest.

One walk'd between his wife and child,
With measured footfall firm and mild,
And now and then he gravely smiled.

The prudent partner of his blood
Lean'd on him, faithful, gentle, good,
Wearing the rose of womanhood.

And in their double love secure,
The little maiden walk'd demure,
Pacing with downward eyelids pure.   420

These three made unity so sweet,
My frozen heart began to beat,
Remembering its ancient heat.

I blest them, and they wander'd on;
I spoke, but answer came there none;
The dull and bitter voice was gone.

A second voice was at mine ear,
A little whisper silver-clear,
A murmur, 'Be of better cheer.'

As from some blissful neighborhood,   430
A notice faintly understood,
'I see the end, and know the good.'

A little hint to solace woe,
A hint, a whisper breathing low,
'I may not speak of what I know.'

Like an Æolian harp that wakes
No certain air, but overtakes
Far thought with music that it makes;

Such seem'd the whisper at my side:
'What is it thou knowest, sweet voice?' I cried.   440
'A hidden hope,' the voice replied;

So heavenly-toned, that in that hour
From out my sullen heart a power
Broke, like the rainbow from the shower,

To feel, altho' no tongue can prove,
That every cloud, that spreads above
And veileth love, itself is love.

And forth into the fields I went,
And Nature's living motion lent
The pulse of hope to discontent.   450

I wonder'd at the bounteous hours,
The slow result of winter showers;
You scarce could see the grass for flowers.

I wonder'd, while I paced along;
The woods were fill'd so full with song,
There seem'd no room for sense of wrong;

And all so variously wrought,
I marvell'd how the mind was brought
To anchor by one gloomy thought;

And wherefore rather I made choice   460
To commune with that barren voice,
Than him that said, 'Rejoice! Rejoice!'

THE MILLER'S DAUGHTER

I SEE the wealthy miller yet,
    His double chin, his portly size,
And who that knew him could forget
    The busy wrinkles round his eyes?
The slow wise smile that, round about
    His dusty forehead drily curl'd,
Seem'd half-within and half-without,
    And full of dealings with the world?

In yonder chair I see him sit,
    Three fingers round the old silver cup—
I see his gray eyes twinkle yet   10
    At his own jest—gray eyes lit up
With summer lightnings of a soul
    So full of summer warmth, so glad,
So healthy, sound, and clear and whole,
    His memory scarce can make me sad.

Yet fill my glass; give me one kiss:
    My own sweet Alice, we must die.
There's somewhat in this world amiss

Shall be unriddled by and by.
There's somewhat flows to us in life,
    But more is taken quite away.
Pray, Alice, pray, my darling wife,
    That we may die the self-same day.

Have I not found a happy earth?
    I least should breathe a thought of pain
Would God renew me from my birth,
    I'd almost live my life again;
So sweet it seems with thee to walk,
    And once again to woo thee mine—
It seems in after-dinner talk
    Across the walnuts and the wine—

To be the long and listless boy
    Late-left an orphan of the squire,
Where this old mansion mounted high
    Looks down upon the village spire;
For even here, where I and you
    Have lived and loved alone so long,
Each morn my sleep was broken thro'
    By some wild skylark's matin song.

And oft I heard the tender dove
    In firry woodlands making moan;
But ere I saw your eyes, my love,
    I had no motion of my own.
For scarce my life with fancy play'd
    Before I dream'd that pleasant dream—
Still hither thither idly sway'd
    Like those long mosses in the stream.

Or from the bridge I lean'd to hear
    The milldam rushing down with noise,
And see the minnows everywhere
    In crystal eddies glance and poise,
The tall flag-flowers when they sprung
    Below the range of stepping-stones,
Or those three chestnuts near, that hung
    In masses thick with milky cones.

But, Alice, what an hour was that,
    When after roving in the woods
('T was April then), I came and sat
    Below the chestnuts, when their buds
Were glistening to the breezy blue;
    And on the slope, an absent fool,

30

40

50

60

I cast me down, nor thought of you,
    But angled in the higher pool.

A love-song I had somewhere read,
    An echo from a measured strain,
Beat time to nothing in my head
    From some odd corner of the brain.
It haunted me, the morning long,
    With weary sameness in the rhymes,   70
The phantom of a silent song,
    That went and came a thousand times.

Then leapt a trout. In lazy mood
    I watch'd the little circles die;
They past into the level flood,
    And there a vision caught my eye;
The reflex of a beauteous form,
    A glowing arm, a gleaming neck,
As when a sunbeam wavers warm
    Within the dark and dimpled beck.   80

For you remember, you had set,
    That morning, on the casement-edge
A long green box of mignonette,
    And you were leaning from the ledge;
And when I raised my eyes, above
    They met with two so full and bright—
Such eyes! I swear to you, my love,
    That these have never lost their light.

I loved, and love dispell'd the fear
    That I should die an early death;   90
For love possess'd the atmosphere,
    And fill'd the breast with purer breath.
My mother thought, What ails the boy?
    For I was alter'd, and began
To move about the house with joy,
    And with the certain step of man.

I loved the brimming wave that swam
    Thro' quiet meadows round the mill,
The sleepy pool above the dam,
    The pool beneath it never still,   100
The meal-sacks on the whiten'd floor,
    The dark round of the dripping wheel,
The very air about the door
    Made misty with the floating meal.

And oft in ramblings on the wold,
   When April nights began to blow,
And April's crescent glimmer'd cold,
   I saw the village lights below;
I knew your taper far away,
   And full at heart of trembling hope,   110
From off the wold I came, and lay
   Upon the freshly-flower'd slope.

The deep brook groan'd beneath the mill;
   And 'by that lamp,' I thought, 'she sits!'
The white chalk-quarry from the hill
   Gleam'd to the flying moon by fits.
'O, that I were beside her now!
   O, will she answer if I call?
O, would she give me vow for vow,
   Sweet Alice, if I told her all?'   120

Sometimes I saw you sit and spin;
   And, in the pauses of the wind,
Sometimes I heard you sing within;
   Sometimes your shadow cross'd the blind.
At last you rose and moved the light,
   And the long shadow of the chair
Flitted across into the night,
   And all the casement darken'd there.

But when at last I dared to speak,
   The lanes, you know, were white with may;   130
Your ripe lips moved not, but your cheek
   Flush'd like the coming of the day;
And so it was—half-sly, half-shy,
   You would, and would not, little one!
Although I pleaded tenderly,
   And you and I were all alone.

And slowly was my mother brought
   To yield consent to my desire:
She wish'd me happy, but she thought
   I might have look'd a little higher;   140
And I was young—too young to wed:
   'Yet must I love her for your sake;
Go fetch your Alice here,' she said:
   Her eyelid quiver'd as she spake.

And down I went to fetch my bride:
   But, Alice, you were ill at ease;
This dress and that by turns you tried,

Too fearful that you should not please.
I loved you better for your fears,
   I knew you could not look but well;   **150**
And dews, that would have fallen in tears,
   I kiss'd away before they fell.

I watch'd the little flutterings,
   The doubt my mother would not see;
She spoke at large of many things,
   And at the last she spoke of me;
And turning look'd upon your face,
   As near this door you sat apart,
And rose, and, with a silent grace
   Approaching, press'd you heart to heart.   **160**

Ah, well—but sing the foolish song
   I gave you, Alice, on the day
When, arm in arm, we went along,
   A pensive pair, and you were gay
With bridal flowers—that I may seem,
   As in the nights of old, to lie
Beside the mill-wheel in the stream,
   While those full chestnuts whisper by.

  It is the miller's daughter,
    And she is grown so dear, so dear,   **170**
  That I would be the jewel
    That trembles in her ear;
  For hid in ringlets day and night,
  I'd touch her neck so warm and white.

  And I would be the girdle
    About her dainty dainty waist,
  And her heart would beat against me,
    In sorrow and in rest;
  And I should know if it beat right,
  I'd clasp it round so close and tight.   **180**

  And I would be the necklace,
    And all day long to fall and rise
  Upon her balmy bosom,
    With her laughter or her sighs;
  And I would lie so light, so light,
  I scarce should be unclasp'd at night.

A trifle, sweet! which true love spells—
   True love interprets—right alone.
His light upon the letter dwells,
   For all the spirit is his own.   **190**
So, if I waste words now, in truth
   You must blame Love. His early rage

Had force to make me rhyme in youth,
   And makes me talk too much in age.

And now those vivid hours are gone,
   Like mine own life to me thou art,
Where Past and Present, wound in one,
   Do make a garland for the heart;
So sing that other song I made,
   Half-anger'd with my happy lot,   200
The day, when in the chestnut shade
   I found the blue forget-me-not.

      Love that hath us in the net,
      Can he pass, and we forget?
      Many suns arise and set;
      Many a chance the years beget;
      Love the gift is Love the debt.
            Even so.
      Love is hurt with jar and fret;
      Love is made a vague regret;   210
      Eyes with idle tears are wet;
      Idle habit links us yet.
      What is love? for we forget:
            Ah, no! no!

Look thro' mine eyes with thine. True wife,
   Round my true heart thine arms entwine;
My other dearer life in life,
   Look thro' my very soul with thine!
Untouch'd with any shade of years,
   May those kind eyes for ever dwell!   220
They have not shed a many tears,
   Dear eyes, since first I knew them well.

Yet tears they shed; they had their part
   Of sorrow; for when time was ripe,
The still affection of the heart,
   Became an outward breathing type,
That into stillness past again,
   And left a want unknown before;
Although the loss had brought us pain,
   That loss but made us love the more,   230

With farther lookings on. The kiss,
   The woven arms, seem but to be
Weak symbols of the settled bliss,
   The comfort, I have found in thee;
But that God bless thee, dear—who wrought
   Two spirits to one equal mind—
With blessings beyond hope or thought,
   With blessings which no words can find.

Arise, and let us wander forth
    To yon old mill across the wolds;
For look, the sunset, south and north,
    Winds all the vale in rosy folds,
And fires your narrow casement glass,
    Touching the sullen pool below;
On the chalk-hill the bearded grass
    Is dry and dewless. Let us go.

240

FATIMA

Φαινεταί μοι κῆνος ἴσος θεοῖσιν
Ἔμμεν ἀνήρ.—SAPPHO.

O Love, Love, Love! O withering might!
O sun, that from thy noonday height
Shudderest when I strain my sight,
Throbbing thro' all thy heat and light,
    Lo, falling from my constant mind,
    Lo, parch'd and wither'd, deaf and blind,
    I whirl like leaves in roaring wind.

Last night I wasted hateful hours
Below the city's eastern towers;
I thirsted for the brooks, the showers;
I roll'd among the tender flowers;
    I crush'd them on my breast, my mouth;
    I look'd athwart the burning drouth
    Of that long desert to the south.

Last night, when some one spoke his name,
From my swift blood that went and came
A thousand little shafts of flame
Were shiver'd in my narrow frame.
    O Love, O fire! once he drew
    With one long kiss my whole soul thro'
    My lips, as sunlight drinketh dew.

Before he mounts the hill, I know
He cometh quickly; from below
Sweet gales, as from deep gardens, blow
Before him, striking on my brow.
    In my dry brain my spirit soon,
    Down-deepening from swoon to swoon,
    Faints like a dazzled morning moon.

The wind sounds like a silver wire,
And from beyond the noon a fire

Is pour'd upon the hills, and nigher
The skies stoop down in their desire;
   And, isled in sudden seas of light,
   My heart, pierced thro' with fierce delight,
   Burst into blossom in his sight.

My whole soul waiting silently,
All naked in a sultry sky,
Droops blinded with his shining eye;
I *will* possess him or will die.
   I will grow round him in his place,
   Grow, live, die looking on his face,
   Die, dying clasp'd in his embrace.

ŒNONE

THERE lies a vale in Ida, lovelier
Than all the valleys of Ionian hills.
The swimming vapor slopes athwart the glen,
Puts forth an arm, and creeps from pine to pine,
And loiters, slowly drawn. On either hand
The lawns and meadow-ledges midway down
Hang rich in flowers, and far below them roars
The long brook falling thro' the cloven ravine
In cataract after cataract to the sea.
Behind the valley topmost Gargarus   10
Stands up and takes the morning; but in front
The gorges, opening wide apart, reveal
Troas and Ilion's column'd citadel,
The crown of Troas.
             Hither came at noon
Mournful Œnone, wandering forlorn
Of Paris, once her playmate on the hills.
Her cheek had lost the rose, and round her neck
Floated her hair or seem'd to float in rest.
She, leaning on a fragment twined with vine,
Sang to the stillness, till the mountain-shade   20
Sloped downward to her seat from the upper cliff.

   'O mother Ida, many-fountain'd Ida,
Dear mother Ida, harken ere I die.
For now the noonday quiet holds the hill;
The grasshopper is silent in the grass;
The lizard, with his shadow on the stone,
Rests like a shadow, and the winds are dead.
The purple flower droops, the golden bee
Is lily-cradled; I alone awake.

My eyes are full of tears, my heart of love,   30
My heart is breaking, and my eyes are dim,
And I am all aweary of my life.

   'O mother Ida, many-fountain'd Ida,
Dear mother Ida, harken ere I die.
Hear me, O earth, hear me, O hills, O caves
That house the cold crown'd snake! O mountain brooks,
I am the daughter of a River-God,
Hear me, for I will speak, and build up all
My sorrow with my song, as yonder walls
Rose slowly to a music slowly breathed,   40
A cloud that gather'd shape; for it may be
That, while I speak of it, a little while
My heart may wander from its deeper woe.

   'O mother Ida, many-fountain'd Ida,
Dear mother Ida, harken ere I die.
I waited underneath the dawning hills;
Aloft the mountain lawn was dewy-dark,
And dewy dark aloft the mountain pine.
Beautiful Paris, evil-hearted Paris,
Leading a jet-black goat white-horn'd, white-hooved,   50
Came up from reedy Simois all alone.

   'O mother Ida, harken ere I die.
Far-off the torrent call'd me from the cleft;
Far up the solitary morning smote
The streaks of virgin snow. With down-dropt eyes
I sat alone; white-breasted like a star
Fronting the dawn he moved; a leopard skin
Droop'd from his shoulder, but his sunny hair
Cluster'd about his temples like a God's;
And his cheek brighten'd as the foam-bow brightens   60
When the wind blows the foam, and all my heart
Went forth to embrace him coming ere he came.

   'Dear mother Ida, harken ere I die.
He smiled, and opening out his milk-white palm
Disclosed a fruit of pure Hesperian gold,
That smelt ambrosially, and while I look'd
And listen'd, the full-flowing river of speech
Came down upon my heart:
                ' "My own Œnone,
Beautiful-brow'd Œnone, my own soul,
Behold this fruit, whose gleaming rind ingraven   70
'For the most fair,' would seem to award it thine,
As lovelier than whatever Oread haunt

The knolls of Ida, loveliest in all grace
Of movement, and the charm of married brows."

'Dear mother Ida, harken ere I die.
He prest the blossom of his lips to mine,
And added, "This was cast upon the board,
When all the full-faced presence of the Gods
Ranged in the halls of Peleus; whereupon
Rose feud, with question unto whom 't were due;
But light-foot Iris brought it yester-eve,
Delivering, that to me, by common voice
Elected umpire, Herè comes to-day,
Pallas and Aphrodite, claiming each
This meed of fairest. Thou, within the cave
Behind yon whispering tuft of oldest pine
Mayst well behold them unbeheld, unheard
Hear all, and see thy Paris judge of Gods."

'Dear mother Ida, harken ere I die.
It was the deep midnoon; one silvery cloud
Had lost his way between the piny sides
Of this long glen. Then to the bower they came,
Naked they came to that smooth-swarded bower,
And at their feet the crocus brake like fire,
Violet, amaracus, and asphodel,
Lotos and lilies; and a wind arose,
And overhead the wandering ivy and vine,
This way and that, in many a wild festoon
Ran riot, garlanding the gnarled boughs
With bunch and berry and flower thro' and thro'.

'O mother Ida, harken ere I die.
On the tree-tops a crested peacock lit,
And o'er him flow'd a golden cloud, and lean'd
Upon him, slowly dropping fragrant dew.
Then first I heard the voice of her to whom
Coming thro' heaven, like a light that grows
Larger and clearer, with one mind the Gods
Rise up for reverence. She to Paris made
Proffer of royal power, ample rule
Unquestion'd, overflowing revenue
Wherewith to embellish state, "from many a vale
And river-sunder'd champaign clothed with corn,
Or labor'd mine undrainable of ore.
Honor," she said, "and homage, tax and toll
From many an inland town and haven large,
Mast-throng'd beneath her shadowing citadel
In glassy bays among her tallest towers."

'O mother Ida, harken ere I die.
Still she spake on and still she spake of power,
"Which in all action is the end of all;   120
Power fitted to the season; wisdom-bred
And throned of wisdom—from all neighbor crowns
Alliance and allegiance, till thy hand
Fail from the sceptre-staff. Such boon from me,
From me, heaven's queen, Paris, to thee king-born,
A shepherd all thy life but yet king-born,
Should come most welcome, seeing men, in power
Only, are likest Gods, who have attain'd
Rest in a happy place and quiet seats
Above the thunder, with undying bliss   130
In knowledge of their own supremacy."

'Dear mother Ida, harken ere I die.
She ceased, and Paris held the costly fruit
Out at arm's-length, so much the thought of power
Flatter'd his spirit; but Pallas where she stood
Somewhat apart, her clear and bared limbs
O'erthwarted with the brazen-headed spear
Upon her pearly shoulder leaning cold,
The while, above, her full and earnest eye
Over her snow-cold breast and angry cheek   140
Kept watch, waiting decision, made reply:

' "Self-reverence, self-knowledge, self-control,
These three alone lead life to sovereign power.
Yet not for power (power of herself
Would come uncall'd for) but to live by law,
Acting the law we live by without fear;
And, because right is right, to follow right
Were wisdom in the scorn of consequence."

'Dear mother Ida, harken ere I die.
Again she said: "I woo thee not with gifts.   150
Sequel of guerdon could not alter me
To fairer. Judge thou me by what I am,
So shalt thou find me fairest.
                           Yet, indeed,
If gazing on divinity disrobed
Thy mortal eyes are frail to judge of fair,
Unbias'd by self-profit, O, rest thee sure
That I shall love thee well and cleave to thee,
So that my vigor, wedded to thy blood,
Shall strike within thy pulses, like a God's,
To push thee forward thro' a life of shocks,   160
Dangers, and deeds, until endurance grow

Sinew'd with action, and the full-grown will,
Circled thro' all experiences, pure law,
Commeasure perfect freedom."

'Here she ceas'd,
And Paris ponder'd, and I cried, "O Paris,
Give it to Pallas!" but he heard me not,
Or hearing would not hear me, woe is me!

'O mother Ida, many-fountain'd Ida,
Dear mother Ida, harken ere I die.
Idalian Aphrodite beautiful,   170
Fresh as the foam, new-bathed in Paphian wells,
With rosy slender fingers backward drew
From her warm brows and bosom her deep hair
Ambrosial, golden round her lucid throat
And shoulder; from the violets her light foot
Shone rosy-white, and o'er her rounded form
Between the shadows of the vine-bunches
Floated the glowing sunlights, as she moved.

'Dear mother Ida, harken ere I die.
She with a subtle smile in her mild eyes,   180
The herald of her triumph, drawing nigh
Half-whisper'd in his ear, "I promise thee
The fairest and most loving wife in Greece."
She spoke and laugh'd; I shut my sight for fear;
But when I look'd, Paris had raised his arm,
And I beheld great Herè's angry eyes,
As she withdrew into the golden cloud,
And I was left alone within the bower;
And from that time to this I am alone,
And I shall be alone until I die.   190

'Yet, mother Ida, harken ere I die.
Fairest—why fairest wife? am I not fair?
My love hath told me so a thousand times.
Methinks I must be fair, for yesterday,
When I past by, a wild and wanton pard,
Eyed like the evening star, with playful tail
Crouch'd fawning in the weed. Most loving is she?
Ah me, my mountain shepherd, that my arms
Were wound about thee, and my hot lips prest
Close, close to thine in that quick-falling dew   200
Of fruitful kisses, thick as autumn rains
Flash in the pools of whirling Simois!

'O mother, hear me yet before I die.
They came, they cut away my tallest pines,
My tall dark pines, that plumed the craggy ledge,

High over the blue gorge, and all between
The snowy peak and snow-white cataract
Foster'd the callow eaglet—from beneath
Whose thick mysterious boughs in the dark morn
The panther's roar came muffled, while I sat   210
Low in the valley. Never, never more
Shall lone Œnone see the morning mist
Sweep thro' them; never see them overlaid
With narrow moonlit slips of silver cloud,
Between the loud stream and the trembling stars.

   'O mother, hear me yet before I die.
I wish that somewhere in the ruin'd folds,
Among the fragments tumbled from the glens,
Or the dry thickets, I could meet with her
The Abominable, that uninvited came   220
Into the fair Peleïan banquet-hall,
And cast the golden fruit upon the board,
And bred this change; that I might speak my mind,
And tell her to her face how much I hate
Her presence, hated both of Gods and men.

   'O mother, hear me yet before I die.
Hath he not sworn his love a thousand times,
In this green valley, under this green hill,
Even on this hand, and sitting on this stone?
Seal'd it with kisses? water'd it with tears?   230
O happy tears, and how unlike to these!
O happy heaven, how canst thou see my face?
O happy earth, how canst thou bear my weight?
O death, death, death, thou ever-floating cloud,
There are enough unhappy on this earth,
Pass by the happy souls, that love to live;
I pray thee, pass before my light of life,
And shadow all my soul, that I may die.
Thou weighest heavy on the heart within,
Weigh heavy on my eyelids; let me die.   240

   'O mother, hear me yet before I die.
I will not die alone, for fiery thoughts
Do shape themselves within me, more and more,
Whereof I catch the issue, as I hear
Dead sounds at night come from the inmost hills,
Like footsteps upon wool. I dimly see
My far-off doubtful purpose, as a mother
Conjectures of the features of her child
Ere it is born. Her child!—a shudder comes

Across me: never child be born of me,
Unblest, to vex me with his father's eyes!

'O mother, hear me yet before I die.
Hear me, O earth. I will not die alone,
Lest their shrill happy laughter come to me
Walking the cold and starless road of death
Uncomforted, leaving my ancient love
With the Greek woman. I will rise and go
Down into Troy, and ere the stars come forth
Talk with the wild Cassandra, for she says
A fire dances before her, and a sound
Rings ever in her ears of armed men.
What this may be I know not, but I know
That, whereso'er I am by night and day,
All earth and air seem only burning fire.'

THE SISTERS

WE were two daughters of one race;
She was the fairest in the face.
   The wind is howling in turret and tree.
They were together, and she fell;
Therefore revenge became me well.
   O, the earl was fair to see!

She died; she went to burning flame;
She mix'd her ancient blood with shame.
   The wind is howling in turret and tree.
Whole weeks and months, and early and late,
To win his love I lay in wait.
   O, the earl was fair to see!

I made a feast; I bade him come;
I won his love, I brought him home.
   The wind is roaring in turret and tree.
And after supper, on a bed,
Upon my lap he laid his head.
   O, the earl was fair to see!

I kiss'd his eyelids into rest,
His ruddy cheek upon my breast.
   The wind is roaring in turret and tree.
I hated him with the hate of hell,
But I loved his beauty passing well.
   O, the earl was fair to see!

I rose up in the silent night;
I made my dagger sharp and bright.
  The wind is raving in turret and tree.
As half-asleep his breath he drew,
Three times I stabb'd him thro' and thro'.
  O, the earl was fair to see!

I curl'd and com'b his comely head,
He look'd so grand when he was dead.
  The wind is blowing in turret and tree.
I wrap't his body in the sheet,
And laid him at his mother's feet.
  O, the earl was fair to see!

TO ——

WITH THE FOLLOWING POEM

I SEND you here a sort of allegory—
For you will understand it—of a soul,
A sinful soul possess'd of many gifts,
A spacious garden full of flowering weeds,
A glorious devil, large in heart and brain,
That did love beauty only—beauty seen
In all varieties of mould and mind—
And knowledge for its beauty; or if good,
Good only for its beauty, seeing not
That Beauty, Good, and Knowledge are three sisters
That doat upon each other, friends to man,
Living together under the same roof,
And never can be sunder'd without tears.
And he that shuts Love out, in turn shall be
Shut out from Love, and on her threshold lie
Howling in outer darkness. Not for this
Was common clay ta'en from the common earth
Moulded by God, and temper'd with the tears
Of angels to the perfect shape of man.

THE PALACE OF ART

I BUILT my soul a lordly pleasure-house,
  Wherein at ease for aye to dwell.
I said, 'O Soul, make merry and carouse,
  Dear soul, for all is well.'

A huge crag-platform, smooth as burnish'd brass,
    I chose. The ranged ramparts bright
From level meadow-bases of deep grass
    Suddenly scaled the light.

Thereon I built it firm. Of ledge or shelf
    The rock rose clear, or winding stair.   10
My soul would live alone unto herself
    In her high palace there.

And 'while the world runs round and round,' I said
    'Reign thou apart, a quiet king,
Still as, while Saturn whirls, his steadfast shade
    Sleeps on his luminous ring.'

To which my soul made answer readily:
    'Trust me, in bliss I shall abide
In this great mansion, that is built for me,
    So royal-rich and wide.'   20

.   .   .   .   .   .

Four courts I made, East, West and South and North,
    In each a squared lawn, wherefrom
The golden gorge of dragons spouted forth
    A flood of fountain-foam.

And round the cool green courts there ran a row
    Of cloisters, branch'd like mighty woods,
Echoing all night to that sonorous flow
    Of spouted fountain-floods;

And round the roofs a gilded gallery
    That lent broad verge to distant lands,   30
Far as the wild swan wings, to where the sky
    Dipt down to sea and sands.

From those four jets four currents in one swell
    Across the mountain stream'd below
In misty folds, that floating as they fell
    Lit up a torrent-bow.

And high on every peak a statue seem'd
    To hang on tiptoe, tossing up
A cloud of incense of all odor steam'd
    From out a golden cup.   40

So that she thought, 'And who shall gaze upon
    My palace with unblinded eyes,

While this great bow will waver in the sun,
    And that sweet incense rise?'

For that sweet incense rose and never fail'd,
    And, while day sank or mounted higher,
The light aerial gallery, golden-rail'd,
    Burnt like a fringe of fire.

Likewise the deep-set windows, stain'd and traced,
    Would seem slow-flaming crimson fires   50
From shadow'd grots of arches interlaced,
    And tipt with frost-like spires.

Full of long-sounding corridors it was,
    That over-vaulted grateful gloom,
Thro' which the livelong day my soul did pass,
    Well-pleased, from room to room.

Full of great rooms and small the palace stood,
    All various, each a perfect whole
From living Nature, fit for every mood
    And change of my still soul.   60

For some were hung with arras green and blue,
    Showing a gaudy summer-morn,
Where with puff'd cheek the belted hunter blew
    His wreathed bugle-horn.

One seem'd all dark and red—a tract of sand,
    And some one pacing there alone,
Who paced for ever in a glimmering land,
    Lit with a low large moon.

One show'd an iron coast and angry waves.
    You seem'd to hear them climb and fall   70
And roar rock-thwarted under bellowing caves,
    Beneath the windy wall.

And one, a full-fed river winding slow
    By herds upon an endless plain,
The ragged rims of thunder brooding low,
    With shadow-streaks of rain.

And one, the reapers at their sultry toil.
    In front they bound the sheaves. Behind
Were realms of upland, prodigal in oil,
    And hoary to the wind.   80

And one a foreground black with stones and slags;
   Beyond, a line of heights; and higher
All barr'd with long white cloud the scornful crags;
   And highest, snow and fire.

And one, an English home—gray twilight pour'd
   On dewy pastures, dewy trees,
Softer than sleep—all things in order stored,
   A haunt of ancient Peace.

Nor these alone, but every landscape fair,
   As fit for every mood of mind,   90
Or gay, or grave, or sweet, or stern, was there,
   Not less than truth design'd.

Or the maid-mother by a crucifix,
   In tracts of pasture sunny-warm,
Beneath branch-work of costly sardonyx
   Sat smiling, babe in arm.

Or in a clear-wall'd city on the sea,
   Near gilded organ-pipes, her hair
Wound with white roses, slept Saint Cecily;
   An angel look'd at her.   100

Or thronging all one porch of Paradise
   A group of Houris bow'd to see
The dying Islamite, with hands and eyes
   That said, We wait for thee.

Or mythic Uther's deeply-wounded son
   In some fair space of sloping greens
Lay, dozing in the vale of Avalon,
   And watch'd by weeping queens.

Or hollowing one hand against his ear,
   To list a foot-fall, ere he saw   110
The wood-nymph, stay'd the Ausonian king to hear
   Of wisdom and of law.

Or over hills with peaky tops engrail'd,
   And many a tract of palm and rice,
The throne of Indian Cama slowly sail'd
   A summer fann'd with spice.

Or sweet Europa's mantle blew unclasp'd,
   From off her shoulder backward borne;

From one hand droop'd a crocus; one hand grasp'd
    The mild bull's golden horn.   120

Or else flush'd Ganymede, his rosy thigh
    Half-buried in the eagle's down,
Sole as a flying star shot thro' the sky
    Above the pillar'd town.

Nor these alone; but every legend fair
    Which the supreme Caucasian mind
Carved out of Nature for itself was there,
    Not less than life design'd.

    .   .   .   .   .   .

Then in the towers I placed great bells that swung,
    Moved of themselves, with silver sound;   130
And with choice paintings of wise men I hung
    The royal dais round.

For there was Milton like a seraph strong,
    Beside him Shakespeare bland and mild;
And there the world-worn Dante grasp'd his song,
    And somewhat grimly smiled.

And there the Ionian father of the rest;
    A million wrinkles carved his skin;
A hundred winters snow'd upon his breast,
    From cheek and throat and chin.   140

Above, the fair hall-ceiling stately-set
    Many an arch high up did lift,
And angels rising and descending met
    With interchange of gift.

Below was all mosaic choicely plann'd
    With cycles of the human tale
Of this wide world, the times of every land
    So wrought they will not fail.

The people here, a beast of burden slow,
    Toil'd onward, prick'd with goads and stings;   150
Here play'd, a tiger, rolling to and fro
    The heads and crowns of kings;

Here rose, an athlete, strong to break or bind
    All force in bonds that might endure,
And here once more like some sick man declined,
    And trusted any cure.

But over these she trod; and those great bells
   Began to chime. She took her throne;
She sat betwixt the shining oriels,
    To sing her songs alone.   160

And thro' the topmost oriels' colored flame
   Two godlike faces gazed below;
Plato the wise, and large-brow'd Verulam,
    The first of those who know.

And all those names that in their motion were
   Full-welling fountain-heads of change,
Betwixt the slender shafts were blazon'd fair
    In diverse raiment strange;

Thro' which the lights, rose, amber, emerald, blue,
   Flush'd in her temples and her eyes,   170
And from her lips, as morn from Memnon, drew
    Rivers of melodies.

No nightingale delighteth to prolong
   Her low preamble all alone,
More than my soul to hear her echo'd song
    Throb thro' the ribbed stone;

Singing and murmuring in her feastful mirth,
   Joying to feel herself alive,
Lord over Nature, lord of the visible earth,
    Lord of the senses five;   180

Communing with herself: 'All these are mine,
   And let the world have peace or wars,
'T is one to me.' She—when young night divine
    Crown'd dying day with stars,

Making sweet close of his delicious toils—
   Lit light in wreaths and anadems,
And pure quintessences of precious oils
    In hallow'd moons of gems,

To mimic heaven; and clapt her hands and cried,
   'I marvel if my still delight   190
In this great house so royal-rich and wide
    Be flatter'd to the height.

'O all things fair to sate my various eyes!
   O shapes and hues that please me well!

O silent faces of the Great and Wise,
　My Gods, with whom I dwell!

'O Godlike isolation which art mine,
　I can but count thee perfect gain,
What time I watch the darkening droves of swine
　That range on yonder plain.   200

'In filthy sloughs they roll a prurient skin,
　They graze and wallow, breed and sleep;
And oft some brainless devil enters in,
　And drives them to the deep.'

Then of the moral instinct would she prate
　And of the rising from the dead,
As hers by right of full-accomplish'd Fate;
　And at the last she said:

'I take possession of man's mind and deed.
　I care not what the sects may brawl.   210
I sit as God holding no form of creed,
　But contemplating all.'

　　　·　·　·　·　·　·

Full oft the riddle of the painful earth
　Flash'd thro' her as she sat alone,
Yet not the less held she her solemn mirth,
　And intellectual throne.

And so she throve and prosper'd; so three years
　She prosper'd; on the fourth she fell,
Like Herod, when the shout was in his ears,
　Struck thro' with pangs of hell.   220

Lest she should fail and perish utterly,
　God, before whom ever lie bare
The abysmal deeps of personality,
　Plagued her with sore despair.

When she would think, where'er she turn'd her sight
　The airy hand confusion wrought,
Wrote, 'Mene, mene,' and divided quite
　The kingdom of her thought.

Deep dread and loathing of her solitude
　Fell on her, from which mood was born   230
Scorn of herself; again, from out that mood
　Laughter at her self-scorn.

'What! is not this my place of strength,' she said,
   'My spacious mansion built for me,
Whereof the strong foundation-stones were laid
    Since my first memory?'

But in dark corners of her palace stood
   Uncertain shapes; and unawares
On white-eyed phantasms weeping tears of blood,
    And horrible nightmares,   240

And hollow shades enclosing hearts of flame,
   And, with dim fretted foreheads all,
On corpses three-months-old at noon she came,
    That stood against the wall.

A spot of dull stagnation, without light
   Or power of movement, seem'd my soul,
Mid onward-sloping motions infinite
    Making for one sure goal;

A still salt pool, lock'd in with bars of sand,
   Left on the shore, that hears all night   250
The plunging seas draw backward from the land
    Their moon-led waters white;

A star that with the choral starry dance
   Join'd not, but stood, and standing saw
The hollow orb of moving Circumstance
    Roll'd round by one fix'd law.

Back on herself her serpent pride had curl'd.
   'No voice,' she shriek'd in that lone hall,
'No voice breaks thro' the stillness of this world;   260
    One deep, deep silence all!'

She, mouldering with the dull earth's mouldering sod,
   Inwrapt tenfold in slothful shame,
Lay there exiled from eternal God,
    Lost to her place and name;

And death and life she hated equally,
   And nothing saw, for her despair,
But dreadful time, dreadful eternity,
    No comfort anywhere;

Remaining utterly confused with fears,
   And ever worse with growing time,   270

And ever unrelieved by dismal tears,
    And all alone in crime.

Shut up as in a crumbling tomb, girt round
    With blackness as a solid wall,
Far off she seem'd to hear the dully sound
    Of human footsteps fall:

As in strange lands a traveller walking slow,
    In doubt and great perplexity,
A little before moonrise hears the low
    Moan of an unknown sea;   280

And knows not if it be thunder, or a sound
    Of rocks thrown down, or one deep cry
Of great wild beasts; then thinketh, 'I have found
    A new land, but I die.'

She howl'd aloud, 'I am on fire within.
    There comes no murmur of reply.
What is it that will take away my sin,
    And save me lest I die?'

So when four years were wholly finished,
    She threw her royal robes away.   290
'Make me a cottage in the vale,' she said,
    'Where I may mourn and pray.

'Yet pull not down my palace towers, that are
    So lightly, beautifully built;
Perchance I may return with others there
    When I have purged my guilt.'

LADY CLARA VERE DE VERE

LADY Clara Vere de Vere,
  Of me you shall not win renown:
You thought to break a country heart
  For pastime, ere you went to town.
At me you smiled, but unbeguiled
  I saw the snare, and I retired;
The daughter of a hundred earls,
  You are not one to be desired.

Lady Clara Vere de Vere,
  I know you proud to bear your name,
Your pride is yet no mate for mine,
  Too proud to care from whence I came.
Nor would I break for your sweet sake
  A heart that dotes on truer charms.
A simple maiden in her flower
  Is worth a hundred coats-of-arms.

Lady Clara Vere de Vere,
  Some meeker pupil you must find,
For, were you queen of all that is,
  I could not stoop to such a mind.
You sought to prove how I could love,
  And my disdain is my reply.
The lion on your old stone gates
  Is not more cold to you than I.

Lady Clara Vere de Vere,
  You put strange memories in my head.
Not thrice your branching limes have blown
  Since I beheld young Laurence dead.
O, your sweet eyes, your low replies!
  A great enchantress you may be;
But there was that across his throat
  Which you had hardly cared to see.

Lady Clara Vere de Vere,
  When thus he met his mother's view,
She had the passions of her kind,
  She spake some certain truths of you.
Indeed I heard one bitter word
  That scarce is fit for you to hear;
Her manners had not that repose
  Which stamps the caste of Vere de Vere.

Lady Clara Vere de Vere,
   There stands a spectre in your hall;
The guilt of blood is at your door;
   You changed a wholesome heart to gall.
You held your course without remorse,
   To make him trust his modest worth,
And, last, you fix'd a vacant stare,
   And slew him with your noble birth.

Trust me, Clara Vere de Vere,
   From you blue heavens above us bent
The gardener Adam and his wife
   Smile at the claims of long descent.
Howe'er it be, it seems to me,
   'T is only noble to be good.
Kind hearts are more than coronets,
   And simple faith than Norman blood.

I know you, Clara Vere de Vere,
   You pine among your halls and towers;
The languid light of your proud eyes
   Is wearied of the rolling hours.
In glowing health, with boundless wealth,
   But sickening of a vague disease,
You know so ill to deal with time,
   You needs must play such pranks as these.

Clara, Clara Vere de Vere,
   If time be heavy on your hands,
Are there no beggars at your gate,
   Nor any poor about your lands?
O, teach the orphan-boy to read,
   Or teach the orphan-girl to sew;
Pray Heaven for a human heart,
   And let the foolish yeoman go.

THE MAY QUEEN

You must wake and call me early, call me early, mother dear;
To-morrow 'ill be the happiest time of all the glad New-year;
Of all the glad New-year, mother, the maddest merriest day,
For I'm to be Queen o' the May, mother, I'm to be Queen o' the May.

There's many a black, black eye, they say, but none so bright as mine;
There's Margaret and Mary, there's Kate and Caroline;
But none so fair as little Alice in all the land they say,
So I'm to be Queen o' the May, mother, I'm to be Queen o' the May.

I sleep so sound all night, mother, that I shall never wake,
If you do not call me loud when the day begins to break; 10
But I must gather knots of flowers, and buds and garlands gay,
For I'm to be Queen o' the May, mother, I'm to be Queen o' the May.

As I came up the valley whom think ye should I see
But Robin leaning on the bridge beneath the hazel-tree?
He thought of that sharp look, mother, I gave him yesterday,
But I'm to be Queen o' the May, mother, I'm to be Queen o' the May.

He thought I was a ghost, mother, for I was all in white,
And I ran by him without speaking, like a flash of light.
They call me cruel-hearted, but I care not what they say,
For I'm to be Queen o' the May, mother, I'm to be Queen o' the May.²⁰

They say he's dying all for love, but that can never be;
They say his heart is breaking, mother—what is that to me?
There's many a bolder lad 'ill woo me any summer day,
And I'm to be Queen o' the May, mother, I'm to be Queen o' the May.

Little Effie shall go with me to-morrow to the green,
And you'll be there, too, mother, to see me made the Queen;
For the shepherd lads on every side 'ill come from far away,
And I'm to be Queen o' the May, mother, I'm to be Queen o' the May.

The honeysuckle round the porch has woven its wavy bowers,
And by the meadow-trenches blow the faint sweet cuckoo-flowers; 30
And the wild marsh-marigold shines like fire in swamps and hollows gray,
And I'm to be Queen o' the May, mother, I'm to be Queen o' the May.

The night-winds come and go, mother, upon the meadow-grass,
And the happy stars above them seem to brighten as they pass;
There will not be a drop of rain the whole of the livelong day,
And I'm to be Queen o' the May, mother, I'm to be Queen o' the May.

All the valley, mother, 'ill be fresh and green and still,
And the cowslip and the crowfoot are over all the hill,
And the rivulet in the flowery dale 'ill merrily glance and play,
For I'm to be Queen o' the May, mother, I'm to be Queen o' the May.⁴⁰

So you must wake and call me early, call me early, mother dear,
To-morrow 'ill be the happiest time of all the glad New-year;
To-morrow 'ill be of all the year the maddest merriest day,
For I'm to be Queen o' the May, mother, I'm to be Queen o' the May.

NEW-YEAR'S EVE

IF you're waking call me early, call me early, mother dear,
For I would see the sun rise upon the glad New-year.
It is the last New-year that I shall ever see,
Then you may lay me low i' the mould and think no more of me.

To-night I saw the sun set; he set and left behind
The good old year, the dear old time, and all my peace of mind;
And the New-year's coming up, mother, but I shall never see
The blossom on the blackthorn, the leaf upon the tree.

Last May we made a crown of flowers; we had a merry day;
Beneath the hawthorn on the green they made me Queen of May;   10
And we danced about the may-pole and in the hazel copse,
Till Charles's Wain came out above the tall white chimney-tops.

There's not a flower on all the hills; the frost is on the pane.
I only wish to live till the snowdrops come again;
I wish the snow would melt and the sun come out on high;
I long to see a flower so before the day I die.

The building rook 'll caw from the windy tall elm-tree,
And the tufted plover pipe along the fallow lea,
And the swallow 'ill come back again with summer o'er the wave,
But I shall lie alone, mother, within the mouldering grave.   20

Upon the chancel-casement, and upon that grave of mine,
In the early early morning the summer sun 'ill shine,
Before the red cock crows from the farm upon the hill,
When you are warm-asleep, mother, and all the world is still.

When the flowers come again, mother, beneath the waning light
You'll never see me more in the long gray fields at night;
When from the dry dark wold the summer airs blow cool
On the oat-grass and the sword-grass, and the bulrush in the pool.

You'll bury me, my mother, just beneath the hawthorn shade,
And you'll come sometimes and see me where I am lowly laid.   30
I shall not forget you, mother, I shall hear you when you pass,
With your feet above my head in the long and pleasant grass.

I have been wild and wayward, but you'll forgive me now;
You'll kiss me, my own mother, and forgive me ere I go;
Nay, nay, you must not weep, nor let your grief be wild;
You should not fret for me, mother, you have another child.

If I can I'll come again, mother, from out my resting-place;
Tho' you'll not see me, mother, I shall look upon your face;
Tho' I cannot speak a word, I shall harken what you say,
And be often, often with you when you think I'm far away. 40

Good-night, good-night, when I have said good-night for evermore,
And you see me carried out from the threshold of the door,
Don't let Effie come to see me till my grave be growing green.
She'll be a better child to you than ever I have been.

She'll find my garden-tools upon the granary floor.
Let her take 'em, they are hers; I shall never garden more;
But tell her, when I'm gone, to train the rosebush that I set
About the parlor-window and the box of mignonette.

Good night, sweet mother; call me before the day is born.
All night I lie awake, but I fall asleep at morn, 50
But I would see the sun rise upon the glad New-year,
So, if you're waking, call me, call me early, mother dear.

CONCLUSION

I THOUGHT to pass away before, and yet alive I am;
And in the fields all round I hear the bleating of the lamb.
How sadly, I remember, rose the morning of the year!
To die before the snowdrop came, and now the violet's here.

O, sweet is the new violet, that comes beneath the skies,
And sweeter is the young lamb's voice to me that cannot rise,
And sweet is all the land about, and all the flowers that blow,
And sweeter far is death than life to me that long to go.

It seem'd so hard at first, mother, to leave the blessed sun,
And now it seems as hard to stay, and yet His will be done! 10
But still I think it can't be long before I find release;
And that good man, the clergyman, has told me words of peace.

O, blessings on his kindly voice and on his silver hair!
And blessings on his whole life long, until he meet me there!
O, blessings on his kindly heart and on his silver head!
A thousand times I blest him, as he knelt beside my bed.

He taught me all the mercy, for he show'd me all the sin.
Now, tho' my lamp was lighted late, there's One will let me in;
Nor would I now be well, mother, again, if that could be,
For my desire is but to pass to Him that died for me. 20

I did not hear the dog howl, mother, or the death-watch beat,
There came a sweeter token when the night and morning meet;
But sit beside my bed, mother, and put your hand in mine,
And Effie on the other side, and I will tell the sign.

All in the wild March-morning I heard the angels call;
It was when the moon was setting, and the dark was over all;
The trees began to whisper, and the wind began to roll,
And in the wild March-morning I heard them call my soul.

For lying broad awake I thought of you and Effie dear;
I saw you sitting in the house, and I no longer here;   30
With all my strength I pray'd for both, and so I felt resign'd,
And up the valley came a swell of music on the wind.

I thought that it was fancy, and I listen'd in my bed,
And then did something speak to me—I know not what was said;
For great delight and shuddering took hold of all my mind,
And up the valley came again the music on the wind.

But you were sleeping; and I said, 'It's not for them, it's mine.'
And if it come three times, I thought, I take it for a sign.
And once again it came, and close beside the window-bars,
Then seem'd to go right up to heaven and die among the stars.   40

So now I think my time is near. I trust it is. I know
The blessed music went that way my soul will have to go.
And for myself, indeed, I care not if I go to-day;
But, Effie, you must comfort *her* when I am past away.

And say to Robin a kind word, and tell him not to fret;
There's many a worthier than I, would make him happy yet.
If I had lived—I cannot tell—I might have been his wife;
But all these things have ceased to be, with my desire of life.

O, look! the sun begins to rise, the heavens are in a glow;
He shines upon a hundred fields, and all of them I know.   50
And there I move no longer now, and there his light may shine—
Wild flowers in the valley for other hands than mine.

O, sweet and strange it seems to me, that ere this day is done
The voice, that now is speaking, may be beyond the sun—
For ever and for ever with those just souls and true—
And what is life, that we should moan? why make we such ado?

For ever and for ever, all in a blessed home—
And there to wait a little while till you and Effie come—

To lie within the light of God, as I lie upon your breast—
And the wicked cease from troubling, and the weary are at rest.   60

THE LOTOS-EATERS

'COURAGE!' he said, and pointed toward the land,
'This mounting wave will roll us shoreward soon.'
In the afternoon they came unto a land
In which it seemed always afternoon.
All round the coast the languid air did swoon,
Breathing like one that hath a weary dream.
Full-faced above the valley stood the moon;
And, like a downward smoke, the slender stream
Along the cliff to fall and pause and fall did seem.

A land of streams! some, like a downward smoke,
Slow-dropping veils of thinnest lawn, did go;
And some thro' wavering lights and shadows broke,
Rolling a slumbrous sheet of foam below.
They saw the gleaming river seaward flow
From the inner land; far off, three mountain-tops,
Three silent pinnacles of aged snow,
Stood sunset-flush'd; and dew'd with showery drops,
Up-clomb the shadowy pine above the woven copse.

The charmed sunset linger'd low adown
In the red West; thro' mountain clefts the dale
Was seen far inland, and the yellow down
Border'd with palm, and many a winding vale
And meadow, set with slender galingale;
A land where all things always seem'd the same!
And round about the keel with faces pale,
Dark faces pale against that rosy flame,
The mild-eyed melancholy Lotos-eaters came.

Branches they bore of that enchanted stem,
Laden with flower and fruit, whereof they gave
To each, but whoso did receive of them
And taste, to him the gushing of the wave
Far far away did seem to mourn and rave
On alien shores; and if his fellow spake,
His voice was thin, as voices from the grave;
And deep-asleep he seem'd, yet all awake,
And music in his ears his beating heart did make.

They sat them down upon the yellow sand,
Between the sun and the moon upon the shore;
And sweet it was to dream of Fatherland,
Of child, and wife, and slave; but evermore
Most weary seem'd the sea, weary the oar,
Weary the wandering fields of barren foam.
Then some one said, 'We will return no more;'
And all at once they sang, 'Our island home
Is far beyond the wave; we will no longer roam.'

CHORIC SONG

I

THERE is sweet music here that softer falls
Than petals from blown roses on the grass,
Or night-dews on still waters between walls
Of shadowy granite, in a gleaming pass;
Music that gentlier on the spirit lies,
Than tired eyelids upon tired eyes;
Music that brings sweet sleep down from the blissful skies.
Here are cool mosses deep,
And thro' the moss the ivies creep,
And in the stream the long-leaved flowers weep,   10
And from the craggy ledge the poppy hangs in sleep.

II

Why are we weigh'd upon with heaviness,
And utterly consumed with sharp distress,
While all things else have rest from weariness?
All things have rest: why should we toil alone,
We only toil, who are the first of things,
And make perpetual moan,
Still from one sorrow to another thrown;
Nor ever fold our wings,
And cease from wanderings,   20
Nor steep our brows in slumber's holy balm;
Nor harken what the inner spirit sings,
'There is no joy but calm!'—
Why should we only toil, the roof and crown of things?

III

Lo! in the middle of the wood,
The folded leaf is woo'd from out the bud
With winds upon the branch, and there

Grows green and broad, and takes no care,
Sun-steep'd at noon, and in the moon
Nightly dew-fed; and turning yellow   30
Falls, and floats adown the air.
Lo! sweeten'd with the summer light,
The full-juiced apple, waxing over-mellow,
Drops in a silent autumn night.
All its allotted length of days
The flower ripens in its place,
Ripens and fades, and falls, and hath no toil,
Fast-rooted in the fruitful soil.

IV

Hateful is the dark-blue sky,
Vaulted o'er the dark-blue sea.   40
Death is the end of life; ah, why
Should life all labor be?
Let us alone. Time driveth onward fast,
And in a little while our lips are dumb.
Let us alone. What is it that will last?
All things are taken from us, and become
Portions and parcels of the dreadful past.
Let us alone. What pleasure can we have
To war with evil? Is there any peace
In ever climbing up a climbing wave?   50
All things have rest, and ripen toward the grave
In silence—ripen, fall, and cease:
Give us long rest or death, dark death, or dreamful ease.

V

How sweet it were, hearing the downward stream,
With half-shut eyes ever to seem
Falling asleep in a half-dream!
To dream and dream, like yonder amber light,
Which will not leave the myrrh-bush on the height;
To hear each other's whisper'd speech;
Eating the Lotos day by day,   60
To watch the crisping ripples on the beach,
And tender curving lines of creamy spray;
To lend our hearts and spirits wholly
To the influence of mild-minded melancholy;
To muse and brood and live again in memory,
With those old faces of our infancy
Heap'd over with a mound of grass,
Two handfuls of white dust, shut in an urn of brass!

VI

Dear is the memory of our wedded lives,
And dear the last embraces of our wives   70
And their warm tears; but all hath suffer'd change;
For surely now our household hearths are cold,
Our sons inherit us, our looks are strange,
And we should come like ghosts to trouble joy.
Or else the island princes over-bold
Have eat our substance, and the minstrel sings
Before them of the ten years' war in Troy,
And our great deeds, as half-forgotten things.
Is there confusion in the little isle?
Let what is broken so remain.   80
The Gods are hard to reconcile;
'T is hard to settle order once again.
There *is* confusion worse than death,
Trouble on trouble, pain on pain,
Long labor unto aged breath,
Sore task to hearts worn out by many wars
And eyes grown dim with gazing on the pilot-stars.

VII

But, propt on beds of amaranth and moly,
How sweet—while warm airs lull us, blowing lowly—
With half-dropt eyelid still,   90
Beneath a heaven dark and holy,
To watch the long bright river drawing slowly
His waters from the purple hill—
To hear the dewy echoes calling
From cave to cave thro' the thick-twined vine—
To watch the emerald-color'd water falling
Thro' many a woven acanthus-wreath divine!
Only to hear and see the far-off sparkling brine,
Only to hear were sweet, stretch'd out beneath the pine.

VIII

The Lotos blooms below the barren peak,   100
The Lotos blows by every winding creek;
All day the wind breathes low with mellower tone;
Thro' every hollow cave and alley lone
Round and round the spicy downs the yellow Lotus-dust is blown.
We have had enough of action, and of motion we,
Roll'd to starboard, roll'd to larboard, when the surge was seething free,
Where the wallowing monster spouted his foam-fountains in the sea.

Let us swear an oath, and keep it with an equal mind,
In the hollow Lotos-land to live and lie reclined
On the hills like Gods together, careless of mankind.   110
For they lie beside their nectar, and the bolts are hurl'd
Far below them in the valleys, and the clouds are lightly curl'd
Round their golden houses, girdled with the gleaming world;
Where they smile in secret, looking over wasted lands,
Blight and famine, plague and earthquake, roaring deeps and fiery sands,
Clanging fights, and flaming towns, and sinking ships, and praying hands.
But they smile, they find a music centred in a doleful song
Steaming up, a lamentation and an ancient tale of wrong,
Like a tale of little meaning tho' the words are strong;
Chanted from an ill-used race of men that cleave the soil,   12?
Sow the seed, and reap the harvest with enduring toil,
Storing yearly little dues of wheat, and wine and oil;
Till they perish and they suffer—some, 't is whisper'd—down in hell
Suffer endless anguish, others in Elysian valleys dwell,
Resting weary limbs at last on beds of asphodel.
Surely, surely, slumber is more sweet than toil, the shore
Than labor in the deep mid-ocean, wind and wave and oar;
O, rest ye, brother mariners, we will not wander more.

A DREAM OF FAIR WOMEN

I READ, before my eyelids dropt their shade,
    'The Legend of Good Women,' long ago
Sung by the morning star of song, who made
        His music heard below;

Dan Chaucer, the first warbler, whose sweet breath
    Preluded those melodious bursts that fill
The spacious times of great Elizabeth
        With sounds that echo still.

And, for a while, the knowledge of his art
    Held me above the subject, as strong gales   10
Hold swollen clouds from raining, tho' my heart,
        Brimful of those wild tales,

Charged both mine eyes with tears. In every land
    I saw, wherever light illumineth,
Beauty and anguish walking hand in hand
        The downward slope to death.

Those far-renowned brides of ancient song
    Peopled the hollow dark, like burning stars,

And I heard sounds of insult, shame, and wrong,
    And trumpets blown for wars;   20

And clattering flints batter'd with clanging hoofs;
    And I saw crowds in column'd sanctuaries,
And forms that pass'd at windows and on roofs
    Of marble palaces;

Corpses across the threshold, heroes tall
    Dislodging pinnacle and parapet
Upon the tortoise creeping to the wall,
    Lances in ambush set;

And high shrine-doors burst thro' with heated blasts
    That run before the fluttering tongues of fire; 30
White surf wind-scatter'd over sails and masts,
    And ever climbing higher;

Squadrons and squares of men in brazen plates,
    Scaffolds, still sheets of water, divers woes,
Ranges of glimmering vaults with iron grates,
    And hush'd seraglios.

So shape chased shape as swift as, when to land
    Bluster the winds and tides the selfsame way,
Crisp foam-flakes scud along the level sand,
    Torn from the fringe of spray.   40

I started once, or seem'd to start in pain,
    Resolved on noble things, and strove to speak,
As when a great thought strikes along the brain
    And flushes all the cheek.

And once my arm was lifted to hew down
    A cavalier from off his saddle-bow,
That bore a lady from a leaguer'd town;
    And then, I know not how,

All those sharp fancies, by down-lapsing thought
    Stream'd onward, lost their edges, and did creep 50
Roll'd on each other, rounded, smooth'd, and brought
    Into the gulfs of sleep.

At last methought that I had wander'd far
    In an old wood; fresh-wash'd in coolest dew
The maiden splendors of the morning star
    Shook in the steadfast blue.

Enormous elm-tree boles did stoop and lean
  Upon the dusky brushwood underneath
Their broad curved branches, fledged with clearest green,
    New from its silken sheath.   60

The dim red Morn had died, her journey done,
  And with dead lips smiled at the twilight plain,
Half-fallen across the threshold of the sun,
    Never to rise again.

There was no motion in the dumb dead air,
  Not any song of bird or sound of rill;
Gross darkness of the inner sepulchre
    Is not so deadly still

As that wide forest. Growths of jasmine turn'd
  Their humid arms festooning tree to tree,   70
And at the root thro' lush green grasses burn'd
    The red anemone.

I knew the flowers, I knew the leaves, I knew
  The tearful glimmer of the languid dawn
On those long, rank, dark wood-walks drench'd in dew,
    Leading from lawn to lawn.

The smell of violets, hidden in the green,
  Pour'd back into my empty soul and frame
The times when I remembered to have been
    Joyful and free from blame.   80

And from within me a clear undertone
  Thrill'd thro' mine ears in that unblissful clime,
'Pass freely thro'; the wood is all thine own
    Until the end of time.'

At length I saw a lady within call,
  Stiller than chisell'd marble, standing there;
A daughter of the gods, divinely tall,
    And most divinely fair.

Her loveliness with shame and with surprise
  Froze my swift speech; she turning on my face   90
The star-like sorrows of immortal eyes,
    Spoke slowly in her place:

'I had great beauty; ask thou not my name:
  No one can be more wise than destiny.

Many drew swords and died. Where'er I came
   I brought calamity.'

'No marvel, sovereign lady: in fair field
   Myself for such a face had boldly died,
I answer'd free; and turning I appeal'd
   To one that stood beside.   100

But she, with sick and scornful looks averse,
   To her full height her stately stature draws;
'My youth,' she said, 'was blasted with a curse:
   This woman was the cause.

'I was cut off from hope in that sad place
   Which men call'd Aulis in those iron years:
My father held his hand upon his face;
   I, blinded with my tears,

'Still strove to speak: my voice was thick with sighs
   As in a dream. Dimly I could descry   110
The stern black-bearded kings with wolfish eyes,
   Waiting to see me die.

'The high masts flicker'd as they lay afloat;
   The crowds, the temples, waver'd, and the shore;
The bright death quiver'd at the victim's throat—
   Touch'd—and I knew no more.'

Whereto the other with a downward brow:
   'I would the white cold heavy-plunging foam,
Whirl'd by the wind, had roll'd me deep below,
   Then when I left my home.'   120

Her slow full words sank thro' the silence drear,
   As thunder drops fall on a sleeping sea:
Sudden I heard a voice that cried, 'Come here,
   That I may look on thee.'

I turning saw, throned on a flowery rise,
   One sitting on a crimson scarf unroll'd;
A queen, with swarthy cheeks and bold black eyes,
   Brow-bound with burning gold.

She, flashing forth a haughty smile, began:
   'I govern'd men by change, and so I sway'd   130
All moods. 'T is long since I have seen a man.
   Once, like the moon, I made

The ever-shifting currents of the blood
    According to my humor ebb and flow.
I have no men to govern in this wood:
    That makes my only woe.

'Nay—yet it chafes me that I could not bend
    One will; nor tame and tutor with mine eye
That dull cold-blooded Cæsar. Prythee, friend,
    Where is Mark Antony?   140

'The man, my lover, with whom I rode sublime
    On Fortune's neck; we sat as God by God:
The Nilus would have risen before his time
    And flooded at our nod.

'We drank the Libyan Sun to sleep, and lit
    Lamps which out-burn'd Canopus. O, my life
In Egypt! O, the dalliance and the wit,
    The flattery and the strife,

'And the wild kiss, when fresh from war's alarms,
    My Hercules, my Roman Antony,   150
My mailed Bacchus leapt into my arms,
    Contented there to die!

'And there he died: and when I heard my name
    Sigh'd forth with life I would not brook my fear
Of the other; with a worm I balk'd his fame.
    What else was left? look here!'—

With that she tore her robe apart, and half
    The polish'd argent of her breast to sight
Laid bare. Thereto she pointed with a laugh,
    Showing the aspick's bite.—   160

'I died a Queen. The Roman soldier found
    Me lying dead, my crown about my brows,
A name for ever!—lying robed and crown'd,
    Worthy a Roman spouse.'

Her warbling voice, a lyre of widest range
    Struck by all passion, did fall down and glance
From tone to tone, and glided thro' all change
    Of liveliest utterance.

When she made pause I knew not for delight;
    Because with sudden motion from the ground   170

She raised her piercing orbs, and fill'd with light
    The interval of sound.

Still with their fires Love tipt his keenest darts;
    As once they drew into two burning rings
All beams of Love, melting the mighty hearts
    Of captains and of kings.

Slowly my sense undazzled. Then I heard
    A noise of some one coming thro' the lawn,
And singing clearer than the crested bird
    That claps his wings at dawn: 180

'The torrent brooks of hallow'd Israel
    From craggy hollows pouring, late and soon,
Sound all night long, in falling thro' the dell,
    Far-heard beneath the moon.

'The balmy moon of blessed Israel
    Floods all the deep-blue gloom with beams divine;
All night the splinter'd crags that wall the dell
    With spires of silver shine.'

As one that museth where broad sunshine laves
    The lawn by some cathedral, thro' the door   190
Hearing the holy organ rolling waves
    Of sound on roof and floor

Within, and anthem sung, is charm'd and tied
    To where he stands,—so stood I, when that flow
Of music left the lips of her that died
    To save her father's vow;

The daughter of the warrior Gileadite,
    A maiden pure; as when she went along
From Mizpeh's tower'd gate with welcome light
    With timbrel and with song.   200

My words leapt forth: 'Heaven heads the count of crimes
    With that wild oath.' She render'd answer high:
'Not so, nor once alone; a thousand times
    I would be born and die.

'Single I grew, like some green plant, whose root
    Creeps to the garden water-pipes beneath,
Feeding the flower; but ere my flower to fruit
    Changed, I was ripe for death.

'My God, my land, my father—these did move
   Me from my bliss of life that Nature gave,   210
Lower'd softly with a threefold cord of love
     Down to a silent grave.

'And I went mourning, "No fair Hebrew boy
   Shall smile away my maiden blame among
The Hebrew mothers"—emptied of all joy,
     Leaving the dance and song,

'Leaving the olive-gardens far below,
   Leaving the promise of my bridal bower,
The valleys of grape-loaded vines that glow
     Beneath the battled tower.   220

'The light white cloud swam over us. Anon
   We heard the lion roaring from his den;
We saw the large white stars rise one by one,
     Or, from the darken'd glen,

'Saw God divide the night with flying flame,
   And thunder on the everlasting hills.
I heard Him, for He spake, and grief became
     A solemn scorn of ills.

'When the next moon was roll'd into the sky,
   Strength came to me that equall'd my desire.   230
How beautiful a thing it was to die
     For God and for my sire!

'It comforts me in this one thought to dwell,
   That I subdued me to my father's will;
Because the kiss he gave me, ere I fell,
     Sweetens the spirit still.

'Moreover it is written that my race
   Hew'd Ammon, hip and thigh, from Aroer
On Arnon unto Minneth.' Here her face
     Glow'd, as I look'd at her.   240

She lock'd her lips; she left me where I stood:
   'Glory to God,' she sang, and past afar,
Thridding the sombre boskage of the wood,
     Toward the morning-star.

Losing her carol I stood pensively,
   As one that from a casement leans his head,
When midnight bells cease ringing suddenly,
     And the old year is dead.

'Alas! alas!' a low voice, full of care,   250
    Murmur'd beside me: 'Turn and look on me;
I am that Rosamond, whom men call fair,
    If what I was I be.

'Would I had been some maiden coarse and poor!
    O me, that I should ever see the light!
Those dragon eyes of anger'd Eleanor
    Do hunt me, day and night.'

She ceased in tears, fallen from hope and trust;
    To whom the Egyptian: 'O, you tamely died!
You should have clung to Fulvia's waist, and thrust   260
    The dagger thro' her side.'

With that sharp sound the white dawn's creeping beams,
    Stolen to my brain, dissolved the mystery
Of folded sleep. The captain of my dreams
    Ruled in the eastern sky.

Morn broaden'd on the borders of the dark
    Ere I saw her who clasp'd in her last trance
Her murder'd father's head, or Joan of Arc,
    A light of ancient France;

Or her who knew that Love can vanquish Death,   270
    Who kneeling, with one arm about her king,
Drew forth the poison with her balmy breath,
    Sweet as new buds in spring.

No memory labors longer from the deep
    Gold-mines of thought to lift the hidden ore
That glimpses, moving up, than I from sleep
    To gather and tell o'er

Each little sound and sight. With what dull pain
    Compass'd, how eagerly I sought to strike
Into that wondrous track of dreams again!   280
    But no two dreams are like.

As when a soul laments, which hath been blest,
    Desiring what is mingled with past years,
In yearnings that can never be exprest
    By signs or groans or tears;

Because all words, tho' cull'd with choicest art,
    Failing to give the bitter of the sweet,
Wither beneath the palate, and the heart
    Faints, faded by its heat.

THE BLACKBIRD

O BLACKBIRD! sing me something well:
   While all the neighbors shoot thee round,
   I keep smooth plats of fruitful ground,
Where thou mayst warble, eat, and dwell.

The espaliers and the standards all
   Are thine; the range of lawn and park;
   The unnetted black-hearts ripen dark,
All thine, against the garden wall.

Yet, tho' I spared thee all the spring,
   Thy sole delight is, sitting still,
   With that gold dagger of thy bill
To fret the summer jenneting.

A golden bill! the silver tongue,
   Cold February loved, is dry;
   Plenty corrupts the melody
That made thee famous once when young;

And in the sultry garden-squares,
   Now thy flute-notes are changed to coarse,
   I hear thee not at all, or hoarse
As when a hawker hawks his wares.

Take warning! he that will not sing
   While yon sun prospers in the blue,
   Shall sing for want, ere leaves are new,
Caught in the frozen palms of Spring.

THE DEATH OF THE OLD YEAR

FULL knee-deep lies the winter snow,
And the winter winds are wearily sighing;
Toll ye the church-bell sad and slow,
And tread softly and speak low,
For the old year lies a-dying.
     Old year, you must not die;
     You came to us so readily,
     You lived with us so steadily,
     Old year, you shall not die.

He lieth still, he doth not move;
He will not see the dawn of day.

He hath no other life above.
He gave me a friend, and a true true-love,
And the New-year will take 'em away.
  Old year, you must not go;
  So long as you have been with us,
  Such joy as you have seen with us,
  Old year, you shall not go.

He froth'd his bumpers to the brim;
A jollier year we shall not see.
But tho' his eyes are waxing dim,
And tho' his foes speak ill of him,
He was a friend to me.
  Old year, you shall not die;
  We did so laugh and cry with you,
  I've half a mind to die with you,
  Old year, if you must die.

He was full of joke and jest,
But all his merry quips are o'er.
To see him die, across the waste
His son and heir doth ride post-haste,
But he'll be dead before.
  Every one for his own.
  The night is starry and cold, my friend,
  And the New-year blithe and bold, my friend,
  Comes up to take his own.

How hard he breathes! over the snow
I heard just now the crowing cock.
The shadows flicker to and fro;
The cricket chirps; the light burns low;
'T is nearly twelve o'clock.
  Shake hands, before you die.
  Old year, we'll dearly rue for you.
  What is it we can do for you?
  Speak out before you die.

His face is growing sharp and thin.
Alack! our friend is gone.
Close up his eyes; tie up his chin;
Step from the corpse, and let him in
That standeth there alone,
  And waiteth at the door.
  There's a new foot on the floor, my friend,
  And a new face at the door, my friend,
  A new face at the door.

TO J. S.

THE wind that beats the mountain blows
  More softly round the open wold,
And gently comes the world to those
  That are cast in gentle mould.

And me this knowledge bolder made,
  Or else I had not dared to flow
In these words toward you, and invade
  Even with a verse your holy woe.

'T is strange that those we lean on most,
  Those in whose laps our limbs are nursed,
Fall into shadow, soonest lost;
  Those we love first are taken first.

God gives us love. Something to love
  He lends us; but, when love is grown
To ripeness, that on which it throve
  Falls off, and love is left alone.

This is the curse of time. Alas!
  In grief I am not all unlearn'd;
Once thro' mine own doors Death did pass;
  One went who never hath return'd.

He will not smile—not speak to me
  Once more. Two years his chair is seen
Empty before us. That was he
  Without whose life I had not been.

Your loss is rarer; for this star
  Rose with you thro' a little arc
Of heaven, nor having wander'd far
  Shot on the sudden into dark.

I knew your brother; his mute dust
  I honor and his living worth;
A man more pure and bold and just
  Was never born into the earth.

I have not look'd upon you nigh
  Since that dear soul hath fallen asleep.
Great Nature is more wise than I;
  I will not tell you not to weep.

And tho' mine own eyes fill with dew,
    Drawn from the spirit thro' the brain,
I will not even preach to you,
    'Weep, weeping dulls the inward pain.'

Let Grief be her own mistress still.
    She loveth her own anguish deep
More than much pleasure. Let her will
    Be done—to weep or not to weep.

I will not say, 'God's ordinance
    Of death is blown in every wind;'
For that is not a common chance
    That takes away a noble mind.

His memory long will live alone
    In all our hearts, as mournful light
That broods above the fallen sun,
    And dwells in heaven half the night.

Vain solace! Memory standing near
    Cast down her eyes, and in her throat
Her voice seem'd distant, and a tear
    Dropt on the letters as I wrote.

I wrote I know not what. In truth,
    How *should* I soothe you any way,
Who miss the brother of your youth?
    Yet something I did wish to say;

For he too was a friend to me.
    Both are my friends, and my true breast
Bleedeth for both; yet it may be
    That only silence suiteth best.

Words weaker than your grief would make
    Grief more. 'T were better I should cease
Although myself could almost take
    The place of him that sleeps in peace.

Sleep sweetly, tender heart, in peace;
    Sleep, holy spirit, blessed soul,
While the stars burn, the moons increase,
    And the great ages onward roll.

Sleep till the end, true soul and sweet.
    Nothing comes to thee new or strange.
Sleep full of rest from head to feet;
    Lie still, dry dust, secure of change.

ON A MOURNER

I

NATURE, so far as in her lies,
   Imitates God, and turns her face
To every land beneath the skies,
   Counts nothing that she meets with base,
   But lives and loves in every place;

II

Fills out the homely quickset-screens,
   And makes the purple lilac ripe,
Steps from her airy hill, and greens
   The swamp, where humm'd the dropping snipe,
   With moss and braided marish-pipe;

III

And on thy heart a finger lays,
   Saying, 'Beat quicker, for the time
Is pleasant, and the woods and ways
   Are pleasant, and the beech and lime
   Put forth and feel a gladder clime.'

IV

And murmurs of a deeper voice,
   Going before to some far shrine,
Teach that sick heart the stronger choice,
   Till all thy life one way incline
   With one wide Will that closes thine.

V

And when the zoning eve has died
   Where yon dark valleys wind forlorn,
Come Hope and Memory, spouse and bride,
   From out the borders of the morn,
   With that fair child betwixt them born.

VI

And when no mortal motion jars
   The blackness round the tombing sod,
Thro' silence and the trembling stars

Comes Faith from tracts no feet have trod,
And Virtue, like a household god

VII

Promising empire; such as those
　　Once heard at dead of night to greet
Troy's wandering prince, so that he rose
　　With sacrifice, while all the fleet
　　Had rest by stony hills of Crete.

———

You ask me, why, tho' ill at ease,
　　Within this region I subsist,
　　Whose spirits falter in the mist,
And languish for the purple seas.

It is the land that freemen till,
　　That sober-suited Freedom chose,
　　The land, where girt with friends or foes
A man may speak the thing he will;

A land of settled government,
　　A land of just and old renown,
　　Where Freedom slowly broadens down
From precedent to precedent;

Where faction seldom gathers head,
　　But, by degrees to fullness wrought,
　　The strength of some diffusive thought
Hath time and space to work and spread.

Should banded unions persecute
　　Opinion, and induce a time
　　When single thought is civil crime,
And individual freedom mute,

Tho' power should make from land to land
　　The name of Britain trebly great—
　　Tho' every channel of the State
Should fill and choke with golden sand—

Yet waft me from the harbor-mouth,
　　Wild wind! I seek a warmer sky,
　　And I will see before I die
The palms and temples of the South.

———

Of old sat Freedom on the heights,
　The thunders breaking at her feet;
Above her shook the starry lights;
　She heard the torrents meet.

There in her place she did rejoice,
　Self-gather'd in her prophet-mind,
But fragments of her mighty voice
　Came rolling on the wind.

Then stept she down thro' town and field
　To mingle with the human race,
And part by part to men reveal'd
　The fullness of her face—

Grave mother of majestic works,
　From her isle-altar gazing down,
Who, Godlike, grasps the triple forks,
　And, king-like, wears the crown.

Her open eyes desire the truth.
　The wisdom of a thousand years
Is in them. May perpetual youth
　Keep dry their light from tears;

That her fair form may stand and shine,
　Make bright our days and light our dreams,
Turning to scorn with lips divine
　The falsehood of extremes!

———

Love thou thy land, with love far-brought
　From out the storied past, and used
　Within the present, but transfused
Thro' future time by power of thought;

True love turn'd round on fixed poles,
　Love, that endures not sordid ends,
　For English natures, freemen, friends,
Thy brothers and immortal souls.

But pamper not a hasty time,
　Nor feed with crude imaginings
　The herd, wild hearts and feeble wings
That every sophister can lime.

Deliver not the tasks of might
  To weakness, neither hide the ray
  From those, not blind, who wait for day,
Tho' sitting girt with doubtful light.

Make knowledge circle with the winds;
  But let her herald, Reverence, fly
  Before her to whatever sky
Bear seed of men and growth of minds.   20

Watch what main-currents draw the years;
  Cut Prejudice against the grain.
  But gentle words are always gain;
Regard the weakness of thy peers.

Nor toil for title, place, or touch
  Of pension, neither count on praise—
  It grows to guerdon after-days.
Nor deal in watch-words overmuch;

Not clinging to some ancient saw,
  Not master'd by some modern term,   30
  Not swift nor slow to change, but firm;
And in its season bring the law,

That from Discussion's lip may fall
  With Life that, working strongly, binds—
  Set in all lights by many minds,
To close the interests of all.

For Nature also, cold and warm,
  And moist and dry, devising long,
  Thro' many agents making strong,
Matures the individual form.   40

Meet is it changes should control
  Our being, lest we rust in ease.
  We all are changed by still degrees,
All but the basis of the soul.

So let the change which comes be free
  To ingroove itself with that which flies,
  And work, a joint of state, that plies
Its office, moved with sympathy.

A saying hard to shape in act;
  For all the past of Time reveals   50

A bridal dawn of thunder-peals,
Wherever Thought hath wedded Fact.

Even now we hear with inward strife
   A motion toiling in the gloom—
   The Spirit of the years to come
Yearning to mix himself with Life.

A slow-develop'd strength awaits
   Completion in a painful school;
   Phantoms of other forms of rule,
New Majesties of mighty States—

The warders of the growing hour,
   But vague in vapor, hard to mark;
   And round them sea and air are dark
With great contrivances of Power.

Of many changes, aptly join'd,
   Is bodied forth the second whole.
   Regard gradation, lest the soul
Of Discord race the rising wind;

A wind to puff your idol-fires,
   And heap their ashes on the head;
   To shame the boast so often made,
That we are wiser than our sires.

O, yet, if Nature's evil star
   Drive men in manhood, as in youth,
   To follow flying steps of Truth
Across the brazen bridge of war—

If New and Old, disastrous feud,
   Must ever shock, like armed foes,
   And this be true, till Time shall close,
That Principles are rain'd in blood;

Not yet the wise of heart would cease
   To hold his hope thro' shame and guilt,
   But with his hand against the hilt,
Would pace the troubled land, like Peace;

Not less, tho' dogs of Faction bay,
   Would serve his kind in deed and word,
   Certain, if knowledge bring the sword,
That knowledge takes the sword away—

Would love the gleams of good that broke
  From either side, nor veil his eyes;
  And if some dreadful need should rise
Would strike, and firmly, and one stroke.

To-morrow yet would reap to-day,
  As we bear blossom of the dead;
  Earn well the thrifty months, nor wed
Raw Haste, half-sister to Delay.

ENGLAND AND AMERICA IN 1782

O THOU that sendest out the man
  To rule by land and sea,
Strong mother of a Lion-line,
Be proud of those strong sons of thine
  Who wrench'd their rights from thee!

What wonder if in noble heat
  Those men thine arms withstood,
Retaught the lesson thou hadst taught,
And in thy spirit with thee fought—
  Who sprang from English blood!

But thou rejoice with liberal joy,
  Lift up thy rocky face,
And shatter, when the storms are black,
In many a streaming torrent back,
  The seas that shock thy base!

Whatever harmonies of law
  The growing world assume,
Thy work is thine—the single note
From that deep chord which Hampden smote
  Will vibrate to the doom.

THE GOOSE

I KNEW an old wife lean and poor,
  Her rags scarce held together;
There strode a stranger to the door,
  And it was windy weather.

He held a goose upon his arm,
  He utter'd rhyme and reason:

'Here, take the goose, and keep you warm,
    It is a stormy season.'

She caught the white goose by the leg,
    A goose—'t was no great matter.
The goose let fall a golden egg
    With cackle and with clatter.

She dropt the goose, and caught the pelf,
    And ran to tell her neighbors,
And bless'd herself, and cursed herself,
    And rested from her labors;

And feeding high, and living soft,
    Grew plump and able-bodied,
Until the grave churchwarden doff'd,
    The parson smirk'd and nodded.

So sitting, served by man and maid,
    She felt her heart grow prouder;
But ah! the more the white goose laid
    It clack'd and cackled louder.

It clutter'd here, it chuckled there,
    It stirr'd the old wife's mettle;
She shifted in her elbow-chair,
    And hurl'd the pan and kettle.

'A quinsy choke thy cursed note!'
    Then wax'd her anger stronger.
'Go, take the goose, and wring her throat,
    I will not bear it longer.'

Then yelp'd the cur, and yawl'd the cat,
    Ran Gaffer, stumbled Gammer.
The goose flew this way and flew that,
    And fill'd the house with clamor.

As head and heels upon the floor
    They flounder'd all together,
There rode a stranger to the door,
    And it was windy weather.

He took the goose upon his arm,
    He utter'd words of scorning:
'So keep you cold, or keep you warm,
    It is a stormy morning.'

The wild wind rang from park and plain,
  And round the attics rumbled,
Till all the tables danced again,
  And half the chimneys tumbled.

The glass blew in, the fire blew out,
  The blast was hard and harder.
Her cap blew off, her gown blew up,
  And a whirlwind clear'd the larder;

And while on all sides breaking loose
  Her household fled the danger,
Quoth she, 'The devil take the goose,
  And God forget the stranger!'

ENGLISH IDYLS
AND OTHER POEMS

THE EPIC

Written in 1835, but not published until 1842.

AT Francis Allen's on the Christmas-eve,—
The game of forfeits done—the girls all kiss'd
Beneath the sacred bush and past away—
The parson Holmes, the poet Everard Hall,
The host, and I sat round the wassail-bowl,
Then half-way ebb'd; and there we held a talk,
How all the old honor had from Christmas gone,
Or gone or dwindled down to some odd games
In some odd nooks like this; till I, tired out
With cutting eights that day upon the pond,   10
Where, three times slipping from the outer edge,
I bump'd the ice into three several stars,
Fell in a doze; and half-awake I heard
The parson taking wide and wider sweeps,
Now harping on the church-commissioners,
Now hawking at geology and schism;
Until I woke, and found him settled down
Upon the general decay of faith
Right thro' the world: 'at home was little left,
And none abroad; there was no anchor, none,   20
To hold by.' Francis, laughing, clapt his hand
On Everard's shoulder, with 'I hold by him.'
'And I,' quoth Everard, 'by the wassail-bowl.'
'Why yes,' I said, 'we knew your gift that way
At college; but another which you had—
I mean of verse (for so we held it then),
What came of that?' 'You know,' said Frank, 'he burnt
His epic, his King Arthur, some twelve books'—
And then to me demanding why: 'O, sir,
He thought that nothing new was said, or else   30
Something so said 't was nothing—that a truth
Looks freshest in the fashion of the day;
God knows; he has a mint of reasons; ask.
It pleased *me* well enough.' 'Nay, nay,' said Hall,
'Why take the style of those heroic times?

For nature brings not back the mastodon,
Nor we those times; and why should any man
Remodel models? these twelve books of mine
Were faint Homeric echoes, nothing-worth,
Mere chaff and draff, much better burnt.' 'But I,'   40
Said Francis, 'pick'd the eleventh from this hearth,
And have it; keep a thing, its use will come.
I hoard it as a sugar-plum for Holmes.'
He laugh'd, and I, tho' sleepy, like a horse
That hears the corn-bin open, prick'd my ears;
For I remember'd Everard's college fame
When we were Freshmen. Then at my request
He brought it; and the poet, little urged,
But with some prelude of disparagement,
Read, mouthing out his hollow oes and aes,   50
Deep-chested music, and to this result.

MORTE D'ARTHUR

So all day long the noise of battle roll'd
Among the mountains by the winter sea,
Until King Arthur's table, man by man,
Had fallen in Lyonness about their lord,
King Arthur; then, because his wound was deep,
The bold Sir Bedivere uplifted him,
Sir Bedivere, the last of all his knights,
And bore him to a chapel nigh the field,
A broken chancel with a broken cross,   60
That stood on a dark strait of barren land.
On one side lay the ocean, and on one
Lay a great water, and the moon was full.
    Then spake King Arthur to Sir Bedivere:
'The sequel of to-day unsolders all
The goodliest fellowship of famous knights
Whereof this world holds record. Such a sleep
They sleep—the men I loved. I think that we
Shall never more, at any future time,
Delight our souls with talk of knightly deeds,   70
Walking about the gardens and the halls
Of Camelot, as in the days that were.
I perish by this people which I made,—
Tho' Merlin sware that I should come again
To rule once more—but let what will be be,
I am so deeply smitten thro' the helm
That without help I cannot last till morn.
Thou therefore take my brand Excalibur,
Which was my pride; for thou rememberest how

In those old days, one summer noon, an arm   80
Rose up from out the bosom of the lake,
Clothed in white samite, mystic, wonderful
Holding the sword—and how I row'd across
And took it, and have worn it, like a king
And, wheresoever I am sung or told
In aftertime, this also shall be known.
But now delay not; take Excalibur,
And fling him far into the middle mere;
Watch what thou seest, and lightly bring me word.'

    To him replied the bold Sir Bedivere: 90
'It is not meet, Sir King, to leave thee thus,
Aidless, alone, and smitten thro' the helm.
A little thing may harm a wounded man.
Yet I thy hest will all perform at full,
Watch what I see, and lightly bring thee word.'

    So saying, from the ruin'd shrine he stept
And in the moon athwart the place of tombs,
Where lay the mighty bones of ancient men,
Old knights, and over them the sea-wind sang
Shrill, chill, with flakes of foam. He, stepping down   100
By zigzag paths and juts of pointed rock,
Came on the shining levels of the lake.

    There drew he forth the brand Excalibur,
And o'er him, drawing it, the winter moon,
Brightening the skirts of a long cloud, ran forth
And sparkled keen with frost against the hilt;
For all the haft twinkled with diamond sparks,
Myriads of topaz-lights, and jacinth-work
Of subtlest jewellery. He gazed so long
That both his eyes were dazzled, as he stood,   110
This way and that dividing the swift mind,
In act to throw; but at the last it seem'd
Better to leave Excalibur conceal'd
There in the many-knotted water-flags,
That whistled stiff and dry about the marge.
So strode he back slow to the wounded king.

    Then spake King Arthur to Sir Bedivere:
'Hast thou perform'd my mission which I gave?
What is it thou hast seen, or what hast heard?'

    And answer made the bold Sir Bedivere: 120
'I heard the ripple washing in the reeds,
And the wild water lapping on the crag.'

    To whom replied King Arthur, faint and pale:
'Thou hast betray'd thy nature and thy name,
Not rendering true answer, as beseem'd
Thy fealty, nor like a noble knight;
For surer sign had follow'd, either hand,

Or voice, or else a motion of the mere.
This is a shameful thing for men to lie.
Yet now, I charge thee, quickly go again   130
As thou art lief and dear, and do the thing
I bade thee, watch, and lightly bring me word.'
      Then went Sir Bedivere the second time
Across the ridge, and paced beside the mere,
Counting the dewy pebbles, fix'd in thought;
But when he saw the wonder of the hilt,
How curiously and strangely chased, he smote
His palms together, and he cried aloud:
      'And if indeed I cast the brand away,
Surely a precious thing, one worthy note,   140
Should thus be lost forever from the earth,
Which might have pleased the eyes of many men.
What good should follow this, if this were done?
What harm, undone? deep harm to disobey,
Seeing obedience is the bond of rule.
Were it well to obey then, if a king demand
An act unprofitable, against himself?
The king is sick, and knows not what he does.
What record, or what relic of my lord
Should be to aftertime, but empty breath   150
And rumors of a doubt? but were this kept,
Stored in some treasure-house of mighty kings,
Some one might show it at a joust of arms,
Saying, "King Arthur's sword, Excalibur,
Wrought by the lonely maiden of the lake;
Nine years she wrought it, sitting in the deeps
Upon the hidden bases of the hills."
So might some old man speak in the aftertime
To all the people, winning reverence;
But now much honor and much fame were lost.'   160
      So spake he, clouded with his own conceit,
And hid Excalibur the second time,
And so strode back slow to the wounded king.
      Then spoke King Arthur, breathing heavily:
'What is it thou hast seen, or what hast heard?'
      And answer made the bold Sir Bedivere:
'I heard the water lapping on the crag,
And the long ripple washing in the reeds.'
      To whom replied King Arthur, much in wrath:
'Ah, miserable and unkind, untrue,   170
Unknightly, traitor-hearted! Woe is me!
Authority forgets a dying king,
Laid widow'd of the power in his eye
That bow'd the will. I see thee what thou art,
For thou, the latest-left of all my knights,

In whom should meet the offices of all,
Thou wouldst betray me for the precious hilt;
Either from lust of gold, or like a girl
Valuing the giddy pleasure of the eyes.
Yet, for a man may fail in duty twice,   180
And the third time may prosper, get thee hence;
But, if thou spare to fling Excalibur,
I will arise and slay thee with my hands.'
    Then quickly rose Sir Bedivere, and ran,
And, leaping down the ridges lightly, plunged
Among the bulrush-beds, and clutch'd the sword,
And strongly wheel'd and threw it. The great brand
Made lightnings in the splendor of the moon,
And flashing round and round, and whirl'd in an arch,
Shot like a streamer of the northern morn,   190
Seen where the moving isles of winter shock
By night, with noises of the northern sea.
So flash'd and fell the brand Excalibur;
But ere he dipt the surface, rose an arm
Cloth'd in white samite, mystic, wonderful,
And caught him by the hilt, and brandish'd him
Three times, and drew him under in the mere.
And lightly went the other to the king.
    Then spoke King Arthur, drawing thicker breath:
'Now see I by thine eyes that this is done.   200
Speak out; what is it thou hast heard, or seen?'
    And answer made the bold Sir Bedivere:
'Sir King, I closed mine eyelids, lest the gems
Should blind my purpose, for I never saw,
Nor shall see, here or elsewhere, till I die,
Not tho' I live three lives of mortal men,
So great a miracle as yonder hilt.
Then with both hands I flung him, wheeling him;
But when I look'd again, behold an arm,
Clothed in white samite, mystic, wonderful,   210
That caught him by the hilt, and brandish'd him
Three times, and drew him under in the mere.'
    And answer made King Arthur, breathing hard:
'My end draws nigh; 't is time that I were gone.
Make broad thy shoulders to receive my weight,
And bear me to the margin; yet I fear
My wound hath taken cold, and I shall die.'
    So saying, from the pavement he half rose,
Slowly, with pain, reclining on his arm,
And looking wistfully with wide blue eyes   220
As in a picture. Him Sir Bedivere
Remorsefully regarded thro' his tears,
And would have spoken, but he found not words,

Then took with care, and kneeling on one knee,
O'er both his shoulders drew the languid hands,
And rising bore him thro' the place of tombs.

But, as he walk'd, King Arthur panted hard,
Like one that feels a nightmare on his bed
When all the house is mute. So sigh'd the king,
Muttering and murmuring at his ear, 'Quick, quick!   230
I fear it is too late, and I shall die.'
But the other swiftly strode from ridge to ridge,
Clothed with his breath, and looking, as he walk'd,
Larger than human on the frozen hills.
He heard the deep behind him, and a cry
Before. His own thought drove him like a goad.
Dry clash'd his harness in the icy caves
And barren chasms, and all to left and right
The bare black cliff clang'd round him, as he based
His feet on juts of slippery crag that rang   240
Sharp-smitten with the dint of armed heels—
And on a sudden, lo! the level lake,
And the long glories of the winter moon.

Then saw they how there hove a dusky barge,
Dark as a funeral scarf from stem to stern
Beneath them; and descending they were ware
That all the decks were dense with stately forms
Black-stoled, black-hooded, like a dream—by these
Three queens with crowns of gold—and from them rose
A cry that shiver'd to the tingling stars,   250
And, as it were one voice, an agony
Of lamentation, like a wind that shrills
All night in a waste land, where no one comes,
Or hath come, since the making of the world.

Then murmur'd Arthur, 'Place me in the barge,'
And to the barge they came. There those three queens
Put forth their hands, and took the king, and wept.
But she that rose the tallest of them all
And fairest laid his head upon her lap,
And loosed the shatter'd casque, and chafed his hands,   260
And call'd him by his name, complaining loud,
And dropping bitter tears against his brow
Striped with dark blood; for all his face was white
And colorless, and like the wither'd moon
Smote by the fresh beam of the springing east;
And all his greaves and cuisses dash'd with drops
Of onset; and the light and lustrous curls—
That made his forehead like a rising sun
High from the dais-throne—were parch'd with dust;
Or, clotted into points and hanging loose,   270
Mix'd with the knightly growth that fringed his lips.

So like a shatter'd column lay the king;
Not like that Arthur who, with lance in rest,
From spur to plume a star of tournament,
Shot thro' the lists at Camelot, and charged
Before the eyes of ladies and of kings.
    Then loudly cried the bold Sir Bedivere:
'Ah! my Lord Arthur, whither shall I go?
Where shall I hide my forehead and my eyes?
For now I see the true old times are dead,   280
When every morning brought a noble chance,
And every chance brought out a noble knight.
Such times have been not since the light that led
The holy Elders with the gift of myrrh.
But now the whole ROUND TABLE is dissolved
Which was an image of the mighty world;
And I, the last, go forth companionless,
And the days darken round me, and the years,
Among new men, strange faces, other minds.'
    And slowly answer'd Arthur from the barge: 290
'The old order changeth, yielding place to new,
And God fulfils himself in many ways,
Lest one good custom should corrupt the world.
Comfort thyself: what comfort is in me?
I have lived my life, and that which I have done
May He within himself make pure! but thou,
If thou shouldst never see my face again,
Pray for my soul. More things are wrought by prayer
Than this world dreams of. Wherefore, let thy voice
Rise like a fountain for me night and day.   300
For what are men better than sheep or goats
That nourish a blind life within the brain,
If, knowing God, they lift not hands of prayer
Both for themselves and those who call them friend?
For so the whole round earth is every way
Bound by gold chains about the feet of God.
But now farewell. I am going a long way
With these thou seest—if indeed I go—
For all my mind is clouded with a doubt—
To the island-valley of Avilion;   310
Where falls not hail, or rain, or any snow,
Nor ever wind blows loudly, but it lies
Deep-meadow'd, happy, fair with orchard lawns
And bowery hollows crown'd with summer sea,
Where I will heal me of my grievous wound.'
    So said he, and the barge with oar and sail
Moved from the brink, like some full-breasted swan
That, fluting a wild carol ere her death,
Ruffles her pure cold plume, and takes the flood

With swarthy webs. Long stood Sir Bedivere   320
Revolving many memories, till the hull
Look'd one black dot against the verge of dawn,
And on the mere the wailing died away.

Here ended Hall, and our last light, that long
Had wink'd and threaten'd darkness, flared and fell;
At which the parson, sent to sleep with sound,
And waked with silence, grunted 'Good!' but we
Sat rapt: it was the tone with which he read—
Perhaps some modern touches here and there
Redeem'd it from the charge of nothingness—   330
Or else we loved the man, and prized his work;
I know not; but we sitting, as I said,
The cock crew loud, as at that time of year
The lusty bird takes every hour for dawn.
Then Francis, muttering, like a man ill-used,
'There now—that's nothing!' drew a little back,
And drove his heel into the smoulder'd log,
That sent a blast of sparkles up the flue.
And so to bed, where yet in sleep I seem'd
To sail with Arthur under looming shores,   340
Point after point; till on to dawn, when dreams
Begin to feel the truth and stir of day,
To me, methought, who waited with the crowd,
There came a bark that, blowing forward, bore
King Arthur, like a modern gentleman
Of stateliest port; and all the people cried,
'Arthur is come again: he cannot die.'
Then those that stood upon the hills behind
Repeated—'Come again, and thrice as fair;'
And, further inland, voices echoed—'Come   350
With all good things, and war shall be no more.'
At this a hundred bells began to peal,
That with the sound I woke, and heard indeed
The clear church-bells ring in the Christmas morn.

THE GARDENER'S DAUGHTER

OR, THE PICTURES

THIS morning is the morning of the day,
When I and Eustace from the city went
To see the Gardener's daughter; I and he,
Brothers in Art; a friendship so complete
Portion'd in halves between us, that we grew
The fable of the city where we dwelt.

My Eustace might have sat for Hercules;
So muscular he spread, so broad of breast.
He, by some law that holds in love, and draws
The greater to the lesser, long desired   10
A certain miracle of symmetry,
A miniature of loveliness, all grace
Summ'd up and closed in little;—Juliet, she
So light of foot, so light of spirit—O, she
To me myself, for some three careless moons,
The summer pilot of an empty heart
Unto the shores of nothing! Know you not
Such touches are but embassies of Love,
To tamper with the feelings, ere he found
Empire for life? but Eustace painted her,   20
And said to me, she sitting with us then,
'When will *you* paint like this?' and I replied—
My words were half in earnest, half in jest:
' 'T is not your work, but Love's. Love, unperceived,
A more ideal artist he than all,
Came, drew your pencil from you, made those eyes
Darker than darkest pansies, and that hair
More black than ashbuds in the front of March.'
And Juliet answer'd laughing, 'Go and see
The Gardener's daughter; trust me, after that,   30
You scarce can fail to match his masterpiece.'
And up we rose, and on the spur we went.
    Not wholly in the busy world, nor quite
Beyond it, blooms the garden that I love.
News from the humming city comes to it
In sound of funeral or of marriage bells;
And, sitting muffled in dark leaves, you hear
The windy clanging of the minster clock;
Altho' between it and the garden lies
A league of grass, wash'd by a slow broad stream,   40
That, stirr'd with languid pulses of the oar,
Waves all its lazy lilies, and creeps on,
Barge-laden, to three arches of a bridge
Crown'd with the minster-towers.
                                        The fields between
Are dewy-fresh, browsed by deep-udder'd kine,
And all about the large lime feathers low—
The lime a summer home of murmurous wings.
    In that still place she, hoarded in herself,
Grew, seldom seen; not less among us lived
Her fame from lip to lip. Who had not heard   50
Of Rose, the Gardener's daughter? Where was he,
So blunt in memory, so old at heart,
At such a distance from his youth in grief,

That, having seen, forgot? The common mouth,
So gross to express delight, in praise of her
Grew oratory. Such a lord is Love,
And Beauty such a mistress of the world.

And if I said that Fancy, led by Love,
Would play with flying forms and images,
Yet this is also true, that, long before   60
I look'd upon her, when I heard her name
My heart was like a prophet to my heart,
And told me I should love. A crowd of hopes,
That sought to sow themselves like winged seeds,
Born out of everything I heard and saw,
Flutter'd about my senses and my soul;
And vague desires, like fitful blasts of balm
To one that travels quickly, made the air
Of life delicious, and all kinds of thought,
That verged upon them, sweeter than the dream   70
Dream'd by a happy man, when the dark East,
Unseen, is brightening to his bridal morn.

And sure this orbit of the memory folds
For ever in itself the day we went
To see her. All the land in flowery squares,
Beneath a broad and equal-blowing wind,
Smelt of the coming summer, as one large cloud
Drew downward; but all else of heaven was pure
Up to the sun, and May from verge to verge,
And May with me from head to heel. And now,   80
As tho' 't were yesterday, as tho' it were
The hour just flown, that morn with all its sound—
For those old Mays had thrice the life of these—
Rings in mine ears. The steer forgot to graze,
And, where the hedge-row cuts the pathway, stood,
Leaning his horns into the neighbor field
And lowing to his fellows. From the woods
Came voices of the well-contented doves.
The lark could scarce get out his notes for joy,
But shook his song together as he near'd   90
His happy home, the ground. To left and right,
The cuckoo told his name to all the hills;
The mellow ouzel fluted in the elm;
The redcap whistled; and the nightingale
Sang loud, as tho' he were the bird of day.

And Eustace turn'd, and smiling said to me:
'Hear how the bushes echo! by my life,
These birds have joyful thoughts. Think you they sing
Like poets, from the vanity of song?
Or have they any sense of why they sing?   100
And would they praise the heavens for what they have?'

And I made answer: 'Were there nothing else
For which to praise the heavens but only love,
That only love were cause enough for praise.'

Lightly he laugh'd, as one that read my thought,
And on we went; but ere an hour had pass'd,
We reach'd a meadow slanting to the North,
Down which a well-worn pathway courted us
To one green wicket in a privet hedge.
This, yielding, gave into a grassy walk 110
Thro' crowded lilac-ambush trimly pruned;
And one warm gust, full-fed with perfume, blew
Beyond us, as we enter'd in the cool.
The garden stretches southward. In the midst
A cedar spreads his dark-green layers of shade.
The garden-glasses shone, and momently
The twinkling laurel scatter'd silver lights.

'Eustace,' I said, 'this wonder keeps the house.'
He nodded, but a moment afterwards
He cried, 'Look! look!' Before he ceased I turn'd, 120
And, ere a star can wink, beheld her there.

For up the porch there grew an Eastern rose,
That, flowering high, the last night's gale had caught
And blown across the walk. One arm aloft—
Gown'd in pure white that fitted to the shape—
Holding the bush, to fix it back, she stood,
A single stream of all her soft brown hair
Pour'd on one side; the shadow of the flowers
Stole all the golden gloss, and, wavering
Lovingly lower, trembled on her waist— 130
Ah, happy shade!—and still went wavering down,
But, ere it touch'd a foot, that might have danced
The greensward into greener circles, dipt,
And mix'd with shadows of the common ground.
But the full day dwelt on her brows, and sunn'd
Her violet eyes, and all her Hebe bloom,
And doubled his own warmth against her lips,
And on the bounteous wave of such a breast
As never pencil drew. Half light, half shade,
She stood, a sight to make an old man young. 140

So rapt, we near'd the house; but she, a Rose
In roses, mingled with her fragrant toil,
Nor heard us come, nor from her tendance turn'd
Into the world without; till close at hand,
And almost ere I knew mine own intent,
This murmur broke the stillness of that air
Which brooded round about her:

'Ah, one rose,
One rose, but one, by those fair fingers cull'd,

Were worth a hundred kisses press'd on lips
Less exquisite than thine.'
               She look'd; but all   150
Suffused with blushes—neither self-possess'd
Nor startled, but betwixt this mood and that,
Divided in a graceful quiet—paused,
And dropt the branch she held, and turning wound
Her looser hair in braid, and stirr'd her lips
For some sweet answer, tho' no answer came,
Nor yet refused the rose, but granted it,
And moved away, and left me, statue-like,
In act to render thanks.
              I, that whole day,
Saw her no more, altho' I linger'd there   160
Till every daisy slept, and Love's white star
Beam'd thro' the thicken'd cedar in the dusk.

So home we went, and all the livelong way
With solemn gibe did Eustace banter me.
'Now,' said he, 'will you climb the top of art.
You cannot fail but work in hues to dim
The Titianic Flora. Will you match
My Juliet? you, not you,—the master, Love,
A more ideal artist he than all.'

So home I went, but could not sleep for joy,   170
Reading her perfect features in the gloom,
Kissing the rose she gave me o'er and o'er,
And shaping faithful record of the glance
That graced the giving—such a noise of life
Swarm'd in the golden present, such a voice
Call'd to me from the years to come, and such
A length of bright horizon rimm'd the dark.
And all that night I heard the watchman peal
The sliding season; all that night I heard
The heavy clocks knolling the drowsy hours.   180
The drowsy hours, dispensers of all good,
O'er the mute city stole with folded wings,
Distilling odors on me as they went
To greet their fairer sisters of the East.

Love at first sight, first-born, and heir to all,
Made this night thus. Henceforward squall nor storm
Could keep me from that Eden where she dwelt.
Light pretexts drew me: sometimes a Dutch love
For tulips; then for roses, moss or musk,
To grace my city rooms; or fruits and cream   190
Served in the weeping elm; and more and more
A word could bring the color to my cheek;
A thought would fill my eyes with happy dew;
Love troubled life within me, and with each

The year increased.
    The daughters of the year,
One after one, thro' that still garden pass'd;
Each garlanded with her peculiar flower
Danced into light, and died into the shade;
And each in passing touch'd with some new grace
Or seem'd to touch her, so that day by day,   200
Like one that never can be wholly known,
Her beauty grew; till Autumn brought an hour
For Eustace, when I heard his deep 'I will,'
Breathed, like a covenant of a God, to hold
From thence thro' all the worlds; but I rose up
Full of his bliss, and following her dark eyes
Felt earth as air beneath me, till I reach'd
The wicket-gate, and found her standing there.

 There sat we down upon a garden mound,
Two mutually enfolded; Love, the third,   210
Between us, in the circle of his arms
Enwound us both; and over many a range
Of waning lime the gray cathedral towers,
Across a hazy glimmer of the west,
Reveal'd their shining windows. From them clash'd
The bells; we listen'd; with the time we play'd,
We spoke of other things; we coursed about
The subject most at heart, more near and near,
Like doves about a dovecote, wheeling round
The central wish, until we settled there.   220

 Then, in that time and place, I spoke to her,
Requiring, tho' I knew it was mine own,
Yet for the pleasure that I took to hear,
Requiring at her hand the greatest gift,
A woman's heart, the heart of her I loved;
And in that time and place she answer'd me,
And in the compass of three little words,
More musical than ever came in one,
The silver fragments of a broken voice,
Made me most happy, faltering, 'I am thine.'   230

 Shall I cease here? Is this enough to say
That my desire, like all strongest hopes,
By its own energy fulfill'd itself,
Merged in completion? Would you learn at full
How passion rose thro' circumstantial grades
Beyond all grades develop'd? and indeed
I had not staid so long to tell you all,
But while I mused came Memory with sad eyes,
Holding the folded annals of my youth;
And while I mused, Love with knit brows went by,   240
And with a flying finger swept my lips,

And spake, 'Be wise: not easily forgiven
Are those who, setting wide the doors that bar
The secret bridal chambers of the heart,
Let in the day.' Here then, my words have end.

Yet might I tell of meetings, of farewells—
Of that which came between, more sweet than each,
In whispers, like the whispers of the leaves
That tremble round a nightingale—in sighs
Which perfect Joy, perplex'd for utterance,   250
Stole from her sister Sorrow. Might I not tell
Of difference, reconcilement, pledges given,
And vows, where there was never need of vows,
And kisses, where the heart on one wild leap
Hung tranced from all pulsation, as above
The heavens between their fairy fleeces pale
Sow'd all their mystic gulfs with fleeting stars;
Or while the balmy glooming, crescent-lit,
Spread the light haze along the river-shores,
And in the hollows; or as once we met   260
Unheedful, tho' beneath a whispering rain
Night slid down one long stream of sighing wind,
And in her bosom bore the baby, Sleep?

But this whole hour your eyes have been intent
On that veil'd picture—veil'd, for what it holds
May not be dwelt on by the common day.
This prelude has prepared thee. Raise thy soul,
Make thine heart ready with thine eyes; the time
Is come to raise the veil.
                            Behold her there,
As I beheld her ere she knew my heart,   270
My first, last love; the idol of my youth,
The darling of my manhood, and alas!
Now the most blessed memory of mine age.

DORA

WITH farmer Allan at the farm abode
William and Dora. William was his son,
And she his niece. He often look'd at them,
And often thought, 'I'll make them man and wife.'
Now Dora felt her uncle's will in all,
And yearn'd toward William; but the youth, because
He had been always with her in the house,
Thought not of Dora.
                    Then there came a day
When Allan call'd his son, and said: 'My son,
I married late, but I would wish to see   10

My grandchild on my knees before I die;
And I have set my heart upon a match.
Now therefore look to Dora; she is well
To look to; thrifty too beyond her age.
She is my brother's daughter; he and I
Had once hard words, and parted, and he died
In foreign lands; but for his sake I bred
His daughter Dora. Take her for your wife;
For I have wish'd this marriage, night and day,
For many years.' But William answer'd short: 20
'I cannot marry Dora; by my life,
I will not marry Dora!' Then the old man
Was wroth, and doubled up his hands, and said:
'You will not, boy! you dare to answer thus!
But in my time a father's word was law,
And so it shall be now for me. Look to it;
Consider, William, take a month to think,
And let me have an answer to my wish,
Or, by the Lord that made me, you shall pack,
And never more darken my doors again.'   30
But William answer'd madly, bit his lips,
And broke away. The more he look'd at her
The less he liked her; and his ways were harsh;
But Dora bore them meekly. Then before
The month was out he left his father's house,
And hired himself to work within the fields;
And half in love, half spite, he woo'd and wed
A laborer's daughter, Mary Morrison.

   Then, when the bells were ringing, Allan call'd
His niece and said: 'My girl, I love you well;   40
But if you speak with him that was my son,
Or change a word with her he calls his wife,
My home is none of yours. My will is law.'
And Dora promised, being meek. She thought,
'It cannot be; my uncle's mind will change!'

   And days went on, and there was born a boy
To William; then distresses came on him,
And day by day he pass'd his father's gate,
Heart-broken, and his father help'd him not.
But Dora stored what little she could save,   50
And sent it them by stealth, nor did they know
Who sent it; till at last a fever seized
On William, and in harvest time he died.
   Then Dora went to Mary. Mary sat
And look'd with tears upon her boy, and thought
Hard things of Dora. Dora came and said:
   'I have obey'd my uncle until now,
And I have sinn'd, for it was all thro' me

This evil came on William at the first.
But, Mary, for the sake of him, that's gone,   60
And for your sake, the woman that he chose,
And for this orphan, I am come to you.
You know there has not been for these five years
So full a harvest. Let me take the boy,
And I will set him in my uncle's eye
Among the wheat; that when his heart is glad
Of the full harvest, he may see the boy,
And bless him for the sake of him that's gone.'

    And Dora took the child, and went her way
Across the wheat, and sat upon a mound   70
That was unsown, where many poppies grew.
Far off the farmer came into the field
And spied her not, for none of all his men
Dare tell him Dora waited with the child;
And Dora would have risen and gone to him,
But her heart fail'd her; and the reapers reap'd,
And the sun fell, and all the land was dark.

    But when the morrow came, she rose and took
The child once more, and sat upon the mound;
And made a little wreath of all the flowers   80
That grew about, and tied it round his hat
To make him pleasing in her uncle's eye.
Then when the farmer pass'd into the field
He spied her, and he left his men at work,
And came and said: 'Where were you yesterday?
Whose child is that? What are you doing here?'
So Dora cast her eyes upon the ground,
And answer'd softly, 'This is William's child!'
'And did I not,' said Allan, 'did I not
Forbid you, Dora?' Dora said again: 90
'Do with me as you will, but take the child,
And bless him for the sake of him that's gone!'
And Allan said: 'I see it is a trick
Got up betwixt you and the woman there.
I must be taught my duty, and by you!
You knew my word was law, and yet you dared
To slight it. Well—for I will take the boy;
But go you hence, and never see me more.'

    So saying, he took the boy that cried aloud
And struggled hard. The wreath of flowers fell   100
As Dora's feet. She bow'd upon her hands,
And the boy's cry came to her from the field
More and more distant. She bow'd down her head,
Remembering the day when first she came,
And all the things that had been. She bow'd down
And wept in secret; and the reapers reap'd,

And the sun fell, and all the land was dark.

Then Dora went to Mary's house, and stood
Upon the threshold. Mary saw the boy
Was not with Dora. She broke out in praise   114
To God, that help'd her in her widowhood.
And Dora said: 'My uncle took the boy;
But, Mary, let me live and work with you:
He says that he will never see me more.'
Then answer'd Mary: 'This shall never be,
That thou shouldst take my trouble on thyself;
And, now I think, he shall not have the boy,
For he will teach him hardness, and to slight
His mother. Therefore thou and I will go,
And I will have my boy, and bring him home;   120
And I will beg of him to take thee back.
But if he will not take thee back again,
Then thou and I will live within one house,
And work for William's child, until he grows
Of age to help us.'
                    So the women kiss'd
Each other, and set out, and reach'd the farm.
The door was off the latch; they peep'd, and saw
The boy set up betwixt his grandsire's knees,
Who thrust him in the hollow of his arm,
And clapt him on the hands and on the cheeks,   130
Like one that loved him; and the lad stretch'd out
And babbled for the golden seal, that hung
From Allan's watch and sparkled by the fire.
Then they came in; but when the boy beheld
His mother, he cried out to come to her;
And Allan set him down, and Mary said:

'O father!—if you will let me call you so—
I never came a-begging for myself,
Or William, or this child; but now I come
For Dora; take her back, she loves you well.   140
O Sir, when William died, he died at peace
With all men; for I ask'd him, and he said,
He could not ever rue his marrying me—
I had been a patient wife; but, Sir, he said
That he was wrong to cross his father thus.
"God bless him!" he said, "and may he never know
The troubles I have gone thro' !" Then he turn'd
His face and pass'd—unhappy that I am!
But now, Sir, let me have my boy, for you
Will make him hard, and he will learn to slight   150
His father's memory; and take Dora back,
And let all this be as it was before.'

    So Mary said, and Dora hid her face

By Mary. There was silence in the room;
And all at once the old man burst in sobs:
  'I have been to blame—to blame. I have kill'd my son.
I have kill'd him—but I loved him—my dear son.
May God forgive me!—I have been to blame.
Kiss me, my children.'
                  Then they clung about
The old man's neck, and kiss'd him many times.   160
And all the man was broken with remorse;
And all his love came back a hundred-fold;
And for three hours he sobb'd o'er William's child
Thinking of William.
              So those four abode
Within one house together, and as years
Went forward Mary took another mate;
But Dora lived unmarried till her death.

AUDLEY COURT

'The Bull, the Fleece are cramm'd, and not a room
For love or money. Let us picnic there
At Audley Court.'
            I spoke, while Audley feast
Humm'd like a hive all round the narrow quay,
To Francis, with a basket on his arm,
To Francis just alighted from the boat
And breathing of the sea. 'With all my heart,'
Said Francis. Then we shoulder'd thro' the swarm,
And rounded by the stillness of the beach
To where the bay runs up its latest horn.   10
  We left the dying ebb that faintly lipp'd
The flat red granite; so by many a sweep
Of meadow smooth from aftermath we reach'd
The griffin-guarded gates, and pass'd thro' all
The pillar'd dusk of sounding sycamores,
And cross'd the garden to the gardener's lodge,
With all its casements bedded, and its walls
And chimneys muffled in the leafy vine.
  There, on a slope of orchard, Francis laid
A damask napkin wrought with horse and hound,   20
Brought out a dusky loaf that smelt of home,
And half-cut-down, a pasty costly-made,
Where quail and pigeon, lark and leveret lay,
Like fossils of the rock, with golden yolks
Imbedded and injellied; last, with these,
A flask of cider from his father's vats,
Prime, which I knew; and so we sat and eat

And talk'd old matters over,—who was dead,
Who married, who was like to be, and how
The races went, and who would rent the hall;   30
Then touch'd upon the game, how scarce it was
This season; glancing thence, discuss'd the farm,
The four-field system, and the price of grain;
And struck upon the corn-laws, where we split,
And came again together on the king
With heated faces; till he laugh'd aloud,
And, while the blackbird on the pippin hung
To hear him, clapt his hand in mine and sang:
    'O, who would fight and march and countermarch,
Be shot for sixpence in a battle-field,   40
And shovell'd up into some bloody trench
Where no one knows? but let me live my life.
    'O, who would cast and balance at a desk,
Perch'd like a crow upon a three-legg'd stool,
Till all his juice is dried, and all his joints
Are full of chalk? but let me live my life.
    'Who'd serve the state? for if I carved my name
Upon the cliffs that guard my native land,
I might as well have traced it in the sands;
The sea wastes all; but let me live my life.   50
    'O, who would love? I woo'd a woman once,
But she was sharper than an eastern wind,
And all my heart turn'd from her, as a thorn
Turns from the sea; but let me live my life.'
    He sang his song, and I replied with mine.
I found it in a volume, all of songs,
Knock'd down to me, when old Sir Robert's pride,
His books—the more the pity, so I said—
Came to the hammer here in March—and this—
I set the words, and added names I knew: 60
    'Sleep, Ellen Aubrey, sleep, and dream of me:
Sleep, Ellen, folded in thy sister's arm,
And sleeping, haply dream her arm is mine.
    'Sleep, Ellen, folded in Emilia's arm;
Emilia, fairer than all else but thou,
For thou art fairer than all else that is.
    'Sleep, breathing health and peace upon her breast;
Sleep, breathing love and trust against her lip.
I go to-night; I come to-morrow morn.
    'I go, but I return; I would I were   70
The pilot of the darkness and the dream.
Sleep, Ellen Aubrey, love, and dream of me.'
    So sang we each to either, Francis Hale,
The farmer's son, who lived across the bay,
My friend; and I, that having wherewithal,

And in the fallow leisure of my life
A rolling stone of here and everywhere,
Did what I would. But ere the night we rose
And saunter'd home beneath a moon that, just
In crescent, dimly rain'd about the leaf
Twilights of airy silver, till we reach'd
The limit of the hills; and as we sank
From rock to rock upon the glooming quay,
The town was hush'd beneath us; lower down
The bay was oily calm; the harbor-buoy,
Sole star of phosphorescence in the calm,
With one green sparkle ever and anon
Dipt by itself, and we were glad at heart.

WALKING TO THE MAIL

John.   I'm glad I walk'd. How fresh the meadows look
Above the river, and, but a month ago,
The whole hillside was redder than a fox!
Is yon plantation where this byway joins
The turnpike?
   James.   Yes.
   John.   And when does this come by?
   James.   The mail? At one o'clock.
   John.   What is it now?
   James.   A quarter to.
   John.   Whose house is that I see?
No, not the County Member's with the vane.
Up higher with the yew-tree by it, and half
A score of gables.
   James.   That? Sir Edward Head's.
But he's abroad; the place is to be sold.
   John.   O, his! He was not broken.
   James.   No, sir, he,
Vext with a morbid devil in his blood
That veil'd the world with jaundice, hid his face
From all men, and commercing with himself,
He lost the sense that handles daily life—
That keeps us all in order more or less—
And sick of home went overseas for change.
   John.   And whither?
   James.   Nay, who knows? he's here and there.
But let him go; his devil goes with him,
As well as with his tenant, Jocky Dawes.
   John.   What's that?
   James.   You saw the man—on Monday, was it?—
There by the humpback'd willow; half stands up

And bristles, half has fallen and made a bridge;
And there he caught the younker tickling trout—
Caught in *flagrante*—what's the Latin word?—
Delicto; but his house, for so they say,
Was haunted with a jolly ghost, that shook
The curtains, whined in lobbies, tapt at doors,
And rummaged like a rat; no servant stay'd.   30
The farmer vext packs up his beds and chairs,
And all his household stuff; and with his boy
Betwixt his knees, his wife upon the tilt,
Sets out, and meets a friend who hails him, 'What!
You're flitting!' 'Yes, we're flitting,' says the ghost—
For they had pack'd the thing among the beds.
'O, well,' says he, 'you flitting with us too!—
Jack, turn the horses' heads and home again.'
   John. He left *his* wife behind; for so I heard.
   James. He left her, yes. I met my lady once;   40
A woman like a butt, and harsh as crabs.
   John. O, yet but I remember, ten years back—
'T is now at least ten years—and then she was—
You could not light upon a sweeter thing;
A body slight and round, and like a pear
In growing, modest eyes, a hand, a foot
Lessening in perfect cadence, and a skin
As clean and white as privet when it flowers.
   James. Ay, ay, the blossom fades, and they that loved
At first like dove and dove were cat and dog.   50
She was the daughter of a cottager,
Out of her sphere. What betwixt shame and pride,
New things and old, himself and her, she sour'd
To what she is; a nature never kind!
Like men, like manners; like breeds like, they say.
Kind nature is the best; those manners next
That fit us like a nature second-hand—
Which are indeed the manners of the great.
   John. But I had heard it was this bill that past,
And fear of change at home, that drove him hence.   60
   James. That was the last drop in the cup of gall.
I once was near him, when his bailiff brought
A Chartist pike. You should have seen him wince
As from a venomous thing; he thought himself
A mark for all, and shudder'd, lest a cry
Should break his sleep by night, and his nice eyes
Should see the raw mechanic's bloody thumbs
Sweat on his blazon'd chairs. But sir, you know
That these two parties still divide the world—
Of those that want, and those that have; and still   70
The same old sore breaks out from age to age

With much the same result. Now I myself,
A Tory to the quick, was as a boy
Destructive, when I had not what I would.
I was at school,—a college in the South.
There lived a flayflint near; we stole his fruit,
His hens, his eggs; but there was a law for *us;*
We paid in person. He had a sow, sir. She,
With meditative grunts of much content,
Lay great with pig, wallowing in sun and mud.   30
By night we dragg'd her to the college tower
From her warm bed, and up the corkscrew stair
With hand and rope we haled the groaning sow,
And on the leads we kept her till she pigg'd.
Large range of prospect had the mother sow,
And but for daily loss of one she loved
As one by one we took them—but for this—
As never sow was higher in this world—
Might have been happy; but what lot is pure?
We took them all, till she was left alone   90
Upon her tower, the Niobe of swine,
And so return'd unfarrow'd to her sty.

    John.   They found you out?
    James.   Not they.
    John.   Well—after all—
What know we of the secret of a man?
His nerves were wrong. What ails us who are sound,
That we should mimic this raw fool the world,
Which charts us all in its coarse blacks or whites,
As ruthless as a baby with a worm,
As cruel as a schoolboy ere he grows
To pity—more from ignorance than will.   100
    But put your best foot forward, or I fear
That we shall miss the mail; and here it comes
With five at top, as quaint a four-in-hand
As you shall see,—three pyebalds and a roan.

EDWIN MORRIS

OR, THE LAKE

O ME, my pleasant rambles by the lake,
My sweet, wild, fresh three quarters of a year,
My one oasis in the dust and drouth
Of city life! I was a sketcher then.
See here, my doing: curves of mountain, bridge,
Boat, island, ruins of a castle, built
When men knew how to build, upon a rock

With turrets lichen-gilded like a rock;
And here, new-comers in an ancient hold,
New-comers from the Mersey, millionaires,   10
Here lived the Hills—a Tudor-chimney'd bulk
Of mellow brickwork on an isle of bowers.
  O me, my pleasant rambles by the lake
With Edwin Morris and with Edward Bull
The curate—he was fatter than his cure!
  But Edwin Morris, he that knew the names,
Long learned names of agaric, moss, and fern,
Who forged a thousand theories of the rocks,
Who taught me how to skate, to row, to swim,
Who read me rhymes elaborately good,   20
His own—I call'd him Crichton, for he seem'd
All perfect, finish'd to the finger-nail.
  And once I ask'd him of his early life,
And his first passion; and he answer'd me,
And well his words became him—was he not
A full-cell'd honeycomb of eloquence
Stored from all flowers? Poet-like he spoke:
  'My love for Nature is as old as I;
But thirty moons, one honeymoon to that,
And three rich sennights more, my love for her.   30
My love for Nature and my love for her,
Of different ages, like twin-sisters grew,
Twin-sisters differently beautiful.
To some full music rose and sank the sun,
And some full music seem'd to move and change
With all the varied changes of the dark,
And either twilight and the day between;
For daily hope fulfill'd, to rise again
Revolving toward fulfilment, made it sweet
To walk, to sit, to sleep, to wake, to breathe.'   40
  Or this or something like to this he spoke.
Then said the fat-faced curate Edward Bull:
  'I take it, God made the woman for the man,
And for the good and increase of the world.
A pretty face is well, and this is well,
To have a dame indoors, that trims us up,
And keeps us tight; but these unreal ways
Seem but the theme of writers, and indeed
Worn threadbare. Man is made of solid stuff
I say, God made the woman for the man,   50
And for the good and increase of the world.'
  'Parson,' said I, 'you pitch the pipe too low.
But I have sudden touches, and can run
My faith beyond my practice into his;
Tho' if, in dancing after Letty Hill,

I do not hear the bells upon my cap,
I scarce have other music—yet say on.
What should one give to light on such a dream?'
I ask'd him half-sardonically.

                   'Give?
Give all thou art,' he answer'd, and a light   60
Of laughter dimpled in his swarthy cheek;
'I would have hid her needle in my heart,
To save her little finger from a scratch
No deeper than the skin; my ears could hear
Her lightest breath; her least remark was worth
The experience of the wise. I went and came;
Her voice fled always thro' the summer land;
I spoke her name alone. Thrice-happy days!
The flower of each, those moments when we met,
The crown of all, we met to part no more.'   70
    Were not his words delicious, I a beast
To take them as I did? but something jarr'd;
Whether he spoke too largely, that there seem'd
A touch of something false, some self-conceit,
Or over-smoothness; howsoe'er it was,
He scarcely hit my humor, and I said:
    'Friend Edwin, do not think yourself alone
Of all men happy. Shall not Love to me,
As in the Latin song I learnt at school,
Sneeze out a full God-bless-you right and left?   80
But you can talk, yours is a kindly vein;
I have, I think,—Heaven knows,—as much within;
Have, or should have, but for a thought or two,
That like a purple beech among the greens
Looks out of place. 'T is from no want in her;
It is my shyness, or my self-distrust,
Or something of a wayward modern mind
Dissecting passion. Time will set me right.'
    So spoke I, knowing not the things that were.
Then said the fat-faced curate, Edward Bull: 90
    'God made the woman for the use of man,
And for the good and increase of the world.'
And I and Edwin laughed; and now we paused
About the windings of the marge to hear
The soft wind blowing over meadowy holms
And alders, garden-isles; and now we left
The clerk behind us, I and he, and ran
By ripply shallows of the lisping lake,
Delighted with the freshness and the sound.
    But when the bracken rusted on their crags,   100
My suit had wither'd, nipt to death by him
That was a god, and is a lawyer's clerk,

The rent-roll Cupid of our rainy isles.
'T is true, we met; one hour I had, no more:
She sent a note, the seal an *Elle vous suit*,
The close, 'Your Letty, only yours;' and this
Thrice underscored. The friendly mist of morn
Clung to the lake. I boated over, ran
My craft aground, and heard with beating heart
The sweet-gale rustle round the shelving keel;   110
And out I stept, and up I crept. She moved,
Like Proserpine in Enna, gathering flowers.
Then low and sweet I whistled thrice; and she,
She turn'd, we closed, we kiss'd, swore faith, I breathed
In some new planet. A silent cousin stole
Upon us and departed. 'Leave,' she cried,
'O, leave me!' 'Never, dearest, never: here
I brave the worst;' and while we stood like fools
Embracing, all at once a score of pugs
And poodles yell'd within, and out they came,   120
Trustees and aunts and uncles. 'What, with him!
Go,' shrill'd the cotton-spinning chorus; 'him!'
I choked. Again they shriek'd the burthen, 'Him!'
Again with hands of wild rejection, 'Go!—
Girl, get you in!' She went—and in one month
They wedded her to sixty thousand pounds,
To lands in Kent and messuages in York,
And slight Sir Robert with his watery smile
And educated whisker. But for me,
They set an ancient creditor to work;   130
It seems I broke a close with force and arms:
There came a mystic token from the king
To greet the sheriff, needless courtesy!
I read, and fled by night, and flying turn'd;
Her taper glimmer'd in the lake below;
I turn'd once more, close-button'd to the storm;
So left the place, left Edwin, nor have seen
Him since, nor heard of her, nor cared to hear.

  Nor cared to hear? perhaps; yet long ago
I have pardon'd little Letty; not indeed,   140
It may be, for her own dear sake, but this,—
She seems a part of those fresh days to me;
For in the dust and drouth of London life
She moves among my visions of the lake,
While the prime swallow dips his wing, or then
While the gold-lily blows, and overhead
The light cloud smoulders on the summer crag.

SAINT SIMEON STYLITES

ALTHO' I be the basest of mankind,
From scalp to sole one slough and crust of sin,
Unfit for earth, unfit for heaven, scarce meet
For troops of devils, mad with blasphemy,
I will not cease to grasp the hope I hold
Of saintdom, and to clamor, mourn, and sob,
Battering the gates of heaven with storms of prayer,
Have mercy, Lord, and take away my sin!
    Let this avail, just, dreadful, mighty God,
This not be all in vain that thrice ten years,   10
Thrice multiplied by superhuman pangs,
In hungers and in thirsts, fevers and cold,
In coughs, aches, stitches, ulcerous throes and cramps,
A sign betwixt the meadow and the cloud,
Patient on this tall pillar I have borne
Rain, wind, frost, heat, hail, damp, and sleet, and snow;
And I had hoped that ere this period closed
Thou wouldst have caught me up into thy rest,
Denying not these weather-beaten limbs
The meed of saints, the white robe and the palm.   20
    O, take the meaning, Lord! I do not breathe,
Not whisper, any murmur of complaint.
Pain heap'd ten-hundred-fold to this, were still
Less burthen, by ten-hundred-fold, to bear,
Than were those lead-like tons of sin that crush'd
My spirit flat before thee.
                    O Lord, Lord,
Thou knowest I bore this letter at the first,
For I was strong and hale of body then;
And tho' my teeth, which now are dropt away,
Would chatter with the cold, and all my beard   30
Was tagg'd with icy fringes in the moon,
I drown'd the whoopings of the owl with sound
Of pious hymns and psalms, and sometimes saw
An angel stand and watch me, as I sang.
Now am I feeble grown; my end draws nigh.
I hope my end draws nigh; half deaf I am,
So that I scarce can hear the people hum
About the column's base, and almost blind,
And scarce can recognize the fields I know;
And both my thighs are rotted with the dew;   40
Yet cease I not to clamor and to cry,
While my stiff spine can hold my weary head,
Till all my limbs drop piecemeal from the stone,
Have mercy, mercy! take away my sin!

O Jesus, if thou wilt not save my soul,
Who may be saved? who is it may be saved?
Who may be made a saint if I fail here?
Show me the man hath suffer'd more than I.
For did not all thy martyrs die one death?
For either they were stoned, or crucified,   50
Or burn'd in fire, or boil'd in oil, or sawn
In twain beneath the ribs; but I die here
To-day, and whole years long, a life of death.
Bear witness, if I could have found a way—
And heedfully I sifted all my thought—
More slowly-painful to subdue this home
Of sin, my flesh, which I despise and hate,
I had not stinted practice, O my God!

 For not alone this pillar-punishment,
Not this alone I bore; but while I lived   60
In the white convent down the valley there,
For many weeks about my loins I wore
The rope that haled the buckets from the well,
Twisted as tight as I could knot the noose,
And spake not of it to a single soul,
Until the ulcer, eating thro' my skin,
Betray'd my secret penance, so that all
My brethren marvell'd greatly. More than this
I bore, whereof, O God, thou knowest all.

 Three winters, that my soul might grow to thee,   70
I lived up there on yonder mountain-side.
My right leg chain'd into the crag, I lay
Pent in a roofless close of ragged stones;
Inswathed sometimes in wandering mist, and twice
Black'd with thy branding thunder, and sometimes
Sucking the damps for drink, and eating not,
Except the spare chance-gift of those that came
To touch my body and be heal'd, and live.
And they say then that I work'd miracles,
Whereof my fame is loud amongst mankind,   80
Cured lameness, palsies, cancers. Thou, O God,
Knowest alone whether this was or no.
Have mercy, mercy! cover all my sin!
 Then, that I might be more alone with thee,
Three years I lived upon a pillar, high
Six cubits, and three years on one of twelve;
And twice three years I crouch'd on one that rose
Twenty by measure; last of all, I grew
Twice ten long weary, weary years to this,
That numbers forty cubits from the soil.   90
 I think that I have borne as much as this—
Or else I dream—and for so long a time,

If I may measure time by yon slow light,
And this high dial, which my sorrow crowns—
So much—even so.

          And yet I know not well,
For that the evil ones come here, and say,
'Fall down, O Simeon; thou hast suffer'd long
For ages and for ages!' then they prate
Of penances I cannot have gone thro',
Perplexing me with lies; and oft I fall,   100
Maybe for months, in such blind lethargies
That Heaven, and Earth, and Time are choked.

              But yet
Bethink thee, Lord, while thou and all the saints
Enjoy themselves in heaven, and men on earth
House in the shade of comfortable roofs,
Sit with their wives by fires, eat wholesome food,
And wear warm clothes, and even beasts have stalls,
I, 'tween the spring and downfall of the light,
Bow down one thousand and two hundred times,
To Christ, the Virgin Mother, and the saints;   110
Or in the night, after a little sleep,
I wake; the chill stars sparkle; I am wet
With drenching dews, or stiff with crackling frost.
I wear an undress'd goatskin on my back;
A grazing iron collar grinds my neck;
And in my weak, lean arms I lift the cross,
And strive and wrestle with thee till I die.
O, mercy, mercy! wash away my sin!

    O Lord, thou knowest what a man I am;
A sinful man, conceived and born in sin.   120
'T is their own doing; this is none of mine;
Lay it not to me. Am I to blame for this,
That here come those that worship me? Ha! ha!
They think that I am somewhat. What am I?
The silly people take me for a saint,
And bring me offerings of fruit and flowers;
And I, in truth—thou wilt bear witness here—
Have all in all endured as much, and more
Than many just and holy men, whose names
Are register'd and calendar'd for saints.   130

    Good people, you do ill to kneel to me.
What is it I can have done to merit this?
I am a sinner viler than you all.
It may be I have wrought some miracles,
And cured some halt and maim'd; but what of that?
It may be no one, even among the saints,
May match his pains with mine; but what of that?
Yet do not rise; for you may look on me,

And in your looking you may kneel to God.
Speak! is there any of you halt or maim'd? 140
I think you know I have some power with Heaven
From my long penance; let him speak his wish.
    Yes, I can heal him. Power goes forth from me.
They say that they are heal'd. Ah, hark! they shout
'Saint Simeon Stylites.' Why, if so,
God reaps a harvest in me. O my soul,
God reaps a harvest in thee! If this be,
Can I work miracles and not be saved?
This is not told of any. They were saints.
It cannot be but that I shall be saved, 150
Yea, crown'd a saint. They shout, 'Behold a saint!'
And lower voices saint me from above.
Courage, Saint Simeon! This dull chrysalis
Cracks into shining wings, and hope ere death
Spreads more and more and more, that God hath now
Sponged and made blank of crimeful record all
My mortal archives.
                    O my sons, my sons,
I, Simeon of the pillar, by surname
Stylites, among men; I, Simeon,
The watcher on the column till the end; 160
I, Simeon, whose brain the sunshine bakes;
I, whose bald brows in silent hours become
Unnaturally hoar with rime, do now
From my high nest of penance here proclaim
That Pontius and Iscariot by my side
Show'd like fair seraphs. On the coals I lay,
A vessel full of sin; all hell beneath
Made me boil over. Devils pluck'd my sleeve,
Abaddon and Asmodeus caught at me.
I smote them with the cross; they swarm'd again. 170
In bed like monstrous apes they crush'd my chest;
They flapp'd my light out as I read; I saw
Their faces grow between me and my book;
With coltlike whinny and with hoggish whine
They burst my prayer. Yet this way was left,
And by this way I 'scaped them. Mortify
Your flesh, like me, with scourges and with thorns;
Smite, shrink not, spare not. If it may be, fast
Whole Lents, and pray. I hardly, with slow steps,
With slow, faint steps, and much exceeding pain, 180
Have scrambled past those pits of fire, that still
Sing in mine ears. But yield not me the praise;
God only thro' his bounty hath thought fit,
Among the powers and princes of this world,
To make me an example to mankind,

Which few can reach to. Yet I do not say
But that a time may come—yea, even now,
Now, now, his footsteps smite the threshold stairs
Of life—I say, that time is at the doors
When you may worship me without reproach;   190
For I will leave my relics in your land,
And you may carve a shrine about my dust,
And burn a fragrant lamp before my bones,
When I am gather'd to the glorious saints.

    While I spake then, a sting of shrewdest pain
Ran shrivelling thro' me, and a cloudlike change,
In passing, with a grosser film made thick
These heavy, horny eyes. The end! the end!
Surely the end! What's here? a shape, a shade,
A flash of light. Is that the angel there   200
That holds a crown? Come blessed brother, come!
I know thy glittering face. I waited long;
My brows are ready. What! deny it now?
Nay, draw, draw, draw nigh. So I clutch it. Christ!
'T is gone; 't is here again; the crown! the crown!
So now 't is fitted on and grows to me,
And from it melt the dews of Paradise,
Sweet! sweet! spikenard, and balm, and frankincense.
Ah! let me not be fool'd, sweet saints; I trust
That I am whole, and clean, and meet for Heaven.   210

    Speak, if there be a priest, a man of God,
Among you there, and let him presently
Approach, and lean a ladder on the shaft,
And climbing up into my airy home,
Deliver me the blessed sacrament;
For by the warning of the Holy Ghost,
I prophesy that I shall die to-night,
A quarter before twelve.
               But thou, O Lord,
Aid all this foolish people; let them take
Example, pattern; lead them to thy light.   220

THE TALKING OAK

ONCE more the gate behind me falls;
   Once more before my face
I see the moulder'd Abbey-walls,
       and within the chace.

   Beyon   e the city lies,
   Beneath   drift of smoke;

And ah! with what delighted eyes
    I turn to yonder oak.

For when my passion first began,
    Ere that which in me burn'd,
The love that makes me thrice a man,
    Could hope itself return'd,

To yonder oak within the field
    I spoke without restraint,
And with a larger faith appeal'd
    Than Papist unto Saint.

For oft I talk'd with him apart,
    And told him of my choice,
Until he plagiarized a heart,
    And answer'd with a voice.

Tho' what he whisper'd under heaven
    None else could understand,
I found him garrulously given,
    A babbler in the land.

But since I heard him make reply
    Is many a weary hour;
'T were well to question him, and try
    If yet he keeps the power.

Hail, hidden to the knees in fern,
    Broad Oak of Sumner-chace,
Whose topmost branches can discern
    The roofs of Sumner-place!

Say, thou, whereon I carved her name,
    If ever maid or spouse,
As fair as my Olivia, came
    To rest beneath thy boughs.

'O Walter, I have shelter'd here
    Whatever maiden grace
The good old summers, year by year,
    Made ripe in Sumner-chace;

'Old summers, when the monk was fat,
    And, issuing shorn and sleek,
Would twist his girdle tight, and pat
    The girls upon the cheek.

10

20

30

40

'Ere yet, in scorn of Peter's-pence,
 And number'd bead, and shrift,
Bluff Harry broke into the spence
 And turn'd the cowls adrift.

'And I have seen some score of those
 Fresh faces that would thrive   50
When his man-minded offset rose
 To chase the deer at five;

'And all that from the town would stroll,
 Till that wild wind made work
In which the gloomy brewer's soul
 Went by me, like a stork;

'The slight she-slips of loyal blood,
 And others, passing praise,
Strait-laced, but all-too-full in bud
 For puritanic stays.   60

'And I have shadow'd many a group
 Of beauties that were born
In teacup-times of hood and hoop,
 Or while the patch was worn;

'And leg and arm with love-knots gay,
 About me leap'd and laugh'd
The modish Cupid of the day,
 And shrill'd his tinsel shaft.

'I swear—and else may insects prick
 Each leaf into a gall!—   70
This girl, for whom your heart is sick,
 Is three times worth them all;

'For those and theirs, by Nature's law,
 Have faded long ago;
But in these latter springs I saw
 Your own Olivia blow,

'From when she gamboll'd on the greens
 A baby-germ, to when
The maiden blossoms of her teens
 Could number five from ten.   80

'I swear, by leaf, and wind, and rain—
 And hear me with thine ears—

That, tho' I circle in the grain
    Five hundred rings of years,

'Yet, since I first could cast a shade,
    Did never creature pass
So slightly, musically made,
    So light upon the grass;

'For as to fairies, that will flit
    To make the greensward fresh,
I hold them exquisitely knit,
    But far too spare of flesh.'

O, hide thy knotted knees in fern,
    And overlook the chace,
And from thy topmost branch discern
    The roofs of Sumner-place!

But thou, whereon I carved her name,
    That oft has heard my vows,
Declare when last Olivia came
    To sport beneath thy boughs.

'O, yesterday, you know, the fair
    Was holden at the town;
Her father left his good arm-chair,
    And rode his hunter down.

'And with him Albert came on his.
    I look'd at him with joy;
As cowslip unto oxlip is,
    So seems she to the boy.

'An hour had past—and, sitting straight
    Within the low-wheel'd chaise,
Her mother trundled to the gate
    Behind the dappled grays.

'But as for her, she staid at home,
    And on the roof she went,
And down the way you used to come,
    She look'd with discontent.

'She left the novel half-uncut
    Upon the rosewood shelf;
She left the new piano shut;
    She could not please herself.

'Then ran she, gamesome as the colt,
    And livelier than a lark
She sent her voice thro' all the holt
    Before her, and the park.

'A light wind chased her on the wing,
    And in the chase grew wild,
As close as might be would he cling
    About the darling child;

'But light as any wind that blows
    So fleetly did she stir,   130
The flower she touch'd on dipt and rose,
    And turn'd to look at her.

'And here she came, and round me play'd,
    And sang to me the whole
Of those three stanzas that you made
    About my "giant bole;"

'And in a fit of frolic mirth
    She strove to span my waist.
Alas! I was so broad of girth,
    I could not be embraced.   140

'I wish'd myself the fair young beech
    That here beside me stands,
That round me, clasping each in each,
    She might have lock'd her hands.

'Yet seem'd the pressure thrice as sweet
    As woodbine's fragile hold,
Or when I feel about my feet
    The berried briony fold.'

O, muffle round thy knees with fern,
    And shadow Sumner-chace!   150
Long may thy topmost branch discern
    The roofs of Sumner-place!

But tell me, did she read the name
    I carved with many vows
When last with throbbing heart I came
    To rest beneath thy boughs?

'O, yes, she wander'd round and round
    These knotted knees of mine,

And found, and kiss'd the name she found,
    And sweetly murmur'd thine.   160

'A teardrop trembled from its source,
    And down my surface crept.
My sense of touch is something coarse,
    But I believe she wept.

'Then flush'd her cheek with rosy light,
    She glanced across the plain,
But not a creature was in sight;
    She kiss'd me once again.

'Her kisses were so close and kind
    That, trust me on my word,   170
Hard wood I am, and wrinkled rind,
    But yet my sap was stirr'd;

'And even into my inmost ring
    A pleasure I discern'd,
Like those blind motions of the spring
    That show the year is turn'd.

'Thrice-happy he that may caress
    The ringlet's waving balm—
The cushions of whose touch may press
    The maiden's tender palm.   180

'I, rooted here among the groves,
    But languidly adjust
My vapid vegetable loves
    With anthers and with dust;

'For ah! my friend, the days were brief
    Whereof the poets talk,
When that which breathes within the leaf
    Could slip its bark and walk.

'But could I, as in times foregone,
    From spray and branch and stem   190
Have suck'd and gather'd into one
    The life that spreads in them,

'She had not found me so remiss;
    But lightly issuing thro',
I would have paid her kiss for kiss,
    With usury thereto.'

O, flourish high, with leafy towers,
    And overlook the lea!
Pursue thy loves among the bowers,
    But leave thou mine to me.   200

  O, flourish, hidden deep in fern,
    Old oak, I love thee well!
A thousand thanks for what I learn
    And what remains to tell.

' 'T is little more: the day was warm;
    At last, tired out with play,
She sank her head upon her arm
    And at my feet she lay.

'Her eyelids dropp'd their silken eaves.
    I breathed upon her eyes   210
Thro' all the summer of my leaves
    A welcome mix'd with sighs.

'I took the swarming sound of life—
    The music from the town—
The murmurs of the drum and fife,
    And lull'd them in my own.

'Sometimes I let a sunbeam slip,
    To light her shaded eye;
A second flutter'd round her lip
    Like a golden butterfly;   220

'A third would glimmer on her neck
    To make the necklace shine;
Another slid, a sunny fleck,
    From head to ankle fine.

'Then close and dark my arms I spread,
    And shadow'd all her rest—
Dropt dews upon her golden head,
    An acorn in her breast.

'But in a pet she started up,
    And pluck'd it out, and drew   230
My little oakling from the cup,
    And flung him in the dew.

'And yet it was a graceful gift—
    I felt a pang within

As when I see the woodman lift
　　His axe to slay my kin.

'I shook him down because he was
　　The finest on the tree.
He lies beside thee on the grass.
　　O, kiss him once for me! 240

'O, kiss him twice and thrice for me,
　　That have no lips to kiss!
For never yet was oak on lea
　　Shall grow so fair as this.'

Step deeper yet in herb and fern,
　　Look further thro' the chace,
Spread upward till thy boughs discern
　　The front of Sumner-place.

This fruit of thine by Love is blest,
　　That but a moment lay 250
Where fairer fruit of Love may rest
　　Some happy future day.

I kiss it twice, I kiss it thrice,
　　The warmth it thence shall win
To riper life may magnetize
　　The baby-oak within.

But thou, while kingdoms overset,
　　Or lapse from hand to hand,
Thy leaf shall never fail, nor yet
　　Thine acorn in the land. 260

May never saw dismember thee,
　　Nor wielded axe disjoint,
That art the fairest-spoken tree
　　From here to Lizard-point.

O, rock upon thy towery top
　　All throats that gurgle sweet!
All starry culmination drop
　　Balm-dews to bathe thy feet!

All grass of silky feather grow—
　　And while he sinks or swells 270
The full south-breeze around thee blow
　　The sound of minster bells!

The fat earth feed thy branchy root,
  That under deeply strikes!
The northern morning o'er thee shoot
  High up, in silver spikes!

Nor ever lightning char thy grain,
  But, rolling as in sleep,
Low thunders bring the mellow rain,
  That makes thee broad and deep!   280

And hear me swear a solemn oath,
  That only by thy side
Will I to Olive plight my troth,
  And gain her for my bride.

And when my marriage morn may fall,
  She, Dryad-like, shall wear
Alternate leaf and acorn-ball
  In wreath about her hair.

And I will work in prose and rhyme,
  And praise thee more in both   290
Than bard has honor'd beech or lime,
  Or that Thessalian growth

In which the swarthy ringdove sat,
  And mystic sentence spoke;
And more than England honors that,
  Thy famous brother-oak,

Wherein the younger Charles abode
  Till all the paths were dim,
And far below the Roundhead rode,
  And humm'd a surly hymn.   300

LOVE AND DUTY

Of love that never found his earthly close,
What sequel? Streaming eyes and breaking hearts?
Or all the same as if he had not been?
  Not so. Shall Error in the round of time
Still father Truth? O, shall the braggart shout
For some blind glimpse of freedom work itself
Thro' madness, hated by the wise, to law,
System, and empire? Sin itself be found
The cloudy porch oft opening on the sun?
And only he, this wonder, dead, become   10

Mere highway dust? or year by year alone
Sit brooding in the ruins of a life,
Nightmare of youth, the spectre of himself?
    If this were thus, if this, indeed, were all,
Better the narrow brain, the stony heart,
The staring eye glazed o'er with sapless days,
The long mechanic pacings to and fro,
The set gray life, and apathetic end.
But am I not the nobler thro' thy love?
O, three times less unworthy! likewise thou   20
Art more thro' Love, and greater than thy years,
The sun will run his orbit, and the moon
Her circle. Wait, and Love himself will bring
The drooping flower of knowledge changed to fruit
Of wisdom. Wait; my faith is large in Time,
And that which shapes it to some perfect end.
    Will some one say, Then why not ill for good?
Why took ye not your pastime? To that man
My work shall answer, since I knew the right
And did it; for a man is not as God,   30
But then most Godlike being most a man.—
So let me think 't is well for thee and me—
Ill-fated that I am, what lot is mine
Whose foresight preaches peace, my heart so slow
To feel it! For how hard it seem'd to me,
When eyes, love-languid thro' half tears would dwell
One earnest, earnest moment upon mine,
Then not to dare to see! what thy low voice,
Faltering, would break its syllables, to keep
My own full-tuned,—hold passion in a leash,   40
And not leap forth and fall about thy neck,
And on thy bosom—deep desired relief!—
Rain out the heavy mist of tears, that weigh'd
Upon my brain, my senses, and my soul!
    For Love himself took part against himself
To warn us off, and Duty loved of Love—
O, this world's curse—beloved but hated—came
Like Death betwixt thy dear embrace and mine,
And crying, 'Who is this? behold thy bride,'
She push'd me from thee.
                   If the sense is hard   50
To alien ears, I did not speak to these—
No, not to thee, but to thyself in me.
Hard is my doom and thine; thou knowest it all.
    Could Love part thus? was it not well to speak,
To have spoken once? It could not but be well.
The slow sweet hours that bring us all things good,
The slow sad hours that bring us all things ill,

And all good things from evil, brought the night
In which we sat together and alone,
And to the want that hollow'd all the heart   60
Gave utterance by the yearning of an eye,
That burn'd upon its object thro' such tears
As flow but once a life.
                 The trance gave way
To those caresses, when a hundred times
In that last kiss, which never was the last,
Farewell, like endless welcome, lived and died.
Then follow'd counsel, comfort, and the words
That make a man feel strong in speaking truth;
Till now the dark was worn, and overhead
The lights of sunset and of sunrise mix'd   70
In that brief night, the summer night, that paused
Among her stars to hear us, stars that hung
Love-charm'd to listen; all the wheels of Time
Spun round in station, but the end had come.
   O, then, like those who clench their nerves to rush
Upon their dissolution, we two rose,
There—closing like an individual life—
In one blind cry of passion and of pain,
Like bitter accusation even to death,
Caught up the whole of love and utter'd it,   80
And bade adieu for ever.
                Live—yet live—
Shall sharpest pathos blight us, knowing all
Life needs for life is possible to will?—
Live happy; tend thy flowers; be tended by
My blessing! Should my Shadow cross thy thoughts
Too sadly for their peace, remand it thou
For calmer hours to Memory's darkest hold,
If not to be forgotten—not at once—
Not all forgotten. Should it cross thy dreams,
O, might it come like one that looks content,   90
With quiet eyes unfaithful to the truth,
And point thee forward to a distant light,
Or seem to lift a burthen from thy heart
And leave thee freer, till thou wake refresh'd
Then when the first low matin-chirp hath grown
Full quire, and morning driven her plow of pearl
Far furrowing into light the mounded rack,
Beyond the fair green field and eastern sea.

THE GOLDEN YEAR

WELL, you shall have that song which Leonard wrote:
It was last summer on a tour in Wales.
Old James was with me; we that day had been
Up Snowden; and I wish'd for Leonard there,
And found him in Llanberis. Then we crost
Between the lakes, and clamber'd half-way up
The counter side; and that same song of his
He told me, for I banter'd him and swore
They said he lived shut up within himself,
A tongue-tied poet in the feverous days   10
That, setting the *how much* before the *how*,
Cry, like the daughters of the horseleech, 'Give,
Cram us with all,' but count not me the herd!

   To which 'They call me what they will,' he said:
'But I was born too late; the fair new forms,
That float about the threshold of an age,
Like truths of Science waiting to be caught—
Catch me who can, and make the catcher crown'd—
Are taken by the forelock. Let it be.
But if you care indeed to listen, hear   20
These measured words, my work of yester-morn:

   'We sleep and wake and sleep, but all things move;
The sun flies forward to his brother sun;
The dark earth follows wheel'd in her ellipse;
And human things returning on themselves
Move onward, leading up the golden year.

   'Ah, tho' the times when some new thought can bud
Are but as poets' seasons when they flower
Yet seas that daily gain upon the shore
Have ebb and flow conditioning their march,   30
And slow and sure comes up the golden year;

   'When wealth no more shall rest in mounded heaps,
But smit with freer light shall slowly melt
In many streams to fatten lower lands,
And light shall spread, and man be liker man
Thro' all the season of the golden year.

   'Shall eagles not be eagles? wrens be wrens?
If all the world were falcons, what of that?
The wonder of the eagle were the less,
But he not less the eagle. Happy days   41
Roll onward, leading up the golden year.

   'Fly, happy, happy sails, and bear the Press;
Fly happy with the mission of the Cross;
Knit land to land, and blowing havenward
With silks, and fruits, and spices, clear of toll,

Enrich the markets of the golden year.
'But we grow old. Ah! when shall all men's good
Be each man's rule, and universal Peace
Lie like a shaft of light across the land,
And like a lane of beams athwart the sea,   50
Thro' all the circle of the golden year?'
    Thus far he flow'd, and ended; whereupon
'Ah, folly!' in mimic cadence answer'd James—
'Ah, folly! for it lies so far away,
Not in our time, nor in our children's time,
'T is like the second world to us that live;
'T were all as one to fix our hopes on heaven
As on this vision of the golden year.'
    With that he struck his staff against the rocks
And broke it,—James,—you know him,—old, but full   60
Of force and choler, and firm upon his feet,
And like an oaken stock in winter woods,
O'erflourish'd with the hoary clematis;
Then added, all in heat
                'What stuff is this!
Old writers push'd the happy season back,—
The more fools they,—we forward; dreamers both—
You most, that, in an age when every hour
Must sweat her sixty minutes to the death,
Live on, God love us, as if the seedsman, rapt
Upon the teeming harvest, should not plunge   70
His hand into the bag; but well I know
That unto him who works, and feels he works,
This same grand year is ever at the doors.'
    He spoke; and, high above, I heard them blast
The steep slate-quarry, and the great echo flap
And buffet round the hills, from bluff to bluff.

ULYSSES

It little profits that an idle king,
By this still hearth, among these barren crags,
Match'd with an aged wife, I mete and dole
Unequal laws unto a savage race,
That hoard, and sleep, and feed, and know not me.
I cannot rest from travel; I will drink
Life to the lees. All times I have enjoy'd
Greatly, have suffer'd greatly, both with those
That loved me, and alone; on shore, and when
Thro' scudding drifts the rainy Hyades   10
Vext the dim sea. I am become a name;
For always roaming with a hungry heart
Much have I seen and known,—cities of men

And manners, climates, councils, governments,
Myself not least, but honor'd of them all,—
And drunk delight of battle with my peers,
Far on the ringing plains of windy Troy.
I am a part of all that I have met;
Yet all experience is an arch wherethro'
Gleams that untravell'd world whose margin fades 20
For ever and for ever when I move.
How dull it is to pause, to make an end,
To rust unburnish'd, not to shine in use!
As tho' to breathe were life! Life piled on life
Were all too little, and of one to me
Little remains; but every hour is saved
From that eternal silence, something more,
A bringer of new things; and vile it were
For some three suns to store and hoard myself,
And this gray spirit yearning in desire 30
To follow knowledge like a sinking star,
Beyond the utmost bound of human thought.

This is my son, mine own Telemachus,
To whom I leave the sceptre and the isle,—
Well-loved of me, discerning to fulfill
This labor, by slow prudence to make mild
A rugged people, and thro' soft degrees
Subdue them to the useful and the good.
Most blameless is he, centred in the sphere
Of common duties, decent not to fail 40
In offices of tenderness, and pay
Meet adoration to my household gods,
When I am gone. He works his work, I mine.

There lies the port; the vessel puffs her sail;
There gloom the dark, broad seas. My mariners,
Souls that have toil'd, and wrought, and thought with me,—
That ever with a frolic welcome took
The thunder and the sunshine, and opposed
Free hearts, free foreheads,—you and I are old;
Old age hath yet his honor and his toil. 50
Death closes all; but something ere the end,
Some work of noble note, may yet be done,
Not unbecoming men that strove with Gods.
The lights begin to twinkle from the rocks;
The long day wanes; the slow moon climbs; the deep
Moans round with many voices. Come, my friends.
'T is not too late to seek a newer world.
Push off, and sitting well in order smite
The sounding furrows; for my purpose holds
To sail beyond the sunset, and the baths 60
Of all the western stars, until I die.

It may be that the gulfs will wash us down;
It may be we shall touch the Happy Isles,
And see the great Achilles, whom we knew.
Tho' much is taken, much abides; and tho'
We are not now that strength which in old days
Moved earth and heaven, that which we are, we are,—
One equal temper of heroic hearts,
Made weak by time and fate, but strong in will
To strive, to seek, to find, and not to yield.   70

TITHONUS

THE woods decay, the woods decay and fall,
The vapors weep their burthen to the ground,
Man comes and tills the field and lies beneath,
And after many a summer dies the swan.
Me only cruel immortality
Consumes; I wither slowly in thine arms,
Here at the quiet limit of the world,
A white-hair'd shadow roaming like a dream
The ever-silent spaces of the East,
Far-folded mists, and gleaming halls of morn.   10
    Alas! for this gray shadow, once a man—
So glorious in his beauty and thy choice,
Who madest him thy chosen, that he seem'd
To his great heart none other than a God!
I ask'd thee, 'Give me immortality.'
Then didst thou grant mine asking with a smile,
Like wealthy men who care not how they give.
But thy strong Hours indignant work'd their wills,
And beat me down and marr'd and wasted me,
And tho' they could not end me, left me maim'd   20
To dwell in presence of immortal youth,
Immortal age beside immortal youth,
And all I was in ashes. Can thy love,
Thy beauty, make amends, tho' even now,
Close over us, the silver star, thy guide,
Shines in those tremulous eyes that fill with tears
To hear me? Let me go; take back thy gift.
Why should a man desire in any way
To vary from the kindly race of men,
Or pass beyond the goal of ordinance   30
Where all should pause, as is most meet for all?
    A soft air fans the cloud apart; there comes
A glimpse of that dark world where I was born.
Once more the old mysterious glimmer steals
From thy pure brows, and from thy shoulders pure,

And bosom beating with a heart renew'd.
Thy cheek begins to redden thro' the gloom,
Thy sweet eyes brighten slowly close to mine,
Ere yet they blind the stars, and the wild team   40
Which love thee, yearning for thy yoke, arise
And shake the darkness from their loosen'd manes,
And beat the twilight into flakes of fire.

　　Lo! ever thus thou growest beautiful
In silence, then before thine answer given
Departest, and thy tears are on my cheek.

　　Why wilt thou ever scare me with thy tears,
And make me tremble lest a saying learnt,
In days far-off, on that dark earth, be true?
'The Gods themselves cannot recall their gifts.'

　　Ay me! ay me! with what another heart   50
In days far-off, and with what other eyes
I used to watch—if I be he that watch'd—
The lucid outline forming round thee; saw
The dim curls kindle into sunny rings;
Changed with thy mystic change, and felt my blood
Glow with the glow that slowly crimson'd all
Thy presence and thy portals, while I lay,
Mouth, forehead, eyelids, growing dewy-warm
With kisses balmier than half-opening buds
Of April, and could hear the lips that kiss'd   60
Whispering I knew not what of wild and sweet,
Like that strange song I heard Apollo sing,
While Ilion like a mist rose into towers.

　　Yet hold me not for ever in thine East;
How can my nature longer mix with thine?
Coldly thy rosy shadows bathe me, cold
Are all thy lights, and cold my wrinkled feet
Upon thy glimmering thresholds, when the steam
Floats up from those dim fields about the homes
Of happy men that have the power to die,   70
And grassy barrows of the happier dead.
Release me, and restore me to the ground.
Thou seest all things, thou wilt see my grave;
Thou wilt renew thy beauty morn by morn,
I earth in earth forget these empty courts,
And thee returning on thy silver wheels.

LOCKSLEY HALL

COMRADES, leave me here a little, while as yet 't is early morn;
Leave me here, and when you want me, sound upon the bugle-horn.

'T is the place, and all around it, as of old, the curlews call,
Dreary gleams about the moorland flying over Locksley Hall;

Locksley Hall, that in the distance overlooks the sandy tracts,
And the hollow ocean-ridges roaring into cataracts.

Many a night from yonder ivied casement, ere I went to rest,
Did I look on great Orion sloping slowly to the west.

Many a night I saw the Pleiads, rising thro' the mellow shade,
Glitter like a swarm of fireflies tangled in a sliver braid.　　10

Here about the beach I wander'd, nourishing a youth sublime
With the fairy tales of science, and the long result of time;

When the centuries behind me like a fruitful land reposed;
When I clung to all the present for the promise that it closed;

When I dipt into the future far as human eye could see,
Saw the vision of the world and all the wonder that would be.—

In the spring a fuller crimson comes upon the robin's breast;
In the spring the wanton lapwing gets himself another crest;

In the spring a livelier iris changes on the burnish'd dove;
In the spring a young man's fancy lightly turns to thoughts of love.　　20

Then her cheek was pale and thinner than should be for one so young,
And her eyes on all my motions with a mute observance hung.

And I said, 'My cousin Amy, speak, and speak the truth to me,
Trust me, cousin, all the current of my being sets to thee.'

On her pallid cheek and forehead came a color and a light,
As I have seen the rosy red flushing in the northern night.

And she turn'd—her bosom shaken with a sudden storm of sighs—
All the spirit deeply dawning in the dark of hazel eyes—

Saying, 'I have hid my feelings, fearing they should do me wrong;'
Saying, 'Dost thou love me, cousin?' weeping, 'I have loved thee long.'' 30

Love took up the glass of Time, and turn'd it in his glowing hands;
Every moment, lightly shaken, ran itself in golden sands.

Love took up the harp of Life, and smote on all the chords with might;
Smote the chord of Self, that, trembling, past in music out of sight.

Many a morning on the moorland did we hear the copses ring,
And her whisper throng'd my pulses with the fulness of the spring.

Many an evening by the waters did we watch the stately ships,
And our spirits rush'd together at the touching of the lips.

O my cousin, shallow-hearted! O my Amy, mine no more!
O the dreary, dreary moorland! O the barren, barren shore!   40

Falser than all fancy fathoms, falser than all songs have sung,
Puppet to a father's threat, and servile to a shrewish tongue!

Is it well to wish the happy?—having known me—to decline
On a range of lower feelings and a narrower heart than mine!

Yet it shall be; thou shalt lower to his level day by day,
What is fine within thee growing coarse to sympathize with clay.

As the husband is, the wife is; thou art mated with a clown,
And the grossness of his nature will have weight to drag thee down.

He will hold thee, when his passion shall have spent its novel force,
Something better than his dog, a little dearer than his horse.   50

What is this? his eyes are heavy; think not they are glazed with wine.
Go to him, it is thy duty; kiss him, take his hand in thine.

It may be my lord is weary, that his brain is overwrought;
Soothe him with thy finer fancies, touch him with thy lighter thought.

He will answer to the purpose, easy things to understand—
Better thou wert dead before me, tho' I slew thee with my hand!

Better thou and I were lying, hidden from the heart's disgrace,
Roll'd in one another's arms, and silent in a last embrace.

Cursed be the social wants that sin against the strength of youth!
Cursed be the social lies that warp us from the living truth!   60

Cursed be the sickly forms that err from honest Nature's rule!
Cursed be the gold that gilds the straiten'd forehead of the fool!

Well—'t is well that I should bluster!—Hadst thou less unworthy proved
Would to God—for I had loved thee more than ever wife was loved.

Am I mad, that I should cherish that which bears but bitter fruit?
I will pluck it from my bosom, tho' my heart be at the root.

Never, tho' my mortal summers to such length of years should come
As the many-winter'd crow that leads the clanging rookery home.

Where is comfort? in division of the records of the mind?
Can I part her from herself, and love her, as I knew her, kind?   70

I remember one that perish'd; sweetly did she speak and move;
Such a one do I remember, whom to look at was to love.

Can I think of her as dead, and love her for the love she bore?
No—she never loved me truly; love is love for evermore.

Comfort? comfort scorn'd of devils! this is truth the poet sings,
That a sorrow's crown of sorrow is remembering happier things.

Drug thy memories, lest thou learn it, lest thy heart be put to proof,
In the dead unhappy night, and when the rain is on the roof.

Like a dog, he hunts in dreams, and thou art staring at the wall,
Where the dying night-lamp flickers, and the shadows rise and fall.   80

Then a hand shall pass before thee, pointing to his drunken sleep,
To thy widow'd marriage-pillows, to the tears that thou wilt weep.

Thou shalt hear the 'Never, never,' whisper'd by the phantom years,
And a song from out the distance in the ringing of thine ears;

And an eye shall vex thee, looking ancient kindness on thy pain.
Turn thee, turn thee on thy pillow; get thee to thy rest again.

Nay, but Nature brings thee solace; for a tender voice will cry.
'T is a purer life than thine, a lip to drain thy trouble dry.

Baby lips will laugh me down; my latest rival brings thee rest.
Baby fingers, waxen touches, press me from the mother's breast.   90

O, the child too clothes the father with a dearness not his due.
Half is thine and half is his; it will be worthy of the two.

O, I see thee old and formal, fitted to thy petty part,
With a little hoard of maxims preaching down a daughter's heart.

'They were dangerous guides the feelings—she herself was not exempt—
Truly, she herself had suffer'd'—Perish in thy self-contempt!

Overlive it—lower yet—be happy! wherefore should I care?
I myself must mix with action, lest I wither by despair.

What is that which I should turn to, lighting upon days like these?
Every door is barr'd with gold, and opens but to golden keys. 100

Every gate is throng'd with suitors, all the markets overflow.
I have but an angry fancy; what is that which I should do?

I had been content to perish, falling on the foeman's ground,
When the ranks are roll'd in vapor, and the winds are laid with sound.

But the jingling of the guinea helps the hurt that Honor feels,
And the nations do but murmur, snarling at each other's heels.

Can I but relive in sadness? I will turn that earlier page.
Hide me from my deep emotion, O thou wondrous Mother-Age!

Make me feel the wild pulsation that I felt before the strife,
When I heard my days before me, and the tumult of my life; 110

Yearning for the large excitement that the coming years would yield,
Eager-hearted as a boy when first he leaves his father's field,

And at night along the dusky highway near and nearer drawn,
Sees in heaven the light of London flaring like a dreary dawn;

And his spirit leaps within him to be gone before him then,
Underneath the light he looks at, in among the throngs of men;

Men, my brothers, men the workers, ever reaping something new;
That which they have done but earnest of the things that they shall do.

For I dipt into the future, far as human eye could see,
Saw the Vision of the world, and all the wonder that would be; 120

Saw the heavens fill with commerce, argosies of magic sails,
Pilots of the purple twilight, dropping down with costly bales;

Heard the heavens fill with shouting, and there rain'd a ghastly dew
From the nations' airy navies grappling in the central blue;

Far along the world-wide whisper of the south-wind rushing warm,
With the standards of the peoples plunging thro' the thunder-storm;

Till the war-drum throbb'd no longer, and the battle-flags were furl'd
In the Parliament of man, the Federation of the world.

There the common sense of most shall hold a fretful realm in awe,
And the kindly earth shall slumber, lapt in universal law. 130

So I triumph'd ere my passion sweeping thro' me left me dry,
Left me with the palsied heart, and left me with the jaundiced eye;

Eye, to which all order festers, all things here are out of joint.
Science moves, but slowly, slowly, creeping on from point to point;

Slowly comes a hungry people, as a lion, creeping nigher,
Glares at one that nods and winks behind a slowly-dying fire.

Yet I doubt not thro' the ages one increasing purpose runs,
And the thoughts of men are widen'd with the process of the suns.

What is that to him that reaps not harvest of his youthful joys,
Tho' the deep heart of existence beat for ever like a boy's?   140

Knowledge comes, but wisdom lingers, and I linger on the shore,
And the individual withers, and the world is more and more.

Knowledge comes, but wisdom lingers, and he bears a laden breast,
Full of sad experience, moving toward the stillness of his rest.

Hark, my merry comrades call me, sounding on the bugle-horn,
They to whom my foolish passion were a target for their scorn.

Shall it not be scorn to me to harp on such a moulder'd string?
I am shamed thro' all my nature to have loved so slight a thing.

Weakness to be wroth with weakness! woman's pleasure, woman's pain—
Nature made them blinder motions bounded in a shallower brain.   150

Woman is the lesser man, and all thy passions, match'd with mine,
Are as moonlight unto sunlight, and as water unto wine—

Here at least, where nature sickens, nothing. Ah, for some retreat
Deep in yonder shining Orient, where my life began to beat,

Where in wild Mahratta-battle fell my father evil-starr'd;—
I was left a trampled orphan, and a selfish uncle's ward.

Or to burst all links of habit—there to wander far away,
On from island unto island at the gateways of the day.

Larger constellations burning, mellow moons and happy skies,
Breadths of tropic shade and palms in cluster knots of Paradise.   160

Never comes the trader, never floats an European flag,
Slides the bird o'er lustrous woodland, swings the trailer from the crag;

Droops the heavy-blossom'd bower, hangs the heavy-fruited tree—
Summer isles of Eden lying in dark-purple spheres of sea.

There methinks would be enjoyment more than in this march of mind,
In the steamship, in the railway, in the thoughts that shake mankind.

There the passions cramp'd no longer shall have scope and breathing
        space;
I will take some savage woman, she shall rear my dusky race.

Iron-jointed, supple-sinew'd, they shall dive, and they shall run,
Catch the wild goat by the hair, and hurl their lances in the sun;   170

Whistle back the parrot's call, and leap the rainbows of the brooks,
Not with blinded eyesight poring over miserable books—

Fool, again the dream, the fancy! but I *know* my words are wild,
But I count the gray barbarian lower than the Christian child.

I, to herd with narrow foreheads, vacant of our glorious gains,
Like a beast with lower pleasures, like a beast with lower pains!

Mated with a squalid savage—what to me were sun or clime?
I the heir of all the ages, in the foremost files of time—

I that rather held it better men should perish one by one,
Then that earth should stand at gaze like Joshua's moon in Ajalon!   180

Not in vain the distance beacons. Forward, forward let us range,
Let the great world spin for ever down the ringing grooves of change.

Thro' the shadow of the globe we sweep into the younger day;
Better fifty years of Europe than a cycle of Cathay.

Mother-Age,—for mine I knew not,—help me as when life begun;
Rift the hills, and roll the waters, flash the lightnings, weigh the sun.

O, I see the crescent promise of my spirit hath not set.
Ancient founts of inspiration well thro' all my fancy yet.

Howsoever these things be, a long farewell to Locksley Hall!
Now for me the woods may wither, now for me the roof-tree fall.   190

Comes a vapor from the margin, blackening over heath and holt,
Cramming all the blast before it, in its breast a thunderbolt.

Let it fall on Locksley Hall, with rain or hail, or fire or snow;
For the mighty wind arises, roaring seaward, and I go.

GODIVA

I waited for the train at Coventry;
I hung with grooms and porters on the bridge,
To watch the three tall spires; and there I shaped
The city's ancient legend into this:—
　Not only we, the latest seed of Time,
New men, that in the flying of a wheel
Cry down the past, not only we, that prate
Of rights and wrongs, have loved the people well,
And loathed to see them overtax'd; but she
Did more, and underwent, and overcame,　　10
The woman of a thousand summers back,
Godiva, wife to that grim Earl, who ruled
In Coventry; for when he laid a tax
Upon his town, and all the mothers brought
Their children, clamoring, 'If we pay, we starve!'
She sought her lord, and found him, where he strode
About the hall, among his dogs, alone,
His beard a foot before him, and his hair
A yard behind. She told him of their tears,
And pray'd him, 'If they pay this tax, they starve.'　　20
Whereat he stared, replying, half-amazed,
'You would not let your little finger ache
For such as *these?*'—'But I would die,' said she.
He laugh'd, and swore by Peter and by Paul,
Then fillip'd at the diamond in her ear:
'O, ay, ay, ay, you talk!'—'Alas!' she said,
'But prove me what it is I would not do.'
And from a heart as rough as Esau's hand,
He answer'd, 'Ride you naked thro' the town,
And I repeal it;' and nodding, as in scorn,　　30
He parted, with great strides among his dogs.
　So left alone, the passions of her mind,
As winds from all the compass shift and blow,
Made war upon each other for an hour,
Till pity won. She sent a herald forth,
And bade him cry, with sound of trumpet, all
The hard condition, but that she would loose
The people; therefore, as they loved her well,
From then till noon no foot should pace the street,
No eye look down, she passing, but that all　　40
Should keep within, door shut, and window barr'd.
　Then fled she to her inmost bower, and there
Unclasp'd the wedded eagles of her belt,
The grim Earl's gift; but ever at a breath
She linger'd, looking like a summer moon

Half-dipt in cloud. Anon she shook her head,
And shower'd the rippled ringlets to her knee;
Unclad herself in haste; adown the stair
Stole on; and like a creeping sunbeam slid
From pillar unto pillar, until she reach'd   50
The gateway; there she found her palfrey trapt
In purple blazon'd with armorial gold.
    Then she rode forth, clothed on with chastity.
The deep air listen'd round her as she rode,
And all the low wind hardly breathed for fear.
The little wide-mouth'd heads upon the spout
Had cunning eyes to see; the barking cur
Made her cheek flame; her palfrey's foot-fall shot
Light horrors thro' her pulses; the blind walls
Were full of chinks and holes; and overhead   60
Fantastic gables, crowding, stared; but she
Not less thro' all bore up, till, last, she saw
The white-flower'd elder-thicket from the field
Gleam thro' the Gothic archway in the wall.
    Then she rode back, clothed on with chastity.
And one low churl, compact of thankless earth,
The fatal byword of all years to come,
Boring a little auger-hole in fear,
Peep'd—but his eyes, before they had their will,
Were shrivell'd into darkness in his head,   70
And dropt before him. So the Powers, who wait
On noble deeds, cancell'd a sense misused;
And she, that knew not, pass'd; and all at once,
With twelve great shocks of sound, the shameless noon
Was clash'd and hammer'd from a hundred towers,
One after one; but even then she gain'd
Her bower, whence reissuing, robed and crown'd,
To meet her lord, she took the tax away
And built herself an everlasting name.

THE DAY-DREAM

PROLOGUE

O Lady Flora, let me speak;
    A pleasant hour has passed away
While, dreaming on your damask cheek,
    The dewy sister-eyelids lay.
As by the lattice you reclined,
    I went thro' many wayward moods
To see you dreaming—and, behind,
    A summer crisp with shining woods.

And I too dream'd, until at last
　Across my fancy, brooding warm,
The reflex of a legend past,
　And loosely settled into form.
And would you have the thought I had,
　And see the vision that I saw,
Then take the broidery-frame, and add
　A crimson to the quaint macaw,
And I will tell it. Turn your face,
　Nor look with that too-earnest eye—
The rhymes are dazzled from their place
　And order'd words asunder fly.

THE SLEEPING PALACE

I

THE varying year with blade and sheaf
　Clothes and reclothes the happy plains,
Here rests the sap within the leaf,
　Here stays the blood along the veins.
Faint shadows, vapors lightly curl'd,
　Faint murmurs from the meadows come,
Like hints and echoes of the world
　To spirits folded in the womb.

II

Soft lustre bathes the range of urns
　On every slanting terrace-lawn.
The fountain to his place returns
　Deep in the garden lake withdrawn.
Here droops the banner on the tower,
　On the hall-hearths the festal fires,
The peacock in his laurel bower,
　The parrot in his gilded wires.

III

Roof-haunting martins warm their eggs;
　In these, in those the life is stay'd.
The mantles from the golden pegs
　Droop sleepily; no sound is made,
Not even of a gnat that sings.
　More like a picture seemeth all
Than those old portraits of old kings,
　That watch the sleepers from the wall.

IV

Here sits the butler with a flask
    Between his knees, half-drain'd; and there
The wrinkled steward at his task,
    The maid-of-honor blooming fair.
The page has caught her hand in his;
    Her lips are sever'd as to speak;   50
His own are pouted to a kiss;
    The blush is fix'd upon her cheek.

V

Till all the hundred summers pass,
    The beams that thro' the oriel shine
Make prisms in every carven glass
    And beaker brimm'd with noble wine.
Each baron at the banquet sleeps,
    Grave faces gather'd in a ring.
His state the king reposing keeps.
    He must have been a jovial king.   60

VI

All round a hedge upshoots, and shows
    At distance like a little wood;
Thorns, ivies, woodbine, mistletoes,
    And grapes with bunches red as blood;
All creeping plants, a wall of green
    Close-matted, bur and brake and brier,
And glimpsing over these, just seen,
    High up, the topmost palace spire.

VII

When will the hundred summers die,   70
    And thought and time be born again,
And newer knowledge, drawing nigh,
    Bring truth that sways the soul of men?
Here all things in their place remain,
    As all were order'd, ages since.
Come, Care and Pleasure, Hope and Pain,
    And bring the fated fairy Prince.

THE SLEEPING BEAUTY

I

YEAR after year unto her feet,
  She lying on her couch alone,
Across the purple coverlet
  The maiden's jet-black hair has grown,
On either side her tranced form
  Forth streaming from a braid of pearl;
The slumbrous light is rich and warm,
  And moves not on the rounded curl.

II

The silk star-broider'd coverlid
  Unto her limbs itself doth mould
Languidly ever; and, amid
  Her full black ringlets downward roll'd,
Glows forth each softly-shadow'd arm
  With bracelets of the diamond bright.
Her constant beauty doth inform
  Stillness with love, and day with light.

III

She sleeps; her breathings are not heard
  In palace chambers far apart.
The fragrant tresses are not stirr'd
  That lie upon her charmed heart.
She sleeps; on either hand upswells
  The gold-fringed pillow lightly prest;
She sleeps, nor dreams, but ever dwells
  A perfect form in perfect rest.

THE ARRIVAL

I

ALL precious things, discover'd late,
  To those that seek them issue forth;
For love in sequel works with fate,
  And draws the veil from hidden worth.
He travels far from other skies—
  His mantle glitters on the rocks—
A fairy Prince, with joyful eyes,
  And lighter-footed than the fox.

80

90

100

II

The bodies and the bones of those
    That strove in other days to pass 110
Are wither'd in the thorny close,
    Or scatter'd blanching on the grass.
He gazes on the silent dead:
    'They perish'd in their daring deeds.'
This proverb flashes thro' his head,
    'The many fail, the one succeeds.'

III

He comes, scarce knowing what he seeks;
    He breaks the hedge; he enters there;
The color flies into his cheeks;
    He trusts to light on something fair; 120
For all his life the charm did talk
    About his path, and hover near
With words of promise in his walk,
    And whisper'd voices at his ear.

IV

More close and close his footsteps wind;
    The Magic Music in his heart,
Beats quick and quicker, till he find
    The quiet chamber far apart.
His spirit flutters like a lark,
    He stoops—to kiss her—on his knee. 130
'Love, if thy tresses be so dark,
    How dark those hidden eyes must be!'

THE REVIVAL

I

A TOUCH, a kiss! the charm was snapt.
    There rose a noise of striking clocks,
And feet that ran, and doors that clapt,
    And barking dogs, and crowing cocks;
A fuller light illumined all,
    A breeze thro' all the garden swept,
A sudden hubbub shook the hall,
    And sixty feet the fountain leapt. 140

II

The hedge broke in, the banner blew,
   The butler drank, the steward scrawl'd,
The fire shot up, the martin flew,
   The parrot scream'd, the peacock squall'd,
The maid and page renew'd their strife,
   The palace bang'd and buzz'd and clackt,
And all the long-pent stream of life
   Dash'd downward in a cataract.

III

And last with these the king awoke,
   And in his chair himself uprear'd,   150
And yawn'd, and rubb'd his face, and spoke,
   'By holy rood, a royal beard!
How say you? we have slept, my lords.
   My beard has grown into my lap.'
The barons swore, with many words,
   'T was but an after-dinner's nap.

IV

'Pardy,' return'd the king, 'but still
   My joints are somewhat stiff or so.
My lord, and shall we pass the bill
   I mention'd half an hour ago?'   160
The chancellor, sedate and vain,
   In courteous words return'd reply,
But dallied with his golden chain,
   And, smiling, put the question by.

THE DEPARTURE

I

And on her lover's arms she leant,
   And round her waist she felt it fold,
And far across the hills they went
   In that new world which is the old;
Across the hills, and far away
   Beyond their utmost purple rim,   170
And deep into the dying day
   The happy princess follow'd him.

II

'I'd sleep another hundred years,
    O love, for such another kiss';
'O, wake for ever, love,' she hears;
    'O love, 't was such as this and this.'
And o'er them many a sliding star
    And many a merry wind was borne,
And, stream'd thro' many a golden bar,
    The twilight melted into morn.   180

III

'O eyes long laid in happy sleep!'
    'O happy sleep, that lightly fled!'
'O happy kiss, that woke thy sleep!'
    'O love, thy kiss would wake the dead!'
And o'er them many a flowing range
    Of vapor buoy'd the crescent-bark,
And, rapt thro' many a rosy change,
    The twilight died into the dark.

IV

'A hundred summers! can it be?
    And whither goest thou, tell me where?'   190
'O, seek my father's court with me,
    For there are greater wonders there.'
And o'er the hills, and far away
    Beyond their utmost purple rim,
Beyond the night, across the day,
    Thro' all the world she follow'd him.

MORAL

I

So, Lady Flora, take my lay,
    And if you find no moral there,
Go, look in any glass and say,
    What moral is in being fair.   200
O, to what uses shall we put
    The wildweed-flower that simply blows?
And is there any moral shut
    Within the bosom of the rose?

II

But any man that walks the mead,
  In bud or blade or bloom, may find,
According as his humors lead,
  A meaning suited to his mind.
And liberal applications lie
  In Art like Nature, dearest friend;   210
So 't were to cramp its use if I
  Should hook it to some useful end.

L'ENVOI

I

You shake your head. A random string
  Your finer female sense offends.
Well—were it not a pleasant thing
  To fall asleep with all one's friends;
To pass with all our social ties
  To silence from the paths of men,
And every hundred years to rise
  And learn the world, and sleep again;   220
To sleep thro' terms of mighty wars,
  And wake on science grown to more,
On secrets of the brain, the stars,
  As wild as aught of fairy lore;
And all that else the years will show,
  The Poet-forms of stronger hours,
The vast Republics that may grow,
  The Federations and the Powers;
Titantic forces taking birth
  In divers seasons, divers climes?   230
For we are Ancients of the earth,
  And in the morning of the times.

II

So sleeping, so aroused from sleep
  Thro' sunny decads new and strange,
Or gay quinquenniads, would we reap
  The flower and quintessence of change.

III

Ah, yet would I—and would I might!
  So much your eyes my fancy take—
Be still the first to leap to light
  That I might kiss those eyes awake!   240

For, am I right, or am I wrong,
   To choose your own you did not care;
You'd have *my* moral from the song,
   And I will take my pleasure there;
And, am I right or am I wrong,
   My fancy, ranging thro' and thro',
To search a meaning for the song,
   Perforce will still revert to you,
Nor finds a closer truth than this
   All-graceful head, so richly curl'd,   **250**
And evermore a costly kiss
   The prelude to some brighter world.

IV

For since the time when Adam first
   Embraced his Eve in happy hour,
And every bird of Eden burst
   In carol, every bud to flower,
What eyes, like thine, have waken'd hopes,
   What lips, like thine, so sweetly join'd?
Where on the double rosebud droops
   The fulness of the pensive mind;   **260**
Which, all too dearly self-involved,
   Yet sleeps a dreamless sleep to me,—
A sleep by kisses undissolved,
   That lets thee neither hear nor see:
But break it. In the name of wife,
   And in the rights that name may **give**,
Are clasp'd the moral of thy life,
   And that for which I care to live.

EPILOGUE

So, Lady Flora, take my lay,
   And if you find a meaning there,   **270**
O, whisper to your glass, and say,
   'What wonder if he thinks me fair?'
What wonder I was all unwise,
   To shape the song for your delight
Like long-tail'd birds of Paradise
   That float thro' heaven, and cannot **light?**
Or old-world trains, upheld at court
   By Cupid-boys of blooming hue—
But take it—earnest wed with sport,
   And either sacred unto you.   **280**

AMPHION

My father left a park to me,
   But it is wild and barren,
A garden too with scarce a tree,
   And waster than a warren;
Yet say the neighbors when they call
   It is not bad but good land,
And in it is the germ of all
   That grows within the woodland.

O, had I lived when song was great
   In days of old Amphion,   10
And ta'en my fiddle to the gate,
   Nor cared for seed or scion!
And had I lived when song was great,
   And legs of trees were limber,
And ta'en my fiddle to the gate,
   And fiddled in the timber!

'T is said he had a tuneful tongue,
   Such happy intonation,
Wherever he sat down and sung
   He left a small plantation;   20
Wherever in a lonely grove
   He set up his forlorn pipes,
The gouty oak began to move,
   And flounder into hornpipes.

The mountain stirr'd its bushy crown,
   And, as tradition teaches,
Young ashes pirouetted down
   Coquetting with young beeches;
And briony-vine and ivy-wreath
   Ran forward to his rhyming,   30
And from the valleys underneath
   Came little copses climbing.

The linden broke her ranks and rent
   The woodbine wreaths that bind her,
And down the middle, buzz! she went
   With all her bees behind her;
The poplars, in long order due,
   With cypress promenaded,
The shock-head willows two and two
   By rivers gallopaded.   40

Came wet-shod alder from the wave,
   Came yews, a dismal coterie;
Each pluck'd his one foot from the grave,
   Poussetting with a sloe-tree;
Old elms came breaking from the vine,
   The vine stream'd out to follow,
And, sweating rosin, plump'd the pine
   From many a cloudy hollow.

And was n't it a sight to see,
   When, ere his song was ended,   50
Like some great landslip, tree by tree,
   The country-side descended;
And shepherds from the mountain-eaves
   Look'd down, half-pleased, half-frighten'd,
As dash'd about the drunken leaves
   The random sunshine lighten'd?

O, Nature first was fresh to men,
   And wanton without measure;
So youthful and so flexile then,
   You moved her at your pleasure.   60
Twang out, my fiddle! shake the twigs!
   And make her dance attendance;
Blow, flute, and stir the stiff-set sprigs,
   And scirrhous roots and tendons!

'T is vain! in such a brassy age
   I could not move a thistle;
The very sparrows in the hedge
   Scarce answer to my whistle;
Or at the most, when three-parts-sick
   With strumming and with scraping,   70
A jackass heehaws from the rick,
   The passive oxen gaping.

But what is that I hear? a sound
   Like sleepy counsel pleading;
O Lord!—'t is in my neighbor's ground,
   The modern Muses reading.
They read Botanic Treatises,
   And Works on Gardening thro' there,
And Methods of Transplanting Trees
   To look as if they grew there.   80

The wither'd Misses! how they prose
   O'er books of travell'd seamen,
And show you slips of all that grows

From England to Van Diemen.
They read in arbors clipt and cut,
    And alleys, faded places,
By squares of tropic summer shut
    And warm'd in crystal cases.

But these, tho' fed with careful dirt,
    Are neither green nor sappy;   90
Half-conscious of the garden-squirt,
    The spindlings look unhappy.
Better to me the meanest weed
    That blows upon its mountain,
The vilest herb that runs to seed
    Beside its native fountain.

And I must work thro' months of toil,
    And years of cultivation,
Upon my proper patch of soil
    To grow my own plantation.   100
I'll take the showers as they fall,
    I will not vex my bosom;
Enough if at the end of all
    A little garden blossom.

SAINT AGNES' EVE

DEEP on the convent-roof the snows
    Are sparkling to the moon;
My breath to heaven like vapor goes;
    May my soul follow soon!
The shadows of the convent-towers
    Slant down the snowy sward,
Still creeping with the creeping hours
    That lead me to my Lord.
Make Thou my spirit pure and clear
    As are the frosty skies,
Or this first snowdrop of the year
    That in my bosom lies.

As these white robes are soil'd and dark,
    To yonder shining ground;
As this pale taper's earthly spark,
    To yonder argent round;
So shows my soul before the Lamb,
    My spirit before Thee;
So in mine earthly house I am,
    To that I hope to be.

Break up the heavens, O Lord! and far,
    Thro' all yon starlight keen,
Draw me, thy bride, a glittering star,
    In raiment white and clean.

He lifts me to the golden doors;
    The flashes come and go;
All heaven bursts her starry floors,
    And strows her lights below,
And deepens on and up! the gates
    Roll back, and far within
For me the Heavenly Bridegroom waits,
    To make me pure of sin.
The Sabbaths of Eternity,
    One Sabbath deep and wide—
A light upon the shining sea—
    The Bridegroom with his bride!

SIR GALAHAD

My good blade carves the casques of men,
    My tough lance thrusteth sure,
My strength is as the strength of ten,
    Because my heart is pure.
The shattering trumpet shrilleth high,
    The hard brands shiver on the steel,
The splinter'd spear-shafts crack and fly,
    The horse and rider reel;
They reel, they roll in clanging lists,
    And when the tide of combat stands,   10
Perfume and flowers fall in showers,
    That lightly rain from ladies' hands.

How sweet are looks that ladies bend
    On whom their favors fall!
For them I battle till the end,
    To save from shame and thrall;
But all my heart is drawn above,
    My knees are bow'd in crypt and shrine;
I never felt the kiss of love,
    Nor maiden's hand in mine.   20
More bounteous aspects on me beam,
    Me mightier transports move and thrill;
So keep I fair thro' faith and prayer
    A virgin heart in work and will.

When down the stormy crescent goes,
    A light before me swims,
Between dark stems the forest glows,
    I hear a noise of hymns.
Then by some secret shrine I ride;
    I hear a voice, but none are there;   30
The stalls are void, the doors are wide,
    The tapers burning fair.
Fair gleams the snowy altar-cloth,
    The silver vessels sparkle clean,
The shrill bell rings, the censer swings,
    And solemn chaunts resound between.

Sometimes on lonely mountain-meres
    I find a magic bark.
I leap on board; no helmsman steers;
    I float till all is dark.   40
A gentle sound, an awful light!
    Three angels bear the Holy Grail;
With folded feet, in stoles of white,
    On sleeping wings they sail.
Ah, blessed vision! blood of God!
    My spirit beats her mortal bars,
As down dark tides the glory slides,
    And starlike mingles with the stars.

When on my goodly charger borne
    Thro' dreaming towns I go,   50
The cock crows ere the Christmas morn,
    The streets are dumb with snow.
The tempest crackles on the leads,
    And, ringing, springs from brand and mail;
But o'er the dark a glory spreads,
    And gilds the driving hail.
I leave the plain, I climb the height;
    No branchy thicket shelter yields;
But blessed forms in whistling storms
    Fly o'er waste fens and windy fields.   60
A maiden knight—to me is given
    Such hope, I know not fear;
I yearn to breathe the airs of heaven
    That often meet me here.
I muse on joy that will not cease,
    Pure spaces clothed in living beams,
Pure lilies of eternal peace,
    Whose odors haunt my dreams;
And, stricken by an angel's hand,
    This mortal armor that I wear,   70

This weight and size, this heart and eyes,
   Are touch'd, are turn'd to finest air.

The clouds are broken in the sky,
   And thro' the mountain-walls
A rolling organ-harmony
   Swells up and shakes and falls.
Then move the trees, the copses nod,
   Wings flutter, voices hover clear:
'O just and faithful knight of God!
   Ride on! the prize is near.'
So pass I hostel, hall, and grange;
   By bridge and ford, by park and pale,
All-arm'd I ride, whate'er betide,
   Until I find the Holy Grail.

80

EDWARD GRAY

Sweet Emma Moreland of yonder town
   Met me walking on yonder way;
'And have you lost your heart?' she said;
   'And are you married yet, Edward Gray?'

Sweet Emma Moreland spoke to me;
   Bitterly weeping I turn'd away:
'Sweet Emma Moreland, love no more
   Can touch the heart of Edward Gray.

'Ellen Adair she loved me well,
   Against her father's and mother's will;
To-day I sat for an hour and wept
   By Ellen's grave, on the windy hill.

'Shy she was, and I thought her cold,
   Thought her proud, and fled over the sea;
Fill'd I was with folly and spite,
   When Ellen Adair was dying for me.

'Cruel, cruel the words I said!
   Cruelly came they back to-day:
"You're too slight and fickle," I said,
   "To trouble the heart of Edward Gray."

'There I put my face in the grass—
   Whisper'd, "Listen to my despair;
I repent me of all I did;
   Speak a little, Ellen Adair!"

'Then I took a pencil, and wrote
  On the mossy stone, as I lay,
"Here lies the body of Ellen Adair;
  And here the heart of Edward Gray!"

'Love may come, and love may go,
  And fly, like a bird, from tree to tree;
But I will love no more, no more,
  Till Ellen Adair come back to me.

'Bitterly wept I over the stone;
  Bitterly weeping I turn'd away.
There lies the body of Ellen Adair!
  And there the heart of Edward Gray!'

WILL WATERPROOF'S LYRICAL MONOLOGUE

MADE AT THE COCK

O PLUMP head-waiter at The Cock,
  To which I most resort,
How goes the time? 'T is five o'clock.
  Go fetch a pint of port;
But let it not be such as that
  You set before chance-comers,
But such whose father-grape grew fat
  On Lusitanian summers.

No vain libation to the Muse,
  But may she still be kind,
And whisper lovely words, and use
  Her influence on the mind,   10
To make me write my random rhymes,
  Ere they be half-forgotten;
Nor add and alter, many times,
  Till all be ripe and rotten.

I pledge her, and she comes and dips
  Her laurel in the wine,
And lays it thrice upon my lips,
  These favor'd lips of mine;   20
Until the charm have power to make
  New life-blood warm the bosom,
And barren commonplaces break
  In full and kindly blossom.

I pledge her silent at the board;
    Her gradual fingers steal
And touch upon the master-chord
    Of all I felt and feel.
Old wishes, ghosts of broken plans,
    And phantom hopes assemble;   30
And that child's heart within the man's
    Begins to move and tremble.

Thro' many an hour of summer suns,
    By many pleasant ways,
Against its fountain upward runs
    The current of my days.
I kiss the lips I once have kiss'd;
    The gaslight wavers dimmer;
And softly, thro' a vinous mist,
    My college friendships glimmer.   40

I grow in worth and wit and sense,
    Unboding critic-pen,
Or that eternal want of pence
    Which vexes public men,
Who hold their hands to all, and cry
    For that which all deny them—
Who sweep the crossings, wet or dry,
    And all the world go by them.

Ah! yet, tho' all the world forsake,
    Tho' fortune clip my wings,   50
I will not cramp my heart, nor take
    Half-views of men and things.
Let Whig and Tory stir their blood;
    There must be stormy weather;
But for some true result of good
    All parties work together.

Let there be thistles, there are grapes;
    If old things, there are new;
Ten thousand broken lights and shapes,
    Yet glimpses of the true.   60
Let raffs be rife in prose and rhyme,
    We lack not rhymes and reasons,
As on this whirligig of Time
    We circle with the seasons.

This earth is rich in man and maid,
    With fair horizons bound;
This whole wide earth of light and shade
    Comes out a perfect round.

High over roaring Temple-bar,
　　And set in heaven's third story,   70
I look at all things as they are,
　　But thro' a kind of glory.

Head-waiter, honor'd by the guest
　　Half-mused, or reeling ripe,
The pint you brought me was the best
　　That ever came from pipe.
But tho' the port surpasses praise,
　　My nerves have dealt with stiffer.
Is there some magic in the place?
　　Or do my peptics differ?   80

For since I came to live and learn,
　　No pint of white or red
Had ever half the power to turn
　　This wheel within my head,
Which bears a season'd brain about,
　　Unsubject to confusion,
Tho' soak'd and saturate, out and out,
　　Thro' every convolution.

For I am of a numerous house,
　　With many kinsmen gay,   90
Where long and largely we carouse
　　As who shall say me nay?
Each month, a birthday coming on,
　　We drink, defying trouble,
Or sometimes two would meet in one,
　　And then we drank it double;

Whether the vintage, yet unkept,
　　Had relish fiery-new,
Or elbow-deep in sawdust slept,
　　As old as Waterloo,   100
Or, stow'd when classic Canning died,
　　In musty bins and chambers,
Had cast upon its crusty side
　　The gloom of ten Decembers.

The Muse, the jolly Muse, it is!
　　She answer'd to my call;
She changes with that mood or this,
　　Is all-in-all to all;
She lit the spark within my throat,
　　To make my blood run quicker,   110

Used all her fiery will, and smote
   Her life into the liquor.

And hence this halo lives about
   The waiter's hands, that reach
To each his perfect pint of stout,
   His proper chop to each.
He looks not like the common breed
   That with the napkin dally;
I think he came, like Ganymede,
   From some delightful valley.   120

The Cock was of a larger egg
   Than modern poultry drop,
Stept forward on a firmer leg,
   And cramm'd a plumper crop,
Upon an ampler dunghill trod,
   Crow'd lustier late and early,
Sipt wine from silver, praising God,
   And raked in golden barley.

A private life was all his joy,
   Till in a court he saw   130
A something-pottle-bodied boy
   That knuckled at the taw.
He stoop'd and clutch'd him, fair and good,
   Flew over roof and casement;
His brothers of the weather stood
   Stock-still for sheer amazement.

But he, by farmstead, thorpe, and spire,
   And follow'd with acclaims,
A sign to many a staring shire,
   Came crowing over Thames.   140
Right down by smoky Paul's they bore,
   Till, where the street grows straiter,
One fix'd for ever at the door,
   And one became head-waiter.

But whither would my fancy go?
   How out of place she makes
The violet of a legend blow
   Among the chops and steaks!
'T is but a steward of the can,
   One shade more plump than common;   150
As just and mere a serving-man
   As any born of woman.

I ranged too high: what draws me down
　　Into the common day?
Is it the weight of that half-crown
　　Which I shall have to pay?
For, something duller than at first,
　　Nor wholly comfortable,
I sit, my empty glass reversed,
　　And thrumming on the table;   160

Half fearful that, with self at strife,
　　I take myself to task,
Lest of the fulness of my life
　　I leave an empty flask;
For I had hope, by something rare,
　　To prove myself a poet,
But, while I plan and plan, my hair
　　Is gray before I know it.

So fares it since the years began,
　　Till they be gather'd up;   170
The truth, that flies the flowing can,
　　Will haunt the vacant cup;
And others' follies teach us not,
　　Nor much their wisdom teaches;
And most, of sterling worth, is what
　　Our own experience preaches.

Ah, let the rusty theme alone!
　　We know not what we know.
But for my pleasant hour, 't is gone;
　　'T is gone, and let it go.   180
'T is gone: a thousand such have slipt
　　Away from my embraces,
And fall'n into the dusty crypt
　　Of darken'd forms and faces.

Go, therefore, thou! thy betters went
　　Long since, and came no more;
With peals of genial clamor sent
　　From many a tavern-door,
With twisted quirks and happy hits,
　　From misty men of letters;   190
The tavern-hours of mighty wits,—
　　Thine elders and thy betters;

Hours when the Poet's words and looks
　　Had yet their native glow,
Nor yet the fear of little books
　　Had made him talk for show;

But, all his vast heart sherris-warm'd,
   He flash'd his random speeches,
Ere days that deal in ana swarm'd
   His literary leeches.   200

So mix for ever with the past,
   Like all good things on earth!
For should I prize thee, couldst thou last,
   At half thy real worth?
I hold it good, good things should pass;
   With time I will not quarrel;
It is but yonder empty glass
   That makes me maudlin-moral.

———

Head-waiter of the chop-house here,
   To which I most resort,   210
I too must part; I hold thee dear
   For this good pint of port.
For this, thou shalt from all things suck
   Marrow of mirth and laughter;
And wheresoe'er thou move, good luck
   Shall fling her old shoe after.

But thou wilt never move from hence,
   The sphere thy fate allots;
Thy latter days increased with pence
   Go down among the pots;   220
Thou battenest by the greasy gleam
   In haunts of hungry sinners,
Old boxes, larded with the steam
   Of thirty thousand dinners.

We fret, we fume, would shift our skins,
   Would quarrel with our lot;
Thy care is, under polish'd tins,
   To serve the hot-and-hot;
To come and go, and come again,
   Returning like the pewit,   230
And watch'd by silent gentlemen,
   That trifle with the cruet.

Live long, ere from thy topmost head
   The thick-set hazel dies;
Long, ere the hateful crow shall tread
   The corners of thine eyes;
Live long, nor feel in head or chest
   Our changeful equinoxes,

Till mellow Death, like some late guest,
　　Shall call thee from the boxes.   240

But when he calls, and thou shalt cease
　　To pace the gritted floor,
And, laying down an unctuous lease
　　Of life, shalt earn no more,
No carved cross-bones, the types of Death,
　　Shall show thee past to heaven,
But carved cross-pipes, and, underneath,
　　A pint-pot neatly graven.

LADY CLARE

IT was the time when lilies blow,
　　And clouds are highest up in air,
Lord Ronald brought a lily-white doe
　　To give his cousin, Lady Clare.

I trow they did not part in scorn;
　　Lovers long-betroth'd were they;
They two will wed the morrow morn—
　　God's blessing on the day!

'He does not love me for my birth,
　　Nor for my lands so broad and fair;   10
He loves me for my own true worth,
　　And that is well,' said Lady Clare.

In there came old Alice the nurse,
　　Said, 'Who was this that went from thee?'
'It was my cousin,' said Lady Clare;
　　'To-morrow he weds with me.'

'O, God be thank'd,' said Alice the nurse,
　　'That all comes round so just and fair!
Lord Ronald is heir of all your lands,
　　And you are *not* the Lady Clare.'   20

'Are ye out of your mind, my nurse, my nurse,'
　　Said Lady Clare, 'that ye speak so wild?'
'As God's above,' said Alice the nurse,
　　'I speak the truth: you are my child.

'The old earl's daughter died at my breast;
　　I speak the truth, as I live by bread!

I buried her like my own sweet child,
   And put my child in her stead.'
'Falsely, falsely have ye done,
   O mother,' she said, 'if this be true,   30
To keep the best man under the sun
   So many years from his due.'

'Nay now, my child,' said Alice the nurse,
   'But keep the secret for your life,
And all you have will be Lord Ronald's,
   When you are man and wife.'

'If I'm a begger born,' she said,
   'I will speak out, for I dare not lie.
Pull off, pull off, the brooch of gold,
   And fling the diamond necklace by.'   40

'Nay now, my child,' said Alice the nurse,
   'But keep the secret all ye can.'
She said, 'Not so; but I will know
   If there be any faith in man.'

'Nay now, what faith?' said Alice the nurse;
   'The man will cleave unto his right.'
'And he shall have it,' the lady replied,
   'Tho' I should die to-night.'

'Yet give one kiss to your mother dear!
   Alas, my child, I sinn'd for thee!'   50
'O mother, mother, mother,' she said,
   'So strange it seems to me.

'Yet here's a kiss for my mother dear,
   My mother dear, if this be so,
And lay your hand upon my head,
   And bless me, mother, ere I go.'

She clad herself in a russet gown,
   She was no longer Lady Clare;
She went by dale, and she went by down,
   With a single rose in her hair.   60

The lily-white doe Lord Ronald had brought
   Leapt up from where she lay,
Dropt her head in the maiden's hand,
   And follow'd her all the way.

Down stept Lord Ronald from his tower:
  'O Lady Clare, you shame your worth!
Why come you drest like a village maid,
  That are the flower of the earth?'

'If I come drest like a village maid,
  I am but as my fortunes are;
I am a beggar born,' she said,   70
  'And not the Lady Clare.'

'Play me no tricks,' said Lord Ronald,
  'For I am yours in word and in deed.
Play me no tricks,' said Lord Ronald,
  'Your riddle is hard to read.'

O, and proudly stood she up!
  Her heart within her did not fail;
She look'd into Lord Ronald's eyes,
  And told him all her nurse's tale.   80

He laugh'd a laugh of mercy scorn;
  He turn'd and kiss'd her where she stood;
'If you are not the heiress born,
  And I,' said he, 'the next in blood,—

'If you are not the heiress born,
  And I,' said he, 'the lawful heir,
We two will wed to-morrow morn,
  And you shall still be Lady Clare.'

THE CAPTAIN

A LEGEND OF THE NAVY

He that only rules by terror
  Doeth grievous wrong.
Deep as hell I count his error.
  Let him hear my song.
Brave the Captain was; the seamen
  Made a gallant crew,
Gallant sons of English freemen,
  Sailors bold and true.
But they hated his oppression;
  Stern he was and rash,
So for every light transgression
  Doom'd them to the lash.
Day by day more harsh and cruel

Seem'd the Captain's mood.
Secret wrath like smother'd fuel
   Burnt in each man's blood.
Yet he hoped to purchase glory,
   Hoped to make the name
Of his vessel great in story,
   Wheresoe'er he came.
So they past by capes and islands,
   Many a harbor-mouth,
Sailing under palmy highlands
   Far within the South.
On a day when they were going
   O'er the lone expanse,
In the north, her canvas flowing,
   Rose a ship of France.
Then the Captain's color heighten'd,
   Joyful came his speech;
But a cloudy gladness lighten'd
   In the eyes of each.
'Chase,' he said; the ship flew forward,
   And the wind did blow;
Stately, lightly, went she norward,
   Till she near'd the foe.
Then they look'd at him they hated,
   Had what they desired;
Mute with folded arms they waited—
   Not a gun was fired.
But they heard the foeman's thunder
   Roaring out their doom;
All the air was torn in sunder,
   Crashing went the boom,
Spars were splinter'd, decks were shatter'd,
   Bullets fell like rain;
Over mast and deck were scatter'd
   Blood and brains of men.
Spars were splinter'd; decks were broken;
   Every mother's son—
Down they dropt—no word was spoken—
   Each beside his gun.
On the decks as they were lying,
   Were their faces grim.
In their blood, as they lay dying,
   Did they smile on him.
Those in whom he had reliance
   For his noble name
With one smile of still defiance
   Sold him unto shame.
Shame and wrath his heart confounded,

Pale he turn'd and red,
Till himself was deadly wounded
Falling on the dead.
Dismal error! fearful slaughter!
Years have wander'd by;
Side by side beneath the water
Crew and Captain lie;
There the sunlit ocean tosses
O'er them mouldering,
And the lonely seabird crosses
With one waft of the wing.

THE LORD OF BURLEIGH

IN her ear he whispers gaily,
'If my heart by signs can tell,
Maiden, I have watch'd thee daily,
And I think thou lov'st me well.'
She replies, in accents fainter,
'There is none I love like thee.'
He is but a landscape-painter,
And a village maiden she.
He to lips that fondly falter
Presses his without reproof,   10
Leads her to the village altar,
And they leave her father's roof.
'I can make no marriage present;
Little can I give my wife.
Love will make our cottage pleasant,
And I love thee more than life.'
They by parks and lodges going
See the lordly castles stand;
Summer woods, about them blowing,
Made a murmur in the land.   20
From deep thought himself he rouses,
Says to her that loves him well,
'Let us see these handsome houses
Where the wealthy nobles dwell.'
So she goes by him attended,
Hears him lovingly converse,
Sees whatever fair and splendid
Lay betwixt his home and hers;
Parks with oak and chestnut shady,
Parks and order'd gardens great,   30
Ancient homes of lord and lady,
Built for pleasure and for state.
All he shows her makes him dearer;

Evermore she seems to gaze
On that cottage growing nearer,
 Where they twain will spend their days.
O, but she will love him truly!
 He shall have a cheerful home;
She will order all things duly,
 When beneath his roof they come.   40
Thus her heart rejoices greatly,
 Till a gateway she discerns
With armorial bearings stately,
 And beneath the gate she turns,
Sees a mansion more majestic
 Than all those she saw before.
Many a gallant gay domestic
 Bows before him at the door;
And they speak in gentle murmur,
 When they answer to his call,   50
While he treads with footstep firmer,
 Leading on from hall to hall.
And, while now she wonders blindly,
 Nor the meaning can divine,
Proudly turns he round and kindly,
 'All of this is mine and thine.'
Here he lives in state and bounty,
 Lord of Burleigh, fair and free;
Not a lord in all the county
 Is so great a lord as he.   60
All at once the color flushes
 Her sweet face from brow to chin;
As it were with shame she blushes,
 And her spirit changed within.
Then her countenance all over
 Pale again as death did prove;
But he clasp'd her like a lover,
 And he cheer'd her soul with love.
So she strove against her weakness,
 Tho' at times her spirit sank,   70
Shaped her heart with woman's meekness
 To all duties of her rank;
And a gentle consort made he,
 And her gentle mind was such
That she grew a noble lady,
 And the people loved her much.
But a trouble weigh'd upon her,
 And perplex'd her, night and morn,
With the burthen of an honor
 Unto which she was not born.   80
Faint she grew, and ever fainter,

And she murmur'd, 'O, that he
  Were once more that landscape-painter
    Which did win my heart from me!'
So she droop'd and droop'd before him,
  Fading slowly from his side;
Three fair children first she bore him,
  Then before her time she died.
Weeping, weeping late and early,
  Walking up and pacing down,   90
Deeply mourn'd the Lord of Burleigh,
  Burleigh-house by Stamford-town.
And he came to look upon her,
  And he look'd at her and said,
'Bring the dress and put it on her,
  That she wore when she was wed.'
Then her people, softly treading,
  Bore to earth her body, drest
In the dress that she was wed in
  That her spirit might have rest.   100

THE VOYAGE

I

We left behind the painted buoy
  That tosses at the harbor-mouth;
And madly danced our hearts with joy,
  As fast we fleeted to the south.
How fresh was every sight and sound
  On open main or winding shore!
We knew the merry world was round,
  And we might sail for evermore.

II

Warm broke the breeze against the brow,
  Dry sang the tackle, sang the sail;   10
The Lady's-head upon the prow
  Caught the shrill salt, and sheer'd the gale.
The broad seas swell'd to meet the keel,
  And swept behind; so quick the run,
We felt the good ship shake and reel,
  We seem'd to sail into the sun!

III

How oft we saw the sun retire,
    And burn the threshold of the night,
Fall from his Ocean-lane of fire,
    And sleep beneath his pillar'd light!   20
How oft the purple-skirted robe
    Of twilight slowly downward drawn,
As thro' the slumber of the globe
    Again we dash'd into the dawn!

IV

New stars all night above the brim
    Of waters lighten'd into view;
They climb'd as quickly, for the rim
    Changed every moment as we flew.
Far ran the naked moon across
    The houseless ocean's heaving field,   30
Or flying shone, the silver boss
    Of her own halo's dusky shield.

V

The peaky islet shifted shapes,
    High towns on hills were dimly seen;
We past long lines of Northern capes
    And dewy Northern meadows green.
We came to warmer waves, and deep
    Across the boundless east we drove,
Where those long swells of breaker sweep
    The nutmeg rocks and isles of clove.   40

VI

By peaks that flamed, or, all in shade,
    Gloom'd the low coast and quivering brine
With ashy rains, that spreading made
    Fantastic plume or sable pine;
By sands and steaming flats, and floods
    Of mighty mouth, we scudded fast,
And hills and scarlet-mingled woods
    Glow'd for a moment as we past.

VII

O hundred shores of happy climes,
    How swiftly stream'd ye by the bark!   50
At times the whole sea burn'd, at times
    With wakes of fire we tore the dark;

At times a carven craft would shoot
  From havens hid in fairy bowers,
With naked limbs and flowers and fruit,
  But we nor paused for fruit nor flowers.

VIII

For one fair Vision ever fled
  Down the waste waters day and night,
And still we follow'd where she led,
  In hope to gain upon her flight.   60
Her face was evermore unseen,
  And fixt upon the far sea-line;
But each man murmur'd, 'O my Queen,
  I follow till I make thee mine.'

IX

And now we lost her, now she gleam'd
  Like Fancy made of golden air,
Now nearer to the prow she seem'd
  Like Virtue firm, like Knowledge fair,
Now high on waves that idly burst
  Like Heavenly Hope she crown'd the sea,   70
And now, the bloodless point reversed,
  She bore the blade of Liberty.

X

And only one among us—him
  We pleased not—he was seldom pleased;
He saw not far, his eyes were dim,
  But ours he swore were all diseased.
'A ship of fools,' he shriek'd in spite,
  'A ship of fools,' he sneer'd and wept.
And overboard one stormy night
  He cast his body, and on we swept.   80

XI

And never sail of ours was furl'd,
  Nor anchor dropt at eve or morn;
We loved the glories of the world,
  But laws of nature were our scorn.
For blasts would rise and rave and cease,
  But whence were those that drove the sail
Across the whirlwind's heart of peace,
  And to and thro' the counter gale?

XII

Again to colder climes we came,
    For still we follow'd where she led;
Now mate is blind and captain lame,
    And half the crew are sick or dead,
But, blind or lame or sick or sound,
    We follow that which flies before;
We know the merry world is round,
    And we may sail for evermore.

90

SIR LAUNCELOT AND QUEEN GUINEVERE

A FRAGMENT

Like souls that balance joy and pain,
With tears and smiles from heaven again
The maiden Spring upon the plain
Came in a sunlit fall of rain.
    In crystal vapor everywhere
Blue isles of heaven laugh'd between,
And far, in forest-deeps unseen,
The topmost elm-tree gather'd green
    From draughts of balmy air.

Sometimes the linnet piped his song;
Sometimes the throstle whistled strong;
Sometimes the sparhawk, wheel'd along,
Hush'd all the groves from fear of wrong;
    By grassy capes with fuller sound
In curves the yellowing river ran,
And drooping chestnut-buds began
To spread into the perfect fan,
    Above the teeming ground.

Then, in the boyhood of the year,
Sir Launcelot and Queen Guinevere
Rode thro' the coverts of the deer,
With blissful treble ringing clear.
    She seem'd a part of joyous Spring;
A gown of grass-green silk she wore,
Buckled with golden clasps before;
A light-green tuft of plumes she bore
    Closed in a golden ring.

Now on some twisted ivy-net,
Now by some tinkling rivulet,
In mosses mixt with violet
Her cream-white mule his pastern set;
    And fleeter now she skimm'd the plains
Than she whose elfin prancer springs
By night to eery warblings,
When all the glimmering moorland rings
    With jingling bridle-reins.

As she fled fast thro' sun and shade,
The happy winds upon her play'd,
Blowing the ringlet from the braid.
She look'd so lovely, as she sway'd
    The rein with dainty finger-tips,
A man had given all other bliss,
And all his worldly worth for this,
To waste his whole heart in one kiss
    Upon her perfect lips.

A FAREWELL

Flow down, cold rivulet, to the sea,
    Thy tribute wave deliver;
No more by thee my steps shall be,
    For ever and for ever.

Flow, softly flow, by lawn and lea,
    A rivulet, then a river;
Nowhere by thee my steps shall be,
    For ever and for ever.

But here will sigh thine alder-tree,
    And here thine aspen shiver;
And here by thee will hum the bee,
    For ever and for ever.

A thousand suns will stream on thee,
    A thousand moons will quiver;
But not by thee my steps shall be,
    For ever and for ever.

THE BEGGAR MAID

HER arms across her breast she laid;
  She was more fair than words can say;
Barefooted came the beggar maid
  Before the king Cophetua.
In robe and crown the king stept down,
  To meet and greet her on her way;
'It is no wonder,' said the lords,
  'She is more beautiful than day.'

As shines the moon in clouded skies,
  She in her poor attire was seen;
One praised her ankles, one her eyes,
  One her dark hair and lovesome mien.
So sweet a face, such angel grace,
  In all that land had never been.
Cophetua sware a royal oath:
  'This beggar maid shall be my queen!'

THE EAGLE

FRAGMENT

HE clasps the crag with crooked hands;
Close to the sun in lonely lands,
Ring'd with the azure world, he stands.

The wrinkled sea beneath him crawls;
He watches from his mountain walls,
And like a thunderbolt he falls.

'MOVE EASTWARD, HAPPY EARTH'

MOVE eastward, happy earth, and leave
  Yon orange sunset waning slow;
From fringes of the faded eve,
  O happy planet, eastward go,
Till over thy dark shoulder glow
  Thy silver sister-world, and rise
  To glass herself in dewy eyes
That watch me from the glen below.

Ah, bear me with thee, smoothly borne,
  Dip forward under starry light,

And move me to my marriage-morn,
And round again to happy night.

'COME NOT, WHEN I AM DEAD'

Come not, when I am dead,
  To drop thy foolish tears upon my grave,
To trample round my fallen head,
  And vex the unhappy dust thou wouldst not save.
There let the wind sweep and the plover cry;
    But thou, go by.

Child, if it were thine error or thy crime
  I care no longer, being all unblest:
Wed whom thou wilt, but I am sick of time,
  And I desire to rest.
Pass on, weak heart, and leave me where I lie;
    Go by, go by.

THE LETTERS

I

Still on the tower stood the vane,
  A black yew gloom'd the stagnant air,
I peer'd athwart the chancel pane
  And saw the altar cold and bare.
A clog of lead was round my feet,
  A band of pain across my brow;
'Cold altar, heaven and earth shall meet
  Before you hear my marriage vow.'

II

I turn'd and humm'd a bitter song
  That mock'd the wholesome human heart,
And then we met in wrath and wrong,
  We met, but only met to part.
Full cold my greeting was and dry;
  She faintly smiled, she hardly moved;
I saw with half-unconscious eye
  She wore the colors I approved.

III

She took the little ivory chest,
    With half a sigh she turn'd the key,
Then raised her head with lips comprest,
    And gave my letters back to me;
And gave the trinkets and the rings,
    My gifts, when gifts of mine could please.
As looks a father on the things
    Of his dead son, I look'd on these.

IV

She told me all her friends had said;
    I raged against the public liar;
She talk'd as if her love were dead,
    But in my words were seeds of fire.
'No more of love, your sex is known;
    I never will be twice deceived.
Henceforth I trust the man alone,
    The woman cannot be believed.

V

'Thro' slander, meanest spawn of hell,—
    And women's slander is the worst,—
And you, whom once I loved so well,
    Thro' you my life will be accurst.'
I spoke with heart and heat and force,
    I shook her breast with vague alarms—
Like torrents from a mountain source
    We rush'd into each other's arms.

VI

We parted; sweetly gleam'd the stars,
    And sweet the vapor-braided blue;
Low breezes fann'd the belfry bars,
    As homeward by the church I drew.
The very graves appear'd to smile,
    So fresh they rose in shadow'd swells;
'Dark porch,' I said, 'and silent aisle,
    There comes a sound of marriage bells.'

THE VISION OF SIN

I

I HAD a vision when the night was late;
A youth came riding toward a palace-gate.
He rode a horse with wings, that would have flown,
But that his heavy rider kept him down.
And from the palace came a child of sin,
And took him by the curls, and led him in,
Where sat a company with heated eyes,
Expecting when a fountain should arise.
A sleepy light upon their brows and lips—
As when the sun, a crescent of eclipse,   10
Dreams over lake and lawn, and isles and capes—
Suffused them, sitting, lying, languid shapes,
By heaps of gourds, and skins of wine, and piles of grapes.

II

Then methought I heard a mellow sound,
Gathering up from all the lower ground;
Narrowing in to where they sat assembled,
Low voluptuous music winding trembled,
Woven in circles. They that heard it sigh'd,
Panted hand-in-hand with faces pale,
Swung themselves, and in low tones replied;   20
Till the fountain spouted, showering wide
Sleet of diamond-drift and pearly hail.
Then the music touch'd the gates and died,
Rose again from where it seem'd to fail,
Storm'd in orbs of song, a growing gale;
Till thronging in and in, to where they waited,
As 't were a hundred-throated nightingale,
The strong tempestuous treble throbb'd and palpitated;
Ran into its giddiest whirl of sound,
Caught the sparkles, and in circles,   30
Purple gauzes, golden hazes, liquid mazes,
Flung the torrent rainbow round.
Then they started from their places,
Moved with violence, changed in hue,
Caught each other with wild grimaces,
Half-invisible to the view,
Wheeling with precipitate paces
To the melody, till they flew,
Hair and eyes and limbs and faces,
Twisted hard in fierce embraces,   40

Like to Furies, like to Graces,
Dash'd together in blinding dew;
Till, kill'd with some luxurious agony,
The nerve-dissolving melody
Flutter'd headlong from the sky.

III

And then I look'd up toward a mountain-tract,
That girt the region with high cliff and lawn.
I saw that every morning, far withdrawn
Beyond the darkness and the cataract,
God made Himself an awful rose of dawn,   50
Unheeded; and detaching, fold by fold,
From those still heights, and, slowly drawing near,
A vapor heavy, hueless, formless, cold,
Came floating on for many a month and year,
Unheeded; and I thought I would have spoken,
And warn'd that madman ere it grew too late,
But, as in dreams, I could not. Mine was broken,
When that cold vapor touch'd the palace-gate,
And link'd again. I saw within my head
A gray and gap-tooth'd man as lean as death,   60
Who slowly rode across a wither'd heath,
And lighted at a ruin'd inn, and said:

IV

'Wrinkled ostler, grim and thin!
    Here is custom come your way;
Take my brute, and lead him in,
    Stuff his ribs with mouldy hay.

'Bitter barmaid, waning fast!
    See that sheets are on my bed.
What! the flower of life is past;
    It is long before you wed.   70

'Slip-shod waiter, lank and sour,
    At the Dragon on the heath!
Let us have a quiet hour,
    Let us hob-and-nob with Death.

'I am old, but let me drink;
    Bring me spices, bring me wine;
I remember, when I think,
    That my youth was half divine.

'Wine is good for shrivell'd lips,
    When a blanket wraps the day,   80
When the rotten woodland drips,
    And the leaf is stamp'd in clay.

'Sit thee down, and have no shame,
    Cheek by jowl, and knee by knee;
What care I for any name?
    What for order or degree?

'Let me screw thee up a peg;
    Let me loose thy tongue with wine;
Callest thou that thing a leg?
    Which is thinnest? thine or mine?   90

'Thou shalt not be saved by works,
    Thou hast been a sinner too;
Ruin'd trunks on wither'd forks,
    Empty scarecrows, I and you!

'Fill the cup and fill the can,
    Have a rouse before the morn;
Every moment dies a man,
    Every moment one is born.

'We are men of ruin'd blood;
    Therefore comes it we are wise.   100
Fish are we that love the mud,
    Rising to no fancy-flies.

'Name and fame! to fly sublime
    Thro' the courts, the camps, the schools
Is to be the ball of Time,
    Bandied by the hands of fools.

'Friendship!—to be two in one—
    Let the canting liar pack!
Well I know, when I am gone,
    How she mouths behind my back.   110

'Virtue!—to be good and just—
    Every heart, when sifted well,
Is a clot of warmer dust,
    Mix'd with cunning sparks of hell.

'O, we two as well can look
    Whited thought and cleanly life

As the priest, above his book
   Leering at his neighbor's wife.

'Fill the cup and fill the can,
   Have a rouse before the morn: 120
Every moment dies a man,
   Every moment one is born.

'Drink, and let the parties rave;
   They are fill'd with idle spleen,
Rising, falling, like a wave,
   For they know not what they mean.

'He that roars for liberty
   Faster binds a tyrant's power,
And the tyrant's cruel glee   130
   Forces on the freer hour.

'Fill the can and fill the cup;
   All the windy ways of men
Are but dust that rises up,
   And is lightly laid again.

'Greet her with applausive breath,
   Freedom, gaily doth she tread;
In her right a civic wreath,
   In her left a human head.

'No, I love not what is new;
   She is of an ancient house,   140
And I think we know the hue
   Of that cap upon her brows.

'Let her go! her thirst she slakes
   Where the bloody conduit runs,
Then her sweetest meal she makes
   On the first-born of her sons.

'Drink to lofty hopes that cool,—
   Visions of a perfect State;
Drink we, last, the public fool,
   Frantic love and frantic hate.   150

'Chant me now some wicked stave,
   Till thy drooping courage rise,
And the glow-worm of the grave
   Glimmer in thy rheumy eyes.

'Fear not thou to loose thy tongue,
    Set thy hoary fancies free;
What is loathsome to the young
    Savors well to thee and me.

'Change, reverting to the years,
    When thy nerves could understand   **160**
What there is in loving tears,
    And the warmth of hand in hand.

'Tell me tales of thy first love—
    April hopes, the fools of chance—
Till the graves begin to move,
    And the dead begin to dance.

'Fill the can and fill the cup;
    All the windy ways of men
Are but dust that rises up,
    And is lightly laid again.   **170**

'Trooping from their mouldy dens
    The chap-fallen circle spreads—
Welcome, fellow-citizens,
    Hollow hearts and empty heads!

'You are bones, and what of that?
    Every face, however full,
Padded round with flesh and fat,
    Is but modell'd on a skull.

'Death is king, and Vivat Rex!
    Tread a measure on the stones,   **180**
Madam—if I know your sex
    From the fashion of your bones.

'No, I cannot praise the fire
    In your eye—nor yet your lip;
All the more do I admire
    Joints of cunning workmanship.

'Lo! God's likeness—the ground-plan—
    Neither modell'd, glazed, nor framed;
Buss me, thou rough sketch of man,
    Far too naked to be shamed!   **190**

'Drink to Fortune, drink to Chance,
    While we keep a little breath!

Drink to heavy Ignorance!
   Hob-and-nob with brother Death!

'Thou art mazed, the night is long,
   And the longer night is near—
What! I am not all as wrong
   As a bitter jest is dear.

'Youthful hopes, by scores, to all,
   When the locks are crisp and curl'd;   200
Unto me my maudlin gall
   And my mockeries of the world.

'Fill the cup and fill the can;
   Mingle madness, mingle scorn!
Dregs of life, and lees of man;
   Yet we will not die forlorn.'

V

The voice grew faint; there came a further change;
Once more uprose the mystic mountain-range.
Below were men and horses pierced with worms,
And slowly quickening into lower forms;   210
By shards and scurf of salt, and scum of dross,
Old plash of rains, and refuse patch'd with moss.
Then some one spake: 'Behold! it was a crime
Of sense avenged by sense that wore with time.'
Another said: 'The crime of sense became
The crime of malice, and is equal blame.'
And one: 'He had not wholly quench'd his power;
A little grain of conscience made him sour.'
At last I heard a voice upon the slope
Cry to the summit, 'Is there any hope?'   220
To which an answer peal'd from that high land,
But in a tongue no man could understand;
And on the glimmering limit far withdrawn
God made Himself an awful rose of dawn.

TO ——

AFTER READING A LIFE AND LETTERS

'Cursed be he that moves my bones.'

Shakespeare's Epitaph

You might have won the Poet's name,
 If such be worth the winning now,
 And gain'd a laurel for your brow
Of sounder leaf than I can claim;

But you have made the wiser choice,
 A life that moves to gracious ends
 Thro' troops of unrecording friends,
A deedful life, a silent voice.

And you have miss'd the irreverent doom
 Of those that wear the Poet's crown;
 Hereafter, neither knave nor clown
Shall hold their orgies at your tomb.

For now the Poet cannot die,
 Nor leave his music as of old,
 But round him ere he scarce be cold
Begins the scandal and the cry:

'Proclaim the faults he would not show;
 Break lock and seal, betray the trust;
 Keep nothing sacred, 't is but just
The many-headed beast should know.'

Ah, shameless! for he did but sing
 A song that pleased us from its worth;
 No public life was his on earth,
No blazon'd statesman he, nor king.

He gave the people of his best;
 His worst he kept, his best he gave.
 My Shakespeare's curse on clown and **knave**
Who will not let his ashes rest!

Who make it seem more sweet to be
 The little life of bank and brier,
 The bird that pipes his lone desire
And dies unheard within his tree,

Than he that warbles long and loud
    And drops at Glory's temple-gates,
    For whom the carrion vulture waits
To tear his heart before the crowd!

TO E. L., ON HIS TRAVELS IN GREECE

ILLYRIAN woodlands, echoing falls
    Of water, sheets of summer glass,
    The long divine Peneïan pass,
The vast Akrokeraunian walls,

Tomohrit, Athos, all things fair,
    With such a pencil, such a pen,
    You shadow forth to distant men,
I read and felt that I was there.

And trust me while I turn'd the page,
    And track'd you still on classic ground,
    I grew in gladness till I found
My spirits in the golden age.

For me the torrent ever pour'd
    And glisten'd—here and there alone
    The broad-limb'd Gods at random thrown
By fountain-urns;—and Naiads oar'd

A glimmering shoulder under gloom
    Of cavern pillars; on the swell
    The silver lily heaved and fell;
And many a slope was rich in bloom,

From him that on the mountain lea
    By dancing rivulets fed his flocks
    To him who sat upon the rocks
And fluted to the morning sea.

———

BREAK, break, break,
    On thy cold gray stones, O Sea!
And I would that my tongue could utter
    The thoughts that arise in me.

O, well for the fisherman's boy,
    That he shouts with his sister at play!
O, well for the sailor lad,
    That he sings in his boat on the bay!

And the stately ships go on
   To their haven under the hill;
But O for the touch of a vanish'd hand,
   And the sound of a voice that is still!

Break, break, break,
   At the foot of thy crags, O Sea!
But the tender grace of a day that is dead
   Will never come back to me.

THE POET'S SONG

THE rain had fallen, the Poet arose,
   He pass'd by the town and out of the street;
A light wind blew from the gates of the sun,
   And waves of shadow went over the wheat;
And he sat him down in a lonely place,
   And chanted a melody loud and sweet,
That made the wild-swan pause in her cloud,
   And the lark drop down at his feet.

The swallow stopt as he hunted the fly,
   The snake slipt under a spray,
The wild hawk stood with the down on his beak,
   And stared, with his foot on the prey;
And the nightingale thought, 'I have sung many songs,
   But never a one so gay,
For he sings of what the world will be
   When the years have died away.'

THE PRINCESS; A MEDLEY

PROLOGUE

Sir Walter Vivian all a summer's day
Gave his broad lawns until the set of sun
Up to the people; thither flock'd at noon
His tenants, wife and child, and thither half
The neighboring borough with their Institute,
Of which he was the patron. I was there
From college, visiting the son,—the son
A Walter too,—with others of our set,
Five others; we were seven at Vivian-place.

And me that morning Walter show'd the house,   10
Greek, set with busts. From vases in the hall
Flowers of all heavens, and lovelier than their names,
Grew side by side; and on the pavement lay
Carved stones of the Abbey-ruin in the park,
Huge Ammonites, and the first bones of Time;
And on the tables every clime and age
Jumbled together; celts and calumets,
Claymore and snow-shoe, toys in lava, fans
Of sandal, amber, ancient rosaries,
Laborious orient ivory sphere in sphere,   20
The cursed Malayan crease, and battle-clubs
From the isles of palm; and higher on the walls,
Betwixt the monstrous horns of elk and deer,
His own forefathers' arms and armor hung.

And 'this,' he said, 'was Hugh's at Agincourt;
And that was old Sir Ralph's at Ascalon.
A good knight he! we keep a chronicle
With all about him,'—which he brought, and I
Dived in a hoard of tales that dealt with knights
Half-legend, half-historic, counts and kings   30
Who laid about them at their wills and died;
And mixt with these a lady, one that arm'd
Her own fair head, and sallying thro' the gate,
Had beat her foes with slaughter from her walls.

'O miracle of women,' said the book,
'O noble heart who, being strait-besieged
By this wild king to force her to his wish,
Nor bent, nor broke, nor shunn'd a soldier's death,
But now when all was lost or seem'd as lost—
Her stature more than mortal in the burst   40
Of sunrise, her arm lifted, eyes on fire—
Brake with a blast of trumpets from the gate,
And, falling on them like a thunderbolt,
She trampled some beneath her horses' heels,
And some were whelm'd with missiles of the wall,
And some were push'd with lances from the rock,
And part were drown'd within the whirling brook;
O miracle of noble womanhood!'

So sang the gallant glorious chronicle;
And, I all rapt in this, 'Come out,' he said,   50
'To the Abbey; there is Aunt Elizabeth
And Sister Lilia with the rest.' We went—
I kept the book and had my finger in it—
Down thro' the park. Strange was the sight to me;
For all the sloping pasture murmur'd, sown
With happy faces and with holiday.
There moved the multitude, a thousand heads;
The patient leaders of their Institute
Taught them with facts. One rear'd a font of stone
And drew, from butts of water on the slope,   60
The fountain of the moment, playing, now
A twisted snake, and now a rain of pearls,
Or steep-up spout whereon the gilded ball
Danced like a wisp; and somewhat lower down
A man with knobs and wires and vials fired
A cannon; Echo answer'd in her sleep
From hollow fields; and here were telescopes
For azure views; and there a group of girls
In circle waited, whom the electric shock
Dislink'd with shrieks and laughter; round the lake   70
A little clock-work steamer paddling plied
And shook the lilies; perch'd about the knolls
A dozen angry models jetted steam;
A petty railway ran; a fire-balloon
Rose gem-like up before the dusky groves
And dropt a fairy parachute and past;
And there thro' twenty posts of telegraph
They flash'd a saucy message to and fro
Between the mimic stations; so that sport
Went hand in hand with science; otherwhere   80
Pure sport; a herd of boys with clamor bowl'd

And stump'd the wicket; babies roll'd about
Like tumbled fruit in grass; and men and maids
Arranged a country dance, and flew thro' light
And shadow, while the twangling violin
Struck up with Soldier-laddie, and overhead
The broad ambrosial aisles of lofty lime
Made noise with bees and breeze from end to end.

Strange was the sight and smacking of the time;
And long we gazed, but satiated at length   90
Came to the ruins. High-arch'd and ivy-claspt,
Of finest Gothic lighter than a fire,
Thro' one wide chasm of time and frost they gave
The park, the crowd, the house; but all within
The sward was trim as any garden lawn.
And here we lit on Aunt Elizabeth,
And Lilia with the rest, and lady friends
From neighbor seats; and there was Ralph himself,
A broken statue propt against the wall,
As gay as any. Lilia, wild with sport,   100
Half child, half woman as she was, had wound
A scarf of orange round the stony helm,
And robed the shoulders in a rosy silk,
That made the old warrior from his ivied nook
Glow like a sunbeam. Near his tomb a feast
Shone, silver-set; about it lay the guests,
And there we join'd them; then the maiden aunt
Took this fair day for text, and from it preach'd
An universal culture for the crowd,
And all things great. But we, unworthier, told   110
Of college: he had climb'd across the spikes,
And he had squeezed himself betwixt the bars,
And he had breathed the Proctor's dogs; and one
Discuss'd his tutor, rough to common men,
But honeying at the whisper of a lord;
And one the Master, as a rogue in grain
Veneer'd with sanctimonious theory.

But while they talk'd, above their heads I saw
The feudal warrior lady-clad; which brought
My book to mind, and opening this I read   120
Of old Sir Ralph a page or two that rang
With tilt and tourney; then the tale of her
That drove her foes with slaughter from her walls,
And much I praised her nobleness, and 'Where,'
Ask'd Walter, patting Lilia's head—she lay
Beside him—'lives there such a woman now?'

Quick answer'd Lilia: 'There are thousands now
Such women, but convention beats them down;
It is but bringing up; no more than that.
You men have done it—how I hate you all!   130
Ah, were I something great! I wish I were
Some mighty poetess, I would shame you then,
That love to keep us children! O, I wish
That I were some great princess, I would build
Far off from men a college like a man's,
And I would teach them all that men are taught;
We are twice as quick!' And here she shook aside
The hand that play'd the patron with her curls.

And one said smiling: 'Pretty were the sight
If our old halls could change their sex, and flaunt   140
With prudes for proctors, dowagers for deans,
And sweet girl-graduates in their golden hair.
I think they should not wear our rusty gowns,
But move as rich as Emperor-moths, or Ralph
Who shines so in the corner; yet I fear,
If there were many Lilias in the brood,
However deep you might embower the nest,
Some boy would spy it.'
                          At this upon the sward
She tapt her tiny silken-sandall'd foot:
'That's your light way; but I would make it death   150
For any male thing but to peep at us.'

Petulant she spoke, and at herself she laugh'd;
A rosebud set with little wilful thorns,
And sweet as English air could make her, she!
But Walter hail'd a score of names upon her,
And 'petty Ogress,' and 'ungrateful Puss,'
And swore he long'd at college, only long'd,
All else was well, for she-society.
They boated and they cricketed; they talk'd
At wine, in clubs, of art, of politics;   160
They lost their weeks; they vext the souls of deans;
They rode; they betted; made a hundred friends,
And caught the blossom of the flying terms,
But miss'd the mignonette of Vivian-place,
The little hearth-flower Lilia. Thus he spoke,
Part banter, part affection.
                           'True,' she said,
'We doubt not that. O, yes, you miss'd us much!
I'll stake my ruby ring upon it you did.'

She held it out; and as a parrot turns
Up thro' gilt wires a crafty loving eye,   170
And takes a lady's finger with all care,
And bites it for true heart and not for harm,
So he with Lilia's. Daintily she shriek'd
And wrung it. 'Doubt my word again!' he said.
'Come, listen! here is proof that you were miss'd:
We seven stay'd at Christmas up to read;
And there we took one tutor as to read:
The hard-grain'd Muses of the cube and square
Were out of season; never man, I think,
So moulder'd in a sinecure as he;   180
For while our cloisters echo'd frosty feet,
And our long walks were stript as bare as brooms,
We did but talk you over, pledge you all
In wassail; often, like as many girls—
Sick for the hollies and the yews of home—
As many little trifling Lilias—play'd
Charades and riddles as at Christmas here,
And *what's my thought* and *when and where and how,*
And often told a tale from mouth to mouth
As here at Christmas.'
                              She remember'd that;   190
A pleasant game, she thought. She liked it more
Than magic music, forfeits, all the rest.
But these—what kind of tales did men tell men,
She wonder'd, by themselves?
                              A half-disdain
Perch'd on the pouted blossom of her lips;
And Walter nodded at me: '*He* began,
The rest would follow, each in turn; and so
We forged a sevenfold story. Kind? what kind?
Chimeras, crotchets, Christmas solecisms;
Seven-headed monsters only made to kill   200
Time by the fire in winter.'
                              'Kill him now,
The tyrant! kill him in the summer too,'
Said Lilia; 'Why not now?' the maiden aunt.
'Why not a summer's as a winter's tale?
A tale for summer as befits the time,
And something it should be to suit the place,
Heroic, for a hero lies beneath,
Grave, solemn!'
                              Walter warp'd his mouth at this
To something so mock-solemn, that I laugh'd
And Lilia woke with sudden-shrilling mirth   210
An echo like a ghostly woodpecker
Hid in the ruins; till the maiden aunt—

A little sense of wrong had touch'd her face
With color—turn'd to me with 'As you will;
Heroic if you will, or what you will,
Or be yourself your hero if you will.'

'Take Lilia, then, for heroine,' clamor'd he,
'And make her some great princess, six feet high,
Grand, epic, homicidal; and be you
The prince to win her!'
                             'Then follow me, the prince,'   220
I answer'd, 'each be hero in his turn!
Seven and yet one, like shadows in a dream.—
Heroic seems our princess as required—
But something made to suit with time and place,
A Gothic ruin and a Grecian house,
A talk of college and of ladies' rights,
A feudal knight in silken masquerade,
And, yonder, shrieks and strange experiments
For which the good Sir Ralph had burnt them all—
This *were* a medley! we should have him back   230
Who told the "Winter's Tale" to do it for us.
No matter; we will say whatever comes.
And let the ladies sing us, if they will,
From time to time, some ballad or a song
To give us breathing-space.'
                             So I began,
And the rest follow'd; and the women sang
Between the rougher voices of the men,
Like linnets in the pauses of the wind:
And here I give the story and the songs.

I

A Prince I was, blue-eyed, and fair in face,
Of temper amorous as the first of May,
With lengths of yellow ringlet, like a girl,
For on my cradle shone the Northern star.

There lived an ancient legend in our house.
Some sorcerer, whom a far-off grandsire burnt
Because he cast no shadow, had foretold,
Dying, that none of all our blood should know
The shadow from the substance, and that one
Should come to fight with shadows and to fall;   10
For so, my mother said, the story ran.
And, truly, waking dreams were, more or less,
An old and strange affection of the house.
Myself too had weird seizures, Heaven knows what!

On a sudden in the midst of men and day,
And while I walk'd and talk'd as heretofore,
I seem'd to move among a world of ghosts,
And feel myself the shadow of a dream.
Our great court-Galen poised his gilt-head cane,
And paw'd his beard, and mutter'd 'catalepsy.'   20
My mother pitying made a thousand prayers.
My mother was as mild as any saint,
Half-canonized by all that look'd on her,
So gracious was her tact and tenderness;
But my good father thought a king a king.
He cared not for the affection of the house;
He held his sceptre like a pedant's wand
To lash offence, and with long arms and hands
Reach'd out and pick'd offenders from the mass
For judgment.
                    Now it chanced that I had been,   30
While life was yet in bud and blade, betroth'd
To one, a neighboring Princess. She to me
Was proxy-wedded with a bootless calf
At eight years old; and still from time to time
Came murmurs of her beauty from the South,
And of her brethren, youths of puissance;
And still I wore her picture by my heart,
And one dark tress; and all around them both
Sweet thoughts would swarm as bees about their queen.

But when the days drew nigh that I should wed,   40
My father sent ambassadors with furs
And jewels, gifts, to fetch her. These brought back
A present, a great labor of the loom;
And therewithal an answer vague as wind.
Besides, they saw the king; he took the gifts;
He said there was a compact; that was true;
But then she had a will; was he to blame?
And maiden fancies; loved to live alone
Among her women; certain, would not wed.

That morning in the presence room I stood   50
With Cyril and with Florian, my two friends:
The first, a gentleman of broken means—
His father's fault—but given to starts and bursts
Of revel; and the last, my other heart,
And almost my half-self, for still we moved
Together, twinn'd as horse's ear and eye.

Now, while they spake, I saw my father's face
Grow long and troubled like a rising moon,

Inflamed with wrath. He started on his feet,
Tore the king's letter, snow'd it down, and rent   60
The wonder of the loom thro' warp and woof
From skirt to skirt; and at the last he sware
That he would send a hundred thousand men,
And bring her in a whirlwind; then he chew'd
The thrice-turn'd cud of wrath, and cook'd his spleen,
Communing with his captains of the war.

    At last I spoke: 'My father, let me go.
It cannot be but some gross error lies
In this report, this answer of a king
Whom all men rate as kind and hospitable;   70
Or, maybe, I myself, my bride once seen,
Whate'er my grief to find her less than fame,
May rue the bargain made.' And Florian said:
'I have a sister at the foreign court,
Who moves about the Princess; she, you know,
Who wedded with a nobleman from thence.
He, dying lately, left her, as I hear,
The lady of three castles in that land;
Thro' her this matter might be sifted clean.'
And Cyril whisper'd: 'Take me with you too.'   80
Then laughing, 'What if these weird seizures come
Upon you in those lands, and no one near
To point you out the shadow from the truth!
Take me; I'll serve you better in a strait;
I grate on rusty hinges here.' But 'No!'
Roar'd the rough king, 'you shall not; we ourself
Will crush her pretty maiden fancies dead
In iron gauntlets; break the council up.'

    But when the council broke, I rose and past
Thro' the wild woods that hung about the town;   90
Found a still place, and pluck'd her likeness out;
Laid it on flowers, and watch'd it lying bathed
In the green gleam of dewy-tassell'd trees.
What were those fancies? wherefore break her troth?
Proud look'd the lips; but while I meditated
A wind arose and rush'd upon the South,
And shook the songs, the whispers, and the shrieks
Of the wild woods together, and a Voice
Went with it, 'Follow, follow, thou shalt win.'

    Then, ere the silver sickle of that month   100
Became her golden shield, I stole from court
With Cyril and with Florian, unperceived,
Cat-footed thro' the town and half in dread

To hear my father's clamor at our backs
With 'Ho!' from some bay-window shake the night;
But all was quiet. From the bastion'd walls
Like threaded spiders, one by one, we dropt,
And flying reach'd the frontier; then we crost
To a livelier land; and so by tilth and grange,
And vines, and blowing bosks of wilderness,   110
We gain'd the mother-city thick with towers,
And in the imperial palace found the king.

   His name was Gama; crack'd and small his voice,
But bland the smile that like a wrinkling wind
On glassy water drove his cheek in lines;
A little dry old man, without a star,
Not like a king. Three days he feasted us
And on the fourth I spake of why we came
And my betroth'd. 'You do us, Prince,' he said,
Airing a snowy hand and signet gem,   120
'All honor. We remember love ourself
In our sweet youth. There did a compact pass
Long summers back, a kind of ceremony—
I think the year in which our olives fail'd.
I would you had her, Prince, with all my heart,
With my full heart; but there were widows here,
Two widows, Lady Psyche, Lady Blanche;
They fed her theories, in and out of place
Maintaining that with equal husbandry
The woman were an equal to the man.   130
They harp'd on this; with this our banquets rang;
Our dances broke and buzz'd in knots of talk;
Nothing but this; my very ears were hot
To hear them. Knowledge, so my daughter held,
Was all in all; they had but been, she thought,
As children; they must lose the child, assume
The woman. Then, sir, awful odes she wrote,
Too awful, sure, for what they treated of,
But all she is and does is awful; odes
About this losing of the child; and rhymes   140
And dismal lyrics, prophesying change
Beyond all reason. These the women sang;
And they that know such things—I sought but peace;
No critic I—would call them masterpieces.
They master'd *me*. At last she begg'd a boon,
A certain summer-palace which I have
Hard by your father's frontier. I said no,
Yet being an easy man, gave it; and there,
All wild to found an University
For maidens, on the spur she fled; and more   150

We know not,—only this: they see no men,
Not even her brother Arac, nor the twins
Her brethren, tho' they love her, look upon her
As on a kind of paragon; and I—
Pardon me saying it—were much loth to breed
Dispute betwixt myself and mine; but since—
And I confess with right—you think me bound
In some sort, I can give you letters to her;
And yet, to speak the truth, I rate your chance
Almost at naked nothing.'
                    Thus the king;   160
And I, tho' nettled that he seem'd to slur
With garrulous ease and oily courtesies
Our formal compact, yet, not less—all frets
But chafing me on fire to find my bride—
Went forth again with both my friends. We rode
Many a long league back to the North. At last
From hills that look'd across a land of hope
We dropt with evening on a rustic town
Set in a gleaming river's crescent-curve,
Close at the boundary of the liberties;   170
There, enter'd an old hostel, call'd mine host
To council, plied him with his richest wines,
And show'd the late-writ letters of the king.

He with a long low sibilation, stared
As blank as death in marble; then exclaim'd,
Averring it was clear against all rules
For any man to go; but as his brain
Began to mellow, 'If the king,' he said,
'Had given us letters, was he bound to speak?
The king would bear him out;' and at the last—   180
The summer of the vine in all his veins—
'No doubt that we might make it worth his while.
She once had past that way; he heard her speak;
She scared him; life! he never saw the like;
She look'd as grand as doomsday and as grave!
And he, he reverenced his liege-lady there;
He always made a point to post with mares;
His daughter and his housemaid were the boys;
The land, he understood, for miles about
Was till'd by women; all the swine were sows,   190
And all the dogs'—
                But while he jested thus,
A thought flash'd thro' me which I clothed in act,
Remembering how we three presented Maid,
Or Nymph, or Goddess, at high tide of feast,
In masque or pageant at my father's court.

We sent mine host to purchase female gear;
He brought it, and himself, a sight to shake
The midriff of despair with laughter, holp
To lace us up, till each in maiden plumes
We rustled; him we gave a costly bribe 200
To guerdon silence, mounted our good steeds,
And boldly ventured on the liberties.

We follow'd up the river as we rode,
And rode till midnight, when the college lights
Began to glitter firefly-like in copse
And linden alley; then we past an arch,
Whereon a woman-statue rose with wings
From four wing'd horses dark against the stars,
And some inscription ran along the front,
But deep in shadow. Further on we gain'd 210
A little street half garden and half house,
But scarce could hear each other speak for noise
Of clocks and chimes, like silver hammers falling
On silver anvils, and the splash and stir
Of fountains spouted up and showering down
In meshes of the jasmine and the rose;
And all about us peal'd the nightingale,
Rapt in her song and careless of the snare.

There stood a bust of Pallas for a sign,
By two sphere lamps blazon'd like Heaven and Earth 220
With constellation and with continent,
Above an entry. Riding in, we call'd;
A plump-arm'd ostleress and a stable wench
Came running at the call, and help'd us down.
Then stept a buxom hostess forth, and sail'd,
Full-blown, before us into rooms which gave
Upon a pillar'd porch, the bases lost
In laurel. Here we ask'd of that and this,
And who were tutors. 'Lady Blanche,' she said,
'And Lady Psyche.' 'Which was prettiest, 230
Best natured?' 'Lady Psyche.' 'Hers are we,'
One voice, we cried; and I sat down and wrote
In such a hand as when a field of corn
Bows all its ears before the roaring East:

'Three ladies of the Northern empire pray
Your Highness would enroll them with your own,
As Lady Psyche's pupils.'
                          This I seal'd;
The seal was Cupid bent above a scroll,
And o'er his head Uranian Venus hung,

And raised the blinding bandage from his eyes.   240
I gave the letter to be sent with dawn;
And then to bed, where half in doze I seem'd
To float about a glimmering night, and watch
A full sea glazed with muffled moonlight swell
On some dark shore just seen that it was rich.

> As thro' the land at eve we went,
>   And pluck'd the ripen'd ears,
> We fell out, my wife and I,
> O, we fell out, I know not why,   250
>   And kiss'd again with tears.
> And blessings on the falling out
>   That all the more endears,
> When we fall out with those we love
>   And kiss again with tears!
> For when we came where lies the child
>   We lost in other years,
> There above the little grave,
> O, there above the little grave,
>   We kiss'd again with tears.

II

At break of day the College Portress came;
She brought us academic silks, in hue
The lilac, with a silken hood to each,
And zoned with gold; and now when these were on,
And we as rich as moths from dusk cocoons,
She, curtseying her obeisance, let us know
The Princess Ida waited. Out we paced,
I first, and following thro' the porch that sang
All round with laurel, issued in a court
Compact of lucid marbles, boss'd with lengths   10
Of classic frieze, with ample awnings gay
Betwixt the pillars, and with great urns of flowers.
The Muses and the Graces, group'd in threes,
Enring'd a billowing fountain in the midst,
And here and there on lattice edges lay
Or book or lute; but hastily we past,
And up a flight of stairs into the hall.

There at a board by tome and paper sat,
With two tame leopards couch'd beside her throne,
All beauty compass'd in a female form,   20
The Princess; liker to the inhabitant
Of some clear planet close upon the sun,
Than our man's earth; such eyes were in her head,
And so much grace and power, breathing down
From over her arch'd brows, with every turn
Lived thro' her to the tips of her long hands,
And to her feet. She rose her height, and said:

'We give you welcome; not without redound
Of use and glory to yourselves ye come,
The first-fruits of the stranger; aftertime,   30
And that full voice which circles round the grave,
Will rank you nobly, mingled up with me.
What! are the ladies of your land so tall?'
'We of the court,' said Cyril. 'From the court,'
She answer'd, 'then ye know the Prince?' and he:
'The climax of his age! as tho' there were
One rose in all the world, your Highness that,
He worships your ideal.' She replied:
'We scarcely thought in our own hall to hear
This barren verbiage, current among men,   40
Light coin, the tinsel clink of compliment.
Your flight from out your bookless wilds would seem
As arguing love of knowledge and of power;
Your language proves you still the child. Indeed,
We dream not of him; when we set our hand
To this great work, we purposed with ourself
Never to wed. You likewise will do well,
Ladies, in entering here, to cast and fling
The tricks which make us toys of men, that so
Some future time, if so indeed you will,   50
You may with those self-styled our lords ally
Your fortunes, justlier balanced, scale with scale.'

    At those high words, we, conscious of ourselves,
Perused the matting; then an officer
Rose up, and read the statutes, such as these:
Not for three years to correspond with home;
Not for three years to cross the liberties;
Not for three years to speak with any men;
And many more, which hastily subscribed,
We enter'd on the boards. And 'Now,' she cried,   60
'Ye are green wood, see ye warp not. Look, our hall!
Our statues!—not of those that men desire,
Sleek Odalisques, or oracles of mode,
Nor stunted squaws of West or East; but she
That taught the Sabine how to rule, and she
The foundress of the Babylonian wall,
The Carian Artemisia strong in war,
The Rhodope that built the pyramid,
Clelia, Cornelia, with the Palmyrene
That fought Aurelian, and the Roman brows   70
Of Agrippina. Dwell with these, and lose
Convention, since to look on noble forms
Makes noble thro' the sensuous organism
That which is higher. O, lift your natures up;

Embrace our aims; work out your freedom. Girls,
Knowledge is now no more a fountain seal'd!
Drink deep, until the habits of the slave,
The sins of emptiness, gossip and spite
And slander, die. Better not be at all
Than not be noble. Leave us; you may go.   80
To-day the Lady Psyche will harangue
The fresh arrivals of the week before;
For they press in from all the provinces,
And fill the hive.'

                  She spoke, and bowing waved
Dismissal; back again we crost the court
To Lady Psyche's. As we enter'd in,
There sat along the forms, like morning doves
That sun their milky bosoms on the thatch,
A patient range of pupils; she herself
Erect behind a desk of satin-wood,   90
A quick brunette, well-moulded, falcon-eyed,
And on the hither side, or so she look'd,
Of twenty summers. At her left, a child,
In shining draperies, headed like a star,
Her maiden babe, a double April old,
Aglaïa slept. We sat; the lady glanced;
Then Florian, but no livelier than the dame
That whisper'd 'Asses' ears' among the sedge,
'My sister.' 'Comely, too, by all that's fair,'
Said Cyril. 'O, hush, hush!' and she began.   100

  'This world was once a fluid haze of light,
Till toward the centre set the starry tides,
And eddied into suns, that wheeling cast
The planets; then the monster, then the man;
Tattoo'd or woaded, winter-clad in skins,
Raw from the prime, and crushing down his mate,
As yet we find in barbarous isles, and here
Among the lowest.'

                Thereupon she took
A bird's-eye view of all the ungracious past;
Glanced at the legendary Amazon   110
As emblematic of a nobler age;
Appraised the Lycian custom, spoke of those
That lay at wine with Lar and Lucumo;
Ran down the Persian, Grecian, Roman lines
Of empire, and the woman's state in each,
How far from just; till warming with her theme
She fulmined out her scorn of laws Salique
And little-footed China, touch'd on Mahomet
With much contempt, and came to chivalry,

When some respect, however slight, was paid   120
To woman, superstition all awry.
However, then commenced the dawn; a beam
Had slanted forward, falling in a land
Of promise; fruit would follow. Deep, indeed,
Their debt of thanks to her who first had dared
To leap the rotten pales of prejudice,
Disyoke their necks from custom, and assert
None lordier than themselves but that which made
Woman and man. She had founded; they must build.
Here might they learn whatever men were taught.   130
Let them not fear, some said their heads were less;
Some men's were small, not they the least of men;
For often fineness compensated size.
Besides the brain was like the hand, and grew
With using: thence the man's, if more was more.
He took advantage of his strength to be
First in the field; some ages had been lost;
But woman ripen'd earlier, and her life
Was longer; and albeit their glorious names
Were fewer, scatter'd stars, yet since in truth   140
The highest is the measure of the man,
And not the Kaffir, Hottentot, Malay,
Nor those horn-handed breakers of the glebe,
But Homer, Plato, Verulam, even so
With woman; and in arts of government
Elizabeth and others, arts of war
The peasant Joan and others, arts of grace
Sappho and others vied with any man;
And, last not least, she who had left her place,
And bow'd her state to them, that they might grow   150
To use and power on this oasis, lapt
In the arms of leisure, sacred from the blight
Of ancient influence and scorn.
                                        At last
She rose upon a wind of prophecy
Dilating on the future: 'everywhere
Two heads in council, two beside the hearth,
Two in the tangled business of the world,
Two in the liberal offices of life,
Two plummets dropt for one to sound the abyss
Of science and the secrets of the mind;   160
Musician, painter, sculptor, critic, more;
And everywhere the broad and bounteous Earth
Should bear a double growth of those rare souls,
Poets, whose thoughts enrich the blood of the world.'

She ended here, and beckon'd us; the rest
Parted; and, glowing full-faced welcome, she
Began to address us, and was moving on
In gratulation, till as when a boat
Tacks and the slacken'd sail flaps, all her voice
Faltering and fluttering in her throat, she cried,   170
'My brother!' 'Well, my sister.' 'O,' she said,
'What do you here? and in this dress? and these?
Why, who are these? a wolf within the fold!
A pack of wolves! the Lord be gracious to me!
A plot, a plot, a plot, to ruin all!'
'No plot, no plot,' he answer'd. 'Wretched boy,
How saw you not the inscription on the gate,
LET NO MAN ENTER IN ON PAIN OF DEATH?'
'And if I had,' he answer'd, 'who could think
The softer Adams of your Academe,   180
O sister, Sirens tho' they be, were such
As chanted on the blanching bones of men?'
'But you will find it otherwise,' she said.
'You jest; ill jesting with edge-tools! my vow
Binds me to speak, and O that iron will,
That axelike edge unturnable, our Head,
The Princess!' 'Well then, Psyche, take my life,
And nail me like a weasel on a grange
For warning; bury me beside the gate,
And cut this epitaph above my bones: 190
Here lies a brother by a sister slain,
All for the common good of womankind.'
'Let me die too,' said Cyril, 'having seen
And heard the Lady Psyche.'
                                I struck in:
'Albeit so mask'd, madam, I love the truth;
Receive it, and in me behold the Prince
Your countryman, affianced years ago
To the Lady Ida. Here, for here she was,
And thus—what other way was left?—I came.'
'O sir, O Prince, I have no country, none;   200
If any, this; but none. Whate'er I was
Disrooted, what I am is grafted here.
Affianced, sir? love-whispers may not breathe
Within this vestal limit, and how should I,
Who am not mine, say, live? The thunderbolt
Hangs silent; but prepare. I speak, it falls.'
'Yet pause,' I said: 'for that inscription there,
I think no more of deadly lurks therein,
Than in a clapper clapping in a garth,
To scare the fowl from fruit; if more there be,   210
If more and acted on, what follows? war;

Your own work marr'd; for this your Academe,
Whichever side be victor, in the halloo
Will topple to the trumpet down, and pass
With all fair theories only made to gild
A stormless summer.' 'Let the Princess judge
Of that,' she said: 'farewell, sir—and to you.
I shudder at the sequel, but I go.'

   'Are you that Lady Psyche,' I rejoin'd,
'The fifth in line from that old Florian,   220
Yet hangs his portrait in my father's hall—
The gaunt old baron with his beetle brow
Sun-shaded in the heat of dusty fights—
As he bestrode my grandsire, when he fell,
And all else fled? we point to it, and we say,
The loyal warmth of Florian is not cold,
But branches current yet in kindred veins.'
'Are you that Psyche,' Florian added; 'she
With whom I sang about the morning hills,
Flung ball, flew kite, and raced the purple fly,   230
And snared the squirrel of the glen? are you
That Psyche, wont to bind my throbbing brow,
To smooth my pillow, mix the foaming draught
Of fever, tell me pleasant tales, and read
My sickness down to happy dreams? are you
That brother-sister Psyche, both in one?
You were that Psyche, but what are you now?'
'You are that Psyche,' Cyril said, 'for whom
I would be that forever which I seem,
Woman, if I might sit beside your feet,   240
And glean your scatter'd sapience.'
                    Then once more,
'Are you that Lady Psyche,' I began,
'That on her bridal morn before she past
From all her old companions, when the king
Kiss'd her pale cheek, declared that ancient ties
Would still be dear beyond the southern hills;
That were there any of our people there
In want or peril, there was one to hear
And help them? look! for such are these and I.'
'Are you that Psyche,' Florian ask'd, 'to whom,   250
In gentler days, your arrow-wounded fawn
Came flying while you sat beside the well?
The creature laid his muzzle on your lap
And sobb'd and you sobb'd with it, and the blood
Was sprinkled on your kirtle, and you wept.
That was fawn's blood, not brother's, yet you wept.
O, by the bright head of my little niece,

You were that Psyche, and what are you now?'
'You are that Psyche,' Cyril said again,
'The mother of the sweetest little maid   260
That ever crow'd for kisses.'
                              'Out upon it!'
She answer'd, 'peace! and why should I not play
The Spartan Mother with emotion, be
The Lucius Junius Brutus of my kind?
Him you call great; he for the common weal,
The fading politics of mortal Rome,
As I might slay this child, if good need were,
Slew both his sons; and I, shall I, on whom
The secular emancipation turns
Of half this world, be swerved from right to save   270
A prince, a brother? a little will I yield.
Best so, perchance, for us, and well for you.
O, hard when love and duty clash! I fear
My conscience will not count me fleckless; yet—
Hear my conditions: promise—otherwise
You perish—as you came, to slip away
To-day, to-morrow, soon. It shall be said,
These women were too barbarous, would not learn;
They fled, who might have shamed us. Promise, all.'

What could we else, we promised each; and she,   280
Like some wild creature newly-caged, commenced
A to-and-fro, so pacing till she paused
By Florian; holding out her lily arms
Took both his hands, and smiling faintly said:
'I knew you at the first; tho' you have grown
You scarce have alter'd. I am sad and glad
To see you, Florian. I give thee to death,
My brother! it was duty spoke, not I.
My needful seeming harshness, pardon it.
Our mother, is she well?'
                          With that she kiss'd   290
His forehead, then, a moment after, clung
About him, and betwixt them blossom'd up
From out a common vein of memory
Sweet household talk, and phrases of the hearth,
And far allusion, till the gracious dews
Began to glisten and to fall; and while
They stood, so rapt, we gazing, came a voice,
'I brought a message here from Lady Blanche.'
Back started she, and turning round we saw
The Lady Blanche's daughter where she stood,   300
Melissa, with her hand upon the lock,
A rosy blonde, and in a college gown,

That clad her like an April daffodilly—
Her mother's color—with her lips apart,
And all her thoughts as fair within her eyes,
As bottom agates seen to wave and float
In crystal currents of clear morning seas.

 So stood that same fair creature at the door.
Then Lady Psyche, 'Ah—Melissa—you!
You heard us?' and Melissa, 'O, pardon me!   310
I heard, I could not help it, did not wish;
But, dearest lady, pray you fear me not,
Nor think I bear that heart within my breast,
To give three gallant gentlemen to death.'
'I trust you,' said the other, 'for we two
Were always friends, none closer, elm and vine;
But yet your mother's jealous temperament—
Let not your prudence, dearest, drowse, or prove
The Danaïd of a leaky vase, for fear
This whole foundation ruin, and I lose   320
My honor, these their lives.' 'Ah, fear me not,'
Replied Melissa; 'no—I would not tell,
No, not for all Aspasia's cleverness,
No, not to answer, madam, all those hard things
That Sheba came to ask of Solomon.'
'Be it so,' the other, 'that we still may lead
The new light up, and culminate in peace,
For Solomon may come to Sheba yet.'
Said Cyril, 'Madam, he the wisest man
Feasted the woman wisest then, in halls   330
Of Lebanonian cedar; nor should you—
Tho', madam, *you* should answer, *we* would ask—
Less welcome find among us, if you came
Among us, debtors for our lives to you,
Myself for something more.' He said not what,
But 'Thanks,' she answer'd, 'go; we have been too long
Together; keep your hoods about the face;
They do so that affect abstraction here.
Speak little; mix not with the rest; and hold
Your promise. All, I trust, may yet be well.'   340

 We turn'd to go, but Cyril took the child,
And held her round the knees against his waist,
And blew the swollen cheek of a trumpeter,
While Psyche watch'd them, smiling, and the child
Push'd her flat hand against his face and laugh'd;
And thus our conference closed.
       And then we strolled
For half the day thro' stately theatres

Bench'd crescent-wise. In each we sat, we heard
The grave professor. On the lecture slate
The circle rounded under female hands   350
With flawless demonstration; follow'd then
A classic lecture, rich in sentiment,
With scraps of thunderous epic lilted out
By violet-hooded Doctors, elegies
And quoted odes, and jewels five-words-long
That on the stretch'd forefinger of all Time
Sparkle forever. Then we dipt in all
That treats of whatsoever is, the state,
The total chronicles of man, the mind,
The morals, something of the frame, the rock,   360
The star, the bird, the fish, the shell, the flower,
Electric, chemic laws, and all the rest,
And whatsoever can be taught and known;
Till like three horses that have broken fence,
And glutted all night long breast-deep in corn,
We issued gorged with knowledge, and I spoke:
'Why, sirs, they do all this as well as we.'
'They hunt old trails,' said Cyril, 'very well;
But when did woman ever yet invent?'
'Ungracious!' answer'd Florian; 'have you learnt   370
No more from Psyche's lecture, you that talk'd
The trash that made me sick, and almost sad?'
'O, trash,' he said, 'but with a kernel in it!
Should I not call her wise who made me wise?
And learnt? I learnt more from her in a flash
Than if my brainpan were an empty hull,
And every Muse tumbled a science in.
A thousand hearts lie fallow in these halls,
And round these halls a thousand baby loves
Fly twanging headless arrows at the hearts,   380
Whence follows many a vacant pang; but O,
With me, sir, enter'd in the bigger boy,
The head of all the golden-shafted firm,
The long-limb'd lad that had a Psyche too;
He cleft me thro' the stomacher. And now
What think you of it, Florian? do I chase
The substance or the shadow? will it hold?
I have no sorcerer's malison on me,
No ghostly hauntings like his Highness. I
Flatter myself that always everywhere   390
I know the substance when I see it. Well,
Are castles shadows? Three of them? Is she
The sweet proprietress a shadow? If not,
Shall those three castles patch my tatter'd coat?
For dear are those three castles to my wants,

And dear is sister Psyche to my heart,
And two dear things are one of double worth;
And much I might have said, but that my zone
Unmann'd me. Then the Doctors! O, to hear
The Doctors! O, to watch the thirsty plants   400
Imbibing! once or twice I thought to roar,
To break my chain, to shake my mane; but thou,
Modulate me, soul of mincing mimicry!
Make liquid treble of that bassoon, my throat;
Abase those eyes that ever loved to meet
Star-sisters answering under crescent brows;
Abate the stride which speaks of man, and loose
A flying charm of blushes o'er this cheek,
Where they like swallows coming out of time
Will wonder why they came. But hark the bell   410
For dinner, let us go!'
                          And in we stream'd
Among the columns, pacing staid and still
By twos and threes, till all from end to end
With beauties every shade of brown and fair
In colors gayer than the morning mist,
The long hall glitter'd like a bed of flowers.
How might a man not wander from his wits
Pierced thro' with eyes, but that I kept mine own
Intent on her, who rapt in glorious dreams,
The second-sight of some Astræan age,   420
Sat compass'd with professors; they, the while,
Discuss'd a doubt and tost it to and fro.
A clamor thicken'd, mixt with inmost terms
Of art and science; Lady Blanche alone
Of faded form and haughtiest lineaments,
With all her autumn tresses falsely brown,
Shot sidelong daggers at us, a tiger-cat
In act to spring.
                  At last a solemn grace
Concluded, and we sought the gardens. There
One walk'd reciting by herself, and one   430
In this hand held a volume as to read,
And smoothed a petted peacock down with that.
Some to a low song oar'd a shallop by,
Or under arches of the marble bridge
Hung, shadow'd from the heat; some hid and sought
In the orange thickets; others tost a ball
Above the fountain-jets, and back again
With laughter; others lay about the lawns,
Of the older sort, and murmur'd that their May
Was passing—what was learning unto them?   440
They wish'd to marry; they could rule a house;

Men hated learned women. But we three
Sat muffled like the Fates; and often came
Melissa hitting all we saw with shafts
Of gentle satire, kin to charity,
That harm'd not. Then day droopt; the chapel bells
Call'd us; we left the walks; we mixt with those
Six hundred maidens clad in purest white,
Before two streams of light from wall to wall,
While the great organ almost burst his pipes,   450
Groaning for power, and rolling thro' the court
A long melodious thunder to the sound
Of solemn psalms and silver litanies,
The work of Ida, to call down from heaven
A blessing on her labors for the world.

Sweet and low, sweet and low,
      Wind of the western sea,
Low, low, breathe and blow,
      Wind of the western sea!
Over the rolling waters go,
Come from the dying moon, and blow,
      Blow him again to me;
While my little one, while my pretty one sleeps.

Sleep and rest, sleep and rest,
      Father will come to thee soon;
Rest, rest, on mother's breast,
      Father will come to thee soon;
Father will come to his babe in the nest,
Silver sails all out of the west
      Under the silver moon;
Sleep, my little one, sleep, my pretty one, sleep.

III

Morn in the white wake of the morning star
Came furrowing all the orient into gold.
We rose, and each by other drest with care
Descended to the court that lay three parts
In shadow, but the Muses' heads were touch'd
Above the darkness from their native East.

There while we stood beside the fount, and watch'd
Or seem'd to watch the dancing bubble, approach'd
Melissa, tinged with wan from lack of sleep,
Or grief, and glowing round her dewy eyes   10
The circled Iris of a night of tears;
And 'Fly,' she cried, 'O fly, while yet you may!
My mother knows.' And when I ask'd her 'how,'
'My fault,' she wept, 'my fault! and yet not mine;
Yet mine in part. O, hear me, pardon me!

My mother, 't is her wont from night to night
To rail at Lady Psyche and her side.
She says the Princess should have been the Head,
Herself and Lady Psyche the two arms;
And so it was agreed when first they came;   20
But Lady Psyche was the right hand now,
And she the left, or not or seldom used;
Hers more than half the students, all the love.
And so last night she fell to canvass you,
Her countrywomen! she did not envy her.
"Who ever saw such wild barbarians?
Girls?—more like men!" and at these words the snake,
My secret, seem'd to stir within my breast;
And O, sirs, could I help it, but my cheek
Began to burn and burn, and her lynx eye   30
To fix and make me hotter, till she laugh'd:
"O marvellously modest maiden, you!
Men! girls, like men! why, if they had been men
You need not set your thoughts in rubric thus
For wholesale comment." Pardon, I am shamed
That I must needs repeat for my excuse
What looks so little graceful: "men"—for still
My mother went revolving on the word—
"And so they are,—very like men indeed—
And with that woman closeted for hours!"   40
Then came these dreadful words out one by one,
"Why—these—*are*—men;" I shudder'd; "and you know it."
"O, ask me nothing," I said. "And she knows too,
And she conceals it." So my mother clutch'd
The truth at once, but with no word from me;
And now thus early risen she goes to inform
The Princess. Lady Psyche will be crush'd;
But you may yet be saved, and therefore fly;
But heal me with your pardon ere you go.'

'What pardon, sweet Melissa, for a blush?'   50
Said Cyril: 'Pale one, blush again; than wear
Those lilies, better blush our lives away.
Yet let us breathe for one hour more in heaven,'
He added, 'lest some classic angel speak
In scorn of us, "They mounted, Ganymedes,
To tumble, Vulcans, on the second morn."
But I will melt this marble into wax
To yield us farther furlough;' and he went.

Melissa shook her doubtful curls, and thought
He scarce would prosper. 'Tell us,' Florian ask'd,   60
'How grew this feud betwixt the right and left.'

'O, long ago,' she said, 'betwixt these two
Division smoulders hidden; 't is my mother,
Too jealous, often fretful as the wind
Pent in a crevice: much I bear with her.
I never knew my father, but she says—
God help her!—she was wedded to a fool;
And still she rail'd against the state of things.
She had the care of Lady Ida's youth,
And from the Queen's decease she brought her up.   70
But when your sister came she won the heart
Of Ida; they were still together, grew—
For so they said themselves—inosculated;
Consonant chords that shiver to one note;
One mind in all things. Yet my mother still
Affirms your Psyche thieved her theories,
And angled with them for her pupil's love;
She calls her plagiarist, I know not what.
But I must go; I dare not tarry,' and light,
As flies the shadow of a bird, she fled.   80

Then murmur'd Florian, gazing after her:
'An open-hearted maiden, true and pure.
If I could love, why this were she. How pretty
Her blushing was, and how she blush'd again,
As if to close with Cyril's random wish!
Not like your Princess cramm'd with erring pride,
Nor like poor Psyche whom she drags in tow.'

'The crane,' I said, 'may chatter of the crane,
The dove may murmur of the dove, but I
An eagle clang an eagle to the sphere.   90
My princess, O my princess! true she errs,
But in her own grand way; being herself
Three times more noble than three score of men,
She sees herself in every woman else,
And so she wears her error like a crown
To blind the truth and me. For her, and her,
Hebes are they to hand ambrosia, mix
The nectar; but—ah, she—whene'er she moves
The Samian Herè rises, and she speaks
A Memnon smitten with the morning sun.'   100

So saying from the court we paced, and gain'd
The terrace ranged along the northern front,
And leaning there on those balusters, high
Above the empurpled champain, drank the gale
That blown about the foliage underneath,
And sated with the innumerable rose,

Beat balm upon our eyelids. Hither came
Cyril, and yawning, 'O hard task,' he cried:
'No fighting shadows here. I forced a way
Thro' solid opposition crabb'd and gnarl'd. 110
Better to clear prime forests, heave and thump
A league of street in summer solstice down,
Than hammer at this reverend gentlewoman.
I knock'd and, bidden, enter'd; found her there
At point to move, and settled in her eyes
The green malignant light of coming storm.
Sir, I was courteous, every phrase well-oil'd,
As man's could be; yet maiden-meek I pray'd
Concealment. She demanded who we were,
And why we came? I fabled nothing fair, 120
But, your example pilot, told her all.
Up went the hush'd amaze of hand and eye,
But when I dwelt upon your old affiance,
She answer'd sharply that I talk'd astray.
I urged the fierce inscription on the gate,
And our three lives. True—we had limed ourselves
With open eyes, and we must take the chance.
But such extremes, I told her, well might harm
The woman's cause. "Not more than now," she said,
"So puddled as it is with favoritism." 130
I tried the mother's heart. Shame might befall
Melissa, knowing, saying not she knew;
Her answer was, "Leave me to deal with that."
I spoke of war to come and many deaths,
And she replied, her duty was to speak,
And duty duty, clear of consequences.
I grew discouraged, sir; but since I knew
No rock so hard but that a little wave
May beat admission in a thousand years,
I recommenced: "Decide not ere you pause. 140
I find you here but in the second place,
Some say the third—the authentic foundress you.
I offer boldly; we will seat you highest.
Wink at our advent; help my prince to gain
His rightful bride, and here I promise you
Some palace in our land, where you shall reign
The head and heart of all our fair she-world,
And your great name flow on with broadening time
For ever." Well, she balanced this a little,
And told me she would answer us to-day, 150
Meantime be mute; thus much, nor more I gain'd.'

He ceasing, came a message from the Head.
'That afternoon the Princess rode to take

The dip of certain strata to the north.
Would we go with her? we should find the land
Worth seeing, and the river made a fall
Out yonder;' then she pointed on to where
A double hill ran up his furrowy forks
Beyond the thick-leaved platans of the vale.

Agreed to, this, the day fled on thro' all 160
Its range of duties to the appointed hour.
Then summon'd to the porch we went. She stood
Among her maidens, higher by the head,
Her back against a pillar, her foot on one
Of those tame leopards. Kitten-like he roll'd
And paw'd about her sandal. I drew near;
I gazed. On a sudden my strange seizure came
Upon me, the weird vision of our house.
The Princess Ida seem'd a hollow show,
Her gay-furr'd cats a painted fantasy, 170
Her college and her maidens empty masks,
And I myself the shadow of a dream,
For all things were and were not. Yet I felt
My heart beat thick with passion and with awe;
Then from my breast the involuntary sigh
Brake, as she smote me with the light of eyes
That lent my knee desire to kneel, and shook
My pulses, till to horse we got, and so
Went forth in long retinue following up
The river as it narrow'd to the hills. 180

I rode beside her and to me she said:
'O friend, we trust that you esteem'd us not
Too harsh to your companion yestermorn;
Unwillingly we spake.' 'No—not to her,'
I answer'd, 'but to one of whom we spake
Your Highness might have seem'd the thing you say.'
'Again?' she cried, 'are you ambassadresses
From him to me? we give you, being strange,
A license; speak, and let the topic die.'

I stammer'd that I knew him—could have wish'd— 190
'Our king expects—was there no precontract?
There is no truer-hearted—ah, you seem
All he prefigured, and he could not see
The bird of passage flying south but long'd
To follow. Surely, if your Highness keep
Your purport, you will shock him even to death,
Or baser courses, children of despair.'

'Poor boy,' she said, can he not read—no books?
Quoit, tennis, ball—no games? nor deals in that
Which men delight in, martial exercise?   200
To nurse a blind ideal like a girl,
Methinks he seems no better than a girl;
As girls were once, as we ourself have been.
We had our dreams; perhaps he mixt with them.
We touch on our dead self, nor shun to do it,
Being other—since we learnt our meaning here,
To lift the woman's fallen divinity
Upon an even pedestal with man.'

      She paused, and added with a haughtier smile,
'And as to precontracts, we move, my friend,   210
At no man's beck, but know ourself and thee,
O Vashti, noble Vashti! Summon'd out
She kept her state, and left the drunken king
To brawl at Sushan underneath the palms.'

      'Alas, your Highness breathes full East,' I said,
'On that which leans to you! I know the Prince,
I prize his truth. And then how vast a work
To assail this gray preëminence of man!
You grant me license; might I use it? think;
Ere half be done perchance your life may fail;   220
Then comes the feebler heiress of your plan,
And takes and ruins all; and thus your pains
May only make that footprint upon sand
Which old-recurring waves of prejudice
Resmooth to nothing. Might I dread that you,
With only Fame for spouse and your great deeds
For issue, yet may live in vain, and miss
Meanwhile what every woman counts her due,
Love, children, happiness?'

                        And she exclaim'd,
'Peace, you young savage of the Northern wild!   230
What! tho' your Prince's love were like a god's,
Have we not made ourself the sacrifice?
You are bold indeed; we are not talk'd to thus.
Yet will we say for children, would they grew
Like field-flowers everywhere! we like them well:
But children die; and let me tell you, girl,
Howe'er you babble, great deeds cannot die;
They with the sun and moon renew their light
For ever, blessing those that look on them.
Children—that men may pluck them from our hearts,   240
Kill us with pity, break us with ourselves—
O—children—there is nothing upon earth

More miserable than she that has a son
And sees him err. Nor would we work for fame;
Tho' she perhaps might reap the applause of Great,
Who learns the one POU STO whence after-hands
May move the world, tho' she herself effect
But little; wherefore up and act, nor shrink
For fear our solid aim be dissipated
By frail successors. Would, indeed, we had been,   250
In lieu of many mortal flies, a race
Of giants living each a thousand years,
That we might see our own work out, and watch
The sandy footprint harden into stone.'

I answer'd nothing, doubtful in myself
If that strange poet-princess with her grand
Imaginations might at all be won.
And she broke out interpreting my thoughts:

'No doubt we seem a kind of monster to you;
We are used to that; for women, up till this   260
Cramp'd under worse than South-sea-isle taboo,
Dwarfs of the gynæceum, fail so far
In high desire, they know not, cannot guess
How much their welfare is a passion to us.
If we could give them surer, quicker proof—
O, if our end were less achievable
By slow approaches than by single act
Of immolation, any phase of death,
We were as prompt to spring against the pikes,
Or down the fiery gulf as talk of it,   270
To compass our dear sisters' liberties.'

She bow'd as if to veil a noble tear;
And up we came to where the river sloped
To plunge in cataract, shattering on black blocks
A breadth of thunder. O'er it shook the woods,
And danced the color, and, below, stuck out
The bones of some vast bulk that lived and roar'd
Before man was. She gazed awhile and said,
'As these rude bones to us, are we to her
That will be.' 'Dare we dream of that,' I ask'd,   280
'Which wrought us, as the workman and his work,
That practice betters?' 'How,' she cried, 'you love
The metaphysics! read and earn our prize,
The golden brooch. Beneath an emerald plane
Sits Diotima, teaching him that died
Of hemlock—our device, wrought to the life—
She rapt upon her subject, he on her;

For there are schools for all.' 'And yet,' I said,
'Methinks I have not found among them all
One anatomic.' 'Nay, we thought of that,'   290
She answer'd, 'but it pleased us not; in truth
We shudder but to dream our maids should ape
Those monstrous males that carve the living hound,
And cram him with the fragments of the grave,
Or in the dark dissolving human heart,
And holy secrets of this microcosm,
Dabbling a shameless hand with shameful jest,
Encarnalize their spirits. Yet we know
Knowledge is knowledge, and this matter hangs.
Howbeit ourself, foreseeing casualty,   300
Nor willing men should come among us, learnt,
For many weary moons before we came,
This craft of healing. Were you sick, ourself
Would tend upon you. To your question now,
Which touches on the workman and his work.
Let there be light and there was light; 't is so,
For was, and is, and will be, are but is,
And all creation is one act at once,
The birth of light; but we that are not all,
As parts, can see but parts, now this, now that,   310
And live, perforce, from thought to thought, and **make**
One act a phantom of succession. Thus
Our weakness somehow shapes the shadow, Time;
But in the shadow will we work, and mould
The woman to the fuller day.'
                                                    She spake
With kindled eyes: we rode a league beyond,
And, o'er a bridge of pinewood crossing, came
On flowery levels underneath the crag,
Full of all beauty. 'O, how sweet,' I said,—
For I was half-oblivious of my mask,—   320
'To linger here with one that loved us!' 'Yea,'
She answer'd, 'or with fair philosophies
That lift the fancy; for indeed these fields
Are lovely, lovelier not the Elysian lawns,
Where paced the demigods of old, and saw
The soft white vapor streak the crowned towers
Built to the Sun.' Then, turning to her maids,
'Pitch our pavilion here upon the sward;
Lay out the viands.' At the word, they raised
A tent of satin, elaborately wrought   330
With fair Corinna's triumph; here she stood,
Engirt with many a florid maiden-cheek,
The woman-conqueror; woman-conquer'd there
The bearded Victor of ten-thousand hymns,

And all the men mourn'd at his side. But we
Set forth to climb; then, climbing, Cyril kept
With Psyche, with Melissa Florian, I
With mine affianced. Many a little hand
Glanced like a touch of sunshine on the rocks,
Many a light foot shone like a jewel set   340
In the dark crag. And then we turn'd, we wound
About the cliffs, the copses, out and in,
Hammering and clinking, chattering stony names
Of shale and hornblende, rag and trap and tuff,
Amygdaloid and trachyte, till the sun
Grew broader toward his death and fell, and all
The rosy heights came out above the lawns.

    The splendor falls on castle walls
      And snowy summits old in story;
    The long light shakes across the lakes,
      And the wild cataract leaps in glory.
Blow, bugle, blow, set the wild echoes flying,
Blow, bugle; answer, echoes, dying, dying, dying.

    O, hark, O, hear! how thin and clear,
      And thinner, clearer, farther going!
    O, sweet and far from cliff and scar
      The horns of Elfland faintly blowing!
Blow, let us hear the purple glens replying,
Blow, bugle; answer, echoes, dying, dying, dying.

    O love, they die in yon rich sky,
      They faint on hill or field or river;
    Our echoes roll from soul to soul,
      And grow for ever and for ever.
Blow, bugle, blow, set the wild echoes flying,
And answer, echoes, answer, dying, dying, dying.

IV

'There sinks the nebulous star we call the sun,
If that hypothesis of theirs be sound,'
Said Ida; 'let us down and rest;' and we
Down from the lean and wrinkled precipices,
By every coppice-feather'd chasm and cleft,
Dropt thro' the ambrosial gloom to where below
No bigger than a glowworm shone the tent
Lamp-lit from the inner. Once she lean'd on me,
Descending; once or twice she lent her hand,
And blissful palpitations in the blood   10
Stirring a sudden transport rose and fell.

    But when we planted level feet, and dipt
Beneath the satin dome and enter'd in,
There leaning deep in broider'd down we sank

Our elbows; on a tripod in the midst
A fragrant flame rose, and before us glow'd
Fruit, blossom, viand, amber wine, and gold.

Then she, 'Let some one sing to us; lightlier move
The minutes fledged with music;' and a maid,
Of those beside her, smote her harp and sang.   20

'Tears, idle tears, I know not what they mean,
Tears from the depth of some divine despair
Rise in the heart, and gather to the eyes,
In looking on the happy autumn-fields,
And thinking of the days that are no more.

'Fresh as the first beam glittering on a sail,
That brings our friends up from the underworld,
Sad as the last which reddens over one
That sinks with all we love below the verge;
So sad, so fresh, the days that are no more.   30

'Ah, sad and strange, as in dark summer dawns
The earliest pipe of half-awaken'd birds
To dying ears, when unto dying eyes
The casement slowly grows a glimmering square;
So sad, so strange, the days that are no more.

'Dear as remember'd kisses after death,
And sweet as those by hopeless fancy feign'd
On lips that are for others; deep as love,
Deep as first love, and wild with all regret;
O Death in Life, the days that are no more!'   40

She ended with such passion that the tear
She sang of shook and fell, an erring pearl
Lost in her bosom; but with some disdain
Answer'd the Princess: 'If indeed there haunt
About the moulder'd lodges of the past
So sweet a voice and vague, fatal to men,
Well needs it we should cram our ears with wool
And so pace by. But thine are fancies hatch'd
In silken-folded idleness; nor is it
Wiser to weep a true occasion lost,   50
But trim our sails, and let old bygones be,
While down the streams that float us each and all
To the issue, goes, like glittering bergs of ice,
Throne after throne, and molten on the waste
Becomes a cloud; for all things serve their time
Toward that great year of equal mights and rights.
Nor would I fight with iron laws, in the end
Found golden. Let the past be past, let be
Their cancell'd Babels; tho' the rough kex break
The starr'd mosaic, and the beard-blown goat   60
Hang on the shaft, and the wild fig-tree split

Their monstrous idols, care not while we hear
A trumpet in the distance pealing news
Of better, and Hope, a poising eagle, burns
Above the unrisen morrow.' Then to me,
'Know you no song of your own land,' she said,
'Not such as moans about the retrospect,
But deals with the other distance and the hues
Of promise; not a death's-head at the wine?'

Then I remember'd one myself had made,   70
What time I watch'd the swallow winging south
From mine own land, part made long since, and part
Now while I sang, and maiden-like as far
As I could ape their treble did I sing.

'O Swallow, Swallow, flying, flying south,
Fly to her, and fall upon her gilded eaves,
And tell her, tell her, what I tell to thee.

'O, tell her, Swallow, thou that knowest each,
That bright and fierce and fickle is the South,
And dark and true and tender is the North.   80

'O Swallow, Swallow, if I could follow, and light
Upon her lattice, I would pipe and trill,
And cheep and twitter twenty million loves.

'O, were I thou that she might take me in,
And lay me on her bosom, and her heart
Would rock the snowy cradle till I died!

'Why lingereth she to clothe her heart with love,
Delaying as the tender ash delays
To clothe herself, when all the woods are green?

'O, tell her, Swallow, that thy brood is flown;   90
Say to her, I do but wanton in the South,
But in the North long since my nest is made.

'O, tell her, brief is life but love is long,
And brief the sun of summer in the North,
And brief the moon of beauty in the South.

'O Swallow, flying from the golden woods,
Fly to her, and pipe and woo her, and make her mine,
And tell her, tell her, that I follow thee.'

I ceased, and all the ladies, each at each,
Like the Ithacensian suitors in old time,   100
Stared with great eyes, and laugh'd with alien lips,
And knew not what they meant; for still my voice
Rang false. But smiling, 'Not for thee,' she said,
'O Bulbul, any rose of Gulistan
Shall burst her veil; marsh-divers, rather, maid,

Shall croak thee sister, or the meadow-crake
Grate her harsh kindred in the grass—and this
A mere love-poem! O, for such, my friend,
We hold them slight; they mind us of the time
When we made bricks in Egypt. Knaves are men, 110
That lute and flute fantastic tenderness,
And dress the victim to the offering up,
And paint the gates of Hell with Paradise,
And play the slave to gain the tyranny.
Poor soul! I had a maid of honor once;
She wept her true eyes blind for such a one,
A rogue of canzonets and serenades.
I loved her. Peace be with her. She is dead.
So, they blaspheme the muse! But great is song
Used to great ends; ourself have often tried 120
Valkyrian hymns, or into rhythm have dash'd
The passion of the prophetess; for song
Is duer unto freedom, force and growth
Of spirit, than to junketing and love.
Love is it? Would this same mock-love and this
Mock-Hymen were laid up like winter bats,
Till all men grew to rate us at our worth,
Not vassals to be beat, nor pretty babes
To be dandled, no, but living wills, and sphered
Whole in ourselves and owed to none. Enough! 130
But now to leaven play with profit, you,
Know you no song, the true growth of your soil,
That gives the manners of your country-women?'

  She spoke and turn'd her sumptuous head with eyes
Of shining expectation fixt on mine.
Then while I dragg'd my brains for such a song,
Cyril, with whom the bell-mouth'd glass had wrought,
Or master'd by the sense of sport, began
To troll a careless, careless tavern-catch
Of Moll and Meg, and strange experiences 140
Unmeet for ladies. Florian nodded at him,
I frowning; Psyche flush'd and wann'd and shook;
The lilylike Melissa droop'd her brows.
'Forbear,' the Princess cried; 'Forbear, sir,' I;
And heated thro' and thro' with wrath and love,
I smote him on the breast. He started up;
There rose a shriek as of a city sack'd;
Melissa clamor'd, 'Flee the death;' 'To horse!'
Said Ida, 'home! to horse!' and fled, as flies
A troop of snowy doves athwart the dusk 150
When some one batters at the dovecote doors,
Disorderly the women. Alone I stood

With Florian, cursing Cyril, vext at heart
In the pavilion. There like parting hopes
I heard them passing from me; hoof by hoof,
And every hoof a knell to my desires,
Clang'd on the bridge; and then another shriek,
'The Head, the Head, the Princess, O the Head!'
For blind with rage, she miss'd the plank, and roll'd
In the river. Out I sprang from glow to gloom;   160
There whirl'd her white robe like a blossom'd branch
Rapt to the horrible fall. A glance I gave,
No more, but woman-vested as I was
Plunged, and the flood drew; yet I caught her; then
Oaring one arm, and bearing in my left
The weight of all the hopes of half the world,
Strove to buffet to land in vain. A tree
Was half-disrooted from his place and stoop'd
To drench his dark locks in the gurgling wave
Mid-channel. Right on this we drove and caught,   170
And grasping down the boughs I gain'd the shore.

There stood her maidens glimmeringly group'd
In the hollow bank. One reaching forward drew
My burthen from mine arms; they cried, 'She lives.'
They bore her back into the tent: but I,
So much a kind of shame within me wrought,
Not yet endured to meet her opening eyes,
Nor found my friends; but push'd alone on foot—
For since her horse was lost I left her mine—
Across the woods, and less from Indian craft   180
Than beelike instinct hiveward, found at length
The garden portals. Two great statues, Art
And Science, Caryatids, lifted up
A weight of emblem, and betwixt were valves
Of open-work in which the hunter rued
His rash intrusion, manlike, but his brows
Had sprouted, and the branches thereupon
Spread out at top, and grimly spiked the gates.

A little space was left between the horns,
Thro' which I clamber'd o'er at top with pain,   190
Dropt on the sward, and up the linden walks,
And, tost on thoughts that changed from hue to hue,
Now poring on the glowworm, now the star,
I paced the terrace, till the Bear had wheel'd
Thro' a great arc his seven slow suns.
                                          A step
Of lightest echo, then a loftier form
Than female, moving thro' the uncertain gloom,

Disturb'd me with the doubt 'if this were she,'
But it was Florian. 'Hist, O, hist!' he said,
'They seek us; out so late is out of rules.   200
Moreover, "Seize the strangers" is the cry.
How came you here?' I told him. 'I,' said he,
'Last of the train, a moral leper, I,
To whom none spake, half-sick at heart, return'd.
Arriving all confused among the rest
With hooded brows I crept into the hall,
And, couch'd behind a Judith, underneath
The head of Holofernes peep'd and saw.
Girl after girl was call'd to trial; each
Disclaim'd all knowledge of us; last of all,   210
Melissa; trust me, sir, I pitied her.
She, question'd if she knew us men, at first
Was silent; closer prest, denied it not,
And then, demanded if her mother knew,
Or Psyche, she affirm'd not, or denied;
From whence the Royal mind, familiar with her,
Easily gather'd either guilt. She sent
For Psyche, but she was not there; she call'd
For Psyche's child to cast it from the doors;
She sent for Blanche to accuse her face to face;   220
And I slipt out. But whither will you now?
And where are Psyche, Cyril? both are fled;
What, if together? that were not so well.
Would rather we had never come! I dread
His wildness, and the chances of the dark.'

'And yet,' I said, 'you wrong him more than I
That struck him; this is proper to the clown,
Tho' smock'd, or furr'd and purpled, still the clown,
To harm the thing that trusts him, and to shame
That which he says he loves. For Cyril, howe'er   230
He deal in frolic, as to-night—the song
Might have been worse and sinn'd in grosser lips
Beyond all pardon—as it is, I hold
These flashes on the surface are not he.
He has a solid base of temperament;
But as the water-lily starts and slides
Upon the level in little puffs of wind,
Tho' anchor'd to the bottom, such is he.'

Scarce had I ceased when from a tamarisk near
Two Proctors leapt upon us, crying, 'Names!'   240
He, standing still, was clutch'd; but I began
To thrid the musky-circled mazes, wind
And double in and out the boles, and race

By all the fountains. Fleet I was of foot;
Before me shower'd the rose in flakes; behind
I heard the puff'd pursuer; at mine ear
Bubbled the nightingale and heeded not,
And secret laughter tickled all my soul.
At last I hook'd my ankle in a vine
That claspt the feet of a Mnemosyne,   250
And falling on my face was caught and known.

They haled us to the Princess where she sat
High in the hall; above her droop'd a lamp,
And made the single jewel on her brow
Burn like the mystic fire on a mast-head,
Prophet of storm; a handmaid on each side
Bow'd toward her, combing out her long black hair
Damp from the river; and close behind her stood
Eight daughters of the plough, stronger than men,
Huge women blowzed with health, and wind, and rain,   260
And labor. Each was like a Druid rock;
Or like a spire of land that stands apart
Cleft from the main, and wail'd about with mews.

Then, as we came, the crowd dividing clove
An advent to the throne; and therebeside,
Half-naked as if caught at once from bed
And tumbled on the purple footcloth, lay
The lily-shining child; and on the left,
Bow'd on her palms and folded up from wrong,
Her round white shoulder shaken with her sobs,   270
Melissa knelt; but Lady Blanche erect
Stood up and spake, an affluent orator:

'It was not thus, O Princess, in old days;
You prized my counsel, lived upon my lips.
I led you then to all the Castalies;
I fed you with the milk of every Muse;
I loved you like this kneeler, and you me
Your second mother, those were gracious times.
Then came your new friend; you began to change—
I saw it and grieved—to slacken and to cool;   280
Till taken with her seeming openness
You turn'd your warmer currents all to her,
To me you froze; this was my meed for all.
Yet I bore up in part from ancient love,
And partly that I hoped to win you back,
And partly conscious of my own deserts,
And partly that you were my civil head,
And chiefly you were born for something great,

In which I might your fellow-worker be,
When time should serve; and thus a noble scheme   290
Grew up from seed we two long since had sown;
In us true growth, in her a Jonah's gourd,
Up in one night and due to sudden sun.
We took this palace; but even from the first
You stood in your own light and darken'd mine.
What student came but that you planed her path
To Lady Psyche, younger, not so wise,
A foreigner, and I your countrywoman,
I your old friend and tried, she new in all?
But still her lists were swell'd and mine were lean;   300
Yet I bore up in hope she would be known.
Then came these wolves; *they* knew her; *they* endured,
Long-closeted with her the yestermorn,
To tell her what they were, and she to hear.
And me none told. Not less to an eye like mine,
A lidless watcher of the public weal,
Last night, their mask was patent, and my foot
Was to you. But I thought again; I fear'd
To meet a cold "We thank you, we shall hear of it
From Lady Psyche;" you had gone to her,   310
She told, perforce, and winning easy grace,
No doubt, for slight delay, remain'd among us
In our young nursery still unknown, the stem
Less grain than touchwood, while my honest heat
Were all miscounted as malignant haste
To push my rival out of place and power.
But public use required she should be known;
And since my oath was ta'en for public use,
I broke the letter of it to keep the sense.
I spoke not then at first, but watch'd them well,   320
Saw that they kept apart, no mischief done;
And yet this day—tho' you should hate me for it—
I came to tell you; found that you had gone,
Ridden to the hills, she likewise. Now, I thought,
That surely she will speak; if not, then I.
Did she? These monsters blazon'd what they were,
According to the coarseness of their kind,
For thus I hear; and known at last—my work—
And full of cowardice and guilty shame—
I grant in her some sense of shame—she flies;   330
And I remain on whom to wreak your rage,
I, that have lent my life to build up yours,
I, that have wasted here health, wealth, and time,
And talent, I—you know it—I will not boast;
Dismiss me, and I prophesy your plan,
Divorced from my experience, will be chaff

For every gust of chance, and men will say
We did not know the real light, but chased
The wisp that flickers where no foot can tread.'

    She ceased; the Princess answer'd coldly, 'Good;   340
Your oath is broken; we dismiss you, go.
For this lost lamb'—she pointed to the child—
'Our mind is changed; we take it to ourself.'

    Thereat the lady stretch'd a vulture throat,
And shot from crooked lips a haggard smile.
'The plan was mine. I built the nest,' she said,
'To hatch the cuckoo. Rise!' and stoop'd to updrag
Melissa. She, half on her mother propt,
Half-drooping from her, turn'd her face, and cast
A liquid look on Ida, full of prayer,   350
Which melted Florian's fancy as she hung,
A Niobeän daughter, one arm out,
Appealing to the bolts of heaven; and while
We gazed upon her came a little stir
About the doors, and on a sudden rush'd
Among us, out of breath, as one pursued,
A woman-post in flying raiment. Fear
Stared in her eyes, and chalk'd her face, and wing'd
Her transit to the throne, whereby she fell
Delivering seal'd dispatches which the Head   360
Took half-amazed, and in her lion's mood
Tore open, silent we with blind surmise
Regarding, while she read, till over brow
And cheek and bosom brake the wrathful bloom
As of some fire against a stormy cloud,
When the wild peasant rights himself, the rick
Flames, and his anger reddens in the heavens;
For anger most it seem'd, while now her breast,
Beaten with some great passion at her heart,
Palpitated, her hand shook, and we heard   370
In the dead hush the papers that she held
Rustle. At once the lost lamb at her feet
Sent out a bitter bleating for its dam.
The plaintive cry jarr'd on her ire; she crush'd
The scrolls together, made a sudden turn
As if to speak, but, utterance failing her,
She whirl'd them on to me, as who should say
'Read,' and I read—two letters—one her sire's:

    'Fair daughter, when we sent the Prince your way
We knew not your ungracious laws, which learnt,   380
We, conscious of what temper you are built,

Came all in haste to hinder wrong, but fell
Into his father's hand, who has this night,
You lying close upon his territory,
Slipt round and in the dark invested you,
And here he keeps me hostage for his son.'

The second was my father's running thus:
'You have our son; touch not a hair of his head;
Render him up unscathed; give him your hand;
Cleave to your contract—tho' indeed we hear   390
You hold the woman is the better man;
A rampant heresy, such as if it spread
Would make all women kick against their lords
Thro' all the world, and which might well deserve
That we this night should pluck your palace down;
And we will do it, unless you send us back
Our son, on the instant, whole.'
                              So far I read;
And then stood up and spoke impetuously:

'O, not to pry and peer on your reserve,
But led by golden wishes, and a hope   400
The child of regal compact, did I break
Your precinct; not a scorner of your sex
But venerator, zealous it should be
All that it might be. Hear me, for I bear,
Tho' man, yet human, whatsoe'er your wrongs,
From the flaxen curl to the gray lock a life
Less mine than yours. My nurse would tell me of you;
I babbled for you, as babies for the moon,
Vague brightness; when a boy, you stoop'd to me
From all high places, lived in all fair lights,   410
Came in long breezes rapt from inmost south
And blown to inmost north; at eve and dawn
With Ida, Ida, Ida, rang the woods;
The leader wild-swan in among the stars
Would clang it, and lapt in wreaths of glowworm light
The mellow breaker murmur'd Ida. Now,
Because I would have reach'd you, had you been
Sphered up with Cassiopeia, or the enthroned
Persephone in Hades, now at length,
Those winters of abeyance all worn out,   420
A man I came to see you; but, indeed,
Not in this frequence can I lend full tongue,
O noble Ida, to those thoughts that wait
On you, their centre. Let me say but this,
That many a famous man and woman, town
And landskip, have I heard of, after seen

The dwarfs of presage; tho' when known, there grew
Another kind of beauty in detail
Made them worth knowing; but in you I found
My boyish dream involved and dazzled down   430
And master'd, while that after-beauty makes
Such head from act to act, from hour to hour,
Within me, that except you slay me here,
According to your bitter statute-book,
I cannot cease to follow you, as they say
The seal does music; who desire you more
Than growing boys their manhood; dying lips,
With many thousand matters left to do,
The breath of life; O, more than poor men wealth,
Than sick men health—yours, yours, not mine—but half 440
Without you; with you, whole; and of those halves
You worthiest; and howe'er you block and bar
Your heart with system out from mine, I hold
That it becomes no man to nurse despair,
But in the teeth of clench'd antagonisms
To follow up the worthiest till he die.
Yet that I came not all unauthorized
Behold your father's letter.'
                              On one knee
Kneeling, I gave it, which she caught, and dash'd
Unopen'd at her feet. A tide of fierce   450
Invective seem'd to wait behind her lips,
As waits a river level with the dam
Ready to burst and flood the world with foam;
And so she would have spoken, but there rose
A hubbub in the court of half the maids
Gather'd together; from the illumined hall
Long lanes of splendor slanted o'er the press
Of snowy shoulders, thick as herded ewes,
And rainbow robes, and gems and gemlike eyes,
And gold and golden heads. They to and fro   460
Fluctuated, as flowers in storm, some red, some pale,
All open-mouth'd, all gazing to the light,
Some crying there was an army in the land,
And some that men were in the very walls,
And some they cared not; till a clamor grew
As of a new-world Babel, woman-built,
And worse-confounded. High above them stood
The placid marble Muses, looking peace.

Not peace she look'd, the Head, but rising up
Robed in the long night of her deep hair, so   470
To the open window moved, remaining there
Fixt like a beacon-tower above the waves

Of tempest, when the crimson-rolling eye
Glares ruin, and the wild birds on the light
Dash themselves dead. She stretch'd her arms and call'd
Across the tumult, and the tumult fell.

'What fear ye, brawlers? am not I your Head?
On me, me, me, the storm first breaks; *I* dare
All these male thunderbolts; what is it ye fear?
Peace! there are those to avenge us and they come;   480
If not,—myself were like enough, O girls,
To unfurl the maiden banner of our rights
And clad in iron burst the ranks of war,
Or, falling, protomartyr of our cause,
Die; yet I blame you not so much for fear;
Six thousand years of fear have made you that
From which I would redeem you. But for those
That stir this hubbub—you and you—I know
Your faces there in the crowd—to-morrow morn
We hold a great convention; then shall they   490
That love their voices more than duty, learn
With whom they deal, dismiss'd in shame to live
No wiser than their mothers, household stuff,
Live chattels, mincers of each other's fame,
Full of weak poison, turnspits for the clown,
The drunkard's football, laughing-stocks of Time,
Whose brains are in their hands and in their heels,
But fit to flaunt, to dress, to dance, to thrum,
To tramp, to scream, to burnish, and to scour,
For ever slaves at home and fools abroad.'   500

She, ending, waved her hands; thereat the crowd
Muttering, dissolved; then with a smile, that look'd
A stroke of cruel sunshine on the cliff,
When all the glens are drown'd in azure gloom
O thunder-shower, she floated to us and said:

'You have done well and like a gentleman,
And like a prince; you have our thanks for all.
And you look well too in your woman's dress.
Well have you done and like a gentleman.
You saved our life; we owe you bitter thanks.   510
Better have died and spilt our bones in the flood—
Then men had said—but now—what hinders me
To take such bloody vengeance on you both?—
Yet since our father—wasps in our good hive,
You would-be quenchers of the light to be,
Barbarians, grosser than your native bears—
O, would I had his sceptre for one hour!

You that have dared to break our bound, and gull'd
Our servants, wrong'd and lied and thwarted us—
I wed with thee! *I* bound by precontract   520
Your bride, your bondslave! not tho' all the gold
That veins the world were pack'd to make your crown,
And every spoken tongue should lord you. Sir,
Your falsehood and yourself are hateful to us;
I trample on your offers and on you.
Begone; we will not look upon you more.
Here, push them out at gates.'

                              In wrath she spake.
Then those eight mighty daughters of the plough
Bent their broad faces toward us and address'd
Their motion. Twice I sought to plead my cause,   530
But on my shoulder hung their heavy hands,
The weight of destiny; so from her face
They push'd us, down the steps, and thro' the court,
And with grim laughter thrust us out at gates.

     We cross'd the street and gain'd a petty mound
Beyond it, whence we saw the lights and heard
The voices murmuring. While I listen'd came
On a sudden a weird seizure and the doubt.
I seem'd to move among a world of ghosts;
The Princess with her monstrous woman-guard,   540
The jest and earnest working side by side,
The cataract and the tumult and the kings
Were shadows; and the long fantastic night
With all its doings had and had not been,
And all things were and were not.

                              This went by
As strangely as it came, and on my spirits
Settled a gentle cloud of melancholy—
Not long; I shook it off; for spite of doubts
And sudden ghostly shadowings I was one
To whom the touch of all mischance but came   550
As night to him that sitting on a hill
Sees the midsummer, midnight, Norway sun
Set into sunrise; then we moved away.

INTERLUDE

Thy voice is heard thro' rolling drums
    That beat to battle where he stands;
Thy face across his fancy comes,
    And gives the battle to his hands.
A moment, while the trumpets blow,
    He sees his brood about thy knee;
The next, like fire he meets the foe,
    And strikes him dead for thine and thee.

So Lilia sang. We thought her half-possess'd,
She struck such warbling fury thro' the words;   10
And, after, feigning pique at what she call'd
The raillery, or grotesque, or false sublime—
Like one that wishes at a dance to change
The music—clapt her hands and cried for war,
Or some grand fight to kill and make an end.
And he that next inherited the tale,
Half turning to the broken statue, said,
'Sir Ralph has got your colors; if I prove
Your knight, and fight your battle, what for me?'
It chanced, her empty glove upon the tomb   20
Lay by her like a model of her hand.
She took it and she flung it. 'Fight,' she said,
'And make us all we would be, great and good.'
He knightlike in his cap instead of casque,
A cap of Tyrol borrow'd from the hall,
Arranged the favor, and assumed the Prince.

V

Now, scarce three paces measured from the mound,
We stumbled on a stationary voice,
And 'Stand, who goes?' 'Two from the palace,' I.
'The second two; they wait,' he said, 'pass on;
His Highness wakes;' and one, that clash'd in arms,
By glimmering lanes and walls of canvas led
Threading the soldier-city, till we heard
The drowsy folds of our great ensign shake
From blazon'd lions o'er the imperial tent
Whispers of war.
                    Entering, the sudden light   10
Dazed me half-blind. I stood and seem'd to hear,
As in a poplar grove when a light wind wakes
A lisping of the innumerous leaf and dies,
Each hissing in his neighbor's ear; and then
A strangled titter, out of which there brake
On all sides, clamoring etiquette to death,
Unmeasured mirth; while now the two old kings
Began to wag their baldness up and down,
The fresh young captains flash'd their glittering teeth,
The huge bush-bearded barons heaved and blew,   20
And slain with laughter roll'd the gilded squire.

At length my sire, his rough cheek wet with tears,
Panted from weary sides, 'King, you are free!
We did but keep you surety for our son,
If this be he,—or a draggled mawkin, thou,

That tends her bristled grunters in the sludge;'
For I was drench'd with ooze, and torn with briers,
More crumbled than a poppy from the sheath,
And all one rag, disprinced from head to heel.
Then some one sent beneath his vaulted palm   30
A whisper'd jest to some one near him, 'Look,
He has been among his shadows.' 'Satan take
The old women and their shadows!'—thus the king
Roar'd—'make yourself a man to fight with men.
Go; Cyril told us all.'
                              As boys that slink
From ferule and the trespass-chiding eye,
Away we stole, and transient in a trice
From what was left of faded woman-slough
To sheathing splendors and the golden scale
Of harness, issued in the sun, that now   40
Leapt from the dewy shoulders of the earth,
And hit the Northern hills. Here Cyril met us,
A little shy at first, but by and by
We twain, with mutual pardon ask'd and given
For stroke and song, resolder'd peace, whereon
Follow'd his tale. Amazed he fled away
Thro' the dark land, and later in the night
Had come cn Psyche weeping: 'then we fell
Into your father's hand, and there she lies,
But will not speak nor stir.'
                              He show'd a tent   50
A stone-shot off; we enter'd in, and there
Among piled arms and rough accoutrements,
Pitiful sight, wrapp'd in a soldier's cloak,
Like some sweet sculpture draped from head to foot,
And push'd by rude hands from its pedestal,
All her fair length upon the ground she lay;
And at her head a follower of the camp,
A charr'd and wrinkled piece of womanhood,
Sat watching like a watcher by the dead.

    Then Florian knelt, and 'Come,' he whisper'd to her,   60
'Lift up your head, sweet sister; lie not thus,
What have you done but right? you could not slay
Me, nor your prince; look up, be comforted.
Sweet is it to have done the thing one ought,
When fallen in darker ways.' And likewise I:
'Be comforted; have I not lost her too,
In whose least act abides the nameless charm
That none has else for me?' She heard, she moved,
She moan'd, a folded voice; and up she sat,
And raised the cloak from brows as pale and smooth   70

As those that mourn half-shrouded over death
In deathless marble. 'Her,' she said, 'my friend—
Parted from her—betray'd her cause and mine—
Where shall I breathe? why kept ye not your faith?
O base and bad! what comfort? none for me!'
To whom remorseful Cyril, 'Yet I pray
Take comfort; live, dear lady, for your child!'
At which she lifted up her voice and cried:

'Ah me, my babe, my blossom, ah, my child,
My one sweet child, whom I shall see no more!
For now will cruel Ida keep her back;
And either she will die from want of care,
Or sicken with ill-usage, when they say
The child is hers—for every little fault,
The child is hers; and they will beat my girl
Remembering her mother—O my flower!
Or they will take her, they will make her hard,
And she will pass me by in after-life
With some cold reverence worse than were she dead.
Ill mother that I was to leave her there,
To lag behind, scared by the cry they made,
The horror of the shame among them all.
But I will go and sit beside the doors,
And make a wild petition night and day,
Until they hate to hear me like a wind
Wailing for ever, till they open to me,
And lay my little blossom at my feet,
My babe, my sweet Aglaïa, my one child;
And I will take her up and go my way,
And satisfy my soul with kissing her.
Ah! what might that man not deserve of me
Who gave me back my child?' 'Be comforted,'
Said Cyril, 'you shall have it!' but again
She vail'd her brows, and prone she sank, and so,
Like tender things that being caught feign death,
Spoke not, nor stirr'd.

                              By this a murmur ran
Thro' all the camp, and inward raced the scouts
With rumor of Prince Arac hard at hand.
We left her by the woman, and without
Found the gray kings at parle; and 'Look you,' cried
My father, 'that our compact be fulfill'd.
You have spoilt this child; she laughs at you and man;
She wrongs herself, her sex, and me, and him.
But red-faced war has rods of steel and fire;
She yields, or war.'

                   Then Gama turn'd to me:

'We fear, indeed, you spent a stormy time
With our strange girl; and yet they say that still
You love her. Give us, then, your mind at large:
How say you, war or not?'
                              'Not war, if possible,   120
O king,' I said, 'lest from the abuse of war,
The desecrated shrine, the trampled year,
The smouldering homestead, and the household flower
Torn from the lintel—all the common wrong—
A smoke go up thro' which I loom to her
Three times a monster. Now she lightens scorn
At him that mars her plan, but then would hate—
And every voice she talk'd with ratify it,
And every face she look'd on justify it—
The general foe. More soluble is this knot
By gentleness than war. I want her love.   130
What were I nigher this altho' we dash'd
Your cities into shards with catapults?—
She would not love—or brought her chain'd, a slave
The lifting of whose eyelash is my lord?
Not ever would she love, but brooding turn
The book of scorn, till all my flitting chance
Were caught within the record of her wrongs
And crush'd to death; and rather, Sire, than this
I would the old god of war himself were dead,
Forgotten, rusting on his iron hills,   140
Rotting on some wild shore with ribs of wreck,
Or like an old-world mammoth bulk'd in ice,
Not to be molten out.'
                        And roughly spake
My father: 'Tut, you know them not, the girls.
Boy, when I hear you prate I almost think
That idiot legend credible. Look you, sir!
Man is the hunter; woman is his game.
The sleek and shining creatures of the chase,
We hunt them for the beauty of their skins;
They love us for it, and we ride them down.   150
Wheedling and siding with them! Out! for shame!
Boy, there's no rose that's half so dear to them
As he that does the thing they dare not do,
Breathing and sounding beauteous battle, comes
With the air of the trumpet round him, and leaps in
Among the women, snares them by the score
Flatter'd and fluster'd, wins, tho' dash'd with death
He reddens what he kisses. Thus I won
Your mother, a good mother, a good wife,
Worth winning; but this firebrand—gentleness   160
To such as her; if Cyril spake her true,

To catch a dragon in a cherry net,
To trip a tigress with a gossamer,
Were wisdom to it.'

             'Yea, but, Sire,' I cried,
'Wild natures need wise curbs. The soldier? No!
What dares not Ida do that she should prize
The soldier? I beheld her, when she rose
The yesternight, and storming in extremes
Stood for her cause, and flung defiance down
Gagelike to man, and had not shunn'd the death,   170
No, not the soldier's; yet I hold her, king,
True woman; but you clash them all in one,
That have as many differences as we.
The violet varies from the lily as far
As oak from elm. One loves the soldier, one
The silken priest of peace, one this, one that,
And some unworthily; their sinless faith,
A maiden moon that sparkles on a sty,
Glorifying clown and satyr; whence they need
More breadth of culture. Is not Ida right?   180
They worth it? truer to the law within?
Severer in the logic of a life?
Twice as magnetic to sweet influences
Of earth and heaven? and she of whom you speak,
My mother, looks as whole as some serene
Creation minted in the golden moods
Of sovereign artists; not a thought, a touch,
But pure as lines of green that streak the white
Of the first snowdrop's inner leaves; I say,
Not like the piebald miscellany, man,   190
Bursts of great heart and slips in sensual mire,
But whole and one; and take them all-in-all,
Were we ourselves but half as good, as kind,
As truthful, much that Ida claims as right
Had ne'er been mooted, but as frankly theirs
As dues of Nature. To our point; not war,
Lest I lose all.'

            'Nay, nay, you spake but sense,'
Said Gama. 'We remember love ourself
In our sweet youth; we did not rate him then
This red-hot iron to be shaped with blows.   200
You talk almost like Ida; *she* can talk;
And there is something in it as you say:
But you talk kindlier; we esteem you for it.—
He seems a gracious and a gallant Prince,
I would he had our daughter. For the rest,
Our own detention, why, the causes weigh'd,
Fatherly fears—you used us courteously—

We would do much to gratify your Prince—
We pardon it; and your ingress here
Upon the skirt and fringe of our fair land,　　　　　　210
You did but come as goblins in the night,
Nor in the furrow broke the ploughman's head,
Nor burnt the grange, nor buss'd the milking-maid,
Nor robb'd the farmer of his bowl of cream.
But let your Prince—our royal word upon it,
He comes back safe—ride with us to our lines,
And speak with Arac. Arac's word is thrice
As ours with Ida; something may be done—
I know not what—and ours shall see us friends.
You, likewise, our late guests, if so you will,　　　　　220
Follow us. Who knows? we four may build some plan
Foursquare to opposition.'
　　　　　　　　　　　Here he reach'd
White hands of farewell to my sire, who growl'd
An answer which, half-muffled in his beard,
Let so much out as gave us leave to go.

　　Then rode we with the old king across the lawns
Beneath huge trees, a thousand rings of Spring
In every bole, a song on every spray
Of birds that piped their Valentines, and woke
Desire in me to infuse my tale of love　　　　　　230
In the old king's ears, who promised help and oozed
All o'er with honey'd answer as we rode;
And blossom-fragrant slipt the heavy dews
Gather'd by night and peace, with each light air
On our mail'd heads. But other thoughts than peace
Burnt in us, when we saw the embattled squares
And squadrons of the Prince, trampling the flowers
With clamor; for among them rose a cry
As if to greet the king; they made a halt;
The horses yell'd; they clash'd their arms; the drum　　240
Beat; merrily-blowing shrill'd the martial fife;
And in the blast and bray of the long horn
And serpent-throated bugle, undulated
The banner. Anon to meet us lightly pranced
Three captains out; nor ever had I seen
Such thews of men. The midmost and the highest
Was Arac; all about his motion clung
The shadow of his sister, as the beam
Of the East, that play'd upon them, made them glance
Like those three stars of the airy Giant's zone,　　　　250
That glitter burnish'd by the frosty dark;
And as the fiery Sirius alters hue,

And bickers into red and emerald, shone
Their morions, wash'd with morning, as they came.

And I that prated peace, when first I heard
War-music, felt the blind wild-beast of force,
Whose home is in the sinews of a man,
Stir in me as to strike. Then took the king
His three broad sons; with now a wandering hand
And now a pointed finger, told them all.   260
A common light of smiles at our disguise
Broke from their lips, and, ere the windy jest
Had labor'd down within his ample lungs,
The genial giant, Arac, roll'd himself
Thrice in the saddle, then burst out in words:

'Our land invaded, 'sdeath! and he himself
Your captive, yet my father wills not war!
And, 'sdeath! myself, what care I, war or no?
But then this question of your troth remains;
And there's a downright honest meaning in her.   270
She flies too high, she flies too high! and yet
She ask'd but space and fair-play for her scheme;
She prest and prest it on me—I myself,
What know I of these things? but, life and soul!
I thought her half-right talking of her wrongs;
I say she flies too high, 'sdeath! what of that?
I take her for the flower of womankind,
And so I often told her, right or wrong;
And, Prince, she can be sweet to those she loves,
And, right or wrong, I care not; this is all,   280
I stand upon her side; she made me swear it—
'Sdeath!—and with solemn rites by candle-light—
Swear by Saint something—I forget her name—
Her that talk'd down the fifty wisest men;
She was a princess too; and so I swore.
Come, this is all; she will not; waive your claim.
If not, the foughten field, what else, at once
Decides it, 'sdeath! against my father's will.'

I lagg'd in answer, loth to render up
My precontract, and loth by brainless war   290
To cleave the rift of difference deeper yet;
Till one of those two brothers, half aside
And fingering at the hair about his lip,
To prick us on to combat, 'Like to like!
The woman's garment hid the woman's heart.'
A taunt that clench'd his purpose like a blow!
For fiery-short was Cyril's counter-scoff,

And sharp I answer'd, touch'd upon the point
Where idle boys are cowards to their shame,
'Decide it here; why not? we are three to three.'   300

Then spake the third: 'But three to three? no more?
No more, and in our noble sister's cause?
More, more, for honor! every captain waits
Hungry for honor, angry for his king.
More, more, some fifty on a side, that each
May breathe himself, and quick! by overthrow
Of these or those, the question settled die.'

'Yea,' answer'd I, 'for this wild wreath of air,
This flake of rainbow flying on the highest
Foam of men's deeds—this honor, if ye will.   310
It needs must be for honor if at all;
Since, what decision? if we fail we fail,
And if we win we fail; she would not keep
Her compact.' ' 'Sdeath! but we will send to her,'
Said Arac, 'worthy reasons why she should
Bide by this issue; let our missive thro',
And you shall have her answer by the word.'

'Boys!' shriek'd the old king, but vainlier than a hen
To her false daughters in the pool; for none
Regarded; neither seem'd there more to say.   320
Back rode we to my father's camp, and found
He thrice had sent a herald to the gates,
To learn if Ida yet would cede our claim,
Or by denial flush her babbling wells
With her own people's life; three times he went.
The first, he blew and blew, but none appear'd;
He batter'd at the doors, none came; the next,
An awful voice within had warn'd him thence;
The third, and those eight daughters of the plough
Came sallying thro' the gates, and caught his hair,   330
And so belabor'd him on rib and cheek
They made him wild. Not less one glance he caught
Thro' open doors of Ida station'd there
Unshaken, clinging to her purpose, firm
Tho' compass'd by two armies and the noise
Of arms; and standing like a stately pine
Set in a cataract on an island-crag,
When storm is on the heights, and right and left
Suck'd from the dark heart of the long hills roll
The torrents, dash'd to the vale; and yet her will   340
Bred will in me to overcome it or fall.

But when I told the king that I was pledged
To fight in tourney for my bride, he clash'd
His iron palms together with a cry;
Himself would tilt it out among the lads;
But overborne by all his bearded lords
With reasons drawn from age and state, perforce
He yielded, wroth and red, with fierce demur;
And many a bold knight started up in heat,
And sware to combat for my claim till death.   350

All on this side the palace ran the field
Flat to the garden-wall; and likewise here,
Above the garden's glowing blossom-belts,
A column'd entry shone and marble stairs,
And great bronze valves, emboss'd with Tomyris
And what she did to Cyrus after fight,
But now fast barr'd. So here upon the flat
All that long morn the lists were hammer'd up,
And all that morn the heralds to and fro,
With message and defiance, went and came;   360
Last, Ida's answer, in a royal hand,
But shaken here and there, and rolling words
Oration-like. I kiss'd it and I read:

'O brother, you have known the pangs we felt,
What heats of indignation when we heard
Of those that iron-cramp'd their women's feet;
Of lands in which at the altar the poor bride
Gives her harsh groom for bridal-gift a scourge;
Of living hearts that crack within the fire
Where smoulder their dead despots; and of those,—   370
Mothers,—that, all prophetic pity, fling
Their pretty maids in the running flood, and swoops
The vulture, beak and talon, at the heart
Made for all noble motion. And I saw
That equal baseness lived in sleeker times
With smoother men; the old leaven leaven'd all;
Millions of throats would bawl for civil rights,
No woman named; therefore I set my face
Against all men, and lived but for mine own.
Far off from men I built a fold for them;   380
I stored it full of rich memorial;
I fenced it round with gallant institutes,
And biting laws to scare the beasts of prey,
And prosper'd, till a rout of saucy boys
Brake on us at our books, and marr'd our peace,
Mask'd like our maids, blustering I know not what
Of insolence and love, some pretext held

Of baby troth, invalid, since my will
Seal'd not the bond—the striplings!—for their sport!—
I tamed my leopards; shall I not tame these?   390
Or you? or I? for since you think me touch'd
In honor—what! I would not aught of false—
Is not our cause pure? and whereas I know
Your prowess, Arac, and what mother's blood
You draw from fight! You failing, I abide
What end soever; fail you will not. Still,
Take not his life, he risk'd it for my own;
His mother lives. Yet whatsoe'er you do,
Fight and fight well; strike and strike home. O dear
Brothers, the woman's angel guards you, you   400
The sole men to be mingled with our cause,
The sole men we shall prize in the aftertime,
Your very armor hallow'd and your statues
Rear'd, sung to, when, this gadfly brush'd aside,
We plant a solid foot into the Time,
And mould a generation strong to move
With claim on claim from right to right, till she
Whose name is yoked with children's know herself;
And Knowledge in our own land make her free,
And, ever following those two crowned twins,   410
Commerce and Conquest, shower the fiery grain
Of freedom broadcast over all that orbs
Between the Northern and the Southern morn.'

    Then came a postscript dash'd across the rest:
'See that there be no traitors in your camp.
We seem a nest of traitors—none to trust
Since our arms fail'd—this Egypt-plague of men!
Almost our maids were better at their homes,
Than thus man-girdled here. Indeed I think
Our chiefest comfort is the little child   420
Of one unworthy mother, which she left.
She shall not have it back; the child shall grow
To prize the authentic mother of her mind.
I took it for an hour in mine own bed
This morning; there the tender orphan hands
Felt at my heart, and seem'd to charm from thence
The wrath I nursed against the world. Farewell.'

    I ceased; he said, 'Stubborn, but she may sit
Upon a king's right hand in thunderstorms,
And breed up warriors! See now, tho' yourself   430
Be dazzled by the wildfire Love to sloughs
That swallow common sense, the spindling king,
This Gama swamp'd in lazy tolerance.

When the man wants weight, the woman takes it up,
And topples down the scales; but this is fixt
As are the roots of earth and base of all,—
Man for the field and woman for the hearth;
Man for the sword, and for the needle she;
Man with the head, and woman with the heart;
Man to command, and woman to obey;   440
All else confusion. Look you! the gray mare
Is ill to live with, when her whinny shrills
From tile to scullery, and her small good-man
Shrinks in his arm-chair while the fires of hell
Mix with his hearth. But you—she's yet a colt—
Take, break her; strongly groom'd and straitly curb'd
She might not rank with those detestable
That let the bantling scald at home, and brawl
Their rights or wrongs like potherbs in the street.
They say she's comely; there's the fairer chance.   450
I like her none the less for rating at her!
Besides, the woman wed is not as we,
But suffers change of frame. A lusty brace
Of twins may weed her of her folly. Boy,
The bearing and the training of a child
Is woman's wisdom.' Thus the hard old king.
I took my leave, for it was nearly noon;
I pored upon her letter which I held,
And on the little clause, 'take not his life;'
I mused on that wild morning in the woods,   460
And on the 'Follow, follow, thou shalt win;'
I thought on all the wrathful king had said,
And how the strange betrothment was to end.
Then I remember'd that burnt sorcerer's curse
That one should fight with shadows and should fall;
And like a flash the weird affection came.
King, camp, and college turn'd to hollow shows;
I seem'd to move in old memorial tilts,
And doing battle with forgotten ghosts,
To dream myself the shadow of a dream;   470
And ere I woke it was the point of noon,
The lists were ready. Empanoplied and plumed
We enter'd in, and waited, fifty there
Opposed to fifty, till the trumpet blared
At the barrier like a wild horn in a land
Of echoes, and a moment, and once more
The trumpet, and again; at which the storm
Of galloping hoofs bare on the ridge of spears
And riders front to front, until they closed
In conflict with the crash of shivering points,   480
And thunder. Yet it seem'd a dream, I dream'd

Of fighting. On his hunches rose the steed,
And into fiery splinters leapt the lance,
And out of stricken helmets sprang the fire.
Part sat like rocks; part reel'd but kept their seats;
Part roll'd on the earth and rose again and drew;
Part stumbled mixt with floundering horses. Down
From those two bulks at Arac's side, and down
From Arac's arm, as from a giant's flail,
The large blows rain'd, as here and everywhere   490
He rode the mellay, lord of the ringing lists,
And all the plain—brand, mace, and shaft, and shield—
Shock'd, like an iron-clinging anvil bang'd
With hammers; till I thought, can this be he
From Gama's dwarfish loins? if this be so,
The mother makes us most—and in my dream
I glanced aside, and saw the palace-front
Alive with fluttering scarfs and ladies' eyes,
And highest, among the statues, statue-like,
Between a cymbal's Miriam and a Jael,   500
With Psyche, babe, was Ida watching us,
A single band of gold about her hair,
Like a saint's glory up in heaven; but she,
No saint—inexorable—no tenderness—
Too hard, too cruel. Yet she sees me fight,
Yea, let her see me fall. With that I drave
Among the thickest and bore down a prince,
And Cyril one. Yea, let me make my dream
All that I would. But that large-moulded man,
His visage all agrin as at a wake,   510
Made at me thro' the press, and, staggering back
With stroke on stroke the horse and horseman, came
As comes a pillar of electric cloud,
Flaying the roofs and sucking up the drains,
And shadowing down the champaign till it strikes
On a wood, and takes, and breaks, and cracks, and splits,
And twists the grain with such a roar that Earth
Reels, and the herdsmen cry; for everything
Gave way before him. Only Florian, he
That loved me closer than his own right eye,   520
Thrust in between; but Arac rode him down.
And Cyril seeing it, push'd against the Prince,
With Psyche's color round his helmet, tough,
Strong, supple, sinew-corded, apt at arms;
But tougher, heavier, stronger, he that smote
And threw him. Last I spurr'd; I felt my veins
Stretch with fierce heat; a moment hand to hand,
And sword to sword, and horse to horse we hung,
Till I struck out and shouted; the blade glanced,

I did but shear a feather, and dream and truth
Flow'd from me; darkness closed me, and I fell.

> Home they brought her warrior dead;
>   She nor swoon'd nor utter'd cry.
> All her maidens, watching, said,
>   'She must weep or she will die.'
>
> Then they praised him, soft and low,
>   Call'd him worthy to be loved,
> Truest friend and noblest foe;
>   Yet she neither spoke nor moved.
>
> Stole a maiden from her place,
>   Lightly to the warrior stept,
> Took the face-cloth from the face;
>   Yet she neither moved nor wept.
>
> Rose a nurse of ninety years,
>   Set his child upon her knee—
> Like summer tempest came her tears—
>   'Sweet my child, I live for thee.'

VI

My dream had never died or lived again;
As in some mystic middle state I lay.
Seeing I saw not, hearing not I heard;
Tho', if I saw not, yet they told me all
So often that I speak as having seen.

For so it seem'd, or so they said to me,
That all things grew more tragic and more strange;
That when our side was vanquish'd and my cause
For ever lost, there went up a great cry,
'The Prince is slain!' My father heard and ran   10
In on the lists, and there unlaced my casque
And grovell'd on my body, and after him
Came Psyche, sorrowing for Aglaïa.

But high upon the palace Ida stood
With Psyche's babe in arm; there on the roofs
Like that great dame of Lapidoth she sang.

> 'Our enemies have fallen, have fallen: the seed,
> The little seed they laugh'd at in the dark,
> Has risen and cleft the soil, and grown a bulk
> Of spanless girth, that lays on every side   20
> A thousand arms and rushes to the sun.
>
> 'Our enemies have fallen, have fallen: they came;
> The leaves were wet with women's tears; they heard
> A noise of songs they would not understand;
> They mark'd it with the red cross to the fall,
> And would have strown it, and are fallen themselves.

'Our enemies have fallen, have fallen: they came,
The woodmen with their axes: lo the tree!
But we will make it faggots for the hearth,
And shape it plank and beam for roof and floor,
And boats and bridges for the use of men.   30

'Our enemies have fallen, have fallen; they struck;
With their own blows they hurt themselves, nor knew
There dwelt an iron nature in the grain;
The glittering axe was broken in their arms,
Their arms were shatter'd to the shoulder blade.

'Our enemies have fallen, but this shall grow
A night of Summer from the heat, a breadth
Of Autumn, dropping fruits of power; and roll'd
With music in the growing breeze of Time,   40
The tops shall strike from star to star, the fangs
Shall move the stony bases of the world.

'And now, O maids, behold our sanctuary
Is violate, our laws broken; fear we not
To break them more in their behoof, whose arms
Champion'd our cause and won it with a day
Blanch'd in our annals, and perpetual feast,
When dames and heroines of the golden year
Shall strip a hundred hollows bare of Spring,
To rain an April of ovation round   50
Their statues, borne aloft, the three; but come,
We will be liberal, since our rights are won.
Let them not lie in the tents with coarse mankind,
Ill nurses; but descend, and proffer these
The brethren of our blood and cause, that there
Lie bruised and maim'd, the tender ministries
Of female hands and hospitality.'

She spoke, and with the babe yet in her arms,
Descending, burst the great bronze valves, and led
A hundred maids in train across the park.   60
Some cowl'd, and some bare-headed, on they came,
Their feet in flowers, her loveliest. By them went
The enamor'd air sighing, and on their curls
From the high tree the blossom wavering fell,
And over them the tremulous isles of light
Slided, they moving under shade; but Blanche
At distance follow'd. So they came: anon
Thro' open field into the lists they wound
Timorously; and as the leader of the herd
That holds a stately fretwork to the sun,   70
And follow'd up by a hundred airy does,
Steps with a tender foot, light as on air,
The lovely, lordly creature floated on
To where her wounded brethren lay; there stay'd,

Knelt on one knee,—the child on one,—and prest
Their hands, and call'd them dear deliverers,
And happy warriors, and immortal names,
And said, 'You shall not lie in the tents, but here,
And nursed by those for whom you fought, and served
With female hands and hospitality.'   80

Then, whether moved by this, or was it chance,
She past my way. Up started from my side
The old lion, glaring with his whelpless eye,
Silent; but when she saw me lying stark,
Dishelm'd and mute, and motionlessly pale,
Cold even to her, she sigh'd; and when she saw
The haggard father's face and reverend beard
Of grisly twine, all dabbled with the blood
Of his own son, shudder'd, a twitch of pain
Tortured her mouth, and o'er her forehead past   90
A shadow, and her hue changed, and she said:
'He saved my life; my brother slew him for it.'
No more; at which the king in bitter scorn
Drew from my neck the painting and the tress,
And held them up. She saw them, and a day
Rose from the distance on her memory,
When the good queen, her mother, shore the tress
With kisses, ere the days of Lady Blanche.
And then once more she look'd at my pale face;
Till understanding all the foolish work   100
Of Fancy, and the bitter close of all,
Her iron will was broken in her mind;
Her noble heart was molten in her breast;
She bow'd, she set the child on the earth; she laid
A feeling finger on my brows, and presently
'O Sire,' she said, 'he lives; he is not dead!
O, let me have him with my brethren here
In our own palace; we will tend on him
Like one of these; if so, by any means,
To lighten this great clog of thanks, that make   110
Our progress falter to the woman's goal.'

She said; but at the happy word 'he lives!'
My father stoop'd, re-father'd o'er my wounds.
So those two foes above my fallen life,
With brow to brow like night and evening mixt
Their dark and gray, while Psyche ever stole
A little nearer, till the babe that by us,
Half-lapt in glowing gauze and golden brede,
Lay like a new-fallen meteor on the grass,
Uncared for, spied its mother and began   120

A blind and babbling laughter, and to dance
Its body, and reach its fatling innocent arms
And lazy lingering fingers. She the appeal
Brook'd not, but clamoring out 'Mine—mine—not yours!
It is not yours, but mine; give me the child!'
Ceased all on tremble; piteous was the cry.
So stood the unhappy mother open-mouth'd,
And turn'd each face her way. Wan was her cheek
With hollow watch, her blooming mantle torn,
Red grief and mother's hunger in her eye,   130
And down dead-heavy sank her curls, and half
The sacred mother's bosom, panting, burst
The laces toward her babe; but she nor cared
Nor knew it, clamoring on, till Ida heard,
Look'd up, and rising slowly from me, stood
Erect and silent, striking with her glance
The mother, me, the child. But he that lay
Beside us, Cyril, batter'd as he was,
Trail'd himself up on one knee; then he drew
Her robe to meet his lips, and down she look'd   140
At the arm'd man sideways, pitying as it seem'd,
Or self-involved; but when she learnt his face,
Remembering his ill-omen'd song, arose
Once more thro' all her height, and o'er him grew
Tall as a figure lengthen'd on the sand
When the tide ebbs in sunshine, and he said:

'O fair and strong and terrible! Lioness
That with your long locks play the lion's mane!
But Love and Nature, these are two more terrible
And stronger. See, your foot is on our necks,   150
We vanquish'd, you the victor of your will.
What would you more? give her the child! remain
Orb'd in your isolation; he is dead,
Or all as dead: henceforth we let you be.
Win you the hearts of women; and beware
Lest, where you seek the common love of these,
The common hate with the revolving wheel
Should drag you down, and some great Nemesis
Break from a darken'd future, crown'd with fire,
And tread you out for ever. But howsoe'er   160
Fixt in yourself, never in your own arms
To hold your own, deny not hers to her,
Give her the child! O, if, I say, you keep
One pulse that beats true woman, if you loved
The breast that fed or arm that dandled you,
Or own one port of sense not flint to prayer,

Give her the child! or if you scorn to lay it,
Yourself, in hands so lately claspt with yours,
Or speak to her, your dearest, her one fault
The tenderness, not yours, that could not kill,   170
Give *me* it; *I* will give it her.'
                                        He said.
At first her eye with slow dilation roll'd
Dry flame, she listening; after sank and sank
And, into mournful twilight mellowing, dwelt
Full on the child. She took it: 'Pretty bud!
Lily of the vale! half-open'd bell of the woods!
Sole comfort of my dark hour, when a world
Of traitorous friend and broken system made
No purple in the distance, mystery,
Pledge of a love not to be mine, farewell!   180
These men are hard upon us as of old,
We two must part; and yet how fain was I
To dream thy cause embraced in mine, to think
I might be something to thee, when I felt
Thy helpless warmth about my barren breast
In the dead prime; but may thy mother prove
As true to thee as false, false, false to me!
And, if thou needs must bear the yoke, I wish it
Gentle as freedom'—here she kiss'd it; then—
'All good go with thee! take it, sir,' and so   190
Laid the soft babe in his hard-mailed hands,
Who turn'd half-round to Psyche as she sprang
To meet it, with an eye that swum in thanks;
Then felt it sound and whole from head to foot,
And hugg'd and never hugg'd it close enough,
And in her hunger mouth'd and mumbled it,
And hid her bosom with it; after that
Put on more calm and added suppliantly:

'We two were friends: I go to mine own land
For ever. Find some other; as for me   200
I scarce am fit for your great plans: yet speak to me,
Say one soft word and let me part forgiven.'

But Ida spoke not, rapt upon the child.
Then Arac: 'Ida—'sdeath! you blame the man;
You wrong yourselves—the woman is so hard
Upon the woman. Come, a grace to me!
I am your warrior; I and mine have fought
Your battle. Kiss her; take her hand, she weeps.
'Sdeath! I would sooner fight thrice o'er than see it.'

But Ida spoke not, gazing on the ground;   210
And reddening in the furrows of his chin,
And moved beyond his custom, Gama said:

'I've heard that there is iron in the blood,
And I believe it. Not one word? not one?
Whence drew you this steel temper? not from me,
Not from your mother, now a saint with saints.
She said you had a heart—I heard her say it—
"Our Ida has a heart"—just ere she died—
"But see that some one with authority
Be near her still;" and I—I sought for one—   220
All people said she had authority—
The Lady Blanche—much profit! Not one word;
No! tho' your father sues. See how you stand
Stiff as Lot's wife, and all the good knights maim'd,
I trust that there is no one hurt to death,
For your wild whim. And was it then for this,
Was it for this we gave our palace up,
Where we withdrew from summer heats and state,
And had our wine and chess beneath the planes,
And many a pleasant hour with her that's gone,   230
Ere you were born to vex us? Is it kind?
Speak to her, I say; is this not she of whom,
When first she came, all flush'd you said to me,
Now had you got a friend of your own age,
Now could you share your thought, now should men see
Two women faster welded in one love
Than pairs of wedlock? she you walk'd with, she
You talk'd with, whole nights long, up in the tower,
Of sine and arc, spheroid and azimuth,
And right ascension, heaven knows what; and now   240
A word, but one, one little kindly word,
Not one to spare her! Out upon you, flint!'
You love nor her, nor me, nor any; nay,
You shame your mother's judgment too. Not one?
You will not? well—no heart have you, or such
As fancies like the vermin in a nut
Have fretted all to dust and bitterness.'
So said the small king moved beyond his wont.

But Ida stood nor spoke, drain'd of her force
By many a varying influence and so long.   250
Down thro' her limbs a drooping languor wept;
Her head a little bent; and on her mouth
A doubtful smile dwelt like a clouded moon
In a still water. Then brake out my sire,
Lifting his grim head from my wounds: 'O you,

Woman, whom we thought woman even now,
And were half fool'd to let you tend our son,
Because he might have wish'd it—but we see
The accomplice of your madness unforgiven,
And think that you might mix his draught with death,   260
When your skies change again; the rougher hand
Is safer. On to the tents; take up the Prince.'

He rose, and while each ear was prick'd to attend
A tempest, thro' the cloud that dimm'd her broke
A genial warmth and light once more, and shone
Thro' glittering drops on her sad friend.

                                                'Come hither,
O Psyche,' she cried out, 'embrace me, come,
Quick while I melt; make reconcilement sure
With one that cannot keep her mind an hour;
Come to the hollow heart they slander so!   270
Kiss and be friends, like children being chid!
I seem no more, *I* want forgiveness too;
I should have had to do with none but maids,
That have no links with men. Ah false but dear,
Dear traitor, too much loved, why?—why?—yet see
Before these kings we embrace you yet once more
With all forgiveness, all oblivion,
And trust, not love, you less.

                                And now, O sire,
Grant me your son, to nurse, to wait upon him,
Like mine own brother. For my debt to him,   280
This nightmare weight of gratitude, I know it.
Taunt me no more; yourself and yours shall have
Free adit; we will scatter all our maids
Till happier times each to her proper hearth.
What use to keep them here—now? grant my prayer.
Help, father, brother, help; speak to the king;
Thaw this male nature to some touch of that
Which kills me with myself, and drags me down
From my fixt height to mob me up with all
The soft and milky rabble of womankind,   290
Poor weakling even as they are.'

                                Passionate tears
Follow'd; the king replied not; Cyril said:
'Your brother, lady,—Florian,—ask for him
Of your great Head—for he is wounded too—
That you may tend upon him with the Prince.'
'Ay, so,' said Ida with a bitter smile,
'Our laws are broken; let him enter too.'
Then Violet, she that sang the mournful song,
And had a cousin tumbled on the plain,

Petition'd too for him. 'Ay, so,' she said,
'I stagger in the stream; I cannot keep
My heart an eddy from the brawling hour.
We break our laws with ease, but let it be.'
'Ay, so?' said Blanche: 'Amazed am I to hear
Your Highness; but your Highness breaks with ease
The law your Highness did not make; 't was I.
I had been wedded wife, I knew mankind,
And block'd them out; but these men came to woo
Your Highness,—verily I think to win.'

So she, and turn'd askance a wintry eye;
But Ida, with a voice that, like a bell
Toll'd by an earthquake in a trembling tower,
Rang ruin, answer'd full of grief and scorn.

'Fling our doors wide! all, all, not one, but all,
Not only he, but by my mother's soul,
Whatever man lies wounded, friend or foe,
Shall enter, if he will! Let our girls flit,
Till the storm die! but had you stood by us,
The roar that breaks the Pharos from his base
Had left us rock. She fain would sting us too,
But shall not. Pass, and mingle with your likes.
We brook no further insult, but are gone.'

She turn'd; the very nape of her white neck
Was rosed with indignation; but the Prince
Her brother came; the king her father charm'd
Her wounded soul with word; nor did mine own
Refuse her proffer, lastly gave his hand.

Then us they lifted up, dead weights, and bare
Straight to the doors; to them the doors gave way
Groaning, and in the vestal entry shriek'd
The virgin marble under iron heels.
And on they moved and gain'd the hall, and there
Rested; but great the crush was, and each base,
To left and right, of those tall columns drown'd
In silken fluctuation and the swarm
Of female whisperers. At the further end
Was Ida by the throne, the two great cats
Close by her, like supporters on a shield,
Bow-back'd with fear; but in the centre stood
The common men with rolling eyes; amazed
They glared upon the women, and aghast
The women stared at these, all silent, save
When armor clash'd or jingled, while the day,

Descending, struck athwart the hall, and shot
A flying splendor out of brass and steel,
That o'er the statues leapt from head to head,
Now fired an angry Pallas on the helm,
Now set a wrathful Dian's moon on flame;
And now and then an echo started up,
And shuddering fled from room to room, and died   350
Of fright in far apartments.
                        Then the voice
Of Ida sounded, issuing ordinance;
And me they bore up the broad stairs, and thro'
The long-laid galleries past a hundred doors
To one deep chamber shut from sound, and due
To languid limbs and sickness, left me in it;
And others otherwise they laid; and all
That afternoon a sound arose of hoof
And chariot, many a maiden passing home
Till happier times; but some were left of those   360
Held sagest, and the great lords out and in,
From those two hosts that lay beside the wall,
Walk'd at their will, and everything was changed.

> Ask me no more: the moon may draw the sea;
>   The cloud may stoop from heaven and take the shape,
>   With fold to fold, of mountain or of cape;
> But O too fond, when have I answer'd thee?
>   Ask me no more.

> Ask me no more: what answer should I give?
>   I love not hollow cheek or faded eye:
>   Yet, O my friend, I will not have thee die!
> Ask me no more, lest I should bid thee live;
>   Ask me no more.

> Ask me no more: thy fate and mine are seal'd,
>   I strove against the stream and all in vain;
>   Let the great river take me to the main.
> No more, dear love, for at a touch I yield;
>   Ask me no more.

VII

So was their sanctuary violated,
So their fair college turn'd to hospital,
At first with all confusion; by and by
Sweet order lived again with other laws,
A kindlier influence reign'd, and everywhere
Low voices with the ministering hand
Hung round the sick. The maidens came, they talk'd,
They sang, they read; till she not fair began
To gather light, and she that was became
Her former beauty treble; and to and fro   10

With books, with flowers, with angel offices,
Like creatures native unto gracious act,
And in their own clear element, they moved.

But sadness on the soul of Ida fell,
And hatred of her weakness, blent with shame.
Old studies fail'd; seldom she spoke; but oft
Clomb to the roofs, and gazed alone for hours
On that disastrous leaguer, swarms of men
Darkening her female field. Void was her use,
And she as one that climbs a peak to gaze   20
O'er land and main, and sees a great black cloud
Drag inward from the deeps, a wall of night,
Blot out the slope of sea from verge to shore,
And suck the blinding splendor from the sand,
And quenching lake by lake and tarn by tarn
Expunge the world; so fared she gazing there,
So blacken'd all her world in secret, blank
And waste it seem'd and vain; till down she came,
And found fair peace once more among the sick.

And twilight dawn'd; and morn by morn the lark   30
Shot up and shrill'd in flickering gyres, but I
Lay silent in the muffled cage of life.
And twilight gloom'd, and broader-grown the bowers
Drew the great night into themselves, and heaven,
Star after star, arose and fell; but I,
Deeper than those weird doubts could reach me, lay
Quite sunder'd from the moving Universe,
Nor knew what eye was on me, nor the hand
That nursed me, more than infants in their sleep.

But Psyche tended Florian; with her oft   40
Melissa came, for Blanche had gone, but left
Her child among us, willing she should keep
Court-favor. Here and there the small bright head,
A light of healing, glanced about the couch,
Or thro' the parted silks the tender face
Peep'd, shining in upon the wounded man
With blush and smile, a medicine in themselves
To wile the length from languorous hours, and draw
The sting from pain; nor seem'd it strange that soon
He rose up whole, and those fair charities   50
Join'd at her side; nor stranger seem'd that hearts
So gentle, so employ'd, should close in love,
Than when two dewdrops on the petal shake
To the same sweet air, and tremble deeper down,
And slip at once all-fragrant into one.

Less prosperously the second suit obtain'd
At first with Psyche. Not tho' Blanche had sworn
That after that dark night among the fields
She needs must wed him for her own good name;
Not tho' he built upon the babe restored;   60
Not tho' she liked him, yielded she, but fear'd
To incense the Head once more; till on a day
When Cyril pleaded, Ida came behind
Seen but of Psyche; on her foot she hung
A moment, and she heard, at which her face
A little flush'd, and she past on; but each
Assumed from thence a half-consent involved
In stillness, plighted troth, and were at peace.

Nor only these; Love in the sacred halls
Held carnival at will, and flying struck   70
With showers of random sweet on maid and man.
Nor did her father cease to press my claim,
Nor did mine own now reconciled; nor yet
Did those twin brothers, risen again and whole;
Nor Arac, satiate with his victory.

But I lay still, and with me oft she sat.
Then came a change; for sometimes I would catch
Her hand in wild delirium, gripe it hard,
And fling it like a viper off, and shriek,
'You are not Ida;' clasp it once again,   80
And call her Ida, tho' I knew her not,
And call her sweet, as if in irony,
And call her hard and cold, which seem'd a truth;
And still she fear'd that I should lose my mind,
And often she believed that I should die;
Till out of long frustration of her care,
And pensive tendance in the all-weary noons,
And watches in the dead, the dark, when clocks
Throbb'd thunder thro' the palace floors, or call'd
On flying Time from all their silver tongues—   90
And out of memories of her kindlier days,
And sidelong glances at my father's grief,
And at the happy lovers heart in heart—
And out of hauntings of my spoken love,
And lonely listenings to my mutter'd dream,
And often feeling of the helpless hands,
And wordless broodings on the wasted cheek—
From all a closer interest flourish'd up,
Tenderness touch by touch, and last, to these,
Love, like an Alpine harebell hung with tears   100
By some cold morning glacier; frail at first

And feeble, all unconscious of itself,
But such as gather'd color day by day.

Last I woke sane, but well-nigh close to death
For weakness. It was evening; silent light
Slept on the painted walls, wherein were wrought
Two grand designs; for on one side arose
The women up in wild revolt, and storm'd
At the Oppian law. Titanic shapes, they cramm'd
The forum, and half-crush'd among the rest   110
A dwarf-like Cato cower'd. On the other side
Hortensia spoke against the tax; behind,
A train of dames. By axe and eagle sat,
With all their foreheads drawn in Roman scowls,
And half the wolf's-milk curdled in their veins,
The fierce triumvirs; and before them paused
Hortensia, pleading; angry was her face.

I saw the forms; I knew not where I was.
They did but look like hollow shows; nor more
Sweet Ida. Palm to palm she sat; the dew   120
Dwelt in her eyes, and softer all her shape
And rounder seem'd. I moved, I sigh'd; a touch
Came round my wrist, and tears upon my hand.
Then all for languor and self pity ran
Mine down my face, and with what life I had,
And like a flower that cannot all unfold,
So drench'd it is with tempest, to the sun,
Yet, as it may, turns toward him, I on her
Fixt my faint eyes, and utter'd whisperingly:

'If you be what I think you, some sweet dream,   130
I would but ask you to fulfil yourself;
But if you be that Ida whom I knew,
I ask you nothing; only, if a dream,
Sweet dream, be perfect. I shall die tonight.
Stoop down and seem to kiss me ere I die.'

I could no more, but lay like one in trance,
That hears his burial talk'd of by his friends,
And cannot speak, nor move, nor make one sign,
But lies and dreads his doom. She turn'd, she paused,
She stoop'd; and out of languor leapt a cry,   140
Leapt fiery Passion from the brinks of death,
And I believed that in the living world
My spirit closed with Ida's at the lips;
Till back I fell, and from mine arms she rose
Glowing all over noble shame; and all

Her falser self slipt from her like a robe,
And left her woman, lovelier in her mood
Than in her mould that other, when she came
From barren deeps to conquer all with love,
And down the streaming crystal dropt; and she   150
Far-fleeted by the purple island-sides,
Naked, a double light in air and wave,
To meet her Graces, where they deck'd her out
For worship without end—nor end of mine,
Stateliest, for thee! but mute she glided forth,
Nor glanced behind her, and I sank and slept,
Fill'd thro' and thro' with love, a happy sleep.

Deep in the night I woke: she, near me, held
A volume of the poets of her land.
There to herself, all in low tones, she read: 160

    'Now sleeps the crimson petal, now the white;
    Nor waves the cypress in the palace walk;
    Nor winks the gold fin in the porphyry font.
    The fire-fly wakens; waken thou with me.

    'Now droops the milk-white peacock like a ghost,
    And like a ghost she glimmers on to me.

    'Now lies the Earth all Danaë to the stars,
    And all thy heart lies open unto me.

    'Now slides the silent meteor on, and leaves
    A shining furrow, as thy thoughts in me.   170

    'Now folds the lily all her sweetness up,
    And slips into the bosom of the lake.
    So fold thyself, my dearest, thou, and slip
    Into my bosom and be lost in me.'

I heard her turn the page; she found a small
Sweet idyl, and once more, as low, she read:

    'Come down, O maid, from yonder mountain height.
    What pleasure lives in height (the shepherd sang),
    In height and cold, the splendor of the hills?
    But cease to move so near the heavens and cease   180
    To glide a sunbeam by the blasted pine,
    To sit a star upon the sparkling spire;
    And come, for Love is of the valley, come,
    For Love is of the valley, come thou down
    And find him; by the happy threshold, he,
    Or hand in hand with Plenty in the maize,
    Or red with spirted purple of the vats,
    Or foxlike in the vine; nor cares to walk
    With Death and Morning on the Silver Horns,
    Nor wilt thou snare him in the white ravine,   190
    Nor find him dropt upon the firths of ice,
    That huddling slant in furrow-cloven falls

To roll the torrent out of dusky doors.
But follow; let the torrent dance thee down
To find him in the valley; let the wild
Lean-headed eagles yelp alone, and leave
The monstrous ledges there to slope, and spill
Their thousand wreaths of dangling water-smoke,
That like a broken purpose waste in air.
So waste not thou, but come; for all the vales   200
Await thee; azure pillars of the hearth
Arise to thee; the children call, and I
Thy shepherd pipe, and sweet is every sound,
Sweeter thy voice, but every sound is sweet;
Myriads of rivulets hurrying thro' the lawn,
The moan of doves in immemorial elms,
And murmuring of innumerable bees.'

So she low-toned, while with shut eyes I lay
Listening, then look'd. Pale was the perfect face;
The bosom with long sighs labor'd; and meek   210
Seem'd the full lips, and mild the luminous eyes,
And the voice trembled and the hand. She said
Brokenly, that she knew it, she had fail'd
In sweet humility, had fail'd in all;
That all her labor was but as a block
Left in the quarry; but she still were loth,
She still were loth to yield herself to one
That wholly scorn'd to help their equal rights
Against the sons of men and barbarous laws.
She pray'd me not to judge their cause from her   220
That wrong'd it, sought far less for truth than power
In knowledge. Something wild within her breast,
A greater than all knowledge, beat her down.
And she had nursed me there from week to week;
Much she learnt in little time. In part
It was ill counsel had misled the girl
To vex true hearts; yet was she but a girl—
'Ah fool, and made myself a queen of farce!
When comes another such? never, I think,
Till the sun drop, dead, from the signs.'

                                    Her voice   230
Choked, and her forehead sank upon her hands,
And her great heart thro' all the faultful past
Went sorrowing in a pause I dared not break;
Till notice of a change in the dark world
Was lispt about the acacias, and a bird,
That early woke to feed her little ones,
Sent from a dewy breast a cry for light.
She moved, and at her feet the volume fell.

'Blame not thyself too much,' I said, 'nor blame
Too much the sons of men and barbarous laws;   240

These were the rough ways of the world till now.
Henceforth thou hast a helper, me, that know
The woman's cause is man's; they rise or sink
Together, dwarf'd or godlike, bond or free.
For she that out of Lethe scales with man
The shining steps of Nature, shares with man
His nights, his days, moves with him to one goal,
Stays all the fair young planet in her hands—
If she be small, slight-natured, miserable,
How shall men grow? but work no more alone!   **250**
Our place is much; as far as in us lies
We two will serve them both in aiding her—
Will clear away the parasitic forms
That seem to keep her up but drag her down—
Will leave her space to burgeon out of all
Within her—let her make herself her own
To give or keep, to live and learn and be
All that not harms distinctive womanhood.
For woman is not undevelopt man,
But diverse. Could we make her as the man,   **260**
Sweet Love were slain; his dearest bond is this,
Not like to like, but like in difference.
Yet in the long years liker must they grow;
The man be more of woman, she of man;
He gain in sweetness and in moral height,
Nor lose the wrestling thews that throw the world;
She mental breadth, nor fail in childward care,
Nor lose the childlike in the larger mind;
Till at the last she set herself to man,
Like perfect music unto noble words;   **270**
And so these twain, upon the skirts of Time,
Sit side by side, full-summ'd in all their powers,
Dispensing harvest, sowing the to-be,
Self-reverent each and reverencing each,
Distinct in individualities,
But like each other even as those who love.
Then comes the statelier Eden back to men;
Then reign the world's great bridals, chaste and calm;
Then springs the crowning race of human-kind.
May these things be!'

                          Sighing she spoke: 'I fear   **280**
They will not.'

                  'Dear, but let us type them now
In our own lives, and this proud watch-word rest
Of equal; seeing either sex alone
Is half itself, and in true marriage lies
Nor equal, nor unequal. Each fulfils
Defect in each, and always thought in thought,

Purpose in purpose, will in will, they grow,
The single pure and perfect animal,
The two-cell'd heart beating, with one full stroke,
Life.'

      And again sighing she spoke: 'A dream   290
That once was mine! what woman taught you this?'

'Alone,' I said, 'from earlier than I know,
Immersed in rich foreshadowings of the world,
I loved the woman. He, that doth not, lives
A drowning life, besotted in sweet self,
Or pines in sad experience worse than death,
Or keeps his wing'd affections clipt with crime.
Yet was there one thro' whom I loved her, one
Not learned, save in gracious household ways,
Not perfect, nay, but full of tender wants,   300
No angel, but a dearer being, all dipt
In angel instincts, breathing Paradise,
Interpreter between the gods and men,
Who look'd all native to her place, and yet
On tiptoe seem'd to touch upon a sphere
Too gross to tread, and all male minds perforce
Sway'd to her from their orbits as they moved,
And girdled her with music. Happy he
With such a mother! faith in womankind
Beats with his blood, and trust in all things high   310
Comes easy to him, and tho' he trip and fall
He shall not blind his soul with clay.'

                                    'But I,'
Said Ida, tremulously, 'so all unlike—
It seems you love to cheat yourself with words;
This mother is your model. I have heard
Of your strange doubts; they well might be; I seem
A mockery to my own self. Never, Prince!
You cannot love me.'

                         'Nay, but thee,' I said,
'From yearlong poring on thy pictured eyes,
Ere seen I loved, and loved thee seen, and saw   320
Thee woman thro' the crust of iron moods
That mask'd thee from men's reverence up, and forced
Sweet love on pranks of saucy boyhood; now,
Given back to life, to life indeed, thro' thee,
Indeed I love. The new day comes, the light
Dearer for night, as dearer thou for faults
Lived over. Lift thine eyes; my doubts are dead,
My haunting sense of hollow shows; the change,
This truthful change in thee has kill'd it. Dear,
Look up, and let thy nature strike on mine,   330

Like yonder morning on the blind half-world.
Approach and fear not; breathe upon my brows;
In that fine air I tremble, all the past
Melts mist-like into this bright hour, and this
Is morn to more, and all the rich to-come
Reels, as the golden Autumn woodland reels
Athwart the smoke of burning weeds. Forgive me,
I waste my heart in signs; let be. My bride,
My wife, my life! O, we will walk this world,
Yoked in all exercise of noble end,   340
And so thro' those dark gates across the wild
That no man knows. Indeed I love thee; come,
Yield thyself up; my hopes and thine are one.
Accomplish thou my manhood and thyself;
Lay thy sweet hands in mine and trust to me.'

CONCLUSION

So closed our tale, of which I give you all
The random scheme as wildly as it rose.
The words are mostly mine; for when we ceased
There came a minute's pause, and Walter said,
'I wish she had not yielded!' then to me,
'What if you drest it up poetically!'
So pray'd the men, the women; I gave assent.
Yet how to bind the scatter'd scheme of seven
Together in one sheaf? What style could suit?
The men required that I should give throughout   10
The sort of mock-heroic gigantesque,
With which we banter'd little Lilia first;
The women—and perhaps they felt their power,
For something in the ballads which they sang,
Or in their silent influence as they sat,
Had ever seem'd to wrestle with burlesque,
And drove us, last, to quite a solemn close—
They hated banter, wish'd for something real,
A gallant fight, a noble princess—why
Not make her true-heroic—true-sublime?   24
Or all, they said, as earnest as the close?
Which yet with such a framework scarce could be.
Then rose a little feud betwixt the two,
Betwixt the mockers and the realists;
And I, betwixt them both, to please them both,
And yet to give the story as it rose,
I moved as in a strange diagonal,
And maybe neither pleased myself nor them.

But Lilia pleased me, for she took no part
In our dispute; the sequel of the tale   30
Had touch'd her, and she sat, she pluck'd the grass,
She flung it from her, thinking; last, she fixt
A showery glance upon her aunt, and said,
'You—tell us what we are'—who might have told,
For she was cramm'd with theories out of books,
But that there rose a shout. The gates were closed
At sunset, and the crowd were swarming now,
To take their leave, about the garden rails.

So I and some went out to these; we climb'd
The slope to Vivian-place, and turning saw   40
The happy valleys, half in light, and half
Far-shadowing from the west, a land of peace;
Gray halls alone among their massive groves;
Trim hamlets; here and there a rustic tower
Half-lost in belts of hop and breadths of wheat;
The shimmering glimpses of a stream; the seas;
A red sail, or a white; and far beyond,
Imagined more than seen, the skirts of France.

'Look there, a garden!' said my college friend,
The Tory member's elder son, 'and there!   50
God bless the narrow sea which keeps her off,
And keeps our Britain, whole within herself,
A nation yet, the rulers and the ruled—
Some sense of duty, something of a faith,
Some reverence for the laws ourselves have made,
Some patient force to change them when we will,
Some civic manhood firm against the crowd—
But yonder, whiff! there comes a sudden heat,
The gravest citizen seems to lose his head,
The king is scared, the soldier will not fight,   60
The little boys begin to shoot and stab,
A kingdom topples over with a shriek
Like an old woman, and down rolls the world
In mock heroics stranger than our own;
Revolts, republics, revolutions, most
No graver than a schoolboys' barring out;
Too comic for the solemn things they are,
Too solemn for the comic touches in them,
Like our wild Princess with as wise a dream
As some of theirs—God bless the narrow seas!   70
I wish they were a whole Atlantic broad.'

'Have patience,' I replied, 'ourselves are full
Of social wrong; and maybe wildest dreams

Are but the needful preludes of the truth.
For me, the genial day, the happy crowd,
The sport half-science, fill me with a faith,
This fine old world of ours is but a child
Yet in the go-cart. Patience! Give it time
To learn its limbs; there is a hand that guides.'

In such discourse we gain'd the garden rails,   80
And there we saw Sir Walter where he stood,
Before a tower of crimson holly-oaks,
Among six boys, head under head, and look'd
No little lily-handed baronet he,
A great broad-shoulder'd genial Englishman,
A lord of fat prize-oxen and of sheep,
A raiser of huge melons and of pine,
A patron of some thirty charities,
A pamphleteer on guano and on grain,
A quarter-sessions chairman, abler none;   90
Fair-hair'd and redder than a windy morn;
Now shaking hands with him, now him, of those
That stood the nearest—now address'd to speech—
Who spoke few words and pithy, such as closed
Welcome, farewell, and welcome for the year
To follow. A shout rose again, and made
The long line of the approaching rookery swerve
From the elms, and shook the branches of the deer
From slope to slope thro' distant ferns, and rang
Beyond the bourn of sunset—O, a shout   105
More joyful than the city-roar that hails
Premier or king! Why should not these great sirs
Give up their parks some dozen times a year
To let the people breathe? So thrice they cried,
I likewise, and in groups they stream'd away.

But we went back to the Abbey, and sat on,
So much the gathering darkness charm'd; we sat
But spoke not, rapt in nameless reverie,
Perchance upon the future man. The walls
Blacken'd about us, bats wheel'd, and owls whoop'd,   110
And gradually the powers of the night,
That range above the region of the wind,
Deepening the courts of twilight broke them up
Thro' all the silent spaces of the worlds,
Beyond all thought into the heaven of heavens.

Last little Lilia, rising quietly,
Disrobed the glimmering statue of Sir Ralph
From those rich silks, and home well-pleased we went.

IN MEMORIAM A. H. H.

OBIIT MDCCCXXXIII

STRONG Son of God, immortal Love,
  Whom we, that have not seen thy face,
  By faith, and faith alone, embrace,
Believing where we cannot prove;

Thine are these orbs of light and shade;
  Thou madest Life in man and brute;
  Thou madest Death; and lo, thy foot
Is on the skull which thou hast made.

Thou wilt not leave us in the dust:
  Thou madest man, he knows not why,
  He thinks he was not made to die;
And thou hast made him: thou art just.

Thou seemest human and divine,
  The highest, holiest manhood, thou.
  Our wills are ours, we know not how;
Our wills are ours, to make them thine.

Our little systems have their day;
  They have their day and cease to be;
  They are but broken lights of thee,
And thou, O Lord, art more than they.

We have but faith: we cannot know,
  For knowledge is of things we see;
  And yet we trust it comes from thee,
A beam in darkness: let it grow.

Let knowledge grow from more to more,
  But more of reverence in us dwell;
  That mind and soul, according well,
May make one music as before,

But vaster. We are fools and slight;
  We mock thee when we do not fear:
  But help thy foolish ones to bear;
Help thy vain worlds to bear thy light.

Forgive what seem'd my sin in me,
    What seem'd my worth since I began;
    For merit lives from man to man,
And not from man, O Lord, to thee.

Forgive my grief for one removed,
    Thy creature, whom I found so fair.
    I trust he lives in thee, and there
I find him worthier to be loved.

Forgive these wild and wandering cries,
    Confusions of a wasted youth;
    Forgive them where they fail in truth,
And in thy wisdom make me wise.
        1849.

I

I held it truth, with him who sings
    To one clear harp in divers tones,
    That men may rise on stepping-stones
Of their dead selves to higher things.

But who shall so forecast the years
    And find in loss a gain to match?
    Or reach a hand thro' time to catch
The far-off interest of tears?

Let Love clasp Grief lest both be drown'd,
    Let darkness keep her raven gloss.
    Ah, sweeter to be drunk with loss,
To dance with Death, to beat the ground,

Than that the victor Hours should scorn
    The long result of love, and boast,
    'Behold the man that loved and lost,
But all he was is overworn.'

II

Old yew, which graspest at the stones
    That name the underlying dead,
    Thy fibres net the dreamless head,
Thy roots are wrapt about the bones.

The seasons bring the flower again,
    And bring the firstling to the flock;
    And in the dusk of thee the clock
Beats out the little lives of men.

O, not for thee the glow, the bloom,
　Who changest not in any gale,
　Nor branding summer suns avail
To touch thy thousand years of gloom;

And gazing on thee, sullen tree,
　Sick for thy stubborn hardihood,
　I seem to fail from out my blood
And grow incorporate into thee.

III

O Sorrow, cruel fellowship,
　O Priestess in the vaults of Death,
　O sweet and bitter in a breath,
What whispers from thy lying lip?

'The stars,' she whispers, 'blindly run;
　A web is woven across the sky;
　From out waste places comes a cry,
And murmurs from the dying sun;

'And all the phantom, Nature, stands—
　With all the music in her tone,
　A hollow echo of my own,—
A hollow form with empty hands.'

And shall I take a thing so blind,
　Embrace her as my natural good;
　Or crush her, like a vice of blood,
Upon the threshold of the mind?

IV

To Sleep I give my powers away;
　My will is bondsman to the dark;
　I sit within a helmless bark,
And with my heart I muse and say:

O heart, how fares it with thee now,
　That thou shouldst fail from thy desire,
　Who scarcely darest to inquire,
'What is it makes me beat so low?'

Something it is which thou hast lost,
　Some pleasure from thine early years.
　Break, thou deep vase of chilling tears,
That grief hath shaken into frost!

Such clouds of nameless trouble cross
  All night below the darken'd eyes;
  With morning wakes the will, and cries,
'Thou shalt not be the fool of loss.'

V

I sometimes hold it half a sin
  To put in words the grief I feel;
  For words, like Nature, half reveal
And half conceal the Soul within.

But, for the unquiet heart and brain,
  A use in measured language lies;
  The sad mechanic exercise,
Like dull narcotics, numbing pain.

In words, like weeds, I'll wrap me o'er,
  Like coarsest clothes against the cold;
  But that large grief which these enfold
Is given in outline and no more.

VI

One writes, that 'other friends remain,'
  That 'loss is common to the race'—
  And common is the commonplace,
And vacant chaff well meant for grain.

That loss is common would not make
  My own less bitter, rather more.
  Too common! Never morning wore
To evening, but some heart did break.

O father, wheresoe'er thou be,
  Who pledgest now thy gallant son,
  A shot, ere half thy draught be done,
Hath still'd the life that beat from thee.

O mother, praying God will save
  Thy sailor,—while thy head is bow'd,
  His heavy-shotted hammock-shroud
Drops in his vast and wandering grave.

Ye know no more than I who wrought
  At that last hour to please him well;
  Who mused on all I had to tell,
And something written, something thought;

Expecting still his advent home;
  And ever met him on his way
  With wishes, thinking, 'here to-day,'
Or 'to-morrow will he come.'

O, somewhere, meek, unconscious dove,
  That sittest ranging golden hair;
  And glad to find thyself so fair,
Poor child, that waitest for thy love!

For now her father's chimney glows
  In expectation of a guest;
  And thinking 'this will please him best,'
She takes a riband or a rose;

For he will see them on to-night;
  And with the thought her color burns;
  And, having left the glass, she turns
Once more to set a ringlet right;

And, even when she turn'd, the curse
  Had fallen, and her future lord
  Was drown'd in passing thro' the ford,
Or kill'd in falling from his horse.

O, what to her shall be the end?
  And what to me remains of good?
  To her perpetual maidenhood,
And unto me no second friend.

VII

Dark house, by which once more I stand
  Here in the long unlovely street,
  Doors, where my heart was used to beat
So quickly, waiting for a hand,

A hand that can be clasp'd no more—
  Behold me, for I cannot sleep,
  And like a guilty thing I creep
At earliest morning to the door.

He is not here; but far away
  The noise of life begins again,
  And ghastly thro' the drizzling rain
On the bald street breaks the blank day.

VIII

A happy lover who has come
　　To look on her that loves him well,
　　Who 'lights and rings the gateway bell,
And learns her gone and far from home;

He saddens, all the magic light
　　Dies off at once from bower and hall,
　　And all the place is dark, and all
The chambers emptied of delight:

So find I every pleasant spot
　　In which we two were wont to meet,
　　The field, the chamber, and the street,
For all is dark where thou are not.

Yet as that other, wandering there
　　In those deserted walks, may find
　　A flower beat with rain and wind,
Which once she foster'd up with care;

So seems it in my deep regret,
　　O my forsaken heart, with thee
　　And this poor flower of poesy
Which, little cared for, fades not yet.

But since it pleased a vanish'd eye,
　　I go to plant in on his tomb,
　　That if it can it there may bloom,
Or, dying, there at least may die.

IX

Fair ship, that from the Italian shore
　　Sailest the placid ocean-plains
　　With my lost Arthur's loved remains,
Spread thy full wings, and waft him o'er.

So draw him home to those that mourn
　　In vain; a favorable speed
　　Ruffle thy mirror'd mast, and lead
Thro' prosperous floods his holy urn.

All night no ruder air perplex
　　Thy sliding keel, till Phosphor, bright
　　As our pure love, thro' early light
Shall glimmer on the dewy decks.

Sphere all your lights around, above;
　Sleep, gentle heavens, before the prow;
　Sleep, gentle winds, as he sleeps now,
My friend, the brother of my love;

My Arthur, whom I shall not see
　Till all my widow'd race be run;
　Dear as the mother to the son,
More than my brothers are to me.

X

I hear the noise about thy keel;
　I hear the bell struck in the night;
　I see the cabin-window bright;
I see the sailor at the wheel.

Thou bring'st the sailor to his wife,
　And travell'd men from foreign lands;
　And letters unto trembling hands;
And, thy dark freight, a vanish'd life.

So bring him; we have idle dreams;
　This look of quiet flatters thus
　Our home-bred fancies. O, to us,
The fools of habit, sweeter seems

To rest beneath the clover sod,
　That takes the sunshine and the rains,
　Oh where the kneeling hamlet drains
The chalice of the grapes of God;

Than if with thee the roaring wells
　Should gulf him fathom-deep in brine,
　And hands so often clasp'd in mine,
Should toss with tangle and with shells.

XI

Calm is the morn without a sound,
　Calm as to suit a calmer grief,
　And only thro' the faded leaf
The chestnut pattering to the ground;

Calm and deep peace on this high wold,
　And on these dews that drench the furze,
　And all the silvery gossamers
That twinkle into green and gold;

Calm and still light on yon great plain
  That sweeps with all its autumn bowers,
  And crowded farms and lessening towers,
To mingle with the bounding main;

Calm and deep peace in this wide air,
  These leaves that redden to the fall,
  And in my heart, if calm at all,
If any calm, a calm despair;

Calm on the seas, and silver sleep,
  And waves that sway themselves in rest,
  And dead calm in that noble breast
Which heaves but with the heaving deep.

XII

Lo, as a dove when up she springs
  To bear thro' heaven a tale of woe,
  Some dolorous message knit below
The wild pulsation of her wings;

Like her I go, I cannot stay;
  I leave this mortal ark behind,
  A weight of nerves without a mind,
And leave the cliffs, and haste away

O'er ocean-mirrors rounded large,
  And reach the glow of southern skies,
  And see the sails at distance rise,
And linger weeping on the marge,

And saying, 'Comes he thus, my friend?
  Is this the end of all my care?'
  And circle moaning in the air,
'Is this the end? Is this the end?'

And forward dart again, and play
  About the prow, and back return
  To where the body sits, and learn
That I have been an hour away.

XIII

Tears of the widower, when he sees
  A late-lost form that sleep reveals,
  And moves his doubtful arms, and feels
Her place is empty, fall like these;

Which weep a loss for ever new,
   A void where heart on heart reposed;
   And, where warm hands have prest and closed,
Silence, till I be silent too;

Which weep the comrade of my choice,
   An awful thought, a life removed,
   The human-hearted man I loved,
A Spirit, not a breathing voice.

Come, Time, and teach me, many years,
   I do not suffer in a dream;
   For now so strange do these things seem,
Mine eyes have leisure for their tears,

My fancies time to rise on wing,
   And glance about the approaching sails,
   As tho' they brought but merchants' bales,
And not the burthen that they bring.

XIV

If one should bring me this report,
   That thou hadst touch'd the land to-day
   And I went down unto the quay,
And found thee lying in the port;

And standing, muffled round with woe,
   Should see thy passengers in rank
   Come stepping lightly down the plank,
And beckoning unto those they know;

And if along with these should come
   The man I held as half-divine,
   Should strike a sudden hand in mine,
And ask a thousand things of home;

And I should tell him all my pain,
   And how my life had droop'd of late,
   And he should sorrow o'er my state
And marvel what possess'd my brain;

And I perceived no touch of change,
   No hint of death in all his frame,
   But found him all in all the same,
I should not feel it to be strange.

XV

To-night the winds begin to rise
    And roar from yonder dropping day;
    The last red leaf is whirl'd away,
The rooks are blown about the skies;

The forest crack'd, the waters curl'd,
    The cattle huddled on the lea;
    And wildly dash'd on tower and tree
The sunbeam strikes along the world:

And but for fancies, which aver
    That all thy motions gently pass
    Athwart a plane of molten glass,
I scarce could brook the strain and stir

That makes the barren branches loud;
    And but for fear it is not so,
    The wild unrest that lives in woe
Would dote and pore on yonder cloud

That rises upward always higher,
    And onward drags a laboring breast,
    And topples round the dreary west,
A looming bastion fringed with fire.

XVI

What words are these have fallen from me?
    Can calm despair and wild unrest
    Be tenants of a single breast,
Or Sorrow such a changeling be?

Or doth she only seem to take
    The touch of change in calm or storm
    But knows no more of transient form
In her deep self, than some dead lake

That holds the shadow of a lark
    Hung in the shadow of a heaven?
    Or has the shock, so harshly given,
Confused me like the unhappy bark

That strikes by night a craggy shelf,
    And staggers blindly ere she sink?
    And stunn'd me from my power to think
And all my knowledge of myself;

And made me that delirious man
   Whose fancy fuses old and new,
   And flashes into false and true,
And mingles all without a plan?

XVII

Thou comest, much wept for; such a breeze
   Compell'd thy canvas, and my prayer
   Was as the whisper of an air
To breathe thee over lonely seas.

For I in spirit saw thee move
   Thro' circles of the bounding sky,
   Week after week; the days go by;
Come quick, thou bringest all I love.

Henceforth, wherever thou mayst roam,
   My blessing, like a line of light,
   Is on the waters day and night,
And like a beacon guards thee home.

So may whatever tempest mars
   Mid-ocean spare thee, sacred bark,
   And balmy drops in summer dark
Slide from the bosom of the stars;

So kind an office hath been done,
   Such precious relics brought by thee,
   The dust of him I shall not see
Till all my widow'd race be run.

XVIII

'T is well; 't is something; we may stand
   Where he in English earth is laid,
   And from his ashes may be made
The violet of his native land.

'T is little; but it looks in truth
   As if the quiet bones were blest
   Among familiar names to rest
And in the places of his youth.

Come then, pure hands, and bear the head
   That sleeps or wears the mask of sleep,
   And come, whatever loves to weep,
And hear the ritual of the dead.

Ah yet, even yet, if this might be,
    I, falling on his faithful heart,
    Would breathing thro' his lips impart
The life that almost dies in me;

That dies not, but endures with pain,
    And slowly forms the firmer mind,
    Treasuring the look it cannot find,
The words that are not heard again.

XIX

The Danube to the Severn gave
    The darken'd heart that beat no more;
    They laid him by the pleasant shore,
And in the hearing of the wave.

There twice a day the Severn fills;
    The salt sea-water passes by,
    And hushes half the babbling Wye,
And makes a silence in the hills.

The Wye is hush'd nor moved along,
    And hush'd my deepest grief of all,
    When fill'd with tears that cannot fall,
I brim with sorrow drowning song.

The tide flows down, the wave again
    Is vocal in its wooded walls;
    My deeper anguish also falls,
And I can speak a little then.

XX

The lesser griefs that may be said,
    That breathe a thousand tender vows,
    Are but as servants in a house
Where lies the master newly dead;

Who speak their feeling as it is,
    And weep the fulness from the mind.
    'It will be hard,' they say, 'to find
Another service such as this.'

My lighter moods are like to these,
    That out of words a comfort win;
    But there are other griefs within,
And tears that at their fountain freeze;

For by the hearth the children sit
　　Cold in that atmosphere of death,
　　And scarce endure to draw the breath,
Or like to noiseless phantoms flit;

But open converse is there none,
　　So much the vital spirits sink
　　To see the vacant chair, and think,
'How good! how kind! and he is gone.'

XXI

I sing to him that rests below,
　　And, since the grasses round me wave,
　　I take the grasses of the grave,
And make them pipes whereon to blow.

The traveller hears me now and then,
　　And sometimes harshly will he speak:
　　'This fellow would make weakness weak,
And melt the waxen hearts of men.'

Another answers: 'Let him be,
　　He loves to make parade of pain,
　　That with his piping he may gain
The praise that comes to constancy.'

A third is wroth: 'Is this an hour
　　For private sorrow's barren song,
　　When more and more the people throng
The chairs and thrones of civil power?

'A time to sicken and to swoon,
　　When Science reaches forth her arms
　　To feel from world to world, and charms
Her secret from the latest moon?'

Behold, ye speak an idle thing;
　　Ye never knew the sacred dust.
　　I do but sing because I must,
And pipe but as the linnets sing;

And one is glad; her note is gay,
　　For now her little ones have ranged;
　　And one is sad; her note is changed,
Because her brood is stolen away.

XXII

The path by which we twain did go,
    Which led by tracts that pleased us well,
    Thro' four sweet years arose and fell,
From flower to flower, from snow to snow;

And we with singing cheer'd the way,
    And, crown'd with all the season lent,
    From April on to April went,
And glad at heart from May to May.

But where the path we walk'd began
    To slant the fifth autumnal slope,
    As we descended following Hope,
There sat the Shadow fear'd of man;

Who broke our fair companionship,
    And spread his mantle dark and cold,
    And wrapt thee formless in the fold,
And dull'd the murmur on thy lip,

And bore thee where I could not see
    Nor follow, tho' I walk in haste,
    And think that somewhere in the waste
The Shadow sits and waits for me.

XXIII

Now, sometimes in my sorrow shut,
    Or breaking into song by fits,
    Alone, alone, to where he sits,
The Shadow cloak'd from head to foot,

Who keeps the keys of all the creeds,
    I wander, often falling lame,
    And looking back to whence I came,
Or on to where the pathway leads;

And crying, How changed from where it ran
    Thro' lands where not a leaf was dumb,
    But all the lavish hills would hum
The murmur of a happy Pan;

When each by turns was guide to each,
    And Fancy light from Fancy caught,
    And Thought leapt out to wed with Thought
Ere Thought could wed itself with Speech;

And all we met was fair and good,
　　And all was good that Time could bring,
　　And all the secret of the Spring
Moved in the chambers of the blood;

And many an old philosophy
　　On Argive heights divinely sang,
　　And round us all the thicket rang
To many a flute of Arcady.

XXIV

And was the day of my delight
　　As pure and perfect as I say?
　　The very source and fount of day
Is dash'd with wandering isles of night.

If all was good and fair we met,
　　This earth had been the Paradise
　　It never look'd to human eyes
Since our first sun arose and set.

And is it that the haze of grief
　　Makes former gladness loom so great?
　　The lowness of the present state,
That sets the past in this relief?

Or that the past will always win
　　A glory from its being far,
　　And orb into the perfect star
We saw not when we moved therein?

XXV

I know that this was Life,—the track
　　Whereon with equal feet we fared;
　　And then, as now, the day prepared
The daily burden for the back.

But this it was that made me move
　　As light as carrier-birds in air;
　　I loved the weight I had to bear,
Because it needed help of Love;

Nor could I weary, heart or limb,
　　When mighty Love would cleave in twain
　　The lading of a single pain,
And part it, giving half to him.

XXVI

Still onward winds the dreary way;
    I with it, for I long to prove
    No lapse of moons can canker Love,
Whatever fickle tongues may say.

And if that eye which watches guilt
    And goodness, and hath power to see
    Within the green the moulder'd tree,
And towers fallen as soon as built—

O, if indeed that eye foresee
    Or see—in Him is no before—
    In more of life true life no more
And Love the indifference to be,

Then might I find, ere yet the morn
    Breaks hither over Indian seas,
    That Shadow waiting with the keys,
To shroud me from my proper scorn.

XXVII

I envy not in any moods
    The captive void of noble rage,
    The linnet born within the cage,
That never knew the summer woods;

I envy not the beast that takes
    His license in the field of time,
    Unfetter'd by the sense of crime,
To whom a conscience never wakes;

Nor, what may count itself as blest,
    The heart that never plighted troth
    But stagnates in the weeds of sloth;
Nor any want-begotten rest.

I hold it true, whate'er befall;
    I feel it, when I sorrow most;
    'Tis better to have loved and lost
Than never to have loved at all.

XXVIII

The time draws near the birth of Christ.
    The moon is hid, the night is still;
    The Christmas bells from hill to hill
Answer each other in the mist.

Four voices of four hamlets round,
  From far and near, on mead and moor,
  Swell out and fail, as if a door
Were shut between me and the sound;

Each voice four changes on the wind,
  That now dilate, and now decrease,
  Peace and goodwill, goodwill and peace,
Peace and goodwill, to all mankind.

This year I slept and woke with pain,
  I almost wish'd no more to wake,
  And that my hold on life would break
Before I heard those bells again;

But they my troubled spirit rule,
  For they controll'd me when a boy;
  They bring me sorrow touch'd with joy,
The merry, merry bells of Yule.

XXIX

With such compelling cause to grieve
  As daily vexes household peace,
  And chains regret to his decease,
How dare we keep our Christmas-eve,

Which brings no more a welcome guest
  To enrich the threshold of the night
  With shower'd largess of delight
In dance and song and game and jest?

Yet go, and while the holly boughs
  Entwine the cold baptismal font,
  Make one wreath more for Use and Wont,
That guard the portals of the house;

Old sisters of a day gone by,
  Gray nurses, loving nothing new—
  Why should they miss their yearly due
Before their time? They too will die.

XXX

With trembling fingers did we weave
  The holly round the Christmas hearth;
  A rainy cloud possess'd the earth,
And sadly fell our Christmas-eve.

At our old pastimes in the hall
  We gamboll'd, making vain pretence
  Of gladness, with an awful sense
Of one mute Shadow watching all.

We paused: the winds were in the beech;
  We heard them sweep the winter land;
  And in a circle hand-in-hand
Sat silent, looking each at each.

Then echo-like our voices rang;
  We sung, tho' every eye was dim,
  A merry song we sang with him
Last year; impetuously we sang.

We ceased; a gentler feeling crept
  Upon us: surely rest is meet.
  'They rest,' we said, 'their sleep is sweet,'
And silence follow'd, and we wept.

Our voices took a higher range;
  Once more we sang: 'They do not die
  Nor lose their mortal sympathy,
Nor change to us, although they change;

'Rapt from the fickle and the frail
  With gather'd power, yet the same,
  Pierces the keen seraphic flame
From orb to orb, from veil to veil.'

Rise, happy morn, rise, holy morn,
  Draw forth the cheerful day from night:
  O Father, touch the east, and light
The light that shone when Hope was born.

XXXI

When Lazarus left his charnel-cave
  And home to Mary's house return'd,
  Was this demanded—if he yearn'd
To hear her weeping by his grave?

'Where wert thou, brother, those four days?
  There lives no record of reply,
  Which telling what it is to die
Had surely added praise to praise.

From every house the neighbors met,
  The streets were fill'd with joyful sound,
  A solemn gladness even crown'd
The purple brows of Olivet.

Behold a man raised up by Christ!
  The rest remaineth unreveal'd;
  He told it not, or something seal'd
The lips of that Evangelist.

XXXII

Her eyes are homes of silent prayer,
  Nor other thought her mind admits
  But, he was dead, and there he sits,
And he that brought him back is there.

Then one deep love doth supersede
  All other, when her ardent gaze
  Roves from the living brother's face,
And rests upon the Life indeed.

All subtle thought, all curious fears,
  Borne down by gladness so complete,
  She bows, she bathes the Saviour's feet
With costly spikenard and with tears.

Thrice blest whose lives are faithful prayers,
  Whose loves in higher love endure;
  What souls possess themselves so pure,
Or is there blessedness like theirs?

XXXIII

O thou that after toil and storm
  Mayst seem to have reach'd a purer air,
  Whose faith has centre everywhere,
Nor cares to fix itself to form,

Leave thou thy sister when she prays
  Her early heaven, her happy views;
  Nor thou with shadow'd hint confuse
A life that leads melodious days.

Her faith thro' form is pure as thine,
  Her hands are quicker unto good.
  O, sacred be the flesh and blood
To which she links a truth divine!

See thou, that countest reason ripe
　　In holding by the law within,
　　Thou fail not in a world of sin,
And even for want of such a type.

XXXIV

My own dim life should teach me this,
　　That life shall live for evermore,
　　Else earth is darkness at the core,
And dust and ashes all that is;

This round of green, this orb of flame,
　　Fantastic beauty; such as lurks
　　In some wild poet, when he works
Without a conscience or an aim.

What then were God to such as I?
　　'T were hardly worth my while to choose
　　Of things all mortal, or to use
A little patience ere I die;

'T were best at once to sink to peace,
　　Like birds the charming serpent draws,
　　To drop head-foremost in the jaws
Of vacant darkness and to cease.

XXXV

Yet if some voice that man could trust
　　Should murmur from the narrow house,
　　'The cheeks drop in, the body bows;
Man dies, nor is there hope in dust;'

Might I not say? 'Yet even here,
　　But for one hour, O Love, I strive
　　To keep so sweet a thing alive.'
But I should turn mine ears and hear

The moanings of the homeless sea,
　　The sound of streams that swift or slow
　　Draw down Æonian hills, and sow
The dust of continents to be;

And Love would answer with a sigh,
　　'The sound of that forgetful shore
　　Will change my sweetness more and more,
Half-dead to know that I shall die.'

O me, what profits it to put
　　An idle case? If Death were seen
　　At first as Death, Love had not been,
Or been in narrowest working shut,

Mere fellowship of sluggish moods,
　　Or in his coarsest Satyr-shape
　　Had bruised the herb and crush'd the grape,
And bask'd and batten'd in the woods.

XXXVI

Tho' truths in manhood darkly join,
　　Deep-seated in our mystic frame,
　　We yield all blessing to the name
Of Him that made them current coin;

For Wisdom dealt with mortal powers,
　　Where truth in closest words shall fail,
　　When truth embodied in a tale
Shall enter in at lowly doors.

And so the Word had breath, and wrought
　　With human hands the creed of creeds
　　In loveliness of perfect deeds,
More strong than all poetic thought;

Which he may read that binds the sheaf,
　　Or builds the house, or digs the grave,
　　And those wild eyes that watch the wave
In roarings round the coral reef.

XXXVII

Urania speaks with darken'd brow:
　　'Thou pratest here where thou art least;
　　This faith has many a purer priest,
And many an abler voice than thou.

'Go down beside thy native rill,
　　On thy Parnassus set thy feet,
　　And hear thy laurel whisper sweet
About the ledges of the hill.'

And my Melpomene replies,
　　A touch of shame upon her cheek:
　　'I am not worthy even to speak
Of thy prevailing mysteries;

'For I am but an earthly Muse,
　　And owning but a little art
　　To lull with song an aching heart,
And render human love his dues;

'But brooding on the dear one dead,
　　And all he said of things divine,—
　　And dear to me as sacred wine
To dying lips is all he said,—

'I murmur'd, as I came along,
　　Of comfort clasp'd in truth reveal'd,
　　And loiter'd in the master's field,
And darken'd sanctities with song.'

XXXVIII

With weary steps I loiter on,
　　Tho' always under alter'd skies
　　The purple from the distance dies,
My prospect and horizon gone.

No joy the blowing season gives,
　　The herald melodies of spring,
　　But in the songs I love to sing
A doubtful gleam of solace lives.

If any care for what is here
　　Survive in spirits render'd free,
　　Then are these songs I sing of thee
Not all ungrateful to thine ear.

XXXIX

Old warder of these buried bones,
　　And answering now my random stroke
　　With fruitful cloud and living smoke,
Dark yew, that graspest at the stones

And dippest toward the dreamless head,
　　To thee too comes the golden hour
　　When flower is feeling after flower;
But Sorrow,—fixt upon the dead,

And darkening the dark graves of men,—
　　What whisper'd from her lying lips?
　　Thy gloom is kindled at the tips,
And passes into gloom again.

XL

Could we forget the widow'd hour
   And look on Spirits breathed away,
   As on a maiden in the day
When first she wears her orange-flower!

When crown'd with blessing she doth rise
   To take her latest leave of home,
   And hopes and light regrets that come
Make April of her tender eyes;

And doubtful joys the father move,
   And tears are on the mother's face,
   As parting with a long embrace
She enters other realms of love;

Her office there to rear, to teach,
   Becoming as is meet and fit
   A link among the days, to knit
The generations each with each;

And, doubtless, unto thee is given
   A life that bears immortal fruit
   In those great offices that suit
The full-grown energies of heaven.

Ay me, the difference I discern!
   How often shall her old fireside
   Be cheer'd with tidings of the bride,
How often she herself return,

And tell them all they would have told,
   And bring her babe, and make her boast,
   Till even those that miss'd her most
Shall count new things as dear as old;

But thou and I have shaken hands,
   Till growing winters lay me low;
   My paths are in the fields I know,
And thine in undiscover'd lands.

XLI

Thy spirit ere our fatal loss
   Did ever rise from high to higher,
   As mounts the heavenward altar-fire,
As flies the lighter thro' the gross.

But thou art turn'd to something strange,
    And I have lost the links that bound
    Thy changes; here upon the ground,
No more partaker of thy change.

Deep folly! yet that this could be—
    That I could wing my will with might
    To leap the grades of life and light,
And flash at once, my friend, to thee!

For tho' my nature rarely yields
    To that vague fear implied in death,
    Nor shudders at the gulfs beneath,
The howlings from forgotten fields;

Yet oft when sundown skirts the moor
    An inner trouble I behold,
    A spectral doubt which makes me cold,
That I shall be thy mate no more,

Tho' following with an upward mind
    The wonders that have come to thee,
    Thro' all the secular to-be,
But evermore a life behind.

XLII

I vex my heart with fancies dim.
    He still outstript me in the race;
    It was but unity of place
That made me dream I rank'd with him.

And so may Place retain us still,
    And he the much-beloved again,
    A lord of large experience, train
To riper growth the mind and will;

And what delights can equal those
    That stir the spirit's inner deeps,
    When one that loves, but knows not, reaps
A truth from one that loves and knows?

XLIII

If Sleep and Death be truly one,
    And every spirit's folded bloom
    Thro' all its intervital gloom
In some long trance should slumber on;

Unconscious of the sliding hour,
    Bare of the body, might it last,
    And silent traces of the past
Be all the color of the flower:

So then were nothing lost to man;
    So that still garden of the souls
    In many a figured leaf enrolls
The total world since life began;

And love will last as pure and whole
    As when he loved me here in Time,
    And at the spiritual prime
Rewaken with the dawning soul.

XLIV

How fares it with the happy dead?
    For here the man is more and more;
    But he forgets the days before
God shut the doorways of his head.

The days have vanish'd, tone and tint,
    And yet perhaps the hoarding sense
    Gives out at times—he knows not whence—
A little flash, a mystic hint;

And in the long harmonious years—
    If Death so taste Lethean springs—
    May some dim touch of earthly things
Surprise thee ranging with thy peers.

If such a dreamy touch should fall,
    O, turn thee round, resolve the doubt;
    My guardian angel will speak out
In that high place, and tell thee all.

XLV

The baby new to earth and sky,
    What time his tender palm is prest
    Against the circle of the breast,
Has never thought that 'this is I;'

But as he grows he gathers much,
    And learns the use of 'I' and 'me,'
    And finds 'I am not what I see,
And other than the things I touch.'

So rounds he to a separate mind
   From whence clear memory may begin,
   As thro' the frame that binds him in
His isolation grows defined.

This use may lie in blood and breath,
   Which else were fruitless of their due,
   Had man to learn himself anew
Beyond the second birth of death.

XLVI

We ranging down this lower track,
   The path we came by, thorn and flower,
   Is shadow'd by the growing hour,
Lest life should fail in looking back.

So be it: there no shade can last
   In that deep dawn behind the tomb,
   But clear from marge to marge shall bloom.
The eternal landscape of the past;

A lifelong tract of time reveal'd,
   The fruitful hours of still increase;
   Days order'd in a wealthy peace,
And those five years its richest field.

O Love, thy province were not large,
   A bounded field, nor stretching far;
   Look also, Love, a brooding star,
A rosy warmth from marge to marge.

XLVII

That each, who seems a separate whole,
   Should move his rounds, and fusing all
   The skirts of self again, should fall
Remerging in the general Soul,

Is faith as vague as all unsweet.
   Eternal form shall still divide
   The eternal soul from all beside;
And I shall know him when we meet;

And we shall sit at endless feast,
   Enjoying each the other's good.
   What vaster dream can hit the mood
Of Love on earth? He seeks at least

Upon the last and sharpest height,
  Before the spirits fade away,
  Some landing-place, to clasp and say,
'Farewell! We lose ourselves in light.'

XLVIII

If these brief lays, of Sorrow born,
  Were taken to be such as closed
  Grave doubts and answers here proposed,
Then these were such as men might scorn.

Her care is not to part and prove;
  She takes, when harsher moods remit,
  What slender shade of doubt may flit,
And makes it vassal unto love;

And hence, indeed, she sports with words,
  But better serves a wholesome law,
  And holds it sin and shame to draw
The deepest measure from the chords;

Nor dare she trust a larger lay,
  But rather loosens from the lip
  Short swallow-flights of song, that dip
Their wings in tears, and skim away.

XLIX

From art, from nature, from the schools,
  Let random influences glance,
  Like light in many a shiver'd lance
That breaks about the dappled pools.

The lightest wave of thought shall lisp,
  The fancy's tenderest eddy wreathe,
  The slightest air of song shall breathe
To make the sullen surface crisp.

And look thy look, and go thy way,
  But blame not thou the winds that make
  The seeming-wanton ripple break,
The tender-pencil'd shadow play.

Beneath all fancied hopes and fears
  Ay me, the sorrow deepens down,
  Whose muffled motions blindly drown
The bases of my life in tears.

L

Be near me when my light is low,
    When the blood creeps, and the nerves prick
    And tingle; and the heart is sick,
And all the wheels of being slow.

Be near me when the sensuous frame
    Is rack'd with pangs that conquer trust;
    And Time, a maniac scattering dust,
And Life, a Fury slinging flame.

Be near me when my faith is dry,
    And men the flies of latter spring,
    That lay their eggs, and sting and sing
And weave their petty cells and die.

Be near me when I fade away,
    To point the term of human strife,
    And on the low dark verge of life
The twilight of eternal day.

LI

Do we indeed desire the dead
    Should still be near us at our side?
    Is there no baseness we would hide?
No inner vileness that we dread?

Shall he for whose applause I strove,
    I had such reverence for his blame,
    See with clear eye some hidden shame
And I be lessen'd in his love?

I wrong the grave with fears untrue.
    Shall love be blamed for want of faith?
    There must be wisdom with great Death;
The dead shall look me thro' and thro'.

Be near us when we climb or fall;
    Ye watch, like God, the rolling hours
    With larger other eyes than ours,
To make allowance for us all.

LII

I cannot love thee as I ought,
    For love reflects the thing beloved;
    My words are only words, and moved
Upon the topmost froth of thought.

'Yet blame not thou, thy plaintive song,'
  The Spirit of true love replied;
  'Thou canst not move me from thy side,
Nor human frailty do me wrong.

'What keeps a spirit wholly true
  To that ideal which he bears?
  What record? not the sinless years
That breathed beneath the Syrian blue;

'So fret not, like an idle girl,
  That life is dash'd with flecks of sin.
  Abide; thy wealth is gather'd in,
When Time hath sunder'd shell from pearl.'

LIII

How many a father have I seen,
  A sober man, among his boys,
  Whose youth was full of foolish noise,
Who wears his manhood hale and green;

And dare we to this fancy give,
  That had the wild oat not been sown,
  The soil, left barren, scarce had grown
The grain by which a man may live?

Or, if we held the doctrine sound
  For life outliving heats of youth,
  Yet who would preach it as a truth
To those that eddy round and round?

Hold thou the good, define it well;
  For fear divine Philosophy
  Should push beyond her mark, and be
Procuress to the Lords of Hell.

LIV

O, yet we trust that somehow good
  Will be the final goal of ill,
  To pangs of nature, sins of will,
Defects of doubt, and taints of blood;

That nothing walks with aimless feet;
  That not one life shall be destroy'd,
  Or cast as rubbish to the void,
When God hath made the pile complete;

That not a worm is cloven in vain;
   That not a moth with vain desire
   Is shrivell'd in a fruitless fire,
Or but subserves another's gain.

Behold, we know not anything;
   I can but trust that good shall fall
   At last—far off—at last, to all,
And every winter change to spring.

So runs my dream; but what am I?
   An infant crying in the night;
   An infant crying for the light,
And with no language but a cry.

LV

The wish, that of the living whole
   No life may fail beyond the grave,
   Derives it not from what we have
The likest God within the soul?

Are God and Nature then at strife,
   That Nature lends such evil dreams?
   So careful of the type she seems,
So careless of the single life,

That I, considering everywhere
   Her secret meaning in her deeds,
   And finding that of fifty seeds
She often brings but one to bear,

I falter where I firmly trod,
   And falling with my weight of cares
   Upon the great world's altar-stairs
That slope thro' darkness up to God,

I stretch lame hands of faith, and grope,
   And gather dust and chaff, and call
   To what I feel is Lord of all,
And faintly trust the larger hope.

LVI

'So careful of the type?' but no.
   From scarped cliff and quarried stone
   She cries, 'A thousand types are gone;
I care for nothing, all shall go.

'Thou makest thine appeal to me:
    I bring to life, I bring to death;
    The spirit does but mean the breath:
I know no more.' And he, shall he,

Man, her last work, who seem'd so fair,
    Such splendid purpose in his eyes,
    Who roll'd the psalm to wintry skies,
Who built him fanes of fruitless prayer,

Who trusted God was love indeed
    And love Creation's final law—
    Tho' Nature, red in tooth and claw
With ravine, shriek'd against his creed—

Who loved, who suffer'd countless ills,
    Who battled for the True, the Just,
    Be blown about the desert dust,
Or seal'd within the iron hills?

No more? A monster then, a dream,
    A discord. Dragons of the prime,
    That tare each other in their slime,
Were mellow music match'd with him.

O life as futile, then, as frail!
    O for thy voice to soothe and bless!
    What hope of answer, or redress?
Behind the veil, behind the veil.

LVII

Peace; come away: the song of woe
    Is after all an earthly song.
    Peace; come away: we do him wrong
To sing so wildly: let us go.

Come; let us go: your cheeks are pale;
    But half my life I leave behind.
    Methinks my friend is richly shrined;
But I shall pass, my work will fail.

Yet in these ears, till hearing dies,
    One set slow bell will seem to toll
    The passing of the sweetest soul
That ever look'd with human eyes.

I hear it now, and o'er and o'er,
    Eternal greetings to the dead;
    And 'Ave, Ave, Ave, said,
'Adieu, adieu,' for evermore.

LVIII

In those sad words I took farewell.
    Like echoes in sepulchral halls,
    As drop by drop the water falls
In vaults and catacombs, they fell;

And, falling, idly broke the peace
    Of hearts that beat from day to day,
    Half-conscious of their dying clay,
And those cold crypts where they shall cease.

The high Muse answer'd: 'Wherefore grieve
    Thy brethren with a fruitless tear?
    Abide a little longer here,
And thou shalt take a nobler leave.'

LIX

O Sorrow, wilt thou live with me
    No casual mistress, but a wife,
    My bosom-friend and half of life;
As I confess it needs must be?

O Sorrow, wilt thou rule my blood,
    Be sometimes lovely like a bride,
    And put thy harsher moods aside,
If thou wilt have me wise and good?

My centred passion cannot move,
    Nor will it lessen from to-day;
    But I'll have leave at times to play
As with the creature of my love;

And set thee forth, for thou art mine,
    With so much hope for years to come,
    That, howsoe'er I know thee, some
Could hardly tell what name were thine.

LX

He past, a soul of nobler tone;
    My spirit loved and loves him yet,
    Like some poor girl whose heart is set
On one whose rank exceeds her own.

He mixing with his proper sphere,
 She finds the baseness of her lot,
 Half jealous of she knows not what,
And envying all that meet him there.

The little village looks forlorn;
 She sighs amid her narrow days,
 Moving about the household ways,
In that dark house where she was born.

The foolish neighbors come and go,
 And tease her till the day draws by;
 At night she weeps, 'How vain am I!
How should he love a thing so low?'

LXI

If, in thy second state sublime,
 Thy ransom'd reason change replies
 With all the circle of the wise,
The perfect flower of human time;

And if thou cast thine eyes below,
 How dimly character'd and slight,
 How dwarf'd a growth of cold and night,
How blanch'd with darkness must I grow!

Yet turn thee to the doubtful shore,
 Where thy first form was made a man;
 I loved thee, Spirit, and love, nor can
The soul of Shakespeare love thee more.

LXII

Tho' if an eye that's downward cast
 Could make thee somewhat blench or fail,
 Then be my love an idle tale
And fading legend of the past;

And thou, as one that once declined,
 When he was little more than boy,
 On some unworthy heart with joy,
But lives to wed an equal mind,

And breathes a novel world, the while
 His other passion wholly dies,
 Or in the light of deeper eyes
Is matter for a flying smile.

LXIII

Yet pity for a horse o'er-driven,
    And love in which my hound has part,
    Can hang no weight upon my heart
In its assumptions up to heaven;

And I am so much more than these,
    As thou, perchance, art more than I,
    And yet I spare them sympathy,
And I would set their pains at ease.

So mayst thou watch me where I weep,
    As, unto vaster motions bound,
    The circuits of thine orbit round
A higher height, a deeper deep.

LXIV

Dost thou look back on what hath been,
    As some divinely gifted man,
    Whose life in low estate began
And on a simple village green;

Who breaks his birth's invidious bar,
    And grasps the skirts of happy chance,
    And breasts the blows of circumstance,
And grapples with his evil star;

Who makes by force his merit known
    And lives to clutch the golden keys,
    To mould a mighty state's decrees,
And shape the whisper of the throne;

And moving up from high to higher,
    Becomes on Fortune's crowning slope
    The pillar of a people's hope,
The centre of a world's desire;

Yet feels, as in a pensive dream,
    When all his active powers are still,
    A distant dearness in the hill,
A secret sweetness in the stream,

The limit of his narrower fate,
    While yet beside its vocal springs
    He play'd at counsellors and kings,
With one that was his earliest mate;

Who ploughs with pain his native lea
  And reaps the labor of his hands,
  Or in the furrow musing stands:
'Does my old friend remember me?'

LXV

Sweet soul, do with me as thou wilt;
  I lull a fancy trouble-tost
  With 'Love's too precious to be lost,
A little grain shall not be spilt.'

And in that solace can I sing,
  Till out of painful phases wrought
  There flutters up a happy thought,
Self-balanced on a lightsome wing;

Since we deserved the name of friends,
  And thine effect so lives in me,
  A part of mine may live in thee
And move thee on to noble ends.

LXVI

You thought my heart too far diseased;
  You wonder when my fancies play
  To find me gay among the gay,
Like one with any trifle pleased.

The shade by which my life was crost,
  Which makes a desert in the mind,
  Has made me kindly with my kind,
And like to him whose sight is lost;

Whose feet are guided thro' the land,
  Whose jest among his friends is free,
  Who takes the children on his knee,
And winds their curls about his hand.

He plays with threads, he beats his chair
  For pastime, dreaming of the sky;
  His inner day can never die,
His night of loss is always there.

LXVII

When on my bed the moonlight falls,
  I know that in thy place of rest
  By that broad water of the west
There comes a glory on the walls:

Thy marble bright in dark appears,
  As slowly steals a silver flame
  Along the letters of thy name,
And o'er the number of thy years.

The mystic glory swims away,
  From off my bed the moonlight dies;
  And closing eaves of wearied eyes
I sleep till dusk is dipt in gray;

And then I know the mist is drawn
  A lucid veil from coast to coast,
  And in the dark church like a ghost
Thy tablet glimmers in the dawn.

LXVIII

When in the down I sink my head,
  Sleep, Death's twin-brother, times my breath;
  Sleep, Death's twin-brother, knows not Death,
Nor can I dream of thee as dead.

I walk as ere I walk'd forlorn,
  When all our path was fresh with dew,
  And all the bugle breezes blew
Reveillée to the breaking morn.

But what is this? I turn about,
  I find a trouble in thine eye,
  Which makes me sad I know not why,
Nor can my dream resolve the doubt;

But ere the lark hath left the lea
  I wake, and I discern the truth;
  It is the trouble of my youth
That foolish sleep transfers to thee.

LXIX

I dream'd there would be Spring no more,
  That Nature's ancient power was lost;
  The streets were black with smoke and frost,
They chatter'd trifles at the door;

I wander'd from the noisy town,
  I found a wood with thorny boughs;
  I took the thorns to bind my brows,
I wore them like a civic crown;

I met with scoffs, I met with scorns
From youth and babe and hoary hairs:
They call'd me in the public squares
The fool that wears a crown of thorns.

They call'd me fool, they call'd me child:
I found an angel of the night;
The voice was low, the look was bright;
He look'd upon my crown and smiled.

He reach'd the glory of a hand,
That seem'd to touch it into leaf;
The voice was not the voice of grief,
The words were hard to understand.

LXX

I cannot see the features right,
When on the gloom I strive to paint
The face I know; the hues are faint
And mix with hollow masks of night;

Cloud-towers by ghostly masons wrought,
A gulf that ever shuts and gapes,
A hand that points, and palled shapes
In shadowy thoroughfares of thought;

And crowds that stream from yawning doors,
And shoals of pucker'd faces drive;
Dark bulks that tumble half alive,
And lazy lengths on boundless shores;

Till all at once beyond the will
I hear a wizard music roll,
And thro' a lattice on the soul
Looks thy fair face and makes it still.

LXXI

Sleep, kinsman thou to death and trance
And madness, thou hast forged at last
A night-long present of the past
In which we went thro' summer France.

Hadst thou such credit with the soul?
Then bring an opiate trebly strong,
Drug down the blindfold sense of wrong,
That so my pleasure may be whole;

While now we talk as once we talk'd
    Of men and minds, the dust of change,
    The days that grow to something strange,
In walking as of old we walk'd

Beside the river's wooded reach,
    The fortress, and the mountain ridge,
    The cataract flashing from the bridge,
The breaker breaking on the beach.

LXXII

Risest thou thus, dim dawn, again,
    And howlest, issuing out of night,
    With blasts that blow the poplar white,
And lash with storm the streaming pane?

Day, when my crown'd estate begun
    To pine in that reverse of doom,
    Which sicken'd every living bloom,
And blurr'd the splendor of the sun;

Who usherest in the dolorous hour
    With thy quick tears that make the rose
    Pull sideways, and the daisy close
Her crimson fringes to the shower;

Who mightst have heaved a windless flame
    Up the deep East, or, whispering, play'd
    A chequer-work of beam and shade
Along the hills, yet look'd the same,

As wan, as chill, as wild as now;
    Day, mark'd as with some hideous crime,
    When the dark hand struck down thro' time,
And cancell'd nature's best: but thou,

Lift as thou mayst thy burthen'd brows
    Thro' clouds that drench the morning star,
    And whirl the ungarner'd sheaf afar,
And sow the sky with flying boughs,

And up thy vault with roaring sound
    Climb thy thick noon, disastrous day;
    Touch thy dull goal of joyless gray,
And hide thy shame beneath the ground.

LXXIII

So many worlds, so much to do,
　　So little done, such things to be,
　　How know I what had need of thee,
For thou wert strong as thou wert true?

The fame is quench'd that I foresaw,
　　The head hath miss'd an earthly wreath:
　　I curse not Nature, no, nor Death;
For nothing is that errs from law.

We pass; the path that each man trod
　　Is dim, or will be dim, with weeds.
　　What fame is left for human deeds
In endless age? It rests with God.

O hollow wraith of dying fame,
　　Fade wholly, while the soul exults,
　　And self-infolds the large results
Of force that would have forged a name.

LXXIV

As sometimes in a dead man's face,
　　To those that watch it more and more,
　　A likeness, hardly seen before,
Comes out—to some one of his race;

So, dearest, now thy brows are cold,
　　I see thee what thou art, and know
　　Thy likeness to the wise below,
Thy kindred with the great of old.

But there is more than I can see,
　　And what I see I leave unsaid,
　　Nor speak it, knowing Death has made
His darkness beautiful with thee.

LXXV

I leave thy praises unexpress'd
　　In verse that brings myself relief,
　　And by the measure of my grief
I leave thy greatness to be guess'd.

What practice howsoe'er expert
  In fitting aptest words to things,
  Or voice the richest-toned that sings,
Hath power to give thee as thou wert?

I care not in these fading days
  To raise a cry that lasts not long,
  And round thee with the breeze of song
To stir a little dust of praise.

Thy leaf has perish'd in the green,
  And, while we breathe beneath the sun,
  The world which credits what is done
Is cold to all that might have been.

So here shall silence guard thy fame;
  But somewhere, out of human view,
  Whate'er thy hands are set to do
Is wrought with tumult of acclaim.

LXXVI

Take wings of fancy, and ascend,
  And in a moment set thy face
  Where all the starry heavens of space
Are sharpen'd to a needle's end;

Take wings of foresight; lighten thro'
  The secular abyss to come,
  And lo, thy deepest lays are dumb
Before the mouldering of a yew;

And if the matin songs, that woke
  The darkness of our planet, last,
  Thine own shall wither in the vast,
Ere half the lifetime of an oak.

Ere these have clothed their branchy bowers
  With fifty Mays, thy songs are vain;
  And what are they when these remain
The ruin'd shells of hollow towers?

LXXVII

What hope is here for modern rhyme
  To him who turns a musing eye
  On songs, and deeds, and lives, that lie
Foreshorten'd in the tract of time?

These mortal lullabies of pain
  May bind a book, may line a box,
  May serve to curl a maiden's locks;
Or when a thousand moons shall wane

A man upon a stall may find,
  And, passing, turn the page that tells
  A grief, then changed to something else,
Sung by a long-forgotten mind.

But what of that? My darken'd ways
  Shall ring with music all the same;
  To breathe my loss is more than fame,
To utter love more sweet than praise.

LXXVIII

Again at Christmas did we weave
  The holly round the Christmas hearth;
  The silent snow possess'd the earth,
And calmly fell our Christmas-eve.

The yule-clog sparkled keen with frost,
  No wing of wind the region swept,
  But over all things brooding slept
The quiet sense of something lost.

As in the winters left behind,
  Again our ancient games had place,
  The mimic picture's breathing grace,
And dance and song and hoodman-blind.

Who show'd a token of distress?
  No single tear, no mark of pain—
  O sorrow, then can sorrow wane?
O grief, can grief be changed to less?

O last regret, regret can die!
  No—mixt with all this mystic frame,
  Her deep relations are the same,
But with long use her tears are dry.

LXXIX

'More than my brothers are to me,'—
  Let this not vex thee, noble heart!
  I know thee of what force thou art
To hold the costliest love in fee.

But thou and I are one in kind,
  As moulded like in Nature's mint;
  And hill and wood and field did print
The same sweet forms in either mind.

For us the same cold streamlet curl'd
  Thro' all his eddying coves, the same
  All winds that roam the twilight came
In whispers of the beauteous world.

At one dear knee we proffer'd vows,
  One lesson from one book we learn'd,
  Ere childhood's flaxen ringlet turn'd
To black and brown on kindred brows.

And so my wealth resembles thine,
  But he was rich where I was poor,
  And he supplied my want the more
As his unlikeness fitted mine.

LXXX

If any vague desire should rise,
  That holy Death ere Arthur died
  Had moved me kindly from his side,
And dropt the dust on tearless eyes;

Then fancy shapes, as fancy can,
  The grief my loss in him had wrought,
  A grief as deep as life or thought,
But stay'd in peace with God and man.

I make a picture in the brain;
  I hear the sentence that he speaks;
  He bears the burthen of the weeks,
But turns his burthen into gain.

His credit thus shall set me free;
  And, influence-rich to soothe and save,
  Unused example from the grave
Reach out dead hands to comfort me.

LXXXI

Could I have said while he was here,
  'My love shall now no further range;
  There cannot come a mellower change,
For now is love mature in ear'?

Love, then, had hope of richer store:
What end is here to my complaint?
This haunting whisper makes me faint,
'More years had made me love thee more.'

But Death returns an answer sweet:
'My sudden frost was sudden gain,
And gave all ripeness to the grain
It might have drawn from after-heat.'

LXXXII

I wage not any feud with Death
For changes wrought on form and face;
No lower life that earth's embrace
May breed with him can fright my faith.

Eternal process moving on,
From state to state the spirit walks;
And these are but the shatter'd stalks,
Or ruin'd chrysalis of one.

Nor blame I Death, because he bare
The use of virtue out of earth;
I know transplanted human worth
Will bloom to profit, otherwhere.

For this alone on Death I wreak
The wrath that garners in my heart:
He put our lives so far apart
We cannot hear each other speak.

LXXXIII

Dip down upon the northern shore,
O sweet new-year delaying long;
Thou doest expectant Nature wrong;
Delaying long, delay no more.

What stays thee from the clouded noons
Thy sweetness from its proper place?
Can trouble live with April days,
Or sadness in the summer moons?

Bring orchis, bring the foxglove spire,
The little speedwell's darling blue,
Deep tulips dash'd with fiery dew,
Laburnums, dropping-wells of fire.

O thou, new-year, delaying long,
  Delayest the sorrow in my blood,
  That longs to burst a frozen bud
And flood a fresher throat with song.

LXXXIV

When I contemplate all alone
  The life that had been thine below,
  And fix my thoughts on all the glow
To which thy crescent would have grown;

I see thee sitting crown'd with good,
  A central warmth diffusing bliss
  In glance and smile, and clasp and kiss,
On all the branches of thy blood;

Thy blood, my friend, and partly mine;
  For now the day was drawing on,
  When thou shouldst link thy life with one
Of mine own house, and boys of thine

Had babbled 'Uncle' on my knee;
  But that remorseless iron hour
  Made cypress of her orange flower,
Despair of hope, and earth of thee.

I seem to meet their least desire,
  To clap their cheeks, to call them mine.
  I see their unborn faces shine
Beside the never-lighted fire.

I see myself an honor'd guest,
  Thy partner in the flowery walk
  Of letters, genial table-talk,
Or deep dispute, and graceful jest;

While now thy prosperous labor fills
  The lips of men with honest praise,
  And sun by sun the happy days
Descend below the golden hills

With promise of a morn as fair;
  And all the train of bounteous hours
  Conduct, by paths of growing powers,
To reverence and the silver hair;

Till slowly worn her earthly robe,
　　Her lavish mission richly wrought,
　　Leaving great legacies of thought,
Thy spirit should fail from off the globe;

What time mine own might also flee,
　　As link'd with thine in love and fate,
　　And, hovering o'er the dolorous strait
To the other shore, involved in thee,

Arrive at last the blessed goal,
　　And He that died in Holy Land
　　Would reach us out the shining hand,
And take us as a single soul.

What reed was that on which I leant?
　　Ah, backward fancy, wherefore wake
　　The old bitterness again, and break
The low beginnings of content?

LXXXV

This truth came borne with bier and pall,
　　I felt it, when I sorrow'd most,
　　'Tis better to have loved and lost,
Than never to have loved at all—

O true in word, and tried in deed,
　　Demanding, so to bring relief
　　To this which is our common grief,
What kind of life is that I lead;

And whether trust in things above
　　Be dimm'd of sorrow, or sustain'd;
　　And whether love for him have drain'd
My capabilities of love;

Your words have virtue such as draws
　　A faithful answer from the breast,
　　Thro' light reproaches, half exprest,
And loyal unto kindly laws.

My blood an even tenor kept,
　　Till on mine ear this message falls,
　　That in Vienna's fatal walls
God's finger touch'd him, and he slept.

The great Intelligences fair
  That range above our mortal state,
  In circle round the blessed gate,
Received and gave him welcome there;

And led him thro' the blissful climes,
  And show'd him in the fountain fresh
  All knowledge that the sons of flesh
Shall gather in the cycled times.

But I remain'd, whose hopes were dim,
  Whose life, whose thoughts were little worth,
  To wander on a darken'd earth,
Where all things round me breathed of him.

O friendship, equal-poised control,
  O heart, with kindliest motion warm,
  O sacred essence, other form,
O solemn ghost, O crowned soul!

Yet none could better know than I,
  How much of act at human hands
  The sense of human will demands
By which we dare to live or die.

Whatever way my days decline,
  I felt and feel, tho' left alone,
  His being working in mine own,
The footsteps of his life in mine;

A life that all the Muses deck'd
  With gifts of grace, that might express
  All-comprehensive tenderness,
All-subtilizing intellect:

And so my passion hath not swerved
  To works of weakness, but I find
  An image comforting the mind,
And in my grief a strength reserved.

Likewise the imaginative woe,
  That loved to handle spiritual strife,
  Diffused the shock thro' all my life,
But in the present broke the blow.

My pulses therefore beat again
  For other friends that once I met;
  Nor can it suit me to forget
The mighty hopes that make us men.

I woo your love: I count it crime
  To mourn for any overmuch;
  I, the divided half of such
A friendship as had master'd Time;

Which masters Time indeed, and is
  Eternal, separate from fears.
  The all-assuming months and years
Can take no part away from this;

But Summer on the steaming floods,
  And Spring that swells the narrow brooks,
  And Autumn, with a noise of rooks,
That gather in the waning woods,

And every pulse of wind and wave
  Recalls, in change of light or gloom,
  My old affection of the tomb,
And my prime passion in the grave.

My old affection of the tomb,
  A part of stillness, yearns to speak:
  'Arise, and get thee forth and seek
A friendship for the years to come.

'I watch thee from the quiet shore;
  Thy spirit up to mine can reach;
  But in dear words of human speech
We two communicate no more.'

And I, 'Can clouds of nature stain
  The starry clearness of the free?
  How is it? Canst thou feel for me
Some painless sympathy with pain?'

And lightly does the whisper fall:
  ' 'Tis hard for thee to fathom this;
  I triumph in conclusive bliss,
And that serene result of all.'

So hold I commerce with the dead;
  Or so methinks the dead would say;
  Or so shall grief with symbols play
And pining life be fancy-fed.

Now looking to some settled end,
  That these things pass, and I shall prove
  A meeting somewhere, love with love,
I crave your pardon, O my friend;

If not so fresh, with love as true,
   I, clasping brother-hands, aver
   I could not, if I would, transfer
The whole I felt for him to you.

For which be they that hold apart
   The promise of the golden hours?
   First love, first friendship, equal powers
That marry with the virgin heart.

Still mine, that cannot but deplore,
   That beats within a lonely place,
   That yet remembers his embrace,
But at his footstep leaps no more,

My heart, tho' widow'd, may not rest
   Quite in the love of what is gone,
   But seeks to beat in time with one
That warms another living breast.

Ah, take the imperfect gift I bring,
   Knowing the primrose yet is dear,
   The primrose of the later year,
As not unlike to that of Spring.

LXXXVI

Sweet after showers, ambrosial air,
   That rollest from the gorgeous gloom
   Of evening over brake and bloom
And meadow, slowly breathing bare

The round of space, and rapt below
   Thro' all the dewy tassell'd wood,
   And shadowing down the horned flood
In ripples, fan my brows and blow

The fever from my cheek, and sigh
   The full new life that feeds thy breath
   Throughout my frame, till Doubt and Death,
Ill brethren, let the fancy fly

From belt to belt of crimson seas
   On leagues of odor streaming far,
   To where in yonder orient star
A hundred spirits whisper 'Peace.'

LXXXVII

I past beside the reverend walls
   In which of old I wore the gown;
   I roved at random thro' the town,
And saw the tumult of the halls;

And heard once more in college fanes
   The storm their high-built organs make,
   And thunder-music, rolling, shake
The prophet blazon'd on the panes;

And caught once more the distant shout,
   The measured pulse of racing oars
   Among the willows; paced the shores
And many a bridge, and all about

The same gray flats again, and felt
   The same, but not the same; and last
   Up that long walk of limes I past
To see the rooms in which he dwelt.

Another name was on the door.
   I linger'd; all within was noise
   Of songs, and clapping hands, and boys
That crash'd the glass and beat the floor;

Where once we held debate, a band
   Of youthful friends, on mind and art,
   And labor, and the changing mart,
And all the framework of the land;

When one would aim an arrow fair,
   But send it slackly from the string;
   And one would pierce an outer ring,
And one an inner, here and there;

And last the master-bowman, he,
   Would cleave the mark. A willing ear
   We lent him. Who but hung to hear
The rapt oration flowing free

From point to point, with power and grace
   And music in the bounds of law,
   To those conclusions when we saw
The God within him light his face,

And seem to lift the form, and glow
   In azure orbits heavenly-wise;
   And over those ethereal eyes
The bar of Michael Angelo?

LXXXVIII

Wild bird, whose warble, liquid sweet,
   Rings Eden thro' the budded quicks,
   O, tell me where the senses mix,
O, tell me where the passions meet,

Whence radiate: fierce extremes employ
   Thy spirits in the darkening leaf,
   And in the midmost heart of grief
Thy passion clasps a secret joy;

And I—my harp would prelude woe—
   I cannot all command the strings;
   The glory of the sum of things
Will flash along the chords and go.

LXXXIX

Witch-elms that counterchange the floor
   Of this flat lawn with dusk and bright;
   And thou, with all thy breadth and height
Of foliage, towering sycamore;

How often, hither wandering down,
   My Arthur found your shadows fair,
   And shook to all the liberal air
The dust and din and steam of town!

He brought an eye for all he saw;
   He mixt in all our simple sports;
   They pleased him, fresh from brawling courts
And dusty purlieus of the law.

O joy to him in this retreat,
   Immantled in ambrosial dark,
   To drink the cooler air, and mark
The landscape winking thro' the heat!

O sound to rout the brood of cares,
   The sweep of scythe in morning dew,
   The gust that round the garden flew,
And tumbled half the mellowing pears!

O bliss, when all in circle drawn
  About him, heart and ear were fed
  To hear him, as he lay and read
The Tuscan poets on the lawn!

Or in the all-golden afternoon
  A guest, or happy sister, sung,
  Or here she brought the harp and flung
A ballad to the brightening moon.

Nor less it pleased in livelier moods,
  Beyond the bounding hill to stray,
  And break the livelong summer day
With banquet in the distant woods;

Whereat we glanced from theme to theme,
  Discuss'd the books to love or hate,
  Or touch'd the changes of the state,
Or threaded some Socratic dream;

But if I praised the busy town,
  He loved to rail against it still,
  For 'ground in yonder social mill
We rub each other's angles down,

'And merge,' he said, 'in form and gloss
  The picturesque of man and man.'
  We talk'd: the stream beneath us ran,
The wine-flask lying couch'd in moss,

Or cool'd within the glooming wave;
  And last, returning from afar,
  Before the crimson-circled star
Had fall'n into her father's grave,

And brushing ankle-deep in flowers,
  We heard behind the woodbine veil
  The milk that bubbled in the pail,
And buzzings of the honeyed hours.

XC

He tasted love with half his mind,
  Nor ever drank the inviolate spring
  Where nighest heaven, who first could fling
This bitter seed among mankind:

That could the dead, whose dying eyes
   Were closed with wail, resume their life,
   They would but find in child and wife
An iron welcome when they rise.

'Twas well, indeed, when warm with wine,
   To pledge them with a kindly tear,
   To talk them o'er, to wish them here,
To count their memories half divine;

But if they came who past away,
   Behold their brides in other hands;
   The hard heir strides about their lands,
And will not yield them for a day.

Yea, tho' their sons were none of these,
   Not less the yet-loved sire would make
   Confusion worse than death, and shake
The pillars of domestic peace.

Ah, dear, but come thou back to me!
   Whatever change the years have wrought,
   I find not yet one lonely thought
That cries against my wish for thee.

XCI

When rosy plumelets tuft the larch,
   And rarely pipes the mounted thrush,
   Or underneath the barren bush
Flits by the sea-blue bird of March;

Come, wear the form by which I know
   Thy spirit in time among thy peers;
   The hope of unaccomplish'd years
Be large and lucid round thy brow.

When summer's hourly-mellowing change
   May breathe, with many roses sweet,
   Upon the thousand waves of wheat
That ripple round the lowly grange,

Come; not in watches of the night,
   But where the sunbeam broodeth warm.
   Come, beauteous in thine after form,
And like a finer light in light.

XCII

If any vision should reveal
   Thy likeness, I might count it vain
   As but the canker of the brain;
Yea, tho' it spake and made appeal

To chances where our lots were cast
   Together in the days behind,
   I might but say, I hear a wind
Of memory murmuring the past.

Yea, tho' it spake and bared to view
   A fact within the coming year;
   And tho' the months, revolving near,
Should prove the phantom-warning true,

They might not seem thy prophecies,
   But spiritual presentiments,
   And such refraction of events
As often rises ere they rise.

XCIII

I shall not see thee. Dare I say
   No spirit ever brake the band
   That stays him from the native land
Where first he walk'd when claspt in clay?

No visual shade of some one lost,
   But he, the Spirit himself, may come
   Where all the nerve of sense is numb,
Spirit to Spirit, Ghost to Ghost.

O, therefore from thy sightless range
   With gods in unconjectured bliss,
   O, from the distance of the abyss
Of tenfold-complicated change,

Descend, and touch, and enter; hear
   The wish too strong for words to name,
   That in this blindness of the frame
My Ghost may feel that thine is near.

XCIV

How pure at heart and sound in head,
　　With what divine affections bold
　　Should be the man whose thought would hold
An hour's communion with the dead.

In vain shalt thou, or any, call
　　The spirits from their golden day,
　　Except, like them, thou too canst say,
My spirit is at peace with all.

They haunt the silence of the breast,
　　Imaginations calm and fair,
　　The memory like a cloudless air,
The conscience as a sea at rest;

But when the heart is full of din,
　　And doubt beside the portal waits,
　　They can but listen at the gates,
And hear the household jar within.

XCV

By night we linger'd on the lawn,
　　For underfoot the herb was dry;
　　And genial warmth; and o'er the sky
The silvery haze of summer drawn;

And calm that let the tapers burn
　　Unwavering: not a cricket chirr'd;
　　The brook alone far-off was heard,
And on the board the fluttering urn.

And bats went round in fragrant skies,
　　And wheel'd or lit the filmy shapes
　　That haunt the dusk, with ermine capes
And woolly breasts and beaded eyes;

While now we sang old songs that peal'd
　　From knoll to knoll, where, couch'd at ease,
　　The white kine glimmer'd, and the trees
Laid their dark arms about the field.

But when those others, one by one,
　　Withdrew themselves from me and night,
　　And in the house light after light
Went out, and I was all alone,

A hunger seized my heart; I read
   Of that glad year which once had been,
   In those fall'n leaves which kept their green,
The noble letters of the dead.

And strangely on the silence broke
   The silent-speaking words, and strange
   Was love's dumb cry defying change
To test his worth; and strangely spoke

The faith, the vigor, bold to dwell
   On doubts that drive the coward back,
   And keen thro' wordy snares to track
Suggestion to her inmost cell.

So word by word, and line by line,
   The dead man touch'd me from the past,
   And all at once it seem'd at last
The living soul was flash'd on mine,

And mine in this was wound, and whirl'd
   About empyreal heights of thought,
   And came on that which is, and caught
The deep pulsations of the world,

Æonian music measuring out
   The steps of Time—the shocks of Chance—
   The blows of Death. At length my trance
Was cancell'd, stricken thro' with doubt.

Vague words! but ah, how hard to frame
   In matter-moulded forms of speech,
   Or even for intellect to reach
Thro' memory that which I became;

Till now the doubtful dusk reveal'd
   The knolls once more where, couch'd at ease,
   The white kine glimmer'd, and the trees
Laid their dark arms about the field;

And suck'd from out the distant gloom
   A breeze began to tremble o'er
   The large leaves of the sycamore,
And fluctuate all the still perfume,

And gathering freshlier overhead,
   Rock'd the full-foliaged elms, and swung
   The heavy-folded rose, and flung
The lilies to and fro, and said,

'The dawn, the dawn,' and died away;
   And East and West, without a breath,
   Mixt their dim lights, like life and death,
To broaden into boundless day.

XCVI

You say, but with no touch of scorn,
   Sweet-hearted, you, whose light-blue eyes
   Are tender over drowning flies,
You tell me, doubt is Devil-born.

I know not: one indeed I knew
   In many a subtle question versed,
   Who touch'd a jarring lyre at first,
But ever strove to make it true;

Perplext in faith, but pure in deeds,
   At last he beat his music out.
   There lives more faith in honest doubt,
Believe me, than in half the creeds.

He fought his doubts and gather'd strength,
   He would not make his judgment blind,
   He faced the spectres of the mind
And laid them; thus he came at length

To find a stronger faith his own,
   And Power was with him in the night,
   Which makes the darkness and the light,
And dwells not in the light alone,

But in the darkness and the cloud,
   As over Sinai's peaks of old,
   While Israel made their gods of gold,
Altho' the trumpet blew so loud.

XCVII

My love has talk'd with rocks and trees;
   He finds on misty mountain-ground
   His own vast shadow glory-crown'd;
He sees himself in all he sees.

Two partners of a married life—
   I look'd on these and thought of thee
   In vastness and in mystery,
And of my spirit as of a wife.

These two—they dwelt with eye on eye,
  Their hearts of old have beat in tune,
  Their meetings made December June,
Their every parting was to die.

Their love has never past away;
  The days she never can forget
  Are earnest that he loves her yet,
Whate'er the faithless people say.

Her life is lone, he sits apart,
  He loves her yet, she will not weep,
  Tho' rapt in matters dark and deep
He seems to slight her simple heart.

He thrids the labyrinth of the mind,
  He reads the secret of the star,
  He seems so near and yet so far,
He looks so cold: she thinks him kind.

She keeps the gift of years before,
  A wither'd violet is her bliss;
  She knows not what his greatness is,
For that, for all, she loves him more.

For him she plays, to him she sings
  Of early faith and plighted vows;
  She knows but matters of the house,
And he, he knows a thousand things.

Her faith is fixt and cannot move,
  She darkly feels him great and wise,
  She dwells on him with faithful eyes,
'I cannot understand; I love.'

XCVIII

You leave us: you will see the Rhine,
  And those fair hills I sail'd below,
  When I was there with him; and go
By summer belts of wheat and vine

To where he breathed his latest breath,
  That city. All her splendor seems
  No livelier than the wisp that gleams
On Lethe in the eyes of Death.

Let her great Danube rolling fair
　　Enwind her isles, unmark'd of me;
　　I have not seen, I will not see
Vienna; rather dream that there,

A treble darkness, Evil haunts
　　The birth, the bridal; friend from friend
　　Is oftener parted, fathers bend
Above more graves, a thousand wants

Gnarr at the heels of men, and prey
　　By each cold hearth, and sadness flings
　　Her shadow on the blaze of kings.
And yet myself have heard him say,

That not in any mother town
　　With statelier progress to and fro
　　The double tides of chariots flow
By park and suburb under brown

Of lustier leaves; nor more content,
　　He told me, lives in any crowd,
　　When all is gay with lamps, and loud
With sport and song, in booth and tent,

Imperial halls, or open plain;
　　And wheels the circled dance, and breaks
　　The rocket molten into flakes
Of crimson or in emerald rain.

XCIX

Risest thou thus, dim dawn, again,
　　So loud with voices of the birds,
　　So thick with lowings of the herds,
Day, when I lost the flower of men;

Who tremblest thro' thy darkling red
　　On yon swoll'n brook that bubbles fast
　　By meadows breathing of the past,
And woodlands holy to the dead;

Who murmurest in the foliaged eaves
　　A song that slights the coming care,
　　And Autumn laying here and there
A fiery finger on the leaves;

Who wakenest with thy balmy breath
    To myriads on the genial earth,
    Memories of bridal, or of birth,
And unto myriads more, of death.

O, wheresoever those may be,
    Betwixt the slumber of the poles,
    To-day they count as kindred souls;
They know me not, but mourn with me.

C

I climb the hill: from end to end
    Of all the landscape underneath,
    I find no place that does not breathe
Some gracious memory of my friend;

No gray old grange, or lonely fold,
    Or low morass and whispering reed,
    Or simple stile from mead to mead,
Or sheepwalk up the windy wold;

Nor hoary knoll of ash and haw
    That hears the latest linnet trill,
    Nor quarry trench'd along the hill
And haunted by the wrangling daw;

Nor runlet tinkling from the rock;
    Nor pastoral rivulet that swerves
    To left and right thro' meadowy curves,
That feed the mothers of the flock;

But each has pleased a kindred eye,
    And each reflects a kindlier day;
    And, leaving these, to pass away,
I think once more he seems to die.

CI

Unwatch'd, the garden bough shall sway,
    The tender blossom flutter down,
    Unloved, that beech will gather brown,
This maple burn itself away;

Unloved, the sunflower, shining fair,
    Ray round with flames her disk of seed,
    And many a rose-carnation feed
With summer spice the humming air;

Unloved, by many a sandy bar,
　　The brook shall babble down the plain,
　　At noon or when the Lesser Wain
Is twisting round the polar star;

Uncared for, gird the windy grove,
　　And flood the haunts of hern and crake,
　　Or into silver arrows break
The sailing moon in creek and cove;

Till from the garden and the wild
　　A fresh association blow,
　　And year by year the landscape grow
Familiar to the stranger's child;

As year by year the laborer tills
　　His wonted glebe, or lops the glades,
　　And year by year our memory fades
From all the circle of the hills.

CII

We leave the well-beloved place
　　Where first we gazed upon the sky;
　　The roofs that heard our earliest cry
Will shelter one of stranger race.

We go, but ere we go from home,
　　As down the garden-walks I move,
　　Two spirits of a diverse love
Contend for loving masterdom.

One whispers, 'Here thy boyhood sung
　　Long since its matin song, and heard
　　The low love-language of the bird
In native hazels tassel-hung.'

The other answers, 'Yea, but here
　　Thy feet have stray'd in after hours
　　With thy lost friend among the bowers,
And this hath made them trebly dear.'

These two have striven half the day,
　　And each prefers his separate claim,
　　Poor rivals in a losing game,
That will not yield each other way.

I turn to go; my feet are set
　To leave the pleasant fields and farms;
　They mix in one another's arms
To one pure image of regret.

CIII

On that last night before we went
　From out the doors where I was bred,
　I dream'd a vision of the dead,
Which left my after-morn content.

Methought I dwelt within a hall,
　And maidens with me; distant hills
　From hidden summits fed with rills
A river sliding by the wall.

The hall with harp and carol rang.
　They sang of what is wise and good
　And graceful. In the centre stood
A statue veil'd, to which they sang;

And which, tho' veil'd, was known to me,
　The shape of him I loved, and love
　For ever. Then flew in a dove
And brought a summons from the sea;

And when they learnt that I must go,
　They wept and wail'd, but led the way
　To where a little shallop lay
At anchor in the flood below;

And on by many a level mead,
　And shadowing bluff that made the banks,
　We glided winding under ranks
Of iris and the golden reed;

And still as vaster grew the shore
　And roll'd the floods in grander space,
　The maidens gather'd strength and grace
And presence, lordlier than before;

And I myself, who sat apart
　And watch'd them, wax'd in every limb;
　I felt the thews of Anakim,
The pulses of a Titan's heart;

As one would sing the death of war,
    And one would chant the history
    Of that great race which is to be,
And one the shaping of a star;

Until the forward-creeping tides
    Began to foam, and we to draw
    From deep to deep, to where we saw
A great ship lift her shining sides.

The man we loved was there on deck,
    But thrice as large as man he bent
    To greet us. Up the side I went,
And fell in silence on his neck;

Whereat those maidens with one mind
    Bewail'd their lot; I did them wrong:
    'We served thee here,' they said, 'so long,
And wilt thou leave us now behind?'

So rapt I was, they could not win
    An answer from my lips, but he
    Replying, 'Enter likewise ye
And go with us:' they enter'd in.

And while the wind began to sweep
    A music out of sheet and shroud,
    We steer'd her toward a crimson cloud
That landlike slept along the deep.

CIV

The time draws near the birth of Christ;
    The moon is hid, the night is still;
    A single church below the hill
Is pealing, folded in the mist.

A single peal of bells below,
    That wakens at this hour of rest
    A single murmur in the breast,
That these are not the bells I know.

Like strangers' voices here they sound,
    In lands where not a memory strays,
    Nor landmark breathes of other days,
But all is new unhallow'd ground.

CV

To-night ungather'd let us leave
  This laurel, let this holly stand:
  We live within the stranger's land,
And strangely falls our Christmas-eve.

Our father's dust is left alone
  And silent under other snows:
  There in due time the woodbine blows,
The violet comes, but we are gone.

No more shall wayward grief abuse
  The genial hour with mask and mime;
  For change of place, like growth of time,
Has broke the bond of dying use.

Let cares that petty shadows cast,
  By which our lives are chiefly proved,
  A little spare the night I loved,
And hold it solemn to the past.

But let no footstep beat the floor,
  Nor bowl of wassail mantle warm;
  For who would keep an ancient form
Thro' which the spirit breathes no more?

Be neither song, nor game, nor feast;
  Nor harp be touch'd, nor flute be blown;
  No dance, no motion, save alone
What lightens in the lucid East

Of rising worlds by yonder wood.
  Long sleeps the summer in the seed;
  Run out your measured arcs, and lead
The closing cycle rich in good.

CVI

Ring out, wild bells, to the wild sky,
  The flying cloud, the frosty light:
  The year is dying in the night;
Ring out, wild bells, and let him die.

Ring out the old, ring in the new,
  Ring, happy bells, across the snow:
  The year is going, let him go;
Ring out the false, ring in the true.

Ring out the grief that saps the mind,
    For those that here we see no more;
    Ring out the feud of rich and poor,
Ring in redress to all mankind.

Ring out a slowly dying cause,
    And ancient forms of party strife;
    Ring in the nobler modes of life,
With sweeter manners, purer laws.

Ring out the want, the care, the sin,
    The faithless coldness of the times;
    Ring out, ring out my mournful rhymes,
But ring the fuller minstrel in.

Ring out false pride in place and blood,
    The civic slander and the spite;
    Ring in the love of truth and right,
Ring in the common love of good.

Ring out old shapes of foul disease;
    Ring out the narrowing lust of gold;
    Ring out the thousand wars of old,
Ring in the thousand years of peace.

Ring in the valiant man and free,
    The larger heart, the kindlier hand;
    Ring out the darkness of the land,
Ring in the Christ that is to be.

CVII

It is the day when he was born,
    A bitter day that early sank
    Behind a purple-frosty bank
Of vapor, leaving night forlorn.

The time admits not flowers or leaves
    To deck the banquet. Fiercely flies
    The blast of North and East, and ice
Makes daggers at the sharpen'd eaves,

And bristles all the brakes and thorns
    To yon hard crescent, as she hangs
    Above the wood which grides and clangs
Its leafless ribs and iron horns

Together, in the drifts that pass
　　To darken on the rolling brine
　　That breaks the coast. But fetch the wine,
Arrange the board and brim the glass;

Bring in great logs and let them lie,
　　To make a solid core of heat;
　　Be cheerful-minded, talk and treat
Of all things ev'n as he were by;

We keep the day. With festal cheer,
　　With books and music, surely we
　　Will drink to him, whate'er he be,
And sing the songs he loved to hear.

CVIII

I will not shut me from my kind,
　　And, lest I stiffen into stone,
　　I will not eat my heart alone,
Nor feed with sighs a passing wind:

What profit lies in barren faith,
　　And vacant yearning, tho' with might
　　To scale the heaven's highest height,
Or dive below the wells of death?

What find I in the highest place,
　　But mine own phantom chanting hymns?
　　And on the depths of death there swims
The reflex of a human face.

I'll rather take what fruit may be
　　Of sorrow under human skies:
　　'T is held that sorrow makes us wise,
Whatever wisdom sleep with thee.

CIX

Heart-affluence in discursive talk
　　From household fountains never dry;
　　The critic clearness of an eye
That saw thro' all the Muses' walk;

Seraphic intellect and force
　　To seize and throw the doubts of man;
　　Impassion'd logic, which outran
The hearer in its fiery course;

High nature amorous of the good,
    But touch'd with no ascetic gloom;
    And passion pure in snowy bloom
Thro' all the years of April blood;

A love of freedom rarely felt,
    Of freedom in her regal seat
    Of England; not the schoolboy heat,
The blind hysterics of the Celt;

And manhood fused with female grace
    In such a sort, the child would twine
    A trustful hand, unask'd, in thine,
And find his comfort in thy face;

All these have been, and thee mine eyes
    Have look'd on: if they look'd in vain,
    My shame is greater who remain,
Nor let thy wisdom make me wise.

CX

Thy converse drew us with delight,
    The men of rathe and riper years;
    The feeble soul, a haunt of fears,
Forgot his weakness in thy sight.

On thee the loyal-hearted hung,
    The proud was half disarm'd of pride,
    Nor cared the serpent at thy side
To flicker with his double tongue.

The stern were mild when thou wert by,
    The flippant put himself to school
    And heard thee, and the brazen fool
Was soften'd, and he knew not why;

While I, thy nearest, sat apart,
    And felt thy triumph was as mine;
    And loved them more, that they were thine,
The graceful tact, the Christian art;

Nor mine the sweetness or the skill,
    But mine the love that will not tire,
    And, born of love, the vague desire
That spurs an imitative will.

CXI

The churl in spirit, up or down
  Along the scale of ranks, thro' all,
  To him who grasps a golden ball,
By blood a king, at heart a clown,—

The churl in spirit, howe'er he veil
  His want in forms for fashion's sake,
  Will let his coltish nature break
At season's thro' the gilded pale;

For who can always act? but he,
  To whom a thousand memories call,
  Not being less but more than all
The gentleness he seem'd to be,

Best seem'd the thing he was, and join'd
  Each office of the social hour
  To noble manners, as the flower
And native growth of noble mind;

Nor ever narrowness or spite,
  Or villain fancy fleeting by,
  Drew in the expression of an eye
Where God and Nature met in light;

And thus he bore without abuse
  The grand old name of gentleman,
  Defamed by every charlatan,
And soil'd with all ignoble use.

CXII

High wisdom holds my wisdom less,
  That I, who gaze with temperate eyes
  On glorious insufficiencies,
Set light by narrower perfectness.

But thou, that fillest all the room
  Of all my love, art reason why
  I seem to cast a careless eye
On souls, the lesser lords of doom.

For what wert thou? some novel power
  Sprang up for ever at a touch,
  And hope could never hope too much,
In watching thee from hour to hour,

Large elements in order brought,
    And tracts of calm from tempest made,
    And world-wide fluctuation sway'd
In vassal tides that follow'd thought.

CXIII

'T is held that sorrow makes us wise;
    Yet how much wisdom sleeps with thee
    Which not alone had guided me,
But served the seasons that may rise;

For can I doubt, who knew thee keen
    In intellect, with force and skill
    To strive, to fashion, to fulfil—
I doubt not what thou wouldst have been:

A life in civic action warm,
    A soul on highest mission sent,
    A potent voice of Parliament,
A pillar steadfast in the storm,

Should licensed boldness gather force,
    Becoming, when the time has birth,
    A lever to uplift the earth
And roll it in another course,

With thousand shocks that come and go,
    With agonies, with energies,
    With overthrowings, and with cries,
And undulations to and fro.

CXIV

Who loves not Knowledge? Who shall rail
    Against her beauty? May she mix
    With men and prosper! Who shall fix
Her pillars? Let her work prevail.

But on her forehead sits a fire;
    She sets her forward countenance
    And leaps into the future chance,
Submitting all things to desire.

Half-grown as yet, a child, and vain—
    She cannot fight the fear of death.
    What is she, cut from love and faith,
But some wild Pallas from the brain

Of demons? fiery-hot to burst
  All barriers in her onward race
  For power. Let her know her place;
She is the second, not the first.

A higher hand must make her mild,
  If all be not in vain, and guide
  Her footsteps, moving side by side
With Wisdom, like the younger child;

For she is earthly of the mind,
  But Wisdom heavenly of the soul.
  O friend, who camest to thy goal
So early, leaving me behind,

I would the great world grew like thee,
  Who grewest not alone in power
  And knowledge, but by year and hour
In reverence and in charity.

CXV

Now fades the last long streak of snow,
  Now burgeons every maze of quick
  About the flowering squares, and thick
By ashen roots the violets blow.

Now rings the woodland loud and long,
  The distance takes a lovelier hue,
  And drown'd in yonder living blue
The lark becomes a sightless song.

Now dance the lights on lawn and lea,
  The flocks are whiter down the vale,
  And milkier every milky sail
On winding stream or distant sea;

Where now the seamew pipes, or dives
  In yonder greening gleam, and fly
  The happy birds, that change their sky
To build and brood, that live their lives

From land to land; and in my breast
  Spring wakens too, and my regret
  Becomes an April violet,
And buds and blossoms like the rest.

CXVI

Is it, then, regret for buried time
    That keenlier in sweet April wakes,
    And meets the year, and gives and takes
The colors of the crescent prime?

Not all: the songs, the stirring air,
    The life re-orient out of dust,
    Cry thro' the sense to hearten trust
In that which made the world so fair.

Not all regret: the face will shine
    Upon me, while I muse alone,
    And that dear voice, I once have known,
Still speak to me of me and mine.

Yet less of sorrow lives in me
    For days of happy commune dead,
    Less yearning for the friendship fled
Than some strong bond which is to be.

CXVII

O days and hours, your work is this,
    To hold me from my proper place,
    A little while from his embrace,
For fuller gain of after bliss;

That out of distance might ensue
    Desire of nearness doubly sweet,
    And unto meeting, when we meet,
Delight a hundredfold accrue,

For every grain of sand that runs,
    And every span of shade that steals,
    And every kiss of toothed wheels,
And all the courses of the suns.

CXVIII

Contemplate all this work of Time,
    The giant laboring in his youth;
    Nor dream of human love and truth,
As dying Nature's earth and lime;

But trust that those we call the dead
   Are breathers of an ampler day
   For ever nobler ends. They say,
The solid earth whereon we tread

In tracts of fluent heat began,
   And grew to seeming-random forms,
   The seeming prey of cyclic storms,
Till at the last arose the man;

Who throve and branch'd from clime to clime,
   The herald of a higher race,
   And of himself in higher place,
If so he type this work of time

Within himself, from more to more;
   Or, crown'd with attributes of woe
   Like glories, move his course, and show
That life is not as idle ore,

But iron dug from central gloom,
   And heated hot with burning fears,
   And dipt in baths of hissing tears,
And batter'd with the shocks of doom

To shape and use. Arise and fly
   The reeling Faun, the sensual feast;
   Move upward, working out the beast,
And let the ape and tiger die.

CXIX

Doors, where my heart was used to beat
   So quickly, not as one that weeps
   I come once more; the city sleeps;
I smell the meadow in the street;

I hear a chirp of birds; I see
   Betwixt the black fronts long-withdrawn
   A light-blue lane of early dawn,
And think of early days and thee,

And bless thee, for thy lips are bland,
   And bright the friendship of thine eye;
   And in my thoughts with scarce a sigh
I take the pressure of thine hand.

CXX

I trust I have not wasted breath:
  I think we are not wholly brain,
  Magnetic mockeries; not in vain,
Like Paul with beasts, I fought with Death;

Not only cunning casts in clay:
  Let Science prove we are, and then
  What matters Science unto men,
At least to me? I would not stay.

Let him, the wiser man who springs
  Hereafter, up from childhood shape
  His action like the greater ape,
But I was *born* to other things.

CXXI

Sad Hesper o'er the buried sun
  And ready, thou, to die with him,
  Thou watchest all things ever dim
And dimmer, and a glory done.

The team is loosen'd from the wain,
  The boat is drawn upon the shore;
  Thou listenest to the closing door,
And life is darken'd in the brain.

Bright Phosphor, fresher for the night,
  By thee the world's great work is heard
  Beginning, and the wakeful bird;
Behind thee comes the greater light.

The market boat is on the stream,
  And voices hail it from the brink;
  Thou hear'st the village hammer clink,
And see'st the moving of the team.

Sweet Hesper-Phosphor, double name
  For what is one, the first, the last,
  Thou, like my present and my past,
Thy place is changed; thou art the same.

CXXII

O, wast thou with me, dearest, then,
  While I rose up against my doom,
  And yearn'd to burst the folded gloom,
To bare the eternal heavens again,

To feel once more, in placid awe,
  The strong imagination roll
  A sphere of stars about my soul,
In all her motion one with law?

If thou wert with me, and the grave
  Divide us not, be with me now,
  And enter in at breast and brow,
Till all my blood, a fuller wave,

Be quicken'd with a livelier breath,
  And like an inconsiderate boy,
  As in the former flash of joy,
I slip the thoughts of life and death;

And all the breeze of Fancy blows,
  And every dewdrop paints a bow,
  The wizard lightnings deeply glow,
And every thought breaks out a rose.

CXXIII

There rolls the deep where grew the tree.
  O earth, what changes hast thou seen!
  There where the long street roars hath been
The stillness of the central sea.

The hills are shadows, and they flow
  From form to form, and nothing stands;
  They melt like mist, the solid lands,
Like clouds they shape themselves and go.

But in my spirit will I dwell,
  And dream my dream, and hold it true;
  For tho' my lips may breathe adieu,
I cannot think the thing farewell.

CXXIV

That which we dare invoke to bless;
    Our dearest faith; our ghastliest doubt;
    He, They, One, All; within, without;
The Power in darkness whom we guess,—

I found Him not in world or sun,
    Or eagle's wing, or insect's eye,
    Nor thro' the questions men may try,
The petty cobwebs we have spun.

If e'er when faith had fallen asleep,
    I heard a voice, 'believe no more,'
    And heard an ever-breaking shore
That tumbled in the Godless deep,

A warmth within the breast would melt
    The freezing reason's colder part,
    And like a man in wrath the heart
Stood up and answer'd, 'I have felt.'

No, like a child in doubt and fear:
    But that blind clamor made me wise;
    Then was I as a child that cries,
But, crying, knows his father near;

And what I am beheld again
    What is, and no man understands;
    And out of darkness came the hands
That reach thro' nature, moulding men.

CXXV

Whatever I have said or sung,
    Some bitter notes my harp would give,
    Yea, tho' there often seem'd to live
A contradiction on the tongue,

Yet Hope had never lost her youth,
    She did but look through dimmer eyes;
    Or Love but play'd with gracious lies,
Because he felt so fix'd in truth;

And if the song were full of care,
    He breathed the spirit of the song;
    And if the words were sweet and strong
He set his royal signet there;

Abiding with me till I sail
 To seek thee on the mystic deeps,
 And this electric force, that keeps
A thousand pulses dancing, fail.

CXXVI

Love is and was my lord and king,
 And in his presence I attend
 To hear the tidings of my friend,
Which every hour his couriers bring.

Love is and was my king and lord,
 And will be, tho' as yet I keep
 Within the court on earth, and sleep
Encompass'd by his faithful guard,

And hear at times a sentinel
 Who moves about from place to place,
 And whispers to the worlds of space,
In the deep night, that all is well.

CXXVII

And all is well, tho' faith and form
 Be sunder'd in the night of fear;
 Well roars the storm to those that hear
A deeper voice across the storm,

Proclaiming social truth shall spread,
 And justice, even tho' thrice again
 The red fool-fury of the Seine
Should pile her barricades with dead.

But ill for him that wears a crown,
 And him, the lazar, in his rags!
 They tremble, the sustaining crags;
The spires of ice are toppled down,

And molten up, and roar in flood;
 The fortress crashes from on high,
 The brute earth lightens to the sky,
And the great Æon sinks in blood,

And compass'd by the fires of hell;
 While thou, dear spirit, happy star,
 O'erlook'st the tumult from afar,
And smilest, knowing all is well.

CXXVIII

The love that rose on stronger wings,
  Unpalsied when he met with Death,
  Is comrade of the lesser faith
That sees the course of human things.

No doubt vast eddies in the flood
  Of onward time shall yet be made,
  And throned races may degrade;
Yet, O ye mysteries of good,

Wild Hours that fly with Hope and Fear,
  If all your office had to do
  With old results that look like new—
If this were all your mission here,

To draw, to sheathe a useless sword,
  To fool the crowd with glorious lies,
  To cleave a creed in sects and cries,
To change the bearing of a word,

To shift an arbitrary power,
  To camp the student at his desk,
  To make old bareness picturesque
And tuft with grass a feudal tower,

Why, then my scorn might well descend
  On you and yours. I see in part
  That all, as in some piece of art,
Is toil coöperant to an end.

CXXIX

Dear friend, far off, my lost desire,
  So far, so near in woe and weal,
  O loved the most, when most I feel
There is a lower and a higher;

Known and unknown, human, divine;
  Sweet human hand and lips and eye;
  Dear heavenly friend that canst not die,
Mine, mine, for ever, ever mine;

Strange friend, past, present, and to be;
  Loved deeplier, darklier understood;
  Behold, I dream a dream of good,
And mingle all the world with thee.

CXXX

Thy voice is on the rolling air;
  I hear thee where the waters run;
  Thou standest in the rising sun,
And in the setting thou art fair.

What art thou then? I cannot guess;
  But tho' I seem in star and flower
  To feel thee some diffusive power,
I do not therefore love thee less.

My love involves the love before;
  My love is vaster passion now;
  Tho' mix'd with God and Nature thou,
I seem to love thee more and more.

Far off thou art, but ever nigh;
  I have thee still, and I rejoice;
  I prosper, circled with thy voice;
I shall not lose thee tho' I die.

CXXXI

O living will that shalt endure
  When all that seems shall suffer shock,
  Rise in the spiritual rock,
Flow thro' our deeds and make them pure,

That we may lift from out of dust
  A voice as unto him that hears,
  A cry above the conquer'd years
To one that with us works, and trust,

With faith that comes of self-control,
  The truths that never can be proved
  Until we close with all we loved,
And all we flow from, soul in soul.

———

O true and tried, so well and long,
  Demand not thou a marriage lay;
  In that it is thy marriage day
Is music more than any song.

Nor have I felt so much of bliss
  Since first he told me that he loved
  A daughter of our house, nor proved
Since that dark day a day like this;

Tho' I since then have number'd o'er
   Some thrice three years; they went and came,
   Remade the blood and changed the frame,
And yet is love not less, but more;

No longer caring to embalm
   In dying songs a dead regret,
   But like a statue solid-set,
And moulded in colossal calm.

Regret is dead, but love is more
   Than in the summers that are flown,
   For I myself with these have grown
To something greater than before;

Which makes appear the songs I made
   As echoes out of weaker times,
   As half but idle brawling rhymes,
The sport of random sun and shade.

But where is she, the bridal flower,
   That must be made a wife ere noon?
   She enters, glowing like the moon
Of Eden on its bridal bower.

On me she bends her blissful eyes
   And then on thee; they meet thy look
   And brighten like the star that shook
Betwixt the palms of Paradise.

O, when her life was yet in bud,
   He too foretold the perfect rose.
   For thee she grew, for thee she grows
For ever, and as fair as good.

And thou art worthy, full of power;
   As gentle: liberal-minded, great,
   Consistent; wearing all that weight
Of learning lightly like a flower.

But now set out: the noon is near,
   And I must give away the bride;
   She fears not, or with thee beside
And me behind her, will not fear.

For I that danced her on my knee,
   That watch'd her on her nurse's arm,
   That shielded all her life from harm,
At last must part with her to thee;

Now waiting to be made a wife,
  Her feet, my darling, on the dead;
  Their pensive tablets round her head,
And the most living words of life

Breathed in her ear. The ring is on,
  The 'Wilt thou?' answer'd, and again
  The 'Wilt thou?' ask'd, till out of twain
Her sweet 'I will' has made you one.

Now sign your names, which shall be read,
  Mute symbols of a joyful morn,
  By village eyes as yet unborn.
The names are sign'd, and overhead

Begins the clash and clang that tells
  The joy to every wandering breeze;
  The blind wall rocks, and on the trees
The dead leaf trembles to the bells.

O happy hour, and happier hours
  Await them. Many a merry face
  Salutes them—maidens of the place,
That pelt us in the porch with flowers.

O happy hour, behold the bride
  With him to whom her hand I gave.
  They leave the porch, they pass the grave
That has to-day its sunny side.

To-day the grave is bright for me,
  For them the light of life increased,
  Who stay to share the morning feast,
Who rest to-night beside the sea.

Let all my genial spirits advance
  To meet and greet a whiter sun;
  My drooping memory will not shun
The foaming grape of eastern France.

It circles round, and fancy plays,
  And hearts are warm'd and faces bloom,
  As drinking health to bride and groom
We wish them store of happy days.

Nor count me all to blame if I
  Conjecture of a stiller guest,
  Perchance, perchance, among the rest,
And, tho' in silence, wishing joy.

But they must go, the time draws on,
  And those white-favor'd horses wait;
  They rise, but linger; it is late;
Farewell, we kiss, and they are gone.

A shade falls on us like the dark
  From little cloudlets on the grass,
  But sweeps away as out we pass
To range the woods, to roam the park,

Discussing how their courtship grew,
  And talk of others that are wed,
  And how she look'd, and what he said,
And back we come at fall of dew.

Again the feast, the speech, the glee,
  The shade of passing thought, the wealth
  Of words and wit, the double health,
The crowning cup, the three-times-three,

And last the dance;—till I retire.
  Dumb is that tower which spake so loud,
  And high in heaven the streaming cloud,
And on the downs a rising fire:

And rise, O moon, from yonder down,
  Till over down and over dale
  All night the shining vapor sail
And pass the silent-lighted town,

The white-faced halls, the glancing rills,
  And catch at every mountain head,
  And o'er the friths that branch and spread
Their sleeping silver thro' the hills;

And touch with shade the bridal doors,
  With tender gloom the roof, the wall;
  And breaking let the splendor fall
To spangle all the happy shores

By which they rest, and ocean sounds,
  And, star and system rolling past,
  A soul shall draw from out the vast
And strike his being into bounds,

And moved thro' life of lower phase,
  Result in man, be born and think,
  And act and love, a closer link
Betwixt us and the crowning race

Of those that, eye to eye, shall look
  On knowledge; under whose command
  Is Earth and Earth's, and in their hand
Is Nature like an open book;

No longer half-akin to brute,
  For all we thought and loved and did,
  And hoped, and suffer'd, is but seed
Of what in them is flower and fruit;

Whereof the man that with me trod
  This planet was a noble type
  Appearing ere the times were ripe,
That friend of mine who lives in God,

That God, which ever lives and loves,
  One God, one law, one element,
  And one far-off divine event,
To which the whole creation moves.

MAUD, AND OTHER POEMS

MAUD; A MONODRAMA

PART I

I

I

I HATE the dreadful hollow behind the little wood;
Its lips in the field above are dabbled with blood-red heath,
The red-ribb'd ledges drip with a silent horror of blood,
An Echo there, whatever is ask'd her, answers 'Death.'

II

For there in the ghastly pit long since a body was found,
His who had given me life—O father! O God! was it well?—
Mangled, and flatten'd, and crush'd, and dinted into the ground;
There yet lies the rock that fell with him when he fell.

III

Did he fling himself down? who knows? for a vast speculation had fail'd,
And ever he mutter'd and madden'd, and ever wann'd with despair,   10
And out he walk'd when the wind like a broken worldling wail'd,
And the flying gold of the ruin'd woodlands drove thro' the air.

IV

I remember the time, for the roots of my hair were stirr'd
By a shuffled step, by a dead weight trail'd, by a whisper'd fright,
And my pulses closed their gates with a shock on my heart as I heard
The shrill-edged shriek of a mother divide the shuddering night.

V

Villainy somewhere! whose? One says, we are villains all.
Not he; his honest fame should at least by me be maintained;
But that old man, now lord of the broad estate and the Hall,
Dropt off gorged from a scheme that had left us flaccid and drain'd.   20

375

VI

Why do they prate of the blessings of peace? we have made them a curse,
Pickpockets, each hand lusting for all that is not its own;
And lust of gain, in the spirit of Cain, is it better or worse
Than the heart of the citizen hissing in war on his own hearthstone?

VII

But these are the days of advance, the works of the men of mind,
When who but a fool would have faith in a tradesman's ware or his word?
Is it peace or war? Civil war, as I think, and that of a kind
The viler, as underhand, not openly bearing the sword.

VIII

Sooner or later I too may passively take the print
Of the golden age—why not? I have neither hope nor trust;   30
May make my heart as a millstone, set my face as a flint,
Cheat and be cheated, and die—who knows? we are ashes and dust.

IX

Peace sitting under her olive, and slurring the days gone by,
When the poor are hovell'd and hustled together, each sex, like swine,
When only the ledger lives, and when only not all men lie;
Peace in her vineyard—yes!—but a company forges the wine.

X

And the vitriol madness flushes up in the ruffian's head,
Till the filthy by-lane rings to the yell of the trampled wife,
And chalk and alum and plaster are sold to the poor for bread,
And the spirit of murder works in the very means of life,   40

XI

And Sleep must lie down arm'd, for the villainous centre-bits
Grind on the wakeful ear in the hush of the moonless nights,
While another is cheating the sick of a few last gasps, as he sits
To pestle a poison'd poison behind his crimson lights.

XII

When a Mammonite mother kills her babe for a burial fee,
And Timour-Mammon grins on a pile of children's bones,
Is it peace or war? better, war! loud war by land and by sea,
War with a thousand battles, and shaking a hundred thrones!

XIII

For I trust if an enemy's fleet came yonder round by the hill,
And the rushing battle-bolt sang from the three-decker out of the foam, 50
That the smooth-faced, snub-nosed rogue would leap from his counter and till,
And strike, if he could, were it but with his cheating yardwand, home.—

XIV

What! am I raging alone as my father raged in his mood?
Must *I* too creep to the hollow and dash myself down and die
Rather than hold by the law that I made, nevermore to brood
On a horror of shatter'd limbs and a wretched swindler's lie?

XV

Would there be sorrow for *me?* there was *love* in the passionate shriek,
Love for the silent thing that had made false haste to the grave—
Wrapt in a cloak, as I saw him, and thought he would rise and speak
And rave at the lie and the liar, ah God, as he used to rave. 60

XVI

I am sick of the Hall and the hill, I am sick of the moor and the main.
Why should I stay? can a sweeter chance ever come to me here?
O, having the nerves of motion as well as the nerves of pain,
Were it not wise if I fled from the place and the pit and the fear?

XVII

Workmen up at the Hall!—they are coming back from abroad;
The dark old place will be gilt by the touch of a millionaire.
I have heard, I know not whence, of the singular beauty of Maud;
I play'd with the girl when a child; she promised then to be fair.

XVIII

Maud, with her venturous climbings and tumbles and childish escapes,
Maud, the delight of the village, the ringing joy of the Hall, 70
Maud, with her sweet purse-mouth when my father dangled the grapes,
Maud, the beloved of my mother, the moon-faced darling of all,—

XIX

What is she now? My dreams are bad. She may bring me a curse.
No, there is fatter game on the moor; she will let me alone.
Thanks; for the fiend best knows whether woman or man be the worse.
I will bury myself in myself, and the Devil may pipe to his own.

II

Long have I sigh'd for a calm; God grant I may find it at last!
It will never be broken by Maud; she has neither savor nor salt,
But a cold and clear-cut face, as I found when her carriage past,
Perfectly beautiful; let it be granted her; where is the fault?   80
All that I saw—for her eyes were downcast, not to be seen—
Faultily faultless, icily regular, splendidly null,
Dead perfection, no more; nothing more, if it had not been
For a chance of travel, a paleness, an hour's defect of the rose,
Or an underlip, you may call it a little too ripe, too full,
Or the least little delicate aquiline curve in a sensitive nose,
From which I escaped heart-free, with the least little touch of spleen.

III

Cold and clear-cut face, why come you so cruelly meek,
Breaking a slumber in which all spleenful folly was drown'd?
Pale with the golden beam of an eyelash dead on the cheek,   90
Passionless, pale, cold face, star-sweet on a gloom profound;
Womanlike, taking revenge too deep for a transient wrong
Done but in thought to your beauty, and ever as pale as before
Growing and fading and growing upon me without a sound,
Luminous, gemlike, ghostlike, deathlike, half the night long
Growing and fading and growing, till I could bear it no more,
But arose, and all by myself in my own dark garden ground,
Listening now to the tide in its broad-flung shipwrecking roar,
Now to the scream of a madden'd beach dragg'd down by the wave,
Walk'd in a wintry wind by a ghastly glimmer, and found   100
The shining daffodil dead, and Orion low in his grave.

IV

I

A million emeralds break from the ruby-budded lime
In the little grove where I sit—ah, wherefore cannot I be
Like things of the season gay, like the bountiful season bland,
When the far-off sail is blown by the breeze of a softer clime,
Half-lost in the liquid azure bloom of a crescent of sea,
The silent sapphire-spangled marriage ring of the land?

II

Below me, there, is the village, and looks how quiet and small!
And yet bubbles o'er like a city, with gossip, scandal, and spite;
And Jack on his ale-house bench has as many lies as a Czar;   110
And here on the landward side, by a red rock, glimmers the Hall;
And up in the high Hall-garden I see her pass like a light;
But sorrow seize me if ever that light be my leading star!

III

When have I bow'd to her father, the wrinkled head of the race?
I met her to-day with her brother, but not to her brother I bow'd;
I bow'd to his lady-sister as she rode by on the moor,
But the fire of a foolish pride flash'd over her beautiful face.
O child, you wrong your beauty, believe it, in being so proud;
Your father has wealth well-gotten, and I am nameless and poor.

IV

I keep but a man and a maid, ever ready to slander and steal;   120
I know it, and smile a hard-set smile, like a stoic, or like
A wiser epicurean, and let the world have its way.
For nature is one with rapine, a harm no preacher can heal;
The Mayfly is torn by the swallow, the sparrow spear'd by the shrike,
And the whole little wood where I sit is a world of plunder and prey.

V

We are puppets, Man in his pride, and Beauty fair in her flower;
Do we move ourselves, or are moved by an unseen hand at a game
That pushes us off from the board, and others ever succeed?
Ah yet, we cannot be kind to each other here for an hour;
We whisper, and hint, and chuckle, and grin at a brother's shame;   130
However we brave it out, we men are a little breed.

VI

A monstrous eft was of old the lord and master of earth,
For him did his high sun flame, and his river billowing ran,
And he felt himself in his force to be Nature's crowning race.
As nine months go to the shaping an infant ripe for his birth,
So many a million of ages have gone to the making of man:
He now is first, but is he the last? is he not too base?

VII

The man of science himself is fonder of glory, and vain,
An eye well-practised in nature, a spirit bounded and poor;
The passionate heart of the poet is whirl'd into folly and vice.   140
I would not marvel at either, but keep a temperate brain;
For not to desire or admire, if a man could learn it, were more
Than to walk all day like the sultan of old in a garden of spice.

VIII

For the drift of the Maker is dark, an Isis hid by the veil.
Who knows the ways of the world, how God will bring them about?
Our planet is one, the suns are many, the world is wide.
Shall I weep if a Poland fall? shall I shriek if a Hungary fail?
Or an infant civilization be ruled with rod or with knout?
I have not made the world, and He that made it will guide.

IX

Be mine a philosopher's life in the quiet woodland ways,   150
Where if I cannot be gay let a passionless peace be my lot,
Far-off from the clamor of liars belied in the hubbub of lies;
From the long-neck'd geese of the world that are ever hissing dispraise
Because their natures are little, and, whether he heed it or not,
Where each man walks with his head in a cloud of poisonous flies.

X

And most of all would I flee from the cruel madness of love
The honey of poison-flowers and all the measureless ill.
Ah, Maud, you milk-white fawn, you are all unmeet for a wife.
Your mother is mute in her grave as her image in marble above;
Your father is ever in London, you wander about at your will;   160
You have but fed on the roses and lain in the lilies of life.

V

I

A voice by the cedar tree
In the meadow under the Hall!
She is singing an air that is known to me,
A passionate ballad gallant and gay,
A martial song like a trumpet's call!
Singing alone in the morning of life,
In the happy morning of life and of May,

Singing of men that in battle array,
Ready in heart and ready in hand,   170
March with banner and bugle and fife
To the death, for their native land.

II

Maud with her exquisite face,
And wild voice pealing up to the sunny sky,
And feet like sunny gems on an English green,
Maud in the light of her youth and her grace,
Singing of Death, and of Honor that cannot die,
Till I well could weep for a time so sordid and mean,
And myself so languid and base.

III

Silence, beautiful voice!   180
Be still, for you only trouble the mind
With a joy in which I cannot rejoice,
A glory I shall not find.
Still! I will hear you no more,
For your sweetness hardly leaves me a choice
But to move to the meadow and fall before
Her feet on the meadow grass, and adore,
Not her, who is neither courtly nor kind,
Not her, not her, but a voice.

VI

I

Morning arises stormy and pale,   190
No sun, but a wannish glare
In fold upon fold of hueless cloud;
And the budded peaks of the wood are bow'd,
Caught, and cuff'd by the gale:
I had fancied it would be fair.

II

Whom but Maud should I meet
Last night, when the sunset burn'd
On the blossom'd gable-ends
At the head of the village street,
Whom but Maud should I meet?   200
And she touch'd my hand with a smile so sweet,
She made me divine amends
For a courtesy not return'd.

III

And thus a delicate spark
Of glowing and growing light
Thro' the livelong hours of the dark
Kept itself warm in the heart of my dreams,
Ready to burst in a color'd flame;
Till at last, when the morning came
In a cloud, it faded, and seems   210
But an ashen-gray delight.

IV

What if with her sunny hair,
And smile as sunny as cold,
She meant to weave me a snare
Of some coquettish deceit,
Cleopatra-like as of old
To entangle me when we met,
To have her lion roll in a silken net
And fawn at a victor's feet.

V

Ah, what shall I be at fifty   220
Should Nature keep me alive,
If I find the world so bitter
When I am but twenty-five?
Yet, if she were not a cheat,
If Maud were all that she seem'd,
And her smile were all that I dream'd,
Then the world were not so bitter
But a smile could make it sweet.

VI

What if, tho' her eye seem'd full
Of a kind intent to me,   230
What if that dandy-despot, he,
That jewell'd mass of millinery,
That oil'd and curl'd Assyrian bull
Smelling of musk and of insolence,
Her brother, from whom I keep aloof,
Who wants the finer politic sense
To mask, tho' but in his own behoof,
With a glassy smile his brutal scorn—
What if he had told her yestermorn

How prettily for his own sweet sake
A face of tenderness might be feign'd,
And a moist mirage in desert eyes,
That so, when the rotten hustings shake
In another month to his brazen lies,
A wretched vote may be gain'd?

VII

For a raven ever croaks, at my side,
Keep watch and ward, keep watch and ward,
Or thou wilt prove their tool.
Yea, too, myself from myself I guard,
For often a man's own angry pride   250
Is cap and bells for a fool.

VIII

Perhaps the smile and tender tone
Came out of her pitying womanhood,
For am I not, am I not, here alone
So many a summer since she died,
My mother, who was so gentle and good?
Living alone in an empty house,
Here half-hid in the gleaming wood,
Where I hear the dead at midday moan,
And the shrieking rush of the wainscot mouse,   260
And my own sad name in corners cried,
When the shiver of dancing leaves is thrown
About its echoing chambers wide,
Till a morbid hate and horror have grown
Of a world in which I have hardly mixt,
And a morbid eating lichen fixt
On a heart half-turned to stone.

IX

O heart of stone, are you flesh, and caught
By that you swore to withstand?
For what was it else within me wrought   270
But, I fear, the new strong wine of love,
That made my tongue so stammer and trip
When I saw the treasured splendor, her hand,
Come sliding out of her sacred glove,
And the sunlight broke from her lip?

X

I have play'd with her when a child;
She remembers it now we meet.
Ah, well, well, well, I *may* be beguiled
By some coquettish deceit.
Yet, if she were not a cheat,   280
If Maud were all that she seem'd,
And her smile had all that I dream'd,
Then the world were not so bitter
But a smile could make it sweet.

VII

I

Did I hear it half in a doze
    Long since, I know not where?
Did I dream it an hour ago,
    When asleep in this arm-chair?

II

Men were drinking together,
    Drinking and talking of me: 290
'Well, if it prove a girl, the boy
    Will have plenty; so let it be.'

III

Is it an echo of something
    Read with a boy's delight,
Viziers nodding together
    In some Arabian night?

IV

Strange, that I hear two men,
    Somewhere, talking of me:
'Well, if it prove a girl, my boy
    Will have plenty; so let it be.'   300

VIII

She came to the village church,
And sat by a pillar alone;
An angel watching an urn

Wept over her, carved in stone;
And once, but once, she lifted her eyes,
And suddenly, sweetly, strangely blush'd
To find they were met by my own;
And suddenly, sweetly, my heart beat stronger
And thicker, until I heard no longer
The snowy-banded, dilettante,   310
Delicate-handed priest intone;
And thought, is it pride? and mused and sigh'd,
'No surely, now it cannot be pride.'

IX

I was walking a mile,
More than a mile from the shore,
The sun look'd out with a smile
Betwixt the cloud and the moor;
And riding at set of day
Over the dark moor land,
Rapidly riding far away,   320
She waved to me with her hand.
There were two at her side,
Something flash'd in the sun,
Down by the hill I saw them ride,
In a moment they were gone;
Like a sudden spark
Struck vainly in the night,
Then returns the dark
With no more hope of light.

X

I

Sick, am I sick of a jealous dread?   330
Was not one of the two at her side
This new-made lord, whose splendor plucks
The slavish hat from the villager's head?
Whose old grandfather has lately died,
Gone to a blacker pit, for whom
Grimy nakedness dragging his trucks
And laying his trams in a poison'd gloom
Wrought, till he crept from a gutted mine
Master of half a servile shire,
And left his coal all turn'd into gold   340
To a grandson, first of his noble line,
Rich in the grace all women desire,
Strong in the power that all men adore,

And simper and set their voices lower,
And soften as if to a girl, and hold
Awe-stricken breaths at a work divine,
Seeing his gewgaw castle shine,
New as his title, built last year,
There amid perky larches and pine,
And over the sullen-purple moor—   350
Look at it—pricking a cockney ear.

II

What, has he found my jewel out?
For one of the two that rode at her side
Bound for the Hall, I am sure was he;
Bound for the Hall, and I think for a bride.
Blithe would her brother's acceptance be.
Maud could be gracious too, no doubt,
To a lord, a captain, a padded shape,
A bought commission, a waxen face,
A rabbit mouth that is ever agape—   360
Bought? what is it he cannot buy?
And therefore splenetic, personal, base,
A wounded thing with a rancorous cry,
At war with myself and a wretched race,
Sick, sick to the heart of life, am I.

III

Last week came one to the county town,
To preach our poor little army down,
And play the game of the despot kings,
Tho' the state has done it and thrice as well
This broad-brimm'd hawker of holy things,   370
Whose ear is cramm'd with his cotton, and rings
Even in dreams to the chink of his pence,
This huckster put down war! can he tell
Whether war be a cause or a consequence?
Put down the passions that make earth hell!
Down with ambition, avarice, pride,
Jealousy, down! cut off from the mind
The bitter springs of anger and fear!
Down too, down at your own fireside,
With the evil tongue and the evil ear,   380
For each is at war with mankind!

IV

I wish I could hear again
The chivalrous battle-song
That she warbled alone in her joy!
I might persuade myself then
She would not do herself this great wrong,
To take a wanton dissolute boy
For a man and leader of men.

V

Ah God, for a man with heart, head, hand,
Like some of the simple great ones gone   390
For ever and ever by,
One still strong man in a blatant land,
Whatever they call him—what care I?—
Aristocrat, democrat, autocrat—one
Who can rule and dare not lie!

VI

And ah for a man to arise in me,
That the man I am may cease to be!

XI

I

O, let the solid ground
    Not fail beneath my feet
Before my life has found   400
    What some have found so sweet!
Then let come what come may,
What matter if I go mad,
I shall have had my day.

II

Let the sweet heavens endure,
    Not close and darken above me
Before I am quite quite sure
    That there is one to love me!
Then let come what come may
To a life that has been so sad,   410
I shall have had my day.

XII

I

Birds in the high Hall-garden
  When twilight was falling,
Maud, Maud, Maud, Maud,
  They were crying and calling.

II

Where was Maud? in our wood;
  And I—who else?—was with her,
Gathering woodland lilies,
  Myriads blow together.

III

Birds in our wood sang
  Ringing thro' the valleys,
Maud is here, here, here
  In among the lilies.

420

IV

I kiss'd her slender hand,
  She took the kiss sedately;
Maud is not seventeen,
  But she is tall and stately.

V

I to cry out on pride
  Who have won her favor!
O, Maud were sure of heaven
  If lowliness could save her!

430

VI

I know the way she went
  Home with her maiden posy,
For her feet have touch'd the meadows
  And left the daisies rosy.

VII

Birds in the high Hall-garden
    Were crying and calling to her,
Where is Maud, Maud, Maud?
    One is come to woo her.

VIII

Look, a horse at the door,   440
    And little King Charley snarling!
Go back, my lord, across the moor,
    You are not her darling.

XIII

I

Scorn'd, to be scorn'd by one that I scorn,
Is that a matter to make me fret?
That a calamity hard to be borne?
Well, he may live to hate me yet.
Fool that I am to be vext with his pride!
I past him, I was crossing his lands;
He stood on the path a little aside;   450
His face, as I grant, in spite of spite,
Has a broad-blown comeliness, red and white,
And six feet two, as I think, he stands;
But his essences turn'd the live air sick,
And barbarous opulence jewel-thick
Sunn'd itself on his breast and his hands.

II

Who shall call me ungentle, unfair?
I long'd so heartily then and there
To give him the grasp of fellowship;
But while I past he was humming an air,   460
Stopt, and then with a riding-whip
Leisurely tapping a glossy boot,
And curving a contumelious lip,
Gorgonized me from head to foot
With a stony British stare.

III

Why sits he here in his father's chair?
That old man never comes to his place;
Shall I believe him ashamed to be seen?
For only once, in the village street,
Last year, I caught a glimpse of his face,   470
A gray old wolf and a lean.
Scarcely, now, would I call him a cheat;
For then, perhaps, as a child of deceit,
She might by a true descent be untrue;
And Maud is as true as Maud is sweet,
Tho' I fancy her sweetness only due
To the sweeter blood by the other side;
Her mother has been a thing complete,
However she came to be so allied.
And fair without, faithful within,   480
Maud to him is nothing akin.
Some peculiar mystic grace
Made her only the child of her mother,
And heap'd the whole inherited sin
On that huge scapegoat of the race,
All, all upon the brother.

IV

Peace, angry spirit, and let him be!
Has not his sister smiled on me?

XIV

I

Maud has a garden of roses
And lilies fair on a lawn;   490
There she walks in her state
And tends upon bed and bower,
And thither I climb'd at dawn
And stood by her garden-gate.
A lion ramps at the top,
He is claspt by a passion-flower.

II

Maud's own little oak-room—
Which Maud, like a precious stone
Set in the heart of the carven gloom,

Lights with herself, when alone   500
She sits by her music and books
And her brother lingers late
With a roystering company—looks
Upon Maud's own garden-gate;
And I thought as I stood, if a hand, as white
As ocean-foam in the moon, were laid
On the hasp of the window, and my Delight
Had a sudden desire, like a glorious ghost, to glide,
Like a beam of the seventh heaven, down to my side,
There were but a step to be made.   510

III

The fancy flatter'd my mind,
And again seem'd overbold;
Now I thought that she cared for me,
Now I thought she was kind
Only because she was cold.

IV

I heard no sound where I stood
But the rivulet on from the lawn
Running down to my own dark wood,
Or the voice of the long sea-wave as it swell'd
Now and then in the dim-gray dawn;   520
But I look'd, and round, all round the house I beheld
The death-white curtain drawn,
Felt a horror over me creep,
Prickle my skin and catch my breath,
Knew that the death-white curtain meant but sleep,
Yet I shudder'd and thought like a fool of the sleep of death.

XV

So dark a mind within me dwells,
  And I make myself such evil cheer,
That if *I* be dear to some one else,
  Then some one else may have much to fear;   530
But if *I* be dear to some one else,
  Then I should be to myself more dear.
Shall I not take care of all that I think,
Yea, even of wretched meat and drink,
If I be dear,
If I be dear to some one else?

XVI

I

This lump of earth has left his estate
The lighter by the loss of his weight;
And so that he find what he went to seek,
And fulsome pleasure clog him, and drown   540
His heart in the gross mud-honey of town,
He may stay for a year who has gone for a week.
But this is the day when I must speak,
And I see my Oread coming down,
O, this is the day!
O beautiful creature, what am I
That I dare to look her way?
Think I may hold dominion sweet,
Lord of the pulse that is lord of her breast.
And dream of her beauty with tender dread,   550
From the delicate Arab arch of her feet
To the grace that, bright and light as the crest
Of a peacock, sits on her shining head,
And she knows it not—O, if she knew it,
To know her beauty might half undo it!
I know it the one bright thing to save
My yet young life in the wilds of Time,
Perhaps from madness, perhaps from crime,
Perhaps from a selfish grave.

II

What, if she be fasten'd to this fool lord,   560
Dare I bid her abide by her word?
Should I love her so well if she
Had given her word to a thing so low?
Shall I love her as well if she
Can break her word were it even for me?
I trust that it is not so.

III

Catch not my breath, O clamorous heart,
Let not my tongue be a thrall to my eye,
For I must tell her before we part,
I must tell her, or die.   570

XVII

Go not, happy day,
   From the shining fields,
Go not, happy day,
   Till the maiden yields.
Rosy is the West,
   Rosy is the South,
Roses are her cheeks,
   And a rose her mouth.
When the happy Yes
   Falters from her lips,   580
Pass and blush the news
   Over glowing ships;
Over blowing seas,
   Over seas at rest,
Pass the happy news,
   Blush it thro' the West;
Till the red man dance
   By his red cedar-tree,
And the red man's babe
   Leap, beyond the sea.   590
Blush from West to East,
   Blush from East to West,
Till the West is East,
   Blush it thro' the West.
Rosy is the West,
   Rosy is the South,
Roses are her cheeks,
   And a rose her mouth.

XVIII

I

I have led her home, my love, my only friend.
There is none like her, none.   600
And never yet so warmly ran my blood
And sweetly, on and on
Calming itself to the long-wish'd-for end,
Full to the banks, close on the promised good.

II

None like her, none.
Just now the dry-tongued laurels' pattering talk
Seem'd her light foot along the garden walk,

And shook my heart to think she comes once more.
But even then I heard her close the door;
The gates of heaven are closed, and she is gone.   610

III

There is none like her, none,
Nor will be when our summers have deceased.
O, art thou sighing for Lebanon
In the long breeze that streams to thy delicious East,
Sighing for Lebanon,
Dark cedar, tho' thy limbs have here increased,
Upon a pastoral slope as fair,
And looking to the South and fed
With honey'd rain and delicate air,
And haunted by the starry head   620
Of her whose gentle will has changed my fate,
And made my life a perfumed altar-flame;
And over whom thy darkness must have spread
With such delight as theirs of old, thy great
Forefathers of the thornless garden, there
Shadowing the snow-limb'd Eve from whom she came?

IV

Here will I lie, while these long branches sway,
And you fair stars that crown a happy day
Go in and out as if at merry play,
Who am no more so all forlorn   630
As when it seem'd far better to be born
To labor and the mattock-harden'd hand
Than nursed at ease and brought to understand
A sad astrology, the boundless plan
That makes you tyrants in your iron skies,
Innumerable, pitiless, passionless eyes,
Cold fires, yet with power to burn and brand
His nothingness into man.

V

But now shine on, and what care I,
Who in this stormy gulf have found a pearl   640
The countercharm of space and hollow sky,
And do accept my madness, and would die
To save from some slight shame one simple girl?—

VI

Would die, for sullen-seeming Death may give
More life to Love than is or ever was
In our low world, where yet 't is sweet to live.
Let no one ask me how it came to pass;
It seems that I am happy, that to me
A livelier emerald twinkles in the grass,
A purer sapphire melts into the sea.   650

VII

Not die, but live a life of truest breath,
And teach true life to fight with mortal wrongs.
O, why should Love, like men in drinking-songs,
Spice his fair banquet with the dust of death?
Make answer, Maud my bliss,
Maud made my Maud by that long loving kiss,
Life of my life, wilt thou not answer this?
'The dusky strand of Death inwoven here
With dear Love's tie, makes Love himself more dear.'

VIII

Is that enchanted moan only the swell   660
Of the long waves that roll in yonder bay?
And hark the clock within, the silver knell
Of twelve sweet hours that past in bridal white,
And died to live, long as my pulses play;
But now by this my love has closed her sight
And given false death her hand, and stol'n away
To dreamful wastes where footless fancies dwell
Among the fragments of the golden day.
May nothing there her maiden grace affright!
Dear heart, I feel with thee the drowsy spell.   670
My bride to be, my evermore delight,
My own heart's heart, my ownest own, farewell;
It is but for a little space I go.
And ye meanwhile far over moor and fell
Beat to the noiseless music of the night!
Has our whole earth gone nearer to the glow
Of your soft splendors that you look so bright?
I have climb'd nearer out of lonely hell.
Beat, happy stars, timing with things below,
Beat with my heart more blest than heart can tell,   680
Blest, but for some dark undercurrent woe
That seems to draw—but it shall not be so;
Let all be well, be well.

XIX

I

Her brother is coming back to-night,
Breaking up my dream of delight.

II

My dream? do I dream of bliss?
I have walk'd awake with Truth.
O, when did a morning shine
So rich in atonement as this
For my dark-dawning youth,   690

Darken'd watching a mother decline
And that dead man at her heart and mine;
For who was left to watch her but I?
Yet so did I let my freshness die.

III

I trust that I did not talk
To gentle Maud in our walk—
For often in lonely wanderings
I have cursed him even to lifeless things—
But I trust that I did not talk,
Not touch on her father's sin.   700
I am sure I did but speak
Of my mother's faded cheek
When it slowly grew so thin
That I felt she was slowly dying
Vext with lawyers and harass'd with debt;
For how often I caught her with eyes all wet,
Shaking her head at her son and sighing
A world of trouble within!

IV

And Maud too, Maud was moved
To speak of the mother she loved   710
As one scarce less forlorn,
Dying abroad and it seems apart
From him who had ceased to share her heart,
And ever mourning over the feud,
The household Fury sprinkled with blood
By which our houses are torn.

How strange was what she said,
When only Maud and the brother
Hung over her dying bed—
That Maud's dark father and mine   720
Had bound us one to the other,
Betrothed us over their wine,
On the day when Maud was born;
Seal'd her mine from her first sweet breath!
Mine, mine by a right, from birth till death!
Mine, mine—our fathers have sworn!

V

But the true blood spilt had in it a heat
To dissolve the precious seal on a bound,
That, if left uncancell'd, had been so sweet;
And none of us thought of a something beyond,   730
A desire that awoke in the heart of the child,
As it were a duty done to the tomb,
To be friends for her sake, to be reconciled;
And I was cursing them and my doom,
And letting a dangerous thought run wild
While often abroad in the fragrant gloom
Of foreign churches—I see her there,
Bright English lily, breathing a prayer
To be friends, to be reconciled!

VI

But then what a flint is he!   740
Abroad, at Florence, at Rome,
I find whenever she touch'd on me
This brother had laugh'd her down,
And at last, when each came home,
He had darken'd into a frown,
Chid her, and forbid her to speak
To me, her friend of the years before;
And this was what had redden'd her cheek
When I bow'd to her on the moor.

VII

Yet Maud, altho' not blind   750
To the faults of his heart and mind,
I see she cannot but love him,
And says he is rough but kind,
And wishes me to approve him,
And tells me, when she lay

Sick once, with a fear of worse,
That he left his wine and horses and play,
Sat with her, read to her, night and day,
And tended her like a nurse.

VIII

Kind? but the death-bed desire
Spurn'd by this heir of the liar—
Rough but kind? yet I know
He has plotted against me in this,
That he plots against me still.
Kind to Maud? that were not amiss.
Well, rough but kind; why, let it be so,
For shall not Maud have her will?

IX

For Maud, so tender and true,
As long as my life endures
I feel I shall owe you a debt
That I never can hope to pay;
And if ever I should forget
That I owe this debt to you
And for your sweet sake to yours,
O, then, what then shall I say?—
If ever I *should* forget,
May God make me more wretched
Than ever I have been yet!

X

So now I have sworn to bury
All this dead body of hate,
I feel so free and so clear
By the loss of that dead weight,
That I should grow light-headed, I fear,
Fantastically merry,
But that her brother comes, like a blight
On my fresh hope, to the Hall to-night.

XX

I

Strange, that I felt so gay,
Strange, that *I* tried to-day
To beguile her melancholy;
The Sultan, as we name him—

760

770

780

790

She did not wish to blame him—
But he vext her and perplext her
With his worldly talk and folly.
Was it gentle to reprove her
For stealing out of view
From a little lazy lover
Who but claims her as his due?
Or for chilling his caresses
By the coldness of her manners,
Nay, the plainness of her dresses? 800
Now I know her but in two,
Nor can pronounce upon it
If one should ask me whether
The habit, hat, and feather,
Or the frock and gipsy bonnet
Be the neater and completer;
For nothing can be sweeter
Than maiden Maud in either.

II

But to-morrow, if we live,
Our ponderous squire will give 810
A grand political dinner
To half the squirelings near;
And Maud will wear her jewels,
And the bird of prey will hover,
And the titmouse hope to win her
With his chirrup at her ear.

III

A grand political dinner
To the men of many acres,
A gathering of the Tory,
A dinner and then a dance 820
For the maids and marriage-makers,
And every eye but mine will glance
At Maud in all her glory.

IV

For I am not invited,
But, with the Sultan's pardon,
I am all as well delighted,
For I know her own rose-garden,
And mean to linger in it

Till the dancing will be over;
And then, O, then, come out to me   830
For a minute, but for a minute,
Come out to your own true lover,
That your true lover may see
Your glory also, and render
All homage to his own darling,
Queen Maud in all her splendor.

XXI

Rivulet crossing my ground,
And bringing me down from the Hall
This garden-rose that I found,
Forgetful of Maud and me,   840
And lost in trouble and moving round
Here at the head of a tinkling fall,
And trying to pass to the sea;
O rivulet, born at the Hall,
My Maud has sent it by thee—
If I read her sweet will right—
On a blushing mission to me,
Saying in odor and color, 'Ah, be
Among the roses to-night.'

XXII

I

Come into the garden, Maud,   850
    For the black bat, night, has flown,
Come into the garden, Maud,
    I am here at the gate alone;
And the woodbine spices are wafted abroad,
    And the musk of the rose is blown.

II

For a breeze of morning moves,
    And the planet of Love is on high,
Beginning to faint in the light that she loves
    On a bed of daffodil sky,
To faint in the light of the sun she loves,   860
    To faint in his light, and to die.

III

All night have the roses heard
  The flute, violin, bassoon;
All night has the casement jessamine stirr'd
  To the dancers dancing in tune;
Till a silence fell with the waking bird,
  And a hush with the setting moon.

IV

I said to the lily, 'There is but one,
  With whom she has heart to be gay.
When will the dancers leave her alone?   870
  She is weary of dance and play.'
Now half to the setting moon are gone,
  And half to the rising day;
Low on the sand and loud on the stone
  The last wheel echoes away.

V

I said to the rose, 'The brief night goes
  In babble and revel and wine.
O young lord-lover, what sighs are those,
  For one that will never be thine?
But mine, but mine,' so I sware to the rose,   880
  'For ever and ever, mine.'

VI

And the soul of the rose went into my blood,
  As the music clash'd in the hall;
And long by the garden lake I stood,
  For I heard your rivulet fall
From the lake to the meadow and on to the wood,
  Our wood, that is dearer than all;

VII

From the meadow your walks have left so sweet
  That whenever a March-wind sighs
He sets the jewel-print of your feet   890
  In violets blue as your eyes,
To the woody hollows in which we meet
  And the valleys of Paradise.

VIII

The slender acacia would not shake
  One long milk-bloom on the tree;
That white lake-blossom fell into the lake
  As the pimpernel dozed on the lea;
But the rose was awake all night for your sake,
  Knowing your promise to me;
The lilies and roses were all awake,   900
  They sigh'd for the dawn and thee.

IX

Queen rose of the rosebud garden of girls,
  Come hither, the dancers are done,
In gloss of satin and glimmer of pearls,
  Queen lily and rose in one;
Shine out, little head, sunning over with curls,
  To the flowers, and be their sun.

X

There has fallen a splendid tear
  From the passion-flower at the gate.
She is coming, my dove, my dear;   910
  She is coming, my life, my fate.
The red rose cries, 'She is near, she is near;'
  And the white rose weeps, 'She is late;'
The larkspur listens, 'I hear, I hear;'
  And the lily whispers, 'I wait.'

XI

She is coming, my own, my sweet;
  Were it ever so airy a tread,
My heart would hear her and beat,
  Were it earth in an earthy bed;
My dust would hear her and beat,   920
  Had I lain for a century dead,
Would start and tremble under her feet,
  And blossom in purple and red.

PART II

I

1

'The fault was mine, the fault was mine'—
Why am I sitting here so stunn'd and still,
Plucking the harmless wild-flower on the hill?—
It is this guilty hand!—
And there arises ever a passionate cry
From underneath in the darkening land—
What is it, that has been done?
O dawn of Eden bright over earth and sky,
The fires of hell brake out of thy rising sun,
The fires of hell and of hate;   10
For she, sweet soul, had hardly spoken a word,
When her brother ran in his rage to the gate,
He came with the babe-faced lord,
Heap'd on her terms of disgrace;
And while she wept, and I strove to be cool,
He fiercely gave me the lie,
Till I with as fierce an anger spoke,
And he struck me, madman, over the face,
Struck me before the languid fool,
Who was gaping and grinning by;   20
Struck for himself an evil stroke,
Wrought for his house an irredeemable woe.
For front to front in an hour we stood,
And a million horrible bellowing echoes broke
From the red-ribb'd hollow behind the wood,
And thunder'd up into heaven the Christless code
That must have life for a blow.
Ever and ever afresh they seem'd to grow.
Was it he lay there with a fading eye?
'The fault was mine,' he whisper'd, 'fly!'   30
Then glided out of the joyous wood
The ghastly Wraith of one that I know,
And there rang on a sudden a passionate cry,
A cry for a brother's blood;
It will ring in my heart and my ears, till I die, till I die.

II

Is it gone? my pulses beat—
What was it? a lying trick of the brain?
Yet I thought I saw her stand,

A shadow there at my feet,
High over the shadowy land.
It is gone; and the heavens fall in a gentle rain,
When they should burst and drown with deluging storms
The feeble vassals of wine and anger and lust,
The little hearts that know not how to forgive.
Arise, my God, and strike, for we hold Thee just,
Strike dead the whole weak race of venomous worms,
That sting each other here in the dust;
We are not worthy to live.

II

I

See what a lovely shell,
Small and pure as a pearl,
Lying close to my foot,
Frail, but a work divine,
Made so fairly well
With delicate spire and whorl,
How exquisitely minute,
A miracle of design!

II

What is it? a learned man
Could give it a clumsy name.
Let him name it who can,
The beauty would be the same.

III

The tiny cell is forlorn,
Void of the little living will
That made it stir on the shore.
Did he stand at the diamond door
Of this house in a rainbow frill?
Did he push, when he was uncurl'd,
A golden foot or a fairy horn
Thro' his dim water-world?

IV

Slight, to be crush'd with a tap
Of my finger-nail on the sand,
Small, but a work divine,
Frail, but of force to withstand,

Year upon year, the shock
Of cataract seas that snap
The three-decker's oaken spine
Athwart the ledges of rock,
Here on the Breton strand!

V

Breton, not Briton; here
Like a shipwreck'd man on a coast
Of ancient fable and fear—
Plagued with a flitting to and fro,
A disease, a hard mechanic ghost
That never came from on high
Nor ever arose from below,
But only moves with the moving eye,
Flying along the land and the main—
Why should it look like Maud?
Am I to be overawed
By what I cannot but know
Is a juggle born of the brain?

VI

Back from the Breton coast,
Sick of a nameless fear,
Back to the dark sea-line
Looking, thinking of all I have lost;
An old song vexes my ear,
But that of Lamech is mine.

VII

For years, a measureless ill,
For years, for ever, to part—
But she, she would love me still;
And as long, O God, as she
Have a grain of love for me,
So long, no doubt, no doubt,
Shall I nurse in my dark heart,
However weary, a spark of will
Not to be trampled out.

VIII

Strange, that the mind, when fraught
With a passion so intense
One would think that it well

Might drown all life in the eye,—
That it should, by being so overwrought,   110
Suddenly strike on a sharper sense
For a shell, or a flower, little things
Which else would have been past by!
And now I remember, I,
When he lay dying there,
I noticed one of his many rings—
For he had many, poor worm—and thought,
It is his mother's hair.

IX

Who knows if he be dead?
Whether I need have fled?   120
Am I guilty of blood?
However this may be,
Comfort her, comfort her, all things good,
While I am over the sea!
Let me and my passionate love go by,
But speak to her all things holy and high,
Whatever happen to me!
Me and my harmful love go by;
But come to her waking, find her asleep,
Powers of the height, Powers of the deep,   130
And comfort her tho' I die!

III

Courage, poor heart of stone!
I will not ask thee why
Thou canst not understand
That thou art left for ever alone;
Courage, poor stupid heart of stone!—
Or if I ask thee why,
Care not thou to reply:
She is but dead, and the time is at hand
When thou shalt more than die.   140

IV

I

O that 'twere possible
After long grief and pain
To find the arms of my true love
Round me once again!

II

When I was wont to meet her
In the silent woody places
By the home that gave me birth,
We stood tranced in long embraces
Mixt with kisses sweeter, sweeter
Than anything on earth.   150

III

A shadow flits before me,
Not thou, but like to thee.
Ah, Christ, that it were possible
For one short hour to see
The souls we loved, that they might tell us
What and where they be!

IV

It leads me forth at evening,
It lightly winds and steals
In a cold white robe before me,
When all my spirit reels   160
At the shouts, the leagues of lights,
And the roaring of the wheels.

V

Half the night I waste in sighs,
Half in dreams I sorrow after
The delight of early skies;
In a wakeful doze I sorrow
For the hand, the lips, the eyes,
For the meeting of the morrow,
The delight of happy laughter,
The delight of low replies.   170

VI

'Tis a morning pure and sweet,
And a dewy splendor falls
On the little flower that clings
To the turrets and the walls;
'Tis a morning pure and sweet,
And the light and shadow fleet.
She is walking in the meadow,

And the woodland echo rings;
In a moment we shall meet.
She is singing in the meadow,   180
And the rivulet at her feet
Ripples on in light and shadow
To the ballad that she sings.

VII

Do I hear her sing as of old,
My bird with the shining head,
My own dove with the tender eye?
But there rings on a sudden a passionate cry,
There is some one dying or dead,
And a sullen thunder is roll'd;
For a tumult shakes the city,   190
And I wake, my dream is fled.
In the shuddering dawn, behold,
Without knowledge, without pity,
By the curtains of my bed
That abiding phantom cold!

VIII

Get thee hence, nor come again,
Mix not memory with doubt,
Pass, thou deathlike type of pain,
Pass and cease to move about!
'Tis the blot upon the brain   200
That *will* show itself without.

IX

Then I rise, the eve-drops fall,
And the yellow vapors choke
The great city sounding wide;
The day comes, a dull red ball
Wrapt in drifts of lurid smoke
On the misty river-tide.

X

Thro' the hubbub of the market
I steal, a wasted frame;
It crosses here, it crosses there,   210
Thro' all that crowd confused and loud,
The shadow still the same;
And on my heavy eyelids
My anguish hangs like shame.

XI

Alas for her that met me,
That heard me softly call,
Came glimmering thro' the laurels
At the quiet evenfall,
In the garden by the turrets
Of the old manorial hall!   220

XII

Would the happy spirit descend
From the realms of light and song,
In the chamber or the street,
As she looks among the blest,
Should I fear to greet my friend
Or to say 'Forgive the wrong,'
Or to ask her, 'Take me, sweet,
To the regions of thy rest'?

XIII

But the broad light glares and beats,
And the shadow flits and fleets   230
And will not let me be;
And I loathe the squares and streets,
And the faces that one meets,
Hearts with no love for me.
Always I long to creep
Into some still cavern deep,
There to weep, and weep, and weep
My whole soul out to thee.

V

I

Dead, long dead,
Long dead!   240
And my heart is a handful of dust,
And the wheels go over my head,
And my bones are shaken with pain,
For into a shallow grave they are thrust,
Only a yard beneath the street,
And the hoofs of the horses beat, beat,
The hoofs of the horses beat,
Beat into my scalp and my brain,

With never an end to the stream of passing feet,
Driving, hurrying, marrying, burying,   250
Clamor and rumble, and ringing and clatter;
And here beneath it is all as bad,
For I thought the dead had peace, but it is not so.
To have no peace in the grave, is that not sad?
But up and down and to and fro,
Ever about me the dead men go;
And then to hear a dead man chatter
Is enough to drive one mad.

II

Wretchedest age, since Time began,
They cannot even bury a man;   260
And tho' we paid our tithes in the days that are gone,
Not a bell was rung, not a prayer was read.
It is that which makes us loud in the world of the dead;
There is none that does his work, not one.
A touch of their office might have sufficed,
But the churchmen fain would kill their church,
As the churches have kill'd their Christ.

III

See, there is one of us sobbing,
No limit to his distress;
And another, a lord of all things, praying   270
To his own great self, as I guess;
And another, a statesman there, betraying
His party-secret, fool, to the press;
And yonder a vile physician, blabbing
The case of his patient—all for what?
To tickle the maggot born in an empty head,
And wheedle a world that loves him not,
For it is but a world of the dead.

IV

Nothing but idiot gabble!
For the prophecy given of old   280
And then not understood,
Has come to pass as foretold;
Not let any man think for the public good,
But babble, merely for babble.
For I never whisper'd a private affair
Within the hearing of cat or mouse,
No, not to myself in the closet alone,

But I heard it shouted at once from the top of the house;
Everything came to be known.
Who told *him* we were there?   290

V

Not that gray old wolf, for he came not back
From the wilderness, full of wolves, where he used to lie;
He has gather'd the bones for his o'ergrown whelp to crack—
Crack them now for yourself, and howl, and die.

VI

Prophet, curse me the blabbing lip,
And curse me the British vermin, the rat;
I know not whether he came in the Hanover ship,
But I know that he lies and listens mute
In an ancient mansion's crannies and holes.
Arsenic, arsenic, sure, would do it,   300
Except that now we poison our babes, poor souls!
It is all used up for that.

VII

Tell him now: she is standing here at my head;
Not beautiful now, not even kind;
He may take her now; for she never speaks her mind,
But is ever the one thing silent here.
She is not *of* us, as I divine,
She comes from another stiller world of the dead,
Stiller, not fairer than mine.

VIII

But I know where a garden grows,   310
Fairer than aught in the world beside,
All made up of the lily and rose
That blow by night, when the season is good,
To the sound of dancing music and flutes:
It is only flowers, they had no fruits,
And I almost fear they are not roses, but blood;
For the keeper was one, so full of pride,
He linkt a dead man there to a spectral bride;
For he, if he had not been a Sultan of brutes,
Would he have that hole in his side?   320

IX

But what will the old man say?
He laid a cruel snare in a pit
To catch a friend of mine one stormy day;
Yet now I could even weep to think of it;
For what will the old man say
When he comes to the second corpse in the pit?

X

Friend, to be struck by the public foe,
Then to strike him and lay him low,
That were a public merit, far,
Whatever the Quaker holds, from sin;   330
But the red life spilt for a private blow—
I swear to you, lawful and lawless war
Are scarcely even akin.

XI

O me, why have they not buried me deep enough?
Is it kind to have made me a grave so rough,
Me, that was never a quiet sleeper?
Maybe still I am but half-dead;
Then I cannot be wholly dumb.
I will cry to the steps above my head
And somebody, surely, some kind heart will come   340
To bury me, bury me
Deeper, ever so little deeper.

PART III

I

My life has crept so long on a broken wing
Thro' cells of madness, haunts of horror and fear,
That I come to be grateful at last for a little thing.
My mood is changed, for it fell at a time of year
When the face of night is fair on the dewy downs,
And the shining daffodil dies, and the Charioteer
And starry Gemini hang like glorious crowns
Over Orion's grave low down in the west,
That like a silent lightning under the stars
She seem'd to divide in a dream from a band of the blest,   10
And spoke of a hope for the world in the coming wars—

'And in that hope, dear soul, let trouble have rest,
Knowing I tarry for thee,' and pointed to Mars
As he glow'd like a ruddy shield on the Lion's breast.

II

And it was but a dream, yet it yielded a dear delight
To have look'd, tho' but in a dream, upon eyes so fair,
That had been in a weary world my one thing bright;
And it was but a dream, yet it lighten'd my despair
When I thought that a war would arise in defence of the right,
That an iron tyranny now should bend or cease,   20
The glory of manhood stand on his ancient height,
Nor Britain's one sole God be the millionaire.
No more shall commerce be all in all, and Peace
Pipe on her pastoral hillock a languid note,
And watch her harvest ripen, her herd increase,
Nor the cannon-bullet rust on a slothful shore,
And the cobweb woven across the cannon's throat
Shall shake its threaded tears in the wind no more.

III

And as months ran on and rumor of battle grew,
'It is time, it is time, O passionate heart,' said I,—   30
For I cleaved to a cause that I felt to be pure and true,—
'It is time, O passionate heart and morbid eye,
That old hysterical mock-disease should die.'
And I stood on a giant deck and mixt my breath
With a loyal people shouting a battle-cry,
Till I saw the dreary phantom arise and fly
Far into the North, and battle, and seas of death.

IV

Let it go or stay, so I wake to the higher aims
Of a land that has lost for a little her lust of gold,
And love of a peace that was full of wrongs and shames,   40
Horrible, hateful, monstrous, not to be told;
And hail once more to the banner of battle unroll'd!
Tho' many a light shall darken, and many shall weep
For those that are crush'd in the clash of jarring claims,
Yet God's just wrath shall be wreak'd on a giant liar,
And many a darkness into the light shall leap,
And shine in the sudden making of splendid names,
And noble thought be freer under the sun,
And the heart of a people beat with one desire;
For the peace, that I deem'd no peace, is over and done,   50

And now by the side of the Black and the Baltic deep,
And deathful-grinning mouths of the fortress, flames
The blood-red blossom of war with a heart of fire.

V

Let it flame or fade, and the war roll down like a wind,
We have proved we have hearts in a cause, we are noble still,
And myself have awaked, as it seems, to the better mind.
It is better to fight for the good than to rail at the ill;
I have felt with my native land, I am one with my kind,
I embrace the purpose of God, and the doom assign'd.

THE BROOK

'HERE by this brook we parted, I to the East
And he for Italy—too late—too late:
One whom the strong sons of the world despise;
For lucky rhymes to him were scrip and share,
And mellow metres more than cent for cent.
Nor could he understand how money breeds,
Thought it a dead thing; yet himself could make
The thing that is not as the thing that is.
O, had he lived! In our schoolbooks we say
Of those that held their heads above the crowd,   10
They flourish'd then or then; but life in him
Could scarce be said to flourish, only touch'd
On such a time as goes before the leaf,
When all the wood stands in a mist of green,
And nothing perfect. Yet the brook he loved,
For which, in branding summers of Bengal,
Or even the sweet half-English Neilgherry air,
I panted, seems, as I re-listen to it,
Prattling the primrose fancies of the boy
To me that loved him; for "O brook," he says,   20
"O babbling brook," says Edmund in his rhyme,
"Whence come you?" and the brook—why not?—replies:

　　　I come from haunts of coot and hern,
　　　　　I make a sudden sally,
　　　And sparkle out among the fern,
　　　　　To bicker down a valley.

　　　By thirty hills I hurry down,
　　　　　Or slip between the ridges,
　　　By twenty thorps, a little town,
　　　　　And half a hundred bridges.   30

Till last by Philip's farm I flow
    To join the brimming river,
For men may come and men may go,
    But I go on for ever.

'Poor lad, he died at Florence, quite worn out,
Travelling to Naples. There is Darnley bridge,
It has more ivy; there the river; and there
Stands Philip's farm where brook and river meet.

I chatter over stony ways,
    In little sharps and trebles,
I bubble into eddying bays,
    I babble on the pebbles.

With many a curve my banks I fret
    By many a field and fallow,
And many a fairy foreland set
    With willow-weed and mallow.

I chatter, chatter, as I flow
    To join the brimming river,
For men may come and men may go,
    But I go on for ever.

'But Philip chatter'd more than brook or bird,
Old Philip; all about the fields you caught
His weary daylong chirping, like the dry
High-elbow'd grigs that leap in summer grass.

I wind about, and in and out,
    With here a blossom sailing,
And here and there a lusty trout,
    And here and there a grayling,

And here and there a foamy flake
    Upon me, as I travel
With many a silvery water-break
    Above the golden gravel,

And draw them all along, and flow
    To join the brimming river,
For men may come and men may go,
    But I go on for ever.

'O darling Katie Willows, his one child!
A maiden of our century, yet most meek;
A daughter of our meadows, yet not coarse;
Straight, but as lissome as a hazel wand;
Her eyes a bashful azure, and her hair
In gloss and hue the chestnut, when the shell
Divides threefold to show the fruit within.

'Sweet Katie, once I did her a good turn,
Her and her far-off cousin and betrothed,
James Willows, of one name and heart with her.
For here I came, twenty years back—the week
Before I parted with poor Edmund—crost
By that old bridge which, half in ruins then,
Still makes a hoary eyebrow for the gleam   80
Beyond it, where the waters marry—crost,
Whistling a random bar of Bonny Doon,
And push'd at Philip's garden-gate. The gate,
Half-parted from a weak and scolding hinge,
Stuck; and he clamor'd from a casement, "Run,"
To Katie somewhere in the walks below,
"Run, Katie!" Katie never ran; she moved
To meet me, winding under woodbine bowers,
A little flutter'd, with her eyelids down,
Fresh apple-blossom, blushing for a boon.   90

'What was it? less of sentiment than sense
Had Katie; not illiterate, nor of those
Who dabbling in the fount of fictive tears,
And nursed by mealy-mouth'd philanthropies,
Divorce the Feeling from her mate the Deed.

'She told me. She and James had quarrell'd. Why?
What cause of quarrel? None, she said, no cause;
James had no cause: but when I prest the cause,
I learnt that James had flickering jealousies
Which anger'd her. Who anger'd James? I said.   100
But Katie snatch'd her eyes at once from mine,
And sketching with her slender pointed foot
Some figure like a wizard pentagram
On garden gravel, let my query pass
Unclaim'd, in flushing silence, till I ask'd
If James were coming. "Coming every day,"
She answer'd, "ever longing to explain,
But evermore her father came across
With some long-winded tale, and broke him short;
And James departed vext with him and her."   110
How could I help her? "Would I—was it wrong?"—
Claspt hands and that petitionary grace
Of sweet seventeen subdued me ere she spoke—
"O, would I take her father for one hour,
For one half-hour, and let him talk to me!"
And even while she spoke, I saw where James
Made toward us, like a wader in the surf,
Beyond the brook, waist-deep in meadow-sweet.

'O Katie, what I suffer'd for your sake!
For in I went, and call'd old Philip out   120
To show the farm. Full willingly he rose;
He led me thro' the short sweet-smelling lanes
Of his wheat-suburb, babbling as he went.
He praised his land, his horses, his machines;
He praised his ploughs, his cows, his hogs, his dogs;
He praised his hens, his geese, his guinea-hens,
His pigeons, who in session on their roofs
Approved him, bowing at their own deserts.
Then from the plaintive mother's teat he took
Her blind and shuddering puppies, naming each,   130
And naming those, his friends, for whom they were;
Then crost the common into Darnley chase
To show Sir Arthur's deer. In copse and fern
Twinkled the innumerable ear and tail.
Then, seated on a serpent-rooted beech,
He pointed out a pasturing colt, and said,
"That was the four-year-old I sold the Squire."
And there he told a long, long-winded tale
Of how the Squire had seen the colt at grass,
And how it was the thing his daughter wish'd,   140
And how he sent the bailiff to the farm
To learn the price, and what the price he ask'd,
And how the bailiff swore that he was mad,
But he stood firm, and so the matter hung;
He gave them line; and five days after that
He met the bailiff at the Golden Fleece,
Who then and there had offer'd something more,
But he stood firm, and so the matter hung;
He knew the man, the colt would fetch its price;
He gave them line; and how by chance at last—   156
It might be May or April, he forgot,
The last of April or the first of May—
He found the bailiff riding by the farm,
And, talking from the point, he drew him in,
And there he mellow'd all his heart with ale,
Until they closed a bargain, hand in hand.

'Then, while I breathed in sight of haven, he—
Poor fellow, could he help it?—recommenced.
And ran thro' all the coltish chronicle,
Wild Will, Black Bess, Tantivy, Tallyho,   160
Reform, White Rose, Bellerophon, the Jilt,
Arbaces, and Phenomenon, and the rest,
Till, not to die a listener, I arose,
And with me Philip, talking still; and so
We turn'd our foreheads from the falling sun,

And following our own shadows thrice as long
As when they follow'd us from Philip's door,
Arrived, and found the sun of sweet content
Re-risen in Katie's eyes, and all things well.

    I steal by lawns and grassy plots,   170
      I slide by hazel covers;
    I move the sweet forget-me-nots
      That grow for happy lovers.

    I slip, I slide, I gloom, I glance,
      Among my skimming swallows;
    I make the netted sunbeam dance
      Against my sandy shallows.

    I murmur under moon and stars
      In brambly wildernesses;
    I linger by my shingly bars,   180
      I loiter round my cresses;

    And out again I curve and flow
      To join the brimming river,
    For men may come and men may go,
      But I go on for ever.

Yes, men may come and go; and these are gone,
All gone. My dearest brother, Edmund, sleeps,
Not by the well-known stream and rustic spire,
But unfamiliar Arno, and the dome
Of Brunelleschi, sleeps in peace; and he,   190
Poor Philip, of all his lavish waste of words
Remains the lean P. W. on his tomb;
I scraped the lichen from it. Katie walks
By the long wash of Australasian seas
Far off, and holds her head to other stars,
And breathes in April-autumns. All are gone.'

    So Lawrence Aylmer, seated on a stile
In the long hedge, and rolling in his mind
Old waifs of rhyme, and bowing o'er the brook
A tonsured head in middle age forlorn,   200
Mused, and was mute. On a sudden a low breath
Of tender air made tremble in the hedge
The fragile bindweed-bells and briony rings;
And he look'd up. There stood a maiden near,
Waiting to pass. In much amaze he stared
On eyes a bashful azure, and on hair
In gloss and hue the chestnut, when the shell
Divides threefold to show the fruit within;
Then, wondering, ask'd her, 'Are you from the farm?'
'Yes,' answer'd she. 'Pray stay a little; pardon me,   210
What do they call you?' 'Katie.' 'That were strange.

What surname?' 'Willows.' 'No!' 'That is my name.'
'Indeed!' and here he look'd so self-perplext,
That Katie laugh'd, and laughing blush'd, till he
Laugh'd also, but as one before he wakes,
Who feels a glimmering strangeness in his dream.
Then looking at her: 'Too happy, fresh and fair,
Too fresh and fair in our sad world's best bloom,
To be the ghost of one who bore your name
About these meadows, twenty years ago.'   220

    'Have you not heard?' said Katie, 'we came back.
We bought the farm we tenanted before.
Am I so like her? so they said on board.
Sir, if you knew her in her English days,
My mother, as it seems you did, the days
That most she loves to talk of, come with me.
My brother James is in the harvest-field;
But she—you will be welcome—O, come in!'

THE DAISY

WRITTEN AT EDINBURGH

O LOVE, what hours were thine and mine,
In lands of palm and southern pine;
   In lands of palm, or orange-blossom,
Of olive, aloe, and maize and vine!

What Roman strength Turbìa show'd
In ruin, by the mountain road;
   How like a gem, beneath, the city
Of little Monaco, basking, glow'd!

How richly down the rocky dell
The torrent vineyard streaming fell   10
   To meet the sun and sunny waters,
That only heaved with a summer swell!

What slender campanili grew
By bays, the peacock's neck in hue;
   Where, here and there, on sandy beaches
A milky-bell'd amaryllis blew!

How young Columbus seem'd to rove,
Yet present in his natal grove,
   Now watching high on mountain cornice,
And steering, now, from a purple cove,   20

Now pacing mute by ocean's rim;
Till, in a narrow street and dim,
 I stay'd the wheels at Cogoletto,
And drank, and loyally drank to him!

Nor knew we well what pleased us most;
Not the clipt palm of which they boast,
 But distant color, happy hamlet,
A moulder'd citadel on the coast,

Or tower, or high hill-convent, seen
A light amid its olives green;
 Or olive-hoary cape in ocean;
Or rosy blossom in hot ravine,   30

Where oleanders flush'd the bed
Of silent torrents, gravel-spread;
 And, crossing, oft we saw the glisten
Of ice, far up on a mountain head.

We loved that hall, tho' white and cold,
Those niched shapes of noble mould,
 A princely people's awful princes,
The grave, severe Genovese of old.   40

At Florence too what golden hours,
In those long galleries, were ours;
 What drives about the fresh Cascinè,
Or walks in Boboli's ducal bowers!

In bright vignettes, and each complete,
Of tower or duomo, sunny-sweet,
 Or palace, how the city glitter'd,
Thro' cypress avenues, at our feet!

But when we crost the Lombard plain
Remember what a plague of rain;   50
 Of rain at Reggio, rain at Parma,
At Lodi rain, Piacenza rain.

And stern and sad—so rare the smiles
Of sunlight—look'd the Lombard piles;
 Porch-pillars on the lion resting,
And sombre, old, colonnaded aisles.

O Milan, O the chanting quires,
The giant windows' blazon'd fires,
 The height, the space, the gloom, the glory!
A mount of marble, a hundred spires!   60

I climb'd the roofs at break of day;
Sun-smitten Alps before me lay.
    I stood among the silent statues,
And statued pinnacles, mute as they.

How faintly-flush'd, how phantom-fair,
Was Monte Rosa, hanging there
    A thousand shadowy-pencill'd valleys
And snowy dells in a golden air!

Remember how we came at last
To Como; shower and storm and blast   70
    Had blown the lake beyond his limit,
And all was flooded; and how we past

From Como, when the light was gray,
And in my head, for half the day,
    The rich Virgilian rustic measure
Of 'Lari Maxume,' all the way,

Like ballad-burthen music, kept,
As on the Lariano crept
    To that fair port below the castle
Of Queen Theodolind, where we slept;   80

Or hardly slept, but watch'd awake
A cypress in the moonlight shake,
    The moonlight touching o'er a terrace
One tall agavè above the lake.

What more? we took our last adieu,
And up the snowy Splügen drew;
    But ere we reach'd the highest summit
I pluck'd a daisy, I gave it you.

It told of England then to me,
And now it tells of Italy.   90
    O love, we two shall go no longer
To lands of summer across the sea,

So dear a life your arms enfold
Whose crying is a cry for gold;
    Yet here to-night in this dark city,
When ill and weary, alone and cold,

I found, tho' crush'd to hard and dry,
This nursling of another sky
    Still in the little book you lent me,
And where you tenderly laid it by;   100

And I forgot the clouded Forth,
The gloom that saddens heaven and earth,
  The bitter east, the misty summer
And gray metropolis of the North.

Perchance to lull the throbs of pain,
Perchance to charm a vacant brain,
  Perchance to dream you still beside me,
My fancy fled to the South again.

TO THE REV. F. D. MAURICE

COME, when no graver cares employ,
Godfather, come and see your boy;
  Your presence will be sun in winter,
Making the little one leap for joy.

For, being of that honest few
Who give the Fiend himself his due,
  Should eighty thousand college-councils
Thunder 'Anathema.' friend, at you,

Should all our churchmen foam in spite
At you, so careful of the right,   10
  Yet one lay-hearth would give you welcome—
Take it and come—to the Isle of Wight;

Where, far from noise and smoke of town,
I watch the twilight falling brown
  All round a careless-order'd garden
Close to the ridge of a noble down.

You'll have no scandal while you dine,
But honest talk and wholesome wine,
  And only hear the magpie gossip
Garrulous under a roof of pine;   20

For groves of pine on either hand,
To break the blast of winter, stand,
  And further on, the hoary Channel
Tumbles a billow on chalk and sand;

Where, if below the milky steep
Some ship of battle slowly creep,
  And on thro' zones of light and shadow
Glimmer away to the lonely deep,

We might discuss the Northern sin
Which made a selfish war begin, 30
   Dispute the claims, arrange the chances,—
Emperor, Ottoman, which shall win;

Or whether war's avenging rod
Shall lash all Europe into blood;
   Till you should turn to dearer matters,
Dear to the man that is dear to God,—

How best to help the slender store,
How mend the dwellings, of the poor,
   How gain in life, as life advances, 40
Valor and charity more and more.

Come, Maurice, come; the lawn as yet
Is hoar with rime or spongy-wet,
   But when the wreath of March has blossom'd,—
Crocus, anemone, violet,—

Or later, pay one visit here,
For those are few we hold as dear;
   Nor pay but one, but come for many,
Many and many a happy year.
January, 1854.

WILL

I

O, WELL for him whose will is strong!
He suffers, but he will not suffer long;
He suffers, but he cannot suffer wrong.
For him nor moves the loud world's random mock,
Nor all Calamity's hugest waves confound,
Who seems a promontory of rock,
That, compass'd round with turbulent sound,
In middle ocean meets the surging shock,
Tempest-buffeted, citadel-crown'd.

II

But ill for him who, bettering not with time,
Corrupts the strength of heaven-descended Will,
And ever weaker grows thro' acted crime,
Or seeming-genial venial fault,
Recurring and suggesting still!

He seems as one whose footsteps halt,
Toiling in immeasurable sand,
And o'er a weary sultry land,
Far beneath a blazing vault,
Sown in a wrinkle of the monstrous hill,
The city sparkles like a grain of salt.

ODE ON THE DEATH OF THE DUKE OF WELLINGTON

I

BURY the Great Duke
  With an empire's lamentation;
Let us bury the Great Duke
  To the noise of the mourning of a mighty nation;
Mourning when their leaders fall,
Warriors carry the warrior's pall,
And sorrow darkens hamlet and hall.

II

Where shall we lay the man whom we deplore?
Here, in streaming London's central roar.
Let the sound of those he wrought for,   10
And the feet of those he fought for,
Echo round his bones for evermore.

III

Lead out the pageant: sad and slow,
As fits an universal woe,
Let the long, long procession go,
And let the sorrowing crowd about it grow,
And let the mournful martial music blow;
The last great Englishman is low.

IV

Mourn, for to us he seems the last,
Remembering all his greatness in the past.   20
No more in soldier fashion will he greet
With lifted hand the gazer in the street.
O friends, our chief state-oracle is mute!
Mourn for the man of long-enduring blood,
The statesman-warrior, moderate, resolute,
Whole in himself, a common good.

Mourn for the man of amplest influence,
Yet clearest of ambitious crime,
Our greatest yet with least pretence,
Great in council and great in war,   30
Foremost captain of his time,
Rich in saving common-sense,
And, as the greatest only are,
In his simplicity sublime.
O good gray head which all men knew,
O voice from which their omens all men drew,
O iron nerve to true occasion true,
O fallen at length that tower of strength
Which stood four-square to all the winds that blew!
Such was he whom we deplore.   40
The long self-sacrifice of life is o'er.
The great World-victor's victor will be seen no more.

V

All is over and done.
Render thanks to the Giver,
England, for thy son.
Let the bell be toll'd.
Render thank to the Giver.
And render him to the mould.
Under the cross of gold
That shines over city and river,   50
There he shall rest for ever
Among the wise and the bold.
Let the bell be toll'd,
And a reverent people behold
The towering car, the sable steeds.
Bright let it be with its blazon'd deeds,
Dark in its funeral fold.
Let the bell be toll'd,
And a deeper knell in the heart be knoll'd;
And the sound of the sorrowing anthem roll'd   60
Thro' the dome of the golden cross;
And the volleying cannon thunder his loss;
He knew their voices of old.
For many a time in many a clime
His captain's-ear has heard them boom
Bellowing victory, bellowing doom.
When he with those deep voices wrought,
Guarding realms and kings from shame,
With those deep voices our dead captain taught
The tyrant, and asserts his claim   70

In that dread sound to the great name
Which he has worn so pure of blame,
In praise and in dispraise the same,
A man of well-attemper'd frame.
O civic muse, to such a name,
To such a name for ages long,
To such a name,
Preserve a broad approach of fame,
And ever-echoing avenues of song!

VI

'Who is he that cometh, like an honor'd guest,   80
With banner and with music, with soldier and with priest,
With a nation weeping, and breaking on my rest?'—
Mighty Seaman, this is he
Was great by land as thou by sea.
Thine island loves thee well, thou famous man,
The greatest sailor since our world began.
Now, to the roll of muffled drums,
To thee the greatest soldier comes;
For this is he
Was great by land as thou by sea.   90
His foes were thine; he kept us free;
O, give him welcome, this is he
Worthy of our gorgeous rites,
And worthy to be laid by thee;
For this is England's greatest son,
He that gain'd a hundred fights,
Nor ever lost an English gun;
This is he that far away
Against the myriads of Assaye
Clash'd with his fiery few and won;   100
And underneath another sun,
Warring on a later day,
Round affrighted Lisbon drew
The treble works, the vast designs
Of his labor'd rampart-lines,
Where he greatly stood at bay,
Whence he issued forth anew,
And ever great and greater grew,
Beating from the wasted vines
Back to France her banded swarms,   110
Back to France with countless blows,
Till o'er the hills her eagles flew
Beyond the Pyrenean pines,

Follow'd up in valley and glen
With blare of bugle, clamor of men,
Roll of cannon and clash of arms,
And England pouring on her foes.
Such a war had such a close.
Again their ravening eagle rose   120
In anger, wheel'd on Europe-shadowing wings,
And barking for the thrones of kings;
Till one that sought but Duty's iron crown
On that loud Sabbath shook the spoiler down;
A day of onsets of despair!
Dash'd on every rocky square,
Their surging charges foam'd themselves away;
Last, the Prussian trumpet blew;
Thro' the long-tormented air
Heaven flash'd a sudden jubilant ray,
And down we swept and charged and overthrew.   130
So great a soldier taught us there
What long-enduring hearts could do
In that world-earthquake, Waterloo!
Mighty Seaman, tender and true,
And pure as he from taint of craven guile,
O saviour of the silver-coasted isle,
O shaker of the Baltic and the Nile,
If aught of things that here befall
Touch a spirit among things divine,
If love of country move thee there at all,   140
Be glad, because his bones are laid by thine!
And thro' the centuries let a people's voice
In full acclaim,
A people's voice,
The proof and echo of all human fame,
A people's voice, when they rejoice
At civic revel and pomp and game,
Attest their great commander's claim
With honor, honor, honor, honor to him,
Eternal honor to his name.   150

VII

A people's voice! we are a people yet.
Tho' all men else their nobler dreams forget,
Confused by brainless mobs and lawless Powers,
Thank Him who isled us here, and roughly set
His Briton in blown seas and storming showers,
We have a voice with which to pay the debt
Of boundless love and reverence and regret
To those great men who fought, and kept it ours.

And keep it ours, O God, from brute control!
O statesmen, guard us, guard the eye, the soul   160
Of Europe, keep our noble England whole,
And save the one true seed of freedom sown
Betwixt a people and their ancient throne,
That sober freedom out of which there springs
Our loyal passion for our temperate kings!
For, saving that, ye help to save mankind
Till public wrong be crumbled into dust,
And drill the raw world for the march of mind,
Till crowds at length be sane and crowns be just.
But wink no more in slothful overtrust.   170
Remember him who led your hosts;
He bade you guard the sacred coasts.
Your cannons moulder on the seaward wall;
His voice is silent in your council-hall
For ever; and whatever tempests lour
For ever silent; even if they broke
In thunder, silent; yet remember all
He spoke among you, and the Man who spoke;
Who never sold the truth to serve the hour,
Nor palter'd with Eternal God for power;   180
Who let the turbid streams of rumor flow
Thro' either babbling world of high and low;
Whose life was work, whose language rife
With rugged maxims hewn from life;
Who never spoke against a foe;
Whose eighty winters freeze with one rebuke
All great self-seekers trampling on the right.
Truth-teller was our England's Alfred named;
Truth-lover was our English Duke;
Whatever record leap to light   190
He never shall be shamed.

VIII

Lo! the leader in these glorious wars
Now to glorious burial slowly borne,
Follow'd by the brave of other lands,
He, on whom from both her open hands
Lavish Honor shower'd all her stars,
And affluent Fortune emptied all her horn.
Yea, let all good things await
Him who cares not to be great
But as he saves or serves the state.   200
Not once or twice in our rough island-story
The path of duty was the way to glory.

He that walks it, only thirsting
For the right, and learns to deaden
Love of self, before his journey closes,
He shall find the stubborn thistle bursting
Into glossy purples, which outredden
All voluptuous garden-roses.
Not once or twice in our fair island-story
The path of duty was the way to glory.   210
He, that ever following her commands,
On with toil of heart and knees and hands,
Thro' the long gorge to the far light has won
His path upward, and prevail'd,
Shall find the toppling crags of Duty scaled
Are close upon the shining table-lands
To which our God Himself is moon and sun.
Such was he: his work is done.
But while the races of mankind endure
Let his great example stand   220
Colossal, seen of every land,
And keep the soldier firm, the statesman pure;
Till in all lands and thro' all human story
The path of duty be the way to glory.
And let the land whose hearths he saved from shame
For many and many an age proclaim
At civic revel and pomp and game,
And when the long-illumined cities flame,
Their ever-loyal iron leader's fame,
With honor, honor, honor, honor to him,   230
Eternal honor to his name.

IX

Peace, his triumph will be sung
By some yet unmoulded tongue
Far on in summers that we shall not see.
Peace, it is a day of pain
For one about whose patriarchal knee
Late the little children clung.
O peace, it is a day of pain
For one upon whose hand and heart and brain
Once the weight and fate of Europe hung.   240
Ours the pain, be his the gain!
More than is of man's degree
Must be with us, watching here
At this, our great solemnity
Whom we see not we revere;
We revere, and we refrain
From talk of battles loud and vain,

And brawling memories all too free
For such a wise humility
As befits a solemn fane: 250
We revere, and while we hear
The tides of Music's golden sea
Setting toward eternity,
Uplifted high in heart and hope are we,
Until we doubt not that for one so true
There must be other nobler work to do
Than when he fought at Waterloo,
And Victor he must ever be.
For tho' the Giant Ages heave the hill
And break the shore, and evermore   260
Make and break, and work their will,
Tho' world on world in myriad myriads roll
Round us, each with different powers,
And other forms of life than ours,
What know we greater than the soul?
On God and Godlike men we build our trust.
Hush, the Dead March wails in the people's ears;
The dark crowd moves, and there are sobs and tears;
The black earth yawns; the mortal disappears;
Ashes to ashes, dust to dust;   270
He is gone who seem'd so great.—
Gone, but nothing can bereave him
Of the force he made his own
Being here, and we believe him
Something far advanced in State,
And that he wears a truer crown
Than any wreath that man can weave him.
Speak no more of his renown,
Lay your earthly fancies down,
And in the vast cathedral leave him,   280
God accept him, Christ receive him!
　　1852.

THE CHARGE OF THE LIGHT BRIGADE

I

HALF a league, half a league,
Half a league onward,
All in the valley of Death
　　Rode the six hundred.
'Forward the Light Brigade!
Charge for the guns!' he said.
Into the valley of Death
　　Rode the six hundred.

II

'Forward the Light Brigade!'
Was there a man dismay'd?
Not tho' the soldier knew
   Some one had blunder'd.
Theirs not to make reply,
Theirs not to reason why,
Theirs but to do and die.
Into the valley of Death
   Rode the six hundred.

III

Cannon to right of them,
Cannon to left of them,
Cannon in front of them
   Volley'd and thunder'd;
Storm'd at with shot and shell,
Boldly they rode and well,
Into the jaws of Death,
Into the mouth of hell,
   Rode the six hundred.

IV

Flash'd all their sabres bare,
Flash'd as they turn'd in air
Sabring the gunners there,
Charging an army, while
   All the world wonder'd.
Plunged in the battery-smoke
Right thro' the line they broke;
Cossack and Russian
Reel'd from the sabre-stroke
   Shatter'd and sunder'd.
Then they rode back, but not,
   Not the six hundred.

V

Cannon to right of them,
Cannon to left of them,
Cannon behind them
   Volley'd and thunder'd;
Storm'd at with shot and shell,
While horse and hero fell,

They that had fought so well
Came thro' the jaws of Death,
Back from the mouth of hell,
All that was left of them,
    Left of six hundred.

VI

When can their glory fade?
O the wild charge they made!
    All the world wonder'd.
Honor the charge they made!
Honor the Light Brigade,
    Noble six hundred!

IDYLLS OF THE KING

IN TWELVE BOOKS

'Flos Regum Arthurus.'—JOSEPH OF EXETER

DEDICATION

THESE to His Memory—since he held them dear,
Perchance as finding there unconsciously
Some image of himself—I dedicate,
I dedicate, I consecrate with tears—
These Idylls.
           And indeed he seems to me.
Scarce other than my king's ideal knight,
'Who reverenced his conscience as his king;
Whose glory was, redressing human wrong;
Who spake no slander, no, nor listen'd to it;
Who loved one only and who clave to her—'   **10**
Her—over all whose realms to their last isle,
Commingled with the gloom of imminent war,
The shadow of his loss drew like eclipse,
Darkening the world. We have lost him; he is gone.
We know him now; all narrow jealousies
Are silent, and we see him as he moved,
How modest, kindly, all-accomplish'd, wise,
With what sublime repression of himself,
And in what limits, and how tenderly;
Not swaying to this faction or to that;   **20**
Not making his high place the lawless perch
Of wing'd ambitions, nor a vantage-ground
For pleasure; but thro' all this tract of years
Wearing the white flower of a blameless life,
Before a thousand peering littlenesses,

In that fierce light which beats upon a throne
And blackens every blot; for where is he
Who dares foreshadow for an only son
A lovelier life, a more unstain'd, than his?
Or how should England dreaming of *his* sons   30
Hope more for these than some inheritance
Of such a life, a heart, a mind as thine,
Thou noble Father of her Kings to be,
Laborious for her people and her poor—
Voice in the rich dawn of an ampler day—
Far-sighted summoner of War and Waste
To fruitful strifes and rivalries of peace—
Sweet nature gilded by the gracious gleam
Of letters, dear to Science, dear to Art,
Dear to thy land and ours, a Prince indeed,   40
Beyond all titles, and a household name,
Hereafter, thro' all times, Albert the Good.

Break not, O woman's-heart but still endure;
Break not, for thou art royal, but endure,
Remembering all the beauty of that star
Which shone so close beside thee that ye made
One light together, but has past and leaves
The Crown a lonely splendor.
                              May all love,
His love, unseen but felt, o'ershadow thee,
The love of all thy sons encompass thee,   50
The love of all thy daughters cherish thee,
The love of all thy people comfort thee,
Till God's love set thee at his side again!

THE COMING OF ARTHUR

LEODOGRAN, the king of Cameliard,
Had one fair daughter, and none other child;
And she was fairest of all flesh on earth,
Guinevere, and in her his one delight.

For many a petty king ere Arthur came
Ruled in this isle and, ever waging war
Each upon other wasted all the land;
And still from time to time the heathen host
Swarm'd over-seas, and harried what was left.
And so there grew great tracts of wilderness,   10
Wherein the beast was ever more and more,
But man was less and less, till Arthur came.

For first Aurelius lived and fought and died,
And after him King Uther fought and died,
But either fail'd to make the kingdom one.
And after these King Arthur for a space,
And thro' the puissance of his Table Round,
Drew all their petty princedoms under him,
Their king and head, and made a realm and reign'd.

And thus the land of Cameliard was waste,   20
Thick with wet woods, and many a beast therein,
And none or few to scare or chase the beast;
So that wild dog and wolf and boar and bear
Came night and day, and rooted in the fields,
And wallow'd in the gardens of the King.
And ever and anon the wolf would steal
The children and devour, but now and then,
Her own brood lost or dead, lent her fierce teat
To human sucklings; and the children, housed
In her foul den, there at their meat would growl,   30
And mock their foster-mother on four feet,
Till, straighten'd, they grew up to wolf-like men,
Worse than the wolves. And King Leodogran
Groan'd for the Roman legions here again
And Cæsar's eagle. Then his brother king,
Urien, assail'd him; last a heathen horde,
Reddening the sun with smoke and earth with blood,
And on the spike that split the mother's heart
Spitting the child, brake on him, till, amazed,
He knew not whither he should turn for aid.   40

But—for he heard of Arthur newly crown'd,
Tho' not without an uproar made by those
Who cried, 'He is not Uther's son'—the King
Sent to him, saying, 'Arise, and help us thou!
For here between the man and beast we die.'

And Arthur yet had done no deed of arms,
But heard the call and came; and Guinevere
Stood by the castle walls to watch him pass;
But since he neither wore on helm or shield
The golden symbol of his kinglyhood,   50
But rode a simple knight among his knights,
And many of these in richer arms than he,
She saw him not, or mark'd not, if she saw,
One among many, tho' his face was bare.
But Arthur, looking downward as he past,
Felt the light of her eyes into his life

Smite on the sudden, yet rode on, and pitch'd
His tents beside the forest. Then he drave
The heathen; after, slew the beast, and fell'd
The forest, letting in the sun, and made   60
Broad pathways for the hunter and the knight,
And so return'd.
                    For while he linger'd there,
A doubt that ever smoulder'd in the hearts
Of those great lords and barons of his realm
Flash'd forth and into war; for most of these,
Colleaguing with a score of petty kings,
Made head against him, crying: 'Who is he
That he should rule us? who hath proven him
King Uther's son? for lo! we look at him,
And find nor face nor bearing, limbs nor voice,   70
Are like to those of Uther whom we knew.
This is the son of Gorloïs, not the King;
This is the son of Anton, not the King.'

    And Arthur, passing thence to battle, felt
Travail, and throes and agonies of the life,
Desiring to be join'd with Guinevere,
And thinking as he rode: 'Her father said
That there between the man and beast they die.
Shall I not lift her from this land of beasts
Up to my throne and side by side with me?   80
What happiness to reign a lonely king,
Vext—O ye stars that shudder over me,
O earth that soundest hollow under me,
Vext with waste dreams? for saving I be join'd
To her that is the fairest under heaven,
I seem as nothing in the mighty world,
And cannot will my will nor work my work
Wholly, nor make myself in mine own realm
Victor and lord. But were I join'd with her,
Then might we live together as one life,   90
And reigning with one will in everything
Have power on this dark land to lighten it,
And power on this dead world to make it live.'

    Thereafter—as he speaks who tells the tale—
When Arthur reach'd a field of battle bright
With pitch'd pavilions of his foe, the world
Was all so clear about him that he saw
The smallest rock far on the faintest hill,
And even in high day the morning star.
So when the King had set his banner broad,   100
At once from either side, with trumpet-blast,

And shouts and clarions shrilling unto blood,
The long-lanced battle let their horses run.
And now the barons and the kings prevail'd,
And now the King, as here and there that war
Went swaying; but the Powers who walk the world
Made lightnings and great thunders over him,
And dazed all eyes, till Arthur by main might,
And mightier of his hands with every blow,
And leading all his knighthood threw the kings,   110
Carádos, Urien, Cradlemont of Wales,
Claudius, and Clariance of Northumberland,
The King Brandagoras of Latangor,
With Anguisant of Erin, Morganore,
And Lot of Orkney. Then, before a voice
As dreadful as the shout of one who sees
To one who sins, and deems himself alone
And all the world asleep, they swerved and brake
Flying, and Arthur call'd to stay the brands
That hack'd among the flyers, 'Ho! they yield!'   120
So like a painted battle the war stood
Silenced, the living quiet as the dead,
And in the heart of Arthur joy was lord.
He laugh'd upon his warrior whom he loved
And honor'd most. 'Thou dost not doubt me King,
So well thine arm hath wrought for me to-day.'
'Sir and my liege,' he cried, 'the fire of God
Descends upon thee in the battle-field.
I know thee for my King!' Whereat the two,
For each had warded either in the fight,   130
Sware on the field of death a deathless love.
And Arthur said, 'Man's word is God in man;
Let chance what will, I trust thee to the death.'

Then quickly from the foughten field he sent
Ulfius, and Brastias, and Bedivere,
His new-made knights, to King Leodogran,
Saying, 'If I in aught have served thee well,
Give me thy daughter Guinevere to wife.'

Whom when he heard, Leodogran in heart
Debating—'How should I that am a king,   140
However much he holp me at my need,
Give my one daughter saving to a king,
And a king's son?'—lifted his voice, and call'd
A hoary man, his chamberlain, to whom
He trusted all things, and of him required
His counsel: 'Knowest thou aught of Arthur's birth?'

Then spake the hoary chamberlain and said:
Sir King, there be but two old men that know;
And each is twice as old as I; and one
Is Merlin, the wise man that ever served   150
King Uther thro' his magic art, and one
Is Merlin's master—so they call him—Bleys,
Who taught him magic; but the scholar ran
Before the master, and so far that Bleys
Laid magic by, and sat him down, and wrote
All things and whatsoever Merlin did
In one great annal-book, where after-years
Will learn the secret of our Arthur's birth.'

To whom the King Leodogran replied:
'O friend, had I been holpen half as well   160
By this King Arthur as by thee to-day,
Then beast and man had had their share of me;
But summon here before us yet once more
Ulfius, and Brastias, and Bedivere.'

Then, when they came before him, the king said:
'I have seen the cuckoo chased by lesser fowl,
And reason in the chase; but wherefore now
Do these your lords stir up the heat of war,
Some calling Arthur born of Gorloïs,
Others of Anton? Tell me, ye yourselves,   170
Hold ye this Arthur for King Uther's son?'

And Ulfius and Brastias answer'd, 'Ay.'
Then Bedivere, the first of all his knights
Knighted by Arthur at his crowning, spake—
For bold in heart and act and word was he,
Whenever slander breathed against the King—

'Sir, there be many rumors on this head;
For there be those who hate him in their hearts,
Call him baseborn, and since his ways are sweet,
And theirs are bestial, hold him less than man;   180
And there be those who deem him more than man,
And dream he dropt from heaven. But my belief
In all this matter—so ye care to learn—
Sir, for ye know that in King Uther's time
The prince and warrior Gorloïs, he that held
Tintagil castle by the Cornish sea,
Was wedded with a winsome wife, Ygerne;
And daughters had she borne him,—one whereof,
Lot's wife, the Queen of Orkney, Bellicent,
Hath ever like a loyal sister cleaved   190
To Arthur,—but a son she had not borne.

And Uther cast upon her eyes of love;
But she, a stainless wife to Gorloïs,
So loathed the bright dishonor of his love
That Gorloïs and King Uther went to war,
And overthrown was Gorloïs and slain.
Then Uther in his wrath and heat besieged
Ygerne within Tintagil, where her men,
Seeing the mighty swarm about their walls,
Left her and fled, and Uther enter'd in,   200
And there was none to call to but himself.
So, compass'd by the power of the king,
Enforced she was to wed him in her tears,
And with a shameful swiftness; afterward,
Not many moons, King Uther died himself,
Moaning and wailing for an heir to rule
After him, lest the realm should go to wrack.
And that same night, the night of the new year,
By reason of the bitterness and grief
That vext his mother, all before his time   210
Was Arthur born, and all as soon as born
Deliver'd at a secret postern-gate
To Merlin, to be holden far apart
Until his hour should come, because the lords
Of that fierce day were as the lords of this,
Wild beasts, and surely would have torn the child
Piecemeal among them, had they known; for each
But sought to rule for his own self and hand,
And many hated Uther for the sake
Of Gorloïs. Wherefore Merlin took the child,   220
And gave him to Sir Anton, an old knight
And ancient friend of Uther; and his wife
Nursed the young prince, and rear'd him with her own;
And no man knew. And ever since the lords
Have foughten like wild beasts among themselves,
So that the realm has gone to wrack; but now,
This year, when Merlin—for his hour had come—
Brought Arthur forth, and set him in the hall,
Proclaiming, "Here is Uther's heir, your king,"
A hundred voices cried: "Away with him!   230
No king of ours! a son of Gorloïs he,
Or else the child of Anton, and no king,
Or else baseborn." Yet Merlin thro' his craft,
And while the people clamor'd for a king,
Had Arthur crown'd; but after, the great lords
Banded, and so brake out in open war.'

    Then while the king debated with himself
If Arthur were the child of shamefulness,

Or born the son of Gorloïs after death,
Or Uther's son and born before his time,   240
Or whether there were truth in anything
Said by these three, there came to Cameliard,
With Gawain and young Modred, her two sons,
Lot's wife, the Queen of Orkney, Bellicent;
Whom as he could, not as he would, the king
Made feast for, saying, as they sat at meat:
'A doubtful throne is ice on summer seas.
Ye come from Arthur's court. Victor his men
Report him! Yea, but ye—think ye this king—
So many those that hate him, and so strong,   250
So few his knights, however brave they be—
Hath body enow to hold his foemen down?'

'O King,' she cried, 'and I will tell thee: few,
Few, but all brave, all of one mind with him;
For I was near him when the savage yells
Of Uther's peerage died, and Arthur sat
Crowned on the daïs, and his warriors cried,
"Be thou the king, and we will work thy will
Who love thee." Then the King in low deep tones,
And simple words of great authority,   260
Bound them by so strait vows to his own self
That when they rose, knighted from kneeling, some
Were pale as at the passing of a ghost,
Some flush'd, and others dazed, as one who wakes
Half-blinded at the coming of a light.

'But when he spake, and cheer'd his Table Round
With large, divine, and comfortable words,
Beyond my tongue to tell thee—I beheld
From eye to eye thro' all their Order flash
A momentary likeness of the King;   270
And ere it left their faces, thro' the cross
And those around it and the Crucified,
Down from the casement over Arthur, smote
Flame-color, vert, and azure, in three rays,
One falling upon each of three fair queens
Who stood in silence near his throne, the friends
Of Arthur, gazing on him, tall, with bright
Sweet faces, who will help him at his need.

'And there I saw mage Merlin, whose vast wit
And hundred winters are but as the hands   280
Of loyal vassals toiling for their liége.

'And near him stood the Lady of the Lake,
Who knows a subtler magic than his own—
Clothed in white samite, mystic, wonderful.
She gave the King his huge cross-hilted sword,
Whereby to drive the heathen out. A mist
Of incense curl'd about her, and her face
Wellnigh was hidden in the minster gloom;
But there was heard among the holy hymns
A voice as of the waters, for she dwells   290
Down in a deep—calm, whatsoever storms
May shake the world—and when the surface rolls,
Hath power to walk the waters like our Lord.

   'There likewise I beheld Excalibur
Before him at his crowning borne, the sword
That rose from out the bosom of the lake,
And Arthur row'd across and took it—rich
With jewels, elfin Urim, on the hilt,
Bewildering heart and eye—the blade so bright
That men are blinded by it—on one side,   300
Graven in the oldest tongue of all this world,
"Take me," but turn the blade and ye shall see,
And written in the speech ye speak yourself,
"Cast me away!" And sad was Arthur's face
Taking it, but old Merlin counsell'd him,
"Take thou and strike! the time to cast away
Is yet far-off." So this great brand the king
Took, and by this will beat his foemen down.'

   Thereat Leodogran rejoiced, but thought
To sift his doubtings to the last, and ask'd,   310
Fixing full eyes of question on her face,
'The swallow and the swift are near akin,
But thou art closer to this noble prince,
Being his own dear sister;' and she said,
'Daughter of Gorloïs and Ygerne am I;'
'And therefore Arthur's sister?' ask'd the king.
She answer'd, 'These be secret things,' and sign'd
To those two sons to pass, and let them be.
And Gawain went, and breaking into song
Sprang out, and follow'd by his flying hair   320
Ran like a colt, and leapt at all he saw;
But Modred laid his ear beside the doors,
And there half-heard—the same that afterward
Struck for the throne, and striking found his doom.

   And then the Queen made answer: 'What know I?
For dark my mother was in eyes and hair,

And dark in hair and eyes am I; and dark
Was Gorloïs, yea, and dark was Uther too,
Wellnigh to blackness; but this king is fair
Beyond the race of Britons and of men.   330
Moreover, always in my mind I hear
A cry from out the dawning of my life,
A mother weeping, and I hear her say,
"O that ye had some brother, pretty one,
To guard thee on the rough ways of the world."'

'Ay,' said the king, 'and hear ye such a cry?
But when did Arthur chance upon thee first?'

'O King!' she cried, 'and I will tell thee true.
He found me first when yet a little maid.
Beaten I had been for a little fault   340
Whereof I was not guilty; and out I ran
And flung myself down on a bank of heath,
And hated this fair world and all therein,
And wept, and wish'd that I were dead; and he—
I know not whether of himself he came,
Or brought by Merlin, who, they say, can walk
Unseen at pleasure—he was at my side,
And spake sweet words, and comforted my heart,
And dried my tears, being a child with me.
And many a time he came, and evermore   350
As I grew greater grew with me; and sad
At times he seem'd, and sad with him was I,
Stern too at times, and then I loved him not,
But sweet again, and then I loved him well.
And now of late I see him less and less,
But those first days had golden hours for me,
For then I surely thought he would be king.

'But let me tell thee now another tale:
For Bleys, our Merlin's master, as they say,
Died but of late, and sent his cry to me,   360
To hear him speak before he left his life.
Shrunk like a fairy changeling lay the mage;
And when I enter'd told me that himself
And Merlin ever served about the king,
Uther, before he died; and on the night
When Uther in Tintagil past away
Moaning and wailing for an heir, the two
Left the still king, and passing forth to breathe,
Then from the castle gateway by the chasm
Descending thro' the dismal night—a night   370
In which the bounds of heaven and earth were lost—

Beheld, so high upon the dreary deeps
It seem'd in heaven, a ship, the shape thereof
A dragon wing'd, and all from stem to stern
Bright with a shining people on the decks,
And gone as soon as seen. And then the two
Dropt to the cove, and watch'd the great sea fall,
Wave after wave, each mightier than the last,
Till last, a ninth one, gathering half the deep
And full of voices, slowly rose and plunged   380
Roaring, and all the wave was in a flame;
And down the wave and in the flame was borne
A naked babe, and rode to Merlin's feet,
Who stoopt and caught the babe, and cried, "The King!
Here is an heir for Uther!" And the fringe
Of that great breaker, sweeping up the strand,
Lash'd at the wizard as he spake the word,
And all at once all round him rose in fire,
So that the child and he were clothed in fire.
And presently thereafter follow'd calm,   390
Free sky and stars. "And this same child," he said,
"Is he who reigns; nor could I part in peace
Till this were told." And saying this the seer
Went thro' the strait and dreadful pass of death,
Not ever to be question'd any more
Save on the further side; but when I met
Merlin, and ask'd him if these things were truth—
The shining dragon and the naked child
Descending in the glory of the seas—
He laugh'd as is his wont, and answer'd me   400
In riddling triplets of old time, and said:—

 '"Rain, rain, and sun! a rainbow in the sky!
A young man will be wiser by and by;
An old man's wit may wander ere he die.

 '"Rain, rain, and sun! a rainbow on the lea!
And the truth is this to me, and that to thee;
And truth or clothed or naked let it be.

 '"Rain, sun, and rain! and the free blossom blows;
Sun, rain, and sun! and where is he who knows?
From the great deep to the great deep he goes."   410

 'So Merlin riddling anger'd me; but thou
Fear not to give this King thine only child,
Guinevere; so great bards of him will sing
Hereafter, and dark sayings from of old
Ranging and ringing thro' the minds of men,
And echo'd by old folk beside their fires
For comfort after their wage-work is done,
Speak of the King; and Merlin in our time

Hath spoken also, not in jest, and sworn
Tho' men may wound him that he will not die,   420
But pass, again to come, and then or now
Utterly smite the heathen underfoot,
Till these and all men hail him for their king.'

She spake and King Leodogran rejoiced,
But musing 'Shall I answer yea or nay?'
Doubted, and drowsed, nodded and slept, and saw,
Dreaming, a slope of land that ever grew,
Field after field, up to a height, the peak
Haze-hidden, and thereon a phantom king,
Now looming, and now lost; and on the slope   430
The sword rose, the hind fell, the herd was driven,
Fire glimpsed; and all the land from roof and rick,
In drifts of smoke before a rolling wind,
Stream'd to the peak, and mingled with the haze
And made it thicker; while the phantom king
Sent out at times a voice; and here or there
Stood one who pointed toward the voice, the rest
Slew on and burnt, crying, 'No king of ours,
No son of Uther, and no king of ours;'
Till with a wink his dream was changed, the haze   440
Descended, and the solid earth became
As nothing, but the King stood out in heaven,
Crown'd. And Leodogran awoke, and sent
Ulfius, and Brastias, and Bedivere,
Back to the court of Arthur answering yea.

Then Arthur charged his warrior whom he loved
And honor'd most, Sir Lancelot, to ride forth
And bring the Queen, and watch'd him from the gates;
And Lancelot past away among the flowers—
For then was latter April—and return'd   450
Among the flowers, in May, with Guinevere.
To whom arrived, by Dubric the high saint,
Chief of the church in Britain, and before
The stateliest of her altar-shrines, the King
That morn was married, while in stainless white,
The fair beginners of a nobler time,
And glorying in their vows and him, his knights
Stood round him, and rejoicing in his joy.
Far shone the fields of May thro' open door,
The sacred altar blossom'd white with May,   460
The sun of May descended on their King,
They gazed on all earth's beauty in their Queen,
Roll'd incense, and there past along the hymns
A voice as of the waters, while the two

Sware at the shrine of Christ a deathless love.
And Arthur said, 'Behold, thy doom is mine.
Let chance what will, I love thee to the death!'
To whom the Queen replied with drooping eyes,
'King and my lord, I love thee to the death!'
And holy Dubric spread his hands and spake: 470
'Reign ye, and live and love, and make the world
Other, and may thy Queen be one with thee,
And all this Order of thy Table Round
Fulfil the boundless purpose of their King!'

So Dubric said; but when they left the shrine
Great lords from Rome before the portal stood,
In scornful stillness gazing as they past;
Then while they paced a city all on fire
With sun and cloth of gold, the trumpets blew,
And Arthur's knighthood sang before the King:—   480

'Blow trumpet, for the world is white with May!
Blow trumpet, the long night hath roll'd away!
Blow thro' the living world—"Let the King reign!"

'Shall Rome or Heathen rule in Arthur's realm?
Flash brand and lance, fall battle-axe upon helm,
Fall battle-axe, and flash brand! Let the King reign!

'Strike for the King and live! his knights have heard
That God hath told the King a secret word.
Fall battle-axe, and flash brand! Let the King reign!

'Blow trumpet! he will lift us from the dust.   490
Blow trumpet! live the strength, and die the lust!
Clang battle-axe, and clash brand! Let the King reign!

'Strike for the King and die! and if thou diest,
The King is king, and ever wills the highest.
Clang battle-axe, and clash brand! Let the King reign!

'Blow, for our Sun is mighty in his May!
Blow, for our Sun is mightier day by day!
Clang battle-axe, and clash brand! Let the King reign!

'The King will follow Christ, and we the King,
In whom high God hath breathed a secret thing.   500
Fall battle-axe, and clash brand! Let the King reign!'

So sang the knighthood, moving to their hall.
There at the banquet those great lords from Rome,
The slowly-fading mistress of the world,
Strode in and claim'd their tribute as of yore.
But Arthur spake: 'Behold, for these have sworn
To wage my wars, and worship me their King;
The old order changeth, yielding place to new,
And we that fight for our fair father Christ,

Seeing that ye be grown too weak and old
To drive the heathen from your Roman wall,
No tribute will we pay.' So those great lords
Drew back in wrath, and Arthur strove with Rome.

And Arthur and his knighthood for a space
Were all one will, and thro' that strength the King
Drew in the petty princedoms under him,
Fought, and in twelve great battles overcame
The heathen hordes, and made a realm and reign'd.

THE ROUND TABLE

GARETH AND LYNETTE

THE last tall son of Lot and Bellicent,
And tallest, Gareth, in a showerful spring
Stared at the spate. A slender-shafted pine
Lost footing, fell, and so was whirl'd away.
'How he went down,' said Gareth, 'as a false knight
Or evil king before my lance, if lance
Were mine to use—O senseless cataract,
Bearing all down in thy precipitancy—
And yet thou art but swollen with cold snows
And mine is living blood. Thou dost His will,   10
The Maker's, and not knowest, and I that know,
Have strength and wit, in my good mother's hall
Linger with vacillating obedience,
Prison'd, and kept and coax'd and whistled to—
Since the good mother holds me still a child!
Good mother is bad mother unto me!
A worse were better; yet no worse would I.
Heaven yield her for it, but in me put force
To weary her ears with one continuous prayer,
Until she let me fly discaged to sweep   20
In ever-highering eagle-circles up
To the great Sun of Glory, and thence swoop
Down upon all things base, and dash them dead,
A knight of Arthur, working out his will,
To cleanse the world. Why, Gawain, when he came
With Modred hither in the summer-time,

Ask'd me to tilt with him, the proven knight.
Modred for want of worthier was the judge.
Then I so shook him in the saddle, he said,
"Thou hast half prevail'd against me," said so—he— 39
Tho' Modred biting his thin lips was mute,
For he is always sullen—what care I?'

And Gareth went, and hovering round her chair
Ask'd, 'Mother, tho' ye count me still the child,
Sweet mother, do ye love the child?' She laugh'd,
'Thou art but a wild-goose, to question it.'
'Then, mother, an ye love the child,' he said,
'Being a goose and rather tame than wild,
Hear the child's story.' 'Yea, my well-beloved,
An 't were but of the goose and golden eggs.' 40

And Gareth answer'd her with kindling eyes:
'Nay, nay, good mother, but this egg of mine
Was finer gold than any goose can lay;
For this an eagle, a royal eagle, laid
Almost beyond eye-reach, on such a palm
As glitters gilded in thy Book of Hours.
And there was ever haunting round the palm
A lusty youth, but poor, who often saw
The splendor sparkling from aloft, and thought,
"An I could climb and lay my hand upon it, 50
Then were I wealthier than a leash of kings."
But ever when he reach'd a hand to climb,
One that had loved him from his childhood caught
And stay'd him, "Climb not lest thou break thy neck,
I charge thee by my love," and so the boy,
Sweet mother, neither clomb nor brake his neck,
But brake his very heart in pining for it,
And past away.'

　　　　　　　To whom the mother said,
'True love, sweet son, had risk'd himself and climb'd,
And handed down the golden treasure to him.' 60

And Gareth answer'd her with kindling eyes:
'Gold? said I gold?—ay then, why he, or she,
Or whosoe'er it was, or half the world
Had ventured—*had* the thing I spake of been
Mere gold—but this was all of that true steel
Whereof they forged the brand Excalibur,
And lightnings play'd about it in the storm,
And all the little fowl were flurried at it,

And there were cries and clashings in the nest,
That sent him from his senses. Let me go.'   70

    Then Bellicent bemoan'd herself and said:
'Hast thou no pity upon my loneliness?
Lo, where thy father Lot beside the hearth
Lies like a dog, and all but smoulder'd out!
For ever since when traitor to the King
He fought against him in the barons' war,
And Arthur gave him back his territory,
His age hath slowly droopt, and now lies there
A yet-warm corpse, and yet unburiable,
No more; nor sees, nor hears, nor speaks, nor knows.   80
And both thy brethren are in Arthur's hall,
Albeit neither loved with that full love
I feel for thee, nor worthy such a love.
Stay therefore thou; red berries charm the bird,
And thee, mine innocent, the jousts, the wars,
Who never knewest finger-ache, nor pang
Or wrench'd or broken limb—an often chance
In those brain-stunning shocks, and tourney-falls,
Frights to my heart. But stay; follow the deer
By these tall firs and our fast-falling burns;   90
So make thy manhood mightier day by day.
Sweet is the chase; and I will seek thee out
Some comfortable bride and fair, to grace
Thy climbing life, and cherish my prone year,
Till falling into Lot's forgetfulness
I know not thee, myself, nor anything.
Stay, my best son! ye are yet more boy than man.'

    Then Gareth: 'An ye hold me yet for child,
Hear yet once more the story of the child.
For, mother, there was once a king, like ours.   100
The prince his heir, when tall and marriageable,
Ask'd for a bride; and thereupon the king
Set two before him. One was fair, strong, arm'd—
But to be won by force—and many men
Desired her; one, good lack, no man desired.
And these were the conditions of the king:
That save he won the first by force, he needs
Must wed that other, whom no man desired,
A red-faced bride who know herself so vile
That evermore she long'd to hide herself,   110
Nor fronted man or woman, eye to eye—
Yea—some she cleaved to, but they died of her.
And one—they call'd her Fame; and one—O mother,'
How can ye keep me tether'd to you?—Shame.

Man am I grown, a man's work must I do.
Follow the deer? follow the Christ, the King,
Live pure, speak true, right wrong, follow the King—
Else, wherefore born?'

            To whom the mother said:
'Sweet son, for there be many who deem him not,
Or will not deem him, wholly proven king— 120
Albeit in mine own heart I knew him King
When I was frequent with him in my youth,
And heard him kingly speak, and doubted him
No more than he, himself; but felt him mine,
Of closest kin to me. Yet—wilt thou leave
Thine easeful biding here, and risk thine all,
Life, limbs, for one that is not proven king?
Stay, till the cloud that settles round his birth
Hath lifted but a little. Stay, sweet son.'

    And Gareth answer'd quickly: 'Not an hour, 130
So that ye yield me—I will walk thro' fire,
Mother, to gain it—your full leave to go.
Not proven, who swept the dust of ruin'd Rome
From off the threshold of the realm, and crush'd
The idolaters, and made the people free?
Who should be king save him who makes us free?'

    So when the Queen, who long had sought in vain
To break him from the intent to which he grew,
Found her son's will unwaveringly one,
She answer'd craftily: 'Will ye walk thro' fire? 140
Who walks thro' fire will hardly heed the smoke.
Ay, go then, an ye must; only one proof,
Before thou ask the King to make thee knight,
Of thine obedience and thy love to me,
Thy mother,—I demand.'

            And Gareth cried:
'A hard one, or a hundred, so I go.
Nay—quick! the proof to prove me to the quick!'

    But slowly spake the mother looking at him:
'Prince, thou shalt go disguised to Arthur's hall,
And hire thyself to serve for meats and drinks 150
Among the scullions and the kitchen-knaves,
And those that hand the dish across the bar.
Nor shalt thou tell thy name to any one.
And thou shalt serve a twelvemonth and a day.'

For so the Queen believed that when her son
Beheld his only way to glory lead
Low down thro' villain kitchen-vassalage,
Her own true Gareth was too princely-proud
To pass thereby; so should he rest with her,
Closed in her castle from the sound of arms.   160

Silent awhile was Gareth, then replied:
'The thrall in person may be free in soul,
And I shall see the jousts. Thy son am I,
And, since thou art my mother, must obey.
I therefore yield me freely to thy will;
For hence will I, disguised, and hire myself
To serve with scullions and with kitchen-knaves;
Nor tell my name to any—no, not the King.'

Gareth awhile linger'd. The mother's eye
Full of the wistful fear that he would go,   170
And turning toward him wheresoe'er he turn'd,
Perplext his outward purpose, till an hour
When, waken'd by the wind which with full voice
Swept bellowing thro' the darkness on to dawn,
He rose, and out of slumber calling two
That still had tended on him from his birth,
Before the wakeful mother heard him, went.

The three were clad like tillers of the soil.
Southward they set their faces. The birds made
Melody on branch and melody in mid air.   180
The damp hill-slopes were quicken'd into green,
And the live green had kindled into flowers,
For it was past the time of Easter-day.

So, when their feet were planted on the plain
That broaden'd toward the base of Camelot,
Far off they saw the silver-misty morn
Rolling her smoke about the royal mount,
That rose between the forest and the field.
At times the summit of the high city flash'd;
At times the spires and turrets half-way down   190
Prick'd thro' the mist; at times the great gate shone
Only, that open'd on the field below;
Anon, the whole fair city had disappear'd.

Then those who went with Gareth were amazed,
One crying, 'Let us go no further, lord;
Here is a city of enchanters, built
By fairy kings.' The second echo'd him,

'Lord, we have heard from our wise man at home
To northward, that this king is not the King,
But only changeling out of Fairyland,   200
Who drave the heathen hence by sorcery
And Merlin's glamour.' Then the first again,
'Lord, there is no such city anywhere,
But all a vision.'

          Gareth answer'd them
With laughter, swearing he had glamour enow
In his own blood, his princedom, youth, and hopes,
To plunge old Merlin in the Arabian sea;
So push'd them all unwilling toward the gate.
And there was no gate like it under heaven.
For barefoot on the keystone, which was lined   210
And rippled like an ever-fleeting wave,
The Lady of the Lake stood; all her dress
Wept from her sides as water flowing away;
But like the cross her great and goodly arms
Stretch'd under all the cornice and upheld.
And drops of water fell from either hand;
And down from one a sword was hung, from one
A censer, either worn with wind and storm;
And o'er her breast floated the sacred fish;
And in the space to left of her, and right,   220
Were Arthur's wars in weird devices done,
New things and old co-twisted, as if Time
Were nothing, so inveterately that men
Were giddy gazing there; and over all
High on the top were those three queens, the friends
Or Arthur, who should help him at his need.

      Then those with Gareth for so long a space
Stared at the figures that at last it seem'd
The dragon-boughts and elvish emblemings
Began to move, seethe, twine, and curl. They call'd   230
To Gareth, 'Lord, the gateway is alive.'

      And Gareth likewise on them fixt his eyes
So long that even to him they seem'd to move.
Out of the city a blast of music peal'd.
Back from the gate started the three, to whom
From out thereunder came an ancient man,
Long-bearded, saying, 'Who be ye, my sons?'

      Then Gareth: 'We be tillers of the soil,
Who leaving share in furrow come to see
The glories of our King; but these, my men,—   240

Your city moved so weirdly in the mist—
Doubt if the King be king at all, or come
From Fairyland; and whether this be built
By magic, and by fairy kings and queens;
Or whether there be any city at all,
Or all a vision; and this music now
Hath scared them both, but tell thou these the truth.'

Then that old Seer made answer, playing on him
And saying: 'Son, I have seen the good ship sail   250
Keel upward, and mast downward, in the heavens,
And solid turrets topsy-turvy in air;
And here is truth, but an it please thee not,
Take thou the truth as thou hast told it me.
For truly, as thou sayest, a fairy king
And fairy queens have built the city, son;
They came from out a sacred mountain-cleft
Toward the sunrise, each with harp in hand,
And built it to the music of their harps.
And, as thou sayest, it is enchanted, son   260
For there is nothing in it as it seems
Saving the King; tho' some there be that hold
The King a shadow, and the city real.
Yet take thou heed of him, for, so thou pass
Beneath this archway, then wilt thou become
A thrall to his enchantments, for the King
Will bind thee by such vows as is a shame
A man should not be bound by, yet the which
No man can keep; but, so thou dread to swear,
Pass not beneath this gateway, but abide
Without, among the cattle of the field.   270
For an ye heard a music, like enow
They are building still, seeing the city is built
To music, therefore never built at all,
And therefore built for ever.'

                              Gareth spake
Anger'd: 'Old master, reverence thine own beard
That looks as white as utter truth, and seems
Wellnigh as long as thou art statured tall!
Why mockest thou the stranger that hath been
To thee fair-spoken?'

                              But the Seer replied:
'Know ye not then the Riddling of the Bards: 280
"Confusion and illusion, and relation,
Elusion, and occasion, and evasion"?
I mock thee not but as thou mockest me,

And all that see thee, for thou art not who
Thou seemest, but I know thee who thou art.
And now thou goest up to mock the King,
Who cannot brook the shadow of any lie.'

Unmockingly the mocker ending here
Turned to the right, and past along the plain;
Whom Gareth looking after said: 'My men,   290
Our one white lie sits like a little ghost
Here on the threshold of our enterprise.
Let love be blamed for it, not she, nor I.
Well, we will make amends.'

                                With all good cheer
He spake and laugh'd, then enter'd with his twain
Camelot, a city of shadowy palaces
And stately, rich in emblem and the work
Of ancient kings who did their days in stone;
Which Merlin's hand, the Mage at Arthur's court,
Knowing all arts, had touch'd, and everywhere,   300
At Arthur's ordinance, tipt with lessening peak
And pinnacle, and had made it spire to heaven.
And ever and anon a knight would pass
Outward, or inward to the hall; his arms
Clash'd, and the sound was good to Gareth's ear.
And out of bower and casement shyly glanced
Eyes of pure women, wholesome stars of love;
And all about a healthful people stept
As in the presence of a gracious king.

Then into hall Gareth ascending heard   310
A voice, the voice of Arthur, and beheld
Far over heads in that long-vaulted hall
The splendor of the presence of the King
Throned, and delivering doom—and look'd no more—
But felt his young heart hammering in his ears,
And thought, 'For this half-shadow of a lie
The truthful King will doom me when I speak.'
Yet pressing on, tho' all in fear to find
Sir Gawain or Sir Modred, saw nor one
Nor other, but in all the listening eyes   320
Of those tall knights that ranged about the throne
Clear honor shining like the dewy star
Of dawn, and faith in their great King, with pure
Affection, and the light of victory,
And glory gain'd, and evermore to gain.

Then came a widow crying to the King:
'A boon, Sir King! Thy father, Uther, reft
From my dead lord a field with violence;
For howsoe'er at first he proffer'd gold,
Yet, for the field was pleasant in our eyes,   330
We yielded not; and then he reft us of it
Perforce and left us neither gold nor field.'

Said Arthur, 'Whether would ye? gold or field?'
To whom the women weeping, 'Nay, my lord,
The field was pleasant in my husband's eye.'

And Arthur: 'Have thy pleasant field again,
And thrice the gold for Uther's use thereof,
According to the years. No boon is here,
But justice, so thy say be proven true.
Accursed, who from the wrongs his father did   340
Would shape himself a right!'

                   And while she past,
Came yet another widow crying to him:
'A boon, Sir King! Thine enemy, King, am I.
With thine own hand thou slewest my dear lord,
A knight of Uther in the barons' war,
When Lot and many another rose and fought
Against thee, saying thou wert basely born.
I held with these, and loathe to ask thee aught.
Yet lo! my husband's brother had my son
Thrall'd in his castle, and hath starved him dead,   350
And standeth seized of that inheritance
Which thou that slewest the sire hast left the son.
So, tho' I scarce can ask it thee for hate,
Grant me some knight to do the battle for me,
Kill the foul thief, and wreak me for my son.'

Then strode a good knight forward, crying to him,
'A boon, Sir King! I am her kinsman, I.
Give me to right her wrong, and slay the man.'

Then came Sir Kay, the seneschal, and cried,
'A boon, Sir King! even that thou grant her none,   360
This railer, that hath mock'd thee in full hall—
None; or the wholesome boon of gyve and gag.'

But Arthur: 'We sit King, to help the wrong'd
Thro' all our realm. The woman loves her lord.
Peace to thee, woman, with thy loves and hates!
The kings of old had doom'd thee to the flames;

Aurelius Emrys would have scourged thee dead,
And Uther slit thy tongue; but get thee hence—
Lest that rough humor of the kings of old
Return upon me! Thou that art her kin,   370
Go likewise; lay him low and slay him not,
But bring him here, that I may judge the right,
According to the justice of the King.
Then, be he guilty, by that deathless King
Who lived and died for men, the man shall die.'

    Then came in hall the messenger of Mark,
A name of evil savor in the land,
The Cornish king. In either hand he bore
What dazzl'd all, and shone far-off as shines
A field of charlock in the sudden sun   380
Between two showers, a cloth of palest gold,
Which down he laid before the throne, and knelt,
Delivering that his lord, the vassal king,
Was ev'n upon his way to Camelot;
For having heard that Arthur of his grace
Had made his goodly cousin Tristram knight,
And, for himself was of the greater state,
Being a king, he trusted his liege-lord
Would yield him this large honor all the more;
So pray'd him well to accept this cloth of gold,   390
In token of true heart and fealty.

    Then Arthur cried to rend the cloth, to rend
In pieces, and so cast it on the hearth.
An oak-tree smoulder'd there. 'The goodly knight!
What! shall the shield of Mark stand among these?'
For, midway down the side of that long hall,
A stately pile,—whereof along the front,
Some blazon'd, some but carven, and some blank,
There ran a treble range of stony shields,—
Rose, and high-arching overbrow'd the hearth.   400
And under every shield a knight was named.
For this was Arthur's custom in his hall:
When some good knight had done one noble deed,
His arms were carven only; but if twain,
His arms were blazon'd also; but if none,
The shield was blank and bare, without a sign
Saving the name beneath. And Gareth saw
The shield of Gawain blazon'd rich and bright,
And Modred's blank as death; and Arthur cried
To rend the cloth and cast it on the hearth.   410

'More like are we to reave him of his crown
Than make him knight because men call him king.
The kings we found, ye know we stay'd their hands
From war among themselves, but left them kings;
Of whom were any bounteous, merciful,
Truth-speaking, brave, good livers, them we enroll'd
Among us, and they sit within our hall.
But Mark hath tarnish'd the great name of king,
As Mark would sully the low state of churl;
And, seeing he hath sent us cloth of gold,   420
Return, and meet, and hold him from our eyes,
Lest we should lap him up in cloth of lead,
Silenced for ever—craven—a man of plots,
Craft, poisonous counsels, wayside ambushings—
No fault of thine; let Kay the seneschal
Look to thy wants, and send thee satisfied—
Accursed, who strikes nor lets the hand be seen!'

And many another suppliant crying came
With noise of ravage wrought by beast and man,
And evermore a knight would ride away.   430

Last, Gareth leaning both hands heavily
Down on the shoulders of the twain, his men,
Approach'd between them toward the King, and ask'd,
'A boon, Sir King,'—his voice was all ashamed,—
'For see ye not how weak and hunger-worn
I seem—leaning on these? grant me to serve
For meat and drink among thy kitchen-knaves
A twelvemonth and a day, nor seek my name.
Hereafter I will fight.'

                         To him the King:
'A goodly youth and worth a goodlier boon!   440
But so thou wilt no goodlier, then must Kay,
The master of the meats and drinks, be thine.'

He rose and past; then Kay, a man of mien
Wan-sallow as the plant that feels itself
Root-bitten by white lichen:

                         'Lo ye now!
This fellow hath broken from some abbey, where,
God wot, he had not beef and brewis enow,
However that might chance! but an he work,
Like any pigeon will I cram his crop,
And sleeker shall he shine than any hog.'   450

Then Lancelot standing near: 'Sir Seneschal,
Sleuth-hound thou knowest, and gray, and all the hounds;
A horse thou knowest, a man thou dost not know.
Broad brows and fair, a fluent hair and fine,
High nose, a nostril large and fine, and hands
Large, fair, and fine!—Some young lad's mystery—
But, or from sheepcot or king's hall, the boy
Is noble-natured. Treat him with all grace,
Lest he should come to shame thy judging of him.'

Then Kay: 'What murmurest thou of mystery?   460
Think ye this fellow will poison the King's dish?
Nay, for he spake too fool-like—mystery!
Tut, an the lad were noble, he had ask'd
For horse and armor. Fair and fine, forsooth!
Sir Fine-face, Sir Fair-hands? but see thou to it
That thine own fineness, Lancelot, some fine day
Undo thee not—and leave my man to me.'

So Gareth all for glory underwent
The sooty yoke of kitchen-vassalage,
Ate with young lads his portion by the door,   470
And couch'd at night with grimy kitchen-knaves.
And Lancelot ever spake him pleasantly,
But Kay the seneschal, who loved him not,
Would hustle and harry him, and labor him
Beyond his comrade of the hearth, and set
To turn the broach, draw water, or hew wood,
Or grosser tasks; and Gareth bow'd himself
With all obedience to the King, and wrought
All kind of service with a noble ease
That graced the lowliest act in doing it.   480
And when the thralls had talk among themselves,
And one would praise the love that linkt the King
And Lancelot—how the King had saved his life
In battle twice, and Lancelot once the King's—
For Lancelot was the first in tournament,
But Arthur mightiest on the battle-field—
Gareth was glad. Or if some other told
How once the wandering forester at dawn,
Far over the blue tarns and hazy seas,
On Caer-Eryri's highest found the King,   490
A naked babe, of whom the Prophet spake,
'He passes to the Isle Avilion,
He passes and is heal'd and cannot die'—
Gareth was glad. But if their talk were foul,
Then would he whistle rapid as any lark,
Or carol some old roundelay, and so loud

That first they mock'd, but, after, reverenced him.
Or Gareth, telling some prodigious tale
Of knights who sliced a red life-bubbling way
Thro' twenty folds of twisted dragon, held   500
All in a gap-mouth'd circle his good mates
Lying or sitting round him, idle hands,
Charm'd; till Sir Kay, the seneschal, would come
Blustering upon them, like a sudden wind
Among dead leaves, and drive them all apart.
Or when the thralls had sport among themselves,
So there were any trial of mastery,
He, by two yards in casting bar or stone,
Was counted best; and if there chanced a joust,
So that Sir Kay nodded him leave to go,   510
Would hurry thither, and when he saw the knights
Clash like the coming and retiring wave,
And the spear spring, and good horse reel, the boy
Was half beyond himself for ecstasy.

So for a month he wrought among the thralls;
But in the weeks that follow'd, the good Queen,
Repentant of the word she made him swear,
And saddening in her childless castle, sent,
Between the in-crescent and de-crescent moon,
Arms for her son, and loosed him from his vow.   520

This, Gareth hearing from a squire of Lot
With whom he used to play at tourney once,
When both were children, and in lonely haunts
Would scratch a ragged oval on the sand,
And each at either dash from either end—
Shame never made girl redder than Gareth joy.
He laugh'd, he sprang. 'Out of the smoke, at once
I leap from Satan's foot to Peter's knee—
These news be mine, none other's—nay, the King's—
Descend into the city;' whereon he sought   530
The King alone, and found, and told him all.

'I have stagger'd thy strong Gawain in a tilt
For pastime; yea, he said it; joust can I.
Make me thy knight—in secret! let my name
Be hidden, and give me the first quest, I spring
Like flame from ashes.'

Here the King's calm eye
Fell on, and check'd, and made him flush, and bow
Lowly, to kiss his hand, who answer'd him:
'Son, the good mother let me know thee here,

And sent her wish that I would yield thee thine.   540
Make thee my knight? my knights are sworn to vows
Of utter hardihood, utter gentleness,
And, loving, utter faithfulness in love,
And uttermost obedience to the King.'

  Then Gareth, lightly springing from his knees:
'My King, for hardihood I can promise thee.
For uttermost obedience make demand
Of whom ye gave me to, the Seneschal,
No mellow master of the meats and drinks!
And as for love, God wot, I love not yet,   550
But love I shall, God willing.'
                          And the King:
'Make thee my knight in secret? yea, but he,
Our noblest brother, and our truest man,
And one with me in all, he needs must know.'

  'Let Lancelot know, my King, let Lancelot know,
Thy noblest and thy truest!'

                          And the King:
'But wherefore would ye men should wonder at you?
Nay, rather for the sake of me, their King,
And the deed's sake my knighthood do the deed,
Than to be noised of.'

                 Merrily Gareth ask'd: 560
'Have I not earn'd my cake in baking of it?
Let be my name until I make my name!
My deeds will speak; it is but for a day.'
So with a kindly hand on Gareth's arm
Smiled the great King, and half-unwillingly
Loving his lusty youthhood yielded to him.
Then, after summoning Lancelot privily:
'I have given him the first quest; he is not proven.
Look therefore, when he calls for this in hall,
Thou get to horse and follow him far away.   570
Cover the lions on thy shield, and see,
Far as thou mayest, he be nor ta'en nor slain.'

  Then that same day there past into the hall
A damsel of high lineage, and a brow
May-blossom, and a cheek of apple-blossom,
Hawk-eyes; and lightly was her slender nose
Tip-tilted like the petal of a flower.
She into hall past with her page and cried:

'O King, for thou hast driven the foe without,
See to the foe within! bridge, ford, beset   580
By bandits, every one that owns a tower
The lord for half a league. Why sit ye there?
Rest would I not, Sir King, an I were king,
Till even the lonest hold were all as free
From cursed bloodshed as thine altar-cloth
From that best blood it is a sin to spill.'

'Comfort thyself,' said Arthur, 'I nor mine
Rest; so my knighthood keep the vows they swore,
The wastest moorland of our realm shall be
Safe, damsel, as the centre of this hall.   590
What is thy name? thy need?'

                                       'My name?' she said—
'Lynette, my name; noble; my need, a knight
To combat for my sister, Lyonors,
A lady of high lineage, of great lands,
And comely, yea, and comelier than myself.
She lives in Castle Perilous. A river
Runs in three loops about her living-place;
And o'er it are three passings, and three knights
Defend the passings, brethren, and a fourth,
And of that four the mightiest, holds her stay'd   600
In her own castle, and so besieges her
To break her will, and make her wed with him;
And but delays his purport till thou send
To do the battle with him thy chief man
Sir Lancelot, whom he trusts to overthrow,
Then wed, with glory; but she will not wed
Save whom she loveth, or a holy life.
Now therefore have I come for Lancelot.'

Then Arthur mindful of Sir Gareth ask'd:
'Damsel, ye know this Order lives to crush   610
All wrongers of the realm. But say, these four,
Who be they? What the fashion of the men?'

'They be of foolish fashion, O Sir King,
The fashion of that old knight-errantry
Who ride abroad, and do but what they will;
Courteous or bestial from the moment, such
As have nor law nor king; and three of these
Proud in their fantasy call themselves the Day,
Morning-Star, and Noon-Sun, and Evening-Star,
Being strong fools; and never a whit more wise   620
The fourth, who always rideth arm'd in black,

A huge man-beast of boundless savagery.
He names himself the Night and oftener Death,
And wears a helmet mounted with a skull,
And bears a skeleton figured on his arms,
To show that who may slay or scape the three,
Slain by himself, shall enter endless night.
And all these four be fools, but mighty men,
And therefore am I come for Lancelot.'

Hereat Sir Gareth call'd from where he rose,   630
A head with kindling eyes above the throng,
'A boon, Sir King—this quest!' then—for he mark'd
Kay near him groaning like a wounded bull—
'Yea, King, thou knowest thy kitchen-knave am I,
And mighty thro' thy meats and drinks am I,
And I can topple over a hundred such.
Thy promise, King,' and Arthur glancing at him,
Brought down a momentary brow. 'Rough, sudden,
And pardonable, worthy to be knight—
Go therefore,' and all hearers were amazed.   640

But on the damsel's forehead shame, pride, wrath
Slew the may-white. She lifted either arm,
'Fie on thee, King! I ask'd for thy chief knight,
And thou hast given me but a kitchen-knave.'
Then ere a man in hall could stay her, turn'd,
Fled down the lane of access to the King,
Took horse, descended the slope street, and past
The weird white gate, and paused without, beside
The field of tourney, murmuring, 'kitchen-knave!'

Now two great entries open'd from the hall,   650
At one end one that gave upon a range
Of level pavement where the King would pace
At sunrise, gazing over plain and wood;
And down from this a lordly stairway sloped
Till lost in blowing trees and tops of towers;
And out by this main doorway past the King.
But one was counter to the hearth, and rose
High that the highest-crested helm could ride
Therethro' nor graze; and by this entry fled
The damsel in her wrath, and on to this   660
Sir Gareth strode, and saw without the door
King Arthur's gift, the worth of half a town,
A war-horse of the best, and near it stood
The two that out of north had follow'd him.
This bare a maiden shield, a casque; that held
The horse, the spear; whereat Sir Gareth loosed

A cloak that dropt from collar-bone to heel,
A cloth of roughest web, and cast it down,
And from it, like a fuel-smother'd fire
That lookt half-dead, brake bright, and flash'd as those   670
Dull-coated things, that making slide apart
Their dusk wing-cases, all beneath there burns
A jewell'd harness, ere they pass and fly.
So Gareth ere he parted flash'd in arms.
Then as he donn'd the helm, and took the shield
And mounted horse and graspt a spear, of grain
Storm-strengthen'd on a windy site, and tipt
With trenchant steel, around him slowly prest
The people, while from out of kitchen came
The thralls in throng, and seeing who had work'd   680
Lustier than any, and whom they could but love,
Mounted in arms, threw up their caps and cried,
'God bless the King, and all his fellowship!'
And on thro' lanes of shouting Gareth rode
Down the slope street, and past without the gate.

   So Gareth past with joy; but as the cur
Pluckt from the cur he fights with, ere his cause
Be cool'd by fighting, follows, being named,
His owner, but remembers all, and growls
Remembering, so Sir Kay beside the door   690
Mutter'd in scorn of Gareth whom he used
To harry and hustle.

                    'Bound upon a quest
With horse and arms—the King hath past his time—
My scullion knave! Thralls, to your work again,
For an your fire be low ye kindle mine!
Will there be dawn in West and eve in East?
Begone!—my knave!—belike and like enow
Some old head-blow not heeded in his youth
So shook his wits they wander in his prime—
Crazed! How the villain lifted up his voice,   700
Nor shamed to bawl himself a kitchen-knave!
Tut, he was tame and meek enow with me,
Till peacock'd up with Lancelot's noticing.
Well—I will after my loud knave, and learn
Whether he know me for his master yet.
Out of the smoke he came, and so my lance
Hold, by God's grace, he shall into the mire—
Thence, if the King awaken from his craze,
Into the smoke again.'

But Lancelot said:
'Kay, wherefore wilt thou go against the King, 710
For that did never he whereon ye rail,
But ever meekly served the King in thee?
Abide; take counsel, for this lad is great
And lusty, and knowing both of lance and sword.'
'Tut, tell not me,' said Kay, 'ye are overfine
To mar stout knaves with foolish courtesies;'
Then mounted, on thro' silent faces rode
Down the slope city, and out beyond the gate.

But by the field of tourney lingering yet
Mutter'd the damsel: 'Wherefore did the King 720
Scorn me? for, were Sir Lancelot lackt, at least
He might have yielded to me one of those
Who tilt for lady's love and glory here,
Rather than—O sweet heaven! O, fie upon him!—
His kitchen-knave.'

To whom Sir Gareth drew—
And there were none but few goodlier than he—
Shining in arms, 'Damsel, the quest is mine.
Lead, and I follow.' She thereat, as one
That smells a foul-flesh'd agaric in the holt,
And deems it carrion of some woodland thing, 730
Or shrew or weasel, nipt her slender nose
With petulant thumb and finger, shrilling, 'Hence!
Avoid, thou smellest all of kitchen-grease.
And look who comes behind;' for there was Kay.
'Knowest thou not me? thy master? I am Kay.
We lack thee by the hearth.'

And Gareth to him,
'Master no more! too well I know thee, ay—
The most ungentle knight in Arthur's hall.'
'Have at thee then,' said Kay; they shock'd, and Kay
Fell shoulder-slipt, and Gareth cried again, 740
'Lead, and I follow,' and fast away she fled.

But after sod and shingle ceased to fly
Behind her, and the heart of her good horse
Was nigh to burst with violence of the beat,
Perforce she stay'd, and overtaken spoke:

'What doest thou, scullion, in my fellowship?
Deem'st thou that I accept thee aught the more
Or love thee better, that by some device
Full cowardly, or by mere unhappiness,

Thou hast overthrown and slain thy master—thou!—   750
Dish-washer and broach-turner, loon!—to me
Thou smellest all of kitchen as before.'

'Damsel,' Sir Gareth answer'd gently, 'say
Whate'er ye will, but whatsoe'er ye say,
I leave not till I finish this fair quest,
Or die therefore.'

                              'Ay, wilt thou finish it?
Sweet lord, how like a noble knight he talks!
The listening rogue hath caught the manner of it.
But, knave, anon thou shalt be met with, knave,
And then by such a one that thou for all   760
The kitchen brewis that was ever supt
Shalt not once dare to look him in the face.'

'I shall assay,' said Gareth with a smile
That madden'd her, and away she flash'd again
Down the long avenues of a boundless wood;
And Gareth following was again beknaved:

'Sir Kitchen-knave, I have miss'd the only way
Where Arthur's men are set along the wood;
The wood is nigh as full of thieves as leaves.
If both be slain, I am rid of thee; but yet,   770
Sir Scullion, canst thou use that spit of thine?
Fight, an thou canst; I have miss'd the only way.'

So till the dusk that follow'd evensong
Rode on the two, reviler and reviled;
Then after one long slope was mounted, saw,
Bowl-shaped, thro' tops of many thousand pines
A gloomy-gladed hollow slowly sink
To westward—in the deeps whereof a mere,
Round as the red eye of an eagle-owl,
Under the half-dead sunset glared; and shouts   780
Ascended, and there brake a servingman
Flying from out of the black wood, and crying,
'They have bound my lord to cast him in the mere.'
Then Gareth, 'Bound am I to right the wrong'd,
But straitlier bound am I to bide with thee.'
And when the damsel spake contemptuously,
'Lead, and I follow,' Gareth cried again,
'Follow, I lead!' so down among the pines
He plunged; and there, black-shadow'd nigh the mere,
And mid-thigh-deep in bulrushes and reed,   790
Saw six tall men haling a seventh along,

A stone about his neck to drown him in it.
Three with good blows he quieted, but three
Fled thro' the pines; and Gareth loosed the stone
From off his neck, then in the mere beside
Tumbled it; oilily bubbled up the mere.
Last, Gareth loosed his bonds and on free feet
Set him, a stalwart baron, Arthur's friend.

'Well that ye came, or else these caitiff rogues
Had wreak'd themselves on me; good cause is theirs   800
To hate me, for my wont hath ever been
To catch my thief, and then like vermin here
Drown him, and with a stone about his neck;
And under this wan water many of them
Lie rotting, but at night let go the stone,
And rise, and flickering in a grimly light
Dance on the mere. Good now, ye have saved a life
Worth somewhat as the cleanser of this wood.
And fain would I reward thee worshipfully.
What guerdon will ye?'

                    Gareth sharply spake: 810
'None! for the deed's sake have I done the deed,
In uttermost obedience to the King.
But wilt thou yield this damsel harborage?'

Whereat the baron saying, 'I well believe
You be of Arthur's Table,' a light laugh
Broke from Lynette: 'Ay, truly of a truth,
And in a sort, being Arthur's kitchen-knave!—
But deem not I accept thee aught the more,
Scullion, for running sharply with thy spit
Down on a rout of craven foresters.   820
A thresher with his flail had scatter'd them.
Nay—for thou smellest of the kitchen still.
But an this lord will yield us harborage,
Well.'

                    So she spake. A league beyond the wood,
All in a full-fair manor and a rich,
His towers, where that day a feast had been
Held in high hall, and many a viand left,
And many a costly cate, received the three.
And there they placed a peacock in his pride
Before the damsel, and the baron set   830
Gareth beside her, but at once she rose.

'Meseems, that here is much discourtesy,
Setting this knave, Lord Baron, at my side.
Hear me—this morn I stood in Arthur's hall,
And pray'd the King would grant me Lancelot
To fight the brotherhood of Day and Night—
The last a monster unsubduable
Of any save of him for whom I call'd—
Suddenly bawls this frontless kitchen-knave,
"The quest is mine; thy kitchen-knave am I,   840
And mighty thro' thy meats and drinks am I."
Then Arthur all at once gone mad replies,
"Go therefore," and so gives the quest to him—
Him—here—a villain fitter to stick swine
Than ride abroad redressing women's wrong,
Or sit beside a noble gentlewoman.'

Then half-ashamed and part-amazed, the lord
Now look'd at one and now at other, left
The damsel by the peacock in his pride,
And, seating Gareth at another board,   850
Sat down beside him, ate and then began:

'Friend, whether thou be kitchen-knave, or not,
Or whether it be the maiden's fantasy,
And whether she be mad, or else the King,
Or both or neither, or thyself be mad,
I ask not; but thou strikest a strong stroke,
For strong thou art and goodly therewithal,
And saver of my life; and therefore now,
For here be mighty men to joust with, weigh
Whether thou wilt not with thy damsel back   860
To crave again Sir Lancelot of the King.
Thy pardon; I but speak for thine avail,
The saver of my life.'

                              And Gareth said,
'Full pardon, but I follow up the quest,
Despite of Day and Night and Death and Hell.'

So when, next morn, the lord whose life he saved
Had, some brief space, convey'd them on their way
And left them with God-speed, Sir Gareth spake,
'Lead, and I follow.' Haughtily she replied:

'I fly no more; I allow thee for an hour.   870
Lion and stoat have isled together, knave,
In time of flood. Nay, furthermore, methinks
Some ruth is mine for thee. Back wilt thou, fool?

For hard by here is one will overthrow
And slay thee; then will I to court again,
And shame the King for only yielding me
My champion from the ashes of his hearth.'

To whom Sir Gareth answer'd courteously:
'Say thou thy say, and I will do my deed.
Allow me for mine hour, and thou wilt find   880
My fortunes all as fair as hers who lay
Among the ashes and wedded the King's son.'

Then to the shore of one of those long loops
Wherethro' the serpent river coil'd, they came.
Rough-thicketed were the banks and steep; the stream
Full, narrow; this a bridge of single arc
Took at a leap; and on the further side
Arose a silk pavilion, gay with gold
In streaks and rays, and all Lent-lily in hue,
Save that the dome was purple, and above,   890
Crimson, a slender banneret fluttering.
And therebefore the lawless warrior paced
Unarm'd, and calling, 'Damsel, is this he,
The champion thou hast brought from Arthur's hall,
For whom we let thee pass?' 'Nay, nay,' she said,
'Sir Morning-Star. The King in utter scorn
Of thee and thy much folly hath sent thee here
His kitchen-knave; and look thou to thyself.
See that he fall not on thee suddenly,
And slay thee unarm'd; he is not knight but knave.'   900

Then at his call, 'O daughters of the Dawn,
And servants of the Morning-Star, approach,
Arm me,' from out the silken curtain-folds
Bare-footed and bare-headed three fair girls
In gilt and rosy raiment came. Their feet
In dewy grasses glisten'd; and the hair
All over glanced with dewdrop or with gem
Like sparkles in the stone Avanturine.
These arm'd him in blue arms, and gave a shield
Blue also, and thereon the morning star.   910
And Gareth silent gazed upon the knight,
Who stood a moment, ere his horse was brought,
Glorying; and in the stream beneath him shone,
Immingled with heaven's azure waveringly,
The gay pavilion and the naked feet,
His arms, the rosy raiment, and the star.

Then she that watch'd him: 'Wherefore stare ye so?
Thou shakest in thy fear. There yet is time;
Flee down the valley before he get to horse.
Who will cry shame? Thou art not knight but knave.'   920

Said Gareth: 'Damsel, whether knave or knight,
Far liefer had I fight a score of times
Than hear thee so missay me and revile.
Fair words were best for him who fights for thee;
But truly foul are better, for they send
That strength of anger thro' mine arms, I know
That I shall overthrow him.'

                              And he that bore
The star, when mounted, cried from o'er the bridge:
'A kitchen-knave, and sent in scorn of me!
Such fight not I, but answer scorn with scorn.   930
For this were shame to do him further wrong
Than set him on his feet, and take his horse
And arms, and so return him to the King.
Come, therefore, leave thy lady lightly, knave.
Avoid; for it beseemeth not a knave
To ride with such a lady.'

                              'Dog, thou liest!
I spring from loftier lineage than thine own.'
He spake; and all at fiery speed the two
Shock'd on the central bridge, and either spear
Bent but not brake, and either knight at once,   940
Hurl'd as a stone from out of a catapult
Beyond his horse's crupper and the bridge,
Fell, as if dead; but quickly rose and drew,
And Gareth lash'd so fiercely with his brand
He drave his enemy backward down the bridge,
The damsel crying, 'Well-stricken, kitchen-knave!'
Till Gareth's shield was cloven; but one stroke
Laid him that clove it grovelling on the ground.

Then cried the fall'n, 'Take not my life; I yield.'
And Gareth, 'So this damsel ask it of me   950
Good—I accord it easily as a grace.'
She reddening, 'Insolent scullion! I of thee?
I bound to thee for any favor ask'd!'
'Then shall he die.' And Gareth there unlaced
His helmet as to slay him, but she shriek'd,
'Be not so hardy, scullion, as to slay
One nobler than thyself.' 'Damsel, thy charge
Is an abounding pleasure to me. Knight,

Thy life is thine at her command. Arise
And quickly pass to Arthur's hall, and say 960
His kitchen-knave hath sent thee. See thou crave
His pardon for thy breaking of his laws.
Myself when I return will plead for thee.
Thy shield is mine—farewell; and, damsel, thou,
Lead, and I follow.'

             And fast away she fled;
Then when he came upon her, spake: 'Methought,
Knave, when I watch'd thee striking on the bridge,
The savor of thy kitchen came upon me
A little faintlier; but the wind hath changed,
I scent it twenty-fold.' And then she sang, 970
' "O morning star"—not that tall felon there
Whom thou, by sorcery or unhappiness
Or some device, hast foully overthrown,—

    "O morning star that smilest in the blue,
    O star, my morning dream hath proven true,
    Smile sweetly, thou! my love hath smiled on me."

   'But thou begone, take counsel, and away,
For hard by here is one that guards a ford—
The second brother in their fool's parable—
Will pay thee all thy wages, and to boot. 980
Care not for shame; thou art not knight but knave.'

   To whom Sir Gareth answer'd, laughingly:
'Parables? Hear a parable of the knave.
When I was kitchen-knave among the rest,
Fierce was the hearth, and one of my co-mates
Own'd a rough dog, to whom he cast his coat,
"Guard it," and there was none to meddle with it.
And such a coat art thou, and thee the King
Gave me to guard, and such a dog am I,
To worry, and not to flee—and—knight or knave— 990
The knave that doth thee service as full knight
Is all as good, meseems, as any knight
Toward thy sister's freeing.'

               Ay, Sir Knave!
Ay, knave, because thou strikest as a knight,
Being but knave, I hate thee all the more.'

   'Fair damsel, you should worship me the more,
That, being but knave, I throw thine enemies.'

   'Ay, ay,' she said, 'but thou shalt meet thy match.'

So when they touch'd the second river-loop,
Huge on a huge red horse, and all in mail   1000
Burnish'd to blinding, shone the Noonday Sun
Beyond a raging shallow. As if the flower
That blows a globe of after arrowlets
Ten-thousand-fold had grown, flash'd the fierce shield,
All sun; and Gareth's eyes had flying blots
Before them when he turn'd from watching him.
He from beyond the roaring shallow roar'd,
'What doest thou, brother, in my marches here?'
And she athwart the shallow shrill'd again,
'Here is a kitchen-knave from Arthur's hall   1010
Hath overthrown thy brother, and hath his arms.'
'Ugh!' cried the Sun, and, vizoring up a red
And cipher face of rounded foolishness,
Push'd horse across the foamings of the ford,
Whom Gareth met mid-stream; no room was there
For lance or tourney-skill. Four strokes they struck
With sword, and these were mighty; the new knight
Had fear he might be shamed; but as the Sun
Heaved up a ponderous arm to strike the fifth,
The hoof of his horse slipt in the stream, the stream   1020
Descended, and the Sun was wash'd away.

Then Gareth laid his lance athwart the ford;
So drew him home; but he that fought no more,
As being all bone-batter'd on the rock,
Yielded, and Gareth sent him to the King.
'Myself when I return will plead for thee.
Lead, and I follow.' Quietly she led.
'Hath not the good wind, damsel changed again?'
'Nay, not a point; nor art thou victor here.
There lies a ridge of slate across the ford;   1030
His horse thereon stumbled—ay, for I saw it.

' "O sun"—not this strong fool whom thou, Sir Knave,
Hast overthrown thro' mere unhappiness—

' "O sun, that wakenest all to bliss or pain,
O moon, that layest all to sleep again,
Shine sweetly; twice my love hath smiled on me."

'What knowest thou of love-song or of love?
Nay, nay, God wot, so thou wert nobly born,
Thou hast a pleasant presence. Yea, perchance,—

' "O dewy flowers that open to the sun,   1040
O dewy flowers that close when day is done,
Blow sweetly; twice my love hath smiled on me."

'What knowest thou of flowers, except, belike,
To garnish meats with? hath not our good King
Who lent me thee, the flower of kitchendom,
A foolish love for flowers? what stick ye round
The pasty? wherewithal deck the boar's head?
Flowers? nay, the boar hath rosemaries and bay.

> ' "O birds that warble to the morning sky,
> O birds that warble as the day goes by,   1050
> Sing sweetly; twice my love hath smiled on me."

'What knowest thou of birds, lark, mavis, merle,
Linnet? what dream ye when they utter forth
May-music growing with the growing light,
Their sweet sun-worship? these be for the snare—
So runs thy fancy—these be for the spit,
Larding and basting. See thou have not now
Larded thy last, except thou turn and fly.
There stands the third fool of their allegory.'

For there beyond a bridge of treble bow,   1060
All in a rose-red from the west, and all
Naked it seem'd, and glowing in the broad
Deep-dimpled current underneath, the knight
That named himself the Star of Evening stood.

And Gareth, 'Wherefore waits the madman there
Naked in open dayshine?' 'Nay,' she cried,
'Not naked, only wrapt in harden'd skins
That fit him like his own; and so ye cleave
His armor off him, these will turn the blade.'

Then the third brother shouted o'er the bridge,   1070
'O brother-star, why shine ye here so low?
Thy ward is higher up; but have ye slain
The damsel's champion?' and the damsel cried:

'No star of thine, but shot from Arthur's heaven
With all disaster unto thine and thee!
For both thy younger brethren have gone down
Before this youth; and so wilt thou, Sir Star.
Art thou not old?'

                              'Old, damsel, old and hard,
Old, with the might and breath of twenty boys.'
Said Gareth, 'Old, and over-bold in brag!   1080
But that same strength which threw the Morning Star
Can throw the Evening.'

                              Then that other blew
A hard and deadly note upon the horn.
'Approach and arm me!' With slow steps from out
An old storm-beaten, russet, many-stain'd
Pavilion, forth a grizzled damsel came,
And arm'd him in old arms, and brought a helm
With but a drying evergreen for crest,
And gave a shield whereon the star of even
Half-tarnish'd and half-bright, his emblem, shone.   1090
But when it glitter'd o'er the saddle-bow,
They madly hurl'd together on the bridge;
And Gareth overthrew him, lighted, drew,
There met him drawn, and overthrew him again,
But up like fire he started; and as oft
As Gareth brought him grovelling on his knees,
So many a time he vaulted up again;
Till Gareth panted hard, and his great heart,
Foredooming all his trouble was in vain,
Labor'd within him, for he seem'd as one   1100
That all in later, sadder age begins
To war against ill uses of a life,
But these from all his life arise, and cry,
'Thou hast made us lords, and canst not put us down!'
He half despairs; so Gareth seem'd to strike
Vainly, the damsel clamoring all the while,
'Well done, knave-knight, well stricken, O good knight-knave—
O knave, as noble as any of all the knights—
Shame me not, shame me not. I have prophesied—
Strike, thou art worthy of the Table Round—   1110
His arms are old, he trusts the harden'd skin—
Strike—strike—the wind will never change again.'
And Gareth hearing ever stronglier smote,
And hew'd great pieces of his armor off him,
But lash'd in vain against the harden'd skin,
And could not wholly bring him under, more
Than loud Southwesterns, rolling ridge on ridge,
The buoy that rides at sea, and dips and springs
For ever; till at length Sir Gareth's brand
Clash'd his, and brake it utterly to the hilt.   1120
'I have thee now;' but forth that other sprang,
And, all unknightlike, writhed his wiry arms
Around him, till he felt, despite his mail,
Strangled, but straining even his uttermost
Cast, and so hurl'd him headlong o'er the bridge
Down to the river, sink or swim, and cried,
'Lead, and I follow.'

But the damsel said:
'I lead no longer; ride thou at my side;
Thou art the kingliest of all kitchen-knaves.

 ' "O trefoil, sparkling on the rainy plain,   1130
  O rainbow with three colors after rain,
  Shine sweetly; thrice my love hath smiled on me."

'Sir,—and, good faith, I fain had added—Knight,
But that I heard thee call thyself a knave,—
Shamed am I that I so rebuked, reviled,
Missaid thee. Noble I am, and thought the King
Scorn'd me and mine; and now thy pardon, friend,
For thou hast ever answer'd courteously,
And wholly bold thou art, and meek withal
As any of Arthur's best, but, being knave,   1140
Hast maz'd my wit. I marvel what thou art.'

'Damsel,' he said, 'you be not all to blame,
Saving that you mistrusted our good King
Would handle scorn, or yield you, asking, one
Not fit to cope your quest. You said your say;
Mine answer was my deed. Good sooth! I hold
He scarce is knight, yea but half-man, nor meet
To fight for gentle damsel, he, who lets
His heart be stirr'd with any foolish heat
At any gentle damsel's waywardness.   1150
Shamed? care not! thy foul sayings fought for me;
And seeing now thy words are fair, methinks
There rides no knight, not Lancelot, his great self,
Hath force to quell me.'

       Nigh upon that hour
When the lone hern forgets his melancholy,
Lets down his other leg, and stretching dreams
Of goodly supper in the distant pool,
Then turn'd the noble damsel smiling at him,
And told him of a cavern hard at hand,
Where bread and baken meats and good red wine   1160
Of Southland, which the Lady Lyonors
Had sent her coming champion, waited him.

Anon they past a narrow comb wherein
Where slabs of rock with figures, knights on horse
Sculptured, and deckt in slowly-waning hues.
'Sir Knave, my knight, a hermit once was here,
Whose holy hand hath fashion'd on the rock
The war of Time against the soul of man.
And yon four fools have suck'd their allegory

From these damp walls, and taken but the form.   1170
Know ye not these?' and Gareth lookt and read—
In letters like to those the vexillary
Hath left crag-carven o'er the streaming Gelt—
'PHOSPHORUS,' then 'MERIDIES,'—'HESPERUS'—
'NOX'—'MORS,' beneath five figures, armed men,
Slab after slab, their faces forward all,
And running down the Soul, a shape that fled
With broken wings, torn raiment, and loose hair,
For help and shelter to the hermit's cave.
'Follow the faces, and we find it. Look,   1180
Who comes behind?'

                              For one—delay'd at first
Thro' helping back the dislocated Kay
To Camelot, then by what thereafter chanced,
The damsel's headlong error thro' the wood—
Sir Lancelot, having swum the river-loops—
His blue shield-lions cover'd—softly drew
Behind the twain, and when he saw the star
Gleam, on Sir Gareth's turning to him, cried,
'Stay, felon knight, I avenge me for my friend.'
And Gareth crying prick'd against the cry;   1190
But when they closed—in a moment—at one touch
Of that skill'd spear, the wonder of the world—
Went sliding down so easily, and fell,
That when he found the grass within his hands
He laughed. The laughter jarr'd upon Lynette.
Harshly she ask'd him, 'Shamed and overthrown,
And tumbled back into the kitchen-knave,
Why laugh ye? that ye blew your boast in vain?'
'Nay, noble damsel, but that I, the son
Of old King Lot and good Queen Bellicent,   1200
And victor of the bridges and the ford,
And knight of Arthur, here lie thrown by whom
I know not, all thro' mere unhappiness—
Device and sorcery and unhappiness—
Out, sword; we are thrown!' And Lancelot answer'd: 'Prince,
O Gareth—thro' the mere unhappiness
Of one who came to help thee, not to harm,
Lancelot, and all as glad to find thee whole
As on the day when Arthur knighted him.'

      Then Gareth: 'Thou—Lancelot!—thine the hand   1210
That threw me? An some chance to mar the boast
Thy brethren of thee make—which could not chance—
Had sent thee down before a lesser spear,
Shamed had I been, and sad—O Lancelot—thou!'

Whereat the maiden, petulant: 'Lancelot,
Why came ye not, when call'd? and wherefore now
Come ye, not call'd? I gloried in my knave,
Who being still rebuked would answer still
Courteous as any knight—but now, if knight,
The marvel dies, and leaves me fool'd and trick'd,   1220
And only wondering wherefore play'd upon;
And doubtful whether I and mine be scorn'd.
Where should be truth if not in Arthur's hall,
In Arthur's presence? Knight, knave, prince and fool,
I hate thee and forever.'

          And Lancelot said:
'Bless'd be thou, Sir Gareth! knight art thou
To the King's best wish. O damsel, be you wise,
To call him shamed who is but overthrown?
Thrown have I been, nor once, but many a time.
Victor from vanquish'd issues at the last,   1230
And overthrower from being overthrown.
With sword we have not striven, and thy good horse
And thou are weary; yet not less I felt
Thy manhood thro' that wearied lance of thine.
Well hast thou done; for all the stream is freed,
And thou hast wreak'd his justice on his foes,
And when reviled hast answer'd graciously,
And makest merry when overthrown. Prince, knight,
Hail, knight and prince, and of our Table Round!'

    And then when turning to Lynette he told   1240
The tale of Gareth, petulantly she said:
'Ay, well—ay, well—for worse than being fool'd
Of others, is to fool one's self. A cave,
Sir Lancelot, is hard by, with meats and drinks
And forage for the horse, and flint for fire.
But all about it flies a honeysuckle.
Seek, till we find.' And when they sought and found,
Sir Gareth drank and ate, and all his life
Past into sleep; on whom the maiden gazed:
'Sound sleep be thine! sound cause to sleep hast thou.   1250
Wake lusty! Seem I not as tender to him
As any mother? Ay, but such a one
As all day long hath rated at her child,
And vext his day, but blesses him asleep—
Good lord, how sweetly smells the honeysuckle
In the hush'd night, as if the world were one
Of utter peace, and love, and gentleness!
O Lancelot, Lancelot,'—and she clapt her hands—
'Full merry am I to find my goodly knave

Is knight and noble. See now, sworn have I,   1260
Else yon black felon had not let me pass,
To bring thee back to do the battle with him.
Thus an thou goest, he will fight thee first;
Who doubts thee victor? so will my knight-knave
Miss the full flower of this accomplishment.'

Said Lancelot: 'Peradventure he you name
May know my shield. Let Gareth, an he will,
Change his for mine, and take my charger, fresh,
Not to be spurr'd, loving the battle as well
As he that rides him.' 'Lancelot-like,' she said,   1270
'Courteous in this, Lord Lancelot, as in all.'

And Gareth, wakening, fiercely clutch'd the shield:
'Ramp, ye lance-splintering lions, on whom all spears
Are rotten sticks! ye seem agape to roar!
Yea, ramp and roar at leaving of your lord!—
Care not, good beasts, so well I care for you.
O noble Lancelot, from my hold on these
Streams virtue—fire—thro' one that will not shame
Even the shadow of Lancelot under shield.
Hence; let us go.'

             Silent the silent field   1280
They traversed. Arthur's Harp tho' summer-wan,
In counter motion to the clouds, allured
The glance of Gareth dreaming on his liege.
A star shot: 'Lo,' said Gareth, 'the foe falls!'
An owl whoopt: 'Hark the victor pealing there!'
Suddenly she that rode upon his left
Clung to the shield that Lancelot lent him, crying:
'Yield, yield him this again; 't is he must fight:
I curse the tongue that all thro' yesterday
Reviled thee, and hath wrought on Lancelot now   1290
To lend thee horse and shield. Wonders ye have done,
Miracles ye cannot. Here is glory enow
In having flung the three. I see thee maim'd,
Mangled; I swear thou canst not fling the fourth.'

'And wherefore, damsel? tell me all ye know.
You cannot scare me; nor rough face, or voice,
Brute bulk of limb, or boundless savagery
Appal me from the quest.'

                     'Nay, prince,' she cried,
'God wot, I never look'd upon the face,
Seeing he never rides abroad by day,   1300

But watch'd him have I like a phantom pass
Chilling the night; nor have I heard the voice.
Always he made his mouthpiece of a page
Who came and went, and still reported him
As closing in himself the strength of ten,
And when his anger tare him, massacring
Man, woman, lad, and girl—yea, the soft babe!
Some hold that he hath swallow'd infant flesh,
Monster! O prince, I went for Lancelot first,
The quest is Lancelot's; give him back the shield.'   1310

    Said Gareth laughing, 'An he fight for this,
Belike he wins it as the better man;
Thus—and not else!'

                    But Lancelot on him urged
All the devisings of their chivalry
When one might meet a mightier than himself;
How best to manage horse, lance, sword, and shield,
And so fill up the gap where force might fail
With skill and fineness. Instant were his words.

    Then Gareth: 'Here be rules. I know but one—
To dash against mine enemy and to win.   1320
Yet have I watch'd thee victor in the joust,
And seen thy way.' 'Heaven help thee!' sigh'd Lynette.

    Then for a space, and under cloud that grew
To thunder-gloom palling all stars, they rode
In converse till she made her palfrey halt,
Lifted an arm, and softly whisper'd, 'There.'
And all the three were silent seeing, pitch'd
Beside the Castle Perilous on flat field,
A huge pavilion like a mountain peak
Sunder the glooming crimson on the marge,   1330
Black, with black banner, and a long black horn
Beside it hanging; which Sir Gareth graspt,
And so, before the two could hinder him,
Sent all his heart and breath thro' all the horn.
Echo'd the walls; a light twinkled; anon
Came lights and lights, and once again he blew;
Whereon were hollow tramplings up and down
And muffled voices heard, and shadows past;
Till high above him, circled with her maids,
The Lady Lyonors at a window stood,   1340
Beautiful among lights, and waving to him
White hands and courtesy. But when the prince
Three times had blown—after long hush—at last—
The huge pavilion slowly yielded up,

Thro' those black foldings, that which housed therein.
High on a night-black horse, in night-black arms,
With white breast-bone, and barren ribs of Death,
And crown'd with fleshless laughter—some ten steps—
In the half-light—thro' the dim dawn—advanced
The monster, and then paused, and spake no word.   1350

But Gareth spake and all indignantly:
'Fool, for thou hast, men say, the strength of ten,
Canst thou not trust the limbs thy God hath given,
But must, to make the terror of thee more,
Trick thyself out in ghastly imageries
Of that which Life hath done with, and the clod,
Less dull than thou, will hide with mantling flowers
As if for pity?' But he spake no word;
Which set the horror higher. A maiden swoon'd;
The Lady Lyonors wrung her hands and wept,   1360
As doom'd to be the bride of Night and Death;
Sir Gareth's head prickled beneath his helm;
And even Sir Lancelot thro' his warm blood felt
Ice strike, and all that mark'd him were aghast.

At once Sir Lancelot's charger fiercely neigh'd,
And Death's dark war-horse bounded forward with him.
Then those that did not blink the terror saw
That Death was cast to ground, and slowly rose.
But with one stroke Sir Gareth split the skull.
Half fell to right and half to left and lay.   1370
Then with a stronger buffet he clove the helm
As throughly as the skull; and out from this
Issued the bright face of a blooming boy
Fresh as a flower new-born, and crying, 'Knight,
Slay me not; my three brethren bade me do it,
To make a horror all about the house,
And stay the world from Lady Lyonors.
They never dream'd the passes would be past.'
Answer'd Sir Gareth graciously to one
Not many a moon his younger, 'My fair child,   1380
What madness made thee challenge the chief knight
Of Arthur's hall?' 'Fair Sir, they bade me do it.
They hate the King and Lancelot, the King's friend;
They hoped to slay him somewhere on the stream,
They never dream'd the passes could be past.'

Then sprang the happier day from underground;
And Lady Lyonors and her house, with dance
And revel and song, made merry over Death,
As being after all their foolish fears

And horrors only proven a blooming boy.
So large mirth lived, and Gareth won the quest.

And he that told the tale in older times
Says that Sir Gareth wedded Lyonors,
But he that told it later says Lynette.

THE MARRIAGE OF GERAINT

THE brave Geraint, a knight of Arthur's court,
A tributary prince of Devon, one
Of that great Order of the Table Round,
Had married Enid, Yniol's only child,
And loved her as he loved the light of heaven.
And as the light of heaven varies, now
At sunrise, now at sunset, now by night
With moon and trembling stars, so loved Geraint
To make her beauty vary day by day,
In crimsons and in purples and in gems.   10
And Enid, but to please her husband's eye,
Who first had found and loved her in a state
Of broken fortunes, daily fronted him
In some fresh splendor; and the Queen herself,
Grateful to Prince Geraint for service done,
Loved her, and often with her own white hands
Array'd and deck'd her, as the loveliest,
Next after her own self, in all the court.
And Enid loved the Queen, and with true heart
Adored her, as the stateliest and the best   20
And loveliest of all women upon earth.
And seeing them so tender and so close,
Long in their common love rejoiced Geraint.
But when a rumor rose about the Queen,
Touching her guilty love for Lancelot,
Tho' yet there lived no proof, nor yet was heard
The world's loud whisper breaking into storm,
Not less Geraint believed it; and there fell
A horror on him lest his gentle wife,
Thro' that great tenderness for Guinevere,   30
Had suffer'd or should suffer any taint
In nature. Wherefore, going to the King,
He made this pretext, that his princedom lay
Close on the borders of a territory
Wherein were bandit earls, and caitiff knights,
Assassins, and all flyers from the hand
Of Justice, and whatever loathes a law;
And therefore, till the King himself should please

To cleanse this common sewer of all his realm,
He craved a fair permission to depart,   40
And there defend his marches. And the King
Mused for a little on his plea, but, last,
Allowing it, the prince and Enid rode,
And fifty knights rode with them, to the shores
Of Severn, and they past to their own land;
Where, thinking that, if ever yet was wife
True to her lord, mine shall be so to me,
He compass'd her with sweet observances
And worship, never leaving her, and grew
Forgetful of his promise to the King,   50
Forgetful of the falcon and the hunt,
Forgetful of the tilt and tournament,
Forgetful of his glory and his name,
Forgetful of his princedom and its cares.
And this forgetfulness was hateful to her.
And by and by the people, when they met
In twos and threes, or fuller companies,
Began to scoff and jeer and babble of him
As of a prince whose manhood was all gone,
And molten down in mere uxoriousness.   60
And this she gather'd from the people's eyes;
This too the women who attired her head,
To please her, dwelling on his boundless love,
Told Enid, and they sadden'd her the more;
And day by day she thought to tell Geraint,
But could not out of bashful delicacy,
While he, that watch'd her sadden, was the more
Suspicious that her nature had a taint.

At last, it chanced that on a summer morn—
They sleeping each by either—the new sun   70
Beat thro' the blindless casement of the room,
And heated the strong warrior in his dreams;
Who, moving, cast the coverlet aside,
And bared the knotted column of his throat,
The massive square of his heroic breast,
And arms on which the standing muscle sloped,
As slopes a wild brook o'er a little stone,
Running too vehemently to break upon it.
And Enid woke and sat beside the couch,
Admiring him, and thought within herself,   80
Was ever man so grandly made as he?
Then, like a shadow, past the people's talk
And accusation of uxoriousness
Across her mind, and, bowing over him,
Low to her own heart piteously she said:

'O noble breast and all-puissant arms,
Am I the cause, I the poor cause that men
Reproach you, saying all your force is gone?
I *am* the cause, because I dare not speak
And tell him what I think and what they say.   90
And yet I hate that he should linger here;
I cannot love my lord and not his name.
Far liefer had I gird his harness on him,
And ride with him to battle and stand by,
And watch his mightful hand striking great blows
At caitiffs and at wrongers of the world.
Far better were I laid in the dark earth,
Not hearing any more his noble voice,
Not to be folded more in these dear arms,
And darken'd from the high light in his eyes,   100
Than that my lord thro' me should suffer shame.
Am I so bold, and could I so stand by,
And see my dear lord wounded in the strife,
Or maybe pierced to death before mine eyes,
And yet not dare to tell him what I think,
And how men slur him, saying all his force
Is melted into mere effeminacy?
O me, I fear that I am no true wife!'

    Half inwardly, half audibly she spoke,
And the strong passion in her made her weep   110
True tears upon his broad and naked breast,
And these awoke him, and by great mischance
He heard but fragments of her later words,
And that she fear'd she was not a true wife.
And then he thought, 'In spite of all my care,
For all my pains, poor man, for all my pains,
She is not faithful to me, and I see her
Weeping for some gay knight in Arthur's hall.'
Then, tho' he loved and reverenced her too much
To dream she could be guilty of foul act,   120
Right thro' his manful breast darted the pang
That makes a man, in the sweet face of her
Whom he loves most, lonely and miserable.
At this he hurl'd his huge limbs out of bed,
And shook his drowsy squire awake and cried,
'My charger and her palfrey;' then to her,
'I will ride forth into the wilderness,
For, tho' it seems my spurs are yet to win,
I have not fallen so low as some would wish.
And thou, put on thy worst and meanest dress   130
And ride with me.' And Enid ask'd, amazed,
'If Enid errs, let Enid learn her fault.'

But he, 'I charge thee, ask not, but obey.'
Then she bethought her of a faded silk,
A faded mantle and a faded veil,
And moving toward a cedarn cabinet,
Wherein she kept them folded reverently
With sprigs of summer laid between the folds,
She took them, and array'd herself therein,
Remembering when first he came on her   140
Drest in that dress, and how he loved her in it,
And all her foolish fears about the dress,
And all his journey to her, as himself
Had told her, and their coming to the court.

    For Arthur on the Whitsuntide before
Held court at old Caerleon upon Usk.
There on a day, he sitting high in hall,
Before him came a forester of Dean,
Wet from the woods, with notice of a hart
Taller than all his fellows, milky-white,   150
First seen that day; these things he told the King.
Then the good King gave order to let blow
His horns for hunting on the morrow morn,
And when the Queen petition'd for his leave
To see the hunt, allow'd it easily.
So with the morning all the court were gone.
But Guinevere lay late into the morn,
Lost in sweet dreams, and dreaming of her love
For Lancelot, and forgetful of the hunt,
But rose at last, a single maiden with her,   160
Took horse, and forded Usk, and gain'd the wood;
There, on a little knoll beside it, stay'd
Waiting to hear the hounds, but heard instead
A sudden sound of hoofs, for Prince Geraint,
Late also, wearing neither hunting-dress
Nor weapon save a golden-hilted brand,
Came quickly flashing thro' the shallow ford
Behind them, and so gallop'd up the knoll.
A purple scarf, at either end whereof
There swung an apple of the purest gold,   170
Sway'd round about him, as he gallop'd up
To join them, glancing like a dragon-fly
In summer suit and silks of holiday.
Low bow'd the tributary prince, and she,
Sweetly and stately, and with all grace
Of womanhood and queenhood, answer'd him:
'Late, late, Sir Prince,' she said, 'later than we!'
'Yea, noble Queen,' he answer'd, 'and so late
That I but come like you to see the hunt,

Not join it.' 'Therefore wait with me,' she said;   180
'For on this little knoll, if anywhere,
There is good chance that we shall hear the hounds:
Here often they break covert at our feet.'

And while they listen'd for the distant hunt,
And chiefly for the baying of Cavall,
King Arthur's hound of deepest mouth, there rode
Full slowly by a knight, lady, and dwarf;
Whereof the dwarf lagg'd latest, and the knight
Had vizor up, and show'd a youthful face,
Imperious, and of haughtiest lineaments.   190
And Guinevere, not mindful of his face
In the King's hall, desired his name, and sent
Her maiden to demand it of the dwarf,
Who being vicious, old, and irritable,
And doubling all his master's vice of pride,
Made answer sharply that she should not know.
'Then will I ask it of himself,' she said.
'Nay, by my faith, thou shalt not,' cried the dwarf;
'Thou art not worthy even to speak of him;'
And when she put her horse toward the knight,   200
Struck at her with his whip, and she return'd
Indignant to the Queen; whereat Geraint
Exclaiming, 'Surely I will learn the name,'
Made sharply to the dwarf, and ask'd it of him,
Who answer'd as before; and when the prince
Had put his horse in motion toward the knight,
Struck at him with his whip, and cut his cheek.
The prince's blood spirted upon the scarf,
Dyeing it; and his quick, instinctive hand
Caught at the hilt, as to abolish him: 210
But he, from his exceeding manfulness
And pure nobility of temperament,
Wroth to be wroth at such a worm, refrain'd
From even a word, and so returning said:

'I will avenge this insult, noble Queen,
Done in your maiden's person to yourself,
And I will track this vermin to their earths;
For tho' I ride unarm'd, I do not doubt
To find, at some place I shall come at, arms
On loan, or else for pledge; and, being found,   220
Then will I fight him, and will break his pride,
And on the third day will again be here,
So that I be not fall'n in fight. Farewell.'

Farewell, fair prince,' answer'd the stately Queen.
'Be prosperous in this journey, as in all;
And may you light on all things that you love,
And live to wed with her whom first you love.
But ere you wed with any, bring your bride,
And I, were she the daughter of a king,
Yea, tho' she were a beggar from the hedge,   230
Will clothe her for her bridals like the sun.'

And Prince Geraint, now thinking that he heard
The noble hart at bay, now the far horn,
A little vext at losing of the hunt,
A little at the vile occasion, rode,
By ups and downs, thro' many a grassy glade
And valley, with fixt eye following the three.
At last they issued from the world of wood,
And climb'd upon a fair and even ridge,
And show'd themselves against the sky, and sank.   240
And thither came Geraint, and underneath
Beheld the long street of a little town
In a long valley, on one side whereof,
White from the mason's hand, a fortress rose;
And on one side a castle in decay,
Beyond a bridge that spann'd a dry ravine.
And out of town and valley came a noise
As of a broad brook o'er a shingly bed
Brawling, or like a clamor of the rooks
At distance, ere they settle for the night.   250

And onward to the fortress rode the three,
And enter'd, and were lost behind the walls.
'So,' thought Geraint, 'I have track'd him to his earth.'
And down the long street riding wearily,
Found every hostel full, and everywhere
Was hammer laid to hoof, and the hot hiss
And bustling whistle of the youth who scour'd
His master's armor; and of such a one
He ask'd, 'What means the tumult in the town?'
Who told him, scouring still, 'The sparrow-hawk!'   260
Then riding close behind an ancient churl,
Who, smitten by the dusty sloping beam,
Went sweating underneath a sack of corn,
Ask'd yet once more what meant the hubbub here?
Who answer'd gruffly, 'Ugh! the sparrow-hawk!'
Then riding further past an armorer's,
Who, with back turn'd, and bow'd above his work,
Sat riveting a helmet on his knee,
He put the selfsame query, but the man

Not turning round, nor looking at him, said: 270
'Friend, he that labors for the sparrow-hawk
Has little time for idle questioners.'
Whereat Geraint flash'd into sudden spleen:
'A thousand pips eat up your sparrow-hawk!
Tits, wrens, and all wing'd nothings peck him dead!
Ye think the rustic cackle of your bourg
The murmur of the world! What is it to me?
O wretched set of sparrows, one and all,
Who pipe of nothing but of sparrow-hawks!
Speak, if ye be not like the rest, hawk-mad,   280
Where can I get me harborage for the night?
And arms, arms, arms to fight my enemy? Speak!'
Whereat the armorer turning all amazed
And seeing one so gay in purple silks,
Came forward with the helmet yet in hand
And answer'd: 'Pardon me, O stranger knight;
We hold a tourney here to-morrow morn,
And there is scantly time for half the work.
Arms? truth! I know not; all are wanted here.
Harborage? truth, good truth, I know not, save,   290
It may be, at Earl Yniol's, o'er the bridge
Yonder.' He spoke and fell to work again.

Then rode Geraint, a little spleenful yet,
Across the bridge that spann'd the dry ravine.
There musing sat the hoary-headed earl—
His dress a suit of fray'd magnificence,
Once fit for feasts of ceremony—and said:
'Whither, fair son?' to whom Geraint replied,
'O friend, I seek a harborage for the night.'
Then Yniol, 'Enter therefore and partake   300
The slender entertainment of a house
Once rich, now poor, but ever open-door'd.'
'Thanks, venerable friend,' replied Geraint;
'So that ye do not serve me sparrow-hawks
For supper, I will enter, I will eat
With all the passion of a twelve hours' fast.'
Then sigh'd and smiled the hoary-headed earl,
And answer'd, 'Graver cause than yours is mine
To curse this hedgerow thief, the sparrow-hawk.
But in, go in; for save yourself desire it,   310
We will not touch upon him even in jest.'

Then rode Geraint into the castle court,
His charger trampling many a prickly star
Of sprouted thistle on the broken stones.
He look'd and saw that all was ruinous.

Here stood a shatter'd archway plumed with fern;
And here had fallen a great part of a tower,
Whole, like a crag that tumbles from the cliff,
And like a crag was gay with wilding flowers;
And high above a piece of turret stair,   320
Worn by the feet that now were silent, wound
Bare to the sun, and monstrous ivy-stems
Claspt the gray walls with hairy-fibred arms,
And suck'd the joining of the stones, and look'd
A knot, beneath, of snakes, aloft, a grove.

And while he waited in the castle court,
The voice of Enid, Yniol's daughter, rang
Clear thro' the open casement of the hall,
Singing; and as the sweet voice of a bird,
Heard by the lander in a lonely isle,   330
Moves him to think what kind of bird it is
That sings so delicately clear, and make
Conjecture of the plumage and the form,
So the sweet voice of Enid moved Geraint,
And made him like a man abroad at morn
When first the liquid note beloved of men
Comes flying over many a windy wave
To Britain, and in April suddenly
Breaks from a coppice gemm'd with green and red,
And he suspends his converse with a friend,   340
Or it may be the labor of his hands,
To think or say, 'There is the nightingale:'
So fared it with Geraint, who thought and said,
'Here, by God's grace, is the one voice for me.'

It chanced the song that Enid sang was one
Of Fortune and her wheel, and Enid sang:

'Turn, Fortune, turn thy wheel, and lower the proud;
Turn thy wild wheel thro' sunshine, storm, and cloud;
Thy wheel and thee we neither love nor hate.

'Turn, Fortune, turn thy wheel with smile or frown;   350
With that wild wheel we go not up or down;
Our hoard is little, but our hearts are great.

'Smile and we smile, the lords of many lands;
Frown and we smile, the lords of our own hands;
For man is man and master of his fate.

'Turn, turn thy wheel above the staring crowd;
Thy wheel and thou are shadows in the cloud;
Thy wheel and thee we neither love nor hate.'

'Hark, by the bird's song ye may learn the nest,'
Said Yniol; 'enter quickly.' Entering then, 360
Right o'er a mount of newly-fallen stones,
The dusky-rafter'd many-cobweb'd hall,
He found an ancient dame in dim brocade;
And near her, like a blossom vermeil-white
That lightly breaks a faded flower-sheath,
Moved the fair Enid, all in faded silk,
Her daughter. In a moment thought Geraint,
'Here, by God's rood, is the one maid for me.'
But none spake word except the hoary earl:
'Enid, the good knight's horse stands in the court; 370
Take him to stall, and give him corn, and then
Go to the town and buy us flesh and wine;
And we will make us merry as we may.
Our hoard is little, but our hearts are great.'

He spake; the prince, as Enid past him, fain
To follow, strode a stride, but Yniol caught
His purple scarf, and held, and said, 'Forbear!
Rest! the good house, tho' ruin'd, O my son,
Endures not that her guest should serve himself.'
And reverencing the custom of the house 380
Geraint, from utter courtesy, forebore.

So Enid took his charger to the stall,
And after went her way across the bridge,
And reach'd the town, and while the prince and earl
Yet spoke together, came again with one,
A youth that, following with a costrel, bore
The means of goodly welcome, flesh and wine.
And Enid brought sweet cakes to make them cheer,
And, in her veil enfolded, manchet bread.
And then, because their hall must also serve 390
For kitchen, boil'd the flesh, and spread the board,
And stood behind, and waited on the three.
And, seeing her so sweet and serviceable,
Geraint had longing in him evermore
To stoop and kiss the tender little thumb
That crost the trencher as she laid it down.
But after all had eaten, then Geraint,
For now the wine made summer in his veins,
Let his eye rove in following, or rest
On Enid at her lowly handmaid-work, 400
Now here, now there, about the dusky hall;
Then suddenly addrest the hoary earl:

'Fair host and earl, I pray your courtesy;
This sparrow-hawk, what is he? tell me of him.
His name? but no, good faith, I will not have it;
For if he be the knight whom late I saw
Ride into that new fortress by your town,
White from the mason's hand, then have I sworn
From his own lips to have it—I am Geraint
Of Devon—for this morning when the Queen   410
Sent her own maiden to demand the name,
His dwarf, a vicious under-shapen thing,
Struck at her with his whip, and she return'd
Indignant to the Queen; and then I swore
That I would track this caitiff to his hold,
And fight and break his pride, and have it of him.
And all unarm'd I rode, and thought to find
Arms in your town, where all the men are mad;
They take the rustic murmur of their bourg
For the great wave that echoes round the world.   420
They would not hear me speak; but if ye know
Where I can light on arms, or if yourself
Should have them, tell me, seeing I have sworn
That I will break his pride and learn his name,
Avenging this great insult done the Queen.'

Then cried Earl Yniol: 'Art thou he indeed,
Geraint, a name far-sounded among men
For noble deeds? and truly I, when first
I saw you moving by me on the bridge,
Felt ye were somewhat, yea, and by your state   430
And presence might have guess'd you one of those
That eat in Arthur's hall at Camelot.
Nor speak I now from foolish flattery;
For this dear child hath often heard me praise
Your feats of arms, and often when I paused
Hath ask'd again, and ever loved to hear;
So grateful is the noise of noble deeds
To noble hearts who see but acts of wrong.
O, never yet had woman such a pair
Of suitors as this maiden; first Limours,   440
A creature wholly given to brawls and wine,
Drunk even when he woo'd; and be he dead
I know not, but he past to the wild land.
The second was your foe, the sparrow-hawk,
My curse, my nephew—I will not let his name
Slip from my lips if I can help it—he,
When I that knew him fierce and turbulent
Refused her to him, then his pride awoke;
And since the proud man often is the mean,

He sow'd a slander in the common ear,
Affirming that his father left him gold,
And in my charge, which was not render'd to him;
Bribed with large promises the men who served
About my person, the more easily
Because my means were somewhat broken into
Thro' open doors and hospitality;
Raised my own town against me in the night
Before my Enid's birthday, sack'd my house;
From mine own earldom foully ousted me;
Built that new fort to overawe my friends,   460
For truly there are those who love me yet;
And keeps me in this ruinous castle here,
Where doubtless he would put me soon to death
But that his pride too much despises me.
And I myself sometimes despise myself;
For I have let men be and have their way,
Am much too gentle, have not used my power;
Nor know I whether I be very base
Or very manful, whether very wise
Or very foolish; only this I know,   470
That whatsoever evil happen to me,
I seem to suffer nothing heart or limb,
But can endure it all most patiently.'

'Well said, true heart,' replied Geraint, 'but arms,
That if the sparrow-hawk, this nephew, fight
In next day's tourney I may break his pride.'

And Yniol answer'd: 'Arms, indeed, but old
And rusty, old and rusty, Prince Geraint,
Are mine, and therefore, at thine asking, thine.
But in this tournament can no man tilt,   480
Except the lady he loves best be there.
Two forks are fixt into the meadow ground,
And over these is placed a silver wand,
And over that a golden sparrow-hawk,
The prize of beauty for the fairest there.
And this, what knight soever be in field
Lays claim to for the lady at his side,
And tilts with my good nephew thereupon,
Who being apt at arms and big of bone
Has ever won it for the lady with him,   490
And toppling over all antagonism
Has earn'd himself the name of sparrow-hawk.
But thou, that hast no lady, canst not fight.'

To whom Geraint with eyes all bright replied,
Leaning a little toward him: 'Thy leave!
Let *me* lay lance in rest, O noble host,
For this dear child, because I never saw,
Tho' having seen all beauties of our time,
Nor can see elsewhere, anything so fair.
And if I fall her name will yet remain   500
Untarnish'd as before; but if I live,
So aid me heaven when at mine uttermost
As I will make her truly my true wife!'

Then, howsoever patient, Yniol's heart
Danced in his bosom, seeing better days.
And looking round he saw not Enid there—
Who hearing her own name had stol'n away—
But that old dame, to whom full tenderly
And fondling all her hand in his he said:
'Mother, a maiden is a tender thing,   510
And best by her that bore her understood.
Go thou to rest, but ere thou go to rest,
Tell her, and prove her heart toward the prince.'

So spake the kindly-hearted earl, and she
With frequent smile and nod departing found,
Half disarray'd as to her rest, the girl;
Whom first she kiss'd on either cheek, and then
On either shining shoulder laid a hand,
And kept her off and gazed upon her face,
And told her all their converse in the hall,   520
Proving her heart. But never light and shade
Coursed one another more on open ground
Beneath a troubled heaven than red and pale
Across the face of Enid hearing her;
While slowly falling as a scale that falls,
When weight is added only grain by grain,
Sank her sweet head upon her gentle breast;
Nor did she lift an eye nor speak a word,
Rapt in the fear and in the wonder of it.
So moving without answer to her rest   530
She found no rest, and ever fail'd to draw
The quiet night into her blood, but lay
Contemplating her own unworthiness;
And when the pale and bloodless east began
To quicken to the sun, arose, and raised
Her mother too, and hand in hand they moved
Down to the meadow where the jousts were held,
And waited there for Yniol and Geraint.

And thither came the twain, and when Geraint
Beheld her first in field, awaiting him, 540
He felt, were she the prize of bodily force,
Himself beyond the rest pushing could move
The Chair of Idris. Yniol's rusted arms
Were on his princely person, but thro' these
Prince-like his bearing shone; and errant knights
And ladies came, and by and by the town
Flow'd in and settling circled all the lists.
And there they fixt the forks into the ground,
And over these they placed the silver wand,
And over that the golden sparrow-hawk. 550
Then Yniol's nephew, after trumpet blown,
Spake to the lady with him and proclaim'd,
'Advance and take, the fairest of the fair,
What I these two years past have won for thee,
The prize of beauty.' Loudly spake the prince,
'Forbear; there is a worthier,' and the knight
With some surprise and thrice as much disdain
Turn'd, and beheld the four, and all his face
Glow'd like the heart of a great fire at Yule,
So burnt he was with passion, crying out, 560
'Do battle for it then,' no more; and thrice
They clash'd together, and thrice they brake their spears.
Then each, dishorsed and drawing, lash'd at each
So often and with such blows that all the crowd
Wonder'd, and now and then from distant walls
There came a clapping as of phantom hands.
So twice they fought, and twice they breathed, and still
The dew of their great labor and the blood
Of their strong bodies, flowing, drain'd their force.
But either's force was match'd till Yniol's cry, 570
'Remember that great insult done the Queen,'
Increased Geraint's, who heaved his blade aloft,
And crack'd the helmet thro', and bit the bone,
And fell'd him, and set foot upon his breast,
And said, 'Thy name?' To whom the fallen man
Made answer, groaning: 'Edyrn, son of Nudd!
Ashamed am I that I should tell it thee.
My pride is broken; men have seen my fall.'
'Then, Edyrn, son of Nudd,' replied Geraint,
'These two things shalt thou do, or else thou diest. 580
First, thou thyself, with damsel and with dwarf,
Shalt ride to Arthur's court and, coming there,
Crave pardon for that insult done the Queen,
And shalt abide her judgment on it; next,
Thou shalt give back their earldom to thy kin.
These two things shalt thou do, or thou shalt die.'

And Edyrn answer'd, 'These things will I do,
For I have never yet been overthrown,
And thou hast overthrown me, and my pride
Is broken down, for Enid sees my fall!'   590
And rising up he rode to Arthur's court,
And there the Queen forgave him easily.
And, being young, he changed and came to loathe
His crime of traitor, slowly drew himself
Bright from his old dark life, and fell at last
In the great battle fighting for the King.

    But when the third day from the hunting-morn
Made a low splendor in the world, and wings
Moved in her ivy, Enid, for she lay
With her fair head in the dim-yellow light,   600
Among the dancing shadows of the birds,
Woke and bethought her of her promise given
No later than last eve to Prince Geraint—
So bent he seem'd on going the third day,
He would not leave her till her promise given—
To ride with him this morning to the court,
And there be made known to the stately Queen,
And there be wedded with all ceremony.
At this she cast her eyes upon her dress,
And thought it never yet had look'd so mean.   610
For as a leaf in mid-November is
To what it was in mid-October, seem'd
The dress that now she look'd on to the dress
She look'd on ere the coming of Geraint.
And still she look'd, and still the terror grew
Of that strange bright and dreadful thing, a court,
All staring at her in her faded silk;
And softly to her own sweet heart she said:

    'This noble prince who won our earldom back,
So splendid in his acts and his attire,   620
Sweet heaven, how much I shall discredit him!
Would he could tarry with us here awhile,
But being so beholden to the prince,
It were but little grace in any of us,
Bent as he seem'd on going this third day,
To seek a second favor at his hands.
Yet if he could but tarry a day or two,
Myself would work eye dim and finger lame
Far liefer than so much discredit him.'

    And Enid fell in longing for a dress   630
All branch'd and flower'd with gold, a costly gift

Of her good mother, given her on the night
Before her birthday, three sad years ago,
That night of fire, when Edyrn sack'd their house
And scatter'd all they had to all the winds;
For while the mother show'd it, and the two
Were turning and admiring it, the work
To both appear'd so costly, rose a cry
That Edyrn's men were on them, and they fled
With little save the jewels they had on,   640
Which being sold and sold had bought them bread.
And Edyrn's men had caught them in their flight,
And placed them in this ruin; and she wish'd
The prince had found her in her ancient home;
Then let her fancy flit across the past,
And roam the goodly places that she knew;
And last bethought her how she used to watch,
Near that old home, a pool of golden carp;
And one was patch'd and blurr'd and lustreless
Among his burnish'd brethren of the pool;   650
And half asleep she made comparison
Of that and these to her own faded self
And the gay court, and fell asleep again,
And dreamt herself was such a faded form
Among her burnish'd sisters of the pool.
But this was in the garden of a king,
And tho' she lay dark in the pool she knew
That all was bright; that all about were birds
Of sunny plume in gilded trellis-work;
That all the turf was rich in plots that look'd   660
Each like a garnet or a turkis in it;
And lords and ladies of the high court went
In silver tissue talking things of state;
And children of the King in cloth of gold
Glanced at the doors or gambol'd down the walks.
And while she thought, 'They will not see me,' came
A stately queen whose name was Guinevere,
And all the children in their cloth of gold
Ran to her, crying, 'If we have fish at all
Let them be gold; and charge the gardeners now   670
To pick the faded creature from the pool,
And cast it on the mixen that it die.'
And therewithal one came and seized on her,
And Enid started waking, with her heart
All overshadowed by the foolish dream,
And lo! it was her mother grasping her
To get her well awake; and in her hand
A suit of bright apparel, which she laid
Flat on the couch, and spoke exultingly:

'See here, my child, how fresh the colors look,   680
How fast they hold, like colors of a shell
That keeps the wear and polish of the wave.
Why not? It never yet was worn, I trow:
Look on it, child, and tell me if ye know it.'

And Enid look'd, but, all confused at first,
Could scarce divide it from her foolish dream.
Then suddenly she knew it and rejoiced,
And answer'd, 'Yea, I know it; your good gift,
So sadly lost on that unhappy night;
Your own good gift!' 'Yea, surely,' said the dame,   690
'And gladly given again this happy morn.
For when the jousts were ended yesterday,
Went Yniol thro' the town, and everywhere
He found the sack and plunder of our house
All scatter'd thro' the houses of the town,
And gave command that all which once was ours
Should now be ours again; and yester-eve,
While ye were talking sweetly with your prince,
Came one with this and laid it in my hand,
For love or fear, or seeking favor of us,   700
Because we have our earldom back again.
And yester-eve I would not tell you of it,
But kept it for a sweet surprise at morn.
Yea, truly is it not a sweet surprise?
For I myself unwillingly have worn
My faded suit, as you, my child, have yours,
And, howsoever patient, Yniol his.
Ah, dear, he took me from a goodly house,
With store of rich apparel, sumptuous fare,
And page, and maid, and squire, and seneschal,   710
And pastime both of hawk and hound, and all
That appertains to noble maintenance.
Yea, and he brought me to a goodly house;
But since our fortune swerved from sun to shade,
And all thro' that young traitor, cruel need
Constrain'd us, but a better time has come.
So clothe yourself in this, that better fits
Our mended fortunes and a prince's bride;
For tho' ye won the prize of fairest fair,
And tho' I heard him call you fairest fair,   720
Let never maiden think, however fair,
She is not fairer in new clothes than old.
And should some great court-lady say, the prince
Hath pick'd a ragged-robin from the hedge,
And like a madman brought her to the court,
Then were ye shamed, and, worse, might shame the prince

To whom we are beholden; but I know,
When my dear child is set forth at her best,
That neither court nor country, tho' they sought
Thro' all the provinces like those of old   730
That lighted on Queen Esther, has her match.'

Here ceased the kindly mother out of breath,
And Enid listen'd brightening as she lay;
Then, as the white and glittering star of morn
Parts from a bank of snow, and by and by
Slips into golden cloud, the maiden rose,
And left her maiden couch, and robed herself,
Help'd by the mother's careful hand and eye,
Without a mirror, in the gorgeous gown;
Who, after, turn'd her daughter round, and said   740
She never yet had seen her half so fair;
And call'd her like that maiden in the tale,
Whom Gwydion made by glamour out of flowers,
And sweeter than the bride of Cassivelaun,
Flur, for whose love the Roman Cæsar first
Invaded Britain: 'But we beat him back,
As this great prince invaded us, and we,
Not beat him back, but welcomed him with joy.
And I can scarcely ride with you to court,
For old am I, and rough the ways and wild;   750
But Yniol goes, and I full oft shall dream
I see my princess as I see her now,
Clothed with my gift and gay among the gay.'

But while the women thus rejoiced, Geraint
Woke where he slept in the high hall, and call'd
For Enid, and when Yniol made report
Of that good mother making Enid gay
In such apparel as might well beseem
His princess, or indeed the stately Queen,
He answer'd: 'Earl, entreat her by my love,   760
Albeit I give no reason but my wish,
That she ride with me in her faded silk.'
Yniol with that hard message went; it fell
Like flaws in summer laying lusty corn;
For Enid, all abash'd she knew not why,
Dared not to glance at her good mother's face,
But silently, in all obedience,
Her mother silent too, nor helping her,
Laid from her limbs the costly-broider'd gift,
And robed them in her ancient suit again,   770
And so descended. Never man rejoiced
More than Geraint to greet her thus attired;

And glancing all at once as keenly at her
As careful robins eye the delver's toil,
Made her cheek burn and either eyelid fall,
But rested with her sweet face satisfied;
Then seeing cloud upon the mother's brow,
Her by both hands he caught, and sweetly said:

'O my new mother, be not wroth or grieved
At thy new son, for my petition to her.   780
When late I left Caerleon, our great Queen,
In words whose echo lasts, they were so sweet,
Made promise that, whatever bride I brought,
Herself would clothe her like the sun in heaven.
Thereafter, when I reach'd this ruin'd hall,
Beholding one so bright in dark estate,
I vow'd that, could I gain her, our fair Queen,
No hand but hers, should make your Enid burst
Sunlike from cloud—and likewise thought perhaps,
That service done so graciously would bind   790
The two together; fain I would the two
Should love each other. How can Enid find
A nobler friend? Another thought was mine:
I came among you here so suddenly
That tho' her gentle presence at the lists
Might well have served for proof that I was loved,
I doubted whether daughter's tenderness,
Or easy nature, might not let itself
Be moulded by your wishes for her weal;
Or whether some false sense in her own self   800
Of my contrasting brightness overbore
Her fancy dwelling in this dusky hall,
And such a sense might make her long for court
And all its perilous glories; and I thought,
That could I someway prove such force in her
Link'd with such love for me that at a word,
No reason given her, she could cast aside
A splendor dear to women, new to her,
And therefore dearer; or if not so new,
Yet therefore tenfold dearer by the power   810
Of intermitted usage; then I felt
That I could rest, a rock in ebbs and flows,
Fixt on her faith. Now, therefore, I do rest,
A prophet certain of my prophecy,
That never shadow of mistrust can cross
Between us. Grant me pardon for my thoughts;
And for my strange petition I will make
Amends hereafter by some gaudy-day,
When your fair child shall wear your costly gift

Beside your own warm hearth, with, on her knees,
Who knows? another gift of the high God,
Which, maybe, shall have learn'd to lisp you thanks.'

He spoke; the mother smiled, but half in tears,
Then brought a mantle down and wrapt her in it,
And claspt and kiss'd her, and they rode away.

Now thrice that morning Guinevere had climb'd
The giant tower, from whose high crest, they say,
Men saw the goodly hills of Somerset,
And white sails flying on the yellow sea;
But not to goodly hill or yellow sea
Look'd the fair Queen, but up the vale of Usk,
By the flat meadow, till she saw them come;
And then descending met them at the gates,
Embraced her with all welcome as a friend,
And did her honor as the prince's bride,
And clothed her for her bridals like the sun;
And all that week was old Caerleon gay,
For by the hands of Dubric, the high saint,
They twain were wedded with all ceremony.

And this was on the last year's Whitsuntide.
But Enid ever kept the faded silk,
Remembering how first he came on her
Drest in that dress, and how he loved her in it,
And all her foolish fears about the dress,
And all his journey toward her, as himself
Had told her, and their coming to the court.

And now this morning when he said to her,
'Put on your worst and meanest dress,' she found
And took it, and array'd herself therein.

GERAINT AND ENID

O PURBLIND race of miserable men,
How many among us at this very hour
Do forge a lifelong trouble for ourselves,
By taking true for false, or false for true;
Here, thro' the feeble twilight of this world
Groping, how many, until we pass and reach
That other where we see as we are seen!

So fared it with Geraint, who issuing forth
That morning, when they both had got to horse,

Perhaps because he loved her passionately,   10
And felt that tempest brooding round his heart
Which, if he spoke at all, would break perforce
Upon a head so dear in thunder, said:
'Not at my side. I charge thee ride before,
Ever a good way on before; and this
I charge thee, on thy duty as a wife,
Whatever happens, not to speak to me,
No, not a word!' and Enid was aghast;
And forth they rode, but scarce three paces on,
When crying out, 'Effeminate as I am,   20
I will not fight my way with gilded arms,
All shall be iron;' he loosed a mighty purse,
Hung at his belt, and hurl'd it toward the squire.
So the last sight that Enid had of home
Was all the marble threshold flashing, strown
With gold and scatter'd coinage, and the squire
Chafing his shoulder. Then he cried again,
'To the wilds!' and Enid leading down the tracks
Thro' which he bade her lead him on, they past
The marches, and by bandit-haunted holds,   30
Gray swamps and pools, waste places of the hern,
And wildernesses, perilous paths, they rode.
Round was their pace at first, but slacken'd soon.
A stranger meeting them had surely thought,
They rode so slowly and they look'd so pale,
That each had suffer'd some exceeding wrong.
For he was ever saying to himself,
'O, I that wasted time to tend upon her,
To compass her with sweet observances,
To dress her beautifully and keep her true'—   40
And there he broke the sentence in his heart
Abruptly, as a man upon his tongue
May break it when his passion masters him.
And she was ever praying the sweet heavens
To save her dear lord whole from any wound.
And ever in her mind she cast about
For that unnoticed failing in herself
Which made him look so cloudy and so cold;
Till the great plover's human whistle amazed
Her heart, and glancing round the waste she fear'd   50
In every wavering brake an ambuscade;
Then thought again, 'If there be such in me,
I might amend it by the grace of Heaven,
If he would only speak and tell me of it.'

But when the fourth part of the day was gone,
Then Enid was aware of three tall knights

On horseback, wholly arm'd, behind a rock
In shadow, waiting for them, caitiffs all;
And heard one crying to his fellow, 'Look,
Here comes a laggard hanging down his head, 60
Who seems no bolder than a beaten hound;
Come, we will slay him and will have his horse
And armor, and his damsel shall be ours.'

Then Enid ponder'd in her heart, and said:
'I will go back a little to my lord,
And I will tell him all their caitiff talk;
For, be he wroth even to slaying me,
Far liefer by his dear hand had I die
Than that my lord should suffer loss or shame.'

Then she went back some paces of return, 70
Met his full frown timidly firm, and said:
'My lord, I saw three bandits by the rock
Waiting to fall on you, and heard them boast
That they would slay you, and possess your horse
And armor, and your damsel should be theirs.'

He made a wrathful answer: 'Did I wish
Your warning or your silence? one command
I laid upon you, not to speak to me,
And thus ye keep it! Well then, look—for now,
Whether ye wish me victory or defeat, 80
Long for my life or hunger for my death,
Yourself shall see my vigor is not lost.'

Then Enid waited pale and sorrowful,
And down upon him bare the bandit three.
And at the midmost charging, Prince Geraint
Drave the long spear a cubit thro' his breast
And out beyond; and then against his brace
Of comrades, each of whom had broken on him
A lance that splinter'd like an icicle,
Swung from his brand a windy buffet out 90
Once, twice, to right, to left, and stunn'd the twain
Or slew them, and dismounting, like a man
That skins the wild beast after slaying him,
Stript from the three dead wolves of woman born
The three gay suits of armor which they wore,
And let the bodies lie, but bound the suits
Of armor on their horses, each on each,
And tied the bridle-reins of all the three
Together, and said to her, 'Drive them on
Before you;' and she drove them thro' the waste. 100

He follow'd nearer; ruth began to work
Against his anger in him, while he watch'd
The being he loved best in all the world,
With difficulty in mild obedience
Driving them on. He fain had spoken to her,
And loosed in words of sudden fire the wrath
And smoulder'd wrong that burnt him all within;
But evermore it seem'd an easier thing
At once without remorse to strike her dead
Than to cry 'Halt,' and to her own bright face   110
Accuse her of the least immodesty:
And thus tongue-tied, it made him wroth the more
That she *could* speak whom his own ear had heard
Call herself false, and suffering thus he made
Minutes an age; but in scarce longer time
Than at Caerleon the full-tided Usk,
Before he turn to fall seaward again,
Pauses, did Enid, keeping watch, behold
In the first shallow shade of a deep wood,
Before a gloom of stubborn-shafted oaks,   120
Three other horsemen waiting, wholly arm'd,
Whereof one seem'd far larger than her lord,
And shook her pulses, crying, 'Look, a prize!
Three horses and three goodly suits of arms,
And all in charge of whom? a girl! set on.'
'Nay,' said the second, 'yonder comes a knight.'
The third, 'A craven; how he hangs his head!'
The giant answer'd merrily, 'Yea, but one?
Wait here, and when he passes fall upon him!'

And Enid ponder'd in her heart and said: 130
'I will abide the coming of my lord,
And I will tell him all their villainy.
My lord is weary with the fight before,
And they will fall upon him unawares.
I needs must disobey him for his good;
How should I dare obey him to his harm?
Needs must I speak, and tho' he kill me for it,
I save a life dearer to me than mine.'

And she abode his coming, and said to him
With timid firmness, 'Have I leave to speak?'   140
He said, 'Ye take it, speaking,' and she spoke:

'There lurk three villains yonder in the wood,
And each of them is wholly arm'd, and one
Is larger-limb'd than you are, and they say
That they will fall upon you while ye pass.'

To which he flung a wrathful answer back:
'And if there were an hundred in the wood,
And every man were larger-limb'd than I,
And all at once should sally out upon me,
I swear it would not ruffle me so much 150
As you that not obey me. Stand aside,
And if I fall, cleave to the better man.'

And Enid stood aside to wait the event,
Not dare to watch the combat, only breathe
Short fits of prayer, at every stroke a breath.
And he she dreaded most bare down upon him.
Aim'd at the helm, his lance err'd; but Geraint's,
A little in the late encounter strain'd,
Struck thro' the bulky bandit's corselet home,
And then brake short, and down his enemy roll'd, 160
And there lay still; as he that tells the tale
Saw once a great piece of a promontory,
That had a sapling growing on it, slide
From the long shore-cliff's windy walls to the beach,
And there lie still, and yet the sapling grew;
So lay the man transfixt. His craven pair
Of comrades making slowlier at the prince,
When now they saw their bulwark fallen, stood;
On whom the victor, to confound them more,
Spurr'd with his terrible war-cry; for as one, 170
That listens near a torrent mountain-brook,
All thro' the crash of the near cataract hears
The drumming thunder of the huger fall
At distance, were the soldiers wont to hear
His voice in battle, and be kindled by it,
And foemen scared, like that false pair who turn'd
Flying, but, overtaken, died the death
Themselves had wrought on many an innocent.

Thereon Geraint, dismounting, pick'd the lance
That pleased him best, and drew from those dead wolves 180
Their three gay suits of armor, each from each,
And bound them on their horses, each on each,
And tied the bridle-reins of all the three
Together, and said to her, 'Drive them on
Before you,' and she drove them thro' the wood.

He follow'd nearer still. The pain she had
To keep them in the wild ways of the wood,
Two sets of three laden with jingling arms,
Together, served a little to disedge
The sharpness of that pain about her heart; 190

And they themselves, like creatures gently born
But into bad hands fallen, and now so long
By bandits groom'd, prick'd their light ears, and felt
Her low firm voice and tender government.

So thro' the green gloom of the wood they past,
And issuing under open heavens beheld
A little town with towers, upon a rock,
And close beneath, a meadow gemlike chased
In the brown wild, and mowers mowing in it;
And down a rocky pathway from the place   200
There came a fair-hair'd youth, that in his hand
Bare victual for the mowers; and Geraint
Had ruth again on Enid looking pale.
Then, moving downward to the meadow ground,
He, when the fair-hair'd youth came by him, said,
'Friend, let her eat; the damsel is so faint.'
'Yea, willingly,' replied the youth; 'and thou,
My lord, eat also, tho' the fare is coarse,
And only meet for mowers;' then set down
His basket, and dismounting on the sward   210
They let the horses graze, and ate themselves.
And Enid took a little delicately,
Less having stomach for it than desire
To close with her lord's pleasure, but Geraint
Ate all the mowers' victual unawares,
And when he found all empty was amazed;
And 'Boy,' said he, 'I have eaten all, but take
A horse and arms for guerdon; choose the best.'
He, reddening in extremity of delight,
'My lord, you overpay me fifty-fold.'   220
'Ye will be all the wealthier,' cried the prince.
'I take it as free gift, then,' said the boy,
'Not guerdon; for myself can easily,
While your good damsel rests, return and fetch
Fresh victual for these mowers of our earl;
For these are his, and all the field is his,
And I myself am his; and I will tell him
How great a man thou art. He loves to know
When men of mark are in his territory;
And he will have thee to his palace here,   230
And serve thee costlier than with mowers' fare.'

Then said Geraint: 'I wish no better fare;
I never ate with angrier appetite
Than when I left your mowers dinnerless.
And into no earl's palace will I go.
I know, God knows, too much of palaces!

And if he want me, let him come to me.
But hire us some fair chamber for the night,
And stalling for the horses, and return
With victual for these men, and let us know.'   240

'Yea, my kind lord,' said the glad youth, and went,
Held his head high, and thought himself a knight,
And up the rocky pathway disappear'd,
Leading the horse, and they were left alone.

But when the prince had brought his errant eyes
Home from the rock, sideways he let them glance
At Enid, where she droopt. His own false doom,
That shadow of mistrust should never cross
Betwixt them, came upon him, and he sigh'd;
Then with another humorous ruth remark'd   250
The lusty mowers laboring dinnerless,
And watch'd the sun blaze on the turning scythe,
And after nodded sleepily in the heat.
But she, remembering her old ruin'd hall,
And all the windy clamor of the daws
About her hollow turret, pluck'd the grass
There growing longest by the meadow's edge,
And into many a listless annulet,
Now over, now beneath her marriage ring,
Wove and unwove it, till the boy return'd   260
And told them of a chamber, and they went;
Where, after saying to her, 'If ye will,
Call for the woman of the house,' to which
She answer'd, 'Thanks, my lord;' the two remain'd
Apart by all the chamber's width, and mute
As creatures voiceless thro' the fault of birth,
Or two wild men supporters of a shield,
Painted, who stare at open space, nor glance
The one at other, parted by the shield.

On a sudden, many a voice along the street,   270
And heel against the pavement echoing, burst
Their drowse; and either started while the door,
Push'd from without, drave backward to the wall,
And midmost of a rout of roisterers,
Femininely fair and dissolutely pale,
Her suitor in old years before Geraint
Enter'd, the wild lord of the place, Limours.
He moving up with pliant courtliness
Greeted Geraint full face, but stealthily,
In the mid-warmth of welcome and graspt hand,   280
Found Enid with the corner of his eye,

And knew her sitting sad and solitary.
Then cried Geraint for wine and goodly cheer
To feed the sudden guest, and sumptuously,
According to his fashion, bade the host
Call in what men soever were his friends,
And feast with these in honor of their earl;
'And care not for the cost; the cost is mine.'

And wine and food were brought, and Earl Limours   290
Drank till he jested with all ease, and told
Free tales, and took the word and play'd upon it,
And made it of two colors; for his talk,
When wine and free companions kindled him,
Was wont to glance and sparkle like a gem
Of fifty facets; thus he moved the prince
To laughter and his comrades to applause.
Then, when the prince was merry, ask'd Limours,
'Your leave, my lord, to cross the room, and speak
To your good damsel there who sits apart,
And seems so lonely?' 'My free leave,' he said;   300
'Get her to speak; she doth not speak to me.'
Then rose Limours, and looking at his feet,
Like him who tries the bridge he fears may fail,
Crost and came near, lifted adoring eyes,
Bow'd at her side and utter'd whisperingly:

'Enid, the pilot star of my lone life,
Enid, my early and my only love,
Enid, the loss of whom hath turn'd me wild—
What chance is this? how is it I see you here?
Ye are in my power at last, are in my power.   310
Yet fear me not; I call mine own self wild,
But keep a touch of sweet civility
Here in the heart of waste and wilderness.
I thought, but that your father came between,
In former days you saw me favorably.
And if it were so do not keep it back.
Make me a little happier; let me know it.
Owe you me nothing for a life half-lost?
Yea, yea, the whole dear debt of all you are.
And, Enid, you and he, I see with joy,   320
Ye sit apart, you do not speak to him,
You come with no attendance, page or maid,
To serve you—doth he love you as of old?
For, call it lovers' quarrels, yet I know
Tho' men may bicker with the things they love,
They would not make them laughable in all eyes,
Not while they loved them; and your wretched dress,

A wretched insult on you, dumbly speaks
Your story, that this man loves you no more.
Your beauty is no beauty to him now. 330
A common chance—right well I know it—pall'd—
For I know men; nor will ye win him back,
For the man's love once gone never returns.
But here is one who loves you as of old;
With more exceeding passion than of old.
Good, speak the word; my followers ring him round.
He sits unarm'd; I hold a finger up;
They understand. Nay, I do not mean blood;
Nor need ye look so scared at what I say.
My malice is no deeper than a moat, 340
No stronger than a wall. There is the keep;
He shall not cross us more; speak but the word.
Or speak it not; but then by Him that made me
The one true lover whom you ever own'd,
I will make use of all the power I have.
O, pardon me! the madness of that hour
When first I parted from thee moves me yet.'

At this the tender sound of his own voice
And sweet self-pity, or the fancy of it,
Made his eye moist; but Enid fear'd his eyes, 350
Moist as they were, wine-heated from the feast,
And answer'd with such craft as women use,
Guilty or guiltless, to stave off a chance
That breaks upon them perilously, and said:

'Earl, if you love me as in former years,
And do not practise on me, come with morn,
And snatch me from him as by violence.
Leave me to-night; I am weary to the death.'

Low at leave-taking, with his brandish'd plume
Brushing his instep, bow'd the all-amorous earl, 360
And the stout prince bade him a loud good-night.
He moving homeward babbled to his men,
How Enid never loved a man but him,
Nor cared a broken egg-shell for her lord.

But Enid left alone with Prince Geraint,
Debating his command of silence given,
And that she now perforce must violate it,
Held commune with herself, and while she held
He fell asleep, and Enid had no heart
To wake him, but hung o'er him, wholly pleased 370
To find him yet unwounded after fight,

And hear him breathing low and equally.
Anon she rose and, stepping lightly, heap'd
The pieces of his armor in one place,
All to be there against a sudden need;
Then dozed awhile herself, but, overtoil'd
By that day's grief and travel, evermore
Seem'd catching at a rootless thorn, and then
Went slipping down horrible precipices,
And strongly striking out her limbs awoke;   380
Then thought she heard the wild earl at the door,
With all this rout of random followers,
Sound on a dreadful trumpet, summoning her;
Which was the red cock shouting to the light,
As the gray dawn stole o'er the dewy world
And glimmer'd on his armor in the room.
And once again she rose to look at it,
But touch'd it unawares; jangling, the casque
Fell, and he started up and stared at her.
Then breaking his command of silence given,   390
She told him all that Earl Limours had said,
Except the passage that he loved her not;
Nor left untold the craft herself had used,
But ended with apology so sweet,
Low-spoken, and of so few words, and seem'd
So justified by that necessity,
That tho' he thought, 'Was it for him she wept
In Devon?' he but gave a wrathful groan,
Saying, 'Your sweet faces make good fellows fools
And traitors. Call the host and bid him bring   400
Charger and palfrey.' So she glided out
Among the heavy breathings of the house,
And like a household spirit at the walls
Beat, till she woke the sleepers, and return'd;
Then tending her rough lord, tho' all unask'd,
In silence, did him service as a squire;
Till issuing arm'd he found the host and cried,
'Thy reckoning, friend?' and ere he learnt it, 'Take
Five horses and their armors;' and the host,
Suddenly honest, answer'd in amaze,   410
'My lord, I scarce have spent the worth of one!'
'Ye will be all the wealthier,' said the prince,
And then to Enid, 'Forward! and to-day
I charge you, Enid, more especially,
What thing soever ye may hear, or see,
Or fancy—tho' I count it of small use
To charge you—that ye speak not but obey.'

And Enid answer'd :'Yea, my lord, I know
Your wish and would obey; but, riding first,
I hear the violent threats you do not hear,
I see the danger which you cannot see.
Then not to give you warning, that seems hard,
Almost beyond me; yet I would obey.'

'Yea so,' said he, 'do it; be not too wise,
Seeing that ye are wedded to a man,
Not all mismated with a yawning clown,
But one with arms to guard his head and yours,
With eyes to find you out however far,
And ears to hear you even in his dreams.'

With that he turn'd and look'd as keenly at her
As careful robins eye the delver's toil;
And that within her which a wanton fool
Or hasty judger would have call'd her guilt
Made her cheek burn and either eyelid fall.
And Geraint look'd and was not satisfied.

Then forward by a way which, beaten broad,
Led from the territory of false Limours
To the waste earldom of another earl,
Doorm, whom his shaking vassals call'd the Bull,
Went Enid with her sullen follower on.
Once she look'd back, and when she saw him ride
More near by many a rood than yestermorn,
It wellnigh made her cheerful; till Geraint,
Waving an angry hand as who should say,
'Ye watch me,' sadden'd all her heart again.
But while the sun yet beat a dewy blade,
The sound of many a heavily-galloping hoof
Smote on her ear, and turning round she saw
Dust, and the points of lances bicker in it.
Then, not to disobey her lord's behest,
And yet to give him warning, for he rode
As if he heard not, moving back she held
Her finger up, and pointed to the dust.
At which the warrior in his obstinacy,
Because she kept the letter of his word,
Was in a manner pleased, and turning stood.
And in the moment after, wild Limours,
Borne on a black horse, like a thundercloud
Whose skirts are loosen'd by the breaking storm,
Half ridden off with by the thing he rode,
And all in passion uttering a dry shriek,
Dash'd on Geraint, who closed with him, and bore

420

430

440

450

460

Down by the length of lance and arm beyond
The crupper, and so left him stunn'd or dead,
And overthrew the next that follow'd him,
And blindly rush'd on all the rout behind.
But at the flash and motion of the man
They vanish'd panic-stricken, like a shoal
Of darting fish, that on a summer morn
Adown the crystal dykes at Camelot   470
Come slipping o'er their shadows on the sand,
But if a man who stands upon the brink
But lift a shining hand against the sun,
There is not left the twinkle of a fin
Betwixt the cressy islets white in flower;
So, scared but at the motion of the man,
Fled all the boon companions of the earl,
And left him lying in the public way;
So vanish friendships only made in wine.

Then like a stormy sunlight smiled Geraint,   480
Who saw the chargers of the two that fell
Start from their fallen lords and wildly fly,
Mixt with the flyers. 'Horse and man,' he said,
'All of one mind and all right-honest friends!
Not a hoof left! and I methinks till now
Was honest—paid with horses and with arms;
I cannot steal or plunder, no, nor beg.
And so what say ye, shall we strip him there,
Your lover? has your palfrey heart enough
To bear his armor? shall we fast or dine?   490
No?—then do thou, being right honest, pray
That we may meet the horsemen of Earl Doorm;
I too would still be honest.' Thus he said;
And sadly gazing on her bridle-reins,
And answering not one word, she led the way.

But as a man to whom a dreadful loss
Falls in a far land and he knows it not,
But coming back he learns it, and the loss
So pains him that he sickens nigh to death;
So fared it with Geraint, who, being prick'd   500
In combat with the followers of Limours,
Bled underneath his armor secretly,
And so rode on, nor told his gentle wife
What ail'd him, hardly knowing it himself,
Till his eye darken'd and his helmet wagg'd;
And at a sudden swerving of the road,
Tho' happily down on a bank of grass,
The prince, without a word, from his horse fell.

And Enid heard the clashing of his fall,
Suddenly came, and at his side all pale   510
Dismounting loosed the fastenings of his arms,
Nor let her true hand falter, nor blue eye
Moisten, till she had lighted on his wound,
And tearing off her veil of faded silk
Had bared her forehead to the blistering sun,
And swathed the hurt that drain'd her dear lord's life.
Then, after all was done that hand could do,
She rested, and her desolation came
Upon her, and she wept beside the way.

And many past, but none regarded her,   520
For in that realm of lawless turbulence
A woman weeping for her murder'd mate
Was cared as much for as a summer shower.
One took him for a victim of Earl Doorm,
Nor dared to waste a perilous pity on him.
Another hurrying past, a man-at-arms,
Rode on a mission to the bandit earl;
Half whistling and half singing a coarse song,
He drove the dust against her veilless eyes.
Another, flying from the wrath of Doorm   530
Before an ever-fancied arrow, made
The long way smoke beneath him in his fear;
At which her palfrey whinnying lifted heel,
And scour'd into the coppices and was lost,
While the great charger stood, grieved like a man.

But at the point of noon the huge Earl Doorm,
Broad-faced with under-fringe of russet beard,
Bound on a foray, rolling eyes of prey,
Came riding with a hundred lances up;
But ere he came, like one that hails a ship,   540
Cried out with a big voice, 'What, is he dead?'
'No, no, not dead!' she answer'd in all haste.
'Would some of your kind people take him up,
And bear him hence out of this cruel sun?
Most sure am I, quite sure, he is not dead.'

Then said Earl Doorm: 'Well, if he be not dead,
Why wail ye for him thus? ye seem a child.
And be he dead, I count you for a fool;
Your wailing will not quicken him; dead or not,
Ye mar a comely face with idiot tears.   550
Yet, since the face is comely—some of you,
Here, take him up, and bear him to our hall.
An if he live, we will have him of our band;

And if he die, why earth has earth enough
To hide him. See ye take the charger too,
A noble one.'
                    He spake and past away,
But left two brawny spearmen, who advanced,
Each growling like a dog, when his good bone
Seems to be pluck'd at by the village boys
Who love to vex him eating, and he fears   560
To lose his bone, and lays his foot upon it,
Gnawing and growling; so the ruffians growl'd,
Fearing to lose, and all for a dead man,
Their chance of booty from the morning's raid,
Yet raised and laid him on a litter-bier,
Such as they brought upon their forays out
For those that might be wounded; laid him on it
All in the hollow of his shield, and took
And bore him to the naked hall of Doorm—
His gentle charger following him unled—   570
And cast him and the bier in which he lay
Down on an oaken settle in the hall,
And then departed, hot in haste to join
Their luckier mates, but growling as before,
And cursing their lost time, and the dead man,
And their own earl, and their own souls, and her.
They might as well have blest her; she was deaf
To blessing or to cursing save from one.

So for long hours sat Enid by her lord
There in the naked hall, propping his head,   580
And chafing his pale hands, and calling to him,
Till at the last he waken'd from his swoon,
And found his own dear bride propping his head,
And chafing his faint hands, and calling to him;
And felt the warm tears falling on his face,
And said to his own heart, 'She weeps for me;'
And yet lay still, and feign'd himself as dead,
That he might prove her to the uttermost,
And say to his own heart, 'She weeps for me.'

But in the falling afternoon return'd   590
The huge Earl Doorm with plunder to the hall.
His lusty spearmen follow'd him with noise:
Each hurling down a heap of things that rang
Against the pavement, cast his lance aside,
And doff'd his helm; and then there flutter'd in,
Half-bold, half-frighted, with dilated eyes,
A tribe of women, dress'd in many hues,
And mingled with the spearmen; and Earl Doorm

Struck with a knife's haft hard against the board,
And call'd for flesh and wine to feed his spears. 600
And men brought in whole hogs and quarter beeves,
And all the hall was dim with steam of flesh.
And none spake word, but all sat down at once,
And ate with tumult in the naked hall,
Feeding like horses when you hear them feed;
Till Enid shrank far back into herself,
To shun the wild ways of the lawless tribe.
But when Earl Doorm had eaten all he would,
He roll'd his eyes about the hall, and found
A damsel drooping in a corner of it. 610
Then he remember'd her and how she wept,
And out of her there came a power upon him;
And rising on the sudden he said: 'Eat!
I never yet beheld a thing so pale.
God's curse, it makes me mad to see you weep.
Eat! Look yourself. Good luck had your good man,
For were I dead who is it would weep for me?
Sweet lady, never since I first drew breath
Have I beheld a lily like yourself.
And so there lived some color in your cheek, 620
There is not one among my gentlewomen
Were fit to wear your slipper for a glove.
But listen to me, and by me be ruled,
And I will do the thing I have not done,
For ye shall share my earldom with me, girl.
And we will live like two birds in one nest,
And I will fetch you forage from all fields,
For I compel all creatures to my will.'

He spoke; the brawny spearman let his cheek
Bulge with the unswallow'd piece, and turning stared; 630
While some, whose souls the old serpent long had drawn
Down, as the worm draws in the wither'd leaf
And makes it earth, hiss'd each at other's ear
What shall not be recorded—women they,
Women, or what had been those gracious things,
But now desired the humbling of their best,
Yea, would have help'd him to it; and all at once
They hated her, who took no thought of them,
But answer'd in low voice, her meek head yet
Drooping, 'I pray you of your courtesy, 640
He being as he is, to let me be.'

She spake so low he hardly heard her speak,
But like a mighty patron, satisfied
With what himself had done so graciously,

Assumed that she had thank'd him, adding, 'Yea,
Eat and be glad, for I account you mine.'

She answer'd meekly, 'How should I be glad
Henceforth in all the world at anything,
Until my lord arise and look upon me?'

Here the huge earl cried out upon her talk,   650
As all but empty heart and weariness
And sickly nothing; suddenly seized on her,
And bare her by main violence to the board,
And thrust the dish before her, crying, 'Eat.'

'No, no,' said Enid, vext, 'I will not eat
Till yonder man upon the bier arise,
And eat with me.' 'Drink, then,' he answer'd. 'Here!'—
And fill'd a horn with wine and held it to her,—
'Lo! I, myself, when flush'd with fight or hot,
God's curse, with anger—often I myself,   660
Before I well have drunken, scarce can eat;
Drink therefore, and the wine will change your will.'

'Not so,' she cried, 'by Heaven, I will not drink
Till my dear lord arise and bid me do it,
And drink with me; and if he rise no more,
I will not look at wine until I die.'

At this he turn'd all red and paced his hall,
Now gnaw'd his under, now his upper lip,
And coming up close to her, said at last:
'Girl, for I see ye scorn my courtesies,   670
Take warning; yonder man is surely dead,
And I compel all creatures to my will.
Not eat nor drink? And wherefore wail for one
Who put your beauty to this flout and scorn
By dressing it in rags? Amazed am I,
Beholding how ye butt against my wish,
That I forbear you thus; cross me no more.
At least put off to please me this poor gown,
This silken rag, this beggar-woman's weed.
I love that beauty should go beautifully;   680
For see ye not my gentlewomen here,
How gay, how suited to the house of one
Who loves that beauty should go beautifully?
Rise therefore; robe yourself in this; obey.'

He spoke, and one among his gentlewomen
Display'd a splendid silk of foreign loom,

Where like a shoaling sea the lovely blue
Play'd into green, and thicker down the front
With jewels than the sward with drops of dew,
When all night long a cloud clings to the hill,   690
And with the dawn ascending lets the day
Strike where it clung; so thickly shone the gems.

But Enid answer'd, harder to be moved
Than hardest tyrants in their day of power,
With lifelong injuries burning unavenged,
And now their hour has come; and Enid said:

'In this poor gown my dear lord found me first,
And loved me serving in my father's hall;
In this poor gown I rode with him to court,
And there the Queen array'd me like the sun;   700
In this poor gown he bade me clothe myself,
When now we rode upon this fatal quest
Of honor, where no honor can be gain'd;
And this poor gown I will not cast aside
Until himself arise a living man,
And bid me cast it. I have griefs enough;
Pray you be gentle, pray you let me be.
I never loved, can never love but him.
Yea, God, I pray you of your gentleness,
He being as he is, to let me be.'   710

Then strode the brute earl up and down his hall,
And took his russet beard between his teeth;
Last, coming up quite close, and in his mood
Crying, 'I count it of no more avail,
Dame, to be gentle than ungentle with you;
Take my salute,' unknightly with flat hand,
However lightly, smote her on the cheek.

Then Enid, in her utter helplessness,
And since she thought, 'He had not dared to do it,
Except he surely knew my lord was dead,'   720
Sent forth a sudden sharp and bitter cry,
As of a wild thing taken in the trap,
Which sees the trapper coming thro' the wood.

This heard Geraint, and grasping at his sword,—
It lay beside him in the hollow shield,—
Made but a single bound, and with a sweep of it
Shore thro' the swarthy neck, and like a ball
The russet-bearded head roll'd on the floor.
So died Earl Doorm by him he counted dead.
And all the men and women in the hall   730

Rose when they saw the dead man rise, and fled
Yelling as from a spectre, and the two
Were left alone together, and he said:

'Enid, I have used you worse than that dead man,
Done you more wrong; we both have undergone
That trouble which has left me thrice your own.
Henceforward I will rather die than doubt.
And here I lay this penance on myself,
Not, tho' mine own ears heard you yestermorn—
You thought me sleeping, but I heard you say,   740
I heard you say, that you were no true wife,
I swear I will not ask your meaning in it.
I do believe yourself against yourself,
And will henceforward rather die than doubt.'

And Enid could not say one tender word,
She felt so blunt and stupid at the heart.
She only pray'd him, 'Fly, they will return
And slay you; fly, your charger is without,
My palfrey lost.' 'Then, Enid, shall you ride
Behind me.' 'Yea,' said Enid, 'let us go.'   750
And moving out they found the stately horse,
Who now no more a vassal to the thief,
But free to stretch his limbs in lawful fight,
Neigh'd with all gladness as they came, and stoop'd
With a low whinny toward the pair; and she
Kiss'd the white star upon his noble front,
Glad also; then Geraint upon the horse
Mounted, and reach'd a hand, and on his foot
She set her own and climb'd; he turn'd his face
And kiss'd her climbing, and she cast her arms   760
About him, and at once they rode away.

And never yet, since high in Paradise
O'er the four rivers the first roses blew,
Came purer pleasure unto mortal kind
Than lived thro' her who in that perilous hour
Put hand to hand beneath her husband's heart,
And felt him hers again. She did not weep,
But o'er her meek eyes came a happy mist
Like that which kept the heart of Eden green
Before the useful trouble of the rain.   770
Yet not so misty were her meek blue eyes
As not to see before them on the path,
Right in the gateway of the bandit hold,
A knight of Arthur's court, who laid his lance
In rest and made as if to fall upon him.

Then, fearing for his hurt and loss of blood,
She, with her mind all full of what had chanced,
Shriek'd to the stranger, 'Slay not a dead man!'
'The voice of Enid,' said the knight; but she,
Beholding it was Edyrn, son of Nudd, 780
Was moved so much the more, and shriek'd again,
'O cousin, slay not him who gave you life.'
And Edyrn moving frankly forward spake:
'My lord Geraint, I greet you with all love;
I took you for a bandit knight of Doorm;
And fear not, Enid, I should fall upon him,
Who love you, prince, with something of the love
Wherewith we love the Heaven that chastens us.
For once, when I was up so high in pride
That I was halfway down the slope to hell, 790
By overthrowing me you threw me higher.
Now, made a knight of Arthur's Table Round,
And since I knew this earl when I myself
Was half a bandit in my lawless hour,
I come the mouthpiece of our King to Doorm—
The King is close behind me—bidding him
Disband himself, and scatter all his powers,
Submit, and hear the judgment of the King.'

'He hears the judgment of the King of kings,'
Cried the wan prince; 'and lo, the powers of Doorm 800
Are scatter'd!' and he pointed to the field,
Where, huddled here and there on mound and knoll,
Were men and women staring and aghast,
While some yet fled; and then he plainlier told
How the huge earl lay slain within his hall.
But when the knight besought him, 'Follow me,
Prince, to the camp, and in the King's own ear
Speak what has chanced; ye surely have endured
Strange chances here alone;' that other flush'd,
And hung his head, and halted in reply, 810
Fearing the mild face of the blameless King,
And after madness acted question ask'd;
Till Edyrn crying, 'If ye will not go
To Arthur, then will Arthur come to you.'
'Enough,' he said, 'I follow,' and they went.
But Enid in their going had two fears,
One from the bandit scatter'd in the field,
And one from Edyrn. Every now and then,
When Edyrn rein'd his charger at her side,
She shrank a little. In a hollow land, 820
From which old fires have broken, men may fear
Fresh fire and ruin. He, perceiving, said:

'Fair and dear cousin, you that most had cause
To fear me, fear no longer, I am changed.
Yourself were first the blameless cause to make
My nature's prideful sparkle in the blood
Break into furious flame; being repulsed
By Yniol and yourself, I schemed and wrought
Until I overturn'd him; then set up—
With one main purpose ever at my heart—   830
My haughty jousts, and took a paramour;
Did her mock-honor as the fairest fair,
And, toppling over all antagonism,
So wax'd in pride that I believed myself
Unconquerable, for I was wellnigh mad;
And, but for my main purpose in these jousts,
I should have slain your father, seized yourself.
I lived in hope that sometime you would come
To these my lists with him whom best you loved,
And there, poor cousin, with your meek blue eyes,   840
The truest eyes that ever answer'd heaven,
Behold me overturn and trample on him.
Then, had you cried, or knelt, or pray'd to me,
I should not less have kill'd him. And you came,—
But once you came,—and with your own true eyes
Beheld the man you loved—I speak as one
Speaks of a service done him—overthrow
My proud self, and my purpose three years old,
And set his foot upon me, and give me life.
There was I broken down, there was I saved;   850
Tho' thence I rode all-shamed, hating the life
He gave me, meaning to be rid of it.
And all the penance the Queen laid upon me
Was but to rest awhile within her court;
Where first as sullen as a beast new-caged,
And waiting to be treated like a wolf,
Because I knew my deeds were known, I found,
Instead of scornful pity or pure scorn,
Such fine reserve and noble reticence,
Manners so kind, yet stately, such a grace   860
Of tenderest courtesy, that I began
To glance behind me at my former life,
And find that it had been the wolf's indeed.
And oft I talk'd with Dubric, the high saint,
Who, with mild heat of holy oratory,
Subdued me somewhat to that gentleness
Which, when it weds with manhood, makes a man.
And you were often there about the Queen,
But saw me not, or mark'd not if you saw;

Nor did I care or dare to speak with you, 870
But kept myself aloof till I was changed;
And fear not, cousin, I am changed indeed.'

He spoke, and Enid easily believed,
Like simple noble natures, credulous
Of what they long for, good in friend or foe,
There most in those who most have done them ill.
And when they reach'd the camp the King himself
Advanced to greet them, and beholding her
Tho' pale, yet happy, ask'd her not a word,
But went apart with Edyrn, whom he held 880
In converse for a little, and return'd,
And, gravely smiling, lifted her from horse,
And kiss'd her with all pureness, brother-like,
And show'd an empty tent allotted her,
And glancing for a minute, till he saw her
Pass into it, turn'd to the prince, and said:

'Prince, when of late ye pray'd me for my leave
To move to your own land and there defend
Your marches, I was prick'd with some reproof,
As one that let foul wrong stagnate and be, 890
By having look'd too much thro' alien eyes,
And wrought too long with delegated hands,
Not used mine own; but now behold me come
To cleanse this common sewer of all my realm,
With Edyrn and with others. Have ye look'd
At Edyrn? have ye seen how nobly changed?
This work of his is great and wonderful.
His very face with change of heart is changed.
The world will not believe a man repents;
And this wise world of ours is mainly right. 900
Full seldom doth a man repent, or use
Both grace and will to pick the vicious quitch
Of blood and custom wholly out of him,
And make all clean, and plant himself afresh.
Edyrn has done it, weeding all his heart
As I will weed this land before I go.
I, therefore, made him of our Table Round,
Not rashly, but have proved him every way
One of our noblest, our most valorous,
Sanest and most obedient; and indeed 910
This work of Edyrn, wrought upon himself
After a life of violence, seems to me
A thousand-fold more great and wonderful
Than if some knight of mine, risking his life,
My subject with my subjects under him,

Should make an onslaught single on a realm
Of robbers, tho' he slew them one by one,
And were himself nigh wounded to the death.'

So spake the King; low bow'd the prince, and felt
His work was neither great nor wonderful,   920
And past to Enid's tent; and thither came
The King's own leech to look into his hurt;
And Enid tended on him there; and there
Her constant motion round him, and the breath
Of her sweet tendance hovering over him,
Fill'd all the genial courses of his blood
With deeper and with ever deeper love,
As the Southwest that blowing Bala lake
Fills all the sacred Dee. So past the days.

But while Geraint lay healing of his hurt,   930
The blameless King went forth and cast his eyes
On each of all whom Uther left in charge
Long since, to guard the justice of the King.
He look'd and found them wanting; and as now
Men weed the White Horse on the Berkshire hills,
To keep him bright and clean as heretofore,
He rooted out the slothful officer
Or guilty, which for bribe had wink'd at wrong,
And in their chairs set up a stronger race
With hearts and hands, and sent a thousand men   940
To till the wastes, and moving everywhere
Clear'd the dark places and let in the law,
And broke the bandit holds and cleansed the land.

Then, when Geraint was whole again, they past
With Arthur to Caerleon upon Usk.
There the great Queen once more embraced her friend,
And clothed her in apparel like the day.
And tho' Geraint could never take again
That comfort from their converse which he took
Before the Queen's fair name was breathed upon,   950
He rested well content that all was well.
Thence after tarrying for a space they rode,
And fifty knights rode with them to the shores
Of Severn, and they past to their own land.
And there he kept the justice of the King
So vigorously yet mildly that all hearts
Applauded, and the spiteful whisper died;
And being ever foremost in the chase,
And victor at the tilt and tournament,
They call'd him the great prince and man of men.   960

But Enid, whom her ladies loved to call
Enid the Fair, a grateful people named
Enid the Good; and in their halls arose
The cry of children, Enids and Geraints
Of times to be; nor did he doubt her more,
But rested in her fealty till he crown'd
A happy life with a fair death, and fell
Against the heathen of the Northern Sea
In battle, fighting for the blameless King.

BALIN AND BALAN

PELLAM the king, who held and lost with Lot
In that first war, and had his realm restored
But render'd tributary, fail'd of late
To send his tribute; wherefore Arthur call'd
His treasurer, one of many years, and spake:
'Go thou with him and him and bring it to us,
Lest we should set one truer on his throne.
Man's word is God in man.'

               His baron said:
'We go, but harken: there be two strange knights
Who sit near Camelot at a fountain side   10
A mile beneath the forest, challenging
And overthrowing every knight who comes.
Wilt thou I undertake them as we pass,
And send them to thee?'

             Arthur laugh'd upon him:
'Old friend, too old to be so young, depart,
Delay not thou for aught, but let them sit,
Until they find a lustier than themselves.'

    So these departed. Early, one fair dawn,
The light-wing'd spirit of his youth return'd
On Arthur's heart; he arm'd himself and went,   20
So coming to the fountain-side beheld
Balin and Balan sitting statue-like,
Brethren, to right and left the spring, that down,
From underneath a plume of lady-fern,
Sang, and the sand danced at the bottom of it.
And on the right of Balin Balin's horse
Was fast beside an alder, on the left
Of Balan Balan's near a poplar-tree.
'Fair sirs,' said Arthur, 'wherefore sit ye here?'
Balin and Balan answer'd: 'For the sake   30

Of glory; we be mightier men than all
In Arthur's court; that also have we proved,
For whatsoever knight against us came
Or I or he have easily overthrown.'
'I too,' said Arthur, 'am of Arthur's hall,
But rather proven in his Paynim wars
Than famous jousts; but see, or proven or not,
Whether me likewise ye can overthrow.'
And Arthur lightly smote the brethren down,
And lightly so return'd, and no man knew.   40

Then Balin rose, and Balan, and beside
The carolling water set themselves again,
And spake no word until the shadow turn'd;
When from the fringe of coppice round them burst
A spangled pursuivant, and crying, 'Sirs,
Rise, follow! ye be sent for by the King,'
They follow'd; whom when Arthur seeing ask'd,
'Tell me your names; why sat ye by the well?'
Balin the stillness of a minute broke
Saying, 'An unmelodious name to thee,   50
Balin, "the Savage"—that addition thine—
My brother and my better, this man here,
Balan. I smote upon the naked skull
A thrall of thine in open hall; my hand
Was gauntleted, half slew him, for I heard
He had spoken evil of me; thy just wrath
Sent me a three-years' exile from thine eyes.
I have not lived my life delightsomely;
For I that did that violence to thy thrall,
Had often wrought some fury on myself,   60
Saving for Balan. Those three kingless years
Have past—were wormwood-bitter to me, King,
Methought that if we sat beside the well,
And hurl'd to ground what knight soever spurr'd
Against us, thou would'st take me gladlier back,
And make, as ten times worthier to be thine
Than twenty Balins, Balan knight. I have said.
Not so—not all. A man of thine to-day
Abash'd us both, and brake my boast. Thy will?'
Said Arthur: 'Thou hast ever spoken truth;   67
Thy too fierce manhood would not let thee lie.
Rise, my true knight. As children learn, be thou
Wiser for falling! walk with me, and move
To music with thine Order and the King.
Thy chair, a grief to all the brethren, stands
Vacant, but thou retake it, mine again!'

Thereafter, when Sir Balin enter'd hall,
The lost one found was greeted as in heaven
With joy that blazed itself in woodland wealth
Of leaf, and gayest garlandage of flowers,   80
Along the walls and down the board; they sat,
And cup clash'd cup; they drank, and some one sang,
Sweet-voiced, a song of welcome, whereupon
Their common shout in chorus, mounting, made
Those banners of twelve battles overhead
Stir as they stirr'd of old, when Arthur's host
Proclaim'd him victor and the day was won.

Then Balan added to their Order lived
A wealthier life than heretofore with these
And Balin, till their embassage return'd.   90

'Sir King,' they brought report, 'we hardly found,
So bush'd about it is with gloom, the hall
Of him to whom ye sent us, Pellam, once
A Christless foe of thine as ever dash'd
Horse against horse; but seeing that thy realm
Hath prosper'd in the name of Christ, the King
Took, as in rival heat, to holy things,
And finds himself descended from the Saint
Arimathæan Joseph, him who first
Brought the great faith to Britain over seas.   100
He boasts his life as purer than thine own;
Eats scarce enow to keep his pulse a-beat;
Hath push'd aside his faithful wife, nor lets
Or dame or damsel enter at his gates
Lest he should be polluted. This gray king
Show'd us a shrine wherein were wonders—yea,
Rich arks with priceless bones of martyrdom,
Thorns of the crown and shivers of the cross,
And therewithal,—for thus he told us,—brought
By holy Joseph hither, that same spear   110
Wherewith the Roman pierced the side of Christ.
He much amazed us; after, when we sought
The tribute, answer'd, "I have quite foregone
All matters of this world. Garlon, mine heir,
Of him demand it," which this Garlon gave
With much ado, railing at thine and thee.

'But when we left, in those deep woods we found
A knight of thine spear-stricken from behind,
Dead, whom we buried; more than one of us
Cried out on Garlon, but a woodman there   120
Reported of some demon in the woods

Was once a man, who, driven by evil tongues
From all his fellows, lived alone, and came
To learn black magic, and to hate his kind
With such a hate that when he died his soul
Became a fiend, which, as the man in life
Was wounded by blind tongues he saw not whence,
Strikes from behind. This woodman show'd the cave
From which he sallies and wherein he dwelt.
We saw the hoof-print of a horse, no more.'   130

Then Arthur, 'Let who goes before me see
He do not fall behind me. Foully slain
And villainously! who will hunt for me
This demon of the woods?' Said Balan, 'I!'
So claim'd the quest and rode away, but first,
Embracing Balin: 'Good my brother, hear!
Let not thy moods prevail when I am gone
Who used to lay them! hold them outer fiends,
Who leap at thee to tear thee; shake them aside,
Dreams ruling when wit sleeps! yea, but to dream   140
That any of these would wrong thee wrongs thyself.
Witness their flowery welcome. Bound are they
To speak no evil. Truly, save for fears,
My fears for thee, so rich a fellowship
Would make me wholly blest; thou one of them,
Be one indeed. Consider them, and all
Their bearing in their common bond of love,
No more of hatred than in heaven itself,
No more of jealousy than in Paradise.'

So Balan warn'd, and went; Balin remain'd,   150
Who—for but three brief moons had glanced away
From being knighted till he smote the thrall,
And faded from the presence into years
Of exile—now would strictlier set himself
To learn what Arthur meant by courtesy,
Manhood, and knighthood; wherefore hover'd round
Lancelot, but when he mark'd his high sweet smile
In passing, and a transitory word
Make knight or churl or child or damsel seem
From being smiled at happier in themselves—   160
Sigh'd, as a boy, lame-born beneath a height
That glooms his valley, sighs to see the peak
Sun-flushed or touch at night the northern star;
For one from out his village lately climb'd
And brought report of azure lands and fair,
Far seen to left and right; and he himself
Hath hardly scaled with help a hundred feet

Up from the base. So Balin, marvelling oft
How far beyond him Lancelot seem'd to move,
Groan'd and at times would mutter: 'These be gifts,   170
Born with the blood, not learnable, divine,
Beyond *my* reach. Well had I foughten—well—
In those fierce wars, struck hard—and had I crown'd
With my slain self the heaps of whom I slew—
So—better!—But this worship of the Queen,
That honor too wherein she holds him—this,
This was the sunshine that hath given the man
A growth, a name that branches o'er the rest,
And strength against all odds, and what the King
So prizes—overprizes—gentleness.   180
Her likewise would I worship an I might.
I never can be close with her, as he
That brought her hither. Shall I pray the King
To let me bear some token of his Queen
Whereon to gaze, remembering her—forget
My heats and violences? live afresh?
What if the Queen disdain'd to grant it! nay,
Being so stately-gentle, would she make
My darkness blackness? and with how sweet grace
She greeted my return! Bold will I be—   190
Some goodly cognizance of Guinevere,
In lieu of this rough beast upon my shield,
Langued gules, and tooth'd with grinning savagery.'

     And Arthur, when Sir Balin sought him, said,
'What wilt thou bear?' Balin was bold, and ask'd
To bear her own crown-royal upon shield,
Whereat she smiled and turn'd her to the King,
Who answer'd; 'Thou shalt put the crown to use.
The crown is but the shadow of the king,
And this a shadow's shadow, let him have it,   200
So this will help him of his violences!'
'No shadow,' said Sir Balin, 'O my Queen,
But light to me! no shadow, O my King,
But golden earnest of a gentler life!'

     So Balin bare the crown, and all the knights
Approved him, and the Queen; and all the world
Made music, and he felt his being move
In music with his Order and the King.

     The nightingale, full-toned in middle May,
Hath ever and anon a note so thin   210
It seems another voice in other groves;
Thus, after some quick burst of sudden wrath,

The music in him seem'd to change and grow
Faint and far-off.
                           And once he saw the thrall
His passion half had gauntleted to death,
That causer of his banishment and shame,
Smile at him, as he deem'd, presumptuously.
His arm half rose to strike again, but fell;
The memory of that cognizance on shield
Weighted it down, but in himself he moan'd: 220

'Too high this mount of Camelot for me;
These high-set courtesies are not for me.
Shall I not rather prove the worse for these?
Fierier and stormier from restraining, break
Into some madness even before the Queen?'

Thus, as a hearth lit in a mountain home,
And glancing on the window, when the gloom
Of twilight deepens round it, seems a flame
That rages in the woodland far below,
So when his moods were darken'd, court and king   230
And all the kindly warmth of Arthur's hall
Shadow'd an angry distance; yet he strove
To learn the graces of their Table, fought
Hard with himself, and seem'd at length in peace.

Then chanced, one morning, that Sir Balin sat
Close-bower'd in that garden nigh the hall.
A walk of roses ran from door to door,
A walk of lilies crost it to the bower;
And down that range of roses the great Queen
Came with slow steps, the morning on her face;   240
And all in shadow from the counter door
Sir Lancelot as to meet her, then at once,
As if he saw not, glanced aside, and paced
The long white walk of lilies toward the bower.
Follow'd the Queen; Sir Balin heard her 'Prince,
Art thou so little loyal to thy Queen
As pass without good morrow to thy Queen?'
To whom Sir Lancelot with his eyes on earth,
'Fain would I still be loyal to the Queen.'
'Yea, so,' she said; 'but so to pass me by—   250
So loyal scarce is loyal to thyself,
Whom all men rate the king of courtesy.
Let be; ye stand, fair lord, as in a dream.'

Then Lancelot with his hand among the flowers:
'Yea—for a dream. Last night methought I saw

That maiden Saint who stands with lily in hand
In yonder shrine. All round her prest the dark,
And all the light upon her silver face
Flow'd from the spiritual lily that she held.
Lo! these her emblems drew mine eyes—away;   260
For see, how perfect-pure! As light a flush
As hardly tints the blossom of the quince
Would mar their charm of stainless maidenhood.'

'Sweeter to me,' she said, 'this garden rose
Deep-hued and many-folded! sweeter still
The wild-wood hyacinth and the bloom of May!
Prince, we have ridden before among the flowers
In those fair days—not all as cool as these,
Tho' season-earlier. Art thou sad? or sick?
Our noble King will send thee his own leech—   270
Sick? or for any matter anger'd at me?'

Then Lancelot lifted his large eyes; they dwelt
Deep-tranced on hers, and could not fall. Her hue
Changed at his gaze; so turning side by side
They past, and Balin started from his bower.

'Queen? subject? but I see not what I see.
Damsel and lover? hear not what I hear.
My father hath begotten me in his wrath.
I suffer from the things before me, know,
Learn nothing; am not worthy to be knight—   280
A churl, a clown!' and in him gloom on gloom
Deepen'd; he sharply caught his lance and shield,
Nor stay'd to crave permission of the King,
But mad for strange adventure, dash'd away.

He took the selfsame track as Balan, saw
The fountain where they sat together, sigh'd,
'Was I not better there with him?' and rode
The skyless woods, but under open blue
Came on the hoar-head woodman at a bough
Wearily hewing. 'Churl, thine axe!' he cried,   290
Descended, and disjointed it at a blow;
To whom the woodman utter'd wonderingly,
'Lord, thou couldst lay the devil of these woods
If arm of flesh could lay him!' Balin cried,
'Him, or the viler devil who plays his part;
To lay that devil would lay the devil in me.'
'Nay,' said the churl, 'our devil is a truth,
I saw the flash of him but yester-even.
And some *do* say that our Sir Garlon too

Hath learn'd black magic, and to ride unseen.   300
Look to the cave.' But Balin answer'd him,
'Old fabler, these be fancies of the churl;
Look to thy woodcraft,' and so leaving him,
Now with slack rein and careless of himself,
Now with dug spur and raving at himself,
Now with droopt brow down the long glades he rode;
So mark'd not on his right a cavern-chasm
Yawn over darkness, where, nor far within,
The whole day died, but, dying, gleam'd on rocks
Roof-pendent, sharp; and others from the floor,   310
Tusklike, arising, made that mouth of night
Whereout the demon issued up from hell.
He mark'd not this, but, blind and deaf to all
Save that chain'd rage which ever yelpt within,
Past eastward from the falling sun. At once
He felt the hollow-beaten mosses thud
And tremble, and then the shadow of a spear,
Shot from behind him, ran along the ground.
Sideways he started from the path, and saw,
With pointed lance as if to pierce, a shape,   320
A light of armor by him flash, and pass
And vanish in the woods; and follow'd this,
But all so blind in rage that unawares
He burst his lance against a forest bough,
Dishorsed himself, and rose again, and fled
Far, till the castle of a king, the hall
Of Pellam, lichen-bearded, grayly draped
With streaming grass, appear'd, low-built but strong;
The ruinous donjon as a knoll of moss,
The battlement overtopt with ivy-tods,   330
A home of bats, in every tower an owl.

Then spake the men of Pellam crying, 'Lord,
Why wear ye this crown-royal upon shield?'
Said Balin, 'For the fairest and the best
Of ladies living gave me this to bear.'
So stall'd his horse, and strode across the court,
But found the greetings both of knight and king
Faint in the low dark hall of banquet. Leaves
Laid their green faces flat against the panes,
Sprays grated, and the canker'd boughs without   340
Whined in the wood; for all was hush'd within,
Till when at feast Sir Garlon likewise ask'd,
'Why wear ye that crown-royal?' Balin said,
'The Queen we worship, Lancelot, I, and all,
As fairest, best, and purest, granted me
To bear it!' Such a sound—for Arthur's knights

Were hated strangers in the hall—as makes
The white swan-mother, sitting, when she hears
A strange knee rustle thro' her secret reeds,
Made Garlon, hissing; then he sourly smiled: 350
'Fairest I grant her—I have seen; but best,
Best, purest? *thou* from Arthur's hall, and yet
So simple! hast thou eyes, or if, are these
So far besotted that they fail to see
This fair wife-worship cloaks a secret shame?
Truly, ye men of Arthur be but babes.'

A goblet on the board by Balin, boss'd
With holy Joseph's legend, on his right
Stood, all of massiest bronze. One side had sea
And ship and sail and angels blowing on it;   360
And one was rough with wattling, and the walls
Of that low church he built at Glastonbury.
This Balin graspt, but while in act to hurl,
Thro' memory of that token on the shield
Relax'd his hold. 'I will be gentle,' he thought,
'And passing gentle;' caught his hand away,
Then fiercely to Sir Garlon: 'Eyes have I
That saw to-day the shadow of a spear,
Shot from behind me, run along the ground;
Eyes too that long have watch'd how Lancelot draws   370
From homage to the best and purest, might,
Name, manhood, and a grace, but scantly thine
Who, sitting in thine own hall, canst endure
To mouth so huge a foulness—to thy guest,
Me, me of Arthur's Table. Felon talk!
Let be! no more!'
                    But not the less by night
The scorn of Garlon, poisoning all his rest,
Stung him in dreams. At length, and dim thro' leaves
Blinkt the white morn, sprays grated, and old boughs
Whined in the wood. He rose, descended, met   380
The scorner in the castle court, and fain,
For hate and loathing, would have past him by;
But when Sir Garlon utter'd mocking-wise,
'What, wear ye still that same crown-scandalous?'
His countenance blacken'd, and his forehead veins
Bloated and branch'd; and tearing out of sheath
The brand, Sir Balin with a fiery, 'Ha!
So thou be shadow, here I make thee ghost,'
Hard upon helm smote him, and the blade flew
Splintering in six, and clinkt upon the stones.   390
Then Garlon, reeling slowly backward, fell,
And Balin by the banneret of his helm

Dragg'd him, and struck, but from the castle a cry
Sounded across the court, and—men-at-arms,
A score with pointed lances, making at him—
He dash'd the pummel at the foremost face,
Beneath a low door dipt, and made his feet
Wings thro' a glimmering gallery, till he mark'd
The portal of King Pellam's chapel wide   400
And inward to the wall; he stept behind;
Thence in a moment heard them pass like wolves
Howling; but while he stared about the shrine,
In which he scarce could spy the Christ for Saints,
Beheld before a golden altar lie
The longest lance his eyes had ever seen,
Point-painted red; and seizing thereupon
Push'd thro' an open casement down, lean'd on it,
Leapt in a semicircle, and lit on earth;
Then hand at ear, and harkening from what side   410
The blindfold rummage buried in the walls
Might echo, ran the counter path, and found
His charger, mounted on him and away.
An arrow whizz'd to the right, one to the left,
One overhead; and Pellam's feeble cry,
'Stay, stay him! he defileth heavenly things
With earthly uses!' made him quickly dive
Beneath the boughs, and race thro' many a mile
Of dense and open, till his goodly horse,
Arising wearily at a fallen oak,   420
Stumbled headlong, and cast him face to ground.

      Half-wroth he had not ended, but all glad,
Knightlike, to find his charger yet unlamed,
Sir Balin drew the shield from off his neck,
Stared at the priceless cognizance, and thought,
'I have shamed thee so that now thou shamest me,
Thee will I bear no more,' high on a branch
Hung it, and turn'd aside into the woods,
And there in gloom cast himself all along,
Moaning, 'My violences, my violences!'

      But now the wholesome music of the wood   430
Was dumb'd by one from out the hall of Mark.
A damsel-errant, warbling, as she rode
The woodland alleys, Vivien, with her squire.

      'The fire of heaven has kill'd the barren cold,
And kindled all the plain and all the wold.
The new leaf ever pushes off the old.
The fire of heaven is not the flame of hell.

'Old priest, who mumble worship in your quire—
Old monk and nun, ye scorn the world's desire,
Yet in your frosty cells ye feel the fire!
The fire of heaven is not the flame of hell.   440

'The fire of heaven is on the dusty ways.
The wayside blossoms open to the blaze.
The whole wood-world is one full peal of praise.
The fire of heaven is not the flame of hell.

'The fire of heaven is lord of all things good,
And starve not thou this fire within thy blood,
But follow Vivien thro' the fiery flood!
The fire of heaven is not the flame of hell!'

Then turning to her squire, 'This fire of heaven,   450
This old sun-worship, boy, will rise again,
And beat the Cross to earth, and break the King
And all his Table.'

                    Then they reach'd a glade,
Where under one long lane of cloudless air
Before another wood, the royal crown
Sparkled, and swaying upon a restless elm
Drew the vague glance of Vivien and her squire.
Amazed were these; 'Lo there,' she cried—'a crown—
Borne by some high lord-prince of Arthur's hall,
And there a horse! the rider? where is he?   460
See, yonder lies one dead within the wood.
Not dead; he stirs!—but sleeping. I will speak.
Hail, royal knight, we break on thy sweet rest,
Not, doubtless, all unearn'd by noble deeds.
But bounden art thou, if from Arthur's hall,
To help the weak. Behold, I fly from shame,
A lustful king, who sought to win my love
Thro' evil ways. The knight with whom I rode
Hath suffer'd misadventure, and my squire
Hath in him small defence; but thou, Sir Prince,   470
Wilt surely guide me to the warrior King,
Arthur the blameless, pure as any maid,
To get me shelter for my maidenhood.
I charge thee by that crown upon thy shield,
And by the great Queen's name, arise and hence.'

And Balin rose: 'Thither no more! nor prince
Nor knight am I, but one that hath defamed
The cognizance she gave me. Here I dwell
Savage among the savage woods, here die—
Die—let the wolves' black maws ensepulchre   480
Their brother beast, whose anger was his lord!
O me, that such a name as Guinevere's,

Which our high Lancelot hath so lifted up,
And been thereby uplifted, should thro' me,
My violence, and my villainy, come to shame!'

Thereat she suddenly laugh'd and shrill, anon
Sigh'd all as suddenly. Said Balin to her:
'Is this thy courtesy—to mock me, ha?
Hence, for I will not with thee.' Again she sigh'd: 490
'Pardon, sweet lord! we maidens often laugh
When sick at heart, when rather we should weep.
I knew thee wrong'd. I brake upon thy rest,
And now full loth am I to break thy dream,
But thou art man, and canst abide a truth,
Tho' bitter. Hither, boy—and mark me well.
Dost thou remember at Caerleon once—
A year ago—nay, then I love thee not—
Ay, thou rememberest well—one summer dawn—
By the great tower—Caerleon upon Usk—   500
Nay, truly we were hidden—this fair lord,
The flower of all their vestal knighthood, knelt
In amorous homage—knelt—what else?—O, ay,
Knelt, and drew down from out his night-black hair
And mumbled that white hand whose ring'd caress
Had wander'd from her own King's golden head,
And lost itself in darkness, till she cried—
I thought the great tower would crash down on both—
"Rise, my sweet King, and kiss me on the lips,
Thou art my King." This lad, whose lightest word   510
Is mere white truth in simple nakedness,
Saw them embrace; he reddens, cannot speak,
So bashful, he! but all the maiden Saints,
The deathless mother-maidenhood of heaven,
Cry out upon her. Up then, ride with me!
Talk not of shame! thou canst not, an thou wouldst,
Do these more shame than these have done themselves.'

She lied with ease; but horror-stricken he,
Remembering that dark bower at Camelot,
Breathed in a dismal whisper, 'It is truth.'

Sunnily she smiled: 'And even in this lone wood,   520
Sweet lord, ye do right well to whisper this.
Fools prate, and perish traitors. Woods have tongues,
As walls have ears; but thou shalt go with me,
And we will speak at first exceeding low.
Meet is it the good King be not deceived.
See now, I set thee high on vantage ground,
From whence to watch the time, and eagle-like
Stoop at thy will on Lancelot and the Queen.'

She ceased; his evil spirit upon him leapt,
He ground his teeth together, sprang with a yell,   530
Tore from the branch and cast on earth the shield,
Drove his mail'd heel athwart the royal crown,
Stampt all into defacement, hurl'd it from him
Among the forest weeds, and cursed the tale,
The told-of, and the teller.

                         That weird yell,
Unearthlier than all shriek of bird or beast,
Thrill'd thro' the woods; and Balan lurking there—
His quest was unaccomplish'd—heard and thought
'The scream of that wood-devil I came to quell!'
Then nearing: 'Lo! he hath slain some brother-knight,   540
And tramples on the goodly shield to show
His loathing of our Order and the Queen.
My quest, meseems, is here. Or devil or man,
Guard thou thine head.' Sir Balin spake not word,
But snatch'd a sudden buckler from the squire,
And vaulted on his horse, and so they crash'd
In onset, and King Pellam's holy spear,
Reputed to be red with sinless blood,
Redden'd at once with sinful, for the point
Across the maiden shield of Balan prick'd   550
The hauberk to the flesh; and Balin's horse
Was wearied to the death, and, when they crash'd,
Rolling back upon Balin, crush'd the man
Inward, and either fell and swoon'd away.

Then to her squire mutter'd the damsel: 'Fools!
This fellow hath wrought some foulness with his Queen;
Else never had he borne her crown, nor raved
And thus foam'd over at a rival name.
But thou, Sir Chick, that scarce hast broken shell,
Art yet half-yolk, not even come to down—   560
Who never sawest Caerleon upon Usk—
And yet hast often pleaded for my love—
See what I see, be thou where I have been,
Or else, Sir Chick—dismount and loose their casques;
I fain would know what manner of men they be.'
And when the squire had loosed them, 'Goodly!—look!
They might have cropt the myriad flower of May,
And butt each other here, like brainless bulls,
Dead for one heifer!'

                         Then the gentle squire:
'I hold them happy, so they died for love;   570
And, Vivien, tho' ye beat me like your dog,
I too could die, as now I live, for thee.'

'Live on, Sir Boy,' she cried; 'I better prize
The living dog than the dead lion. Away!
I cannot brook to gaze upon the dead.'
Then leapt her palfrey o'er the fallen oak,
And bounding forward, 'Leave them to the wolves.'

But when their foreheads felt the cooling air,
Balin first woke, and seeing that true face,
Familiar up from cradle-time, so wan,   580
Crawl'd slowly with low moans to where he lay,
And on his dying brother cast himself
Dying; and *he* lifted faint eyes; he felt
One near him; all at once they found the world,
Staring wild-wide; then with a childlike wail,
And drawing down the dim disastrous brow
That o'er him hung, he kiss'd it, moan'd, and spake:

'O Balin, Balin, I that fain had died
To save thy life, have brought thee to thy death.
Why had ye not the shield I knew? and why   590
Trampled ye thus on that which bare the crown?'

Then Balin told him brokenly and in gasps
All that had chanced, and Balan moan'd again:

'Brother, I dwelt a day in Pellam's hall;
This Garlon mock'd me, but I heeded not.
And one said, "Eat in peace! a liar is he,
And hates thee for the tribute!" This good knight
Told me that twice a wanton damsel came,
And sought for Garlon at the castle-gates,
Whom Pellam drove away with holy heat.   600
I well believe this damsel, and the one
Who stood beside thee even now, the same.
"She dwells among the woods," he said, "and meets
And dallies with him in the Mouth of Hell."
Foul are their lives, foul are their lips; they lied.
Pure as our own true mother is our Queen.'

'O brother,' answer'd Balin, 'woe is me!
My madness all thy life has been thy doom,
Thy curse, and darken'd all thy day; and now
The night has come. I scarce can see thee now.   610
Good night! for we shall never bid again
Good morrow—Dark my doom was here, and dark
It will be there. I see thee now no more.
I would not mine again should darken thine;
Good night, true brother.'

Balan answer'd low,

'Good night, true brother, here! good morrow there!
We two were born together, and we die
Together by one doom:' and while he spoke
Closed his death-drowsing eyes, and slept the sleep
With Balin, either lock'd in either's arm. 620

MERLIN AND VIVIEN

A STORM was coming, but the winds were still,
And in the wild woods of Broceliande,
Before an oak, so hollow, huge, and old
It look'd a tower of ivied masonwork,
At Merlin's feet the wily Vivien lay.

For he that always bare in bitter grudge
The slights of Arthur and his Table, Mark
The Cornish King, had heard a wandering voice,
A minstrel of Caerleon by strong storm
Blown into shelter at Tintagil, say 10
That out of naked knight-like purity
Sir Lancelot worshipt no unmarried girl,
But the great Queen herself, fought in her name,
Sware by her—vows like theirs that high in heaven
Love most, but neither marry nor are given
In marriage, angels of our Lord's report.

He ceased, and then—for Vivien sweetly said—
She sat beside the banquet nearest Mark,—
'And is the fair example follow'd, sir,
In Arthur's household?'—answer'd innocently: 20

'Ay, by some few—ay, truly—youths that hold
It more beseems the perfect virgin knight
To worship woman as true wife beyond
All hopes of gaining, than as maiden girl.
They place their pride in Lancelot and the Queen.
So passionate for an utter purity
Beyond the limit of their bond are these,
For Arthur bound them not to singleness.
Brave hearts and clean! and yet—God guide them!—young.'

Then Mark was half in heart to hurl his cup 30
Straight at the speaker, but forbore. He rose
To leave the hall, and, Vivien following him,
Turn'd to her: 'Here are snakes within the grass;
And you methinks, O Vivien, save ye fear

The monkish manhood, and the mask of pure
Worn by this court, can stir them till they sting.'

    And Vivien answer'd, smiling scornfully:
'Why fear? because that foster'd at *thy* court
I savor of thy—virtues? fear them? no,
As love, if love be perfect, casts out fear,   40
So hate, if hate be perfect, casts out fear.
My father died in battle against the King,
My mother on his corpse in open field;
She bore me there, for born from death was I
Among the dead and sown upon the wind—
And then on thee! and shown the truth betimes,
That old true filth, and bottom of the well,
Where Truth is hidden. Gracious lessons thine,
And maxims of the mud! "This Arthur pure!
Great Nature thrò' the flesh herself hath made   50
Gives him the lie! There is no being pure,
My cherub; saith not Holy Writ the same?"—
If I were Arthur, I would have thy blood.
Thy blessing, stainless King! I bring thee back,
When I have ferreted out their burrowings,
The hearts of all this Order in mine hand—
Ay—so that fate and craft and folly close,
Perchance, one curl of Arthur's golden beard.
To me this narrow grizzled fork of thine
Is cleaner-fashion'd— Well, I loved thee first;   60
That warps the wit.'

                Loud laugh'd the graceless Mark.
But Vivien, into Camelot stealing, lodged
Low in the city, and on a festal day
When Guinevere was crossing the great hall
Cast herself down, knelt to the Queen, and wail'd.

    'Why kneel ye there? What evil have ye wrought?
Rise!' and the damsel bidden rise arose
And stood with folded hands and downward eyes
Of glancing corner and all meekly said:
'None wrought, but suffer'd much, an orphan maid!   70
My father died in battle for thy King,
My mother on his corpse—in open field,
The sad sea-sounding wastes of Lyonnesse—
Poor wretch—no friend!—and now by Mark the king,
For that small charm of feature mine, pursued—
If any such be mine—I fly to thee.
Save, save me thou! Woman of women—thine
The wreath of beauty, thine the crown of power,

Be thine the balm of pity, O heaven's own white
Earth-angel, stainless bride of stainless King— 80
Help, for he follows! take me to thyself!
O yield me shelter for mine innocency
Among thy maidens!'

       Here her slow sweet eyes
Fear-tremulous, but humbly hopeful, rose
Fixt on her hearer's, while the Queen who stood
All glittering like May sunshine on May leaves
In green and gold, and plumed with green replied:
'Peace, child! of over-praise and over-blame
We choose the last. Our noble Arthur, him
Ye scarce can overpraise, will hear and know. 90
Nay—we believe all evil of thy Mark—
Well, we shall test thee farther; but this hour
We ride a-hawking with Sir Lancelot.
He hath given us a fair falcon which he train'd;
We go to prove it. Bide ye here the while.'

  She past; and Vivien murmur'd after, 'Go!
I bide the while.' Then thro' the portal-arch
Peering askance, and muttering broken-wise,
As one that labors with an evil dream,
Beheld the Queen and Lancelot get to horse. 100

  'Is that the Lancelot? goodly—ay, but gaunt;
Courteous—amends for gauntness—takes her hand—
That glance of theirs, but for the street, had been
A clinging kiss—how hand lingers in hand!
Let go at last!—they ride away—to hawk
For waterfowl. Royaller game is mine.
For such a supersensual sensual bond
As that gray cricket chirpt of at our hearth—
Touch flax with flame—a glance will serve—the liars!
Ah little rat that borest in the dyke 110
Thy hole by night to let the boundless deep
Down upon far-off cities while they dance—
Or dream—of thee they dream'd not—nor of me
These—ay, but each of either; ride, and dream
The mortal dream that never yet was mine—
Ride, ride and dream until ye wake—to me!
Then, narrow court and lubber King, farewell!
For Lancelot will be gracious to the rat,
And our wise Queen, if knowing that I know,
Will hate, loathe, fear—but honor me the more.' 120

Yet while they rode together down the plain,
Their talk was all of training, terms of art,
Diet and seeling, jesses, leash and lure.
'She is too noble,' he said, 'to check at pies,
Nor will she rake: there is no baseness in her.'
Here when the Queen demanded as by chance,
'Know ye the stranger woman?' 'Let her be,'
Said Lancelot, and unhooded casting off
The goodly falcon free; she tower'd; her bells,
Tone under tone, shrill'd; and they lifted up   130
Their eager faces, wondering at the strength,
Boldness, and royal knighthood of the bird,
Who pounced her quarry and slew it. Many a time
As once—of old—among the flowers—they rode.

But Vivien half-forgotten of the Queen
Among her damsels broidering sat, heard, watch'd,
And whisper'd. Thro' the peaceful court she crept
And whisper'd; then, as Arthur in the highest
Leaven'd the world, so Vivien in the lowest,
Arriving at a time of golden rest,   140
And sowing one ill hint from ear to ear,
While all the heathen lay at Arthur's feet,
And no quest came, but all was joust and play,
Leaven'd his hall. They heard and let her be.

Thereafter, as an enemy that has left
Death in the living waters and withdrawn,
The wily Vivien stole from Arthur's court.

She hated all the knights, and heard in thought
Their lavish comment when her name was named.
For once, when Arthur walking all alone,   150
Vext at a rumor issued from herself
Of some corruption crept among his knights,
Had met her, Vivien, being greeted fair,
Would fain have wrought upon his cloudy mood
With reverent eyes mock-loyal, shaken voice,
And flutter'd adoration, and at last
With dark sweet hints of some who prized him more
Than who should prize him most; at which the King
Had gazed upon her blankly and gone by.
But one had watch'd, and had not held his peace;   160
It made the laughter of an afternoon
That Vivien should attempt the blameless King.
And after that, she set herself to gain
Him, the most famous man of all those times,
Merlin, who knew the range of all their arts,
Had built the King his havens, ships, and halls,

Was also bard, and knew the starry heavens;
The people call'd him wizard; whom at first
She play'd about with slight and sprightly talk,
And vivid smiles, and faintly-venom'd points   170
Of slander, glancing here and grazing there;
And yielding to his kindlier moods, the seer
Would watch her at her petulance and play,
Even when they seem'd unlovable, and laugh
As those that watch a kitten. Thus he grew
Tolerant of what he half disdain'd, and she,
Perceiving that she was but half disdain'd,
Began to break her sports with graver fits,
Turn red or pale, would often when they met
Sigh fully, or all-silent gaze upon him   180
With such a fixt devotion that the old man,
Tho' doubtful, felt the flattery, and at times
Would flatter his own wish in age for love,
And half believe her true; for thus at times
He waver'd, but that other clung to him,
Fixt in her will, and so the seasons went.

    Then fell on Merlin a great melancholy;
He walk'd with dreams and darkness, and he found
A doom that ever poised itself to fall,
An ever-moaning battle in the mist,   190
World-war of dying flesh against the life,
Death in all life and lying in all love,
The meanest having power upon the highest,
And the high purpose broken by the worm.

    So leaving Arthur's court he gain'd the beach,
There found a little boat and stept into it;
And Vivien follow'd, but he mark'd her not.
She took the helm and he the sail; the boat
Drave with a sudden wind across the deeps,
And, touching Breton sands, they disembark'd.   200
And then she follow'd Merlin all the way,
Even to the wild woods of Broceliande.
For Merlin once had told her of a charm,
The which if any wrought on any one
With woven paces and with waving arms,
The man so wrought on ever seem'd to lie
Closed in the four walls of a hollow tower,
From which was no escape for evermore;
And none could find that man for evermore,
Nor could he see but him who wrought the charm   210
Coming and going, and he lay as dead
And lost to life and use and name and fame.

And Vivien ever sought to work the charm
Upon the great enchanter of the time,
As fancying that her glory would be great
According to his greatness whom she quench'd.

There lay she all her length and kiss'd his feet,
As if in deepest reverence and in love.
A twist of gold was round her hair; a robe
Of samite without price, that more exprest   220
Than hid her, clung about her lissome limbs,
In color like the satin-shining palm
On sallows in the windy gleams of March.
And while she kiss'd them, crying, 'Trample me,
Dear feet, that I have follow'd thro' the world,
And I will pay you worship; tread me down
And I will kiss you for it;' he was mute.
So dark a forethought roll'd about his brain,
As on a dull day in an ocean cave
The blind wave feeling round his long sea-hall   230
In silence; wherefore, when she lifted up
A face of sad appeal, and spake and said,
'O Merlin, do ye love me?' and again,
'O Merlin, do ye love me?' and once more,
'Great Master, do ye love me?' he was mute.
And lissome Vivien, holding by his heel,
Writhed toward him, slided up his knee and sat,
Behind his ankle twined her hollow feet
Together, curved an arm about his neck,
Clung like a snake; and letting her left hand   240
Droop from his mighty shoulder, as a leaf,
Made with her right a comb of pearl to part
The lists of such a beard as youth gone out
Had left in ashes. Then he spoke and said,
Not looking at her, 'Who are wise in love
Love most, say least,' and Vivien answer'd quick:
'I saw the little elf-god eyeless once
In Arthur's arras hall at Camelot;
But neither eyes nor tongue—O stupid child!
Yet you are wise who say it; let me think   250
Silence is wisdom. I am silent then,
And ask no kiss;' then adding all at once,
'And lo, I clothe myself with wisdom,' drew
The vast and shaggy mantle of his beard
Across her neck and bosom to her knee,
And call'd herself a gilded summer fly
Caught in a great old tyrant spider's web,
Who meant to eat her up in that wild wood
Without one word. So Vivien call'd herself,

260

But rather seem'd a lovely baleful star
Veil'd in gray vapor; till he sadly smiled:
'To what request for what strange boon,' he said,
'Are these your pretty tricks and fooleries,
O Vivien, the preamble? yet my thanks,
For these have broken up my melancholy.'

And Vivien answer'd smiling saucily:
'What, O my Master, have ye found your voice?
I bid the stranger welcome. Thanks at last!
But yesterday you never open'd lip,
Except indeed to drink. No cup had we;
In mine own lady palms I cull'd the spring
That gather'd trickling dropwise from the cleft,
And made a pretty cup of both my hands
And offer'd you it kneeling. Then you drank
And knew no more, nor gave me one poor word;
O, no more thanks than might a goat have given
With no more sign of reverence than a beard.
And when we halted at that other well,
And I was faint to swooning, and you lay
Foot-gilt with all the blossom-dust of those
Deep meadows we have traversed, did you know
That Vivien bathed your feet before her own?
And yet no thanks; and all thro' this wild wood
And all this morning when I fondled you.
Boon, ay, there was a boon, one not so strange—
How had I wrong'd you? surely ye are wise,
But such a silence is more wise than kind.'

And Merlin lock'd his hand in hers and said:
'O, did ye never lie upon the shore,
And watch the curl'd white of the coming wave
Glass'd in the slippery sand before it breaks?
Even such a wave, but not so pleasurable,
Dark in the glass of some presageful mood,
Had I for three days seen, ready to fall.
And then I rose and fled from Arthur's court
To break the mood. You follow'd me unask'd;
And when I look'd, and saw you following still,
My mind involved yourself the nearest thing
In that mind-mist—for shall I tell you truth?
You seem'd that wave about to break upon me
And sweep me from my hold upon the world,
My use and name and fame. Your pardon, child.
Your pretty sports have brighten'd all again.
And ask your boon, for boon I owe you thrice,
Once for wrong done you by confusion, next

270

280

290

300

For thanks it seems till now neglected, last
For these your dainty gambols; wherefore ask,
And take this boon so strange and not so strange.'

And Vivien answer'd smiling mournfully:
'O, not so strange as my long asking it,   310
Not yet so strange as you yourself are strange,
Nor half so strange as that dark mood of yours.
I ever fear'd ye were not wholly mine;
And see, yourself have own'd ye did me wrong.
The people call you prophet; let it be;
But not of those that can expound themselves.
Take Vivien for expounder; she will call
That three-days-long presageful gloom of yours
No presage, but the same mistrustful mood
That makes you seem less noble than yourself,   320
Whenever I have ask'd this very boon,
Now ask'd again; for see you not, dear love,
That such a mood as that which lately gloom'd
Your fancy when ye saw me following you
Must make me fear still more you are not mine,
Must make me yearn still more to prove you mine,
And make me wish still more to learn this charm
Of woven paces and of waving hands,
As proof of trust. O Merlin, teach it me!
The charm so taught will charm us both to rest.   330
For, grant me some slight power upon your fate,
I, feeling that you felt me worthy trust,
Should rest and let you rest, knowing you mine.
And therefore be as great as ye are named,
Not muffled round with selfish reticence.
How hard you look and how denyingly!
O, if you think this wickedness in me,
That I should prove it on you unawares,
That makes me passing wrathful; then our bond
Had best be loosed for ever; but think or not,   340
By Heaven that hears, I tell you the clean truth,
As clean as blood of babes, as white as milk!
O Merlin, may this earth, if ever I,
If these unwitty wandering wits of mine,
Even in the jumbled rubbish of a dream,
Have tript on such conjectural treachery—
May this hard earth cleave to the nadir hell
Down, down, and close again and nip me flat,
If I be such a traitress! Yield my boon,
Till which I scarce can yield you all I am;   350
And grant my re-reiterated wish,

The great proof of your love; because I think,
However wise, ye hardly know me yet.'

And Merlin loosed his hand from hers and said:
'I never was less wise, however wise,
Too curious Vivien, tho' you talk of trust,
Than when I told you first of such a charm.
Yea, if ye talk of trust I tell you this,
Too much I trusted when I told you that,
And stirr'd this vice in you which ruin'd man   360
Thro' woman the first hour; for howsoe'er
In children a great curiousness be well,
Who have to learn themselves and all the world,
In you, that are no child, for still I find
Your face is practised when I spell the lines,
I call it,—well, I will not call it vice;
But since you name yourself the summer fly,
I well could wish a cobweb for the gnat
That settles beaten back, and beaten back
Settles, till one could yield for weariness.   370
But since I will not yield to give you power
Upon my life and use and name and fame,
Why will ye never ask some other boon?
Yea, by God's rood, I trusted you too much!'

And Vivien, like the tenderest-hearted maid
That ever bided tryst at village stile,
Made answer, either eyelid wet with tears:
'Nay, Master, be not wrathful with your maid;
Caress her, let her feel herself forgiven
Who feels no heart to ask another boon.   380
I think ye hardly know the tender rhyme
Of "trust me not at all or all in all."
I heard the great Sir Lancelot sing it once,
And it shall answer for me. Listen to it.

   ' "In love, if love be love, if love be ours,
  Faith and unfaith can ne'er be equal powers:
  Unfaith in aught is want of faith in all.

   ' "It is the little rift within the lute,
  That by and by will make the music mute,
  And ever widening slowly silence all.   390

   ' "The little rift within the lover's lute,
  Or little pitted speck in garner'd fruit,
  That rotting inward slowly moulders all.

   ' "It is not worth the keeping; let it go:
  But shall it? answer, darling, answer, no.
  And trust me not at all or all in all."

'O master, do ye love my tender rhyme?'

And Merlin look'd and half believed her true,
So tender was her voice, so fair her face,
So sweetly gleam'd her eyes behind her tears   400
Like sunlight on the plain behind a shower;
And yet he answer'd half indignantly:

'Far other was the song that once I heard
By this huge oak, sung nearly where we sit;
For here we met, some ten or twelve of us,
To chase a creature that was current then
In these wild woods, the hart with golden horns.
It was the time when first the question rose
About the founding of a Table Round,
That was to be, for love of God and men   410
And noble deeds, the flower of all the world;
And each incited each to noble deeds.
And while we waited, one, the youngest of us,
We could not keep him silent, out he flash'd,
And into such a song, such fire for fame,
Such trumpet-blowings in it, coming down
To such a stern and iron-clashing close,
That when he stopt we long'd to hurl together,
And should have done it, but the beauteous beast
Scared by the noise upstarted at our feet,   420
And like a silver shadow slipt away
Thro' the dim land. And all day long we rode
Thro' the dim land against a rushing wind,
That glorious roundel echoing in our ears,
And chased the flashes of his golden horns
Until they vanish'd by the fairy well
That laughs at iron—as our warriors did—
Where children cast their pins and nails, and cry,
"Laugh, little well!" but touch it with a sword,
It buzzes fiercely round the point; and there   430
We lost him—such a noble song was that.
But, Vivien, when you sang me that sweet rhyme,
I felt as tho' you knew this cursed charm,
Were proving it on me, and that I lay
And felt them slowly ebbing, name and fame.'

And Vivien answer'd smiling mournfully:
'O, mine have ebb'd away for evermore,
And all thro' following you to this wild wood,
Because I saw you sad, to comfort you.
Lo now, what hearts have men! they never mount   440
As high as woman in her selfless mood.

And touching fame, howe'er ye scorn my song,
Take one verse more—the lady speaks it—this:

> ' "My name, once mine, now thine, is closelier mine,
> For fame, could fame be mine, that fame were thine,
> And shame, could shame be thine, that shame were mine.
> So trust me not at all or all in all."

'Says she not well? and there is more—this rhyme
Is like the fair pearl-necklace of the Queen,
That burst in dancing and the pearls were spilt;   450
Some lost, some stolen, some as relics kept;
But nevermore the same two sister pearls
Ran down the silken thread to kiss each other
On her white neck—so is it with this rhyme.
It lives dispersedly in many hands,
And every minstrel sings it differently;
Yet is there one true line, the pearl of pearls:
"Man dreams of fame while woman wakes to love."
Yea! love, tho' love were of the grossest, carves
A portion from the solid present, eats   460
And uses, careless of the rest; but fame,
The fame that follows death is nothing to us;
And what is fame in life but half-disfame
And counterchanged with darkness? ye yourself
Know well that envy calls you devil's son,
And since ye seem the master of all art,
They fain would make you master of all vice.'

And Merlin lock'd his hand in hers and said:
'I once was looking for a magic weed,
And found a fair young squire who sat alone,   470
Had carved himself a knightly shield of wood,
And then was painting on it fancied arms,
Azure, an eagle rising or, the sun
In dexter chief; the scroll, "I follow fame."
And speaking not, but leaning over him,
I took his brush and blotted out the bird,
And made a gardener putting in a graff,
With this for motto, "Rather use than fame."
You should have seen him blush; but afterwards
He made a stalwart knight. O Vivien,   480
For you, methinks you think you love me well;
For me, I love you somewhat. Rest; and Love
Should have some rest and pleasure in himself,
Not ever be too curious for a boon,
Too prurient for a proof against the grain
Of him ye say ye love. But Fame with men,
Being but ampler means to serve mankind,

Should have small rest or pleasure in herself,
But work as vassal to the larger love
That dwarfs the petty love of one to one.   49
Use gave me fame at first, and fame again
Increasing gave me use. Lo, there my boon!
What other? for men sought to prove me vile,
Because I fain had given them greater wits;
And then did envy call me devil's son.
The sick weak beast, seeking to help herself
By striking at her better, miss'd, and brought
Her own claw back, and wounded her own heart.
Sweet were the days when I was all unknown,
But when my name was lifted up the storm   500
Brake on the mountain and I cared not for it.
Right well know I that fame is half-disfame,
Yet needs must work my work. That other fame,
To one at least who hath not children vague,
The cackle of the unborn about the grave,
I cared not for it. A single misty star,
Which is the second in a line of stars
That seem a sword beneath a belt of three,
I never gazed upon it but I dreamt
Of some vast charm concluded in that star   510
To make fame nothing. Wherefore, if I fear,
Giving you power upon me thro' this charm,
That you might play me falsely, having power,
However well ye think ye love me now—
As sons of kings loving in pupilage
Have turn'd to tyrants when they came to power—
I rather dread the loss of use than fame;
If you—and not so much from wickedness,
As some wild turn of anger, or a mood
Of overstrain'd affection, it may be,   520
To keep me all to your own self,—or else
A sudden spurt of woman's jealousy,—
Should try this charm on whom ye say ye love.'

And Vivien answer'd smiling as in wrath:
'Have I not sworn? I am not trusted. Good!
Well, hide it, hide it; I shall find it out,
And being found take heed of Vivien.
A woman and not trusted, doubtless I
Might feel some sudden turn of anger born
Of your misfaith; and your fine epithet   530
Is accurate too, for this full love of mine
Without the full heart back may merit well
Your term of overstrain'd. So used as I,
My daily wonder is, I love at all.

And as to woman's jealousy, O, why not?
O, to what end, except a jealous one,
And one to make me jealous if I love,
Was this fair charm invented by yourself?
I well believe that all about this world
Ye cage a buxom captive here and there, 540
Closed in the four walls of a hollow tower
From which is no escape for evermore.'

Then the great master merrily answer'd her:
'Full many a love in loving youth was mine;
I needed then no charm to keep them mine
But youth and love; and that full heart of yours
Whereof ye prattle, may now assure you mine;
So live uncharm'd. For those who wrought it first,
The wrist is parted from the hand that waved,
The feet unmortised from their ankle-bones 550
Who paced it, ages back—but will ye hear
The legend as in guerdon for your rhyme?

'There lived a king in the most eastern East,
Less old than I, yet older, for my blood
Hath earnest in it of far springs to be.
A tawny pirate anchor'd in his port,
Whose bark had plunder'd twenty nameless isles;
And passing one, at the high peep of dawn,
He saw two cities in a thousand boats
All fighting for a woman on the sea. 560
And pushing his black craft among them all,
He lightly scatter'd theirs and brought her off,
With loss of half his people arrow-slain;
A maid so smooth, so white, so wonderful,
They said a light came from her when she moved.
And since the pirate would not yield her up,
The king impaled him for his piracy,
Then made her queen. But those isle-nurtured eyes
Waged such unwilling tho' successful war
On all the youth, they sicken'd; councils thinn'd, 570
And armies waned, for magnet-like she drew
The rustiest iron of old fighters' hearts;
And beasts themselves would worship; camels knelt
Unbidden, and the brutes of mountain back
That carry kings in castles bow'd black knees
Of homage, ringing with their serpent hands,
To make her smile, her golden ankle-bells.
What wonder, being jealous, that he sent
His horns of proclamation out thro' all
The hundred under-kingdoms that he sway'd 586

To find a wizard who might teach the king
Some charm which, being wrought upon the queen,
Might keep her all his own. To such a one
He promised more than ever king has given,
A league of mountain full of golden mines,
A province with a hundred miles of coast,
A palace and a princess, all for him;
But on all those who tried and fail'd the king
Pronounced a dismal sentence, meaning by it   590
To keep the list low and pretenders back,
Or, like a king, not to be trifled with—
Their heads should moulder on the city gates.
And many tried and fail'd, because the charm
Of nature in her overbore their own;
And many a wizard brow bleach'd on the walls,
And many weeks a troop of carrion crows
Hung like a cloud above the gateway towers.'

    And Vivien breaking in upon him, said:
'I sit and gather honey; yet, methinks,
Thy tongue has tript a little; ask thyself.   600
The lady never made *unwilling* war
With those fine eyes; she had her pleasure in it,
And made her good man jealous with good cause.
And lived there neither dame nor damsel then
Wroth at a lover's loss? were all as tame,
I mean, as noble, as their queen was fair?
Not one to flirt a venom at her eyes,
Or pinch a murderous dust into her drink,
Or make her paler with a poison'd rose?
Well, those were not our days—but did they find   610
A wizard? Tell me, was he like to thee?'

    She ceased, and made her lithe arm round his neck
Tighten, and then drew back, and let her eyes
Speak for her, glowing on him, like a bride's
On her new lord, her own, the first of men.

    He answer'd laughing: 'Nay, not like to me.
At last they found—his foragers for charms—
A little glassy-headed hairless man,
Who lived alone in a great wild on grass,
Read but one book, and ever reading grew   620
So grated down and filed away with thought,
So lean his eyes were monstrous; while the skin
Clung but to crate and basket, ribs and spine.
And since he kept his mind on one sole aim,
Nor ever touch'd fierce wine, nor tasted flesh,

Nor own'd a sensual wish, to him the wall
That sunders ghosts and shadow-casting men
Became a crystal, and he saw them thro' it,
And heard their voices talk behind the wall,
And learnt their elemental secrets, powers   630
And forces; often o'er the sun's bright eye
Drew the vast eyelid of an inky cloud,
And lash'd it at the base with slanting storm;
Or in the noon of mist and driving rain,
When the lake whiten'd and the pinewood roar'd,
And the cairn'd mountain was a shadow, sunn'd
The world to peace again. Here was the man;
And so by force they dragg'd him to the king.
And then he taught the king to charm the queen
In such-wise that no man could see her more,   640
Nor saw she save the king, who wrought the charm,
Coming and going, and she lay as dead,
And lost all use of life. But when the king
Made proffer of the league of golden mines,
The province with a hundred miles of coast,
The palace and the princess, that old man
Went back to his old wild, and lived on grass,
And vanish'd, and his book came down to me.'

    And Vivien answer'd smiling saucily:
'Ye have the book; the charm is written in it.   650
Good! take my counsel, let me know it at once;
For keep it like a puzzle chest in chest,
With each chest lock'd and padlock'd thirty-fold,
And whelm all this beneath as vast a mound
As after furious battle turfs the slain
On some wild down above the windy deep,
I yet should strike upon a sudden means
To dig, pick, open, find and read the charm;
Then, if I tried it, who should blame me then?'

    And smiling as a master smiles at one   660
That is not of his school, nor any school
But that where blind and naked Ignorance
Delivers brawling judgments, unashamed,
On all things all day long, he answer'd her:

    'Thou read the book, my pretty Vivien!
O, ay, it is but twenty pages long,
But every page having an ample marge,
And every marge enclosing in the midst
A square of text that looks a little blot,
The text no larger than the limbs of fleas;   670

And every square of text an awful charm,
Writ in a language that has long gone by,
So long that mountains have arisen since
With cities on their flanks—thou read the book!
And every margin scribbled, crost, and cramm'd
With comment, densest condensation, hard
To mind and eye; but the long sleepless nights
Of my long life have made it easy to me.
And none can read the text, not even I;
And none can read the comment but myself;   680
And in the comment did I find the charm.
O, the results are simple; a mere child
Might use it to the harm of any one,
And never could undo it. Ask no more;
For tho' you should not prove it upon me,
But keep that oath ye sware, ye might, perchance,
Assay it on some one of the Table Round,
And all because ye dream they babble of you.'

      And Vivien, frowning in true anger, said:
'What dare the full-fed liars say of me?   690
They ride abroad redressing human wrongs!
They sit with knife in meat and wine in horn.
They bound to holy vows of chastity!
Were I not woman, I could tell a tale.
But you are man, you well can understand
The shame that cannot be explain'd for shame.
Not one of all the drove should touch me—swine!'

      Then answer'd Merlin careless of her words:
'You breathe but accusation vast and vague,
Spleen-born, I think, and proofless. If ye know,   700
Set up the charge ye know, to stand or fall!'

      And Vivien answer'd frowning wrathfully:
'O, ay, what say ye to Sir Valence, him
Whose kinsman left him watcher o'er his wife
And two fair babes, and went to distant lands,
Was one year gone, and on returning found
Not two but three? there lay the reckling, one
But one hour old! What said the happy sire?
A seven-months' babe had been a truer gift.
Those twelve sweet moons confused his fatherhood.'   710

      Then answer'd Merlin: 'Nay, I know the tale.
Sir Valence wedded with an outland dame;
Some cause had kept him sunder'd from his wife.
One child they had; it lived with her; she died.

His kinsman travelling on his own affair
Was charged by Valence to bring home the child.
He brought, not found it therefore; take the truth.'

'O, ay,' said Vivien, 'over-true a tale!
What say ye then to sweet Sir Sagramore,
That ardent man? "To pluck the flower in season,"   720
So says the song, "I trow it is no treason."
O Master, shall we call him over-quick
To crop his own sweet rose before the hour?'

    And Merlin answer'd: 'Over-quick art thou
To catch a loathly plume fallen from the wing
Of that foul bird of rapine whose whole prey
Is man's good name. He never wrong'd his bride.
I know the tale. An angry gust of wind
Puff'd out his torch among the myriad-room'd
And many-corridor'd complexities   730
Of Arthur's palace. Then he found a door,
And darkling felt the sculptured ornament
That wreathen round it made it seem his own,
And wearied out made for the couch and slept,
A stainless man beside a stainless maid;
And either slept, nor knew of other there,
Till the high dawn piercing the royal rose
In Arthur's casement glimmer'd chastely down,
Blushing upon them blushing, and at once
He rose without a word and parted from her.   740
But when the thing was blazed about the court,
The brute world howling forced them into bonds,
And as it chanced they are happy, being pure.'

    'O, ay,' said Vivien, 'that were likely too!
What say ye then to fair Sir Percivale
And of the horrid foulness that he wrought,
The saintly youth, the spotless lamb of Christ,
Or some black wether of Saint Satan's fold?
What, in the precincts of the chapel-yard,
Among the knightly brasses of the graves,   750
And by the cold Hic Jacets of the dead!'

    And Merlin answer'd careless of her charge:
'A sober man is Percivale and pure,
But once in life was fluster'd with new wine,
Then paced for coolness in the chapel-yard,
Where one of Satan's shepherdesses caught
And meant to stamp him with her master's mark.
And that he sinn'd is not believable;

For, look upon his face!—but if he sinn'd,   760
The sin that practice burns into the blood,
And not the one dark hour which brings remorse,
Will brand us, after, of whose fold we be;
Or else were he, the holy king whose hymns
Are chanted in the minster, worse than all.
But is your spleen froth'd out, or have ye more?'

And Vivien answer'd frowning yet in wrath:
'O, ay; what say ye to Sir Lancelot, friend,
Traitor or true? that commerce with the Queen,
I ask you, is it clamor'd by the child,   770
Or whisper'd in the corner? do ye know it?'

To which he answer'd sadly: 'Yea, I know it.
Sir Lancelot went ambassador, at first,
To fetch her, and she watch'd him from her walls.
A rumor runs, she took him for the King,
So fixt her fancy on him; let them be.
But have ye no one word of loyal praise
For Arthur, blameless king and stainless man?'

She answer'd with a low and chuckling laugh:
'Man! is he man at all, who knows and winks?
Sees what his fair bride is and does, and winks?   780
By which the good King means to blind himself,
And blinds himself and all the Table Round
To all the foulness that they work. Myself
Could call him—were it not for womanhood—
The pretty, popular name such manhood earns,
Could call him the main cause of all their crime,
Yea, were he not crown'd king, coward and fool.'

Then Merlin to his own heart, loathing, said:
'O true and tender! O my liege and King!
O selfless man and stainless gentleman,   790
Who wouldst against thine own eye-witness fain
Have all men true and leal, all women pure!
How, in the mouths of base interpreters,
From over-fineness not intelligible
To things with every sense as false and foul
As the poach'd filth that floods the middle street,
Is thy white blamelessness accounted blame!'

But Vivien, deeming Merlin overborne
By instance, recommenced, and let her tongue
Rage like a fire among the noblest names,   800

Polluting, and imputing her whole self,
Defaming and defacing, till she left
Not even Lancelot brave nor Galahad clean.

Her words had issue other than she will'd.
He dragged his eyebrow bushes down, and made
A snowy pent-house for his hollow eyes,
And mutter'd in himself: 'Tell *her* the charm!
So, if she had it, would she rail on me
To snare the next, and if she have it not
So will she rail. What did the wanton say?   810
"Not mount as high!" we scarce can sink as low;
For men at most differ as heaven and earth,
But women, worst and best, as heaven and hell.
I know the Table Round, my friends of old;
All brave, and many generous, and some chaste.
She cloaks the scar of some repulse with lies.
I well believe she tempted them and fail'd,
Being so bitter; for fine plots may fail,
Tho' harlots paint their talk as well as face
With colors of the heart that are not theirs.   820
I will not let her know; nine tithes of times
Face-flatterer and backbiter are the same.
And they, sweet soul, that most impute a crime
Are pronest to it, and impute themselves,
Wanting the mental range, or low desire
Not to feel lowest makes them level all;
Yea, they would pare the mountain to the plain,
To leave an equal baseness; and in this
Are harlots like the crowd that if they find
Some stain or blemish in a name of note,   830
Not grieving that their greatest are so small,
Inflate themselves with some insane delight,
And judge all nature from her feet of clay,
Without the will to lift their eyes, and see
Her godlike head crown'd with spiritual fire,
And touching other worlds. I am weary of her.'

He spoke in words part heard, in whispers part,
Half-suffocated in the hoary fell
And many-winter'd fleece of throat and chin.
But Vivien, gathering somewhat of his mood,   840
And hearing 'harlot' mutter'd twice or thrice,
Leapt from her session on his lap, and stood
Stiff as a viper frozen; loathsome sight,
How from the rosy lips of life and love
Flash'd the bare-grinning skeleton of death!
White was her cheek; sharp breaths of anger puff'd

Her fairy nostril out; her hand half-clench'd
Went faltering sideways downward to her belt,
And feeling. Had she found a dagger there—
For in a wink the false love turns to hate—   850
She would have stabb'd him; but she found it not.
His eye was calm, and suddenly she took
To bitter weeping like a beaten child,
A long, long weeping, not consolable.
Then her false voice made way, broken with sobs:

'O crueller than was ever told in tale
Or sung in song! O vainly lavish'd love!
O cruel, there was nothing wild or strange,
Or seeming shameful—for what shame in love,
So love be true, and not as yours is?—nothing   860
Poor Vivien had not done to win his trust
Who call'd her what he call'd her—all her crime,
All—all—the wish to prove him wholly hers.'

She mused a little, and then clapt her hands
Together with a wailing shriek, and said:
'Stabb'd through the heart's affections to the heart!
Seethed like the kid in its own mother's milk!
Kill'd with a word worse than a life of blows!
I thought that he was gentle, being great;
O God, that I had loved a smaller man!   870
I should have found in him a greater heart.
O, I, that flattering my true passion, saw
The knights, the court, the King, dark in your light,
Who loved to make men darker than they are,
Because of that high pleasure which I had
To seat you sole upon my pedestal
Of worship—I am answer'd, and henceforth
The course of life that seem'd so flowery to me
With you for guide and master, only you,
Becomes the sea-cliff pathway broken short,   880
And ending in a ruin—nothing left
But into some low cave to crawl, and there,
If the wolf spare me, weep my life away,
Kill'd with inutterable unkindliness.'

She paused, she turn'd away, she hung her head,
The snake of gold slid from her hair, the braid
Slipt and uncoil'd itself, she wept afresh,
And the dark wood grew darker toward the storm
In silence, while his anger slowly died
Within him, till he let his wisdom go   890
For ease of heart, and half believed her true;

Call'd her to shelter in the hollow oak,
'Come from the storm,' and having no reply,
Gazed at the heaving shoulder and the face
Hand-hidden, as for utmost grief or shame;
Then thrice essay'd, by tenderest-touching terms,
To sleek her ruffled peace of mind, in vain.
At last she let herself be conquer'd by him,
And as the cageling newly flown returns,
The seeming-injured simple-hearted thing   900
Came to her old perch back, and settled there.
There while she sat, half-falling from his knees,
Half-nestled at his heart, and since he saw
The slow tear creep from her closed eyelid yet,
About her, more in kindness than in love,
The gentle wizard cast a shielding arm.
But she dislink'd herself at once and rose,
Her arms upon her breast across, and stood,
A virtuous gentlewoman deeply wrong'd,
Upright and flush'd before him; then she said: 910

'There must be now no passages of love
Betwixt us twain henceforward evermore;
Since, if I be what I am grossly call'd,
What should be granted which your own gross heart
Would reckon worth the taking? I will go.
In truth, but one thing now—better have died
Thrice than have ask'd it once—could make me stay—
That proof of trust—so often ask'd in vain!
How justly, after that vile term of yours,
I find with grief! I might believe you then,   920
Who knows? once more. Lo! what was once to me
Mere matter of the fancy, now hath grown
The vast necessity of heart and life.
Farewell; think gently of me, for I fear
My fate or folly, passing gayer youth
For one so old, must be to love thee still.
But ere I leave thee let me swear once more
That if I schemed against thy peace in this,
May yon just heaven, that darkens o'er me, send
One flash that, missing all things else, may make   930
My scheming brain a cinder, if I lie.'

Scarce had she ceased, when out of heaven a bolt—
For now the storm was close above them—struck,
Furrowing a giant oak, and javelining
With darted spikes and splinters of the wood
The dark earth round. He raised his eyes and saw
The tree that shone white-listed thro' the gloom.

But Vivien, fearing heaven had heard her oath,
And dazzled by the livid-flickering fork,
And deafen'd with the stammering cracks and claps   940
That follow'd, flying back and crying out,
'O Merlin, tho' you do not love me, save,
Yet save me!' clung to him and hugg'd him close;
And call'd him dear protector in her fright,
Nor yet forgot her practice in her fright,
But wrought upon his mood and hugg'd him close.
The pale blood of the wizard at her touch
Took gayer colors, like an opal warm'd.
She blamed herself for telling hearsay tales;
She shook from fear, and for her fault she wept   950
Of petulancy; she call'd him lord and liege,
Her seer, her bard, her silver star of eve,
Her God, her Merlin, the one passionate love
Of her whole life; and ever overhead
Bellow'd the tempest, and the rotten branch
Snapt in the rushing of the river-rain
Above them; and in change of glare and gloom
Her eyes and neck glittering went and came;
Till now the storm, its burst of passion spent,
Moaning and calling out of other lands,   960
Had left the ravaged woodland yet once more
To peace; and what should not have been had been,
For Merlin, overtalk'd and overworn,
Had yielded, told her all the charm, and slept.

      Then, in one moment, she put forth the charm
Of woven paces and of waving hands,
And in the hollow oak he lay as dead,
And lost to life and use and name and fame.

      Then crying, 'I have made his glory mine,'
And shrieking out, 'O fool!' the harlot leapt   970
Adown the forest, and the thicket closed
Behind her, and the forest echo'd 'fool.'

LANCELOT AND ELAINE

ELAINE the fair, Elaine the lovable,
Elaine, the lily maid of Astolat,
High in her chamber up a tower to the east
Guarded the sacred shield of Lancelot;
Which first she placed where morning's earliest ray
Might strike it, and awake her with the gleam;
Then fearing rust or soilure fashion'd for it

A case of silk, and braided thereupon
All the devices blazon'd on the shield
In their own tinct, and added, of her wit,   10
A border fantasy of branch and flower,
And yellow-throated nestling in the nest.
Nor rested thus content, but day by day,
Leaving her household and good father, climb'd
That eastern tower, and entering barr'd her door,
Stript off the case, and read the naked shield,
Now guess'd a hidden meaning in his arms,
Now made a pretty history to herself
Of every dint a sword had beaten in it,
And every scratch a lance had made upon it,   20
Conjecturing when and where: this cut is fresh,
That ten years back; this dealt him at Caerlyle,
That at Caerleon—this at Camelot—
And ah, God's mercy, what a stroke was there!
And here a thrust that might have kill'd, but God
Broke the strong lance, and roll'd his enemy down,
And saved him: so she lived in fantasy.

How came the lily maid by that good shield
Of Lancelot, she that knew not even his name?
He left it with her, when he rode to tilt   30
For the great diamond in the diamond jousts,
Which Arthur had ordain'd, and by that name
Had named them, since a diamond was the prize.

For Arthur, long before they crown'd him king,
Roving the trackless realms of Lyonnesse,
Had found a glen, gray boulder and black tarn.
A horror lived about the tarn, and clave
Like its own mists to all the mountain side;
For here two brothers, one a king, had met
And fought together, but their names were lost;   40
And each had slain his brother at a blow;
And down they fell and made the glen abhorr'd.
And there they lay till all their bones were bleach'd,
And lichen'd into color with the crags.
And he that once was king had on a crown
Of diamonds, one in front and four aside.
And Arthur came, and laboring up the pass,
All in a misty moonshine, unawares
Had trodden that crown'd skeleton, and the skull
Brake from the nape, and from the skull the crown   50
Roll'd into light, and turning on its rims
Fled like a glittering rivulet to the tarn.

And down the shingly scaur he plunged, and caught,
And set it on his head, and in his heart
Heard murmurs, 'Lo, thou likewise shalt be king.'

Thereafter, when a king, he had the gems
Pluck'd from the crown, and show'd them to his knights
Saying: 'These jewels, whereupon I chanced
Divinely, are the kingdom's, not the King's—
For public use. Henceforward let there be,   60
Once every year, a joust for one of these;
For so by nine years' proof we needs must learn
Which is our mightiest, and ourselves shall grow
In use of arms and manhood, till we drive
The heathen, who, some say, shall rule the land
Hereafter, which God hinder!' Thus he spoke.
And eight years past, eight jousts had been, and still
Had Lancelot won the diamond of the year,
With purpose to present them to the Queen
When all were won; but, meaning all at once   70
To snare her royal fancy with a boon
Worth half her realm, had never spoken word.

Now for the central diamond and the last
And largest, Arthur, holding then his court
Hard on the river nigh the place which now
Is this world's hugest, let proclaim a joust
At Camelot, and when the time drew nigh
Spake—for she had been sick—to Guinevere:
'Are you so sick, my Queen, you cannot move
To these fair jousts?' 'Yea, lord,' she said, 'ye know it.'   80
'Then will ye miss,' he answer'd, 'the great deeds
Of Lancelot, and his prowess in the lists,
A sight ye love to look on.' And the Queen
Lifted her eyes, and they dwelt languidly
On Lancelot, where he stood beside the King.
He, thinking that he read her meaning there,
'Stay with me, I am sick; my love is more
Than many diamonds,' yielded; and a heart
Love-loyal to the least wish of the Queen—
However much he yearn'd to make complete   90
The tale of diamonds for his destined boon—
Urged him to speak against the truth, and say,
'Sir King, mine ancient wound is hardly whole,
And lets me from the saddle;' and the King
Glanced first at him, then her, and went his way.
No sooner gone than suddenly she began:

'To blame, my lord Sir Lancelot, much to blame!
Why go ye not to these fair jousts? the knights
Are half of them our enemies, and the crowd
Will murmur, "Lo the shameless ones, who take   100
Their pastime now the trustful King is gone!" '
Then Lancelot, vext at having lied in vain:
'Are ye so wise? ye were not once so wise,
My Queen, that summer when ye loved me first.
Then of the crowd ye took no more account
Than of the myriad cricket of the mead,
When its own voice clings to each blade of grass,
And every voice is nothing. As to knights,
Them surely can I silence with all ease.
But now my loyal worship is allow'd   110
Of all men; many a bard, without offence,
Has link'd our names together in his lay,
Lancelot, the flower of bravery, Guinevere,
The pearl of beauty; and our knights at feast
Have pledged us in this union, while the King
Would listen smiling. How then? is there more?
Has Arthur spoken aught? or would yourself,
Now weary of my service and devoir,
Henceforth be truer to your faultless lord?'

She broke into a little scornful laugh: 120
'Arthur, my lord, Arthur, the faultless King,
That passionate perfection, my good lord—
But who can gaze upon the sun in heaven?
He never spake word of reproach to me,
He never had a glimpse of mine untruth,
He cares not for me. Only here to-day
There gleamed a vague suspicion in his eyes;
Some meddling rogue has tamper'd with him—else
Rapt in this fancy of his Table Round,
And swearing men to vows impossible,   130
To make them like himself; but, friend, to me
He is all fault who hath no fault at all.
For who loves me must have a touch of earth;
The low sun makes the color. I am yours,
Not Arthur's, as ye know, save by the bond.
And therefore hear my words: go to the jousts;
The tiny-trumpeting gnat can break our dream
When sweetest; and the vermin voices here
May buzz so loud—we scorn them, but they sting.'

Then answer'd Lancelot, the chief of knights: 140
'And with what face, after my pretext made,
Shall I appear, O Queen, at Camelot, I

Before a king who honors his own word
As if it were his God's?'

                           'Yea,' said the Queen,
'A moral child without the craft to rule,
Else had he not lost me; but listen to me,
If I must find you wit. We hear it said
That men go down before your spear at a touch,
But knowing you are Lancelot; your great name,
This conquers. Hide it therefore; go unknown.   150
Win! by this kiss you will; and our true King
Will then allow your pretext, O my knight,
As all for glory; for to speak him true,
Ye know right well, how meek soe'er he seem,
No keener hunter after glory breathes.
He loves it in his knights more than himself;
They prove to him his work. Win and return.'

    Then got Sir Lancelot suddenly to horse,
Wroth at himself. Not willing to be known,
He left the barren-beaten thoroughfare,   160
Chose the green path that show'd the rarer foot,
And there among the solitary downs,
Full often lost in fancy, lost his way;
Till as he traced a faintly-shadow'd track,
That all in loops and links among the dales
Ran to the Castle of Astolat, he saw
Fired from the west, far on a hill, the towers.
Thither he made, and blew the gateway horn.
Then came an old, dumb, myriad-wrinkled man,
Who let him into lodging and disarm'd.   170
And Lancelot marvell'd at the wordless man;
And issuing found the Lord of Astolat
With two strong sons, Sir Torre and Sir Lavaine,
Moving to meet him in the castle court;
And close behind them stept the lily maid
Elaine, his daughter; mother of the house
There was not. Some light jest among them rose
With laughter dying down as the great knight
Approach'd them; then the Lord of Astolat:
'Whence comest thou, my guest, and by what name   180
Livest between the lips? for by thy state
And presence I might guess thee chief of those,
After the King, who eat in Arthur's halls.
Him have I seen; the rest, his Table Round,
Known as they are, to me they are unknown.'

Then answer'd Lancelot, the chief of knights:
'Known am I, and of Arthur's hall, and known,
What I by mere mischance have brought, my shield.
But since I go to joust as one unknown
At Camelot for the diamond, ask me not; 190
Hereafter ye shall know me—and the shield—
I pray you lend me one, if such you have,
Blank, or at least with some device not mine.'

Then said the Lord of Astolat: 'Here is Torre's:
Hurt in his first tilt was my son, Sir Torre,
And so, God wot, his shield is blank enough.
His ye can have.' Then added plain Sir Torre,
'Yea, since I cannot use it, ye may have it.'
Here laugh'd the father saying: 'Fie, Sir Churl,
Is that an answer for a noble knight? 200
Allow him! but Lavaine, my younger here,
He is so full of lustihood, he will ride,
Joust for it, and win, and bring it in an hour,
And set it in this damsel's golden hair,
To make her thrice as wilful as before.'

'Nay, father, nay, good father, shame me not
Before this noble knight,' said young Lavaine,
'For nothing. Surely I but play'd on Torre,
He seem'd so sullen, vext he could not go;
A jest, no more! for, knight, the maiden dreamt 210
That some one put this diamond in her hand,
And that it was too slippery to be held,
And slipt and fell into some pool or stream,
The castle-well, belike; and then I said
That if I went and if I fought and won it—
But all was jest and joke among ourselves—
Then must she keep it safelier. All was jest.
But, father, give me leave, an if he will,
To ride to Camelot with this noble knight.
Win shall I not, but do my best to win; 220
Young as I am, yet would I do my best.'

'So ye will grace me,' answer'd Lancelot,
Smiling a moment, 'with your fellowship
O'er these waste downs whereon I lost myself,
Then were I glad of you as guide and friend;
And you shall win this diamond,—as I hear,
It is a fair large diamond,—if ye may,
And yield it to this maiden, if ye will.'
'A fair large diamond,' added plain Sir Torre,
'Such be for queens, and not for simple maids.' 230

Then she, who held her eyes upon the ground,
Elaine, and heard her name so tost about,
Flush'd slightly at the slight disparagement
Before the stranger knight, who, looking at her,
Full courtly, yet not falsely, thus return'd:
'If what is fair be but for what is fair,
And only queens are to be counted so,
Rash were my judgment then, who deem this maid
Might wear as fair a jewel as is on earth,
Not violating the bond of like to like.'   240

He spoke and ceased; the lily maid Elaine,
Won by the mellow voice before she look'd,
Lifted her eyes and read his lineaments.
The great and guilty love he bare the Queen,
In battle with the love he bare his lord,
Had marr'd his face, and mark'd it ere his time.
Another sinning on such heights with one,
The flower of all the west and all the world,
Had been the sleeker for it; but in him
His mood was often like a fiend, and rose   250
And drove him into wastes and solitudes
For agony, who was yet a living soul.
Marr'd as he was, he seem'd the goodliest man
That ever among ladies ate in hall,
And noblest, when she lifted up her eyes.
However marr'd, of more than twice her years,
Seam'd with an ancient sword-cut on the cheek,
And bruised and bronzed, she lifted up her eyes
And loved him, with that love which was her doom.

Then the great knight, the darling of the court,   260
Loved of the loveliest, into that rude hall
Stept with all grace, and not with half disdain
Hid under grace, as in a smaller time,
But kindly man moving among his kind;
Whom they with meats and vintage of their best
And talk and minstrel melody entertain'd.
And much they ask'd of court and Table Round,
And ever well and readily answer'd he;
But Lancelot, when they glanced at Guinevere,
Suddenly speaking of the wordless man,   270
Heard from the baron that, ten years before,
The heathen caught and reft him of his tongue.
'He learnt and warn'd me of their fierce design
Against my house, and him they caught and maim'd;
But I, my sons, and little daughter fled
From bonds or death, and dwelt among the woods

By the great river in a boatman's hut.
Dull days were those, till our good Arthur broke
The Pagan yet once more on Badon hill.'

'O, there, great lord, doubtless,' Lavaine said, rapt   280
By all the sweet and sudden passion of youth
Toward greatness in its elder, 'you have fought.
O, tell us—for we live apart—you know
Of Arthur's glorious wars.' And Lancelot spoke
And answer'd him at full, as having been
With Arthur in the fight which all day long
Rang by the white mouth of the violent Glem;
And in the four loud battles by the shore
Of Duglas; that on Bassa; then the war
That thunder'd in and out the gloomy skirts   290
Of Celidon the forest; and again
By Castle Gurnion, where the glorious King
Had on his cuirass worn our Lady's Head,
Carved of one emerald centred in a sun
Of silver rays, that lighten'd as he breathed;
And at Caerleon had he help'd his lord,
When the strong neighings of the wild White Horse
Set every gilded parapet shuddering;
And up in Agned-Cathregonion too,
And down the waste sand-shores of Trath Treroit,   300
Where many a heathen fell; 'and on the mount
Of Badon I myself beheld the King
Charge at the head of all his Table Round,
And all his legions crying Christ and him,
And break them; and I saw him, after, stand
High on a heap of slain, from spur to plume
Red as the rising sun with heathen blood,
And seeing me, with a great voice he cried,
"They are broken, they are broken!" for the King,
However mild he seems at home, nor cares   310
For triumph in our mimic wars, the jousts—
For if his own knight casts him down, he laughs,
Saying his knights are better men than he—
Yet in this heathen war the fire of God
Fills him. I never saw his like; there lives
No greater leader.'

        While he utter'd this,
Low to her own heart said the lily maid,
'Save your great self, fair lord;' and when he fell
From talk of war to traits of pleasantry—
Being mirthful he, but in a stately kind—   320
She still took note that when the living smile

Died from his lips, across him came a cloud
Of melancholy severe, from which again,
Whenever in her hovering to and fro
The lily maid had striven to make him cheer,
There brake a sudden-beaming tenderness
Of manners and of nature; and she thought
That all was nature, all, perchance, for her.
And all night long his face before her lived,
As when a painter, poring on a face,   330
Divinely thro' all hindrance finds the man
Behind it, and so paints him that his face,
The shape and color of a mind and life,
Lives for his children, ever at its best
And fullest; so the face before her lived,
Dark-splendid, speaking in the silence, full
Of noble things, and held her from her sleep,
Till rathe she rose, half-cheated in the thought
She needs must bid farewell to sweet Lavaine.
First as in fear, step after step, she stole   340
Down the long tower-stairs, hesitating.
Anon, she heard Sir Lancelot cry in the court,
'This shield, my friend, where is it?' and Lavaine
Past inward, as she came from out the tower.
There to his proud horse Lancelot turn'd, and smooth'd
The glossy shoulder, humming to himself.
Half-envious of the flattering hand, she drew
Nearer and stood. He look'd, and, more amazed
Than if seven men had set upon him, saw
The maiden standing in the dewy light.   350
He had not dream'd she was so beautiful.
Then came on him a sort of sacred fear,
For silent, tho' he greeted her, she stood
Rapt on his face as if it were a god's.
Suddenly flash'd on her a wild desire
That he should wear her favor at the tilt.
She braved a riotous heart in asking for it.
'Fair lord, whose name I know not—noble it is,
I well believe, the noblest—will you wear
My favor at this tourney?' 'Nay,' said he,   360
'Fair lady, since I never yet have worn
Favor of any lady in the lists.
Such is my wont, as those who know me know.'
'Yea, so,' she answer'd; 'then in wearing mine
Needs must be lesser likelihood, noble lord,
That those who know should know you.' And he turn'd
Her counsel up and down within his mind,
And found it true, and answer'd: 'True, my child.
Well, I will wear it; fetch it out to me.

What is it?' and she told him, 'A red sleeve   370
Broider'd with pearls,' and brought it. Then he bound
Her token on his helmet, with a smile
Saying, 'I never yet have done so much
For any maiden living,' and the blood
Sprang to her face and fill'd her with delight;
But left her all the paler when Lavaine
Returning brought the yet-unblazon'd shield,
His brother's, which he gave to Lancelot,
Who parted with his own to fair Elaine:
'Do me this grace, my child, to have my shield   380
In keeping till I come.' 'A grace to me,'
She answer'd, 'twice to-day. I am your squire!'
Whereat Lavaine said laughing: 'Lily maid,
For fear our people call you lily maid
In earnest, let me bring your color back;
Once, twice, and thrice. Now get you hence to bed;'
So kiss'd her, and Sir Lancelot his own hand,
And thus they moved away. She staid a minute,
Then made a sudden step to the gate, and there—
Her bright hair blown about the serious face   390
Yet rosy-kindled with her brother's kiss—
Paused by the gateway, standing near the shield
In silence, while she watch'd their arms far-off
Sparkle, until they dipt below the downs.
Then to her tower she climb'd, and took the shield,
There kept it, and so lived in fantasy.

Meanwhile the new companions past away
Far o'er the long backs of the bushless downs,
To where Sir Lancelot knew there lived a knight
Not far from Camelot, now for forty years   400
A hermit, who had pray'd, labor'd and pray'd,
And ever laboring had scoop'd himself
In the white rock a chapel and a hall
On massive columns, like a shore-cliff cave,
And cells and chambers. All were fair and dry;
The green light from the meadows underneath
Struck up and lived along the milky roofs;
And in the meadows tremulous aspen-trees
And poplars made a noise of falling showers.
And thither wending there that night they bode.   410

But when the next day broke from underground,
And shot red fire and shadows thro' the cave,
They rose, heard mass, broke fast, and rode away.
Then Lancelot saying, 'Hear, but hold my name
Hidden, you ride with Lancelot of the Lake,'

Abash'd Lavaine, whose instant reverence,
Dearer to true young hearts than their own praise,
But left him leave to stammer, 'Is it indeed?'
And after muttering, 'The great Lancelot,'
At last he got his breath and answer'd: 'One,   420
One have I seen—that other, our liege lord,
The dread Pendragon, Britain's King of kings,
Of whom the people talk mysteriously,
He will be there—then were I stricken blind
That minute, I might say that I had seen.'

So spake Lavaine, and when they reach'd the lists
By Camelot in the meadow, let his eyes
Run thro' the peopled gallery which half round
Lay like a rainbow fallen upon the grass,
Until they found the clear-faced King, who sat   430
Robed in red samite, easily to be known,
Since to his crown the golden dragon clung,
And down his robe the dragon writhed in gold,
And from the carven-work behind him crept
Two dragons gilded, sloping down to make
Arms for his chair, while all the rest of them
Thro' knots and loops and folds innumerable
Fled ever thro' the woodwork, till they found
The new design wherein they lost themselves,
Yet with all ease, so tender was the work,   440
And, in the costly canopy o'er him set,
Blazed the last diamond of the nameless king.

Then Lancelot answer'd young Lavaine and said:
'Me you call great; mine is the firmer seat,
The truer lance; but there is many a youth
Now crescent, who will come to all I am
And overcome it; and in me there dwells
No greatness, save it be some far-off touch
Of greatness to know well I am not great.
There is the man.' And Lavaine gaped upon him   450
As on a thing miraculous, and anon
The trumpets blew; and then did either side,
They that assail'd, and they that held the lists,
Set lance in rest, strike spur, suddenly move,
Meet in the midst, and there so furiously
Shock that a man far-off might well perceive,
If any man that day were left afield,
The hard earth shake, and a low thunder of arms.
And Lancelot bode a little, till he saw
Which were the weaker; then he hurl'd into it   460

Against the stronger. Little need to speak
Of Lancelot in his glory! King, duke, earl,
Count, baron—whom he smote, he overthrew.

But in the field were Lancelot's kith and kin,
Ranged with the Table Round that held the lists,
Strong men, and wrathful that a stranger knight
Should do and almost overdo the deeds
Of Lancelot; and one said to the other, 'Lo!
What is he? I do not mean the force alone—
The grace and versatility of the man!   470
Is it not Lancelot?' 'When has Lancelot worn
Favor of any lady in the lists?
Not such his wont, as we that know him know.'
'How then? who then?' a fury seized them all,
A fiery family passion for the name
Of Lancelot, and a glory one with theirs.
They couch'd their spears and prick'd their steeds, and thus,
Their plumes driven backward by the wind they made
In moving, all together down upon him
Bare, as a wild wave in the wide North Sea,   480
Green-glimmering toward the summit, bears, with all
Its stormy crests that smoke against the skies,
Down on a bark, and overbears the bark
And him that helms it; so they overbore
Sir Lancelot and his charger, and a spear
Down-glancing lamed the charger, and a spear
Prick'd sharply his own cuirass, and the head
Pierced thro' his side, and there snapt and remain'd.

Then Sir Lavaine did well and worshipfully.
He bore a knight of old repute to the earth,   490
And brought his horse to Lancelot where he lay.
He up the side, sweating with agony, got,
But thought to do while he might yet endure,
And being lustily holpen by the rest,
His party,—tho' it seem'd half-miracle
To those he fought with,—drave his kith and kin,
And all the Table Round that held the lists,
Back to the barrier; then the trumpets blew
Proclaiming his the prize who wore the sleeve
Of scarlet and the pearls; and all the knights,   500
His party, cried, 'Advance and take thy prize
The diamond;' but he answer'd: 'Diamond me
No diamonds! for God's love, a little air!
Prize me no prizes, for my prize is death!
Hence will I, and I charge you, follow me not.'

He spoke, and vanish'd suddenly from the field
With young Lavaine into the poplar grove.
There from his charger down he slid, and sat,
Gasping to Sir Lavaine, 'Draw the lance-head.'
'Ah, my sweet lord Sir Lancelot,' said Lavaine,   510
'I dread me, if I draw it, you will die.'
But he, 'I die already with it; draw—
Draw,'—and Lavaine drew, and Sir Lancelot gave
A marvellous great shriek and ghastly groan,
And half his blood burst forth, and down he sank
For the pure pain, and wholly swoon'd away.
Then came the hermit out and bare him in,
There stanch'd his wound; and there, in daily doubt
Whether to live or die, for many a week
Hid from the wild world's rumor by the grove   520
Of poplars with their noise of falling showers,
And ever-tremulous aspen-trees, he lay.

But on that day when Lancelot fled the lists,
His party, knights of utmost North and West,
Lords of waste marches, kings of desolate isles,
Came round their great Pendragon, saying to him,
'Lo, Sire, our knight, thro' whom we won the day,
Hath gone sore wounded, and hath left his prize
Untaken, crying that his prize is death.'
'Heaven hinder,' said the King, 'that such an one,   530
So great a knight as we have seen to-day—
He seem'd to me another Lancelot—
Yea, twenty times I thought him Lancelot—
He must not pass uncared for. Wherefore rise,
O Gawain, and ride forth and find the knight.
Wounded and wearied, needs must he be near.
I charge you that you get at once to horse.
And, knights and kings, there breathes not one of you
Will deem this prize of ours is rashly given;
His prowess was too wondrous. We will do him   540
No customary honor; since the knight
Came not to us, of us to claim the prize,
Ourselves will send it after. Rise and take
This diamond, and deliver it, and return,
And bring us where he is, and how he fares,
And cease not from your quest until ye find.'

So saying, from the carven flower above,
To which it made a restless heart, he took
And gave the diamond. Then from where he sat
At Arthur's right, with smiling face arose,   550
With smiling face and frowning heart, a prince

In the mid might and flourish of his May,
Gawain, surnamed the Courteous, fair and strong,
And after Lancelot, Tristram, and Geraint,
And Gareth, a good knight, but therewithal
Sir Modred's brother, and the child of Lot,
Nor often loyal to his word, and now
Wroth that the King's command to sally forth
In quest of whom he knew not, made him leave
The banquet and concourse of knights and kings.   560

So all in wrath he got to horse and went;
While Arthur to the banquet, dark in mood,
Past, thinking, 'Is it Lancelot who hath come
Despite the wound he spake of, all for gain
Of glory, and hath added wound to wound,
And ridden away to die?' So fear'd the King,
And, after two days' tarriance there, return'd.
Then when he saw the Queen, embracing ask'd,
'Love, are you yet so sick?' 'Nay, lord,' she said.
'And where is Lancelot?' Then the Queen amazed,   570
'Was he not with you? won he not your prize?'
'Nay, but one like him.' 'Why, that like was he.'
And when the King demanded how she knew,
Said: 'Lord, no sooner had ye parted from us
Than Lancelot told me of a common talk
That men went down before his spear at a touch,
But knowing he was Lancelot; his great name
Conquer'd; and therefore would he hide his name
From all men, even the King, and to this end
Had made the pretext of a hindering wound,   580
That he might joust unknown of all, and learn
If his old prowess were in aught decay'd;
And added, "Our true Arthur, when he learns,
Will well allow my pretext, as for gain
Of purer glory." '

Then replied the King:
'Far lovelier in our Lancelot had it been,
In lieu of idly dallying with the truth,
To have trusted me as he hath trusted thee.
Surely his King and most familiar friend
Might well have kept his secret. True, indeed,   590
Albeit I know my knights fantastical,
So fine a fear in our large Lancelot
Must needs have moved my laughter; now remains
But little cause for laughter. His own kin—
Ill news, my Queen, for all who love him, this!—
His kith and kin, not knowing, set upon him;

So that he went sore wounded from the field.
Yet good news too; for goodly hopes are mine
That Lancelot is no more a lonely heart.
He wore, against his wont, upon his helm   600
A sleeve of scarlet, broider'd with great pearls,
Some gentle maiden's gift.'

                           'Yea, lord,' she said,
'Thy hopes are mine,' and saying that, she choked,
And sharply turn'd about to hide her face,
Past to her chamber, and there flung herself
Down on the great King's couch, and writhed upon it,
And clench'd her fingers till they bit the palm,
And shriek'd out 'Traitor!' to the unhearing wall,
Then flash'd into wild tears, and rose again,
And moved about her palace, proud and pale.   610

    Gawain the while thro' all the region round
Rode with his diamond, wearied of the quest,
Touch'd at all points except the poplar grove,
And came at last, tho' late, to Astolat;
Whom glittering in enamell'd arms the maid
Glanced at, and cried, 'What news from Camelot, lord?
What of the knight with the red sleeve?' 'He won.'
'I knew it,' she said. 'But parted from the jousts
Hurt in the side;' whereat she caught her breath.
Thro' her own side she felt the sharp lance go.   620
Thereon she smote her hand; wellnigh she swoon'd.
And, while he gazed wonderingly at her, came
The Lord of Astolat out, to whom the prince
Reported who he was, and on what quest
Sent, that he bore the prize and could not find
The victor, but had ridden a random round
To seek him, and had wearied of the search.
To whom the Lord of Astolat: 'Bide with us,
And ride no more at random, noble prince!
Here was the knight, and here he left a shield;   630
This will he send or come for. Furthermore
Our son is with him; we shall hear anon,
Needs must we hear.' To this the courteous prince
Accorded with his wonted courtesy,
Courtesy with a touch of traitor in it,
And staid; and cast his eyes on fair Elaine;
Where could be found face daintier? then her shape
From forehead down to foot, perfect—again
From foot to forehead exquisitely turn'd:
'Well—if I bide, lo! this wild flower for me!'   640
And oft they met among the garden yews,

And there he set himself to play upon her
With sallying wit, free flashes from a height
Above her, graces of the court, and songs,
Sighs, and low smiles, and golden eloquence
And amorous adulation, till the maid
Rebell'd against it, saying to him: 'Prince,
O loyal nephew of our noble King,
Why ask you not to see the shield he left,
Whence you might learn his name? Why slight your King,   650
And lose the quest he sent you on, and prove
No surer than our falcon yesterday,
Who lost the hern we slipt her at, and went
To all the winds?' 'Nay, by mine head,' said he,
'I lose it, as we lose the lark in heaven,
O damsel, in the light of your blue eyes;
But an ye will it let me see the shield.'
And when the shield was brought, and Gawain saw
Sir Lancelot's azure lions, crown'd with gold,
Ramp in the field, he smote his thigh, and mock'd: 660
'Right was the King! our Lancelot! that true man!'
'And right was I,' she answer'd merrily, 'I,
Who dream'd my knight the greatest knight of all.'
'And if *I* dream'd,' said Gawain, 'that you love
This greatest knight, your pardon! lo, ye know it!
Speak therefore; shall I waste myself in vain?'
Full simple was her answer: 'What know I?
My brethren have been all my fellowship;
And I, when often they have talk'd of love,
Wish'd it had been my mother, for they talk'd,   670
Meseem'd, of what they knew not; so myself—
I know not if I know what true love is,
But if I know, then, if I love not him,
I know there is none other I can love.'
'Yea, by God's death,' said he, 'ye love him well,
But would not, knew ye what all others know,
And whom he loves.' 'So be it,' cried Elaine,
And lifted her fair face and moved away;
But he pursued her, calling, 'Stay a little!
One golden minute's grace! he wore your sleeve.   680
Would he break faith with one I may not name?
Must our true man change like a leaf at last?
Nay—like enow. Why then, far be it from me
To cross our mighty Lancelot in his loves!
And, damsel, for I deem you know full well
Where your great knight is hidden, let me leave
My quest with you; the diamond also—here!
For if you love, it will be sweet to give it;
And if he love, it will be sweet to have it

From your own hand; and whether he love or not,
A diamond is a diamond. Fare you well
A thousand times!—a thousand times farewell!
Yet, if he love, and his love hold, we two
May meet at court hereafter! there, I think,
So ye will learn the courtesies of the court,
We two shall know each other.'

                      Then he gave,
And slightly kiss'd the hand to which he gave,
The diamond, and all wearied of the quest
Leapt on his horse, and carolling as he went
A true-love ballad, lightly rode away.

    Thence to the court he past; there told the King
What the King knew, 'Sir Lancelot is the knight.'
And added, 'Sire, my liege, so much I learnt,
But fail'd to find him, tho' I rode all round
The region; but I lighted on the maid
Whose sleeve he wore. She loves him; and to her,
Deeming our courtesy is the truest law,
I gave the diamond. She will render it;
For by mine head she knows his hiding-place.'

    The seldom-frowning King frown'd, and replied,
'Too courteous truly! ye shall go no more
On quest of mine, seeing that ye forget
Obedience is the courtesy due to kings.'

    He spake and parted. Wroth, but all in awe,
For twenty strokes of the blood, without a word,
Linger'd that other, staring after him;
Then shook his hair, strode off, and buzz'd abroad
About the maid of Astolat, and her love.
All ears were prick'd at once, all tongues were loosed:
'The maid of Astolat loves Sir Lancelot,
Sir Lancelot loves the maid of Astolat.'
Some read the King's face, some the Queen's, and all
Had marvel what the maid might be, but most
Predoom'd her as unworthy. One old dame
Came suddenly on the Queen with the sharp news.
She, that had heard the noise of it before,
But sorrowing Lancelot should have stoop'd so low,
Marr'd her friend's aim with pale tranquillity.
So ran the tale like fire about the court,
Fire in dry stubble a nine-days' wonder flared;
Till even the knights at banquet twice or thrice
Forgot to drink to Lancelot and the Queen,

And pledging Lancelot and the lily maid
Smiled at each other, while the Queen, who sat
With lips severely placid, felt the knot
Climb in her throat, and with her feet unseen
Crush'd the wild passion out against the floor
Beneath the banquet, where the meats became
As wormwood and she hated all who pledged.

But far away the maid in Astolat,   740
Her guiltless rival, she that ever kept
The one-day-seen Sir Lancelot in her heart,
Crept to her father, while he mused alone,
Sat on his knee, stroked his gray face and said:
'Father, you call me wilful, and the fault
Is yours who let me have my will, and now,
Sweet father, will you let me lose my wits?'
'Nay,' said he, 'surely.' 'Wherefore, let me hence,'
She answer'd, 'and find out our dear Lavaine.'
'Ye will not lose your wits for dear Lavaine.   750
Bide,' answer'd he: 'we needs must hear anon
Of him, and of that other.' 'Ay,' she said,
'And of that other, for I needs must hence
And find that other, wheresoë'er he be,
And with mine own hand give his diamond to him,
Lest I be found as faithless in the quest
As yon proud prince who left the quest to me.
Sweet father, I behold him in my dreams
Gaunt as it were the skeleton of himself,
Death-pale, for the lack of gentle maiden's aid.   760
The gentler-born the maiden, the more bound,
My father, to be sweet and serviceable
To noble knights in sickness, as ye know,
When these have worn their tokens. Let me hence,
I pray you.' Then her father nodding said:
'Ay, ay, the diamond. Wit ye well, my child,
Right fain were I to learn this knight were whole,
Being our greatest. Yea, and you must give it—
And sure I think this fruit is hung too high
For any mouth to gape for save a queen's—   770
Nay, I mean nothing; so then, get you gone,
Being so very wilful you must go.'

Lightly, her suit allow'd, she slipt away,
And while she made her ready for her ride
Her father's latest word humm'd in her ear,
'Being so very wilful you must go,'
And changed itself and echo'd in her heart,
'Being so very wilful you must die.'

But she was happy enough and shook it off,
As we shake off the bee that buzzes at us;   780
And in her heart she answer'd it and said,
'What matter, so I help him back to life?'
Then far away with good Sir Torre for guide
Rode o'er the long backs of the bushless downs
To Camelot, and before the city-gates
Came on her brother with a happy face
Making a roan horse caper and curvet
For pleasure all about a field of flowers;
Whom when she saw, 'Lavaine', she cried, 'Lavaine,
How fares my lord Sir Lancelot?' He amazed,   790
'Torre and Elaine! why here? Sir Lancelot!
How know ye my lord's name is Lancelot?'
But when the maid had told him all her tale,
Then turn'd Sir Torre, and being in his moods
Left them, and under the strange-statued gate,
Where Arthur's wars were render'd mystically,
Past up the still rich city to his kin,
His own far blood, which dwelt at Camelot;
And her, Lavaine across the poplar grove
Led to the caves. There first she saw the casque   800
Of Lancelot on the wall; her scarlet sleeve,
Tho' carved and cut, and half the pearls away,
Stream'd from it still; and in her heart she laugh'd,
Because he had not loosed it from his helm,
But meant once more perchance to tourney in it.
And when they gain'd the cell wherein he slept,
His battle-writhen arms and mighty hands
Lay naked on the wolf-skin, and a dream
Of dragging down his enemy made them move.
Then she that saw him lying unsleek, unshorn,   810
Gaunt as it were the skeleton of himself,
Utter'd a little tender dolorous cry.
The sound not wonted in a place so still
Woke the sick knight, and while he roll'd his eyes
Yet blank from sleep, she started to him, saying,
'Your prize the diamond sent you by the King.'
His eyes glisten'd; she fancied, 'Is it for me?'
And when the maid had told him all the tale
Of king and prince, the diamond sent, the quest
Assign'd to her not worthy of it, she knelt   820
Full lowly by the corners of his bed,
And laid the diamond in his open hand.
Her face was near, and as we kiss the child
That does the task assign'd, he kiss'd her face.
At once she slipt like water to the floor.
'Alas,' he said, 'your ride hath wearied you.

Rest must you have.' 'No rest for me,' she said;
'Nay, for near you, fair lord, I am at rest.'
What might she mean by that? his large black eyes,
Yet larger thro' his leanness, dwelt upon her,   830
Till all her heart's sad secret blazed itself
In the heart's colors on her simple face;
And Lancelot look'd and was perplext in mind,
And being weak in body said no more,
But did not love the color; woman's love,
Save one, he not regarded, and so turn'd
Sighing, and feign'd a sleep until he slept.

Then rose Elaine and glided thro' the fields,
And past beneath the weirdly-sculptured gates
Far up the dim rich city to her kin;   840
There bode the night, but woke with dawn, and past
Down thro' the dim rich city to the fields,
Thence to the cave. So day by day she past
In either twilight ghost-like to and fro
Gliding, and every day she tended him,
And likewise many a night; and Lancelot
Would, tho' he call'd his wound a little hurt
Whereof he should be quickly whole, at times
Brain-feverous in his heat and agony, seem
Uncourteous, even he. But the meek maid   850
Sweetly forbore him ever, being to him
Meeker than any child to a rough nurse,
Milder than any mother to a sick child,
And never woman yet, since man's first fall,
Did kindlier unto man, but her deep love
Upbore her; till the hermit, skill'd in all
The simples and the science of that time,
Told him that her fine care had saved his life.
And the sick man forgot her simple blush,
Would call her friend and sister, sweet Elaine,   860
Would listen for her coming and regret
Her parting step, and held her tenderly,
And loved her with all love except the love
Of man and woman when they love their best,
Closest and sweetest, and had died the death
In any knightly fashion for her sake.
And peradventure had he seen her first
She might have made this and that other world
Another world for the sick man; but now
The shackles of an old love straiten'd him,   870
His honor rooted in dishonor stood,
And faith unfaithful kept him falsely true.

Yet the great knight in his mid-sickness made
Full many a holy vow and pure resolve.
These, as but born of sickness, could not live;
For when the blood ran lustier in him again,
Full often the bright image of one face,
Making a treacherous quiet in his heart,
Dispersed his resolution like a cloud.
Then if the maiden, while that ghostly grace   880
Beam'd on his fancy, spoke, he answer'd not,
Or short and coldly, and she knew right well
What the rough sickness meant, but what this meant
She knew not, and the sorrow dimm'd her sight,
And drave her ere her time across the fields
Far into the rich city, where alone
She murmur'd, 'Vain, in vain! it cannot be.
He will not love me. How then? must I die?'
Then as a little helpless innocent bird,
That has but one plain message of few notes,   890
Will sing the simple passage o'er and o'er
For all an April morning, till the ear
Wearies to hear it, so the simple maid
Went half the night repeating, 'Must I die?'
And now to right she turn'd, and now to left,
And found no ease in turning or in rest;
And 'Him or death,' she mutter'd, 'death or him,'
Again and like a burthen, 'Him or death.'

But when Sir Lancelot's deadly hurt was whole,
To Astolat returning rode the three.   900
There morn by morn, arraying her sweet self
In that wherein she deem'd she look'd her best,
She came before Sir Lancelot, for she thought,
'If I be loved, these are my festal robes,
If not, the victim's flowers before he fall.'
And Lancelot ever prest upon the maid
That she should ask some goodly gift of him
For her own self or hers: 'and do not shun
To speak the wish most near to your true heart;
Such service have ye done me that I make   910
My will of yours, and prince and lord am I
In mine own land, and what I will I can.'
Then like a ghost she lifted up her face,
But like a ghost without the power to speak.
And Lancelot saw that she withheld her wish,
And bode among them yet a little space
Till he should learn it; and one morn it chanced
He found her in among the garden yews,

And said, 'Delay no longer, speak your wish,
Seeing I go to-day.' Then out she brake: 920
'Going? and we shall never see you more.
And I must die for want of one bold word.'
'Speak; that I live to hear,' he said, 'is yours.'
Then suddenly and passionately she spoke:
'I have gone mad. I love you; let me die.'
'Ah, sister,' answer'd Lancelot, 'what is this?'
And innocently extending her white arms,
'Your love,' she said, 'your love—to be your wife.'
And Lancelot answer'd, 'Had I chosen to wed,
I had been wedded earlier, sweet Elaine;   930
But now there never will be wife of mine.'
'No, no,' she cried, 'I care not to be wife,
But to be with you still, to see your face,
To serve you, and to follow you thro' the world.'
And Lancelot answer'd: 'Nay, the world, the world,
All ear and eye, with such a stupid heart
To interpret ear and eye, and such a tongue
To blare its own interpretation—nay,
Full ill then should I quit your brother's love,
And your good father's kindness.' And she said,   940
'Not to be with you, not to see your face—
Alas for me then, my good days are done!'
'Nay, noble maid,' he answer'd, 'ten times nay!
This is not love, but love's first flash in youth,
Most common; yea, I know it of mine own self,
And you yourself will smile at your own self
Hereafter, when you yield your flower of life
To one more fitly yours, not thrice your age.
And then will I, for true you are and sweet
Beyond mine old belief in womanhood,   950
More specially should your good knight be poor,
Endow you with broad land and territory
Even to the half my realm beyond the seas,
So that would make you happy; furthermore,
Even to the death, as tho' ye were my blood,
In all your quarrels will I be your knight.
This will I do, dear damsel, for your sake,
And more than this I cannot.'

                               While he spoke
She neither blush'd nor shook, but deathly-pale
Stood grasping what was nearest, then replied,   960
'Of all this will I nothing;' and so fell,
And thus they bore her swooning to her tower.

Then spake, to whom thro' those black walls of yew
Their talk had pierced, her father: 'Ay, a flash,
I fear me, that will strike my blossom dead.
Too courteous are ye, fair Lord Lancelot.
I pray you, use some rough discourtesy
To blunt or break her passion.'

                    Lancelot said,
'That were against me; what I can I will;'
And there that day remain'd, and toward even   970
Sent for his shield. Full meekly rose the maid,
Stript off the case, and gave the naked shield;
Then, when she heard his horse upon the stones,
Unclasping flung the casement back, and look'd
Down on his helm, from which her sleeve had gone.
And Lancelot knew the little clinking sound;
And she by tact of love was well aware
That Lancelot knew that she was looking at him.
And yet he glanced not up, nor waved his hand,
Nor bade farewell, but sadly rode away.   980
This was the one discourtesy that he used.

So in her tower alone the maiden sat.
His very shield was gone; only the case,
Her own poor work, her empty labor, left.
But still she heard him, still his picture form'd
And grew between her and the pictured wall.
Then came her father, saying in low tones,
'Have comfort,' whom she greeted quietly.
Then came her brethren saying 'Peace to thee,
Sweet sister,' whom she answer'd with all calm.   990
But when they left her to herself again,
Death, like a friend's voice from a distant field
Approaching thro' the darkness, call'd; the owls
Wailing had power upon her, and she mixt
Her fancies with the sallow-rifted glooms
Of evening and the moanings of the wind.

And in those days she made a little song,
And call'd her song 'The Song of Love and Death,'
And sang it; sweetly could she make and sing.

     'Sweet is true love tho' given in vain, in vain;   1000
     And sweet is death who puts an end to pain.
     I know not which is sweeter, no, not I.

     'Love, art thou sweet? then bitter death must be.
     Love, thou art bitter; sweet is death to me.
     O Love, if death be sweeter, let me die.

'Sweet love, that seems not made to fade away;
Sweet death, that seems to make us loveless clay;
I know not which is sweeter, no, not I.

'I fain would follow love, if that could be;
I needs must follow death, who calls for me;   1010
Call and I follow, I follow! let me die.'

High with the last line scaled her voice, and this,
All in a fiery dawning wild with wind
That shook her tower, the brothers heard, and thought
With shuddering, 'Hark the Phantom of the house
That ever shrieks before a death,' and call'd
The father, and all three in hurry and fear
Ran to her, and lo! the blood-red light of dawn
Flared on her face, she shrilling, 'Let me die!'

As when we dwell upon a word we know,   1020
Repeating, till the word we know so well
Becomes a wonder, and we know not why,
So dwelt the father on her face, and thought,
'Is this Elaine?' till back the maiden fell,
Then gave a languid hand to each, and lay,
Speaking a still good-morrow with her eyes.
At last she said: "Sweet brothers, yester-night
I seem'd a curious little maid again,
As happy as when we dwelt among the woods
And when ye used to take me with the flood   1030
Up the great river in the boatman's boat.
Only ye would not pass beyond the cape
That has the poplar on it; there ye fixt
Your limit, oft returning with the tide.
And yet I cried because ye would not pass
Beyond it, and far up the shining flood
Until we found the palace of the King.
And yet ye would not; but this night I dream'd
That I was all alone upon the flood,
And then I said, "Now shall I have my will;"   1040
And there I woke, but still the wish remain'd.
So let me hence that I may pass at last
Beyond the poplar and far up the flood,
Until I find the palace of the King.
There will I enter in among them all,
And no man there will dare to mock at me;
But there the fine Gawain will wonder at me,
And there the great Sir Lancelot muse at me;
Gawain, who bade a thousand farewells to me,
Lancelot, who coldly went, nor bade me one.   1050
And there the King will know me and my love,

And there the Queen herself will pity me,
And all the gentle court will welcome me,
And after my long voyage I shall rest!'

'Peace,' said her father, 'O my child, ye seem
Light-headed, for what force is yours to go
So far, being sick? and wherefore would ye look
On this proud fellow again, who scorns us all?'
Then the rough Torre began to heave and move,   1060
And bluster into stormy sobs and say:
'I never loved him; an I meet with him,
I care not howsoever great he be,
Then will I strike at him and strike him down.
Give me good fortune, I will strike him dead,
For this discomfort he hath done the house.'

To whom the gentle sister made reply:
'Fret not yourself, dear brother, nor be wroth,
Seeing it is no more Sir Lancelot's fault
Not to love me than it is mine to love
Him of all men who seems to me the highest.'   1070

'Highest?' the father answer'd, echoing 'highest?'—
He meant to break the passion in her—'nay,
Daughter, I know not what you call the highest;
But this I know, for all the people know it,
He loves the Queen, and in an open shame,
And she returns his love in open shame;
If this be high, what is it to be low?'

Then spake the lily maid of Astolat:
'Sweet father, all too faint and sick am I
For anger. These are slanders; never yet   1080
Was noble man but made ignoble talk.
He makes no friend who never made a foe.
But now it is my glory to have loved
One peerless, without stain; so let me pass,
My father, howsoe'er I seem to you,
Not all unhappy, having loved God's best
And greatest, tho' my love had no return.
Yet, seeing you desire your child to live,
Thanks, but you work against your own desire,
For if I could believe the things you say   1090
I should but die the sooner; wherefore cease,
Sweet father, and bid call the ghostly man
Hither, and let me shrive me clean and die.'

So when the ghostly man had come and gone,
She, with a face bright as for sin forgiven,
Besought Lavaine to write as she devised
A letter, word for word; and when he ask'd,
'Is it for Lancelot, is it for my dear lord?
Then will I bear it gladly;' she replied,
'For Lancelot and the Queen and all the world,   1100
But I myself must bear it.' Then he wrote
The letter she devised; which being writ
And folded, 'O sweet father, tender and true,
Deny me not,' she said—'ye never yet
Denied my fancies—this, however strange,
My latest. Lay the letter in my hand
A little ere I die, and close the hand
Upon it; I shall guard it even in death.
And when the heat has gone from out my heart,
Then take the little bed on which I died   1110
For Lancelot's love, and deck it like the Queen's
For richness, and me also like the Queen
In all I have of rich, and lay me on it.
And let there be prepared a chariot-bier
To take me to the river, and a barge
Be ready on the river, clothed in black.
I go in state to court, to meet the Queen.
There surely I shall speak for mine own self,
And none of you can speak for me so well.
And therefore let our dumb old man alone   1120
Go with me; he can steer and row, and he
Will guide me to that palace, to the doors.'

She ceased. Her father promised; whereupon
She grew so cheerful that they deem'd her death
Was rather in the fantasy than the blood.
But ten slow mornings past, and on the eleventh
Her father laid the letter in her hand,
And closed the hand upon it, and she died.
So that day there was dole in Astolat.

But when the next sun brake from underground,   1130
Then, those two brethren slowly with bent brows
Accompanying, the sad chariot-bier
Past like a shadow thro' the field, that shone
Full-summer, to that stream whereon the barge,
Pall'd all its length in blackest samite, lay.
There sat the lifelong creature of the house,
Loyal, the dumb old servitor, on deck,
Winking his eyes, and twisted all his face.
So those two brethren from the chariot took

And on the black decks laid her in her bed,   1140
Set in her hand a lily, o'er her hung
The silken case with braided blazonings,
And kiss'd her quiet brows, and saying to her,
'Sister, farewell forever,' and again,
'Farewell, sweet sister,' parted all in tears.
Then rose the dumb old servitor, and the dead,
Oar'd by the dumb, went upward with the flood—
In her right hand the lily, in her left
The letter—all her bright hair streaming down—
And all the coverlid was cloth of gold   1150
Drawn to her waist, and she herself in white
All but her face, and that clear-featured face
Was lovely, for she did not seem as dead,
But fast asleep, and lay as tho' she smiled.

     That day Sir Lancelot at the palace craved
Audience of Guinevere, to give at last
The price of half a realm, his costly gift,
Hard-won and hardly won with bruise and blow,
With deaths of others, and almost his own,
The nine-years-fought-for diamonds; for he saw   1160
One of her house, and sent him to the Queen
Bearing his wish, whereto the Queen agreed
With such and so unmoved a majesty
She might have seem'd her statue, but that he,
Low-drooping till he wellnigh kiss'd her feet
For loyal awe, saw with a sidelong eye
The shadow of some piece of pointed lace,
In the Queen's shadow, vibrate on the walls,
And parted, laughing in his courtly heart.

     All in an oriel on the summer side,   1170
Vine-clad, of Arthur's palace toward the stream,
They met, and Lancelot kneeling utter'd: 'Queen,
Lady, my liege, in whom I have my joy,
Take, what I had not won except for you,
These jewels, and make me happy, making them
An armlet for the roundest arm on earth,
Or necklace for a neck to which the swan's
Is tawnier than her cygnet's. These are words;
Your beauty is your beauty, and I sin
In speaking, yet O, grant my worship of it   1180
Words, as we grant grief tears. Such sin in words
Perchance, we both can pardon; but, my Queen,
I hear of rumors flying thro' your court.
Our bond, as not the bond of man and wife,
Should have in it an absoluter trust

To make up that defect: let rumors be.
When did not rumors fly? these, as I trust
That you trust me in your own nobleness,
I may not well believe that you believe.'

While thus he spoke, half turn'd away, the Queen   1190
Brake from the vast oriel-embowering vine
Leaf after leaf, and tore, and cast them off,
Till all the place whereon she stood was green;
Then, when he ceased, in one cold passive hand
Received at once and laid aside the gems
There on a table near her, and replied:

'It may be I am quicker of belief
Than you believe me, Lancelot of the Lake,
Our bond is not the bond of man and wife.
This good is in it, whatsoe'er of ill,   1200
It can be broken easier. I for you
This many a year have done despite and wrong
To one whom ever in my heart of hearts
I did acknowledge nobler. What are these?
Diamonds for me! they had been thrice their worth
Being your gift, had you not lost your own.
To loyal hearts the value of all gifts
Must vary as the giver's. Not for me!
For her! for your new fancy. Only this
Grant me, I pray you; have your joys apart.   1210
I doubt not that, however changed, you keep
So much of what is graceful; and myself
Would shun to break those bounds of courtesy
In which as Arthur's Queen I move and rule,
So cannot speak my mind. An end to this!
A strange one! yet I take it with Amen.
So pray you, add my diamonds to her pearls;
Deck her with these; tell her, she shines me down:
An armlet for an arm to which the Queen's
Is haggard, or a necklace for a neck   1220
O, as much fairer—as a faith once fair
Was richer than these diamonds—hers not mine—
Nay, by the mother of our Lord himself,
Or hers or mine, mine now to work my will—
She shall not have them.'

                              Saying which she seized,
And, thro' the casement standing wide for heat,
Flung them, and down they flash'd, and smote the stream.
Then from the smitten surface flash'd, as it were,
Diamonds to meet them, and they past away.

Then while Sir Lancelot leant, in half disdain   1230
At love, life, all things, on the window ledge,
Close underneath his eyes, and right across
Where these had fallen, slowly past the barge
Whereon the lily maid of Astolat
Lay smiling, like a star in blackest night.

     But the wild Queen, who saw not, burst away
To weep and wail in secret; and the barge,
On to the palace-doorway sliding, paused.
There two stood arm'd, and kept the door; to whom,
All up the marble stair, tier over tier,   1240
Were added mouths that gaped, and eyes that ask'd,
'What is it?' but that oarsman's haggard face,
As hard and still as is the face that men
Shape to their fancy's eye from broken rocks
On some cliff-side, appall'd them, and they said:
'He is enchanted, cannot speak—and she,
Look how she sleeps—the Fairy Queen, so fair!
Yea, but how pale! what are they? flesh and blood?
Or come to take the King to Fairyland?
For some do hold our Arthur cannot die,   1250
But that he passes into Fairyland.'

     While thus they babbled of the King, the King
Came girt with knights. Then turn'd the tongueless man
From the half-face to the full eye, and rose
And pointed to the damsel and the doors.
So Arthur bade the meek Sir Percivale
And pure Sir Galahad to uplift the maid;
And reverently they bore her into hall.
Then came the fine Gawain and wonder'd at her,
And Lancelot later came and mused at her,   1260
And last the Queen herself, and pitied her;
But Arthur spied the letter in her hand,
Stoopt, took, brake seal, and read it; this was all:

     'Most noble lord, Sir Lancelot of the Lake,
I, sometimes call'd the maid of Astolat,
Come, for you left me taking no farewell,
Hither, to take my last farewell of you.
I loved you, and my love had no return,
And therefore my true love has been my death.
And therefore to our Lady Guinevere,   1270
And to all other ladies, I make moan:
Pray for my soul, and yield me burial.
Pray for my soul thou too, Sir Lancelot,
As thou art a knight peerless.'

Thus he read;
And ever in the reading lords and dames
Wept, looking often from his face who read
To hers which lay so silent, and at times,
So touch'd were they, half-thinking that her lips
Who had devised the letter moved again.

Then freely spoke Sir Lancelot to them all: 1280
'My lord liege Arthur, and all ye that hear,
Know that for this most gentle maiden's death
Right heavy am I; for good she was and true,
But loved me with a love beyond all love
In women, whomsoever I have known.
Yet to be loved makes not to love again;
Not at my years, however it hold in youth.
I swear by truth and knighthood that I gave
No cause, not willingly, for such a love.
To this I call my friends in testimony,   1290
Her brethren, and her father, who himself
Besought me to be plain and blunt, and use,
To break her passion, some discourtesy
Against my nature; what I could, I did.
I left her and I bade her no farewell;
Tho', had I dreamt the damsel would have died,
I might have put my wits to some rough use,
And help'd her from herself.'

Then said the Queen—
Sea was her wrath, yet working after storm:
'Ye might at least have done her so much grace,   1300
Fair lord, as would have help'd her from her death.'
He raised his head, their eyes met and hers fell,
He adding: 'Queen, she would not be content
Save that I wedded her, which could not be.
Then might she follow me thro' the world, she ask'd;
It could not be. I told her that her love
Was but the flash of youth, would darken down,
To rise hereafter in a stiller flame
Toward one more worthy of her—then would I,
More specially were he she wedded poor,   1310
Estate them with large land and territory
In mine own realm beyond the narrow seas,
To keep them in all joyance. More than this
I could not; this she would not, and she died.'

He pausing, Arthur answer'd: 'O my knight,
It will be to thy worship, as my knight,
And mine, as head of all our Table Round,
To see that she be buried worshipfully.'

So toward that shrine which then in all the realm
Was richest, Arthur leading, slowly went   1320
The marshall'd Order of their Table Round,
And Lancelot sad beyond his wont, to see
The maiden buried, not as one unknown,
Nor meanly, but with gorgeous obsequies,
And mass, and rolling music, like a queen.
And when the knights had laid her comely head
Low in the dust of half-forgotten kings,
Then Arthur spake among them: 'Let her tomb
Be costly, and her image thereupon,
And let the shield of Lancelot at her feet   1330
Be carven, and her lily in her hand.
And let the story of her dolorous voyage
For all true hearts be blazon'd on her tomb
In letters gold and azure!' which was wrought
Thereafter; but when now the lords and dames
And people, from the high door streaming, brake
Disorderly, as homeward each, the Queen,
Who mark'd Sir Lancelot where he moved apart,
Drew near, and sigh'd in passing, 'Lancelot,
Forgive me; mine was jealousy in love.'   1340
He answer'd with his eyes upon the ground,
'That is love's curse; pass on, my Queen, forgiven.'
But Arthur, who beheld his cloudy brows,
Approach'd him, and with full affection said:

'Lancelot, my Lancelot, thou in whom I have
Most joy and most affiance, for I know
What thou hast been in battle by my side,
And many a time have watch'd thee at the tilt
Strike down the lusty and long practised knight
And let the younger and unskill'd go by   1350
To win his honor and to make his name,
And loved thy courtesies and thee, a man
Made to be loved; but now I would to God,
Seeing the homeless trouble in thine eyes,
Thou couldst have loved this maiden, shaped, it seems,
By God for thee alone, and from her face,
If one may judge the living by the dead,
Delicately pure and marvelously fair,
Who might have brought thee, now a lonely man
Wifeless and heirless, noble issue, sons   1360
Born to the glory of thy name and fame,
My knight, the great Sir Lancelot of the Lake.'

Then answer'd Lancelot: 'Fair she was, my King,
Pure, as you ever wish your knights to be.

To doubt her fairness were to want an eye,
To doubt her pureness were to want a heart—
Yea, to be loved, if what is worthy love
Could bind him, but free love will not be bound.'

'Free love, so bound, were freest,' said the King.
'Let love be free; free love is for the best.   1370
And, after heaven, on our dull side of death,
What should be best, if not so pure a love
Clothed in so pure a loveliness? yet thee
She fail'd to bind, tho' being, as I think,
Unbound as yet, and gentle, as I know.'

And Lancelot answer'd nothing, but he went,
And at the inrunning of a little brook
Sat by the river in a cove, and watch'd
The high reed wave, and lifted up his eyes
And saw the barge that brought her moving down,   1380
Far-off, a blot upon the stream, and said
Low in himself: 'Ah, simple heart and sweet,
Ye loved me, damsel, surely with a love
Far tenderer than my Queen's. Pray for thy soul?
Ay, that will I. Farewell too—now at last—
Farewell, fair lily. "Jealousy in love?"
Not rather dead love's harsh heir, jealous pride?
Queen, if I grant the jealousy as of love,
May not your crescent fear for name and fame
Speak, as it waxes, of a love that wanes?   1390
Why did the King dwell on my name to me?
Mine own name shames me, seeming a reproach,
Lancelot, whom the Lady of the Lake
Caught from his mother's arms—the wondrous one
Who passes thro' the vision of the night—
She chanted snatches of mysterious hymns
Heard on the winding waters, eve and morn
She kiss'd me saying, "Thou art fair, my child,
As a king's son," and often in her arms
She bare me, pacing on the dusky mere.   1400
Would she had drown'd me in it, where'er it be!
For what am I? what profits me my name
Of greatest knight? I fought for it, and have it.
Pleasure to have it, none; to lose it, pain;
Now grown a part of me; but what use in it?
To make men worse by making my sin known?
Or sin seem less, the sinner seeming great?
Alas for Arthur's greatest knight, a man
Not after Arthur's heart! I needs must break
These bonds that so defame me. Not without   1410

She wills it—would I, if she will'd it? nay,
Who knows? but if I would not, then may God,
I pray him, send a sudden angel down
To seize me by the hair and bear me far,
And fling me deep in that forgotten mere,
Among the tumbled fragments of the hills.'

So groan'd Sir Lancelot in remorseful pain,
Not knowing he should die a holy man.

THE HOLY GRAIL

FROM noiseful arms, and acts of prowess done
In tournament or tilt, Sir Percivale
Whom Arthur and his knighthood call'd the Pure,
Had past into the silent life of prayer,
Praise, fast, and alms; and leaving for the cowl
The helmet in an abbey far away
From Camelot, there, and not long after, died.

And one, a fellow-monk among the rest,
Ambrosius, loved him much beyond the rest,
And honor'd him, and wrought into his heart   10
A way by love that waken'd love within,
To answer that which came; and as they sat
Beneath a world-old yew-tree, darkening half
The cloisters, on a gustful April morn
That puff'd the swaying branches into smoke
Above them, ere the summer when he died,
The monk Ambrosius question'd Percivale:

'O brother, I have seen this yew-tree smoke,
Spring after spring, for half a hundred years;
For never have I known the world without,   20
Nor ever stray'd beyond the pale. But thee,
When first thou camest—such a courtesy
Spake thro' the limbs and in the voice—I knew
For one of those who eat in Arthur's hall;
For good ye are and bad, and like to coins,
Some true, some light, but every one of you
Stamp'd with the image of the King; and now
Tell me, what drove thee from the Table Round,
My brother? was it earthly passion crost?'

'Nay,' said the knight; 'for no such passion mine.   30
But the sweet vision of the Holy Grail
Drove me from all vainglories, rivalries,

And earthly heats that spring and sparkle out
Among us in the jousts, while women watch
Who wins, who falls, and waste the spiritual strength
Within us, better offer'd up to heaven.'

To whom the monk: 'The Holy Grail!—I trust
We are green in Heaven's eyes; but here too much
We moulder—as to things without I mean—
Yet one of your own knights, a guest of ours,   40
Told us of this in our refectory,
But spake with such a sadness and so low
We heard not half of what he said. What is it?
The phantom of a cup that comes and goes?'

'Nay, monk! what phantom?' answer'd Percivale.
'The cup, the cup itself, from which our Lord
Drank at the last sad supper with his own.
This, from the blessed land of Aromat—
After the day of darkness, when the dead
Went wandering o'er Moriah—the good saint   50
Arimathæan Joseph, journeying brought
To Glastonbury, where the winter thorn
Blossoms at Christmas, mindful of our Lord.
And there awhile it bode; and if a man
Could touch or see it, he was heal'd at once,
By faith, of all his ills. But then the times
Grew to such evil that the holy cup
Was caught away to heaven, and disappear'd.'

To whom the monk: 'From our old books I know
That Joseph came of old to Glastonbury,   60
And there the heathen Prince, Arviragus,
Gave him an isle of marsh whereon to build;
And there he built with wattles from the marsh
A little lonely church in days of yore,
For so they say, these books of ours, but seem
Mute of this miracle, far as I have read.
But who first saw the holy thing to-day?'

'A woman,' answer'd Percivale, 'a nun,
And one no further off in blood from me
Than sister; and if ever holy maid   70
With knees of adoration wore the stone,
A holy maid; tho' never maiden glow'd,
But that was in her earlier maidenhood,
With such a fervent flame of human love,
Which, being rudely blunted, glanced and shot
Only to holy things; to prayer and praise

She gave herself, to fast and alms. And yet,
Nun as she was, the scandal of the Court,
Sin against Arthur and the Table Round,
And the strange sound of an adulterous race,   80
Across the iron grating of her cell
Beat, and she pray'd and fasted all the more.

'And he to whom she told her sins, or what
Her all but utter whiteness held for sin,
A man wellnigh a hundred winters old,
Spake often with her of the Holy Grail,
A legend handed down thro' five or six,
And each of these a hundred winters old,
From our Lord's time. And when King Arthur made
His Table Round, and all men's hearts became   90
Clean for a season, surely he had thought
That now the Holy Grail would come again;
But sin broke out. Ah, Christ, that it would come,
And heal the world of all their wickedness!
"O Father!" ask'd the maiden, "might it come
To me by prayer and fasting?" "Nay," said he,
"I know not, for thy heart is pure as snow."
And so she pray'd and fasted, till the sun
Shone, and the wind blew, thro' her, and I thought
She might have risen and floated when I saw her.   100

'For on a day she sent to speak with me.
And when she came to speak, behold her eyes
Beyond my knowing of them, beautiful,
Beyond all knowing of them, wonderful,
Beautiful in the light of holiness!
And "O my brother Percivale," she said,
"Sweet brother, I have seen the Holy Grail;
For, waked at dead of night, I heard a sound
As of a silver horn from o'er the hills
Blown, and I thought, 'It is not Arthur's use   110
To hunt by moonlight.' And the slender sound
As from a distance beyond distance grew
Coming upon me—O never harp nor horn,
Nor aught we blow with breath, or touch with hand,
Was like that music as it came; and then
Stream'd thro' my cell a cold and silver beam,
And down the long beam stole the Holy Grail,
Rose-red with beatings in it, as if alive,
Till all the white walls of my cell were dyed
With rosy colors leaping on the wall;   120
And then the music faded, and the Grail
Past, and the beam decay'd, and from the walls

The rosy quiverings died into the night.
So now the Holy Thing is here again
Among us, brother, fast thou too and pray,
And tell thy brother knights to fast and pray,
That so perchance the vision may be seen
By thee and those, and all the world be heal'd."

'Then leaving the pale nun, I spake of this
To all men; and myself fasted and pray'd   130
Always, and many among us many a week
Fasted and pray'd even to the uttermost,
Expectant of the wonder that would be.

'And one there was among us, ever moved
Among us in white armor, Galahad.
"God make thee good as thou art beautiful!"
Said Arthur, when he dubb'd him knight, and none
In so young youth was ever made a knight
Till Galahad; and this Galahad, when he heard
My sister's vision, fill'd me with amaze;   140
His eyes became so like her own, they seem'd
Hers, and himself her brother more than I.

'Sister or brother none had he; but some
Call'd him a son of Lancelot, and some said
Begotten by enchantment—chatterers they,
Like birds of passage piping up and down,
That gape for flies—we know not whence they come;
For when was Lancelot wanderingly lewd?

'But she, the wan sweet maiden, shore away
Clean from her forehead all that wealth of hair   150
Which made a silken mat-work for her feet;
And out of this she plaited broad and long
A strong sword-belt, and wove with silver thread
And crimson in the belt a strange device,
A crimson grail within a silver beam;
And saw the bright boy-knight, and bound it on him,
Saying: "My knight, my love, my knight of heaven,
O thou, my love, whose love is one with mine,
I, maiden, round thee, maiden, bind my belt.
Go forth, for thou shalt see what I have seen,   160
And break thro' all, till one will crown thee king
Far in the spiritual city;" and as she spake
She sent the deathless passion in her eyes
Thro' him, and made him hers, and laid her mind
On him, and he believed in her belief.

'Then came a year of miracle. O brother,
In our great hall there stood a vacant chair,
Fashion'd by Merlin ere he past away,
And carven with strange figures; and in and out
The figures, like a serpent, ran a scroll
Of letters in a tongue no man could read.
And Merlin call'd it "the Siege Perilous,"
Perilous for good and ill; "for there," he said,
"No man could sit but he should lose himself."
And once by misadverture Merlin sat
In his own chair, and so was lost; but he,
Galahad, when he heard of Merlin's doom,
Cried, "If I lose myself, I save myself!"

'Then on a summer night it came to pass,
While the great banquet lay along the hall,
That Galahad would sit in Merlin's chair.

'And all at once, as there we sat, we heard
A cracking and a riving of the roofs,
And rending, and a blast, and overhead
Thunder, and in the thunder was a cry.
And in the blast there smote along the hall
A beam of light seven times more clear than day;
And down the long beam stole the Holy Grail
All over cover'd with a luminous cloud,
And none might see who bare it, and it past.
But every knight beheld his fellow's face
As in a glory, and all the knights arose,
And staring each at other like dumb men
Stood, till I found a voice and sware a vow.

'I sware a vow before them all, that I,
Because I had not seen the Grail, would ride
A twelvemonth and a day in quest of it,
Until I found and saw it, as the nun
My sister saw it; and Galahad sware the vow,
And good Sir Bors, our Lancelot's cousin, sware,
And Lancelot sware, and many among the knights,
And Gawain sware, and louder than the rest.'

Then spake the monk Ambrosius, asking him,
'What said the King? Did Arthur take the vow?

'Nay, for my lord,' said Percivale, 'the King,
Was not in hall; for early that same day,
Scaped thro' a cavern from a bandit bold,
An outraged maiden sprang into the hall

Crying on help; for all her shining hair
Was smear'd with earth, and either milky arm   210
Red-rent with hooks of bramble, and all she wore
Torn as a sail that leaves the rope is torn
In tempest. So the King arose and went
To smoke the scandalous hive of those wild bees
That made such honey in his realm. Howbeit
Some little of this marvel he too saw,
Returning o'er the plain that then began
To darken under Camelot; whence the King
Look'd up, calling aloud, "Lo there! the roofs
Of our great hall are roll'd in thunder-smoke!   220
Pray heaven, they be not smitten by the bolt!"
For dear to Arthur was that hall of ours,
As having there so oft with all his knights
Feasted, and as the stateliest under heaven.

'O brother, had you known our mighty hall,
Which Merlin built for Arthur long ago!
For all the sacred mount of Camelot,
And all the dim rich city, roof by roof,
Tower after tower, spire beyond spire,
By grove, and garden-lawn, and rushing brook,   230
Climbs to the mighty hall that Merlin built.
And four great zones of sculpture, set betwixt
With many a mystic symbol, gird the hall;
And in the lowest beasts are slaying men,
And in the second men are slaying beasts,
And on the third are warriors, perfect men,
And on the fourth are men with growing wings,
And over all one statue in the mould
Of Arthur, made by Merlin, with a crown,
And peak'd wings pointed to the Northern Star.   240
And eastward fronts the statue, and the crown
And both the wings are made of gold, and flame
At sunrise till the people in far fields,
Wasted so often by the heathen hordes,
Behold it, crying, "We have still a king."

'And, brother, had you known our hall within,
Broader and higher than any in all the lands!
Where twelve great windows blazon Arthur's wars,
And all the light that falls upon the board
Streams thro' the twelve great battles of our King.   250
Nay, one there is, and at the eastern end,
Wealthy with wandering lines of mount and mere,
Where Arthur finds the brand Excalibur.
And also one to the west, and counter to it,

And blank; and who shall blazon it? when and how?—
O, there, perchance, when all our wars are done,
The brand Excalibur will be cast away!

'So to this hall full quickly rode the King,
In horror lest the work by Merlin wrought,
Dreamlike, should on the sudden vanish, wrapt   260
In unremorseful folds of rolling fire.
And in he rode, and up I glanced, and saw
The golden dragon sparkling over all;
And many of those who burnt the hold, their arms
Hack'd, and their foreheads grimed with smoke and sear'd,
Follow'd, and in among bright faces, ours,
Full of the vision, prest; and then the King
Spake to me, being nearest, "Percivale,"—
Because the hall was all in tumult—some
Vowing, and some protesting,—"what is this?"   270

'O brother, when I told him what had chanced,
My sister's vision and the rest, his face
Darken'd, as I have seen it more than once,
When some brave deed seem'd to be done in vain,
Darken; and "Woe is me, my knights," he cried,
"Had I been here, ye had not sworn the vow."
Bold was mine answer, "Had thyself been here,
My King, thou wouldst have sworn." "Yea, yea," said he,
"Art thou so bold and hast not seen the Grail?"

' "Nay, lord, I heard the sound, I saw the light,   280
But since I did not see the holy thing,
I sware a vow to follow it till I saw."

'Then when he ask'd us, knight by knight, if any
Had seen it, all their answers were as one:
"Nay, lord, and therefore have we sworn our vows."

' "Lo, now," said Arthur, "have ye seen a cloud?
What go ye into the wilderness to see?"

'Then Galahad on the sudden, and in a voice
Shrilling along the hall to Arthur, call'd,
"But I, Sir Arthur, saw the Holy Grail,   290
I saw the Holy Grail and heard a cry—
'O Galahad, and O Galahad, follow me!' " '

' "Ah, Galahad, Galahad," said the King, "for such
As thou art is the vision, not for these.
Thy holy nun and thou have seen a sign—

Holier is none, my Percivale, than she—
A sign to maim this Order which I made.
But ye that follow but the leader's bell,"—
Brother, the King was hard upon his knights,—
"Taliessin is our fullest throat of song,   300
And one hath sung and all the dumb will sing.
Lancelot is Lancelot, and hath overborne
Five knights at once, and every younger knight,
Unproven, holds himself as Lancelot,
Till overborne by one, he learns—and ye,
What are ye? Galahads?—no, nor Percivales"—
For thus it pleased the King to range me close
After Sir Galahad;—"nay," said he, "but men
With strength and will to right the wrong'd, of power
To lay the sudden heads of violence flat,   310
Knights that in twelve great battles splash'd and dyed
The strong White Horse in his own heathen blood—
But one hath seen, and all the blind will see.
Go, since your vows are sacred, being made.
Yet—for ye know the cries of all my realm
Pass thro' this hall—how often, O my knights,
Your places being vacant at my side,
This chance of noble deeds will come and go
Unchallenged, while ye follow wandering fires
Lost in the quagmire! Many of you, yea most,   320
Return no more. Ye think I show myself
Too dark a prophet. Come now, let us meet
The morrow morn once more in one full field
Of gracious pastime, that once more the King,
Before ye leave him for this quest, may count
The yet-unbroken strength of all his knights,
Rejoicing in that Order which he made."

'So when the sun broke next from underground,
All the great Table of our Arthur closed
And clash'd in such a tourney and so full,   330
So many lances broken—never yet
Had Camelot seen the like since Arthur came;
And I myself and Galahad, for a strength
Was in us from the vision, overthrew
So many knights that all the people cried,
And almost burst the barriers in their heat,
Shouting, "Sir Galahad and Sir Percivale!"

'But when the next day brake from underground—
O brother, had you known our Camelot,
Built by old kings, age after age, so old   340
The King himself had fears that it would fall,

So strange, and rich, and dim; for where the roofs
Totter'd toward each other in the sky,
Met foreheads all along the street of those
Who watch'd us pass; and lower, and where the long
Rich galleries, lady-laden, weigh'd the necks
Of dragons clinging to the crazy walls,
Thicker than drops from thunder, showers of flowers
Fell as we past; and men and boys astride
On wyvern, lion, dragon, griffin, swan,   350
At all the corners, named us each by name,
Calling "God speed!" but in the ways below
The knights and ladies wept, and rich and poor
Wept, and the King himself could hardly speak
For grief, and all in middle street the Queen,
Who rode by Lancelot, wail'd and shriek'd aloud,
"This madness has come on us for our sins."
So to the Gate of the Three Queens we came,
Where Arthur's wars are render'd mystically,
And thence departed every one his way.   360

'And I was lifted up in heart, and thought
Of all my late-shown prowess in the lists,
How my strong lance had beaten down the knights,
So many and famous names; and never yet
Had heaven appear'd so blue, nor earth so green,
For all my blood danced in me, and I knew
That I should light upon the Holy Grail.

'Thereafter, the dark warning of our King,
That most of us would follow wandering fires,
Came like a driving gloom across my mind.   370
Then every evil word I had spoken once,
And every evil thought I had thought of old,
And every evil deed I ever did,
Awoke and cried, "This quest is not for thee."
And lifting up mine eyes, I found myself
Alone, and in a land of sand and thorns,
And I was thirsty even unto death;
And I, too, cried, "This quest is not for thee."

'And on I rode, and when I thought my thirst
Would slay me, saw deep lawns, and then a brook,   380
With one sharp rapid, where the crisping white
Play'd ever back upon the sloping wave
And took both ear and eye; and o'er the brook
Were apple-trees, and apples by the brook
Fallen, and on the lawns. "I will rest here,"
I said, "I am not worthy of the quest;"

But even while I drank the brook, and ate
The goodly apples, all these things at once
Fell into dust, and I was left alone
And thirsting in a land of sand and thorns.   390

    'And then behold a woman at a door
Spinning; and fair the house whereby she sat,
And kind the woman's eyes and innocent,
And all her bearing gracious; and she rose
Opening her arms to meet me, as who should say,
"Rest here;" but when I touch'd her, lo! she, too,
Fell into dust and nothing, and the house
Became no better than a broken shed,
And in it a dead babe; and also this
Fell into dust, and I was left alone.   400

    'And on I rode, and greater was my thirst.
Then flash'd a yellow gleam across the world,
And where it smote the plowshare in the field
The plowman left his plowing and fell down
Before it; where it glitter'd on her pail
The milkmaid left her milking and fell down
Before it, and I knew not why, but thought
"The sun is rising," tho' the sun had risen.
Then was I ware of one that on me moved
In golden armor with a crown of gold   410
About a casque all jewels, and his horse
In golden armor jewelled everywhere;
And on the splendor came, flashing me blind,
And seem'd to me the lord of all the world,
Being so huge. But when I thought he meant
To crush me, moving on me, lo! he, too,
Open'd his arms to embrace me as he came,
And up I went and touch'd him, and he, too,
Fell into dust, and I was left alone
And wearying in a land of sand and thorns.   420

    'And I rode on and found a mighty hill,
And on the top a city wall'd; the spires
Prick'd with incredible pinnacles into heaven.
And by the gateway stirr'd a crowd; and these
Cried to me climbing, "Welcome, Percivale!
Thou mightiest and thou purest among men!"
And glad was I and clomb, but found at top
No man, nor any voice. And thence I past
Far thro' a ruinous city, and I saw
That man had once dwelt there; but there I found   430
Only one man of an exceeding age.

"Where is that goodly company," said I,
"That so cried out upon me?" and he had
Scarce any voice to answer, and yet gasp'd,
"Whence and what art thou?" and even as he spoke
Fell into dust and disappear'd, and I
Was left alone once more and cried in grief,
"Lo, if I find the Holy Grail itself
And touch it, it will crumble into dust!"

'And thence I dropt into a lowly vale,   440
Low as the hill was high, and where the vale
Was lowest found a chapel, and thereby
A holy hermit in a hermitage,
To whom I told my phantoms, and he said:

' "O son, thou hast not true humility,
The highest virtue, mother of them all;
For when the Lord of all things made Himself
Naked of glory for His mortal change,
'Take thou my robe,' she said, 'for all is thine,'
And all her form shone forth with sudden light   450
So that the angels were amazed, and she
Follow'd Him down, and like a flying star
Led on the gray-hair'd wisdom of the east.
But her thou hast not known; for what is this
Thou thoughtest of thy prowess and thy sins?
Thou hast not lost thyself to save thyself
As Galahad." When the hermit made an end,
In silver armor suddenly Galahad shone
Before us, and against the chapel door
Laid lance and enter'd, and we knelt in prayer   460
And there the hermit slaked my burning thirst,
And at the sacring of the mass I saw
The holy elements alone; but he,
"Saw ye no more? I, Galahad, saw the Grail,
The Holy Grail, descend upon the shrine.
I saw the fiery face as of a child
That smote itself into the bread and went;
And hither am I come; and never yet
Hath what thy sister taught me first to see,
This holy thing, fail'd from my side, nor come   470
Cover'd, but moving with me night and day,
Fainter by day, but always in the night
Blood-red, and sliding down the blacken'd marsh
Blood-red, and on the naked mountain top
Blood-red, and in the sleeping mere below
Blood-red. And in the strength of this I rode,
Shattering all evil customs everywhere,

And past thro' Pagan realms, and made them mine,
And clash'd with Pagan hordes, and bore them down,
And broke thro' all, and in the strength of this   480
Come victor. But my time is hard at hand,
And hence I go, and one will crown me king
Far in the spiritual city; and come thou, too,
For thou shalt see the vision when I go."

'While thus he spake, his eye, dwelling on mine,
Drew me, with power upon me, till I grew
One with him, to believe as he believed.
Then, when the day began to wane, we went.

'There rose a hill that none but man could climb,
Scarr'd with a hundred wintry water-courses—   490
Storm at the top, and when we gain'd it, storm
Round us and death; for every moment glanced
His silver arms and gloom'd, so quick and thick
The lightnings here and there to left and right
Struck, till the dry old trunks about us, dead,
Yea, rotten with a hundred years of death,
Sprang into fire. And at the base we found
On either hand, as far as eye could see,
A great black swamp and of an evil smell,
Part black, part whiten'd with the bones of men,   500
Not to be crost, save that some ancient king
Had built a way, where, link'd with many a bridge,
A thousand piers ran into the great Sea.
And Galahad fled along them bridge by bridge,
And every bridge as quickly as he crost
Sprang into fire and vanish'd, tho' I yearn'd
To follow; and thrice above him all the heavens
Open'd and blazed with thunder such as seem'd
Shoutings of all the sons of God. And first
At once I saw him far on the great Sea,   510
In silver-shining armor starry-clear;
And o'er his head the Holy Vessel hung
Clothed in white samite or a luminous cloud.
And with exceeding swiftness ran the boat,
If boat it were—I saw not whence it came.
And when the heavens open'd and blazed again
Roaring, I saw him like a silver star—
And had he set the sail, or had the boat
Become a living creature clad with wings?
And o'er his head the Holy Vessel hung   520
Redder than any rose, a joy to me,
For now I knew the veil had been withdrawn.
Then in a moment when they blazed again

Opening, I saw the least of little stars
Down on the waste, and straight beyond the star
I saw the spiritual city and all her spires
And gateways in a glory like one pearl—
No larger, tho' the goal of all the saints—
Strike from the sea; and from the star there shot
A rose-red sparkle to the city, and there   530
Dwelt, and I knew it was the Holy Grail,
Which never eyes on earth again shall see.
Then fell the floods of heaven drowning the deep,
And how my feet recrost the deathful ridge
No memory in me lives; but that I touch'd
The chapel-doors at dawn I know, and thence
Taking my war-horse from the holy man,
Glad that no phantom vext me more, return'd
To whence I came, the gate of Arthur's wars.'

    'O brother,' ask'd Ambrosius,—'for in sooth   540
These ancient books—and they would win thee—teem,
Only I find not there this Holy Grail,
With miracles and marvels like to these,
Not all unlike; which oftentime I read,
Who read but on my breviary with ease,
Till my head swims, and then go forth and pass
Down to the little thorpe that lies so close,
And almost plaster'd like a martin's nest
To these old walls—and mingle with our folk;
And knowing every honest face of theirs   550
As well as ever shepherd knew his sheep,
And every homely secret in their hearts,
Delight myself with gossip and old wives,
And ills and aches, and teethings, lyings-in,
And mirthful sayings, children of the place,
That have no meaning half a league away;
Or lulling random squabbles when they rise,
Chafferings and chatterings at the market-cross,
Rejoice, small man, in this small world of mine,
Yea, even in their hens and in their eggs—   560
O brother, saving this Sir Galahad,
Came ye on none but phantoms in your quest,
No man, no woman?'

                    Then Sir Percivale:
'All men, to one so bound by such a vow,
And women were as phantoms. O, my brother,
Why wilt thou shame me to confess to thee
How far I falter'd from my quest and vow?
For after I had lain so many nights,

A bed-mate of the snail and eft and snake,
In grass and burdock, I was changed to wan 570
And meagre, and the vision had not come;
And then I chanced upon a goodly town
With one great dwelling in the middle of it.
Thither I made, and there was I disarm'd
By maidens each as fair as any flower;
But when they led me into hall, behold,
The princess of that castle was the one,
Brother, and that one only, who had ever
Made my heart leap; for when I moved of old
A slender page about her father's hall, 580
And she a slender maiden, all my heart
Went after her with longing, yet we twain
Had never kiss'd a kiss or vow'd a vow.
And now I came upon her once again,
And one had wedded her, and he was dead,
And all his land and wealth and state were hers.
And while I tarried, every day she set
A banquet richer than the day before
By me, for all her longing and her will
Was toward me as of old; till one fair morn, 590
I walking to and fro beside a stream
That flash'd across her orchard underneath
Her castle-walls, she stole upon my walk,
And calling me the greatest of all knights,
Embraced me, and so kiss'd me the first time,
And gave herself and all her wealth to me.
Then I remember'd Arthur's warning word,
That most of us would follow wandering fires,
And the quest faded in my heart. Anon,
The heads of all her people drew to me, 600
With supplication both of knees and tongue:
"We have heard of thee; thou art our greatest knight,
Our Lady says it, and we well believe.
Wed thou our Lady, and rule over us,
And thou shalt be as Arthur in our land."
O me, my brother! but one night my vow
Burnt me within, so that I rose and fled,
But wail'd and wept, and hated mine own self,
And even the holy quest, and all but her;
Then after I was join'd with Galahad 610
Cared not for her nor anything upon earth.'

Then said the monk: 'Poor men, when yule is cold,
Must be content to sit by little fires.
And this am I, so that ye care for me
Ever so little; yea, and blest be heaven

That brought thee here to this poor house of ours
Where all the brethren are so hard, to warm
My cold heart with a friend; but O the pity
To find thine own first love once more—to hold,
Hold her a wealthy bride within thine arms,   620
Or all but hold, and then—cast her aside,
Foregoing all her sweetness, like a weed!
For we that want the warmth of double life,
We that are plagued with dreams of something sweet
Beyond all sweetness in a life so rich,—
Ah, blessed Lord, I speak too earthly-wise,
Seeing I never stray'd beyond the cell,
But live like an old badger in his earth,
With earth about him everywhere, despite
All fast and penance. Saw ye none beside,   630
None of your knights?'

                                    'Yea, so,' said Percivale:
'One night my pathway swerving east, I saw
The pelican on the casque of our Sir Bors
All in the middle of the rising moon,
And toward him spurr'd, and hail'd him, and he me,
And each made joy of either. Then he ask'd:
"Where is he? hast thou seen him—Lancelot?—Once,"
Said good Sir Bors, "he dash'd across me—mad,
And maddening what he rode; and when I cried,
'Ridest thou then so hotly on a quest   640
So holy?' Lancelot shouted, 'Stay me not!
I have been the sluggard, and I ride apace,
For now there is a lion in the way!'
So vanish'd."

                                    'Then Sir Bors had ridden on
Softly, and sorrowing for our Lancelot,
Because his former madness, once the talk
And scandal of our table, had return'd;
For Lancelot's kith and kin so worship him
That ill to him is ill to them, to Bors
Beyond the rest. He well had been content   650
Not to have seen, so Lancelot might have seen,
The Holy Cup of healing; and, indeed,
Being so clouded with his grief and love,
Small heart was his after the holy quest.
If God would send the vision, well; if not,
The quest and he were in the hands of Heaven.

                                    'And then, with small adventure met, Sir Bors
Rode to the lonest tract of all the realm,

And found a people there among their crags,
Our race and blood, a remnant that were left 660
Paynim amid their circles, and the stones
They pitch up straight to heaven; and their wise men
Were strong in that old magic which can trace
The wandering of the stars, and scoff'd at him
And this high quest as at a simple thing,
Told him he follow'd—almost Arthur's words—
A mocking fire: "what other fire than he,
Whereby the blood beats, and the blossom blows,
And the sea rolls, and all the world is warm'd?"
And when his answer chafed them, the rough crowd, 670
Hearing he had a difference with their priests,
Seized him, and bound and plunged him into a cell
Of great piled stones; and lying bounden there
In darkness thro' innumerable hours
He heard the hollow-ringing heavens sweep
Over him till by miracle—what else?—
Heavy as it was, a great stone slipt and fell,
Such as no wind could move; and thro' the gap
Glimmer'd the streaming scud. Then came a night
Still as the day was loud, and thro' the gap 680
The seven clear stars of Arthur's Table Round—
For, brother, so one night, because they roll
Thro' such a round in heaven, we named the stars,
Rejoicing in ourselves and in our King—
And these, like bright eyes of familiar friends,
In on him shone: "And then to me, to me,"
Said good Sir Bors, "beyond all hopes of mine,
Who scarce had pray'd or ask'd it for myself—
Across the seven clear stars—O grace to me!—
In color like the fingers of a hand 690
Before a burning taper, the sweet Grail
Glided and past, and close upon it peal'd
A sharp quick thunder." Afterwards, a maid,
Who kept our holy faith among her kin
In secret, entering, loosed and let him go.'

To whom the monk: 'And I remember now
That pelican on the casque. Sir Bors it was
Who spake so low and sadly at our board,
And mighty reverent at our grace was he;
A square-set man and honest, and his eyes, 700
An outdoor sign of all the warmth within,
Smiled with his lips—a smile beneath a cloud,
But heaven had meant it for a sunny one.
Ay, ay, Sir Bors, who else? But when ye reach'd

The city, found ye all your knights return'd,
Or was there sooth in Arthur's prophecy,
Tell me, and what said each, and what the King?'

Then answer'd Percivale: 'And that can I,
Brother, and truly; since the living words
Of so great men as Lancelot and our King   710
Pass not from door to door and out again,
But sit within the house. O, when we reach'd
The city, our horses stumbling as they trode
On heaps of ruin, hornless unicorns,
Crack'd basilisks, and splinter'd cockatrices,
And shatter'd talbots, which had left the stones
Raw that they fell from, brought us to the hall.

'And there sat Arthur on the dais-throne,
And those that had gone out upon the quest,
Wasted and worn, and but a tithe of them.   720
And those that had not, stood before the King,
Who, when he saw me, rose and bade me hail,
Saying: "A welfare in thine eyes reproves
Our fear of some disastrous chance for thee
On hill or plain, at sea or flooding ford.
So fierce a gale made havoc here of late
Among the strange devices of our kings,
Yea, shook this newer, stronger hall of ours,
And from the statue Merlin moulded for us
Half-wrench'd a golden wing; but now—the quest,   730
This vision—hast thou seen the Holy Cup
That Joseph brought of old to Glastonbury?"

'So when I told him all thyself hast heard,
Ambrosius, and my fresh but fixt resolve
To pass away into the quiet life,
He answer'd not, but, sharply turning, ask'd
Of Gawain, "Gawain, was this quest for thee?"

' "Nay, lord," said Gawain, "not for such as I.
Therefore I communed with a saintly man,
Who made me sure the quest was not for me;   740
For I was much a-wearied of the quest,
But found a silk pavilion in a field,
And merry maidens in it; and then this gale
Tore my pavilion from the tenting-pin,
And blew my merry maidens all about
With all discomfort; yea, and but for this,
My twelvemonth and a day were pleasant to me."

'He ceased; and Arthur turn'd to whom at first
He saw not, for Sir Bors, on entering, push'd
Athwart the throng to Lancelot, caught his hand,   750
Held it, and there, half-hidden by him, stood,
Until the King espied him, saying to him,
"Hail, Bors! if ever loyal man and true
Could see it, thou hast seen the Grail;" and Bors,
"Ask me not, for I may not speak of it;
I saw it;" and the tears were in his eyes.

'Then there remain'd but Lancelot, for the rest
Spake but of sundry perils in the storm.
Perhaps, like him of Cana in Holy Writ,
Our Arthur kept his best until the last;   760
"Thou, too, my Lancelot," ask'd the King, "my friend,
Our mightiest, hath this quest avail'd for thee?"
    ' "Our mightiest!" answer'd Lancelot, with a groan;
"O King!"—and when he paused methought I spied
A dying fire of madness in his eyes—
"O King, my friend, if friend of thine I be,
Happier are those that welter in their sin,
Swine in the mud, that cannot see for slime,
Slime of the ditch; but in me lived a sin
So strange, of such a kind, that all of pure,   770
Noble, and knightly in me twined and clung
Round that one sin, until the wholesome flower
And poisonous grew together, each as each,
Not to be pluck'd asunder; and when thy knights
Sware, I sware with them only in the hope
That could I touch or see the Holy Grail
They might be pluck'd asunder. Then I spake
To one most holy saint, who wept and said
That, save they could be pluck'd asunder, all
My quest were but in vain; to whom I vow'd   780
That I would work according as he will'd.
And forth I went, and while I yearn'd and strove
To tear the twain asunder in my heart,
My madness came upon me as of old,
And whipt me into waste fields far away.
There was I beaten down by little men,
Mean knights, to whom the moving of my sword
And shadow of my spear had been enow
To scare them from me once; and then I came
All in my folly to the naked shore,   790
Wide flats, where nothing but coarse grasses grew;
But such a blast, my King, began to blow,
So loud a blast along the shore and sea,
Ye could not hear the waters for the blast,

Tho' heapt in mounds and ridges all the sea
Drove like a cataract, and all the sand
Swept like a river, and the clouded heavens
Were shaken with the motion and the sound.
And blackening in the sea-foam sway'd a boat,
Half-swallow'd in it, anchor'd with a chain;   800
And in my madness to myself I said,
'I will embark and I will lose myself,
And in the great sea wash away my sin.'
I burst the chain, I sprang into the boat.
Seven days I drove along the dreary deep,
And with me drove the moon and all the stars;
And the wind fell, and on the seventh night
I heard the shingle grinding in the surge,
And felt the boat shock earth, and looking up,
Behold, the enchanted towers of Carbonek,   810
A castle like a rock upon a rock,
With chasm-like portals open to the sea,
And steps that met the breaker! There was none
Stood near it but a lion on each side
That kept the entry, and the moon was full.
Then from the boat I leapt, and up the stairs,
There drew my sword. With sudden-flaring manes
Those two great beasts rose upright like a man,
Each gript a shoulder, and I stood between,
And, when I would have smitten them, heard a voice,   820
'Doubt not, go forward; if thou doubt, the beasts
Will tear thee piecemeal.' Then with violence
The sword was dash'd from out my hand, and fell.
And up into the sounding hall I past;
But nothing in the sounding hall I saw,
No bench nor table, painting on the wall
Or shield of knight, only the rounded moon
Thro' the tall oriel on the rolling sea.
But always in the quiet house I heard,
Clear as a lark, high o'er me as a lark,   830
A sweet voice singing in the topmost tower
To the eastward. Up I climb'd a thousand steps
With pain; as in a dream I seem'd to climb
For ever; at the last I reach'd a door,
A light was in the crannies, and I heard,
'Glory and joy and honor to our Lord
And to the Holy Vessel of the Grail!'
Then in my madness I essay'd the door;
It gave, and thro' a stormy glare, a heat
As from a seven-times-heated furnace, I,   840
Blasted and burnt, and blinded as I was,
With such a fierceness that I swoon'd away—

O, yet methought I saw the Holy Grail,
All pall'd in crimson samite, and around
Great angels, awful shapes, and wings and eyes!
And but for all my madness and my sin,
And then my swooning, I had sworn I saw
That which I saw; but what I saw was veil'd
And cover'd, and this quest was not for me."

  'So speaking, and here ceasing, Lancelot left   850
The hall long silent, till Sir Gawain—nay,
Brother, I need not tell thee foolish words,—
A reckless and irreverent knight was he,
Now bolden'd by the silence of his King,—
Well, I will tell thee: "O King, my liege," he said,
"Hath Gawain fail'd in any quest of thine?
When have I stinted stroke in foughten field?
But as for thine, my good friend Percivale,
Thy holy nun and thou have driven men mad,
Yea, made our mightiest madder than our least.   860
But by mine eyes and by mine ears I swear,
I will be deafer than the blue-eyed cat,
And thrice as blind as any noonday owl,
To holy virgins in their ecstasies,
Henceforward."

              ' "Deafer," said the blameless King,
"Gawain, and blinder unto holy things,
Hope not to make thyself by idle vows,
Being too blind to have desire to see.
But if indeed there came a sign from heaven,
Blessed are Bors, Lancelot, and Percivale,   870
For these have seen according to their sight.
For every fiery prophet in old times,
And all the sacred madness of the bard,
When God made music thro' them, could but speak
His music by the framework and the chord;
And as ye saw it ye have spoken truth.

  ' "Nay—but thou errest, Lancelot; never yet
Could all of true and noble in knight and man
Twine round one sin, whatever it might be,
With such a closeness but apart there grew,   880
Save that he were the swine thou spakest of,
Some root of knighthood and pure nobleness;
Whereto see thou, that it may bear its flower.

  ' "And spake I not too truly, O my knights?
Was I too dark a prophet when I said

To those who went upon the Holy Quest,
That most of them would follow wandering fires,
Lost in the quagmire?—lost to me and gone,
And left me gazing at a barren board,
And a lean Order—scarce return'd a tithe—   890
And out of those to whom the vision came
My greatest hardly will believe he saw.
Another hath beheld it afar off,
And, leaving human wrongs to right themselves,
Cares but to pass into the silent life.
And one hath had the vision face to face,
And now his chair desires him here in vain,
However they may crown him otherwhere.

  ' "And some among you held that if the King
Had seen the sight he would have sworn the vow.   900
Not easily, seeing that the King must guard
That which he rules, and is but as the hind
To whom a space of land is given to plow,
Who may not wander from the allotted field
Before his work be done, but, being done,
Let visions of the night or of the day
Come as they will; and many a time they come,
Until this earth he walks on seems not earth,
This light that strikes his eyeball is not light,
This air that smites his forehead is not air   910
But vision—yea, his very hand and foot—
In moments when he feels he cannot die,
And knows himself no vision to himself,
Nor the high God a vision, nor that One
Who rose again. Ye have seen what ye have seen."

  'So spake the King; I knew not all he meant.'

PELLEAS AND ETTARRE

KING ARTHUR made new knights to fill the gap
Left by the Holy Quest; and as he sat
In hall at old Caerleon, the high doors
Were softly sunder'd, and thro' these a youth,
Pelleas, and the sweet smell of the fields
Past, and the sunshine came along with him.

  'Make me thy knight, because I know, Sir King,
All that belongs to knighthood, and I love.'
Such was his cry; for having heard the King

Had let proclaim a tournament—the prize
A golden circlet and a knightly sword,
Full fain had Pelleas for his lady won
The golden circlet, for himself the sword.
And there were those who knew him near the King,
And promised for him; and Arthur made him knight.

And this new knight, Sir Pelleas of the Isles—
But lately come to his inheritance,
And lord of many a barren isle was he—
Riding at noon, a day or twain before,
Across the forest call'd of Dean, to find
Caerleon and the King, had felt the sun
Beat like a strong knight on his helm and reel'd
Almost to falling from his horse, but saw
Near him a mound of even-sloping side
Whereon a hundred stately beeches grew,
And here and there great hollies under them;
But for a mile all round was open space
And fern and heath. And slowly Pelleas drew
To that dim day, then, binding his good horse
To a tree, cast himself down; and as he lay
At random looking over the brown earth
Thro' that green-glooming twilight of the grove,
It seem'd to Pelleas that the fern without
Burnt as a living fire of emeralds,
So that his eyes were dazzled looking at it.
Then o'er it crost the dimness of a cloud
Floating, and once the shadow of a bird
Flying, and then a fawn; and his eyes closed.
And since he loved all maidens, but no maid
In special, half-awake he whisper'd: 'Where?
O, where? I love thee, tho' I know thee not.
For fair thou art and pure as Guinevere,
And I will make thee with my spear and sword
As famous—O my Queen, my Guinevere,
For I will be thine Arthur when we meet.'

Suddenly waken'd with a sound of talk
And laughter at the limit of the wood,
And glancing thro' the hoary boles, he saw,
Strange as to some old prophet might have seem'd
A vision hovering on a sea of fire,
Damsels in divers colors like the cloud
Of sunset and sunrise, and all of them
On horses, and the horses richly trapt
Breast-high in that bright line of bracken stood;

20

30

40

50

And all the damsels talk'd confusedly,
And one was pointing this way and one that,
Because the way was lost.

                              And Pelleas rose,
And loosed his horse, and led him to the light.
There she that seem'd the chief among them said:
'In happy time behold our pilot-star!   60
Youth, we are damsels-errant, and we ride,
Arm'd as ye see, to tilt against the knights
There at Caerleon, but have lost our way.
To right? to left? straight forward? back again?
Which? tell us quickly.'

                              Pelleas gazing thought,
'Is Guinevere herself so beautiful?'
For large her violet eyes look'd, and her bloom
A rosy dawn kindled in stainless heavens,
And round her limbs, mature in womanhood;
And slender was her hand and small her shape;   70
And but for those large eyes, the haunts of scorn,
She might have seem'd a toy to trifle with,
And pass and care no more. But while he gazed
The beauty of her flesh abash'd the boy,
As tho' it were the beauty of her soul;
For as the base man, judging of the good,
Puts his own baseness in him by default
Of will and nature, so did Pelleas lend
All the young beauty of his own soul to hers,
Believing her, and when she spake to him   80
Stammer'd, and could not make her a reply.
For out of the waste islands had he come,
Where saving his own sisters he had known
Scarce any but the women of his isles,
Rough wives, that laugh'd and scream'd against the gulls,
Makers of nets, and living from the sea.

    Then with a slow smile turn'd the lady round
And look'd upon her people; and, as when
A stone is flung into some sleeping tarn
The circle widens till it lip the marge,   90
Spread the slow smile thro' all her company.
Three knights were thereamong, and they too smiled,
Scorning him; for the lady was Ettarre,
And she was a great lady in her land.

    Again she said: 'O wild and of the woods,
Knowest thou not the fashion of our speech?

Or have the Heavens but given thee a fair face,
Lacking a tongue?'

'O damsel,' answer'd he,
'I woke from dreams, and coming out of gloom
Was dazzled by the sudden light, and crave   100
Pardon; but will ye to Caerleon? I
Go likewise; shall I lead you to the King?'

'Lead then,' she said; and thro' the woods they went.
And while they rode, the meaning in his eyes,
His tenderness of manner, and chaste awe,
His broken utterances and bashfulness,
Were all a burthen to her, and in her heart
She mutter'd, 'I have lighted on a fool,
Raw, yet so stale!' But since her mind was bent
On hearing, after trumpet blown, her name   110
And title, 'Queen of Beauty,' in the lists
Cried—and beholding him so strong she thought
That peradventure he will fight for me,
And win the circlet—therefore flatter'd him,
Being so gracious that he wellnigh deem'd
His wish by hers was echo'd; and her knights
And all her damsels too were gracious to him,
For she was a great lady.

                              And when they reach'd
Caerleon, ere they past to lodging, she,
Taking his hand, 'O the strong hand,' she said,   120
'See! look at mine! but wilt thou fight for me,
And win me this fine circlet, Pelleas,
That I may love thee?'

                         Then his helpless heart
Leapt, and he cried, 'Ay! wilt thou if I win?'
'Ay, that will I,' she answer'd, and she laugh'd,
And straitly nipt the hand, and flung it from her;
Then glanced askew at those three knights of hers,
Till all her ladies laugh'd along with her.

'O happy world,' thought Pelleas, 'all, meseems,
Are happy; I the happiest of them all!'   130
Nor slept that night for pleasure in his blood,
And green wood-ways, and eyes among the leaves;
Then being on the morrow knighted, sware
To love one only. And as he came away,
The men who met him rounded on their heels
And wonder'd after him, because his face

Shone like the countenance of a priest of old
Against the flame about a sacrifice
Kindled by fire from heaven; so glad was he.

Then Arthur made vast banquets, and strange knights   140
From the four winds came in; and each one sat,
Tho' served with choice from air, land, stream, and sea,
Oft in mid-banquet measuring with his eyes
His neighbor's make and might; and Pelleas look'd
Noble among the noble, for he dream'd
His lady loved him, and he knew himself
Loved of the King; and him his new-made knight
Worshipt, whose lightest whisper moved him more
Than all the ranged reasons of the world.

Then blush'd and brake the morning of the jousts,   150
And this was call'd 'The Tournament of Youth;'
For Arthur, loving his young knight, withheld
His older and his mightier from the lists,
That Pelleas might obtain his lady's love,
According to her promise, and remain
Lord of the tourney. And Arthur had the jousts
Down in the flat field by the shore of Usk
Holden; the gilded parapets were crown'd
With faces, and the great tower fill'd with eyes
Up to the summit, and the trumpets blew.   160
There all day long Sir Pelleas kept the field
With honor; so by that strong hand of his
The sword and golden circlet were achieved.

Then rang the shout his lady loved; the heat
Of pride and glory fired her face, her eye
Sparkled; she caught the circlet from his lance,
And there before the people crown'd herself.
So for the last time she was gracious to him.

Then at Caerleon for a space—her look
Bright for all others, cloudier on her knight—   170
Linger'd Ettarre; and, seeing Pelleas droop,
Said Guinevere, 'We marvel at thee much,
O damsel, wearing this unsunny face
To him who won thee glory!' And she said,
'Had ye not held your Lancelot in your bower,
My Queen, he had not won.' Whereat the Queen,
As one whose foot is bitten by an ant,
Glanced down upon her, turn'd and went her way.

But after, when her damsels, and herself,
And those three knights all set their faces home, 180
Sir Pelleas follow'd. She that saw him cried:
'Damsels—and yet I should be shamed to say it—
I cannot bide Sir Baby. Keep him back
Among yourselves. Would rather that we had
Some rough old knight who knew the worldly way,
Albeit grizzlier than a bear, to ride
And jest with! Take him to you, keep him off,
And pamper him with papmeat, if ye will,
Old milky fables of the wolf and sheep,
Such as the wholesome mothers tell their boys. 190
Nay, should ye try him with a merry one
To find his mettle, good; and if he fly us,
Small matter! let him.' This her damsels heard,
And, mindful of her small and cruel hand,
They, closing round him thro' the journey home,
Acted her hest, and always from her side
Restrain'd him with all manner of device,
So that he could not come to speech with her.
And when she gain'd her castle, upsprang the bridge,
Down rang the grate of iron thro' the groove, 200
And he was left alone in open field.

'These be the ways of ladies,' Pelleas thought,
'To those who love them, trials of our faith.
Yea, let her prove me to the uttermost,
For loyal to the uttermost am I.'
So made his moan, and, darkness falling, sought
A priory not far off, there lodged, but rose
With morning every day, and, moist or dry,
Full-arm'd upon his charger all day long
Sat by the walls, and no one open'd to him. 210

And this persistence turn'd her scorn to wrath.
Then, calling her three knights, she charged them, 'Out!
And drive him from the walls.' And out they came,
But Pelleas overthrew them as they dash'd
Against him one by one; and these return'd,
But still he kept his watch beneath the wall.

Thereon her wrath became a hate; and once,
A week beyond, while walking on the walls
With her three knights, she pointed downward, 'Look,
He haunts me—I cannot breathe—besieges me! 220
Down! strike him! put my hate into your strokes,
And drive him from my walls.' And down they went,
And Pelleas overthrew them one by one;

And from the tower above him cried Ettarre,
'Bind him, and bring him in.'
                                He heard her voice;
Then let the strong hand, which had overthrown
Her minion-knights, by those he overthrew
Be bounden straight, and so they brought him in.

Then when he came before Ettarre, the sight
Of her rich beauty made him at one glance   230
More bondsman in his heart than in his bonds.
Yet with good cheer he spake: 'Behold me, lady,
A prisoner, and the vassal of thy will;
And if thou keep me in thy donjon here,
Content am I so that I see thy face
But once a day; for I have sworn my vows,
And thou hast given thy promise, and I know
That all these pains are trials of my faith,
And that thyself, when thou hast seen me strain'd
And sifted to the utmost, wilt at length   240
Yield me thy love and know me for thy knight.'

Then she began to rail so bitterly,
With all her damsels, he was stricken mute,
But, when she mock'd his vows and the great King,
Lighted on words: 'For pity of thine own self,
Peace, lady, peace; is he not thine and mine?'
'Thou fool,' she said, 'I never heard his voice
But long'd to break away. Unbind him now,
And thrust him out of doors; for save he be
Fool to the midmost marrow of his bones,   250
He will return no more.' And those, her three,
Laugh'd, and unbound, and thrust him from the gate.

And after this, a week beyond, again
She call'd them, saying: 'There he watches yet,
There like a dog before his master's door!
Kick'd, he returns; do ye not hate him, ye?
Ye know yourselves; how can ye bide at peace,
Affronted with his fulsome innocence?
Are ye but creatures of the board and bed,
No men to strike? Fall on him all at once,   260
And if ye slay him I reck not; if ye fail,
Give ye the slave mine order to be bound,
Bind him as heretofore, and bring him in.
It may be ye shall slay him in his bonds.'

She spake, and at her will they couch'd their spears.
Three against one; and Gawain passing by,

Bound upon solitary adventure, saw
Low down beneath the shadow of those towers
A villainy, three to one; and thro' his heart
The fire of honor and all noble deeds   270
Flash'd, and he call'd, 'I strike upon thy side—
The caitiffs!' 'Nay,' said Pelleas, 'but forbear;
He needs no aid who doth his lady's will.'

So Gawain, looking at the villainly done,
Forbore, but in his heat and eagerness
Trembled and quiver'd, as the dog, withheld
A moment from the vermin that he sees
Before him, shivers ere he springs and kills.

And Pelleas overthrew them, one to three;
And they rose up, and bound, and brought him in.   280
Then first her anger, leaving Pelleas, burn'd
Full on her knights in many an evil name
Of craven, weakling, and thrice-beaten hound:
'Yet, take him, ye that scarce are fit to touch,
Far less to bind, your victor, and thrust him out,
And let who will release him from his bonds.
And if he comes again'—there she brake short;
And Pelleas answer'd: 'Lady, for indeed
I loved you and I deem'd you beautiful,
I cannot brook to see your beauty marr'd   290
Thro' evil spite; and if ye love me not,
I cannot bear to dream you so forsworn.
I had liefer ye were worthy of my love
Than to be loved again of you—farewell.
And tho' ye kill my hope, not yet my love,
Vex not yourself; ye will not see me more.'

While thus he spake, she gazed upon the man
Of princely bearing, tho' in bonds, and thought:
'Why have I push'd him from me? this man loves,
If love there be; yet him I love not. Why?   300
I deem'd him fool? yea, so? or that in him
A something—was it nobler than myself?—
Seem'd my reproach? He is not of my kind.
He could not love me, did he know me well.
Nay, let him go—and quickly.' And her knights
Laugh'd not, but thrust him bounden out of door.

Forth sprang Gawain, and loosed him from his bounds,
And flung them o'er the walls; and afterward,
Shaking his hands, as from a lazar's rag,
'Faith of my body,' he said, 'and art thou not—   310

Yea thou art he, whom late our Arthur made
Knight of his table; yea, and he that won
The circlet? wherefore hast thou so defamed
Thy brotherhood in me and all the rest
As let these caitiffs on thee work their will?'

And Pelleas answer'd: 'O, their wills are hers
For whom I won the circlet; and mine, hers,
Thus to be bounden, so to see her face,
Marr'd tho' it be with spite and mockery now,
Other than when I found her in the woods;   320
And tho' she hath me bounden but in spite,
And all to flout me, when they bring me in,
Let me be bounden, I shall see her face;
Else must I die thro' mine unhappiness.'

And Gawain answer'd kindly tho' in scorn:
'Why, let my lady bind me if she will,
And let my lady beat me if she will;
But an she send her delegate to thrall
These fighting hands of mine—Christ kill me then
But I will slice him handless by the wrist,   330
And let my lady sear the stump for him,
Howl as he may! But hold me for your friend.
Come, ye know nothing; here I pledge my troth,
Yea, by the honor of the Table Round,
I will be leal to thee and work thy work,
And tame thy jailing princess to thine hand.
Lend me thine horse and arms, and I will say
That I have slain thee. She will let me in
To hear the manner of thy fight and fall;
Then, when I come within her counsels, then   340
From prime to vespers will I chant thy praise
As prowest knight and truest lover, more
Than any have sung thee living, till she long
To have thee back in lusty life again,
Not to be bound, save by white bonds and warm,
Dearer than freedom. Wherefore now thy horse
And armor; let me go; be comforted.
Give me three days to melt her fancy, and hope
The third night hence will bring thee news of gold.'

Then Pelleas lent his horse and all his arms,   350
Saving the goodly sword, his prize, and took
Gawain's, and said, 'Betray me not, but help—
Art thou not he whom men call light-of-love?'

'Ay,' said Gawain, 'for women be so light;'
Then bounded forward to the castle walls,
And raised a bugle hanging from his neck,
And winded it, and that so musically
That all the old echoes hidden in the wall
Rang out like hollow woods at hunting-tide

Up ran a score of damsels to the tower;   360
'Avaunt,' they cried, 'our lady loves thee not!'
But Gawain lifting up his vizor said:
'Gawain am I, Gawain of Arthur's court,
And I have slain this Pelleas whom ye hate.
Behold his horse and armor. Open gates,
And I will make you merry.'

                        And down they ran,
Her damsels, crying to their lady, 'Lo!
Pelleas is dead—he told us—he that hath
His horse and armor; will ye let him in?
He slew him! Gawain, Gawain of the court,   370
Sir Gawain—there he waits below the wall,
Blowing his bugle as who should say him nay.'

And so, leave given, straight on thro' open door
Rode Gawain, whom she greeted courteously.
'Dead, is it so?' she ask'd. 'Ay, ay,' said he,
'And oft in dying cried upon your name.'
'Pity on him,' she answer'd, 'a good knight,
But never let me bide one hour at peace.'
'Ay,' thought Gawain, 'and you be fair enow;
But I to your dead man have given my troth,   380
That whom ye loathe, him will I make you love.'

So those three days, aimless about the land,
Lost in a doubt, Pelleas wandering
Waited, until the third night brought a moon
With promise of large light on woods and ways.

Hot was the night and silent; but a sound
Of Gawain ever coming, and this lay—
Which Pelleas had heard sung before the Queen,
And seen her sadden listening—vext his heart,
And marr'd his rest—'A worm within the rose.'   390

     'A rose, but one, none other rose had I,
    A rose, one rose, and this was wondrous fair,
    One rose, a rose that gladden'd earth and sky,
    One rose, my rose, that sweeten'd all mine air—
    I cared not for the thorns; the thorns were there.

'One rose, a rose to gather by and by,
One rose, a rose, to gather and to wear,
No rose but one—what other rose had I?
One rose, my rose; a rose that will not die,—
He dies who loves it,—if the worm be there.'   400

This tender rhyme, and evermore the doubt,
'Why lingers Gawain with his golden news?'
So shook him that he could not rest, but rode
Ere midnight to her walls, and bound his horse
Hard by the gates. Wide open were the gates,
And no watch kept; and in thro' these he past,
And heard but his own steps, and his own heart
Beating, for nothing moved but his own self
And his own shadow. Then he crost the court,
And spied not any light in hall or bower,   410
But saw the postern portal also wide
Yawning; and up a slope of garden, all
Of roses white and red, and brambles mixt
And overgrowing them, went on, and found,
Here too, all hush'd below the mellow moon,
Save that one rivulet from a tiny cave
Came lightening downward, and so spilt itself
Among the roses and was lost again.

Then was he ware of three pavilions rear'd
Above the bushes, gilden-peakt. In one,   420
Red after revel, droned her lurdane knights
Slumbering, and their three squires across their feet;
In one, their malice on the placid lip
Frozen by sweet sleep, four of her damsels lay;
And in the third, the circlet of the jousts
Bound on her brow, were Gawain and Ettarre.

Back, as a hand that pushes thro' the leaf
To find a nest and feels a snake, he drew;
Back, as a coward slinks from what he fears
To cope with, or a traitor proven, or hound   430
Beaten, did Pelleas in an utter shame
Creep with his shadow thro' the court again,
Fingering at his sword-handle until he stood
There on the castle-bridge once more, and thought,
'I will go back, and slay them where they lie.'

And so went back, and seeing them yet in sleep
Said, 'Ye, that so dishallow the holy sleep,
Your sleep is death,' and drew the sword, and thought,
'What! slay a sleeping knight? the King hath bound
And sworn me to this brotherhood;' again,   440

'Alas that ever a knight should be so false!'
Then turn'd, and so return'd, and groaning laid
The naked sword athwart their naked throats,
There left it, and them sleeping; and she lay,
The circlet of the tourney round her brows,
And the sword of the tourney across her throat.

And forth he past, and mounting on his horse
Stared at her towers that, larger than themselves
In their own darkness, throng'd into the moon;
Then crush'd the saddle with his thighs, and clench'd   450
His hands, and madden'd with himself and moan'd:

'Would they have risen against me in their blood
At the last day? I might have answer'd them
Even before high God. O towers so strong,
Huge, solid, would that even while I gaze
The crack of earthquake shivering to your base
Split you, and hell burst up your harlot roofs
Bellowing, and charr'd you thro' and thro' within,
Black as the harlot's heart—hollow as a skull!
Let the fierce east scream thro' your eyelet-holes,   460
And whirl the dust of harlots round and round
In dung and nettles! hiss, snake—I saw him there—
Let the fox bark, let the wolf yell! Who yells
Here in the still sweet summer night but I—
I, the poor Pelleas whom she call'd her fool?
Fool, beast—he, she, or I? myself most fool;
Beast too, as lacking human wit—disgraced,
Dishonor'd all for trial of true love—
Love?—we be all alike; only the King
Hath made us fools and liars. O noble vows!   470
O great and sane and simple race of brutes
That own no lust because they have no law!
For why should I have loved her to my shame?
I loathe her, as I loved her to my shame.
I never loved her, I but lusted for her—
Away!'—

He dash'd the rowel into his horse,
And bounded forth and vanish'd thro' the night.

Then she, that felt the cold touch on her throat,
Awakening knew the sword, and turn'd herself
To Gawain: 'Liar, for thou hast not slain   480
This Pelleas! here he stood, and might have slain
Me and thyself.' And he that tells the tale
Says that her ever-veering fancy turn'd

To Pelleas, as the one true knight on earth
And only lover; and thro' her love her life
Wasted and pined, desiring him in vain.

But he by wild and way, for half the night,
And over hard and soft, striking the sod
From out the soft, the spark from off the hard,
Rode till the star above the wakening sun,   490
Beside that tower where Percivale was cowl'd,
Glanced from the rosy forehead of the dawn.
For so the words were flash'd into his heart
He knew not whence or wherefore: 'O sweet star,
Pure on the virgin forehead of the dawn!'
And there he would have wept, but felt his eyes
Harder and drier than a fountain bed
In summer. Thither came the village girls
And linger'd talking, and they come no more
Till the sweet heavens have fill'd it from the heights   500
Again with living waters in the change
Of seasons. Hard his eyes, harder his heart
Seem'd; but so weary were his limbs that he,
Gasping, 'Of Arthur's hall am I, but here,
Here let me rest and die,' cast himself down,
And gulf'd his griefs in inmost sleep; so lay,
Till shaken by a dream, that Gawain fired
The hall of Merlin, and the morning star
Reel'd in the smoke, brake into flame, and fell.

He woke, and being ware of some one nigh,   510
Sent hands upon him, as to tear him, crying,
'False! and I held thee pure as Guinevere.'

But Percivale stood near him and replied,
'Am I but false as Guinevere is pure?
Or art thou mazed with dreams? or being one
Of our free-spoken Table hast not heard
That Lancelot'—there he check'd himself and paused.

Then fared it with Sir Pelleas as with one
Who gets a wound in battle, and the sword
That made it plunges thro' the wound again,   520
And pricks it deeper; and he shrank and wail'd,
'Is the Queen false?' and Percivale was mute.
'Have any of our Round Table held their vows?'
And Percivale made answer not a word.
'Is the King true?' 'The King!' said Percivale.
'Why, then let men couple at once with wolves.
What! art thou mad?'

But Pelleas, leaping up,
Ran thro' the doors and vaulted on his horse
And fled. Small pity upon his horse had he,
Or on himself, or any, and when he met   530
A cripple, one that held a hand for alms—
Hunch'd as he was, and like an old dwarf-elm
That turns its back on the salt blast, the boy
Paused not, but overrode him, shouting, 'False,
And false with Gawain!' and so left him bruised
And batter'd, and fled on, and hill and wood
Went ever streaming by him till the gloom
That follows on the turning of the world
Darken'd the common path. He twitch'd the reins,
And made his beast, that better knew it, swerve   540
Now off it and now on; but when he saw
High up in heaven the hall that Merlin built,
Blackening against the dead-green stripes of even,
'Black nest of rats,' he groan'd, 'ye build too high.'

   Not long thereafter from the city gates
Issued Sir Lancelot riding airily,
Warm with a gracious parting from the Queen,
Peace at his heart, and gazing at a star
And marvelling what it was; on whom the boy,
Across the silent seeded meadow-grass   550
Borne, clash'd; and Lancelot, saying, 'What name hast thou
That ridest here so blindly and so hard?'
'No name, no name,' he shouted, 'a scourge am I
To lash the treasons of the Table Round.'
'Yea, but thy name?' 'I have many names,' he cried:
'I am wrath and shame and hate and evil fame,
And like a poisonous wind I pass to blast
And blaze the crime of Lancelot and the Queen.'
'First over me,' said Lancelot, 'shalt thou pass.'
'Fight therefore,' yell'd the youth, and either knight   560
Drew back a space, and when they closed, at once
The weary steed of Pelleas floundering flung
His rider, who call'd out from the dark field,
'Thou art false as hell; slay me, I have no sword.'
Then Lancelot, 'Yea, between thy lips—and sharp;
But here will I disedge it by thy death.'
'Slay then,' he shriek'd, 'my will is to be slain,'
And Lancelot, with his heel upon the fallen,
Rolling his eyes, a moment stood, then spake:
'Rise, weakling; I am Lancelot; say thy say.'   570

   And Lancelot slowly rode his war-horse back
To Camelot, and Sir Pelleas in brief while

Caught his unbroken limbs from the dark field,
And follow'd to the city. It chanced that both
Brake into hall together, worn and pale.
There with her knights and dames was Guinevere.
Full wonderingly she gazed on Lancelot
So soon return'd, and then on Pelleas, him
Who had not greeted her, but cast himself
Down on a bench, hard-breathing. 'Have ye fought?'   580
She ask'd of Lancelot. 'Ay, my Queen,' he said.
'And thou hast overthrown him?' 'Ay, my Queen.'
Then she, turning to Pelleas, 'O young knight,
Hath the great heart of knighthood in thee fail'd
So far thou canst not bide, unfrowardly,
A fall from *him?*' Then, for he answer'd not,
'Or hast thou other griefs? If I, the Queen,
May help them, loose thy tongue, and let me know.'
But Pelleas lifted up an eye so fierce
She quail'd; and he, hissing 'I have no sword,'   590
Sprang from the door into the dark. The Queen
Look'd hard upon her lover, he on her,
And each foresaw the dolorous day to be;
And all talk died, as in a grove all song
Beneath the shadow of some bird of prey.
Then a long silence came upon the hall,
And Modred thought, 'The time is hard at hand.'

THE LAST TOURNAMENT

DAGONET, the fool, whom Gawain in his mood
Had made mock-knight of Arthur's Table Round,
At Camelot, high above the yellowing woods,
Danced like a wither'd leaf before the hall.
And toward him from the hall, with harp in hand,
And from the crown thereof a carcanet
Of ruby swaying to and fro, the prize
Of Tristram in the jousts of yesterday,
Came Tristram, saying, 'Why skip ye so, Sir Fool?'

For Arthur and Sir Lancelot riding once   10
Far down beneath a winding wall of rock
Heard a child wail. A stump of oak half-dead,
From roots like some black coil of carven snakes,
Clutch'd at the crag, and started thro' mid air
Bearing an eagle's nest; and thro' the tree
Rush'd ever a rainy wind, and thro' the wind
Pierced ever a child's cry; and crag and tree
Scaling, Sir Lancelot from the perilous nest,

This ruby necklace thrice around her neck,
And all unscarr'd from beak or talon, brought   20
A maiden babe, which Arthur pitying took,
Then gave it to his Queen to rear. The Queen,
But coldly acquiescing, in her white arms
Received, and after loved it tenderly,
And named it Nestling; so forgot herself
A moment, and her cares; till that young life
Being smitten in mid heaven with mortal cold
Past from her, and in time the carcanet
Vext her with plaintive memories of the child.
So she, delivering it to Arthur, said,   30
'Take thou the jewels of this dead innocence,
And make them, an thou wilt, a tourney-prize.'

   To whom the King: 'Peace to thine eagle-borne
Dead nestling, and this honor after death,
Following thy will! but, O my Queen, I muse
Why ye not wear on arm, or neck, or zone
Those diamonds that I rescued from the tarn,
And Lancelot won, methought, for thee to wear.'

   'Would rather you had let them fall,' she cried,
'Plunge and be lost—ill-fated as they were,   40
A bitterness to me!—ye look amazed,
Not knowing they were lost as soon as given—
Slid from my hands when I was leaning out
Above the river—that unhappy child
Past in her barge; but rosier luck will go
With these rich jewels, seeing that they came
Not from the skeleton of a brother-slayer,
But the sweet body of a maiden babe.
Perchance—who knows?—the purest of thy knights
May win them for the purest of my maids.'   50

   She ended, and the cry of a great jousts
With trumpet-blowings ran on all the ways
From Camelot in among the faded fields
To furthest towers; and everywhere the knights
Arm'd for a day of glory before the King.

   But on the hither side of that loud morn
Into the hall stagger'd, his visage ribb'd
From ear to ear with dogwhip-weals, his nose
Bridge-broken, one eye out, and one hand off,
And one with shatter'd fingers dangling lame,   60
A churl, to whom indignantly the King:

'My churl, for whom Christ died, what evil beast
Hath drawn his claws athwart thy face? or fiend?
Man was it who marr'd heaven's image in thee thus?'

Then, sputtering thro' the hedge of splinter'd teeth,
Yet strangers to the tongue, and with blunt stump
Pitch-blacken'd sawing the air, said the maim'd churl:

'He took them and he drave them to his tower—
Some hold he was a table-knight of thine—
A hundred goodly ones—the Red Knight, he—   70
Lord, I was tending swine, and the Red Knight
Brake in upon me and drave them to his tower;
And when I call'd upon thy name as one
That doest right by gentle and by churl,
Maim'd me and maul'd, and would outright have slain,
Save that he sware me to a message, saying:
"Tell thou the King and all his liars that I
Have founded my Round Table in the North,
And whatsoever his own knights have sworn
My knights have sworn the counter to it—and say   80
My tower is full of harlots, like his court,
But mine are worthier, seeing they profess
To be none other than themselves—and say
My knights are all adulterers like his own,
But mine are truer, seeing they profess
To be none other; and say his hour is come,
The heathen are upon him, his long lance
Broken, and his Excalibur a straw." '

Then Arthur turn'd to Kay the seneschal:
'Take thou my churl, and tend him curiously   90
Like a king's heir, till all his hurts be whole.
The heathen—but that ever-climbing wave,
Hurl'd back again so often in empty foam,
Hath lain for years at rest—and renegades,
Thieves, bandits, leavings of confusion, whom
The wholesome realm is purged of otherwhere,
Friends, thro' your manhood and your fealty,—now
Make their last head like Satan in the North.
My younger knights, new-made, in whom your flower
Waits to be solid fruit of golden deeds,   100
Move with me toward their quelling, which achieved,
The loneliest ways are safe from shore to shore.
But thou, Sir Lancelot, sitting in my place
Enchair'd to-morrow, arbitrate the field;
For wherefore shouldst thou care to mingle with it,
Only to yield my Queen her own again?
Speak, Lancelot, thou art silent; is it well?'

Thereto Sir Lancelot answer'd: 'It is well;
Yet better if the King abide, and leave
The leading of his younger knights to me. 110
Else, for the King has will'd it, it is well.'

Then Arthur rose and Lancelot follow'd him,
And while they stood without the doors, the King
Turn'd to him saying: 'Is it then so well?
Or mine the blame that oft I seem as he
Of whom was written, "A sound is in his ears"?
The foot that loiters, bidden go,—the glance
That only seems half-loyal to command,—
A manner somewhat fallen from reverence—
Or have I dream'd the bearing of our knights 120
Tells of a manhood ever less and lower?
Or whence the fear lest this my realm, uprear'd,
By noble deeds at one with noble vows,
From flat confusion and brute violences,
Reel back into the beast, and be no more?'

He spoke, and taking all his younger knights,
Down the slope city rode, and sharply turn'd
North by the gate. In her high bower the Queen,
Working a tapestry, lifted up her head,
Watch'd her lord pass, and knew not that she sigh'd. 130
Then ran across her memory the strange rhyme
Of bygone Merlin, 'Where is he who knows?
From the great deep to the great deep he goes.'

But when the morning of a tournament,
By these in earnest those in mockery call'd
The Tournament of the Dead Innocence,
Brake with a wet wind blowing, Lancelot,
Round whose sick head all night, like birds of prey,
The words of Arthur flying shriek'd, arose,
And down a streetway hung with folds of pure 140
White samite, and by fountains running wine,
Where children sat in white with cups of gold,
Moved to the lists, and there, with slow sad steps
Ascending, fill'd his double-dragon'd chair.

He glanced and saw the stately galleries,
Dame, damsel, each thro' worship of their Queen
White-robed in honor of the stainless child,
And some with scatter'd jewels, like a bank
Of maiden snow mingled with sparks of fire.
He looked but once, and vail'd his eyes again. 150

The sudden trumpet sounded as in a dream
To ears but half-awaked, then one low roll
Of autumn thunder, and the jousts began;
And ever the wind blew, and yellowing leaf,
And gloom and gleam, and shower and shorn plume
Went down it. Sighing weariedly, as one
Who sits and gazes on a faded fire,
When all the goodlier guests are past away,
Sat their great umpire looking o'er the lists.
He saw the laws that ruled the tournament   160
Broken, but spake not; once, a knight cast down
Before his throne of arbitration cursed
The dead babe and follies of the King;
And once the laces of a helmet crack'd,
And show'd him, like a vermin in its hole,
Modred, a narrow face. Anon he heard
The voice that billow'd round the barriers roar
An ocean-sounding welcome to one knight,
But newly-enter'd, taller than the rest,
And armor'd all in forest green, whereon   170
There tript a hundred tiny silver deer,
And wearing but a holly-spray for crest,
With ever-scattering berries, and on shield
A spear, a harp, a bugle—Tristram—late
From over-seas in Brittany return'd,
And marriage with a princess of that realm,
Isolt the White—Sir Tristram of the Woods—
Whom Lancelot knew, had held sometime with pain
His own against him, and now yearn'd to shake
The burthen off his heart in one full shock   180
With Tristram even to death. His strong hands gript
And dinted the gilt dragons right and left,
Until he groan'd for wrath—so many of those
That ware their ladies' colors on the casque
Drew from before Sir Tristram to the bounds,
And there with gibes and flickering mockeries
Stood, while he mutter'd, 'Craven crests! O shame!
What faith have these in whom they sware to love?
The glory of our Round Table is no more.'

So Tristram won, and Lancelot gave, the gems,   190
Not speaking other word than, 'Hast thou won?
Art thou the purest, brother? See, the hand
Wherewith thou takest this is red!' to whom
Tristram, half plagued by Lancelot's languorous mood,
Made answer: 'Ay, but wherefore toss me this
Like a dry bone cast to some hungry hound?
Let be thy fair Queen's fantasy. Strength of heart

And might of limb, but mainly use and skill,
Are winners in this pastime of our King.
My hand—belike the lance hath dript upon it—   206
No blood of mine, I trow; but O chief knight,
Right arm of Arthur in the battle-field,
Great brother, thou nor I have made the world;
Be happy in thy fair Queen as I in mine.'

And Tristram round the gallery made his horse
Caracole; then bow'd his homage, bluntly saying,
'Fair damsels, each to him who worships each
Sole Queen of Beauty and of love, behold
This day my Queen of Beauty is not here.'
And most of these were mute, some anger'd, one   210
Murmuring, 'All courtesy is dead,' and one,
'The glory of our Round Table is no more.'

Then fell thick rain, plume droopt and mantle clung,
And pettish cries awoke, and the wan day
Went glooming down in wet and weariness;
But under her black brows a swarthy one
Laugh'd shrilly, crying: 'Praise the patient saints,
Our one white day of Innocence hath past,
Tho' somewhat draggled at the skirt. So be it.
The snowdrop only, flowering thro' the year,   220
Would make the world as blank as winter-tide.
Come—let us gladden their sad eyes, our Queen's
And Lancelot's, at this night's solemnity
With all the kindlier colors of the field.'

So dame and damsel glitter'd at the feast
Variously gay; for he that tells the tale
Liken'd them, saying, as when an hour of cold
Falls on the mountain in midsummer snows,
And all the purple slopes of mountain flowers
Pass under white, till the warm hour returns   230
With veer of wind and all are flowers again,
So dame and damsel cast the simple white,
And glowing in all colors, the live grass,
Rose-campion, bluebell, kingcup, poppy, glanced
About the revels, and with mirth so loud
Beyond all use, that, half-amazed, the Queen,
And wroth at Tristram and the lawless jousts,
Brake up their sports, then slowly to her bower
Parted, and in her bosom pain was lord.

And little Dagonet on the morrow morn,   240
High over all the yellowing autumn-tide,

Danced like a wither'd leaf before the hall.
Then Tristram saying, 'Why skip ye so, Sir Fool?'
Wheel'd round on either heel, Dagonet replied,
'Belike for lack of wiser company;
Or being fool, and seeing too much wit
Makes the world rotten, why, belike I skip
To know myself the wisest knight of all.'
'Ay, fool,' said Tristram, 'but 'tis eating dry
To dance without a catch, a roundelay   250
To dance to.' Then he twangled on his harp,
And while he twangled little Dagonet stood
Quiet as any water-sodden log
Stay'd in the wandering warble of a brook,
But when the twangling ended, skipt again;
And being ask'd, 'Why skipt ye not, Sir Fool?'
Made answer, 'I had liefer twenty years
Skip to the broken music of my brains
Than any broken music thou canst make.'
Then Tristram, waiting for the quip to come,   260
'Good now, what music have I broken, fool?'
And little Dagonet, skipping, 'Arthur, the King's;
For when thou playest that air with Queen Isolt,
Thou makest broken music with thy bride,
Her daintier namesake down in Brittany—
And so thou breakest Arthur's music too.'
'Save for that broken music in thy brains,
Sir Fool,' said Tristram, 'I would break thy head.
Fool, I came late, the heathen wars were o'er,
The life had flown, we sware but by the shell—   270
I am but a fool to reason with a fool—
Come, thou art crabb'd and sour; but lean me down,
Sir Dagonet, one of thy long asses' ears,
And harken if my music be not true.

> ' "Free love—free field—we love but while we may.
> The woods are hush'd, their music is no more;
> The leaf is dead, the yearning past away.
> New leaf, new life—the days of frost are o'er;
> New life, new love, to suit the newer day;
> New loves are sweet as those that went before.   280
> Free love—free field—we love but while we may."

'Ye might have moved slow-measure to my tune,
Not stood stock-still. I made it in the woods,
And heard it ring as true as tested gold.'

But Dagonet with one foot poised in his hand:
'Friend, did ye mark that fountain yesterday,
Made to run wine?—but this had run itself
All out like a long life to a sour end—

And them that round it sat with golden cups
To hand the wine to whosoever came—   290
The twelve small damosels white as Innocence,
In honor of poor Innocence the babe,
Who left the gems which Innocence the Queen
Lent to the King, and Innocence the King
Gave for a prize—and one of those white slips
Handed her cup and piped, the pretty one,
"Drink, drink, Sir Fool," and thereupon I drank,
Spat—pish—the cup was gold, the draught was mud.'

    And Tristram: 'Was it muddier than thy gibes?
Is all the laughter gone dead out of thee?—   300
Not marking how the knighthood mock thee, fool—
"Fear God: honor the King—his one true knight—
Sole follower of the vows"—for here be they
Who knew thee swine enow before I came,
Smuttier than blasted grain. But when the King
Had made thee fool, thy vanity so shot up
It frighted all free fool from out thy heart;
Which left thee less than fool, and less than swine,
A naked aught—yet swine I hold thee still,
For I have flung thee pearls and find thee swine.'   310

    And little Dagonet mincing with his feet:
'Knight, an ye fling those rubies round my neck
In lieu of hers, I'll hold thou hast some touch
Of music, since I care not for thy pearls.
Swine? I have wallow'd, I have wash'd—the world
Is flesh and shadow—I have had my day.
The dirty nurse, Experience, in her kind
Hath foul'd me—an I wallow'd, then I wash'd—
I have had my day and my philosophies—
And thank the Lord I am King Arthur's fool.   320
Swine, say ye? swine, goats, asses, rams, and geese
Troop'd round a Paynim harper once, who thrumm'd
On such a wire as musically as thou
Some such fine song—but never a king's fool.'

    And Tristram, 'Then were swine, goats, asses, geese
The wiser fools, seeing thy Paynim bard
Had such a mastery of his mystery
That he could harp his wife up out of hell.'

    Then Dagonet, turning on the ball of his foot,
'And whither harp'st thou thine? down! and thyself   330
Down! and two more; a helpful harper thou,
That harpest downward! Dost thou know the star
We call the Harp of Arthur up in heaven?'

And Tristram, 'Ay, Sir Fool, for when our King
Was victor wellnigh day by day, the knights,
Glorying in each new glory, set his name
High on all hills and in the signs of heaven.'

And Dagonet answer'd: 'Ay, and when the land
Was freed, and the Queen false, ye set yourself
To babble about him, all to show your wit—   340
And whether he were king by courtesy,
Or king by right—and so went harping down
The black king's highway, got so far and grew
So witty that ye play'd at ducks and drakes
With Arthur's vows on the great lake of fire.
Tuwhoo! do ye see it? do ye see the star?'

'Nay, fool,' said Tristram, 'not in open day.'
And Dagonet: 'Nay, nor will; I see it and hear.
It makes a silent music up in heaven,
And I and Arthur and the angels hear,   350
And then we skip.' 'Lo, fool,' he said, 'ye talk
Fool's treason; is the King thy brother fool?'
Then little Dagonet clapt his hands and shrill'd:
'Ay, ay, my brother fool, the king of fools!
Conceits himself as God that he can make
Figs out of thistles, silk from bristles, milk
From burning spurge, honey from hornet-combs,
And men from beasts—Long live the king of fools!'

And down the city Dagonet danced away;
But thro' the slowly-mellowing avenues   360
And solitary passes of the wood
Rode Tristram toward Lyonnesse and the west.
Before him fled the face of Queen Isolt
With ruby-circled neck, but evermore
Past, as a rustle or twitter in the wood
Made dull his inner, keen his outer eye
For all that walk'd, or crept, or perch'd, or flew.
Anon the face, as, when a gust hath blown,
Unruffling waters re-collect the shape
Of one that in them sees himself, return'd;   370
But at the slot or fewmets of a deer,
Or even a fallen feather, vanish'd again.

So on for all that day from lawn to lawn
Thro' many a league-long bower he rode. At length
A lodge of intertwisted beechen-boughs,
Furze-cramm'd and bracken-rooft, the which himself
Built for a summer day with Queen Isolt

Against a shower, dark in the golden grove
Appearing, sent his fancy back to where
She lived a moon in that low lodge with him;   380
Till Mark her lord had past, the Cornish King,
With six or seven, when Tristram was away,
And snatch'd her thence, yet, dreading worse than shame
Her warrior Tristram, spake not any word,
But bode his hour, devising wretchedness.

    And now that desert lodge to Tristram lookt
So sweet that, halting, in he past and sank
Down on a drift of foliage random-blown;
But could not rest for musing how to smooth
And sleek his marriage over to the queen.   390
Perchance in lone Tintagil far from all
The tonguesters of the court she had not heard.
But then what folly had sent him over-seas
After she left him lonely here? a name?
Was it the name of one in Brittany
Isolt, the daughter of the king? 'Isolt
Of the White Hands,' they call'd her: the sweet name
Allured him first, and then the maid herself,
Who served him well with those white hands of hers,
And loved him well, until himself had thought   400
He loved her also, wedded easily,
But left her all as easily, and return'd.
The black-blue Irish hair and Irish eyes
Had drawn him home—what marvel? then he laid
His brows upon the drifted leaf and dream'd.

    He seem'd to pace the strand of Brittany
Between Isolt of Britain and his bride,
And show'd them both the ruby-chain, and both
Began to struggle for it, till his queen
Graspt it so hard that all her hand was red.   410
Then cried the Breton, 'Look, her hand is red!
These be no rubies, this is frozen blood,
And melts within her hand—her hand is hot
With ill desires, but this I gave thee, look,
Is all as cool and white as any flower.'
Follow'd a rush of eagle's wings, and then
A whimpering of the spirit of the child,
Because the twain had spoil'd her carcanet.

    He dream'd; but Arthur with a hundred spears
Rode far, till o'er the illimitable reed,   420
And many a glancing plash and sallowy isle,
The wide-wing'd sunset of the misty marsh

Glared on a huge machicolated tower
That stood with open doors, whereout was roll'd
A roar of riot, as from men secure
Amid their marshes, ruffians at their ease
Among their harlot-brides, an evil song.
'Lo there,' said one of Arthur's youth, for there,
High on a grim dead tree before the tower,
A goodly brother of the Table Round   430
Swung by the neck; and on the boughs a shield
Showing a shower of blood in a field noir,
And there beside a horn, inflamed the knights
At that dishonor done the gilded spur,
Till each would clash the shield and blow the horn.
But Arthur waved them back. Alone he rode.
Then at the dry harsh roar of the great horn,
That sent the face of all the marsh aloft
An ever upward-rushing storm and cloud
Of shriek and plume, the Red Knight heard, and all,   440
Even to tipmost lance and topmost helm,
In blood-red armor sallying, howl'd to the King:

'The teeth of Hell flay bare and gnash thee flat!—
Lo! art thou not that eunuch-hearted king
Who fain had clipt free manhood from the world—
The woman-worshipper? Yea, God's curse, and I!
Slain was the brother of my paramour
By a knight of thine, and I that heard her whine
And snivel, being eunuch-hearted too,
Sware by the scorpion-worm that twists in hell   450
And stings itself to everlasting death,
To hang whatever knight of thine I fought
And tumbled. Art thou king?—Look to thy life!'

He ended. Arthur knew the voice; the face
Wellnigh was helmet-hidden, and the name
Went wandering somewhere darkling in his mind.
And Arthur deign'd not use of word or sword,
But let the drunkard, as he stretch'd from horse
To strike him, overbalancing his bulk,
Down from the causeway heavily to the swamp   460
Fall, as the crest of some slow-arching wave,
Heard in dead night along that table-shore,
Drops flat, and after the great waters break
Whitening for half a league, and thin themselves,
Far over sands marbled with moon and cloud,
From less and less to nothing; thus he fell
Head-heavy. Then the knights, who watch'd him, roar'd
And shouted and leapt down upon the fallen,

There trampled out his face from being known,
And sank his head in mire, and slimed themselves;   470
Nor heard the King for their own cries, but sprang
Thro' open doors, and swording right and left
Men, women, on their sodden faces, hurl'd
The tables over and the wines, and slew
Till all the rafters rang with woman-yells,
And all the pavement stream'd with massacre.
Then, echoing yell with yell, they fired the tower,
Which half that autumn night, like the live North,
Red-pulsing up thro' Alioth and Alcor,
Made all above it, and a hundred meres   480
About it, as the water Moab saw
Come round by the east, and out beyond them flush'd
The long low dune and lazy-plunging sea.

  So all the ways were safe from shore to shore,
But in the heart of Arthur pain was lord.

  Then, out of Tristram waking, the red dream
Fled with a shout, and that low lodge return'd,
Mid-forest, and the wind among the boughs.
He whistled his good war-horse left to graze
Among the forest greens, vaulted upon him,   490
And rode beneath an ever-showering leaf,
Till one lone woman, weeping near a cross,
Stay'd him. 'Why weep ye?' 'Lord,' she said, 'my man
Hath left me or is dead;' whereon he thought—
'What, if she hate me now? I would not this.
What, if she love me still? I would not that.
I know not what I would'—but said to her,
'Yet weep not thou, lest, if thy mate return,
He find thy favor changed and love thee not'—
Then pressing day by day thro' Lyonnesse   500
Last in a rocky hollow, belling, heard
The hounds of Mark, and felt the goodly hounds
Yelp at his heart, but, turning, past and gain'd
Tintagil, half in sea and high on land,
A crown of towers.

                          Down in a casement sat,
A low sea-sunset glorying round her hair
And glossy-throated grace, Isolt the queen.
And when she heard the feet of Tristram grind
The spiring stone that scaled about her tower,
Flush'd, started, met him at the doors, and there   510
Belted his body with her white embrace,
Crying aloud: 'Not Mark—not Mark, my soul!

The footstep flutter'd me at first—not he!
Catlike thro' his own castle steals my Mark,
But warrior-wise thou stridest thro' his halls
Who hates thee, as I him—even to the death.
My soul, I felt my hatred for my Mark
Quicken within me, and knew that thou wert nigh,'
To whom Sir Tristram smiling, 'I am here;
Let be thy Mark, seeing he is not thine.'   520

And drawing somewhat backward she replied:
'Can he be wrong'd who is not even his own,
But save for dread of thee had beaten me,
Scratch'd, bitten, blinded, marr'd me somehow—Mark?
What rights are his that dare not strike for them?
Not lift a hand—not, tho' he found me thus!
But harken! have ye met him? hence he went
To-day for three days' hunting—as he said—
And so returns belike within an hour.
Mark's way, my soul!—but eat not thou with Mark,   530
Because he hates thee even more than fears,
Nor drink; and when thou passest any wood
Close vizor, lest an arrow from the bush
Should leave me all alone with Mark and hell.
My God, the measure of my hate for Mark
Is as the measure of my love for thee!'

So, pluck'd one way by hate and one by love,
Drain'd of her force, again she sat, and spake
To Tristram, as he knelt before her, saying:
'O hunter, and O blower of the horn,   540
Harper, and thou hast been a rover too,
For, ere I mated with my shambling king,
Ye twain had fallen out about the bride
Of one—his name is out of me—the prize,
If prize she were—what marvel?—she could see—
Thine, friend; and ever since my craven seeks
To wreck thee villainously—but, O Sir Knight,
What dame or damsel have ye kneel'd to last?'

And Tristram, 'Last to my Queen Paramount,
Here now to my queen paramount of love   550
And loveliness—ay, lovelier than when first
Her light feet fell on our rough Lyonnesse,
Sailing from Ireland.'

Softly laugh'd Isolt:
'Flatter me not, for hath not our great Queen
My dole of beauty trebled?' and he said:

'Her beauty is her beauty, and thine thine,
And thine is more to me—soft, gracious, kind—
Save when thy Mark is kindled on thy lips
Most gracious; but she, haughty, even to him,
Lancelot; for I have seen him wan enow   560
To make one doubt if ever the great Queen
Have yielded him her love.'

                    To whom Isolt:
'Ah, then, false hunter and false harper, thou
Who brakest thro' the scruple of my bond,
Calling me thy white hind, and saying to me
That Guinevere had sinn'd against the highest,
And I—misyoked with such a want of man—
That I could hardly sin against the lowest.'

    He answer'd: 'O my soul, be comforted!
If this be sweet, to sin in leading-strings,   570
If here be comfort, and if ours be sin,
Crown'd warrant had we for the crowning sin
That made us happy; but how ye greet me—fear
And fault and doubt—no word of that fond tale—
Thy deep heart-yearnings, thy sweet memories
Of Tristram in that year he was away.'

    And, saddening on the sudden, spake Isolt:
'I had forgotten all in my strong joy
To see thee—yearnings?—ay! for, hour by hour,
Here in the never-ended afternoon,   580
O, sweeter than all memories of thee,
Deeper than any yearnings after thee
Seem'd those far-rolling, westward-smiling seas,
Watch'd from this tower. Isolt of Britain dash'd
Before Isolt of Brittany on the strand,
Would that have chill'd her bride-kiss? Wedded her?
Fought in her father's battles? wounded there?
The King was all fulfill'd with gratefulness,
And she, my namesake of the hands, that heal'd
Thy hurt and heart with unguent and caress—   590
Well—can I wish her any huger wrong
Than having known thee? her too hast thou left
To pine and waste in those sweet memories.
O, were I not my Mark's, by whom all men
Are noble, I should hate thee more than love.'

    And Tristram, fondling her light hands, replied:
'Grace, queen, for being loved; she loved me well.
Did I love her? the name at least I loved.

Isolt?—I fought his battles, for Isolt!
The night was dark; the true star set. Isolt!   600
The name was ruler of the dark—Isolt?
Care not for her! patient, and prayerful, meek,
Pale-blooded, she will yield herself to God.'

And Isolt answer'd: 'Yea, and why not I?
Mine is the larger need, who am not meek,
Pale-blooded, prayerful. Let me tell thee now.
Here one black, mute midsummer night I sat,
Lonely, but musing on thee, wondering where,
Murmuring a light song I had heard thee sing,
And once or twice I spake thy name aloud.   610
Then flash'd a levin-brand; and near me stood,
In fuming sulphur blue and green, a fiend—
Mark's way to steal behind one in the dark—
For there was Mark: "He has wedded her," he said,
Not said, but hiss'd it; then this crown of towers
So shook to such a roar of all the sky,
That here in utter dark I swoon'd away,
And woke again in utter dark, and cried,
"I will flee hence and give myself to God"—
And thou wert lying in thy new leman's arms.'   620

Then Tristram, ever dallying with her hand,
'May God be with thee, sweet, when old and gray,
And past desire!' a saying that anger'd her.
' "May God be with thee, sweet, when thou art old,
And sweet no more to me!" I need Him now.
For when had Lancelot utter'd aught so gross
Even to the swineherd's malkin in the mast?
The greater man the greater courtesy.
Far other was the Tristram, Arthur's knight!
But thou, thro' ever harrying thy wild beasts—   630
Save that to touch a harp, tilt with a lance
Becomes thee well—art grown wild beast thyself.
How darest thou, if lover, push me even
In fancy from thy side, and set me far
In the gray distance, half a life away,
Her to be loved no more? Unsay it, unswear!
Flatter me rather, seeing me so weak,
Broken with Mark and hate and solitude,
Thy marriage and mine own, that I should suck
Lies like sweet wines. Lie to me; I believe.   640
Will ye not lie? not swear, as there ye kneel,
And solemnly as when ye sware to him,
The man of men, our King—My God, the power
Was once in vows when men believed the King!

They lied not then who sware, and thro' their vows
The King prevailing made his realm—I say,
Swear to me thou wilt love me even when old,
Gray-hair'd, and past desire, and in despair.'

    Then Tristram, pacing moodily up and down:
'Vows! did you keep the vow you made to Mark   650
More than I mine? Lied, say ye? Nay, but learnt,
The vow that binds too strictly snaps itself—
My knighthood taught me this—ay, being snapt—
We run more counter to the soul thereof
Than had we never sworn. I swear no more.
I swore to the great King, and am forsworn.
For once—even to the height—I honor'd him.
"Man, is he man at all?" methought, when first
I rode from our rough Lyonnesse, and beheld
That victor of the Pagan throned in hall—   660
His hair, a sun that ray'd from off a brow
Like hill-snow high in heaven, the steel-blue eyes,
The golden beard that clothed his lips with light—
Moreover, that weird legend of his birth,
With Merlin's mystic babble about his end
Amazed me; then, his foot was on a stool
Shaped as a dragon; he seem'd to me no man,
But Michael trampling Satan; so I sware,
Being amazed. But this went by—The vows!
O, ay—the wholesome madness of an hour—   670
They served their use, their time; for every knight
Believed himself a greater than himself,
And every follower eyed him as a God;
Till he, being lifted up beyond himself,
Did mightier deeds than elsewise he had done,
And so the realm was made. But then their vows—
First mainly thro' that sullying of our Queen—
Began to gall the knighthood, asking whence
Had Arthur right to bind them to himself?
Dropt down from heaven? wash'd up from out the deep?   680
They fail'd to trace him thro' the flesh and blood
Of our old kings. Whence then? a doubtful lord
To bind them by inviolable vows,
Which flesh and blood perforce would violate;
For feel this arm of mine—the tide within
Red with free chase and heather-scented air,
Pulsing full man. Can Arthur make me pure
As any maiden child? lock up my tongue
From uttering freely what I freely hear?
Bind me to one? The wide world laughs at it.   690
And worldling of the world am I, and know

The ptarmigan that whitens ere his hour
Woos his own end; we are not angels here
Nor shall be. Vows—I am woodman of the woods,
And hear the garnet-headed yaffingale
Mock them—my soul, we love but while we may;
And therefore is my love so large for thee,
Seeing it is not bounded save by love.'

Here ending, he moved toward her, and she said: 700
'Good; an I turn'd away my love for thee
To some one thrice as courteous as thyself—
For courtesy wins woman all as well
As valor may, but he that closes both
Is perfect, he is Lancelot—taller indeed,
Rosier and comelier, thou—but say I loved
This knightliest of all knights, and cast thee back
Thine own small saw, "We love but while we may,"
Well then, what answer?'

                    He that while she spake,
Mindful of what he brought to adorn her with,
The jewels, had let one finger lightly touch   710
The warm white apple of her throat, replied,
'Press this a little closer, sweet, until—
Come, I am hunger'd and half-anger'd—meat,
Wine, wine—and I will love thee to the death,
And out beyond into the dream to come.'

So then, when both were brought to full accord,
She rose, and set before him all he will'd;
And after these had comforted the blood
With meats and wines, and satiated their hearts—
Now talking of their woodland paradise,   720
The deer, the dews, the fern, the founts, the lawns;
Now mocking at the much ungainliness,
And craven shifts, and long crane legs of Mark—
Then Tristram laughing caught the harp and sang:

        'Ay, ay, O, ay—the winds that bend the brier!
    A star in heaven, a star within the mere!
    Ay, ay, O, ay—a star was my desire,
    And one was far apart and one was near.
    Ay, ay, O, ay—the winds that bow the grass!
    And one was water and one star was fire,   730
    And one will ever shine and one will pass.
    Ay, ay, O, ay—the winds that move the mere!'

Then in the light's last glimmer Tristram show'd
And swung the ruby carcanet. She cried,
'The collar of some Order, which our King

Hath newly founded, all for thee, my soul,
For thee, to yield thee grace beyond thy peers.'

'Not so, my queen,' he said, 'but the red fruit
Grown on a magic oak-tree in mid-heaven,
And won by Tristram as a tourney-prize,   740
And hither brought by Tristram for his last
Love-offering and peace-offering unto thee.'

He spoke, he turn'd, then, flinging round her neck,
Claspt it, and cried, 'Thine Order, O my queen!'
But, while he bow'd to kiss the jewell'd throat,
Out of the dark, just as the lips had touch'd,
Behind him rose a shadow and a shriek—
'Mark's way,' said Mark, and clove him thro' the brain.

That night came Arthur home, and while he climb'd,
All in a death-dumb autumn-dripping gloom,   750
The stairway to the hall, and look'd and saw
The great Queen's bower was dark,—about his feet
A voice clung sobbing till he question'd it,
'What art thou?' and the voice about his feet
Sent up an answer, sobbing, 'I am thy fool,
And I shall never make thee smile again.'

GUINEVERE

QUEEN GUINEVERE had fled the court, and sat
There in the holy house at Almesbury
Weeping, none with her save a little maid,
A novice. One low light betwixt them burn'd
Blurr'd by the creeping mist, for all abroad,
Beneath a moon unseen albeit at full,
The white mist, like a face-cloth to the face,
Clung to the dead earth, and the land was still.

For hither had she fled, her cause of flight
Sir Modred; he that like a subtle beast   10
Lay couchant with his eyes upon the throne,
Ready to spring, waiting a chance. For this
He chill'd the popular praises of the King
With silent smiles of slow disparagement;
And tamper'd with the Lords of the White Horse,
Heathen, the brood by Hengist left; and sought
To make disruption in the Table Round
Of Arthur, and to splinter it into feuds
Serving his traitorous end; and all his aims
Were sharpen'd by strong hate for Lancelot.   20

For thus it chanced one morn when all the court,
Green-suited, but with plumes that mock'd the may,
Had been—their wont—a-maying and return'd,
That Modred still in green, all ear and eye,
Climb'd to the high top of the garden-wall
To spy some secret scandal if he might,
And saw the Queen who sat betwixt her best
Enid, and lissome Vivien, of her court
The wiliest and the worst; and more than this
He saw not, for Sir Lancelot passing by   30
Spied where he couch'd, and as the gardener's hand
Picks from the colewort a green caterpillar,
So from the high wall and the flowering grove
Of grasses Lancelot pluck'd him by the heel,
And cast him as a worm upon the way;
But when he knew the prince tho' marr'd with dust,
He, reverencing king's blood in a bad man,
Made such excuses as he might, and these
Full knightly without scorn. For in those days
No knight of Arthur's noblest dealt in scorn;   40
But, if a man were halt, or hunch'd, in him
By those whom God had made full-limb'd and tall,
Scorn was allow'd as part of his defect,
And he was answer'd softly by the King
And all his Table. So Sir Lancelot holp
To raise the prince, who rising twice or thrice
Full sharply smote his knees, and smiled, and went;
But, ever after, the small violence done
Rankled in him and ruffled all his heart,
As the sharp wind that ruffles all day long   50
A little bitter pool about a stone
On the bare coast.

                          But when Sir Lancelot told
This matter to the Queen, at first she laugh'd
Lightly, to think of Modred's dusty fall,
Then shudder'd, as the village wife who cries,
'I shudder, some one steps across my grave;'
Then laugh'd again, but faintlier, for indeed
She half-foresaw that he, the subtle beast,
Would track her guilt until he found, and hers
Would be for evermore a name of scorn.   60
Henceforward rarely could she front in hall,
Or elsewhere, Modred's narrow foxy face,
Heart-hiding smile, and gray persistent eye.
Henceforward too, the Powers that tend the soul,
To help it from the death that cannot die,
And save it even in extremes, began

To vex and plague her. Many a time for hours,
Beside the placid breathings of the King,
In the dead night, grim faces came and went
Before her, or a vague spiritual fear—
Like to some doubtful noise of creaking doors,
Heard by the watcher in a haunted house,
That keeps the rust of murder on the walls—
Held her awake; or if she slept she dream'd
An awful dream, for then she seem'd to stand
On some vast plain before a setting sun,
And from the sun there swiftly made at her
A ghastly something, and its shadow flew
Before it till it touch'd her, and she turn'd—
When lo! her own, that broadening from her feet,
And blackening, swallow'd all the land, and in it
Far cities burnt, and with a cry she woke.
And all this trouble did not pass but grew,
Till even the clear face of the guileless King,
And trustful courtesies of household life,
Became her bane; and at the last she said:
'O Lancelot, get thee hence to thine own land,
For if thou tarry we shall meet again,
And if we meet again some evil chance
Will make the smouldering scandal break and blaze
Before the people and our lord the King.'
And Lancelot ever promised, but remain'd,
And still they met and met. Again she said,
'O Lancelot, if thou love me get thee hence.'
And then they were agreed upon a night—
When the good King should not be there—to meet
And part for ever. Vivien, lurking, heard.
She told Sir Modred. Passion-pale they met
And greeted. Hands in hands, and eye to eye,
Low on the border of her couch they sat
Stammering and staring. It was their last hour,
A madness of farewells. And Modred brought
His creatures to the basement of the tower
For testimony; and crying with full voice,
'Traitor, come out, ye are trapt at last,' aroused
Lancelot, who rushing outward lionlike
Leapt on him, and hurl'd him headlong, and he fell
Stunn'd, and his creatures took and bare him off,
And all was still. Then she, 'The end is come,
And I am ashamed for ever;' and he said:
'Mine be the shame, mine was the sin; but rise,
And fly to my strong castle over-seas.
There will I hide thee till my life shall end,
There hold thee with my life against the world.'

She answer'd: 'Lancelot, wilt thou hold me so?
Nay, friend, for we have taken our farewells.
Would God that thou couldst hide me from myself!
Mine is the shame, for I was wife, and thou
Unwedded; yet rise now, and let us fly,
For I will draw me into sanctuary,   120
And bide my doom.' So Lancelot got her horse,
Set her thereon, and mounted on his own,
And then they rode to the divided way,
There kiss'd, and parted weeping; for he past,
Love-loyal to the least wish of the Queen,
Back to his land; but she to Almesbury
Fled all night long by glimmering waste and weald,
And heard the spirits of the waste and weald
Moan as she fled, or thought she heard them moan.
And in herself she moan'd, 'Too late, too late!'   130
Till in the cold wind that foreruns the morn,
A blot in heaven, the raven, flying high,
Croak'd, and she thought, 'He spies a field of death;
For now the heathen of the Northern Sea,
Lured by the crimes and frailties of the court,
Begin to slay the folk and spoil the land.'

     And when she came to Almesbury she spake
There to the nuns, and said, 'Mine enemies
Pursue me, but, O peaceful Sisterhood,
Receive and yield me sanctuary, nor ask   140
Her name to whom ye yield it till her time
To tell you;' and her beauty, grace, and power
Wrought as a charm upon them, and they spared
To ask it.

          So the stately Queen abode
For many a week, unknown, among the nuns,
Nor with them mix'd, nor told her name, nor sought,
Wrapt in her grief, for housel or for shrift,
But communed only with the little maid,
Who pleased her with a babbling heedlessness
Which often lured her from herself; but now,   150
This night, a rumor wildly blown about
Came that Sir Modred had usurp'd the realm
And leagued him with the heathen, while the King
Was waging war on Lancelot. Then she thought,
'With what a hate the people and the King
Must hate me,' and bow'd down upon her hands
Silent, until the little maid, who brook'd
No silence, brake it, uttering 'Late! so late!
What hour, I wonder now?' and when she drew

No answer, by and by began to hum
An air the nuns had taught her: 'Late, so late!'
Which when she heard, the Queen look'd up, and said,
'O maiden, if indeed ye list to sing,
Sing, and unbind my heart that I may weep.'
Whereat full willingly sang the little maid.

> 'Late, late, so late! and dark the night and chill!
> Late, late, so late! but we can enter still.
> Too late, too late! ye cannot enter now.

> 'No light had we; for that we do repent,
> And learning this, the bridegroom will relent.
> Too late, too late! ye cannot enter now.

> 'No light! so late! and dark and chill the night!
> O, let us in, that we may find the light!
> Too late, too late! ye cannot enter now.

> 'Have we not heard the bridegroom is so sweet?
> O, let us in, tho' late, to kiss his feet!
> No, no, too late! ye cannot enter now.'

So sang the novice, while full passionately,
Her head upon her hands, remembering
Her thought when first she came, wept the sad Queen.
Then said the little novice prattling to her:

'O pray you, noble lady, weep no more;
But let my words—the words of one so small,
Who knowing nothing knows but to obey,
And if I do not there is penance given—
Comfort your sorrows, for they do not flow
From evil done; right sure am I of that,
Who see your tender grace and stateliness.
But weigh your sorrows with our lord the King's
And weighing find them less; for gone is he
To wage grim war against Sir Lancelot there,
Round that strong castle where he holds the Queen;
And Modred whom he left in charge of all,
The traitor—Ah, sweet lady, the King's grief
For his own self, and his own Queen, and realm,
Must needs be thrice as great as any of ours!
For me, I thank the saints, I am not great;
For if there ever come a grief to me
I cry my cry in silence, and have done;
None knows it, and my tears have brought me good.
But even were the griefs of little ones
As great as those of great ones, yet this grief
Is added to the griefs the great must bear,
That, howsoever much they may desire

170

180

190

200

Silence, they cannot weep behind a cloud;
As even here they talk at Almesbury
About the good King and his wicked Queen,
And were I such a King with such a Queen,
Well might I wish to veil her wickedness,
But were I such a King it could not be.'   210

Then to her own sad heart mutter'd the Queen,
'Will the child kill me with her innocent talk?'
But openly she answer'd, 'Must not I,
If this false traitor have displaced his lord,
Grieve with the common grief of all the realm?'

'Yea,' said the maid, 'this all is woman's grief,
That *she* is woman, whose disloyal life
Hath wrought confusion in the Table Round
Which good King Arthur founded, years ago,
With signs and miracles and wonders, there   220
At Camelot, ere the coming of the Queen.'

Then thought the Queen within herself again,
'Will the child kill me with her foolish prate?'
But openly she spake and said to her,
'O little maid, shut in by nunnery walls,
What canst thou know of Kings and Tables Round,
Or what of signs and wonders, but the signs
And simple miracles of thy nunnery?'

To whom the little novice garrulously:
'Yea, but I know; the land was full of signs   230
And wonders ere the coming of the Queen.
So said my father, and himself was knight
Of the great Table—at the founding of it,
And rode thereto from Lyonnesse; and he said
That as he rode, an hour or maybe twain
After the sunset, down the coast, he heard
Strange music, and he paused, and turning—there,
All down the lonely coast of Lyonnesse,
Each with a beacon-star upon his head,
And with a wild sea-light about his feet,   240
He saw them—headland after headland flame
Far on into the rich heart of the west.
And in the light the white mermaiden swam,
And strong man-breasted things stood from the sea,
And sent a deep sea-voice thro' all the land,
To which the little elves of chasm and cleft
Made answer, sounding like a distant horn.
So said my father—yea, and furthermore,

Next morning, while he past the dim-lit woods
Himself beheld three spirits mad with joy   250
Come dashing down on a tall wayside flower,
That shook beneath them as the thistle shakes
When three gray linnets wrangle for the seed.
And still at evenings on before his horse
The flickering fairy-circle wheel'd and broke
Flying, and link'd again, and wheel'd and broke
Flying, for all the land was full of life.
And when at last he came to Camelot,
A wreath of airy dancers hand-in-hand
Swung round the lighted lantern of the hall;   260
And in the hall itself was such a feast
As never man had dream'd; for every knight
Had whatsoever meat he long'd for served
By hands unseen; and even as he said
Down in the cellars merry bloated things
Shoulder'd the spigot, straddling on the butts
While the wine ran; so glad were spirits and men
Before the coming of the sinful Queen.'

    Then spake the Queen and somewhat bitterly,
'Were they so glad? ill prophets were they all,   270
Spirits and men. Could none of them foresee,
Not even thy wise father with his signs
And wonders, what has fallen upon the realm?'

    To whom the novice garrulously again:
'Yea, one, a bard, of whom my father said,
Full many a noble war-song had he sung,
Even in the presence of an enemy's fleet,
Between the steep cliff and the coming wave;
And many a mystic lay of life and death
Had chanted on the smoky mountain-tops,   280
When round him bent the spirits of the hills
With all their dewy hair blown back like flame.
So said my father—and that night the bard
Sang Arthur's glorious wars, and sang the King
As wellnigh more than man, and rail'd at those
Who call'd him the false son of Gorloïs.
For there was no man knew from whence he came;
But after tempest, when the long wave broke
All down the thundering shores of Bude and Bos,
There came a day as still as heaven, and then   290
They found a naked child upon the sands
Of dark Tintagil by the Cornish sea,
And that was Arthur, and they foster'd him
Till he by miracle was approven King;

And that his grave should be a mystery
From all men, like his birth; and could he find
A woman in her womanhood as great
As he was in his manhood, then, he sang,
The twain together well might change the world.
But even in the middle of his song   300
He falter'd, and his hand fell from the harp,
And pale he turn'd, and reel'd, and would have fallen,
But that they stay'd him up; nor would he tell
His vision; but what doubt that he foresaw
This evil work of Lancelot and the Queen?'

    Then thought the Queen, 'Lo! they have set her on,
Our simple-seeming abbess and her nuns,
To play upon me,' and bow'd her head nor spake.
Whereat the novice crying, with clasp'd hands,
Shame on her own garrulity garrulously,   310
Said the good nuns would check her gadding tongue
Full often, 'and, sweet lady, if I seem
To vex an ear too sad to listen to me,
Unmannerly, with prattling and the tales
Which my good father told me, check me too
Nor let me shame my father's memory, one
Of noblest manners, tho' himself would say
Sir Lancelot had the noblest; and he died,
Kill'd in a tilt, come next, five summers back,
And left me; but of others who remain,   320
And of the two first-famed for courtesy—
And pray you check me if I ask amiss—
But pray you, which had noblest, while you moved
Among them, Lancelot or our lord the King?'

    Then the pale Queen look'd up and answer'd her:
'Sir Lancelot, as became a noble knight,
Was gracious to all ladies, and the same
In open battle or the tilting-field
Forbore his own advantage, and the King
In open battle or the tilting-field   330
Forbore his own advantage, and these two
Were the most nobly-manner'd men of all;
For manners are not idle, but the fruit
Of loyal nature and of noble mind.'

    'Yea,' said the maid, 'be manners such fair fruit?
Then Lancelot's needs must be a thousand-fold
Less noble, being, as all rumor runs,
The most disloyal friend in all the world.'

To which a mournful answer made the Queen:
'O, closed about by narrowing nunnery-walls,
What knowest thou of the world and all its lights
And shadows, all the wealth and all the woe?
If ever Lancelot, that most noble knight,
Were for one hour less noble than himself,
Pray for him that he scape the doom of fire,
And weep for her who drew him to his doom.'

'Yea,' said the little novice, 'I pray for both;
But I should all as soon believe that his,
Sir Lancelot's, were as noble as the King's,
As I could think, sweet lady, yours would be
Such as they are, were you the sinful Queen.'

So she, like many another babbler, hurt
Whom she would soothe, and harm'd where she would heal;
For here a sudden flush of wrathful heat
Fired all the pale face of the Queen, who cried:
'Such as thou art be never maiden more
For ever! thou their tool, set on to plague
And play upon and harry me, petty spy
And traitress!' When that storm of anger brake
From Guinevere, aghast the maiden rose,
White as her veil, and stood before the Queen
As tremulously as foam upon the beach
Stands in a wind, ready to break and fly,
And when the Queen had added, 'Get thee hence!'
Fled frighted. Then that other left alone
Sigh'd, and began to gather heart again,
Saying in herself: 'The simple, fearful child
Meant nothing, but my own too-fearful guilt,
Simpler than any child, betrays itself.
But help me, Heaven, for surely I repent!
For what is true repentance but in thought—
Not even in inmost thought to think again
The sins that made the past so pleasant to us?
And I have sworn never to see him more,
To see him more.'
                    And even in saying this,
Her memory from old habit of the mind
Went slipping back upon the golden days
In which she saw him first, when Lancelot came,
Reputed the best knight and goodliest man,
Ambassador, to yield her to his lord
Arthur, and led her forth, and far ahead
Of his and her retinue moving, they,
Rapt in sweet talk or lively, all on love

And sport and tilts and pleasure,—for the time
Was may-time, and as yet no sin was dream'd,—
Rode under groves that look'd a paradise
Of blossom, over sheets of hyacinth
That seem'd the heavens upbreaking thro' the earth,
And on from hill to hill, and every day
Beheld at noon in some delicious dale   390
The silk pavilions of King Arthur raised
For brief repast or afternoon repose
By couriers gone before; and on again,
Till yet once more ere set of sun they saw
The Dragon of the great Pendragonship,
That crown'd the state pavilion of the King,
Blaze by the rushing brook or silent well.

But when the Queen immersed in such a trance,
And moving thro' the past unconsciously,
Came to that point where first she saw the King   400
Ride toward her from the city, sigh'd to find
Her journey done, glanced at him, thought him cold,
High, self-contain'd, and passionless, not like him,
'Not like my Lancelot'—while she brooded thus
And grew half-guilty in her thoughts again,
There rode an armed warrior to the doors.
A murmuring whisper thro' the nunnery ran,
Then on a sudden a cry, 'The King!' She sat
Stiff-stricken, listening; but when armed feet
Thro' the long gallery from the outer doors   410
Rang coming, prone from off her seat she fell,
And grovell'd with her face against the floor.
There with her milk-white arms and shadowy hair
She made her face a darkness from the King,
And in the darkness heard his armed feet
Pause by her; then came silence, then a voice,
Monotonous and hollow like a ghost's
Denouncing judgment, but, tho' changed, the King's:

'Liest thou here so low, the child of one
I honor'd, happy, dead before thy shame?   420
Well is it that no child is born of thee.
The children born of thee are sword and fire,
Red ruin, and the breaking up of laws,
The craft of kindred and the godless hosts
Of heathen swarming o'er the Northern Sea;
Whom I, while yet Sir Lancelot, my right arm,
The mightiest of my knights, abode with me,
Have everywhere about this land of Christ
In twelve great battles ruining overthrown.

And knowest thou now from whence I come—from him, 430
From waging bitter war with him; and he,
That did not shun to smite me in worse way,
Had yet that grace of courtesy in him left,
He spared to lift his hand against the King
Who made him knight. But many a knight was slain;
And many more and all his kith and kin
Clave to him, and abode in his own land.
And many more when Modred raised revolt,
Forgetful of their troth and fealty, clave
To Modred, and a remnant stays with me. 440
And of this remnant will I leave a part,
True men who love me still, for whom I live,
To guard thee in the wild hour coming on,
Lest but a hair of this low head be harm'd.
Fear not; thou shalt be guarded till my death.
Howbeit I know, if ancient prophecies
Have err'd not, that I march to meet my doom.
Thou hast not made my life so sweet to me,
That I the King should greatly care to live;
For thou hast spoilt the purpose of my life. 450
Bear with me for the last time while I show,
Even for thy sake, the sin which thou hast sinn'd.
For when the Roman left us, and their law
Relax'd its hold upon us, and the ways
Were fill'd with rapine, here and there a deed
Of prowess done redress'd a random wrong.
But I was first of all the kings who drew
The knighthood-errant of this realm and all
The realms together under me, their Head,
In that fair Order of my Table Round, 460
A glorious company, the flower of men,
To serve as model for the mighty world,
And be the fair beginning of a time.
I made them lay their hands in mine and swear
To reverence the King, as if he were
Their conscience, and their conscience as their King,
To break the heathen and uphold the Christ,
To ride abroad redressing human wrongs,
To speak no slander, no, nor listen to it,
To honor his own word as if his God's, 470
To lead sweet lives in purest chastity,
To love one maiden only, cleave to her,
And worship her by years of noble deeds,
Until they won her; for indeed I knew
Of no more subtle master under heaven
Than is the maiden passion for a maid,
Not only to keep down the base in man,

But teach high thought, and amiable words
And courtliness, and the desire of fame,
And love of truth, and all that makes a man.   480
And all this throve before I wedded thee,
Believing, "Lo, mine helpmate, one to feel
My purpose and rejoicing in my joy!"
Then came thy shameful sin with Lancelot;
Then came the sin of Tristram and Isolt;
Then others, following these my mightiest knights,
And drawing foul ensample from fair names,
Sinn'd also, till the loathsome opposite
Of all my heart had destined did obtain,
And all thro' thee! so that this life of mine   490
I guard as God's high gift from scathe and wrong,
Not greatly care to lose; but rather think
How sad it were for Arthur, should he live,
To sit once more within his lonely hall,
And miss the wonted number of my knights,
And miss to hear high talk of noble deeds
As in the golden days before thy sin.
For which of us who might be left could speak
Of the pure heart, nor seem to glance at thee?
And in thy bowers of Camelot or of Usk   500
Thy shadow still would glide from room to room,
And I should evermore be vext with thee
In hanging robe or vacant ornament,
Or ghostly footfall echoing on the stair.
For think not, tho' thou wouldst not love thy lord,
Thy lord has wholly lost his love for thee.
I am not made of so slight elements.
Yet must I leave thee, woman, to thy shame.
I hold that man the worst of public foes
Who either for his own or children's sake,   510
To save his blood from scandal, lets the wife
Whom he knows false abide and rule the house:
For being thro' his cowardice allow'd
Her station, taken everywhere for pure,
She like a new disease, unknown to men,
Creeps, no precaution used, among the crowd,
Makes wicked lightnings of her eyes, and saps
The fealty of our friends, and stirs the pulse
With devil's leaps, and poisons half the young.
Worst of the worst were that man he that reigns!   520
Better the King's waste hearth and aching heart
Than thou reseated in thy place of light,
The mockery of my people and their bane!'

He paused, and in the pause she crept an inch
Nearer, and laid her hands about his feet.
Far off a solitary trumpet blew.
Then waiting by the doors the war-horse neigh'd
As at a friend's voice, and he spake again:

'Yet think not that I come to urge thy crimes;
I did not come to curse thee, Guinevere,   530
I, whose vast pity almost makes me die
To see thee, laying there thy golden head,
My pride in happier summers, at my feet.
The wrath which forced my thoughts on that fierce law,
The doom of treason and the flaming death,—
When first I learnt thee hidden here,—is past.
The pang—which, while I weigh'd thy heart with one
Too wholly true to dream untruth in thee,
Made my tears burn—is also past—in part.
And all is past, the sin is sinn'd, and I,   540
Lo, I forgive thee, as Eternal God
Forgives! do thou for thine own soul the rest.
But how to take last leave of all I loved?
O golden hair, with which I used to play
Not knowing! O imperial-moulded form,
And beauty such as never woman wore,
Until it came a kingdom's curse with thee—
I cannot touch thy lips, they are not mine,
But Lancelot's; nay, they never were the King's.
I cannot take thy hand; that too is flesh,   550
And in the flesh thou hast sinn'd; and mine own flesh,
Here looking down on thine polluted, cries,
"I loathe thee;" yet not less, O Guinevere,
For I was ever virgin save for thee,
My love thro' flesh hath wrought into my life
So far that my doom is, I love thee still.
Let no man dream but that I love thee still.
Perchance, and so thou purify thy soul,
And so thou lean on our fair father Christ,
Hereafter in that world where all are pure   560
We two may meet before high God, and thou
Wilt spring to me, and claim me thine, and know
I am thine husband—not a smaller soul,
Nor Lancelot, nor another. Leave me that,
I charge thee, my last hope. Now must I hence.
Thro' the thick night I hear the trumpet blow.
They summon me their King to lead mine hosts
Far down to that great battle in the west,
Where I must strike against the man they call
My sister's son—no kin of mine, who leagues   570

With Lords of the White Horse, heathen, and knights,
Traitors—and strike him dead, and meet myself
Death, or I know not what mysterious doom.
And thou remaining here wilt learn the event;
But hither shall I never come again,
Never lie by thy side, see thee no more—
Farewell!'

           And while she grovell'd at his feet,
She felt the King's breath wander o'er her neck,
And in the darkness o'er her fallen head
Perceived the waving of his hands that blest.   580

Then, listening till those armed steps were gone,
Rose the pale Queen, and in her anguish found
The casement: 'peradventure,' so she thought,
'If I might see his face, and not be seen.'
And lo, he sat on horseback at the door!
And near him the sad nuns with each a light
Stood, and he gave them charge about the Queen,
To guard and foster her for evermore.
And while he spake to these his helm was lower'd,
To which for crest the golden dragon clung   590
Of Britain; so she did not see the face,
Which then was as an angel's, but she saw,
Wet with the mists and smitten by the lights,
The Dragon of the great Pendragonship
Blaze, making all the night a steam of fire.
And even then he turn'd; and more and more
The moony vapor rolling round the King,
Who seem'd the phantom of a giant in it,
Enwound him fold by fold, and made him gray
And grayer, till himself became as mist   600
Before her, moving ghostlike to his doom.

Then she stretch'd out her arms and cried aloud,
'O Arthur!' there her voice brake suddenly,
Then—as a stream that spouting from a cliff
Fails in mid air, but gathering at the base
Re-makes itself, and flashes down the vale—
Went on in passionate utterance:

           'Gone—my lord!
Gone thro' my sin to slay and to be slain!
And he forgave me, and I could not speak.
Farewell? I should have answer'd his farewell.   610
His mercy choked me. Gone, my lord the King,
My own true lord! how dare I call him mine?

The shadow of another cleaves to me,
And makes me one pollution. He, the King,
Call'd me polluted. Shall I kill myself?
What help in that? I cannot kill my sin,
If soul be soul, nor can I kill my shame;
No, nor by living can I live it down.
The days will grow to weeks, the weeks to months,
The months will add themselves and make the years,   620
The years will roll into the centuries,
And mine will ever be a name of scorn.
I must not dwell on that defeat of fame.
Let the world be; that is but of the world—
What else? what hope? I think there was a hope,
Except he mock'd me when he spake of hope;
His hope he call'd it; but he never mocks,
For mockery is the fume of little hearts.
And blessed be the King, who hath forgiven
My wickedness to him, and left me hope   630
That in mine own heart I can live down sin
And be his mate hereafter in the heavens
Before high God! Ah great and gentle lord,
Who wast, as is the conscience of a saint
Among his warring senses, to thy knights—
To whom my false voluptuous pride, that took
Full easily all impressions from below,
Would not look up, or half-despised the height
To which I would not or I could not climb—
I thought I could not breathe in that fine air,   640
That pure severity of perfect light—
I yearn'd for warmth and color which I found
In Lancelot—now I see thee what thou art,
Thou art the highest and most human too,
Not Lancelot, nor another. Is there none
Will tell the King I love him tho' so late?
Now—ere he goes to the great battle? none!
Myself must tell him in that purer life,
But now it were too daring. Ah my God,
What might I not have made of thy fair world,   650
Had I but loved thy highest creature here?
It was my duty to have loved the highest;
It surely was my profit had I known;
It would have been my pleasure had I seen.
We needs must love the highest when we see it,
Not Lancelot, nor another.'
                                        Here her hand
Grasp'd, made her vail her eyes. She look'd and saw
The novice, weeping, suppliant, and said to her,
'Yea, little maid, for am *I* not forgiven?'

Then glancing up beheld the holy nuns
All round her, weeping; and her heart was loosed
Within her, and she wept with these and said:

'Ye know me then, that wicked one, who broke
The vast design and purpose of the King.
O, shut me round with narrowing nunnery-walls,
Meek maidens, from the voices crying, "Shame!"
I must not scorn myself; he loves me still.
Let no one dream but that he loves me still.
So let me, if you do not shudder at me,
Nor shun to call me sister, dwell with you;
Wear black and white, and be a nun like you,
Fast with your fasts, not feasting with your feasts;
Grieve with your griefs, not grieving at your joys,
But not rejoicing; mingle with your rites;
Pray and be pray'd for; lie before your shrines;
Do each low office of your holy house;
Walk your dim cloister, and distribute dole
To poor sick people, richer in His eyes
Who ransom'd us, and haler too than I;
And treat their loathsome hurt and heal mine own;
And so wear out in alms-deed and in prayer
The sombre close of that voluptuous day
Which wrought the ruin of my lord the King.'

She said. They took her to themselves; and she
Still hoping, fearing 'Is it yet too late?'
Dwelt with them, till in time their abbess died.
Then she, for her good deeds and her pure life,
And for the power of ministration in her,
And likewise for the high rank she had borne,
Was chosen abbess, there, an abbess, lived
For three brief years, and there, an abbess, past
To where beyond these voices there is peace.

THE PASSING OF ARTHUR

THAT story which the bold Sir Bedivere,
First made and latest left of all the knights,
Told, when the man was no more than a voice
In the white winter of his age, to those
With whom he dwelt, new faces, other minds.

For on their march to westward, Bedivere,
Who slowly paced among the slumbering host,
Heard in his tent the moanings of the King:

'I found Him in the shining of the stars,
I mark'd Him in the flowering of His fields,
But in His ways with men I find Him not.
I waged His wars, and now I pass and die.
O me! for why is all around us here
As if some lesser god had made the world,
But had not force to shape it as he would,
Till the High God behold it from beyond,
And enter it, and make it beautiful?
Or else as if the world were wholly fair,
But had not force to shape it as he would,
And have not power to see it as it is—
Perchance, because we see not to the close;—
For I, being simple, thought to work His will,
And have but stricken with the sword in vain,
And all whereon I lean'd in wife and friend
Is traitor to my peace, and all my realm
Reels back into the beast, and is no more.
My God, thou hast forgotten me in my death!
Nay—God my Christ—I pass but shall not die.'

Then, ere that last weird battle in the west,
There came on Arthur sleeping, Gawain kill'd
In Lancelot's war, the ghost of Gawain blown
Along a wandering wind, and past his ear
Went shrilling: 'Hollow, hollow all delight!
Hail, King! to-morrow thou shalt pass away.
Farewell! there is an isle of rest for thee.
And I am blown along a wandering wind,
And hollow, hollow, hollow all delight!'
And fainter onward, like wild birds that change
Their season in the night and wail their way
From cloud to cloud, down the long wind the dream
Shrill'd; but in going mingled with dim cries
Far in the moonlit haze among the hills,
As of some lonely city sack'd by night,
When all is lost, and wife and child with wail
Pass to new lords; and Arthur woke and call'd:
'Who spake? A dream. O, light upon the wind,
Thine, Gawain, was the voice—are these dim cries
Thine? or doth all that haunts the waste and wild
Mourn, knowing it will go along with me?'

This heard the bold Sir Bedivere and spake:
'O me, my King, let pass whatever will,
Elves, and the harmless glamour of the field;
But in their stead thy name and glory cling
To all high places like a golden cloud
For ever; but as yet thou shalt not pass.

Light was Gawain in life, and light in death
Is Gawain, for the ghost is as the man;
And care not thou for dreams from him, but rise—
I hear the steps of Modred in the west,
And with him many of thy people, and knights   60
Once thine, whom thou hast loved, but grosser grown
Than heathen, spitting at their vows and thee.
Right well in heart they know thee for the King.
Arise, go forth and conquer as of old.'

    Then spake King Arthur to Sir Bedivere:
'Far other is this battle in the west
Whereto we move than when we strove in youth,
And brake the petty kings, and fought with Rome,
Or thrust the heathen from the Roman wall,
And shook him thro' the north. Ill doom is mine   70
To war against my people and my knights.
The king who fights his people fights himself.
And they my knights, who loved me once, the stroke
That strikes them dead is as my death to me.
Yet let us hence, and find or feel a way
Thro' this blind haze which, ever since I saw
One lying in the dust at Almesbury,
Hath folded in the passes of the world.'

    Then rose the King and moved his host by night,
And ever push'd Sir Modred, league by league,   80
Back to the sunset bound of Lyonnesse—
A land of old upheaven from the abyss
By fire, to sink into the abyss again;
Where fragments of forgotten peoples dwelt,
And the long mountains ended in a coast
Of ever-shifting sand, and far away
The phantom circle of a moaning sea.
There the pursuer could pursue no more,
And he that fled no further fly the King;
And there, that day when the great light of heaven   90
Burn'd at his lowest in the rolling year,
On the waste sand by the waste sea they closed.
Nor ever yet had Arthur fought a fight
Like this last, dim, weird battle of the west.
A death-white mist slept over sand and sea,
Whereof the chill, to him who breathed it, drew
Down with his blood, till all his heart was cold
With formless fear; and even on Arthur fell
Confusion, since he saw not whom he fought.
For friend and foe were shadows in the mist,   100
And friend slew friend not knowing whom he slew;

And some had visions out of golden youth,
And some beheld the faces of old ghosts
Look in upon the battle; and in the mist
Was many a noble deed, many a base,
And chance and craft and strength in single fights,
And ever and anon with host to host
Shocks, and the splintering spear, the hard mail hewn,
Shield-breakings, and the clash of brands, the crash
Of battle-axes on shatter'd helms, and shrieks   110
After the Christ, of those who falling down
Look'd up for heaven, and only saw the mist;
And shouts of heathen and the traitor knights,
Oaths, insult, filth, and monstrous blasphemies,
Sweat, writhings, anguish, laboring of the lungs
In that close mist, and cryings for the light,
Moans of the dying, and voices of the dead.

    Last, as by some one death-bed after wail
Of suffering, silence follows, or thro' death
Or death-like swoon, thus over all that shore,   120
Save for some whisper of the seething seas,
A dead hush fell; but when the dolorous day
Grew drearier toward twilight falling, came
A bitter wind, clear from the north, and blew
The mist aside, and with that wind the tide
Rose, and the pale King glanced across the field
Of battle. But no man was moving there;
Nor any cry of Christian heard thereon,
Nor yet of heathen; only the wan wave
Brake in among dead faces, to and fro   130
Swaying the helpless hands, and up and down
Tumbling the hollow helmets of the fallen,
And shiver'd brands that once had fought with Rome,
And rolling far along the gloomy shores
The voice of days of old and days to be.

    Then spake King Arthur to Sir Bedivere,
And whiter than the mist that all day long
Had held the field of battle was the King:

    'Hearest thou this great voice that shakes the world,
And wastes the narrow realm whereon we move,   140
And beats upon the faces of the dead,
My dead, as tho' they had not died for me?—
O Bedivere, for on my heart hath fallen
Confusion, till I know not what I am,
Nor whence I am, nor whether I be king;
Behold, I seem but king among the dead.'

Then spake the bold Sir Bedivere: 'My King!
King everywhere! and so the dead have kings,
There also will I worship thee as king.
Yet still thy life is whole, and still I live　　　150
Who love thee; but who hates thee, he that brought
The heathen back among us, yonder stands,
Modred, unharm'd, the traitor of thine house.'

Then spake the King: 'My house hath been my doom.
But call not thou this traitor of my house
Who hath but dwelt beneath one roof with me.
My house are rather they who sware my vows,
Yea, even while they brake them, own'd me king.
And well for thee, saying in my dark hour,　　　160
When all the purport of my throne hath fail'd,
That quick or dead thou holdest me for king.
King am I, whatsoever be their cry;
And one last act of kinghood shalt thou see
Yet, ere I pass.' And uttering this the King
Made at the man. Then Modred smote his liege
Hard on that helm which many a heathen sword
Had beaten thin; while Arthur at one blow,
Striking the last stroke with Excalibur,
Slew him, and, all but slain himself, he fell.

So all day long the noise of battle roll'd　　　170
Among the mountains by the winter sea,
Until King Arthur's Table, man by man,
Had fallen in Lyonnesse about their lord,
King Arthur; then, because his wound was deep,
The bold Sir Bedivere uplifted him,
And bore him to a chapel nigh the field,
A broken chancel with a broken cross,
That stood on a dark strait of barren land.
On one side lay the Ocean, and on one　　　180
Lay a great water, and the moon was full.

Then spake King Arthur to Sir Bedivere:
'The sequel of to-day unsolders all
The goodliest fellowship of famous knights
Whereof this world holds record. Such a sleep
They sleep—the men I loved. I think that we
Shall never more, at any future time,
Delight our souls with talk of knightly deeds,
Walking about the gardens and the halls
Of Camelot, as in the days that were.
I perish by this people which I made,—　　　190
Tho' Merlin sware that I should come again

To rule once more—but let what will be be,
I am so deeply smitten thro' the helm
That without help I cannot last till morn.
Thou therefore take my brand Excalibur,
Which was my pride; for thou rememberest how
In those old days, one summer noon, an arm
Rose up from out the bosom of the lake,
Clothed in white samite, mystic, wonderful,
Holding the sword—and how I row'd across   200
And took it, and have worn it, like a king;
And, wheresoever I am sung or told
In aftertime, this also shall be known.
But now delay not; take Excalibur,
And fling him far into the middle mere;
Watch what thou seest, and lightly bring me word.'

      To him replied the bold Sir Bedivere:
'It is not meet, Sir King, to leave thee thus,
Aidless, alone, and smitten thro' the helm—
A little thing may harm a wounded man;   210
Yet I thy hest will all perform at full,
Watch what I see, and lightly bring thee word.'

      So saying, from the ruin'd shrine he stept,
And in the moon athwart the place of tombs,
Where lay the mighty bones of ancient men,
Old knights, and over them the sea-wind sang
Shrill, chill, with flakes of foam. He, stepping down
By zigzag paths and juts of pointed rock,
Came on the shining levels of the lake.

      There drew he forth the brand Excalibur,   220
And o'er him, drawing it, the winter moon,
Brightening the skirts of a long cloud, ran forth
And sparkled keen with frost against the hilt;
For all the haft twinkled with diamond sparks,
Myriads of topaz-lights, and jacinth-work
Of subtlest jewellery. He gazed so long
That both his eyes were dazzled as he stood,
This way and that dividing the swift mind,
In act to throw; but at the last it seem'd
Better to leave Excalibur conceal'd   230
There in the many-knotted water-flags,
That whistled stiff and dry about the marge.
So strode he back slow to the wounded King.

      Then spake King Arthur to Sir Bedivere:
'Hast thou perform'd my mission which I gave?
What is it thou hast seen? or what hast heard?'

And answer made the bold Sir Bedivere:
'I heard the ripple washing in the reeds,
And the wild water lapping on the crag.'

To whom replied King Arthur, faint and pale: 240
'Thou hast betray'd thy nature and thy name,
Not rendering true answer, as beseem'd
Thy fealty, nor like a noble knight;
For surer sign had follow'd, either hand,
Or voice, or else a motion of the mere.
This is a shameful thing for men to lie.
Yet now, I charge thee, quickly go again,
As thou art lief and dear, and do the thing
I bade thee, watch, and lightly bring me word.'

Then went Sir Bedivere the second time   250
Across the ridge, and paced beside the mere,
Counting the dewy pebbles, fixt in thought;
But when he saw the wonder of the hilt,
How curiously and strangely chased, he smote
His palms together, and he cried aloud:

'And if indeed I cast the brand away,
Surely a precious thing, one worthy note,
Should thus be lost for ever from the earth,
Which might have pleasèd the eyes of many men.
What good should follow this, if this were done?   260
What harm, undone? Deep harm to disobey,
Seeing obedience is the bond of rule.
Were it well to obey then, if a king demand
An act unprofitable, against himself?
The King is sick, and knows not what he does.
What record or what relic of my lord
Should be to aftertime, but empty breath
And rumors of a doubt? But were this kept,
Stored in some treasure-house of mighty kings,
Some one might show it at a joust of arms,   270
Saying: "King Arthur's sword, Excalibur,
Wrought by the lonely Maiden of the Lake,
Nine years she wrought it, sitting in the deeps
Upon the hidden bases of the hills."
So might some old man speak in the aftertime
To all the people, winning reverence.
But now much honor and much fame were lost.'

So spake he, clouded with his own conceit,
And hid Excalibur the second time,
And so strode back slow to the wounded King.   280

Then spoke King Arthur, breathing heavily:
'What is it thou hast seen? or what hast heard?'

And answer made the bold Sir Bedivere:
'I heard the water lapping on the crag,
And the long ripple washing in the reeds.'

To whom replied King Arthur, much in wrath:
'Ah miserable, and unkind, untrue,
Unknightly, traitor-hearted! Woe is me!
Authority forgets a dying king,
Laid widow'd of the power in his eye   290
That bow'd the will. I see thee what thou art,
For thou, the latest-left of all my knights,
In whom should meet the offices of all,
Thou wouldst betray me for the precious hilt;
Either from lust of gold, or like a girl
Valuing the giddy pleasure of the eyes.
Yet, for a man may fail in duty twice,
And the third time may prosper, get thee hence;
But, if thou spare to fling Excalibur,
I will arise and slay thee with my hands.'   300

Then quickly rose Sir Bedivere, and ran,
And, leaping down the ridges lightly, plunged
Among the bulrush beds, and clutch'd the sword,
And strongly wheel'd and threw it. The great brand
Made lightnings in the splendor of the moon,
And flashing round and round, and whirl'd in an arch,
Shot like a streamer of the northern morn,
Seen where the moving isles of winter shock
By night, with noises of the Northern Sea.
So flash'd and fell the brand Excalibur;   310
But ere he dipt the surface, rose an arm
Clothed in white samite, mystic, wonderful,
And caught him by the hilt, and brandish'd him
Three times, and drew him under in the mere.
And lightly went the other to the King.

Then spoke King Arthur, drawing thicker breath:
'Now see I by thine eyes that this is done.
Speak out; what is it thou hast heard, or seen?'

And answer made the bold Sir Bedivere:
'Sir King, I closed mine eyelids, lest the gems   320
Should blind my purpose, for I never saw,
Nor shall see, here or elsewhere, till I die,
Not tho' I live three lives of mortal men,

So great a miracle as yonder hilt.
Then with both hands I flung him, wheeling him;
But when I look'd again, behold an arm,
Clothed in white samite, mystic, wonderful,
That caught him by the hilt, and brandish'd him
Three times, and drew him under in the mere.'

And answer made King Arthur, breathing hard: 330
'My end draws nigh; 't is time that I were gone.
Make broad thy shoulders to receive my weight,
And bear me to the margin; yet I fear
My wound hath taken cold, and I shall die.'

So saying, from the pavement he half rose,
Slowly, with pain, reclining on his arm,
And looking wistfully with wide blue eyes
As in a picture. Him Sir Bedivere
Remorsefully regarded thro' his tears,
And would have spoken, but he found not words;   340
Then took with care, and kneeling on one knee,
O'er both his shoulders drew the languid hands,
And rising bore him thro' the place of tombs.

But, as he walk'd, King Arthur panted hard,
Like one that feels a nightmare on his bed
When all the house is mute. So sigh'd the King,
Muttering and murmuring at his ear, 'Quick, quick!
I fear it is too late, and I shall die.'
But the other swiftly strode from ridge to ridge,
Clothed with his breath, and looking, as he walk'd,   350
Larger than human on the frozen hills.
He heard the deep behind him, and a cry
Before. His own thought drove him like a goad.
Dry clash'd his harness in the icy caves
And barren chasms, and all to left and right
The bare black cliff clang'd round him, as he based
His feet on juts of slippery crag that rang
Sharp-smitten with the dint of armed heels—
And on a sudden, lo, the level lake,
And the long glories of the winter moon!   360

Then saw they how there hove a dusky barge,
Dark as a funeral scarf from stem to stern,
Beneath them; and descending they were ware
That all the decks were dense with stately forms,
Black-stoled, black-hooded, like a dream—by these
Three queens with crowns of gold—and from them rose
A cry that shiver'd to the tingling stars,

And, as it were one voice, an agony
Of lamentation, like a wind that shrills
All night in a waste land, where no one comes,   370
Or hath come, since the making of the world.

Then murmur'd Arthur, 'Place me in the barge.'
So to the barge they came. There those three queens
Put forth their hands, and took the King, and wept.
But she that rose the tallest of them all
And fairest laid his head upon her lap,
And loosed the shatter'd casque, and chafed his hands,
And call'd him by his name, complaining loud,
And dropping bitter tears against a brow
Striped with dark blood; for all his face was white   380
And colorless, and like the wither'd moon
Smote by the fresh beam of the springing east;
And all his greaves and cuisses dash'd with drops
Of onset; and the light and lustrous curls—
That made his forehead like a rising sun
High from the dais-throne—were parch'd with dust,
Or, clotted into points and hanging loose,
Mixt with the knightly growth that fringed his lips.
So like a shatter'd column lay the King;
Not like that Arthur who, with lance in rest,   390
From spur to plume a star of tournament,
Shot thro' the lists at Camelot, and charged
Before the eyes of ladies and of kings.

Then loudly cried the bold Sir Bedivere:
'Ah! my Lord Arthur, whither shall I go?
Where shall I hide my forehead and my eyes?
For now I see the true old times are dead,
When every morning brought a noble chance,
And every chance brought out a noble knight.
Such times have been not since the light that led   400
The holy Elders with the gift of myrrh.
But now the whole Round Table is dissolved
Which was an image of the mighty world;
And I, the last, go forth companionless,
And the days darken round me, and the years,
Among new men, strange faces, other minds.'

And slowly answer'd Arthur from the barge:
'The old order changeth, yielding place to new,
And God fulfils himself in many ways,
Lest one good custom should corrupt the world.   410
Comfort thyself; what comfort is in me?
I have lived my life, and that which I have done

May He within himself make pure! but thou,
If thou shouldst never see my face again,
Pray for my soul. More things are wrought by prayer
Than this world dreams of. Wherefore, let thy voice
Rise like a fountain for me night and day.
For what are men better than sheep or goats
That nourish a blind life within the brain,
If, knowing God, they lift not hands of prayer   420
Both for themselves and those who call them friend?
For so the whole round earth is every way
Bound by gold chains about the feet of God.
But now farewell. I am going a long way
With these thou seest—if indeed I go—
For all my mind is clouded with a doubt—
To the island-valley of Avilion;
Where falls not hail, or rain, or any snow,
Nor ever wind blows loudly; but it lies
Deep-meadow'd, happy, fair with orchard lawns   430
And bowery hollows crown'd with summer sea,
Where I will heal me of my grievous wound.'

  So said he, and the barge with oar and sail
Moved from the brink, like some full-breasted swan
That, fluting a wild carol ere her death,
Ruffles her pure cold plume, and takes the flood
With swarthy webs. Long stood Sir Bedivere
Revolving many memories, till the hull
Look'd one black dot against the verge of dawn,
And on the mere the wailing died away.   440

  But when that moan had past for evermore,
The stillness of the dead world's winter dawn
Amazed him, and he groan'd, 'The King is gone.'
And therewithal came on him the weird rhyme,
'From the great deep to the great deep he goes.'

  Whereat he slowly turn'd and slowly clomb
The last hard footstep of that iron crag,
Thence mark'd the black hull moving yet, and cried:
'He passes to be king among the dead,
And after healing of his grievous wound   450
He comes again; but—if he come no more—
O me, be yon dark queens in yon black boat,
Who shriek'd and wail'd, the three whereat we gazed
On that high day, when, clothed with living light,
They stood before his throne in silence, friends
Of Arthur, who should help him at his need?

Then from the dawn it seem'd there came, but faint
As from beyond the limit of the world,
Like the last echo born of a great cry,
Sounds, as if some fair city were one voice   460
Around a king returning from his wars.

Thereat once more he moved about, and clomb
Even to the highest he could climb, and saw,
Straining his eyes beneath an arch of hand,
Or thought he saw, the speck that bare the King,
Down that long water opening on the deep
Somewhere far off, pass on and on, and go
From less to less and vanish into light.
And the new sun rose bringing the new year.

TO THE QUEEN

O LOYAL to the royal in thyself,
And loyal to thy land, as this to thee—
Bear witness, that rememberable day,
When, pale as yet and fever-worn, the Prince
Who scarce had pluck'd his flickering life again
From halfway down the shadow of the grave
Past with thee thro' thy people and their love,
And London roll'd one tide of joy thro' all
Her trebled millions, and loud leagues of man
And welcome! witness, too, the silent cry,   10
The prayer of many a race and creed, and clime—
Thunderless lightnings striking under sea
From sunset and sunrise of all thy realm,
And that true North, whereof we lately heard
A strain to shame us, 'Keep you to yourselves;
So loyal is too costly! friends—your love
Is but a burthen; loose the bond, and go.'
Is this the tone of empire? here the faith
That made us rulers? this, indeed, her voice
And meaning whom the roar of Hougoumont   20
Left mightiest of all peoples under heaven?
What shock has fool'd her since, that she should speak
So feebly? wealthier—wealthier—hour by hour!
The voice of Britain, or a sinking land,
Some third-rate isle half-lost among her seas?
There rang her voice, when the full city peal'd
Thee and thy Prince! The loyal to their crown
Are loyal to their own far sons, who love
Our ocean-empire with her boundless homes
For ever-broadening England, and her throne   30

In our vast Orient, and one isle, one isle,
That knows not her own greatness; if she knows
And dreads it we are fallen.—But thou, my Queen,
Not for itself, but thro' thy living love
For one to whom I made it o'er his grave
Sacred, accept this old imperfect tale,
New-old, and shadowing Sense at war with Soul,
Ideal manhood closed in real man,
Rather than that gray king whose name, a ghost,
Streams like a cloud, man-shaped, from mountain peak,   40
And cleaves to cairn and cromlech still; or him
Of Geoffrey's book, or him of Malleor's, one
Touch'd by the adulterous finger of a time
That hover'd between war and wantonness,
And crownings and dethronements. Take withal
Thy poet's blessing, and his trust that Heaven
Will blow the tempest in the distance back
From thine and ours; for some are scared, who mark,
Or wisely or unwisely, signs of storm,
Waverings of every vane with every wind,   50
And wordy trucklings to the transient hour,
And fierce or careless looseners of the faith,
And Softness breeding scorn of simple life,
Or Cowardice, the child of lust for gold,
Or Labor, with a groan and not a voice,
Or Art with poisonous honey stolen from France,
And that which knows, but careful for itself,
And that which knows not, ruling that which knows
To its own harm. The goal of this great world
Lies beyond sight; yet—if our slowly-grown   60
And crown'd Republic's crowning common-sense,
That saved her many times, not fail—their fears
Are morning shadows huger than the shapes
That cast them, not those gloomier which forego
The darkness of that battle in the west
Where all of high and holy dies away.

ENOCH ARDEN, AND OTHER POEMS

ENOCH ARDEN

Long lines of cliff breaking have
  left a chasm;
And in the chasm are foam and yellow
  sands;
Beyond, red roofs about a narrow
  wharf
In cluster; then a moulder'd church;
  and higher
A long street climbs to one tall-tower'd
  mill;
And high in heaven behind it a gray
  down
With Danish barrows; and a hazel-
  wood,
By autumn nutters haunted, flourishes
Green in a cuplike hollow of the down.
Here on this beach a hundred years
  ago,   10
Three children of three houses, Annie
  Lee,
The prettiest little·damsel in the port,
And Philip Ray, the miller's only son,
And Enoch Arden, a rough sailor's lad
Made orphan by a winter shipwreck,
  play'd
Among the waste and lumber of the
  shore,
Hard coils of cordage, swarthy fishing-
  nets,
Anchors of rusty fluke, and boats up-
  drawn;
And built their castles of dissolving
  sand
To watch them overflow'd, or follow-
  ing up   20
And flying the white breaker, daily
  left
The little footprint daily wash'd away.

A narrow cave ran in beneath the
  cliff;

In this the children play'd at keeping
  house.
Enoch was host one day, Philip the
  next,
While Annie still was mistress; but at
  times
Enoch would hold possession for a
  week:
'This is my house and this my little
  wife.'
'Mine too,' said Philip; 'turn and turn
  about;'
When, if they quarrell'd, Enoch
  stronger-made   30
Was master. Then would Philip, his
  blue eyes
All flooded with the helpless wrath of
  tears,
Shriek out, 'I hate you, Enoch,' and at
  this
The little wife would weep for company,
And pray them not to quarrel for her
  sake,
And say she would be little wife to
  both.

But when the dawn of rosy child-
  hood past,
And the new warmth of life's ascend-
  ing sun
Was felt by either, either fixt his heart
On that one girl; and Enoch spoke his
  love,   40
But Philip loved in silence; and the
  girl
Seem'd kinder unto Philip than to
  him;
But she loved Enoch, tho' she knew it
  not,
And would if ask'd deny it. Enoch set
A purpose evermore before his eyes,
To hoard all savings to the uttermost,

To purchase his own boat, and make a
home
For Annie; and so prosper'd that at
last
A luckier or a bolder fisherman,
A carefuller in peril, did not breathe ⁵⁰
For leagues along that breaker-beaten
coast
Than Enoch. Likewise had he served
a year
On board a merchantman, and made
himself
Full sailor; and he thrice had pluck'd
a life
From the dread sweep of the down-
streaming seas,
And all men look'd upon him favor-
ably.
And ere he touch'd his one-and-twen-
tieth May
He purchased his own boat, and made
a home
For Annie, neat and nestlike, halfway
up
The narrow street that clamber'd to-
ward the mill. ⁶⁰

Then, on a golden autumn eventide,
The younger people making holiday,
With bag and sack and basket, great
and small,
Went nutting to the hazels. Philip
stay'd—
His father lying sick and needing
him—
An hour behind; but as he climb'd the
hill,
Just where the prone edge of the wood
began
To feather toward the hollow, saw the
pair,
Enoch and Annie, sitting hand-in-
hand,
His large gray eyes and weather-
beaten face ⁷⁰
All-kindled by a still and sacred fire,
That burn'd as on an altar. Philip
look'd,
And in their eyes and faces read his
doom;
Then, as their faces drew together,
groan'd,

And slipt aside, and like a wounded
life
Crept down into the hollows of the
wood;
There, while the rest were loud in
merry-making,
Had his dark hour unseen, and rose
and past
Bearing a lifelong hunger in his heart.

So these were wed, and merrily rang
the bells, ⁸⁰
And merrily ran the years, seven
happy years,
Seven happy years of health and com-
petence,
And mutual love and honorable toil,
With children, first a daughter. In him
woke,
With his first babe's first cry, the
noble wish
To save all earnings to the uttermost,
And give his child a better bringing-up
Than his had been, or hers; a wish re-
new'd,
When two years after came a boy to be
The rosy idol of her solitudes, ⁹⁰
While Enoch was abroad on wrathful
seas,
Or often journeying landward; for in
truth
Enoch's white horse, and Enoch's
ocean-spoil
In ocean-smelling osier, and his face,
Rough-redden'd with a thousand win-
ter gales,
Not only to the market-cross were
known,
But in the leafy lanes behind the down,
Far as the portal-warding lion-whelp
And peacock yew-tree of the lonely
Hall,
Whose Friday fare was Enoch's min-
istering. ¹⁰⁰

Then came a change, as all things
human change.
Ten miles to northward of the narrow
port
Open'd a larger haven. Thither used
Enoch at times to go by land or sea;
And once when there, and clambering
on a mast

In harbor, by mischance he slipt and
  fell.
A limb was broken when they lifted
  him;
And while he lay recovering there, his
  wife
Bore him another son, a sickly one.
Another hand crept too across his
  trade   110
Taking her bread and theirs; and on
  him fell,
Altho' a grave and staid God-fearing
  man,
Yet lying thus inactive, doubt and
  gloom.
He seem'd, as in a nightmare of the
  night,
To see his children leading evermore
Low miserable lives of hand-to-mouth,
And her he loved a beggar. Then he
  pray'd,
'Save them from this, whatever comes
  to me.'
And while he pray'd, the master of
  that ship
Enoch had served in, hearing his mis-
  chance,   120
Came, for he knew the man and valued
  him,
Reporting of his vessel China-bound,
And wanting yet a boatswain. Would
  he go?
There yet were many weeks before she
  sail'd,
Sail'd from this port. Would Enoch
  have the place?
And Enoch all at once assented to it,
Rejoicing at that answer to his prayer.

So now that shadow of mischance
  appear'd
No graver than as when some little
  cloud
Cuts off the fiery highway of the sun,
And isles a light in the offing. Yet the
  wife—   131
When he was gone—the children—
  what to do?
Then Enoch lay long-pondering on his
  plans:
To sell the boat—and yet he loved her
  well—

How many a rough sea had he weath-
  er'd in her!
He knew her, as a horseman knows his
  horse—
And yet to sell her—then with what
  she brought
Buy goods and stores—set Annie forth
  in trade
With all that seamen needed or their
  wives—
So might she keep the house while he
  was gone.   140
Should he not trade himself out yon-
  der? go
This voyage more than once? yea,
  twice or thrice—
As oft as needed—last, returning rich,
Become the master of a larger craft,
With fuller profits lead an easier life,
Have all his pretty young ones edu-
  cated,
And pass his days in peace among his
  own.

Thus Enoch in his heart determined
  all;
Then moving homeward came on An-
  nie pale,
Nursing the sickly babe, her latest-
  born.   150
Forward she started with a happy cry,
And laid the feeble infant in his arms;
Whom Enoch took, and handled all his
  limbs,
Appraised his weight and fondled
  father-like,
But had no heart to break his purposes
To Annie, till the morrow, when he
  spoke.

Then first since Enoch's golden
  ring had girt
Her finger, Annie fought against his
  will;
Yet not with brawling opposition she,
But manifold entreaties, many a
  tear,   160
Many a sad kiss by day, by night, re-
  new'd—
Sure that all evil would come out of
  it—
Besought him, supplicating, if he cared
For her or his dear children, not to go.

He not for his own self caring, but
    her,
Her and her children, let her plead in
    vain;
So grieving held his will, and bore it
    thro'.

    For Enoch parted with his old sea-
        friend,
Bought Annie goods and stores, and
    set his hand
To fit their little streetward sitting-
    room   170
With shelf and corner for the goods
    and stores.
So all day long till Enoch's last at
    home,
Shaking their pretty cabin, hammer
    and axe,
Auger and saw, while Annie seem'd
    to hear
Her own death-scaffold raising, shrill'd
    and rang,
Till this was ended, and his careful
    hand,—
The space was narrow,—having or-
    der'd all
Almost as neat and close as Nature
    packs
Her blossom or her seedling, paused;
    and he,
Who needs would work for Annie to
    the last,   180
Ascending tired, heavily slept till
    morn.

    And Enoch faced this morning of
        farewell
Brightly and boldly. All his Annie's
    fears,
Save as his Annie's, were a laughter
    to him.
Yet Enoch as a brave God-fearing
    man
Bow'd himself down, and in that mys-
    tery
Where God-in-man is one with man-
    in-God,
Pray'd for a blessing on his wife and
    babes,
Whatever came to him; and then he
    said:

'Annie, this voyage by the grace of
    God   190
Will bring fair weather yet to all of
    us.
Keep a clean hearth and a clear fire
    for me,
For I'll be back, my girl, before you
    know it;'
Then lightly rocking baby's cradle,
    'and he,
This pretty, puny, weakly little one,—
Nay—for I love him all the better for
    it—
God bless him, he shall sit upon my
    knees
And I will tell him tales of foreign
    parts,
And make him merry, when I come
    home again.
Come, Annie, come, cheer up before
    I go.'   200

    Him running on thus hopefully she
        heard,
And almost hoped herself; but when
    he turn'd
The current of his talk to graver
    things
In sailor fashion roughly sermonizing
On providence and trust in heaven,
    she heard,
Heard and not heard him; as the vil-
    lage girl,
Who sets her pitcher underneath the
    spring,
Musing on him that used to fill it for
    her,
Hears and not hears, and lets it over-
    flow.

    At length she spoke: 'O Enoch, you
        are wise;   210
And yet for all your wisdom well
    know I
That I shall look upon your face no
    more.'

    'Well, then,' said Enoch, 'I shall
        look on yours.
Annie, the ship I sail in passes here'—
He named the day;—'get you a sea-
    man's glass,

Spy out my face, and laugh at all
  your fears.'

But when the last of those last
  moments came:
'Annie, my girl, cheer up, be comforted,
Look to the babes, and till I come
  again
Keep everything shipshape, for I
  must go.   220
And fear no more for me; or if you
  fear,
Cast all your cares on God; that
  anchor holds.
Is He not yonder in those uttermost
Parts of the morning? if I flee to
  these,
Can I go from Him? and the sea is
  His,
The sea is His; He made it.'

                          Enoch rose,
Cast his strong arms about his drooping wife,
And kiss'd his wonder-stricken little
  ones;
But for the third, the sickly one, who
  slept
After a night of feverous wakefulness,   230
When Annie would have raised him
  Enoch said,
'Wake him not, let him sleep; how
  should the child
Remember this?' and kiss'd him in
  his cot.
But Annie from her baby's forehead
  clipt
A tiny curl, and gave it; this he kept
Thro' all his future, but now hastily
  caught
His bundle, waved his hand, and
  went his way.

She, when the day that Enoch mention'd came,
Borrow'd a glass, but all in vain. Perhaps
She could not fix the glass to suit her
  eye;   240
Perhaps her eye was dim, hand tremulous;

She saw him not, and while he stood
  on deck
Waving, the moment and the vessel
  past.

Even to the last dip of the vanishing sail
She watch'd it, and departed weeping
  for him;
Then, tho' she mourn'd his absence
  as his grave,
Set her sad will no less to chime with
  his,
But throve not in her trade, not being bred
To barter, nor compensating the want
By shrewdness, neither capable of
  lies,   250
Nor asking overmuch and taking less,
And still foreboding 'what would
  Enoch say?'
For more than once, in days of difficulty
And pressure, had she sold her wares
  for less
Than what she gave in buying what
  she sold.
She fail'd and sadden'd knowing it;
  and thus,
Expectant of that news which never
  came,
Gain'd for her own a scanty sustenance,
And lived a life of silent melancholy.

Now the third child was sicklyborn and grew   260
Yet sicklier, tho' the mother cared for
  it
With all a mother's care; nevertheless,
Whether her business often call'd her
  from it,
Or thro' the want of what it needed
  most,
Or means to pay the voice who best
  could tell
What most it needed—howsoe'er it
  was,
After a lingering,—ere she was
  aware,—
Like the caged bird escaping suddenly,
The little innocent soul flitted away.

In that same week when Annie
    buried it,   270
Philip's true heart, which hunger'd
    for her peace,—
Since Enoch left he had not look'd
    upon her,—
Smote him, as having kept aloof so
    long.
'Surely,' said Philip, 'I may see her
    now,
May be some little comfort;' there-
    fore went,
Past thro' the solitary room in front,
Paused for a moment at an inner
    door,
Then struck it thrice, and, no one
    opening,
Enter'd, but Annie, seated with her
    grief,
Fresh from the burial of her little
    one,   280
Cared not to look on any human face,
But turn'd her own toward the wall
    and wept.
Then Philip standing up said falter-
    ingly,
'Annie, I came to ask a favor of you.'

He spoke; the passion in her
    moan'd reply,
'Favor from one so sad and so for-
    lorn
As I am!' half abashed him; yet un-
    ask'd,
His bashfulness and tenderness at
    war,
He set himself beside her, saying to
    her:

'I came to speak to you of what he
    wish'd,   290
Enoch, your husband. I have ever
    said
You chose the best among us—a
    strong man;
For where he fixt his heart he set his
    hand
To do the thing he will'd, and bore it
    thro'.
And wherefore did he go this weary
    way,
And leave you lonely? not to see the
    world—

For pleasure?—nay, but for the
    wherewithal
To give his babes a better bringing
    up
Than his had been, or yours; that
    was his wish.
And if he come again, vext will he
    be   300
To find the precious morning hours
    were lost.
And it would vex him even in his
    grave,
If he could know his babes were run-
    ning wild
Like colts about the waste. So, An-
    nie, now—
Have we not known each other all
    our lives?
I do beseech you by the love you bear
Him and his children not to say me
    nay—
For, if you will, when Enoch comes
    again
Why then he shall repay me—if you
    will,
Annie—for I am rich and well-to-
    do.   310
Now let me put the boy and girl to
    school;
This is the favor that I came to ask.'

Then Annie with her brows against
    the wall
Answer'd, 'I cannot look you in the
    face;
I seem so foolish and so broken down.
When you came in my sorrow broke
    me down;
And now I think your kindness
    breaks me down.
But Enoch lives; that is borne in on
    me;
He will repay you. Money can be re-
    paid,
Not kindness such as yours.'

           And Philip ask'd,   320
'Then you will let me, Annie?'

               There she turn'd,
She rose, and fixt her swimming eyes
    upon him,
And dwelt a moment on his kindly
    face,

Then calling down a blessing on his
head
Caught at his hand, and wrung it pas-
sionately,
And past into the little garth beyond.
So lifted up in spirit he moved away.

Then Philip put the boy and girl to
school,
And bought them needful books, and
every way,
Like one who does his duty by his
own,   330
Made himself theirs; and tho' for
Annie's sake,
Fearing the lazy gossip of the port,
He oft denied his heart his dearest
wish,
And seldom crost her threshold, yet
he sent
Gifts by the children, garden-herbs
and fruit,
The late and early roses from his
wall,
Or conies from the down, and now
and then,
With some pretext of fineness in the
meal
To save the offence of charitable,
flour
From his tall mill that whistled on the
waste.   340

But Philip did not fathom Annie's
mind;
Scarce could the woman, when he
came upon her,
Out of a full heart and boundless
gratitude
Light on a broken word to thank him
with.
But Philip was her children's all-in-
all;
From distant corners of the street
they ran
To greet his hearty welcome heartily;
Lords of his house and of his mill
were they,
Worried his passive ear with petty
wrongs
Or pleasures, hung upon him, play'd
with him   350

And call'd him Father Philip. Philip
gain'd
As Enoch lost, for Enoch seem'd to
them
Uncertain as a vision or a dream,
Faint as a figure seen in early dawn
Down at the far end of an avenue,
Going we know not where; and so
ten years,
Since Enoch left his hearth and na-
tive land,
Fled forward, and no news of Enoch
came.

It chanced one evening Annie's
children long'd
To go with others nutting to the
wood,   360
And Annie would go with them; then
they begg'd
For Father Philip, as they call'd him,
too.
Him, like the working bee in blossom-
dust,
Blanch'd with his mill, they found;
and saying to him,
'Come with us, Father Philip,' he
denied;
But when the children pluck'd at him
to go,
He laugh'd, and yielded readily to
their wish,
For was not Annie with them? and
they went.

But after scaling half the weary
down,
Just where the prone edge of the
wood began   370
To feather toward the hollow, all her
force
Fail'd her; and sighing, 'Let me rest,'
she said.
So Philip rested with her well-con-
tent;
While all the younger ones with jubilant cries
Broke from their elders, and tumultu-
ously
Down thro' the whitening hazels
made a plunge
To the bottom, and dispersed, and
bent or broke

The lithe reluctant boughs to tear
    away
Their tawny clusters, crying to each
    other
And calling, here and there, about the
    wood.   380

  But Philip sitting at her side forgot
Her presence, and remember'd one
    dark hour
Here in this wood, when like a
    wounded life
He crept into the shadow. At last he
    said,
Lifting his honest forehead, 'Listen,
    Annie,
How merry they are down yonder in
    the wood.
Tired, Annie?' for she did not speak
    a word.
'Tired?' but her face had fallen upon
    her hands;
At which, as with a kind of anger in
    him,
'The ship was lost,' he said, 'the ship
    was lost!   390
No more of that! why should you kill
    yourself
And make them orphans quite?' And
    Annie said,
'I thought not of it; but—I know not
    why—
Their voices make me feel so soli-
    tary.'

  Then Philip coming somewhat
    closer spoke:
'Annie, there is a thing upon my
    mind,
And it has been upon my mind so
    long
That, tho' I know not when it first
    came there,
I know that it will out at last. O
    Annie,
It is beyond all hope, against all
    chance,   400
That he who left you ten long years
    ago
Should still be living; well, then—let
    me speak.
I grieve to see you poor and wanting
    help;

I cannot help you as I wish to do
Unless—they say that women are so
    quick—
Perhaps you know what I would have
    you know—
I wish you for my wife. I fain would
    prove
A father to your children; I do think
They love me as a father; I am sure
That I love them as if they were
    mine own;   410
And I believe, if you were fast my
    wife,
That after all these sad uncertain
    years
We might be still as happy as God
    grants
To any of his creatures. Think upon
    it;
For I am well-to-do—no kin, no care,
No burthen, save my care for you and
    yours,
And we have known each other all
    our lives,
And I have loved you longer than you
    know.'

  Then answer'd Annie—tenderly she
    spoke:
'You have been as God's good angel
    in our house.   420
God bless you for it, God reward you
    for it,
Philip, with something happier than
    myself.
Can one love twice? can you be ever
    loved
As Enoch was? what is it that you
    ask?'
'I am content,' he answer'd, 'to be
    loved
A little after Enoch.' 'O,' she cried,
Scared as it were, 'dear Philip, wait a
    while.
If Enoch comes—but Enoch will not
    come—
Yet wait a year, a year is not so long.
Surely I shall be wiser in a year.   430
O, wait a little!' Philip sadly said,
'Annie, as I have waited all my life
I well may wait a little.' 'Nay,' she
    cried,

'I am bound: you have my promise—
in a year.
Will you not bide your year as I bide
mine?'
And Philip answer'd, 'I will bide my
year.'

Here both were mute, till Philip
glancing up
Beheld the dead flame of the fallen
day
Pass from the Danish barrow overhead;
Then, fearing night and chill for Annie, rose   440
And sent his voice beneath him thro'
the wood.
Up came the children laden with their
spoil;
Then all descended to the port, and
there
At Annie's door he paused and gave
his hand,
Saying gently, 'Annie, when I spoke
to you,
That was your hour of weakness. I
was wrong,
I am always bound to you, but you
are free.'
Then Annie weeping answer'd, 'I am
bound.'

She spoke; and in one moment as
it were,
While yet she went about her household ways,   450
Even as she dwelt upon his latest
words,
That he had loved her longer than she
knew,
That autumn into autumn flash'd
again,
And there he stood once more before
her face,
Claiming her promise. 'Is it a year?'
she ask'd.
'Yes, if the nuts,' he said, 'be ripe
again;
Come out and see.' But she—she put
him off—
So much to look to—such a change—
a month—

Give her a month—she knew that she
was bound—
A month—no more. Then Philip with
his eyes   460
Full of that lifelong hunger, and his
voice
Shaking a little like a drunkard's
hand,
'Take your own time, Annie, take
your own time.'
And Annie could have wept for pity
of him;
And yet she held him on delayingly
With many a scarce-believable ex-
cuse,
Trying his truth and his long-suf-
ferance,
Till half another year had slipt away.

By this the lazy gossips of the port,
Abhorrent of a calculation crost,   470
Began to chafe as at a personal wrong.
Some thought that Philip did but
trifle with her;
Some that she but held off to draw
him on;
And others laugh'd at her and Philip
too,
As simple folk that knew not their own
minds;
And one, in whom all evil fancies
clung
Like serpent eggs together, laughingly
Would hint at worse in either. Her
own son
Was silent, tho' he often look'd his
wish;
But evermore the daughter prest upon
her   480
To wed the man so dear to all of them
And lift the household out of poverty;
And Philip's rosy face contracting
grew
Careworn and wan; and all these
things fell on her
Sharp as reproach.

                    At last one night it chanced
That Annie could not sleep, but
earnestly
Pray'd for a sign, 'My Enoch, is he
gone?'

Then compass'd round by the blind
  wall of night
Brook'd not the expectant terror of
  her heart,
Started from bed, and struck herself
  a light,   490
Then desperately seized the holy
  Book,
Suddenly set it wide to find a sign,
Suddenly put her finger on the text,
'Under the palm-tree.' That was noth-
  ing to her,
No meaning there; she closed the
  Book and slept.
When lo! her Enoch sitting on a
  height,
Under a palm-tree, over him the sun.
'He is gone,' she thought, 'he is happy,
  he is singing
Hosanna in the highest; yonder shines
The Sun of Righteousness, and these
  be palms   500
Whereof the happy people strowing
  cried
"Hosanna in the highest!" ' Here she
  woke,
Resolved, sent for him and said wildly
  to him,
'There is no reason why we should not
  wed.'
'Then for God's sake,' he answer'd,
  'both our sakes,
So you will wed me, let it be at once.'

So these were wed, and merrily rang
  the bells,
Merrily rang the bells, and they were
  wed.
But never merrily beat Annie's heart.
A footstep seem'd to fall beside her
  path,   510
She knew not whence; a whisper on
  her ear,
She knew not what; nor loved she to
  be left
Alone at home, nor ventured out alone.
What ail'd her then that, ere she en-
  ter'd, often
Her hand dwelt lingeringly on the
  latch,
Fearing to enter? Philip thought he
  knew:

Such doubts and fears were common
  to her state,
Being with child; but when her child
  was born,
Then her new child was as herself renew'd,
Then the new mother came about her
  heart,   520
Then her good Philip was her all-in-
  all,
And that mysterious instinct wholly
  died.

  And where was Enoch? Prosper-
  ously sail'd
The ship 'Good Fortune,' tho' at set-
  ting forth
The Biscay, roughly ridging eastward,
  shook
And almost overwhelm'd her, yet un-
  vext
She slipt across the summer of the
  world,
Then after a long tumble about the
  Cape
And frequent interchange of foul and
  fair,
She passing thro' the summer world
  again,   530
The breath of heaven came contin-
  ually
And sent her sweetly by the golden
  isles,
Till silent in her oriental haven.

  There Enoch traded for himself,
  and bought
Quaint monsters for the market of
  those times,
A gilded dragon also for the babes.

  Less lucky her home-voyage: at
  first indeed
Thro' many a fair sea-circle, day by
  day,
Scarce-rocking, her full-busted figure-
  head
Stared o'er the ripple feathering from
  her bows: 540
Then follow'd calms, and then winds
  variable,
Then baffling, a long course of them;
  and last

Storm, such as drove her under moon-
less heavens
Till hard upon the cry of 'breakers'
came
The crash of ruin, and the loss of all
But Enoch and two others. Half the
night,
Buoy'd upon floating tackle and
broken spars,
These drifted, stranding on an isle at
morn
Rich, but the loneliest in a lonely sea.

No want was there of human suste-
nance,   550
Soft fruitage, mighty nuts, and nour-
ishing roots;
Nor save for pity was it hard to take
The helpless life so wild that it was
tame.
There in a seaward-gazing mountain-
gorge
They built, and thatch'd with leaves
of palm, a hut,
Half hut, half native cavern. So the
three,
Set in this Eden of all plenteousness,
Dwelt with eternal summer, ill-con-
tent.
For one, the youngest, hardly more
than boy,
Hurt in that night of sudden ruin and
wreck,   560
Lay lingering out a five-years' death-
in-life.
They could not leave him. After he
was gone,
The two remaining found a fallen
stem;
And Enoch's comrade, careless of himself,
Fire-hollowing this in Indian fashion,
fell
Sun-stricken, and that other lived
alone.
In those two deaths he read God's
warning 'wait.'

The mountain wooded to the peak,
the lawns
And winding glades high up like ways
to heaven,

The slender coco's drooping crown of
plumes,   570
The lightning flash of insect and of
bird,
The lustre of the long convolvuluses
That coil'd around the stately stems,
and ran
Even to the limit of the land, the
glows
And glories of the broad belt of the
world,—
All these he saw; but what he fain had
seen
He could not see, the kindly human
face,
Nor ever hear a kindly voice, but
heard
The myriad shriek of wheeling ocean-
fowl,
The league-long roller thundering on
the reef,   580
The moving whisper of huge trees that
branch'd
And blossom'd in the zenith, or the
sweep
Of some precipitous rivulet to the
wave,
As down the shore he ranged, or all
day long
Sat often in the seaward-gazing gorge,
A shipwreck'd sailor, waiting for a
sail.
No sail from day to day, but every day
The sunrise broken into scarlet shafts
Among the palms and ferns and preci-
pices;   589
The blaze upon the waters to the east;
The blaze upon his island overhead;
The blaze upon the waters to the west;
Then the great stars that globed them-
selves in heaven,
The hollower-bellowing ocean, and
again
The scarlet shafts of sunrise—but no
sail.

There often as he watch'd or seem'd
to watch,
So still the golden lizard on him
paused,
A phantom made of many phantoms
moved

Before him haunting him, or he him-
    self
Moved haunting people, things, and
    places, known   600
Far in a darker isle beyond the line;
The babes, their babble, Annie, the
    small house,
The climbing street, the mill, the
    leafy lanes,
The peacock yew-tree and the lonely
    Hall,
The horse he drove, the boat he sold,
    the chill
November dawns and dewy-glooming
    downs,
The gentle shower, the smell of dying
    leaves,
And the low moan of leaden-color'd
    seas.

    Once likewise, in the ringing of his
        ears,
Tho' faintly, merrily—far and far
    away—   610
He heard the pealing of his parish
    bells;
Then, tho' he knew not wherefore,
    started up
Shuddering, and when the beauteous
    hateful isle
Return'd upon him, had not his poor
    heart
Spoken with That which being every-
    where
Lets none who speaks with Him seem
    all alone,
Surely the man had died of solitude.

    Thus over Enoch's early-silvering
        head
The sunny and rainy seasons came and
    went
Year after year. His hopes to see his
    own,   620
And pace the sacred old familiar fields,
Not yet had perish'd, when his lonely
    doom
Came suddenly to an end. Another
    ship—
She wanted water—blown by baffling
    winds,
Like the 'Good Fortune,' from her
    destined course,

Stay'd by this isle, not knowing where
    she lay;
For since the mate had seen at early
    dawn
Across a break on the mist-wreathen
    isle
The silent water slipping from the
    hills,
They sent a crew that landing burst
    away   630
In search of stream or fount, and fill'd
    the shores
With clamor. Downward from his
    mountain gorge
Stept the long-hair'd, long-bearded
    solitary,
Brown, looking hardly human,
    strangely clad,
Muttering and mumbling, idiot-like it
    seem'd,
With inarticulate rage, and making
    signs
They knew not what; and yet he led
    the way
To where the rivulets of sweet water
    ran,
And ever as he mingled with the crew,
And heard them talking, his long-
    bounden tongue   640
Was loosen'd, till he made them un-
    derstand;
Whom, when their casks were fill'd,
    they took aboard.
And there the tale he utter'd brokenly,
Scarce-credited at first but more and
    more,
Amazed and melted all who listen'd
    to it;
And clothes they gave him and free
    passage home,
But oft he work'd among the rest and
    shook
His isolation from him. None of these
Came from his country, or could an-
    swer him,
If question'd, aught of what he cared
    to know.   650
And dull the voyage was with long
    delays,
The vessel scarce sea-worthy; but
    ever more
His fancy fled before the lazy wind

Returning, till beneath a clouded moon
He like a lover down thro' all his blood
Drew in the dewy meadowy morning-breath
Of England, blown across her ghostly wall.
And that same morning officers and men
Levied a kindly tax upon themselves,
Pitying the lonely man, and gave him it;   660
Then moving up the coast they landed him,
Even in that harbor whence he sail'd before.

There Enoch spoke no word to any one,
But homeward—home—what home? had he a home?—
His home, he walk'd. Bright was that afternoon,
Sunny but chill; till drawn thro' either chasm,
Where either haven open'd on the deeps,
Roll'd a sea-haze and whelm'd the world in gray,
Cut off the length of highway on before,
And left but narrow breadth to left and right   670
Of wither'd holt or tilth or pasturage.
On the nigh-naked tree the robin piped
Disconsolate, and thro' the dripping haze
The dead weight of the dead leaf bore it down.
Thicker the drizzle grew, deeper the gloom;
Last, as it seem'd, a great mist-blotted light
Flared on him, and he came upon the place.

Then down the long street having slowly stolen,
His heart foreshadowing all calamity,
His eyes upon the stones, he reach'd the home   680
Where Annie lived and loved him, and his babes

In those far-off seven happy years were born;
But finding neither light nor murmur there—
A bill of sale gleam'd thro' the drizzle—crept
Still downward thinking, 'dead or dead to me!'

Down to the pool and narrow wharf he went,
Seeking a tavern which of old he knew,
A front of timber-crost antiquity,
So propt, worm-eaten, ruinously old,
He thought it must have gone; but he was gone   690
Who kept it, and his widow Miriam Lane,
With daily-dwindling profits held the house;
A haunt of brawling seamen once, but now
Stiller, with yet a bed for wandering men.
There Enoch rested silent many days.

But Miriam Lane was good and garrulous,
Nor let him be, but often breaking in,
Told him, with other annals of the port,
Not knowing—Enoch was so brown, so bow'd,   699
So broken—all the story of his house:
His baby's death, her growing poverty,
How Philip put her little ones to school,
And kept them in it, his long wooing her,
Her slow consent and marriage, and the birth
Of Philip's child; and o'er his countenance
No shadow past, nor motion. Any one,
Regarding, well had deem'd he felt the tale
Less than the teller; only when she closed,
'Enoch, poor man, was cast away and lost,'   709
He, shaking his gray head pathetically,

Repeated muttering, 'cast away and
    lost;'
Again in deeper inward whispers,
    'lost!'

But Enoch yearn'd to see her face
    again:
'If I might look on her sweet face
    again,
And know that she is happy.' So the
    thought
Haunted and harass'd him, and drove
    him forth,
At evening when the dull November
    day
Was growing duller twilight, to the
    hill.
There he sat down gazing on all be-
    low;
There did a thousand memories roll
    upon him,   720
Unspeakable for sadness. By and by
The ruddy square of comfortable
    light,
Far-blazing from the rear of Philip's
    house,
Allured him, as the beacon-blaze al-
    lures
The bird of passage, till he madly
    strikes
Against it and beats out his weary
    life.

For Philip's dwelling fronted on the
    street,
The latest house to landward; but be-
    hind,
With one small gate that open'd on the
    waste,
Flourish'd a little garden square and
    wall'd,   730
And in it throve an ancient evergreen,
A yew-tree, and all round it ran a walk
Of shingle, and a walk divided it.
But Enoch shunn'd the middle walk
    and stole
Up by the wall, behind the yew; and
    thence
That which he better might have
    shunn'd, if griefs
Like his have worse or better, Enoch
    saw.

For cups and silver on the burnish'd
    board
Sparkled and shone; so genial was the
    hearth;
And on the right hand of the hearth
    he saw   740
Philip, the slighted suitor of old times,
Stout, rosy, with his babe across his
    knees;
And o'er her second father stoopt a
    girl,
A later but a loftier Annie Lee,
Fair-hair'd and tall, and from her
    lifted hand
Dangled a length of ribbon and a ring
To tempt the babe, who rear'd his
    creasy arms,
Caught at and ever miss'd it, and they
    laugh'd;
And on the left hand of the hearth he
    saw
The mother glancing often toward her
    babe,   750
But turning now and then to speak
    with him,
Her son, who stood beside her tall and
    strong,
And saying that which pleased him,
    for he smiled.

Now when the dead man come to
    life beheld
His wife his wife no more, and saw the
    babe
Hers, yet not his, upon the father's
    knee,
And all the warmth, the peace, the
    happiness,
And his own children tall and beauti-
    ful,
And him, that other, reigning in his
    place,
Lord of his rights and of his children's
    love—   760
Then he, tho' Miriam Lane had told
    him all,
Because things seen are mightier than
    things heard,
Stagger'd and shook, holding the
    branch, and fear'd
To send abroad a shrill and terrible
    cry,

Which in one moment, like the blast
   of doom,
Would shatter all the happiness of the
   hearth.

  He therefore turning softly like a
   thief,
Lest the harsh shingle should grate
   underfoot,
And feeling all along the garden-wall,
Lest he should swoon and tumble and
   be found,   770
Crept to the gate, and open'd it and
   closed,
As lightly as a sick man's chamber-
   door,
Behind him, and came out upon the
   waste.

  And there he would have knelt, but
   that his knees
Were feeble, so that falling prone he
   dug
His fingers into the wet earth, and
   pray'd:

  'Too hard to bear! why did they
   take me thence?
O God Almighty, blessed Saviour,
   Thou
That didst uphold me on my lonely
   isle,   779
Uphold me, Father, in my loneliness
A little longer! aid me, give me
   strength
Not to tell her, never to let her know.
Help me not to break in upon her
   peace.
My children too! must I not speak to
   these?
They know me not. I should betray
   myself.
Never! no father's kiss for me—the
   girl
So like her mother, and the boy, my
   son.'

  There speech and thought and nature fail'd a little,
And he lay tranced; but when he rose
   and paced   789
Back toward his solitary home again,

All down the long and narrow street
   he went
Beating it in upon his weary brain,
As tho' it were the burthen of a song,
'Not to tell her, never to let her
   know.'

  He was not all unhappy. His resolve
Upbore him, and firm faith, and ever-
   more
Prayer from a living source within the
   will,
And beating up thro' all the bitter
   world,
Like fountains of sweet water in the
   sea,
Kept him a living soul. 'This miller's
   wife,'   800
He said to Miriam, 'that you spoke
   about,
Has she no fear that her first husband
   lives?'
'Ay, ay, poor soul,' said Miriam, 'fear
   enow!
If you could tell her you had seen him
   dead,
Why, that would be her comfort;' and
   he thought,
'After the Lord has call'd me she shall
   know,
I wait His time;' and Enoch set him-
   self,
Scorning an alms, to work whereby to
   live.
Almost to all things could he turn his
   hand.
Cooper he was and carpenter, and
   wrought   810
To make the boatmen fishing-nets, or
   help'd
At lading and unlading the tall barks
That brought the stinted commerce of
   those days,
Thus earn'd a scanty living for him-
   self.
Yet since he did but labor for himself,
Work without hope, there was not life
   in it
Whereby the man could live; and as
   the year
Roll'd itself round again to meet the
   day

When Enoch had return'd, a languor came   819
Upon him, gentle sickness, gradually
Weakening the man, till he could do no more,
But kept the house, his chair, and last his bed.
And Enoch bore his weakness cheerfully.
For sure no gladlier does the stranded wreck
See thro' the gray skirts of a lifting squall
The boat that bears the hope of life approach
To save the life despair'd of, than he saw
Death dawning on him, and the close of all.

For thro' that dawning gleam'd a kindlier hope   829
On Enoch thinking, 'after I am gone,
Then may she learn I loved her to the last.'
He call'd aloud for Miriam Lane and said:
'Woman, I have a secret—only swear,
Before I tell you—swear upon the book
Not to reveal it, till you see me dead.'
'Dead,' clamor'd the good woman, 'hear him talk!
I warrant, man, that we shall bring you round.'
'Swear,' added Enoch sternly, 'on the book;'
And on the book, half-frighted, Miriam swore.
Then Enoch rolling his gray eyes upon her,   840
'Did you know Enoch Arden of this town?'
'Know him?' she said, 'I knew him far away.
Ay, ay, I mind him coming down the street;
Held his head high, and cared for no man, he.'
Slowly and sadly Enoch answer'd her:
'His head is low, and no man cares for him.

I think I have not three days more to live;
I am the man.' At which the woman gave
A half-incredulous, half-hysterical cry:
'You Arden, you! nay,—sure he was a foot   850
Higher than you be.' Enoch said again:
'My God has bow'd me down to what I am;
My grief and solitude have broken me;
Nevertheless, know you that I am he
Who married—but that name has twice been changed—
I married her who married Philip Ray.
Sit, listen.' Then he told her of his voyage,
His wreck, his lonely life, his coming back,
His gazing in on Annie, his resolve,
And how he kept it. As the woman heard,   860
Fast flow'd the current of her easy tears,
While in her heart she yearn'd incessantly
To rush abroad all round the little haven,
Proclaiming Enoch Arden and his woes;
But awed and promise-bounden she forbore,
Saying only, 'See your bairns before you go!
Eh, let me fetch 'em, Arden,' and arose
Eager to bring them down, for Enoch hung
A moment on her words, but then replied:

'Woman, disturb me not now at the last,   870
But let me hold my purpose till I die.
Sit down again; mark me and understand,
While I have power to speak. I charge you now,
When you shall see her, tell her that I died

Blessing her, praying for her, loving
  her;
Save for the bar between us, loving
  her
As when she laid her head beside my
  own.
And tell my daughter Annie, whom I
  saw
So like her mother, that my latest
  breath
Was spent in blessing her and praying
  for her.   880
And tell my son that I died blessing
  him.
And say to Philip that I blest him too;
He never meant us anything but good.
But if my children care to see me
  dead,
Who hardly knew me living, let them
  come,
I am their father; but she must not
  come,
For my dead face would vex her after-
  life.
And now there is but one of all my
  blood
Who will embrace me in the world-
  to-be.
This hair is his, she cut it off and gave
  it,   890
And I have borne it with me all these
  years,
And thought to bear it with me to my
  grave;
But now my mind is changed, for I
  shall see him,
My babe in bliss. Wherefore when I
  am gone,
Take, give her this, for it may comfort
  her;
It will moreover be a token to her
That I am he.'

    He ceased; and Miriam Lane
Made such a voluble answer promis-
  ing all,
That once again he roll'd his eyes upon
  her
Repeating all he wish'd, and once
  again   900
She promised.

Then the third night after this,
While Enoch slumber'd motionless
  and pale,
And Miriam watch'd and dozed at in-
  tervals,
There came so loud a calling of the sea
That all the houses in the haven rang.
He woke, he rose, he spread his arms
  abroad,
Crying with a loud voice, 'A sail! a
  sail!
I am saved;' and so fell back and
  spoke no more.

So past the strong heroic soul away.
And when they buried him the little
  port   910
Had seldom seen a costlier funeral.

AYLMER'S FIELD

1793

DUST are our frames; and, gilded
  dust, our pride
Looks only for a moment whole and
  sound,
Like that long-buried body of the
  king,
Found lying with his urns and ornaments,
Which at a touch of light, an air of
  heaven,
Slipt into ashes, and was found no
  more.

  Here is a story which in rougher
  shape
Came from a grizzled cripple, whom I
  saw
Sunning himself in a waste field
  alone—
Old, and a mine of memories—who
  had served,   10
Long since, a bygone rector of the
  place,
And been himself a part of what he
  told.

  SIR AYLMER AYLMER, that almighty
  man,
The county God—in whose capacious
  hall,

Hung with a hundred shields, the
    family tree
Sprang from the midriff of a prostrate
    king—
Whose blazing wyvern weathercock'd
    the spire,
Stood from his walls and wing'd his
    entry-gates,
And swang besides on many a windy
    sign—
Whose eyes from under a pyramidal
    head   20
Saw from his windows nothing save
    his own—
What lovelier of his own had he than
    her,
His only child, his Edith, whom he
    loved
As heiress and not heir regretfully?
But 'he that marries her marries her
    name.'
This fiat somewhat soothed himself
    and wife,
His wife a faded beauty of the Baths,
Insipid as the queen upon a card;
Her all of thought and bearing hardly
    more   29
Than his own shadow in a sickly sun.

A land of hops and poppy-mingled
    corn,
Little about it stirring save a brook!
A sleepy land, where under the same
    wheel
The same old rut would deepen year
    by year;
Where almost all the village had one
    name;
Where Aylmer followed Aylmer at the
    Hall
And Averill Averill at the Rectory
Thrice over; so that rectory and Hall,
Bound in an immemorial intimacy,
Were open to each other; tho' to
    dream   40
That Love could bind them closer well
    had made
The hoar hair of the baronet bristle up
With horror, worse than had he heard
    his priest
Preach an inverted scripture, sons of
    men,

Daughters of God; so sleepy was the
    land.

And might not Averill, had he will'd
    it so,
Somewhere beneath his own low range
    of roofs,
Have also set his many-shielded tree?
There was an Aylmer-Averill marriage
    once,
When the red rose was redder than
    itself,   50
And York's white rose as red as Lan-
    caster's,
With wounded peace which each had
    prick'd to death.
'Not proven,' Averill said, or laugh-
    ingly,
'Some other race of Averills'—proven
    or no,
What cared he? what, if other or the
    same?
He lean'd not on his fathers but him-
    self.
But Leolin, his brother, living oft
With Averill, and a year or two before
Call'd to the bar, but ever call'd away
By one low voice to one dear neigh-
    borhood,   60
Would often, in his walks with Edith,
    claim
A distant kinship to the gracious blood
That shook the heart of Edith hearing
    him.

Sanguine he was; a but less vivid
    hue
Than of that islet in the chestnut-
    bloom
Flamed in his cheek; and eager eyes,
    that still
Took joyful note of all things joyful,
    beam'd,
Beneath a mane-like mass of rolling
    gold,
Their best and brightest when they
    dwelt on hers,
Edith, whose pensive beauty, perfect
    else,   70
But subject to the season or the mood,
Shone like a mystic star between the
    less
And greater glory varying to and fro,

We know not wherefore; bounteously
    made,
And yet so finely, that a troublous
    touch
Thinn'd, or would seem to thin her in
    a day,
A joyous to dilate, as toward the light.
And these had been together from the
    first.
Leolin's first nurse was, five years
    after, hers.
So much the boy foreran; but when
    his date   80
Doubled her own, for want of play-
    mates, he—
Since Averill was a decad and a half
His elder, and their parents under-
    ground—
Had tost his ball and flown his kite,
    and roll'd
His hoop to pleasure Edith, with her
    dipt
Against the rush of the air in the prone
    swing,
Made blossom-ball or daisy-chain, ar-
    ranged
Her garden, sow'd her name and kept
    it green
In living letters, told her fairy-tales,
Show'd her the fairy footings on the
    grass,   90
The little dells of cowslip, fairy palms,
The petty mare's-tail forest, fairy
    pines,
Or from the tiny pitted target blew
What look'd a flight of fairy arrows
    aim'd
All at one mark, all hitting, make-
    believes
For Edith and himself; or else he
    forged,
But that was later, boyish histories
Of battle, bold adventure, dungeon,
    wreck,
Flights, terrors, sudden rescues, and
    true love
Crown'd after trial; sketches rude and
    faint,   100
But where a passion yet unborn per-
    haps
Lay hidden as the music of the moon
Sleeps in the plain eggs of the night-
    ingale.

And thus together, save for college-
    times
Or Temple-eaten terms, a couple, fair
As ever painter painted, poet sang,
Or heaven in lavish bounty moulded,
    grew.
And more and more, the maiden
    woman-grown,
He wasted hours with Averill; there,
    when first   109
The tented winter-field was broken up
Into that phalanx of the summer
    spears
That soon should wear the garland;
    there again
When burr and bine were gather'd;
    lastly there
At Christmas; ever welcome at the
    Hall,
On whose dull sameness his full tide of
    youth
Broke with a phosphorescence charm-
    ing even
My lady, and the baronet yet had laid
No bar between them. Dull and self-
    involved,
Tall and erect, but bending from his
    height
With half-allowing smiles for all the
    world,   120
And mighty courteous in the main—
    his pride
Lay deeper than to wear it as his
    ring—
He, like an Aylmer in his Aylmerism,
Would care no more for Leolin's walk-
    ing with her
Than for his old Newfoundland's,
    when they ran
To loose him at the stables, for he rose
Two-footed at the limit of his chain,
Roaring to make a third; and how
    should Love,
Whom the cross-lightnings of four
    chance-met eyes
Flash into fiery life from nothing, fol-
    low   130
Such dear familiarities of dawn?
Seldom, but when he does, master of
    all.

So these young hearts, not knowing
    that they loved,

Not she at least, nor conscious of a bar
Between them, nor by plight or broken
 ring
Bound, but an immemorial intimacy,
Wander'd at will, and oft accompanied
By Averill; his, a brother's love, that
 hung
With wings of brooding shelter o'er
 her peace,
Might have been other, save for Leo-
 lin's—   140
Who knows? but so they wander'd,
 hour by hour
Gather'd the blossom that re-bloom'd,
 and drank
The magic cup that fill'd itself anew.

A whisper half reveal'd her to her-
 self.
For out beyond her lodges, where the
 brook
Vocal, with here and there a silence,
 ran
By sallowy rims, arose the laborers'
 homes,
A frequent haunt of Edith, on low
 knolls
That dimpling died into each other,
 huts
At random scatter'd, each a nest in
 bloom.   150
Her art, her hand, her counsel, all had
 wrought
About them. Here was one that, sum-
 mer-blanch'd,
Was parcel-bearded with the travel-
 ler's-joy
In autumn, parcel ivy-clad; and here
The warm-blue breathings of a hidden
 hearth
Broke from a bower of vine and
 honeysuckle.
One look'd all rose-tree, and another
 wore
A close-set robe of jasmine sown with
 stars.
This had a rosy sea of gillyflowers
About it; this, a milky-way on earth,
Like visions in the Northern dream-
 er's heavens,   161
A lily-avenue climbing to the doors;
One, almost to the martin-haunted
 eaves

A summer burial deep in hollyhocks;
Each, its own charm; and Edith's
 everywhere;
And Edith ever visitant with him,
He but less loved than Edith, of her
 poor.
For she—so lowly-lovely and so lov-
 ing,
Queenly responsive when the loyal
 hand
Rose from the clay it work'd in as she
 past,   170
Not sowing hedgerow texts and pass-
 ing by,
Nor dealing goodly counsel from a
 height
That makes the lowest hate it, but a
 voice
Of comfort and an open hand of help,
A splendid presence flattering the poor
 roofs
Revered as theirs, but kindlier than
 themselves
To ailing wife or wailing infancy
Or old bedridden palsy,—was adored;
He, loved for her and for himself. A
 grasp
Having the warmth and muscle of the
 heart,   180
A childly way with children, and a
 laugh
Ringing like proven golden coinage
 true,
Were no false passport to that easy
 realm,
Where once with Leolin at her side the
 girl,
Nursing a child, and turning to the
 warmth
The tender pink five-beaded baby-
 soles,
Heard the good mother softly whisper,
 'Bless,
God bless 'em! marriages are made in
 heaven.'

A flash of semi-jealousy clear'd it to
 her.
My lady's Indian kinsman unan-
 nounced   190
With half a score of swarthy faces
 came.

His own, tho' keen and bold and sol-
dierly,
Sear'd by the close ecliptic, was not
fair;
Fairer his talk, a tongue that ruled the
hour,
Tho' seeming boastful. So when first
he dash'd
Into the chronicle of a deedful day,
Sir Aylmer half forgot his lazy smile
Of patron, 'Good! my lady's kinsman!
good!'   198
My lady with her fingers interlock'd,
And rotatory thumbs on silken knees,
Call'd all her vital spirits into each ear
To listen; unawares they flitted off,
Busying themselves about the flower-
age
That stood from out a stiff brocade in
which,
The meteor of a splendid season, she,
Once with this kinsman, ah! so long
ago,
Stept thro' the stately minuet of those
days.
But Edith's eager fancy hurried with
him
Snatch'd thro' the perilous passes of
his life;   209
Till Leolin, ever watchful of her eye,
Hated him with a momentary hate.
Wife-hunting, as the rumor ran, was
he.
I know not, for he spoke not, only
shower'd
His oriental gifts on every one
And most on Edith. Like a storm he
came,
And shook the house, and like a storm
he went.

Among the gifts he left her—pos-
sibly
He flow'd and ebb'd uncertain, to return
When others had been tested—there
was one,
A dagger, in rich sheath with jewels
on it   220
Sprinkled about in gold that branch'd
itself
Fine as ice-ferns on January panes

Made by a breath. I know not whence
at first,
Nor of what race, the work; but as he
told
The story, storming a hill-fort of
thieves
He got it; for their captain after fight,
His comrades having fought their last
below,
Was climbing up the valley, at whom
he shot.
Down from the beetling crag to which
he clung   229
Tumbled the tawny rascal at his feet,
This dagger with him, which, when
now admired
By Edith whom his pleasure was to
please,
At once the costly Sahib yielded to
her.

And Leolin, coming after he was
gone,
Tost over all her presents petulantly;
And when she show'd the wealthy
scabbard, saying,
'Look what a lovely piece of work-
manship!'
Slight was his answer, 'Well—I care
not for it.'
Then playing with the blade he prick'd
his hand,   239
'A gracious gift to give a lady, this!'
'But would it be more gracious,' ask'd
the girl,
'Were I to give this gift of his to one
That is no lady?' 'Gracious? No,' said
he.
'Me?—but I cared not for it. O, par-
don me,
I seem to be ungraciousness itself.'
'Take it,' she added sweetly, 'tho' his
gift;
For I am more ungracious even than
you,
I care not for it either;' and he said,
'Why, then I love it;' but Sir Aylmer
past,
And neither loved nor liked the thing
he heard.   250

The next day came a neighbor.
Blues and reds

They talk'd of; blues were sure of it,
   he thought;
Then of the latest fox—where started
   —kill'd
In such a bottom. 'Peter had the
   brush,
My Peter, first;' and did Sir Aylmer
   know
That great pock-pitten fellow had
   been caught?
Then made his pleasure echo, hand to
   hand,
And rolling as it were the substance
   of it
Between his palms a moment up and
   down—
'The birds were warm, the birds were
   warm upon him;   260
We have him now;' and had Sir
   Aylmer heard—
Nay, but he must—the land was ring-
   ing of it—
This blacksmith border-marriage—
   one they knew—
Raw from the nursery—who could
   trust a child?
That cursed France with her egalities!
And did Sir Aylmer—deferentially
With nearing chair and lower'd accent
   —think—
For people talk'd—that it was wholly
   wise
To let that handsome fellow Averill
   walk
So freely with his daughter? people
   talk'd—   270
The boy might get a notion into him;
The girl might be entangled ere she
   knew
Sir Aylmer Aylmer slowly stiffening
   spoke:
'The girl and boy, sir, know their dif-
   ferences!'
'Good,' said his friend, 'but watch!'
   and he, 'Enough,
More than enough, sir! I can guard
   my own.'
They parted, and Sir Aylmer Aylmer
   watch'd.

Pale, for on her the thunders of the
   house

Had fallen first, was Edith that same
   night;
Pale as the Jephtha's daughter, a
   rough piece   280
Of early rigid color, under which
Withdrawing by the counter door to
   that
Which Leolin open'd, she cast back
   upon him
A piteous glance, and vanish'd. He, as
   one
Caught in a burst of unexpected
   storm,
And pelted with outrageous epithets,
Turning beheld the Powers of the
   House
On either side the hearth, indignant;
   her,
Cooling her false cheek with a feather
   fan,
Him, glaring, by his own stale devil
   spurr'd,   290
And, like a beast hard-ridden, breath-
   ing hard.
'Ungenerous, dishonorable, base,
Presumptuous! trusted as he was with
   her,
The sole succeeder to their wealth,
   their lands,
The last remaining pillar of their
   house,
The one transmitter of their ancient
   name,
Their child.' 'Our child!' 'Our heiress!'
   'Ours!' for still,
Like echoes from beyond a hollow,
   came
Her sicklier iteration. Last he said:
'Boy, mark me! for your fortunes are
   to make.   300
I swear you shall not make them out
   of mine.
Now inasmuch as you have practised
   on her,
Perplext her, made her half forget
   herself,
Swerve from her duty to herself and
   us—
Things in an Aylmer deem'd impos-
   sible,
Far as we track ourselves—I say that
   this—

Else I withdraw favor and counte-
nance
From you and yours for ever—shall
you do,
Sir, when you see her—but you shall
not see her—
No, you shall write, and not to her, but
me; 310
And you shall say that having spoken
with me,
And after look'd into yourself, you
find
That you meant nothing—as indeed
you know
That you meant nothing. Such a match
as this!
Impossible, prodigious!' These were
words,
As meted by his measure of himself,
Arguing boundless forbearance: after
which,
And Leolin's horror-stricken answer,
'I
So foul a traitor to myself and her!
Never, O, never!' for about as long 320
As the wind-hover hangs in balance,
paused
Sir Aylmer reddening from the storm
within,
Then broke all bonds of courtesy, and
crying,
'Boy, should I find you by my doors
again,
My men shall lash you from them like
a dog;
Hence!' with a sudden execration
drove
The footstool from before him, and
arose;
So, stammering 'scoundrel' out of
teeth that ground
As in a dreadful dream, while Leolin
still
Retreated half-aghast, the fierce old
man 330
Follow'd, and under his own lintel
stood
Storming with lifted hands, a hoary
face
Meet for the reverence of the hearth,
but now,
Beneath a pale and unimpassion'd
moon,

Vext with unworthy madness, and de-
form'd.

Slowly and conscious of the rage-
ful eye
That watch'd him, till he heard the
ponderous door
Close, crashing with long echoes thro'
the land,
Went Leolin; then, his passions all in
flood 339
And masters of his motion, furiously
Down thro' the bright lawns to his
brother's ran,
And foam'd away his heart at Averill's
ear;
Whom Averill solaced as he might,
amazed:
The man was his, had been his father's
friend;
He must have seen, himself had seen
it long;
He must have known, himself had
known; besides,
He never yet had set his daughter
forth
Here in the woman-markets of the
west,
Where our Caucasians let themselves
be sold.
Some one, he thought, had slander'd
Leolin to him. 350
'Brother, for I have loved you more
as son
Than brother, let me tell you: I my-
self—
What is their pretty saying? jilted, is
it?
Jilted I was; I say it for your peace.
Pain'd, and, as bearing in myself the
shame
The woman should have borne, humil-
iated,
I lived for years a stunted sunless life;
Till after our good parents past away
Watching your growth, I seem'd again
to grow. 359
Leolin, I almost sin in envying you.
The very whitest lamb in all my fold
Loves you; I know her; the worst
thought she has
Is whiter even than her pretty hand.

She must prove true; for, brother,
    where two fight
The strongest wins, and truth and love
    are strength,
And you are happy; let her parents
    be.'

But Leolin cried out the more upon
    them—
Insolent, brainless, heartless! heiress,
    wealth,
Their wealth, their heiress! wealth
    enough was theirs
For twenty matches. Were he lord of
    this,   ³⁷⁰
Why, twenty boys and girls should
    marry on it,
And forty blest ones bless him, and
    himself
Be wealthy still, ay, wealthier. He be-
    lieved
This filthy marriage-hindering Mam-
    mon made
The harlot of the cities; Nature crost
Was mother of the foul adulteries
That saturate soul with body. Name,
    too! name,
Their ancient name! they *might* be
    proud; its worth
Was being Edith's. Ah, how pale she
    had look'd
Darling, tonight! they must have rated
    her   ³⁸⁰
Beyond all tolerance. These old pheas-
    ant-lords,
These partridge-breeders of a thou-
    sand years,
Who had mildew'd in their thousands,
    doing nothing
Since Egbert—why, the greater their
    disgrace!
Fall back upon a name! rest, rot in
    that!
Not *keep* it noble, make it nobler?
    fools,
With such a vantage-ground for noble-
    ness!
He had known a man, a quintessence
    of man,
The life of all—who madly loved—
    and he,
Thwarted by one of these old father-
    fools,   ³⁹⁰

Had rioted his life out, and made an
    end.
He would not do it! her sweet face
    and faith
Held him from that; but he had pow-
    ers, he knew it.
Back would he to his studies, make a
    name,
Name, fortune too; the world should
    ring of him,
To shame these mouldy Aylmers in
    their graves.
Chancellor, or what is greatest would
    he be—
'O brother, I am grieved to learn your
    grief—
Give me my fling, and let me say my
    say.'

At which, like one that sees his own
    excess,   ⁴⁰⁰
And easily forgives it as his own,
He laugh'd, and then was mute, but
    presently
Wept like a storm; and honest Ave-
    rill, seeing
How low his brother's mood had
    fallen, fetch'd
His richest bee's-wing from a binn re-
    served
For banquets, praised the waning red,
    and told
The vintage—when *this* Aylmer came
    of age—
Then drank and past it; till at length
    the two,
Tho' Leolin flamed and fell again,
    agreed
That much allowance must be made
    for men.   ⁴¹⁰
After an angry dream this kindlier
    glow
Faded with morning, but his purpose
    held.

Yet once by night again the lovers
    met,
A perilous meeting under the tall pines
That darken'd all the northward of
    her Hall.
Him, to her meek and modest bosom
    prest
In agony, she promised that no force,

Persuasion, no, nor death could alter
  her;
He, passionately hopefuller, would go,
Labor for his own Edith, and return
In such a sunlight of prosperity   421
He should not be rejected. 'Write to
  me!
They loved me, and because I love
  their child
They hate me. There is war between
  us, dear,
Which breaks all bonds but ours; we
  must remain
Sacred to one another.' So they talk'd,
Poor children, for their comfort. The
  wind blew,
The rain of heaven and their own bit-
  ter tears,
Tears and the careless rain of heaven,
  mixt
Upon their faces, as they kiss'd each
  other   430
In darkness, and above them roar'd
  the pine.

  So Leolin went; and as we task our-
    selves
To learn a language known but smat-
  teringly
In phrases here and there at random,
  toil'd
Mastering the lawless science of our
  law,
That codeless myriad of precedent,
That wilderness of single instances,
Thro' which a few, by wit or fortune
  led,
May beat a pathway out to wealth and
  fame.
The jests, that flash'd about the plead-
  er's room,   440
Lightning of the hour, the pun, the
  scurrilous tale,—
Old scandals buried now seven decads
  deep
In other scandals that have lived and
  died,
And left the living scandal that shall
  die—
Were dead to him already; bent as he
  was
To make disproof of scorn, and strong
  in hopes,

And prodigal of all brain-labor he,
Charier of sleep, and wine, and exer-
  cise,
Except when for a breathing-while at
  eve,
Some niggard fraction of an hour, he
  ran   450
Beside the river-bank. And then in-
  deed
Harder the times were, and the hands
  of power
Were bloodier, and the according
  hearts of men
Seem'd harder too; but the soft river-
  breeze,
Which fann'd the gardens of that rival
  rose
Yet fragrant in a heart remembering
His former talks with Edith, on him
  breathed
Far purelier in his rushings to and fro,
After his books, to flush his blood with
  air,
Then to his books again. My lady's
  cousin,   460
Half-sickening of his pension'd after-
  noon,
Drove in upon the student once or
  twice,
Ran a Malayan amuck against the
  times,
Had golden hopes for France and all
  mankind,
Answer'd all queries touching those at
  home
With a heaved shoulder and a saucy
  smile,
And fain had haled him out into the
  world,
And air'd him there. His nearer friend
  would say,
'Screw not the chord too sharply lest
  it snap.'
Then left alone he pluck'd her dagger
  forth   470
From where his worldless heart had
  kept it warm,
Kissing his vows upon it like a knight.
And wrinkled benchers often talk'd of
  him
Approvingly, and prophesied his rise;
For heart, I think, help'd head. Her
  letters too,

Tho' far between, and coming fitfully
Like broken music, written as she
    found
Or made occasion, being strictly
    watch'd,
Charm'd him thro' every labyrinth
    till he saw
An end, a hope, a light breaking upon
    him.   480

But they that cast her spirit into
    flesh,
Her worldly-wise begetters, plagued
    themselves
To sell her, those good parents, for
    her good.
Whatever eldest-born of rank or
    wealth
Might lie within their compass, him
    they lured
Into their net made pleasant by the
    baits
Of gold and beauty, wooing him to
    woo.
So month by month the noise about
    their doors,
And distant blaze of those dull ban-
    quets, made
The nightly wirer of their innocent
    hare   490
Falter before he took it. All in vain.
Sullen, defiant, pitying, wroth, re-
    turn'd
Leolin's rejected rivals from their suit
So often, that the folly taking wings
Slipt o'er those lazy limits down the
    wind
With rumor, and became in other
    fields
A mockery to the yeomen over ale,
And laughter to their lords. But those
    at home,
As hunters round a hunted creature
    draw
The cordon close and closer toward
    the death,   500
Narrow'd her goings out and comings
    in;
Forbade her first the house of Ave-
    rill,
Then closed her access to the wealth-
    ier farms,

Last from her own home-circle of the
    poor
They barr'd her. Yet she bore it, yet
    her cheek
Kept color—wondrous! but, O mys-
    tery!
What amulet drew her down to that
    old oak,
So old, that twenty years before, a
    part
Falling had let appear the brand of
    John—
Once grove-like, each huge arm a tree,
    but now   510
The broken base of a black tower, a
    cave
Of touchwood, with a single flourish-
    ing spray.
There the manorial lord too curiously
Raking in that millennial touchwood-
    dust
Found for himself a bitter treasure-
    trove;
Burst his own wyvern on the seal, and
    read
Writhing a letter from his child, for
    which
Came at the moment Leolin's emis-
    sary,
A crippled lad, and coming turn'd to
    fly,
But scared with threats of jail and
    halter gave   520
To him that fluster'd his poor parish
    wits
The letter which he brought, and
    swore besides
To play their go-between as hereto-
    fore
Nor let them know themselves be-
    tray'd; and then,
Soul-stricken at their kindness to him,
    went
Hating his own lean heart and miser-
    able.

Thenceforward oft from out a des-
    pot dream
The father panting woke, and oft, as
    dawn
Aroused the black republic on his
    elms,

Sweeping the froth-fly from the fescue
    brush'd   530
Thro' the dim meadow toward his
    treasure-trove,
Seized it, took home, and to my lady,
    —who made
A downward crescent of her minion
    mouth,
Listless in all despondence,—read;
    and tore,
As if the living passion symboll'd there
Were living nerves to feel the rent;
    and burnt,
Now chafing at his own great self de-
    fied,
Now striking on huge stumbling-
    blocks of scorn
In babyisms and dear diminutives
Scatter'd all over the vocabulary   540
Of such a love as like a chidden child,
After much wailing, hush'd itself at
    last
Hopeless of answer. Then tho' Averill
    wrote
And bade him with good heart sustain
    himself—
All would be well—the lover heeded
    not,
But passionately restless came and
    went,
And rustling once at night about the
    place,
There by a keeper shot at, slightly
    hurt,
Raging return'd. Nor was it well for
    her
Kept to the garden now, and grove of
    pines,   550
Watch'd even there; and one was set
    to watch
The watcher, and Sir Aylmer watch'd
    them all,
Yet bitterer from his readings. Once
    indeed,
Warm'd with his wines, or taking pride
    in her,
She look'd so sweet, he kiss'd her ten-
    derly,
Not knowing what possess'd him.
    That one kiss
Was Leolin's one strong rival upon
    earth;
Seconded, for my lady follow'd suit,

Seem'd hope's returning rose; and
    then ensued   559
A Martin's summer of his faded love,
Or ordeal by kindness. After this
He seldom crost his child without a
    sneer;
The mother flow'd in shallower acri-
    monies,
Never one kindly smile, one kindly
    word;
So that the gentle creature shut from
    all
Her charitable use, and face to face
With twenty months of silence, slowly
    lost,
Nor greatly cared to lose, her hold on
    life.
Last some low fever ranging round to
    spy   569
The weakness of a people or a house,
Like flies that haunt a wound, or deer,
    or men,
Or almost all that is, hurting the
    hurt—
Save Christ as we believe him—found
    the girl
And flung her down upon a couch of
    fire,
Where careless of the household faces
    near,
And crying upon the name of Leolin,
She, and with her the race of Aylmer,
    past.

    Star to star vibrates light; may
       soul to soul
Strike thro' a finer element of her
    own?
So,—from afar,—touch as at once?
    or why   580
That night, that moment, when she
    named his name,
Did the keen shriek, 'Yes, love, yes,
    Edith, yes,'
Shrill, till the comrade of his cham-
    bers woke,
And came upon him half-arisen from
    sleep,
With a weird bright eye, sweating and
    trembling,
His hair as it were crackling into
    flames,

His body half flung forward in pursuit,
And his long arms stretch'd as to grasp
a flyer.
Nor knew he wherefore he had made
the cry;   589
And being much befool'd and idioted
By the rough amity of the other, sank
As into sleep again. The second day,
My lady's Indian kinsman rushing in,
A breaker of the bitter news from
home,
Found a dead man, a letter edged with
death
Beside him, and the dagger which himself
Gave Edith, redden'd with no bandit's
blood;
'From Edith' was engraven on the
blade.

Then Averill went and gazed upon
his death.
And when he came again, his flock
believed—   600
Beholding how the years which are
not Time's
Had blasted him—that many thousand days
Were clipt by horror from his term of
life.
Yet the sad mother, for the second
death
Scarce touch'd her thro' that nearness
of the first,
And being used to find her pastor
texts,
Sent to the harrow'd brother, praying
him
To speak before the people of her
child,
And fixt the Sabbath. Darkly that day
rose.
Autumn's mock sunshine of the faded
woods   610
Was all the life of it; for hard on
these,
A breathless burthen of low-folded
heavens
Stifled and chill'd at once; but every
roof
Sent out a listener. Many too had
known

Edith among the hamlets round, and
since
The parents' harshness and the hapless loves
And double death were widely murmur'd, left
Their own gray tower, or plain-faced
tabernacle,
To hear him; all in mourning these,
and those
With blots of it about them, ribbon,
glove,   620
Or kerchief; while the church,—one
night, except
For greenish glimmerings thro' the
lancets,—made
Still paler the pale head of him, who
tower'd
Above them, with his hopes in either
grave.

Long o'er his bent brows linger'd
Averill,
His face magnetic to the hand from
which
Livid he pluck'd it forth, and labor'd
thro'
His brief prayer-prelude, gave the
verse, 'Behold,
Your house is left unto you desolate!'
But lapsed into so long a pause again
As half amazed, half frighted, all his
flock;   631
Then from his height and loneliness
of grief
Bore down in flood, and dash'd his
angry heart
Against the desolations of the world.

Never since our bad earth became
one sea,
Which rolling o'er the palaces of the
proud,
And all but those who knew the living
God—
Eight that were left to make a purer
world—
When since had flood, fire, earthquake, thunder, wrought   639
Such waste and havoc as the idolatries
Which from the low light of mortality
Shot up their shadows to the heaven
of heavens,

And worshipt their own darkness in
   the Highest?
'Gash thyself, priest, and honor thy
   brute Baäl,
And to thy worst self sacrifice thyself,
For with thy worst self hast thou
   clothed thy God.
Then came a Lord in no wise like to
   Baäl.
The babe shall lead the lion. Surely
   now
The wilderness shall blossom as the
   rose.
Crown thyself, worm, and worship
   thine own lusts!—   650
No coarse and blockish God of acre-
   age
Stands at thy gate for thee to grovel
   to—
Thy God is far diffused in noble
   groves
And princely halls, and farms, and
   flowing lawns,
And heaps of living gold that daily
   grow,
And title-scrolls and gorgeous her-
   aldries.
In such a shape dost thou behold thy
   God.
Thou wilt not gash thy flesh for *him;*
   for thine   658
Fares richly, in fine linen, not a hair
Ruffled upon the scarfskin, even while
The deathless ruler of thy dying house
Is wounded to the death that cannot
   die;
And tho' thou numberest with the fol-
   lowers
Of One who cried, "Leave all and fol-
   low me."
Thee therefore with His light about
   thy feet,
Thee with His message ringing in thine
   ears,
Thee shall thy brother man, the Lord
   from heaven,
Born of a village girl, carpenter's son,
Wonderful, Prince of Peace, the
   Mighty God,
Count the more base idolater of the
   two;   670
Crueller, as not passing thro' the fire

Bodies, but souls—thy children's—
   thro' the smoke,
The blight of low desires—darkening
   thine own
To thine own likeness; or if one of
   these,
Thy better born unhappily from thee,
Should, as by miracle, grow straight
   and fair—
Friends, I was bid to speak of such a
   one
By those who most have cause to sor-
   row for her—
Fairer than Rachel by the palmy well,
Fairer than Ruth among the fields of
   corn,   680
Fair as the Angel that said "Hail!" she
   seem'd,
Who entering fill'd the house with
   sudden light.
For so mine own was brighten'd—
   where indeed
The roof so lowly but that beam of
   heaven
Dawn'd sometime thro' the doorway?
   whose the babe
Too ragged to be fondled on her lap,
Warm'd at her bosom? The poor child
   of shame,
The common care whom no one cared
   for, leapt
To greet her, wasting his forgotten
   heart,
As with the mother he had never
   known,   690
In gambols; for her fresh and inno-
   cent eyes
Had such a star of morning in their
   blue,
That all neglected places of the field
Broke into nature's music when they
   saw her.
Low was her voice, but won mysteri-
   ous way
Thro' the sealed ear to which a louder
   one
Was all but silence—free of alms her
   hand—
The hand that robed your cottage-
   walls with flowers
Has often toil'd to clothe your little
   ones;

How often placed upon the sick man's
 brow   700
Cool'd it, or laid his feverish pillow
 smooth!
Had you one sorrow and she shared it
 not?
One burthen and she would not lighten
 it?
One spiritual doubt she did not
 soothe?
Or when some heat of difference
 sparkled out,
How sweetly would she glide between
 your wraths,
And steal you from each other! for
 she walk'd
Wearing the light yoke of that Lord
 of love
Who still'd the rolling wave of Gali-
 lee!
And one—of him I was not bid to
 speak—   710
Was always with her, whom you also
 knew.
Him too you loved, for he was worthy
 love.
And these had been together from the
 first;
They might have been together till
 the last.
Friends, this frail bark of ours, when
 sorely tried,
May wreck itself without the pilot's
 guilt,
Without the captain's knowledge;
 hope with me.
Whose shame is that, if he went hence
 with shame?
Nor mine the fault, if losing both of
 these
I cry to vacant chairs and widow'd
 walls,   720
"My house is left unto me desolate."'

While thus he spoke, his hearers
 wept; but some,
Sons of the glebe, with other frowns
 than those
That knit themselves for summer
 shadow, scowl'd
At their great lord. He, when it seem'd
 he saw

No pale sheet-lightnings from afar,
 but fork'd
Of the near storm, and aiming at his
 head,
Sat anger-charm'd from sorrow, sol-
 dier-like,
Erect; but when the preacher's cadence flow'd
Softening thro' all the gentle attributes   730
Of his lost child, the wife, who
 watch'd his face,
Paled at a sudden twitch of his iron
 mouth;
And 'O, pray God that he hold up!'
 she thought,
'Or surely I shall shame myself and
 him.'

'Nor yours the blame—for who be-
 side your hearths
Can take her place—if echoing me
 you cry
"Our house is left unto us desolate"?
But thou, O thou that killest, hadst
 thou known,
O thou that stonest, hadst thou under-
 stood
The things belonging to thy peace and
 ours!   740
Is there no prophet but the voice that
 calls
Doom upon kings, or in the waste "Re-
 pent"?
Is not our own child on the narrow
 way,
Who down to those that saunter in the
 broad
Cries, "Come up hither," as a prophet
 to us?
Is there no stoning save with flint and
 rock?
Yes, as the dead we weep for testify—
No desolation but by sword and fire?
Yes, as your moanings witness, and
 myself
Am lonelier, darker, earthlier for my
 loss.   750
Give me your prayers, for he is past
 your prayers,
Not past the living fount of pity in
 heaven.

But I that thought myself long-suffer-
ing, meek,
Exceeding "poor in spirit"—how the
words
Have twisted back upon themselves,
and mean
Vileness, we are grown so proud—I
wish'd my voice
A rushing tempest of the wrath of God
To blow these sacrifices thro' the
world—
Sent like the twelve-divided concu-
bine
To inflame the tribes; but there—out
yonder—earth   760
Lightens from her own central hell—
O, there
The red fruit of an old idolatry—
The heads of chiefs and princes fall
so fast,
They cling together in the ghastly
sack—
The land all shambles—naked mar-
riages
Flash from the bridge, and ever-mur-
der'd France,
By shores that darken with the gather-
ing wolf,
Runs in a river of blood to the sick
sea.
Is this a time to madden madness
then?
Was this a time for these to flaunt
their pride?   770
May Pharaoh's darkness, folds as
dense as those
Which hid the Holiest from the people's eyes
Ere the great death, shroud this great
sin from all!
Doubtless our narrow world must
canvass it.
O, rather pray for those and pity
them,
Who, thro' their own desire accomplish'd, bring
Their own gray hairs with sorrow to
the grave—
Who broke the bond which they desired to break,
Which else had link'd their race with
times to come—

Who wove coarse webs to snare her
purity,   780
Grossly contriving their dear daugh-
ter's good—
Poor souls, and knew not what they
did, but sat
Ignorant, devising their own daugh-
ter's death!
May not that earthly chastisement
suffice?
Have not our love and reverence left
them bare?
Will not another take their heritage?
Will there be children's laughter in
their hall
For ever and for ever, or one stone
Left on another, or is it a light thing
That I, their guest, their host, their
ancient friend,   790
I made by these the last of all my
race,
Must cry to these the last of theirs, as
cried
Christ ere His agony to those that
swore
Not by the temple but the gold, and
made
Their own traditions God, and slew
the Lord,
And left their memories a world's
curse—"Behold,
Your house is left unto you deso-
late"?'

Ended he had not, but she brook'd
no more;
Long since her heart had beat re-
morselessly,
Her crampt-up sorrow pain'd her, and
a sense   800
Of meanness in her unresisting life.
Then their eyes vext her; for on en-
tering
He had cast the curtains of their seat
aside—
Black velvet of the costliest—she her-
self
Had seen to that. Fain had she closed
them now,
Yet dared not stir to do it, only near'd
Her husband inch by inch, but when
she laid,

Wifelike, her hand in one of his, he
    veil'd
His face with the other, and at once,
    as falls
A creeper when the prop is broken,
    fell   810
The woman shrieking at his feet, and
    swoon'd.
Then her own people bore along the
    nave
Her pendent hands, and narrow mea-
    gre face
Seam'd with the shallow cares of fifty
    years.
And her the lord of all the landscape
    round
Even to its last horizon, and of all
Who peer'd at him so keenly, fol-
    low'd out
Tall and erect, but in the middle aisle
Reel'd, as a footsore ox in crowded
    ways
Stumbling across the market to his
    death,   820
Unpitied; for he groped as blind, and
    seem'd
Always about to fall, grasping the
    pews
And oaken finials till he touch'd the
    door;
Yet to the lychgate, where his chariot
    stood,
Strode from the porch, tall and erect
    again.

But nevermore did either pass the
    gate
Save under pall with bearers. In one
    month,
Thro' weary and yet ever wearier
    hours,
The childless mother went to seek her
    child;
And when he felt the silence of his
    house   830
About him, and the change and not
    the change,
And those fixt eyes of painted ances-
    tors
Staring for ever from their gilded
    walls
On him their last descendant, his own
    head

Began to droop, to fall. The man be-
    came
Imbecile; his one word was 'desolate.'
Dead for two years before his death
    was he;
But when the second Christmas came,
    escaped
His keepers, and the silence which he
    felt   839
To find a deeper in the narrow gloom
By wife and child; nor wanted at his
    end
The dark retinue reverencing death
At golden thresholds; nor from ten-
    der hearts,
And those who sorrow'd o'er a van-
    ished race,
Pity, the violet on the tyrant's grave.
Then the great Hall was wholly broken
    down,
And the broad woodland parcell'd into
    farms;
And where the two contrived their
    daughter's good,
Lies the hawk's cast, the mole has
    made his run,
The hedgehog underneath the plan-
    tain bores,   850
The rabbit fondles his own harmless
    face,
The slow-worm creeps, and the thin
    weasel there
Follows the mouse, and all is open
    field.

SEA DREAMS

A CITY clerk, but gently born and
    bred;
His wife, an unknown artist's orphan
    child—
One babe was theirs, a Margaret, three
    years old.
They, thinking that her clear german-
    der eye
Droopt in the giant-factoried city-
    gloom,
Came, with a month's leave given
    them, to the sea;
For which his gains were dock'd, how-
    ever small.

Small were his gains, and hard his
    work; besides,
Their slender household fortunes—for
    the man
Had risk'd his little—like the little
    thrift,   10
Trembled in perilous places o'er a
    deep.
And oft, when sitting all alone, his face
Would darken, as he cursed his credu-
    lousness,
And that one unctuous mouth which
    lured him, rogue,
To buy strange shares in some Peru-
    vian mine.
Now seaward-bound for health they
    gain'd a coast,
All sand and cliff and deep-inrunning
    cave,
At close of day; slept, woke, and went
    the next,
The Sabbath, pious variers from the
    church,   19
To chapel; where a heated pulpiteer,
Not preaching simple Christ to simple
    men,
Announced the coming doom, and ful-
    minated
Against the Scarlet Woman and her
    creed.
For sideways up he swung his arms,
    and shriek'd
'Thus, thus with violence,' even as if
    he held
The Apocalyptic millstone, and him-
    self
Were that great angel; 'Thus with vio-
    lence
Shall Babylon be cast into the sea;
Then comes the close.' The gentle-
    hearted wife   29
Sat shuddering at the ruin of a world,
He at his own; but when the wordy
    storm
Had ended, forth they came and paced
    the shore,
Ran in and out the long sea-framing
    caves,
Drank the large air, and saw, but
    scarce believed—
The soot-flake of so many a summer
    still

Clung to their fancies—that they saw
    the sea.
So now on sand they walk'd, and now
    on cliff,
Lingering about the thymy promon-
    tories,
Till all the sails were darken'd in the
    west,
And rosed in the east, then homeward
    and to bed;   40
Where she, who kept a tender Chris-
    tian hope,
Haunting a holy text, and still to that
Returning, as the bird returns, at
    night,
'Let not the sun go down upon your
    wrath,'
Said, 'Love, forgive him.' But he did
    not speak;
And silenced by that silence lay the
    wife,
Remembering her dear Lord who died
    for all,
And musing on the little lives of men,
And how they mar this little by their
    feuds.

But while the two were sleeping, a
    full tide   50
Rose with ground-swell, which, on the
    foremost rocks
Touching, upjetted in spirits of wild
    sea-smoke,
And scaled in sheets of wasteful foam,
    and fell
In vast sea-cataracts—ever and anon
Dead claps of thunder from within the
    cliffs
Heard thro' the living roar. At this the
    babe,
Their Margaret cradled near them,
    wail'd and woke
The mother, and the father suddenly
    cried,
'A wreck, a wreck!' then turn'd and
    groaning said:

'Forgive! How many will say, "for-
    give," and find   60
A sort of absolution in the sound
To hate a little longer! No; the sin
That neither God nor man can well
    forgive,

Hypocrisy, I saw it in him at once.
Is it so true that second thoughts are
    best?
Not first, and third, which are a riper
    first?
Too ripe, too late! they come too late
    for use.
Ah, love, there surely lives in man and
    beast
Something divine to warn them of
    their foes;
And such a sense, when first I fronted
    him,   70
Said, "Trust him not;" but after, when
    I came
To know him more, I lost it, knew him
    less,
Fought with what seem'd my own
    uncharity,
Sat at his table, drank his costly wines,
Made more and more allowance for
    his talk;
Went further, fool! and trusted him
    with all,
All my poor scrapings from a dozen
    years
Of dust and desk-work. There is no
    such mine,
None; but a gulf of ruin, swallowing
    gold,
Not making. Ruin'd! ruin'd! the sea
    roars   80
Ruin—a fearful night!'

                    'Not fearful; fair,'
Said the good wife, 'if every star in
    heaven
Can make it fair; you do but hear the
    tide.
Had you ill dreams?'

                    'O, yes,' he said, 'I dream'd
Of such a tide swelling toward the
    land,
And I from out the boundless outer
    deep
Swept with it to the shore, and en-
    ter'd one
Of those dark caves that run beneath
    the cliffs.
I thought the motion of the boundless
    deep

Bore thro' the cave, and I was heaved
    upon it   90
In darkness; then I saw one lovely star
Larger and larger. "What a world," I
    thought,
"To live in!" but in moving on I found
Only the landward exit of the cave,
Bright with the sun upon the stream
    beyond;
And near the light a giant woman sat,
All over earthy, like a piece of earth,
A pickaxe in her hand. Then out I slipt
Into a land all sun and blossom, trees
As high as heaven, and every bird that
    sings;   100
And here the night-light flickering in
    my eyes
Awoke me.'

'That was then your dream,' she
    said,
'Not sad, but sweet.'

                    'So sweet, I lay,' said he,
'And mused upon it, drifting up the
    stream
In fancy, till I slept again, and pieced
The broken vision; for I dream'd that
    still
The motion of the great deep bore me
    on,
And that the woman walk'd upon the
    brink.
I wonder'd at her strength, and ask'd
    her of it.
"It came," she said, "by working in
    the mines."   110
O, then to ask her of my shares, I
    thought;
And ask'd; but not a word; she shook
    her head.
And then the motion of the current
    ceased,
And there was rolling thunder; and we
    reach'd
A mountain, like a wall of burs and
    thorns;
But she with her strong feet up the
    steep hill
Trod out a path. I follow'd, and at top
She pointed seaward; there a fleet of
    glass,

That seem'd a fleet of jewels under
   me,
Sailing along before a gloomy cloud [120]
That not one moment ceased to thun-
   der, past
In sunshine. Right across its track
   there lay,
Down in the water, a long reef of
   gold,
Or what seem'd gold; and I was glad
   at first
To think that in our often-ransack'd
   world
Still so much gold was left; and then I
   fear'd
Lest the gay navy there should splinter
   on it,
And fearing waved my arm to warn
   them off;
An idle signal, for the brittle fleet—
I thought I could have died to save it
   —near'd, [130]
Touch'd, clink'd, and clash'd, and van-
   ish'd, and I awoke,
I heard the clash so clearly. Now I see
My dream was Life, the woman honest
   Work,
And my poor venture but a fleet of
   glass
Wreck'd on a reef of visionary gold.'

'Nay,' said the kindly wife to comfort him,
'You raised your arm, you tumbled
   down and broke
The glass with little Margaret's medicine in it;
And, breaking that, you made and
   broke your dream. [139]
A trifle makes a dream, a trifle breaks.'

'No trifle,' groan'd the husband;
   'yesterday
I met him suddenly in the street, and
   ask'd
That which I ask'd the woman in my
   dream.
Like her, he shook his head. "Show me
   the books!"
He dodged me with a long and loose
   account.
"The books, the books!" but he, he
   could not wait,

Bound on a matter he of life and
   death;
When the great Books—see Daniel
   seven and ten—
Were open'd, I should find he meant
   me well;
And then began to bloat himself, and
   ooze [150]
All over with the fat affectionate smile
That makes the widow lean. "My dear-
   est friend,
Have faith, have faith! We live by
   faith," said he;
"And all things work together for the
   good
Of those"—it makes me sick to quote
   him—last
Gript my hand hard, and with God-
   bless-you went.
I stood like one that had received a
   blow.
I found a hard friend in his loose ac-
   counts,
A loose one in the hard grip of his
   hand,
A curse in his God-bless-you; then my
   eyes [160]
Pursued him down the street, and far
   away,
Among the honest shoulders of the
   crowd,
Read rascal in the motions of his back,
And scoundrel in the supple-sliding
   knee.'

'Was he so bound, poor soul?' said
   the good wife;
'So are we all; but do not call him,
   love,
Before you prove him, rogue, and
   proved, forgive.
His gain is loss; for he that wrongs his
   friend
Wrongs himself more, and ever bears
   about [169]
A silent court of justice in his breast,
Himself the judge and jury, and himself
The prisoner at the bar, ever condemn'd.
And that drags down his life; then
   comes what comes

Hereafter; and he meant, he said he
 meant,
Perhaps he meant, or partly meant,
 you well.'

  ' "With all his conscience and one
   eye askew"—
Love, let me quote these lines, that
 you may learn
A man is likewise counsel for himself,
Too often, in that silent court of
 yours—

  ' "With all his conscience and one
   eye askew,   180
So false, he partly took himself for
 true;
Whose pious talk, when most his heart
 was dry,
Made wet the crafty crowsfoot round
 his eye;
Who, never naming God except for
 gain,
So never took that useful name in vain,
Made Him his catspaw and the Cross
 his tool,
And Christ the bait to trap his dupe
 and fool;
Nor deeds of gift, but gifts of grace he
 forged,
And snake-like slimed his victim ere
 he gorged;
And oft at Bible meetings, o'er the
 rest   190
Arising, did his holy oily best,
Dropping the too rough H in Hell and
 Heaven,
To spread the Word by which him-
 self had thriven."
How like you this old satire?'

        'Nay,' she said,
'I loathe it; he had never kindly heart,
Nor ever cared to better his own kind,
Who first wrote satire, with no pity in
 it.
But will you hear *my* dream, for I had
 one
That altogether went to music? Still
It awed me.'

  Then she told it, having dream'd 200
Of that same coast.—

     But round the North, a light,
A belt, it seem'd, of luminous vapor,
 lay,
And ever in it a low musical note
Swell'd up and died; and, as it swell'd
 a ridge
Of breaker issued from the belt, and
 still
Grew with the growing note, and when
 the note
Had reach'd a thunderous fulness, on
 those cliffs
Broke, mixt with awful light—the
 same as that
Living within the belt—whereby she
 saw
That all those lines of cliffs were cliffs
 no more,   210
But huge cathedral fronts of every
 age,
Grave, florid, stern, as far as eye
 could see,
One after one; and then the great
 ridge drew,
Lessening to the lessening music, back,
And past into the belt and swell'd
 again
Slowly to music. Ever when it broke
The statues, king, or saint, or founder
 fell;
Then from the gaps and chasms of
 ruin left
Came men and women in dark clusters
 round,
Some crying, 'Set them up! they shall
 not fall!'   220
And others, 'Let them lie, for they
 have fallen.'
And still they strove and wrangled;
 and she grieved
In her strange dream, she knew not
 why, to find
Their wildest wailings never out of
 tune
With that sweet note; and ever as
 their shrieks
Ran highest up the gamut, that great
 wave
Returning, while none mark'd it, on
 the crowd
Broke, mixt with awful light, and
 show'd their eyes

Glaring, and passionate looks, and
  swept away
The men of flesh and blood, and men
  of stone,   230
To the waste deeps together.

            'Then I fixt
My wistful eyes on two fair images,
Both crown'd with stars and high
  among the stars,—
The Virgin Mother standing with her
  child
High up on one of those dark minster-
  fronts—
Till she began to totter, and the child
Clung to the mother, and sent out a
  cry
Which mixt with little Margaret's,
  and I woke,
And my dream awed me;—well—but
  what are dreams?
Yours came but from the breaking of
  a glass,   240
And mine but from the crying of a
  child.'

  'Child? No!' said he, 'but this tide's
    roar, and his,
Our Boanerges with his threats of
  doom
And   loud-lung'd   Antibabylonian-
  isms—
Altho' I grant but little music there—
Went both to make your dream; but
  if there were
A music harmonizing our wild cries,
Sphere-music such as that you
  dream'd about,
Why, that would make our passions
  far too like
The discords dear to the musician.
  No—   250
One shriek of hate would jar all the
  hymns of heaven.
True devils with no ear, they howl in
  tune
With nothing but the devil!'

                  ' "True" indeed!
One of our town, but later by an hour
Here than ourselves, spoke with me
  on the shore;

While you were running down the
  sands, and made
The dimpled flounce of the sea-fur-
  below flap,
Good man, to please the child. She
  brought strange news.
Why were you silent when I spoke to-
  night?
I had set my heart on your forgiving
  him   260
Before you knew. We *must* forgive the
  dead.'

  'Dead! who is dead?'

            'The man your eye pursued.
A little after you had parted with him,
He suddenly dropt dead of heart-dis-
  ease.'

  'Dead? he? of heart-disease? what
    heart had he
To die of? dead!'

                'Ah, dearest, if there be
A devil in man, there is an angel too,
And if he did that wrong you charge
  him with,
His angel broke his heart. But your
  rough voice—
You spoke so loud—has roused the
  child again.   270
Sleep, little birdie, sleep! will she not
  sleep
Without her "little birdie"? well, then,
  sleep,
And I will sing you "birdie." '

                        Saying this,
The woman half turn'd round from
  him she loved,
Left him one hand, and reaching thro'
  the night
Her other, found—for it was close beside—
And half-embraced the basket cradle-
  head
With one soft arm, which, like the
  pliant bough
That moving moves the nest and nestling, sway'd
The cradle, while she sang this baby-
  song: 280

What does little birdie say
In her nest at peep of day?
Let me fly, says little birdie,
Mother, let me fly away.
Birdie, rest a little longer,
Till the little wings are stronger,
So she rests a little longer,
Then she flies away.

What does little baby say,
In her bed at peep of day?   290
Baby says, like little birdie,
Let me rise and fly away.
Baby, sleep a little longer,
Till the little limbs are stronger;
If she sleeps a little longer,
Baby too shall fly away.

'She sleeps; let us too, let all evil,
    sleep.
He also sleeps—another sleep than
    ours.
He can do no more wrong; forgive
    him, dear,
And I shall sleep the sounder!'

                    Then the man, 300
'His deeds yet live, the worst is yet to
    come.
Yet let your sleep for this one night be
    sound;
I do forgive him!'

            'Thanks, my love,' she said,
'Your own will be the sweeter,' and
    they slept.

ODE SUNG AT THE OPENING OF THE INTERNATIONAL EXHIBITION

I

UPLIFT a thousand voices full and
    sweet,
    In this wide hall with earth's inven-
        tion stored,
    And praise the invisible universal
        Lord,
Who lets once more in peace the na-
    tions meet,
    Where Science, Art, and Labor have
        outpour'd

Their myriad horns of plenty at our
    feet.

II

O silent father of our Kings to be,
Mourn'd in this golden hour of jubilee,
For this, for all, we weep our thanks
    to thee!

III

The world-compelling plan was
        thine,—
And, lo! the long laborious miles
Of Palace; lo! the giant aisles,
Rich in model and design;
Harvest-tool and husbandry,
Loom and wheel and enginery,
Secrets of the sullen mine,
Steel and gold, and corn and wine,
Fabric rough, or fairy-fine,
Sunny tokens of the Line,
Polar marvels, and a feast
Of wonder, out of West and East,
And shapes and hues of Art divine!
All of beauty, all of use,
That one fair planet can produce,
    Brought from under every star,
Blown from over every main,
And mixt, as life is mixt with pain,
    The works of peace with works of
        war.

IV

Is the goal so far away?
Far, how far no tongue can say,
Let us dream our dream to-day.

V

O ye, the wise who think, the wise
        who reign,
From growing Commerce loose her
        latest chain,
And let the fair white-wing'd peace-
    maker fly
To happy heavens under all the sky,
And mix the seasons and the golden
        hours;
Till each man find his own in all men's
        good,

And all men work in noble brotherhood,
Breaking their mailed fleets and armed
towers,
And ruling by obeying Nature's powers,
And gathering all the fruits of earth
and crown'd with all her flowers.

A WELCOME TO ALEXANDRA

MARCH 7, 1863

SEA-KINGS' daughter from over the
sea,
Alexandra!
Saxon and Norman and Dane are we,
But all of us Danes in our welcome of
thee,
Alexandra!
Welcome her, thunders of fort and of
fleet!
Welcome her, thundering cheer of the
street!
Welcome her, all things youthful and
sweet,
Scatter the blossom under her feet!
Break, happy land, into earlier flow-
ers!
Make music, O bird, in the new-
budded bowers!
Blazon your mottoes of blessing and
prayer!
Welcome her, welcome her, all that is
ours!
Warble, O bugle, and trumpet, blare!
Flags, flutter out upon turrets and
towers!
Flames, on the windy headland flare!
Utter your jubilee, steeple and spire!
Clash, ye bells, in the merry March
air!
Flash, ye cities, in rivers of fire!
Rush to the roof, sudden rocket, and
higher
Melt into stars for the land's desire!
Roll and rejoice, jubilant voice,
Roll as a ground-swell dash'd on the
strand,
Roar as the sea when he welcomes the
land,

And welcome her, welcome the land's
desire,
The sea-kings' daughter as happy as
fair,
Blissful bride of a blissful heir,
Bride of the heir of the kings of the
sea—
O joy to the people and joy to the
throne,
Come to us, love us and make us your
own;
For Saxon or Dane or Norman we,
Teuton or Celt, or whatever we be,
We are each all Dane in our welcome
of thee,
Alexandra!

THE GRANDMOTHER

I

AND Willy, my eldest-born, is gone,
you say, little Anne?
Ruddy and white, and strong on his
legs, he looks like a man.
And Willy's wife has written; she
never was over-wise,
Never the wife for Willy; he wouldn't
take my advice.

II

For, Annie, you see, her father was
not the man to save,
Had n't a head to manage, and drank
himself into his grave.
Pretty enough, very pretty! but I was
against it for one.
Eh!—but he would n't hear me—and
Willy, you say, is gone.

III

Willy, my beauty, my eldest-born, the
flower of the flock;
Never a man could fling him, for Willy
stood like a rock.   10
'Here's a leg for a babe of a week!'
says Doctor; and he would be
bound
There was not his like that year in
twenty parishes round.

IV

Strong of his hands, and strong on his
    legs, but still of his tongue!
I ought to have gone before him; I
    wonder he went so young.
I cannot cry for him, Annie; I have
    not long to stay.
Perhaps I shall see him the sooner, for
    he lived far away.

V

Why do you look at me, Annie?
    you think I am hard and cold;
But all my children have gone before
    me, I am so old.
I cannot weep for Willy, nor can I
    weep for the rest;
Only at your age, Annie, I could have
    wept with the best.   20

VI

For I remember a quarrel I had with
    your father, my dear,
All for a slanderous story, that cost
    me many a tear.
I mean your grandfather, Annie; it
    cost me a world of woe,
Seventy years ago, my darling, sev-
    enty years ago.

VII

For Jenny, my cousin, had come to
    the place, and I knew right well
That Jenny had tript in her time; I
    knew, but I would not tell.
And she to be coming and slandering
    me, the base little liar!
But the tongue is a fire, as you know,
    my dear, the tongue is a fire.

VIII

And the parson made it his text that
    week, and he said likewise
That a lie which is half a truth is ever
    the blackest of lies,   30
That a lie which is all a lie may be met
    and fought with outright,

But a lie which is part a truth is a
    harder matter to fight.

IX

And Willy had not been down to the
    farm for a week and a day;
And all things look'd half-dead, tho'
    it was the middle of May.
Jenny, to slander me, who knew what
    Jenny had been!
But soiling another, Annie, will never
    make oneself clean.

X

And I cried myself well-nigh blind,
    and all of an evening late
I climb'd to the top of the garth, and
    stood by the road at the gate.
The moon like a rick on fire was rising
    over the dale,
And whit, whit, whit, in the bush be-
    side me chirrupt the nightin-
    gale.   40

XI

All of a sudden he stopt; there past
    by the gate of the farm
Willy,—he did n't see me,—and Jenny
    hung on his arm.
Out into the road I started, and spoke
    I scarce knew how;
Ah, there's no fool like the old one—
    it makes me angry now.

XII

Willy stood up like a man, and look'd
    the thing that he meant;
Jenny, the viper, made me a mocking
    curtsey and went.
And I said, 'Let us part; in a hundred
    years it'll all be the same.
You cannot love me at all, if you love
    not my good name.'

XIII

And he turn'd, and I saw his eyes all
    wet, in the sweet moonshine:

'Sweetheart, I love you so well that
    your good name is mine.   50
And what do I care for Jane, let her
    speak of you well or ill;
But marry me out of hand; we two
    shall be happy still.'

XIV

'Marry you, Willy!' said I, 'but I
    needs must speak my mind,
And I fear you'll listen to tales, be
    jealous and hard and unkind.'
But he turn'd and claspt me in his
    arms, and answer'd, 'No, love,
    no;'
Seventy years ago, my darling, sev-
    enty years ago.

XV

So Willy and I were wedded. I wore a
    lilac gown;
And the ringers rang with a will, and
    he gave the ringers a crown.
But the first that ever I bare was dead
    before he was born;
Shadow and shine is life, little Annie,
    flower and thorn.   60

XVI

That was the first time, too, that ever
    I thought of death.
There lay the sweet little body that
    never had drawn a breath.
I had not wept, little Anne, not since
    I had been a wife;
But I wept like a child that day, for
    the babe had fought for his life.

XVII

His dear little face was troubled, as if
    with anger or pain;
I look'd at the still little body—his
    trouble had all been in vain.
For Willy I cannot weep, I shall see
    him another morn;
But I wept like a child for the child
    that was dead before he was
    born.

XVIII

But he cheer'd me, my good man, for
    he seldom said me nay.
Kind, like a man, was he; like a man,
    too, would have his way;   70
Never jealous—not he. We had many
    a happy year;
And he died, and I could not weep—
    my own time seem'd so near.

XIX

But I wish'd it had been God's will
    that I, too, then could have
    died;
I began to be tired a little, and fain
    had slept at his side.
And that was ten years back, or more,
    if I don't forget;
But as to the children, Annie, they're
    all about me yet.

XX

Pattering over the boards, my Annie
    who left me at two,
Patter she goes, my own little Annie,
    an Annie like you;
Pattering over the boards, she comes
    and goes at her will,
While Harry is in the five-acre and
    Charlie ploughing the hill.   80

XXI

And Harry and Charlie, I hear them
    too—they sing to their team;
Often they come to the door in a
    pleasant kind of a dream.
They come and sit by my chair, they
    hover about my bed—
I am not always certain if they be
    alive or dead.

XXII

And yet I know for a truth there's
    none of them left alive,
For Harry went at sixty, your father
    at sixty-five;
And Willy, my eldest-born, at nigh
    three-score and ten.

I knew them all as babies, and now
    they're elderly men.

XXIII

For mine is a time of peace, it is not
    often I grieve;
I am oftener sitting at home in my
    father's farm at eve;   90
And the neighbors come and laugh
    and gossip, and so do I;
I find myself often laughing at things
    that have long gone by.

XXIV

To be sure the preacher says, our sins
    should make us sad;
But mine is a time of peace, and there
    is Grace to be had;
And God, not man, is the Judge of us
    all when life shall cease;
And in this Book, little Annie, the
    message is one of peace.

XXV

And age is a time of peace, so it be
    free from pain,
And happy has been my life; but I
    would not live it again.
I seem to be tired a little, that's all,
    and long for rest;
Only at your age, Annie, I could have
    wept with the best.   100

XXVI

So Willy has gone, my beauty, my
    eldest-born, my flower;
But how can I weep for Willy, he has
    but gone for an hour,—
Gone for a minute, my son, from this
    room into the next;
I, too, shall go in a minute. What time
    have I to be vext?

XXVII

And Willy's wife has written, she
    never was over-wise.
Get me my glasses, Annie; thank God
    that I keep my eyes.

There is but a trifle left you, when I
    shall have past away.
But stay with the old woman now;
    you cannot have long to stay.

NORTHERN FARMER

OLD STYLE

I

Wheer 'asta beän saw long and meä
    liggin' 'ere aloän?
Noorse? thoort nowt o' a noorse;
    whoy, Doctor 's abeän an'
    agoän;
Says that I moänt 'a naw moor aäle,
    but I beänt a fool;
Git ma my aäle, fur I beänt a-gawin'
    to breäk my rule.

II

Doctors, they knaws nowt, fur a says
    what 's nawways true;
Naw soort o' koind o' use to saäy the
    things that a do.
I 've 'ed my point o' aäle ivry noight
    sin' I beän 'ere.
An' I 've 'ed my quart ivry market-
    noight for foorty year.

III

Parson 's a beän loikewoise, an' a sit-
    tin' 'ere o' my bed.
'The Amoighty 's a taäkin o' you [1] to
    'issén, my friend,' a said,

An' a towd ma my sins, an' 's toithe
    were due, an' I gied it in hond;
I done moy duty boy 'um, as I 'a done
    boy the lond.

IV

Larn'd a ma' beä. I reckons I 'annot sa
    mooch to larn.
But a cast oop, thot a did, 'bout Bessy
    Marris's barne.

[1] *ou* as in *hour*.

Thaw a knaws I hallus voäted wi'
    Squoire an' choorch an' staäte,
An' i' the woost o' toimes I wur niver
    agin the raäte.

V

An' I hallus coom'd to 's choorch afoor
    moy Sally wur deäd,
An' 'eärd 'um a bummin' awaäy loïke a
    buzzard-clock [1] ower my 'eäd,
An' I niver knaw'd whot a meän'd but
    I thowt a 'ad summut to saäy,
An' I thowt a said whot a owt to 'a
    said, an' I coom'd awaäy.

VI

Bessy Marris's barne! tha knaws she
    laäid it to meä.
Mowt a beän, mayhap, for she wur a
    bad un, sheä.
'Siver, I kep 'um, I kep 'um, my lass,
    tha mun understond;
I done moy duty boy 'um, as I 'a done
    boy the lond.

VII

But Parson a cooms an' a goäs, an' a
    say it eäsy an' freeä:
'The Amoighty 's a taäkin o' you to
    'issén, my friend,' says 'eä.
I weänt saäy men be loiars, thaw sum-
    mun said it in 'aäste;
But 'e reäds wonn sarmin a weeäk, an'
    I 'a stubb'd Thurnaby waäste.

VIII

D' ya moind the waäste, my lass? naw,
    naw, tha was not born then;
Theer wur a boggle in it, I often 'eärd
    'um mysén;
Moäst loike a butter-bump,[2] fur I
    'eärd 'um about an' about,
But I stubb'd 'um oop wi' the lot, an'
    raäved an' rembled 'um out.

IX

Keäper's it wur; fo' they fun 'um
    theer a-laäid of 'is faäce

Down i' the woild 'enemies [1] afoor I
    coom'd to the plaäce.
Noäks or Thimbleby—toäner [2] 'ed
    shot 'um as deäd as a naäil.
Noäks wur' 'ang'd for it oop at 'soize
    —but git ma my aäle.

X

Dubbut looök at the waäste; theer
    warn't not feeäd for a cow;
Nowt at all but bracken an' fuzz, an'
    looök at it now—
Warn't worth nowt a haäcre, an' now
    theer 's lots o' feeäd,
Fourscoor [3] yows upon it, an' some on
    it down i' seeäd.[4]

XI

Nobbut a bit on it 's left, an' I meän'd
    to 'a stubb'd it at fall,
Done it ta-year I meän'd, an' runn'd
    plow thruff it an' all,
If Godamoighty an' parson 'ud nobbut
    let ma aloän,—
Meä, wi' haäte hoonderd haäcre o'
    Squoire's, an' lond o' my oän.

XII

Do Godamoighty knaw what a 's doing
    a-taäkin' o' meä?
I beänt wonn as saws 'ere a beän an'
    yonder a peä;
An' Squoire 'ull be sa mad an' all—a'
    dear, a' dear!
And I 'a managed for Squoire coom
    Michaelmas thutty year.

XIII

A mowt 'a taäen owd Joänes, as 'ant
    not a 'aäpoth o' sense,
Or a mowt 'a taäen young Robins—a
    niver mended a fence;
But Godamoighty a moost taäke meä
    an' taäke ma now,
Wi' aäf the cows to cauve an' Thurn-
    aby hoälms to plow!

---

[1] Cockchafer.   [2] Bittern.
[1] Anemones.   [2] One or other.
[3] ou as in hour.   [4] Clover.

XIV

Looök 'ow quoloty smoiles when they
  seeäs ma a passin' boy,
Says to thessén, naw doubt, 'What a
  man a beä sewer-loy!'
Fur they knaws what I beän to Squoire
  sin' fust a coom'd to the 'All;
I done moy duty by Squoire an' I done
  moy duty boy hall.

XV

Squoire 's i' Lunnon, an' summun I
  reckons 'ull 'a to wroite,
For whoä 's to howd the lond ater meä
  thot muddles ma quoit;
Sartin-sewer I beä thot a weänt niver
  give it to Joänes,
Naw, nor a moänt to Robins—a niver
  rembles the stoäns.

XVI

But summun 'ull come ater meä mayhap wi' 'is kittle o' steäm
Huzzin' an' maäzin' the blessed feälds
  wi' the divil's oän teäm.
Sin' I mun doy I mun doy, thaw loife
  they says is sweet,
But sin' I mun doy I mun doy, for I
  couldn abeär to see it.

XVII

What atta stannin' theer fur, an' doesn
  bring ma the aäle?
Doctor 's a 'toättler, lass, an a 's hallus
  i' the owd taäle;
I weänt breäk rules fur Doctor, a
  knaws naw moor nor a floy;
Git ma my aäle, I tell tha, an' if I mun
  doy I mun doy.

NORTHERN FARMER

NEW STYLE

I

Dosn't thou 'ear my 'erse's legs, as
  they canters awaäy?
Proputty, proputty, proputty—that's
  what I 'ears 'em saäy.

Proputty, proputty, proputty—Sam,
  thou's an ass for thy païns;
Theer's moor sense i' one o' 'is legs,
  nor in all thy braïns.

II

Woä—theer's a craw to pluck wi' tha,
  Sam: yon 's parson's 'ouse—
Dosn't thou knaw that a man mun be
  eäther a man or a mouse?
Time to think on it then; for thou'll
  be twenty to weeäk.[1]
Proputty, proputty—woä then, woä—
  let ma 'ear mysén speäk.

III

Me an' thy muther, Sammy, 'as beän
  a-talkin' o' thee;
Thou 's beän talkin' to muther, an' she
  beän a-tellin' it me.
Thou 'll not marry for munny—thou's
  sweet upo' parson's lass—
Noä—thou 'll marry for luvv—an' we
  boäth on us thinks tha an ass.

IV

Seeä'd her to-daäy goä by—Saäint's-
  daäy—they was ringing the
  bells.
She's a beauty, thou thinks—an' soä
  is scoors o' gells,
Them as 'as munny an' all—wot's a
  beauty?—the flower as blaws.
But proputty, proputty sticks, an'
  proputty, proputty graws.

V

Do'ant be stunt; [2] taäke time. I knaws
  what maäkes tha sa mad.
Warn't I craäzed fur the lasses mysén
  when I wur a lad?
But I knaw'd a Quaäker feller as often
  'as towd ma this:
'Doänt thou marry for munny, but goä
  wheer munny is!'

---

[1] This week.   [2] Obstinate.

VI

An' I went wheer munny war; an' thy
    muther coom to 'and,
Wi' lots o' munny laaïd by, an' a nice-
    tish bit o' land.
Maäybe she warn't a beauty—I niver
    giv it a thowt—
But warn't she as good to cuddle an'
    kiss as a lass as 'ant nowt?

VII

Parson's lass 'ant nowt, an' she weänt
    'a nowt when 'e 's deäd,
Mun be a guvness, lad, or summut,
    and addle [1] her breäd.
Why? fur 'e 's nobbut a curate, an'
    weänt niver get hissén clear,
An' 'e maäde the bed as 'e ligs on afoor
    'e coom'd to the shere.

VIII

An' thin 'e coom'd to the parish wi'
    lots o' Varsity debt,
Stook to his taaïl they did, an' 'e 'ant
    got shut on 'em yet.
An' 'e ligs on 'is back i' the grip, wi'
    noän to lend 'im a shove,
Woorse nor a far-welter'd [2] yowe; fur,
    Sammy, 'e married fur luvv.

IX

Luvv? what's luvv? thou can luvv thy
    lass an' 'er munny too,
Maäkin' 'em goä togither, as they 've
    good right to do.
Couldn I luvv thy muther by cause o'
    'er munny laaïd by?
Naäy—fur I luvv'd 'er a vast sight
    moor fur it; reäson why.

X

Ay, an' thy muther says thou wants to
    marry the lass,
Cooms of a gentleman burn; an' we
    boäth on us thinks tha an ass.

[1] Earn.
[2] Or, fow-welter'd,—said of a sheep lying
on its back in the furrow.

Woä then, proputty, wiltha?—an ass
    as near as mays nowt [1]—
Woä then, wiltha? dangtha!—the bees
    is as fell as owt.[2]

XI

Breäk me a bit o' the esh for his 'eäd,
    lad, out o' the fence!
Gentleman burn! what's gentleman
    burn? is it shillins an' pence?
Proputty, proputty's ivrything 'ere,
    an', Sammy, I 'm blest
If it is n't the saäme oop yonder, fur
    them as 'as it 's the best.

XII

Tis 'n them as 'as munny as breäks
    into 'ouses an' steäls,
Them as 'as coäts to their backs an'
    taäkes their regular meäls.
Noä, but it 's them as niver knaws
    wheer a meäl 's to be 'ad.
Taäke my word for it, Sammy, the
    poor in a loomp is bad.

XIII

Them or thir feythers, tha sees, mun
    'a beän a laäzy lot,
Fur work mun 'a gone to the gittin'
    whiniver munny was got.
Feyther 'ad ammost nowt; leästways
    'is munny was 'id.
But 'e tued an' moil'd issén deäd, an'
    'e died a good un, 'e did.

XIV

Looök thou theer wheer Wrigglesby
    beck cooms out by the 'ill!
Feyther run oop to the farm, an' I
    runs oop to the mill;
An' I 'll run oop to the brig, an' that
    thou 'll live to see;
And if thou marries a good un I'll
    leäve the land to thee.

[1] Makes nothing.
[2] The flies are as fierce as anything.

XV

Thim's my noätions, Sammy, wheerby
  I meäns to stick;
But if thou marries a bad un, I'll leäve
  the land to Dick.—
Coom oop, proputty, proputty—that's
  what I 'ears 'im saäy—
Proputty, proputty, proputty—canter
  an' canter awaäy.

IN THE VALLEY OF CAUTERETZ

ALL along the valley, stream that
  flashest white,
Deepening thy voice with the deepening of the night,
All along the valley, where thy waters
  flow,
I walk'd with one I loved two and
  thirty years ago.
All along the valley, while I walk'd
  to-day,
The two and thirty years were a mist
  that rolls away;
For all along the valley, down thy
  rocky bed,
Thy living voice to me was as the
  voice of the dead,
And all along the valley, by rock and
  cave and tree,
The voice of the dead was a living
  voice to me.

THE FLOWER

ONCE in a golden hour
  I cast to earth a seed.
Up there came a flower,
  The people said, a weed.

To and fro they went
  Thro' my garden-bower,
And muttering discontent
  Cursed me and my flower.

Then it grew so tall
  It wore a crown of light,
But thieves from o'er the wall
  Stole the seed by night;

Sow'd it far and wide
  By every town and tower,
Till all the people cried,
  'Splendid is the flower.'

Read my little fable:
  He that runs may read.
Most can raise the flowers now
  For all have got the seed.

And some are pretty enough,
  And some are poor indeed;
And now again the people
  Call it but a weed.

REQUIESCAT

FAIR is her cottage in its place,
  Where yon broad water sweetly,
    slowly glides.
It sees itself from thatch to base
  Dream in the sliding tides.

And fairer she, but ah, how soon to
    die!
  Her quiet dream of life this hour
    may cease.
Her peaceful being slowly passes by
  To some more perfect peace.

THE SAILOR BOY

HE rose at dawn and, fired with hope,
  Shot o'er the seething harbor-bar,
And reach'd the ship and caught the
    rope,
  And whistled to the morning star.

And while he whistled long and loud
  He heard a fierce mermaiden cry,
'O boy, tho' thou art young and proud,
  I see the place where thou wilt lie.

'The sands and yeasty surges mix
  In caves about the dreary bay,
And on thy ribs the limpet sticks,
  And in thy heart the scrawl shall
    play.'

'Fool,' he answer'd, 'death is sure
　To those that stay and those that
　　roam,
But I will nevermore endure
　To sit with empty hands at home.

'My mother clings about my neck,
　My sisters crying, "Stay for
　　shame;"
My father raves of death and wreck,—
　They are all to blame, they are all
　　to blame.

'God help me! save I take my part
　Of danger on the roaring sea,
A devil rises in my heart,
　Far worse than any death to me.'

THE ISLET

'WHITHER, O whither, love, shall we
　go,
For a score of sweet little summers or
　　so?'
The sweet little wife of the singer said,
On the day that follow'd the day she
　　was wed,
'Whither, O whither, love, shall we
　go?'.
And the singer shaking his curly head
Turn'd as he sat, and struck the keys
There at his right with a sudden crash,
Singing, 'And shall it be over the seas
With a crew that is neither rude nor
　　rash,
But a bevy of Eroses apple-cheek'd,
In a shallop of crystal ivory-beak'd?
With a satin sail of a ruby glow,
To a sweet little Eden on earth that I
　　know,
A mountain islet pointed and peak'd;
Waves on a diamond shingle dash,
Cataract brooks to the ocean run,
Fairily-delicate palaces shine
Mixt with myrtle and clad with vine,
And overstream'd and silvery-streak'd
With many a rivulet high against the
　　sun
The facets of the glorious mountain
　　flash
Above the valleys of palm and pine.'

'Thither, O thither, love, let us go.'

'No, no, no!
For in all that exquisite isle, my dear,
There is but one bird with a musical
　　throat,
And his compass is but of a single
　　note,
That it makes one weary to hear.'

'Mock me not! mock me not! love,
　let us go.'

'No, love, no.
For the bud ever breaks into bloom on
　　the tree,
And a storm never wakes on the lonely
　　sea,
And a worm is there in the lonely
　　wood,
That pierces the liver and blackens the
　　blood,
And makes it a sorrow to be.'

A DEDICATION

DEAR, near and true,—no truer Time
　himself
Can prove you, tho' he make you ever-
　more
Dearer and nearer, as the rapid of life
Shoots to the fall,—take this and pray
　that he
Who wrote it, honoring your sweet
　faith in him,
May trust himself; and after praise
　and scorn,
As one who feels the immeasurable
　world,
Attain the wise indifference of the
　wise;
And after autumn past—if left to pass
His autumn into seeming-leafless
　days—
Draw toward the long frost and
　longest night,
Wearing his wisdom lightly, like the
　fruit
Which in our winter woodland looks a
　flower.[1]

[1] The fruit of the Spindle-tree (*Euony-
mus Europæus*).

EXPERIMENTS

BOÄDICÉA

WHILE about the shore of Mona those
    Neronian legionaries
Burnt and broke the grove and altar
    of the Druid and Druidess,
Far in the East Boädicéa, standing
    loftily charioted,
Mad and maddening all that heard her
    in her fierce volubility,
Girt by half the tribes of Britain, near
    the colony Cámulodúne,
Yell'd and shriek'd between her
    daughters o'er a wild confed-
    eracy.

'They that scorn the tribes and call
    us Britain's barbarous popu-
    laces,
Did they hear me, would they listen,
    did they pity me supplicating?
Shall I heed them in their anguish?
    shall I brook to be supplicated?
Hear, Icenian, Catieuchlanian, hear,
    Coritanian, Trinobant!
Must their ever-ravening eagle's beak
    and talon annihilate us?
Tear the noble heart of Britain, leave
    it gorily quivering?
Bark an answer, Britain's raven! bark
    and blacken innumerable,
Blacken round the Roman carrion,
    make the carcase a skeleton,
Kite and kestrel, wolf and wolfkin,
    from the wilderness, wallow in
    it,
Till the face of Bel be brighten'd, Ta-
    ranis be propitiated.
Lo their colony half-defended! lo their
    colony, Cámulodúne!
There the horde of Roman robbers
    mock at a barbarous adversary.
There the hive of Roman liars wor-
    ship an emperor-idiot.
Such is Rome, and this her deity; hear
    it, Spirit of Cássivëlaún!

'Hear it, Gods! the Gods have heard
    it, O Icenian, O Coritanian!
Doubt not ye the Gods have answer'd,
    Catieuchlanian, Trinobant.
These have told us all their anger in
    miraculous utterances,
Thunder, a flying fire in heaven, a
    murmur heard aërially,
Phantom sound of blows descending,
    moan of an enemy massacred,
Phantom wail of women and children,
    multitudinous agonies.
Bloodily flow'd the Tamesa rolling
    phantom bodies of horses
    and men;
Then a phantom colony smoulder'd
    on the refluent estuary;
Lastly yonder yester-even, suddenly
    giddily tottering—
There was one who watch'd and told
    me—down their statue of Vic-
    tory fell.
Lo their precious Roman bantling, lo
    the colony Cámulodúne,
Shall we teach it a Roman lesson?
    shall we care to be pitiful?
Shall we deal with it as an infant?
    shall we dandle it amorously?

'Hear, Icenian, Catieuchlanian,
    hear, Coritanian, Trinobant!
While I roved about the forest, long
    and bitterly meditating,
There I heard them in the darkness,
    at the mystical ceremony;
Loosely robed in flying raiment, sang
    the terrible prophetesses:
"Fear not, isle of blowing woodland,
    isle of silvery parapets!
Tho' the Roman eagle shadow thee,
    tho' the gathering enemy nar-
    row thee,
Thou shalt wax and he shall dwindle,
    thou shalt be the mighty one
    yet!
Thine the liberty, thine the glory,
    thine the deeds to be cele-
    brated,
Thine the myriad-rolling ocean, light
    and shadow illimitable,
Thine the lands of lasting summer,
    many-blossoming Paradises,
Thine the North and thine the South
    and thine the battle-thunder of
    God."

So they chanted: how shall Britain
  light upon auguries happier?
So they chanted in the darkness, and
  there cometh a victory now.

'Hear,   Icenian,   Catieuchlanian,
  hear, Coritanian, Trinobant!
Me the wife of rich Prasútagus, me
  the lover of liberty,
Me they seized and me they tortured,
  me they lash'd and humiliated,
Me the sport of ribald Veterans, mine
  of ruffian violators!
See, they sit, they hide their faces,
  miserable in ignominy!
Wherefore in me burns an anger, not
  by blood to be satiated.
Lo the palaces and the temple, lo the
  colony Cámulodúne!
There they ruled, and thence they
  wasted all the flourishing territory,
Thither at their will they haled the
  yellow-ringleted Britoness—
Bloodily, bloodily fall the battle-axe,
  unexhausted, inexorable.
Shout, Icenian, Catieuchlanian, shout,
  Coritanian, Trinobant,
Till the victim hear within and yearn
  to hurry precipitously,
Like the leaf in a roaring whirlwind,
  like the smoke in a hurricane
  whirl'd.
Lo the colony, there they rioted in
  the city of Cúnobelíne!
There they drank in cups of emerald,
  there at tables of ebony lay,
Rolling on their purple couches in
  their tender effeminacy.
There they dwelt and there they
  rioted; there — there — they
  dwell no more.
Burst the gates, and burn the palaces,
  break the works of the statu-
  ary,
Take the hoary Roman head and shatter it, hold it abominable,

Cut the Roman boy to pieces in his
  lust and voluptuousness,
Lash the maiden into swooning, me
  they lash'd and humiliated,
Chop the breasts from off the mother,
  dash the brains of the little one
  out,
Up, my Britons! on, my chariot! on,
  my chargers, trample them under us!'

So the Queen Boädicéa, standing
  loftily charioted,
Brandishing in her hand a dart and
  rolling glances lioness-like,
Yell'd   and   shriek'd   between   her
  daughters in her fierce volu-
  bility.
Till her people all around the royal
  chariot agitated,
Madly dash'd the darts together,
  writhing barbarous lineaments,
Made the noise of frosty woodlands,
  when they shiver in January,
Roar'd as when the roaring breakers
  boom and blanch on the precipices,
Yell'd as when the winds of winter
  tear an oak on a promontory.
So the silent colony, hearing her tu-
  multuous adversaries
Clash the darts and on the buckler
  beat   with   rapid   unanimous
  hand,
Thought on all her evil tyrannies, all
  her pitiless avarice,
Till she felt the heart within her fall
  and flutter tremulously,
Then her pulses at the clamoring of
  her enemy fainted away.
Out of evil evil flourishes, out of
  tyranny tyranny buds.
Ran the land with Roman slaughter,
  multitudinous agonies.
Perish'd many a maid and matron,
  many a valorous legionary,
Fell the colony, city, and citadel,
  London, Verulam, Cámulodúne.

IN QUANTITY

ON TRANSLATIONS OF HOMER

(HEXAMETERS AND PENTAMETERS)

THESE lame hexameters the strong-
    wing'd music of Homer!
    No—but a most burlesque barbar-
    ous experiment.
When was a harsher sound ever heard,
    ye Muses, in England?
    When did a frog coarser croak upon
    our Helicon?
Hexameters no worse than daring
    Germany gave us,
    Barbarous experiment, barbarous
    hexameters.

MILTON

(ALCAICS)

O MIGHTY-MOUTH'D inventor of har-
    monies,
O skill'd to sing of Time or Eternity,
    God-gifted organ-voice of England,
    Milton, a name to resound for
    ages;
Whose Titan angels, Gabriel, Abdiel,
Starr'd from Jehovah's gorgeous ar-
    mories,
    Tower, as the deep-domed empy-
    rean
    Rings to the roar of an angel on-
    set!
Me rather all that bowery loneliness,
The brooks of Eden mazily murmur-
    ing,
    And bloom profuse and cedar arches
    Charm, as a wanderer out in
    ocean,
Where some refulgent sunset of India
Streams o'er a rich ambrosial ocean
    isle,
    And crimson-hued the stately palm-
    woods
    Whisper in odorous heights of
    even.

(HENDECASYLLABICS)

O YOU chorus of indolent reviewers,
Irresponsible, indolent reviewers,
Look, I come to the test, a tiny poem
All composed in a metre of Catullus,
All in quantity, careful of my motion,
Like the skater on ice that hardly
    bears him,
Lest I fall unawares before the people,
Waking laughter in indolent review-
    ers.
Should I flounder a while without a
    tumble
Thro' this metrification of Catullus,
They should speak to me not without
    a welcome,
All that chorus of indolent reviewers.
Hard, hard, hard is it, only not to
    tumble,
So fantastical is the dainty metre.
Wherefore slight me not wholly, nor
    believe me
Too presumptuous, indolent review-
    ers.
O blatant Magazines, regard me
    rather—
Since I blush to belaud myself a mo-
    ment—
As some rare little rose, a piece of in-
    most
Horticultural art, or half coquette-
    like
Maiden, not to be greeted unbenignly.

SPECIMEN OF A TRANSLATION OF THE ILIAD IN BLANK VERSE

[ILIAD, VIII. 542–561]

So Hector spake; the Trojans roar'd
    applause;
Then loosed their sweating horses
    from the yoke,
And each beside his chariot bound his
    own;
And oxen from the city, and goodly
    sheep
In haste they drove, and honey-
    hearted wine

And bread from out the houses
  brought and heap'd
Their firewood, and the winds from
  off the plain
Roll'd the rich vapor far into the
  heaven.
And these all night upon the bridge [1]
  of war
Sat glorying; many a fire before them
  blazed.
As when in heaven the stars about the
  moon
Look beautiful, when all the winds
  are laid,
And every height comes out, and jutting peak
And valley, and the immeasurable
  heavens
Break open to their highest, and all
  the stars
Shine, and the shepherd gladdens in
  his heart;
So many a fire between the ships and
  stream
Of Xanthus blazed before the towers
  of Troy,
A thousand on the plain; and close
  by each
Sat fifty in the blaze of burning fire;
And eating hoary grain and pulse the
  steeds,
Fixt by their cars, waited the golden
  dawn.

THE THIRD OF FEBRUARY,
1852

My Lords, we heard you speak: you
  told us all
  That England's honest censure
    went too far,
That our free press should cease to
  brawl,
  Not sting the fiery Frenchman into
    war.
It was our ancient privilege, my
  Lords,
To fling whate'er we felt, not fearing,
  into words.

[1] Or, ridge.

We love not this French God, the
  child of hell,
  Wild War, who breaks the converse
    of the wise;
But though we love kind Peace so
  well,
  We dare not even by silence sanc-
    tion lies.
It might be safe our censures to with-
  draw,
And yet, my Lords, not well; there is
  a higher law.

As long as we remain, we must speak
  free,
  Tho' all the storm of Europe on us
    break.
No little German state are we,
  But the one voice in Europe; we
    must speak,
That if to-night our greatness were
  struck dead,
  There might be left some record of
    the things we said.

If you be fearful, then must we be
  bold.
  Our Britain cannot salve a tyrant
    o'er.
Better the waste Atlantic roll'd
  On her and us and ours for ever-
    more.
What! have we fought for freedom
  from our prime,
At last to dodge and palter with a
  public crime?

Shall we fear *him?* our own we never
  fear'd.
  From our first Charles by force we
    wrung our claims.
Prick'd by the Papal spur, we rear'd,
  We flung the burthen of the second
    James.
I say, we *never* fear'd! and as for
  these,
We broke them on the land, we drove
  them on the seas.

And you, my Lords, you make the
  people muse
  In doubt if you be of our Barons'
    breed—

Were those your sires who fought at
Lewes?
    Is this the manly strain of Runny-
mede?
O fallen nobility that, overawed,
Would lisp in honey'd whispers of
this monstrous fraud!

We feel, at least, that silence here
were sin,
    Not ours the fault if we have
feeble hosts—
If easy patrons of their kin
    Have left the last free race with
naked coasts!
They knew the precious things they
had to guard;
For us, we will not spare the tyrant
one hard word.

Tho' niggard throats of Manchester
may bawl,
    What England was, shall her true
sons forget?
We are not cotton-spinners all,
    But some love England and her
honor yet.
And these in our Thermopylæ shall
stand,
And hold against the world this honor
of the land.

A WELCOME TO HER ROYAL HIGHNESS MARIE ALEXANDROVNA, DUCHESS OF EDINBURGH

MARCH 7, 1874

I

THE Son of him with whom we strove
for power—
    Whose will is lord thro' all his
world-domain—
    Who made the serf a man, and burst
his chain—
Has given our Prince his own imperial Flower,
            Alexandrovna.
And welcome, Russian flower, a people's pride,

To Britain, when her flowers begin
to blow!
    From love to love, from home to
home you go,
From mother unto mother, stately
bride,
            Marie Alexandrovna!

II

The golden news along the steppes is
blown,
    And at thy name the Tartar tents
are stirr'd;
    Elburz and all the Caucasus have
heard;
And all the sultry palms of India
known,
            Alexandrovna.
The voices of our universal sea
    On capes of Afric as on cliffs of
Kent,
    The Maoris and that Isle of Conti-
nent,
And loyal pines of Canada murmur
thee,
            Marie Alexandrovna!

III

Fair empires branching, both, in lusty
life!—
    Yet Harold's England fell to Nor-
man swords;
    Yet thine own land has bow'd to
Tartar hordes
Since English Harold gave its throne
a wife,
           Alexandrovna!
For thrones and peoples are as waifs
that swing,
    And float or fall, in endless ebb and
flow;
    But who love best have best the
grace to know
That Love by right divine is deathless
king,
            Marie Alexandrovna!

IV

And Love has led thee to the stranger
land,

Where men are bold and strongly
say their say;—
See, empire upon empire smiles to-
day,
As thou with thy young lover hand in
hand,
        Alexandrovna!
So now thy fuller life is in the west,
  Whose hand at home was gracious
to thy poor;
  Thy name was blest within the narrow door;
Here also, Marie, shall thy name be
blest,
      Marie Alexandrovna!

v

Shall fears and jealous hatreds flame
again?
  Or at thy coming, Princess, everywhere,
  The blue heaven break, and some
diviner air
Breathe thro' the world and change
the hearts of men,
      Alexandrovna?
But hearts that change not, love that
cannot cease,
  And peace be yours, the peace of
soul in soul!
  And howsoever this wild world may
roll,
Between your peoples truth and manful peace,
      Alfred—Alexandrovna!

IN THE GARDEN AT SWAINS-TON

Nightingales warbled without,
  Within was weeping for thee;
Shadows of three dead men
  Walk'd in the walks with me,
  Shadows of three dead men, and
thou wast one of the three.

Nightingales sang in his woods,
  The Master was far away;
Nightingales warbled and sang
  Of a passion that lasts but a day;

Still in the house in his coffin the
  Prince of courtesy lay.

Two dead men have I known
  In courtesy like to thee;
Two dead men have I loved
  With a love that ever will be;
  Three dead men have I loved, and
thou art last of the three.

CHILD SONGS

I

THE CITY CHILD

Dainty little maiden, whither would
  you wander?
  Whither from this pretty home, the
home where mother dwells?
'Far and far away,' said the dainty
  little maiden,
'All among the gardens, auriculas,
anemones,
  Roses and lilies and Canterbury
bells.'

Dainty little maiden, whither would
  you wander?
  Whither from this pretty house,
this city-house of ours?
'Far and far away,' said the dainty little maiden,
'All among the meadows, the clover
and the clematis,
  Daisies and kingcups and honey-
suckle-flowers.'

II

MINNIE AND WINNIE

Minnie and Winnie
  Slept in a shell.
Sleep, little ladies!
  And they slept well.

Pink was the shell within,
  Silver without;
Sounds of the great sea
  Wander'd about.

Sleep, little ladies!
  Wake not soon!
Echo on echo
  Dies to the moon.

Two bright stars
  Peep'd into the shell.
'What are they dreaming of?
  Who can tell?'

Started a green linnet
  Out of the croft;
Wake, little ladies!
  The sun is aloft!

THE SPITEFUL LETTER

Here, it is here, the close of the year,
  And with it a spiteful letter.
My name in song has done him much
    wrong,
  For himself has done much better.

O little bard, is your lot so hard,
  If men neglect your pages?
I think not much of yours or of mine,
  I hear the roll of the ages.

Rhymes and rhymes in the range of
    the times!
  Are mine for the moment stronger?
Yet hate me not, but abide your lot;
  I last but a moment longer.

This faded leaf, our names are as
    brief;
  What room is left for a hater?
Yet the yellow leaf hates the greener
    leaf,
  For it hangs one moment later.

Greater than I—is that your cry?
  And men will live to see it.
Well—if it be so—so it is, you know;
  And if it be so, so be it.

Brief, brief is a summer leaf,
  But this is the time of hollies.
O hollies and ivies and evergreens,
  How I hate the spites and the fol-
    lies!

LITERARY SQUABBLES

Ah God! the petty fools of rhyme
  That shriek and sweat in pigmy
    wars
Before the stony face of Time,
  And look'd at by the silent stars;

Who hate each other for a song,
  And do their little best to bite
And pinch their brethren in the throng,
  And scratch the very dead for spite;

And strain to make an inch of room
  For their sweet selves, and cannot
    hear
The sullen Lethe rolling doom
  On them and theirs and all things
    here;

When one small touch of Charity
  Could lift them nearer Godlike state
Than if the crowded Orb should cry
  Like those who cried Diana great.

And I too talk, and lose the touch
  I talk of. Surely, after all,
The noblest answer unto such
  Is perfect stillness when they brawl.

THE VICTIM

I

A plague upon the people fell,
  A famine after laid them low;
Then thorpe and byre arose in fire,
  For on them brake the sudden foe;
So thick they died the people cried,
  'The Gods are moved against the
    land.'
The Priest in horror about his altar
  To Thor and Odin lifted a hand:
    'Help us from famine
    And plague and strife!
    What would you have of us?
    Human life?
    Were it our nearest,
    Were it our dearest,—
    Answer, O answer!—
    We give you his life.'

II

But still the foeman spoil'd and
    burn'd,
  And cattle died, and deer in wood,
And bird in air, and fishes turn'd
  And whiten'd all the rolling flood;
And dead men lay all over the way,
  Or down in a furrow scathed with
    flame;
And ever and aye the Priesthood
    moan'd,
  Till at last it seem'd that an answer
    came:
      'The King is happy
      In child and wife;
      Take you his dearest,
      Give us a life.'

III

The Priest went out by heath and hill;
  The King was hunting in the wild;
They found the mother sitting still;
  She cast her arms about the child.
The child was only eight summers old,
  His beauty still with his years in-
    creased,
His face was ruddy, his hair was gold,
  He seem'd a victim due to the
    priest.
      The Priest beheld him,
      And cried with joy.
      'The Gods have answer'd;
      We give them the boy.'

IV

The King return'd from out the wild,
  He bore but little game in hand;
The mother said, 'They have taken the
    child
  To spill his blood and heal the land.
The land is sick, the people diseased,
  And blight and famine on all the
    lea;
The holy Gods, they must be ap-
    peased,
  So I pray you tell the truth to me.
      They have taken our son,
      They will have his life.
      Is *he* your dearest?
      Or I, the wife?'

V

The King bent low, with hand on
    brow,
  He stay'd his arms upon his knee:
'O wife, what use to answer now?
  For now the Priest has judged for
    me.'
The King was shaken with holy fear;
  'The Gods,' he said, 'would have
    chosen well;
Yet both are near, and both are dear,
  And which the dearest I cannot
    tell!'
      But the Priest was happy,
      His victim won:
      'We have his dearest,
      His only son!'

VI

The rites prepared, the victim bared,
  The knife uprising toward the blow,
To the altar-stone she sprang alone:
  'Me, not my darling, no!'
He caught her away with a sudden
    cry;
  Suddenly from him brake his wife,
And shrieking, '*I* am his dearest, I—
  I am his dearest!' rush'd on the
    knife.
      And the Priest was happy:
      'O Father Odin,
      We give you a life.
      Which was his nearest?
      Who was his dearest?
      The Gods have answer'd;
      We give them the wife!'

WAGES

Glory of warrior, glory of orator,
    glory of song,
  Paid with a voice flying by to be
    lost on an endless sea—
Glory of Virtue, to fight, to struggle,
    to right the wrong—
  Nay, but she aim'd not at glory, no
    lover of glory she;
Give her the glory of going on, and
    still to be.

The wages of sin is death: if the wages
of Virtue be dust,
Would she have heart to endure for
the life of the worm and the
fly?
She desires no isles of the blest, no
quiet seats of the just,
To rest in a golden grove, or to bask
in a summer sky;
Give her the wages of going on, and
not to die.

THE HIGHER PANTHEISM

THE sun, the moon, the stars, the seas,
the hills and the plains,—
Are not these, O Soul, the Vision of
Him who reigns?

Is not the Vision He, tho' He be not
that which He seems?
Dreams are true while they last, and
do we not live in dreams?

Earth, these solid stars, this weight of
body and limb,
Are they not sign and symbol of thy
division from Him?

Dark is the world to thee; thyself art
the reason why,
For is He not all but thou, that hast
power to feel 'I am I'?

Glory about thee, without thee; and
thou fulfillest thy doom,
Making Him broken gleams and a
stifled splendor and gloom.

Speak to Him, thou, for He hears, and
Spirit with Spirit can meet—
Closer is He than breathing, and
nearer than hands and feet.

God is law, say the wise; O Soul, and
let us rejoice,
For if He thunder by law the thunder
is yet His voice.

Law is God, say some; no God at all,
says the fool,
For all we have power to see is a
straight staff bent in a pool;

And the ear of man cannot hear, and
the eye of man cannot see;
But if we could see and hear, this
Vision—were it not He?

THE VOICE AND THE PEAK

I

THE voice and the Peak
Far over summit and lawn,
The lone glow and long roar
Green-rushing from the rosy thrones
of dawn!

II

All night have I heard the voice
Rave over the rocky bar,
But thou wert silent in heaven,
Above thee glided the star.

III

Hast thou no voice, O Peak,
That standest high above all?
'I am the voice of the Peak,
I roar and rave, for I fall.

IV

'A thousand voices go
To North, South, East, and West;
They leave the heights and are trou-
bled,
And moan and sink to their rest.

V

'The fields are fair beside them,
The chestnut towers in his bloom;
But they—they feel the desire of the
deep—
Fall, and follow their doom.

VI

'The deep has power on the height,
And the height has power on the
deep;
They are raised for ever and ever,
And sink again into sleep.'

VII

Not raised for ever and ever,
  But when their cycle is o'er,
The valley, the voice, the peak, the
    star
  Pass, and are found no more.

VIII

The Peak is high and flush'd
  At his highest with sunrise fire;
The Peak is high, and the stars are
    high,
  And the thought of a man is higher.

IX

A deep below the deep,
  And a height beyond the height!
Our hearing is not hearing,
  And our seeing is not sight.

X

The voice and the Peak
  Far into heaven withdrawn,
The lone glow and long roar
  Green-rushing from the rosy thrones
    of dawn!

'FLOWER IN THE CRANNIED WALL'

FLOWER in the crannied wall,
I pluck you out of the crannies,
I hold you here, root and all, in my
  hand,
Little flower—but *if* I could under-
  stand
What you are, root and all, and all in
  all,
I should know what God and man is.

LUCRETIUS

LUCILIA, wedded to Lucretius, found
Her master cold; for when the morn-
  ing flush
Of passion and the first embrace had
  died
Between them, tho' he loved her none
  the less,
Yet often when the woman heard his
  foot
Return from pacings in the field, and
  ran
To greet him with a kiss, the master
  took
Small notice, or austerely, for—his
  mind
Half buried in some weightier argu-
  ment   9
Or fancy-born perhaps upon the rise
And long roll of the hexameter—he
  past
To turn and ponder those three hun-
  dred scrolls
Left by the Teacher, whom he held
  divine.
She brook'd it not, but wrathful, petu-
  lant,
Dreaming some rival, sought and
  found a witch
Who brew'd the philtre which had
  power, they said,
To lead an errant passion home again.
And this, at times, she mingled with
  his drink,
And this destroy'd him; for the
  wicked broth
Confused the chemic labor of the
  blood,   20
And tickling the brute brain within
  the man's
Made havoc among those tender cells,
  and check'd
His power to shape. He loathed him-
  self, and once
After a tempest woke upon a morn
That mock'd him with returning calm,
  and cried:

  'Storm in the night! for thrice I
    heard the rain
Rushing; and once the flash of a thun-
  derbolt—
Methought I never saw so fierce a
  fork—
Struck out the streaming mountain-
  side, and show'd   29
A riotous confluence of watercourses

Blanching and billowing in a hollow
   of it,
Where all but yester-eve was dusty-
   dry.

'Storm, and what dreams, ye holy
   Gods, what dreams!
For thrice I waken'd after dreams.
   Perchance
We do but recollect the dreams that
   come
Just ere the waking. Terrible: for it
   seem'd
A void was made in Nature; all her
   bonds
Crack'd; and I saw the flaring atom-
   streams
And torrents of her myriad universe,
Ruining along the illimitable inane,   40
Fly on to clash together again, and
   make
Another and another frame of things
For ever. That was mine, my dream,
   I knew it—
Of and belonging to me, as the dog
With inward yelp and restless forefoot
   plies
His function of the woodland; but the
   next!
I thought that all the blood by Sylla
   shed
Came driving rainlike down again on
   earth,
And where it dash'd the reddening
   meadow, sprang
No dragon warriors from Cadmean
   teeth,   50
For these I thought my dream would
   show to me,
But girls, Hetairai, curious in their art,
Hired animalisms, vile as those that
   made
The mulberry-faced Dictator's orgies
   worse
Than aught they fable of the quiet
   Gods.
And hands they mixt, and yell'd and
   round me drove
In narrowing circles till I yell'd again
Half-suffocated, and sprang up, and
   saw—
Was it the first beam of my latest
   day?

'Then, then, from utter gloom stood
   out the breasts,   60
The breasts of Helen, and hoveringly
   a sword
Now over and now under, now direct,
Pointed itself to pierce, but sank down
   shamed
At all that beauty; and as I stared, a
   fire,
The fire that left a roofless Ilion,
Shot out of them, and scorch'd me
   that I woke.

'Is this thy vengeance, holy Venus,
   thine,
Because I would not one of thine own
   doves
Not even a rose, were offer'd to thee?
   thine,
Forgetful how my rich proœmion
   makes   70
Thy glory fly along the Italian field,
In lays that will outlast thy deity?

'Deity? nay, thy worshippers. My
   tongue
Trips, or I speak profanely. Which of
   these
Angers thee most, or angers thee at
   all?
Not if thou be'st of those who, far
   aloof
From envy, hate and pity, and spite
   and scorn,
Live the great life which all our greatest fain
Would follow, centred in eternal calm.

'Nay, if thou canst, O Goddess, like
   ourselves   80
Touch, and be touch'd, then would I
   cry to thee
To kiss thy Mavors, roll thy tender
   arms
Round him, and keep him from the
   lust of blood
That makes a steaming slaughter-
   house of Rome.

'Ay, but I meant not thee; I meant
   not her
Whom all the pines of Ida shook to
   see

Slide from that quiet heaven of hers,
and tempt
The Trojan, while his neatherds were
abroad;
Nor her that o'er her wounded hunter
wept
Her deity false in human-amorous
tears;   90
Nor whom her beardless apple-arbiter
Decided fairest. Rather, O ye Gods,
Poet-like, as the great Sicilian called
Calliope to grace his golden verse—
Ay, and this Kypris also—did I take
That popular name of thine to shadow
forth
The all-generating powers and genial
heat
Of Nature, when she strikes thro' the
thick blood
Of cattle, and light is large, and lambs
are glad
Nosing the mother's udder, and the
bird   100
Makes his heart voice amid the blaze
of flowers;
Which things appear the work of
mighty Gods.

'The Gods! and if I go my work is
left
Unfinish'd—if I go. The Gods, who
haunt
The lucid interspace of world and
world,
Where never creeps a cloud, or moves
a wind,
Nor ever falls the least white star of
snow,
Nor ever lowest roll of thunder moans,
Nor sound of human sorrow mounts
to mar
Their sacred everlasting calm! and
such,   110
Not all so fine, nor so divine a calm,
Not such, nor all unlike it, man may
gain
Letting his own life go. The Gods, the
Gods!
If all be atoms, how then should the
Gods
Being atomic not be dissoluble,
Not follow the great law? My master
held

That Gods there are, for all men so
believe.
I prest my footsteps into his, and
meant
Surely to lead my Memmius in a train
Of flowery clauses onward to the
proof   120
That Gods there are, and deathless.
Meant? I meant?
I have forgotten what I meant; my
mind
Stumbles, and all my faculties are
lamed.

'Look where another of our Gods,
the Sun,
Apollo, Delius, or of older use
All-seeing Hyperion—what you will—
Has mounted yonder; since he never
sware,
Except his wrath were wreak'd on
wretched man,
That he would only shine among the
dead
Hereafter—tales! for never yet on
earth   130
Could dead flesh creep, or bits of
roasting ox
Moan round the spit—nor knows he
what he sees;
King of the East altho' he seem, and
girt
With song and flame and fragrance,
slowly lifts
His golden feet on those empurpled
stairs
That climb into the windy halls of
heaven
And here he glances on an eye new-
born,
And gets for greeting but a wail of
pain;
And here he stays upon a freezing orb
That fain would gaze upon him to the
last,   140
And here upon a yellow eyelid fallen
And closed by those who mourn a
friend in vain,
Not thankful that his troubles are no
more.
And me, altho' his fire is on my face
Blinding, he sees not, nor at all can tell

Whether I mean this day to end my-
        self,
Or lend an ear to Plato where he says,
That men like soldiers may not quit
        the post
Allotted by the Gods. But he that
        holds
The Gods are careless, wherefore need
        he care   150
Greatly for them, nor rather plunge
        at once,
Being troubled, wholly out of sight,
        and sink
Past earthquake—ay, and gout and
        stone, that break
Body toward death, and palsy, death-
        in-life,
And wretched age—and worst disease
        of all,
These prodigies of myriad naked-
        nesses,
And twisted shapes of lust, unspeak-
        able,
Abominable, strangers at my hearth
Not welcome, harpies miring every
        dish,
The phantom husks of something
        foully done,   160
And fleeting thro' the boundless uni-
        verse,
And blasting the long quiet of my
        breast
With animal heat and dire insanity?

'How should the mind, except it
        loved them, clasp
These idols to herself? or do they fly
Now thinner, and now thicker, like
        the flakes
In a fall of snow, and so press in, per-
        force
Of multitude, as crowds that in an
        hour
Of civic tumult jam the doors, and
        bear
The keepers down, and throng, their
        rags and they   170
The basest, far into that council-hall
Where sit the best and stateliest of the
        land?

'Can I not fling this horror off me
        again,

Seeing with how great ease Nature can
        smile,
Balmier and nobler from her bath of
        storm,
At random ravage? and how easily
The mountain there has cast his
        cloudy slough,
Now towering o'er him in serenest air,
A mountain o'er a mountain,—ay, and
        within
All hollow as the hopes and fears of
        men?   180

'But who was he that in the garden
        snared
Picus and Faunus, rustic Gods? a tale
To laugh at—more to laugh at in my-
        self—
For look! what is it? there? yon arbu-
        tus
Totters; a noiseless riot underneath
Strikes through the wood, sets all the
        tops quivering—
The mountain quickens into Nymph
        and Faun;
And here an Oread—how the sun de-
        lights
To glance and shift about her slippery
        sides,
And rosy knees and supple rounded-
        ness,   190
And budded bosom-peaks—who this
        way runs
Before the rest!—A satyr, a satyr,
        see,
Follows; but him I proved impossible;
Twy-natured is no nature. Yet he
        draws
Nearer and nearer, and I scan him
        now
Beastlier than any phantom of his
        kind
That ever butted his rough brother-
        brute
For lust or lusty blood or provender.
I hate, abhor, spit, sicken at him; and
        she
Loathes him as well; such a precipi-
        tate heel,   200
Fledged as it were with Mercury's
        ankle-wing,
Whirls her to me—but will she fling
        herself

Shameless upon me? Catch her, goat-
    foot! nay,
Hide, hide them, million-myrtled wil-
    derness,
And cavern-shadowing laurels, hide!
    do I wish—
What?—that the bush were leafless?
    or to whelm
All of them in one massacre? O ye
    Gods,
I know you careless, yet, behold, to
    you
From childly wont and ancient use I
    call—
I thought I lived securely as your-
    selves—   210
No lewdness, narrowing envy, mon-
    key-spite,
No madness of ambition, avarice,
    none;
No larger feast than under plane or
    pine
With neighbors laid along the grass,
    to take
Only such cups as left us friendly-
    warm,
Affirming each his own philosophy—
Nothing to mar the sober majesties
Of settled, sweet, Epicurean life.
But now it seems some unseen mon-
    ster lays
His vast and filthy hands upon my
    will,   220
Wrenching it backward into his, and
    spoils
My bliss in being; and it was not
    great,
For save when shutting reasons up in
    rhythm,
Or Heliconian honey in living words,
To make a truth less harsh, I often
    grew
Tired of so much within our little life,
Or of so little in our little life—
Poor little life that toddles half an
    hour
Crown'd with a flower or two, and
    there an end—
And since the nobler pleasure seems
    to fade,   230
Why should I, beastlike as I find my-
    self,

Not manlike end myself?—our privi-
    lege—
What beast has heart to do it? And
    what man,
What Roman would be dragg'd in tri-
    umph thus?
Not I; not he, who bears one name
    with her
Whose death-blow struck the dateless
    doom of kings,
When, brooking not the Tarquin in
    her veins,
She made her blood in sight of Col-
    latine
And all his peers, flushing the guiltless
    air,
Spout from the maiden fountain in
    her heart.   240
And from it sprang the Common-
    wealth, which breaks
As I am breaking now!

                    'And therefore now
Let her, that is the womb and tomb of
    all,
Great Nature, take, and forcing far
    apart
Those blind beginnings that have
    made me man,
Dash then anew together at her will
Thro' all her cycles—into man once
    more,
Or beast or bird or fish, or opulent
    flower.
But till this cosmic order everywhere
Shatter'd into one earthquake in one
    day   250
Cracks all to pieces,—and that hour
    perhaps
Is not so far when momentary man
Shall seem no more a something to
    himself,
But he, his hopes and hates, his homes
    and fanes,
And even his bones long laid within
    the grave,
The very sides of the grave itself shall
    pass,
Vanishing, atom and void, atom and
    void,
Into the unseen for ever,—till that
    hour,

My golden work in which I told a
    truth   259
That stays the rolling Ixionian wheel,
And numbs the Fury's ringlet-snake,
    and plucks
The mortal soul from out immortal
    hell,
Shall stand. Ay, surely; then it fails
    at last
And perishes as I must; for O Thou,
Passionless bride, divine Tranquillity,
Yearn'd after by the wisest of the
    wise,
Who fail to find thee, being as thou
    art
Without one pleasure and without one
    pain,
Howbeit I know thou surely must be
    mine
Or soon or late, yet out of season,
    thus   270

I woo thee roughly, for thou carest
    not
How roughly men may woo thee so
    they win—
Thus—thus—the soul flies out and
    dies in the air.'

    With that he drove the knife into
    his side.
She heard him raging, heard him fall,
    ran in,
Beat breast, tore hair, cried out upon
    herself
As having fail'd in duty to him,
    shriek'd
That she but meant to win him back,
    fell on him,
Clasp'd, kiss'd him, wail'd. He an-
    swer'd, 'Care not thou!
Thy duty? What is duty? Fare thee
    well!'   280

THE WINDOW; OR, THE SONG OF
THE WRENS

Four years ago Mr. Sullivan requested me to write a little song-cycle, German fashion, for him to exercise his art upon. He had been very successful in setting such old songs, as 'Orpheus with his lute,' and I drest up for him, partly in the old style, a puppet, whose almost only merit is, perhaps, that it can dance to Mr. Sullivan's instrument. I am sorry that my four-year-old puppet should have to dance at all in the dark shadow of these days; but the music is now completed, and I am bound by my promise.

December, 1870

A. Tennyson

THE WINDOW

ON THE HILL

The lights and shadows fly!
Yonder it brightens and darkens down
  on the plain.
  A jewel, a jewel dear to a lover's
    eye!
O, is it the brook, or a pool, or her
  window-pane,
    When the winds are up in the
    morning?

Clouds that are racing above,
And winds and lights and shadows
  that cannot be still,
  All running on one way to the home
    of my love,
You are all running on, and I stand on
  the slope of the hill,
    And the winds are up in the
    morning!   10

Follow, follow the chase!
And my thoughts are as quick and as
  quick, ever on, on, on.
  O lights, are you flying over her
    sweet little face?
And my heart is there before you are
  come, and gone,
    When the winds are up in the
    morning!

Follow them down the slope!
And I follow them down to the win-
  dow-pane of my dear,
  And it brightens and darkens and
    brightens like my hope,
And it darkens and brightens and
  darkens like my fear,
    And the winds are up in the morn-
    ing!   20

AT THE WINDOW

Vine, vine and eglantine,
Clasp her window, trail and twine!
Rose, rose and clematis,
Trail and twine and clasp and kiss,
Kiss, kiss—and out of her bower
  All of flowers, and drop me a
    flower,
    Drop me a flower.

Vine, vine and eglantine,
Cannot a flower, a flower, be mine?
Rose, rose and clematis,   36
Drop me a flower, a flower, to kiss,
Kiss, kiss—and out of her bower
  All of flowers, a flower, a flower,
    Dropt, a flower.

GONE

Gone!
Gone, till the end of the year,

Gone, and the light gone with her, and
      left me in shadow here!
         Gone—flitted away,
Taken the stars from the night and
      the sun from the day!
Gone, and a cloud in my heart, and a
      storm in the air!   40
Flown to the east or the west, flitted I
      know not where!
Down in the south is a flash and a
      groan; she is there! she is
      there!

WINTER

The frost is here,
And fuel is dear,
And woods are sear,
And fires burn clear,
And frost is here
And has bitten the heel of the going
      year.

Bite, frost, bite!
You roll up away from the light   50
The blue wood-louse and the plump
      dormouse,
And the bees are still'd, and the flies
      are kill'd,
And you bite far into the heart of the
      house,
But not into mine.

Bite, frost, bite!
The woods are all the searer,
The fuel is all the dearer,
The fires are all the clearer,
My spring is all the nearer,
You have bitten into the heart of the
      earth,   60
But not into mine.

SPRING

Birds' love and birds' song
      Flying here and there,
Birds' song and birds' love,
      And you with gold for hair!
Birds' song and birds' love,
      Passing with the weather,
Men's song and men's love,
      To love once and for ever.

Men's love and birds' love,   70
      And women's love and men's!
And you my wren with a crown of
      gold,
      You my queen of the wrens!
You the queen of the wrens—
      We'll be birds of a feather,
I'll be King of the Queen of the wrens,
      And all in a nest together.

THE LETTER

Where is another sweet as my sweet,
      Fine of the fine, and shy of the shy?
Fine little hands, fine little feet—   80
      Dewy blue eye.
Shall I write to her? shall I go?
      Ask her to marry me by and by?
Somebody said that she'd say no;
      Somebody knows that she'll say ay!

Ay or no, if ask'd to her face?
      Ay or no, from shy of the shy?
Go, little letter, apace, apace,
      Fly;   89
Fly to the light in the valley below—
      Tell my wish to her dewy blue eye.
Somebody said that she'd say no;
      Somebody knows that she'll say ay!

NO ANSWER

The mist and the rain, the mist and
      the rain!
      Is it ay or no? is it ay or no?
And never a glimpse of her window-
      pane!
      And I may die but the grass will
      grow,
And the grass will grow when I am
      gone,
And the wet west wind and the world
      will go on.   99

Ay is the song of the wedded spheres,
      No is trouble and cloud and storm,
Ay is life for a hundred years,
      No will push me down to the worm,
And when I am there and dead and
      gone,
The wet west wind and the world will
      go on.

The wind and the wet, the wind and
   the wet!
  Wet west wind, how you blow, you
    blow!
And never a line from my lady yet!
  Is it ay or no? is it ay or no?   109
Blow then, blow, and when I am gone
The wet west wind and the world may
   go on.

NO ANSWER

Winds are loud and you are dumb,
Take my love, for love will come,
  Love will come but once a life.
Winds are loud and winds will pass!
Spring is here with leaf and grass;
  Take my love and be my wife.
After-loves of maids and men
Are but dainties drest again.   119
Love me now, you'll love me then;
  Love can love but once a life.

THE ANSWER

Two little hands that meet,
Claspt on her seal, my sweet!
Must I take you and break you,
Two little hands that meet?
I must take you, and break you,
And loving hands must part—
Take, take—break, break—
Break—you may break my heart.
  Faint heart never won—   130
  Break, break, and all's done.

AY

Be merry, all birds, to-day,
  Be merry on earth as you never
    were merry before,
Be merry in heaven, O larks, and far
   away,
  And merry for ever and ever, and
    one day more.
          Why?
   For it's easy to find a rhyme.
Look, look, how he flits,
  The fire-crown'd king of the wrens,
    from out of the pine!
Look how they tumble the blossom,
   the mad little tits   140

'Cuck-oo! Cuck-oo!' was ever a
  May so fine?
          Why?
  For it's easy to find a rhyme.
O merry the linnet and dove,
  And swallow and sparrow and thros-
    tle and have your desire!
O merry my heart, you have gotten
   the wings of love,
  And flit like the king of the wrens
    with a crown of fire.
          Why?
   For it's ay ay, ay ay.

WHEN

Sun comes, moon comes,   156
  Time slips away.
Sun sets, moon sets,
  Love, fix a day.

'A year hence, a year hence.'
  'We shall both be gray.'
'A month hence, a month hence.'
  'Far, far away.'

'A week hence, a week hence.'
  'Ah, the long delay!'
'Wait a little, wait a little,   160
  You shall fix a day.'

'To-morrow, love, to-morrow,
  And that's an age away.'
Blaze upon her window, sun,
  And honor all the day.

MARRIAGE MORNING

Light, so low upon earth,
  You send a flash to the sun.
Here is the golden close of love,
  All my wooing is done.
O, the woods and the meadows,   170
  Woods where we hid from the wet,
Stiles where we stay'd to be kind,
  Meadows in which we met!

Light, so low in the vale
  You flash and lighten afar,
For this is the golden morning of love,
  And you are his morning star.

Flash, I am coming, I come,
  By meadow and stile and wood,
O, lighten into my eyes and my heart,
  Into my heart and my blood!   [181]

Heart, are you great enough
  For a love that never tires?

O heart, are you great enough for
  love?
  I have heard of thorns and briers.
Over the thorns and briers,
  Over the meadows and stiles,
Over the world to the end of it
  Flash for a million miles.

THE LOVER'S TALE

The original Preface to 'The Lover's Tale' states that it was composed in my nineteenth year. Two only of the three parts then written were printed, when, feeling the imperfection of the poem, I withdrew it from the press. One of my friends, however, who, boylike, admired the boy's work, distributed among our common associates of that hour some copies of these two parts, without my knowledge, without the omissions and amendments which I had in contemplation, and marred by the many misprints of the compositor. Seeing that these two parts have of late been mercilessly pirated, and that what I had deemed scarce worthy to live is not allowed to die, may I not be pardoned if I suffer the whole poem at last to come into the light—accompanied with a reprint of the sequel—a work of my mature life—'The Golden Supper'?
    May, 1879.

ARGUMENT

Julian, whose cousin and foster-sister, Camilla, has been wedded to his friend and rival, Lionel, endeavors to narrate the story of his own love for her, and the strange sequel. He speaks (in Parts II. and III.) of having been haunted by visions and the sound of bells, tolling for a funeral, and at last ringing for a marriage; but he breaks away, overcome, as he approaches the Event, and a witness to it completes the tale.

I

HERE far away, seen from the topmost
    cliff,
Filling with purple gloom the vacancies
Between the tufted hills, the sloping
    seas
Hung in mid-heaven, and half-way
    down rare sails,
White as white clouds, floated from
    sky to sky.
O pleasant breast of waters, quiet bay,
Like to a quiet mind in the loud world,
Where the chafed breakers of the
    outer sea
Sank powerless, as anger falls aside
And withers on the breast of peaceful
    love!   10
Thou didst receive the growth of pines
    that fledged
The hills that watch'd thee, as Love
    watcheth Love,

In thine own essence, and delight thyself
To make it wholly thine on sunny
    days.
Keep thou thy name of 'Lover's Bay.'
    See, sirs,
Even now the Goddess of the Past,
    that takes
The heart, and sometimes touches but
    one string
That quivers and is silent, and sometimes
Sweeps suddenly all its half-moulder'd
    chords
To some old melody, begins to play   20
That air which pleased her first. I feel
    thy breath;
I come, great Mistress of the ear and
    eye;
Thy breath is of the pine-wood, and
    tho' years
Have hollow'd out a deep and stormy
    strait

Betwixt the native land of Love and
  me,
Breathe but a little on me, and the sail
Will draw me to the rising of the sun,
The lucid chambers of the morning
  star,
And East of Life.

Permit me, friend, I prythee,
To pass my hand across my brows, and
  muse   30
On those dear hills, that nevermore
  will meet
The sight that throbs and aches be-
  neath my touch,
As tho' there beat a heart in either
  eye;
For when the outer lights are darken'd
  thus,
The memory's vision hath a keener
  edge.
It grows upon me now—the semicircle
Of dark-blue waters and the narrow
  fringe
Of curving beach—its wreaths of drip-
  ping green—
Its pale pink shells—the summer-
  house aloft
That open'd on the pines with doors
  of glass,   40
A mountain nest—the pleasure-boat
  that rock'd,
Light-green with its own shadow, keel
  to keel,
Upon the dappled dimplings of the
  wave
That blanch'd upon its side.

O Love, O Hope!
They come, they crowd upon me all at
  once—
Moved from the cloud of unforgotten
  things,
That sometimes on the horizon of the
  mind
Lies folded, often sweeps athwart in
  storm—
Flash upon flash they lighten thro' me
  —days   49
Of dewy dawning and the amber eves
When thou and I, Camilla, thou and I
Were borne about the bay or safely
  moor'd

Beneath a low-brow'd cavern, where
  the tide
Plash'd, sapping its worn ribs; and all
  without
The slowly-ridging rollers on the cliffs
Clash'd, calling to each other, and
  thro' the arch
Down those loud waters, like a setting
  star,
Mixt with the gorgeous west the light-
  house shone,
And silver-smiling Venus ere she fell
Would often loiter in her balmy blue,
To crown it with herself.

Here, too, my love   61
Waver'd at anchor with me, when day
  hung
From his mid-dome in heaven's airy
  halls;
Gleams of the water-circles as they
  broke,
Flicker'd like doubtful smiles about
  her lips,
Quiver'd a flying glory on her hair,
Leapt like a passing thought across her
  eyes;
And mine with one that will not pass,
  till earth
And heaven pass too, dwelt on my
  heaven, a face
Most starry-fair, but kindled from
  within   70
As 't were with dawn. She was dark-
  hair'd, dark-eyed—
O, such dark eyes! a single glance of
  them
Will govern a whole life from birth to
  death,
Careless of all things else, led on with
  light
In trances and in visions. Look at
  them,
You lose yourself in utter ignorance;
You cannot find their depth; for they
  go back,
And farther back, and still withdraw
  themselves
Quite into the deep soul, that ever-
  more
Fresh springing from her fountains in
  the brain,   80

Still pouring thro', floods with redun-
dant life
Her narrow portals.

          Trust me, long ago
I should have died, if it were possible
To die in gazing on that perfectness
Which I do bear within me. I had died,
But from my farthest lapse, my latest
ebb,
Thine image, like a charm of light and
strength
Upon the waters, push'd me back
again
On these deserted sands of barren life.
Tho' from the deep vault where the   90
heart of Hope
Fell into dust, and crumbled in the
dark—
Forgetting how to render beautiful
Her countenance with quick and
healthful blood—
Thou didst not sway me upward;
could I perish
While thou, a meteor of the sepulchre,
Didst swathe thyself all round Hope's
quiet urn
For ever? He that saith it hath o'er-
stept
The slippery footing of his narrow
wit,
And fallen away from judgment. Thou
art light,
To which my spirit leaneth all her
flowers,   100
And length of days, and immortality
Of thought, and freshness ever self-
renew'd.
For Time and Grief abode too long
with Life,
And, like all other friends i' the world,
at last
They grew aweary of her fellowship.
So Time and Grief did beckon unto
Death,
And Death drew nigh and beat the
doors of Life;
But thou didst sit alone in the inner
house,
A wakeful portress, and didst parle
with Death,—
'This is a charmed dwelling which I
hold;'   110

So Death gave back, and would no
further come.
Yet is my life nor in the present time,
Nor in the present place. To me alone,
Push'd from his chair of regal herit-
age,
The Present is the vassal of the Past:
So that, in that I *have* lived, do I live,
And cannot die, and am, in having
been—
A portion of the pleasant yesterday,
Thrust forward on to-day and out of
place;
A body journeying onward, sick with
toil,   120
The weight as if of age upon my limbs,
The grasp of hopeless grief about my
heart,
And all the senses weaken'd, save in
that,
Which long ago they had glean'd and
garner'd up
Into the granaries of memory—
The clear brow, bulwark of the pre-
cious brain,
Chink'd as you see, and seam'd—and
all the while
The light soul twines and mingles with
the growths
Of vigorous early days, attracted, won,
Married, made one with, molten into
all   130
The beautiful in Past of act or place,
And like the all-enduring camel,
driven
Far from the diamond fountain by
the palms,
Who toils across the middle moonlit
nights,
Or when the white heats of the blind-
ing noons
Beat from the concave sand; yet in
him keeps
A draught of that sweet fountain that
he loves,
To stay his feet from falling and his
spirit
From bitterness of death.

          Ye ask me, friends,
When I began to love. How should I
tell you?   140
Or from the after-fulness of my heart,

Flow back again unto my slender
  spring
And first of love, tho' every turn and
  depth
Between is clearer in my life than all
Its present flow. Ye know not what ye
  ask.
How should the broad and open flower
  tell
What sort of bud it was, when, prest
  together
In its green sheath, close-lapt in silken
  folds,
It seem'd to keep its sweetness to it-
  self,
Yet was not the less sweet for that it
  seem'd?   150
For young Life knows not when young
  Life was born,
But takes it all for granted: neither
  Love,
Warm in the heart, his cradle, can re-
  member
Love in the womb, but resteth satis-
  fied,
Looking on her that brought him to
  the light;
Or as men know not when they fall
  asleep
Into delicious dreams, our other life,
So know I not when I began to love.
This is my sum of knowledge—that
  my love
Grew with myself—say rather, was
  my growth,   160
My inward sap, the hold I have on
  earth,
My outward circling air wherewith I
  breathe,
Which yet upholds my life, and ever-
  more
Is to me daily life and daily death.
For how should I have lived and not
  have loved?
Can ye take off the sweetness from the
  flower,
The color and the sweetness from the
  rose,
And place them by themselves; or set
  apart
Their motions and their brightness
  from the stars,

And then point out the flower or the
  star?   170
Or build a wall betwixt my life and
  love,
And tell me where I am? 'T is even
  thus:
In that I live I love; because I love
I live. Whate'er is fountain to the one
Is fountain to the other; and whene'er
Our God unknits the riddle of the one,
There is no shade or fold of mystery
Swathing the other.

                        Many, many years—
For they seem many and my most of
  life,
And well I could have linger'd in that
  porch,   180
So unproportion'd to the dwelling-
  place,—
In the May-dews of childhood, oppo-
  site
The flush and dawn of youth, we lived
  together,
Apart, alone together on those hills.

  Before he saw my day my father
  died,
And he was happy that he saw it not;
But I and the first daisy on his grave
From the same clay came into light at
  once.
As Love and I do number equal years,
So she, my love, is of an age with me.
How like each other was the birth of
  each!   191
On the same morning, almost the same
  hour,
Under the selfsame aspect of the
  stars—
O, falsehood of all star-craft!—we
  were born.
How like each other was the birth of
  each!
The sister of my mother—she that
  bore
Camilla close beneath her beating
  heart,
Which to the imprison'd spirit of the
  child,
With its true-touched pulses in the
  flow
And hourly visitation of the blood, 200

Sent notes of preparation manifold,
And mellow'd echoes of the outer
    world—
My mother's sister, mother of my
    love,
Who had a twofold claim upon my
    heart,
One twofold mightier than the other
    was,
In giving so much beauty to the world,
And so much wealth as God had
    charged her with—
Loathing to put it from herself for
    ever,
Left her own life with it; and dying
    thus,
Crown'd with her highest act the
    placid face   210
And breathless body of her good deeds
    past.

    So were we born, so orphan'd. She
    was motherless,
And I without a father. So from each
Of those two pillars which from earth
    uphold
Our childhood, one had fallen away,
    and all
The careful burthen of our tender
    years
Trembled upon the other. He that
    gave
Her life, to me delightedly fulfill'd
All loving kindnesses, all offices
Of watchful care and trembling ten-
    derness.   220
He waked for both, he pray'd for
    both, he slept
Dreaming of both; nor was his love
    the less
Because it was divided, and shot forth
Boughs on each side, laden with whole-
    some shade,
Wherein we nested sleeping or awake,
And sang aloud the matin-song of life.

    She was my foster-sister. On one
    arm
The flaxen ringlets of our infancies
Wander'd, the while we rested; one
    soft lap
Pillow'd us both; a common light of
    eyes   230

Was on us as we lay; our baby lips,
Kissing one bosom, ever drew from
    thence
The stream of life, one stream, one
    life, one blood,
One sustenance, which, still as thought
    grew large,
Still larger moulding all the house of
    thought,
Made all our tastes and fancies like,
    perhaps—
All—all but one; and strange to me,
    and sweet,
Sweet thro' strange years to know
    that whatsoe'er
Our general mother meant for me
    alone,
Our mutual mother dealt to both of
    us.   240
So what was earliest mine in earliest
    life,
I shared with her in whom myself re-
    mains.

    As was our childhood, so our in-
    fancy,
They tell me that we would not be
Of fellow-feeling and communion.
They tell me that we would not be
    alone,—
We cried when we were parted; when
    I wept,
Her smile lit up the rainbow on my
    tears,
Stay'd on the cloud of sorrow; that we
    loved
The sound of one another's voices
    more   250
Than the gray cuckoo loves his name,
    and learn'd
To lisp in tune together; that we slept
In the same cradle always, face to
    face,
Heart beating time to heart, lip press-
    ing lip,
Folding each other, breathing on each
    other,
Dreaming together—dreaming of each
    other,
They should have added,—till the
    morning light
Sloped thro' the pines, upon the dewy
    pane

Falling, unseal'd our eyelids, and we
  woke
To gaze upon each other. If this be
  true,   260
At thought of which my whole soul
  languishes
And faints, and hath no pulse, no
  breath—as tho'
A man in some still garden should in-
  fuse
Rich atar in the bòsom of the rose,
Till, drunk with its own wine, and
  overfull
Of sweetness, and in smelling of itself,
It fall on its own thorns—if this be
  true—
And that way my wish leads me ever-
  more
Still to believe it, 't is so sweet a
  thought—
Why in the utter stillness of the soul
Doth question'd memory answer not,
  nor tell   271
Of this our earliest, our closest-
  drawn,
Most loveliest, earthly-heavenliest
  harmony?

  O blossom'd portal of the lonely
    house,
Green prelude, April promise, glad
  new-year
Of being, which with earliest violets
And lavish carol of clear-throated
  larks
Fill'd all the March of life!—I will
  not speak of thee,
These have not seen thee, these can
  never know thee,
They cannot understand me. Pass we
  then   280
A term of eighteen years. Ye would
  but laugh
If I should tell you how I hoard in
  thought
The faded rhymes and scraps of an-
  cient crones,
Gray relics of the nurseries of the
  world,
Which are as gems set in my memory,
Because she learnt them with me; or
  what use
To know her father left us just before

The daffodil was blown? or how we
  found
The dead man cast upon the shore?
  All this
Seems to the quiet daylight of your
  minds   290
But cloud and smoke, and in the dark
  of mine
Is traced with flame. Move with me
  to the event.

  There came a glorious morning,
    such a one
As dawns but once a season. Mercury
On such a morning would have flung
  himself
From cloud to cloud, and swum with
  balanced wings
To some tall mountain. When I said
  to her,
'A day for gods to stoop,' she an-
  swered, 'Ay,
And men to soar;' for as that other
  gazed,
Shading his eyes till all the fiery cloud,
The prophet and the chariot and the
  steeds,   301
Suck'd into oneness like a little star
Were drunk into the inmost blue, we
  stood,
When first we came from out the pines
  at noon,
With hands for eaves, uplooking and
  almost
Waiting to see some blessed shape in
  heaven,
So bathed we were in brilliance. Never
  yet
Before or after have I known the
  spring
Pour with such sudden deluges of light
Into the middle summer; for that day
Love, rising, shook his wings, and
  charged the winds   311
With spiced May-sweets from bound
  to bound, and blew
Fresh fire into the sun, and from
  within
Burst thro' the heated buds, and sent
  his soul
Into the songs of birds, and touch'd
  far-off

His mountain-altars, his high hills,
        with flame
Milder and purer.

                    Thro' the rocks we wound;
The great pine shook with lonely
        sounds of joy
That came on the sea-wind. As moun-
        tain streams
Our bloods ran free; the sunshine
        seem'd to brood   320
More warmly on the heart than on the
        brow.
We often paused, and, looking back,
        we saw
The clefts and openings in the moun-
        tains fill'd
With the blue valley and the glistening
        brooks,
And all the low dark groves, a land of
        love!
A land of promise, a land of memory,
A land of promise flowing with the
        milk
And honey of delicious memories!
And down to sea, and far as eye could
        ken,
Each way from verge to verge a Holy
        Land,   330
Still growing holier as you near'd the
        bay,
For there the Temple stood.

                    When we had reach'd
The grassy platform on some hill, I
        stoop'd,
I gather'd the wild herbs, and for her
        brows
And mine made garlands of the self-
        same flower,
Which she took smiling, and with my
        work thus
Crown'd her clear forehead. Once or
        twice she told me—
For I remember all things—to let
        grow
The flowers that run poison in their
        veins.
She said, 'The evil flourish in the
        world.'   340
Then playfully she gave herself the
        lie—
'Nothing in nature is unbeautiful;

So, brother, pluck and spare not.' So
        I wove
Even the dull-blooded poppy-stem,
        'whose flower,
Hued with the scarlet of a fierce sun-
        rise,
Like to the wild youth of an evil
        prince,
Is without sweetness, but who crowns
        himself
Above the naked poisons of his heart
In his old age.' A graceful thought of
        hers
Graven on my fancy! And O, how like
        a nymph,   350
A stately mountain nymph she look'd!
        how native
Unto the hills she trod on! While I
        gazed
My coronal slowly disentwined itself
And fell between us both; tho' while I
        gazed
My spirit leap'd as with those thrills
        of bliss
That strike across the soul in prayer,
        and show us
That we are surely heard. Methought
        a light
Burst from the garland I had woven,
        and stood
A solid glory on her bright black hair;
A light methought broke from her
        dark, dark eyes,   360
And shot itself into the singing winds;
A mystic light flash'd even from her
        white robe
As from a glass in the sun, and fell
        about
My footsteps on the mountains.

                    Last we came
To what our people call 'The Hill of
        Woe.'
A bridge is there, that, look'd at from
        beneath,
Seems but a cobweb filament to link
The yawning of an earthquake-cloven
        chasm.
And thence one night, when all the
        winds were loud,
A woful man—for so the story went—
Had thrust his wife and child and
        dash'd himself   371

Into the dizzy depth below. Below,
Fierce in the strength of far descent, a stream
Flies with a shatter'd foam along the chasm.

The path was perilous, loosely strown with crags.
We mounted slowly; yet to both there came
The joy of life in steepness overcome,
And victories of ascent, and looking down
On all that had look'd down on us; and joy
In breathing nearer heaven; and joy to me,   380
High over all the azure-circled earth,
To breathe with her as if in heaven itself;
And more than joy that I to her became
Her guardian and her angel, raising her
Still higher, past all peril, until she saw
Beneath her feet the region far away,
Beyond the nearest mountain's bosky brows,
Arise in open prospect—heath and hill,
And hollow lined and wooded to the lips,
And steep-down walls of battlemented rock   390
Gilded with broom, or shatter'd into spires,
And glory of broad waters interfused,
Whence rose as it were breath and steam of gold,
And over all the great wood rioting
And climbing, streak'd or starr'd at intervals
With falling brook or blossom'd bush —and last,
Framing the mighty landscape to the west,
A purple range of mountain-cones, between
Whose interspaces gush'd in blinding bursts
The incorporate blaze of sun and sea.

At length
Descending from the point, and standing both   401
There on the tremulous bridge, that from beneath
Had seem'd a gossamer filament up in air,
We paused amid the splendor. All the west
And even unto the middle south was ribb'd
And barr'd with bloom on bloom. The sun below,
Held for a space 'twixt cloud and wave, shower'd down
Rays of a mighty circle, weaving over
That various wilderness a tissue of light
Unparallel'd. On the other side, the moon,   410
Half-melted into thin blue air, stood still,
And pale and fibrous as a wither'd leaf,
Nor yet endured in presence of His eyes
To indue his lustre; most unloverlike,
Since in his absence full of light and joy,
And giving light to others. But this most,
Next to her presence whom I loved so well,
Spoke loudly even into my inmost heart
As to my outward hearing. The loud stream,
Forth issuing from his portals in the crag,—   420
A visible link unto the home of my heart,—
Ran amber toward the west, and nigh the sea
Parting my own loved mountains was received,
Shorn of its strength, into the sympathy
Of that small bay, which out to open main
Glow'd intermingling close beneath the sun.
Spirit of Love! that little hour was bound,

Shut in from Time, and dedicate to
    thee;
Thy fires from heaven had touch'd it,
    and the earth
They fell on became hallow'd ever-
    more.   430

We turn'd, our eyes met; hers were
    bright, and mine
Were dim with floating tears, that shot
    the sunset
In lightnings round me, and my name
    was borne
Upon her breath. Henceforth my
    name has been
A hallow'd memory like the names of
    old,
A centred, glory-circled memory,
And a peculiar treasure, brooking not
Exchange or currency; and in that
    hour
A hope flow'd round me, like a golden
    mist
Charm'd amid eddies of melodious
    airs,   440
A moment, ere the onward whirlwind
    shatter it,
Waver'd and floated—which was less
    than Hope,
Because it lack'd the power of perfect
    Hope;
But which was more and higher than
    all Hope,
Because all other Hope had lower aim;
Even that this name to which her
    gracious lips
Did lend such gentle utterance, this
    one name,
In some obscure hereafter, might in-
    wreathe—
How lovelier, nobler then!—her life,
    her love,
With my life, love, soul, spirit, and
    heart and strength.   450
'Brother,' she said, 'let this be call'd
    henceforth
The Hill of Hope;' and I replied, 'O
    sister,
My will is one with thine; the Hill of
    Hope.'
Nevertheless, we did not change the
    name.

I did not speak; I could not speak
    my love.
Love lieth deep, Love dwells not in
    lip-depths.
Love wraps his wings on either side
    the heart,
Constraining it with kisses close and
    warm,
Absorbing all the incense of sweet
    thoughts
So that they pass not to the shrine of
    sound.   460
Else had the life of that delighted hour
Drunk in the largeness of the utter-
    ance
Of Love; but how should earthly
    measure mete
The heavenly-unmeasured or unlim-
    ited Love,
Who scarce can tune his high majes-
    tic sense
Unto the thunder-song that wheels the
    spheres,
Scarce living in the Æolian harmony,
And flowing odor of the spacious air,
Scarce housed within the circle of this
    earth,
Be cabin'd up in words and syllables,
Which pass with that which breathes
    them? Sooner earth   471
Might go round heaven, and the strait
    girth of Time
Inswathe the fulness of Eternity,
Than language grasp the infinite of
    Love.

O day which did enwomb that
    happy hour,
Thou art blessed in the years, divinest
    day!
O Genius of that hour which dost up-
    hold
Thy coronal of glory like a god,
Amid thy melancholy mates far-seen,
Who walk before thee, ever turning
    round   480
To gaze upon thee till their eyes are
    dim
With dwelling on the light and depth
    of thine,
Thy name is ever worshipp'd among
    hours!

Had I died then, I had not seem'd to
          die,
For bliss stood round me like the light
          of heaven,—
Had I died then, I had not known the
          death;
Yea, had the Power from whose right
          hand the light
Of Life issueth, and from whose left
          hand floweth
The Shadow of Death, perennial ef-
          fluences,
Whereof to all that draw the whole-
          some air,   490
Somewhile the one must overflow the
          other—
Then had he stemm'd my day with
          night, and driven
My current to the fountain whence it
          sprang,—
Even his own abiding excellence—
On me, methinks, that shock of gloom
          had fallen
Unfelt, and in this glory I had merged
The other, like the sun I gazed upon,
Which seeming for the moment due to
          death,
And dipping his head low beneath the
          verge,
Yet bearing round about him his own
          day,   500
In confidence of unabated strength,
Steppeth from heaven to heaven, from
          light to light,
And holdeth his undimmed forehead
          far
Into a clearer zenith, pure of cloud.

We trod the shadow of the down-
          ward hill;
We past from light to dark. On the
          other side
Is scoop'd a cavern and a mountain
          hall,
Which none have fathom'd. If you go
          far in—
The country people rumor—you may
          hear
The moaning of the woman and the
          child,   510
Shut in the secret chambers of the
          rock.

I too have heard a sound—perchance
          of streams
Running far on within its inmost halls,
The home of darkness; but the cav-
          ern-mouth,
Half overtrailed with a wanton weed,
Gives birth to a brawling brook, that
          passing lightly
Adown a natural stair of tangled roots
Is presently received in a sweet grave
Of eglantines, a place of burial
Far lovelier than its cradle; for un-
          seen,   520
But taken with the sweetness of the
          place,
It makes a constant bubbling melody
That drowns the nearer echoes. Lower
          down
Spreads out a little lake, that, flood-
          ing, leaves
Low banks of yellow sand; and from
          the woods
That belt it rise three dark, tall cy-
          presses,—
Three cypresses, symbols of mortal
          woe,
That men plant over graves.

                    Hither we came,
And sitting down upon the golden
          moss,
Held converse sweet and low—low
          converse sweet,   530
In which our voices bore least part.
          The wind
Told a love-tale beside us, how he
          woo'd
The waters, and the waters answering
          lisp'd
To kisses of the wind, that, sick with
          love,
Fainted at intervals, and grew again
To utterance of passion. Ye cannot
          shape
Fancy so fair as is this memory.
Methought all excellence that ever
          was
Had drawn herself from many thou-
          sand years,
And all the separate Edens of this
          earth,   540
To centre in this place and time. I lis-
          ten'd,

And her words stole with most pre-
vailing sweetness
Into my heart, as thronging fancies
come
To boys and girls when summer days
are new,
And soul and heart and body are all
at ease.
What marvel my Camilla told me all?
It was so happy an hour, so sweet a
place,
And I was as the brother of her blood,
And by that name I moved upon her
breath;
Dear name, which had too much of
nearness in it   550
And heralded the distance of this
time!
At first her voice was very sweet and
low,
As if she were afraid of utterance;
But in the onward current of her
speech,—
As echoes of the hollow-banked brooks
Are fashion'd by the channel which
they keep,—
Her words did of their meaning bor-
row sound,
Her cheek did catch the color of her
words.
I heard and trembled, yet I could but
hear;
My heart paused—my raised eyelids
would not fall,   560
But still I kept my eyes upon the sky.
I seem'd the only part of Time stood
still,
And saw the motion of all other
things;
While her words, syllable by syllable,
Like water, drop by drop, upon my
ear
Fell, and I wish'd, yet wish'd her not
to speak;
But she spake on, for I did name no
wish.
What marvel my Camilla told me all
Her maiden dignities of Hope and
Love—
'Perchance,' she said, 'return'd'? Even
then the stars   570
I id tremble in their stations as I
gazed;

But she spake on, for I did name no
wish,
No wish—no hope. Hope was not
wholly dead,
But breathing hard at the approach of
death,—
Camilla, my Camilla, who was mine
No longer in the dearest sense of
mine—
For all the secret of her inmost heart,
And all the maiden empire of her
mind,
Lay like a map before me, and I saw
There, where I hoped myself to reign
as king,   580
There, where that day I crown'd my-
self as king,
There in my realm and even on my
throne,
Another! Then it seem'd as tho' a link
Of some tight chain within my inmost
frame
Was riven in twain; that life I heeded
not
Flow'd from me, and the darkness of
the grave,
The darkness of the grave and utter
night,
Did swallow up my vision; at her
feet,
Even the feet of her I loved, I fell,
Smit with exceeding sorrow unto
death.   590

Then had the earth beneath me
yawning cloven
With such a sound as when an iceberg
splits
From cope to base—had Heaven from
all her doors,
With all her golden thresholds clashing, roll'd
Her heaviest thunder—I had lain as
dead,
Mute, blind, and motionless as then I
lay;
Dead, for henceforth there was no life
for me!
Mute, for henceforth what use were
words to me?
Blind, for the day was as the night to
me!

The night to me was kinder than the
day; 600
The night in pity took away my day,
Because my grief as yet was newly
born
Of eyes too weak to look upon the
light;
And thro' the hasty notice of the ear
Frail Life was startled from the ten-
der love
Of him she brooded over. Would I had
lain
Until the plaited ivy-tress had wound
Round my worn limbs, and the wild
brier had driven
Its knotted thorns thro' my unpain-
ing brows,
Leaning its roses on my faded eyes. 610
The wind had blown above me, and
the rain
Had fallen upon me, and the gilded
snake
Had nestled in this bosom-throne of
Love,
But I had been at rest for evermore.

Long time entrancement held me.
All too soon
Life—like a wanton, too-officious
friend,
Who will not *hear* denial, vain and
rude
With proffer of unwish'd-for serv-
ices—
Entering all the avenues of sense
Past thro' into his citadel, the brain,
With hated warmth of apprehensive-
ness. 621
And first the chillness of the sprinkled
brook
Smote on my brows, and then I seem'd
to hear
Its murmur, as the drowning seaman
hears,
Who with his head below the surface
dropt
Listens the muffled booming indistinct
Of the confused floods, and dimly
knows
His head shall rise no more; and then
came in
The white light of the weary moon
above,

Diffused and molten into flaky cloud.
Was my sight drunk that it did shape
to me 631
Him who should own that name?
Were it not well
If so be that the echo of that name
Ringing within the fancy had updrawn
A fashion and a phantasm of the form
It should attach to? Phantom!—had
the ghastliest
That ever lusted for a body, sucking
The foul steam of the grave to thicken
by it,
There in the shuddering moonlight
brought its face
And what it has for eyes as close to
mine 640
As he did—better that than his, than
he
The friend, the neighbor, Lionel, the
beloved,
The loved, the lover, the happy
Lionel,
The low-voiced, tender-spirited
Lionel,
All joy, to whom my agony was a joy.
O, how her choice did leap forth from
his eyes!
O, how her love did clothe itself in
smiles
About his lips! and—not one mo-
ment's grace—
Then when the effect weigh'd seas
upon my head
To come my way! to twit me with the
cause! 650

Was not the land as free thro' all
her ways
To him as me? Was not his wont to
walk
Between the going light and growing
night?
Had I not learnt my loss before he
came?
Could that be more because he came
my way?
Why should he not come my way if he
would?
And yet to-night, to-night—when all
my wealth
Flash'd from me in a moment and I
fell

Beggar'd for ever—why *should* he
   come my way
Robed in those robes of light I must
   not wear,   660
With that great crown of beams about
   his brows—
Come like an angel to a damned soul,
To tell him of the bliss he had with
   God—
Come like a careless and a greedy heir
That scarce can wait the reading of
   the will
Before he takes possession? Was mine
   a mood
To be invaded rudely, and not rather
A sacred, secret, unapproached woe,
Unspeakable? I was shut up with
   Grief;
She took the body of my past delight,
Narded and swathed and balm'd it for
   herself,   671
And laid it in a sepulchre of rock
Never to rise again. I was led mute
Into her temple like a sacrifice;
I was the High Priest in her holiest
   place,
Not to be loudly broken in upon.

  O friend, thoughts deep and heavy
   as these well-nigh
O'erbore the limits of my brain: but
   he
Bent o'er me, and my neck his arm
   upstay'd.
I thought it was an adder's fold, and
   once   680
I strove to disengage myself, but
   fail'd,
Being so feeble. She bent above me,
   too;
Wan was her cheek, for whatsoe'er of
   blight
Lives in the dewy touch of pity had
   made
The red rose there a pale one—and her
   eyes—
I saw the moonlight glitter on their
   tears—
And some few drops of that distress-
   ful rain
Fell on my face, and her long ringlets
   moved,

Drooping and beaten by the breeze,
   and brush'd   689
My fallen forehead in their to and fro,
For in the sudden anguish of her heart
Loosed from their simple thrall they
   had flow'd abroad,
And floated on and parted round her
   neck,
Mantling her form halfway. She, when
   I woke,
Something she ask'd, I know not what,
   and ask'd,
Unanswer'd, since I spake not; for the
   sound
Of that dear voice so musically low,
And now first heard with any sense of
   pain,
As it had taken life away before,
Choked all the syllables that strove to
   rise   700
From my full heart.

            The blissful lover, too,
From his great hoard of happiness
   distill'd
Some drops of solace; like a vain rich
   man,
That, having always prosper'd in the
   world,
Folding his hands, deals comfortable
   words
To hearts wounded for ever; yet, in
   truth,
Fair speech was his and delicate of
   phrase,
Falling in whispers on the sense, address'd
More to the inward than the outward
   ear,
As rain of the midsummer midnight
   soft,   710
Scarce-heard, recalling fragrance and
   the green
Of the dead spring: but mine was
   wholly dead,
No bud, no leaf, no flower, no fruit for
   me.
Yet who had done, or who had suffer'd
   wrong?
And why was I to darken their pure
   love?
If, as I found, they two did love each
   other,

Because my own was darken'd? Why
    was I
To cross between their happy star and
    them?
To stand a shadow by their shining
    doors,
And vex them with my darkness? Did
    I love her?   720
Ye know that I did love her; to this
    present
My full-orb'd love has waned not.
    Did I love her,
And could I look upon her tearful
    eyes?
What had *she* done to weep? Why
    should *she* weep?
O innocent of spirit—let my heart
Break rather—whom the gentlest airs
    of heaven
Should kiss with an unwonted gentle-
    ness.
Her love did murder mine? What
    then? She deem'd
I wore a brother's mind; she call'd me
    brother,
She told me all her love; she shall not
    weep.   730

    The brightness of a burning
      thought, awhile
In battle with the glooms of my dark
    will,
Moonlike emerged, and to itself lit up
There on the depth of an unfathom'd
    woe
Reflex of action. Starting up at once,
As from a dismal dream of my own
    death,
I, for I loved her, lost my love in
    Love;
I, for I loved her, graspt the hand she
    loved,
And laid it in her own, and sent my
    cry
Thro' the blank night to Him who
    loving made   740
The happy and the unhappy love, that
    He
Would hold the hand of blessing over
    them,
Lionel, the happy, and her, and her,
    his bride!

Let them so love that men and boys
    may say,
'Lo! how they love each other!' till
    their love
Shall ripen to a proverb, unto all
Known, when their faces are forgot in
    the land—
One golden dream of love, from which
    may death
Awake them with heaven's music in a
    life
More living to some happier happi-
    ness,   750
Swallowing its precedent in victory.
And as for me, Camilla, as for me,—
The dew of tears is an unwholesome
    dew;
They will but sicken the sick plant the
    more.
Deem that I love thee but as brothers
    do,
So shalt thou love me still as sisters
    do;
Or if thou dream aught farther, dream
    but how
I could have loved thee, had there
    been none else
To love as lovers, loved again by thee.

    Or this, or somewhat like to this, I
      spake,   760
When I beheld her weep so ruefully;
For sure my love should ne'er indue
    the front
And mask of Hate, who lives on oth-
    ers' moans.
Shall Love pledge Hatred in her bitter
    draughts,
And batten on her poisons? Love for-
    bid!
Love passeth not the threshold of cold
    Hate,
And Hate is strange beneath the roof
    of Love.
O Love, if thou be'st Love, dry up
    these tears
Shed for the love of Love; for tho'
    mine image,
The subject of thy power, be cold in
    her,   770
Yet, like cold snow, it melteth in the
    source

Of these sad tears, and feeds their
　　downward flow.
So Love, arraign'd to judgment and to
　　death,
Received unto himself a part of
　　blame,
Being guiltless, as an innocent pris-
　　oner,
Who, when the woeful sentence hath
　　been past,
And all the clearness of his fame hath
　　gone
Beneath the shadow of the curse of
　　man,
First falls asleep in swoon, wherefrom
　　awaked,
And looking round upon his tearful
　　friends,   780
Forthwith and in his agony conceives
A shameful sense as of a cleaving
　　crime—
For whence without some guilt should
　　such grief be?

So died that hour, and fell into the
　　abysm
Of forms outworn, but not to me out-
　　worn,
Who never hail'd another—was there
　　one?
There might be one—one other, worth
　　the life
That made it sensible. So that hour
　　died
Like odor rapt into the winged wind
Borne into alien lands and far away.

There be some hearts so airily built,
　　that they,   791
They—when their love is wreck'd—if
　　Love can wreck—
On that sharp ridge of utmost doom
　　ride highly
Above the perilous seas of Change and
　　Chance,
Nay, more, hold out the lights of
　　cheerfulness;
As the tall ship, that many a dreary
　　year
Knit to some dismal sandbank far at
　　sea,
All thro' the livelong hours of utter
　　dark,

Showers slanting light upon the dol-
　　orous wave.
For me—what light, what gleam on
　　those black ways   800
Where Love could walk with banish'd
　　Hope no more?

It was ill-done to part you, sisters
　　fair;
Love's arms were wreath'd about the
　　neck of Hope,
And Hope kiss'd Love, and Love drew
　　in her breath
In that close kiss, and drank her whis-
　　per'd tales.
They said that Love would die when
　　Hope was gone,
And Love mourn'd long, and sorrow'd
　　after Hope;
At last she sought out Memory, and
　　they trod
The same old paths where Love had
　　walk'd with Hope,
And Memory fed the soul of Love
　　with tears.   810

II

From that time forth I would not see
　　her more;
But many weary moons I lived alone—
Alone, and in the heart of the great
　　forest.
Sometimes upon the hills beside the
　　sea
All day I watch'd the floating isles of
　　shade,
And sometimes on the shore, upon the
　　sands
Insensibly I drew her name, until
The meaning of the letters shot into
My brain; anon the wanton billow
　　wash'd
Them over, till they faded like my
　　love.   10
The hollow caverns heard me—the
　　black brooks
Of the mid-forest heard me—the soft
　　winds,
Laden with thistle-down and seeds of
　　flowers,
Paused in their course to hear me, for
　　my voice

Was all of thee; the merry linnet knew
   me,
The squirrel knew me, and the
   dragon-fly
Shot by me like a flash of purple fire.
The rough brier tore my bleeding
   palms; the hemlock,
Brow-high, did strike my forehead as
   I past;
Yet trod I not the wild-flower in my
   path,   20
Nor bruised the wild-bird's egg.

                Was this the end?
Why grew we then together in one
   plot?
Why fed we from one fountain? drew
   one sun?
Why were our mothers branches of
   one stem?
Why were we one in all things, save
   in that
Where to have been one had been the
   cope and crown
Of all I hoped and fear'd?—if that
   same nearness
Were father to this distance, and that
   one
Vauntcourier to this *double!* if Affec-
   tion
Living slew Love, and Sympathy
   hew'd out   30
The bosom-sepulchre of Sympathy?

Chiefly I sought the cavern and the
   hill
Where last we roam'd together, for
   the sound
Of the loud stream was pleasant, and
   the wind
Came wooingly with woodbine smells.
   Sometimes
All day I sat within the cavern-mouth,
Fixing my eyes on those three cy-
   press-cones
That spired above the wood; and with
   mad hand
Tearing the bright leaves of the ivy-
   screen,
I cast them in the noisy brook be-
   neath,   40
And watch'd them till they vanish'd
   from my sight

Beneath the bower of wreathed eglantines.
And all the fragments of the living
   rock,—
Huge blocks, which some old trembling of the world
Had loosen'd from the mountain, till
   they fell
Half-digging their own graves,—these
   in my agony
Did I make bare of all the golden
   moss,
Wherewith the dashing runnel in the
   spring
Had liveried them all over. In my
   brain
The spirit seem'd to flag from thought
   to thought,   50
As moonlight wandering thro' a mist;
   my blood
Crept like marsh drains thro' all my
   languid limbs;
The motions of my heart seem'd far
   within me,
Unfrequent, low, as tho' it told its
   pulses;
And yet it shook me, that my frame
   would shudder,
As if 't were drawn asunder by the
   rack.
But over the deep graves of Hope and
   Fear,
And all the broken palaces of the past,
Brooded one master-passion ever-
   more,
Like to a low-hung and a fiery sky   60
Above some fair metropolis, earth-
   shock'd,—
Hung round with ragged rims and
   burning folds,—
Embathing all with wild and woful
   hues,
Great hills of ruins, and collapsed
   masses
Of thunder-shaken columns indistinct,
And fused together in the tyrannous
   light—
Ruins, the ruin of all my life and me!

   Sometimes I thought Camilla was
    no more;
Some one had told me she was dead,
   and ask'd

If I would see her burial. Then I
    seem'd   70
To rise, and through the forest-
    shadow borne
With more than mortal swiftness, I
    ran down
The steepy sea-bank, till I came upon
The rear of a procession, curving
    round
The silver-sheeted bay, in front of
    which
Six stately virgins, all in white, upbare
A broad earth-sweeping pall of whitest
    lawn,
Wreathed round the bier with gar-
    lands. In the distance,
From out the yellow woods upon the
    hill
Look'd forth the summit and the pin-
    nacles   80
Of a gray steeple—thence at intervals
A low bell tolling. All the pageantry,
Save those six virgins which upheld
    the bier,
Were stoled from head to foot in
    flowing black;
One walk'd abreast with me, and
    veil'd his brow,
And he was loud in weeping and in
    praise
Of her we follow'd. A strong sympathy
Shook all my soul; I flung myself upon
    him
In tears and cries. I told him all my
    love,
How I had loved her from the first;
    whereat   90
He shrank and howl'd, and from his
    brow drew back
His hand to push me from him, and
    the face,
The very face and form of Lionel
Flash'd thro' my eyes into my inner-
    most brain,
And at his feet I seem'd to faint and
    fall,
To fall and die away. I could not rise,
Albeit I strove to follow. They past
    on,
The lordly phantasms! in their float-
    ing folds
They past and were no more; but I
    had fallen

Prone by the dashing runnel on the
    grass.   100

    Alway the inaudible, invisible
    thought,
Artificer and subject, lord and slave,
Shaped by the audible and visible,
Moulded the audible and visible.
All crisped sounds of wave and leaf
    and wind
Flatter'd the fancy of my fading
    brain;
The cloud-pavilion'd element, the
    wood,
The mountain, the three cypresses,
    the cave,
Storm, sunset, glows and glories of
    the moon
Below black firs, when silent-creeping
    winds   110
Laid the long night in silver streaks
    and bars,
Were wrought into the tissue of my
    dream.
The moanings in the forest, the loud
    brook,
Cries of the partridge like a rusty key
Turn'd in a lock, owl-whoop and dor-
    hawk-whirr
Awoke me not, but were a part of
    sleep,
And voices in the distance calling to
    me
And in my vision bidding me dream
    on,
Like sounds without the twilight realm
    of dreams,
Which wander round the bases of the
    hills,   120
And murmur at the low-dropt eaves
    of sleep,
Half-entering the portals. Oftentimes
The vision had fair prelude, in the end
Opening on darkness, stately vesti-
    bules
To caves and shows of death—
    whether the mind,
With some revenge—even to itself un-
    known—
Made strange division of its suffering
With her, whom to have suffering
    view'd had been

Extremest pain; or that the clear-
eyed Spirit,
Being blunted in the present, grew at
length   130
Prophetical and prescient of whate'er
The future had in store; or that which
most
Enchains belief, the sorrow of my
spirit
Was of so wide a compass it took in
All I had loved, and my dull agony,
Ideally to her transferr'd, became
Anguish intolerable.

             The day waned;
Alone I sat with her. About my brow
Her warm breath floated in the utter-
ance
Of silver-chorded tones; her lips were
sunder'd   140
With smiles of tranquil bliss, which
broke in light
Like morning from her eyes—her elo-
quent eyes—
As I have seen them many a hundred
times—
Fill'd all with pure clear fire, thro'
mine down rain'd
Their spirit-searching splendors. As a
vision
Unto a haggard prisoner, iron-stay'd
In damp and dismal dungeons under-
ground,
Confined on points of faith, when
strength is shock'd
With torment, and expectancy of
worse
Upon the morrow, thro' the ragged
walls,   150
All unawares before his half-shut
eyes,
Comes in upon him in the dead of
night,
And with the excess of sweetness and
of awe,
Makes the heart tremble, and the sight
run over
Upon his steely gyves; so those fair
eyes
Shone on my darkness, forms which
ever stood
Within the magic cirque of memory,
Invisible but deathless, waiting still

The edict of the will to reassume   159
The semblance of those rare realities
Of which they were the mirrors. Now
the light
Which was their life burst through the
cloud of thought
Keen, irrepressible.

             It was a room
Within the summer-house of which I
spake,
Hung round with paintings of the sea,
and one
A vessel in mid-ocean, her heaved
prow
Clambering, the mast bent and the
ravin wind
In her sail roaring. From the outer
day,
Betwixt the close-set ivies came a
broad
And solid beam of isolated light,   170
Crowded with driving atomies, and
fell
Slanting upon that picture, from prime
youth
Well-known, well-loved. She drew it
long ago
Forthgazing on the waste and open
sea,
One morning when the upblown billow
ran
Shoreward beneath red clouds, and I
had pour'd
Into the shadowing pencil's naked
forms
Color and life. It was a bond and seal
Of friendship, spoken of with tearful
smiles;   179
A monument of childhood and of love;
The poesy of childhood, my lost love
Symboll'd in storm. We gazed on it
together
In mute and glad remembrance, and
each heart
Grew closer to the other, and the eye
Was riveted and charm-bound, gazing
like
The Indian on a still-eyed snake, low-
couch'd—
A beauty which is death; when all at
once
That painted vessel, as with inner life,

Began to heave upon that painted sea.
An earthquake, my loud heart-beats, made the ground   190
Reel under us, and all at once, soul, life
And breath and motion, past and flow'd away
To those unreal billows. Round and round
A whirlwind caught and bore us; mighty gyres
Rapid and vast, of hissing spray wind-driven
Far thro' the dizzy dark. Aloud she shriek'd;
My heart was cloven with pain; I wound my arms
About her; we whirl'd giddily; the wind
Sung, but I clasp'd her without fear. Her weight
Shrank in my grasp, and over my dim eyes,   200
And parted lips which drank her breath, down-hung
The jaws of Death. I, groaning, from me flung
Her empty phantom; all the sway and whirl
Of the storm dropt to windless calm, and I
Down welter'd thro' the dark ever and ever.

III

I came one day and sat among the stones
Strewn in the entry of the moaning cave;
A morning air, sweet after rain, ran over
The rippling levels of the lake, and blew
Coolness and moisture and all smells of bud
And foliage from the dark and dripping woods
Upon my fever'd brows that shook and throbb'd
From temple unto temple. To what height
The day had grown I know not. Then came on me   9

The hollow tolling of the bell, and all
The vision of the bier. As heretofore
I walk'd behind with one who veil'd his brow.
Methought by slow degrees the sullen bell
Toll'd quicker, and the breakers on the shore
Sloped into louder surf. Those that went with me,
And those that held the bier before my face,
Moved with one spirit round about the bay,
Trod swifter steps; and while I walk'd with these
In marvel at that gradual change, I thought
Four bells instead of one began to ring,   20
Four merry bells, four merry marriage-bells,
In clanging cadence jangling peal on peal—
A long loud clash of rapid marriage-bells.
Then those who led the van, and those in rear,
Rush'd into dance, and like wild Bacchanals
Fled onward to the steeple in the woods.
I, too, was borne along and felt the blast
Beat on my heated eyelids. All at once
The front rank made a sudden halt; the bells
Lapsed into frightful stillness; the surge fell   30
From thunder into whispers; those six maids
With shrieks and ringing laughter on the sand
Threw down the bier; the woods upon the hill
Waved with a sudden gust that sweeping down
Took the edges of the pall, and blew it far
Until it hung, a little silver cloud
Over the sounding seas. I turn'd; my heart

Shrank in me, like a snowflake in the
    hand,
Waiting to see the settled countenance
Of her I loved, adorn'd with fading
    flowers.   40
But she from out her death-like chrys-
    alis,
She from her bier, as into fresher life,
My sister, and my cousin, and my
    love,
Leapt lightly clad in bridal white—her
    hair
Studded with one rich Provence rose
    —a light
Of smiling welcome round her lips—
    her eyes
And cheeks as bright as when she
    climb'd the hill.
One hand she reach'd to those that
    came behind,
And while I mused nor yet endured to
    take
So rich a prize, the man who stood
    with me   50
Stept gaily forward, throwing down
    his robes,
And claspt her hand in his. Again the
    bells
Jangled and clang'd; again the stormy
    surf
Crash'd in the shingle; and the whirl-
    ing rout
Led by those two rush'd into dance,
    and fled
Wind-footed to the steeple in the
    woods,
Till they were swallow'd in the leafy
    bowers,
And I stood sole beside the vacant
    bier.

There, there, my latest vision—then
    the event!

IV

THE GOLDEN SUPPER [1]

(*Another speaks*)

He flies the event; he leaves the event
    to me.

[1] This poem is founded upon a story in
Boccaccio. See Argument, page 730.

Poor Julian—how he rush'd away; the
    bells,
Those marriage-bells, echoing in ear
    and heart—
But cast a parting glance at me, you
    saw,
As who should say 'Continue.' Well,
    he had
One golden hour—of triumph shall I
    say?
Solace at least—before he left his
    home.

Would you had seen him in that
    hour of his!
He moved thro' all of it majestically—
Restrain'd himself quite to the close
    —but now—   10
Whether they *were* his lady's mar-
    riage-bells,
Or prophets of them in his fantasy,
I never ask'd; but Lionel and the girl
Were wedded, and our Julian came
    again
Back to his mother's house among the
    pines.
But these, their gloom, the mountains
    and the Bay,
The whole land weigh'd him down as
    Ætna does
The Giant of Mythology; he would
    go,
Would leave the land for ever, and
    had gone   19
Surely, but for a whisper, 'Go not yet,'
Some warning—sent divinely—as it
    seem'd
By that which follow'd—but of this I
    deem
As of the visions that he told—the
    event
Glanced back upon them in his after
    life,
And partly made them—tho' he knew
    it not.

And thus he stay'd and would not
    look at her—
No, not for months; but, when the
    eleventh moon
After their marriage lit the lover's
    Bay,

Heard yet once more the tolling bell,
   and said,
'Would you could toll me out of life!'
   but found—   30
All softly as his mother broke it to
   him—
A crueller reason than a crazy ear
For that low knell tolling his lady
   dead—
Dead—and had lain three days without a pulse;
All that look'd on her had pronounced
   her dead.
And so they bore her—for in Julian's
   land
They never nail a dumb head up in
   elm—
Bore her free-faced to the free airs of
   heaven,
And laid her in the vault of her own
   kin.

What did he then? not die—he is
   here and hale—   40
Not plunge headforemost from the
   mountain there,
And leave the name of Lover's Leap,
   not he.
He knew the meaning of the whisper
   now,
Thought that he knew it. 'This, I
   stay'd for this;
O Love, I have not seen you for so
   long!
Now, now, will I go down into the
   grave,
I will be all alone with all I love,
And kiss her on the lips. She is his no
   more;
The dead returns to me, and I go down
To kiss the dead.'

          The fancy stirr'd him so
He rose and went, and, entering the
   dim vault   51
And making there a sudden light, beheld
All round about him that which all
   will be.
The light was but a flash, and went
   again.
Then at the far end of the vault he
   saw

His lady with the moonlight on her
   face;
Her breast as in a shadow-prison, bars
Of black and bands of silver, which
   the moon
Struck from an open grating overhead
High in the wall, and all the rest of
   her   60
Drown'd in the gloom and horror of
   the vault.

  'It was my wish,' he said, 'to pass,
   to sleep,
To rest, to be with her—till the great
   day
Peal'd on us with that music which
   rights all,
And raised us hand in hand.' And
   kneeling there
Down in the dreadful dust that once
   was man,
'Dust,' as he said, 'that once was lov-
   ing hearts,
Hearts that had beat with such a love
   as mine—
Not such as mine, no, nor for such as
   her,—   69
He softly put his arm about her neck
And kiss'd her more than once, till
   helpless death
And silence made him bold—nay, but
   I wrong him,
He reverenced his dear lady even in
   death;
But, placing his true hand upon her
   heart,
'O you warm heart,' he moan'd, 'not
   even death
Can chill you all at once'—then, start-
   ing, thought
His dreams had come again. 'Do I
   wake or sleep?
Or am I made immortal, or my love
Mortal once more?' It beat—the heart
   —it beat;
Faint—but it beat; at which his own
   began   80
To pulse with such a vehemence that
   it drown'd
The feebler motion underneath his
   hand.

But when at last his doubts were satis-
fied
He raised her softly from the sepul-
chre,
And, wrapping her all over with the
cloak
He came in, and now striding fast, and
now
Sitting awhile to rest, but evermore
Holding his golden burthen in his
arm,
So bore her thro' the solitary land
Back to the mother's house where she
was born.   90

There the good mother's kindly min-
istering,
With half a night's appliances, re-
call'd
Her fluttering life. She rais'd an eye
that ask'd
'Where?' till the things familiar to her
youth
Had made a silent answer; then she
spoke
'Here! and how came I here?' and
learning it—
They told her somewhat rashly, as I
think—
At once began to wander and to wail,
'Ay, but you know that you must give
me back.
Send! bid him come;' but Lionel was
away—   100
Stung by his loss had vanish'd, none
knew where.
'He casts me out,' she wept, 'and goes'
—a wail
That, seeming something, yet was
nothing, born
Not from believing mind but shat-
ter'd nerve,
Yet haunting Julian, as her own re-
proof
At some precipitance in her burial.
Then, when her own true spirit had
return'd,
'O, yes, and you,' she said, 'and none
but you?
For you have given me life and love
again,
And none but you yourself shall tell
him of it,   110

And you shall give me back when he
returns.'
'Stay then a little,' answer'd Julian,
'here,
And keep yourself, none knowing, to
yourself;
And I will do your will. I may not
stay,
No, not an hour; but send me notice
of him
When he returns, and then will I return,
And I will make a solemn offering of
you
To him you love.' And faintly she replied,
'And I will do *your* will, and none shall
know.'

Not know? with such a secret to be
known.   120
But all their house was old and loved
them both,
And all the house had known the loves
of both,
Had died almost to serve them any
way,
And all the land was waste and soli-
tary.
And then he rode away; but after this,
An hour or two, Camilla's travail came
Upon her, and that day a boy was
born,
Heir of his face and land, to Lionel.

And thus our lonely lover rode
away,
And pausing at a hostel in a marsh,
There fever seized upon him. Myself
was then   131
Travelling that land, and meant to
rest an hour;
And sitting down to such a base re-
past,
It makes me angry yet to speak of it—
I heard a groaning overhead, and
climb'd
The moulder'd stairs—for everything
was vile—
And in a loft, with none to wait on
him,
Found, as it seem'd, a skeleton alone,

Raving of dead men's dust and beating hearts.

A dismal hostel in a dismal land, 140
A flat malarial world of reed and
rush!
But there from fever and my care of
him
Sprang up a friendship that may help
us yet.
For while we roam'd along the dreary
coast,
And waited for her message, piece by
piece
I learnt the drearier story of his life;
And, tho' he loved and honor'd Lionel,
Found that the sudden wail his lady
made
Dwelt in his fancy. Did he know her
worth,
Her beauty even? should he not be
taught,   150
Even by the price that others set upon
it,
The value of that jewel he had to
guard?

Suddenly came her notice and we
past,
I with our lover to his native Bay.

This love is of the brain, the mind,
the soul;
That makes the sequel pure, tho' some
of us
Beginning at the sequel know no more.
Not such am I; and yet I say the bird
That will not hear my call, however
sweet,
But if my neighbor whistle answers
him—   160
What matter? there are others in the
wood.
Yet when I saw her—and I thought
him crazed,
Tho' not with such a craziness as needs
A cell and keeper—those dark eyes of
hers—
O, such dark eyes! and not her eyes
alone,
But all from these to where she
touch'd on earth,
For such a craziness as Julian's look'd
No less than one divine apology.

So sweetly and so modestly she
came
To greet us, her young hero in her
arms!   170
'Kiss him,' she said. 'You gave me life
again.
He, but for you, had never seen it
once.
His other father you! Kiss him, and
then
Forgive him, if his name be Julian
too.'

Talk of lost hopes and broken
heart! his own
Sent such a flame into his face, I knew
Some sudden vivid pleasure hit him
there.

But he was all the more resolved to
go,
And sent at once to Lionel, praying
him,
By that great love they both had borne
the dead,   180
To come and revel for one hour with
him
Before he left the land for evermore;
And then to friends—they were not
many—who lived
Scatteringly about that lonely land of
his,
And bade them to a banquet of farewells.

And Julian made a solemn feast; I
never
Sat at a costlier, for all round his hall
From column on to column, as in a
wood,
Not such as here—an equatorial one,
Great garlands swung and blossom'd:
and beneath,   190
Heirlooms, and ancient miracles of
art,
Chalice and salver, wines that, heaven
knows when,
Had suck'd the fire of some forgotten
sun,
And kept it thro' a hundred years of
gloom,
Yet glowing in a heart of ruby—cups

Where nymph and god ran ever round
      in gold—
Others of glass as costly—some with
      gems
Movable and resettable at will,
And trebling all the rest in value—Ah
      heavens!
Why need I tell you all?—suffice to
      say   200
That whatsoever such a house as his,
And his was old, has in it rare or fair
Was brought before the guest. And
      they, the guests,
Wonder'd at some strange light in
      Julian's eyes—
I told you that he had his golden
      hour—
And such a feast, ill-suited as it
      seem'd
To such a time, to Lionel's loss and
      his
And that resolved self-exile from a
      land
He never would revisit, such a feast
So rich, so strange, and stranger even
      than rich,   210
But rich as for the nuptials of a king.

And stranger yet, at one end of the
      hall
Two great funereal curtains, looping
      down,
Parted a little ere they met the floor,
About a picture of his lady, taken
Some years before, and falling hid the
      frame.
And just above the parting was a
      lamp;
So the sweet figure folded round with
      night
Seem'd stepping out of darkness with
      a smile.

Well, then—our solemn feast—we
      ate and drank,   220
And might—the wines being of such
      nobleness—
Have jested also, but for Julian's eyes,
And something weird and wild about
      it all.
What was it? for our lover seldom
      spoke,

Scarce touch'd the meats, but ever and
      anon
A priceless goblet with a priceless
      wine
Arising show'd he drank beyond his
      use;
And when the feast was near an end,
      he said:

'There is a custom in the Orient,
      friends—
I read of it in Persia—when a man   230
Will honor those who feast with him,
      he brings
And shows them whatsoever he ac-
      counts
Of all his treasures the most beautiful,
Gold, jewels, arms, whatever it may
      be.
This custom—'

                  Pausing here a moment, all
The guests broke in upon him with
      meeting hands
And cries about the banquet—'Beau-
      tiful!
Who could desire more beauty at a
      feast?'

      The lover answer'd: 'There is more
      than one
Here sitting who desires. Laud me
      not   240
Before my time, but hear me to the
      close.
This custom steps yet further when
      the guest
Is loved and honor'd to the uttermost.
For after he hath shown him gems or
      gold,
He brings and sets before him in rich
      guise
That which is thrice as beautiful as
      these,
The beauty that is dearest to his
      heart—
"O my heart's lord, would I could
      show you," he says,
"Even my heart too." And I propose
      to-night
To show you what is dearest to my
      heart,   250
And my heart too.

'But solve me first a doubt.
I knew a man, nor many years ago;
He had a faithful servant, one who
    loved
His master more than all on earth be-
    side.
He falling sick, and seeming close on
    death,
His master would not wait until he
    died,
But bade his menials bear him from
    the door,
And leave him in the public way to
    die.
I knew another, not so long ago,
Who found the dying servant, took
    him home,   260
And fed, and cherish'd him, and saved
    his life.
I ask you now, should this first master
    claim
His service, whom does it belong to? him
Who thrust him out, or him who saved
    his life?'

This question, so flung down before
    the guests,
And balanced either way by each, at
    length
When some were doubtful how the
    law would hold,
Was handed over by consent of all
To one who had not spoken, Lionel.

Fair speech was his, and delicate of
    phrase.   270
And he, beginning languidly—his loss
Weigh'd on him yet—but warming as
    he went,
Glanced at the point of law, to pass it
    by,
Affirming that as long as either lived,
By all the laws of love and grateful-
    ness,
The service of the one so saved was
    due
All to the saver—adding, with a smile,
The first for many weeks—a semi-
    smile
As at a strong conclusion—'body and
    soul

And life and limbs, all his to work
    his will.'   280

Then Julian made a secret sign to
    me
To bring Camilla down before them
    all.
And crossing her own picture as she
    came,
And looking as much lovelier than her-
    self
Is lovelier than all others—on her
    head
A diamond circlet, and from under
    this
A veil, that seem'd no more than gilded
    air,
Flying by each fine ear, an Eastern
    gauze
With seeds of gold—so, with that
    grace of hers,
Slow-moving as a wave against the
    wind,   290
That flings a mist behind it in the
    sun—
And bearing high in arms the mighty
    babe,
The younger Julian, who himself was
    crown'd
With roses, none so rosy as himself—
And over all her babe and her the
    jewels
Of many generations of his house
Sparkled and flash'd, for he had
    deck'd them out
As for a solemn sacrifice of love—
So she came in—I am long in telling it,
I never yet beheld a thing so strange,
Sad, sweet, and strange together—
    floated in—   301
While all the guests in mute amaze-
    ment rose—
And slowly pacing to the middle hall,
Before the board, there paused and
    stood, her breast
Hard-heaving, and her eyes upon her
    feet,
Not daring yet to glance at Lionel.
But him she carried, him nor lights
    nor feast
Dazed or amazed, nor eyes of men;
    who cared
Only to use his own, and staring wide

And hungering for the gilt and jewell'd
world   310
About him, look'd, as he is like to
prove,
When Julian goes, the lord of all he
saw.

'My guests,' said Julian, 'you are
honor'd now
Even to the uttermost; in her behold
Of all my treasures the most beautiful,
Of all things upon earth the dearest to
me;'
Then waving us a sign to seat our-
selves,
Led his dear lady to a chair of state.
And I, by Lionel sitting, saw his face
Fire, and dead ashes and all fire again
Thrice in a second, felt him tremble
too,   321
And heard him muttering, 'So like, so
like;
She never had a sister. I knew none.
Some cousin of his and hers—O God,
so like!'
And then he suddenly ask'd her if she
were.
She shook, and cast her eyes down,
and was dumb.
And then some other question'd if she
came
From foreign lands, and still she did
not speak.
Another, if the boy were hers; but she
To all their queries answer'd not a
word,   330
Which made the amazement more, till
one of them
Said, shuddering, 'Her spectre!' But
his friend
Replied, in half a whisper, 'Not at
least
The spectre that will speak if spoken
to.
Terrible pity, if one so beautiful
Prove, as I almost dread to find her,
dumb!'

But Julian, sitting by her, answer'd
all:
'She is but dumb, because in her you
see

That faithful servant whom we spoke
about,   339
Obedient to her second master now;
Which will not last. I have here to-
night a guest
So bound to me by common love and
loss—
What! shall I bind him more? in his
behalf,
Shall I exceed the Persian, giving him
That which of all things is the dearest
to me,
Not only showing? and he himself pro-
nounced
That my rich gift is wholly mine to
give.

'Now all be dumb, and promise all
of you
Not to break in on what I say by word
Or whisper, while I show you all my
heart.'   350
And then began the story of his love
As here to-day, but not so wordily—
The passionate moment would not suf-
fer that—
Past thro' his visions to the burial;
thence
Down to this last strange hour in his
own hall;
And then rose up, and with him all his
guests
Once more as by enchantment; all but
he,
Lionel, who fain had risen, but fell
again,
And sat as if in chains—to whom he
said:

'Take my free gift, my cousin, for
your wife;   360
And were it only for the giver's sake,
And tho' she seem so like the one you
lost,
Yet cast her not away so suddenly,
Lest there be none left here to bring
her back.
I leave this land for ever.' Here he
ceased.

Then taking his dear lady by one
hand,

And bearing on one arm the noble
  babe,
He slowly brought them both to
  Lionel.
And there the widower husband and
  dead wife
Rush'd each at each with a cry that
  rather seem'd   370
For some new death than for a life
  renew'd;
Whereat the very babe began to wail.
At once they turn'd, and caught and
  brought him in
To their charm'd circle, and, half kill-
  ing him
With kisses, round him closed and
  claspt again.

But Lionel, when at last he freed him-
  self
From wife and child, and lifted up a
  face
All over glowing with the sun of life,
And love, and boundless thanks—the
  sight of this
So frighted our good friend that, turn-
  ing to me   380
And saying, 'It is over; let us go'—
There were our horses ready at the
  doors—
We bade them no farewell, but mount-
  ing these
He past for ever from his native land;
And I with him, my Julian, back to
  mine.

TO ALFRED TENNYSON

MY GRANDSON

GOLDEN-HAIR'D Ally whose name is
    one with mine,
Crazy with laughter and babble and
    earth's new wine,
Now that the flower of a year and a
    half is thine,
O little blossom, O mine, and mine of
    mine,
Glorious poet who never hast written
    a line,
Laugh, for the name at the head of
    my verse is thine.
Mayst thou never be wrong'd by the
    name that is mine!

THE FIRST QUARREL

(IN THE ISLE OF WIGHT)

I

'WAIT a little,' you say, 'you are sure
    it'll all come right,'
But the boy was born i' trouble, an'
    looks so wan an' so white;
Wait! an' once I ha' waited—I hadn't
    to wait for long.
Now I wait, wait, wait for Harry.—
    No, no, you are doing me
    wrong!
Harry and I were married; the boy
    can hold up his head,
The boy was born in wedlock, but
    after my man was dead;
I ha' work'd for him fifteen years, an'
    I work an' I wait to the end.
I am all alone in the world, an' you
    are my only friend.

II

Doctor, if *you* can wait, I'll tell you
    the tale o' my life.
When Harry an' I were children, he
    call'd me his own little wife; [10]
I was happy when I was with him, an'
    sorry when he was away,
An' when we play'd together, I loved
    him better than play;
He workt me the daisy chain—he
    made me the cowslip ball,
He fought the boys that were rude,
    an' I loved him better than all.
Passionate girl tho' I was, an' often
    at home in disgrace,
I never could quarrel with Harry—I
    had but to look in his face.

III

There was a farmer in Dorset of
    Harry's kin, that had need
Of a good stout lad at his farm; he
    sent, an' the father agreed;
So Harry was bound to the Dorset-
    shire farm for years an' for
    years;
I walk'd with him down to the quay,
    poor lad, an' we parted in
    tears.   20
The boat was beginning to move, we
    heard them a-ringing the bell,
'I'll never love any but you, God bless
    you, my own little Nell.'

IV

I was a child, an' he was a child, an'
    he came to harm;
There was a girl, a hussy, that workt
    with him up at the farm,

One had deceived her an' left her
    alone with her sin an' her
    shame,
And so she was wicked with Harry;
    the girl was the most to blame.

V

And years went over till I that was
    little had grown so tall
The men would say of the maids, 'Our
    Nelly's the flower of 'em all.'
I did n't take heed o' *them*, but I
    taught myself all I could
To make a good wife for Harry, when
    Harry came home for good. 30

VI

Often I seem'd unhappy, and often as
    happy too,
For I heard it abroad in the fields,
    'I'll never love any but you;'
'I'll never love any but you,' the morn-
    ing song of the lark;
'I'll never love any but you,' the night-
    ingale's hymn in the dark.

VII

And Harry came home at last, but he
    look'd at me sidelong and shy,
Vext me a bit, till he told me that so
    many years had gone by,
I had grown so handsome and tall—
    that I might ha' forgot him
    somehow—
For he thought—there were other lads
    —he was fear'd to look at me
    now.

VIII

Hard was the frost in the field, we
    were married o' Christmas day,
Married among the red berries, an' all
    as merry as May—   40
Those were the pleasant times, my
    house an' my man were my
    pride,
We seem'd like ships i' the Channel
    a-sailing with wind an' tide.

IX

But work was scant in the Isle, tho' he
    tried the villages round,
So Harry went over the Solent to see
    if work could be found;
An' he wrote: 'I ha' six weeks' work,
    little wife, so far as I know;
I'll come for an hour to-morrow, an'
    kiss you before I go.'

X

So I set to righting the house, for
    wasn't he coming that day?
An' I hit on an old deal-box that was
    push'd in a corner away,
It was full of old odds an' ends, an' a
    letter along wi' the rest,
I had better ha' put my naked hand in
    a hornets' nest.   50

XI

'Sweetheart,'—this was the letter—
    this was the letter I read—
'You promised to find me work near
    you, an' I wish I was dead—
Didn't you kiss me an' promise? you
    haven't done it, my lad,
An' I almost died o' your going away,
    an' I wish that I had.'

XII

I too wish that I had—in the pleasant
    times that had past,
Before I quarrell'd with Harry—*my*
    quarrel—the first an' the last.

XIII

For Harry came in, an' I flung him the
    letter that drove me wild,
An' he told it me all at once, as simple
    as any child,
'What can it matter, my lass, what I
    did wi' my single life?
I ha' been as true to you as ever a man
    to his wife;   60
An' *she* wasn't one o' the worst.'
    'Then,' I said, 'I'm none o' the
    best.'

An' he smiled at me, 'Ain't you, my
    love? Come, come, little wife,
    let it rest!
The man isn't like the woman, no need
    to make such a stir.'
But he anger'd me all the more, an' I
    said, 'You were keeping with
    her,
When I was a-loving you all along an'
    the same as before.'
An' he didn't speak for a while, an' he
    anger'd me more and more.
Then he patted my hand in his gentle
    way, 'Let bygones be!'
'Bygones! you kept yours hush'd,' I
    said, 'when you married me!
By-gones ma' be come-agains; an' *she*
    —in her shame an' her sin—
You'll have her to nurse my child, if I
    die o' my lying in!   70
You'll make her its second mother! I
    hate her—an' I hate you!'
Ah, Harry, my man, you had better
    ha' beaten me black an' blue
Then ha' spoken as kind as you did,
    when I were so crazy wi' spite,
'Wait a little, my lass, I am sure it 'ill
    all come right.'

XIV

An' he took three turns in the rain, an'
    I watch'd him, an' when he
    came in
I felt that my heart was hard; he was
    all wet thro' to the skin,
An' I never said, 'off wi' the wet,' I
    never said, 'on wi' the dry,'
So I knew my heart was hard, when he
    came to bid me good-bye.
'You said that you hated me, Ellen,
    but that isn't true, you know;
I am going to leave you a bit—you'll
    kiss me before I go?'   80

XV

'Going! you're going to her—kiss her
    —if you will,' I said—
I was near my time wi' the boy, I must
    ha' been light i' my head—
'I had sooner be cursed than kiss'd!'
    —I didn't know well what I
    meant,

But I turn'd my face from *him*, an' he
    turn'd *his* face an' he went.

XVI

And then he sent me a letter, 'I've
    gotten my work to do;
You wouldn't kiss me, my lass, an' I
    never loved any but you;
I am sorry for all the quarrel an' sorry
    for what she wrote,
I ha' six weeks' work in Jersey an' go
    to-night by the boat.'

XVII

An' the wind began to rise, an' I
    thought of him out at sea,
An' I felt I had been to blame; he was
    always kind to me.   90
'Wait a little, my lass, I am sure it 'ill
    all come right'—
An' the boat went down that night—
    the boat went down that night.

RIZPAH

17—

I

WAILING, wailing, wailing, the wind
    over land and sea—
And Willy's voice in the wind, 'O
    mother, come out to me!'
Why should he call me to-night, when
    he knows that I cannot go?
For the downs are as bright as day,
    and the full moon stares at the
    snow.

II

We should be seen, my dear; they
    would spy us out of the town.
The loud black nights for us, and the
    storm rushing over the down,
When I cannot see my own hand, but
    am led by the creak of the
    chain,
And grovel and grope for my son till
    I find myself drenched with the
    rain.

III

Anything fallen again? nay—what was
    there left to fall?
I have taken them home, I have num-
    ber'd the bones, I have hidden
    them all.   10
What am I saying? and what are *you?*
    do you come as a spy?
Falls? what falls? who knows? As the
    tree falls so must it lie.

IV

Who let her in? how long has she
    been? you—what have you
    heard?
Why did you sit so quiet? you never
    have spoken a word.
O—to pray with me—yes—a lady—
    none of their spies—
But the night has crept into my heart,
    and begun to darken my eyes.

V

Ah—you, that have lived so soft, what
    should *you* know of the night,
The blast and the burning shame and
    the bitter frost and the fright?
I have done it, while you were asleep
    —you were only made for the
    day.
I have gather'd my baby together—
    and now you may go your
    way.   20

VI

Nay—for it's kind of you, madam, to
    sit by an old dying wife.
But say nothing hard of my boy, I
    have only an hour of life.
I kiss'd my boy in the prison, before
    he went out to die.
'They dared me to do it,' he said, and
    he never has told me a lie.
I whipt him for robbing an orchard
    once when he was but a child—
'The farmer dared me to do it,' he
    said; he was always so wild—
And idle—and couldn't be idle—my
    Willy—he never could rest.

The King should have made him a
    soldier, he would have been one
    of his best.

VII

But he lived with a lot of wild mates,
    and they never would let him
    be good;
They swore that he dare not rob the
    mail, and he swore that he
    would;   30
And he took no life, but he took one
    purse, and when all was done
He flung it among his fellows—'I'll
    none of it,' said my son.

VIII

I came into court to the judge and the
    lawyers. I told them my tale,
God's own truth—but they kill'd him,
    they kill'd him for robbing the
    mail.
They hang'd him in chains for a show
    —we had always borne a good
    name—
To be hang'd for a thief—and then
    put away—isn't that enough
    shame?
Dust to dust—low down—let us hide!
    but they set him so high
That all the ships of the world could
    stare at him, passing by.
God 'ill pardon the hell-black raven
    and horrible fowls of the air,
But not the black heart of the lawyer
    who kill'd him and hang'd him
    there.   40

IX

And the jailer forced me away. I had
    bid him my last good-bye;
They had fasten'd the door of his cell
    'O mother!' I heard him cry.
I couldn't get back tho' I tried, he had
    something further to say,
And now I never shall know it. The
    jailer forced me away.

X

Then since I couldn't but hear that cry
    of my boy that was dead,

They seized me and shut me up: they
    fasten'd me down on my bed.
'Mother, O mother!'—he call'd in the
    dark to me year after year—
They beat me for that, they beat me—
    you know that I couldn't but
    hear;
And then at the last they found I had
    grown so stupid and still
They let me abroad again—but the
    creatures had worked their
    will.   50

XI

Flesh of my flesh was gone, but bone
    of my bone was left—
I stole them all from the lawyers—and
    you, will you call it a theft?—
My baby, the bones that had suck'd
    me, the bones that had laughed
    and had cried—
Theirs? O, no! they are mine—not
    theirs—they had moved in my
    side.

XII

Do you think I was scared by the
    bones? I kiss'd 'em, I buried
    'em all—
I can't dig deep, I am old—in the
    night by the churchyard wall.
My Willy 'ill rise up whole when the
    trumpet of judgment 'ill
    sound,
But I charge you never to say that I
    laid him in holy ground.

XIII

They would scratch him up—they
    would hang him again on the
    cursed tree.
Sin? O, yes, we are sinners, I know—
    let all that be,   60
And read me a Bible verse of the
    Lord's goodwill toward men—
'Full of compassion and mercy, the
    Lord'—let me hear it again;
'Full of compassion and mercy—long-
    suffering.' Yes, O, yes!

For the lawyer is born but to murder
    —the Saviour lives but to
    bless.
He 'll never put on the black cap ex-
    cept for the worst of the worst,
And the first may be last—I have
    heard it in church—and the last
    may be first.
Suffering—O, long-suffering—yes, as
    the Lord must know,
Year after year in the mist and the
    wind and the shower and the
    snow.

XIV

Heard, have you? what? they have
    told you he never repented his
    sin.
How do they know it? are *they* his
    mother? are *you* of his kin? 70
Heard! have you ever heard, when
    the storm on the downs began,
The wind that 'ill wail like a child and
    the sea that 'ill moan like a
    man?

XV

Election, Election, and Reprobation—
    it's all very well.
But I go to-night to my boy, and I
    shall not find him in hell.
For I cared so much for my boy that
    the Lord as look'd into my
    care,
And He means me I'm sure to be
    happy with Willy, I know not
    where.

XVI

And if *he* be lost—but to save *my* soul,
    that is all your desire—
Do you think that I care for *my* soul
    if my boy be gone to the fire?
I have been with God in the dark—
    go, go, you may leave me
    alone—
You never have borne a child—you
    are just as hard as a stone. 80

XVII

Madam, I beg your pardon! I think
    that you mean to be kind,
But I cannot hear what you say for
    my Willy's voice in the wind—
The snow and the sky so bright—he
    used but to call in the dark,
And he calls to me now from the
    church and not from the gibbet
    —for hark!
Nay—you can hear it yourself—it is
    coming—shaking the walls—
Willy—the moon's in a cloud—Good-
    night. I am going. He calls.

THE NORTHERN COBBLER

I

Waäit till our Sally cooms in, fur thou
    mun a' sights [1] to tell.
Eh, but I be maäin glad to seeä tha sa'
    'arty an' well.
'Cast awaäy on a disolut land wi' a
    vartical soon [2]!'
Strange fur to goä fur to think what
    saäilors a' seëan an' a' doon;
'Summat to drink—sa 'ot?' I 'a nowt
    but Adam's wine:
What's the 'eät o' this little 'ill-side to
    the 'eät o' the line?

II

'What's i' tha bottle a-stanning theer?'
    I'll tell tha. Gin.
But if thou wants thy grog, tha mun
    goä fur it down to the inn.
Naäy—fur I be maäin-glad, but thaw
    tha was iver sa dry,

[1] The vowels *aï*, pronounced separately
though in the closest conjunction, best
render the sound of the long *i* and *y* in
this dialect. But since such words as
craïin', *daïin'*, *whaï*, *aï* (I), etc., look
awkward except in a page of express
phonetics, I have thought it better to
leave the simple *i* and *y*, and to trust that
my readers will give them the broader
pronunciation.
[2] The *oo* short, as in 'wood.'

Thou gits naw gin fro' the bottle theer,
    an' I'll tell tha why.   10

III

Meä an' thy sister was married, when
    wur it? back-end o' June,
Ten year sin', and wa 'greed as well as
    a fiddle i' tune.
I could fettle and clump owd booöts
    and shoes wi' the best on 'em
    all,
As fer as fro' Thursby thurn hup to
    Harmsby and Hutterby Hall.
We was busy as beeäs i' the bloom an'
    as 'appy as 'art could think,
An' then the babby wur burn, and then
    I taäkes to the drink.

IV

An' I weänt gaäinsaäy it, my lad, thaw
    I be hafe shaämed on it now,
We could sing a good song at the Plow,
    we could sing a good song at
    the Plow;
Thaw once of a frosty night I slither'd
    an' hurted my huck, [1]
An' I coom'd neck-an-crop soomtimes
    slaäpe down i' the squad an'
    the muck: 20
An' once I fowt wi' the taäilor—not
    hafe ov a man, my lad—
Fur he scrawm'd an' scratted my faäce
    like a cat, an' it maäde 'er sa
    mad
That Sally she turn'd a tongue-
    banger, [2] an' raäted ma, 'Sot-
    tin' thy braäins
Guzzlin' an' soäkin' an' smoäkin' an'
    hawmin' [3] about i' the laänes,
Soä sow-droonk that tha doesn not
    touch thy 'at to the Squire;'
An' I looök'd cock-eyed at my noäse
    an' I seeäd 'im a-gittin' o' fire;
But sin' I wur hallus i' liquor an' hal-
    lus as droonk as a king,
Foälks' coostom flitted awaäy like a
    kite wi' a brokken string.

[1] Hip.   [2] Scold.
[3] Lounging.

V

An' Sally she wesh'd foälks' cloäths to
keep the wolf fro' the door,
Eh, but the moor she riled me, she
druv me to drink the moor, 30
Fur I fun', when 'er back wur turn'd,
wheer Sally's owd stockin' wur
'id,
An' I grabb'd the munny she maäde,
and I weär'd it o' liquor, I did.

VI

An' one night I cooms 'oäm like a bull
gotten loose at a faäir,
An' she wur a-waäitin' fo'mma, an'
cryin' and teärin' 'er aäir,
An' I tummled athurt the craädle an'
sweär'd as I'd breäk ivry stick
O' furnitur 'ere i' the 'ouse, an' I gied
our Sally a kick,
An' I mash'd the taäbles an' chairs,
an' she an' the babby beäl'd,[1]
Fur I knaw'd naw moor what I did nor
a mortal beäst o' the feäld.

VII

An' when I waäked i' the murnin' I
seeäd that our Sally went laämed
Cos' o' the kick as I gied 'er, an' I wur
dreädful ashaämed; 40
An' Sally wur sloomy[2] an' draggle-
taäil'd in an owd turn gown,
An' the babby's faäce wurn't wesh'd,
an' the 'ole 'ouse hupside down.

VIII

An' then I minded our Sally sa pratty
an' neät an' sweeät,
Straät as a pole an' cleän as a flower
fro' 'eäd to feeät:
An' then I minded the fust kiss I gied
'er by Thursday thurn;
Theer wur a lark a-singin' 'is best of a
Sunday at murn,
Couldn't see 'im, we 'eärd 'im
a-mountin' oop 'igher an'
'igher,

[1] Bellowed, cried out.
[2] Sluggish, out of spirits.

An' then 'e turn'd to the sun, an' 'e
shined like a sparkle o' fire.
'Doesn't tha see 'im?' she axes, 'fur I
can see 'im;' an' I 49
Seeäd nobbut the smile o' the sun as
danced in 'er pratty blue eye;
An' I says, 'I mun gie tha a kiss,' an'
Sally says, 'Noä, thou moänt,'
But I gied 'er a kiss, an' then anoother,
an' Sally says, 'doänt!'

IX

An' when we coom'd into meeätin', at
fust she wur all in a tew,
But, arter, we sing'd the 'ymn togither
like birds on a beugh;
An' Muggins 'e preäch'd o' hell-fire an'
the loov o' God fur men,
An' then upo' coomin' awaäy Sally
gied me a kiss ov 'ersen.

X

Heer wur a fall fro' a kiss to a kick like
Saätan as fell
Down out o' heaven i' hell-fire—thaw
theer's naw drinkin' i' hell;
Meä fur to kick our Sally as kep the
wolf fro' the door,
All along o' the drink, fur I loov'd 'er
as well as afoor. 60

XI

Sa like a graät num-cumpus I blub-
ber'd awaäy o' the bed—
'Weänt niver do it naw moor;' an'
Sally loöokt up an' she said,
'I'll upowd it[1] tha weänt; thou 'rt
like the rest o' the men,
Thou'll goä sniffin' about the tap till
tha does it ageän.
Theer's thy hennemy, man, an' I
knaws, as knaws tha sa well,
That, if tha seeäs 'im an' smells 'im
tha 'll foller 'im slick into hell.'

XII

'Naäy,' says I, 'fur I weänt goä sniffin'
about the tap.'

[1] I'll uphold it.

'Weänt tha?' she says, an' mysen I
  thowt i' mysen 'mayhap.'
'Noä:' an' I started awaäy like a shot,
  an' down to the hinn,
An' I browt what tha seeäs stannin'
  theer, yon big black bottle o'
  gin.   70

XIII

'That caps owt,'[1] says Sally, an' saw
  she begins to cry,
But I puts it inter 'er 'ands an' I says
  to 'er, 'Sally,' says I,
'Stan' 'im theer i' the naäme o' the
  Lord an' the power ov 'is
  graäce,
Stan' 'im theer, fur I'll looök my hennemy straäit i' the faäce,
Stan' 'im theer i' the winder, an' let
  ma looök at 'im then,
'E seeäms naw moor nor watter, an'
  'e 's the divil's oän sen.'

XIV

An' I wur down i' tha mouth, couldn't
  do naw work an' all,
Nasty an' snaggy an' shaäky, an'
  poonch'd my 'and wi' the hawl,
But she wur a power o' coomfut, an'
  sattled 'ersen o' my knee,
An' coäxd an' coodled me oop till
  ageän I feel'd mysen free.   80

XV

An' Sally she tell'd it about, an' foälk
  stood a-gawmin'[2] in,
As thaw it wur summat bewitch'd
  istead of a quart o' gin;
An' some on 'em said it wur watter—
  an' I wur chousin' the wife,
Fur I couldn't 'owd 'ands off gin, wur
  it nobbut to saäve my life;
An' blacksmith 'e strips me the thick
  ov 'is airm, an' 'e shaws it to
  me,
'Feeäl thou this! thou can't graw this
  upo' watter!' says he.

[1] That 's beyond everything.
[2] Staring vacantly.

An' Doctor 'e calls o' Sunday an' just
  as candles was lit,
'Thou moänt do it,' he says, 'tha mun
  breäk 'im off bit by bit.'
'Thou 'rt but a Methody-man,' says
  Parson, and laäys down 'is 'at,
An' 'e points to the bottle o' gin, 'but I
  respecks tha fur that;'   90
An' Squire, his oän very sen, walks
  down fro' the 'All to see,
An' 'e spanks 'is 'and into mine, 'fur I
  respecks tha,' says 'e;
An' coostom ageän draw'd in like a
  wind fro' far an' wide,
And browt me the booöts to be cob-
  bled fro' hafe the coontryside.

XVI

An' theer 'e stans an' theer 'e shall
  stan' to my dying daäy;
I 'a gotten to loov 'im ageän in anoother kind of a waäy,
Proud on 'im, like, my lad, an' I
  keeäps 'im cleän an' bright,
Loovs 'im, an' roobs 'im, an' doosts
  'im, an' puts 'im back i' the
  light.

XVII

Wouldn't a pint a' sarved as well as a
  quart? Naw doubt;
But I liked a bigger feller to fight wi'
  an' fowt it out.   100
Fine an' meller 'e mun be by this, if I
  cared to taäste,
But I moänt, my lad, and I weänt, fur
  I'd feäl mysen cleän dis-
  graäced.

XVIII

An' once I said to the Missis, 'My
  lass, when I cooms to die,
Smash the bottle to smithers, the
  divil's in 'im,' said I.
But arter I chaänged my mind, an' if
  Sally be left aloän,
I'll hev 'im a-buried wi'mma an' taäke
  'im afoor the Throän.

XIX

Coom thou 'eer—yon laädy a-steppin'
    along the streeät,
Doesn't tha knaw 'er—sa pratty, an'
    feät, an' neät, an' sweeät?
Look at the cloäths on 'er back, thebbe
    ammost spick-span-new,
An' Tommy's faäce be as fresh as a
    codlin wesh'd i' the dew.   110

XX

'Ere be our Sally an' Tommy, an' we
    be a-goin to dine,
Baäcon an' taätes, an' a beslings-pud-
    din' [1] an' Adam's wine;
But if tha wants ony grog tha mun
    goä fur it down to the Hinn,
Fur I weänt shed a drop on 'is blood,
    noä, not fur Sally's oän kin.

THE REVENGE

A BALLAD OF THE FLEET

I

At Flores in the Azores Sir Richard
    Grenville lay,
And a pinnace, like a flutter'd bird,
    came flying from far away:
'Spanish ships of war at sea! we have
    sighted fifty-three!'
Then sware Lord Thomas Howard:
    ' 'Fore God I am no coward;
But I cannot meet them here, for my
    ships are out of gear,
And the half my men are sick. I must
    fly, but follow quick.
We are six ships of the line; can we
    fight with fifty-three?'

II

Then spake Sir Richard Grenville: 'I
    know you are no coward;
You fly them for a moment to fight
    with them again.

[1] A pudding made with the first milk of
the cow after calving.

But I've ninety men and more that are
    lying sick ashore.   10
I should count myself the coward if I
    left them, my Lord Howard,
To these Inquisition dogs and the
    devildoms of Spain.'

III

So Lord Howard past away with five
    ships of war that day,
Till he melted like a cloud in the
    silent summer heaven;
But Sir Richard bore in hand all his
    sick men from the land
Very carefully and slow,
Men of Bideford in Devon,
And we laid them on the ballast down
    below;
For we brought them all aboard,
And they blest him in their pain, that
    they were not left to Spain, 20
To the thumb-screw and the stake, for
    the glory of the Lord.

IV

He had only a hundred seamen to
    work the ship and to fight,
And he sailed away from Flores till
    the Spaniard came in sight,
With his huge sea-castles heaving upon
    the weather bow.
'Shall we fight or shall we fly?
Good Sir Richard, tell us now,
For to fight is but to die!
There'll be little of us left by the time
    this sun be set.'
And Sir Richard said again: 'We be
    all good English men.
Let us bang these dogs of Seville, the
    children of the devil, 30
For I never turn'd my back upon Don
    or devil yet.'

V

Sir Richard spoke and he laugh'd, and
    we roar'd a hurrah, and so
The little Revenge ran on sheer into
    the heart of the foe,
With her hundred fighters on deck,
    and her ninety sick below;

For half of their fleet to the right and
    half to the left were seen,
And the little Revenge ran on thro' the
    long sea-lane between.

VI

Thousands of their soldiers look'd
    down from their decks and
    laugh'd,
Thousands of their seamen made mock
    at the mad little craft
Running on and on, till delay'd
By their mountain-like San Philip
    that, of fifteen hundred tons, 40
And up-shadowing high above us with
    her yawning tiers of guns,
Took the breath from our sails, and
    we stay'd.

VII

And while now the great San Philip
    hung above us like a cloud
Whence the thunderbolt will fall
Long and loud,
Four galleons drew away
From the Spanish fleet that day,
And two upon the larboard and two
    upon the starboard lay,
And the battle-thunder broke from
    them all.

VIII

But anon the great San Philip, she be-
    thought herself and went,   50
Having that within her womb that had
    left her ill content;
And the rest they came aboard us, and
    they fought us hand to hand,
For a dozen times they came with
    their pikes and musqueteers,
And a dozen times we shook 'em off as
    a dog that shakes his ears
When he leaps from the water to the
    land.

IX

And the sun went down, and the stars
    came out far over the summer
    sea,

But never a moment ceased the fight
    of the one and the fifty-three.
Ship after ship, the whole night long,
    their high-built galleons came,
Ship after ship, the whole night long,
    with her battle-thunder and
    flame;
Ship after ship, the whole night long,
    drew back with her dead and
    her shame.   60
For some were sunk and many were
    shatter'd, and so could fight us
    no more—
God of battles, was ever a battle like
    this in the world before?

X

For he said, 'Fight on! fight on!'
Tho' his vessel was all but a wreck;
And it chanced that, when half of the
    short summer night was gone,
With a grisly wound to be drest he had
    left the deck,
But a bullet struck him that was
    dressing it suddenly dead,
And himself he was wounded again in
    the side and the head,
And he said, 'Fight on! fight on!'

XI

And the night went down, and the sun
    smiled out far over the summer
    sea,   70
And the Spanish fleet with broken
    sides lay round us all in a ring;
But they dared not touch us again,
    for they fear'd that we still
    could sting,
So they watch'd what the end would
    be.
And we had not fought them in vain,
But in perilous plight were we,
Seeing forty of our poor hundred were
    slain,
And half of the rest of us maim'd for
    life
In the crash of the cannonades and
    the desperate strife;
And the sick men down in the hold
    were most of them stark and
    cold,

And the pikes were all broken or
    bent, and the powder was all
    of it spent;   80
And the masts and the rigging were
    lying over the side;
But Sir Richard cried in his English
    pride:
'We have fought such a fight for a
    day and a night
As may never be fought again!
We have won great glory, my men!
And a day less or more
At sea or ashore,
We die—does it matter when?
Sink me the ship, Master Gunner—
    sink her, split her in twain!
Fall into the hands of God, not into
    the hands of Spain!'   90

XII

And the gunner said, 'Ay, ay,' but the
    seamen made reply:
'We have children, we have wives,
And the Lord hath spared our lives.
We will make the Spaniard promise,
    if we yield, to let us go;
We shall live to fight again and to
    strike another blow.'
And the lion there lay dying, and they
    yielded to the foe.

XIII

And the stately Spanish men to their
    flagship bore him then,
Where they laid him by the mast, old
    Sir Richard caught at last,
And they praised him to his face with
    their courtly foreign grace;
But he rose upon their decks, and he
    cried: 100
'I have fought for Queen and Faith
    like a valiant man and true;
I have only done my duty as a man is
    bound to do.
With a joyful spirit I Sir Richard
    Grenville die!'
And he fell upon their decks, and he
    died.

XIV

And they stared at the dead that had
    been so valiant and true,
And had holden the power and glory
    of Spain so cheap
That he dared her with one little ship
    and his English few;
Was he devil or man? He was devil
    for aught they knew,
But they sank his body with honor
    down into the deep,
And they mann'd the Revenge with a
    swarthier alien crew,   110
And away she sail'd with her loss and
    long'd for her own;
When a wind from the lands they had
    ruin'd awoke from sleep,
And the water began to heave and the
    weather to moan,
And or ever that evening ended a great
    gale blew,
And a wave like the wave that is
    raised by an earthquake grew,
Till it smote on their hulls and their
    sails and their masts and their
    flags,
And the whole sea plunged and fell on
    the shot-shatter'd navy of
    Spain,
And the little Revenge herself went
    down by the island crags
To be lost evermore in the main.

THE SISTERS

They have left the doors ajar; and by
    their clash,
And prelude on the keys, I know the
    song,
Their favorite—which I call 'The
    Tables Turn'd.'
Evelyn begins it, 'O diviner Air.'

EVELYN

    O diviner Air,
    Thro' the heat, the drowth, the dust,
      the glare,
    Far from out the west in shadowing
      showers,
    Over all the meadow baked and bare,

Making fresh and fair
All the bowers and the flowers,   10
Fainting flowers, faded bowers,
Over all this weary world of ours,
Breathe, diviner Air!

A sweet voice that—you scarce could
      better that!
Now follows Edith echoing Evelyn.

EDITH

O diviner light,
Thro' the cloud that roofs our noon
      with night,
Thro' the blotting mist, the blinding
      showers,
Far from out a sky for ever bright,
Over all the woodland's flooded
      bowers,   20
Over all the meadow's drowning
      flowers,
Over all this ruin'd world of ours,
Break, diviner light!

Marvellously like, their voices—and
      themselves!
Tho' one is somewhat deeper than the
      other,
As one is somewhat graver than the
      other—
Edith than Evelyn. Your good uncle,
      whom
You count the father of your for-
      tune, longs
For this alliance. Let me ask you then,
Which voice most takes you? for I do
      not doubt,   30
Being a watchful parent, you are
      taken
With one or other; tho' sometimes I
      fear
You may be flickering, fluttering in a
      doubt
Between the two—which must not be
      —which might
Be death to one. They both are beau-
      tiful;
Evelyn is gayer, wittier, prettier, says
The common voice, if one may trust
      it, she?
No! but the paler and the graver,
      Edith.
Woo her and gain her then; no waver-
      ing, boy!

The graver is perhaps the one for
      you   40
Who jest and laugh so easily and so
      well.
For love will go by contrast, as by
      likes.

No sisters ever prized each other
      more.
Not so; their mother and her sister
      loved
More passionately still.
                  But that my best
And oldest friend, your uncle, wishes
      it,
And that I know you worthy every
      way
To be my son, I might, perchance, be
      loath
To part them, or part from them; and
      yet one
Should marry, or all the broad lands
      in your view   50
From this bay-window—which our
      house has held
Three hundred years—will pass col-
      laterally.

My father with a child on either
      knee,
A hand upon the head of either child,
Smoothing their locks, as golden as
      his own
Were silver, 'get them wedded' would
      he say.
And once my prattling Edith ask'd
      him 'why?'
'Ay, why?' said he, 'for why should I
      go lame?'
Then told them of his wars, and of his
      wound.
For see—this wine—the grape from
      whence it flow'd   60
Was blackening on the slopes of Por-
      tugal,
When that brave soldier, down the
      terrible ridge
Plunged in the last fierce charge at
      Waterloo,
And caught the laming bullet. He left
      me this,
Which yet retains a memory of its
      youth,

As I of mine, and my first passion.
   Come!
Here's to your happy union with my
   child!

Yet must you change your name—
   no fault of mine!
You say that you can do it as willingly
As birds make ready for their bridal-
   time   70
By change of feather; for all that, my
   boy,
Some birds are sick and sullen when
   they moult.
An old and worthy name! but mine
   that stirr'd
Among our civil wars and earlier too
Among the Roses, the more venerable.
I care not for a name—no fault of
   mine.
Once more—a happier marriage than
   my own!

You see yon Lombard poplar on the
   plain.
The highway running by it leaves a
   breadth
Of sward to left and right, where, long
   ago,   80
One bright May morning in a world
   of song,
I lay at leisure, watching overhead
The aerial poplar wave, an amber
   spire.

I dozed; I woke. An open landaulet
Whirl'd by, which, after it had past
   me, show'd
Turning my way, the loveliest face on
   earth.
The face of one there sitting oppo-
   site,
On whom I brought a strange unhap-
   piness,
That time I did not see.

                    Love at first sight
May seem—with goodly rhyme and
   reason for it—   90
Possible—at first glimpse, and for a
   face
Gone in a moment—strange. Yet
   once, when first

I came on lake Llanberris in the dark,
A moonless night with storm—one
   lightning-fork
Flash'd out the lake; and tho' I loi-
   ter'd there
The full day after, yet in retrospect
That less than momentary thunder-
   sketch
Of lake and mountain conquers all the
   day.

The sun himself has limn'd the face
   for me.
Not quite so quickly, no, nor half as
   well.   100
For look you here—the shadows are
   too deep,
And like the critic's blurring comment
   make
The veriest beauties of the work appear
The darkest faults; the sweet eyes
   frown, the lips
Seem but a gash. My sole memorial
Of Edith—no, the other,—both indeed.

So that bright face was flash'd thro'
   sense and soul
And by the poplar vanish'd—to be
   found
Long after, as it seem'd, beneath the
   tall
Tree-bowers, and those long-sweeping
   beechen boughs   110
Of our New Forest. I was there alone.
The phantom of the whirling landaulet
For ever past me by; when one quick
   peal
Of laughter drew me thro' the glimmering glades
Down to the snowlike sparkle of a
   cloth
On fern and foxglove. Lo, the face
   again,
My Rosalind in this Arden—Edith—
   all
One bloom of youth, health, beauty,
   happiness,
And moved to merriment at a passing
   jest.

There one of those about her know-
ing me   120
Call'd me to join them; so with these
I spent
What seem'd my crowning hour, my
day of days.

I woo'd her then, nor unsuccess-
fully,
The worse for her, for me! Was I con-
tent?
Ay—no, not quite; for now and then
I thought
Laziness, vague love-longings, the
bright May,
Had made a heated haze to magnify
The charm of Edith—that a man's
ideal
Is high in heaven, and lodged with
Plato's God,
Not findable here—content, and not
content,   130
In some such fashion as a man may be
That having had the portrait of his
friend
Drawn by an artist, looks at it, and
says,
'Good! very like! not altogether he.'

As yet I had not bound myself by
words,
Only, believing I loved Edith, made
Edith love *me*. Then came the day
when I,
Flattering myself that all my doubts
were fools
Born of the fool this Age that doubts
of all—
Not I that day of Edith's love or
mine—   140
Had braced my purpose to declare
myself.
I stood upon the stairs of Paradise.
The golden gates would open at a
word.
I spoke it—told her of my passion,
seen
And lost and found again, had got so
far,
Had caught her hand, her eyelids fell
—I heard
Wheels, and a noise of welcome at the
doors—

On a sudden after two Italian years
Had set the blossom of her health
again,
The younger sister, Evelyn, enter'd—
there,   150
There was the face, and altogether
she.
The mother fell about the daughter's
neck,
The sisters closed in one another's
arms,
Their people throng'd about them
from the hall,
And in the thick of question and reply
I fled the house, driven by one angel
face,
And all the Furies.

                    I was bound to her;
I could not free myself in honor—
bound
Not by the sounded letter of the word,
But counter-pressures of the yielded
hand   160
That timorously and faintly echoed
mine,
Quick blushes, the sweet dwelling of
her eyes
Upon me when she thought I did not
see—
Were these not bonds? nay, nay, but
could I wed her
Loving the other? do her that great
wrong?
Had I not dream'd I loved her yester-
morn?
Had I not known where Love, at first
a fear,
Grew after marriage to full height and
form?
Yet after marriage, that mock-sister
there—
Brother-in-law—the fiery nearness of
it—   170
Unlawful and disloyal brotherhood—
What end but darkness could ensue
from this
For all the three? So Love and Honor
jarr'd,
Tho' Love and Honor join'd to raise
the full
High-tide of doubt that sway'd me up
and down

Advancing nor retreating.

Edith wrote:
'My mother bids me ask'—I did not
   tell you—
A widow with less guile than many a
   child.
God help the wrinkled children that
   are Christ's
As well as the plump cheek—she
   wrought us harm,   180
Poor soul, not knowing!—'Are you
   ill?'—so ran
The letter—'you have not been here
   of late.
You will not find me here. At last I go
On that long-promised visit to the
   North.
I told your wayside story to my
   mother
And Evelyn. She remembers you.
   Farewell.
Pray come and see my mother. Almost
   blind
With ever-growing cataract, yet she
   thinks
She sees you when she hears. Again
   farewell.'

Cold words from one I had hoped
   to warm so far   190
That I could stamp my image on her
   heart!
'Pray come and see my mother, and
   farewell.'
Cold, but as welcome as free airs of
   heaven
After a dungeon's closeness. Selfish,
   strange!
What dwarfs are men! my strangled
   vanity
Utter'd a stifled cry—to have vext
   myself
And all in vain for her—cold heart or
   none—
No bride for me. Yet so my path was
   clear
To win the sister.
         Whom I woo'd and won.

For Evelyn knew not of my former
   suit,   200

Because the simple mother work'd
   upon
By Edith pray'd me not to whisper of
   it.
And Edith would be bridesmaid on the
   day.

But on that day, not being all at
   ease,
I from the altar glancing back upon
   her,
Before the first 'I will' was utter'd,
   saw
The bridesmaid pale, statue-like, passionless—
'No harm, no harm'—I turn'd again,
   and placed
My ring upon the finger of my bride.

So, when we parted, Edith spoke no
   word,   210
She wept no tear, but round my Evelyn clung
In utter silence for so long, I thought,
'What, will she never set her sister
   free?'

We left her, happy each in each,
   and then,
As tho' the happiness of each in each
Were not enough, must fain have tor-
   rents, lakes,
Hills, the great things of Nature and
   the fair,
To lift us as it were from common-
   place,
And help us to our joy. Better have
   sent
Our Edith thro' the glories of the
   earth,   220
To change with her horizon, if true
   Love
Were not his own imperial all-in-all.

Far off we went. My God, I would
   not live
Save that I think this gross hard-seem-
   ing world
Is our misshaping vision of the Powers
Behind the world, that make our
   griefs our gains.

For on the dark night of our mar-
 riage-day
The great tragedian, that had
 quench'd herself
In that assumption of the bridesmaid—she
That loved me—our true Edith—her
 brain broke   230
With over-acting, till she rose and
 fled
Beneath a pitiless rush of autumn
 rain
To the deaf church—to be let in—to
 pray
Before *that* altar—so I think; and
 there
They found her beating the hard Protestant doors.
She died and she was buried ere we
 knew.

I learnt it first. I had to speak. At
 once
The bright quick smile of Evelyn,
 that had sunn'd
The morning of our marriage, past
 away.
And on our home-return the daily
 want   240
Of Edith in the house, the garden,
 still
Haunted us like her ghost; and by and
 by,
Either from that necessity for talk
Which lives with blindness, or plain
 innocence
Of nature, or desire that her lost child
Should earn from both the praise of
 heroism,
The mother broke her promise to the
 dead,
And told the living daughter with
 what love
Edith had welcomed my brief wooing
 of her,
And all her sweet self-sacrifice and
 death.   250

Henceforth that mystic bond betwixt the twins—
Did I not tell you they were twins?—
 prevail'd

So far that no caress could win my
 wife
Back to that passionate answer of full
 heart
I had from her at first. Not that her
 love,
Tho' scarce as great as Edith's power
 of love,
Had lessen'd but the mother's gar-
 rulous wail
For ever woke the unhappy Past
 again,
Till that dead bridesmaid, meant to be
 my bride,
Put forth cold hands between us, and
 I fear'd   260
The very fountains of her life were
 chill'd;
So took her thence, and brought her
 here, and here
She bore a child, whom reverently we
 call'd
Edith; and in the second year was
 born
A second—this I named from her own
 self,
Evelyn; then two weeks—no more—
 she join'd,
In and beyond the grave, that one she
 loved.

Now in this quiet of declining life,
Thro' dreams by night and trances of
 the day,
The sisters glide about me hand in
 hand,   270
Both beautiful alike, nor can I tell
One from the other, no, nor care to
 tell
One from the other, only know they
 come,
They smile upon me, till, remembering
 all
The love they both have borne me,
 and the love
I bore them both—divided as I am
From either by the stillness of the
 grave—
I know not which of these I love the
 best.

But *you* love Edith; and her own
 true eyes

Are traitors to her; our quick Eve-
lyn— 280
The merrier, prettier, wittier, as they
talk,
And not without good reason, my good
son—
Is yet untouch'd. And I that hold
them both
Dearest of all things—well, I am not
sure—
But if there lie a preference either
way,
And in the rich vocabulary of Love
'Most dearest' be a true superlative—
I think *I* likewise love your Edith
most.

THE VILLAGE WIFE; OR, THE ENTAIL [1]

I

'OUSE-KEEPER sent tha, my lass, fur
new Squire coom'd last night.
Butter an' heggs—yis—yis. I'll goä
wi' tha back; all right;
Butter I warrants be prime, an' I warrants the heggs be as well,
Hafe a pint o' milk runs out when ya
breäks the shell.

II

Sit thysen down fur a bit; hev a glass
o' cowslip wine!
I liked the owd Squire an' 'is gells as
thaw they was gells o' mine,
Fur then we was all es one, the Squire
an' 'is darters an' me,
Hall but Miss Annie, the heldest, I
niver not took to she.
But Nelly, the last of the cletch,[2] I
liked 'er the fust on 'em all,
Fur hoffens we talkt o' my darter es
died o' the fever at fall; 10
An' I thowt 't wur the will o' the Lord,
but Miss Annie she said it wur
draäins,
Fur she hed n't naw coomfut in 'er,
an' arn'd naw thanks fur 'er
paäins.

[1] See note on pronunciation, p. 762.
[2] A brood of chickens.

Eh! thebbe all wi' the Lord, my
childer, I han't gotten none!
Sa new Squire 's coom'd wi' 'is taäil in
'is 'and, an' owd Squire 's gone.

III

Fur 'staäte be i' taäil, my lass—tha
dosn' knaw what that be?
But I knaws the law, I does, for the
lawyer ha towd it me.
'When theer 's naw 'eäd to a 'Ouse by
the fault o' that ere maäle—
The gells they counts fur nowt, and
the next un he taäkes the taäil.'

IV

What be the next un like? can tha tell
ony harm on 'im, lass?—
Naäy sit down—naw 'urry—sa cowd!
—hev another glass! 20
Straänge an' cowd fur the time! we
may happen a fall o' snaw—
Not es I cares fur to hear ony harm,
but I likes to knaw.
An' I oäps es 'e beänt booöklarn'd;
but 'e dosn' not coom fro' the
shere;
We 'd anew o' that wi' the Squire, an'
we haätes booöklarnin' ere.

V

Fur Squire wur a Varsity scholard, an'
niver lookt arter the land—
Whoäts or turmuts or taätes—'e 'd
hallus a booök i' 'is 'and,
Hallus aloän wi' 'is booöks, thaw nigh
upo' seventy year.
An' booöks, what 's booöks? thou
knaws thebbe neyther 'ere nor
theer.

VI

An' the gells, they hed n't naw taäils,
an' the lawyer he towd it me
That 'is taäil were soä tied up es he
could n't cut down a tree! 30
'Drat the trees,' says I, to be sewer I
haätes 'em, my lass,

Fur we puts the muck o' the land, an'
    they sucks the muck fro' the
    grass.

VII

An' Squire wur hallus a-smilin', an'
    gied to the tramps goin' by—
An' all o' the wust i' the parish—wi'
    hoffens a drop in 'is eye.
An' ivry darter o' Squire 's hed her
    awn ridin-erse to 'ersen,
An' they rampaged about wi' their
    grooms, an' wus 'untin' arter
    the men,
An' hallus a-dallackt [1] an' dizen'd out,
    an' a-buyin' new cloäthes,
While 'e sit like a greät glimmer-
    gowk [2] wi' 'is glasses athurt 'is
    noäse,
An' 'is noäse sa grufted wi' snuff as it
    could n't be scroob'd awaäy,
Fur 'atween 'is readin' an' writin' 'e
    snifft up a box in a daäy,   40
An' 'e niver runn'd arter the fox, nor
    arter the birds wi' 'is gun,
An' 'e niver not shot one 'are, but 'e
    leäved it to Charlie 'is son,
An' 'e niver not fish'd 'is awn ponds,
    but Charlie 'e cotch'd the pike,
Fur 'e warn't not burn to the land, an'
    'e did n't take kind to it like;
But I 'eärs es 'e 'd gie fur a howry [3]
    owd book thutty pound an'
    moor,
An' 'e 'd wrote an' owd book, his awn
    sen, sa I knaw'd es 'e 'd coom
    to be poor;
An' 'e gied—I be fear'd fur to tell tha
    'ow much—fur an owd scrat-
    ted stoän,
An' 'e digg'd up a loomp i' the land an'
    'e got a brown pot an' a boän,
An' 'e bowt owd money, es would n't
    goä, wi' good gowd o' the
    Queen,
An' 'e bowt little statutes all naäkt an'
    which was a shaäme to be
    seen;   50
But 'e niver loöokt ower a bill, nor 'e
    niver not seed to owt,

[1] Overdrest in gay colors.
[2] Owl.   [3] Filthy.

An' 'e niver knawd nowt but booöks,
    an' booöks, as thou knaws,
    beänt nowt.

VIII

But owd Squire's laädy es long es she
    lived she kep' 'em all clear,
Thaw es long es she lived I niver hed
    none of 'er darters 'ere;
But arter she died we was all es one,
    the childer an' me,
An' sarvints runn'd in an' out, an' of-
    fens we hed 'em to tea.
Lawk! 'ow I laugh'd when the lasses
    'ud talk o' their Missis's waäys,
An' the Missisis talk'd o' the lasses.—
    I'll tell tha some o' these daäys.
Hoänly Miss Annie were saw stuck
    oop, like 'er mother afoor—
'Er an' 'er blessed darter—they niver
    derken'd my door.   60

IX

An' Squire 'e smiled an' 'e smiled till
    'e 'd gotten a fright at last,
An' 'e calls fur 'is son, fur the 'turney's
    letters they foller'd sa fast;
But Squire wur afear'd o' 'is son, an' 'e
    says to 'im, meek as a mouse,
'Lad, thou mun cut off thy taäil, or the
    gells 'ull goä to the 'Ouse,
Fur I finds es I be that i' debt, es I
    oäps es thou 'll 'elp me a bit,
An' if thou 'll 'gree to cut off thy taäil
    I may saäve mysen yit.'

X

But Charlie 'e sets back 'is ears, an' 'e
    sweärs, an' 'e says to 'im, 'Noä.
I've gotten the 'staäte by the taäil an'
    be dang'd if I iver let goä!
Coom! coom! feyther,' 'e says, 'why
    shouldn't thy booöks be sowd!
I hears es soom o' thy booöks mebbe
    worth their weight i' gowd.'   70

XI

Heäps an' heäps o' booöks, I ha' seed
    'em, belong'd to the Squire,

But the lasses 'ed teärd out leäves i'
    the middle to kindle the fire;
Sa moäst on 'is owd big boooks fetch'd
    nigh to nowt at the saäle,
And Squire were at Charlie ageän to
    git 'im to cut off 'is taäil.

XII

Ya would n't find Charlie's likes—'e
    were that outdacious at 'oäm,
Not thaw ye went fur to raäke out hell
    wi' a small-tooth coämb—
Droonk wi' the Quoloty's wine, an'
    droonk wi' the farmer's ääle,
Mad wi' the lasses an' all—an' 'e
    would n't cut off the taäil.

XIII

Thou 's coom'd oop by the beck; and
    a thurn be a-grawin' theer,
I niver ha seed it sa white wi' the maäy
    es I seed it to-year—   80
Theerabouts Charlie joompt—and it
    gied me a scare tother night,
Fur I thowt it wur Charlie's ghoäst i'
    the derk, fur it looökt sa white.
'Billy,' says 'e, 'hev a joomp!'—thaw
    the banks o' the beck be sa
    high,
Fur he ca'd 'is 'erse Billy-rough-un,
    thaw niver a hair wur awry;
But Billy fell bakkuds o' Charlie, an'
    Charlie 'e brok 'is neck,
Sa theer wur a hend o' the taäil, fur 'e
    lost 'is taäil i' the beck.

XIV

Sa 'is taäil wur lost an' 'is boooks wur
    gone an' 'is boy wur deäd,
An' Squire 'e smiled an' 'e smiled, but
    'e niver not lift oop 'is 'eäd.
Hallus a soft un, Squire! an' 'e smiled,
    fur 'e hed n't naw friend,
Sa feyther an' son was buried togither,
    an' this wur the hend.   90

XV

An' Parson as hes n't the call, nor the
    mooney, but hes the pride,
'E reäds of a sewer an' sartan 'oäp o'
    the tother side;
But I beänt that sewer es the Lord,
    howsiver they praäy'd an'
    praäy'd,
Lets them inter 'eaven eäsy es leäves
    their debts to be paäid.
Siver the mou'ds rattled down upo'
    poor owd Squire i' the wood,
An' I cried along wi' the gells, fur they
    weänt niver coom to naw good.

XVI

Fur Molly the long un she walkt
    awaäy wi' a hofficer lad,
An' nawbody 'eärd on 'er sin', sa o'
    coorse she be gone to the bad!
An' Lucy wur laäme o' one leg, sweet-
    'arts she niver 'ed none—
Straänge an' unheppen [1] Miss Lucy!
    we naämed her 'Dot an' gaw
    one!'   100
An' Hetty wur weak i' the hattics,
    wi'out ony harm i' the legs,
An' the fever 'ed baäked Jinny's 'eäd
    as bald as one o' them heggs,
An' Nelly wur up fro' the craädle as
    big i' the mouth as a cow,
An' saw she mun hammergrate,[2] lass,
    or she weänt git a maäte ony-
    how!
An' es for Miss Annie es call'd me
    afoor my awn foälks to my
    faäce,
'A hignorant village wife es 'ud hev to
    be larn'd her awn plaäce,'
Hes fur Miss Hannie the heldest hes
    now be a-grawin' sa howd,
I knaws that mooch o' sheä, es it beänt
    not fit to be towd!

XVII

Sa I did n't not taäke it kindly ov owd
    Miss Annie to saäy
Es I should be talkin' ageän 'em, es
    soon es they went awaäy,   110
Fur lawks! 'ow I cried when they
    went, an' our Nelly she gied me
    'er 'and,

[1] Ungainly, awkward.
[2] Emigrate.

Fur I 'd ha done owt for the Squire an'
    'is gells es belong'd to the land;
Boooks es I said afoor, thebbe neyther
    'ere nor theer!
But I sarved 'em wi' butter an' heggs
    fur huppuds o' twenty year.

XVIII

An' they hallus paäid what I hax'd, sa
    I hallus deal'd wi' the Hall,
An' they knaw'd what butter wur, an'
    they knaw'd what a hegg wur,
    an' all;
Hugger-mugger they lived, but they
    was n't that eäsy to pleäse,
Till I gied 'em Hinjian curn, an' they
    laäid big heggs es tha seeäs;
An' I niver puts saäme [1] i' *my* butter
    —they does it at Willis's farm;
Taäste another drop o' the wine—
    tweänt do tha naw harm.   120

XIX

Sa new Squire 's coom'd wi' 'is taäil in
    'is 'and, an' owd Squire 's gone;
I heard 'im a roomlin' by, but arter
    my night-cap wur on;
Sa I han't clapt eyes on 'im yit, fur he
    coom'd last night sa laäte—
Pluksh!!! [2] the hens i' the peäs! why
    didn't tha hesp the gaäte?

IN THE CHILDREN'S
HOSPITAL

EMMIE

'It should be remembered that this is a
little drama, in which the Hospital Nurse,
not the Poet, is supposed to be speaking
throughout' (Palgrave).

I

Our doctor had call'd in another, I
    never had seen him before,
But he sent a chill to my heart when
    I saw him come in at the door,

[1] Lard.
[2] A cry accompanied by a clapping of
hands to scare trespassing fowl.

Fresh from the surgery-schools of
    France and of other lands—
Harsh red hair, big voice, big chest,
    big merciless hands!
Wonderful cures he had done, O, yes,
    but they said too of him
He was happier using the knife than
    in trying to save the limb,
And that I can well believe, for he
    look'd so coarse and so red,
I could think he was one of those who
    would break their jests on the
    dead,
And mangle the living dog that had
    loved him and fawn'd at his
    knee—
Drench'd with the hellish oorali—
    that ever such things should
    be!

II

Here was a boy—I am sure that some
    of our children would die
But for the voice of love, and the
    smile, and the comforting
    eye—
Here was a boy in the ward, every
    bone seem'd out of its place—
Caught in a mill and crush'd—it was
    all but a hopeless case;
And he handled him gently enough:
    but his voice and his face were
    not kind,
And it was but a hopeless case, he had
    seen it and made up his mind,
And he said to me roughly, 'The lad
    will need little more of your
    care.'
'All the more need,' I told him, 'to
    seek the Lord Jesus in prayer;
They are all His children here, and I
    pray for them all as my own.'
But he turn'd to me, 'Ay, good
    woman, can prayer set a
    broken bone?'
Then he mutter'd half to himself, but
    I know that I heard him say,
'All very well—but the good Lord
    Jesus has had his day.'

III

Had? has it come? It has only dawn'd.
     It will come by and by.
O, how could I serve in the wards if
     the hope of the world were a
     lie?
How could I bear with the sights and
     the loathsome smells of disease
But that He said, 'Ye do it to me,
     when ye do it to these'?

IV

So he went. And we past to this ward
     where the younger children are
     laid.
Here is the cot of our orphan, our
     darling, our meek little maid;
Empty, you see, just now! We have
     lost her who loved her so
     much—
Patient of pain tho' as quick as a sen-
     sitive plant to the touch.
Hers was the prettiest prattle, it often
     moved me to tears,
Hers was the gratefullest heart I have
     found in a child of her years—
Nay you remember our Emmie; you
     used to send her the flowers.
How she would smile at 'em, play with
     'em, talk to 'em hours after
     hours!
They that can wander at will where
     the works of the Lord are re-
     veal'd
Little guess what joy can be got from
     a cowslip out of the field;
Flowers to these 'spirits in prison' are
     all they can know of the spring,
They freshen and sweeten the wards
     like the waft of an angel's
     wing.
And she lay with a flower in one hand
     and her thin hands crost on her
     breast—
Wan, but as pretty as heart can de-
     sire, and we thought her at rest,
Quietly sleeping—so quiet, our doctor
     said, 'Poor little dear,
Nurse, I must do it to-morrow; she 'll
     never live thro' it, I fear.'

V

I walk'd with our kindly old doctor as
     far as the head of the stair,
Then I return'd to the ward; the child
     did n't see I was there.

VI

Never since I was nurse had I been so
     grieved and so vext!
Emmie had heard him. Softly she
     call'd from her cot to the next,
'He says I shall never live thro' it; O
     Annie, what shall I do?'
Annie consider'd. 'If I,' said the wise
     little Annie, 'was you,
I should cry to the dear Lord Jesus to
     help me, for, Emmie, you see,
It's all in the picture there: "Little
     children should come to
     me" '—
Meaning the print that you gave us,
     I find that it always can please
Our children, the dear Lord Jesus
     with children about his knees.
'Yes, and I will,' said Emmie, 'but
     then if I call to the Lord,
How should he know that it's me?
     such a lot of beds in the ward!'
That was a puzzle for Annie. Again
     she consider'd and said:
'Emmie, you put out your arms, and
     you leave 'em outside on the
     bed—
The Lord has so *much* to see to! but,
     Emmie, you tell it him plain,
It's the little girl with her arms lying
     out on the counterpane.'

VII

I had sat three nights by the child—
     I could not watch her for
     four—
My brain had begun to reel—I felt I
     could do it no more.
That was my sleeping-night, but I
     thought that it never would
     pass.
There was a thunderclap once, and a
     clatter of hail on the glass,

And there was a phantom cry that I
    heard as I tost about,
The motherless bleat of a lamb in the
    storm and the darkness with-
    out;
My sleep was broken besides with
    dreams of the dreadful knife
And fears for our delicate Emmie who
    scarce would escape with her
    life;
Then in the gray of the morning it
    seem'd she stood by me and
    smiled,
And the doctor came at his hour, and
    we went to see to the child.

VIII

He had brought his ghastly tools; we
    believed her asleep again—
Her dear, long, lean, little arms lying
    out on the counterpane—
Say that His day is done! Ah, why
    should we care what they say?
The Lord of the children had heard
    her, and Emmie had past away.

DEDICATORY POEM OF THE PRINCESS ALICE

The Princess Alice, Grand Duchess of
Hesse-Darmstadt, died on the 14th of
December, 1878, aged thirty-five years.

DEAD PRINCESS, living Power, if that
    which lived
True life live on—and if the fatal kiss,
Born of true life and love, divorce
    thee not
From earthly love and life—if what
    we call
The spirit flash not all at once from
    out
This shadow into Substance—then
    perhaps
The mellow'd murmur of the people's
    praise
From thine own State, and all our
    breadth of realm,
Where Love and Longing dress thy
    deeds in light,
Ascends to thee; and this March morn
    that sees

Thy Soldier-brother's bridal orange-
    bloom
Break thro' the yews and cypress of
    thy grave,
And thine Imperial mother smile
    again,
May send one ray to thee! and who
    can tell—
Thou — England's England - loving
    daughter—thou
Dying so English thou wouldst have
    her flag
Borne on thy coffin—where is he can
    swear
But that some broken gleam from our
    poor earth
May touch thee, while, remembering
    thee, I lay
At thy pale feet this ballad of the
    deeds
Of England, and her banner in the
    East?

THE DEFENCE OF LUCKNOW

This poem tells of happenings which
took place in 1857 during the Sepoy Rebellion in India. 'Sir Henry Lawrence
took charge of Lucknow as Resident in
March of that year. The spread of rebellion in June confined him to the
defence of the city, where he died of
wounds on July 4. Brigadier Inglis, in
succession, then defended Lucknow for
twelve weeks until it was relieved on
September 25 by General Havelock, to
whom Sir James Outram (who accompanied as volunteer) had generously
ceded the exploit' (Palgrave).

I

BANNER of England, not for a season,
    O banner of Britain, hast thou
Floated in conquering battle or flapt
    to the battle-cry!
Never with mightier glory than when
    we had rear'd thee on high
Flying at top of the roofs in the
    ghastly siege of Lucknow—
Shot thro' the staff or the halyard, but
    ever we raised thee anew,
And ever upon the topmost roof our
    banner of England blew.

II

Frail were the works that defended
the hold that we held with our
lives—
Women and children among us, God
help them, our children and
wives!
Hold it we might—and for fifteen
days or for twenty at most.
'Never surrender, I charge you, but
every man die at his post!' 10
Voice of the dead whom we loved, our
Lawrence the best of the
brave;
Cold were his brows when we kiss'd
him—we laid him that night in
his grave.
'Every man die at his post!' and there
hail'd on our houses and halls
Death from their rifle-bullets, and
death from their cannon-balls,
Death in our innermost chamber, and
death at our slight barricade,
Death while we stood with the mus-
ket, and death while we stoopt
to the spade,
Death to the dying, and wounds to the
wounded, for often there fell,
Striking the hospital wall, crashing
thro' it, their shot and their
shell,
Death—for their spies were among
us, their marksmen were told
of our best,
So that the brute bullet broke thro'
the brain that could think for
the rest; 20
Bullets would sing by our foreheads,
and bullets would rain at our
feet—
Fire from ten thousand at once of the
rebels that girdled us round—
Death at the glimpse of a finger from
over the breadth of a street,
Death from the heights of the mosque
and the palace, and death in
the ground!
Mine? yes, a mine! Countermine!
down, down! and creep thro'
the hole!
Keep the revolver in hand! you can
hear him — the murderous
mole!
Quiet, ah! quiet—wait till the point of
the pickaxe be thro'!
Click with the pick, coming nearer
and nearer again than before—
Now let it speak, and you fire, and the
dark pioneer is no more;
And ever upon the topmost roof our
banner of England blew! 30

III

Ay, but the foe sprung his mine many
times, and it chanced on a day
Soon as the blast of that underground
thunder-clap echo'd away,
Dark thro' the smoke and the sulphur
like so many fiends in their
hell—
Cannon-shot, musket-shot, volley on
volley, and yell upon yell—
Fiercely on all the defences our
myriad enemy fell.
What have they done? where is it?
Out yonder. Guard the Redan!
Storm at the Water-gate! storm at the
Bailey-gate! storm, and it ran
Surging and swaying all round us, as
ocean on every side
Plunges and heaves at a bank that is
daily drown'd by the tide—
So many thousands that, if they be
bold enough, who shall escape? 40
Kill or be kill'd, live or die, they shall
know we are soldiers and men!
Ready! take aim at their leaders—
their masses are gapp'd with
our grape—
Backward they reel like the wave, like
the wave flinging forward
again,
Flying and foil'd at the last by the
handful they could not subdue;
And ever upon the topmost roof our
banner of England blew.

IV

Handful of men as we were, we were
English in heart and in limb,

Strong with the strength of the race
    to command, to obey, to en-
    dure,
Each of us fought as if hope for the
    garrison hung but on him;
Still—could we watch at all points?
    we were every day fewer and
    fewer.
There was a whisper among us, but
    only a whisper that past: 50
'Children and wives—if the tigers leap
    into the fold unawares—
Every man die at his post—and the
    foe may outlive us at last—
Better to fall by the hands that they
    love, than to fall into theirs!'
Roar upon roar in a moment two
    mines by the enemy sprung
Clove into perilous chasms our walls
    and our poor palisades.
Rifleman, true is your heart, but be
    sure that your hand be as true!
Sharp is the fire of assault, better
    aimed are your flank fusil-
    lades—
Twice do we hurl them to earth from
    the ladders to which they had
    clung,
Twice from the ditch where they shel-
    ter we drive them with hand-
    grenades;
And ever upon the topmost roof our
    banner of England blew.   60

V

Then on another wild morning an-
    other wild earthquake out-tore
Clean from our lines of defence ten or
    twelve good paces or more.
Rifleman, high on the roof, hidden
    there from the light of the
    sun—
One has leapt up on the breach, crying
    out: 'Follow me, follow me!'—
Mark him—he falls! then another,
    and him too, and down goes he.
Had they been bold enough then, who
    can tell but the traitors had
    won?
Boardings and rafters and door—an
    embrasure! make way for the
    gun!

Now double-charge it with grape! It
    is charged and we fire, and they
    run.
Praise to our Indian brothers, and let
    the dark face have his due!
Thanks to the kindly dark faces who
    fought with us, faithful and
    few,   70
Fought with the bravest among us,
    and drove them, and smote
    them, and slew,
That ever upon the topmost roof our
    banner in India blew.

VI

Men will forget what we suffer and
    not what we do. We can fight!
But to be soldier all day, and be sen-
    tinel all thro' the night—
Ever the mine and assault, our sallies,
    their lying alarms,
Bugles and drums in the darkness, and
    shoutings and soundings to
    arms,
Ever the labor of fifty that had to be
    done by five,
Ever the marvel among us that one
    should be left alive,
Ever the day with its traitorous death
    from the loopholes around,
Ever the night with its coffinless
    corpse to be laid in the ground,
Heat like the mouth of a hell, or a
    deluge of cataract skies,   81
Stench of old offal decaying, and in-
    finite torment of flies,
Thoughts of the breezes of May blow-
    ing over an English field,
Cholera, scurvy, and fever, the wound
    that would not be heal'd,
Lopping away of the limb by the piti-
    ful-pitiless knife,—
Torture and trouble in vain,—for it
    never could save us a life.
Valor of delicate women who tended
    the hospital bed,
Horror of women in travail among the
    dying and dead,
Grief for our perishing children, and
    never a moment for grief,
Toil and ineffable weariness, faltering
    hopes of relief,   90

Havelock baffled, or beaten, or butcher'd for all that we knew—
Then day and night, day and night,
 coming down on the still-shat-
 ter'd walls
Millions of musket-bullets, and thousands of cannon-balls—
But ever upon the topmost roof our
 banner of England blew.

VII

Hark cannonade, fusillade! is it true
 what was told by the scout,
Outram and Havelock breaking their
 way through the fell muti-
 neers?
Surely the pibroch of Europe is ring-
 ing again in our ears!
All on a sudden the garrison utter a
 jubilant shout,
Havelock's glorious Highlanders an-
 swer with conquering cheers,
Sick from the hospital echo them,
 women and children come out,
Blessing the wholesome white faces of
 Havelock's good fusileers, 101
Kissing the war-harden'd hand of the
 Highlander wet with their
 tears!
Dance to the pibroch!—saved! we are
 saved!—is it you? is it you?
Saved by the valor of Havelock, saved
 by the blessing of heaven!
'Hold it for fifteen days!' we have
 held it for eighty-seven!
And ever aloft on the palace roof the
 old banner of England blew.

SIR JOHN OLDCASTLE, LORD COBHAM

(IN WALES)

The subject of this poem was thrown
into the Tower during the reign of Henry
V on a charge of heresy. He escaped to
Wales, where he was captured four years
later and burnt on the gallows as a traitor and heretic.

My friend should meet me somewhere
 hereabout

To take me to that hiding in the hills.

I have broke their cage, no gilded
 one, I trow—
I read no more the prisoner's mute
 wail
Scribbled or carved upon the pitiless
 stone;
I find hard rocks, hard life, hard cheer,
 or none,
For I am emptier than a friar's brains;
But God is with me in this wilderness,
These wet black passes and foam-
 churning chasms—
And God's free air, and hope of bet-
 ter things.   10

I would I knew their speech; not
 now to glean,
Not now—I hope to do it—some scat-
 ter'd ears,
Some ears for Christ in this wild field
 of Wales—
But, bread, merely for bread. This
 tongue that wagg'd
They said with such heretical arro-
 gance
Against the proud archbishop Arun-
 del—
So much God's cause was fluent in it
 —is here
But as a Latin Bible to the crowd;
'Bara!'—what use? The shepherd,
 when I speak,
Vailing a sudden eyelid with his hard
'Dim Saesneg,' passes, wroth at things
 of old—   21
No fault of mine. Had he God's word
 in Welsh
He might be kindlier; happily come
 the day!

Not least art thou, thou little Beth-
 lehem
In Judah, for in thee the Lord was
 born;
Nor thou in Britain, little Lutter-
 worth,
Least, for in thee the word was born
 again.

Heaven-sweet Evangel, ever-living
 word,

Who whilome spakest to the South in
    Greek   29
About the soft Mediterranean shores,
And then in Latin to the Latin crowd,
As good need was—thou hast come to
    talk our isle.
Hereafter thou, fulfilling Pentecost,
Must learn to use the tongues of all
    the world.
Yet art thou thine own witness that
    thou bringest
Not peace, a sword, a fire.
                What did he say,
My frighted Wiclif-preacher whom I
    crost
In flying hither? that one night a
    crowd
Throng'd the waste field about the
    city gates;
The king was on them suddenly with
    a host.   40
Why there? they came to hear their
    preacher. Then
Some cried on Cobham, on the good
    Lord Cobham;
Ay, for they love me! but the king—
    nor voice
Nor finger raised against him—took
    and hang'd,
Took, hang'd and burnt—how many
    —thirty-nine—
Call'd it rebellion—hang'd, poor
    friends, as rebels
And burn'd alive as heretics! for your
    priest
Labels—to take the king along with
    him—
All heresy, treason; but to call men
    traitors
May make men traitors.
               Rose of Lancaster,
Red in thy birth, redder with house-
    hold war,   51
Now reddest with the blood of holy
    men,
Redder to be, red rose of Lancaster,
If somewhere in the North, as Rumor
    sang
Fluttering the hawks of this crown-
    lusting line—
By firth and loch thy silver sister
    grow,[1]

[1] Richard II.

That were my rose, there my alle-
    giance due.
Self-starved, they say—nay, mur-
    der'd, doubtless dead.
So to this king I cleaved. My friend
    was he,
Once my fast friend; I would have
    given my life   60
To help his own from scathe, a thou-
    sand lives
To save his soul. He might have come
    to learn
Our Wiclif's learning; but the worldly
    priests,
Who fear the king's hard common-
    sense should find
What rotten piles uphold their mason-
    work,
Urge him to foreign war. O, had he
    will'd
I might have stricken a lusty stroke
    for him,
But he would not; far liever led my
    friend
Back to the pure and universal
    church,
But he would not—whether that heir-
    less flaw   70
In his throne's title make him feel so
    frail,
He leans on Antichrist; or that his
    mind,
So quick, so capable in soldiership,
In matters of the faith, alas the while!
More worth than all the kingdoms of
    this world,
Runs in the rut, a coward to the priest.

    Burnt—good Sir Roger Acton, my
    dear friend!
Burnt too, my faithful preacher, Bev-
    erley!
Lord, give thou power to thy two wit-
    nesses,
Lest the false faith make merry over
    them!   80
Two—nay, but thirty-nine have risen
    and stand,
Dark with the smoke of human sacri-
    fice,
Before thy light, and cry continu-
    ally—

Cry—against whom?
        Him, who should bear the sword
Of Justice—what! the kingly, kindly
        boy;
Who took the world so easily hereto-
        fore,
My boon companion, tavern-fellow—
        him
Who jibed and japed—in many a
        merry tale
That shook our sides—at pardoners,
        summoners,
Friars, absolution-sellers, monkeries
And nunneries, when the wild hour
        and the wine   91
Had set the wits aflame.
                    Harry of Monmouth,
Or Amurath of the East?
                        Better to sink
Thy fleurs-de-lys in slime again, and
        fling
Thy royalty back into the riotous fits
Of wine and harlotry—thy shame, and
        mine,
Thy comrade—than to persecute the
        Lord,
And play the Saul that never will be
        Paul.

    Burnt, burnt! and while this mitred
        Arundel
Dooms our unlicensed preacher to the
        flame,   100
The mitre-sanction'd harlot draws his
        clerks
Into the suburb—their hard celibacy,
Sworn to be veriest ice of pureness,
        molten
Into adulterous living, or such crimes
As holy Paul—a shame to speak of
        them—
Among the heathen—
                    Sanctuary granted
To bandit, thief, assassin—yea, to
        him
Who hacks his mother's throat—de-
        nied to him
Who finds the Saviour in his mother
        tongue.
The Gospel, the priest's pearl, flung
        down to swine—   110
The swine, lay-men, lay-women, who
        will come,

God willing, to outlearn the filthy
        friar.
Ah, rather, Lord, than that thy Gos-
        pel, meant
To course and range thro' all the
        world, should be
Tether'd to these dead pillars of the
        Church—
Rather than so, if thou wilt have it so,
Burst vein, snap sinew, and crack
        heart, and life
Pass in the fire of Babylon! but how
        long,
O Lord, how long!
            My friend should meet me here.
Here is the copse, the fountain and—
        a cross!   120
To thee, dead wood, I bow not head
        nor knees.
Rather to thee, green boscage, work
        of God,
Black holly, and white-flower'd way-
        faring-tree!
Rather to thee, thou living water,
        drawn
By this good Wiclif mountain down
        from heaven,
And speaking clearly in thy native
        tongue—
No Latin—He that thirsteth, come
        and drink!

    Eh! how I anger'd Arundel asking
        me
To worship Holy Cross! I spread mine
        arms,
God's work, I said, a cross of flesh and
        blood   30
And holier. That was heresy.—My
        good friend
By this time should be with me.—'Im-
        ages?'
'Bury them as God's truer images
Are daily buried.' 'Heresy.—Pen-
        ance?' 'Fast,
Hair-shirt and scourge—nay, let a
        man repent,
Do penance in his heart, God hears
        him.' 'Heresy—
Not shriven, not saved?' 'What prof-
        its an ill priest
Between me and my God? I would not
        spurn

Good counsel of good friends, but
    shrive myself—
No, not to an Apostle.' 'Heresy.'— 140
My friend is long in coming.—'Pil-
    grimages?'
'Drink, bagpipes, revelling, devil's-
    dances, vice.
The poor man's money gone to fat the
    friar.
Who reads of begging saints in Scrip-
    ture?'—'Heresy'—
Hath he been here—not found me—
    gone again?
Have I mislearnt our place of meet-
    ing?—'Bread—
Bread left after the blessing?' how
    they stared,
That was their main test-question—
    glared at me!
'He veil'd Himself in flesh, and now
    He veils
His flesh in bread, body and bread to-
    gether.'   150
Then rose the howl of all the cassock'd
    wolves,
'No bread, no bread. God's body!'
    Archbishop, bishop,
Priors, canons, friars, bell-ringers,
    parish-clerks—
'No bread, no bread!'—'Authority of
    the Church,
Power of the keys!'—Then I, God
    help me, I
So mock'd, so spurn'd, so baited two
    whole days—
I lost myself and fell from evenness,
And rail'd at all the Popes that, ever
    since
Sylvester shed the venom of world-
    wealth
Into the church, had only proven   160
    themselves
Poisoners, murderers. Well—God par-
    don all—
Me, them, and all the world—yea,
    that proud priest,
That mock-meek mouth of utter An-
    tichrist,
That traitor to King Richard and the
    truth,
Who rose and doom'd me to the fire.
            Amen!

Nay, I can burn, so that the Lord of
    life
Be by me in my death.
          Those three! the fourth
Was like the Son of God! Not burnt
    were they.
On *them* the smell of burning had not
    past.
That was a miracle to convert the   170
    king.
These Pharisees, this Caiaphas-Arun-
    del
What miracle could turn? *He* here
    again,
He thwarting their traditions of Him-
    self,
He would be found a heretic to Him-
    self,
And doom'd to burn alive.
          So, caught, I burn.
Burn? heathen men have borne as
    much as this,
For freedom, or the sake of those
    they loved,
Or some less cause, some cause far less
    than mine;
For every other cause is less than
    mine.
The moth will singe her wings, and   180
    singed return,
Her love of light quenching her fear
    of pain—
How now, my soul, we do not heed the
    fire?
Faint-hearted? tut!—faint-stom-
    ach'd! faint as I am,
God willing, I will burn for Him.
          Who comes?
A thousand marks are set upon my
    head.
Friend?—foe perhaps—a tussle for it
    then!
Nay, but my friend. Thou art so well
    disguised,
I knew thee not. Hast thou brought
    bread with thee?
I have not broken bread for fifty
    hours.
None? I am damn'd already by the   190
    priest
For holding there was bread where
    bread was none—

No bread. My friends await me yon-
    der? Yes.
Lead on then. *Up* the mountain? Is it
    far?
Not far. Climb first and reach me
    down thy hand.
I am not like to die for lack of bread,
For I must live to testify by fire.[1]

COLUMBUS

CHAINS, my good lord! In your raised
    brows I read
Some wonder at our chamber orna-
    ments.
We brought this iron from our isles of
    gold.

Does the King know you deign to
    visit him
Whom once he rose from off his
    throne to greet
Before his people, like his brother
    king?
I saw your face that morning in the
    crowd.

At Barcelona—tho' you were not
    then
So bearded. Yes. The city deck'd her-
    self
To meet me, roar'd my name; the
    King, the Queen,   10
Bade me be seated, speak, and tell
    them all
The story of my voyage, and while I
    spoke
The crowd's roar fell as at the 'Peace,
    be still!'
And when I ceased to speak, the King,
    the Queen,
Sank from their thrones, and melted
    into tears,
And knelt, and lifted hand and heart
    and voice
In praise to God who led me thro' the
    waste.
And then the great 'Laudamus' rose to
    heaven.

[1] He was burnt on Christmas Day, 1417.

Chains for the Admiral of the
    Ocean! chains
For him who gave a new heaven, a
    new earth,   20
As holy John had prophesied of me,
Gave glory and more empire to the
    kings
Of Spain than all their battles! chains
    for him
Who push'd his prows into the setting
    sun,
And made West East, and sail'd the
    Dragon's Mouth,
And came upon the Mountain of the
    World,
And saw the rivers roll from Paradise!

Chains! we are Admirals of the
    Ocean, we,
We and our sons for ever. Ferdinand
Hath sign'd it and our Holy Catholic
    Queen—   30
Of the Ocean—of the Indies—Ad-
    mirals we—
Our title, which we never mean to
    yield,
Our guerdon not alone for what we
    did,
But our amends for all we might have
    done—
The vast occasion of our stronger
    life—
Eighteen long years of waste, seven in
    your Spain,
Lost, showing courts and kings a truth
    the babe
Will suck in with his milk hereafter—
    earth
A sphere.

    Were *you* at Salamanca? No.
We fronted there the learning of all
    Spain,   40
All their cosmogonies, their astrono-
    mies.
Guess-work *they* guess'd it, but the
    golden guess
Is morning-star to the full round of
    truth.
No guess-work! I was certain of my
    goal;
Some thought it heresy, but that
    would not hold.

King David call'd the heavens a hide,
    a tent
Spread over earth, and so this earth
    was flat.
Some cited old Lactantius; could it be
That trees grew downward, rain fell
    upward, men
Walk'd like the fly on ceilings? and be-
    sides,   50
The great Augustine wrote that none
    could breathe
Within the zone of heat; so might
    there be
Two Adams, two mankinds, and that
    was clean
Against God's word. Thus was I beaten
    back,
And chiefly to my sorrow by the
    Church,
And thought to turn my face from
    Spain, appeal
Once more to France or England; but
    our Queen
Recall'd me, for at last their High-
    nesses
Were half-assured this earth might be
    a sphere.   59

All glory to the all-blessed Trinity,
All glory to the mother of our Lord,
And Holy Church, from whom I never
    swerved
Not even by one hair's-breadth of
    heresy,
I have accomplish'd what I came to
    do.

    Not yet—not all—last night a
    dream—I sail'd
On my first voyage, harass'd by the
    frights
Of my first crew, their curses and their
    groans.
The great flame-banner borne by
    Teneriffe,
The compass, like an old friend false
    at last
In our most need, appall'd them, and
    the wind   70
Still westward, and the weedy seas—
    at length
The land-bird, and the branch with
    berries on it,

The carven staff—and last the light,
    the light
On Guanahani! but I changed the
    name;
San Salvador I call'd it; and the light
Grew as I gazed, and brought out a
    broad sky
Of dawning over—not those alien
    palms,
The marvel of that fair new nature—
    not
That Indian isle, but our most ancient
    East,   79
Moriah with Jerusalem; and I saw
The glory of the Lord flash up, and
    beat
Thro' all the homely town from jas-
    per, sapphire,
Chalcedony, emerald, sardonyx, sar-
    dius,
Chrysolite, beryl, topaz, chrysoprase,
Jacynth, and amethyst—and those
    twelve gates,
Pearl—and I woke, and thought—
    death—I shall die—
I am written in the Lamb's own Book
    of Life
To walk within the glory of the Lord
Sunless and moonless, utter light—
    but no!
The Lord had sent this bright strange
    dream to me   90
To mind me of the secret vow I made
When Spain was waging war against
    the Moor—
I strove myself with Spain against the
    Moor.
There came two voices from the Sep-
    ulchre,
Two friars crying that, if Spain should
    oust
The Moslem from her limit, he, the
    fierce
Soldan of Egypt, would break down
    and raze
The blessed tomb of Christ; whereon
    I vow'd
That, if our princes harken'd to my
    prayer,
Whatever wealth I brought from that
    new world   100
Should, in this old, be consecrate to
    lead

A new crusade against the Saracen,
And free the Holy Sepulchre from
   thrall.

  Gold? I had brought your princes
   gold enough
If left alone! Being but a Genovese,
I am handled worse than had I been
   a Moor,
And breach'd the belting wall of
   Cambalu,
And given the Great Khan's palaces to
   the Moor,
Or clutch'd the sacred crown of Pres-
   ter John,
And cast it to the Moor. But *had* I
   brought   110
From Solomon's now-recover'd Ophir
   all
The gold that Solomon's navies car-
   ried home,
Would that have gilded *me?* Blue
   blood of Spain,
Tho' quartering your own royal arms
   of Spain,
I have not; blue blood and black blood
   of Spain,
The noble and the convict of Castile,
Howl'd me from Hispaniola. For you
   know
The flies at home, that ever swarm
   about
And cloud the highest heads, and mur-
   mur down
Truth in the distance—these out-
   buzz'd me so   120
That even our prudent King, our
   righteous Queen—
I pray'd them being so calumniated
They would commission one of weight
   and worth
To judge between my slander'd self
   and me—
Fonseca my main enemy at their
   court,
They sent me out *his* tool, Bovadilla,
   one
As ignorant and impolitic as a beast—
Blockish irreverence, brainless greed
   —who sack'd
My dwelling, seized upon my papers,
   loosed

My captives, feed the rebels of the
   crown,   130
Sold the crown-farms for all but noth-
   ing, gave
All but free leave for all to work the
   mines,
Drove me and my good brothers home
   in chains,
And gathering ruthless gold—a single
   piece
Weigh'd nigh four thousand Castil-
   lanos—so
They tell me—weigh'd him down into
   the abysm—
The hurricane of the latitude on him
   fell,
The seas of our discovering over-roll
Him and his gold; the frailer caravel,
With what was mine, came happily to
   the shore.   140
There was a glimmering of God's
   hand.

              And God
Hath more than glimmer'd on me. O
   my lord,
I swear to you I heard His voice be-
   tween
The thunders in the black Veragua
   nights,
'O soul of little faith, slow to believe!
Have I not been about thee from thy
   birth?
Given thee the keys of the great
   Ocean-sea?
Set thee in light till time shall be no
   more?
Is it I who have deceived thee or the
   world?
Endure! thou hast done so well for
   men, that men   150
Cry out against thee. Was it otherwise
With mine own Son?'

          And more than once in days
Of doubt and cloud and storm, when
   drowning hope
Sank all but out of sight, I heard His
   voice,
'Be not cast down. I lead thee by the
   hand,
Fear not.' And I shall hear His voice
   again—

I know that He has led me all my life,
I am not yet too old to work His
    will—
His voice again.

Still for all that, my lord,
I lying here bedridden and alone, [160]
Cast off, put by, scouted by court and
    king—
The first discoverer starves—his fol-
    lowers, all
Flower into fortune—our world's way
    —and I,
Without a roof that I can call mine
    own,
With scarce a coin to buy a meal
    withal,
And seeing what a door for scoundrel
    scum
I open'd to the West, thro' which the
    lust,
Villainy, violence, avarice, of your
    Spain
Pour'd in on all those happy naked
    isles—
Their kindly native princes slain or
    slaved, [170]
Their wives and children Spanish con-
    cubines,
Their innocent hospitalities quench'd
    in blood,
Some dead of hunger, some beneath
    the scourge,
Some over-labor'd, some by their own
    hands,—
Yea, the dear mothers, crazing Na-
    ture, kill
Their babies at the breast for hate of
    Spain—
Ah God, the harmless people whom we
    found
In Hispaniola's island-Paradise!
Who took us for the very gods from
    heaven,
And we have sent them very fiends
    from hell; [180]
And I myself, myself not blameless, I
Could sometimes wish I had never led
    the way.

Only the ghost of our great Catholic
    Queen

Smiles on me, saying, 'Be thou com-
    forted!
This creedless people will be brought
    to Christ
And own the holy governance of
    Rome.'

But who could dream that we, who
    bore the Cross
Thither, were excommunicated there,
For curbing crimes that scandalized
    the Cross,
By him, the Catalonian Minorite, [190]
Rome's Vicar in our Indies? who be-
    lieve
These hard memorials of our truth to
    Spain
Clung closer to us for a longer term
Than any friend of ours at Court? and
    yet
Pardon—too harsh, unjust. I am
    rack'd with pains.

You see that I have hung them by
    my bed,
And I will have them buried in my
    grave.

Sir, in that flight of ages which are
    God's
Own voice to justify the dead—per-
    chance
Spain, once the most chivalric race on
    earth, [200]
Spain, then the mightiest, wealthiest
    realm on earth,
So made by me, may seek to unbury
    me,
To lay me in some shrine of this old
    Spain,
Or in that vaster Spain I leave to
    Spain.
Then some one standing by my grave
    will say,
'Behold the bones of Christopher Co-
    lòn'—
'Ay, but the chains, what do *they*
    mean—the chains?'—
I sorrow for that kindly child of Spain
Who then will have to answer, 'These
    same chains
Bound these same bones back thro'
    the Atlantic sea, [210]

Which he unchain'd for all the world
    to come.'

    O Queen of Heaven who seest the
        souls in hell
And purgatory, I suffer all as much
As they do—for the moment. Stay,
    my son
Is here anon; my son will speak for
    me
Ablier than I can in these spasms that
    grind
Bone against bone. You will not. One
    last word.

    You move about the Court; I pray
        you tell
King Ferdinand who plays with me,
    that one
Whose life has been no play with him
    and his   220
    vers, fights,
Hidalgos—shipwrecks, famines, fe-
Mutinies, treacheries—wink'd at, and
    condoned—
That I am loyal to him till the death,
And ready—tho' our Holy Catholic
    Queen,
Who fain had pledged her jewels on
    my first voyage,
Whose hope was mine to spread the
    Catholic faith,
Who wept with me when I return'd in
    chains,
Who sits beside the blessed Virgin
    now,
To whom I send my prayer by night
    and day—
She is gone—but you will tell the
    King, that I,   230
Rack'd as I am with gout, and
    wrench'd with pains
Gain'd in the service of His Highness,
    yet
Am ready to sail forth on one last
    voyage,
And readier, if the King would hear,
    to lead
One last crusade against the Saracen,
And save the Holy Sepulchre from
    thrall.

    Going? I am old and slighted; you
    have dared

Somewhat perhaps in coming? my
    poor thanks!
I am but an alien and a Genovese.

THE VOYAGE OF MAELDUNE

(FOUNDED ON AN IRISH LEGEND.
A. D. 700)

I

I was the chief of the race—he had
    stricken my father dead—
But I gather'd my fellows together, I
    swore I would strike off his
    head.
Each of them look'd like a king, and
    was noble in birth as in worth,
And each of them boasted he sprang
    from the oldest race upon
    earth.
Each was as brave in the fight as the
    bravest hero of song,
And each of them liefer had died than
    have done one another a
    wrong.
He lived on an isle in the ocean—we
    sail'd on a Friday morn—
He that had slain my father the day
    before I was born.

II

And we came to the isle in the ocean,
    and there on the shore was he.
But a sudden blast blew us out and
    away thro' a boundless sea.   10

III

And we came to the Silent Isle that we
    never had touch'd at before,
Where a silent ocean always broke on
    a silent shore,
And the brooks glitter'd on in the light
    without sound, and the long
    waterfalls
Pour'd in a thunderless plunge to the
    base of the mountain walls,
And the poplar and cypress unshaken
    by storm flourish'd up beyond
    sight,

And the pine shot aloft from the crag
    to an unbelievable height,
And high in the heaven above it there
    flicker'd a songless lark,
And the cock could n't crow, and the
    bull could n't low, and the dog
    could n't bark.
And round it we went, and thro' it, but
    never a murmur, a breath—
It was all of it fair as life, it was all
    of it quiet as death,   20
And we hated the beautiful isle, for
    whenever we strove to speak
Our voices were thinner and fainter
    than any flittermouse-shriek;
And the men that were mighty of
    tongue and could raise such a
    battle-cry
That a hundred who heard it would
    rush on a thousand lances and
    die—
O, they to be dumb'd by the charm!—
    so fluster'd with anger were
    they
They almost fell on each other; but
    after we sail'd away.

IV

And we came to the Isle of Shouting;
    we landed, a score of wild birds
Cried from the topmost summit with
    human voices and words.
Once in an hour they cried, and when-
    ever their voices peal'd
The steer fell down at the plow and
    the harvest died from the field,
And the men dropt dead in the valleys
    and half of the cattle went
    lame,   31
And the roof sank in on the hearth,
    and the dwelling broke into
    flame;
And the shouting of these wild birds
    ran into the hearts of my crew,
Till they shouted along with the shout-
    ing and seized one another and
    slew.
But I drew them the one from the
    other; I saw that we could not
    stay,
And we left the dead to the birds, and
    we sail'd with our wounded
    away.

V

And we came to the Isle of Flowers;
    their breath met us out on the
    seas,
For the Spring and the middle Sum-
    mer sat each on the lap of the
    breeze;
And the red passion-flower to the
    cliffs, and the dark-blue clem-
    atis, clung,
And starr'd with a myriad blossom the
    long convolvulus hung;   40
And the topmost spire of the moun-
    tain was lilies in lieu of snow,
And the lilies like glaciers winded
    down, running out below
Thro' the fire of the tulip and poppy,
    the blaze of gorse, and the
    blush
Of millions of roses that sprang with-
    out leaf or a thorn from the
    bush;
And the whole isle-side flashing down
    from the peak without ever a
    tree
Swept like a torrent of gems from the
    sky to the blue of the sea.
And we roll'd upon capes of crocus
    and vaunted our kith and our
    kin,
And we wallow'd in beds of lilies, and
    chanted the triumph of Finn,
Till each like a golden image was pol-
    len'd from head to feet
And each was as dry as a cricket, with
    thirst in the middle-day heat.
Blossom and blossom, and promise of
    blossom, but never a fruit!   51
And we hated the Flowering Isle, as
    we hated the isle that was
    mute,
And we tore up the flowers by the mil-
    lion and flung them in bight
    and bay,
And we left but a naked rock, and in
    anger we sail'd away.

VI

And we came to the Isle of Fruits; all
    round from the cliffs and the
    capes,

Purple or amber, dangled a hundred
    fathom of grapes,
And the warm melon lay like a little
    sun on the tawny sand,
And the fig ran up from the beach and
    rioted over the land,
And the mountain arose like a jewell'd
    throne thro' the fragrant air,
Glowing with all-color'd plums and
    with golden masses of pear,   60
And the crimson and scarlet of berries
    that flamed upon bine and vine,
But in every berry and fruit was the
    poisonous pleasure of wine;
And the peak of the mountain was ap-
    ples, the hugest that ever were
    seen,
And they prest, as they grew, on each
    other, with hardly a leaflet be-
    tween,
And all of them redder than rosiest
    health or than utterest shame,
And setting, when Even descended,
    the very sunset aflame.
And we stay'd three days, and we
    gorged and we madden'd, till
    every one drew
His sword on his fellow to slay him,
    and ever they struck and they
    slew;
And myself, I had eaten but sparely,
    and fought till I sunder'd the
    fray,
Then I bade them remember my
    father's death, and we sail'd
    away.   70

VII

And we came to the Isle of Fire; we
    were lured by the light from
    afar,
For the peak sent up one league of fire
    to the Northern Star;
Lured by the glare and the blare, but
    scarcely could stand upright,
For the whole isle shudder'd and shook
    like a man in a mortal affright.
We were giddy besides with the fruits
    we had gorged, and so crazed
    that at last
There were some leap'd into the fire;
    and away we sail'd, and we past

Over that undersea isle, where the
    water is clearer than air.
Down we look'd—what a garden! O
    bliss, what a Paradise there!
Towers of a happier time, low down
    in a rainbow deep
Silent palaces, quiet fields of eternal
    sleep!   80
And three of the gentlest and best of
    my people, whate'er I could
    say,
Plunged head-down in the sea, and the
    Paradise trembled away.

VIII

And we came to the Bounteous Isle,
    where the heavens lean low on
    the land,
And ever at dawn from the cloud glit-
    ter'd o'er us a sun-bright hand,
Then it open'd and dropt at the side
    of each man, as he rose from
    his rest,
Bread enough for his need till the
    laborless day dipt under the
    west;
And we wander'd about it and thro'
    it. O, never was time so good!
And we sang of the triumphs of Finn,
    and the boast of our ancient
    blood,
And we gazed at the wandering wave
    as we sat by the gurgle of
    springs,
And we chanted the songs of the
    Bards and the glories of fairy
    kings.   90
But at length we began to be weary,
    to sigh, and to stretch and
    yawn,
Till we hated the Bounteous Isle and
    the sun-bright hand of the
    dawn,
For there was not an enemy near, but
    the whole green isle was our
    own,
And we took to playing at ball, and
    we took to throwing the stone,
And we took to playing at battle, but
    that was a perilous play,
For the passion of battle was in us, we
    slew and we sail'd away.

IX

And we came to the Isle of Witches
    and heard their musical cry—
'Come to us, O come, come!' in the
    stormy red of a sky
Dashing the fires and the shadows of
    dawn on the beautiful shapes,
For a wild witch naked as heaven
    stood on each of the loftiest
    capes,   100
And a hundred ranged on the rock like
    white sea-birds in a row,
And a hundred gamboll'd and pranced
    on the wrecks in the sand be-
    low,
And a hundred splash'd from the
    ledges, and bosom'd the burst
    of the spray;
But I knew we should fall on each
    other, and hastily sail'd away.

X

And we came in an evil time to the
    Isle of the Double Towers,
One was of smooth-cut stone, one
    carved all over with flowers,
But an earthquake always moved in
    the hollows under the dells,
And they shock'd on each other and
    butted each other with clash-
    ing of bells,
And the daws flew out of the towers
    and jangled and wrangled in
    vain,
And the clash and boom of the bells
    rang into the heart and the
    brain,   110
Till the passion of battle was on us,
    and all took sides with the
    towers,
There were some for the clean-cut
    stone, there were more for the
    carven flowers,
And the wrathful thunder of God
    peal'd over us all the day,
For the one half slew the other, and
    after we sail'd away.

XI

And we came to the Isle of a Saint
    who had sail'd with Saint Bren-
    dan of yore,
He had lived ever since on the isle and
    his winters were fifteen score,
And his voice was low as from other
    worlds, and his eyes were
    sweet,
And his white hair sank to his heels,
    and his white beard fell to his
    feet,
And he spake to me: 'O Maeldune, let
    be this purpose of thine!
Remember the words of the Lord
    when he told us, "Vengeance is
    mine!"   120
His fathers have slain thy fathers in
    war or in single strife,
Thy fathers have slain his fathers,
    each taken a life for a life,
Thy father had slain his father, how
    long shall the murder last?
Go back to the Isle of Finn and suffer
    the Past to be Past.'
And we kiss'd the fringe of his beard,
    and we pray'd as we heard him
    pray,
And the holy man he assoil'd us, and
    sadly we sail'd away.

XII

And we came to the isle we were
    blown from, and there on the
    shore was he,
The man that had slain my father. I
    saw him and let him be.
O, weary was I of the travel, the trou-
    ble, the strife, and the sin,   129
When I landed again with a tithe of
    my men, on the Isle of Finn!

DE PROFUNDIS:

THE TWO GREETINGS

I

OUT of the deep, my child, out of the
    deep,

Where all that was to be, in all that
    was,
Whirl'd for a million æons thro' the
    vast
Waste dawn of multitudinous-eddy-
    ing light—
Out of the deep, my child, out of the
    deep,
Thro' all this changing world of
    changeless law,
And every phase of ever-heightening
    life,
And nine long months of antenatal
    gloom,
With this last moon, this crescent—
    her dark orb
Touch'd with earth's light—thou com-
    est, darling boy;
Our own; a babe in lineament and
    limb
Perfect, and prophet of the perfect
    man;
Whose face and form are hers and
    mine in one,
Indissolubly married like our love.
Live, and be happy in thyself, and
    serve
This mortal race thy kin so well that
    men
May bless thee as we bless thee, O
    young life
Breaking with laughter from the dark;
    and may
The fated channel where thy motion
    lives
Be prosperously shaped, and sway thy
    course
Along the years of haste and random
    youth
Unshatter'd; then full-current thro'
    full man;
And last in kindly curves, with gen-
    tlest fall,
By quiet fields, a slowly-dying power,
To that last deep where we and thou
    are still.

II

I

Out of the deep, my child, out of the
    deep,

From that great deep, before our
    world begins,
Whereon the Spirit of God moves as
    he will—
Out of the deep, my child, out of the
    deep,
From that true world within the world
    we see,
Whereof our world is but the bound-
    ing shore—
Out of the deep, Spirit, out of the
    deep,
With this ninth moon, that sends the
    hidden sun
Down yon dark sea, thou comest, dar-
    ling boy.

II

For in the world which is not ours
    They said,
'Let us make man,' and that which
    should be man,
From that one light no man can look
    upon,
Drew to this shore lit by the suns and
    moons
And all the shadows. O dear Spirit,
    half-lost
In thine own shadow and this fleshly
    sign
That thou art thou—who wailest be-
    ing born
And banish'd into mystery, and the
    pain
Of this divisible-indivisible world
Among the numerable-innumerable
Sun, sun, and sun, thro' finite-infinite
    space
In finite-infinite Time—our mortal
    veil
And shatter'd phantom of that infinite
    One,
Who made thee unconceivably Thy-
    self
Out of His whole World-self and all in
    all—
Live thou! and of the grain and husk,
    the grape
And ivy-berry, choose; and still de-
    part
From death to death thro' life and life,
    and find

Nearer and ever nearer Him, who wrought
Not matter, nor the finite-infinite,
But this main-miracle, that thou art thou,
With power on thine own act and on the world.

THE HUMAN CRY

I

HALLOWED be Thy name—Hallelu-
        iah!—
    Infinite Ideality!
    Immeasurable Realty!
    Infinite Personality!
Hallowed be Thy name—Halleluiah!

II

We feel we are nothing—for all is Thou and in Thee;
We feel we are something—*that* also has come from Thee;
We know we are nothing—but Thou wilt help us to be.
Hallowed be Thy name—Halleluiah!

SONNETS

PREFATORY SONNET

TO 'THE NINETEENTH CENTURY'

THOSE that of late had fleeted far and fast
To touch all shores, now leaving to the skill
Of others their old craft seaworthy still,
Have charter'd this; where, mindful of the past,
Our true co-mates regather round the mast;
Of diverse tongue, but with a common will
Here, in this roaring moon of daffodil
And crocus, to put forth and brave the blast.
For some, descending from the sacred peak

Of hoar high-templed Faith, have leagued again
Their lot with ours to rove the world about;
And some are wilder comrades, sworn to seek
If any golden harbor be for men
In seas of Death and sunless gulfs of Doubt.

TO THE REV. W. H. BROOK-
FIELD

BROOKS, for they call'd you so that knew you best,
Old Brooks, who loved so well to mouth my rhymes,
How oft we two have heard Saint Mary's chimes!
How oft the Cantab supper, host and guest,
Would echo helpless laughter to your jest!
How oft with him we paced that walk of limes,
Him, the lost light of those dawn-golden times,
Who loved you well! Now both are gone to rest.
You man of humorous-melancholy mark,
Dead of some inward agony—is it so?
Our kindlier, trustier Jaques, past away!
I cannot laud this life, it looks so dark.
Σκιᾶς ὄναρ—dream of a shadow, go—
God bless you! I shall join you in a day.

MONTENEGRO

THEY rose to where their sovran eagle sails,
They kept their faith, their freedom, on the height,
Chaste, frugal, savage, arm'd by day and night
Against the Turk; whose inroad no-where scales

Their headlong passes, but his foot-
     step fails,
And red with blood the Crescent reels
     from fight
Before their dauntless hundreds, in
     prone flight
By thousands down the crags and
     thro' the vales.
O smallest among peoples! rough
     rock-throne
Of Freedom! warriors beating back
     the swarm
Of Turkish Islam for five hundred
     years,
Great Tsernogora! never since thine
     own
Black ridges drew the cloud and brake
     the storm
Has breathed a race of mightier moun-
     taineers.

TO VICTOR HUGO

VICTOR in Drama, Victor in Romance,
Cloud-weaver of phantasmal hopes
     and fears,
French of the French, and Lord of
     human tears;
Child-lover; Bard whose fame-lit lau-
     rels glance
Darkening the wreaths of all that
     would advance,
Beyond our strait, their claim to be
     thy peers;
Weird Titan by thy winter weight of
     years
As yet unbroken, stormy voice of
     France!
Who dost not love our England—so
     they say;
I know not—England, France, all man
     to be
Will make one people ere man's race
     be run:
And I, desiring that diviner day,
Yield thee full thanks for thy full
     courtesy
To younger England in the boy my
     son.

TRANSLATIONS, ETC.

BATTLE OF BRUNANBURH

'Constantinus, King of the Scots, after
having sworn allegiance to Athelstan, allied himself with the Danes of Ireland
under Anlaf, and invading England, was
defeated by Athelstan and his brother
Edmund with great slaughter at Brunanburh in the year 937.'

I

[1] ATHELSTAN King,
Lord among Earls,
Bracelet-bestower and
Baron of Barons,
He with his brother,
Edmund Atheling,
Gaining a lifelong
Glory in battle,
Slew with the sword-edge
There by Brunanburh,
Brake the shield-wall,
Hew'd the linden-wood,[2]
Hack'd the battle-shield,
Sons of Edward with hammer'd
     brands

II

Theirs was a greatness
Got from their grandsires—
Theirs that so often in
Strife with their enemies
Struck for their hoards and their
     hearts and their homes.

III

Bow'd the spoiler,
Bent the Scotsman,
Fell the ship-crews
Doom'd to the death.
All the field with blood of the fighters
     Flow'd, from when first the great
     Sun-star of morning-tide,

[1] I have more or less availed myself of
my son's prose translation of this poem
in the *Contemporary Review* (November, 1876).
     [2] Shields of lindenwood.

Lamp of the Lord God
Lord everlasting,
Glode over earth till the glorious crea-
ture
Sank to his setting.

IV

There lay many a man
Marr'd by the javelin,
Men of the Northland
Shot over shield.
There was the Scotsman
Weary of war.

V

We the West-Saxons,
Long as the daylight
Lasted, in companies
Troubled the track of the host that we
hated;
Grimly with swords that were sharp
from the grindstone,
Fiercely we hack'd at the flyers before
us.

VI

Mighty the Mercian,
Hard was his hand-play,
Sparing not any of
Those that with Anlaf,
Warriors over the
Weltering waters
Borne in the bark's-bosom,
Drew to this island—
Doom'd to the death.

VII

Five young kings put asleep by the
sword-stroke,
Seven strong earls of the army of
Anlaf
Fell on the war-field, numberless num-
bers,
Shipmen and Scotsmen.

VIII

Then the Norse leader—
Dire was his need of it,

Few were his following—
Fled to his war-ship;
Fleeted his vessel to sea with the king
in it,
Saving his life on the fallow flood.

IX

Also the crafty one
Constantinus,
Crept to his North again,
Hoar-headed hero!

X

Slender warrant had
He to be proud of
The welcome of war-knives—
He that was reft of his
Folk and his friends that had
Fallen in conflict,
Leaving his son too
Lost in the carnage,
Mangled to morsels,
A youngster in war!

XI

Slender reason had
He to be glad of
The clash of the war-glaive—
Traitor and trickster
And spurner of treaties—
He nor had Anlaf
With armies so broken
A reason for bragging
That they had the better
In perils of battle
On places of slaughter—
The struggle of standards,
The rush of the javelins,
The crash of the charges,[1]
The wielding of weapons—
The play that they play'd with
The children of Edward.

XII

Then with their nail'd prows
Parted the Norsemen, a
Blood-redden'd relic of
Javelins over

[1] Lit. 'the gathering of men.'

The jarring breaker, the deep-sea billow,
Shaping their way toward Dyflen [1]
again,
Shamed in their souls.

XIII

Also the brethren,
King and Atheling,
Each in his glory,
Went to his own in his own West-
Saxon-land,
Glad of the war.

XIV

Many a carcase they left to be carrion,
Many a livid one, many a sallow-
skin—
Left for the white-tail'd eagle to tear
it, and
Left for the horny-nibb'd raven to
rend it, and
Gave to the garbaging war-hawk to
gorge it, and
That gray beast, the wolf of the weald.

XV

Never had huger
Slaughter of heroes
Slain by the sword-edge—
Such as old writers
Have writ of in histories—
Hapt in this isle, since
Up from the East hither
Saxon and Angle from
Over the broad billow
Broke into Britain with
Haughty war-workers who
Harried the Welshman, when
Earls that were lured by the
Hunger of glory gat
Hold of the land.

ACHILLES OVER THE TRENCH

[ILIAD, XVIII. 202]

So SAYING, light-foot Iris pass'd away.
Then rose Achilles dear to Zeus; and
round

[1] Dublin.

The warrior's puissant shoulders Pal-
las flung
Her fringed ægis, and around his head
The glorious goddess wreath'd a
golden cloud,
And from it lighted an all-shining
flame.
As when a smoke from a city goes to
heaven
Far off from out an island girt by foes,
All day the men contend in grievous
war
From their own city, but with set of
sun
Their fires flame thickly, and aloft the
glare
Flies streaming, if perchance the
neighbors round
May see, and sail to help them in the
war;
So from his head the splendor went to
heaven.
From wall to dyke he stept, he stood,
nor join'd
The Achæans—honoring his wise
mother's word—
There standing, shouted, and Pallas
far away
Call'd; and a boundless panic shook
the foe.
For like the clear voice when a trum-
pet shrills,
Blown by the fierce beleaguerers of a
town,
So rang the clear voice of Æakidês;
And when the brazen cry of Æakidês
Was heard among the Trojans, all
their hearts
Were troubled, and the full-maned
horses whirl'd
The chariots backward, knowing griefs
at hand;
And sheer-astounded were the chari-
oteers
To see the dread, unweariable fire
That always o'er the great Peleion's
head
Burn'd, for the bright-eyed goddess
made it burn.
Thrice from the dyke he sent his
mighty shout,
Thrice backward reel'd the Trojans
and allies;

And there and then twelve of their
noblest died
Among their spears and chariots.

TO PRINCESS FREDERICA ON
HER MARRIAGE

O you that were eyes and light to the
King till he past away
From the darkness of life—
He saw not his daughter—he blest
her: the blind King sees you
to-day,
He blesses the wife.

SIR JOHN FRANKLIN

ON THE CENOTAPH IN WESTMINSTER
ABBEY

Not here! the white North has thy
bones; and thou,

Heroic sailor-soul,
Art passing on thine happier voyage
now
Toward no earthly pole.

TO DANTE

(WRITTEN AT REQUEST OF THE
FLORENTINES)

King, that hast reign'd six hundred
years, and grown
In power, and ever growest, since
thine own
Fair Florence honoring thy nativity,
Thy Florence now the crown of Italy,
Hath sought the tribute of a verse
from me,
I, wearing but the garland of a day,
Cast at thy feet one flower that fades
away.

TIRESIAS AND OTHER POEMS

DEDICATION

TO MY GOOD FRIEND

ROBERT BROWNING

WHOSE GENIUS AND GENIALITY
WILL BEST APPRECIATE WHAT MAY BE BEST
AND MAKE MOST ALLOWANCE FOR WHAT MAY BE WORST
THIS VOLUME
IS
AFFECTIONATELY DEDICATED

TO E. FITZGERALD

Fitzgerald was seventy-five when this
was written in 1883. He died shortly
after, before it was published.

OLD FITZ, who from your suburb
    grange,
  Where once I tarried for a while,
Glance at the wheeling orb of change,
  And greet it with a kindly smile;
Whom yet I see as there you sit
  Beneath your sheltering garden-
    tree,
And watch your doves about you flit,
  And plant on shoulder, hand, and
    knee,
Or on your head their rosy feet,
  As if they knew your diet spares
Whatever moved in that full sheet
  Let down to Peter at his prayers;
Who live on milk and meal and grass;
  And once for ten long weeks I tried
Your table of Pythagoras,
  And seem'd at first 'a thing enskied,'
As Shakespeare has it, airy-light
  To float above the ways of men,
Then fell from that half-spiritual
    height
  Chill'd, till I tasted flesh again
One night when earth was winter-
    black,
  And all the heavens flash'd in frost;

And on me, half-asleep, came back
  That wholesome heat the blood had
    lost,
And set me climbing icy capes
  And glaciers, over which there
    roll'd
To meet me long-arm'd vines with
    grapes
  Of Eshcol hugeness; for the cold
Without, and warmth within me,
    wrought
  To mould the dream; but none can
    say
That Lenten fare makes Lenten
    thought,
  Who reads your golden Eastern lay,
Than which I know no version done
  In English more divinely well;
A planet equal to the sun
  Which cast it, that large infidel
Your Omar; and your Omar drew
  Full-handed plaudits from our best
In modern letters, and from two,
  Old friends outvaluing all the rest,
Two voices heard on earth no more;
  But we old friends are still alive,
And I am nearing seventy-four,
  While you have touch'd at seventy-
    five,
And so I send a birthday line
  Of greeting; and my son, who dipt
In some forgotten book of mine
  With sallow scraps of manuscript,

And dating many a year ago,
  Has hit on this, which you will take,
My Fitz, and welcome, as I know,
  Less for its own than for the sake
Of one recalling gracious times,
  When, in our younger London days,
You found some merit in my rhymes,
  And I more pleasure in your praise.

TIRESIAS

I WISH I were as in the years of old,
While yet the blessed daylight made
  itself
Ruddy thro' both the roofs of sight,
  and woke
These eyes, now dull, but then so keen
  to seek
The meanings ambush'd under all they
  saw,
The flight of birds, the flame of sacri-
  fice,
What omens may foreshadow fate to
  man
And woman, and the secret of the
  Gods.
  My son, the Gods, despite of human
    prayer,
Are slower to forgive than human
  kings.   10
The great God Arês burns in anger
  still
Against the guiltless heirs of him from
  Tyre,
Our Cadmus, out of whom thou art,
  who found
Beside the springs of Dircê, smote,
  and still'd
Thro' all its folds the multitudinous
  beast,
The dragon, which our trembling
  fathers call'd
The God's own son.
        A tale, that told to me,
When but thine age, by age as winter-
  white
As mine is now, amazed, but made me
  yearn
For larger glimpses of that more than
  man   20
Which rolls the heavens, and lifts and
  lays the deep,

Yet loves and hates with mortal hates
  and loves,
And moves unseen among the ways of
  men.
  Then, in my wanderings all the
    lands that lie
Subjected to the Heliconian ridge
Have heard this footstep fall, altho'
  my wont
Was more to scale the highest of the
  heights
With some strange hope to see the
  nearer God.
  One naked peak—the sister of the
    Sun
Would climb from out the dark, and
  linger there   30
To silver all the valleys with her
  shafts—
There once, but long ago, five-fold thy
  term
Of years, I lay; the winds were dead
  for heat;
The noonday crag made the hand
  burn; and sick
For shadow—not one bush was near—
  I rose,
Following a torrent till its myriad falls
Found silence in the hollows under-
  neath.
  There in a secret olive-glade I saw
Pallas Athene climbing from the bath
In anger; yet one glittering foot dis-
  turb'd   40
The lucid well; one snowy knee was
  prest
Against the margin flowers; a dreadful
  light
Came from her golden hair, her golden
  helm
And all her golden armor on the grass,
And from her virgin breast, and virgin
  eyes
Remaining fixt on mine, till mine
  grew dark
For ever, and I heard a voice that said,
'Henceforth be blind, for thou hast
  seen too much,
And speak the truth that no man may
  believe.'
  Son, in the hidden world of sight
    that lives   50

Behind this darkness, I behold her
    still,
Beyond all work of those who carve
    the stone,
Beyond all dreams of Godlike woman-
    hood,
Ineffable beauty, out of whom, at a
    glance,
And as it were, perforce, upon me
    flash'd
The power of prophesying—but to me
No power—so chain'd and coupled
    with the curse
Of blindness and their unbelief who
    heard
And heard not, when I spake of
    famine, plague,
Shrine-shattering earthquake, fire,
    flood, thunderbolt,   60
And angers of the Gods for evil done
And expiation lack'd—no power on
    Fate
Theirs, or mine own! for when the
    crowd would roar
For blood, for war, whose issue was
    their doom,
To cast wise words among the multi-
    tude
Was flinging fruit to lions; nor, in
    hours
Of civil outbreak, when I knew the
    twain
Would each waste each, and bring on
    both the yoke
Of stronger states, was mine the voice
    to curb
The madness of our cities and their
    kings.   70
    Who ever turn'd upon his heel to
    hear
My warning that the tyranny of one
Was prelude to the tyranny of all?
My counsel that the tyranny of all
Led backward to the tyranny of one?
    This power hath work'd no good to
    aught that lives,
And these blind hands were useless in
    their wars.
O, therefore, that the unfulfill'd desire,
The grief for ever born from griefs to
    be,
The boundless yearning of the proph-
    et's heart—   80

Could *that* stand forth, and like a
    statue, rear'd
To some great citizen, win all praise
    from all
Who past it, saying, 'That was he!'
                            In vain!
Virtue must shape itself in deed, and
    those
Whom weakness or necessity have
    cramp'd
Within themselves, immerging, each,
    his urn
In his own well, draws solace as he
    may.
    Menœceus, thou hast eyes, and I
    can hear
Too plainly what full tides of onset
    sap
Our seven high gates, and what a
    weight of war   90
Rides on those ringing axles! jingle of
    bits,
Shouts, arrows, tramp of the horn-
    footed horse
That grind the glebe to powder! Stony
    showers
Of that ear-stunning hail of Arês crash
Along the sounding walls. Above, be-
    low,
Shock after shock, the song-built
    towers and gates
Reel, bruised and butted with the
    shuddering
War-thunder of iron rams; and from
    within
The city comes a murmur void of joy,
Lest she be taken captive—maidens,
    wives,   100
And mothers with their babblers of
    the dawn,
And oldest age in shadow from the
    night,
Falling about their shrines before
    their Gods,
And wailing, 'Save us.'
                    And they wail to thee!
These eyeless eyes, that cannot see
    thine own,
See this, that only in thy virtue lies
The saving of our Thebes; for, yester-
    night,
To me, the great God Arês, whose
    one bliss

Is war and human sacrifice—himself
Blood-red from battle, spear and hel-
    met tipt   110
With stormy light as on a mast at sea,
Stood out before a darkness, crying,
    'Thebes,
Thy Thebes shall fall and perish, for I
    loathe
The seed of Cadmus—yet if one of
    these
By his own hand—if one of these—'
                              My son,
No sound is breathed so potent to
    coerce,
And to conciliate, as their names who
    dare
For that sweet mother land which
  . gave them birth
Nobly to do, nobly to die. Their
    names,
Graven on memorial columns, are a
    song   120
Heard in the future; few, but more
    than wall
And rampart, their examples reach a
    hand
Far thro' all years, and everywhere
    they meet
And kindle generous purpose, and the
    strength
To mould it into action pure as theirs.
    Fairer thy fate than mine, if life's
    best end
Be to end well! and thou refusing this,
Unvenerable will thy memory be
While men shall move the lips; but if
    thou dare—
Thou, one of these, the race of Cad-
    mus—then   130
No stone is fitted in yon marble girth
Whose echo shall not tongue thy glo-
    rious doom,
Nor in this pavement but shall ring
    thy name
To every hoof that clangs it, and the
    springs
Of Dircê laving yonder battle-plain,
Heard from the roofs by night, will
    murmur thee
To thine own Thebes, while Thebes
    thro' thee shall stand
Firm-based with all her Gods.
                  The Dragon's cave

Half hid, they tell me, now in flowing
    vines—
Where once he dwelt and whence he
    roll'd himself   140
At dead of night—thou knowest, and
    that smooth rock
Before it, altar-fashion'd, where of
    late
The woman-breasted Sphinx, with
    wings drawn back,
Folded her lion paws, and look'd to
    Thebes.
There blanch the bones of whom she
    slew, and these
Mixt with her own, because the fierce
    beast found
A wiser than herself, and dash'd her-
    self
Dead in her rage; but thou art wise
    enough,
Tho' young, to love thy wiser, blunt
    the curse
Of Pallas, hear, and tho' I speak the
    truth   150
Believe I speak it, let thine own hand
    strike
Thy youthful pulses into rest and
    quench
The red God's anger, fearing not to
    plunge
Thy torch of life in darkness, rather—
    thou
Rejoicing that the sun, the moon, the
    stars
Send no such light upon the ways of
    men
As one great deed.
                  Thither, my son, and there
Thou, that hast never known the em-
    brace of love,
Offer thy maiden life.
                  This useless hand!
I felt one warm tear fall upon it.
    Gone!   160
He will achieve his greatness.
                  But for me,
I would that I were gather'd to my
    rest,
And mingled with the famous kings of
    old,
On whom about their ocean-islets
    flash

The faces of the Gods—the wise man's
    word,
Here trampled by the populace under-
    foot,
There crown'd with worship—and
    these eyes will find
The men I knew, and watch the char-
    iot whirl
About the goal again, and hunters race
The shadowy lion, and the warrior-
    kings,   170
In height and prowess more than hu-
    man, strive
Again for glory, while the golden lyre
Is ever sounding in heroic ears
Heroic hymns, and every way the
    vales
Wind, clouded with the grateful in-
    cense fume
Of those who mix all odor to the Gods
On one far height in one far-shining
    fire.

———

'One height and one far-shining fire!
    And while I fancied that my friend
For this brief idyll would require   180
    A less diffuse and opulent end,
And would defend his judgment well,
    If I should deem it over nice—
The tolling of his funeral bell
    Broke on my Pagan Paradise,
And mixt the dream of classic times,
    And all the phantoms of the dream,
With present grief, and made the
    rhymes,
    That miss'd his living welcome,
    seem   189
Like would-be guests an hour too late,
    Who down the highway moving on
With easy laughter find the gate
    Is bolted, and the master gone.
Gone into darkness, that full light
    Of friendship! past, in sleep, away
By night, into the deeper night!
    The deeper night? A clearer day
Than our poor twilight dawn on
    earth—
    If night, what barren toil to be!
What life, so maim'd by night, were
    worth   200
    Our living out? Not mine to me

Remembering all the golden hours
    Now silent, and so many dead,
And him the last; and laying flowers,
    This wreath, above his honor'd
    head,
And praying that, when I from hence
    Shall fade with him into the un-
    known,
My close of earth's experience
    May prove as peaceful as his own.

THE WRECK

I

HIDE me, mother! my fathers belong'd
    to the church of old,
I am driven by storm and sin and
    death to the ancient fold,
I cling to the Catholic Cross once
    more, to the Faith that saves.
My brain is full of the crash of wrecks,
    and the roar of waves,
My life itself is a wreck, I have sullied
    a noble name,
I am flung from the rushing tide of the
    world as a waif of shame,
I am roused by the wail of a child, and
    awake to a livid light,
And a ghastlier face than ever has
    haunted a grave by night.
I would hide from the storm without,
    I would flee from the storm
    within,
I would make my life one prayer for a
    soul that died in his sin,   10
I was the tempter, mother, and mine
    was the deeper fall;
I will sit at your feet, I will hide my
    face, I will tell you all.

II

He that they gave me to, mother, a
    heedless and innocent bride—
I never have wrong'd his heart, I have
    only wounded his pride—
Spain in his blood and the Jew—dark-
    visaged, stately and tall—
A princelier-looking man never stept
    thro' a prince's hall.

And who, when his anger was kindled,
    would venture to give him the
    nay?
And a man men fear is a man to be
    loved by the women, they say.
And I could have loved him too, if the
    blossom can dote on the blight,
Or the young green leaf rejoice in the
    frost that sears it at night;   20
He would open the books that I prized,
    and toss them away with a
    yawn,
Repell'd by the magnet of Art to the
    which my nature was drawn,
The word of the Poet by whom the
    deeps of the world are stirr'd,
The music that robes it in language
    beneath and beyond the word!
My Shelley would fall from my hands
    when he cast a contemptuous
    glance
From where he was poring over his
    Tables of Trade and Finance;
My hands, when I heard him coming,
    would drop from the chords or
    the keys,
But ever I fail'd to please him, how-
    ever I strove to please—
All day long far-off in the cloud of the
    city, and there   29
Lost, head and heart, in the chances of
    dividend, consol, and share—
And at home if I sought for a kindly
    caress, being woman and weak,
His formal kiss fell chill as a flake of
    snow on the cheek.
And so, when I bore him a girl, when I
    held it aloft in my joy,
He look'd at it coldly, and said to me,
    'Pity it isn't a boy.'
The one thing given me, to love and to
    live for, glanced at in scorn!
The child that I felt I could die for—
    as if she were basely born!
I had lived a wild-flower life, I was
    planted now in a tomb;
The daisy will shut to the shadow, I
    closed my heart to the gloom;
I threw myself all abroad—I would
    play my part with the young
By the low foot-lights of the world—
    and I caught the wreath that
    was flung.   40

III

Mother, I have not—however their
    tongues may have babbled of
    me—
Sinn'd thro' an animal vileness, for all
    but a dwarf was he,
And all but a hunchback too; and I
    look'd at him, first, askance,
With pity—not he the knight for an
    amorous girl's romance!
Tho' wealthy enough to have bask'd in
    the light of a dowerless smile,
Having lands at home and abroad in a
    rich West-Indian isle;
But I came on him once at a ball, the
    heart of a listening crowd—
Why, what a brow was there! he was
    seated—speaking aloud
To women, the flower of the time, and
    men at the helm of state—   49
Flowing with easy greatness and
    touching on all things great,
Science, philosophy, song—till I felt
    myself ready to weep
For I knew not what, when I heard
    that voice,—as mellow and
    deep
As a psalm by a mighty master and
    peal'd from an organ,—roll
Rising and falling—for, mother, the
    voice was the voice of the soul;
And the sun of the soul made day in
    the dark of his wonderful eyes.
Here was the hand that would help
    me, would heal me—the heart
    that was wise!
And he, poor man, when he learnt that
    I hated the ring I wore,
He helpt me with death, and he heal'd
    me with sorrow for evermore.

IV

For I broke the bond. That day my
    nurse had brought me the
    child.
The small sweet face was flush'd, but
    it coo'd to the mother and
    smiled.   60
'Anything ailing,' I ask'd her, 'with
    baby?' She shook her head,

And the motherless mother kiss'd it,
    and turn'd in her haste and fled.

V

Low warm winds had gently breathed
    us away from the land—
Ten long sweet summer days upon
    deck, sitting hand in hand—
When he clothed a naked mind with
    the wisdom and wealth of his
    own,
And I bow'd myself down as a slave to
    his intellectual throne,
When he coin'd into English gold some
    treasure of classical song,
When he flouted a statesman's error,
    or flamed at a public wrong,
When he rose as it were on the wings
    of an eagle beyond me, and
    past   69
Over the range and the change of the
    world from the first to the last,
When he spoke of his tropical home in
    the canes by the purple tide,
And the high star-crowns of his palms
    on the deep-wooded mountain-
    side,
And cliffs all robed in lianas that dropt
    to the brink of his bay,
And trees like the towers of a minster,
    the sons of a winterless day.
'Paradise there!' so he said, but I
    seem'd in Paradise then
With the first great love I had felt for
    the first and greatest of men;
Ten long days of summer and sin—if
    it must be so—
But days of a larger light than I ever
    again shall know—
Days that will glimmer, I fear, thro'
    life to my latest breath;
'No frost there,' so he said, 'as in tru-
    est love no death.'   80

VI

Mother, one morning a bird with a
    warble plaintively sweet
Perch'd on the shrouds, and then fell
    fluttering down at my feet;
I took it, he made it a cage, we fon-
    dled it, Stephen and I,

But it died, and I thought of the child
    for a moment, I scarce know
    why.

VII

But if sin be sin, not inherited fate, as
    many will say,
My sin to my desolate little one found
    me at sea on a day,
When her orphan wail came borne in
    the shriek of a growing wind,
And a voice rang out in the thunders
    of ocean and heaven, 'Thou
    hast sinn'd.'
And down in the cabin were we, for
    the towering crest of the tides
Plunged on the vessel and swept in a
    cataract off from her sides,   90
And ever the great storm grew with a
    howl and a hoot of the blast
In the rigging, voices of hell—then
    came the crash of the mast.
'The wages of sin is death,' and there
    I began to weep,
'I am the Jonah, the crew should cast
    me into the deep,
For, ah, God! what a heart was mine
    to forsake her even for you!'
'Never the heart among women,' he
    said, 'more tender and true.'
'The heart! not a mother's heart, when
    I left my darling alone.'
'Comfort yourself, for the heart of the
    father will care for his own.'
'The heart of the father will spurn
    her,' I cried, 'for the sin of the
    wife,   99
The cloud of the mother's shame will
    enfold her and darken her life.'
Then his pale face twitch'd. 'O
    Stephen, I love you, I love you,
    and yet'—
As I lean'd away from his arms—
    'would God, we had never
    met!'
And he spoke not—only the storm;
    till after a little, I yearn'd
For his voice again, and he call'd to
    me, 'Kiss me!' and there—as I
    turn'd—
'The heart, the heart!' I kiss'd him, I
    clung to the sinking form,

And the storm went roaring above us,
   and he—was out of the storm.

VIII

And then, then, mother, the ship stagger'd under a thunderous shock,
That shook us asunder, as if she had
   struck and crash'd on a rock;
For a huge sea smote every soul from
   the decks of the Falcon but
   one;   ¹⁰⁹ 109
All of them, all but the man that was
   lash'd to the helm had gone;
And I fell—and the storm and the
   days went by, but I knew no
   more—
Lost myself—lay like the dead by the
   dead on the cabin floor,
Dead to the death beside me, and lost
   to the loss that was mine,
With a dim dream, now and then, of a
   hand giving bread and wine,
Till I woke from the trance, and the
   ship stood still, and the skies
   were blue,
But the face I had known, O mother,
   was not the face that I knew.

IX

The strange misfeaturing mask that I
   saw so amazed me that I
Stumbled on deck, half mad. I would
   fling myself over and die!
But one—he was waving a flag—the
   one man left on the wreck—
'Woman,'—he graspt at my arm,—
   'stay there!'—I crouch'd upon
   deck—   120
'We are sinking, and yet there's hope:
   look yonder,' he cried, 'a sail!'
In a tone so rough that I broke into
   passionate tears, and the wail
Of a beaten babe, till I saw that a boat
   was nearing us—then
All on a sudden I thought, I shall look
   on the child again.

X

They lower'd me down the side, and
   there in the boat I lay

With sad eyes fixt on the lost sea-
   home, as we glided away,
And I sigh'd as the low dark hull dipt
   under the smiling main,
'Had I stay'd with *him*, I had now—
   with *him*—been out of my
   pain.'

XI

They took us aboard. The crew were
   gentle, the captain kind,
But *I* was the lonely slave of an often-
   wandering mind;   130
For whenever a rougher gust might
   tumble a stormier wave,
'O Stephen,' I moan'd, 'I'm coming to
   thee in thine ocean-grave.'
And again, when a balmier breeze
   curl'd over a peacefuller sea,
I found myself moaning again, 'O
   child, I am coming to thee.'

XII

The broad white brow of the isle—
   that bay with the color'd
   sand—
Rich was the rose of sunset there, as
   we drew to the land;
All so quiet the ripple would hardly
   blanch into spray
At the feet of the cliff; and I pray'd—
   'My child,'—for I still could
   pray,—
'May her life be as blissfully calm, be
   never gloom'd by the curse ¹³⁹
Of a sin, not hers!'
       Was it well with the child?
         I wrote to the nurse
Who had borne my flower on her hire-
   ling heart; and an answer came
Not from the nurse—nor yet to the
   wife—to her maiden name!
I shook as I open'd the letter—I knew
   that hand too well—
And from it a scrap, clipt out of the
   'deaths' in a paper, fell.
'Ten long sweet summer days' of
   fever, and want of care!
And gone—that day of the storm—O
   mother, she came to me there!

DESPAIR

'A man and his wife having lost faith in a God, and hope of a life to come, and being utterly miserable in this, resolve to end themselves by drowning. The woman is drowned, but the man rescued by a minister of the sect he had abandoned.'

I

Is it you, that preach'd in the chapel
    there looking over the sand?
Follow'd us too that night, and dogg'd
    us, and drew me to land?

II

What did I feel that night? You are
    curious. How should I tell?
Does it matter so much what I felt?
    You rescued me—yet—was it
    well
That you came unwish'd for, uncall'd,
    between me and the deep and
    my doom,
Three days since, three more dark
    days of the Godless gloom
Of a life without sun, without health,
    without hope, without any de-
    light
In anything here upon earth? but, ah,
    God! that night, that night
When the rolling eyes of the light-
    house there on the fatal neck
Of land running out into rock—they
    had saved many hundreds from
    wreck—   10
Glared on our way toward death, I re-
    member I thought, as we past,
Does it matter how many they saved?
    we are all of us wreck'd at
    last—
'Do you fear?' and there came thro'
    the roar of the breaker a whis-
    per, a breath,
'Fear? am I not with you? I am
    frighted at life, not death.'

III

And the suns of the limitless universe
    sparkled and shone in the sky,
Flashing with fires as of God, but we
    knew that their light was a
    lie—
Bright as with deathless hope—but,
    however they sparkled and
    shone,
The dark little worlds running round
    them were worlds of woe like
    our own—
No soul in the heaven above, no soul
    on the earth below,
A fiery scroll written over with lamen-
    tation and woe.   20

IV

See, we were nursed in the drear
    night-fold of your fatalist
    creed,
And we turn'd to the growing dawn,
    we had hoped for a dawn in-
    deed,
When the light of a sun that was com-
    ing would scatter the ghosts of
    the past,
And the cramping creeds that had
    madden'd the peoples would
    vanish at last,
And we broke away from the Christ,
    our human brother and friend,
For He spoke, or it seem'd that He
    spoke, of a hell without help,
    without end.

V

Hoped for a dawn, and it came, but
    the promise had faded away;
We had past from a cheerless night to
    the glare of a drearier day;
He is only a cloud and a smoke who
    was once a pillar of fire,
The guess of a worm in the dust and
    the shadow of its desire—   30
Of a worm as it writhes in a world of
    the weak trodden down by the
    strong,
Of a dying worm in a world, all mas-
    sacre, murder, and wrong.

VI

O, we poor orphans of nothing—alone
    on that lonely shore—

Born of the brainless Nature who
    knew not that which she bore!
Trusting no longer that earthly flower
    would be heavenly fruit—
Come from the brute, poor souls—no
    souls—and to die with the
    brute—

VII

Nay, but I am not claiming your pity;
    I know you of old—
Small pity for those that have ranged
    from the narrow warmth of
    your fold,
Where you bawl'd the dark side of
    your faith and a God of eternal
    rage,
Till you flung us back on ourselves,
    and the human heart, and the
    Age.　　40

VIII

But pity—the Pagan held it a vice—
    was in her and in me,
Helpless, taking the place of the pity-
    ing God that should be!
Pity for all that aches in the grasp of
    an idiot power,
And pity for our own selves on an
    earth that bore not a flower;
Pity for all that suffers on land or in
    air or the deep,
And pity for our own selves till we
    long'd for eternal sleep.　　.

IX

'Lightly step over the sands! the
    waters—you hear them call!
Life with its anguish, and horrors, and
    errors—away with it all!'
And she laid her hand in my own—she
    was always loyal and sweet—
Till the points of the foam in the dusk
    came playing about our feet.
There was a strong sea-current would
    sweep us out to the main.　51
'Ah, God!' tho' I felt as I spoke I was
    taking the name in vain—
'Ah, God!' and we turn'd to each
    other, we kiss'd, we embraced,
    she and I,

Knowing the love we were used to be-
    lieve everlasting would die.
We had read their know-nothing
    books, and we lean'd to the
    darker side—
Ah, God, should we find Him, per-
    haps, perhaps, if we died, if we
    died;
We never had found Him on earth,
    this earth is a fatherless hell—
'Dear love, for ever and ever, for ever
    and ever farewell!'
Never a cry so desolate, not since the
    world began,
Never a kiss so sad, no, not since the
    coming of man!　　60

X

But the blind wave cast me ashore,
    and you saved me, a valueless
    life.
Not a grain of gratitude mine! You
    have parted the man from the
    wife.
I am left alone on the land, she is all
    alone in the sea;
If a curse meant aught, I would curse
    you for not having let me be.

XI

Visions of youth—for my brain was
    drunk with the water, it seems;
I had past into perfect quiet at length
    out of pleasant dreams,
And the transient trouble of drown-
    ing—what was it when match'd
    with the pains
Of the hellish heat of a wretched life
    rushing back thro' the veins?

XII

Why should I live? one son had forged
    on his father and fled,　69
And if I believed in a God, I would
    thank Him, the other is dead,
And there was a baby-girl, that had
    never look'd on the light;
Happiest she of us all, for she past
    from the night to the night.

XIII

But the crime, if a crime, of her eld-
    est-born, her glory, her boast,
Struck hard at the tender heart of the
    mother, and broke it almost;
Tho' glory and shame dying out for
    ever in endless time,
Does it matter so much whether
    crown'd for a virtue, or hang'd
    for a crime?

XIV

And ruin'd by *him*, by *him*, I stood
    there, naked, amazed
In a world of arrogant opulence, fear'd
    myself turning crazed,
And I would not be mock'd, in a mad-
    house! and she, the delicate
    wife,
With a grief that could only be cured,
    if cured, by the surgeon's
    knife,—   80

XV

Why should we bear with an hour of
    torture, a moment of pain,
If every man die for ever, if all his
    griefs are in vain,
And the homeless planet at length will
    be wheel'd thro' the silence of
    space,
Motherless evermore of an ever-van-
    ishing race,
When the worm shall have writhed its
    last, and its last brother-worm
    will have fled
From the dead fossil skull that is left
    in the rocks of an earth that is
    dead?

XVI

Have I crazed myself over their hor-
    rible infidel writings? O, yes,
For these are the new dark ages, you
    see, of the popular press,
When the bat comes out of his cave,
    and the owls are whooping at
    noon,

And Doubt is the lord of this dunghill
    and crows to the sun and the
    moon,   90
Till the sun and the moon of our sci-
    ence are both of them turn'd
    into blood,
And Hope will have broken her heart,
    running after a shadow of
    good;
For their knowing and know-nothing
    books are scatter'd from hand
    to hand—
We have knelt in your know-all chapel
    too, looking over the sand.

XVII

What! I should call on that Infinite
    Love that has served us so
    well?
Infinite cruelty rather that made ever-
    lasting hell,
Made us, foreknew us, foredoom'd us,
    and does what he will with his
    own;
Better our dead brute mother who
    never has heard us groan!

XVIII

Hell? if the souls of men were im-
    mortal, as men have been told,
The lecher would cleave to his lusts,
    and the miser would yearn for
    his gold,   100
And so there were hell for ever! but
    were there a God, as you say,
His love would have power over hell
    till it utterly vanish'd away.

XIX

Ah, yet—I have had some glimmer, at
    times, in my gloomiest woe,
Of a God behind all—after all—the
    great God, for aught that I
    know;
But the God of love and of hell
    together—they cannot be
    thought,
If there be such a God, may the Great
    God curse him and bring him
    to nought!

XX

Blasphemy! whose is the fault? is it
    mine? for why would you save
A madman to vex you with wretched
    words, who is best in his grave?
Blasphemy! ay, why not, being
    damn'd beyond hope of grace?
O, would I were yonder with her, and
    away from your faith and your
    face!   110
Blasphemy! true! I have scared you
    pale with my scandalous talk,
But the blasphemy to *my* mind lies all
    in the way that you walk.

XXI

Hence! she is gone! can I stay? can I
    breathe divorced from the
    past?
You needs must have good lynx-eyes
    if I do not escape you at last.
Our orthodox coroner doubtless will
    find it a felo-de-se,
And the stake and the cross-road, fool,
    if you will , does it matter to
    me?

THE ANCIENT SAGE

A THOUSAND summers ere the time of
    Christ,
From out his ancient city came a Seer
Whom one that loved and honor'd
    him, and yet
Was no disciple, richly garb'd, but
    worn
From wasteful living, follow'd—in his
    hand
A scroll of verse—till that old man be-
    fore
A cavern whence an affluent fountain
    pour'd
From darkness into daylight, turn'd
    and spoke:

'This wealth of waters might but
    seem to draw
From yon dark cave, but, son, the
    source is higher,   10

Yon summit half-a-league in air—and
    higher
The cloud that hides it—higher still
    the heavens
Whereby the cloud was moulded, and
    whereout
The cloud descended. Force is from
    the heights.
I am wearied of our city, son, and go
To spend my one last year among the
    hills.
What hast thou there? Some death-
    song for the Ghouls
To make their banquet relish? let me
    read.

' "How far thro' all the bloom and brake
    That nightingale is heard!   20
What power but the bird's could make
    This music in the bird?
How summer-bright are yonder skies,
    And earth as fair in hue!
And yet what sign of aught that lies
    Behind the green and blue?
But man to-day is fancy's fool
    As man hath ever been.
The nameless Power, or Powers, that rule
    Were never heard or seen."   30

If thou wouldst hear the Nameless,
    and wilt dive
Into the temple-cave of thine own
    self,
There, brooding by the central altar,
    thou
Mayst haply learn the Nameless hath
    a voice,
By which thou wilt abide, if thou be
    wise,
As if thou knewest, tho' thou canst
    not know;
For knowledge is the swallow on the
    lake
That sees and stirs the surface-shadow
    there
But never yet hath dipt into the
    abysm,
The abysm of all abysms, beneath,
    within   40
The blue of sky and sea, the green of
    earth,
And in the million-millionth of a grain
Which cleft and cleft again for ever-
    more,

And ever vanishing, never vanishes,
To me, my son, more mystic than my-
    self,
Or even than the Nameless is to me.
    'And when thou sendest thy free
        soul thro' heaven,
Nor understandest bound nor bound-
    lessness,
Thou seest the Nameless of the hun-
    dred names.
    'And if the Nameless should with-
        draw from all   50
Thy frailty counts most real, all thy
    world
Might vanish like thy shadow in the
    dark.

  '"And since—from when this earth be-
    gan—
   The Nameless never came
Among us, never spake with man,
    And never named the Name"—

Thou canst not prove the Nameless, O
    my son,
Nor canst thou prove the world thou
    movest in,
Thou canst not prove that thou art
    body alone,
Nor canst thou prove that thou art
    spirit alone,   60
Nor canst thou prove that thou art
    both in one.
Thou canst not prove thou art immor-
    tal, no,
Nor yet that thou art mortal—nay,
    my son,
Thou canst not prove that I, who
    speak with thee,
Am not thyself in converse with thy-
    self,
For nothing worthy proving can be
    proven,
Nor yet disproven. Wherefore thou be
    wise,
Cleave ever to the sunnier side of
    doubt,
And cling to Faith beyond the forms
    of Faith!
She reels not in the storm of warring
    words,   70
She brightens at the clash of "Yes"
    and "No,"

She sees the best that glimmers thro'
    the worst,
She feels the sun is hid but for a
    night,
She spies the summer thro' the winter
    bud,
She tastes the fruit before the blossom
    falls,
She hears the lark within the songless
    egg,
She finds the fountain where they
    wail'd "Mirage!"

  '"What Power? aught akin to Mind,
    The mind in me and you?
Or power as of the Gods gone blind   80
    Who see not what they do?"

But some in yonder city hold, my son,
That none but gods could build this
    house of ours,
So beautiful, vast, various, so beyond
All work of man, yet, like all work of
    man,
A beauty with defect—till That which
    knows,
And is not known, but felt thro' what
    we feel
Within ourselves is highest, shall de-
    scend
On this half-deed, and shape it at the
    last
According to the Highest in the High-
    est.   90

  '"What Power but the Years that make
    And break the vase of clay,
And stir the sleeping earth, and wake
    The bloom that fades away?
What rulers but the Days and Hours
    That cancel weal with woe,
And wind the front of youth with flow-
    ers,
    And cap our age with snow?"

The days and hours are ever glancing
    by,
And seem to flicker past thro' sun and
    shade,   100
Or short, or long, as Pleasure leads, or
    Pain,
But with the Nameless is nor day nor
    hour;
Tho' we, thin minds, who creep from
    thought to thought,

Break into "Thens" and "Whens" the
    Eternal Now—
This double seeming of the single
    world!—
My words are like the babblings in a
    dream
Of nightmare, when the babblings
    break the dream.
But thou be wise in this dream-world
    of ours,
Nor take thy dial for thy deity,
But make the passing shadow serve
    thy will.   110

' "The years that made the stripling wise
    Undo their work again,
And leave him, blind of heart and eyes,
    The last and least of men;
Who clings to earth, and once would dare
    Hell-heat or Arctic cold,
And now one breath of cooler air
    Would loose him from his hold.
His winter chills him to the root,
    He withers marrow and mind;   120
The kernel of the shrivell'd fruit
    Is jutting thro' the rind;
The tiger spasms tear his chest,
    The palsy wags his head;
The wife, the sons, who love him best
    Would fain that he were dead;
The griefs by which he once was wrung
    Were never worth the while"—

Who knows? or whether this earth-
    narrow life
Be yet but yolk, and forming in the
    shell?   130

' "The shaft of scorn that once had stung
    But wakes a dotard smile."

The placid gleam of sunset after
    storm!

' "The statesman's brain that sway'd the
    past
    Is feebler than his knees;
The passive sailor wrecks at last
    In ever-silent seas;
The warrior hath forgot his arms,
    The learned all his lore;
The changing market frets or charms 140
    The merchant's hope no more:
The prophet's beacon burn'd in vain,
    And now is lost in cloud;
The plowman passes, bent with pain,
    To mix with what he plow'd;

The poet whom his age would quote
    As heir of endless fame—
He knows not even the book he wrote,
    Not even his own name.
For man has overlived his day,   150
    And, darkening in the light,
Scarce feels the senses break away
    To mix with ancient Night."

The shell must break before the bird
    can fly.

' "The years that when my youth began
    Had set the lily and rose
By all my ways where'er they ran,
    Have ended mortal foes;
My rose of love for ever gone,
    My lily of truth and trust—   160
They made her lily and rose in one,
    And changed her into dust.
O rose-tree planted in my grief,
    And growing on her tomb,
Her dust is greening in your leaf,
    Her blood is in your bloom.
O slender lily waving there,
    And laughing back the light,
In vain you tell me 'Earth is fair'
    When all is dark as night."   170

My son, the world is dark with griefs
    and graves,
So dark that men cry out against the
    heavens.
Who knows but that the darkness is in
    man?
The doors of Night may be the gates
    of Light;
For wert thou born or blind or deaf,
    and then
Suddenly heal'd, how wouldst thou
    glory in all
The splendors and the voices of the
    world!
And we, the poor earth's dying race,
    and yet
No phantoms, watching from a phan-
    tom shore
Await the last and largest sense to
    make   180
The phantom walls of this illusion
    fade,
And show us that the world is wholly
    fair.

' "But vain the tears for darken'd years
    As laughter over wine,

And vain the laughter as the tears,
 O brother, mine or thine,
For all that laugh, and all that weep
 And all that breathe are one
Slight ripple on the boundless deep   190
 That moves, and all is gone."

But that one ripple on the boundless
  deep
Feels that the deep is boundless, and
  itself
For ever changing form, but evermore
One with the boundless motion of the
  deep.

' "Yet wine and laughter, friends! and set
 The lamps alight, and call
For golden music, and forget
 The darkness of the pall."

If utter darkness closed the day, my
  son—
But earth's dark forehead flings
 athwart the heavens   200
Her shadow crown'd with stars—and
 yonder—out
To northward—some that never set,
 but pass
From sight and night to lose themselves in day.
I hate the black negation of the bier,
And wish the dead, as happier than
 ourselves
And higher, having climb'd one step
 beyond
Our village miseries, might be borne
 in white
To burial or to burning, hymn'd from
 hence
With songs in praise of death, and
 crown'd with flowers!

' "O worms and maggots of to-day   210
 Without their hope of wings!"

But louder than thy rhyme the silent
 Word
Of that world-prophet in the heart of
 man.

' "Tho' some have gleams, or so they say,
 Of more than mortal things."

To-day? but what of yesterday? for
 oft

On me, when boy, there came what
 then I call'd,
Who knew no books and no philosophies,
In my boy-phrase, "The Passion of
 the Past."
The first gray streak of earliest sum-
 mer-dawn,   220
The last long strife of waning crim-
 son gloom,
As if the late and early were but
 one—
A height, a broken grange, a grove, a
 flower
Had murmurs, "Lost and gone, and
 lost and gone!"
A breath, a whisper—some divine
 farewell—
Desolate sweetness — far and far
 away—
What had he loved, what had he lost,
 the boy?
I know not, and I speak of what has
 been.
 'And more, my son! for more than
  once when I
Sat all alone, revolving in myself   230
The word that is the symbol of myself,
The mortal limit of the Self was
 loosed,
And past into the Nameless, as a
 cloud
Melts into heaven. I touch'd my limbs,
 the limbs
Were strange, not mine—and yet no
 shade of doubt,
But utter clearness, and thro' loss of
 self
The gain of such large life as match'd
 with ours
Were sun to spark—unshadowable in
 words,
Themselves but shadows of a shadow-
 world.

' "And idle gleams will come and go,   240
 But still the clouds remain;"

The clouds themselves are children of
 the Sun.

' "And Night and Shadow rule below
 When only Day should reign."

And Day and Night are children of
    the Sun,
And idle gleams to thee are light to
    me.
Some say, the Light was father of the
    Night,
And some, the Night was father of the
    Light,
No night, no day!—I touch thy world
    again—
No ill, no good! such counter-terms,
    my son,   250
Are border-races, holding each its own
By endless war. But night enough is
    there
In yon dark city. Get thee back; and
    since
The key to that weird casket, which
    for thee
But holds a skull, is neither thine nor
    mine,
But in the hand of what is more than
    man,
Or in man's hand when man is more
    than man,
Let be thy wail, and help thy fellow-
    men,
And make thy gold thy vassal, not thy
    king,
And fling free alms into the beggar's
    bowl,   260
And send the day into the darken'd
    heart;
Nor list for guerdon in the voice of
    men,
A dying echo from a falling wall;
Nor care—for Hunger hath the evil
    eye—
To vex the noon with fiery gems, or
    fold
Thy presence in the silk of sumptuous
    looms;
Nor roll thy viands on a luscious
    tongue,
Nor drown thyself with flies in
    honeyed wine;
Nor thou be rageful, like a handled
    bee,
And lose thy life by usage of thy
    sting;   270
Nor harm an adder thro' the lust for
    harm,

Nor make a snail's horn shrink for
    wantonness.
And more—think well! Do-well will
    follow thought,
And in the fatal sequence of this world
An evil thought may soil thy chil-
    dren's blood;
But curb the beast would cast thee in
    the mire,
And leave the hot swamp of voluptu-
    ousness,
A cloud between the Nameless and
    thyself,
And lay thine uphill shoulder to the
    wheel,
And climb the Mount of Blessing,
    whence, if thou   280
Look higher, then—perchance—thou
    mayest—beyond
A hundred ever-rising mountain lines,
And past the range of Night and
    Shadow—see
The high-heaven dawn of more than
    mortal day
Strike on the Mount of Vision!
                So, farewell.'

THE FLIGHT

I

ARE you sleeping? have you forgot-
    ten? do not sleep, my sister
    dear!
How *can* you sleep? the morning
    brings the day I hate and fear;
The cock has crow'd already once, he
    crows before his time;
Awake! the creeping glimmer steals,
    the hills are white with rime.

II

Ah, clasp me in your arms, sister, ah,
    fold me to your breast!
Ah, let me weep my fill once more, and
    cry myself to rest!
To rest? to rest and wake no more
    were better rest for me,
Than to waken every morning to that
    face I loathe to see.

III

I envied your sweet slumber, all night
    so calm you lay;
The night was calm, the morn is calm,
    and like another day;   10
But I could wish yon moaning sea
    would rise and burst the shore,
And such a whirlwind blow these
    woods as never blew before.

IV

For, one by one, the stars went down
    across the gleaming pane,
And project after project rose, and all
    of them were vain;
The blackthorn-blossom fades and
    falls and leaves the bitter sloe,
The hope I catch at vanishes, and
    youth is turn'd to woe.

V

Come, speak a little comfort! all night
    I pray'd with tears,
And yet no comfort came to me, and
    now the morn appears,
When he will tear me from your side,
    who bought me for his slave;
This father pays his debt with me, and
    weds me to my grave.   20

VI

What father, this or mine, was he,
    who, on that summer day
When I had fallen from off the crag
    we clamber'd up in play,
Found, fear'd me dead, and groan'd,
    and took and kiss'd me, and
    again
He kiss'd me; and I loved him then;
    he *was* my father then.

VII

No father now, the tyrant vassal of a
    tyrant vice!
The godless Jephtha vows his child
    . . . . to one cast of the dice.
These ancient woods, this Hall at last
    will go—perhaps have gone,

Except his own meek daughter yield
    her life, heart, soul to one—

VIII

To one who knows I scorn him. O, the
    formal mocking bow,
The cruel smile, the courtly phrase
    that masks his malice now—   30
But often in the sidelong eyes a gleam
    of all things ill—
It is not Love but Hate that weds a
    bride against her will;

IX

Hate, that would pluck from this true
    breast the locket that I wear,
The precious crystal into which I
    braided Edwin's hair!
The love that keeps this heart alive
    beats on it night and day—
One golden curl, his golden gift, before
    he past away.

X

He left us weeping in the woods; his
    boat was on the sand;
How slowly down the rocks he went,
    how loth to quit the land!
And all my life was darken'd, as I saw
    the white sail run,
And darken, up that lane of light into
    the setting sun.   40

XI

How often have we watch'd the sun
    fade from us thro' the West,
And follow Edwin to those isles, those
    Islands of the Blest!
Is *he* not there? would I were there,
    the friend, the bride, the wife,
With him, where summer never dies,
    with Love, the sun of life!

XII

O, would I were in Edwin's arms—
    once more—to feel his breath
Upon my cheek—on Edwin's ship,
    with Edwin, even in death,

Tho' all about the shuddering wreck
    the death-white sea should
    rave,
Or if lip were laid to lip on the pillows
    of the wave!

XIII

Shall I take *him?* I kneel with *him?* I
    swear and swear forsworn
To love him most whom most I loathe,
    to honor whom I scorn?   50
The Fiend would yell, the grave would
    yawn, my mother's ghost
    would rise—
To lie, to lie—in God's own house—
    the blackest of all lies!

XIV

Why—rather than that hand in mine,
    tho' every pulse would freeze,
I'd sooner fold an icy corpse dead of
    some foul disease.
Wed him? I will not wed him, let them
    spurn me from the doors,
And I will wander till I die about the
    barren moors.

XV

The dear, mad bride who stabb'd
    her bridegroom on her bridal
    night—
If mad, then I am mad, but sane if
    she were in the right.
My father's madness makes me mad
    —but words are only words!
I am not mad, not yet, not quite—
    There! listen how the birds 60

XVI

Begin to warble yonder in the budding
    orchard trees!
The lark has past from earth to heaven
    upon the morning breeze!
How gladly, were I one of those, how
    early would I wake!
And yet the sorrow that I bear is sor-
    row for *his* sake.

XVII

They love their mates, to whom they
    sing; or else their songs, that
    meet
The morning with such music, would
    never be so sweet!
And tho' these fathers will not hear,
    the blessed Heavens are just,
And Love is fire, and burns the feet
    would trample it to dust.

XVIII

A door was open'd in the house—who?
    who? my father sleeps!
A stealthy foot upon the stair! he—
    some one—this way creeps! 70
If he? yes, he—lurks, listens, fears his
    victim may have fled—
He! where is some sharp-pointed
    thing? he comes, and finds me
    dead.

XIX

Not he, not yet! and time to act—but
    how my temples burn!
And idle fancies flutter me, I know
    not where to turn;
Speak to me, sister, counsel me; this
    marriage must not be.
You only know the love that makes
    the world a world to me!

XX

Our gentle mother, had *she* lived—but
    we were left alone.
That other left us to ourselves, he
    cared not for his own;
So all the summer long we roam'd in
    these wild woods of ours,
My Edwin loved to call us then 'his
    two wild woodland flowers.' 80

XXI

Wild flowers blowing side by side in
    God's free light and air,
Wild flowers of the secret woods, when
    Edwin found us there,

Wild woods in which we roved with
    him, and heard his passionate
    vow,
Wild woods in which we rove no more,
    if we be parted now!

XXII

You will not leave me thus in grief to
    wander forth forlorn;
We never changed a bitter word, not
    once since we were born;
Our dying mother join'd our hands;
    she knew this father well;
She bade us love, like souls in heaven,
    and now I fly from hell,

XXIII

And you with me; and we shall light
    upon some lonely shore,
Some lodge within the waste sea-
    dunes, and hear the waters
    roar,   90
And see the ships from out the West
    go dipping thro' the foam,
And sunshine on that sail at last which
    brings our Edwin home.

XXIV

But look, the morning grows apace,
    and lights the old church-
    tower,
And lights the clock! the hand points
    five—O, me!—it strikes the
    hour—
I bide no more, I meet my fate, what-
    ever ills betide!
Arise, my own true sister, come forth!
    the world is wide.

XXV

And yet my heart is ill at ease, my
    eyes are dim with dew,
I seem to see a new-dug grave up
    yonder by the yew!
If we should never more return, but
    wander hand in hand
With breaking hearts, without a
    friend, and in a distant
    land!   100

XXVI

O sweet, they tell me that the world is
    hard, and harsh of mind,
But can it be so hard, so harsh, as
    those that should be kind?
That matters not. Let come what will;
    at last the end is sure,
And every heart that loves with truth
    is equal to endure.

TO-MORROW

I

Her, that yer Honor was spakin' to?
    Whin, yer Honor? last year—
Standin' here be the bridge, when last
    yer Honor was here?
An' yer Honor ye gev her the top of
    the mornin', 'To-morra,' says
    she.
What did they call her, yer Honor?
    They call'd her Molly Magee.
An' yer Honor 's the thrue ould blood
    that always manes to be kind,
But there 's rason in all things, yer
    Honor, for Molly was out of
    her mind.

II

Shure, an' meself remimbers wan
    night comin' down be the
    sthrame,
An' it seems to me now like a bit of
    yistherday in a dhrame—
Here where yer Honor seen her—
    there was but a slip of a moon,
But I hard thim—Molly Magee
    wid her bachelor, Danny
    O'Roon—   10
'You've been takin' a dhrop o' the cra-
    thur,' an' Danny says, 'Troth,
    an' I been
Dhrinkin' yer health wid Shamus
    O'Shea at Katty's shebeen; [1]
But I must be lavin' ye soon.' 'Ochone,
    are ye goin' away?'

---

[1] Grog-shop.

'Goin' to cut the Sassenach whate,' he
    says, 'over the say'—
'An' whin will ye meet me agin?' an'
    I hard him, 'Molly asthore,
I'll meet you agin to-morra,' says he,
    'be the chapel-door.'
'An' whin are ye goin' to lave me?'
    'O' Monday mornin',' says he;
'An' shure thin ye 'll meet me to-
    morra?' 'To-morra, to-morra,
    machree!'
Thin Molly's ould mother, yer Honor,
    that had no likin' for Dan,
Call'd from her cabin an' tould her to
    come away from the man,   20
An' Molly Magee kem flyin' acrass
    me, as light as a lark,
An' Dan stood there for a minute, an'
    thin wint into the dark.
But wirrah! the storm that night—the
    tundher, an' rain that fell,
An' the sthrames runnin' down at the
    back o' the glin 'ud 'a
    dhrownded hell.

III

But airth was at pace nixt mornin',
    an' hiven in its glory smiled,
As the Holy Mother o' Glory that
    smiles at her sleepin' child—
Ethen—she stept an the chapel-green,
    an' she turn'd herself roun'
Wid a diamond dhrop in her eye, for
    Danny was not to be foun',
An' many 's the time that I watch'd
    her at mass lettin' down the
    tear,
For the divil a Danny was there, yer
    Honor, for forty year.   30

IV

Och, Molly Magee, wid the red o' the
    rose an' the white o' the may,
An' yer hair as black as the night, an'
    yer eyes as bright as the day!
Achora, yer laste little whishper was
    sweet as the lilt of a bird!
Achushla, ye set me heart batin' to
    music wid ivery word!
An' sorra the Queen wid her sceptre in
    sich an illigant han',

An' the fall of yer foot in the dance
    was as light as snow an the lan',
An' the sun kem out of a cloud whin-
    iver ye walkt in the shtreet,
An' Shamus O'Shea was yer shadda,
    an' laid himself undher yer
    feet,
An' I loved ye meself wid a heart an' a
    half, me darlin' and he
'Ud 'a shot his own sowl dead for a
    kiss of ye, Molly Magee.   40

V

But shure we wor betther frinds whin
    I crack'd his skull for her sake,
An' he ped me back wid the best he
    could give at ould Donovan's
    wake—
For the boys wor about her agin whin
    Dan did n't come to the fore,
An' Shamus along wid the rest, but
    she put thim all to the door.
An', afther, I thried her meself av the
    bird 'ud come to me call,
But Molly, begorrah, 'ud listhen to
    naither at all, at all.

VI

An' her nabors an' frinds 'ud consowl
    an' condowl wid her, airly an'
    late,
'Your Danny,' they says, 'niver crasst
    over say to the Sassenach
    whate;
He 's gone to the States, aroon, an'
    he 's married another wife,
An' ye 'll niver set eyes an the face of
    the thraithur agin in life!   50
An' to dhrame of a married man,
    death alive, is a mortial sin.'
But Molly says, 'I 'd his hand-prom-
    ise, an' shure he 'll meet me
    agin.'

VII

An' afther her paärints had inter'd
    glory, an' both in wan day,
She began to spake to herself, the cra-
    thur, an' whishper, an' say,
'To-morra, to-morra!' an' Father Mo-
    lowny he tuk her in han',

'Molly, you 're manin',' he says, 'me
    dear, av I undherstan',
That ye 'll meet your paärints agin an'
    yer Danny O'Roon afore God
Wid his blessed Marthyrs an' Saints;'
    an she gev him a frindly nod,
'To-morra, to-morra,' she says, an' she
    did n't intind to desave,
But her wits wor dead, an' her hair
    was as white as the snow an a
    grave.   60

VIII

Arrah now, here last month they wor
    diggin' the bog, an' they foun'
Dhrownded in black bog-wather a
    corp lyin' undher groun'.

IX

Yer Honor's own agint, he says to me
    wanst, at Katty's shebeen,
'The divil take all the black lan', for
    a blessin' 'ud come wid the
    green!'
An' where 'ud the poor man, thin, cut
    his bit o' turf for the fire?
But och! bad scran to the bogs whin
    they swallies the man intire!
An' sorra the bog, that 's in hiven wid
    all the light an' the glow,
An' there 's hate enough, shure, wid-
    out *thim* in the divil's kitchen
    below.

X

Thim ould blind nagers in Agypt, I
    hard his Riverence say,
Could keep their haithen kings in the
    flesh for the Jidgment day, 70
An' faix, be the piper o' Moses, they
    kep' the cat an' the dog,
But it 'ud 'a been aisier work av they
    lived be an Irish bog.

XI

How-an-iver they laid this body they
    foun' an the grass,
Be the chapel-door, an' the people 'ud
    see it that wint in to mass—

But a frish gineration had riz, an' most
    of the ould was few,
An' I did n't know him meself, an'
    none of the parish knew.

XII

But Molly kem limpin' up wid her
    stick,—she was lamed iv a
    knee,—
Thin a slip of a gossoon call'd, 'Div ye
    know him, Molly Magee?'
An' she stood up strait as the queen
    of the world—she lifted her
    head—
'He said he would meet me to-morra!'
    an' dhropt down dead an the
    dead.   80

XIII

Och, Molly, we thought, machree, ye
    would start back agin into life,
Whin we laid yez, aich be aich, at yer
    wake like husban' an' wife.
Sorra the dhry eye thin but was wet
    for the frinds that was gone!
Sorra the silent throat but we hard it
    cryin', 'Ochone!'
An' Shamus O'Shea that has now ten
    childer, hansome an' tall,
Him an' his childer wor keenin' as if
    he had lost thim all.

XIV

Thin his Riverence buried thim both
    in wan grave be the dead boor-
    tree,[1]
The young man Danny O'Roon wid
    his ould woman, Molly Magee.

XV

May all the flowers o' Jeroosilim blos-
    som an' spring from the grass,
Imbrashin' an' kissin' aich other—as
    ye did—over yer Crass! 90
An' the lark fly out o' the flowers wid
    his song to the sun an' the
    moon,

---

[1] Elder-tree.

An' tell thim in hiven about Molly
    Magee an' her Danny O'Roon,
Till Holy Saint Pether gets up wid his
    kays an' opens the gate!
An' shure, be the Crass, that 's bet-
    ther nor cuttin' the Sassenach
    whate,
To be there wid the Blessed Mother
    an' Saints an' Marthyrs galore,
An' singin' yer 'Aves' an' 'Pathers' for
    iver an' ivermore.

XVI

An' now that I tould yer Honor what-
    iver I hard an' seen,
Yer Honor 'ill give me a thrifle to
    dhrink yer health in potheen.

THE SPINSTER'S SWEET-ARTS

I

Milk for my sweet-arts, Bess! fur it
    mun be the time about now
When Molly cooms in fro' the far-end
    close wi' her paäils fro' the
    cow.
Eh! tha be new to the plaäce—thou 'rt
    gaäpin'—doesn't tha see
I calls 'em arter the fellers es once was
    sweet upo' me?

II

Naäy, to be sewer, it be past 'er time.
    What maäkes 'er sa laäte?
Goä to the laäne at the back, an' looök
    thruf Maddison's gaäte!

III

Sweet-arts! Molly belike may 'a
    lighted to-night upo' one.
Sweet-arts! thanks to the Lord that I
    niver not listen'd to noän!
So I sits i' my oän armchair wi' my
    oän kettle theere o' the hob,
An' Tommy the fust, an' Tommy the
    second, an' Steevie an' Rob. 10

IV

Rob, coom oop 'ere o' my knee. Thou
    sees that i' spite o' the men
I 'a kep' thruf thick an' thin my two
    'oonderd a-year to mysen;
Yis! thaw tha call'd me es pretty es
    ony lass i' the Shere;
An' thou be es pretty a tabby, but
    Robby I seed thruf ye theere.

V

Feyther 'ud saäy I wur ugly es sin, an'
    I beänt not vaäin,
But I niver wur downright hugly,
    thaw soom 'ud 'a thowt ma
    plaäin,
An' I wasn't sa plaäin i' pink ribbons
    —ye said I wur pretty i' pinks,
An' I liked to 'ear it I did, but I beänt
    sich a fool as ye thinks;
Ye was stroäkin' ma down wi' the 'air,
    as I be a-stroäkin' o' you,
But whiniver I looöked i' the glass I
    wur sewer that it couldn't be
    true;   20
Niver wur pretty, not I, but ye knaw'd
    it wur pleasant to 'ear,
Thaw it warn't not me es wur pretty,
    but my two 'oonderd a-year.

VI

D' ya mind the murnin' when we was
    a-walkin' togither, an' stood
By the claäy'd-oop pond, that the
    foälk be sa scared at, i' Gig-
    glesby wood,
Wheer the poor wench drowndid her-
    sen, black Sal, es 'ed been dis-
    graäced?
An' I feel'd thy arm es I stood wur
    a-creeäpin' about my waäist;
An' me es wur allus afear'd of a man's
    gittin' ower fond,
I sidled awaäy an' awaäy till I plumpt
    foot fust i' the pond;
And, Robby, I niver 'a liked tha sa
    well, as I did that daäy,
Fur tha joompt in thysen, an' tha
    hoickt my feet wi' a flop fro'
    the claäy.   30

Ay, stick oop thy back, an' set oop thy
　　taäil, tha may gie ma a kiss,
Fur I walk'd wi' tha all the way hoäm
　　an' wur niver sa nigh saäyin'
　　Yis.
But wa boäth was i' sich a clat we was
　　shaämed to cross Gigglesby
　　Greeän,
Fur a cat may loook at a king, thou
　　knaws, but the cat mun be
　　cleän.
Sa we boäth on us kep' out o' sight
　　o' the winders o' Gigglesby
　　Hinn—
Naäy, but the claws o' tha! quiet!
　　they pricks cleän thruf to the
　　skin—
An' wa boäth slinkt 'oäm by the brok-
　　ken shed i' the laäne at the
　　back,
Weer the poodle runn'd at tha once,
　　an' thou runn'd oop o' the
　　thack,
An' tha squeedg'd my 'and i' the shed,
　　fur theere we was forced to
　　'ide,
Fur I seed that Steevie wur coomin',
　　and one o' the Tommies be-
　　side.   40

VII

Theere now, what art 'a mewin' at,
　　Steevie? for owt I can tell—
Robby wur fust, to be sewer, or I
　　mowt 'a liked tha as well.

VIII

But, Robby, I thowt o' tha all the
　　while I wur chaängin' my
　　gown,
An' I thowt, shall I chaänge my
　　staäte? but, O Lord, upo'
　　coomin' down—
My bran-new carpet es fresh es a mid-
　　der o' flowers i' Maäy—
Why 'ed n't tha wiped thy shoes? it
　　wur clatted all ower wi' claäy.
An' I could 'a cried ammost, fur I seed
　　that it couldn't be,
An', Robby, I gied tha a raätin' that
　　sattled thy coortin' o' me.

An' Molly an' me was agreed, as we
　　was a-cleänin' the floor,   49
That a man be a durty thing an' a
　　trouble an' plague wi' indoor.
But I rued it arter a bit, fur I stuck to
　　tha moor na the rest,
But I couldn't 'a lived wi' a man, an' I
　　knaws it be all fur the best.

IX

Naäy—let ma stroäk tha down till I
　　maäkes tha es smooth es silk,
But if I 'ed married tha, Robby,
　　thou'd not 'a been worth thy
　　milk,
Thou'd niver 'a cotch'd ony mice but
　　'a left me the work to do,
And 'a taäen to the bottle beside, so es
　　all that I 'ears be true;
But I loovs tha to maäke thysen 'appy,
　　an' soä purr awaäy, my dear,
Thou 'ed wellnigh purr'd ma awaäy
　　fro' my oän two 'oonderd
　　a-year.

X

Sweärin' ageän, you Toms, as ye used
　　to do twelve year sin'!
Ye niver eärd Steevie sweär 'cep' it
　　wur at a dog coomin' in,   60
An' boäth o' ye mun be fools to be
　　hallus a-shawin' your claws,
Fur I niver cared nothink for neither
　　—an' one o' ye deäd, ye knaws!
Coom, give hoäver then, weänt ye? I
　　warrant ye soom fine daäy—
Theere, lig down—I shall hev to gie
　　one or tother awaäy.
Can't ye taäke pattern by Steevie? ye
　　shan't hev a drop fro' the paäil.
Steevie be right good manners bang
　　thruf to the tip o' the taäil.

XI

Robby, git down wi' tha, wilt tha? let
　　Steevie coom oop o' my knee.
Steevie, my lad, thou 'ed very nigh
　　been the Steevie fur me!
Robby wur fust, to be sewer, 'e wur
　　burn an' bred i' the 'ouse,

But thou be es 'ansom a tabby es iver
    patted a mouse.   70

XII

An' I beänt not vaäin, but I knaws I
    'ed led tha a quieter life
Nor her wi' the hepitaph yonder! 'A
    faäithful an' loovin' wife!'
An' 'cos o' thy farm by the beck, an'
    thy windmill oop o' the croft,
Tha thowt tha would marry ma, did
    tha? but that wur a bit ower
    soft,
Thaw thou was es soäber es daäy, wi'
    a niced red faäce, an' es cleän
Es a shillin' fresh fro' the mint wi' a
    bran-new 'eäd o' the Queeän,
An' thy farmin' es cleän es thysen, fur,
    Steevie, tha kep' it sa neät
That I niver not spied sa much es a
    poppy along wi' the wheät,
An' the wool of a thistle a-flyin' an'
    seeädin' tha haäted to see; 79
'Twur es bad es a battle-twig [1] 'ere i'
    my oän blue chaumber to me.
Ay, roob thy whiskers ageän ma, fur I
    could 'a taäen to tha well,
But fur thy bairns, poor Steevie, a
    bouncin' boy an' a gell.

XIII

An' thou was es fond o' thy bairns es I
    be mysen o' my cats,
But I niver not wish'd fur childer, I
    hev n't naw likin' fur brats;
Pretty anew when ya dresses 'em oop,
    an' they goäs fur a walk,
Or sits wi' their 'ands afoor 'em, an'
    doesn't not 'inder the talk!
But their bottles o' pap, an' their
    mucky bibs, an' the clats, an'
    the clouts,
An' their mashin' their toys to pieäces
    an' maäkin' ma deäf wi' their
    shouts,
An' hallus a-joompin' about ma as if
    they was set upo' springs,
An' a haxin' ma hawkard questions,
    an' saäyin' ondecent things, 90
An' a-callin' ma 'hugly' mayhap to my
    faäce, or a-teärin' my gown—

[1] Earwig.

Dear! dear! dear! I mun part them
    Tommies—Steevie, git down.

XIV

Ye be wuss nor the men-tommies, you.
    I tell'd ya, na moor o' that!
Tom, lig theere o' the cushion, an'
    tother Tom 'ere o' the mat.

XV

Theere! I ha' master'd *them!* Hed
    I married the Tommies—O
    Lord,
To loove an' obaäy the Tommies! I
    couldn't 'a stuck by my word.
To be horder'd about, an' waäked,
    when Molly'd put out the light,
By a man coomin' in wi' a hiccup at
    ony hour o' the night!
An' the taäble staäin'd wi' 'is aäle, an'
    the mud o' 'is boots o' the
    stairs,
An' the stink o' 'is pipe i' the 'ouse,
    an' the mark o' 'is 'eäd o' the
    chairs! 100
An' noän o' my four sweet-arts 'ud 'a
    let me 'a hed my oän waäy,
Sa I likes 'em best wi' taäils when they
    'ev n't a word to saäy.

XVI

An' I sits i' my oän little parlor, an'
    sarved by my oän little lass,
Wi' my oän little garden outside, an'
    my oän bed o' sparrow-grass,
An' my oän door-poorch wi' the wood-
    bine an' jessmine a-dressin' it
    greeän,
An' my oän fine Jackman i' purple a
    roäbin' the 'ouse like a queeän.

XVII

An' the little gells bobs to ma hoffens
    es I be abroad i' the laänes,
When I goäs fur to coomfut the poor
    es be down wi' their haäches
    an' their paäins:
An' a haäf-pot o' jam, or a mossel o'
    meät when it beänt too dear,

They maäkes ma a graäter lady nor 'er
    i' the mansion theer,   110
Hes 'es hallus to hax of a man how
    much to spare or to spend;
An' a spinster I be an' I will be, if
    soä pleäse God, to the hend.

XVIII

Mew! mew!—Bess wi' the milk! what
    ha maäde our Molly sa laäte?
It should 'a been 'ere by seven, an'
    theere—it be strikin' height—
'Cushie wur craäzed fur 'er cauf,' well
    —I 'eärd 'er a-maäkin' 'er
    moän,
An' I thowt to mysen, 'thank God that
    I hev n't naw cauf o' my oän.'
Theere!
      Set it down!
          Now, Robby!
You Tommies shall waäit to-night
Till Robby an' Steevie 'es 'ed their
    lap—an' it sarves ye right.

THE CHARGE OF THE HEAVY BRIGADE AT BALACLAVA

OCTOBER 25, 1854

Prologue

To General Hamley

OUR birches yellowing and from each
    The light leaf falling fast,
While squirrels from our fiery beech
    Were bearing off the mast,
You came, and look'd and loved the
    view
    Long-known and loved by me,
Green Sussex fading into blue
    With one gray glimpse of sea;
And, gazing from this height alone,
    We spoke of what had been
Most marvellous in the wars your own
    Crimean eyes had seen;
And now—like old-world inns that
    take
    Some warrior for a sign
That therewithin a guest may make
    True cheer with honest wine—
Because you heard the lines I read
    Nor utter'd word of blame,

I dare without your leave to head
    These rhymings with your name,
Who know you but as one of those
    I fain would meet again,
Yet know you, as your England knows
    That you and all your men
Were soldiers to her heart's desire,
    When, in the vanish'd year,
You saw the league-long rampart-fire
    Flare from Tel-el-Kebir
Thro' darkness, and the foe was
    driven,
    And Wolseley overthrew
Arabi, and the stars in heaven
    Paled, and the glory grew.

The Charge

I

THE charge of the gallant three hun-
    dred, the Heavy Brigade!
Down the hill, down the hill, thou-
    sands of Russians,
Thousands of horsemen, drew to the
    valley—and stay'd;
For Scarlett and Scarlett's three hun-
    dred were riding by
When the points of the Russian lances
    arose in the sky;
And he call'd, 'Left wheel into line!'
    and they wheel'd and obey'd.
Then he look'd at the host that had
    halted he knew not why,
And he turn'd half round, and he bade
    his trumpeter sound
To the charge, and he rode on ahead,
    as he waved his blade
To the gallant three hundred whose
    glory will never die—
'Follow,' and up the hill, up the hill,
    up the hill,
Follow'd the Heavy Brigade.

II

The trumpet, the gallop, the charge,
    and the might of the fight!
Thousands of horsemen had gather'd
    there on the height,
With a wing push'd out to the left and
    a wing to the right,
And who shall escape if they close?
    but he dash'd up alone

Thro' the great gray slope of men,
Sway'd his sabre, and held his own
Like an Englishman there and then.
All in a moment follow'd with force
Three that were next in their fiery
    course,
Wedged themselves in between horse
    and horse,
Fought for their lives in the narrow
    gap they had made—
Four amid thousands! and up the hill,
    up the hill,
Gallopt the gallant three hundred, the
    Heavy Brigade.

III

Fell like a cannon-shot,
Burst like a thunderbolt,
Crash'd like a hurricane,
Broke thro' the mass from below,
Drove thro' the midst of the foe,
Plunged up and down, to and fro,
Rode flashing blow upon blow,
Brave Inniskillens and Greys
Whirling their sabres in circles of
    light!
And some of us, all in amaze,
Who were held for a while from the
    fight,
And were only standing at gaze,
When the dark-muffled Russian crowd
Folded its wings from the left and the
    right,
And roll'd them around like a cloud,—
O, mad for the charge and the battle
    were we,
When our own good redcoats sank
    from sight,
Like drops of blood in a dark-gray sea,
And we turn'd to each other, whisper-
    ing, all dismay'd,
'Lost are the gallant three hundred of
    Scarlett's Brigade!'

IV

'Lost one and all' were the words
Mutter'd in our dismay;
But they rode like victors and lords
Thro' the forest of lances and swords
In the heart of the Russian hordes,
They rode, or they stood at bay—

Struck with the sword-hand and slew,
Down with the bridle-hand drew
The foe from the saddle and threw
Underfoot there in the fray—
Ranged like a storm or stood like a
    rock
In the wave of a stormy day;
Till suddenly shock upon shock
Stagger'd the mass from without,
Drove it in wild disarray,
For our men gallop up with a cheer
    and a shout,
And the foeman surged, and waver'd,
    and reel'd
Up the hill, up the hill, up the hill, out
    of the field,
And over the brow and away.

V

Glory to each and to all, and the
    charge that they made!
Glory to all the three hundred, and all
    the Brigade!

NOTE.—The 'three hundred' of the
'Heavy Brigade' who made this famous
charge were the Scots Greys and the 2d
squadron of Inniskillens; the remainder
of the 'Heavy Brigade' subsequently
dashing up to their support.

The 'three' were Scarlett's aide-de-
camp, Elliot, and the trumpeter, and
Shegog the orderly, who had been close
behind him.

Epilogue

IRENE

NOT this way will you set your name
    A star among the stars.

POET

What way?

IRENE

    You praise when you should
    blame
The barbarism of wars.
A juster epoch has begun.

POET

Yet tho' this cheek be gray,
And that bright hair the modern sun,
 Those eyes the blue to-day,
You wrong me, passionate little friend.
 I would that wars should cease,
I would the globe from end to end
 Might sow and reap in peace,
And some new Spirit o'erbear the old,
 Or Trade re-frain the Powers
From war with kindly links of gold,
 Or Love with wreaths of flowers.
Slav, Teuton, Kelt, I count them all
 My friends and brother souls,
With all the peoples, great and small,
 That wheel between the poles.
But since our mortal shadow, Ill,
 To waste this earth began—
Perchance from some abuse of Will
 In worlds before the man
Involving ours—he needs must fight
 To make true peace his own,
He needs must combat might with
  might,
 Or Might would rule alone;
And who loves war for war's own sake
 Is fool, or crazed, or worse;
But let the patriot-soldier take
 His meed of fame in verse;
Nay—tho' that realm were in the
  wrong
 For which her warriors bleed,
It still were right to crown with song
 The warrior's noble deed—
A crown the Singer hopes may last,
 For so the deed endures;
But Song will vanish in the Vast;
 And that large phrase of yours
'A star among the stars,' my dear,
 Is girlish talk at best;
For dare we dally with the sphere
 As he did half in jest,
Old Horace? 'I will strike,' said he,
 'The stars with head sublime,'
But scarce could see, as now we see,
 The man in space and time,
So drew perchance a happier lot
 Than ours, who rhyme to-day.
The fires that arch this dusky dot—
 Yon myriad-worlded way—

The vast sun-clusters' gather'd blaze,
 World-isles in lonely skies,
Whole heavens within themselves,
  amaze
 Our brief humanities.
And so does Earth; for Homer's fame,
 Tho' carved in harder stone—
The falling drop will make his name
 As mortal as my own.

IRENE

No!

POET

Let it live then—ay, till when?
 Earth passes, all is lost
In what they prophesy, our wise men,
 Sun-flame or sunless frost,
And deed and song alike are swept
 Away, and all in vain
As far as man can see, except
 The man himself remain;
And tho', in this lean age forlorn,
 Too many a voice may cry
That man can have no after-morn,
 Not yet of those am I.
The man remains, and whatsoe'er
 He wrought of good or brave
Will mould him thro' the cycle-year
 That dawns behind the grave.

————

And here the Singer for his art
 Not all in vain may plead
'The song that nerves a nation's heart
 Is in itself a deed.'

TO VIRGIL

WRITTEN AT THE REQUEST OF THE
MANTUANS FOR THE NINETEENTH
CENTENARY OF VIRGIL'S DEATH

I

ROMAN VIRGIL, thou that singest
 Ilion's lofty temples robed in
   fire,

Ilion falling, Rome arising,
  wars, and filial faith, and
   Dido's pyre;

II

Landscape-lover, lord of language
  more than he that sang the
   'Works and Days,'
All the chosen coin of fancy
  flashing out from many a
   golden phrase;

III

Thou that singest wheat and woodland,
  tilth and vineyard, hive and
   horse and herd;
All the charm of all the Muses
  often flowering in a lonely
   word;

IV

Poet of the happy Tityrus
  piping underneath his beechen
   bowers;
Poet of the poet-satyr
  whom the laughing shepherd
   bound with flowers;

V

Chanter of the Pollio, glorying
  in the blissful years again to
   be,
Summers of the snakeless meadow,
  unlaborious earth and oarless
   sea;

VI

Thou that seest Universal
  Nature moved by Universal
   Mind;
Thou majestic in thy sadness
  at the doubtful doom of human
   kind;

VII

Light among the vanish'd ages;
  star that gildest yet this phantom shore;

Golden branch amid the shadows,
  kings and realms that pass to
   rise no more;

VIII

Now thy Forum roars no longer,
  fallen every purple Cæsar's
   dome—
Tho' thine ocean-roll of rhythm
  sound forever of Imperial
   Rome—

IX

Now the Rome of slaves hath perish'd,
  and the Rome of freemen
   holds her place,
I, from out the Northern Island
  sunder'd once from all the
   human race,

X

I salute thee, Mantovano,
  I that loved thee since my day
   began,
Wielder of the stateliest measure
  ever moulded by the lips of
   man.

THE DEAD PROPHET

182–

I

DEAD!
  And the Muses cried with a stormy
   cry,
'Send them no more, for evermore.
  Let the people die.'

II

Dead!
  'Is it *he* then brought so low?'
And a careless people flock'd from the
   fields
With a purse to pay for the show.

III

Dead, who had served his time,
  Was one of the people's kings,

Had labor'd in lifting them out of
slime,
And showing them, souls have
wings!

IV

Dumb on the winter heath he lay.
His friends had stript him bare,
And roll'd his nakedness everyway
That all the crowd might stare.

V

A storm-worn signpost not to be read,
And a tree with a moulder'd nest
On its barkless bones, stood stark by
the dead;
And behind him, low in the West,

VI

With shifting ladders of shadow and
light,
And blurr'd in color and form,
The sun hung over the gates of night,
And glared at a coming storm.

VII

Then glided a vulturous beldam forth,
That on dumb death had thriven;
They call'd her 'Reverence' here upon
earth,
And 'The Curse of the Prophet' in
heaven.

VIII

She knelt—'We worship him'—all but
wept—
'So great, so noble, was he!'
She clear'd her sight, she arose, she
swept
The dust of earth from her knee.

IX

'Great! for he spoke and the people
heard,
And his eloquence caught like a
flame
From zone to zone of the world, till
his word
Had won him a noble name.

X

'Noble! he sung, and the sweet sound
ran
Thro' palace and cottage door,
For he touch'd on the whole sad planet
of man,
The kings and the rich and the
poor;

XI

'And he sung not alone of an old sun
set,
But a sun coming up in his youth!
Great and noble—O, yes—but yet—
For man is a lover of truth,

XII

'And bound to follow, wherever she
go
Stark-naked, and up or down,
Thro' her high hill-passes of stainless
snow,
Or the foulest sewer of the town—

XIII

'Noble and great—O, ay—but then,
Tho' a prophet should have his due,
Was he noblier-fashion'd than other
men?
Shall we see to it, I and you?

XIV

'For since he would sit on a prophet's
seat,
As a lord of the human soul,
We needs must scan him from head to
feet,
Were it but for a wart or a mole?'

XV

His wife and his child stood by him in
tears,
But she—she push'd them aside.
'Tho' a name may last for a thousand
years,
Yet a truth is a truth,' she cried.

XVI

And she that had haunted his pathway
     still,
Had often truckled and cower'd
When he rose in his wrath, and had
     yielded her will
To the master, as overpower'd,

XVII

She tumbled his helpless corpse about.
     'Small blemish upon the skin!
But I think we know what is fair with-
     out
If often as foul within.'

XVIII

She crouch'd, she tore him part from
     part,
     And out of his body she drew
The red 'blood-eagle'[1] of liver and
     heart;
     She held them up to the view;

XIX

She gabbled, as she groped in the dead,
     And all the people were pleased;
'See, what a little heart,' she said,
     'And the liver is half-diseased!'

XX

She tore the prophet after death,
     And the people paid her well.
Lightnings flicker'd along the heath;
     One shriek'd, 'The fires of hell!'

EARLY SPRING

I

ONCE more the Heavenly Power
     Makes all things new,
And domes the red-plow'd hills
     With loving blue;
The blackbirds have their wills,
     The throstles too.

[1] Old Viking term for lungs, liver, etc.,
when torn by the conqueror out of the
body of the conquered.

II

Opens a door in heaven;
     From skies of glass
A Jacob's ladder falls
     On greening grass,
And o'er the mountain-walls
     Young angels pass.

III

Before them fleets the shower,
     And burst the buds,
And shine the level lands,
     And flash the floods;
The stars are from their hands
     Flung thro' the woods,

IV

The woods with living airs
     How softly fann'd,
Light airs from where the deep,
     All down the sand,
Is breathing in his sleep,
     Heard by the land.

V

O, follow, leaping blood,
     The season's lure!
O heart, look down and up
     Serene, secure,
Warm as the crocus cup,
     Like snowdrops, pure!

VI

Past, Future glimpse and fade
     Thro' some slight spell,
A gleam from yonder vale,
     Some far blue fell,
And sympathies, how frail,
     In sound and smell!

VII

Till at thy chuckled note,
     Thou twinkling bird,
The fairy fancies range,
     And, lightly stirr'd,
Ring little bells of change
     From word to word.

VIII

For now the Heavenly Power
    Makes all things new,
And thaws the cold, and fills
    The flower with dew;
The blackbirds have their wills,
    The poets too.

PREFATORY POEM TO MY BROTHER'S SONNETS

MIDNIGHT, JUNE 30, 1879

I

MIDNIGHT—in no midsummer tune
The breakers lash the shores;
The cuckoo of a joyless June
Is calling out of doors.

And thou hast vanish'd from thine
        own
To that which looks like rest,
True brother, only to be known
By those who love thee best.

II

Midnight—and joyless June gone by,
And from the deluged park
The cuckoo of a worse July
Is calling thro' the dark;

But thou art silent underground,
And o'er thee streams the rain,
True poet, surely to be found
When Truth is found again.

III

And, now to these unsummer'd skies
The summer bird is still,
Far off a phantom cuckoo cries
From out a phantom hill;

And thro' this midnight breaks the sun
Of sixty years away,
The light of days when life begun,
The days that seem to-day,

When all my griefs were shared with
        thee,
As all my hopes were thine—
As all thou wert was one with me,
May all thou art be mine!

'FRATER AVE ATQUE VALE'

Row us out from Desenzano, to your
        Sirmione row!
So they row'd, and there we landed—
        'O venusta Sirmio!'
There to me thro' all the groves of
        olive in the summer glow,
There beneath the Roman ruin where
        the purple flowers grow,
Came that 'Ave atque Vale' of the
        Poet's hopeless woe,
Tenderest of Roman poets nineteen
        hundred years ago,
'Frater Ave atque Vale'—as we wan-
        der'd to and fro
Gazing at the Lydian laughter of the
        Garda Lake below
Sweet Catullus's all-but-island, olive-
        silvery Sirmio!

HELEN'S TOWER

[Written at the request of my friend,
Lord Dufferin.]

HELEN'S TOWER, here I stand,
Dominant over sea and land.
Son's love built me, and I hold
Mother's love in letter'd gold.
Love is in and out of time,
I am mortal stone and lime.
Would my granite girth were strong
As either love, to last as long!
I should wear my crown entire
To and thro' the Doomsday fire,
And be found of angel eyes
In earth's recurring Paradise.

EPITAPH ON LORD STRATFORD DE REDCLIFFE

IN WESTMINSTER ABBEY

THOU third great Canning, stand
        among our best

And noblest, now thy long day's
    work hath ceased,
Here silent in our Minster of the West
Who wert the voice of England in
    the East.

EPITAPH ON GENERAL GORDON

IN THE GORDON BOYS' NATIONAL
MEMORIAL HOME NEAR WOKING

WARRIOR of God, man's friend, and
    tyrant's foe,
Now somewhere dead far in the
    waste Soudan,
Thou livest in all hearts, for all men
    know
This earth has never borne a nobler
    man.

EPITAPH ON CAXTON

IN ST. MARGARET'S, WESTMINSTER

Fiat Lux (his motto)

THY prayer was 'Light—more Light
    —while Time shall last!'
Thou sawest a glory growing on the
    night,
But not the shadows which that light
    would cast,
Till shadows vanish in the Light of
    Light.

TO THE DUKE OF ARGYLL

O PATRIOT Statesman, be thou wise to
    know
The limits of resistance, and the
    bounds
Determining concession; still be bold
Not only to slight praise but suffer
    scorn;
And be thy heart a fortress to main-
    tain
The day against the moment, and the
    year
Against the day; thy voice, a music
    heard

Thro' all the yells and counter-yells
    of feud
And faction, and thy will, a power to
    make
This ever-changing world of circum-
    stance,
In changing, chime with never-chang-
    ing Law.

HANDS ALL ROUND

FIRST pledge our Queen this solemn
    night,
    Then drink to England, every
        guest;
That man 's the best Cosmopolite
    Who loves his native country best.
May freedom's oak for ever live
    With stronger life from day to day;
That man 's the true Conservative
    Who lops the moulder'd branch
        away.
            Hands all round!
    God the traitor's hope confound!
To this great cause of Freedom drink,
        my friends,
    And the great name of England,
        round and round.
To all the loyal hearts who long
    To keep our English Empire whole!
To all our noble sons, the strong
    New England of the Southern Pole!
To England under Indian skies,
    To those dark millions of her realm!
To Canada whom we love and prize,
    Whatever statesman hold the helm.
            Hands all round!
    God the traitor's hope confound!
To this great name of England drink,
        my friends,
    And all her glorious empire, round
        and round.
To all our statesmen so they be
    True leaders of the land's desire!
To both our Houses, may they see
    Beyond the borough and the shire!
We sail'd wherever ship could sail,
    We founded many a mighty state;
Pray God our greatness may not fail
    Thro' craven fears of being great!
            Hands all round!
    God the traitor's hope confound!

To this great cause of Freedom drink,
    my friends,
    And the great name of England,
    round and round.

FREEDOM

I

O thou so fair in summers gone,
    While yet thy fresh and virgin soul
Inform'd the pillar'd Parthenon,
    The glittering Capitol;

II

So fair in southern sunshine bathed,
    But scarce of such majestic mien
As here with forehead vapor-swathed
    In meadows ever green;

III

For thou—when Athens reign'd and
    Rome,
    Thy glorious eyes were dimm'd with
        pain
To mark in many a freeman's home
    The slave, the scourge, the chain;

IV

O follower of the Vision, still
    In motion to the distant gleam,
Howe'er blind force and brainless will
    May jar thy golden dream

V

Of Knowledge fusing class with class,
    Of civic Hate no more to be,
Of Love to leaven all the mass,
    Till every soul be free;

VI

Who yet, like Nature, wouldst not mar
    By changes all too fierce and fast
This order of her Human Star,
    This heritage of the past;

VII

O scorner of the party cry
    That wanders from the public good,
Thou—when the nations rear on high
    Their idol smear'd with blood,

VIII

And when they roll their idol down—
    Of saner worship sanely proud;
Thou loather of the lawless crown
    As of the lawless crowd;

IX

How long thine ever-growing mind
    Hath still'd the blast and strown the
        wave,
Tho' some of late would raise a wind
    To sing thee to thy grave,

X

Men loud against all forms of power—
    Unfurnish'd brows, tempestuous
        tongues,
Expecting all things in an hour—
    Brass mouths and iron lungs!

POETS AND THEIR BIBLIOGRA-
PHIES

Old poets foster'd under friendlier
        skies,
    Old Virgil who would write ten
        lines, they say,
    At dawn, and lavish all the golden
        day
To make them wealthier in his read-
        ers' eyes;
And you, old popular Horace, you the
        wise
    Adviser of the nine-years-ponder'd
        lay,
    And you, that wear a wreath of
        sweeter bay,
Catullus, whose dead songster never
        dies;
If, glancing downward on the kindly
        sphere

That once had roll'd you round and
    round the sun,
You see your Art still shrined in hu-
    man shelves,
You should be jubilant that you flour-
    ish'd here
Before the Love of Letters, over-
    done,
Had swampt the sacred poets with
    themselves.

TO H. R. H. PRINCESS
BEATRICE

Two Suns of Love make day of human
    life,
Which else with all its pains, and
    griefs, and deaths,
Were utter darkness—one, the Sun of
    dawn
That brightens thro' the Mother's ten-
    der eyes,
And warms the child's awakening
    world—and one
The later-rising Sun of spousal Love,
Which from her household orbit draws
    the child

To move in other spheres. The Mother
    weeps
At that white funeral of the single life,
Her maiden daughter's marriage; and
    her tears
Are half of pleasure, half of pain—the
    child
Is happy—even in leaving *her!* but
    thou,
True daughter, whose all-faithful,
    filial eyes
Have seen the loneliness of earthly
    thrones,
Wilt neither quit the widow'd Crown,
    nor let
This later light of Love have risen in
    vain,
But moving thro' the Mother's home,
    between
The two that love thee, lead a summer
    life,
Sway'd by each Love, and swaying to
    each Love,
Like some conjectured planet in mid
    heaven
Between two suns, and drawing down
    from both
The light and genial warmth of double
    day.

LOCKSLEY HALL SIXTY YEARS AFTER, ETC.

TO MY WIFE
I DEDICATE
THIS DRAMATIC MONOLOGUE
AND
THE POEMS WHICH FOLLOW

LOCKSLEY HALL SIXTY YEARS AFTER

LATE, my grandson! half the morning
    have I paced these sandy
    tracts,
Watch'd again the hollow ridges roar-
    ing into cataracts,

Wander'd back to living boyhood
    while I heard the curlews call,
I myself so close on death, and death
    itself in Locksley Hall.

So—your happy suit was blasted—she
    the faultless, the divine;
And you liken—boyish babble—this
    boy-love of yours with mine.

I myself have often babbled doubtless
    of a foolish past;
Babble, babble; our old England may
    go down in babble at last.

'Curse him!' curse your fellow-vic-
    tim? call him dotard in your
    rage?
Eyes that lured a doting boyhood well
    might fool a dotard's age.   10

Jilted for a wealthier! wealthier? yet
    perhaps she was not wise;
I remember how you kiss'd the min-
    iature with those sweet eyes.

In the hall there hangs a painting—
    Amy's arms about my neck—

Happy children in a sunbeam sitting
    on the ribs of wreck.

In my life there was a picture, she
    that clasp'd my neck had
    flown;
I was left within the shadow sitting on
    the wreck alone.

Yours has been a slighter ailment,
    will you sicken for her sake?
You, not you! your modern amorist is
    of easier, earthlier make.

Amy loved me, Amy fail'd me, Amy
    was a timid child;
But your Judith—but your worldling
    —*she* had never driven me
    wild.   20

She that holds the diamond necklace
    dearer than the golden ring,
She that finds a winter sunset fairer
    than a morn of spring.

She that in her heart is brooding on
    his briefer lease of life,
While she vows 'till death shall part
    us,' she the would-be-widow
    wife.

She the worldling born of worldlings
    —father, mother—be content,
Even the homely farm can teach us
    there is something in descent.

Yonder in that chapel, slowly sinking
    now into the ground,
Lies the warrior, my forefather, with
    his feet upon the hound.

Cross'd! for once he sail'd the sea to
    crush the Moslem in his pride;

Dead the warrior, dead his glory, dead
    the cause in which he died. [30]

Yet how often I and Amy in the
    mouldering aisle have stood,
Gazing for one pensive moment on
    that founder of our blood.

There again I stood to-day, and where
    of old we knelt in prayer,
Close beneath the casement crimson
    with the shield of Locksley—
    there,

All in white Italian marble, looking
    still as if she smiled,
Lies my Amy dead in childbirth, dead
    the mother, dead the child.

Dead—and sixty years ago, and dead
    her aged husband now—
I, this old white-headed dreamer,
    stoopt and kiss'd her marble
    brow.

Gone the fires of youth, the follies,
    furies, curses, passionate tears,
Gone like fires and floods and earth-
    quakes of the planet's dawning
    years.   [40]

Fires that shook me once, but now to
    silent ashes fallen away.
Cold upon the dead volcano sleeps the
    gleam of dying day.

Gone the tyrant of my youth, and
    mute below the chancel stones,
All his virtues—I forgive them—black
    in white above his bones.

Gone the comrades of my bivouac,
    some in fight against the foe,
Some thro' age and slow diseases, gone
    as all on earth will go.

Gone with whom for forty years my
    life in golden sequence ran,
She with all the charm of woman, she
    with all the breadth of man,

Strong in will and rich in wisdom,
    Edith, yet so lowly-sweet,

Woman to her inmost heart, and
    woman to her tender feet, [50]

Very woman of very woman, nurse of
    ailing body and mind,
She that link'd again the broken chain
    that bound me to my kind.

Here to-day was Amy with me, while
    I wander'd down the coast,
Near us Edith's holy shadow, smiling
    at the slighter ghost.

Gone our sailor son thy father, Leon-
    ard early lost at sea;
Thou alone, my boy, of Amy's kin and
    mine art left to me.

Gone thy tender-natured mother,
    wearying to be left alone,
Pining for the stronger heart that once
    had beat beside her own.

Truth, for truth is truth, he worshipt,
    being true as he was brave;
Good, for good is good, he follow'd,
    yet he look'd beyond the grave,

Wiser there than you, that crowning
    barren Death as lord of all, [61]
Deem this over-tragic drama's closing
    curtain is the pall!

Beautiful was death in him, who saw
    the death, but kept the deck,
Saving women and their babes, and
    sinking with the sinking wreck,

Gone for ever! Ever? no—for since
    our dying race began,
Ever, ever, and for ever was the lead-
    ing light of man.

Those that in barbarian burials kill'd
    the slave, and slew the wife
Felt within themselves the sacred pas-
    sion of the second life.

Indian warriors dream of ampler
    hunting grounds beyond the
    night;
Even the black Australian dying hopes
    he shall return, a white. [70]

Truth for truth, and good for good!
    The good, the true, the pure,
        the just—
Take the charm 'For ever' from them,
    and they crumble into dust.

Gone the cry of 'Forward, Forward,'
    lost within a growing gloom;
Lost, or only heard in silence from the
    silence of a tomb.

Half the marvels of my morning, tri-
    umphs over time and space,
Staled by frequence, shrunk by usage
    into commonest commonplace!

'Forward' rang the voices then, and of
    the many mine was one.
Let us hush this cry of 'Forward' till
    ten thousand years have gone.

Far among the vanish'd races, old As-
    syrian kings would flay
Captives whom they caught in battle
    —iron-hearted victors they. 80

Ages after, while in Asia, he that led
    the wild Moguls,
Timur built his ghastly tower of eighty
    thousand human skulls;

Then, and here in Edward's time, an
    age of noblest English names,
Christian conquerors took and flung
    the conquer'd Christian into
    flames.

Love your enemy, bless your haters,
    said the Greatest of the great;
Christian love among the Churches
    look'd the twin of heathen
    hate.

From the golden alms of Blessing man
    had coin'd himself a curse:
Rome of Cæsar, Rome of Peter, which
    was   crueller?   which   was
    worse?

France had shown a light to all men,
    preach'd a Gospel, all men's
    good; 89
Celtic Demos rose a Demon, shriek'd
    and slaked the light with blood.

Hope was ever on her mountain,
    watching till the day begun—
Crown'd with sunlight—over darkness
    —from the still unrisen sun.

Have we grown at last beyond the pas-
    sions of the primal clan?
'Kill your enemy, for you hate him,'
    still, 'your enemy' was a man.

Have we sunk below them? peasants
    maim the helpless horse, and
    drive
Innocent cattle under thatch, and
    burn the kindlier brutes alive.

Brutes, the brutes are not your wrong-
    ers—burnt at midnight, found
    at morn,
Twisted hard in mortal agony with
    their offspring, born-unborn,

Clinging to the silent mother! Are we
    devils? are we men?
Sweet Saint Francis of Assisi, would
    that he were here again, 100

He that in his Catholic wholeness used
    to call the very flowers
Sisters, brothers—and the beasts—
    whose pains are hardly less
    than ours!

Chaos, Cosmos! Cosmos, Chaos! who
    can tell how all will end?
Read the wide world's annals, you,
    and take their wisdom for your
    friend.

Hope the best, but hold the Present
    fatal daughter of the Past,
Shape your heart to front the hour,
    but dream not that the hour
    will last.

Ay, if dynamite and revolver leave
    you courage to be wise—
When was age so cramm'd with men-
    ace? madness? written, spoken
    lies?

Envy wears the mask of Love, and,
    laughing sober fact to scorn,
Cries to weakest as to strongest, 'Ye
    are equals, equal-born.' 110

Equal-born? O, yes, if yonder hill be
    level with the flat.
Charm us, orator, till the lion look no
    larger than the cat,

Till the cat thro' that mirage of over-
    heated language loom
Larger than the lion,—Demos end in
    working its own doom.

Russia bursts our Indian barrier, shall
    we fight her? shall we yield?
Pause! before you sound the trumpet,
    hear the voices from the field.

Those three hundred millions under
    one Imperial sceptre now,
Shall we hold them? shall we loose
    them? take the suffrage of the
    plow.

Nay, but these would feel and follow
    Truth if only you and you,
Rivals of realm-ruining party, when
    you speak were wholly true. 120

Plowmen, shepherds, have I found,
    and more than once, and still
    could find,
Sons of God, and kings of men in utter
    nobleness of mind,

Truthful, trustful, looking upward to
    the practised hustings-liar;
So the higher wields the lower, while
    the lower is the higher.

Here and there a cotter's babe is
    royal-born by right divine;
Here and there my lord is lower than
    his oxen or his swine.

Chaos, Cosmos! Cosmos, Chaos! once
    again the sickening game;
Freedom, free to slay herself, and dy-
    ing while they shout her name.

Step by step we gain'd a freedom
    known to Europe, known to
    all;
Step by step we rose to greatness,—
    thro' the tonguesters we may
    fall. 130

You that woo the Voices—tell them
    'old experience is a fool,'
Teach your flatter'd kings that only
    those who cannot read can
    rule.

Pluck the mighty from their seat, but
    set no meek ones in their place;
Pillory Wisdom in your markets, pelt
    your offal at her face.

Tumble Nature heel o'er head, and,
    yelling with the yelling street,
Set the feet above the brain and swear
    the brain is in the feet.

Bring the old dark ages back without
    the faith, without the hope,
Break the State, the Church, the
    Throne, and roll their ruins
    down the slope.

Authors—essayist, atheist, novelist,
    realist, rhymester, play your
    part,
Paint the mortal shame of nature with
    the living hues of art. 140

Rip your brothers' vices open, strip
    your own foul passions bare;
Down with Reticence, down with
    Reverence — forward — naked
    let them stare.

Feed the budding rose of boyhood
    with the drainage of your
    sewer;
Send the drain into the fountain, lest
    the stream should issue pure.

Set the maiden fancies wallowing in
    the troughs of Zolaism,—
Forward, forward, ay, and backward,
    downward too into the abysm!

Do your best to charm the worst, to
    lower the rising race of men;
Have we risen from out the beast,
    then back into the beast again?

Only 'dust to dust' for me that sicken
    at your lawless din,
Dust in wholesome old-world dust be-
    fore the newer world begin. 150

Heated am I? you—you wonder—
   well, it scarce becomes mine
   age—
Patience! let the dying actor mouth
   his last upon the stage.

Cries of unprogressive dotage ere the
   dotard fall asleep?
Noises of a current narrowing, not the
   music of a deep?

Ay, for doubtless I am old, and think
   gray thoughts, for I am gray;
After all the stormy changes shall we
   find a changeless May?

After madness, after massacre, Jacob-
   ism and Jacquerie,
Some diviner force to guide us thro'
   the days I shall not see?

When the schemes and all the systems, kingdoms and republics
   fall,   159
Something kindlier, higher, holier—
   all for each and each for all?

All the full-brain, half-brain races, led
   by Justice, Love, and Truth;
All the millions one at length with all
   the visions of my youth?

All diseases quench'd by Science, no
   man halt, or deaf, or blind;
Stronger ever born of weaker, lustier
   body, larger mind?

Earth at last a warless world, a single
   race, a single tongue—
I have seen her far away—for is not
   Earth as yet so young?—

Every tiger madness muzzled, every
   serpent passion kill'd,
Every grim ravine a garden, every
   blazing desert till'd,

Robed in universal harvest up to
   either pole she smiles,
Universal ocean softly washing all her
   warless isles.   170

Warless? when her tens are thousands,
   and her thousands millions,
   then—
All her harvest all too narrow—who
   can fancy warless men?

Warless? war will die out late then.
   Will it ever? late or soon?
Can it, till this outworn earth be dead
   as yon dead world the moon?

Dead the new astronomy calls her.—
   On this day and at this hour,
In this gap between the sandhills,
   whence you see the Locksley
   tower,

Here we met, our latest meeting—
   Amy—sixty years ago—
She and I—the moon was falling
   greenish thro' a rosy glow,

Just above the gateway tower, and
   even where you see her now—
Here we stood and claspt each other,
   swore the seeming-deathless
   vow.—   180

Dead, but how her living glory lights
   the hall, the dune, the grass!
Yet the moonlight is the sunlight, and
   the sun himself will pass.

Venus near her! smiling downward at
   this earthlier earth of ours,
Closer on the sun, perhaps a world of
   never fading flowers.

Hesper, whom the poet call'd the
   Bringer home of all good
   things—
All good things may move in Hesper,
   perfect peoples, perfect kings.

Hesper—Venus—were we native to
   that splendor or in Mars,
We should see the globe we groan in,
   fairest of their evening stars.

Could we dream of wars and carnage,
   craft and madness, lust and
   spite,
Roaring London, raving Paris, in that
   point of peaceful light?   190

Might we not in glancing heavenward
    on a star so silver-fair,
Yearn, and clasp the hands and mur-
    mur, 'Would to God that we
    were there'?

Forward, backward, backward, for-
    ward, in the immeasurable sea,
Sway'd by vaster ebbs and flows than
    can be known to you or me.

All the suns—are these but symbols of
    innumerable man,
Man or Mind that sees a shadow of the
    planner or the plan?

Is there evil but on earth? or pain in
    every peopled sphere?
Well, be grateful for the sounding
    watchword 'Evolution' here,

Evolution ever climbing after some
    ideal good,
And Reversion ever dragging Evolu-
    tion in the mud.   200

What are men that He should heed us?
    cried the king of sacred song;
Insects of an hour, that hourly work
    their brother insect wrong,

While the silent heavens roll, and suns
    along their fiery way,
All their planets whirling round them,
    flash a million miles a day.

Many an æon moulded earth before
    her highest, man, was born,
Many an æon too may pass while earth
    is manless and forlorn,

Earth so huge, and yet so bounded—
    pools of salt, and plots of
    land—
Shallow skin of green and azure—
    chains of mountain, grains of
    sand!

Only That which made us meant us to
    be mightier by and by,   209
Set the sphere of all the boundless
    heavens within the human eye,

Sent the shadow of Himself, the
    boundless, thro' the human
    soul;
Boundless inward in the atom, bound-
    less outward in the Whole.

  . . . .

Here is Locksley Hall, my grandson,
    here the lion-guarded gate.
Not to-night in Locksley Hall—to-
    morrow—you, you come so
    late.

Wreck'd—your train—or all but
    wreck'd? a shatter'd wheel? a
    vicious boy!
Good, this forward, you that preach it,
    is it well to wish you joy?

Is it well that while we range with
    Science, glorying in the Time,
City children soak and blacken soul
    and sense in city slime?

There among the glooming alleys
    Progress halts on palsied feet,
Crime and hunger cast our maidens by
    the thousand on the street.   220

There the master scrimps his haggard
    sempstress of her daily bread,
There a single sordid attic holds the
    living and the dead.

There the smouldering fire of fever
    creeps across the rotted floor,
And the crowded couch of incest in the
    warrens of the poor.

Nay, your pardon, cry your 'Forward,'
    yours are hope and youth, but
    I—
Eighty winters leave the dog too lame
    to follow with the cry,

Lame and old, and past his time, and
    passing now into the night;
Yet I would the rising race were half
    as eager for the light.

Light the fading gleam of even? light
    the glimmer of the dawn?   229
Aged eyes may take the growing glim-
    mer for the gleam withdrawn.

Far away beyond her myriad coming
    changes earth will be
Something other than the wildest
    modern guess of you and me.

Earth may reach her earthly-worst,
    or if she gain her earthly-best,
Would she find her human offspring
    this ideal man at rest?

Forward then, but still remember how
    the course of Time will swerve,
Crook and turn upon itself in many a
    backward streaming curve.

Not the Hall to-night, my grandson!
    Death and Silence hold their
    own.
Leave the master in the first dark
    hour of his last sleep alone.

Worthier soul was he than I am, sound
    and honest, rustic Squire,
Kindly landlord, boon companion—
    youthful jealousy is a liar. 240

Cast the poison from your bosom, oust
    the madness from your brain.
Let the trampled serpent show you
    that you have not lived in vain.

Youthful! youth and age are scholars
    yet but in the lower school,
Nor is he the wisest man who never
    proved himself a fool.

Yonder lies our young sea-village—
    Art and Grace are less and
    less:
Science grows and Beauty dwindles—
    roofs of slated hideousness!

There is one old hostel left us where
    they swing the Locksley shield,
Till the peasant cow shall butt the
    'lion passant' from his field.

Poor old Heraldry, poor old History,
    poor old Poetry, passing hence,
In the common deluge drowning old
    political common-sense! 250

Poor old voice of eighty crying after
    voices that have fled!
All I loved are vanish'd voices, all my
    steps are on the dead.

All the world is ghost to me, and as
    the phantom disappears,
Forward far and far from here is all
    the hope of eighty years.

. . . . . .

In this hostel—I remember—I repent
    it o'er his grave—
Like a clown—by chance he met me—
    I refused the hand he gave.

From that casement where the trailer
    mantles all the mouldering
    bricks—
I was then in early boyhood, Edith but
    a child of six—

While I shelter'd in this archway from
    a day of driving showers—
Peept the winsome face of Edith like
    a flower among the flowers. 260

Here to-night! the Hall to-morrow,
    when they toll the chapel bell!
Shall I hear in one dark room a wail-
    ing, 'I have loved thee well'?

Then a peal that shakes the portal—
    one has come to claim his
    bride,
Her that shrank, and put me from her,
    shriek'd, and started from my
    side—

Silent echoes! You, my Leonard, use
    and not abuse your day,
Move among your people, know them,
    follow him who led the way,

Strove for sixty widow'd years to help
    his homelier brother men,
Served the poor, and built the cottage,
    raised the school, and drain'd
    the fen.

Hears he now the voice that wrong'd
    him? who shall swear it can-
    not be?
Earth would never touch her worst,
    were one in fifty such as he. 270

Ere she gain her heavenly-best, a God
    must mingle with the game.
Nay, there may be those about us
    whom we neither see nor name,

Felt within us as ourselves, the Powers
    of Good, the Powers of Ill,
Strowing balm, or shedding poison in
    the fountains of the will.

Follow you the star that lights a desert
    pathway, yours or mine.
Forward, till you see the Highest
    Human Nature is divine.

Follow Light, and do the Right—
    for man can half-control his
    doom—
Till you find the deathless Angel
    seated in the vacant tomb.

Forward, let the stormy moment fly
    and mingle with the past.
I that loathed have come to love him.
    Love will conquer at the
    last.   280

Gone at eighty, mine own age, and I
    and you will bear the pall;
Then I leave thee lord and master,
    latest lord of Locksley Hall.

THE FLEET [1]

I

You, you, *if* you should fail to under-
    stand
    What England is, and what her all-
      in-all,
On you will come the curse of all the
    land,
    Should this old England fall
      Which Nelson left so great.

[1] The speaker said that 'he should like to
be assured that other outlying portions
of the Empire, the Crown colonies, and
important coaling stations were being as
promptly and as thoroughly fortified as
the various capitals of the self-governing
colonies. He was credibly informed this
was not so. It was impossible, also, not
to feel some degree of anxiety about the

II

His isle, the mightiest Ocean-power
    on earth,
    Our own fair isle, the lord of every
      sea—
Her fuller franchise—what would that
    be worth—
    Her ancient fame of Free—
      Were she . . . a fallen state?

III

Her dauntless army scatter'd, and so
    small,
    Her island-myriads fed from alien
      lands—

efficacy of present provision to defend
and protect, by means of swift well-
armed cruisers, the immense mercantile
fleet of the Empire. A third source of
anxiety, so far as the colonies were con-
cerned, was the apparently insufficient
provision for the rapid manufacture of
armaments and their prompt despatch
when ordered to their colonial destina-
tion. Hence the necessity for manufac-
turing appliances equal to the require-
ments, not of Great Britain alone, but of
the whole Empire. But the keystone of
the whole was the necessity for an over-
whelmingly powerful fleet and efficient
defence for all necessary coaling stations.
This was as essential for the colonies as
for Great Britain. It was the one condition for the continuance of the Empire.
All that Continental Powers did with respect to armies England should effect
with her navy. It was essentially a defen-
sive force, and could be moved rapidly
from point to point, but it should be
equal to all that was expected from it.
It was to strengthen the fleet that colo-
nists would first readily tax themselves,
because they realized how essential a
powerful fleet was to the safety, not only
of that extensive commerce sailing in
every sea, but ultimately to the security
of the distant portions of the Empire.
Who could estimate the loss involved in
even a brief period of disaster to the Imperial Navy? Any amount of money
timely expended in preparation would
be quite insignificant when compared
with the possible calamity he had re-
ferred to.'—*Extract from Sir Graham
Berry's Speech at the Colonial Institute*,
9th *November, 1886.*

The fleet of England is her all-in-all;
 Her fleet is in your hands,
  And in her fleet her fate.

IV

You, you, that have the ordering of
  her fleet,
 If you should only compass her dis-
  grace,
When all men starve, the wild mob's
  million feet
 Will kick you from your place,
  But then too late, too late.

OPENING OF THE INDIAN AND COLONIAL EXHIBITION BY THE QUEEN

WRITTEN AT THE REQUEST OF THE PRINCE OF WALES

I

WELCOME, welcome with one voice!
In your welfare we rejoice,
Sons and brothers that have sent,
From isle and cape and continent,
Produce of your field and flood,
Mount and mine, and primal wood;
Works of subtle brain and hand,
And splendors of the morning land,
Gifts from every British zone,
  Britons, hold your own!

II

May we find, as ages run,
The mother featured in the son;
And may yours for ever be
That old strength and constancy
Which has made your fathers great
In our ancient island State,
And wherever her flag fly,
Glorying between sea and sky,
Makes the might of Britain known;
  Britons, hold your own!

III

Britain fought her sons of yore—
Britain fail'd; and never more,
Careless of our growing kin,

Shall we sin our fathers' sin,
Men that in a narrower day—
Unprophetic rulers they—
Drove from out the mother's nest
That young eagle of the West
To forage for herself alone;
  Britons, hold your own!

IV

Sharers of our glorious past,
Brothers, must we part at last?
Shall we not thro' good and ill
Cleave to one another still?
Britain's myriad voices call,
'Sons, be welded each and all
Into one imperial whole,
One with Britain, heart and soul!
One life, one flag, one fleet, one
  throne!'
  Britons, hold your own!

TO W. C. MACREADY

1851

FAREWELL, Macready, since to-night
  we part;
 Full-handed thunders often have
  confessed
 Thy power, well-used to move the
  public breast.
We thank thee with our voice, and
  from the heart.
Farewell, Macready, since this night
  we part,
 Go, take thine honors home; rank
  with the best,
 Garrick and statelier Kemble, and
  the rest
Who made a nation purer through
  their art.
Thine is it that our drama did not die,
 Nor flicker down to brainless pan-
  tomime,
 And those gilt gauds men-children
  swarm to see.
 Farewell, Macready, moral, grave,
  sublime;
Our Shakespeare's bland and universal eye
 Dwells pleased, through twice a
  hundred years, on thee.

DEMETER

AND OTHER POEMS

TO THE MARQUIS OF DUFFERIN AND AVA

I

At times our Britain cannot rest,
  At times her steps are swift and
    rash;
  She moving, at her girdle clash
The golden keys of East and West.

II

Not swift or rash, when late she lent
  The sceptres of her West, her East,
  To one that ruling has increased
Her greatness and her self-content.

III

Your rule has made the people love
  Their ruler. Your viceregal days
  Have added fulness to the phrase
Of 'Gauntlet in the velvet glove.'

IV

But since your name will grow with
    time,
  Not all, as honoring your fair fame
  Of Statesman, have I made the
    name
A golden portal to my rhyme;

V

But more, that you and yours may
    know
  From me and mine, how dear a debt
  We owed you, and are owing yet
To you and yours, and still would owe.

VI

For he—your India was his Fate,
  And drew him over sea to you—
  He fain had ranged her thro' and
    thro',
To serve her myriads and the State,—

VII

A soul that, watch'd from earliest
    youth,
  And on thro' many a brightening
    year,
  Had never swerved for craft or fear,
By one side-path, from simple truth;

VIII

Who might have chased and claspt
    Renown
  And caught her chaplet here—and
    there
  In haunts of jungle-poison'd air
The flame of life went wavering
    down;

IX

But ere he left your fatal shore,
  And lay on that funereal boat,
  Dying, 'Unspeakable,' he wrote,
'Their kindness,' and he wrote no
    more.

X

And sacred is the latest word;
  And now the Was, the Might-have-
    been,
  And those lone rites I have not seen,
And one drear sound I have not heard,

XI

Are dreams that scarce will let me be,
  Not there to bid my boy farewell,
  When That within the coffin fell,
Fell—and flash'd into the Red Sea,

XII

Beneath a hard Arabian moon
  And alien stars. To question why
  The sons before the fathers die,
Not mine! and I may meet him soon;

XIII

But while my life's late eve endures,
  Nor settles into hueless gray,
  My memories of his briefer day
Will mix with love for you and yours.

ON THE JUBILEE OF QUEEN VICTORIA

I

FIFTY times the rose has flower'd and
    faded,
Fifty times the golden harvest fallen,
Since our Queen assumed the globe,
    the sceptre.

II

She beloved for a kindliness
Rare in fable or history,
Queen, and Empress of India,
Crown'd so long with a diadem
Never worn by a worthier,
Now with prosperous auguries
Comes at last to the bounteous
Crowning year of her Jubilee.

III

Nothing of the lawless, of the despot,
Nothing of the vulgar, or vainglorious,
All is gracious, gentle, great and
    queenly.

IV

You then joyfully, all of you,
Set the mountain aflame to-night,
Shoot your stars to the firma-
    ment,
Deck your houses, illuminate
All your towns for a festival,
And in each let a multitude
Loyal, each, to the heart of it,
One full voice of allegiance,
Hail the fair Ceremonial
Of this year of her Jubilee.

V

Queen, as true to womanhood as
    Queenhood,
Glorying in the glories of her people,
Sorrowing with the sorrows of the
    lowest!

VI

You, that wanton in affluence,
Spare not now to be bountiful,
Call your poor to regale with you,
All the lowly, the destitute,
Make their neighborhood health-
    fuller,
Give your gold to the hospital,
Let the weary be comforted,
Let the needy be banqueted,
Let the maim'd in his heart re-
    joice
At this glad Ceremonial,
And this year of her Jubilee.

VII

Henry's fifty years are all in shadow,
Gray with distance Edward's fifty
    summers,
Even her Grandsire's fifty half for-
    gotten.

VIII

You, the Patriot Architect,
You that shape for eternity,
Raise a stately memorial,
Make it regally gorgeous,

Some Imperial Institute,
Rich in symbol, in ornament,
Which may speak to the cen-
    turies,
All the centuries after us,
Of this great Ceremonial,
And this year of her Jubilee.

IX

Fifty years of ever-broadening Com-
    merce!
Fifty years of ever-brightening Sci-
    ence!
Fifty years of ever-widening Empire!

X

You, the Mighty, the Fortunate,
You, the Lord-territorial,
You, the Lord-manufacturer,
You, the hardy, laborious,
Patient children of Albion,
You, Canadian, Indian,
Australasian, African,
All your hearts be in harmony,
All your voices in unison,
Singing, 'Hail to the glorious
Golden year of her Jubilee!'

XI

Are there thunders moaning in the dis-
    tance?
Are there spectres moving in the dark-
    ness?
Trust the Hand of Light will lead her
    people,
Till the thunders pass, the spectres
    vanish,
And the Light is Victor, and the dark-
    ness
Dawns into the Jubilee of the Ages.

TO PROFESSOR JEBB

WITH THE FOLLOWING POEM

FAIR things are slow to fade away,
Bear witness you, that yesterday [1]
    From out the Ghost of Pindar in
    you

[1] In Bologna.

Roll'd an Olympian; and they say [1]
That here the torpid mummy wheat
Of Egypt bore a grain as sweet
    As that which gilds the glebe of
    England,
Sunn'd with a summer of milder heat.

So may this legend for a while,
If greeted by your classic smile,
    Tho' dead in its Trinacrian Enna,
Blossom again on a colder isle.

DEMETER AND PERSEPHONE

(IN ENNA)

FAINT as a climate-changing bird that
    flies
All night across the darkness, and at
    dawn
Falls on the threshold of her native
    land,
And can no more, thou camest, O my
    child,
Led upward by the God of ghosts and
    dreams,
Who laid thee at Eleusis, dazed and
    dumb
With passing thro' at once from state
    to state,
Until I brought thee hither, that the
    day,
When here thy hands let fall the
    gather'd flower,
Might break thro' clouded memories
    once again   10
On thy lost self. A sudden nightingale
Saw thee, and flash'd into a frolic of
    song
And welcome; and a gleam as of the
    moon,
When first she peers along the tremu-
    lous deep,
Fled wavering o'er thy face, and
    chased away
That shadow of a likeness to the king
Of shadows, thy dark mate, Perseph-
    one!
Queen of the dead no more—my
    child! Thine eyes
Again were human-godlike, and the
    Sun

[1] They say, for the fact is doubtful.

Burst from a swimming fleece of win-
    ter gray, 20
And robed thee in his day from head
    to feet—
'Mother!' and I was folded in thine
    arms.

Child, those imperial, disimpas-
    sion'd eyes
Awed even me at first, thy mother—
    eyes
That oft had seen the serpent-wanded
    power
Draw downward into Hades with his
    drift
Of flickering spectres, lighted from
    below
By the red race of fiery Phlegethon;
But when before have Gods or men
    beheld
The Life that had descended re-
    arise, 30
And lighted from above him by the
    Sun?
So mighty was the mother's childless
    cry,
A cry that rang thro' Hades, Earth,
    and Heaven!

So in this pleasant vale we stand
    again,
The field of Enna, now once more
    ablaze
With flowers that brighten as thy foot-
    step falls,
All flowers—but for one black blur of
    earth
Left by that closing chasm, thro'
    which the car
Of dark Aïdoneus rising rapt thee
    hence.
And here, my child, tho' folded in
    thine arms, 40
I feel the deathless heart of mother-
    hood
Within me shudder, lest the naked
    glebe
Should yawn once more into the gulf,
    and thence
The shrilly whinnyings of the team of
    Hell,
Ascending, pierce the glad and songful
    air,

And all at once their arch'd necks,
    midnight-maned,
Jet upward thro' the midday blossom.
    No!
For, see, thy foot has touch'd it; all
    the space
Of blank earth-baldness clothes itself
    afresh,
And breaks into the crocus-purple
    hour 50
That saw thee vanish.

Child, when thou wert gone,
I envied human wives, and nested
    birds,
Yea, the cubb'd lioness; went in
    search of thee
Thro' many a palace, many a cot, and
    gave
Thy breast to ailing infants in the
    night,
And set the mother waking in amaze
To find her sick one whole; and forth
    again
Among the wail of midnight winds,
    and cried,
'Where is my loved one? Wherefore
    do ye wail?'
And out from all the night an answer
    shrill'd, 60
'We know not, and we know not why
    we wail.'
I climb'd on all the cliffs of all the
    seas,
And ask'd the waves that moan about
    the world,
'Where? do ye make your moaning for
    my child?'
And round from all the world the
    voices came,
'We know not, and we know not why
    we moan.'
'Where?' and I stared from every
    eagle-peak,
I thridded the black heart of all the
    woods,
I peer'd thro' tomb and cave, and in
    the storms
Of autumn swept across the city, and
    heard 70
The murmur of their temples chant-
    ing me,

Me, me, the desolate mother!
   'Where?'—and turn'd,
And fled by many a waste, forlorn of
   man,
And grieved for man thro' all my grief
   for thee,—
The jungle rooted in his shatter'd
   hearth,
The serpent coil'd about his broken
   shaft,
The scorpion crawling over naked
   skulls;—
I saw the tiger in the ruin'd fane
Spring from his fallen God, but trace
   of thee
I saw not; and far on, and, following
   out   80
A league of labyrinthine darkness,
   came
On three gray heads beneath a gleam-
   ing rift.
'Where?' and I heard one voice from
   all the three,
'We know not, for we spin the lives
   of men,
And not of Gods, and know not why
   we spin!
There is a Fate beyond us.' Nothing
   knew.

Last as the likeness of a dying man,
Without his knowledge, from him
   flits to warn
A far-off friendship that he comes no
   more,
So he, the God of dreams, who heard
   my cry,   90
Drew from thyself the likeness of thy-
   self
Without thy knowledge, and thy
   shadow past
Before me, crying, 'The Bright one in
   the highest
Is brother of the Dark one in the low-
   est,
And Bright and Dark have sworn that
   I, the child
Of thee, the great Earth-Mother, thee,
   the Power
That lifts her buried life from gloom
   to bloom,
Should be for ever and for evermore
The Bride of Darkness.'

          So the Shadow wail'd.
Then I, Earth-Goddess, cursed the
   Gods of heaven.   100
I would not mingle with their feasts;
   to me
Their nectar smack'd of hemlock on
   the lips,
Their rich ambrosia tasted aconite.
The man, that only lives and loves an
   hour,
Seem'd nobler than their hard eterni-
   ties.
My quick tears kill'd the flower, my
   ravings hush'd
The bird, and lost in utter grief I
   fail'd
To send my life thro' olive-yard and
   vine
And golden-grain, my gift to helpless
   man
Rain-rotten died the wheat, the bar-
   ley-spears   110
Were hollow-husk'd, the leaf fell, and
   the Sun,
Pale at my grief, drew down before
   his time
Sickening, and Ætna kept her winter
   snow.

   Then He, the brother of this Darkness, He
Who still is highest, glancing from his
   height
On earth a fruitless fallow, when he
   miss'd
The wonted steam of sacrifice, the
   praise
And prayer of men, decreed that thou
   shouldst dwell
For nine white moons of each whole
   year with me,
Three dark ones in the shadow with
   thy king.   120

   Once more the reaper in the gleam
   of dawn
Will see me by the landmark far
   away,
Blessing his field, or seated in the dusk
Of even, by the lonely threshing-floor,
Rejoicing in the harvest and the
   grange.

Yet I, Earth-Goddess, am but ill-
    content
With them who still are highest. Those
    gray heads,
What meant they by their 'Fate be-
    yond the Fates'
But younger kindlier Gods to bear us
    down,
As we bore down the Gods before us?
    Gods,   130
To quench, not hurl the thunderbolt,
    to stay,
Not spread the plague, the famine;
    Gods indeed,
To send the noon into the night and
    break
The sunless halls of Hades into
    Heaven?
Till thy dark lord accept and love the
    Sun,
And all the Shadow die into the Light,
When thou shalt dwell the whole
    bright year with me,
And souls of men, who grew beyond
    their race,
And made themselves as Gods against
    the fear
Of Death and Hell; and thou that hast
    from men,   140
As Queen of Death, that worship
    which is Fear,
Henceforth, as having risen from out
    the dead,
Shalt ever send thy life along with
    mine
From buried grain thro' springing
    blade, and bless
Their garner'd autumn also, reap with
    me,
Earth-Mother, in the harvest hymns
    of Earth
The worship which is Love, and see
    no more
The Stone, the Wheel, the dimly-glim-
    mering lawns
Of that Elysium, all the hateful fires
Of torment, and the shadowy warrior
    glide   150
Along the silent field of Asphodel.

OWD ROÄ [1]

NAÄY, noä mander [2] o' use to be callin'
    'im Roä, Roä, Roä,
Fur the dog 's stoän-deäf, an' 'e 's
    blind, 'e can naither stan' nor
    goä.

But I meäns fur to maäke 'is owd aäge
    as 'appy as iver I can,
Fur I owäs owd Roäver moor nor I
    iver owäd, mottal man.

Thou 's rode of 'is back when a
    babby, afoor thou was gotten
    too owd,
Fur 'e 'd fetch an' carry like owt, 'e
    was allus as good as gowd.

Eh, but 'e 'd fight wi' a will *when* 'e
    fowt; 'e could howd [3] 'is oän,
An' Roä was the dog as knaw'd when
    an' wheere to bury his boäne.

An' 'e kep his heäd hoop like a king,
    an' 'e 'd niver not down wi' 'is
    taäil,
Fur 'e 'd niver done nowt to be
    shaämed on, when we was i'
    Howlaby Daäle.   10

An' 'e sarved me sa well when 'e lived,
    that, Dick, when 'e cooms to be
    deäd,
I thinks as I 'd like fur to hev soom
    sort of a sarvice reäd.

Fur 'e 's moor good sense na the Par-
    liament man 'at stans fur us
    'ere,
An' I 'd voät fur 'im, my oän sen, if 'e
    could but stan' for the Shere.

'Faäithful an' True'—them words be
    i' Scriptur—an' Faäithful an'
    True
Ull be fun' [4] upo' four short legs ten
    times fur one upo' two.

---

[1] Old Rover.   [2] Manner.
[3] Hold.   [4] Found.

An' maäybe they 'll walk upo' two, but
    I knaws they runs upo'
    four,[1]—
Bedtime, Dicky! but waäit till tha
    'eärs it be strikin' the hour.

Fur I wants to tell tha o' Roä when
    we lived i' Howlaby Daäle,
Ten year sin'—Naäy—naäy! tha mun
    nobbut hev' one glass of
    aäle.   20

Straänge an' owd-farran'd [2] the 'ouse,
    an' belt [3] long afoor my daäy,
Wi' haäfe o' the chimleys a-twizzen'd [4]
    an' twined like a band o' haäy.

The fellers as maäkes them picturs,
    'ud coom at the fall o' the year,
An' sattle their ends upo' stools to pic-
    tur the door-poorch theere,

An' the Heagle 'as hed two heäds stan-
    nin' theere o' the brokken
    stick; [5]
An' they niver 'ed seed sich ivin' [6] as
    graw'd hall ower the brick;

An' theere i' the 'ouse one night—but
    it 's down, an' all on it now
Goän into mangles an' tonups,[7] an'
    raäved slick thruf by the
    plow—

Theere, when the 'ouse wur a house,
    one night I wur sittin' aloän,
Wi' Roäver athurt my feeät, an'
    sleeäpin' still as a stoän,   30

Of a Christmas Eäve, an' as cowd as
    this, an' the midders [8] as white,
An' the fences all on 'em bolster'd oop
    wi' the windle [9] that night;

An' the cat wur a-sleeäpin' alongside
    Roäver, but I wur awaäke,
An' smoäkin' an' thinkin' o' things—
    Doänt maäke thysen sick wi'
    the caäke.

Fur the men ater supper 'ed sung their
    songs an' 'ed 'ed their beer,
An' 'ed goän their waäys; ther was
    nobbut three, an' noän on 'em
    theere.

They was all on 'em fear'd o' the
    Ghoäst an' duss n't not sleeäp
    i' the 'ouse,
But, Dicky, the Ghoäst moästlins [1]
    was nobbut a rat or a mouse.

An' I looökt out wonst [2] at the night,
    an' the daäle was all of a thaw,
Fur I seed the beck coomin' down like
    a long black snaäke i' the
    snaw,   40

An' I heärd greät heäps o' the snaw
    slushin' down fro' the bank to
    the beck,
An' then as I stood i' the doorwaäy, I
    feeäld it drip o' my neck.

Saw I turn'd in ageän, an' I thowt o'
    the good owd times 'at was
    goän,
An' the munney they maäde by the
    war, an' the times 'at was
    coomin' on;

Fur I thowt if the Staäte was a-gawin'
    to let in furriners' wheät,
Howiver was British farmers to stan'
    ageän o' their feeät?

Howiver was I fur to find my rent an'
    to paäy my men?
An' all along o' the feller [3] as turn'd
    'is back of hissen.

Thou slep i' the chaumber above us,
    we could n't ha' 'eärd tha call,

---

[1] ou as in 'house.'
[2] 'Owd-farran'd,' old-fashioned.
[3] Built.
[4] 'Twizzen'd,' twisted.
[5] On a staff ragulé.
[6] Ivy.
[7] Mangolds and turnips.
[8] Meadows.
[9] Drifted snow.

[1] 'Moästlins,' for the most part, generally.
[2] Once.   [3] Peel.

Sa moother 'ed tell'd ma to bring tha
    down, an' thy craädle an'
    all;   50

Fur the gell o' the farm 'at slep wi' tha
    then 'ed gotten wer leäve,
Fur to goä that night to 'er foälk by
    cause o' the Christmas Eäve;

But I cleän forgot tha, my lad, when
    moother 'ed gotten to bed,
An' I slep i' my chair hup-on-end, an'
    the Freeä Traäde runn'd i' my
    'ead,

Till I dreämed 'at Squire walkt in, an'
    I says to him, 'Squire, ya 're
    laäte,'
Then I seed 'at 'is faäce wur as red as
    the Yule-block theere i' the
    graäte.

An' 'e says, 'Can ya paäy me the rent
    to-night?' an' I says to 'im,
    'Noä,'
An' 'e cotch'd howd hard o' my
    hairm,[1] 'Then hout to-night
    tha shall goä.'

'Tha 'll niver,' says I, 'be a-turnin' ma
    hout upo' Christmas Eäve?'
Then I waäked an' I fun it was
    Roäver a-tuggin' an' teärin' my
    sleäve.   60

An' I thowt as 'e 'd goän cleän-wud,[2]
    fur I noäwaäys knaw'd 'is in-
    tent;
An' I says, 'Git awaäy, ya beast,' an'
    I fetcht 'im a kick, an' 'e went.

Then 'e tummled up stairs, fur I 'eärd
    'im, as if 'e 'd 'a brokken 'is
    neck,
An' I 'd cleär forgot, little Dicky,
    thy chaumber door would n't
    sneck;[3]

An' I slep i' my chair ageän wi' my
    hairm hingin' down to the
    floor,
An' I thowt it was Roäver a-tuggin'
    an' teärin' me wuss nor afoor,

[1] Arm.   [2] Mad.   [3] Latch.

An' I thowt 'at I kick'd 'im ageän, but
    I kick'd thy moother istead.
'What arta snorin' theere fur? the
    house is afire,' she said.

Thy moother 'ed beän a-naggin' about
    the gell o' the farm,
She offens 'ud spy summut wrong
    when there warn't not a mos-
    sel o' harm;   70

An' she did n't not solidly meän I wur
    gawin' that waäy to the bad,
Fur the gell[1] was as howry a trollope
    as iver traäpes'd i' the squad.

But moother was free of 'er tongue, as
    I offens 'ev tell'd 'er mysen,
Sa I kep i' my chair, fur I thowt she
    was nobbut a-rilin' ma then.

An' I says, 'I 'd be good to tha, Bess, if
    tha'd onywaäys let ma be
    good,'
But she skelpt ma haäfe ower i' the
    chair, an' screeäd like a howl
    gone wud[2]—

'Ya mun run fur the lether.[3] Git oop,
    if ya 're onywaäys good for
    owt.'
And I says, 'If I beänt noäwaäys—not
    nowadaäys—good fur nowt—

'Yit I beänt sich a nowt[4] of all nowts
    as 'ull hallus do as 'e 's bid.'
'But the stairs is afire,' she said; then
    I seed 'er a-cryin', I did.   80

An' she beäld, 'Ya mun saäve little
    Dick, an' be sharp about it an'
    all,'
Sa I runs to the yard fur a lether, an'
    sets 'im ageän the wall.

[1] 'The girl was as dirty a slut as ever
trudged in the mud,' but there is a sense
of slatternliness in 'traäpes'd' which is
not expressed in 'trudged.'
[2] 'She half overturned me and shrieked
like an owl gone mad.'
[3] Ladder.
[4] A thoroughly insignificant or worthless
person.

An' I claums an' I mashes the winder
    hin, when I gits to the top,
But the heät druv hout i' my heyes till
    I feäld mysen ready to drop.

Thy moother was howdin' the lether,
    an' tellin' me not to be skeärd,
An' I was n't afeärd, or I thinks leäst-
    waäys as I was n't afeärd;

But I could n't see fur the smoäke
    wheere thou was a-liggin, my
    lad,
An' Roäver was theere i' the chaum-
    ber a-yowlin' an' yaupin' like
    mad;

An' thou was a-beälin' likewise, an'
    a-squeälin', as if tha was bit,
An' it was n't a bite but a burn, fur
    the merk 's[1] o' thy shou'der
    yit;   90

Then I call'd out, 'Roä, Roä, Roä,'
    thaw I did n't haäfe think as 'e
    'd 'ear,
But 'e coom'd thruf the fire wi' my
    bairn i' 'is mouth to the winder
    theere!

He coom'd like a hangel o' marcy as
    soon as 'e 'eärd 'is naäme,
Or like tother hangel i' Scriptur 'at
    summun seed i' the flaäme,

When summun 'ed hax'd fur a son, an'
    'e promised a son to she,
An' Roä was as good as the hangel i'
    saävin' a son fur me.

Sa I browt tha down, an' I says, 'I
    mun gaw up ageän fur Roä.'
'Gaw up ageän fur the varmint?' I
    tell'd 'er, 'Yeäs, I mun goä.'

An' I claumb'd up ageän to the winder,
    an' clemm'd[2] owd Roä by the
    'eäd,   99
An' is 'air coom'd off i' my 'ands an'
    I taäked 'im at fust fur deäd;

[1] Mark.   [2] Clutched.

Fur 'e smell'd like a herse a-singein',
    an' seeäm'd as blind as a poop,
An' haäfe on 'im bare as a bublin'.[1] I
    could n't wakken 'im oop,

But I browt 'im down, an' we got to
    the barn, fur the barn would
    n't burn
Wi' the wind blawin' hard tother
    waäy, an' the wind was n't like
    to turn.

An' *I* kep a-callin' o' Roä till 'e wag-
    gled 'is taäil fur a bit,
But the cocks kep a-crawin' an'
    crawin' all night, an' I 'ears 'em
    yit;

An' the dogs was a-yowlin' all round,
    and thou was a-squeälin' thy-
    sen,
An' moother was naggin' an' groänin'
    an' moänin' an' naggin' ageän;

An' I 'eärd the bricks an' the baulks[2]
    rummle down when the roof
    gev waäy.
Fur the fire was a-raägin' an' raävin'
    an' roarin' like judgment
    daäy.   110

Warm enew theere sewer-ly, but the
    barn was as cowd as owt,
An' we cuddled and huddled togither,
    an' happt wersens[3] oop as we
    mowt.

An' I browt Roä round, but moother
    'ed beän sa soäk'd wi' the thaw
'At she cotch'd 'er death o' cowd that
    night, poor soul, i' the straw.

Haäfe o' the parish runn'd oop when
    the rig-tree[4] was tummlin'
    in—
Too laäte—but it 's all ower now—
    hall hower—an' ten year sin';

[1] 'Bubbling,' a young unfledged bird.
[2] Beams.
[3] Wrapt ourselves.
[4] The beam that runs along the roof of
the house just beneath the ridge.

Too laäte, tha mun git tha to bed, but
    I 'll coom an' I 'll squench the
    light,
Fur we moänt 'ev naw moor fires—
    and soä, little Dick, good-
    night.

VASTNESS

I

MANY a hearth upon our dark globe
    sighs after many a vanish'd
    face,
Many a planet by many a sun may roll
    with the dust of a vanish'd
    race.

II

Raving politics, never at rest—as this
    poor earth's pale history
    runs,—
What is it all but a trouble of ants in
    the gleam of a million million
    of suns?

III

Lies upon this side, lies upon that side,
    truthless violence mourn'd by
    the wise,
Thousands of voices drowning his own
    in a popular torrent of lies
    upon lies;

IV

Stately purposes, valor in battle, glori-
    ous annals of army and fleet,
Death for the right cause, death for
    the wrong cause, trumpets of
    victory, groans of defeat;

V

Innocence seethed in her mother's
    milk, and Charity setting the
    martyr aflame;
Thraldom who walks with the banner
    of Freedom, and recks not to
    ruin a realm in her name.

VI

Faith at her zenith, or all but lost in
    the gloom of doubts that
    darken the schools;
Craft with a bunch of all-heal in her
    hand, follow'd up by her vassal
    legion of fools;

VII

Trade flying over a thousand seas with
    her spice and her vintage, her
    silk and her corn;
Desolate offing, sailorless harbors,
    famishing populace, wharves
    forlorn;

VIII

Star of the morning, Hope in the sun-
    rise; gloom of the evening,
    Life at a close;
Pleasure who flaunts on her wide
    downway with her flying robe
    and her poison'd rose;

IX

Pain, that has crawl'd from the corpse
    of Pleasure, a worm which
    writhes all day, and at night
Stirs up again in the heart of the
    sleeper, and stings him back to
    the curse of the light;

X

Wealth with his wines and his wedded
    harlots; honest Poverty, bare
    to the bone;
Opulent Avarice, lean as Poverty;
    Flattery gilding the rift in a
    throne;

XI

Fame blowing out from her golden
    trumpet a jubilant challenge to
    Time and to Fate;
Slander, her shadow, sowing the
    nettle on all the laurell'd
    graves of the great;

XII

Love, for the maiden, crown'd with
    marriage, no regrets for aught
    that has been,
Household happiness, gracious chil-
    dren, debtless competence,
    golden mean;

XIII

National hatreds of whole generations,
    and pigmy spites of the village
    spire;
Vows that will last to the last death-
    ruckle, and vows that are snapt
    in a moment of fire;

XIV

He that has lived for the lust of the
    minute, and died in the doing
    it, flesh without mind;
He that has nail'd all flesh to the
    Cross, till Self died out in the
    love of his kind;

XV

Spring and Summer and Autumn and
    Winter, and all these old revo-
    lutions of earth;
All new-old revolutions of Empire—
    change of the tide—what is all
    of it worth?

XVI

What the philosophies, all the sci-
    ences, poesy, varying voices of
    prayer,
All that is noblest, all that is basest,
    all that is filthy with all that is
    fair?

XVII

What is it all, if we all of us end but
    in being our own corpse-coffins
    at last?
Swallow'd in Vastness, lost in Silence,
    drown'd in the deeps of a
    meaningless Past?

XVIII

What but a murmur of gnats in the
    gloom, or a moment's anger of
    bees in their hive?—
. . . .

Peace, let it be! for I loved him, and
    love him for ever: the dead are
    not dead but alive.

THE RING

DEDICATED TO THE
HON. J. RUSSELL LOWELL

MIRIAM AND HER FATHER

MIRIAM (*singing*)

MELLOW moon of heaven,
    Bright in blue,
Moon of married hearts,
    Hear me you!

Twelve times in the year
    Bring me bliss,
Globing honey moons
    Bright as this.

Moon, you fade at times
    From the night.   **10**
Young again you grow
    Out of sight.

Silver crescent-curve,
    Coming soon,
Globe again, and make
    Honey moon.

Shall not *my* love last,
    Moon, with you,
For ten thousand years
    Old and new?   **20**

FATHER

And who was he with such love-
    drunken eyes
They made a thousand honey moons
    of one?

MIRIAM

The prophet of his own, my Hubert—
    his

The words, and mine the setting. 'Air
    and words,'
Said Hubert, when I sang the song,
    'are bride
And bridegroom.' Does it please you?

FATHER

            Mainly, child,
Because I hear your mother's voice in
    yours.
She—, why, you shiver tho' the wind
    is west
With all the warmth of summer.

MIRIAM

            Well, I felt
On a sudden I know not what, a
    breath that past   30
With all the cold of winter.

FATHER (*muttering to himself*)

            Even so.
The Ghost in Man, the Ghost that
    once was Man,
But cannot wholly free itself from
    Man,
Are calling to each other thro' a dawn
Stranger than earth has ever seen; the
    veil
Is rending, and the Voices of the day
Are heard across the Voices of the
    dark.
No sudden heaven, nor sudden hell,
    for man,
But thro' the Will of One who knows
    and rules—
And utter knowledge is but utter
    love—   40
Æonian Evolution, swift or slow,
Thro' all the spheres—and ever open-
    ing height,
An ever lessening earth—and she per-
    haps,
My Miriam, breaks her latest earthly
    link
With me to-day.

MIRIAM

    You speak so low; what is it?
Your 'Miriam breaks'—is making a
    new link
Breaking an old one?

FATHER

           No, for we, my child,
Have been till now each other's all-in-
    all.

MIRIAM

And you the lifelong guardian of the
    child.

FATHER

I, and one other whom you have not
    known.   50

MIRIAM

And who? what other?

FATHER

        Whither are you bound?
For Naples which we only left in
    May?

MIRIAM

No, father, Spain, but Hubert brings
    me home
With April and the swallow. Wish me
    joy!

FATHER

What need to wish when Hubert weds
    in you
The heart of love, and you the soul of
    truth
In Hubert?

MIRIAM

      Tho' you used to call me once
The lonely maiden princess of the
    wood,
Who meant to sleep her hundred sum-
    mers out
Before a kiss should wake her.

FATHER

          Ay, but now   60
Your fairy prince has found you, take
    this ring.

MIRIAM

'Io t' amo'—and these diamonds—
    beautiful!
'From Walter,' and for me from you
    then?

FATHER

                        Well,
One way for Miriam.

MIRIAM

                Miriam am I not?

FATHER

This ring bequeath'd you by your
    mother, child
Was to be given you—such her dying
    wish—
Given on the morning when you came
    of age
Or on the day you married. Both the
    days
Now close in one. The ring is doubly
    yours
Why do you look so gravely at the
    tower?   70

MIRIAM

I never saw it yet so all ablaze
With creepers crimsoning to the pin-
    nacles,
As if perpetual sunset linger'd there,
And all ablaze too in the lake below!
And how the birds that circle round
    the tower
Are cheeping to each other of their
    flight
To summer lands!

FATHER

            And that has made you grave?
Fly—care not. Birds and brides must
    leave the nest.
Child, I am happier in your happiness
Than in mine own.

MIRIAM

            It is not that!

FATHER

                    What else? 80

MIRIAM

That chamber in the tower.

FATHER

            What chamber, child?
Your nurse is here?

MIRIAM

            My mother's nurse and mine.
She comes to dress me in my bridal
    veil.

FATHER

What did she say?

MIRIAM

                She said that you and I
Had been abroad for my poor health
    so long
She fear'd I had forgotten her, and I
    ask'd
About my mother, and she said, 'Thy
    hair
Is golden like thy mother's, not so
    fine.'

FATHER

What then? what more?

MIRIAM

                She said—perhaps indeed
She wander'd, having wander'd now so
    far   90
Beyond the common date of death—
    that you,
When I was smaller than the statuette
Of my dear mother on your bracket
    here—

You took me to that chamber in the
tower,
The topmost—a chest there, by which
you knelt—
And there were books and dresses—
left to me,
A ring too which you kiss'd, and I, she
said,
I babbled, 'Mother, mother'—as I
used
To prattle to her picture—stretch'd
my hands
As if I saw her; then a woman came
And caught me from my nurse. I hear
her yet—   101
A sound of anger like a distant storm.

FATHER

Garrulous old crone!

MIRIAM

Poor nurse!

FATHER

I bade her keep,
Like a seal'd book, all mention of the
ring,   •
For I myself would tell you all to-day.

MIRIAM

'She too might speak to-day,' she
mumbled. Still,
I scarce have learnt the title of your
book,
But you will turn the pages.

FATHER

Ay, to-day!
I brought you to that chamber on your
third
September birthday with your nurse,
and felt   110
An icy breath play on me, while I
stoopt
To take and kiss the ring.

MIRIAM

This very ring,
'Io t' amo'?

FATHER

Yes, for some wild hope was mine
That, in the misery of my married life,
Miriam your mother might appear to
me.
She came to you, not me. The storm
you hear
Far-off is Muriel—your stepmother's
voice.

MIRIAM

Vext, that you thought my mother
came to me?
Or at my crying, 'Mother'? or to find
My mother's diamonds hidden from
her there,   120
Like worldly beauties in the cell, not
shown
To dazzle all that see them?

FATHER

Wait a while.
Your mother and stepmother—Miriam Erne
And Muriel Erne—the two were cousins—lived
With Muriel's mother on the down,
that sees
A thousand squares of corn and meadow, far
As the gray deep, a landscape which
your eyes
Have many a time ranged over when
a babe.

MIRIAM

I climb'd the hill with Hubert, yester-
day,
And from the thousand squares, one
silent voice   130
Came on the wind, and seem'd to say,
'Again.'
We saw far off an old forsaken house,
Then home, and past the ruin'd mill.

FATHER

And there
I found these cousins often by the
brook,

For Miriam sketch'd and Muriel
　　threw the fly;
The girls of equal age, but one was
　　fair,
And one was dark, and both were
　　beautiful.
No voice for either spoke within my
　　heart
Then, for the surface eye, that only
　　dotes
On outward beauty, glancing from the
　　one　　　　　　　　　　　　140
To the other, knew not that which
　　pleased it most,
The raven ringlet or the gold; but
　　both
Were dowerless, and myself, I used to
　　walk
This terrace—morbid, melancholy;
　　mine
And yet not mine the hall, the farm,
　　the field;
For all that ample woodland whis-
　　per'd, 'Debt,'
The brook that feeds this lakelet mur-
　　mur'd, 'Debt,'
And in yon arching avenue of old
　　elms,
Tho' mine, not mine, I heard the sober
　　rook
And carrion crow cry, 'Mortgage.'

MIRIAM

　　　　　　　　　　　Father's fault 150
Visited on the children!

FATHER

　　　　　　　　Ay, but then
A kinsman, dying, summon'd me to
　　Rome—
He left me wealth—and while I jour-
　　ney'd hence,
And saw the world fly by me like a
　　dream,
And while I commuв'd with my truest
　　self,
I woke to all of truest in myself,
Till, in the gleam of those midsummer
　　dawns,
The form of Muriel faded, and the
　　face

Of Miriam grew upon me, till I knew;
And past and future mixt in heaven
　　and made　　　　　　　　160
The rosy twilight of a perfect day.

MIRIAM

So glad? no tear for him who left you
　　wealth,
Your kinsman?

FATHER

　　　　　　I had seen the man but once;
He loved my name, not me; and then
　　I pass'd
Home, and thro' Venice, where a jew-
　　eller,
So far gone down, or so far up in life,
That he was nearing his own hundred,
　　sold
This ring to me, then laugh'd, 'The
　　ring is weird.'
And weird and worn and wizard-like
　　was he.
'Why weird?' I ask'd him; and he said,
　　'The souls　　　　　　　170
Of two repentant lovers guard the
　　ring;'
Then with a ribald twinkle in his
　　bleak eyes—
'And if you give the ring to any maid,
They still remember what it cost
　　them here,
And bind the maid to love you by the
　　ring;
And if the ring were stolen from the
　　maid,
The theft were death or madness to
　　the thief,
So sacred those ghost lovers hold the
　　gift.'
And then he told their legend:
　　　　　　　　　　　'Long ago
Two lovers parted by a scurrilous tale
Had quarrell'd, till the man repenting
　　sent　　　　　　　　　181
This ring, "Io t' amo," to his best be-
　　loved,
And sent it on her birthday. She in
　　wrath
Return'd it on her birthday, and that
　　day

His death-day, when, half-frenzied by
    the ring,
He wildly fought a rival suitor, him
The causer of that scandal, fought and
    fell;
And she that came to part them all too
    late,
And found a corpse and silence, drew
    the ring
From his dead finger, wore it till her
    death,   190
Shrined him within the temple of her
    heart,
Made every moment of her after life
A virgin victim to his memory,
And dying rose, and rear'd her arms,
    and cried,
"I see him, Io t' amo, Io t' amo."'

MIRIAM

Legend or true? so tender should be
    true!
Did *he* believe it? did you ask him?

FATHER

                      Ay!
But that half skeleton, like a barren
    ghost
From out the fleshless world of spirits,
    laugh'd—
A hollow laughter!

MIRIAM

             Vile, so near the ghost
Himself, to laugh at love in death!
But you?   201

FATHER

Well, as the bygone lover thro' this
    ring
Had sent his cry for her forgiveness, I
Would call thro' this 'Io t' amo' to the
    heart
Of Miriam; then I bade the man en-
    grave
'From Walter' on the ring, and sent it
    —wrote
Name, surname, all as clear as noon,
    but he—

Some younger hand must have en-
    graven the ring—
His fingers were so stiffen'd by the
    frost
Of seven and ninety winters, that he
    scrawl'd   210
A 'Miriam' that might seem a 'Mu-
    riel';
And Muriel claim'd and open'd what
    I meant
For Miriam, took the ring, and
    flaunted it
Before that other whom I loved and
    love.

A mountain stay'd me here, a min-
    ster there,
A galleried palace, or a battle-field,
Where stood the sheaf of Peace: but—
    coming home—
And on your mother's birthday—all
    but yours—
A week betwixt—and when the tower
    as now
Was all ablaze with crimson to the
    roof,   220
And all ablaze too plunging in the lake
Head-foremost—who were those that
    stood between
The tower and that rich phantom of
    the tower?
Muriel and Miriam, each in white, and
    like
May-blossoms in mid-autumn—was it
    they?
A light shot upward on them from the
    lake.
What sparkled there? whose hand was
    that? they stood
So close together. I am not keen of
    sight,
But coming nearer—Muriel had the
    ring—
'O Miriam! have you given your ring
    to her?   230
O Miriam!' Miriam redden'd, Muriel
    clench'd
The hand that wore it, till I cried
    again:
'O Miriam, if you love me take the
    ring!'
She glanced at me, at Muriel, and was
    mute.

'Nay, if you cannot love me, let it be.'
Then—Muriel standing ever statue-
    like—
She turn'd, and in her soft imperial
    way
And saying gently, 'Muriel, by your
    leave,
Unclosed the hand and from it drew
    the ring,
And gave it me, who pass'd it down
    her own,   240
Io t' amo, all is well then.' Muriel fled.

MIRIAM

Poor Muriel!

FATHER

Ay, poor Muriel, when you hear
What follows! Miriam loved me from
    the first,
Not thro' the ring; but on her mar-
    riage-morn
This birthday, death-day, and be-
    trothal ring,
Laid on her table overnight, was gone;
And after hours of search and doubt
    and threats,
And hubbub, Muriel enter'd with it,
    'See!—
Found in a chink of that old mould-
    er'd floor!'
My Miriam nodded with a pitying
    smile,   250
As who should say that 'those who lose
    can find.'
    Then I and she were married for a
    year,
One year without a storm, or even a
    cloud;
And you, my Miriam, born within the
    year;
And she, my Miriam, dead within the
    year.
    I sat beside her dying, and she
    gaspt:
'The books, the miniature, the lace
    are hers,
My ring too when she comes of age,
    or when
She marries; you—you loved me, kept
    your word.

You love me still, "Io t' amo."—Mu-
    riel—no—   260
She cannot love; she loves her own
    hard self,
Her firm will, her fix'd purpose. Prom-
    ise me,
Miriam, not Muriel—she shall have
    the ring.'
And there the light of other life, which
    lives
Beyond our burial and our buried
    eyes,
Gleam'd for a moment in her own on
    earth.
I swore the vow, then with my latest
    kiss
Upon them, closed her eyes, which
    would not close,
But kept their watch upon the ring
    and you.
Your birthday was her death-day.

MIRIAM

                O poor mother! 270
And you, poor desolate father, and
    poor me,
The little senseless, worthless, word-
    less babe,
Saved when your life was wreck'd!

FATHER

                Desolate? yes!
Desolate as that sailor whom the
    storm
Had parted from his comrade in the
    boat,
And dash'd half dead on barren sands,
    was I.
Nay, you were my one solace; only—
    you
Were always ailing. Muriel's mother,
    sent,
And sure am I, by Muriel, one day
    came
And saw you, shook her head, and
    patted yours,   280
And smiled, and making with a kindly
    pinch
Each poor pale cheek a momentary
    rose—

'*That* should be fix'd,' she said; your
    pretty bud,
So blighted here, would flower into
    full health
Among our health and bracken. Let
    her come!
And we will feed her with our moun-
    tain air,
And send her home to you rejoicing.'
    No—
We could not part. And once, when
    you, my girl,
Rode on my shoulder home—the tiny
    fist
Had graspt a daisy from your
    mother's grave—   290
By the lych-gate was Muriel. 'Ay,' she
    said,
'Among the tombs in this damp vale
    of yours!
You scorn my mother's warning, but
    the child
Is paler than before. We often walk
In open sun, and see beneath our feet
The mist of autumn gather from your
    lake,
And shroud the tower; and once we
    only saw
Your gilded vane, a light above the
    mist'—
Our old bright bird that still is veer-
    ing there
Above his four gold letters—'and the
    light,'   300
She said, 'was like that light'—and
    there she paused,
And long; till I, believing that the
    girl's
Lean fancy, groping for it, could not
    find
One likeness, laugh'd a little and found
    her two—
'A warrior's crest above the cloud of
    war'—
'A fiery phœnix rising from the smoke,
The pyre he burnt in.'—'Nay,' she
    said, 'the light
That glimmers on the marsh and on
    the grave.'
And spoke no more, but turn'd and
    past away.
    Miriam, I am not surely one of
    those   310

Caught by the flower that closes on
    the fly,
But after ten slow weeks her fix'd in-
    tent,
In aiming at an all but hopeless mark
To strike it, struck. I took, I left you
    there;
I came, I went, was happier day by
    day;
For Muriel nursed you with a mother's
    care;
Till on that clear and heather-scented
    height
The rounder cheek had brighten'd into
    bloom.
She always came to meet me carrying
    you,
And all her talk was of the babe she
    loved;   320
So, following her old pastime of the
    brook,
She threw the fly for me; but oftener
    left
That angling to the mother. 'Muriel's
    health
Had weaken'd, nursing little Miriam.
    Strange!
She used to shun the wailing babe, and
    dotes
On this of yours.' But when the ma-
    tron saw
That hinted love was only wasted bait,
Not risen to, she was bolder. 'Ever
    since
You sent the fatal ring'—I told her
    'sent
To 'Miriam,' 'Doubtless—ay, but ever
    since   330
In all the world my dear one sees but
    you—
In your sweet babe she finds but you
    —she makes
Her heart a mirror that reflects but
    you.'
And then the tear fell, the voice broke
    Her heart!
I gazed into the mirror, as a man
Who sees his face in water, and a
    stone,
That glances from the bottom of the
    pool,
Strike upward thro' the shadow; yet
    at last,

Gratitude—loneliness—desire to keep
So skilled a nurse about you always—
 nay!   340
Some half remorseful kind of pity
 too—
Well! well, you know I married Mu-
 riel Erne.
 'I take thee Muriel for my wedded
  wife'—
I had forgotten it was your birthday,
 child—
When all at once with some electric
 thrill
A cold air pass'd between us, and the
 hands
Fell from each other, and were join'd
 again.
 No second cloudless honeymoon
  was mine.
For by and by she sicken'd of the
 farce,
She dropt the gracious mask of moth-
 erhood,   350
She came no more to meet me, carry-
 ing you,
Nor ever cared to set you on her knee,
Nor ever let you gambol in her sight,
Nor ever cheer'd you with a kindly
 smile,
Nor ever ceased to clamor for the
 ring;
Why had I sent the ring at first to
 her?
Why had I made her love me thro' the
 ring,
And then had changed? so fickle are
 men—the best!
Not she—but now my love was hers
 again,
The ring by right, she said, was hers
 again.   360
At times too shrilling in her angrier
 moods,
'That weak and watery nature love
 you? No!
"*Io* t' *amo, Io* t' amo"!' flung herself
Against my heart, but often while her
 lips
Were warm upon my cheek, an icy
 breath,
As from the grating of a sepulchre,
Past over both. I told her of my vow,
No pliable idiot I to break my vow;

But still she made her outcry for the
 ring;
For one monotonous fancy madden'd
 her,   370
Till I myself was madden'd with her
 cry,
And even that 'Io t' amo,' those three
 sweet
Italian words, became a weariness.
 My people too were scared with
  eerie sounds,
A footstep, a low throbbing in the
 walls,
A noise of falling weights that never
 fell,
Weird whispers, bells that rang without a hand,
Door-handles turn'd when none was
 at the door,
And bolted doors that open'd of themselves;
And one betwixt the dark and light
 had seen   380
Her, bending by the cradle of her
 babe.

MIRIAM

And I remember once that being
 waked
By noises in the house—and no one
 near—
I cried for nurse, and felt a gentle
 hand
Fall on my forehead, and a sudden
 face
Look'd in upon me like a gleam and
 pass'd,
And I was quieted, and slept again.
Or is it some half memory of a dream?

FATHER

Your fifth September birthday.

MIRIAM

      And the face,
The hand,—my mother.

FATHER

      Miriam, on that day
Two lovers parted by no scurrilous
 tale—   391

Mere want of gold—and still for
  twenty years
Bound by the golden cord of their first
  love—
Had ask'd us to their marriage, and to
  share
Their marriage-banquet. Muriel, paler
  then
Than ever you were in your cradle,
  moan'd,
'I am fitter for my bed, or for my
  grave,
I cannot go, go you.' And then she
  rose,
She clung to me with such a hard em-
  brace,   399
So lingeringly long, that half-amazed
I parted from her, and I went alone.
And when the bridegroom murmur'd,
  'With this ring,'
I felt for what I could not find, the
  key,
The guardian of her relics, of *her* ring.
I kept it as a sacred amulet
About me,—gone! and gone in that
  embrace!
Then, hurrying home, I found her not
  in house
Or garden—up the tower—an icy air
Fled by me.—There, the chest was
  open—all
The sacred relics tost about the floor—
Among them Muriel lying on her
  face—   411
I raised her, call'd her, 'Muriel, Mu-
  riel, wake!'
The fatal ring lay near her; the glazed
  eye
Glared at me as in horror. Dead! I
  took
And chafed the freezing hand. A red
  mark ran
All round one finger pointed straight,
  the rest
Were crumpled inwards. Dead!—and
  maybe stung
With some remorse, had stolen, worn
  the ring—
Then torn it from her finger, or as
  if—
For never had I seen her show re-
  morse—   420
As if—

MIRIAM

—those two ghost lovers—

FATHER

                    Lovers yet—

MIRIAM

Yes, yes!

FATHER

—but dead so long, gone up so far,
That now their ever-rising life has
  dwarf'd
Or lost the moment of their past on
  earth,
As we forget our wail at being born—
As if—

MIRIAM

—a dearer ghost had—

FATHER

             —wrench'd it away.

MIRIAM

Had floated in with sad reproachful
  eyes,
Till from her own hand she had torn
  the ring
In fright, and fallen dead. And I myself   430
Am half afraid to wear it.

FATHER

             Well, no more!
No bridal music this! but fear not
  you!
You have the ring she guarded; that
  poor link
With earth is broken, and has left her
  free,
Except that, still drawn downward for
  an hour,
Her spirit hovering by the church,
  where she

Was married too, may linger, till she
sees
Her maiden coming like a queen, who
leaves
Some colder province in the North to
gain
Her capital city, where the loyal bells
Clash welcome—linger, till her own,
the babe   440
She lean'd to from her spiritual sphere
Her lonely maiden princess, crowned
with flowers,
Has enter'd on the larger woman-
world
Of wives and mothers.
            But the bridal veil—
Your nurse is waiting. Kiss me, child,
and go.

FORLORN

I

'He is fled—I wish him dead—
    He that wrought my ruin—
O, the flattery and the craft
    Which were my undoing—
        In the night, in the night,
        When the storms are blowing.

II

'Who was witness of the crime?
    Who shall now reveal it?
He is fled, or he is dead,
    Marriage will conceal it—
        In the night, in the night,
        While the gloom is growing.'

III

Catherine, Catherine, in the night,
    What is this you 're dreaming?
There is laughter down in hell
    At your simple scheming—
        In the night, O, the night!
        When the ghosts are fleeting.

IV

You to place a hand in his
    Like an honest woman's,

You that lie with wasted lungs
    Waiting for your summons—
        In the night, O, the night!
        O, the deathwatch beating!

V

There will come a witness soon
    Hard to be confuted,
All the world will hear a voice
    Scream you are polluted—
        In the night! O, the night,
        When the owls are wailing!

VI

Shame and marriage, shame and marriage,
    Fright and foul dissembling,
Bantering bridesman, reddening priest,
    Tower and altar trembling—
        In the night, O, the night,
        When the mind is failing!

VII

Mother, dare you kill your child?
    How your hand is shaking!
Daughter of the seed of Cain,
    What is this you 're taking?—
        In the night, O, the night,
        While the house is sleeping.

VIII

Dreadful! has it come to this,
    O unhappy creature?
You that would not tread on a worm
    For your gentle nature—
        In the night, O, the night,
        O, the night of weeping!

IX

Murder would not veil your sin,
    Marriage will not hide it,
Earth and Hell will brand your name,
    Wretch, you must abide it—
        In the night, O, the night,
        Long before the dawning.

X

Up, get up, and tell him all,
    Tell him you were lying!

Do not die with a lie in your mouth,
 You that know you 're dying—
  In the night, O, the night,
  While the grave is yawning.

XI

No—you will not die before,
 Tho' you 'll ne'er be stronger;
You will live till *that* is born,
 Then a little longer—
  In the night, O, the night,
  While the Fiend is prowling.

XII

Death and marriage, death and mar-
  riage!
 Funeral hearses rolling!
Black with bridal favors mixt!
 Bridal bells with tolling!—
  In the night, O, the night,
  When the wolves are howling.

XIII

Up, get up, the time is short,
 Tell him now or never!
Tell him all before you die,
 Lest you die for ever—
  In the night, O, the night,
  Where there 's no forgetting.

XIV

Up she got, and wrote him all,
 All her tale of sadness,
Blister'd every word with tears,
 And eased her heart of madness—
  In the night, and nigh the dawn,
  And while the moon was setting.

HAPPY

THE LEPER'S BRIDE

I

WHY wail you, pretty plover? and
  what is it that you fear?
 Is he sick, your mate, like mine?
  have you lost him, is he fled?

And there—the heron rises from his
  watch beside the mere,
 And flies above the leper's hut,
  where lives the living-dead.

II

Come back, nor let me know it! would
  he live and die alone?
 And has he not forgiven me yet, his
  overjealous bride,
Who am, and was, and will be, his own
  and only own,
 To share his living death with him,
  die with him side by side?

III

Is that the leper's hut on the solitary
  moor,
 Where noble Ulric dwells forlorn
  and wears the leper's weed? [16]
The door is open. He! is he standing
  at the door,
 My soldier of the Cross? it is he,
  and he indeed!

IV

My roses—will he take them *now*—
  mine, his—from off the tree
 We planted both together, happy in
  our marriage morn?
O God, I could blaspheme, for he
  fought Thy fight for Thee,
 And Thou hast made him leper to
  compass him with scorn—

V

Hast spared the flesh of thousands, the
  coward and the base,
 And set a crueller mark than Cain's
  on him, the good and brave!
He sees me, waves me from him. I will
  front him face to face.
 You need not wave me from you. I
  would leap into your grave. [20]

.   .   .   .

VI

My warrior of the Holy Cross and of
  the conquering sword,

The roses that you cast aside—once
    more I bring you these.
No nearer? do you scorn me when you
    tell me, O my lord,
You would not mar the beauty of
    your bride with your disease.

VII

You say your body is so foul—then
    here I stand apart,
Who yearn to lay my loving head
    upon your leprous breast.
The leper plague may scale my skin,
    but never taint my heart;
Your body is not foul to me, and
    body is foul at best.

VIII

I loved you first when young and fair,
    but now I love you most;
The fairest flesh at last is filth on
    which the worm will feast; 30
This poor rib-grated dungeon of the
    holy human ghost,
This house with all its hateful needs
    no cleaner than the beast,

IX

This coarse diseaseful creature which
    in Eden was divine,
This Satan-haunted ruin, this little
    city of sewers,
This wall of solid flesh that comes be-
    tween your soul and mine,
Will vanish and give place to the
    beauty that endures,

X

The beauty that endures on the Spirit-
    ual height,
When we shall stand transfigured,
    like Christ on Hermon hill,
And moving each to music, soul in soul
    and light in light,
Shall flash thro' one another in a
    moment as we will. 40

XI

Foul! foul! the word was yours not
    mine, I worship that right hand
Which fell'd the foes before you as
    the woodman fells the wood,
And sway'd the sword that lighten'd
    back the sun of Holy Land,
    And clove the Moslem crescent
    moon, and changed it into
    blood.

XII

And once I worshipt all too well this
    creature of decay,
    For age will chink the face, and
    death will freeze the supplest
    limbs—
Yet you in your mid manhood—O,
    the grief when yesterday
They bore the Cross before you to
    the chant of funeral hymns!

XIII

'Libera me, Domine!' you sang the
    Psalm, and when
The priest pronounced you dead,
    and flung the mould upon your
    feet, 50
A beauty came upon your face, not
    that of living men,
But seen upon the silent brow when
    life has ceased to beat.

XIV

'Libera nos, Domine'—you knew not
    one was there
Who saw you kneel beside your
    bier, and weeping scarce could
    see;
May I come a little nearer, I that
    heard, and changed the prayer
And sang the married 'nos' for the
    solitary 'me'?

XV

My beauty marred by you? by you! so
    be it. All is well

If I lose it and myself in the higher
    beauty, yours.
My beauty lured that falcon from his
    eyry on the fell,
Who never caught one gleam of the
    beauty which endures—   60

XVI

The Count who sought to snap the
    bond that link'd us life to life,
Who whisper'd me, 'Your Ulric
    loves'—a little nearer still—
He hiss'd, 'Let us revenge ourselves,
    your Ulric woos my wife'—
A lie by which he thought he could
    subdue me to his will.

XVII

I knew that you were near me when I
    let him kiss my brow;
  Did he touch me on the lips? I was
    jealous, anger'd, vain,
And I meant to make *you* jealous. Are
    you jealous of me now?
    Your pardon, O my love, if I ever
    gave you pain!

XVIII

You never once accused me, but I
    wept alone, and sigh'd
In the winter of the present for the
    summer of the past;   70
That icy winter silence—how it froze
    you from your bride,
    Tho' I made one barren effort to
    break it at the last!

XIX

I brought you, you remember, these
    roses, when I knew
    You were parting for the war, and
    you took them tho' you
    frown'd;
You frown'd and yet you kiss'd them.
    All at once the trumpet blew,
    And you spurr'd your fiery horse,
    and you hurl'd them to the
    ground.

XX

You parted for the Holy War without
    a word to me,
And clear myself unask'd—not I.
    My nature was too proud.
And him I saw but once again, and far
    away was he,   79
    When I was praying in a storm—
    the crash was long and loud—

XXI

That God would ever slant His bolt
    from falling on your head—
    Then I lifted up my eyes, he was
    coming down the fell—
I clapt my hands. The sudden fire
    from heaven had dash'd him
    dead,
    And sent him charr'd and blasted to
    the deathless fire of hell.

XXII

See, I sinn'd but for a moment. I re-
    pented and repent,
    And trust myself forgiven by the
    God to whom I kneel.
A little nearer? Yes. I shall hardly be
    content
    Till I be leper like yourself, my
    love, from head to heel.

XXIII

O foolish dreams, that you, that I,
    would slight our marriage
    oath!
    I held you at that moment even
    dearer than before;   90
Now God has made you leper in His
    loving care for both,
    That we might cling together, never
    doubt each other more.

XXIV

The priest, who join'd you to the dead,
    has join'd our hands of old;
    If man and wife be but one flesh, let
    mine be leprous too,

As dead from all the human race as if
　　beneath the mould;
If you be dead, then I am dead, who
　　only live for you.

XXV

Would Earth tho' hid in cloud not be
　　follow'd by the Moon?
The leech forsake the dying bed for
　　terror of his life?
The Shadow leave the Substance in
　　the brooding light of noon?
Or if *I* had been the leper would you
　　have left the wife?   100

XXVI

Not take them? Still you wave me off
　　—poor roses—must I go—
I have worn them year by year—
　　from the bush we both had
　　set—
What? fling them to you?—well—that
　　were hardly gracious. No!
Your plague but passes by the
　　touch. A little nearer yet!

XXVII

There, there! he buried you, the
　　priest; the priest is not to
　　blame,
He joins us once again, to his either
　　office true.
I thank him. I am happy, happy. Kiss
　　me. In the name
Of the everlasting God, I will live
　　and die with you!

[Dean Milman has remarked that the
protection and care afforded by the
Church to this blighted race of lepers was
among the most beautiful of its offices
during the Middle Ages. The leprosy of
the thirteenth and fourteenth centuries
was supposed to be a legacy of the Cru-
sades, but was in all probability the offspring of meagre and unwholesome diet,
miserable lodging and clothing, physical
and moral degradation. The services of
the Church in the seclusion of these unhappy sufferers were most affecting. The
stern duty of looking to the public welfare is tempered with exquisite compassion for the victims of this loathsome
disease. The ritual for the sequestration
of the leprous differed little from the burial service. After the leper had been
sprinkled with holy water, the priest con-
ducted him into the church, the leper
singing the psalm 'Libera me, Domine,'
and the crucifix and bearer going before.
In the church a black cloth was stretched
over two trestles in front of the altar,
and the leper leaning at its side devoutly
heard mass. The priest, taking up a little
earth in his cloak, threw it on one of the
leper's feet, and put him out of the
church, if it did not rain too heavily;
took him to his hut in the midst of the
fields, and then uttered the prohibitions:
'I forbid you entering the church . . . or
entering the company of others. I forbid
you quitting your home without your
leper's dress.' He concluded: 'Take this
dress, and wear it in token of humility;
take these gloves, take this clapper, as a
sign that you are forbidden to speak to
any one. You are not to be indignant at
being thus separated from others, and as
to your little wants, good people will
provide for you, and God will not desert
you.' Then in this old ritual follow these
sad words: 'When it shall come to pass
that the leper shall pass out of this world,
he shall be buried in his hut, and not in
the churchyard.' At first there was a
doubt whether wives should follow their
husbands who had been leprous, or remain in the world and marry again. The
Church decided that the marriage-tie
was indissoluble, and so bestowed on
these unhappy beings this immense
source of consolation. With a love
stronger than this living death, lepers
were followed into banishment from the
haunts of men by their faithful wives.
Readers of Sir J. Stephen's 'Essays on
Ecclesiastical Biography' will recollect
the description of the founder of the
Franciscan order, how, controlling his
involuntary disgust, Saint Francis of
Assisi washed the feet and dressed the
sores of the lepers, once at least reverently applying his lips to their wounds.
—BOURCHER-JAMES.]

This ceremony of *quasi*-burial varied
considerably at different times and in
different places. In some cases a grave
was dug, and the leper's face was often
covered during the service.

TO ULYSSES [1]

I

ULYSSES, much-experienced man,
    Whose eyes have known this globe
        of ours,
    Her tribes of men, and trees, and
        flowers,
From Corrientes to Japan,

II

To you that bask below the Line,
    I soaking here in winter wet—
    The century's three strong eights
        have met
To drag me down to seventy-nine

III

In summer if I reach my day—
    To you, yet young, who breathe the
        balm
    Of summer-winters by the palm
And orange grove of Paraguay,

IV

I, tolerant of the colder time,
    Who love the winter woods, to trace
    On paler heavens the branching
        grace
Of leafless elm, or naked lime,

V

And see my cedar green, and there
    My giant ilex keeping leaf
    When frost is keen and days are
        brief—
Or marvel how in English air

VI

My yucca, which no winter quells,
    Altho' the months have scarce be-
        gun,
    Has push'd toward our faintest sun
A spike of half-accomplish'd bells—

[1] 'Ulysses,' the title of a number of essays by W. G. Palgrave. He died at
Montevideo before seeing my poem.

VII

Or watch the waving pine which here
    The warrior of Caprera set, [1]
    A name that earth will not forget
Till earth has roll'd her latest year—

VIII

I, once half-crazed for larger light
    On broader zones beyond the foam,
    But chaining fancy now at home
Among the quarried downs of Wight,

IX

Not less would yield full thanks to
        you
    For your rich gift, your tale of
        lands
    I know not, [2] your Arabian sands;
Your cane, your palm, tree-fern, bam-
        boo,

X

The wealth of tropic bower and
        brake;
    Your Oriental Eden-isles, [3]
    Where man, nor only Nature
        smiles;
Your wonder of the boiling lake; [4]

XI

Phra-Chai, the Shadow of the Best, [5]
    Phra-bat [6] the step; your Pontic
        coast;
    Crag-cloister; [7] Anatolian Ghost; [8]

[1] Garibaldi said to me, alluding to his
barren island, 'I wish I had your trees.'
[2] The tale of Nejd.
[3] The Philippines.
[4] In Dominica.
[5] The Shadow of the Lord. Certain obscure markings on a rock in Siam, which
express the image of Buddha to the Bud-
dhist more or less distinctly according to
his faith and his moral worth.
[6] The footstep of the Lord on another
rock.
[7] The monastery of Sumelas.
[8] Anatolian spectre stories.

Hong-Kong,[1] Karnac,[2] and all the rest;

XII

Thro' which I follow'd line by line
    Your leading hand, and came, my friend,
      To prize your various book, and send
A gift of slenderer value, mine.

TO MARY BOYLE

WITH THE FOLLOWING POEM

I

'SPRING-FLOWERS'! While you still de-lay to take
    Your leave of town,
Our elm-tree's ruddy-hearted blos-som-flake
    Is fluttering down.

II

Be truer to your promise. There! I heard
    Our cuckoo call.
Be needle to the magnet of your word,
    Nor wait, till all

III

Our vernal bloom from every vale and plain
    And garden pass,
And all the gold from each laburnum chain
    Drop to the grass.

IV

Is memory with your Marian gone to rest,
    Dead with the dead?
For ere she left us, when we met, you prest
    My hand, and said

[1] The three cities.
[2] Travels in Egypt.

V

'I come with your spring-flowers.' You came not, friend;
    My birds would sing,
You heard not. Take then this spring-flower I send,
    This song of spring,

VI

Found yesterday—forgotten mine own rhyme
    By mine old self,
As I shall be forgotten by old Time,
    Laid on the shelf—

VII

A rhyme that flower'd betwixt the whitening sloe
    And kingcup blaze,
And more than half a hundred years ago,
    In rick-fire days,

VIII

When Dives loathed the times, and paced his land
    In fear of worse,
And sanguine Lazarus felt a vacant hand
    Fill with *his* purse.

IX

For lowly minds were madden'd to the height
    By tonguester tricks,
And once—I well remember that red night
    When thirty ricks,

X

All flaming, made an English home-stead hell—
    These hands of mine
Have helpt to pass a bucket from the well
    Along the line,

XI

When this bare dome had not begun
    to gleam
      Thro' youthful curls,
And you were then a lover's fairy
    dream,
      His girl of girls;

XII

And you, that now are lonely, and with
    Grief
      Sit face to face,
Might find a flickering glimmer of re-
    lief
      In change of place.

XIII

What use to brood? This life of min-
    gled pains
      And joys to me,
Despite of every Faith and Creed,
    remains
      The Mystery.

XIV

Let golden youth bewail the friend,
    the wife,
      For ever gone.
He dreams of that long walk thro'
    desert life
      Without the one

XV

The silver year should cease to mourn
    and sigh—
      Not long to wait—
So close are we, dear Mary, you and I
      To that dim gate.

XVI

Take, read! and be the faults your
    Poet makes
      Or many or few,
He rests content, if his young music
    wakes
      A wish in you

XVII

To change our dark Queen-city, all
    her realm
      Of sound and smoke,
For his clear heaven, and these few
    lanes of elm
      And whispering oak.

THE PROGRESS OF SPRING

I

The ground-flame of the crocus
    breaks the mould,
  Fair Spring slides hither o'er the
    Southern sea,
Wavers on her thin stem the snow-
    drop cold
  That trembles not to kisses of the
    bee.
Come, Spring, for now from all the
    dripping eaves
  The spear of ice has wept itself
    away,
And hour by hour unfolding wood-
    bine leaves
  O'er his uncertain shadow droops
    the day.
She comes! The loosen'd rivulets run;
  The frost-bead melts upon her
    golden hair;
Her mantel, slowly greening in the
    Sun,
  Now wraps her close, now arching
    leaves her bare
  To breaths of balmier air;

II

Up leaps the lark, gone wild to wel-
    come her,
  About her dance the tits, and shriek
    the jays,
Before her skims the jubilant wood-
    pecker,
  The linnet's bosom blushes at her
    gaze,
While round her brows a woodland
    culver flits,

Watching her large light eyes and
  gracious looks,
And in her open palm a halcyon sits
  Patient—the secret splendor of the
  brooks.
Come, Spring! She comes on waste
  and wood,
  On farm and field; but enter also
  here,
Diffuse thyself at will thro' all my
  blood,
  And, tho' thy violet sicken into sere,
Lodge with me all the year!

III

Once more a downy drift against the
  brakes,
  Self-darken'd in the sky, descending
  slow!
But gladly see I thro' the wavering
  flakes
  Yon blanching apricot like snow in
  snow.
These will thine eyes not brook in
  forest-paths,
  On their perpetual pine, nor round
  the beech;
They fuse themselves to little spicy
  baths,
  Solved in the tender blushes of the
  peach;
They lose themselves and die
  On that new life that gems the haw-
  thorn line;
Thy gay lent-lilies wave and put them
  by,
  And out once more in varnish'd
  glory shine
Thy stars of celandine.

IV

She floats across the hamlet. Heaven
  lours,
  But in the tearful splendor of her
  smiles
I see the slowly-thickening chestnut
  towers
  Fill out the spaces by the barren
  tiles.
Now past her feet the swallow circling
  flies,

A clamorous cuckoo stoops to meet
  her hand;
Her light makes rainbows in my closing eyes,
  I hear a charm of song thro' all the
  land.
Come, Spring! She comes, and Earth
  is glad
  To roll her North below thy deepening dome,
But ere thy maiden birk be wholly
  clad,
  And these low bushes dip their
  twigs in foam,
Make all true hearths thy home.

V

Across my garden! and the thicket
  stirs,
  The fountain pulses high in sunnier
  jets,
The blackcap warbles, and the turtle
  purrs,
  The starling claps his tiny castanets.
Still round her forehead wheels the
  woodland dove,
  And scatters on her throat the
  sparks of dew,
The kingcup fills her footprint, and
  above
  Broaden the glowing isles of vernal
  blue.
Hail, ample presence of a Queen,
  Bountiful, beautiful, apparell'd gay,
Whose mantle, every shade of glanc-
  ing green,
  Flies back in fragrant breezes to
  display
A tunic white as May!

VI

She whispers, 'From the South I bring
  you balm,
  For on a tropic mountain was I
  born,
While some dark dweller by the coco-
  palm
  Watch'd my far meadow zoned with
  airy morn;
From under rose a muffled moan of
  floods;

I sat beneath a solitude of snow;
There no one came, the turf was fresh,
    the woods
    Plunged gulf on gulf thro' all their
        vales below.
I saw beyond their silent tops
    The streaming marshes of the scar-
        let cranes,
The slant seas leaning on the man-
        grove copse,
    And summer basking in the sultry
        plains
About a land of cranes.

VII

'Then from my vapor-girdle soaring
    forth
    I scaled the buoyant highway of the
        birds,
And drank the dews and drizzle of the
    North,
    That I might mix with men, and
        hear their words
On pathway'd plains; for—while my
    hand exults
    Within the bloodless heart of lowly
        flowers
To work old laws of Love to fresh re-
    sults,
    Thro' manifold effect of simple
        powers—
I too would teach the man
    Beyond the darker hour to see the
        bright,
That his fresh life may close as it be-
    gan,
    The still-fulfilling promise of a
        light
Narrowing the bounds of night.'

VIII

So wed thee with my soul, that I may
    mark
    The coming year's great good and
        varied ills,
And new developments, whatever
    spark
    Be struck from out the clash of
        warring wills;
Or whether, since our nature cannot
    rest,

The smoke of war's volcano burst
    again
From hoary deeps that belt the
    changeful West,
    Old Empires, dwellings of the kings
        of men;
Or should those fail that hold the
    helm,
    While the long day of knowledge
        grows and warms,
And in the heart of this most ancient
    realm
    A hateful voice be utter'd, and
        alarms
    Sounding 'To arms! to arms!'

IX

A simpler, saner lesson might he learn
    Who reads thy gradual process,
        Holy Spring.
Thy leaves possess the season in their
    turn,
    And in their time thy warblers rise
        on wing.
How surely glidest thou from March
    to May,
    And changest, breathing it, the sul-
        len wind,
Thy scope of operation, day by day,
    Larger and fuller, like the human
        mind!
Thy warmths from bud to bud
    Accomplish that blind model in the
        seed,
And men have hopes, which race the
    restless blood,
    That after many changes may suc-
        ceed
Life which is Life indeed.

MERLIN AND THE GLEAM

I

O young Mariner,
You from the haven
Under the sea-cliff,
You that are watching
The gray Magician
With eyes of wonder,
I am Merlin,

And *I* am dying,
I am Merlin
Who follow the Gleam.

II

Mighty the Wizard
Who found me at sunrise
Sleeping, and woke me
And learn'd me Magic!
Great the Master,
And sweet the Magic,
When over the valley,
In early summers,
Over the mountain,
On human faces,
And all around me,
Moving to melody,
Floated the Gleam.

III

Once at the croak of a Raven who
    crost it
A barbarous people,
Blind to the magic
And deaf to the melody,
Snarl'd at and cursed me.
A demon vext me,
The light retreated,
The landskip darken'd,
The melody deaden'd,
The Master whisper'd,
'Follow the Gleam.'

IV

Then to the melody,
Over a wilderness
Gliding, and glancing at
Elf of the woodland,
Gnome of the cavern,
Griffin and Giant,
And dancing of Fairies
In desolate hollows,
And wraiths of the mountain,
And rolling of dragons
By warble of water,
Or cataract music
Of falling torrents,
Flitted the Gleam.

V

Down from the mountain
And over the level,
And streaming and shining on
Silent river,
Silvery willow,
Pasture and plowland,
Innocent maidens,
Garrulous children,
Homestead and harvest,
Reaper and gleaner,
And rough-ruddy faces
Of lowly labor,
Slided the Gleam—

VI

Then, with a melody
Stronger and statelier,
Led me at length
To the city and palace
Of Arthur the King;
Touch'd at the golden
Cross of the churches,
Flash'd on the tournament,
Flicker'd and bicker'd
From helmet to helmet,
And last on the forehead
Of Arthur the blameless
Rested the Gleam.

VII

Clouds and darkness
Closed upon Camelot;
Arthur had vanish'd
I knew not whither,
The king who loved me,
And cannot die;
Far out of the darkness
Silent and slowly
The Gleam, that had waned to a win-
    try glimmer
On icy fallow
And faded forest,
Drew to the valley
Named of the shadow,
And slowly brightening
Out of the glimmer,
And slowly moving again to a melody
    Yearningly tender,

Fell on the shadow,
No longer a shadow,
But clothed with the Gleam.

VIII

And broader and brighter
The Gleam flying onward,
Wed to the melody,
Sang thro' the world;
And slower and fainter,
Old and weary,
But eager to follow,
I saw, whenever
In passing it glanced upon
Hamlet or city,
That under the Crosses
The dead man's garden,
The mortal hillock,
Would break into blossom;
And so to the land's
Last limit I came—
And can no longer,
But die rejoicing,
For thro' the Magic
Of Him the Mighty,
Who taught me in childhood,
There on the border
Of boundless Ocean,
And all but in Heaven
Hovers the Gleam.

IX

Not of the sunlight,
Not of the moonlight,
Not of the starlight!
O young Mariner,
Down to the haven,
Call your companions,
Launch your vessel,
And crowd your canvas,
And, ere it vanishes
Over the margin,
After it, follow it,
Follow the Gleam.

ROMNEY'S REMORSE

[I read Hayley's Life of Romney the other day—Romney wanted but education and reading to make him a very fine painter: but his ideal was not high nor fixed. How touching is the close of his life! He married at nineteen, and because Sir Joshua and others had said that 'marriage spoilt an artist' almost immediately left his wife in the North and scarce saw her till the end of his life; when old, nearly mad, and quite desolate, he went back to her and she received him and nursed him till he died. This quiet act of hers is worth all Romney's pictures! even as a matter of Art, I am sure.—EDWARD FITZGERALD, 'Letters and Literary Remains,' vol. i.]

'BEAT, little heart—I give you this
and this.'
   Who are you? What! the Lady
      Hamilton?
Good, I am never weary painting you.
To sit once more? Cassandra, Hebe,
      Joan,
Or spinning at your wheel beside the
      vine—
Bacchante, what you will; and if I
      fail
To conjure and concentrate into form
And color all you are, the fault is less
In me than Art. What artist ever yet
Could make pure light live on the
      canvas? Art!
Why should I so disrelish that short
      word?
   Where am I? snow on all the hills!
      so hot,
So fever'd! never colt would more de-
      light
To roll himself in meadow grass than
      I
To wallow in that winter of the hills.
   Nurse, were you hired? or came of
      your own will
To wait on one so broken, so forlorn?
Have I not met you somewhere long
      ago?
I am all but sure I have—in Kendal
      church—
O, yes! I hired you for a season there,
And then we parted; but you look so
      kind
That you will not deny my sultry
      throat
One draught of icy water. There—you
      spill
The drops upon my forehead. Your
      hand shakes.

I am ashamed. I am a trouble to you,
Could kneel for your forgiveness. Are
    they tears?
For me—they do me too much grace
    —for me?
O Mary, Mary!
            Vexing you with words!
Words only, born of fever, or the
    fumes
Of that dark opiate dose you gave me,
    —words,
Wild babble. I have stumbled back
    again
Into the common day, the sounder
    self.
God stay me there, if only for your
    sake,
The truest, kindliest, noblest-hearted
    wife
That ever wore a Christian marriage-
    ring.
    My curse upon the Master's apoth-
    egm,
That wife and children drag an artist
    down!
This seem'd my lodestar in the heaven
    of Art,
And lured me from the household fire
    on earth.
To you my days have been a lifelong
    lie,
Grafted on half a truth; and tho' you
    say,
'Take comfort you have won the
    painter's fame,'
The best in me that sees the worst in
    me,
And groans to see it, finds no comfort
    there.
    What fame? I am not Raphael,
    Titian,—no,
Nor even a Sir Joshua, some will cry.
Wrong there! The painter's fame?
    but mine, that grew
Blown into glittering by the popular
    breath,
May float awhile beneath the sun,
    may roll
The rainbow hues of heaven about
    it—
        There!
The color'd bubble bursts above the
    abyss

Of Darkness, utter Lethe.

                  Is it so?
Her sad eyes plead for my own fame
    with me
To make it dearer.

          Look, the sun has risen
To flame along another dreary day.
Your hand. How bright you keep your
    marriage-ring!
Raise me. I thank you.

          Has your opiate then
Bred this black mood? or am I con-
    scious more
Than other Masters, of the chasm be-
    tween
Work and Ideal? Or does the gloom
    of age
And suffering cloud the height I stand
    upon
Even from myself? stand? stood—no
    more.
        And yet
The world would lose, if such a wife as
    you
Should vanish unrecorded. Might I
    crave
One favor? I am bankrupt of all
    claim
On your obedience, and my strongest
    wish
Falls flat before your least unwilling-
    ness.
Still, would you—if it please you—sit
    to me?
    I dream'd last night of that clear
    summer noon,
When seated on a rock, and foot to
    foot
With your own shadow in the placid
    lake,
You claspt our infant daughter, heart
    to heart.
I had been among the hills, and
    brought you down
A length of staghorn-moss, and this
    you twined
About her cap. I see the picture yet,
Mother and child. A sound from far
    away,
No louder than a bee among the
    flowers,

A fall of water lull'd the noon asleep.
You still'd it for the moment with a
    song
Which often echo'd in me, while I
    stood
Before the great Madonna-master-
    pieces
Of ancient Art in Paris, or in Rome.

Mary, my crayons! if I can, I will.
You should have been—I might have
    made you once,
Had I but known you as I know you
    now—
The true Alcestis of the time. Your
    song—
Sit, listen! I remember it, a proof
That I—even I—at times remember'd
    you.

'Beat upon mine, little heart! beat, beat!
Beat upon mine! you are mine, my
    sweet!
All mine from your pretty blue eyes to
    your feet,
                    My sweet.'

Less profile! turn to me—three-quar-
    ter face.

'Sleep, little blossom, my honey, my
    bliss!
For I give you this, and I give you this!
And I blind your pretty blue eyes with a
    kiss!
                    Sleep!'

Too early blinded by the kiss of
    death—

'Father and Mother will watch you
    grow'—

You watch'd, not I; she did not grow,
    she died.

'Father and Mother will watch you
    grow,
And gather the roses whenever they
    blow,
And find the white heather wherever
    you go,
                    My sweet.'

Ah, my white heather only blooms in
    heaven

With Milton's amaranth. There, there,
    there! a child
Had shamed me at it—Down, you idle
    tools,
Stampt into dust—tremulous, all
    awry,
Blurr'd like a landskip in a ruffled
    pool,—
Not one stroke firm. This Art, that
    harlot-like
Seduced me from you, leaves me har-
    lot-like,
Who love her still, and whimper, im-
    potent
To win her back before I die—and
    then—
Then, in the loud world's bastard
    judgment-day,
One truth will damn me with the
    mindless mob,
Who feel no touch of my temptation,
    more
Than all the myriad lies that blacken
    round
The corpse of every man that gains a
    name;
'This model husband, this fine artist!'
    Fool,
What matters? Six foot deep of burial
    mould
Will dull their comments! Ay, but
    when the shout
Of His descending peals from heaven,
    and throbs
Thro' earth and all her graves, if *He*
    should ask,
'Why left you wife and children? for
    my sake,
According to my word?' and I replied,
'Nay, Lord, for *Art*,' why, that would
    sound so mean
That all the dead, who wait the doom
    of hell
For bolder sins than mine, adulteries,
Wife-murders,—nay, the ruthless
    Mussul-man
Who flings his bowstrung harem in
    the sea,
Would turn, and glare at me, and
    point and jeer,
And gibber at the worm who, living,
    made

The wife of wives a widow-bride, and
  lost
Salvation for a sketch.
                    I am wild again!
The coals of fire you heap upon my
  head
Have crazed me. Some one knocking
  there without?
No! Will my Indian brother come?
  to find
Me or my coffin? Should I know the
  man?
This worn-out Reason dying in her
  house
May leave the windows blinded, and
  if so,
Bid him farewell for me, and tell
  him—Hope!
I hear a death-bed angel whisper,
  'Hope.'
'The miserable have no medicine—
But only hope!' He said it—in the
  play.
His crime was of the senses; of the
  mind
Mine—worse, cold, calculated.
                    Tell my son—
O, let me lean my head upon your
  breast.
'Beat, little heart' on this fool brain of
  mine.
I once had friends—and many—none
  like you.
I love you more than when we mar-
  ried. Hope!
O, yes, I hope, or fancy that, perhaps,
Human forgiveness touches heaven,
  and thence—
For you forgive me, you are sure of
  that—
Reflected, sends a light on the for-
  given.

PARNASSUS

Exegi monumentum . . .
Quod non . . .
Possit diruere . . .
            . . . innumerabilis
Annorum series et fuga temporum.
                    HORACE.

I

WHAT be those crown'd forms high
  over the sacred fountain?
Bards, that the mighty Muses have
  raised to the heights of the
  mountain,
And over the flight of the Ages! O
  Goddesses, help me up thither!
Lightning may shrivel the laurel of
  Cæsar, but mine would not
  wither.
Steep is the mountain, but you, you
  will help me to overcome it,
And stand with my head in the zenith,
  and roll my voice from the
  summit,
Sounding for ever and ever thro'
  Earth and her listening na-
  tions,
And mixt with the great sphere-music
  of stars and of constellations.

II

What be those two shapes high over
  the sacred fountain,
Taller than all the Muses, and huger
  than all the mountain?
On those two known peaks they stand
  ever spreading and heighten-
  ing;
Poet, that evergreen laurel is blasted
  by more than lightning!
Look, in their deep double shadow the
  crown'd ones all disappearing!
Sing like a bird and be happy, nor
  hope for a deathless hearing!
'Sounding for ever and ever?' pass on!
  the sight confuses—
These are Astronomy and Geology,
  terrible Muses!

III

If the lips were touch'd with fire from
  off a pure Pierian altar,
Tho' their music here be mortal need
  the singer greatly care?
Other songs for other worlds! the fire
  within him would not falter;
Let the golden Iliad vanish, Homer
  here is Homer there.

BY AN EVOLUTIONIST

THE Lord let the house of a brute to
  the soul of a man,
  And the man said, 'Am I your
    debtor?'
And the Lord—'Not yet; but make it
  as clean as you can,
And then I will let you a better.'

I

If my body come from brutes, my
  soul uncertain or a fable,
  Why not bask amid the senses while
    the sun of morning shines,
I, the finer brute rejoicing in my
  hounds, and in my stable,
  Youth and health, and birth and
    wealth, and choice of women
    and of wines?

II

What hast thou done for me, grim Old
  Age, save breaking my bones
    on the rack?
  Would I had past in the morning
    that looks so bright from afar!

OLD AGE

Done for thee? starved the wild beast
    that was linkt with thee eighty
    years back.
  Less weight now for the ladder-of-
    heaven that hangs on a star.

I

If my body come from brutes, tho'
  somewhat finer than their own,
  I am heir, and this my kingdom.
    Shall the royal voice be mute?
No, but if the rebel subject seek to
  drag me from the throne,
  Hold the sceptre, Human Soul, and
    rule thy province of the brute.

II

I have climb'd to the snows of Age,
  and I gaze at a field in the
  Past,

Where I sank with the body at
  times in the sloughs of a low
    desire,
But I hear no yelp of the beast, and
  the Man is quiet at last,
  As he stands on the heights of his
    life with a glimpse of a height
    that is higher.

FAR—FAR—AWAY

(FOR MUSIC)

WHAT sight so lured him thro' the
  fields he knew
As where earth's green stole into heav-
  en's own hue,
        Far—far—away?

What sound was dearest in his native
  dells?
The mellow lin-lan-lone of evening
  bells
        Far—far—away.

What vague world-whisper, mystic
  pain or joy,
Thro' those three words would haunt
  him when a boy,
        Far—far—away?

A whisper from his dawn of life? a
  breath
From some fair dawn beyond the
  doors of death
        Far—far—away?

Far, far, how far? from o'er the gates
  of birth,
The faint horizons, all the bounds of
  earth,
        Far—far—away?

What charm in words, a charm no
  words could give?
O dying words, can Music make you
  live
        Far—far—away?

POLITICS

WE move, the wheel must always
    move,
    Nor always on the plain,
And if we move to such a goal
    As Wisdom hopes to gain,
Then you that drive, and know your
    craft,
    Will firmly hold the rein,
Nor lend an ear to random cries,
    Or you may drive in vain;
For some cry 'Quick' and some cry
    'Slow,'
    But, while the hills remain,
Up hill 'Too-slow' will need the whip,
    Down hill 'Too-quick' the chain.

BEAUTIFUL CITY

BEAUTIFUL city the centre and crater
    of European confusion,
O you with your passionate shriek for
    the rights of an equal human-
    ity
How often your Re-volution has
    proven but E-volution
Roll'd again back on itself in the tides
    of a civic insanity!

THE ROSES ON THE TERRACE

ROSE, on this terrace fifty years ago,
    When I was in my June, you in your
    May,
Two words, 'My Rose,' set all your
    face aglow,
    And now that I am white and you
    are gray,
That blush of fifty years ago, my dear,
    Blooms in the past, but close to me
    to-day,
As this red rose, which on our terrace
    here
    Glows in the blue of fifty miles
    away.

THE PLAY

ACT first, this Earth, a stage so
    gloom'd with woe
    You all but sicken at the shifting
    scenes.
And yet be patient. Our Playwright
    may show
    In some fifth act what this wild
    Drama means.

ON ONE WHO AFFECTED AN
EFFEMINATE MANNER

WHILE man and woman still are in-
    complete,
I prize that soul where man and
    woman meet,
Which types all Nature's male and
    female plan,
But, friend, man-woman is not
    woman-man.

TO ONE WHO RAN DOWN THE
ENGLISH

YOU make our faults too gross, and
    thence maintain
Our darker future. May your fears
    be vain!
At times the small black fly upon the
    pane
May seem the black ox of the distant
    plain.

THE SNOWDROP

MANY, many welcomes,
February fair-maid,
Ever as of old time,
Solitary firstling,
Coming in the cold time,
Prophet of the gay time,
Prophet of the May time,
Prophet of the roses,
Many, many welcomes,
February fair-maid!

THE THROSTLE

'SUMMER is coming, summer is com-
       ing.
   I know it, I know it, I know it.
Light again, leaf again, life again, love
       again!'
   Yes, my wild little Poet.

Sing the new year in under the blue.
   Last year you sang it as gladly.
'New, new, new, new!' Is it then *so*
       new
   That you should carol so madly?

'Love again, song again, nest again,
       young again,'
   Never a prophet so crazy!
And hardly a daisy as yet, little
       friend,
   See, there is hardly a daisy.

'Here again, here, here, here, happy
       year!'
   O warble unchidden, unbidden!
Summer is coming, is coming, my
       dear,
   And all the winters are hidden.

THE OAK

LIVE thy Life,
   Young and old,
Like yon oak

Bright in spring,
   Living gold;

Summer-rich
   Then; and then
Autumn-changed,
Soberer-hued
   Gold again.

All his leaves
   Fallen at length,
Look, he stands,
Trunk and bough,
   Naked strength.

IN MEMORIAM

W. G. WARD

FAREWELL, whose like on earth I shall
       not find,
   Whose Faith and Work were bells
       of full accord,
My friend, the most unworldly of
       mankind,
   Most generous of all Ultramon-
       tanes, Ward,
How subtle at tierce and quart of
       mind with mind,
   How loyal in the following of thy
       Lord!

QUEEN MARY

A DRAMA

DRAMATIS PERSONÆ

QUEEN MARY.
PHILIP, *King of Naples and Sicily, afterwards King of Spain.*
THE PRINCESS ELIZABETH.
REGINALD POLE, *Cardinal and Papal Legate.*
SIMON RENARD, *Spanish Ambassador.*
LE SIEUR DE NOAILLES, *French Ambassador.*
THOMAS CRANMER, *Archbishop of Canterbury.*
SIR NICHOLAS HEATH, *Archbishop of York; Lord Chancellor after Gardiner.*
EDWARD COURTENAY, *Earl of Devon.*
LORD WILLIAM HOWARD, *afterwards Lord Howard, and Lord High Admiral.*
LORD WILLIAMS OF THAME.
LORD PAGET.
LORD PETRE.
STEPHEN GARDINER, *Bishop of Winchester and Lord Chancellor.*
EDMUND BONNER, *Bishop of London.*
THOMAS THIRLBY, *Bishop of Ely.*
SIR THOMAS WYATT } *Insurrectionary Leaders.*
SIR THOMAS STAFFORD }
SIR RALPH BAGENHALL.
SIR ROBERT SOUTHWELL.
SIR HENRY BEDINGFIELD.
SIR WILLIAM CECIL.
SIR THOMAS WHITE, *Lord Mayor of London.*
THE DUKE OF ALVA } *attending on Philip.*
THE COUNT DE FERIA }
PETER MARTYR.
FATHER COLE.
FATHER BOURNE.
VILLA GARCIA.
SOTO.
CAPTAIN BRETT } *Adherents of Wyatt.*
ANTHONY KNYVETT }
PETERS, *Gentleman of Lord Howard.*
ROGER, *Servant to Noailles.*
WILLIAM, *Servant to Wyatt.*
STEWARD OF HOUSEHOLD *to the Princess Elizabeth.*
OLD NOKES *and* NOKES.
MARCHIONESS OF EXETER, *Mother of Courtenay.*
LADY CLARENCE }
LADY MAGDALEN DACRES } *Ladies in Waiting to the Queen.*
ALICE }
MAID OF HONOR *to the Princess Elizabeth.*
JOAN } *two Country Wives.*
TIB }

Lords and other Attendants, Members of the Privy Council, Members of Parliament,
two Gentlemen, Aldermen, Citizens, Peasants, Ushers, Messengers, Guards,
Pages, Gospellers, Marshalmen, etc.

QUEEN MARY

ACT I

SCENE I—ALDGATE RICHLY DECORATED

CROWD. MARSHALMEN.

Marshalman. Stand back, keep a clear lane! When will her Majesty pass, say'st thou? why now, even now; wherefore draw back your heads and your horns before I break them, and make what noise you will with your tongues, so it be not treason. Long live Queen Mary, the lawful and legitimate daughter of Harry the Eighth! Shout, knaves!

Citizens. Long live Queen Mary!

First Citizen. That 's a hard word, legitimate; what does it mean?

Second Citizen. It means a bastard.

Third Citizen. Nay, it means trueborn.

First Citizen. Why, did n't the Parliament make her a bastard?

Second Citizen. No; it was the Lady Elizabeth.

Third Citizen. That was after, man; that was after.

First Citizen. Then which is the bastard?

Second Citizen. Troth, they be both bastards by Act of Parliament and Council.

Third Citizen. Ay, the Parliament can make every true-born man of us a bastard. Old Nokes, can't it make thee a bastard? thou shouldst know, for thou art as white as three Christmases.

Old Nokes (*dreamily*). Who 's a-passing? King Edward or King Richard?

Third Citizen. No, old Nokes.

Old Nokes. It 's Harry!

Third Citizen. It 's Queen Mary.

Old Nokes. The blessed Mary 's a-passing!   [*Falls on his knees.*

Nokes. Let father alone, my masters! he 's past your questioning.

Third Citizen. Answer thou for him, then! thou 'rt no such cockerel thyself, for thou was born i' the tail end of old Harry the Seventh.

Nokes. Eh! that was afore bastard-making began. I was born true man at five in the forenoon, i' the tail of old Harry, and so they can't make me a bastard.

Third Citizen. But if Parliament can make the Queen a bastard, why, it follows all the more that they can make thee one, who art fray'd i' the knees, and out at elbow, and bald o' the back, and bursten at the toes, and down at heels.

Nokes. I was born of a true man and a ring'd wife, and I can't argue upon it; but I and my old woman 'ud burn upon it, that would we.

Marshalman. What are you cackling of bastardy under the Queen's own nose? I 'll have you flogg'd and burnt too, by the rood I will.

First Citizen. He swears by the rood. Whew!

Second Citizen. Hark! the trumpets.

[*The Procession passes,* Mary *and* Elizabeth *riding side by side, and disappears under the gate.*

Citizens. Long live Queen Mary! down with all traitors! God save her Grace; and death to Northumberland!   [*Exeunt.*

Manent TWO GENTLEMEN.

First Gentleman. By God's light a noble creature, right royal!

Second Gentleman. She looks comelier than ordinary to-day; but to my mind the Lady Elizabeth is the more noble and royal.

First Gentleman. I mean the Lady Elizabeth. Did you hear (I have a daughter in her service who reported it) that she met the Queen at Wanstead with five hundred horse, and the Queen (tho' some say they be much divided) took her hand, call'd her sweet sister, and kiss'd not her alone, but all the ladies of her following.

Second Gentleman. Ay, that was in her hour of joy. There will be plenty to sunder and unsister them again; this Gardiner for one, who is to be made Lord Chancellor, and will pounce like a wild beast out of his cage to worry Cranmer.

First Gentleman. And, furthermore, my daughter said that when there rose a talk of the late rebellion, she spoke even of Northumberland pitifully, and of the good Lady Jane as a poor innocent child who had but obeyed her father; and, furthermore, she said that no one in her time should be burnt for heresy.

Second Gentleman. Well, sir, I look for happy times.

First Gentleman. There is but one thing against them. I know not if you know.

Second Gentleman. I suppose you touch upon the rumor that Charles, the master of the world, has offer'd her his son Philip, the Pope and the devil. I trust it is but a rumor.

First Gentleman. She is going now to the Tower to loose the prisoners there, and among them Courtenay, to be made Earl of Devon, of royal blood, of splendid feature, whom the council and all her people wish her to marry. May it be so, for we are many of us Catholics, but few Papists, and

the Hot Gospellers will go mad upon it.

Second Gentleman. Was she not betroth'd in her babyhood to the Great Emperor himself?

First Gentleman. Ay, but he's too old.

Second Gentleman. And again to her cousin Reginald Pole, now Cardinal; but I hear that he too is full of aches and broken before his day.

First Gentleman. Oh, the Pope could dispense with his cardinalate, and his achage, and his breakage, if that were all. Will you not follow the procession?

Second Gentleman. No; I have seen enough for this day.

First Gentleman. Well, I shall follow; if I can get near enough I shall judge with my own eyes whether her Grace incline to this splendid scion of Plantagenet.   [*Exeunt.*

SCENE II

A ROOM IN LAMBETH PALACE

Cranmer. To Strasburg, Antwerp, Frankfort, Zurich, Worms,
Geneva, Basle—our bishops from their sees
Or fled, they say, or flying—Poinet, Barlow,
Bale, Scory, Coverdale; besides the deans
Of Christchurch, Durham, Exeter, and Wells—
Ailmer and Bullingham, and hundreds more;
So they report. I shall be left alone.
No; Hooper, Ridley, Latimer, will not fly.

Enter PETER MARTYR.

Peter Martyr. Fly, Cranmer! were there nothing else, your name
Stands first of those who sign'd the letter patent
That gave her royal crown to Lady Jane.

Cranmer. Stand first it may, but it was written last.
Those that are now her privy council sign'd
Before me; nay, the judges had pronounced
That our young Edward might bequeath the crown
Of England, putting by his father's will.
Yet I stood out, till Edward sent for me.
The wan boy-king, with his fast-fading eyes
Fixt hard on mine, his frail transparent hand,
Damp with the sweat of death, and griping mine,
Whisper'd me, if I loved him, not to yield
His Church of England to the Papal wolf
And Mary; then I could no more—I sign'd.
Nay, for bare shame of inconsistency,
She cannot pass her traitor council by,
To make me headless.
    Peter Martyr. That might be forgiven.
I tell you, fly, my lord. You do not own
The bodily presence in the Eucharist,
Their wafer and perpetual sacrifice:
Your creed will be your death.
    Cranmer. Step after step,
Thro' many voices crying right and left,
Have I climb'd back into the primal church,
And stand within the porch, and Christ with me.
My flight were such a scandal to the faith,
The downfall of so many simple souls,
I dare not leave my post.
    Peter Martyr. But you divorced
Queen Catharine and her father; hence, her hate
Will burn till you are burn'd.
    Cranmer. I cannot help it.
The Canonists and Schoolmen were with me.

'Thou shalt not wed thy brother's wife.'—'T is written,
'They shall be childless.' True, Mary was born,
But France would not accept her for a bride
As being born from incest; and this wrought
Upon the King; and child by child, you know,
Were momentary sparkles, out as quick
Almost as kindled; and he brought his doubts
And fears to me. Peter, I 'll swear for him
He *did* believe the bond incestuous.
But wherefore am I trenching on the time
That should already have seen your steps a mile
From me and Lambeth? God be with you! Go.
    Peter Martyr. Ah, but how fierce a letter you wrote against
Their superstition when they slander'd you
For setting up a mass at Canterbury
To please the Queen!
    Cranmer. It was a wheedling monk
Set up the mass.
    Peter Martyr. I know it, my good lord.
But you so bubbled over with hot terms
Of Satan, liars, blasphemy, Antichrist,
She never will forgive you. Fly, my lord, fly!
    Cranmer. I wrote it, and God grant me power to burn!
    Peter Martyr. They have given me a safe conduct; for all that
I dare not stay. I fear, I fear, I see you,
Dear friend, for the last time; farewell, and fly.
    Cranmer. Fly and farewell, and let me die the death.
                    [*Exit* Peter Martyr.

Enter OLD SERVANT.

O, kind and gentle master, the Queen's Officers

Are here in force to take you to the
　　Tower,
Cranmer. Ay, gentle friend, admit
　　them. I will go.
I thank my God it is too late to fly.
　　　　　　　　　　　　　[Exeunt.

SCENE III

ST. PAUL'S CROSS

FATHER BOURNE *in the pulpit. A
crowd.* MARCHIONESS OF EXETER,
COURTENAY. *The* SIEUR DE NOAILLES
and his man ROGER *in front of the
stage.* Hubbub.

Noailles. Hast thou let fall those
　　papers in the palace?
Roger. Ay, sir.
Noailles. 'There will be no peace
for Mary till Elizabeth lose her head.'
Roger. Ay, sir.
Noailles. And the other, 'Long live
Elizabeth the Queen!'
Roger. Ay, sir; she needs must
　　tread upon them.
Noailles.　　　　Well.
These beastly swine make such a
　　grunting here,
I cannot catch what Father Bourne is
　　saying.
Roger. Quiet a moment, my mas-
ters; hear what the shaveling has to
say for himself.
Crowd. Hush—hear!
Bourne. —and so this unhappy
land, long divided in itself, and sev-
er'd from the faith, will return into
the one true fold, seeing that our gracious Virgin Queen hath—
Crowd. No pope! no pope!
*Roger (to those about him, mim-
icking* Bourne).—hath sent for the
holy legate of the holy father the
Pope, Cardinal Pole, to give us all that
holy absolution which—
First Citizen. Old Bourne to the
　　life!
Second Citizen. Holy absolution!
　　holy Inquisition!
Third Citizen. Down with the Pa-
　　pist!　　　　　　　　　　*[Hubbub.*

Bourne. —and now that your good
bishop, Bonner, who hath lain so long
under bonds for the faith— *[Hubbub.*
Noailles. Friend Roger, steal thou
　　in among the crowd,
And get the swine to shout 'Elizabeth.'
Yon gray old Gospeller, sour as mid-
　　winter,
Begin with him.
Roger (goes). By the mass, old
friend, we 'll have no pope here while
the Lady Elizabeth lives.
Gospeller. Art thou of the true
faith, fellow, that swearest by the
mass?
Roger. Ay, that am I, new con-
verted, but the old leaven sticks to
my tongue yet.
First Citizen. He says right; by the
mass, we 'll have no mass here.
Voices of the Crowd. Peace! hear
him; let his own words damn the Papist. From thine own mouth I judge
thee—tear him down!
Bourne. —and since our gracious
Queen, let me call her our second
Virgin Mary, hath begun to re-edify
the true temple—
First Citizen. Virgin Mary! we 'll
have no virgins here—we 'll have the
Lady Elizabeth!
　　*[Swords are drawn, a knife is
　　　hurled and sticks in the pulpit.
　　　The mob throng to the pulpit
　　　stairs.*
Marchioness of Exeter. Son Cour-
　　tenay, wilt thou see the holy
　　father
Murdered before thy face? up, son,
　　and save him!
They love thee, and thou canst not
　　come to harm.
Courtenay (in the pulpit). Shame,
　　shame, my masters! are you
　　English-born,
And set yourselves by hundreds
　　against one?
Crowd. A Courtenay! a Courtenay!
　　*[A train of Spanish servants
　　　crosses at the back of the
　　　stage.*
Noailles. These birds of passage
come before their time.

Stave off the crowd upon the Spaniard there.

Roger. My masters, yonder 's fatter game for you
Than this old gaping gurgoyle; look you there—
The Prince of Spain coming to wed our Queen!
After him, boys! and pelt him from the city.

[*They seize stones and follow the Spaniards. Exeunt on the other side* Marchioness of Exeter *and* Attendants.

Noailles (*to* Roger). Stand from me. If Elizabeth lose her head—
That makes for France.
And if her people, anger'd thereupon,
Arise against her and dethrone the Queen—
That makes for France.
And if I breed confusion any way—
That makes for France.
Good-day, my Lord of Devon;
A bold heart yours to beard that raging mob!

Courtenay. My mother said, Go up; and up I went.
I knew they would not do me any wrong,
For I am mighty popular with them, Noailles.

Noailles. You look'd a king.

Courtenay. Why not? I am king's blood.

Noailles. And in the whirl of change may come to be one.

Courtenay. Ah!

Noailles. But does your gracious Queen entreat you kinglike?

Courtenay. 'Fore God, I think she entreats me like a child.

Noailles. You 've but a dull life in this maiden court,
I fear, my lord?

Courtenay. A life of nods and yawns.

Noailles. So you would honor my poor house to-night,
We might enliven you. Divers honest fellows,

The Duke of Suffolk lately freed from prison,
Sir Peter Carew and Sir Thomas Wyatt,
Sir Thomas Stafford, and some more —we play.

Courtenay. At what?

Noailles. The game of chess.

Courtenay. The game of chess!
I can play well, and I shall beat you there.

Noailles. Ay, but we play with Henry, King of France,
And certain of his court.
His Highness makes his moves across the Channel,
We answer him with ours, and there are messengers
That go between us.

Courtenay. Why, such a game, sir, were whole years a-playing.

Noailles. Nay; not so long I trust.
That all depends
Upon the skill and swiftness of the players.

Courtenay. The King is skilful at it?

Noailles. Very, my Lord.

Courtenay. And the stakes high?

Noailles. But not beyond your means.

Courtenay. Well, I 'm the first of players. I shall win.

Noailles. With our advice and in our company,
And so you well attend to the King's moves,
I think you may.

Courtenay. When do you meet?

Noailles. To-night.

Courtenay (*aside*). I will be there; the fellow 's at his tricks—
Deep—I shall fathom him. (*Aloud.*) Good morning, Noailles.

[*Exit* Courtenay.

Noailles. Good-day, my Lord.
Strange game of chess! a king
That with her own pawns plays against a queen,
Whose play is all to find herself a king.
Ay; but this fine blue-blooded Courtenay seems

Too princely for a pawn. Call him a knight,
That, with an ass's, not a horse's head,
Skips every way, from levity or from fear.
Well, we shall use him somehow, so that Gardiner
And Simon Renard spy not out our game
Too early. Roger, thinkest thou that any one
Suspected thee to be my man?
　　Roger.　　　　　Not one, sir.
　　Noailles. No! the disguise was perfect. Let 's away.　　[*Exeunt.*

SCENE IV

LONDON. A ROOM IN THE PALACE

ELIZABETH. *Enter* COURTENAY.

Courtenay. So yet am I,
Unless my friends and mirrors lie to me,
A goodlier-looking fellow than this Philip.
Pah!
The Queen is ill advised. Shall I turn traitor?
They 've almost talked me into it; yet the word
Affrights me somewhat; to be such a one
As Harry Bolingbroke hath a lure in it.
Good now, my Lady Queen, tho' by your age
And by your looks you are not worth the having,
Yet by your crown you are.
　　　　　　[*Seeing* Elizabeth.
　　　　　　The Princess there?
If I tried her, and la—she 's amorous.
Have we not heard of her in Edward's time,
Her freaks and frolics with the late Lord Admiral?
I do believe she 'd yield. I should be still

A party in the State; and then, who knows—
　　Elizabeth. What are you musing on, my Lord of Devon?
　　Courtenay. Has not the Queen—
　　Elizabeth.　　　Done what, Sir?
　　Courtenay.　　　—made you follow
The Lady Suffolk and the Lady Lennox?—you,
The heir presumptive.
　　Elizabeth. Why do you ask? you know it.
　　Courtenay. You needs must bear it hardly.
　　Elizabeth.　　　　No, indeed!
I am utterly submissive to the Queen.
　　Courtenay. Well, I was musing upon that; the Queen
Is both my foe and yours; we should be friends.
　　Elizabeth. My Lord, the hatred of another to us
Is no true bond of friendship.
　　Courtenay.　　　Might it not
Be the rough preface of some closer bond?
　　Elizabeth. My lord, you late were loosed from out the Tower,
Where, like a butterfly in a chrysalis,
You spent your life; that broken, out you flutter
Thro' the new world, go zigzag, now would settle
Upon this flower, now that. But all things here
At court are known; you have solicited
The Queen, and been rejected.
　　Courtenay.　　　Flower, she!
Half faded! but you, cousin, are fresh and sweet
As the first flower no bee has ever tried.
　　Elizabeth. Are you the bee to try me? why, but now
I called you butterfly.
　　Courtenay.　　You did me wrong,
I love not to be called a butterfly.
Why do you call me butterfly?
　　Elizabeth. Why do you go so gay then?
　　Courtenay.　　　Velvet and gold.

This dress was made me as the Earl of
    Devon
To take my seat in; looks it not right
    royal?
    Elizabeth. So royal that the Queen
        forbade you wearing it.
    Courtenay. I wear it then to spite
    her.
    Elizabeth.   My lord, my lord;
I see you in the Tower again. Her
    Majesty
Hears you affect the Prince—prel-
    ates kneel to you.—
    Courtenay. I am the noblest blood
        in Europe, Madam,
A Courtenay of Devon, and her
    cousin.
    Elizabeth. She hears you make your
        boast that after all
She means to wed you. Folly, my good
    lord.
    Courtenay. How folly? a great
        party in the state
Wills me to wed her.
    Elizabeth.   Failing her, my lord,
Doth not as great a party in the State
Will you to wed me?
    Courtenay.   Even so, fair lady.
    Elizabeth. You know to flatter
        ladies.
    Courtenay.   Nay, I meant
True matters of the heart.
    Elizabeth.   My heart, my lord,
Is no great party in the State as yet.
    Courtenay. Great, said you? nay,
        you shall be great. I love you,
Lay my life in your hands. Can you
    be close?
    Elizabeth. Can you, my lord?
    Courtenay. Close as a miser's
        casket.
Listen:
The King of France, Noailles the Am-
    bassador,
The Duke of Suffolk and Sir Peter
    Carew,
Sir Thomas Wyatt, I myself, some
    others,
Have sworn this Spanish marriage
    shall not be.
If Mary will not hear us—well—con-
    jecture—

Were I in Devon with my wedded
    bride,
The people there so worship me—
    your ear;
You shall be Queen.
    Elizabeth. You speak too low, my
        lord;
I cannot hear you.
    Courtenay.   I 'll repeat it.
    Elizabeth.   No!
Stand further off, or you may lose
    your head.
    Courtenay. I have a head to lose for
        your sweet sake.
    Elizabeth. Have you, my lord? Best
        keep it for your own.
Nay, pout not, cousin.
Not many friends are mine, except in-
    deed
Among the many. I believe you mine;
And so you may continue mine, fare-
    well,
And that at once.

Enter MARY, *behind*.

    Mary.   Whispering—leagued to-
        gether
To bar me from my Philip.
    Courtenay.   Pray—consider—
    Elizabeth (*seeing the Queen*). Well,
        that 's a noble horse of yours,
        my lord.
I trust that he will carry you well to-
    day,
And heal your headache.
    Courtenay. You are wild; what
        headache?
Heartache, perchance, not headache.
    Elizabeth (*aside to* Courtenay),
        Are you blind?
        [Courtenay *sees the* Queen *and
        exit. Exit* Mary.

Enter LORD WILLIAM HOWARD.

    Howard. Was that my lord of
        Devon? do not you
Be seen in corners with my Lord of
    Devon.
He hath fallen out of favor with the
    Queen.

She fears the lords may side with you
    and him
Against her marriage; therefore is he
    dangerous.
And if this Prince of fluff and feather
    come
To woo you, niece, he is dangerous
    everyway.
    Elizabeth. Not very dangerous that
    way, my good uncle.
    Howard. But your own state is full
    of danger here.
The disaffected, heretics, reformers,
Look to you as the one to crown their
    ends.
Mix not yourself with any plot I pray
    you;
Nay, if by chance you hear of any
    such,
Speak not thereof—no, not to your
    best friend,
Lest you should be confounded with
    it. Still—
Perinde ac cadaver—as the priest says,
You know your Latin—quiet as a dead
    body.
What was my Lord of Devon telling
    you?
    Elizabeth. Whether he told me any-
    thing or not,
I follow your good counsel, gracious
    uncle.
Quiet as a dead body.
    Howard.   You do right well.
I do not care to know; but this I
    charge you,
Tell Courtenay nothing. The Lord
    Chancellor—
I count it as a kind of virtue in him,
He hath not many—as a mastiff dog
May love a puppy cur for no more
    reason
Than that the twain have been tied up
    together,
Thus Gardiner—for the two were fel-
    low-prisoners
So many years in yon accursed
    Tower—
Hath taken to this Courtenay. Look
    to it, niece,
He hath no fence when Gardiner ques-
    tions him;

All oozes out; yet him—because they
    know him
The last White Rose, the last Plantag-
    enet—
Nay, there is Cardinal Pole, too—the
    people
Claim as their natural leader—ay,
    some say
That you shall marry him, make him
    king belike.
    Elizabeth. Do they say so, good
    uncle?
    Howard.   Ay, good niece!
You should be plain and open with
    me, niece.
You should not play upon me.
    Elizabeth.   No, good uncle.

Enter GARDINER.

    Gardiner. The Queen would see
    your Grace upon the moment.
    Elizabeth. Why, my lord bishop?
    Gardiner. I think she means to
    counsel your withdrawing
To Ashridge, or some other country
    house.
    Elizabeth. Why, my lord bishop?
    Gardiner. I do but bring the mes-
    sage, know no more.
Your Grace will hear her reasons from
    herself.
    Elizabeth. 'T is mine own wish ful-
    fill'd before the word
Was spoken, for in truth I had meant
    to crave
Permission of her Highness to retire
To Ashridge, and pursue my studies
    there.
    Gardiner. Madam, to have the wish
    before the word
Is man's good fairy—and the Queen is
    yours.
I left her with rich jewels in her hand,
Whereof 't is like enough she means
    to make
A farewell present to your Grace.
    Elizabeth.   My lord,
I have the jewel of a loyal heart.
    Gardiner. I doubt it not, madam,
    most loyal. [*Bows low and exit.*
    Howard.   See,

This comes of parleying with my Lord
of Devon.

Well, well, you must obey; and I myself

Believe it will be better for your welfare.

Your time will come.

Elizabeth.   I think my time will
come.

Uncle,

I am of sovereign nature, that I know,

Not to be quell'd; and I have felt
within me

Stirrings of some great doom when
God's just hour

Peals—but this fierce old Gardiner—
his big baldness,

That irritable forelock which he rubs,

His buzzard beak and deep-incavern'd
eyes

Half fright me.

Howard. You've a bold heart; keep
it so.

He cannot touch you save that you
turn traitor;

And so take heed I pray you—you are
one

Who love that men should smile upon
you, niece.

They'd smile you into treason—some
of them.

Elizabeth. I spy the rock beneath
the smiling sea.

But if this Philip, the proud Catholic
prince,

And this bald priest, and she that hates
me, seek

In that lone house to practise on my
life,

By poison, fire, shot, stab—

Howard.   They will not, niece.

Mine is the fleet and all the power at
sea—

Or will be in a moment. If they dared

To harm you, I would blow this Philip
and all

Your trouble to the dog-star and the
devil.

Elizabeth. To the Pleiads, uncle;
they have lost a sister.

Howard. But why say that? what
have you done to lose her?

Come, come, I will go with you to the
Queen.   [*Exeunt.*

SCENE V

A ROOM IN THE PALACE

MARY *with* PHILIP'S *miniature.* ALICE.

Mary (*kissing the miniature*). Most
goodly, kinglike, and an emperor's son,—

A king to be,—is he not noble, girl?

Alice. Goodly enough, your Grace,
and yet, methinks,

I have seen goodlier.

Mary.   Ay, some waxen doll

Thy baby eyes have rested on, belike;

All red and white, the fashion of our
land.

But my good mother came—God rest
her soul!—

Of Spain, and I am Spanish in myself,

And in my likings.

Alice.   By your Grace's leave,

Your royal mother came of Spain, but
took

To the English red and white. Your
royal father—

For so they say—was all pure lily and
rose

In his youth, and like a lady.

Mary.   O just God!

Sweet mother, you had time and cause
enough

To sicken of his lilies and his roses.

Cast off, betray'd, defamed, divorced,
forlorn!

And then the King—that traitor past
forgiveness,

The false archbishop fawning on him,
married

The mother of Elizabeth—a heretic

Even as *she* is; but God hath sent me
here

To take such order with all heretics

That it shall be, before I die, as tho'

My father and my brother had not
lived.

What wast thou saying of this Lady
Jane,

Now in the Tower?
    Alice.   Why madam, she was passing
Some chapel down in Essex, and with
    her
Lady Anne Wharton, and the Lady
    Anne
Bow'd to the pyx; but Lady Jane
    stood up
Stiff as the very backbone of heresy.
And wherefore bow ye not, says Lady
    Anne,
To him within there who made heaven
    and earth?
I cannot, and I dare not, tell your
    Grace
What Lady Jane replied.
    Mary.   But I will have it.
    Alice. She said—pray pardon me,
    and pity her—
She hath hearken'd evil counsel—ah!
    she said
The baker made him.
    Mary.   Monstrous! blasphemous!
She ought to burn. Hence, thou
                            [*Exit* Alice.
        No—being traitor
Her head will fall. Shall it? she is but
    a child.
We do not kill the child for doing that
His father whipt him into doing—a
    head
So full of grace and beauty! would
    that mine
Were half as gracious! O, my lord to
    be,
My love, for thy sake only!
I am eleven years older than he is.
But will he care for that?
No, by the holy Virgin, being noble,
But love me only. Then the bastard
    sprout,
My sister, is far fairer than myself.
Will he be drawn to her?
No, being of the true faith with my-
    self.
Paget is for him—for to wed with
    Spain
Would treble England—Gardiner is
    against him;
The Council, people, Parliament
    against him;
But I will have him! My hard father
    hated me;

My brother rather hated me than
    loved;
My sister cowers and hates me. Holy
    Virgin,
Plead with thy blessed Son; grant me
    my prayer.
Give me my Philip; and we two will
    lead
The living waters of the Faith again
Back thro' their widow'd channel here,
    and watch
The parch'd banks rolling incense, as
    of old,
To heaven, and kindled with the palms
    of Christ!

            Enter USHER.

Who waits, sir?
    Usher.   Madam, the Lord Chan-
    cellor.
    Mary. Bid him come in.

            Enter GARDINER.

Good morning, my good lord.
                        [*Exit* Usher.
    Gardiner. That every morning of
    your Majesty
May be most good, is every morning's
    prayer
Of your most loyal subject, Stephen
    Gardiner.
    Mary. Come you to tell me this, my
    lord?
    Gardiner.   And more.
Your people have begun to learn your
    worth.
Your pious wish to pay King Ed-
    ward's debts,
Your lavish household curb'd, and the
    remission
Of half that subsidy levied on the peo-
    ple,
Make all tongues praise and all hearts
    beat for you.
I'd have you yet more loved. The
    realm is poor,
The exchequer at neap-tide; we might
    withdraw
Part of our garrison at Calais.
    Mary.   Calais!

Our one point on the main, the gate of
 France!
I am Queen of England; take mine
 eyes, mine heart,
But do not lose me Calais.
 Gardiner.   Do not fear it.
Of that hereafter. I say your Grace is
 loved.
That I may keep you thus, who am
 your friend
And ever faithful counsellor, might I
 speak?
 Mary. I can forespeak your speak-
 ing. Would I marry
Prince Philip, if all England hate him?
 That is
Your question, and I front it with
 another:
Is it England, or a party? Now, your
 answer.
 Gardiner. My answer is, I wear be-
 neath my dress
A shirt of mail; my house hath been
 assaulted,
And when I walk abroad the populace,
With fingers pointed like so many
 daggers,
Stab me in fancy, hissing Spain and
 Philip;
And when I sleep a hundred men-at-
 arms
Guard my poor dreams for England.
 Men would murder me,
Because they think me favorer of this
 marriage.
 Mary. And that were hard upon
 you, my Lord Chancellor.
 Gardiner. But our young Earl of
 Devon—
 Mary.   Earl of Devon?
I freed him from the Tower, placed
 him at Court;
I made him Earl of Devon, and—the
 fool—
He wrecks his health and wealth on
 courtesans,
And rolls himself in carrion like a dog.
 Gardiner. More like a school-boy
 that hath broken bounds
Sickening himself with sweets.
 Mary.   I will not hear of him.
Good, then, they will revolt; but I am
 Tudor,

And shall control them.
 Gardiner. I will help you, madam,
Even to the utmost. All the church is
 grateful.
You have ousted the mock priest, re-
 pulpited
The shepherd of Saint Peter, raised
 the rood again,
And brought us back the mass. I am
 all thanks
To God and to your Grace; yet I
 know well,
Your people, and I go with them so
 far,
Will brook nor Pope nor Spaniard
 here to play
The tyrant, or in commonwealth or
 church.
 Mary (showing the picture). Is this
 the face of one who plays the
 tyrant?
Peruse it; is it not goodly, ay, and
 gentle?
 Gardiner. Madam, methinks a cold
 face and a haughty.
And when your Highness talks of
 Courtenay—
Ay, true—a goodly one. I would his
 life
Were half as goodly *(aside)*.
 Mary. What is that you mutter?
 Gardiner. O, madam, take it
 bluntly; marry Philip,
And be stepmother of a score of sons!
The prince is known in Spain, in
 Flanders, ha!
For Philip—
 Mary. You offend us; you may
 leave us.
You see thro' warping glasses.
 Gardiner. If your Majesty—
 Mary. I have sworn upon the body
 and blood of Christ
I'll none but Philip.
 Gardiner. Hath your Grace so
 sworn?
 Mary. Ay, Simon Renard knows it.
 Gardiner.   News to me!
It then remains for your poor Gar-
 diner,
So you still care to trust him some-
 what less

Than Simon Renard, to compose the event
In some such form as least may harm your Grace.

Mary. I'll have the scandal sounded to the mud.
I know it a scandal.

Gardiner.   All my hope is now
It may be found a scandal.

Mary.   You offend us.

Gardiner (*aside*). These princes are like children, must be phys-ick'd,
The bitter in the sweet. I have lost mine office,
It may be, thro' mine honesty, like a fool.   [*Exit.*

Enter USHER.

Mary. Who waits?

Usher. The ambassador from France, your Grace.

Mary (*sits down*). Bid him come in. Good morning, Sir de Noailles.   [*Exit* Usher.

Noailles (*entering*). A happy morning to your Majesty.

Mary. And I should some time have a happy morning;
I have had none yet. What says the King your master?

Noailles. Madam, my master hears with much alarm
That you may marry Philip, Prince of Spain—
Foreseeing, with whate'er unwilling-ness,
That if this Philip be the titular King
Of England, and at war with him, your Grace
And kingdom will be suck'd into the war,
Ay, tho' you long for peace; where-fore, my master,
If but to prove your Majesty's good-will,
Would fain have some fresh treaty drawn between you.

Mary. Why some fresh treaty? wherefore should I do it?
Sir, if we marry, we shall still main-tain
All former treaties with his Majesty.
Our royal word for that! and your good master,
Pray God he do not be the first to break them,
Must be content with that; and so, farewell.

Noailles (*going, returns*). I would your answer had been other, madam,
For I foresee dark days.

Mary.   And so do I, sir;
Your master works against me in the dark.
I do believe he holp Northumberland
Against me.

Noailles.   Nay, pure phantasy, your Grace.
Why should we move against you?

Mary.   Will you hear why
Mary of Scotland,—for I have not own'd
My sister, and I will not,—after me
Is heir of England; and my royal father,
To make the crown of Scotland one with ours,
Had mark'd her for my brother Ed-ward's bride;
Ay, but your king stole her a babe from Scotland
In order to betroth her to your Dau-phin.
See then:
Mary of Scotland, married to your Dauphin,
Would make our England, France;
Mary of England, joining hands with Spain,
Would be too strong for France.
Yea, were there issue born to her, Spain and we,
One crown, might rule the world. There lies your fear.
That is your drift. You play at hide and seek.
Show me your faces!

Noailles.   Madam, I am amazed.
French, I must needs wish all good things for France.
That must be pardon'd me; but I pro-test

Your Grace's policy hath a farther
    flight
Than mine into the future. We but
    seek
Some settled ground for peace to
    stand upon.
    Mary. Well, we will leave all this,
      sir, to our council.
Have you seen Philip ever?
    Noailles.   Only once.
    Mary. Is this like Philip?
    Noailles. Ay, but nobler-looking.
    Mary. Hath he the large ability of
      the Emperor?
    Noailles. No, surely.
    Mary. I can make allowance for
      thee,
Thou speakest of the enemy of thy
    king.
    Noailles. Make no allowance for
      the naked truth.
He is every way a lesser man than
    Charles;
Stone-hard, ice-cold—no dash of dar-
    ing in him.
    Mary. If cold, his life is pure.
    Noailles. Why (*smiling*), no, in-
      deed.
    Mary. Say'st thou?
    Noailles. A very wanton life indeed
      (*smiling*).
    Mary. Your audience is concluded,
      sir. (*Exit* Noailles.) You can-
      not
Learn a man's nature from his natural
    foe.

Enter USHER.

Who waits?
    Usher. The ambassador of Spain,
      your Grace.   [*Exit.*

Enter SIMON RENARD.

    Mary (*rising to meet him*). Thou
      art ever welcome, Simon Re-
      nard. Hast thou
Brought me the letter which thine
    Emperor promised
Long since, a formal offer of the hand
Of Philip?

    Renard. Nay, your Grace, it hath
      not reach'd me.
I know not wherefore—some mis-
    chance of flood,
And broken bridge, or spavin'd horse,
    or wave
And wind at their old battle; he must
    have written.
    Mary. But Philip never writes me
      one poor word,
Which in his absence had been all my
    wealth.
Strange in a wooer!
    Renard.   Yet I know the Prince,
So your king-parliament suffer him to
    land,
Yearns to set foot upon your island
    shore.
    Mary. God change the pebble which
      his kingly foot
First presses into some more costly
    stone
Than ever blinded eye! I'll have one
    mark it
And bring it me. I'll have it burnish'd
    firelike;
I'll set it round with gold, with pearl,
    with diamond.
Let the great angel of the Church
    come with him,
Stand on the deck and spread his
    wings for sail!
God lay the waves and strow the
    storms at sea,
And here at land among the people!
    O Renard,
I am much beset, I am almost in de-
    spair.
Paget is ours. Gardiner perchance is
    ours;
But for our heretic Parliament—
    Renard.   O madam,
You fly your thoughts like kites. My
    master, Charles,
Bade you so softly with your heretics
    here,
Until your throne had ceased to trem-
    ble. Then
Spit them like larks for aught I care.
    Besides,
When Henry broke the carcase of
    your church

To pieces, there were many wolves
among you
Who dragg'd the scatter'd limbs into
their den.
The Pope would have you make them
render these;
So would your cousin, Cardinal Pole
—ill counsel!
These let them keep at present; stir
not yet
This matter of the Church lands. At
his coming
Your star will rise.
   Mary.   My star! a baleful one.
I see but the black night, and hear the
wolf.
What star?
   Renard. Your star will be your
princely son,
Heir of this England and the Nether-
lands!
And if your wolf the while should
howl for more,
We'll dust him from a bag of Spanish
gold.
I do believe—I have dusted some al-
ready—
That, soon or late, your Parliament is
ours.
   Mary. Why do they talk so foully
of your Prince,
Renard?
   Renard. The lot of princes. To sit
high
Is to be lied about.
   Mary.   They call him cold,
Haughty, ay worse.
   Renard.   Why, doubtless, Philip
shows
Some of the bearing of your blue
blood—still
All within measure—nay, it well be-
comes him.
   Mary. Hath he the large ability of
his father?
   Renard. Nay, some believe that he
will go beyond him.
   Mary. Is this like him?
   Renard. Ay, somewhat; but your
Philip
Is the most princelike prince beneath
the sun.

This is a daub to Philip.
   Mary.   Of a pure life?
   Renard. As an angel among angels.
Yea, by Heaven,
The text—Your Highness knows it,
'Whosoever
Looketh after a woman,' would not
graze
The Prince of Spain. You are happy in
him there,
Chaste as your Grace!
   Mary. I am happy in him there.
   Renard. And would be altogether
happy, madam,
So that your sister were but look'd to
closer.
You have sent her from the court, but
then she goes,
I warrant, not to hear the nightin-
gales,
But hatch you some new treason in
the woods.
   Mary. We have our spies abroad to
catch her tripping,
And then, if caught, to the Tower.
   Renard.   The Tower! the block!
The word has turn'd your Highness
pale; the thing
Was no such scarecrow in your
father's time.
I have heard, the tongue yet quiver'd
with the jest
When the head leapt—so common! I
do think,
To save your crown, that it must
come to this.
   Mary. No, Renard; it must never
come to this.
   Renard. Not yet; but your old trai-
tors of the Tower—
Why, when you put Northumberland
to death,
The sentence having passed upon
them all,
Spared you the Duke of Suffolk,
Guildford Dudley,
Even that young girl who dared to
wear your crown?
   Mary. Dared? nay, not so; the
child obey'd her father.
Spite of her tears her father forced it
on her.

Renard. Good madam, when the Roman wish'd to reign,
He slew not him alone who wore the purple,
But his assessor in the throne, perchance
A child more innocent than Lady Jane.

Mary. I am English Queen, not Roman Emperor.

Renard. Yet too much mercy is a want of mercy,
And wastes more life. Stamp out the fire, or this
Will smoulder and re-flame, and burn the throne
Where you should sit with Philip. He will not come
Till she be gone.

Mary. Indeed, if that were true—
For Philip comes, one hand in mine, and one
Steadying the tremulous pillars of the Church—
But no, no, no! Farewell. I am somewhat faint
With our long talk. Tho' Queen, I am not Queen
Of mine own heart, which every now and then
Beats me half dead. Yet stay, this golden chain—
My father on a birthday gave it me,
And I have broken with my father—take
And wear it as memorial of a morning
Which found me full of foolish doubts, and leaves me
As hopeful.

Renard (*aside*). Whew—the folly of all follies
Is to be lovesick for a shadow.
(*Aloud.*) Madam,
This chains me to your service, not with gold,
But dearest links of love. Farewell, and trust me,
Philip is yours.   [*Exit.*

Mary. Mine—but not yet all mine.

Enter USHER.

Usher. Your Council is in session, please your Majesty.

Mary. Sir, let them sit. I must have time to breathe.
No, say I come. (*Exit* Usher.) I won by boldness once.
The Emperor counsell'd me to fly to Flanders.
I would not; but a hundred miles I rode,
Sent out my letters, call'd my friends together,
Struck home and won.
And when the Council would not crown me—thought
To bind me first by oaths I could not keep,
And keep with Christ and conscience —was it boldness
Or weakness that won there? when I, their Queen,
Cast myself down upon my knees before them,
And those hard men brake into woman-tears,
Even Gardiner, all amazed, and in that passion
Gave me my Crown.

Enter ALICE.

                    Girl, hast thou ever heard
Slanders against Prince Philip in our Court?

Alice. What slanders? I, your Grace? no, never.

Mary.   Nothing?

Alice. Never, your Grace.

Mary. See that you neither hear them nor repeat!

Alice (*aside*). Good Lord! but I have heard a thousand such—
Ay, and repeated them as often— mum!
Why comes that old fox-Fleming back again?

Enter RENARD.

Renard. Madam, I scarce had left your Grace's presence
Before I chanced upon the messenger
Who brings that letter which we waited for—
The formal offer of Prince Philip's hand.

It craves an instant answer, Ay or No.
    Mary. An instant Ay or No! the
        Council sits.
Give it me quick.
    Alice (stepping before her). Your
        Highness is all trembling.
    Mary. Make way.
      [*Exit into the Council Chamber.*
    Alice. O Master Renard, Master
        Renard,
If you have falsely painted your fine
    Prince,
Praised where you should have blamed
    him, I pray God
No woman ever love you, Master Re-
    nard!
It breaks my heart to hear her moan
    at night
As tho' the nightmare never left her
    bed.
    Renard. My pretty maiden, tell me,
        did you ever
Sigh for a beard?
    Alice. That's not a pretty question.
    Renard. Not prettily put? I mean,
        my pretty maiden,
A pretty man for such a pretty
    maiden.
    Alice. My Lord of Devon is a pretty
        man.
I hate him. Well, but if I have, what
    then?
    Renard. Then, pretty maiden, you
        should know that whether
A wind be warm or cold, it serves to
    fan
A kindled fire.
    Alice.   According to the song.

His friends would praise him, I believed
    'em,
  His foes would blame him, and I
      scorn'd 'em,
His friends—as angels I received 'em,
  His foes—the devil had suborn'd 'em.

    Renard. Peace, pretty maiden.
I hear them stirring in the Council
    Chamber.
Lord Paget's 'Ay' is sure—who else?
    and yet,
They are all too much at odds to close
    at once

In one full-throated No! Her High-
    ness comes.

        Enter MARY.

    Alice. How deathly pale!—a chair,
        your Highness.
      [*Bringing one to the* Queen.
    Renard.   Madam,
The Council?
    Mary.   Ay! My Philip is all mine.
      [*Sinks into chair, half fainting.*

ACT II

SCENE I.—ALINGTON CASTLE

Sir Thomas Wyatt. I do not hear
    from Carew or the Duke
Of Suffolk, and till then I should not
    move.
The Duke hath gone to Leicester;
    Carew stirs
In Devon; that fine porcelain Courte-
    nay,
Save that he fears he might be crack'd
    in using—
I have known a semi-madman in my
    time
So fancy-ridden—should be in Devon
    too.

        Enter WILLIAM.

News abroad, William?
    William. None so new, Sir Thomas,
and none so old, Sir Thomas. No new
news that Philip comes to wed Mary,
no old news that all men hate it. Old
Sir Thomas would have hated it. The
bells are ringing at Maidstone. Does
n't your worship hear?
    Wyatt. Ay, for the Saints are come
    to reign again.
Most like it is a Saint's-day. There's
    no call
As yet for me; so in this pause, before
The mine be fired, it were a pious
    work
To string my father's sonnets, left
    about

Like loosely-scatter'd jewels, in fair
    order,
And head them with a lamer rhyme
    of mine,
To grace his memory.
  William. Ay, why not, Sir Thomas?
He was a fine courtier, he; Queen
Anne loved him. All the women loved
him. I loved him, I was in Spain with
him. I could n't eat in Spain, I could
n't sleep in Spain. I hate Spain, Sir
Thomas.
  Wyatt. But thou couldst drink in
    Spain if I remember.
  William. Sir Thomas, we may grant
the wine. Old Sir Thomas always
granted the wine.
  Wyatt. Hand me the casket with
    my father's sonnets.
  William. Ay — sonnets — a fine
courtier of the old Court, old Sir
Thomas.   [*Exit.*
  Wyatt. Courtier of many courts, he
    loved the more
His own gray towers, plain life, and
    letter'd peace,
To read and rhyme in solitary fields,
The lark above, the nightingale below,
And answer them in song. The sire
    begets
Not half his likeness in the son. I fail
Where he was fullest. Yet—to write
    it down.   [*He writes.*

Re-enter WILLIAM.

  William. There *is* news, there *is*
news, and no call for sonnet-sorting
now, nor for sonnet-making either,
but ten thousand men on Penenden
Heath all calling after your worship,
and your worship's name heard into
Maidstone market, and your worship
the first man in Kent and Christendom, for the Queen's down, and the
world's up, and your worship a-top of
it.
  Wyatt. Inverted Æsop—mountain
    out of mouse.
Say for ten thousand ten—and pot-
    house knaves,
Brain-dizzied with a draught of morn-
    ing ale.

Enter ANTONY KNYVETT.

  William. Here's Antony Knyvett.
  Knyvett. Look you, Master Wyatt,
Tear up that woman's work there.
  Wyatt.   No; not these,
Dumb children of my father, that will
    speak
When I and thou and all rebellions lie
Dead bodies without voice. Song flies,
    you know,
For ages.
  Knyvett. Tut, your sonnet's a fly-
    ing ant,
Wing'd for a moment.
  Wyatt.   Well, for mine own work,
        [*Tearing the paper.*
It lies there in six pieces at your feet;
For all that, I can carry it in my head.
  Knyvett. If you can carry your
    head upon your shoulders.
  Wyatt. I fear you come to carry it
    off my shoulders,
And sonnet-making's safer.
  Knyvett.   Why, good lord,
Write you as many sonnets as you
    will.
Ay, but not now; what, have you eyes,
    ears, brains?
This Philip and the black-faced
    swarms of Spain,
The hardest, cruellest people in the
    world,
Come locusting upon us, eat us up,
Confiscate lands, goods, money—
    Wyatt, Wyatt,
Wake, or the stout old island will be-
    come
A rotten limb of Spain. They roar for
    you
On Penenden Heath, a thousand of
    them—more—
All arm'd, waiting a leader; there 's no
    glory
Like his who saves his country. And
    you sit
Sing-songing here; but, if I'm any
    judge,
By God, you are as poor a poet,
    Wyatt,
As a good soldier.
  Wyatt.   You as poor a critic

As an honest friend; you stroke me
    on one cheek,
Buffet the other. Come, you bluster,
    Antony!
You know I know all this. I must not
    move
Until I hear from Carew and the
    Duke.
I fear the mine is fired before the
    time.
    Knyvett (*showing a paper*). But
      here's some Hebrew. Faith, I
      half forgot it.
Look—can you make it English? A
    strange youth
Suddenly thrust it on me, whisper'd,
    'Wyatt,'
And whisking round a corner, show'd
    his back
Before I read his face.
    Wyatt.   Ha! Courtenay's cipher.
                     [*Reads.*
'Sir Peter Carew fled to France; it
is thought the Duke will be taken. I
am with you still; but, for appear-
ances sake, stay with the Queen.
Gardiner knows, but the Council are
all at odds, and the Queen hath no
force for resistance. Move, if you
move, at once.'

Is Peter Carew fled? Is the Duke
    taken?
Down scabbard, and out sword! and
    let Rebellion
Roar till throne rock, and crown fall!
    No, not that;
But we will teach Queen Mary how to
    reign.
Who are those that shout below there?
    Knyvett.   Why, some fifty
That follow'd me from Penenden
    Heath in hope
To hear you speak.
    Wyatt. Open the window, Knyvett;
The mine is fired, and I will speak to
    them.

Men of Kent, England of England,
you that have kept your old customs
upright, while all the rest of England
bowed theirs to the Norman, the cause
that hath brought us together is not
the cause of a county or a shire, but
of this England, in whose crown our
Kent is the fairest jewel. Philip shall
not wed Mary; and ye have called me
to be your leader. I know Spain. I
have been there with my father; I
have seen them in their own land,
have marked the haughtiness of their
nobles, the cruelty of their priests. If
this man marry our Queen, however
the Council and the Commons may
fence round his power with restric-
tion, he will be King, King of England, my masters; and the Queen, and
the laws, and the people, his slaves.
What? shall we have Spain on the
throne and in the parliament; Spain
in the pulpit and on the law-bench;
Spain in all the great offices of state;
Spain in our ships, in our forts, in our
houses, in our beds?
    Crowd. No! no! no Spain!
    William. No Spain in our beds—
that were worse than all. I have been
there with old Sir Thomas, and the
beds I know. I hate Spain.
    A Peasant. But, Sir Thomas, must
we levy war against the Queen's
Grace?
    Wyatt. No, my friend; war *for* the
Queen's Grace—to save her from herself and Philip—war against Spain.
And think not we shall be alone—
thousands will flock to us. The Council, the Court itself, is on our side.
The Lord Chancellor himself is on our
side. The King of France is with us;
the King of Denmark is with us; the
world is with us—war against Spain!
And if we move not now, yet it will
be known that we have moved; and if
Philip come to be King, O my God!
The rope, the rack, the thumbscrew,
the stake, the fire. If we move not
now, Spain moves, bribes our nobles
with her gold, and creeps, creeps
snake-like about our legs till we cannot move at all; and ye know, my
masters, that wherever Spain hath
ruled she hath wither'd all beneath
her. Look at the New World—a para-

dise made hell; the red man, that good
helpless creature, starved, maim'd,
flogg'd, flay'd, burn'd, boil'd, buried
alive, worried by dogs; and here,
nearer home, the Netherlands, Sicily,
Naples, Lombardy. I say no more—
only this, their lot is yours. Forward
to London with me! forward to London! If ye love your liberties or your
skins, forward to London!

Crowd. Forward to London! A
    Wyatt! a Wyatt!
Wyatt. But first to Rochester, to
    take the guns
From out the vessels lying in the river.
Then on.
A Peasant. Ay, but I fear we be too
    few, Sir Thomas.
Wyatt. Not many yet. The world
    as yet, my friend,
Is not half-waked; but every parish
    tower
Shall clang and clash alarum as we
    pass,
And pour along the land, and, swollen
    and fed
With indraughts and side-currents, in
    full force
Roll upon London.
Crowd. A Wyatt! a Wyatt! For-
    ward!
Knyvett. Wyatt, shall we proclaim
    Elizabeth?
Wyatt. I'll think upon it, Knyvett.
Knyvett.   Or Lady Jane?
Wyatt. No, poor soul, no.
Ah, gray old castle Alington, green
    field
Beside the brimming Medway, it may
    chance
That I shall never look upon you
    more.
Knyvett. Come, now, you're son-
    netting again
Wyatt.   Not I.
I'll have my head set higher in the
    State;
Or—if the Lord God will it—on the
    stake.   [*Exeunt.*

SCENE II

GUILDHALL

SIR THOMAS WHITE (*The Lord
    Mayor*), LORD WILLIAM HOWARD,
SIR RALPH BAGENHALL, ALDERMEN
    and CITIZENS.

White. I trust the Queen comes
    hither with her guards.
Howard. Ay, all in arms.
    [*Several of the citizens move
    hastily out of the hall.*
    Why do they hurry out there?
White. My lord, cut out the rotten
    from your apple,
Your apple eats the better. Let them
    go.
They go like those old Pharisees in
    John
Convicted by their conscience, arrant
    cowards,
Or tamperers with that treason out of
    Kent.
When will her Grace be here?
    Howard.   In some few minutes.
She will address your guilds and com-
    panies.
I have striven in vain to raise a man
    for her.
But help her in this exigency, make
Your city loyal, and be the mightiest
    man
This day in England.
    White.   I am Thomas White.
Few things have fail'd to which I set
    my will.
I do my most and best.
    Howard.   You know that after
The Captain Brett, who went with
    your train bands
To fight with Wyatt, had gone over to
    him
With all his men, the Queen in that
    distress
Sent Cornwallis and Hastings to the
    traitor,
Feigning to treat with him about her
    marriage—
Know too what Wyatt said.
    White.   He'd sooner be.

While this same marriage question
      was being argued,
Trusted than trust—the scoundrel—
      and demanded
Possession of her person and the
      Tower.
      Howard. And four of her poor
      Council too, my Lord,
As hostages.
      White. I know it. What do and say
Your Council at this hour?
      Howard.   I will trust you.
We fling ourselves on you, my Lord.
      The Council,
The Parliament as well, are troubled
      waters;
And yet like waters of the fen they
      know not
Which way to flow. All hands on her
      address,
And upon you, Lord Mayor.
      White.   How look'd the city
When now you past it? Quiet?
      Howard.   Like our Council,
Your city is divided. As we past,
Some hail'd, some hiss'd us. There
      were citizens
Stood each before his shut-up booth,
      and look'd
As grim and grave as from a funeral.
And here a knot of ruffians all in rags,
With execrating execrable eyes,
Glared at the citizen. Here was a
      young mother,
Her face on flame, her red hair all
      blown back,
She shrilling 'Wyatt,' while the boy
      she held
Mimick'd and piped her 'Wyatt,' as
      red as she
In hair and cheek; and almost elbow-
      ing her,
So close they stood, another, mute as
      death,
And white as her own milk; her babe
      in arms
Had felt the faltering of his mother's
      heart,
And look'd as bloodless. Here a pious
      Catholic,
Mumbling and mixing up in his scared
      prayers

Heaven and earth's Maries; over his
      bow'd shoulder
Scowl'd that world-hated and world-
      hating beast,
A haggard Anabaptist. Many such
      groups.
The names of Wyatt, Elizabeth,
      Courtenay,
Nay, the Queen's right to reign—'fore
      God, the rogues!—
Were freely buzz'd among them. So I
      say
Your city is divided, and I fear
One scruple, this or that way, of suc-
      cess
Would turn it thither. Wherefore now
      the Queen,
In this low pulse and palsy of the
      state,
Bade me to tell you that she counts
      on you
And on myself as her two hands; on
      you,
In your own city, as her right, my
      lord,
For you are loyal.
      White.   Am I Thomas White?
One word before she comes. Eliza-
      beth—
Her name is much abused among
      these traitors.
Where is she? She is loved by all of
      us.
I scarce have heart to mingle in this
      matter,
If she should be mishandled.
      Howard.   No, she shall not.
The Queen had written her word to
      come to court:
Methought I smelt out Renard in the
      letter,
And fearing for her, sent a secret mis-
      sive,
Which told her to be sick. Happily or
      not,
It found her sick indeed.
      White.   God send her well!
Here comes her Royal Grace.

Enter GUARDS, MARY, *and* GARDINER.
   SIR THOMAS WHITE *leads her to a
   raised seat on the dais.*

White. I, the Lord Mayor, and these our companies
And guilds of London, gathered here, beseech
Your Highness to accept our lowliest thanks
For your most princely presence; and we pray
That we, your true and loyal citizens,
From your own royal lips, at once may know
The wherefore of this coming, and so learn
Your royal will, and do it.—I, Lord Mayor
Of London, and our guilds and companies.

Mary. In mine own person am I come to you,
To tell you what indeed ye see and know,
How traitorously these rebels out of Kent
Have made strong head against ourselves and you.
They would not have me wed the Prince of Spain;
That was their pretext—so they spake at first—
But we sent divers of our Council to them,
And by their answers to the question ask'd,
It doth appear this marriage is the least
Of all their quarrel.
They have betrayed the treason of their hearts,
Seek to possess our person, hold our Tower,
Place and displace our councillors, and use
Both us and them according as they will.
Now what I am ye know right well—your Queen;
To whom, when I was wedded to the realm
And the realm's laws—the spousal ring whereof,
Not ever to be laid aside, I wear
Upon this finger—ye did promise full
Allegiance and obedience to the death.

Ye know my father was the rightful heir
Of England, and his right came down to me,
Corroborate by your acts of Parliament.
And as ye were most loving unto him,
So doubtless will ye show yourselves to me.
Wherefore, ye will not brook that any one
Should seize our person, occupy our state,
More specially a traitor so presumptuous
As this same Wyatt, who hath tamper'd with
A public ignorance, and, under color
Of such a cause as hath no color, seeks
To bend the laws to his own will, and yield
Full scope to persons rascal and forlorn,
To make free spoil and havoc of your goods.
Now, as your Prince, I say,
I, that was never mother, cannot tell
How mothers love their children; yet, methinks,
A prince as naturally may love his people
As these their children; and be sure your Queen
So loves you, and so loving, needs must deem
This love by you return'd as heartily;
And thro' this common knot and bond of love,
Doubt not they will be speedily overthrown.
As to this marriage, ye shall understand
We made thereto no treaty of ourselves,
And set no foot theretoward unadvised
Of all our Privy Council; furthermore,
This marriage had the assent of those to whom
The King, my father, did commit his trust;
Who not alone esteem'd it honorable,

But for the wealth and glory of our
    realm,
And all our loving subjects, most ex-
    pedient.
As to myself,
I am not so set on wedlock as to
    choose
But where I list, nor yet so amorous
That I must needs be husbanded; I
    thank God,
I have lived a virgin, and I noway
    doubt
But that, with God's grace, I can live
    so still.
Yet if it might please God that I
    should leave
Some fruit of mine own body after
    me,
To be your king, ye would rejoice
    thereat,
And it would be your comfort, as I
    trust;
And truly, if I either thought or knew
This marriage should bring loss or
    danger to you,
My subjects, or impair in any way
This royal state of England, I would
    never
Consent thereto, nor marry while I
    live.
Moreover, if this marriage should not
    seem,
Before our own High Court of Par-
    liament,
To be of rich advantage to our realm,
We will refrain, and not alone from
    this,
Likewise from any other, out of which
Looms the least chance of peril to our
    realm.
Wherefore be bold, and with your
    lawful Prince
Stand fast against our enemies and
    yours,
And fear them not. I fear them not.
    My lord,
I leave Lord William Howard in your
    city,
To guard and keep you whole and safe
    from all
The spoil and sackage aim'd at by
    these rebels,

Who mouth and foam against the
    Prince of Spain.
Voices. Long live Queen Mary!
                Down with Wyatt!
                            The Queen!
White. Three voices from our
    guilds and companies!
You are shy and proud like English-
    men, my masters,
And will not trust your voices. Un-
    derstand,
Your lawful Prince hath come to cast
    herself
On loyal hearts and bosoms, hoped to
    fall
Into the wide-spread arms of fealty,
And finds you statues. Speak at once
    —and all!
For whom?
Our Sovereign Lady by King Harry's
    will,
The Queen of England—or the Kent-
    ish Squire?
I know you loyal. Speak! in the name
    of God!
The Queen of England or the rabble
    of Kent?
The reeking dungfork master of the
    mace!
Your havings wasted by the scythe
    and spade—
Your rights and charters hobnail'd
    into slush—
Your houses fired—your gutters bub-
    bling blood—
    Acclamation. No! No! The Queen!
        the Queen!
White.   Your Highness hears
This burst and bass of loyal harmony,
And how we each and all of us abhor
The venomous, bestial, devilish revolt
Of Thomas Wyatt. Hear us now make
    oath
To raise your Highness thirty thou-
    sand men,
And arm and strike as with one hand,
    and brush
This Wyatt from our shoulders, like a
    flea
That might have leapt upon us un-
    awares.
Swear with me, noble fellow-citizens,
    all,

With all your trades, and guilds, and
    companies.
  Citizens. We swear!
  Mary. We thank your lordship and
    your loyal city.
      [*Exit* Mary, *attended.*
  White. I trust this day, thro' God, I
    have saved the crown.
  First Alderman. Ay, so my Lord of
    Pembroke in command
Of all her force be safe; but there are
    doubts.
  Second Alderman. I hear that Gar-
    diner coming with the Queen,
And meeting Pembroke, bent to his
    saddle-bow,
As if to win the man by flattering him.
Is he so safe to fight upon her side?
  First Alderman. If not, there's no
    man safe.
  White.   Yes, Thomas White.
I am safe enough; no man need flatter
    me.
  Second Alderman. Nay, no man
    need; but did you mark our
    Queen?
The color freely play'd into her face,
And the half sight which makes her
    look so stern
Seem'd thro' that dim dilated world of
    hers
To read our faces; I have never seen
    her
So queenly or so goodly.
  White.   Courage, sir,
That makes or man or woman look
    their goodliest.
Die like the torn fox dumb, but never
    whine
Like that poor heart, Northumber-
    land, at the block.
  Bagenhall. The man had children,
    and he whined for those.
Methinks most men are but poor-
    hearted, else
Should we so dote on courage, were it
    commoner?
The Queen stands up, and speaks for
    her own self;
And all men cry, She is queenly, she is
    goodly.
Yet she's no goodlier; tho' my Lord
    Mayor here,

By his own rule, he hath been so bold
    to-day,
Should look more goodly than the rest
    of us.
  White. Goodly? I feel most goodly,
    heart and hand,
And strong to throw ten Wyatts and
    all Kent.
Ha! ha! sir; but you jest; I love it. A
    jest
In time of danger shows the pulses
    even.
Be merry! yet, Sir Ralph, you look
    but sad.
I dare avouch you'd stand up for
    yourself,
Tho' all the world should bay like
    winter wolves.
  Bagenhall. Who knows? the man is
    proven by the hour.
  White. The man should make the
    hour, not this the man;
And Thomas White will prove this
    Thomas Wyatt,
And he will prove an Iden to this
    Cade,
And he will play the Walworth to this
    Wat.
Come, sirs, we prate; hence all—
    gather your men—
Myself must bustle. Wyatt comes to
    Southwark;
I'll have the drawbridge hewn into the
    Thames,
And see the citizens arm'd. Good day;
    good day.   [*Exit* White.
  Bagenhall. One of much outdoor
    bluster.
  Howard. For all that,
Most honest, brave, and skilful; and
    his wealth
A fountain of perennial alms—his
    fault
So thoroughly to believe in his own
    self.
  Bagenhall. Yet thoroughly to be-
    lieve in one's own self,
So one's own self be thorough, were to
    do
Great things, my lord.
  Howard.   It may be.
  Bagenhall.   I have heard

One of your Council fleer and jeer at
  him.
  Howard. The nursery-cocker'd child
    will jeer at aught
That may seem strange beyond his
  nursery.
The statesman that shall jeer and fleer
  at men,
Makes enemies for himself and for his
  king;
And if he jeer, not seeing the true man
Behind his folly, he is thrice the fool;
And if he see the man and still will
  jeer,
He is child and fool, and traitor to the
  State.
Who is he? let me shun him.
  Bagenhall.   Nay, my lord,
He is damn'd enough already.
  Howard.   I must set
The guard at Ludgate. Fare you well,
  Sir Ralph.
  Bagenhall. 'Who knows?' I am for
    England. But who knows,
That knows the Queen, the Spaniard,
  and the Pope,
Whether I be for Wyatt, or the
  Queen?   [*Exeunt.*

SCENE III

LONDON BRIDGE

Enter SIR THOMAS WYATT *and* BRETT.

  Wyatt. Brett, when the Duke of
    Norfolk moved against us
Thou criedst 'A Wyatt!' and flying to
  our side
Left his all bare, for which I love thee,
  Brett.
Have for thine asking aught that I can
  give,
For thro' thine help we are come to
  London Bridge;
But how to cross it balks me. I fear
  we cannot.
  Brett. Nay, hardly, save by boat,
    swimming, or wings.
  Wyatt. Last night I climb'd into the
    gate-house, Brett,
And scared the gray old porter and his
  wife.

And then I crept along the gloom and
  saw
They had hewn the drawbridge down
  into the river.
It roll'd as black as death; and that
  same tide
Which, coming with our coming,
  seem'd to smile
And sparkle like our fortune as thou
  saidest,
Ran sunless down, and moan'd against
  the piers.
But o'er the chasm I saw Lord Wil-
  liam Howard
By torchlight, and his guard; four
  guns gaped at me,
Black, silent mouths. Had Howard
  spied me there
And made them speak, as well he
  might have done,
Their voice had left me none to tell
  you this.
What shall we do?
  Brett.   On somehow. To go back
Were to lose all.
  Wyatt.   On over London Bridge
We cannot; stay we cannot; there is
  ordnance
On the White Tower and on the
  Devil's Tower,
And pointed full at Southwark. We
  must round
By Kingston Bridge.
  Brett.   Ten miles about.
  Wyatt.   Even so.
But I have notice from our partisans
Within the city that they will stand by
  us
If Ludgate can be reach'd by dawn to-
  morrow.

Enter one of WYATT'S *men.*

  Man. Sir Thomas, I've found this
paper; pray your worship read it; I
know not my letters; the old priests
taught me nothing.
  Wyatt (reads). 'Whosoever will apprehend the traitor Thomas Wyatt
shall have a hundred pounds for reward.'
  Man. Is that it? That's a big lot of
  money.

Wyatt. Ay, ay, my friend; not read
  it? 'tis not written
Half plain enough. Give me a piece of
  paper!
  [*Writes* 'THOMAS WYATT' *large.*
There, any man can read that.
  [*Sticks it in his cap.*
Brett. But that's foolhardy.
Wyatt. No! boldness, which will
  give my followers boldness.

Enter MAN *with a prisoner.*

Man. We found him, your worship,
a-plundering o' Bishop Winchester's
house; he says he's a poor gentleman.
Wyatt. Gentleman! a thief! Go
  hang him. Shall we make
Those that we come to serve our
  sharpest foes?
Brett. Sir Thomas—
Wyatt. Hang him, I say.
Brett. Wyatt, but now you prom-
  ised me a boon.
Wyatt. Ay, and I warrant this fine
  fellow's life.
Brett. Even so; he was my neighbor
  once in Kent.
He's poor enough, has drunk and gam-
  bled out
All that he had, and gentleman he was.
We have been glad together; let him
  live.
Wyatt. He has gambled for his life
  and lost, he hangs.
No, no, my word's my word. Take thy
  poor gentleman!
Gamble thyself at once out of my
  sight,
Or I will dig thee with my dagger.
  Away!
Women and children!

Enter a CROWD *of* WOMEN *and* CHIL-
DREN.

First Woman. O Sir Thomas, Sir
Thomas, pray you go away, Sir
Thomas, or you'll make the White
Tower a black 'un for us this blessed
day. He'll be the death on us; and
you'll set the Divil's Tower a-spitting,

and he'll smash all our bits o' things
worse than Philip o' Spain.
Second Woman. Don't ye now go
to think that we be for Philip o'
Spain.
Third Woman. No, we know that ye
be come to kill the Queen, and we'll
pray for you all on our bended knees.
But o' God's mercy don't ye kill the
Queen here, Sir Thomas; look ye,
here's little Dickon, and little Robin,
and little Jenny—though she's but a
side-cousin—and all on our knees, we
pray you to kill the Queen further off,
Sir Thomas.
Wyatt. My friends, I have not come
  to kill the Queen
Or here or there; I come to save you
  all,
And I'll go further off.
Crowd. Thanks, Sir Thomas, we be
beholden to you, and we'll pray for
you on our bended knees till our lives'
end.
Wyatt. Be happy, I am your friend
  To Kingston, forward!
  [*Exeunt*

SCENE IV

ROOM IN THE GATE-HOUSE OF WEST-
MINSTER PALACE

MARY, ALICE, GARDINER, RENARD,
LADIES.

Gardiner. Their cry is, Philip never
  shall be king.
Mary. Lord Pembroke in command
  of all our force
Will front their cry and shatter them
  into dust.
Alice. Was not Lord Pembroke with
  Northumberland?
O madam, if this Pembroke should be
  false!
Mary. No, girl; most brave and
  loyal, brave and loyal.
His breaking with Northumberland
  broke Northumberland.
At the park gate he hovers with our
  guards.

These Kentish plowmen cannot break the guards.

Enter MESSENGER.

Messenger. Wyatt, your Grace, hath broken thro' the guards
And gone to Ludgate.
   Gardiner.   Madam, I much fear
That all is lost; but we can save your Grace.
The river still is free. I do beseech you,
There yet is time, take boat and pass to Windsor.
   Mary. I pass to Windsor and I lose my crown.
   Gardiner. Pass, then, I pray your Highness, to the Tower.
   Mary. I shall but be their prisoner in the Tower.
   Cries without. The traitor! treason! Pembroke!
   Ladies.   Treason! treason!
   Mary. Peace.
False to Northumberland, is he false to me?
Bear witness, Renard, that I live and die
The true and faithful bride of Philip
   —A sound
Of feet and voices thickening hither—blows—
Hark, there is battle at the palace gates,
And I will out upon the gallery.
   Ladies. No, no, your Grace; see there the arrows flying.
   Mary. I am Harry's daughter, Tudor, and not Fear.
      [*Goes out on the gallery.*
The guards are all driven in, skulk into corners
Like rabbits to their holes. A gracious guard
Truly; shame on them! they have shut the gates!

Enter SIR ROBERT SOUTHWELL.

Southwell. The porter, please your Grace, hath shut the gates

On friend and foe. Your gentlemen-at-arms,
If this be not your Grace's order, cry
To have the gates set wide again, and they
With their good battle-axes will do you right
Against all traitors.
   Mary. They are the flower of England; set the gates wide.
      [*Exit* Southwell.

Enter COURTENAY.

   Courtenay. All lost, all lost, all yielded! A barge, a barge!
The Queen must to the Tower.
   Mary.   Whence come you, sir?
   Courtenay. From Charing Cross; the rebels broke us there,
And I sped hither with what haste I might
To save my royal cousin.
   Mary.   Where is Pembroke?
   Courtenay. I left him somewhere in the thick of it.
   Mary. Left him and fled; and thou that wouldst be King,
And hast nor heart nor honor! I myself
Will down into the battle and there bide
The upshot of my quarrel, or die with those
That are no cowards and no Courtenays.
   Courtenay. I do not love your Grace should call me coward.

Enter another MESSENGER.

   Messenger. Over, your Grace, all crush'd; the brave Lord William
Thrust him from Ludgate, and the traitor flying
To Temple Bar, there by Sir Maurice Berkeley
Was taken prisoner.
   Mary.   To the Tower with *him!*
   Messenger. 'Tis said he told Sir Maurice there was one

Cognizant of this, and party there-
    unto,
My Lord of Devon.

Mary.   To the Tower with *him!*

Courtenay. O la, the Tower, the
    Tower, always the Tower,
I shall grow into it—I shall be the
    Tower.

Mary. Your lordship may not have
    so long to wait.

Remove him!

Courtenay. La, to whistle out my
    life,
And carve my coat upon the walls
    again!

            [*Exit* Courtenay, *guarded.*

Messenger. Also this Wyatt did
    confess the Princess
Cognizant thereof, and party there-
    unto.

Mary. What? whom—whom did
    you say?

Messenger. Elizabeth,
Your royal sister.

Mary.   To the Tower with *her!*
My foes are at my feet, and I am
    Queen.

[Gardiner *and her* Ladies *kneel to her.*

Gardiner (*rising*). There let them
    lie, your footstool! (*Aside.*)
    Can I strike
Elizabeth?—not now and save the life
Of Devon. If I save him, he and his
Are bound to me—may strike here-
    after. (*Aloud.*) Madam,
What Wyatt said, or what they said
    he said,
Cries of the moment and the street—

Mary.   He said it.

Gardiner. Your courts of justice
    will determine that.

Renard (*advancing*). I trust by this
    your Highness will allow
Some spice of wisdom in my telling
    you,
When last we talk'd, that Philip would
    not come
Till Guildford Dudley and the Duke
    of Suffolk
And Lady Jane had left us.

Mary.   They shall die.

Renard. And your so loving sister?

Mary.   She shall die.

My foes are at my feet, and Philip
    King.

                        [*Exeunt.*

ACT III

SCENE I.—THE CONDUIT IN GRACE-CHURCH

*Painted with the Nine Worthies,
among them King Henry VIII.
holding a book, on it inscribed
'Verbum Dei.'*

Enter SIR RALPH BAGENHALL *and* SIR
    THOMAS STAFFORD.

Bagenhall. A hundred here and
    hundreds hang'd in Kent.
The tigress had unsheath'd her nails
    at last,
And Renard and the Chancellor
    sharpen'd them.
In every London street a gibbet stood.
They are down to-day. Here by this
    house was one;
The traitor husband dangled at the
    door,
And when the traitor wife came out
    for bread
To still the petty treason therewithin,
Her cap would brush his heels.

Stafford.   It is Sir Ralph,
And muttering to himself as hereto-
    fore.
Sir, see you aught up yonder?

Bagenhall.   I miss something.
The tree that only bears dead fruit is
    gone.

Stafford. What tree, sir?

Bagenhall. Well, the tree in Virgil,
    sir,
That bears not its own apples.

Stafford.   What! the gallows?

Bagenhall. Sir, this dead fruit was
    ripening overmuch,
And had to be removed lest living
    Spain
Should sicken at dead England.

Stafford.   Not so dead
But that a shock may rouse her.

Bagenhall.   I believe

Sir Thomas Stafford?
 Stafford.   I am ill disguised.
 Bagenhall. Well, are you not in peril
  here?
 Stafford. I think so.
I came to feel the pulse of England,
  whether
It beats hard at this marriage. Did
  you see it?
 Bagenhall. Stafford, I am a sad man
  and a serious.
Far liefer had I in my country hall
Been reading some old book, with
  mine old hound
Couch'd at my hearth, and mine old
  flask of wine
Beside me, than have seen it; yet I
  saw it.
 Stafford. Good, was it splendid?
 Bagenhall. Ay, if dukes, and earls,
And counts, and sixty Spanish cava-
  liers,
Some six or seven bishops, diamonds,
  pearls,
That royal commonplace too, cloth of
  gold,
Could make it so.
 Stafford. And what was Mary's
  dress?
 Bagenhall. Good faith, I was too
  sorry for the woman
To mark the dress. She wore red
  shoes!
 Stafford. Red shoes!
 Bagenhall. Scarlet, as if her feet
  were wash'd in blood,
As if she had waded in it.
 Stafford.   Were your eyes
So bashful that you look'd no higher?
 Bagenhall. A diamond,
And Philip's gift, as proof of Philip's
  love,
Who hath not any for any,—tho' a
  true one,
Blazed false upon her heart.
 Stafford. But this proud Prince—
 Bagenhall. Nay, he is King, you
  know, the King of Naples.
The father ceded Naples that the son,
Being a King, might wed a Queen—O,
  he
Flamed in brocade—white satin his
  trunk-hose,

Inwrought with silver,—on his neck a
  collar,
Gold, thick with diamonds; hanging
  down from this
The Golden Fleece—and round his
  knee, misplaced,
Our English Garter, studded with
  great emeralds,
Rubies, I know not what. Have you
  had enough
Of all this gear?
 Stafford. Ay, since you hate the tell-
  ing it.
How look'd the Queen?
 Bagenhall. No fairer for her jewels.
And I could see that as the new-made
  couple
Came from the Minster, moving side
  by side
Beneath one canopy, ever and anon
She cast on him a vassal smile of love,
Which Philip with a glance of some
  distaste,
Or so methought, return'd. I may be
  wrong, sir.
This marriage will not hold.
 Stafford.   I think with you.
The King of France will help to break
  it.
 Bagenhall. France!
We once had half of France, and
  hurl'd our battles
Into the heart of Spain; but England
  now
Is but a ball chuck'd between France
  and Spain,
His in whose hand she drops. Harry of
  Bolingbroke
Had holpen Richard's tottering throne
  to stand,
Could Harry have foreseen that all
  our nobles
Would perish on the civil slaughter-
  field,
And leave the people naked to the
  Crown,
And the Crown naked to the people;
  the Crown
Female, too! Sir, no woman's regi-
  men
Can save us. We are fallen, and, as I
  think,

Never to rise again.

Stafford. You are too black-blooded.
I'd make a move myself to hinder
    that;
I know some lusty fellows there in
    France.

Bagenhall. You would but make us
    weaker, Thomas Stafford.
Wyatt was a good soldier, yet he
    fail'd,
And strengthen'd Philip.

Stafford.   Did not his last breath
Clear Courtenay and the Princess
    from the charge
Of being his co-rebels?

Bagenhall.   Ay, but then
What such a one as Wyatt says is
    nothing;
We have no men among us. The new
    lords
Are quieted with their sop of Abbey-
    lands,
And even before the Queen's face
    Gardiner buys them
With Philip's gold. All greed, no faith,
    no courage!
Why, even the haughty prince, North-
    umberland,
The leader of our Reformation, knelt
And blubber'd like a lad, and on the
    scaffold
Recanted, and resold himself to
    Rome.

Stafford. I swear you do your coun-
    try wrong, Sir Ralph.
I know a set of exiles over there,
Dare-devils, that would eat fire and
    spit it out
At Philip's beard; they pillage Spain
    already.
The French King winks at it. An hour
    will come
When they will sweep her from the
    seas. No men?
Did not Lord Suffolk die like a true
    man?
Is not Lord William Howard a true
    man?
Yea, you yourself, altho' you are
    black-blooded;
And I, by God, believe myself a man.
Ay, even in the church there is a
    man—

Cranmer.
Fly would he not, when all men bade
    him fly.
And what a letter he wrote against
    the Pope!
There's a brave man, if any.

Bagenhall.   Ay; if it hold.

Crowd (*coming on*). God save their
    Graces!

Stafford.   Bagenhall, I see
The Tudor green and white. (*Trum-
    pets.*) They are coming now.
And here's a crowd as thick as her-
    ring-shoals.

Bagenhall. Be limpets to this pillar
    or we are torn
Down the strong wave of brawlers.

Crowd. God save their Graces!

*Procession of Trumpeters, Javelin-
    men, etc.; then Spanish and Flem-
    ish Nobles intermingled.*

Stafford. Worth seeing, Bagenhall!
    These black dog-Dons
Garb themselves bravely. Who's the
    long-face there,
Looks very Spain of very Spain?

Bagenhall.   The Duke
Of Alva, an iron soldier.

Stafford.   And the Dutchman,
Now laughing at some jest?

Bagenhall.   William of Orange,
William the Silent.

Stafford.   Why do they call him so?

Bagenhall. He keeps, they say, some
    secret that may cost
Philip his life.

Stafford. But then he looks so
    merry.

Bagenhall. I cannot tell you why
    they call him so.

[*The* King *and* Queen *pass, at-
    tended by Peers of the Realm,
    Officers of State, etc. Cannon
    shot off.*

Crowd. Philip and Mary, Philip and
    Mary!
Long live the King and Queen, Philip
    and Mary!

Stafford. They smile as if content with one another.

Bagenhall. A smile abroad is oft a scowl at home.

[King *and* Queen *pass on. Procession.*

First Citizen. I thought this Philip had been one of those black devils of Spain, but he hath a yellow beard.

Second Citizen. Not red like Iscariot's.

First Citizen. Like a carrot's, as thou say'st, and English carrot's better than Spanish licorice; but I thought he was a beast.

Third Citizen. Certain I had heard that every Spaniard carries a tail like a devil under his trunk-hose.

Tailor. Ay, but see what trunk-hoses! Lord! they be fine; I never stitch'd none such. They make amends for the tails.

Fourth Citizen. Tut! every Spanish priest will tell you that all English heretics have tails.

Fifth Citizen. Death and the devil —if he find I have one—

Fourth Citizen. Lo! thou hast call'd them up! here they come—a pale horse for Death, and Gardiner for the devil.

Enter GARDINER (*turning back from the procession*).

Gardiner. Knave, wilt thou wear thy cap before the Queen?

Man. My lord, I stand so squeezed among the crowd
I cannot lift my hands unto my head.

Gardiner. Knock off his cap there, some of you about him!
See there be others that can use their hands.
Thou art one of Wyatt's men?

Man.   No, my lord, no.

Gardiner. Thy name, thou knave?

Man.   I am nobody, my lord.

Gardiner (*shouting*). God's passion! knave, thy name?

Man.   I have ears to hear.

Gardiner. Ay, rascal, if I leave thee ears to hear.

Find out his name and bring it me (*to Attendant*).

Attendant.   Ay, my lord.

Gardiner. Knave, thou shalt lose thine ears and find thy tongue,
And shalt be thankful if I leave thee that.

[*Coming before the Conduit.*
The conduit painted—the Nine Worthies—ay!
But then what's here? King Harry with a scroll.
Ha—Verbum Dei—verbum—Word of God!
God's passion! do you know the knave that painted it?

Attendant. I do, my lord.

Gardiner. Tell him to paint it out,
And put some fresh device in lieu of it—
A pair of gloves, a pair of gloves, sir; ha?
There is no heresy there.

Attendant.   I will, my lord;
The man shall paint a pair of gloves. I am sure—
Knowing the man—he wrought it ignorantly,
And not from any malice.

Gardiner.   Word of God
In English! over this the brainless loons
That cannot spell Esaias from Saint Paul,
Make themselves drunk and mad, fly out and flare
Into rebellions. I'll have their Bibles burnt.
The Bible is the priest's. Ay! fellow, what!
Stand staring at me! shout, you gaping rogue!

Man. I have, my lord, shouted till I am hoarse.

Gardiner. What hast thou shouted, knave?

Man.   Long live Queen Mary!

Gardiner. Knave, there be two.
There be both King and Queen, Philip and Mary. Shout!

Man.   Nay, but my lord,
The Queen comes first, Mary and Philip.

Gardiner. Shout, then,
Mary and Philip!
Man. Mary and Philip!
Gardiner. Now,
Thou hast shouted for thy pleasure,
    shout for mine!
Philip and Mary!
Man. Must it be so, my lord?
Gardiner. Ay, knave.
Man. Philip and Mary.
Gardiner. I distrust thee.
Thine is a half voice and a lean as-
    sent.
What is thy name?
Man. Sanders.
Gardiner. What else?
Man. Zerubbabel.
Gardiner. Where dost thou live?
Man. In Cornhill.
Gardiner. Where, knave, where?
Man. Sign of the Talbot.
Gardiner. Come to me to-mor-
    row.—
Rascal!—this land is like a hill of fire,
One crater opens when another shuts.
But so I get the laws against the
    heretic,
Spite of Lord Paget and Lord Wil-
    liam Howard,
And others of our Parliament, re-
    vived,
I will show fire on my side—stake and
    fire—
Sharp work and short. The knaves are
    easily cow'd.
Follow their Majesties.
    [*Exit. The crowd following.*
Bagenhall. As proud as Becket.
Stafford. You would not have him
    murder'd as Becket was?
Bagenhall. No—murder fathers
    murder; but I say
There is no man—there was one
    woman with us—
It was a sin to love her married, dead
I cannot choose but love her.
Stafford. Lady Jane?
Crowd (going off). God save their
    Graces!
Stafford. Did you see her die?
Bagenhall. No, no; her innocent
    blood had blinded me.

You call me too black-blooded—true
    enough,
Her dark, dead blood is in my heart
    with mine.
If ever I cry out against the Pope
Her dark, dead blood that ever moves
    with mine
Will stir the living tongue and make
    the cry.
Stafford. Yet doubtless you can tell
    me how she died?
Bagenhall. Seventeen—and knew
    eight languages—in music
Peerless—her needle perfect, and her
    learning
Beyond the churchmen; yet so meek,
    so modest,
So wife-like humble to the trivial boy
Mismatch'd with her for policy! I
    have heard
She would not take a last farewell of
    him;
She fear'd it might unman him for his
    end.
She could not be unmann'd—no, nor
    out-woman'd—
Seventeen—a rose of grace!
Girl never breathed to rival such a
    rose;
Rose never blew that equall'd such a
    bud.
Stafford. Pray you go on.
Bagenhall. She came upon the scaf-
    fold,
And said she was condemn'd to die
    for treason;
She had but follow'd the device of
    those
Her nearest kin; she thought they
    knew the laws.
But for herself, she knew but little
    law,
And nothing of the titles to the crown;
She had no desire for that, and wrung
    her hands,
And trusted God would save her thro'
    the blood
Of Jesus Christ alone.
Stafford. Pray you go on.
Bagenhall. Then knelt and said the
    Miserere Mei—
But all in English, mark you; rose
    again,

And, when the headsman pray'd to be
    forgiven,
Said, You will give me my true
    crown at last,
But do it quickly;' then all wept but
    she,
Who changed not color when she saw
    the block,
But ask'd him, childlike, 'Will you
    take it off
Before I lay me down?' 'No, madam,'
    he said,
Gasping; and when her innocent eyes
    were bound,
She, with her poor blind hands feeling
    —'Where is it?
Where is it?'—You must fancy that
    which follow'd,
If you have heart to do it!
   Crowd (*in the distance*). God save
    their Graces!
   Stafford. Their Graces, our dis-
    graces! God confound them!
Why, she's grown bloodier! when I
    last was here,
This was against her conscience—
    would be murder!
   Bagenhall. The 'Thou shalt do no
    murder,' which God's hand
Wrote on her conscience, Mary rubb'd
    out pale—
She could not make it white—and
    over that,
Traced in the blackest text of hell—
    'Thou shalt!'
And sign'd it—Mary!
   Stafford.   Philip and the Pope
Must have sign'd too. I hear this
    legate's coming
To bring us absolution from the Pope.
The Lords and Commons will bow
    down before him—
You are of the house? what will you
    do, Sir Ralph?
   Bagenhall. And why should I be
    bolder than the rest,
Or honester than all?
   Stafford.   But, sir, if I—
And over-sea they say this State of
    yours
Hath no more mortise than a tower of
    cards;
And that a puff would do it—then if I

And others made that move I touched
    upon,
Back'd by the power of France, and
    landing here,
Came with a sudden splendor, shout,
    and show,
And dazzled men and deafen'd by
    some bright
Loud venture, and the people so un-
    quiet—
And I the race of murder'd Bucking-
    ham—
Not for myself, but for the kingdom
    —Sir,
I trust that you would fight along with
    us.
   Bagenhall. No; you would fling
    your lives into the gulf.
   Stafford. But if this Philip, as he's
    like to do,
Left Mary a wife-widow here alone,
Set up a viceroy, sent his myriads
    hither
To seize upon the forts and fleet, and
    make us
A Spanish province; would you not
    fight then?
   Bagenhall. I think I should fight
    then.
   Stafford. I am sure of it.
Hist! there's the face coming on here
    of one
Who knows me. I must leave you.
    Fare you well,
You'll hear of me again.
   Bagenhall.   Upon the scaffold.
                 [*Exeunt*.

SCENE II

ROOM IN WHITEHALL PALACE

MARY. *Enter* PHILIP *and* CARDINAL
POLE.

   Pole. Ave Maria, gratia plena, bene-
    dicta tu in mulieribus!
   Mary. Loyal and royal cousin, hum-
    blest thanks.
Had you a pleasant voyage up the
    river?

Pole. We had your royal barge, and
    that same chair,
Or rather throne of purple, on the
    deck.
Our silver cross sparkled before the
    prow,
The ripples twinkled at their dia-
    mond-dance,
The boats that follow'd were as glow-
    ing-gay
As regal gardens, and your flocks of
    swans
As fair and white as angels; and your
    shores
Wore in mine eyes the green of Para-
    dise.
My foreign friends, who dream'd us
    blanketed
In ever-closing fog, were much
    amazed
To find as fair a sun as might have
    flash'd
Upon their lake of Garda fire the
    Thames;
Our voyage by sea was all but mir-
    acle;
And here the river flowing from the
    sea,
Not toward it—for they thought not
    of our tides—
Seem'd as a happy miracle to make
    glide—
In quiet—home your banish'd coun-
    tryman.
    Mary. We heard that you were sick
    in Flanders, cousin.
    Pole. A dizziness.
    Mary. And how came you round
    again?
    Pole. The scarlet thread of Rahab
    saved her life;
And mine, a little letting of the blood.
    Mary. Well? now?
    Pole. Ay, cousin, as the heathen
    giant
Had but to touch the ground, his force
    return'd—
Thus, after twenty years of banish-
    ment,
Feeling my native land beneath my
    foot,
I said thereto: 'Ah, native land of
    mine,

Thou art much beholden to this foot
    of mine,
That hastes with full commission
    from the Pope
To absolve thee from thy guilt of
    heresy.
Thou hast disgraced me and attainted
    me,
And mark'd me even as Cain, and I
    return
As Peter, but to bless thee; make me
    well.'
Methinks the good land heard me, for
    today
My heart beats twenty, when I see
    you, cousin.
Ah, gentle cousin, since your Herod's
    death,
How oft hath Peter knock'd at Mary's
    gate!
And Mary would have risen and let
    him in,
But, Mary, there were those within
    the house
Who would not have it.
    Mary.   True, good cousin Pole;
And there were also those without
    the house
Who would not have it.
    Pole.   I believe so, cousin.
State-policy and church-policy are
    conjoint,
But Janus-faces looking diverse ways.
I fear the Emperor much misvalued
    me.
But all is well; 't was even the will of
    God,
Who, waiting till the time had ripen'd,
    now
Makes me His mouth of holy greet-
    ing, 'Hail,
Daughter of God, and saver of the
    faith.
Sit benedictus fructus ventris tui!'
    Mary. Ah, heaven!
    Pole.   Unwell, your Grace?
    Mary.   No, cousin, happy—
Happy to see you; never yet so happy
Since I was crown'd.
    Pole.   Sweet cousin, you forget
That long low minster where you gave
    your hand
To this great Catholic King.

Philip.   Well said, Lord Legate.

Mary. Nay, not well said; I thought
        of you, my liege,
Even as I spoke.

Philip. Ay, madam; my Lord Paget
Waits to present our Council to the
        legate.
Sit down here, all; madam, between
        us you.

Pole. Lo, now you are enclosed with
        boards of cedar,
Our little sister of the Song of Songs!
You are doubly fenced and shielded
        sitting here
Between the two most high-set
        thrones on earth,
The Emperor's highness happily sym-
        boll'd by
The King your husband, the Pope's
        holiness
By mine own self.

Mary.   True, cousin, I am happy.
When will you that we summon both
        our houses
To take this absolution from your
        lips,
And be re-gather'd to the Papal fold?

Pole. In Britain's calendar the
        brightest day
Beheld our rough forefathers break
        their gods,
And clasp the faith in Christ; but
        after that
Might not Saint Andrew's be her hap-
        piest day?

Mary. Then these shall meet upon
        Saint Andrew's Day.

Enter PAGET, *who presents the Coun-
        cil. Dumb show.*

Pole. I am an old man wearied with
        my journey,
Even with my joy. Permit me to with-
        draw.
To Lambeth?

Philip. Ay, Lambeth has ousted
        Cranmer.
It was not meet the heretic swine
        should live
In Lambeth.

Mary. There or anywhere, or at all.

Philip. We have had it swept and
        garnish'd after him.

Pole. Not for the seven devils to
        enter in?

Philip. No, for we trust they parted
        in the swine.

Pole. True, and I am the Angel of
        the Pope.
Farewell, your Graces.

Philip.   Nay, not here—to me;
I will go with you to the waterside.

Pole. Not be my Charon to the
        counter side?

Philip. No, my Lord Legate, the
        Lord Chancellor goes.

Pole. And unto no dead world, but
        Lambeth Palace,
Henceforth a centre of the living
        faith.
        [*Exeunt* Philip, Pole, Paget, *etc.*

Manet MARY.

Mary. He hath awaked! he hath
        awaked!
He stirs within the darkness!
O Philip, husband! now thy love to
        mine
Will cling more close, and those bleak
        manners thaw,
That make me shamed and tongue-
        tied in my love.
The second Prince of Peace—
The great unborn defender of the
        Faith,
Who will avenge me of mine en-
        emies—
He comes, and my star rises.
The stormy Wyatts and Northumber-
        lands,
The proud ambitions of Elizabeth,
And all her fieriest partisans—are pale
Before my star!
The light of this new learning wanes
        and dies;
The ghosts of Luther and Zuinglius
        fade
Into the deathless hell which is their
        doom
Before my star!
His sceptre shall **go forth from Ind
        to Ind!**

His sword shall hew the heretic peo-
ples down!
His faith shall clothe the world that
will be his,
Like universal air and sunshine!
Open,
Ye everlasting gates! The King is
here!—
My star, my son!

Enter PHILIP, DUKE OF ALVA, *etc.*

O, Philip, come with me!
Good news have I to tell you, news
to make
Both of us happy—ay, the kingdom
too.
Nay, come with me—one moment!
Philip (to Alva). More than that;
There was one here of late—William
the Silent
They call him—he is free enough in
talk,
But tells me nothing. You will be, we
trust,
Sometime the viceroy of those prov-
inces—
He must deserve his surname better.
Alva. Ay, sir;
Inherit the Great Silence.
Philip. True; the provinces
Are hard to rule and must be hardly
ruled;
Most fruitful, yet, indeed, an empty
rind,
All hollow'd out with stinging here-
sies;
And for their heresies, Alva, they
will fight;
You must break them or they break
you.
Alva (proudly). The first.
Philip. Good!
Well, Madam, this new happiness of
mine? [*Exeunt.*

Enter THREE PAGES.

First Page. News, mates! a miracle,
a miracle! news!
The bells must ring; Te Deums must
be sung;
The Queen hath felt the motion of her
babe!
Second Page. Ay; but see here!
First Page. See what?
Second Page. This paper, Dickon.
I found it fluttering at the palace
gates:—
'The Queen of England is delivered of
a dead dog!'
Third Page. These are the things
that madden her. Fie upon it!
First Page. Ay; but I hear she hath
a dropsy, lad,
Or a high-dropsy, as the doctors call
it.
Third Page. Fie on her dropsy, so
she have a dropsy!
I know that she was ever sweet to me.
First Page. For thou and thine are
Roman to the core.
Third Page. So thou and thine must
be. Take heed!
First Page. Not I;
And whether this flash of news be
false or true,
So the wine run, and there be revelry,
Content am I. Let all the steeples
clash,
Till the sun dance, as upon Easter
Day. [*Exeunt.*

SCENE III

GREAT HALL IN WHITEHALL

*At the far end a dais. On this three
chairs, two under one canopy for
MARY and PHILIP, another on the
right of these for POLE. Under the
dais on POLE's side, ranged along
the wall, sit all the Spiritual Peers,
and along the wall opposite all the
Temporal. The Commons on cross
benches in front, a line of approach
to the dais between them. In the
foreground, SIR RALPH BAGENHALL
and other MEMBERS of the COM-
MONS.*

First Member. Saint Andrew's
Day; sit close, sit close, we are
friends.
Is reconciled the word? the Pope
again?

It must be thus; and yet, cocksbody!
    how strange
That Gardiner, once so one with all of
    us
Against this foreign marriage, should
    have yielded
So utterly!—strange! but stranger
    still that he,
So fierce against the headship of the
    Pope,
Should play the second actor in this
    pageant
That brings him in; such a chameleon
    he!
    Second Member. This Gardiner
    turn'd his coat in Henry's
    time;
The serpent that hath slough'd will
    slough again.
    Third Member. Tut, then we all
    are serpents.
    Second Member. Speak for your-
    self.
    Third Member. Ay, and for Gar-
    diner! being English citizen,
How should he bear a bridegroom
    out of Spain?
The Queen would have him! being
    English churchman,
How should he bear the headship of
    the Pope?
The Queen would have it! Statesmen
    that are wise
Shape a necessity, as a sculptor clay,
To their own model.
    Second Member. Statesmen that
    are wise
Take truth herself for model. What
    say you?
        [*To* Sir Ralph Bagenhall.
Bagenhall. We talk and talk.
    First Member. Ay, and what use
    to talk?
Philip's no sudden alien—the Queen's
    husband,
He 's here, and King, or will be—yet,
    cocksbody!
So hated here! I watch'd a hive of
    late;
My seven-years' friend was with me,
    my young boy;
Out crept a wasp, with half the swarm
    behind.

'Philip!' says he. I had to cuff the
    rogue
For infant treason.
    Third Member. But they say that
    bees,
If any creeping life invade their hive
Too gross to be thrust out, will build
    him round,
And bind him in from harming of
    their combs.
And Philip by these articles is bound
From stirring hand or foot to wrong
    the realm.
    Second Member. By bonds of bees-
    wax, like your creeping thing;
But your wise bees had stung him
    first to death.
    Third Member. Hush, hush!
You wrong the Chancellor. The
    clauses added
To that same treaty which the Em-
    peror sent us
Were mainly Gardiner's: that no for-
    eigner
Hold office in the household, fleet,
    forts, army;
That if the Queen should die without
    a child,
The bond between the kingdoms be
    dissolved;
That Philip should not mix us any
    way
With his French wars—
    Second Member. Ay, ay, but what
    security,
Good sir, for this, if Philip—
    Third Member. Peace—the Queen,
Philip, and Pole.   [*All rise, and stand.*

Enter MARY, PHILIP, *and* POLE.

[Gardiner *conducts them to the
    three chairs of state.* Philip *sits
    on the* Queen's *left,* Pole *on
    her right.*

Gardiner. Our short-lived sun, be-
    fore his winter plunge,
Laughs at the last red leaf, and An-
    drew's Day.
    Mary. Should not this day be held
    in after years

More solemn than of old?
Philip.   Madam, my wish
Echoes your Majesty's.
    Pole.   It shall be so.
    Gardiner. Mine echoes both your
        Graces'; (*aside*) but the
        Pope—
Can we not have the Catholic Church
        as well
Without as with the Italian? if we
        cannot,
Why, then the Pope.
        My lords of the upper house,
And ye, my masters, of the lower
        house,
Do ye stand fast by that which ye re-
        solved?
    Voices. We do.
    Gardiner. And be you all one mind
        to supplicate
The legate here for pardon, and
        acknowledge
The primacy of the Pope?
    Voices.   We are all one mind.
    Gardiner. Then must I play the
        vassal to this Pole.   [*Aside.*

[*He draws a paper from under
    his robes and presents it to the
    King and Queen, who look
    through it and return it to
    him; then ascends a tribune,
    and reads.*

We, the Lords Spiritual and Tem-
        poral,
And Commons here in Parliament as-
        sembled,
Presenting the whole body of this
        realm
Of England, and dominions of the
        same,
Do make most humble suit unto your
        Majesties,
In our own name and that of all the
        State,
That by your gracious means and in-
        tercession
Our supplication be exhibited
To the Lord Cardinal Pole, sent here
        as legate
From our most Holy Father Julius,
        Pope,

And from the Apostolic See of Rome;
And do declare our penitence and
        grief
For our long schism and disobedience
Either in making laws and ordinances
Against the Holy Father's primacy,
Or else by doing or by speaking aught
Which might impugn or prejudice the
        same;
By this our supplication promising,
As well for our own selves as all the
        realm,
That now we be and ever shall be
        quick,
Under and with your Majesties' au-
        thorities,
To do to the utmost all that in us lies
Towards the abrogation and repeal
Of all such laws and ordinances made;
Whereon we humbly pray your Maj-
        esties,
As persons undefiled with our offence,
So to set forth this humble suit of
        ours
That we the rather by your interces-
        sion
May from the Apostolic See obtain,
Thro' this most reverend father, abso-
        lution,
And full release from danger of all
        censures
Of Holy Church that we be fallen
        into,
So that we may, as children penitent,
Be once again received into the bosom
And unity of Universal Church;
And that this noble realm thro' after
        years
May in this unity and obedience
Unto the holy see and reigning
        Pope
Serve God and both your Majesties.
    Voices.   Amen. [*All sit.*

[*He again presents the petition
    to the King and Queen, who
    hand it reverentially to Pole.*

Pole (*sitting*). This is the loveliest
        day that ever smiled
On England. All her breath should,
        incense-like,

Rise to the heavens in grateful praise
  of Him
Who now recalls her to His ancient
  fold.
Lo! once again God to this realm hath
  given
A token of His more especial grace;
For as this people were the first of all
The islands call'd into the dawning
  church
Out of the dead, deep night of hea-
  thendom,
So now are these the first whom God
  hath given
Grace to repent and sorrow for their
  schism;
And if your penitence be not mock-
  ery,
O, how the blessed angels who rejoice
Over one saved do triumph at this
  hour
In the re-born salvation of a land
So noble!   [A pause.
      For ourselves we do protest
That our commission is to heal, not
  harm;
We come not to condemn, but recon-
  cile;
We come not to compel, but call
  again;
We come not to destroy, but edify;
Nor yet to question things already
  done;
These are forgiven—matters of the
  past—
And range with jetsam and with offal
  thrown
Into the blind sea of forgetfulness.
      [A pause.
Ye have reversed the attainder laid
  on us
By him who sack'd the house of God;
  and we,
Amplier than any field on our poor
  earth
Can render thanks in fruit for being
  sown,
Do here and now repay you sixty-
  fold,
A hundred, yea, a thousand thousand-
  fold,
With heaven for earth.

[*Rising and stretching forth his
  hands. All kneel but* Sir Ralph
  Bagenhall, *who rises and remains standing.*

  The Lord who hath redeem'd us
With His own blood, and wash'd us
  from our sins,
To purchase for Himself a stainless
  bride;
He, whom the Father hath appointed
  Head
Of all His church, He by His mercy
  absolve you.   [A pause.
And we by that authority Apostolic
Given unto us, his legate, by the Pope,
Our Lord and Holy Father, Julius,
God's Vicar and Vicegerent upon
  earth,
Do here absolve you and deliver you
And every one of you, and all the
  realm
And its dominions from all heresy,
All schism, and from all and every
  censure,
Judgment, and pain accruing there-
  upon;
And also we restore you to the bosom
And unity of Universal Church.
      [*Turning to* Gardiner.
Our letters of commission will declare
  this plainlier.

[Queen *heard sobbing. Cries of*
  Amen! Amen! *Some of the*
  Members *embrace one another. All but* Sir Ralph Bagenhall *pass out into the neighboring chapel, whence is heard the
  Te Deum.*

Bagenhall. We strove against the
  papacy from the first,
In William's time, in our first Ed-
  ward's time,
And in my master Henry's time; but
  now,
The unity of Universal Church,
Mary would have it; and this Gar-
  diner follows!
The unity of Universal Hell,
Philip would have it; and this Gar-
  diner follows!

A Parliament of imitative apes!
Sheep at the gap which Gardiner
  takes, who not
Believes the Pope, nor any of them
  believe—
These spaniel-Spaniard English of the
  time,
Who rub their fawning noses in the
  dust,
For that is Philip's gold-dust, and
  adore
This Vicar of their Vicar. Would I
  had been
Born Spaniard! I had held my head
  up then.
I am ashamed that I am Bagenhall,
English.

Enter OFFICER

Officer. Sir Ralph Bagenhall!
Bagenhall.   What of that?
Officer. You were the one sole man
  in either house
Who stood upright when both the
  houses fell.
Bagenhall. The houses fell!
Officer.   I mean the houses knelt
Before the legate.
Bagenhall. Do not scrimp your
  phrase,
But stretch it wider; say when Eng-
  land fell.
Officer. I say you were the one sole
  man who stood.
Bagenhall. I am the one sole man in
  either house,
Perchance in England, loves her like
  a son.
Officer. Well, you one man, because
  you stood upright,
Her Grace the Queen commands you
  to the Tower.
Bagenhall. As traitor, or as heretic,
  or for what?
Officer. If any man in any way
  would be
The one man, he shall be so to his
  cost.
Bagenhall. What! will she have my
  head?
Officer.   A round fine likelier.

Your pardon.   [*Calling to Attendant.*
  By the river to the Tower.
                              [*Exeunt.*

SCENE IV

WHITEHALL. A ROOM IN THE PALACE

MARY, GARDINER, POLE, PAGET,
  BONNER, *etc.*

Mary. The King and I, my lords,
  now that all traitors
Against our royal state have lost the
  heads
Wherewith they plotted in their trea-
  sonous malice,
Have talk'd together, and are well
  agreed
That those old statutes touching Lol-
  lardism
To bring the heretic to the stake,
  should be
No longer a dead letter, but re-quick-
  en'd.
  One of the Council. Why, what hath
    fluster'd Gardiner? how he
    rubs
His forelock!
  Paget. I have changed a word with
    him
In coming, and may change a word
  again.
  Gardiner. Madam, your Highness
    is our sun, the King
And you together our two suns in
  one;
And so the beams of both may shine
  upon us,
The faith that seem'd to droop will
  feel your light,
Lift head, and flourish; yet not light
  alone,
There must be heat—there must be
  heat enough
To scorch and wither heresy to the
  root.
For what saith Christ? 'Compel them
  to come in.'
And what saith Paul? 'I would they
  were cut off
That trouble you.' Let the dead letter
  live!

Trace it in fire, that all the louts to
   whom
Their A B C is darkness, clowns and
   grooms
May read it! so you quash rebellion
   too,
For heretic and traitor are all one;
Two vipers of one breed—an amphis-
   bæna,
Each end a sting. Let the dead letter
   burn!
   Paget. Yet there be some disloyal
   Catholics,
And many heretics loyal; heretic
   throats
Cried no God-bless-her to the Lady
   Jane,
But shouted in Queen Mary. So there
   be
Some traitor-heretic, there is axe and
   cord.
To take the lives of others that are
   loyal,
And by the churchman's pitiless doom
   of fire,
Were but a thankless policy in this
   crown,
Ay, and against itself; for there are
   many.
   Mary. If we could burn out heresy,
   my Lord Paget,
We reck not tho' we lost this crown
   of England—
Ay! tho' it were ten Englands!
   Gardiner.   Right, your Grace.
Paget, you are all for this poor life
   of ours,
And care but little for the life to be.
   Paget. I have some time, for curi-
   ousness, my lord,
Watch'd children playing at *their* life
   to be,
And cruel at it, killing helpless flies;
Such is our time—all times for aught
   I know.
   Gardiner. We kill the heretics that
   sting the soul—
They, with right reason, flies that
   prick the flesh.
   Paget. They had not reach'd right
   reason, little children!
They kill'd but for their pleasure and
   the power

They felt in killing.
   Gardiner.   A spice of Satan, ha!
Why, good! what then? granted!—we
   are fallen creatures;
Look to your Bible, Paget! we are
   fallen.
   Paget. I am but of the laity, my
   lord bishop,
And may not read your Bible, yet I
   found
One day a wholesome scripture, 'Little
   children,
Love one another.'
   Gardiner. Did you find a scripture,
'I come not to bring peace but a
   sword'? The sword
Is in her Grace's hand to smite with.
   Paget,
You stand up here to fight for heresy,
You are more than guess'd at as a
   heretic,
And on the steep-up track of the true
   faith
Your lapses are far seen.
   Paget.   The faultless Gardiner!
   Mary. You brawl beyond the ques-
   tion; speak, lord legate!
   Pole. Indeed, I cannot follow with
   your Grace;
Rather would say—the shepherd doth
   not kill
The sheep that wander from his flock,
   but sends
His careful dog to bring them to the
   fold.
Look to the Netherlands, wherein
   have been
Such holocausts of heresy! to what
   end?
For yet the faith is not established
   there.
   Gardiner. The end 's not come.
   Pole. No—nor this way will
   come,
Seeing there lie two ways to every
   end,
A better and a worse—the worse is
   here
To persecute, because to persecute
Makes a faith hated, and is further-
   more
No perfect witness of a perfect faith

In him who persecutes. When men are
    tost
On tides of strange opinion, and not
    sure
Of their own selves, they are wroth
    with their own selves,
And thence with others; then, who
    lights the faggot?
Not the full faith, no, but the lurking
    doubt.
Old Rome, that first made martyrs in
    the Church,
Trembled for her own gods, for these
    were trembling—
But when did our Rome tremble?
    Paget.   Did she not
In Henry's time and Edward's?
    Pole.   What, my lord!
The Church on Peter's rock? never! I
    have seen
A pine in Italy that cast its shadow
Athwart a cataract; firm stood the
    pine—
The cataract shook the shadow. To
    my mind,
The cataract typed the headlong
    plunge and fall
Of heresy to the pit; the pine was
    Rome.
You see, my lords,
It was the shadow of the Church that
    trembled;
Your church was but the shadow of a
    church,
Wanting the Papal mitre.
    Gardiner (*muttering*). Here be
    tropes.
    Pole. And tropes are good to clothe
    a naked truth,
And make it look more seemly.
    Gardiner.   Tropes again!
    Pole. You are hard to please. Then
    without tropes, my lord,
An overmuch severeness, I repeat,
When faith is wavering makes the
    waverer pass
Into more settled hatred of the doc-
    trines
Of those who rule, which hatred by
    and by
Involves the ruler—thus there springs
    to light

That Centaur of a monstrous Com-
    monweal,
The traitor-heretic;—then tho' some
    may quail;
Yet others are that dare the stake and
    fire,
And their strong torment bravely
    borne begets
An admiration and an indignation,
And hot desire to imitate; so the
    plague
Of schism spreads. Were there but
    three or four
Of these misleaders, yet I would not
    say
Burn! and we cannot burn whole
    towns; they are many,
As my Lord Paget says.
    Gardiner. Yet, my Lord Cardinal—
    Pole. I am your legate; please you
    let me finish.
Methinks that under our Queen's
    regimen
We might go softlier than with crim-
    son rowel
And streaming lash. When Herod-
    Henry first
Began to batter at your English
    Church,
This was the cause, and hence the
    judgment on her.
She seethed with such adulteries, and
    the lives
Of many among your churchmen were
    so foul
That heaven wept and earth blush'd. I
    would advise
That we should thoroughly cleanse
    the Church within
Before these bitter statutes be re-
    quicken'd
So after that when she once more is
    seen
White as the light, the spotless bride
    of Christ,
Like Christ himself on Tabor, pos-
    sibly
The Lutheran may be won to her
    again;
Till when, my lords, I counsel toler-
    ance.
    Gardiner. What, if a mad dog bit
    your hand, my lord,

Would you not chop the bitten finger off,
Lest your whole body should madden with the poison?
I would not, were I Queen, tolerate the heretic,
No, not an hour. The ruler of a land
Is bounden by his power and place to see
His people be not poison'd. Tolerate them!
Why? do they tolerate you? Nay, many of them
Would burn—have burnt each other; call they not
The one true faith a loathsome idol-worship?
Beware, lord legate, of a heavier crime
Than heresy is itself; beware, I say,
Lest men accuse you of indifference
To all faiths, all religion; for you know
Right well that you yourself have been supposed
Tainted with Lutheranism in Italy.
    Pole (*angered*). But you, my lord, beyond all supposition,
In clear and open day were congruent
With that vile Cranmer in the accursed lie
Of good Queen Catharine's divorce—the spring
Of all those evils that have flow'd upon us;
For you yourself have truckled to the tyrant,
And done your best to bastardize our Queen,
For which God's righteous judgment fell upon you
In your five years of imprisonment, my lord,
Under young Edward. Who so bolster'd up
The gross King's headship of the Church, or more
Denied the Holy Father?
    Gardiner.   Ha! what! eh?
But you, my lord, a polish'd gentleman,
A bookman, flying from the heat and tussle,

You lived among your vines and oranges,
In your soft Italy yonder! You were sent for,
You were appeal'd to, but you still preferr'd
Your learned leisure. As for what I did,
I suffer'd and repented. You, lord, legate
And cardinal-deacon, have not now to learn
That even Saint Peter in his time of fear
Denied his Master, ay, and thrice, my lord.
    Pole. But not for five-and-twenty years, my lord.
    Gardiner. Ha! good! it seems then I was summon'd hither
But to be mock'd and baited. Speak, friend Bonner,
And tell this learned legate he lacks zeal.
The Church's evil is not as the King's,
Cannot be heal'd by stroking. The mad bite
Must have the cautery—tell him—and at once.
What wouldst thou do hadst thou his power, thou
That layest so long in heretic bonds with me?
Wouldst thou not burn and blast them root and branch?
    Bonner. Ay, after you, my lord.
    Gardiner. Nay, God's passion, before me! speak!
    Bonner. I am on fire until I see them flame.
    Gardiner. Ay, the psalm-singing weavers, cobblers, scum—
But this most noble prince Plantagenet,
Our good Queen's cousin—dallying overseas
Even when his brother's nay, his noble mother's,
Head fell—
    Pole.   Peace, madman!
Thou stirrest up a grief thou canst not fathom.

Thou Christian bishop, thou Lord
    Chancellor
Of England! no more rein upon thine
    anger
Than any child! Thou mak'st me
    much ashamed
That I was for a moment wroth at
    thee.
    Mary. I come for counsel and ye
    give me feuds,
Like dogs that, set to watch their mas-
    ter's gate,
Fall, when the thief is even within the
    walls,
To worrying one another. My Lord
    Chancellor,
You have an old trick of offending us;
And but that you are art and part
    with us
In purging heresy, well we might, for
    this
Your violence and much roughness to
    the legate,
Have shut you from our counsels.
    Cousin Pole,
You are fresh from brighter lands.
    Retire with me.
His Highness and myself—so you
    allow us—
Will let you learn in peace and pri-
    vacy
What power this cooler sun of Eng-
    land hath
In breeding godless vermin. And pray
    Heaven
That you may see according to our
    sight!
Come, cousin.
    [*Exeunt* Queen *and* Pole, *etc.*
    Gardiner. Pole has the Plantagenet
    face,
But not the force made them our
    mightiest kings.
Fine eyes—but melancholy, irreso-
    lute—
A fine beard, Bonner, a very full fine
    beard.
But a weak mouth, an indetermi-
    nate—ha?
    Bonner. Well, a weak mouth, per-
    chance.
    Gardiner. And not like thine

To gorge a heretic whole, roasted or
    raw.
    Bonner. I 'd do my best, my Lord;
    but yet the legate
Is here as Pope and Master of the
    Church,
And if he go not with you—
    Gardiner. Tut, Master Bishop,
Our bashful legate, saw'st not how he
    flush'd?
Touch him upon his old heretical talk,
He 'll burn a diocese to prove his
    orthodoxy.
And let him call me truckler. In those
    times,
Thou knowest we had to dodge, or
    duck, or die;
I kept my head for use of Holy
    Church;
And see you, we shall have to dodge
    again,
And let the Pope trample our rights,
    and plunge
His foreign fist into our island Church
To plump the leaner pouch of Italy.
For a time, for a time.
Why? that these statutes may be put
    in force,
And that his fan may thoroughly
    purge his floor.
    Bonner. So then you hold the
    Pope—
    Gardiner. I hold the Pope!
What do I hold him? what do I hold
    the Pope?
Come, come, the morsel stuck—this
    Cardinal's fault—
I have gulpt it down. I am wholly
    for the Pope,
Utterly and altogether for the Pope,
The Eternal Peter of the changeless
    chair,
Crown'd slave of slaves, and mitred
    king of kings,
God upon earth! what more? what
    would you have?
Hence, let 's be gone.

Enter USHER.

    Usher. Well that you be not gone,
My lord. The Queen, most wroth at
    first with you,

Is now content to grant you full for-
    giveness,
So that you crave full pardon of the
    legate.
I am sent to fetch you.
    Gardiner. Doth Pole yield, sir, ha?
Did you hear 'em? were you by?
    Usher.   I cannot tell you,
His bearing is so courtly-delicate;
And yet methinks he falters; their
    two Graces
Do so dear-cousin and royal-cousin
    him,
So press on him the duty which as
    legate
He owes himself, and with such royal
    smiles—
    Gardiner. Smiles that burn men.
    Bonner, it will be carried.
He falters, ha? 'fore God, we change
    and change;
Men now are bow'd and old, the doc-
    tors tell you,
At three-score years; then if we
    change at all
We needs must do it quickly; it is an
    age
Of brief life, and brief purpose, and
    brief patience,
As I have shown to-day. I am sorry
    for it
If Pole be like to turn. Our old friend
    Cranmer,
Your more especial love, hath turn'd
    so often
He knows not where he stands, which,
    if this pass,
We two shall have to teach him; let
    'em look to it,
Cranmer and Hooper, Ridley and
    Latimer,
Rogers and Ferrar, for their time is
    come,
Their hour is hard at hand, their 'dies
    Iræ,'
Their 'dies Illa,' which will test their
    sect.
I feel it but a duty—you will find in it
Pleasure as well as duty, worthy Bon-
    ner,—
To test their sect. Sir, I attend the
    Queen

To crave most humble pardon—of
    her most
Royal, Infallible, Papal Legate-
    cousin.   [*Exeunt.*

SCENE V

WOODSTOCK

ELIZABETH, LADY IN WAITING.

    Elizabeth. So they have sent poor
    Courtenay over-sea.
    Lady. And banish'd us to Wood-
    stock, and the fields.
The colors of our Queen are green and
    white;
These fields are only green, they make
    me gape.
    Elizabeth. There's white-thorn, girl.
    Lady.   Ay, for an hour in May.
But court is always May, buds out in
    masques,
Breaks into feather'd merriments, and
    flowers
In silken pageants. Why do they keep
    us here?
Why still suspect your Grace?
    Elizabeth.   Hard upon both.
    [*Writes on the window with a
    diamond.*

    Much suspected, of me
    Nothing proven can be.
      Quoth Elizabeth, prisoner.

    Lady. What hath your Highness
    written?
    Elizabeth. A true rhyme.
    Lady. Cut with a diamond; so to
    last like truth.
    Elizabeth. Ay, if truth last.
    Lady. But truth, they say, will out;
So it must last. It is not like a word,
That comes and goes in uttering.
    Elizabeth.   Truth, a word!
The very Truth and very Word are
    one.
But truth of story, which I glanced at,
    girl,
Is like a word that comes from olden
    days,

And passes thro' the peoples; every tongue
Alters it passing, till it spells and speaks
Quite other than at first.
Lady.   I do not follow.
Elizabeth. How many names, in the long sweep of time
That so foreshortens greatness, may but hang
On the chance mention of some fool that once
Brake bread with us, perhaps; and my poor chronicle
Is but of glass. Sir Henry Bedingfield
May split it for a spite.
Lady.   God grant it last,
And witness to your Grace's innocence,
Till doomsday melt it!
Elizabeth.   Or a second fire,
Like that which lately crackled underfoot
And in this very chamber, fuse the glass,
And char us back again into the dust
We spring from. Never peacock against rain
Scream'd as you did for water.
Lady.   And I got it.
I woke Sir Henry—and he 's true to you—
I read his honest horror in his eyes.
Elizabeth. Or true to you?
Lady.   Sir Henry Bedingfield!
I will have no man true to me, your Grace,
But one that pares his nails; to me? the clown!
Elizabeth. Out, girl! you wrong a noble gentleman.
Lady. For, like his cloak, his manners want the nap
And gloss of court; but of this fire he says,
Nay swears, it was no wicked wilfulness,
Only a natural chance.
Elizabeth.   A chance—perchance
One of those wicked wilfuls that men make,
Nor shame to call it nature. Nay, I know

They hunt my blood. Save for my daily range
Among the pleasant fields of Holy Writ
I might despair. But there hath some one come;
The house is all in movement. Hence, and see.   [*Exit* Lady.

MILKMAID (*singing without*).

Shame upon you, Robin,
    Shame upon you now!
Kiss me would you? with my hands
    Milking the cow?
    Daisies grow again,
    Kingcups blow again,
And you came and kiss'd me milking the cow.

Robin came behind me,
    Kiss'd me well, I vow.
Cuff him could I? with my hands
    Milking the cow?
    Swallows fly again,
    Cuckoos cry again,
And you came and kiss'd me milking the cow.

Come, Robin, Robin,
    Come and kiss me now;
Help it can I? with my hands
    Milking the cow?
    Ringdoves coo again,
    All things woo again.
Come behind and kiss me milking the cow!

Elizabeth. Right honest and redcheek'd; Robin was violent,
And she was crafty—a sweet violence,
And a sweet craft. I would I were a milkmaid,
To sing, love, marry, churn, brew, bake, and die,
Then have my simple headstone by the church,
And all things lived and ended honestly.
I could not if I would. I am Harry's daughter.
Gardiner would have my head. They are not sweet,
The violence and the craft that do divide
The world of nature; what is weak must lie.

The lion needs but roar to guard his
    young;
The lapwing lies, says 'here' when
    they are there.
Threaten the child, 'I 'll scourge you
    if you did it;'
What weapon hath the child, save his
    soft tongue,
To say 'I did not'? and my rod 's the
    block.
I never lay my head upon the pillow
Put that I think, 'Wilt thou lie there
    to-morrow?'
How oft the falling axe, that never
    fell,
Hath shock'd me back into the day-
    light truth
That it may fall to-day! Those damp,
    black, dead
Nights in the Tower; dead—with the
    fear of death
Too dead even for a death-watch!
    Toll of a bell,
Stroke of a clock, the scurrying of a
    rat
Affrighted me, and then delighted me,
For there was life—And there was life
    in death—
The little murder'd princes, in a pale
    light,
Rose hand in hand, and whisper'd,
    'Come away!
The civil wars are gone for evermore;
Thou last of all the Tudors, come
    away!
With us is peace!' The last? It was a
    dream;
I must not dream, not wink, but
    watch. She has gone,
Maid Marian to her Robin—by and
    by
Both happy! a fox may filch a hen by
    night,
And make a morning outcry in the
    yard;
But there 's no Renard here to 'catch
    her tripping.'
Catch me who can; yet, sometime I
    have wish'd
That I were caught, and kill'd away
    at once
Out of the flutter. The gray rogue,
    Gardiner,

Went on his knees, and pray'd me to
    confess
In Wyatt's business, and to cast my-
    self
Upon the good Queen's mercy; ay,
    when, my lord?
God save the Queen! My jailor—

Enter SIR HENRY BEDINGFIELD.

Bedingfield.   One, whose bolts
That jail you from free life, bar you
    from death.
There haunt some Papist ruffians
    hereabout
Would murder you.
    Elizabeth. I thank you heartily, sir,
But I am royal, tho' your prisoner,
And God hath blest or cursed me with
    a nose—
Your boots are from the horses.
    Bedingfield.   Ay, my lady.
When next there comes a missive
    from the Queen
It shall be all my study for one hour
To rose and lavender my horsiness,
Before I dare to glance upon your
    Grace.
    Elizabeth. A missive from the
        Queen! last time she wrote,
I had like to have lost my life. It takes
    my breath—
O God, sir, do you look upon your
    boots,
Are you so small a man? Help me!
    what think you,
Is it life or death?
    Bedingfield. I thought not on my
        boots;
The devil take all boots were ever
    made
Since man went barefoot! See, I lay
    it here,
For I will come no nearer to your
    Grace;
        [*Laying down the letter.*
And, whether it brings you bitter news
    or sweet,
And God hath given your Grace a
    nose or not,
I 'll help you, if I may.
    Elizabeth.   Your pardon, then;

It is the heat and narrowness of the
  cage
That makes the captive testy; with
  free wing
The world were all one Araby. Leave
  me now,
Will you, companion to myself, sir?
  Bedingfield.   Will I?
With most exceeding willingness, I
  will;
You know I never come till I be
  call'd.   [*Exit.*
  Elizabeth. It lies there folded; is
  there venom in it?
A snake—and if I touch it, it may
  sting.
Come, come, the worst!
Best wisdom is to know the worst at
  once.   [*Reads.*

'It is the King's wish that you
should wed Prince Philibert of Savoy.
You are to come to Court on the instant; and think of this in your coming.

                         'MARY THE QUEEN.'

Think! I have many thoughts;
I think there may be bird-lime here
  for me;
I think they fain would have me from
  the realm;
I think the Queen may never bear a
  child;
I think that I may be some time the
  Queen,
Then, Queen indeed; no foreign
  prince or priest
Should fill my throne, myself upon
  the steps.
I think I will not marry any one,
Specially not this landless Phili-
  bert
Of Savoy; but, if Philip menace me,
I think that I will play with Phili-
  bert,—
As once the Holy Father did with
  mine,
Before my father married my good
  mother,—
For fear of Spain.

                Enter LADY.

  Lady. O Lord! your Grace, Your
  Grace,
I feel so happy. It seems that we shall
  fly
These bald, blank fields, and dance
  into the sun
That shines on princes.
  Elizabeth.   Yet, a moment since,
I wish'd myself the milkmaid singing
  here,
To kiss and cuff among the birds and
  flowers—
A right rough life and healthful.
  Lady.   But the wench
Hath her own troubles; she is weep-
  ing now;
For the wrong Robin took her at her
  word.
Then the cow kick'd, and all her milk
  was spilt.
Your Highness such a milkmaid?
  Elizabeth.   I had kept
My Robins and my cows in sweeter
  order
Had I been such.
  Lady (*slyly*). And had your Grace
  a Robin?
  Elizabeth. Come, come, you are
  chill here; you want the sun
That shines at court; make ready for
  the journey.
Pray God, we 'scape the sunstroke!
  Ready at once.   [*Exeunt.*

                   SCENE VI

      LONDON. A ROOM IN THE PALACE

      LORD PETRE *and* LORD WILLIAM
                 HOWARD.

  Petre. You cannot see the Queen.
  Renard denied her
Even now to me.
  Howard. Their Flemish go-between
And all-in-all. I came to thank her
  Majesty
For freeing my friend Bagenhall from
  the Tower;

A grace to me! Mercy, that herb-of-grace,
Flowers now but seldom.
    Petre.   Only now, perhaps,
Because the Queen hath been three days in tears
For Philip's going—like the wild hedge-rose
Of a soft winter, possible, not probable,
However you have proven it.
    Howard.   I must see her.

Enter RENARD.

    Renard. My lords, you cannot see her Majesty.
    Howard. Why, then the King! for I would have him bring it
Home to the leisure wisdom of his Queen,
Before he go, that since these statutes past,
Gardiner out-Gardiners Gardiner in his heat,
Bonner cannot out-Bonner his own self—
Beast!—but they play with fire as children do,
And burn the house. I know that these are breeding
A fierce resolve and fixt heart-hate in men
Against the King, the Queen, the Holy Father,
The faith itself. Can I not see him?
    Renard.   Not now.
And in all this, my lord, her Majesty
Is flint of flint; you may strike fire from her,
Not hope to melt her. I will give your message.
    [*Exeunt* Petre *and* Howard.

Enter PHILIP (*musing*).

    Philip. She will not have Prince Philibert of Savoy,
I talk'd with her in vain—says she will live
And die true maid—a goodly creature too.

Would *she* had been the Queen! yet she must have him.
She troubles England; that she breathes in England
Is life and lungs to every rebel birth
That passes out of embryo.
              Simon Renard!—
This Howard, whom they fear, what was he saying?
    Renard. What your imperial father said, my liege,
To deal with heresy gentlier. Gardiner burns,
And Bonner burns; and it would seem this people
Care more for our brief life in their wet land
Than yours in happier Spain. I told my lord
He should not vex her Highness; she would say
These are the means God works with, that His church
May flourish.
    Philip. Ay, sir, but in statesmanship
To strike too soon is oft to miss the blow.
Thou knowest I bade my chaplain, Castro, preach
Against these burnings.
    Renard.   And the Emperor
Approved you, and, when last he wrote, declared
His comfort in your Grace that you were bland
And affable to men of all estates,
In hope to charm them from their hate of Spain.
    Philip. In hope to crush all heresy under Spain.
But, Renard, I am sicker staying here
Than any sea could make me passing hence,
Tho' I be ever deadly sick at sea;
So sick am I with biding for this child.
Is it the fashion in this clime for women
To go twelve months in bearing of a child?
The nurses yawn'd, the cradle gaped, they led

Processions, chanted litanies, clash'd
    their bells,
Shot off their lying cannon, and her
    priests
Have preach'd, the fools, of this fair
    prince to come,
Till, by Saint James, I find myself the
    fool.
Why do you lift your eyebrow at me
    thus?
    Renard. I never saw your Highness
    moved till now.
    Philip. So weary am I of this wet
    land of theirs,
And every soul of man that breathes
    therein.
    Renard. My liege, we must not drop
    the mask before
The masquerade is over—
    Philip.   Have I dropt it?
I have but shown a loathing face to
    you,
Who knew it from the first.

Enter MARY.

    Mary (*aside*). With Renard. Still
Parleying with Renard, all the day
    with Renard,
And scarce a greeting all the day for
    me—
And goes to-morrow.   [*Exit* Mary.
    Philip (*to* Renard, *who advances to
    him*). Well, sir, is there more?
    Renard (*who has perceived the*
    Queen). May Simon Renard
    speak a single word?
    Philip. Ay.
    Renard.   And be forgiven for it?
    Philip.   Simon Renard
Knows me too well to speak a single
    word
That could not be forgiven.
    Renard.   Well, my liege,
Your Grace hath a most chaste and
    loving wife.
    Philip. Why not? The Queen of
    Philip should be chaste.
    Renard. Ay, but, my lord, you
    know what Virgil sings,
Woman is various and most mutable.
    Philip. She play the harlot! never.
    Renard.   No, sire, no,

Not dream'd of by the rabidest gos-
    peller.
There was a paper thrown into the
    palace,
'The King hath wearied of his barren
    bride.'
She came upon it, read it, and then
    rent it,
With all the rage of one who hates a
    truth
He cannot but allow. Sire, I would
    have you—
What should I say, I cannot pick my
    words—
Be somewhat less—majestic to your
    Queen.
    Philip. Am I to change my manners,
    Simon Renard,
Because these islanders are brutal
    beasts?
Or would you have me turn a son-
    neteer,
And warble those brief-sighted eyes
    of hers?
    Renard. Brief-sighted tho' they be,
    I have seen them, sire,
When you perchance were trifling
    royally
With some fair dame of court, sud-
    denly fill
With such fierce fire—had it been fire
    indeed
It would have burnt both speakers.
    Philip.   Ay, and then?
    Renard. Sire, might it not be policy
    in some matter
Of small importance now and then to
    cede
A point to her demand?
    Philip.   Well, I am going.
    Renard. For should her love when
    you are gone, my liege,
Witness these papers, there will not
    be wanting
Those that will urge her injury—
    should her love—
And I have known such women more
    than one—
Veer to the counterpoint, and jealousy
Hath in it an alchemic force to fuse
Almost into one metal love and
    hate,—

And she impress her wrongs upon her
    Council,
And these again upon her Parlia-
    ment—
We are not loved here, and would be
    then perhaps
Not so well holpen in our wars with
    France,
As else we might be—here she comes.

Enter MARY.

Mary.   O Philip!
Nay, must you go indeed?
    Philip.   Madam, I must.
    Mary. The parting of a husband
        and a wife
Is like the cleaving of a heart; one
    half
Will flutter here, one there.
    Philip.   You say true, Madam.
    Mary. The Holy Virgin will not
        have me yet
Lose the sweet hope that I may bear
    a prince.
If such a prince were born, and you
    not here!
    Philip. I should be here if such a
        prince were born.
    Mary. But must you go?
    Philip. Madam, you know my
        father,
Retiring into cloistral solitude
To yield the remnant of his years to
    heaven,
Will shift the yoke and weight of all
    the world
From off his neck to mine. We meet
    at Brussels.
But since mine absence will not be for
    long,
Your Majesty shall go to Dover with
    me,
And wait my coming back
    Mary.   To Dover? no,
I am too feeble. I will go to Green-
    wich,
So you will have me with you; and
    there watch
All that is gracious in the breath of
    heaven
Draw with your sails from our poor
    land and pass

And leave me, Philip, with my prayers
    for you.
    Philip. And doubtless I shall profit
        by your prayers.
    Mary. Methinks that would you
        tarry one day more—
The news was sudden—I could mould
    myself
To bear your going better; will you do
    it?
    Philip. Madam, a day may sink or
        save a realm.
    Mary. A day may save a heart from
        breaking too.
    Philip. Well, Simon Renard, shall
        we stop a day?
    Renard. Your Grace's business will
        not suffer, sire,
For one day more, so far as I can tell.
    Philip. Then one day more to please
        her Majesty.
    Mary. The sunshine sweeps across
        my life again.
O, if I knew you felt this parting,
    Philip,
As I do!
    Philip. By Saint James I do protest,
Upon the faith and honor of a Span-
    iard,
I am vastly grieved to leave your
    Majesty.
Simon, is supper ready?
    Renard.   Ay, my liege,
I saw the covers laying.
    Philip.   Let us have it.
                        [*Exeunt.*

ACT IV

SCENE I.—A ROOM IN THE PALACE
    MARY, CARDINAL POLE.

    Mary. What have you there?
    Pole.   So please your Majesty,
A long petition from the foreign exiles
To spare the life of Cranmer. Bishop
    Thrilby,
And my Lord Paget and Lord William
    Howard,
Crave, in the same cause, hearing of
    your Grace.

Hath he not written himself—infat-
uated—
To sue you for his life?
Mary.   His life? O, no;
Not sued for that—he knows it were
in vain.
But so much of the anti-papal leaven
Works in him yet, he hath pray'd me
not to sully
Mine own prerogative, and degrade
the realm
By seeking justice at a stranger's hand
Against my natural subject. King and
Queen,
To whom he owes his loyalty after
God,
Shall these accuse him to a foreign
prince?
Death would not grieve him more. I
cannot be
True to this realm of England and the
Pope
Together, says the heretic.
Pole.   And there errs;
As he hath ever err'd thro' vanity.
A secular kingdom is but as the body
Lacking a soul; and in itself a beast.
The Holy Father in a secular king-
dom
Is as the soul descending out of
heaven
Into a body generate.
Mary.   Write to him, then.
Pole. I will.
Mary. And sharply, Pole.
Pole. Here come the Cranmerites!

Enter THIRLBY, LORD PAGET, LORD WIL-
LIAM HOWARD.

Howard. Health to your Grace!
Good morrow, my Lord Car-
dinal;
We make our humble prayer unto
your Grace
That Cranmer may withdraw to for-
eign parts,
Or into private life within the realm.
In several bills and declarations,
madam,
He hath recanted all his heresies.
Paget. Ay, ay; if Bonner have not
forged the bills.   [*Aside.*

Mary. Did not More die, and
Fisher? he must burn.
Howard. He hath recanted, Madam.
Mary.   The better for him.
He burns in purgatory, not in hell.
Howard. Ay, ay, your Grace; but it
was never seen
That any one recanting thus at full,
As Cranmer hath, came to the fire on
earth.
Mary. It will be seen now, then.
Thrilby.   O madam, madam!
I thus implore you, low upon my
knees,
To reach the hand of mercy to my
friend.
I have err'd with him; with him I
have recanted.
What human reason is there why my
friend
Should meet with lesser mercy than
myself?
Mary. My lord of Ely, this. After a
riot
We hang the leaders, let their follow-
ing go.
Cranmer is head and father of these
heresies,
New learning as they call it; yea, may
God
Forget me at most need when I forget
Her foul divorce—my sainted mother
—No!—
Howard. Ay, ay, but mighty doc-
tors doubted there.
The Pope himself waver'd; and more
than one
Row'd in that galley—Gardiner to
wit,
Whom truly I deny not to have been
Your faithful friend and trusty coun-
cillor.
Hath not your Highness ever read his
book,
His tractate upon True Obedience,
Writ by himself and Bonner?
Mary.   I will take
Such order with all bad, heretical
books
That none shall hold them in his house
and live,
Henceforward. No, my lord.
Howard.   Then never read it.

The truth is here. Your father was a man
Of such colossal kinghood, yet so courteous,
Except when wroth, you scarce could meet his eye
And hold your own; and were he wroth indeed,
You held it less, or not at all. I say,
Your father had a will that beat men down;
Your father had a brain that beat men down—
   Pole. Not me, my lord.
   Howard.   No, for you were not here;
You sit upon this fallen Cranmer's throne;
And it would more become you, my Lord Legate,
To join a voice, so potent with her Highness,
To ours in plea for Cranmer than to stand
On naked self-assertion.
   Mary.   All your voices
Are waves on flint. The heretic must burn.
   Howard. Yet once he saved your Majesty's own life;
Stood out against the King in your behalf,
At his own peril.
   Mary.   I know not if he did;
And if he did I care not, my Lord Howard.
My life is not so happy, no such boon,
That I should spare to take a heretic priest's,
Who saved it or not saved. Why do you vex me?
   Paget. Yet to save Cranmer were to serve the Church,
Your Majesty's I mean; he is effaced,
Self-blotted out; so wounded in his honor,
He can but creep down into some dark hole
Like a hurt beast, and hide himself and die;
But if you burn him,—well, your Highness knows

The saying, 'Martyr's blood—seed of the Church.'
   Mary. Of the true Church; but his is none, nor will be.
You are too politic for me, my Lord Paget.
And if he have to live so loath'd a life,
It were more merciful to burn him now.
   Thirlby. O, yet relent! O, madam, if you knew him
As I do, ever gentle, and so gracious,
With all his learning—
   Mary.   Yet a heretic still.
His learning makes his burning the more just.
   Thirlby. So worshipt of all those that came across him;
The stranger at his hearth, and all his house—
   Mary. His children and his concubine, belike.
   Thirlby. To do him any wrong was to beget
A kindness from him, for his heart was rich,
Of such fine mould that if you sow'd therein
The seed of Hate, it blossom'd Charity.
   Pole. 'After his kind it costs him nothing,' there's
An old world English adage to the point.
These are but natural graces, my good bishop,
Which in the Catholic garden are as flowers,
But on the heretic dunghill only weeds.
   Howard. Such weeds make dunghills gracious.
   Mary.   Enough, my lords.
It is God's will, the Holy Father's will,
And Philip's will, and mine, that he should burn.
He is pronounced anathema.
   Howard.   Farewell, madam,
God grant you ampler mercy at your call
Than you have shown to Cranmer.
               [*Exeunt* Lords.
   Pole,   After this,

Your Grace will hardly care to over-
look
This same petition of the foreign
exiles
For Cranmer's life.
  Mary. Make out the writ to-night.
                             [*Exeunt.*

SCENE II

OXFORD. CRANMER IN PRISON.

  Cranmer. Last night, I dream'd the
    faggots were alight,
And that myself was fasten'd to the
    stake,
And found it all a visionary flame,
Cool as the light in old decaying
    wood;
And then King Harry look'd from out
    a cloud,
And bade me have good courage; and
    I heard
An angel cry, 'There is more joy in
    Heaven,'—
And after that, the trumpet of the
    dead.   [*Trumpets without.*
Why, there are trumpets blowing
    now; what is it?

Enter FATHER COLE.

  Cole. Cranmer, I come to question
    you again.
Have you remain'd in the true Cath-
    olic faith
I left you in?
  Cranmer. In the true Catholic faith,
By Heaven's grace, I am more and
    more confirm'd.
Why are the trumpets blowing, Father
    Cole?
  .*Cole.* Cranmer, it is decided by the
    Council
That you to-day should read your re-
    cantation
Before the people in Saint Mary's
    Church.
And there be many heretics in the
    town,
Who loathe you for your late return
    to Rome,

And might assail you passing through
    the street,
And tear you piecemeal; so you have
    a guard.
  Cranmer. Or seek to rescue me. I
    thank the Council.
  Cole. Do you lack any money?
  Cranmer.   Nay, why should I?
The prison fare is good enough for
    me.
  Cole. Ay, but to give the poor.
  Cranmer.   Hand it me, then!
I thank you.
  Cole. For a little space, farewell;
Until I see you in Saint Mary's
    Church.   [*Exit* Cole.
  Cranmer. It is against all precedent
    to burn
One who recants; they mean to par-
    don me.
To give the poor—they give the poor
    who die.
Well, burn me or not burn me I am
    fixt;
It is but a communion, not a mass,
A holy supper, not a sacrifice;
No man can make his Maker—Villa
    Garcia.

Enter VILLA GARCIA.

  Villa Garcia. Pray you write out
    this paper for me, Cranmer.
  Cranmer. Have I not writ enough
    to satisfy you?
  Villa Garcia. It is the last.
  Cranmer.   Give it me, then.
                   [*He writes.*
  Villa Garcia.   Now sign.
  Cranmer. I have sign'd enough, and
    I will sign no more.
  Villa Garcia. It is no more than
    what you have sign'd already,
The public form thereof.
  Cranmer.   It may be so;
I sign it with my presence, if I read it
  Villa Garcia. But this is idle of you
    Well, sir, well,
You are to beg the people to pray for
    you;
Exhort them to a pure and virtuous
    life;

Declare the Queen's right to the throne; confess
Your faith before all hearers; and retract
That Eucharistic doctrine in your book.
Will you not sign it now?
    Cranmer.   No, Villa Garcia,
I sign no more. Will they have mercy on me?
    Villa Garcia. Have you good hopes of mercy! So, farewell. [*Exit.*
    Cranmer. Good hopes, not theirs, have I that I am fixt,
Fixt beyond fall; however, in strange hours,
After the long brain-dazing colloquies,
And thousand-times recurring argument
Of those two friars ever in my prison,
When left alone in my despondency,
Without a friend, a book, my faith would seem
Dead or half-drown'd, or else swam heavily
Against the huge corruptions of the Church,
Monsters of mistradition, old enough
To scare me into dreaming. 'What am I,
Cranmer, against whole ages?' was it so,
Or am I slandering my most inward friend,
To veil the fault of my most outward foe—
The soft and tremulous coward in the flesh?
O higher, holier, earlier, purer church,
I have found thee and not leave thee any more.
It is but a communion, not a mass—
No sacrifice, but a life-giving feast!
(*Writes.*) So, so; this will I say—thus will I pray. [*Puts up the paper.*

Enter BONNER.

    Bonner. Good day, old friend; what, you look somewhat worn;
And yet it is a day to test your health

Even at the best. I scarce have spoken with you
Since when?—your degradation. At your trial
Never stood up a bolder man than you;
You would not cap the Pope's commissioner—
Your learning, and your stoutness, and your heresy,
Dumbfounded half of us. So, after that,
We had to dis-archbishop and unlord,
And make you simple Cranmer once again,
The common barber clipt your hair, and I
Scraped from your finger-prints the holy oil;
And worse than all, you had to kneel to *me;*
Which was not pleasant for you, Master Cranmer.
Now you, that would not recognize the Pope,
And you, that would not own the Real Presence,
Have found a real presence in the stake,
Which frights you back into the ancient faith;
And so you have recanted to the Pope.
How are the mighty fallen, Master Cranmer!
    Cranmer. You have been more fierce against the Pope than I;
But why fling back the stone he strikes me with?   [*Aside.*
O Bonner, if I ever did you kindness—
Power hath been given you to try faith by fire—
Pray you, remembering how yourself have changed,
Be somewhat pitiful, after I have gone,
To the poor flock—to women and to children—
That when I was archbishop held with me.
    Bonner. Ay—gentle as they call you—live or die!
Pitiful to this pitiful heresy?

I must obey the Queen and Council,
man.
Win thro' this day with honor to yourself,
And I'll say something for you—so—
good-bye.   [*Exit.*
  Cranmer. This hard coarse man of
old hath crouch'd to me
Till I myself was half ashamed for
him.

Enter THIRLBY.

Weep not, good Thirlby.
  Thirlby.   O, my lord, my lord!
My heart is no such block as Bonner's
is:
Who would not weep?
  Cranmer. Why do you so my-lord
me,
Who am disgraced?
  Thirlby. On earth; but saved in
heaven
By your recanting.
  Cranmer. Will they burn me,
Thirlby?
  Thirlby. Alas, they will! these
burnings will not help
The purpose of the faith; but my poor
voice
Against them is a whisper to the roar
Of a spring-tide.
  Cranmer. And they will surely burn
me?
  Thirlby. Ay; and besides will have
you in the church
Repeat your recantation in the ears
Of all men, to the saving of their
souls,
Before your execution. May God help
you
Thro' that hard hour!
  Cranmer. And may God bless you,
Thirlby!
Well, they shall hear my recantation
there.   [*Exit Thirlby.*
Disgraced, dishonor'd!—not by them,
indeed,
By mine own self—by mine own
hand!
O thin-skinn'd hand and jutting veins,
't was you

That sign'd the burning of poor Joan
of Kent;
But then she was a witch. You have
written much,
But you were never raised to plead for
Frith,
Whose dogmas I have reach'd. He was
deliver'd
To the secular arm to burn; and there
was Lambert;
Who can forsee himself? truly these
burnings,
As Thirlby says, are profitless to the
burners,
And help the other side. You shall
burn too,
Burn first when I am burnt.
Fire—inch by inch to die in agony!
Latimer
Had a brief end—not Ridley. Hooper
burn'd
Three-quarters of an hour. Will my
faggots
Be wet as his were? It is a day of rain.
I will not muse upon it.
My fancy takes the burner's part, and
makes
The fire seem even crueller than it is.
No, I not doubt that God will give me
strength,
Albeit I have denied Him.

Enter SOTO *and* VILLA GARCIA.

  Villa Garcia.   We are ready
To take you to Saint Mary's, Master
Cranmer.
  Cranmer. And I. Lead on; ye loose
me from my bonds.   [*Exeunt.*

SCENE III

ST. MARY'S CHURCH

COLE *in the Pulpit,* LORD WILLIAMS OF
THAME *presiding.* LORD WILLIAM
HOWARD, LORD PAGET, *and others.*
CRANMER *enters between* SOTO *and*
VILLA GARCIA, *and the whole Choir
strike up,* 'Nunc Dimittis.' CRAN-
MER *is set upon a Scaffold before
the people.*

Cole. Behold him—
    [*A pause: people in the fore-
      ground.*
People. O, unhappy sight!
First Protestant. See how the tears
    run down his fatherly face.
Second Protestant. James, didst
    thou ever see a carrion crow
Stand watching a sick beast before he
    dies?
    First Protestant. Him perch'd up
    there? I wish some thunder-
    bolt
Would make this Cole a cinder, pulpit
    and all.
    Cole. Behold him, brethren; he
    hath cause to weep!—
So have we all. Weep with him if ye
    will,
Yet—
It is expedient for one man to die,
Yea, for the people, lest the people
    die.
Yet wherefore should he die that hath
    return'd
To the one Catholic Universal
    Church,
Repentant of his errors?
    Protestant Murmurs. Ay, tell us
    that.
    Cole. Those of the wrong side will
    despise the man,
Deeming him one that thro' the fear
    of death
Gave up his cause, except he seal his
    faith
In the sight of all with flaming mar-
    tyrdom.
    Cranmer. Ay.
    Cole. Ye hear him, and albeit there
    may seem
According to the canons pardon due
To him that so repents, yet are there
    causes
Wherefore our Queen and Council at
    this time
Adjudge him to the death. He hath
    been a traitor,
A shaker and confounder of the
    realm;
And when the King's divorce was sued
    at Rome,
He here, this heretic metropolitan.

As if he had been the Holy Father, sat
And judged it. Did I call him heretic?
A huge heresiarch? never was it known
That any man so writing, preaching
    so,
So poisoning the Church, so long con-
    tinuing,
Hath found his pardon; therefore he
    must die,
For warning and example.
               Other reasons
There be for this man's ending, which
    our Queen
And Council at this present deem it
    not
Expedient to be known.
    Protestant Murmurs. I warrant
    you.
    Cole. Take therefore, all, example
    by this man,
For if our Holy Queen not pardon
    him,
Much less shall others in like cause
    escape,
That all of you, the highest as the
    lowest,
May learn there is no power against
    the Lord.
There stands a man, once of so high
    degree,
Chief prelate of our Church, arch-
    bishop, first
In Council, second person in the
    realm,
Friend for so long time of a mighty
    King;
And now ye see downfallen and de-
    based
From councillor to caitiff—fallen so
    low,
The leprous flutterings of the byway,
    scum
And offal of the city, would not change
Estates with him; in brief, so miser-
    able
There is no hope of better left for
    him,
No place for worse.
            Yet, Cranmer, be thou glad.
This is the work of God. He is glori-
    fied
In thy conversion; lo! thou art re-
    claim'd;

He brings thee home; nor fear but
    that to-day
Thou shalt receive the penitent thief's
    award,
And be with Christ the Lord in Para-
    dise
Remember how God made the fierce
    fire seem
To those three children like a pleasant
    dew.
Remember, too,
The triumph of Saint Andrew on his
    cross,
The patience of Saint Lawrence in the
    fire.
Thus, if thou call on God and all the
    Saints
God will beat down the fury of the
    flame,
Or give thee saintly strength to un-
    dergo.
And for thy soul shall masses here be
    sung
By every priest in Oxford. Pray for
    him.
    Cranmer. Ay, one and all, dear
    brothers, pray for me;
Pray with one breath, one heart, one
    soul for me.
    Cole. And now, lest any one among
    you doubt
The man's conversion and remorse of
    heart,
Yourselves shall hear him speak.
    Speak, Master Cranmer,
Fulfil your promise made me, and
    proclaim
Your true undoubted faith, that all
    may hear.
    Cranmer. And that I will. O God,
    Father of Heaven!
O Son of God, Redeemer of the
    world!
O Holy Ghost, proceeding from them
    both!
Three persons and one God, have
    mercy on me,
Most miserable sinner, wretched
    man!
I have offended against heaven and
    earth
More grievously than any tongue can
    tell.

Then whither should I flee for any
    help?
I am ashamed to lift my eyes to
    heaven,
And I can find no refuge upon earth.
Shall I despair then?—God forbid! O
    God,
For Thou art merciful, refusing none
That come to Thee for succor, unto
    Thee,
Therefore, I come; humble myself to
    Thee;
Saying, O Lord God, although my sins
    be great,
For Thy great mercy have mercy! O
    God the Son,
Not for slight faults alone, when Thou
    becamest
Man in the flesh, was the great mys-
    tery wrought;
O God the Father, not for little sins
Didst Thou yield up Thy Son to hu-
    man death!
But for the greatest sin that can be
    sinn'd,
Yea, even such as mine, incalculable,
Unpardonable,—sin against the light,
The truth of God, which I had proven
    and known.
Thy mercy must be greater than all
    sin.
Forgive me, Father, for no merit of
    mine,
But that Thy name by man be glori-
    fied,
And Thy most blessed Son's, who died
    for man.
    Good people, every man at time of
    death
Would fain set forth some saying that
    may live
After his death and better human-
    kind;
For death gives life's word a power to
    live,
And, like the stone-cut epitaph, re-
    main
After the vanish'd voice, and speak to
    men.
God grant me grace to glorify my
    God!
And first I say it is a grievous case,
Many so dote upon this bubble world,

Whose colors in a moment break and
  fly,
They care for nothing else. What
  saith Saint John?
'Love of this world is hatred against
  God.'
Again, I pray you all that, next to
  God,
You do unmurmuringly and willingly
Obey your King and Queen, and not
  for dread
Of these alone, but from the fear of
  Him
Whose ministers they be to govern
  you.
Thirdly, I pray you all to live together
Like brethren; yet what hatred Chris-
  tian men
Bear to each other, seeming not as
  brethren,
But mortal foes! But do you good to
  all
As much as in you lieth. Hurt no man
  more
Than you would harm your loving
  natural brother
Of the same roof, same breast. If any
  do,
Albeit he think himself at home with
  God,
Of this be sure, he is whole worlds
  away.
  Protestant Murmurs. What sort of
    brothers then be those that
    lust
To burn each other?
  Williams. Peace among you, there!
  Cranmer. Fourthly, to those that
    own exceeding wealth,
Remember that sore saying spoken
  once
By Him that was the truth, 'How hard
  it is
For the rich man to enter into
  heaven!'
Let all rich men remember that hard
  word.
I have not time for more; if ever, now
Let them flow forth in charity, seeing
  now
The poor so many, and all food so
  dear.

Long have I lain in prison, yet have
  heard
Of all their wretchedness. Give to the
  poor,
Ye give to God. He is with us in the
  poor.
  And now, and forasmuch as I have
    come
To the last end of life, and thereupon
Hangs all my past, and all my life to
  be,
Either to live with Christ in heaven
  with joy,
Or to be still in pain with devils in
  hell;
And, seeing in a moment I shall find
          [*Pointing upwards.*
Heaven or else hell ready to swallow
  me,
          [*Pointing downwards.*
I shall declare to you my very faith
Without all color.
  Cole.   Hear him, my good
    brethren.
  Cranmer. I do believe in God,
    Father of all;
In every article of the Catholic faith,
And every syllable taught us by our
  Lord,
His prophets, and apostles, in the
  Testaments,
Both Old and New.
  Cole. Be plainer, Master Cranmer.
  Cranmer. And now I come to the
    great cause that weighs
Upon my conscience more than any-
  thing
Or said or done in all my life by me;
For there be writings I have set
  abroad
Against the truth I knew within my
  heart,
Written for fear of death, to save my
  life,
If that might be; the papers by my
  hand
Sign'd since my degradation—by this
  hand
          [*Holding out his right hand.*
Written and sign'd—I here renounce
  them all;
And, since my hand offended, having
  written

Against my heart, my hand shall first
    be burnt,
So I may come to the fire.
                [*Dead silence.*

PROTESTANT MURMURS.

First Protestant. I knew it would
    be so.
Second Protestant. Our prayers are
    heard!
Third Protestant. God bless him!

CATHOLIC MURMURS.

      Out upon him! out upon him!
Liar! dissembler! traitor! to the fire!
  Williams (*raising his voice*). You
    know that you recanted all you
    said
Touching the sacrament in that same
    book
You wrote against my Lord of Win-
    chester;
Dissemble not; play the plain Chris-
    tian man.
  Cranmer. Alas, my lord,
I have been a man loved plainness all
    my life;
I *did* dissemble, but the hour has come
For utter truth and plainness; where-
    fore, I say,
I hold by all I wrote within that book.
Moreover,
As for the Pope, I count him Anti-
    christ,
With all his devil's doctrines, and re-
    fuse,
Reject him, and abhor him. I have
    said.
    [*Cries on all sides,* 'Pull him down!
    Away with him!'
  Cole. Ay, stop the heretic's mouth!
    Hale him away!
  Williams. Harm him not, harm him
    not! have him to the fire!
    [*Cranmer goes out between Two
    Friars, smiling; hands are
    reached to him from the
    crowd.* Lord William Howard
    and Lord Paget *are left alone
    in the church.*
  Paget. The nave and aisles all
    empty as a fool's jest!

No, here 's Lord William Howard.
    What my lord,
You have not gone to see the burning?
  Howard.   Fie!
To stand at ease, and stare as at a
    show,
And watch a good man burn. Never
    again.
I saw the deaths of Latimer and Rid-
    ley.
Moreover, tho' a Catholic, I would
    not,
For the pure honor of our common
    nature,
Hear what I might—another recanta-
    tion
Of Cranmer at the stake.
  Paget.   You'd not hear that.
He pass'd out smiling, and he walk'd
    upright;
His eye was like a soldier's, whom the
    general
He looks to and he leans on as his
    God,
Hath rated for some backwardness
    and bidden him
Charge one against a thousand, and
    the man
Hurls his soil'd life against the pikes
    and dies.
  Howard. Yet that he might not
    after all those papers
Of recantation yield again, who
    knows?
  Paget. Papers of recantation!
Think you then
That Cranmer read all papers that he
    sign'd?
Or sign'd all those they tell us that
    he sign'd?
Nay, I trow not; and you shall see,
    my Lord,
That howsoever hero-like the man
Dies in the fire, this Bonner or an-
    other
Will in some lying fashion misreport
    his ending to the glory of their
    church.
And you saw Latimer and Ridley die?
Latimer was eighty, was he not? his
    best
Of life was over then.
  Howard.   His eighty years

Look'd somewhat crooked on him in
    his frieze;
But after they had stript him to his
    shroud,
He stood upright, a lad of twenty-one,
And gather'd with his hands the start-
    ing flame,
And wash'd his hands and all his face
    therein,
Until the powder suddenly blew him
    dead.
Ridley was longer burning; but he
    died
As manfully and boldly, and, 'fore
    God,
I know them heretics, but right Eng-
    lish ones.
If ever, as heaven grant, we clash with
    Spain,
Our Ridley-soldiers and our Latimer-
    sailors
Will teach her something.
    Paget.   Your mild legate Pole
Will tell you that the devil helpt them
    thro' it.
    [*A murmur of the Crowd in the dis-
        tance.*
Hark, how those Roman wolf-dogs
    howl and bay him!
    Howard. Might it not be the other
    side rejoicing
In his brave end?
    Paget. They are too crush'd, too
    broken,
They can but weep in silence.
    Howard.   Ay, ay, Paget,
They have brought it in large meas-
    ure on themselves.
Have I not heard them mock the
    blessed Host
In songs so lewd the beast might roar
    his claim
To being in God's image, more than
    they?
Have I not seen the gamekeeper, the
    groom,
Gardener, and huntsman, in the par-
    son's place,
The parson from his own spire swung
    out dead,
And Ignorance crying in the streets,
    and all men

Regarding her? I say they have drawn
    the fire
On their own heads; yet, Paget, I do
    hold
The Catholic, if he have the greater
    right,
Hath been the crueller.
    Paget.   Action and reaction,
The miserable see-saw of our child-
    world,
Make us despise it at odd hours, my
    lord.
Heaven help that this reaction not re-
    act
Yet fiercelier under Queen Elizabeth
So that she come to rule us.
    Howard.   The world's mad.
    Paget. My Lord, the world is like a
    drunken man,
Who cannot move straight to his end,
    but reels
Now to the right, then as far to the
    left,
Push'd by the crowd beside—and un-
    derfoot
An earthquake; for since Henry for a
    doubt—
Which a young lust had clapt upon
    the back,
Crying, 'Forward!'—set our old
    church rocking, men
Have hardly known what to believe,
    or whether
They should believe in anything; the
    currents
So shift and change, they see not how
    they are borne,
Nor whither. I conclude the King a
    beast;
Verily a lion if you will—the world
A most obedient beast and fool—my-
    self
Half beast and fool as appertaining to
    it;
Altho' your lordship hath as little of
    each
Cleaving to your original Adam-clay
As may be consonant with mortality.
    Howard. We talk and Cranmer suf-
    fers.
The kindliest man I ever knew; see,
    see,

I speak of him in the past. Unhappy
    land!
Hard-natured Queen, half-Spanish in
    herself,
And grafted on the hard-grain'd stock
    of Spain—
Her life, since Philip left her, and she
    lost
Her fierce desire of bearing him a
    child,
Hath, like a brief and bitter winter's
    day,
Gone narrowing down and darkening
    to a close.
There will be more conspiracies, I
    fear.
    Paget. Ay, ay, beware of France.
    Howard.   O Paget, Paget!
I have seen heretics of the poorer sort,
Expectant of the rack from day to
    day,
To whom the fire were welcome, lying
    chain'd
In breathless dungeons over steaming
    sewers,
Fed with rank bread that crawl'd
    upon the tongue,
And putrid water, every drop a worm,
Until they died of rotted limbs; and
    then
Cast on the dunghill naked, and be-
    come
Hideously alive again from head to
    heel,
Made even the carrion-nosing mon-
    grel vomit
With hate and horror.
    Paget.   Nay, you sicken *me*
To hear you.
    Howard. Fancy-sick; these things
    are done,
Done right against the promise of this
    Queen
Twice given.
    Paget. No faith with heretics, my
    lord!
Hist! there be two old gossips—gos-
    pellers,
'I take it; stand behind the pillar here;
I warrant you they talk about the
    burning.

Enter TWO OLD WOMEN. JOAN, *and
    after her* TIB.

    Joan. Why, it be Tib!
    Tib. I cum behind tha, gall, and
could n't make tha hear. Eh, the wind
and the wet! What a day, what a day!
nigh upo' judgment daay loike.
Pwoaps be pretty things, Joan, but
they wunt set i' the Lord's cheer o'
that daay.
    Joan. I must set down myself, Tib;
it be a var waay vor my owld legs up
vro' Islip. Eh, my rheumatizy be that
bad howiver be I to win to the
burnin'?
    Tib. I should saay 't wur ower by
now. I'd ha' been here avore, but
Dumble wur blow'd wi' the wind, and
Dumble 's the best milcher in Islip.
    Joan. Our Daisy 's as good 'z her.
    Tib. Noa, Joan.
    Joan. Our Daisy's butter 's as good
'z hern.
    Tib. Noa, Joan.
    Joan. Our Daisy's cheeses be better.
    Tib. Noa, Joan.
    Joan. Eh, then ha' thy waay wi' me.
Tib; ez thou hast wi' thy owld man.
    Tib. Ay, Joan, and my owld man
wur up and away betimes wi' dree
hard eggs for a good pleace at the
burnin'; and barrin' the wet, Hodge
'ud ha' been a-harrowin' o' white pea-
sen i' the outfield—and barrin' the
wind, Dumble wur blow'd wi' the
wind, so 'z we was forced to stick her,
but we fetched her round at last.
Thank the Lord therevore. Dumble 's
the best milcher in Islip.
    Joan. Thou 's thy way wi' man and
beast, Tib. I wonder at tha, it beats
me! Eh, but I do know ez Pwoaps and
vires be bad things; tell 'ee now, I
heerd summat as summun towld summun o' owld Bishop Gardiner's end;
there wur an owld lord a-cum to dine
wi' un, and a wur so owld a could n't
bide vor his dinner, but a had to bide
howsomiver, vor 'I wunt dine,' says
my Lord Bishop, says he, 'not till I
hears ez Latimer and Ridley be

a-vire;' and so they bided on and on
till vour o' the clock, till his man cum
in post vro' here, and tells um ez the
vire has tuk holt. 'Now,' says the
Bishop, says he, 'we 'll gwo to dinner;'
and the owld lord fell to 's meat wi' a
will, God bless un! but Gardiner wur
struck down like by the hand o' God
avore a could taste a mossel, and a set
un all a-vire, so 'z the tongue on un
cum a-lolluping out o' 'is mouth as
black as a rat. Thank the Lord therevore!

Paget. The fools!

Tib. Ay, Joan; and Queen Mary
gwoes on a-burnin' and a-burnin', to
get her baaby born; but all her burnin's 'ill never burn out the hypocrisy
that makes the water in her. There's
nought but the vire of God's hell ez
can burn out that.

Joan. Thank the Lord therevore!

Paget. The fools!

Tib. A-burnin', and a-burnin', and
a-makin' o' volk madder and madder;
but tek thou my word vor 't, Joan,—
and I bean't wrong not twice i' ten
year—the burnin' o' the owld archbishop 'll burn the Pwoap out o' this
'ere land vor iver and iver.

Howard. Out of the church, you
    brace of cursed crones,
Or I will have you duck'd! (*Women
    hurry out.*) Said I not right?
For how should reverend prelate or
    throned prince
Brook for an hour such brute malig-
    nity?
Ah, what an acrid wine has Luther
    brew'd!

Paget. Pooh, pooh, my lord! poor
    garrulous country-wives.
Buy you their cheeses, and they'll side
    with you;
You cannot judge the liquor from the
    lees.

Howard. I think that in some sort
    we may. But see,

Enter PETERS.

Peters, my gentleman, an honest
    Catholic,

Who follow'd with the crowd to Cran-
    mer's fire.
One that would neither misreport nor
    lie,
Not to gain paradise; no, nor if the
    Pope
Charged him to do it—he is white as
    death.
Peters, how pale you look! you bring
    the smoke
Of Cranmer's burning with you.

Peters.   Twice or thrice
The smoke of Cranmer's burning
    wrapt me round.

Howard. Peters, you know me
    Catholic, but English.
Did he die bravely? Tell me that, or
    leave
All else untold.

Peters. My lord, he died most
    bravely.

Howard. Then tell me all.

Paget.   Ay, Master Peters, tell us.

Peters. You saw him how he past
    among the crowd;
And ever as he walk'd the Spanish
    friars
Still plied him with entreaty and re-
    proach;
But Cranmer, as the helmsman at the
    helm
Steers, ever looking to the happy
    haven
Where he shall rest at night, moved
    to his death;
And I could see that many silent
    hands
Came from the crowd and met his
    own; and thus,
When we had come where Ridley
    burnt with Latimer,
He, with a cheerful smile, as one
    whose mind
Is all made up, in haste put off the rags
They had mock'd his misery with,
    and all in white,
His long white beard, which he had
    never shaven
Since Henry's death, down-swooping
    to the chain
Wherewith they bound him to the
    stake, he stood

More like an ancient father of the
    Church
Than heretic of these times; and still
    the friars
Plied him, but Cranmer only shook
    his head,
Or answer'd them in smiling nega-
    tives;
Whereat Lord Williams gave a sudden
    cry:—
'Make short! make short!' and so
    they lit the wood.
Then Cranmer lifted his left hand to
    heaven,
And thrust his right into the bitter
    flame;
And crying, in his deep voice, more
    than once,
'This hath offended—this unworthy
    hand!'
So held it till it all was burn'd, before
The flame had reach'd his body; I
    stood near—
Mark'd him—he never uttered moan
    of pain.
He never stirr'd or writhed, but, like a
    statue,
Unmoving in the greatness of the
    flame,
Gave up the ghost; and so past mar-
    tyr-like—
Martyr I may not call him—past—
    but whither?
Paget. To purgatory, man, to pur-
    gatory.
Peters. Nay, but, my lord, he denied
    purgatory.
Paget. Why then to heaven, and
    God ha' mercy on him!
Howard. Paget, despite his fearful
    heresies,
I loved the man, and needs must moan
    for him;
O Cranmer!
Paget. But your moan is useless
    now.
Come out, my lord, it is a world of
    fools.   [*Exeunt.*

ACT V

SCENE I.—LONDON. HALL IN THE PALACE

QUEEN, SIR NICHOLAS HEATH.

Heath. Madam,
I do assure you that it must be look'd
    to.
Calais is but ill-garrison'd, in Guisnes
Are scarce two hundred men, and the
    French fleet
Rule in the narrow seas. It must be
    look'd to,
If war should fall between yourself
    and France;
Or you will lose your Calais.
Mary.   It shall be look'd to;
I wish you a good morning, good Sir
    Nicholas.
Here is the King.   [*Exit* Heath.

Enter PHILIP.

Philip. Sir Nicholas tells you true,
And you must look to Calais when I
    go.
Mary. Go? must you go, indeed—
    again—so soon?
Why, nature's licensed vagabond, the
    swallow,
That might live always in the sun's
    warm heart,
Stays longer here in our poor North
    than you—
Knows where he nested—ever comes
    again.
Philip. And, Madam, so shall I.
Mary.   O, will you? will you?
I am faint with fear that you will
    come no more.
Philip. Ay, ay; but many voices call
    me hence.
Mary. Voices—I hear unhappy ru-
    mors—nay,
I say not, I believe. What voices call
    you
Dearer than mine that should be dear-
    est to you?
Alas, my lord! what voices and how
    many?

Philip. The voices of Castile and
    Aragon,
Granada, Naples, Sicily, and Milan,—
The voices of Franche-Comté, and the
    Netherlands,
The voices of Peru and Mexico,
Tunis, and Oran, and the Philippines,
And all the fair spice-islands of the
    East.
    Mary (admiringly). You are the
    mightiest monarch upon earth,
I but a little Queen; and so, indeed,
Need you the more.
    Philip.   A little Queen! but when
I come to wed your majesty, Lord
    Howard,
Sending an insolent shot that dash'd
    the seas
Upon us, made us lower our kingly
    flag
To yours of England.
    Mary.   Howard is all English!
There is no king, not were he ten
    times king,
Ten times our husband, but must
    lower his flag
To that of England in the seas of
    England.
    Philip. Is that your answer?
    Mary.   Being Queen of England,
I have none other.
    Philip.   So.
    Mary.   But wherefore not
Helm the huge vessel of your State,
    my liege,
Here by the side of her who loves you
    most?
    Philip. No, madam, no! a candle in
    the sun
Is all but smoke—a star beside the
    moon
Is all but lost; your people will not
    crown me—
Your people are as cheerless as your
    clime.
Hate me and mine; witness the
    brawls, the gibbets.
Here swings a Spaniard—there an
    Englishman;
The peoples are unlike as their com-
    plexion;
Yet will I be your swallow and re-
    turn—

But now I cannot bide.
    Mary.   Not to help *me?*
They hate *me* also for my love to
    you,
My Philip; and these judgments on
    the land—
Harvestless autumns, horrible agues,
    plague—
    Philip. The blood and sweat of here-
    tics at the stake
Is God's best dew upon the barren
    field.
Burn more!
    Mary. I will, I will; and you will
    stay?
    Philip. Have I not said? Madam,
    I came to sue
Your Council and yourself to declare
    war.
    Mary. Sir, there are many English
    in your ranks
To help your battle.
    Philip.   So far, good. I say
I came to sue your Council and your-
    self
To declare war against the King of
    France.
    Mary. Not to see me?
    Philip.   Ay, madam, to see you.
Unalterably and pesteringly fond!
                   [*Aside.*
But soon or late you must have war
    with France;
King Henry warms your traitors at
    his hearth.
Carew is there, and Thomas Stafford
    there.
Courtenay, belike—
    Mary.   A fool and featherhead!
    Philip. Ay, but they use his name.
    In brief, this Henry
Stirs up your land against you to the
    intent
That you may lose your English heri-
    tage.
And then, your Scottish namesake
    marrying
The Dauphin, he would weld France,
    England, Scotland,
Into one sword to hack at Spain and
    me.
    Mary. And yet the Pope is now col-
    leagued with France;

You make your wars upon him down
   in Italy—
Philip, can that be well?

Philip.   Content you, madam;
You must abide my judgment, and
   my father's,
Who deems it a most just and holy
   war.
The Pope would cast the Spaniard out
   of Naples;
He calls us worse than Jews, Moors,
   Saracens.
The Pope has pushed his horns be-
   yond his mitre—
Beyond his province. Now,
Duke Alva will but touch him on the
   horns,
And he withdraws; and on his holy
   head—
For Alva is true son of the true
   Church—
No hair is harm'd. Will you not help
   me here?

Mary. Alas! the Council will not
   hear of war.
They say your wars are not the wars
   of England.
They will not lay more taxes on a
   land
So hunger-nipt and wretched; and you
   know
The crown is poor. We have given the
   church-lands back.
The nobles would not; nay, they clapt
   their hands
Upon their swords when ask'd; and
   therefore God
Is hard upon the people. What's to be
   done?
Sir, I will move them in your cause
   again,
And we will raise us loans and sub-
   sidies
Among the merchants; and Sir
   Thomas Gresham
Will aid us. There is Antwerp and the
   Jews.

Philip. Madam, my thanks.

Mary. And you will stay your going?

Philip. And further to discourage
   and lay lame
The plots of France, altho' you love
   her not,
You must proclaim Elizabeth your
   heir.
She stands between you and the Queen
   of Scots.

Mary. The Queen of Scots at least
   is Catholic.

Philip. Ay, madam, Catholic; but I
   will not have
The King of France the King of England too.

Mary. But she's a heretic, and, when
   I am gone,
Brings the new learning back.

Philip.   It must be done.
You must proclaim Elizabeth your
   heir.

Mary. Then it is done; but you will
   stay your going
Somewhat beyond your settled purpose?

Philip.   No!

Mary. What, not one day?

Philip.   You beat upon the rock.

Mary. And I am broken there.

Philip.   Is this a place
To wail in, madam? what! a public
   hall?
Go in, I pray you.

Mary.   Do not seen so changed.
Say go; but only say it lovingly.

Philip. You do mistake. I am not
   one to change.
I never loved you more.

Mary.   Sire, I obey you.
Come quickly.

Philip.   Ay.   [*Exit* Mary.

Enter COUNT DE FERIA

Feria (*aside*). The Queen in tears!

Philip.   Feria!
Hast thou not mark'd—come closer
   to mine ear—
How doubly aged this Queen of ours
   hath grown
Since she lost hope of bearing us a
   child?

Feria. Sire, if your Grace hath
   mark'd it, so have I.

Philip. Hast thou not likewise
   mark'd Elizabeth,

How fair and royal—like a queen, indeed?

Feria. Allow me the same answer as
before—
That if your Grace hath mark'd her,
so have I.

Philip. Good, now; methinks my
Queen is like enough
To leave me by and by.

Feria.   To leave you, sire?

Philip. I mean not like to live. Eliz-
abeth—
To Philibert of Savoy, as you know,
We meant to wed her; but I am not
sure
She will not serve me better—so my
Queen
Would leave me—as—my wife.

Feria.   Sire, even so.

Philip. She will not have Prince
Philibert of Savoy.

Feria. No, sire.

Philip.   I have to pray you, some
odd time,
To sound the Princess carelessly on
this;
Not as from me, but as your phantasy;
And tell me how she takes it.

Feria.   Sire, I will.

Philip. I am not certain but that
Philibert
Shall be the man; and I shall urge his
suit
Upon the Queen, because I am not
certain.
You understand, Feria.

Feria.   Sire, I do.

Philip. And if you be not secret in
this matter,
You understand me there, too?

Feria.   Sire, I do.

Philip. You must be sweet and supple, like a Frenchman.
She is none of those who loathe the
honeycomb.

[*Exit Feria.*

Enter RENARD.

Renard. My liege, I bring you
goodly tidings.

Philip.   Well?

Renard. There *will* be war with
France, at last, my liege;
Sir Thomas Stafford, a bull-headed
ass,
Sailing from France, with thirty Eng-
lishmen,
Hath taken Scarboro' Castle, north of
York;
Proclaims himself protector, and af-
firms
The Queen has forfeited her right to
reign
By marriage with an alien—other
things
As idle; a weak Wyatt! Little doubt
This buzz will soon be silenced; but
the Council—
I have talk'd with some already—are
for war.
This is the fifth conspiracy hatch'd in
France;
They show their teeth upon it; and
your Grace,
So you will take advice of mine, should
stay
Yet for a while, to shape and guide
the event.

Philip. Good! Renard, I will stay
then.

Renard.   Also, sire,
Might I not say—to please your wife,
the Queen?

Philip. Ay, Renard, if you care to
put it so.

[*Exeunt.*

SCENE II

A ROOM IN THE PALACE

MARY, *sitting: a rose in her hand.*
LADY CLARENCE. ALICE *in the background.*

Mary. Look! I have play'd with
this poor rose so long
I have broken off the head.

Lady Clarence.   Your Grace hath
been
More merciful to many a rebel head
That should have fallen, and may rise
again.

Mary. There were not many hang'd
  for Wyatt's rising.
Lady Clarence. Nay, not two hundred.
Mary.   I could weep for them
And her, and mine own self and all the
  world.
Lady Clarence. For her? for whom,
  your Grace?

Enter USHER.

Usher.   The Cardinal.
Enter CARDINAL POLE (MARY *rises*).
Mary. Reginald Pole, what news
  hath plagued thy heart?
What makes thy favor like the blood-
  less head
Fallen on the block, and held up by
  the hair?
Philip?—
Pole. No, Philip is as warm in life
As ever.
Mary. Ay, and then as cold as ever.
Is Calais taken?
Pole. Cousin, there hath chanced
A sharper harm to England and to
  Rome
Than Calais taken. Julius the Third
Was ever just, and mild, and father-
  like;
But this new Pope Caraffa, Paul the
  Fourth,
Not only reft me of that legateship
Which Julius gave me, and the legate-
  ship
Annex'd to Canterbury—nay, but
  worse—
And yet I must obey the Holy Father,
And so must you, good cousin;—
  worse than all,
A passing bell toll'd in a dying ear—
He hath cited me to Rome, for heresy,
Before his Inquisition.
Mary.   I knew it, cousin.
But held from you all papers sent by
  Rome,
That you might rest among us, till the
  Pope,
To compass which I wrote myself to
  Rome,
Reversed his doom, and that you
  might not seem

To disobey his Holiness.
Pole.   He hates Philip;
He is all Italian, and he hates the
  Spaniard;
He cannot dream that *I* advised the
  war;
He strikes thro' me at Philip and your-
  self.
Nay, but I know it of old, he hates
  me too;
So brands me in the stare of Christen-
  dom
A heretic!
Now, even now, when bow'd before
  my time,
The house half-ruin'd ere the lease be
  out;
When I should guide the Church in
  peace at home,
After my twenty years of banishment,
And all my lifelong labor to uphold
The primacy—a heretic! Long ago,
When I was ruler in the patrimony,
I was too lenient to the Lutheran,
And I and learned friends among our-
  selves
Would freely canvass certain Lu-
  theranisms.
What then, he knew I was no Lu-
  theran.
A heretic!
He drew this shaft against me to the
  head,
When it was thought I might be
  chosen Pope,
But then withdrew it. In full consis-
  tory,
When I was made archbishop, he ap-
  proved me.
And how should he have sent me legate
  hither,
Deeming me heretic? and what heresy
  since?
But he was evermore mine enemy,
And hates the Spaniard—fiery-chol-
  eric,
A drinker of black, strong, volcanic
  wines,
That ever made him fierier. I, a here-
  tic?
Your Highness knows that in pursu-
  ing heresy

I have gone beyond your late Lord
   Chancellor,—
He cried 'Enough! enough!' before
   his death,—
Gone beyond him and mine own nat-
   ural man—
It was God's cause—so far they call
   me now
The scourge and butcher of their Eng-
   lish church.
   Mary. Have courage, your reward
   is heaven itself.
   Pole. They groan amen; they swarm
   into the fire
Like flies—for what? no dogma. They
   know nothing;
They burn for nothing.
   Mary.   You have done your best.
   Pole. Have done my best, and as a
   faithful son,
That all day long hath wrought his
   father's work,
When back he comes at evening hath
   the door
Shut on him by the father whom he
   loved,
His early follies cast into his teeth,
And the poor son turn'd out into the
   street
To sleep, to die—I shall die of it,
   cousin.
   Mary. I pray you be not so discon-
   solate;
I still will do mine utmost with the
   Pope.
Poor cousin!
Have not I been the fast friend of
   your life
Since mine began, and it was thought
   we two
Might make one flesh, and cleave unto
   each other
As man and wife?
   Pole.   Ah, cousin, I remember
How I would dandle you upon my
   knee
At lisping-age. I watch'd you dancing
   once
With your huge father; he look'd the
   Great Harry,
You but his cockboat; prettily you did
   it,

And innocently. No—we were not
   made
One flesh in happiness, no happiness
   here;
But now we are made one flesh in mis-
   ery;
Our bridesmaids are not lovely—Dis-
   appointment,
Ingratitude, Injustice, Evil-tongue,
Labor-in-vain.
   Mary.   Surely, not all in vain.
Peace, cousin, peace! I am sad at
   heart myself.
   Pole. Our altar is a mound of dead
   men's clay,
Dug from the grave that yawns for us
   beyond;
And there is one Death stands behind
   the groom,
And there is one Death stands behind
   the bride—
   Mary. Have you been looking at the
   'Dance of Death'?
   Pole. No; but these libellous papers
   which I found
Strewn in your palace. Look you here
   —the Pope
Pointing at me with 'Pole, the heretic,
Thou hast burnt others, do thou burn
   thyself,
Or I will burn thee;' and this other;
   see!—
'We pray continually for the death
Of our accursed Queen and Cardinal
   Pole.'
This last—I dare not read it her.
                     [Aside.
   Mary.   Away!
Why do you bring me these?
I thought you knew me better. I never
   read,
I tear them; they come back upon my
   dreams.
The hands that write them should be
   burnt clean off
As Cranmer's, and the fiends that ut-
   ter them
Tongue-torn with pincers, lash'd to
   death, or lie
Famishing in black cells, while fam-
   ish'd rats
Eat them alive. Why do they bring
   me these?

Do you mean to drive me mad?

Pole. I had forgotten
How these poor libels trouble you.
Your pardon,
Sweet cousin, and farewell! 'O bubble world,
Whose colors in a moment break and fly!'
Why, who said that? I know not—true enough!
[*Puts up the papers, all but the last, which falls. Exit* Pole.

Alice. If Cranmer's spirit were a mocking one,
And heard these two, there might be sport for him. [*Aside.*

Mary. Clarence, they hate me; even while I speak
There lurks a silent dagger, listening
In some dark closet, some long gallery, drawn,
And panting for my blood as I go by.

Lady Clarence. Nay, madam, there be loyal papers too,
And I have often found them.

Mary. Find me one!

Lady Clarence. Ay, madam; but Sir Nicholas Heath, the Chancellor,
Would see your Highness.

Mary. Wherefore should I see him?

Lady Clarence. Well, Madam, he may bring you news from Philip.

Mary. So, Clarence.

Lady Clarence. Let me first put up your hair;
It tumbles all abroad.

Mary. And the gray dawn
Of an old age that never shall be mine
Is all the clearer seen. No, no; what matters?
Forlorn I am, and let me look forlorn.
Enter SIR NICHOLAS HEATH.

Heath. I bring your Majesty such grievous news
I grieve to bring it. Madam, Calais is taken.

Mary. What traitor spoke? Here, let him my cousin Pole
Seize him and burn him for a Lutheran.

Heath. Her highness is unwell. I will retire.

Lady Clarence. Madam, your Chancellor, Sir Nicholas Heath.

Mary. Sir Nicholas! I am stunn'd
—Nicholas Heath?
Methought some traitor smote me on the head.
What said you, my good lord, that our brave English
Had sallied out from Calais and driven back
The Frenchmen from their trenches?

Heath. Alas! no.
That gateway to the mainland over which
Our flag hath floated for two hundred years
Is France again.

Mary. So; but it is not lost—
Not yet. Send out; let England as of old
Rise lionlike, strike hard and deep into
The prey they are rending from her—ay, and rend
The renders too. Send out, send out, and make
Musters in all the counties; gather all
From sixteen years to sixty; collect the fleet;
Let every craft that carries sail and gun
Steer toward Calais. Guisnes is not taken yet?

Heath. Guisnes is not taken yet.

Mary. There yet is hope.

Heath. Ah, madam, but your people are so cold;
I do much fear that England will not care.
Methinks there is no manhood left among us.

Mary. Send out; I am too weak to stir abroad.
Tell my mind to the Council—to the Parliament;
Proclaim it to the winds. Thou art cold thyself
To babble of their coldness. O, would I were
My father for an hour! Away now—quick! [*Exit* Heath.

I hoped I had served God with all my
    might!
It seems I have not. Ah! much heresy
Shelter'd in Calais. Saints, I have re-
    built
Your shrines, set up your broken im-
    ages;
Be comfortable to me. Suffer not
That my brief reign in England be de-
    famed
Thro' all her angry chronicles here-
    after
By loss of Calais. Grant me Calais.
    Philip,
We have made war upon the Holy
    Father
All for your sake. What good could
    come of that?
    Lady Clarence. No, Madam, not
    against the Holy Father;
You did but help King Philip's war
    with France,
Your troops were never down in
    Italy.
    Mary. I am a byword. Heretic and
    rebel
Point at me and make merry. Philip
    gone!
And Calais gone! Time that I were
    gone too!
    Lady Clarence. Nay, if the fetid
    gutter had a voice
And cried I was not clean, what should
    I care?
Or you, for heretic cries? And I be-
    lieve,
Spite of your melancholy Sir Nicholas,
Your England is as loyal as myself.
    Mary (*seeing the paper dropt by*
    Pole). There! there! another
    paper! Said you not
Many of these were loyal? Shall I
    try
If this be one of such?
    Lady Clarence.   Let it be, let it be.
God pardon me! I have never yet
    found one.   [*Aside.*
    Mary (*reads*). 'Your people hate
    you as your husband hates
    you.'
Clarence, Clarence, what have I done?
    what sin

Beyond all grace, all pardon? Mother
    of God,
Thou knowest never woman meant so
    well,
And fared so ill in this disastrous
    world.
My people hate me and desire my
    death.
    Lady Clarence. No, madam, no.
    Mary. My husband hates me, and
    desires my death.
    Lady Clarence. No, madam; these
    are libels.
    Mary. I hate myself, and I desire
    my death.
    Lady Clarence. Long live your Maj-
    esty!
    Shall Alice sing you
One of her pleasant songs? Alice, my
    child,
Bring us your lute (Alice *goes*). They
    say the gloom of Saul
Was lighten'd by young David's harp.
    Mary.   Too young!
And never knew a Philip.

        Re-enter ALICE.

               Give *me* the lute.
He hates me!
      (*She sings.*)
Hapless doom of woman happy in be-
    trothing!
Beauty passes like a breath, and love is
    lost in loathing.
Low, my lute; speak low, my lute, but
    say the world is nothing—
    Low, lute, low!
Love will hover round the flowers when
    they first awaken;
Love will fly the fallen leaf, and not be
    overtaken.
Low, my lute! O, low, my lute! we fade
    and are forsaken—
    Low, dear lute, low!

Take it away! not low enough for me!
    Alice. Your Grace hath a low voice.
    Mary.   How dare you say it?
Even for that he hates me. A low voice
Lost in a wilderness where none can
    hear!
A voice of shipwreck on a shoreless
    sea!

A low voice from the dust and from
the grave!
(*Sitting on the ground*). There, am I
low enough now?
Alice. Good Lord! how grim and
ghastly looks her Grace,
With both her knees drawn upward to
her chin.
There was an old-world tomb beside
my father's,
And this was open'd, and the dead
were found
Sitting, and in this fashion; she looks
a corpse.

Enter LADY MAGDALEN DACRES.

Lady Magdalen. Madam, the Count
de Feria waits without,
In hopes to see your Highness.
Lady Clarence (*pointing to* Mary).
Wait he must—
Her trance again. She neither sees nor
hears,
And may not speak for hours.
Lady Magdalen. Unhappiest
Of queens and wives and women!
Alice (*in the foreground with* Lady
Magdalen). And all along
Of Philip.
Lady Magdalen. Not so loud! Our
Clarence there
Sees ever such an aureole round the
Queen,
It gilds the greatest wronger of her
peace,
Who stands the nearest to her.
Alice. Ay, this Philip;
I used to love the Queen with all my
heart—
God help me, but methinks I love her
less
For such a dotage upon such a man.
I would I were as tall and strong as
you.
Lady Magdalen. I seem half-
shamed at times to be so tall.
Alice. You are the stateliest deer in
all the herd—
Beyond his aim—but I am small and
scandalous,
And love to hear bad tales of Philip.
Lady Magdalen. Why?

I never heard him utter worse of you
Than that you were low-statured.
Alice. Does he think
Low stature is low nature, or all
women's
Low as his own?
Lady Magdalen. There you strike
in the nail.
This coarseness is a want of phan-
tasy.
It is the low man thinks the woman
low;
Sin is too dull to see beyond himself.
Alice. Ah, Magdalen, sin is bold as
well as dull.
How dared he?
Lady Magdalen. Stupid soldiers oft
are bold.
Poor lads, they see not what the gen-
eral sees,
A risk of utter ruin. I am *not*
Beyond his aim, or was not.
Alice. Who? Not you?
Tell, tell me; save my credit with
myself.
Lady Magdalen. I never breathed
it to a bird in the eaves,
Would not for all the stars and maiden
moon
Our drooping Queen should know! In
Hampton Court
My window look'd upon the corridor;
And I was robing;—this poor throat
of mine
Barer than I should wish a man to
see it,—
When he we speak of drove the win-
dow back,
And, like a thief, push'd in his royal
hand;
But by God's providence a good
stout staff
Lay near me, and you know me strong
of arm.
I do believe I lamed his Majesty's
For a day or two, tho', give the devil
his due,
I never found he bore me any spite.
Alice. I would she could have
wedded that poor youth,
My Lord of Devon,—light enough,
God knows,

And mixt with Wyatt's rising,—and
   the boy
Not out of him—but neither cold,
   coarse, cruel,
And more than all—no Spaniard.
   Lady Clarence.   Not so loud.
Lord Devon, girls! what are you whis-
   pering here?
   Alice. Probing an old state-secret—
   how it chanced
That this young earl was sent on for-
   eign travel,
Not lost his head.
   Lady Clarence. There was no proof
   against him.
   Alice. Nay, madam; did not Gar-
   diner intercept
A letter which the Count de Noailles
   wrote
To that dead traitor Wyatt, with full
   proof
Of Courtenay's treason? What be-
   came of that?
   Lady Clarence. Some say that Gar-
   diner, out of love for him,
Burnt it, and some relate that it was
   lost
When Wyatt sack'd the Chancellor's
   house in Southwark.
Let dead things rest.
   Alice. Ay, and with him who died
Alone in Italy.
   Lady Clarence. Much changed, I
   hear,
Had put off levity and put graveness
   on.
The foreign courts report him in his
   manner
Noble as his young person and old
   shield.
It might be so—but all is over now;
He caught a chill in the lagoons of
   Venice,
And died in Padua.
   Mary (looking up suddenly). Died
   in the true faith?
   Lady Clarence. Ay, madam, happily.
   Mary.   Happier he than I.
   Lady Magdalen. It seems her High-
   ness hath awaken'd. Think you
That I might dare to tell her that the
   count—

   Mary. I will see no man hence for
   evermore.
Saving my confessor and my cousin
   Pole.
   Lady Magdalen. It is the Count de
   Feria, my dear lady.
   Mary. What count?
   Lady Magdalen. The Count de Fe-
   ria, from his Majesty
King Philip.
   Mary. Philip! quick! loop up my
   hair!
Throw cushions on that seat, and
   make it thronelike.
Arrange my dress—the gorgeous In-
   dian shawl
That Philip brought me in our happy
   days!—
That covers all. So—am I somewhat
   queenlike,
Bride of the mightiest sovereign upon
   earth?
   Lady Clarence. Ay, so your Grace
   would bide a moment yet.
   Mary. No, no, he brings a letter. I
   may die
Before I read it. Let me see him at
   once.

   Enter COUNT DE FERIA *(kneels).*

   Feria. I trust your Grace is well.
   (Aside.) How her hand burns!
   Mary. I am not well, but it will
   better me,
Sir Count, to read the letter which you
   bring.
   Feria. Madam, I bring no letter.
   Mary.   How! no letter?
   Feria. His Highness is so vex'd with
   strange affairs—
   Mary. That his own wife is no affair
   of his.
   Feria. Nay, madam, nay! he sends
   his veriest love,
And says he will come quickly.
   Mary.   Doth he, indeed?
You, sir, do *you* remember what *you*
   said
When last you came to England?
   Feria.   Madam, I brought
My King's congratulations; it was
   hoped

Your Highness was once more in
    happy state
To give him an heir male.
    Mary.   Sir, you said more;
You said he would come quickly. I
    had horses
On all the road from Dover, day and
    night;
On all the road from Harwich, night
    and day;
But the child came not, and the hus-
    band came not;
And yet he will come quickly.—Thou
    hast learnt
Thy lesson, and I mine. There is no
    need
For Philip so to shame himself again.
    Return,
And tell him that I know he comes no
    more.
Tell him at last I know his love is
    dead,
And that I am in state to bring forth
    death—
Thou art commission'd to Elizabeth,
And not to me!
    Feria. Mere compliments and
    wishes.
But shall I take some message from
    your Grace?
    Mary. Tell her to come and close
    my dying eyes,
And wear my crown, and dance upon
    my grave.
    Feria. Then I may say your Grace
    will see your sister?
Your Grace is too low-spirited. Air
    and sunshine.
I would we had you, madam, in our
    warm Spain.
You droop in your dim London.
    Mary.   Have him away!
I sicken of his readiness.
    Lady Clarence.   My Lord Count,
Her Highness is too ill for colloquy.
    Feria (*kneels and kisses her hand*).
    I wish her Highness better.
    (*Aside.*) How her hand burns!
                  [*Exeunt*

SCENE III

A HOUSE NEAR LONDON

ELIZABETH, STEWARD OF THE HOUSE-
HOLD ATTENDANTS.

    Elizabeth. There's half an angel
    wrong'd in your account;
Methinks I am all angel, that I bear it
Without more ruffling. Cast it o'er
    again.
    Steward. I were whole devil if I
    wrong'd you, madam.
              [*Exit* Steward.
    Attendant. The Count de Feria,
    from the King of Spain.
    Elizabeth. Ah!—let him enter. Nay,
    you need not go:
             [*To her* Ladies.
Remain within the chamber, but
    apart.
We'll have no private conference.
    Welcome to England!

Enter FERIA.

    Feria. Fair island star!
    Elizabeth. I shine! What else, Sir
    Count?
    Feria. As far as France, and into
    Philip's heart.
My King would know if you be fairly
    served,
And lodged, and treated.
    Elizabeth.   You see the lodging, sir.
I am well-served, and am in every-
    thing
Most loyal and most grateful to the
    Queen.
    Feria. You should be grateful to my
    master, too.
He spoke of this; and unto him you
    owe
That Mary hath acknowledged you
    her heir.
    Elizabeth. No, not to her nor him;
    but to the people,
Who know my right, and love me, as
    I love
The people! whom God aid!
    Feria.   You will be Queen,
And, were I Philip—

Elizabeth. Wherefore pause you—
    what?
Feria. Nay, but I speak from mine
    own self, not him.
Your royal sister cannot last; your
    hand
Will be much coveted! What a deli-
    cate one!
Our Spanish ladies have none such—
    and there,
Were you in Spain, this fine fair gos-
    samer gold—
Like sun-gilt breathings on a frosty
    dawn—
That hovers round your shoulder—
    Elizabeth.   Is it so fine?
Troth, some have said so.
Feria. —would be deemed a mir-
    acle.
Elizabeth. Your Philip hath gold
    hair and golden beard;
There must be ladies many with hair
    like mine.
Feria. Some few of Gothic blood
    have golden hair,
But none like yours.
    Elizabeth. I am happy you approve
    it.
Feria. But as to Philip and your
    Grace,—consider,—
If such a one as you should match
    with Spain,
What hinders but that Spain and Eng-
    land join'd
Should make the mightiest empire
    earth has known.
Spain would be England on her seas,
    and England
Mistress of the Indies.
    Elizabeth. It may chance that
    England
Will be the Mistress of the Indies yet,
Without the help of Spain.
    Feria.   Impossible;
Except you put Spain down.
Wide of the mark even for a mad-
    man's dream.
    Elizabeth. Perhaps; but we have
    seamen. Count de Feria.
I take it that the King hath spoken to
    you;
But is Don Carlos such a goodly
    match?

Feria. Don Carlos, Madam, is but
    twelve years old.
    Elizabeth. Ay, tell the King that I
    will muse upon it;
He is my good friend, and I would
    keep him so;
But—he would have me Catholic of
    Rome,
And that I scarce can be; and, sir, till
    now
My sister's marriage, and my father's
    marriages,
Make me full fain to live and die a
    maid.
But I am much beholden to your King.
Have you aught else to tell me?
    Feria.   Nothing, Madam,
Save that methought I gather'd from
    the Queen
That she would see your Grace before
    she—died.
    Elizabeth. God's death! and where-
    fore spake you not before?
We dally with our lazy moments here,
And hers are number'd. Horses there,
    without!
I am much beholden to the King, your
    master.
Why did you keep me prating?
    Horses, there!
            [*Exit* Elizabeth, *etc.*
Feria. So from a clear sky falls the
    thunderbolt!
Don Carlos? Madam, if you marry
    Philip,
Then I and he will snaffle your 'God's
    death,'
And break your paces in, and make
    you tame.
God's death, forsooth—you do not
    know King Philip!   [*Exit.*

SCENE IV

LONDON. BEFORE THE PALACE

A light burning within. Voices *of the
night passing.*

    First. Is not yon light in the Queen's
    chamber?
    Second.   Ay,

They say she's dying.

First.   So is Cardinal Pole.
May the great angels join their wings,
     and make
Down for their heads to heaven!

Second.   Amen. Come on.
                              [*Exeunt.*

TWO OTHERS.

First. There's the Queen's light. I
     hear she cannot live.
Second. God curse her and her le-
     gate! Gardiner burns
Already; but to pay them full in kind,
The hottest hold in all the devil's den
Were but a sort of winter. Sir, in
     Guernsey,
I watch'd a woman burn; and in her
     agony
The mother came upon her—a child
     was born—
And, sir, they hurl'd it back into the
     fire,
That, being but baptized in fire, the
     babe
Might be in fire for ever. Ah, good
     neighbor,
There should be something fierier
     than fire
To yield them their deserts.

First.   Amen to all
Your wish, and further!

A Third Voice. Deserts! Amen to
what? Whose deserts? Yours? You
have a gold ring on your finger, and
soft raiment about your body; and is
not the woman up yonder sleeping
after all she has done, in peace and
quietness, on a soft bed, in a closed
room, with light, fire, physic, tendance; and I have seen the true men
of Christ lying famine-dead by scores,
and under no ceiling but the cloud that
wept on them, not for them.

First. Friend, tho' so late, it is not
safe to preach.
You had best go home. What are you?

Third. What am I? One who cries
continually with sweat and tears to
the Lord God that it would please
Him out of His infinite love to break
down all kingship and queenship, all

priesthood and prelacy; to cancel and
abolish all bonds of human alleigance,
all the magistracy, all the nobles, and
all the wealthy; and to send us again,
according to His promise, the one
King, the Christ, and all things in
common, as in the day of the first
church, when Christ Jesus was King.

First. If ever I heard a madman,—
     let's away!
Why, you long-winded—Sir, you go
     beyond me.
I pride myself on being moderate.
Good night! Go home! Besides, you
     curse so loud,
The watch will hear you. Get you
     home at once.   [*Exeunt.*

SCENE V

LONDON. A ROOM IN THE PALACE

*A Gallery on one side. The moonlight
streaming through a range of win-
dows on the wall opposite.* MARY,
LADY CLARENCE, LADY MAGDALEN
DACRES, ALICE. QUEEN *pacing the
Gallery. A writing-table in front.*
QUEEN *comes to the table and
writes and goes again, pacing the
Gallery.*

Lady Clarence. Mine eyes are dim:
     what hath she written? -read.
Alice. 'I am dying, Philip; come to
     me.'
Lady Magdalen. There—up and
     down, poor lady, up and down.
Alice. And how her shadow crosses
     one by one
The moonlight casements pattern'd
     on the wall,
Following her like her sorrow! She
     turns again.
     [*Queen sits and writes, and goes
     again.*
Lady Clarence. What hath she
     written now?
Alice. Nothing; but 'come, come,
     come,' and all awry,
And blotted by her tears. This can-
     not last.   [*Queen returns.*

Mary. I whistle to the bird has broken cage,
And all in vain.   [*Sitting down.*
Calais gone—Guisnes gone, too—and Philip gone!

Lady Clarence. Dear madam, Philip is but at the wars;
I cannot doubt but that he comes again;
And he is with you in a measure still.
I never look'd upon so fair a likeness
As your great King in armor there, his hand
Upon his helmet.
          [*Pointing to the portrait of Philip on the wall.*

Mary.   Doth he not look noble?
I had heard of him in battle over seas,
And I would have my warrior all in arms.
He said it was not courtly to stand helmeted
Before the Queen. He had his gracious moment,
Altho' you'll not believe me. How he smiles
As if he loved me yet!

Lady Clarence.   And so he does.

Mary. He never loved me—nay, he could not love me.
It was his father's policy against France.
I am eleven years older than he,
Poor boy!   [*Weeps.*

Alice. That was a lusty boy of twenty-seven;   [*Aside.*
Poor enough in God's grace!

Mary.   And all in vain!
The Queen of Scots is married to the Dauphin,
And Charles, the lord of this low world, is gone;
And all his wars and wisdoms past away;
And in a moment I shall follow him.

Lady Clarence. Nay, dearest lady, see your good physician.

Mary. Drugs—but he knows they cannot help me—says
That rest is all—tells me I must not think—
That I must rest—I shall rest by and by.

Catch the wild cat, cage him, and when he springs
And maims himself against the bars, say 'rest.'
Why, you must kill him if you would have him rest—
Dead or alive, you cannot make him happy.

Lady Clarence. Your Majesty has lived so pure a life,
And done such mighty things by Holy Church,
I trust that God will make you happy yet.

Mary. What is the strange thing happiness? Sit down here.
Tell me thine happiest hour.

Lady Clarence.   I will, if that
May make your Grace forget yourself a little.
There runs a shallow brook across our field
For twenty miles, where the black crow flies five,
And doth so bound and babble all the way
As if itself were happy. It was May-time,
And I was walking with the man I loved.
I loved him, but I thought I was not loved.
And both were silent, letting the wild brook
Speak for us—till he stoop'd and gather'd one
From out a bed of thick forget-me-nots,
Look'd hard and sweet at me, and gave it me.
I took it, tho' I did not know I took it,
And put it in my bosom, and all at once
I felt his arms about me, and his lips—

Mary. O God! I have been too slack, too slack;
There are Hot Gospellers even among our guards—
Nobles we dared not touch. We have but burnt
The heretic priest, workmen, and women and children.

Wet, famine, ague, fever, storm,
    wreck, wrath,—
We have so play'd the coward; but by
    God's grace,
We'll follow Philip's leading, and set
    up
The Holy Office here—garner the
    wheat,
And burn the tares with unquenchable
    fire!
Burn!—
Fie, what a savor! tell the cooks to
    close
The doors of all the offices below.
Latimer!
Sir, we are private with our women
    here—
Ever a rough, blunt, and uncourtly
    fellow—
Thou light a torch that never will go
    out!
'Tis out—mine flames. Women, the
    Holy Father
Has ta'en the legateship from our
    cousin Pole—
Was that well done? and poor Pole
    pines of it,
As I do, to the death. I am but a
    woman,
I have no power.—Ah, weak and
    meek old man,
Sevenfold dishonor'd even in the
    sight
Of thine own sectaries—No, no. No
    pardon!—
Why, that was false; there is the right
    hand still
Beckons me hence.
Sir, you were burnt for heresy, not for
    treason,
Remember that! 't was I and Bonner
    did it,
And Pole; we are three to one—Have
    you found mercy there,
Grant it me here—and see, he smiles
    and goes,
Gentle as in life.
    Alice. Madam, who goes? King
Philip?
    Mary. No, Philip comes and goes,
    but never goes.
Women, when I am dead,

Open my heart, and there you will
    find written
Two names, Philip and Calais; open
    his,—
So that he have one,—
You will find Philip only, policy, pol-
    icy,—
Ay, worse than that—not one hour
    true to me!
Foul maggots crawling in a fester'd
    vice!
Adulterous to the very heart of hell!
Hast thou a knife?
    Alice. Ay, madam, but o' God's
        mercy—
    Mary. Fool, think'st thou I would
        peril mine own soul
By slaughter of the body? I could
    not, girl,
Not this way—callous with a con-
    stant stripe,
Unwoundable. The knife!
    Alice.   Take heed, take heed!
The blade is keen as death.
    Mary.   This Philip shall not
Stare in upon me in my haggardness;
Old, miserable, diseased,
Incapable of children. Come thou
    down.
    [*Cuts out the picture and throws
        it down.*
Lie there. (*Wails.*) O God, I have
    kill'd my Philip!
    Alice.   No,
Madam, you have but cut the canvas
    out;
We can replace it.
    Mary.   All is well then; rest—
I will to rest; he said I must have
    rest.
    [*Cries of* 'Elizabeth' *in the street.*
A cry! What's that? Elizabeth? re-
    volt?
A new Northumberland, another
    Wyatt?
I'll fight it on the threshold of the
    grave.
    Lady Clarence. Madam, your royal
    sister comes to see you.
    Mary. I will not see her.
Who knows if Boleyn's daughter be
    my sister?

I will see none except the priest. Your
    arm.   [*To* Lady Clarence.
O Saint of Aragon, with that sweet
    worn smile
Among thy patient wrinkles—help me
    hence.   [*Exeunt.*

The PRIEST *passes. Enter* ELIZABETH
and SIR WILLIAM CECIL.

  Elizabeth. Good counsel yours.—
    No one in waiting? still,
As if the chamberlain were Death
    himself!
The room she sleeps in—is not this
    the way?
No, that way there are voices. Am I
    too late?
Cecil . . . God guide me lest I lose
    the way!   [*Exit* Elizabeth.
  Cecil. Many points weather'd, many
    perilous ones,
At last a harbor opens; but therein
Sunk rocks—they need fine steering—
    much it is
To be nor mad nor bigot—have a
    mind—
Nor let priests' talk, or dream of
    worlds to be,
Miscolor things about her—sudden
    touches
For him, or him—sunk rocks; no pas-
    sionate faith—
But—if let be—balance and com-
    promise;
Brave, wary, sane to the heart of her
    —a Tudor
School'd by the shadow of death—a
    Boleyn, too,
Glancing across the Tudor—not so
    well.

       Enter ALICE.

How is the good Queen now?
  Alice.   Away from Philip.
Back in her childhood—prattling to
    her mother
Of her betrothal to the Emperor
    Charles,
And childlike-jealous of him again—
    and once
She thank'd her father sweetly for his
    book

Against that godless German. Ah,
    those days
Were happy. It was never merry
    world
In England since the Bible came
    among us.
  Cecil. And who says that?
  Alice. It is a saying among the
    Catholics.
  Cecil. It never will be merry world
    in England
Till all men have their Bible, rich and
    poor.
  Alice. The Queen is dying, or you
    dare not say it.

      Enter ELIZABETH.

  Elizabeth. The Queen is dead.
  Cecil. Then here she stands! my
    homage.
  Elizabeth. She knew me, and ac-
    knowledge me her heir,
Pray'd me to pay her debts, and keep
    the Faith;
Then claspt the cross, and pass'd away
    in peace.
I left her lying still and beautiful,
More beautiful than in life. Why
    would you vex yourself,
Poor sister? Sir, I swear I have no
    heart
To be your Queen. To reign is restless
    fence,
Tierce, quart, and trickery. Peace is
    with the dead,
Her life was winter, for her spring was
    nipt;
And she loved much: pray God she be
    forgiven!
  Cecil. Peace with the dead, who
    never were at peace!
Yet she loved one so much—I needs
    must say—
That never English monarch dying
    left
England so little.
  Elizabeth.   But with Cecil's aid
And others, if our person be secured
From traitor stabs—we will make
    England great.

Enter PAGET, *and other* LORDS OF THE COUNCIL, SIR RALPH BAGENHALL, *etc.*

    Lords. God save Elizabeth, the Queen of England!

Bagenhall. God save the Crown! the Papacy is no more.

Paget (aside). Are we so sure of that?

Acclamation. God save the Queen!

HAROLD

A DRAMA

TO HIS EXCELLENCY

THE RIGHT HON. LORD LYTTON,

VICEROY AND GOVERNOR-GENERAL OF INDIA.

MY DEAR LORD LYTTON,—After old-world records—such as Bayeux tapestry and the Roman de Rou,—Edward Freeman's History of the Norman Conquest, and your father's Historical Romance treating of the same times, have been mainly helpful to me in writing this Drama. Your father dedicated his 'Harold' to my father's brother; allow me to dedicate my 'Harold' to yourself.

A. TENNYSON

SHOW-DAY AT BATTLE ABBEY, 1876

A GARDEN here—May breath and bloom of spring—
The cuckoo yonder from an English elm
Crying, 'With my false egg I overwhelm
The native nest'; and fancy hears the ring
Of harness, and that deathful arrow sing,
And Saxon battle-axe clang on Norman helm.
Here rose the dragon-banner of our realm;
Here fought, here fell, our Norman-slander'd king.
O Garden blossoming out of English blood!
O strange hate-healer Time! We stroll and stare
Where might made right eight hundred years ago;
Might, right ay, good, so all things make for good—
But he and he, if soul be soul, are where
Each stands full face with all he did below.

DRAMATIS PERSONÆ

KING EDWARD THE CONFESSOR.
STIGAND, *created Archbishop of Canterbury by the Antipope Benedict.*
ALDRED, *Archbishop of York.*
THE NORMAN BISHOP OF LONDON.
HAROLD, *Earl of Wessex, afterwards King of England*
TOSTIG, *Earl of Northumbria*
GURTH, *Earl of East Anglia*   }Sons of Godwin
LEOFWIN, *Earl of Kent and Essex*
WULFNOTH
COUNT WILLIAM OF NORMANDY.
WILLIAM RUFUS.

WILLIAM MALET, *a Norman Noble.*[1]
EDWIN, *Earl of Mercia*
MORCAR, *Earl of Northumbria after Tostig* } *Sons of Alfgar of Mercia.*
GAMEL, *a Northumbrian Thane.*
GUY, *Count of Ponthieu.*
ROLF, *a Ponthieu Fisherman.*
HUGH MARGOT, *a Norman Monk.*
OSGOD *and* ATHELRIC, *Canons from Waltham.*
THE QUEEN, *Edward the Confessor's Wife, Daughter of Godwin.*
ALDWYTH, *Daughter of Alfgar and Widow of Griffyth, King of Wales.*
EDITH, *Ward of King Edward.*

Courtiers, Earls and Thanes, Men-at-Arms, Canons of Waltham, Fishermen, etc.

[1] . . . quidam partim Normannus et Anglus Compater Heraldi. (*Guy of Amiens,* 587.)

HAROLD

ACT I

SCENE I.—LONDON. THE KING'S
PALACE

(*A comet seen through the open
window.*)

ALDWYTH, GAMEL, COURTIERS *talking
together.*

First Courtier. Lo! there once more
—this is the seventh night!
Yon grimly-glaring, treble-brandish'd
scourge
Of England!
Second Courtier. Horrible!
First Courtier. Look you, there's a
star
That dances in it as mad with agony!
Third Courtier. Ay, like a spirit in
hell who skips and flies
To right and left, and cannot scape
the flame.
Second Courtier. Steam'd upward
from the undescendible
Abysm.
First Courtier. Or floated down-
ward from the throne
Of God Almighty.
Aldwyth.   Gamel, son of Orm,
What thinkest thou this mean?
Gamel.   War, my dear lady!
Aldwyth. Doth this affright thee?
Gamel.   Mightily, my dear lady!
Aldwyth. Stand by me then, and
look upon my face,
Not on the comet.

Enter MORCAR.

            Brother! why so pale?
Morcar. It glares in heaven, it flares
upon the Thames,

The people are as thick as bees be-
low,
They hum like bees,—they cannot
speak—for awe;
Look to the skies, then to the river,
strike
Their hearts, and hold their babies up
to it.
I think that they would Molochize
them too,
To have the heavens clear.
Aldwyth.   They fright not me.

Enter LEOFWIN, *after him* GURTH.

Ask thou Lord Leofwin what he
thinks of this!
Morcar. Lord Leofwin, dost thou
believe that these
Three rods of blood-red fire up yonder
mean
The doom of England and the wrath
of Heaven?
Bishop of London (*passing*). Did
ye not cast with bestial vio-
lence
Our holy Norman bishops down from
all
Their thrones in England? I alone re-
main.
Why should not Heaven be wroth?
Leofwin.   With us, or thee?
Bishop of London. Did ye not out-
law your archbishop Robert,
Robert of Jumièges—well-nigh mur-
der him too?
Is there no reason for the wrath of
Heaven?
Leofwin. Why, then the wrath of
Heaven hath three tails,
The devil only one.
            [*Exit* Bishop of London.

Enter ARCHBISHOP STIGAND.

Ask *our* archbishop.
Stigand should know the purposes of
Heaven.
   Stigand. Not I. I cannot read the
face of heaven;
Perhaps our vines will grow the better
for it.
   Leofwin (*laughing*). He can but
read the King's face on his
coins.
   Stigand. Ay, ay, young lord, *there*
the King's face is power.
   Gurth. O father, mock not at a pub-
lic fear,
But tell us, is this pendent hell in
heaven
A harm to England?
   Stigand.   Ask it of King Edward!
And he may tell thee *I* am a harm to
England.
Old uncanonical Stigand—ask of *me*
Who had my pallium from an Anti-
pope!
Not he the man—for in our windy
world
What 's up is faith, what 's down is
heresy.
Our friends, the Normans, holp to
shake his chair.
I have a Norman fever on me, son,
And cannot answer sanely.—What it
means?
Ask our broad earl.
   [*Pointing to* Harold, *who enters.*
   Harold (*seeing* Gamel). Hail,
Gamel, son of Orm!
Albeit no rolling stone, my good
friend Gamel,
Thou hast rounded since we met. Thy
life at home
Is easier than mine here. Look! am I
not
Work-wan, flesh-fallen?
   Gamel.   Art thou sick, good earl?
   Harold. Sick as an autumn swallow
for a voyage,
Sick for an idle week of hawk and
hound
Beyond the seas—a change! When
camest thou hither?

   Gamel. To-day, good earl.
   Harold. Is the North quiet, Gamel?
   Gamel. Nay, there be murmurs, for
thy brother breaks us
With over-taxing—quiet, ay, as
yet—
Nothing as yet.
   Harold. Stand by him, mine old
friend,
Thou art a great voice in Northum-
berland!
Advise him; speak him sweetly, he
will hear thee.
He is passionate but honest. Stand
thou by him!
More talk of this to-morrow, if yon
weird sign
Not blast us in our dreams.—Well,
father Stigand—
   [*To* Stigand, *who advances to him.*
   Stigand (*pointing to the comet*).
War there, my son? is that the
doom of England?
   Harold. Why not the doom of all
the world as well?
For all the world sees it as well as
England.
These meteors came and went before
our day.
Not harming any; it threatens us no
more
Than French or Norman. War? the
worst that follows
Things that seem jerk'd out of the
common rut
Of Nature is the hot religious fool,
Who, seeing war in heaven, for heav-
en's credit
Makes it on earth—but look, where
Edward draws
A faint foot hither, leaning upon Tos-
tig.
He hath learnt to love our Tostig
much of late.
   Leofwin. And *he* hath learnt, de-
spite the tiger in him,
To sleek and supple himself to the
King's hand.
   Gurth. I trust the kingly touch that
cures the evil
May serve to charm the tiger out of
him.

Leofwin. He hath as much of cat as
    tiger in him.
Our Tostig loves the hand and not the
    man.
Harold. Nay! Better die than lie!

Enter KING, QUEEN, *and* TOSTIG.

Edward.   In heaven signs!
Signs upon earth! signs everywhere!
    your priests
Gross, worldly, simoniacal, unlearn'd!
They scarce can read their Psalter;
    and your churches
Uncloth, unhandsome, while in Nor-
    manland
God speaks thro' abler voices, as He
    dwells
In statelier shrines. I say not this, as
    being
Half Norman-blooded, nor, as some
    have held,
Because I love the Norman better—
    no,
But dreading God's revenge upon this
    realm
For narrowness and coldness; and I
    say it
For the last time perchance, before I
    go
To find the sweet refreshment of the
    Saints.
I have lived a life of utter purity;
I have builded the great church of
    Holy Peter;
I have wrought miracles—to God the
    glory!—
And miracles will in my name be
    wrought
Hereafter.—I have fought the fight
    and go—
I see the flashing of the gates of
    pearl—
And it is well with me, tho' some of
    you
Have scorn'd me—ay—but after I am
    gone
Woe, woe to England! I have had a
    vision;
The Seven Sleepers in the cave at
    Ephesus
Have turn'd from right to left.
    Harold.   My most dear master,

What matters? let them turn from left
    to right
And sleep again.
    Tostig.   Too hardy with thy King!
A life of prayer and fasting well may
    see
Deeper into the mysteries of heaven
Than thou, good brother.
    Aldwyth (*aside*). Sees he into
    thine,
That thou wouldst have his promise
    for the crown?
    Edward. Tostig says true; my son,
    thou art too hard,
Not stagger'd by this ominous earth
    and heaven;
But heaven and earth are threads of
    the same loom,
Play into one another, and weave the
    web
That may confound thee yet.
    Harold.   Nay, I trust not,
For I have served thee long and hon-
    estly.
    Edward. I know it, son! I am not
    thankless; thou
Hast broken all my foes, lighten'd for
    me
The weight of this poor crown, and
    left me time
And peace for prayer to gain a better
    one.
Twelve years of service! England
    loves thee for it.
Thou art the man to rule her!
    Aldwyth (*aside*). So, not Tostig!
    Harold. And after those twelve
    years a boon, my King,
Respite, a holiday,—thyself wast
    wont
To love the chase,—thy leave to set
    my feet
On board, and hunt and hawk beyond
    the seas!
    Edward. What, with this flaming
    horror overhead?
    Harold. Well, when it passes then.
    Edward.   Ay, if it pass
Go not to Normandy—go not to Nor-
    mandy.
    Harold. And wherefore not, my
    King, to Normandy?

Is not my brother Wulfnoth hostage
    there
For my dead father's loyalty to thee?
I pray thee, let me hence and bring
    him home.
    Edward. Not thee, my son; some
      other messenger,
    Harold. And why not me, my lord,
      to Normandy?
Is not the Norman Count thy friend
    and mine?
    Edward. I pray thee, do not go to
      Normandy.
    Harold. Because my father drove
      the Normans out
Of England?—That was many a sum-
    mer gone—
Forgotten and forgiven by them and
    thee.
    Edward. Harold, I will not yield
      thee leave to go.
    Harold. Why, then to Flanders. I
      will hawk and hunt
In Flanders.
    Edward. Be there not fair woods
      and fields
In England? Wilful, wilful! Go—the
    Saints
Pilot and prosper all thy wandering
    out
And homeward!—Tostig, I am faint
    again.—
Son Harold, I will in and pray for
    thee.
    [*Exit, leaning on* Tostig, *and fol-
      lowed by* Stigand, Morcar, *and*
      Courtiers.
    Harold. What lies upon the mind of
      our good King,
That he should harp this way on Nor-
    mandy?
    Queen. Brother, the King is wiser
      than he seems;
And Tostig knows it; Tostig loves the
    King.
    Harold. And love should know; and
      —be the King so wise,—
Then Tostig too were wiser than he
    seems.
I love the man, but not his phantasies.

    Re-enter TOSTIG.

             Well, brother,
When didst thou hear from thy
    Northumbria?
    Tostig. When did I hear aught but
      this '*When*' from thee?
Leave me alone, brother, with my
    Northumbria;
She is *my* mistress, let *me* look to her!
The King hath made me earl; make
    me not fool!
Nor make the King a fool, who made
    me earl!
    Harold. No, Tostig—lest I make
      myself a fool.
Who made the King who made thee
    make thee earl.
    Tostig. Why chafe me then? Thou
      knowest I soon go wild.
    Gurth. Come, come! as yet thou art
      not gone so wild
But thou canst hear the best and
      wisest of us.
    Harold. So says old Gurth, not I;
      yet hear! thine earldom,
Tostig, hath been a kingdom. Their
    old crown
Is yet a force among them, a sun set
But leaving light enough for Alfgar's
    house
To strike thee down by—nay, this
    ghastly glare
May heat their fancies.
    Tostig. My most worthy brother,
Thou art the quietest man in all the
    world—
Ay, ay, and wise in peace and great
    in war—
Pray God the people choose thee for
    their king!
But all the powers of the house of
    Godwin
Are not enframed in thee.
    Harold.   Thank the Saints, no!
But thou hast drain'd them shallow
    by thy tolls,
And thou art ever here about the
    King.
Thine absence well may seem a want
    of care.

Cling to their love; for, now the sons
   of Godwin
Sit topmost in the field of England,
   envy,
Like the rough bear beneath the tree,
   good brother,
Waits till the man let go.
   Tostig.   Good counsel truly!
I heard from my Northumbria yester-
   day.
   Harold. How goes it then with thy
   Northumbria? Well?
   Tostig. And wouldst thou that it
   went aught else than well?
   Harold. I would it went as well as
   with mine earldom,
Leofwin's and Gurth's.
   Tostig.   Ye govern milder men.
   Gurth. We have made them milder
   by just government.
   Tostig. Ay, ever give yourselves
   your own good word.
   Leofwin. An honest gift, by all the
   Saints, if giver
And taker be but honest! but they
   bribe
Each other, and so often, an honest
   world
Will not believe them.
   Harold.   I may tell thee, Tostig,
I heard from thy Northumberland to-
   day.
   Tostig. From spies of thine to spy
   my nakedness
In my poor North.
   Harold. There is a movement there,
A blind one—nothing yet.
   Tostig.   Crush it at once
With all the power I have!—I must
   —I will!—
Crush it half-born! Fool still? or wis-
   dom there,
My wise head-shaking Harold?
   Harold.   Make not thou
The nothing something. Wisdom when
   in power
And wisest should not frown as
   Power, but smile
As kindness, watching all, till the true
   must
Shall make her strike as Power: but
   when to strike—

O Tostig, O dear brother—if they
   prance,
Rein in, not lash them, lest they rear
   and run
And break both neck and axle.
   Tostig.   Good again!
Good counsel tho' scarce needed. Pour
   not water
In the full vessel running out at top
To swamp the house.
   Leofwin. Nor thou be a wild thing
Out of the waste, to turn and bite the
   hand
Would help thee from the trap.
   Tostig.   Thou playest in tune.
   Leofwin. To the deaf adder thee,
   that wilt not dance
However wisely charm'd.
   Tostig.   No more, no more!
   Gurth. I likewise cry 'no more.' Un-
   wholesome talk
For Godwin's house! Leofwin, thou
   hast a tongue!
Tostig, thou look'st as thou wouldst
   spring upon him.
Saint Olaf, not while I am by! Come,
   come,
Join hands, let brethren dwell in
   unity;
Let kith and kin stand close as our
   shield-wall,
Who breaks us then? I say, thou hast
   a tongue,
And Tostig is not stout enough to bear
   it.
Vex him not, Leofwin.
   Tostig.   No, I am not vext,—
Altho' ye seek to vex me, one and all.
I have to make report of my good
   earldom
To the good King who gave it—not to
   you—
Not any of you.—I am not vext at all.
   Harold. The King? the King is ever
   at his prayers;
In all that handles matter of the state
I am the King.
   Tostig.   That shalt thou never be
If I can thwart thee.
   Harold.   Brother, brother!
   Tostig.   Away!
                                 [*Exit* Tostig.

Queen. Spite of this grisly star ye
　　three must gall
Poor Tostig.
　Leofwin. Tostig, sister, galls him-
　　self;
He cannot smell a rose but pricks his
　　nose
Against the thorn, and rails against
　　the rose.
　Queen. I am the only rose of all
　　the stock
That never thorn'd him; Edward
　　loves him, so
Ye hate him. Harold always hated
　　him.
Why—how they fought when boys—
　　and, Holy Mary!
How Harold used to beat him!
　Harold.　　　Why, boys will fight.
Leofwin would often fight me, and I
　　beat him.
Even old Gurth would fight. I had
　　much ado
To hold mine own against old Gurth.
　　Old Gurth,
We fought like great States for grave
　　cause; but Tostig—
On a sudden—at a something—for a
　　nothing—
The boy would fist me hard, and when
　　we fought
I conquer'd, and he loved me none the
　　less,
Till thou wouldst get him all apart,
　　and tell him
That where he was but worsted he was
　　wrong'd.
Ah! thou hast taught the King to spoil
　　him too;
Now the spoilt child sways both. Take
　　heed, take heed;
Thou art the Queen; ye are boy and
　　girl no more.
Side not with Tostig in any violence,
Lest thou be sideways guilty of the
　　violence.
　Queen. Come, fall not foul on me. I
　　leave thee, brother.
　Harold. Nay, my good sister—
　　[*Exeunt* Queen, Harold, Gurth,
　　and Leofwin.
　Aldwyth.　　　Gamel, son of Orm,

What thinkest thou this means?
　　　　　[*Pointing to the comet.*
　Gamel.　　　War, my dear lady,
War, waste, plague, famine, all malig-
　　nities.
　Aldwyth. It means the fall of Tostig
　　from his earldom.
　Gamel. That were too small a mat-
　　ter for a comet!
　Aldwyth. It means the lifting of the
　　house of Alfgar.
　Gamel. Too small! a comet would
　　not show for that!
　Aldwyth. Not small for thee, if thou
　　canst compass it.
　Gamel. Thy love?
　Aldwyth. As much as I can give
　　thee, man;
This Tostig is, or like to be, a ty-
　　rant.
Stir up thy people; oust him!
　Gamel.　　　And thy love?
　Aldwyth. As much as thou canst
　　bear.
　Gamel.　I can bear all,
And not be giddy.
　Aldwyth. No more now; to-
　　morrow.

SCENE II

IN THE GARDEN. THE KING'S HOUSE
NEAR LONDON. SUNSET

　Edith. Mad for thy mate, passion-
　　ate nightingale!—
I love thee for it—ay, but stay a mo-
　　ment;
He can but stay a moment; he is go-
　　ing.
I fain would hear him coming!—near
　　me—near,
Somewhere—to draw him nearer with
　　a charm
Like thine to thine!

　　　　(*Singing.*)

Love is come with a song and a smile,
Welcome Love with a smile and a song.
Love can stay but a little while.
Why cannot he stay? they call him
　　away.

Ye do him wrong, ye do him wrong;
Love will stay for a whole life long.

Enter HAROLD.

Harold. The nightingales in Haver-
    ingatte-Bower
Sang out their loves so loud that Ed-
    ward's prayers
Were deafen'd and he pray'd them
    dumb, and thus
I dumb thee too, my wingless night-
    ingale!   [*Kissing her.*
Edith. Thou art my music! Would
    their wings were mine
To follow thee to Flanders! Must
    thou go?
Harold. Not must, but will. It is
    but for one moon.
Edith. Leaving so many foes in Ed-
    ward's hall
To league against thy weal. The Lady
    Aldwyth
Was here to-day, and when she
    touch'd on thee
She stammer'd in her hate; I am sure
    she hates thee,
Pants for thy blood.
Harold. Well, I have given her
    cause—
I fear no woman.
Edith.   Hate not one who felt
Some pity for thy hater! I am sure
Her morning wanted sunlight, she so
    praised
The convent and lone life—within the
    pale—
Beyond the passion. Nay—she held
    with Edward,
At least methought she held with holy
    Edward,
That marriage was half sin.
Harold.   A lesson worth
Finger and thumb—thus (*snaps his
    fingers*).
          And my answer to it—
See here—an interwoven H and E!
Take thou this ring; I will demand his
    ward
From Edward when I come again. Ay,
    would she?
She to shut up my blossom in the
    dark!

Thou art *my* nun, thy cloister in mine
    arms.
Edith (*taking the ring*). Yea, but
    Earl Tostig—
Harold.   That 's a truer fear!
For if the North take fire, I should
    be back;
I shall be, soon enough.
Edith.   Ay, but last night
An evil dream that ever came and
    went—
Harold. A gnat that vext thy pil-
    low! Had I been by,
I would have spoil'd his horn. My girl,
    what was it?
Edith. O that thou wert not going!
For so methought it was our mar-
    riage-morn,
And while we stood together, a dead
    man
Rose from behind the altar, tore away
My marriage ring, and rent my bridal
    veil;
And then I turn'd, and saw the church
    all fill'd
With dead men upright from their
    graves, and all
The dead men made at thee to murder
    thee,
But thou didst back thyself against a
    pillar,
And strike among them with thy
    battle-axe—
There, what a dream!
Harold. Well, well—a dream—no
    more!
Edith. Did not Heaven speak to
    men in dreams of old?
Harold. Ay—well—of old. I tell
    thee what, my child;
Thou hast misread this merry dream
    of thine,
Taken the rifted pillars of the wood
For smooth stone columns of the
    sanctuary,
The shadows of a hundred fat dead
    deer
For dead men's ghosts. True, that the
    battle-axe
Was out of place; it should have been
    the bow.—
Come, thou shalt dream no more such
    dreams; I swear it,

By mine own eyes—and these two
    sapphires—these
Twin rubies, that are amulets against
    all
The kisses of all kind of womankind
In Flanders, till the sea shall roll me
    back
To tumble at thy feet.

    Edith. That would but shame me,
Rather than make me vain. The sea
    may roll
Sand, shingle, shore-weed, not the liv-
    ing rock
Which guards the land.

    Harold. Except it be a soft one,
And under-eaten to the fall. Mine
    amulet—
This last—upon thine eyelids, to shut
    in
A happier dream. Sleep, sleep, and
    thou shalt see
My greyhounds fleeting like a beam of
    light,
And hear my peregrine and her bells
    in heaven;
And other bells on earth, which yet
    are heaven's;
Guess what they be.

    Edith. He cannot guess who knows.
Farewell, my king.

    Harold. Not yet, but then—my
    queen.   [*Exeunt.*

Enter ALDWYTH *from the thicket.*

    Aldwyth. The kiss that charms
    thine eyelids into sleep
Will hold mine waking. Hate him? I
    could love him
More, tenfold, than this fearful child
    can do;
Griffyth I hated; why not hate the foe
Of England? Griffyth, when I saw him
    flee,
Chased deer-like up his mountains, all
    the blood
That should have only pulsed for
    Griffyth beat
For his pursuer. I love him, or think I
    love him.
If he were King of England, I his
    queen,

I might be sure of it. Nay, I do love
    him.—
She must be cloister'd somehow, lest
    the king
Should yield his ward to Harold's will.
    What harm?
She hath but blood enough to live, not
    love.—
When Harold goes and Tostig, shall I
    play
The craftier Tostig with him? fawn
    upon him?
Chime in with all? 'O thou more saint
    than king!'
And that were true enough. 'O blessed
    relics!'
'O Holy Peter!' If he found me thus,
Harold might hate me; he is broad
    and honest,
Breathing an easy gladness—not like
    Aldwyth—
For which I strangely love him.
    Should not England
Love Aldwyth, if she stay the feuds
    that part
The sons of Godwin from the sons of
    Alfgar
By such a marrying? Courage, noble
    Aldwyth!
Let all thy people bless thee!

                  Our wild Tostig,
Edward hath made him earl; he would
    be king.
The dog that snapt the shadow dropt
    the bone.
I trust he may do well, this Gamel,
    whom
I play upon, that he may play the note
Whereat the dog shall howl and run,
    and Harold
Hear the King's music, all alone with
    him,
Pronounced his heir of England.
I see the goal and half the way to
    it.—
Peace-lover is our Harold for the sake
Of England's wholeness — so — to
    shake the North
With earthquake and disruption—
    some division—
Then fling mine own fair person in
    the gap
A sacrifice to Harold, a peace-offering,

A scapegoat marriage—all the sins of
both
The houses on mine head—then a fair
life
And bless the Queen of England!
 Morcar (coming from the thicket).
  Art thou assured
By this, that Harold loves but Edith?
 Aldwyth.   Morcar!
Why creep'st thou like a timorous
 beast of prey
Out of the bush by night?
 Morcar.   I follow'd thee.
 Aldwyth. Follow my lead, and I will
 make thee earl.
 Morcar. What lead then?
 Aldwyth. Thou shalt flash it se-
 cretly
Among the good Northumbrian folk,
 that I—
That Harold loves me—yea, and pres-
 ently
That I and Harold are betroth'd—and
 last—
Perchance that Harold wrongs me;
 tho' I would not
That it should come to that.
 Morcar.   I will both flash
And thunder for thee.
 Aldwyth.   I said 'secretly;'
It is the flash that murders, the poor
 thunder
Never harm'd head.
 Morcar. But thunder may bring
 down
That which the flash hath stricken.
 Aldwyth.   Down with Tostig!
That first of all.—And when doth
 Harold go?
 Morcar. To-morrow—first to Bos-
 ham, then to Flanders.
 Aldwyth. Not to come back till
 Tostig shall have shown
And redden'd with his people's blood
 the teeth
That shall be broken by us—yea, and
 thou
Chair'd in his place. Good-night, and
 dream thyself
Their chosen earl.   [*Exit* Aldwyth.
 Morcar. Earl first, and after that
Who knows I may not dream myself
 their king?

ACT II

SCENE I.—SEASHORE. PONTHIEU.
    NIGHT

HAROLD *and his* MEN, *wrecked.*

 Harold. Friends, in that last inhos-
 pitable plunge
Our boat hath burst her ribs; but ours
 are whole;
I have but bark'd my hands.
 Attendant.   I dug mine into
My old fast friend the shore, and
 clinging thus
Felt the remorseless outdraught of the
 deep
Haul like a great strong fellow at my
 legs,
And then I rose and ran. The blast
 that came
So suddenly hath fallen as suddenly—
Put thou the comet and this blast to-
 gether—
 Harold. Put thou thyself and
 mother-wit together.
Be not a fool!

Enter FISHERMEN *with torches,*
HAROLD *going up to one of
 them,* ROLF.

    Wicked sea-will-o'-the-wisp!
Wolf of the shore! dog, with thy
 lying lights
Thou hast betray'd us on these rocks
 of thine!
 Rolf. Ay, but thou liest as loud as
the black herring-pond behind thee.
We be fishermen; I came to see after
my nets.
 Harold. To drag us into them. Fishermen? devils!
Who, while ye fish for men with your
 false fires,
Let the great devil fish for your own
 souls.
 Rolf. Nay then, we be liker the
blessed Apostles; *they* were fishers of
men, Father Jean says.
 Harold. I had liefer that the fish
 had swallowed me,

Like Jonah, than have known there
    were such devils.
What 's to be done?
    [*To his* Men—*goes apart with
    them.*
  Fisherman. Rolf, what fish did
swallow Jonah?
  Rolf. A whale!
  Fisherman. Then a whale to a
whelk we have swallowed the King of
England. I saw him over there. Look
thee, Rolf, when I was down in the
fever, *she* was down with the hunger,
and thou didst stand by her and give
her thy crabs, and set her up again,
till now, by the patient Saints, she 's
as crabb'd as ever.
  Rolf. And I 'll give her my crabs
again, when thou art down again.
  Fisherman. I thank thee, Rolf. Run
thou to Count Guy; he is hard at
hand. Tell him what hath crept into
our creel, and he will fee thee as freely
as he will wrench this outlander's ransom out of him—and why not? for
what right had he to get himself
wrecked on another man's land?
  Rolf. Thou art the human-hearted-
est, Christian-charitiest of all crab-
catchers. Share and share alike!
              [*Exit.*
  Harold (*to* Fisherman). Fellow,
    dost thou catch crabs?
  Fisherman. As few as I may in a
wind, and less than I would in a calm.
Ay!
  Harold. I have a mind that thou
    shalt catch no more.
  Fisherman. How?
  Harold. I have a mind to brain thee
    with mine axe.
  Fisherman. Ay, do, do, and our
great count-crab will make his nippers
meet in thine heart; he 'll sweat it
out thee, he 'll sweat it out of thee!
Look, he 's here! He 'll speak for him-
self. Hold thine own, if thou canst!

  Enter GUY, COUNT OF PONTHIEU.

  Harold. Guy, Count of Ponthieu?
  Guy.   Harold, Earl of Wessex!

  Harold. Thy villains with their
    lying lights have wreck'd us!
  Guy. Art thou not Earl of Wessex?
  Harold.   In mine earldom
A man may hang gold bracelets on a
    bush,
And leave them for a year, and com-
    ing back
Find them again.
  Guy.   Thou art a mighty man
In thine own earldom!
  Harold. Were such murderous liars
In Wessex—if I caught them, they
    should hang
Cliff-gibbeted for sea-marks, our sea-
    mew
Winging their only wail!
  Guy.   Ay, but my men
Hold that the shipwreckt are accurst
    of God;—
What hinders me to hold with mine
    own men?
  Harold. The Christian manhood of
    the man who reigns!
  Guy. Ay, rave thy worst, but in our
    oubliettes
Thou shalt or rot or ransom.—Hale
    him hence!
        [*To one of his* Attendants.
Fly thou to William; tell him we have
    Harold.

            SCENE II

        BAYEUX. PALACE

COUNT WILLIAM *and* WILLIAM MALET.

  William. We hold our Saxon wood-
    cock in the springe,
But he begins to flutter. As I think
He was thine host in England when I
    went
To visit Edward.
  Malet.   Yea, and there, my lord,
To make allowance for their rougher
    fashions,
I found him all a noble host should be.
  William. Thou art his friend. Thou
    know'st my claim on England
Thro' Edward's promise. We have him
    in the toils;

And it were well if thou shouldst let
him feel
How dense a fold of danger nets him
round,
So that he bristle himself against my
will.
 Malet. What would I do, my lord,
if I were you?
 William. What wouldst thou do?
 Malet. My lord, he is thy guest.
 William. Nay, by the splendor of
God, no guest of mine.
He came not to see me, had past me
by
To hunt and hawk elsewhere, save for
the fate
Which hunted *him* when that un-
Saxon blast,
And bolts of thunder moulded in high
heaven
To serve the Norman purpose, drave
and crack'd
His boat on Ponthieu beach; where
our friend Guy
Had wrung his ransom from him by
the rack,
But that I stept between and pur-
chased him,
Translating his captivity from Guy
To mine own hearth at Bayeux, where
he sits
My ransom'd prisoner.
 Malet.   Well, if not with gold,
With golden deeds and iron strokes
that brought
Thy war with Brittany to a goodlier
close
Than else had been, he paid his ran-
som back.
 William. So that henceforth they
are not like to league
With Harold against *me*.
 Malet.   A marvel, how
He from the liquid sands of Coesnon
Haled thy shore-swallow'd, armor'd
Normans up
To fight for thee again!
 William.   Perchance against
Their saver, save thou save him from
himself.
 Malet. But I should let him home
again, my lord.

 William. Simple! let fly the bird
within the hand,
To catch the bird again within the
bush!
No.
Smooth thou my way, before he clash
with me;
I want his voice in England for the
crown,
I want thy voice with him to bring
him round;
And being brave he must be subtly
cow'd,
And being truthful wrought upon to
swear
Vows that he dare not break. England
our own
Thro' Harold's help, he shall be my
dear friend
As well as thine, and thou thyself
shalt have
Large lordship there of lands and ter-
ritory.
 Malet. I knew thy purpose; he and
Wulfnoth never
Have met, except in public; shall
they meet
In private? I have often talk'd with
Wulfnoth,
And stuff'd the boy with fears, that
these may act
On Harold when they meet.
 William.   Then let them meet!
 Malet. I can but love this noble,
honest Harold.
 William. Love him! why not? thine
is a loving office,
I have commission'd thee to save the
man.
Help the good ship, showing the
sunken rock,
Or he is wreckt for ever.

   Enter WILLIAM RUFUS.

William Rufus.   Father.
William.   Well, boy.
William Rufus. They have taken
away the toy thou gavest me,
The Norman knight.
 William. Why, boy?
 William Rufus. Because I broke

The horse's leg—it was mine own to
  break;
I like to have my toys, and break
    them too.
  William. Well, thou shalt have an-
    other Norman knight.
  William Rufus. And may I break
    his legs?
  William. Yea,—get thee gone!
  William Rufus. I'll tell them I have
    had my way with thee. [*Exit.*
  Malet. I never knew thee check thy
    will for aught
Save for the prattling of thy little
    ones.
  William. Who shall be kings of
    England. I am heir
Of England by the promise of her
    king.
  Malet. But there the great Assem-
    bly choose their king,
The choice of England is the voice of
    England.
  William. I will be King of England
    by the laws,
The choice, and voice of England.
  Malet.   Can that be?
  William. The voice of any people is
    the sword
That guards them, or the sword that
    beats them down.
Here comes the would-be what I will
    be—kinglike . . .
Tho' scarce at ease; for, save our
    meshes break,
More kinglike he than like to prove a
    king.

Enter HAROLD, *musing, with his eyes
    on the ground.*

He sees me not—and yet he dreams
    of me.
Earl, wilt thou fly my falcons this fair
    day?
They are of the best, strong-wing'd
    against the wind.
  Harold (*looking up suddenly, hav-
    ing caught but the last word*).
    Which way does it blow?
  William. Blowing for England, ha?
Not yet. Thou hast not learnt thy
    quarters here.

The winds so cross and jostle among
    these towers.
  Harold. Count of the Normans,
    thou hast ransom'd us,
Maintain'd, and entertain'd us roy-
    ally,
  William. And thou for us hast
    fought as loyally,
Which binds us friendship-fast for
    ever!
  Harold. Good!
But lest we turn the scale of courtesy
By too much pressure on it, I would
    fain,
Since thou hast promised Wulfnoth
    home with us,
Be home again with Wulfnoth.
  William.   Stay—as yet
Thou hast but seen how Norman
    hands can strike,
But walk'd our Norman field, scarce
    touch'd or tasted
The splendors of our court.
  Harold.   I am in no mood;
I should be as the shadow of a cloud
Crossing your light.
  William. Nay, rest a week or two,
And we will fill thee full of Norman
    sun,
And send thee back among thine is-
    land mists
With laughter.
  Harold. Count, I thank thee, but
    had rather
Breathe the free wind from off our
    Saxon downs,
Tho' charged with all the wet of all
    the west.
  William. Why if thou wilt, so let it
    be—thou shalt.
That were a graceless hospitality
To chain the free guest to the ban-
    quet-board;
To-morrow we will ride with thee to
    Harfleur,
And see thee shipt, and pray in thy
    behalf
For happier homeward winds than
    that which crack'd
Thy bark at Ponthieu,—yet to us, in
    faith,
A happy one—whereby we came to
    know

Thy valor and thy value, noble earl.
Ay, and perchance a happy one for
    thee,
Provided—I will go with thee to-
    morrow—
Nay—but there be conditions, easy
    ones,
So thou, fair friend, will take them
    easily.

Enter PAGE.

Page. My lord, there is a post from
    over seas
With news for thee.   [*Exit* Page.
    William. Come, Malet, let us hear!
[*Exeunt* Count William *and* Malet.
    Harold. Conditions? What condi-
        tions? pay him back
His ransom? 'easy'—that were easy
    —nay—
No money-lover he! What said the
    king?
'I pray you do not go to Normandy.'
And fate hath blown me hither, bound
    me too
With bitter obligation to the Count—
Have I not fought it out? What did
    he mean?
There lodged a gleaming grimness in
    his eyes,
Gave his shorn smile the lie. The walls
    oppress me,
And yon huge keep that hinders half
    the heaven.
Free air! free field!
    [*Moves to go out. A* Man-at-
        arms *follows him.*
    Harold (*to the* Man-at-arms). I
        need thee not. Why dost thou
        follow me?
Man-at-arms. I have the Count's
    commands to follow thee.
Harold. What then? Am I in danger
    in this court?
Man-at-arms. I cannot tell. I have
    the Count's commands.
Harold. Stand out of earshot then,
    and keep me still.
In eyeshot.
    Man-at-arms. Yea, lord Harold.
        [*Withdraws.*
    Harold.   And arm'd men

Ever keep watch beside my chamber
    door,
And if I walk within the lonely wood,
There is an arm'd man ever glides be-
    hind!

Enter MALET.

Why am I follow'd, haunted, har-
    ass'd, watch'd?
See yonder!
    [*Pointing to the* Man-at-arms.
    Malet. 'T is the good Count's care
        for thee!
The Normans love thee not, nor thou
    the Normans,
Or—so they deem.
    Harold. But wherefore is the wind,
Which way soever the vane-arrow
    swing,
Not ever fair for England? Why, but
    now
He said—thou heard'st him—that I
    must not hence
Save on conditions.
    Malet.   So in truth he said.
    Harold. Malet, thy mother was an
        Englishwoman;
There somewhere beats an English
    pulse in thee!
    Malet. Well—for my mother's sake
        I love your England,
But for my father I love Normandy.
    Harold. Speak for thy mother's
        sake, and tell me true.
    Malet. Then for my mother's sake,
        and England's sake
That suffers in the daily want of thee,
Obey the Count's conditions, my
    good friend.
    Harold. How, Malet, if they be not
        honorable!
    Malet. Seem to obey them.
    Harold.   Better die than lie!
    Malet. Choose therefore whether
        thou wilt have thy conscience
White as a maiden's hand, or whether
    England
Be shatter'd into fragments.
    Harold.   News from England?
    Malet. Morcar and Edwin have
        stirr'd up the thanes

Against thy brother Tostig's govern-
ance;
And all the North of Humber is one
storm.
Harold. I should be there, Malet,
I should be there!
Malet. And Tostig in his own hall
on suspicion
Hath massacred the thane that was
his guest,
Gamel, the son of Orm; and there be
more
As villainously slain.
Harold. The wolf! the beast!
Ill news for guests, ha, Malet! More?
What more?
What do they say? did Edward know
of this?
Malet. They say his wife was know-
ing and abetting.
Harold. They say his wife!—To
marry and have no husband
Makes the wife fool. My God, I
should be there!
I'll hack my way to the sea.
Malet. Thou, canst not, Harold;
Our duke is all between thee and the
sea,
Our duke is all about thee like a God;
All passes block'd. Obey him, speak
him fair,
For he is only debonair to those
That follow where he leads, but stark
as death
To those that cross him.—Look thou,
here is Wulfnoth!
I leave thee to thy talk with him
alone;
How wan, poor lad! how sick and sad
for home!   [*Exit* Malet.
Harold (*muttering*). Go not to
Normandy—go not to Nor-
mandy!

Enter WULFNOTH.

Poor brother! still a hostage!
Wulfnoth.   Yea, and I
Shall see the dewy kiss of dawn no
more
Make blush the maiden-white of our
tall cliffs,

Nor mark the sea-bird rouse himself
and hover
Above the windy ripple, and fill the
sky
With free sea-laughter—never—save
indeed
Thou canst make yield this iron-
mooded duke
To let me go.
Harold. Why, brother, so he will;
But on conditions. Canst thou guess
at them?
Wulfnoth. Draw nearer,—I was in
the corridor,
I saw him coming with his brother
Odo
The Bayeux bishop, and I hid myself.
Harold. They did thee wrong who
made thee hostage; thou
Wast ever fearful.
Wulfnoth. And he spoke—I heard
him—
'This Harold is not of the royal blood,
Can have no right to the crown;' and
Odo said,
'Thine is the right, for thine the
might; he is here,
And yonder is thy keep.'
Harold. No, Wulfnoth, no!
Wulfnoth. And William laugh'd
and swore that might was
right,
Far as he knew in this poor world of
ours—
'Marry, the Saints must go along with
us,
And, brother, we will find a way,' said
he—
Yea, yea, he would be King of Eng-
land.
Harold. Never!
Wulfnoth. Yea, but thou must not
this way answer *him.*
Harold. Is it not better still to
speak the truth?
Wulfnoth. Not here, or thou wilt
never hence nor I;
For in the racing toward this golden
goal
He turns not right or left, but tramples flat
Whatever thwarts him; hast thou
never heard

His savagery at Alençon,—the town
Hung out raw hides along their walls,
    and cried,
'Work for the tanner.'
    Harold.   That had anger'd *me*
Had I been William.
    Wulfnoth.   Nay, but he had pris-
    oners,
He tore their eyes out, sliced their
    hands away,
And flung them streaming o'er the
    battlements
Upon the heads of those who walk'd
    within—
O, speak him fair, Harold, for thine
    own sake!
    Harold. Your Welshman says, 'The
    Truth against the World,'
Much more the truth against myself.
    Wulfnoth.   Thyself?
But for my sake, O brother! O, for
    my sake!
    Harold. Poor Wulfnoth! do they
    not entreat thee well?
    Wulfnoth. I see the blackness of
    my dungeon loom
Across their lamps of revel, and be-
    yond
The merriest murmurs of their ban-
    quet clank
The shackles that will bind me to the
    wall.
    Harold. Too fearful still.
    Wulfnoth. O, no, no—speak him
    fair!
Call it to temporize, and not to lie;
Harold, I do not counsel thee to lie.
The man that hath to foil a murder-
    ous aim
May, surely, play with words.
    Harold.   Words are the man.
Not even for thy sake, brother, would
    I lie.
    Wulfnoth. Then for thine Edith?
    Harold. There thou prick'st me
    deep.
    Wulfnoth. And for our Mother
    England?
    Harold. Deeper still.
    Wulfnoth. And deeper still the
    deep-down oubliette,
Down thirty feet below the smiling
    day—

In blackness—dogs' food thrown
    upon thy head.
And over thee the suns arise and set,
And the lark sings, the sweet stars
    come and go,
And men are at their markets, in their
    fields,
And woo their loves and have forgot-
    ten thee;
And thou art upright in thy living
    grave,
Where there is barely room to shift
    thy side,
And all thine England hath forgotten
    thee;
And he our lazy-pious Norman King,
With all his Normans round him once
    again,
Counts his old beads, and hath for-
    gotten thee.
    Harold. Thou art of my blood, and
    so methinks, my boy,
Thy fears infect me beyond reason.
    Peace!
    Wulfnoth. And then our fiery Tos-
    tig, while thy hands
Are palsied here, if his Northum-
    brians rise
And hurl him from them,—I have
    heard the Normans
Count upon this confusion—may he
    not make
A league with William, so to bring
    him back?
    Harold. That lies within the shadow
    of the chance.
    Wulfnoth. And like a river in flood
    thro' a burst dam
Descends the ruthless Norman—our
    good King
Kneels mumbling some old bone—
    our helpless folk
Are wash'd away, wailing, in their
    own blood—
    Harold. Wailing! not warring?
    Boy, thou hast forgotten
That thou art English.
    Wulfnoth.   Then our modest
    women—
I know the Norman license—thine
    own Edith—
    Harold. No more! I will not hear
    thee—William comes.

Wulfnoth. I dare not well be seen in talk with thee.
Make thou not mention that I spake with thee.
[*Moves away to the back of the stage.*

Enter WILLIAM, MALET, *and* OFFICER.

Officer. We have the man that rail'd against thy birth.
William. Tear out his tongue.
Officer. He shall not rail again.
He said that he should see confusion fall
On thee and on thine house.
William. Tear out his eyes,
And plunge him into prison.
Officer. It shall be done.
[*Exit* Officer.
William. Look not amazed, fair earl! Better leave undone
Than do by halves—tongueless and eyeless, prison'd—
Harold. Better methinks have slain the man at once!
William. We have respect for man's immortal soul,
We seldom take man's life, except in war;
It frights the traitor more to maim and blind.
Harold. In mine own land I should have scorn'd the man,
Or lash'd his rascal back, and let him go.
William. And let him go? To slander thee again!
Yet in thine own land in thy father's day
They blinded my young kinsman, Alfred—ay,
Some said it was thy father's deed.
Harold. They lied.
William. But thou and he—whom at thy word, for thou
Art known a speaker of the truth, I free
From this foul charge—
Harold. Nay, nay, he freed himself
By oath and compurgation from the charge.
The King, the lords, the people clear'd him of it.

William. But thou and he drove our good Normans out
From England, and this rankles in us yet.
Archbishop Robert hardly escaped with life.
Harold. Archbishop Robert! Robert the Archbishop!
Robert of Jumièges, he that—
Malet. Quiet! quiet!
Harold. Count! if there sat within the Norman chair
A ruler all for England—one who fill'd
All offices, all bishoprics with English—
We could not move from Dover to the Humber
Saving thro' Norman bishoprics—I say
Ye would applaud that Norman who should drive
The stranger to the fiends!
William. Why, that is reason!
Warrior thou art, and mighty wise withal!
Ay, ay, but many among our Norman lords
Hate thee for this, and press upon me—saying
God and the sea have given thee to our hands—
To plunge thee into lifelong prison here;—
Yet I hold out against them, as I may,
Yea—would hold out, yea, tho' they should revolt—
For thou hast done the battle in my cause.
I am thy fastest friend in Normandy.
Harold. I am doubly bound to thee —if this be so.
William. And I would bind thee more, and would myself
Be bounden to thee more.
Harold. Then let me hence
With Wulfnoth to King Edward.
William. So we will.
We hear he hath not long to live.
Harold. It may be.
William. Why then, the heir of England, who is he?

Harold. The Atheling is nearest to the throne.

William. But sickly, slight, half-witted and a child,
Will England have him king?

Harold.　　　　It may be, no.

William. And hath King Edward not pronounced his heir?

Harold. Not that I know.

William. When he was here in Normandy,
He loved us and we him, because we found him
A Norman of the Normans.

Harold.　　　　So did we.

William. A gentle, gracious, pure and saintly man!
And grateful to the hand that shielded him,
He promised that if ever he were king
In England, he would give his kingly voice
To me as his successor. Knowest thou this?

Harold. I learn it now.

William. Thou knowest I am his cousin,
And that my wife descends from Alfred?

Harold. Ay,

William. Who hath a better claim then to the crown?
So that ye will not crown the Atheling?

Harold. None that I know—if that but hung upon
King Edward's will.

William.　　　　Wilt *thou* uphold my claim?

Malet (aside to Harold). Be careful of thine answer, my good friend.

Wulfnoth (aside to Harold). O Harold, for my sake and for thine own!

Harold. Ay . . . if the King have not revoked his promise.

William. But hath he done it then?

Harold.　　　　Not that I know.

William. Good, good, and thou wilt help me to the crown?

Harold. Ay—if the Witan will consent to this.

William. Thou art the mightiest voice in England, man,
Thy voice will lead the Witan—shall I have it?

Wulfnoth (aside to Harold). O Harold, if thou love thine Edith, ay.

Harold. Ay, if—

Malet (aside to Harold). Thine 'ifs' will sear thine eyes out—ay.

William. I ask thee, wilt thou help me to the crown?
And I will make thee my great earl of earls,
Foremost in England and in Normandy;
Thou shalt be verily king—all but the name—
For I shall most sojourn in Normandy;
And thou be my vice-king in England. Speak.

Wulfnoth (aside to Harold). Ay, brother—for the sake of England—ay.

Harold. My lord—

Malet (aside to Harold). Take heed now.

Harold.　　　　Ay.

William.　　　　I am content,
For thou art truthful, and thy word thy bond.
To-morrow will we ride with thee to Harfleur.　　[*Exit* William.

Malet. Harold, I am thy friend, one life with thee,
And even as I should bless thee saving mine,
I thank thee now for having saved thyself.　　[*Exit* Malet.

Harold. For having lost myself to save myself,
Said 'ay' when I meant 'no,' lied like a lad
That dreads the pendent scourge, said 'ay' for 'no'!
Ay! No!—he hath not bound me by an oath—
Is 'ay' an oath? is 'ay' strong as an oath?
Or is it the same sin to break my word

As break mine oath? He call'd my
  word my bond!
He is a liar who knows I am a liar,
And makes believe that he believes
  my word—
The crime be on his head—not bound-
  en—no.

[*Suddenly doors are flung open,
  discovering in an inner hall*
  Count William *in his state
  robes, seated upon his throne,
  between two Bishops,* Odo of
  Bayeux *being one; in the centre of the hall an ark covered
  with cloth of gold, and on
  either side of it the* Norman
  Barons.

Enter a JAILOR *before* WILLIAM'S
                throne.

William (*to* Jailor). Knave, hast
  thou let thy prisoner scape?
Jailor.   Sir Count,
He had but one foot, he must have
  hopt away,
Yea, some familiar spirit must have
  help'd him.
William. Woe, knave, to thy famil-
  iar and to thee!
Give me thy keys. [*They fall clashing.*
Nay, let them lie. Stand there and
  wait my will.
          [*The* Jailor *stands aside.*
William (*to* Harold). Hast thou
  such trustless jailors in thy
  North?
Harold. We have few prisoners in
  mine earldom there,
So less chance for false keepers.
William.   We have heard
Of thy just, mild, and equal govern-
  ance;
Honor to thee! thou art perfect in all
  honor!
Thy naked word thy bond! confirm it
  now
Before our gather'd Norman baron-
  age,
For they will not believe thee—as I
  believe.
      [*Descends from his throne and
      stands by the ark.*

Let all men here bear witness of our
  bond!
    [*Beckons to* Harold, *who advances.*

      Enter MALET *behind him.*

Lay thou thy hand upon this golden
  pall!
Behold the jewel of Saint Pancratius
Woven into the gold. Swear thou on
  this!
Harold. What should I swear? Why
  should I swear on this?
William (*savagely*). Swear thou to
  help me to the crown of England.
Malet (*whispering* Harold). My
  friend, thou hast gone too far
  to palter now.
Wulfnoth (*whispering* Harold).
  Swear thou to-day, to-morrow
  is thine own.
Harold. I swear to help thee to the
  crown of England—
According as King Edward promises.
William. Thou must swear abso-
  lutely, noble earl.
Malet (*whispering*). Delay is death
  to thee, ruin to England.
Wulfnoth (*whispering*). Swear,
  dearest brother, I beseech
  thee, swear!
Harold (*putting his hand on the
  jewel*). I swear to help thee to
  the crown of England.
William. Thanks, truthful earl; I
  did not doubt thy word,
But that my barons might believe thy
  word,
And that the Holy Saints of Normandy
When thou art home in England, with
  thine own,
Might strengthen thee in keeping of
  thy word,
I made thee swear. Show him by
  whom he hath sworn.
    [*The two* Bishops *advance, and
    raise the cloth of gold. The
    bodies and bones of Saints are
    seen lying in the ark.*
The holy bones of all the canonized

From all the holiest shrines in Nor-
    mandy!
Harold. Horrible!
        [*They let the cloth fall again.*
William. Ay, for thou hast sworn
    an oath
Which, if not kept, would make the
    hard earth rive
To the very devil's horns, the bright
    sky cleave
To the very feet of God, and send her
    hosts
Of injured Saints to scatter sparks of
    plague
Thro' all your cities, blast your in-
    fants, dash
The torch of war among your stand-
    ing corn,
Dabble your hearths with your own
    blood.—Enough!
Thou wilt not break it! I, the count—
    the king—
Thy friend—am grateful for thine
    honest oath,
Not coming fiercely like a conqueror,
    now,
But softly as a bridegroom to his
    own.
For I shall rule according to your
    laws,
And make your ever-jarring earldoms
    move
To music and in order—Angle, Jute,
Dane, Saxon, Norman, help to build a
    throne
Out-towering hers of France.—The
    wind is fair
For England now.—To-night we will
    be merry.
To-morrow will I ride with thee to
    Harfleur.
        [*Exeunt* William *and all the* Nor-
        man Barons, *etc.*
Harold. To-night we will be merry
    —and to-morrow—
Juggler and bastard—bastard—he
    hates that most—
William the tanner's bastard! Would
    he heard me!
O God, that I were in some wide,
    waste field
With nothing but my battle-axe and
    him

To spatter his brains! Why, let earth
    rive, gulf in
These cursed Normans—yea, and
    mine own self!
Cleave heaven, and send thy Saints
    that I may say
Even to their faces, 'If ye side with
    William
Ye are not noble!' How their pointed
    fingers
Glared at me! Am I Harold, Harold,
    son
Of our great Godwin? Lo! I touch
    mine arms,
My limbs—they are not mine—they
    are a liar's—
I mean to be a liar — I am not
    bound—
Stigand shall give me absolution for
    it—
Did the chest move? did it move? I
    am utter craven!
O Wulfnoth, Wulfnoth, brother, thou
    hast betray'd me!
Wulfnoth. Forgive me, brother, I
    will live here and die.

Enter PAGE.

Page. My lord! the duke awaits
    thee at the banquet.
Harold. Where they eat dead men's
    flesh, and drink their blood.
Page. My lord—
Harold. I know your Norman cook-
    ery is so spiced,
It masks all this.
Page. My lord! thou art white as
    death.
Harold. With looking on the dead.
    Am I so white?
Thy duke will seem the darker.
    Hence, I follow.   [*Exeunt.*

ACT III

SCENE I.—THE KING'S PALACE.
LONDON

KING EDWARD, *dying on a couch, and
    by him standing the* QUEEN, HAR-
OLD, ARCHBISHOP STIGAND, GURTH,

LEOFWIN, ARCHBISHOP ALDRED,
ALDWYTH, *and* EDITH.

Stigand. Sleeping or dying there?
    If this be death,
Then our great Council wait to crown
    thee king—
Come hither, I have a power;
                  [*To* Harold.
They call me near, for I am close to
    thee
And England—I, old shrivell'd Sti-
    gand, I,
Dry as an old wood-fungus on a dead
    tree,
I have a power!
See here this little key about my neck!
There lies a treasure buried down in
    Ely.
If e'er the Norman grow too hard for
    thee,
Ask me for this at thy most need, son
    Harold,
At thy most need—not sooner.
    Harold.   So I will.
    Stigand. Red gold—a hundred
    purses—yea, and more!
If thou canst make a wholesome use
    of these
To chink against the Norman, I do
    believe
My old crook'd spine would bud out
    two young wings
To fly to heaven straight with.
    Harold.   Thank thee, father!
Thou art English, Edward too is Eng-
    lish now,
He hath clean repented of his Nor-
    manism.
    Stigand. Ay, as the libertine re-
    pents who cannot
Make done undone, when thro' his
    dying sense
Shrills, 'Lost thro' thee!' They have
    built their castles here;
Our priories are Norman; the Nor-
    man adder
Hath bitten us; we are poison'd; our
    dear England
Is demi-Norman. He!—
    [*Pointing to* King Edward, *sleep-
    ing.*
    Harold.   I would I were

As holy and as passionless as he!
That I might rest as calmly! Look at
    him—
The rosy face, and long down-silver-
    ing beard,
The brows unwrinkled as a summer
    mere.—
    Stigand. A summer mere with sud-
    den wreckful gusts
From a side-gorge. Passionless? How
    he flamed
When Tostig's anger'd earldom flung
    him, nay,
He fain had calcined all Northumbria
To one black ash, but that thy patriot
    passion,
Siding with our great Council against
    Tostig,
Out-passion'd his! Holy? ay, ay, for-
    sooth,
A conscience for his own soul, not his
    realm;
A twilight conscience lighted thro' a
    chink;
Thine by the sun; nay, by some sun
    to be,
When all the world hath learnt to
    speak the truth,
And lying were self-murder by that
    State
Which was the exception.
    Harold. That sun may God speed!
    Stigand. Come, Harold, shake the
    cloud off!
    Harold.   Can I, father?
Our Tostig parted cursing me and
    England;
Our sister hates us for his banish-
    ment;
He hath gone to kindle Norway
    against England,
And Wulfnoth is alone in Normandy.
For when I rode with William down
    to Harfleur,
'Wulfnoth is sick,' he said; 'he cannot
    follow;'
Then with that friendly-fiendly smile
    of his,
'We have learnt to love him, let him
    a little longer
Remain a hostage for the loyalty
Of Godwin's house.' As far as touches
    Wulfnoth

I that so prized plain word and naked
    truth
Have sinn'd against it—all in vain.
    Leofwin.   Good brother,
By all the truths that ever priest hath
    preach'd,
Of all the lies that ever men have lied,
Thine is the pardonablest.
    Harold.   Maybe so!
I think it so, I think I am a fool
To think it can be otherwise than so.
    Stigand. Tut, tut, I have absolved
    thee. Dost thou scorn me,
Because I had my Canterbury pallium
From one whom they dispoped?
    Harold.   No, Stigand, no!
    Stigand. Is naked truth actable in
    true life?
I have heard a saying of thy father
    Godwin,
That, were a man of state nakedly
    true,
Men would but take him for the craft-
    ier liar.
    Leofwin. Be men less delicate than
    the devil himself?
I thought that naked Truth would
    shame the devil,
The devil is so modest.
    Gurth.   He never said it!
    Leofwin. Be thou not stupid-hon-
    est, brother Gurth!
    Harold. Better to be a liar's dog,
    and hold
My master honest, than believe that
    lying
And ruling men are fatal twins that
    cannot
Move one without the other. Edward
    wakes!—
Dazed—he hath seen a vision.
    Edward.   The green tree!
Then a great Angel past along the
    highest
Crying, 'The doom of England!' and
    at once
He stood beside me, in his grasp a
    sword
Of lightnings, wherewithal he cleft
    the tree
From off the bearing trunk, and hurl'd
    it from him

Three fields away, and then he dash'd
    and drench'd,
He dyed, he soak'd the trunk with
    human blood,
And brought the sunder'd tree again,
    and set it
Straight on the trunk, that, thus bap-
    tized in blood,
Grew ever high and higher, beyond
    my seeing,
And shot out sidelong boughs across
    the deep
That dropt themselves, and rooted in
    far isles
Beyond my seeing; and the great
    Angel rose
And past again along the highest, cry-
    ing,
'The doom of England!'—Tostig,
    raise my head!
                    [*Falls back senseless.*
    Harold (raising him). Let Harold
    serve for Tostig!
    Queen.   Harold served
Tostig so ill, he cannot serve for Tos-
    tig!
Ay, raise his head, for thou hast laid
    it low!
The sickness of our saintly King, for
    whom
My prayers go up as fast as my tears
    fall,
I well believe, hath mainly drawn it-
    self
From lack of Tostig—thou hast ban-
    ish'd him.
    Harold. Nay—but the Council, and
    the King himself.
    Queen. Thou hatest him, hatest
    him!
    Harold (coldly). Ay—Stigand, un-
    riddle
This vision, canst thou?
    Stigand.   Dotage!
    Edward (starting up). It is finish'd.
I have built the Lord a house—the
    Lord hath dwelt
In darkness. I have built the Lord a
    house—
Palms, flowers, pomegranates, golden
    cherubim
With twenty-cubit wings from wall to
    wall—

I have built the Lord a house—sing,
Asaph! clash
The cymbal, Heman! blow the trum-
pet, priest!
Fall, cloud, and fill the house—lo! my
two pillars,
Jachin and Boaz!—
[*Seeing* Harold *and* Gurth.
Harold, Gurth,—where am I?
Where is the charter of our West-
minster?
Stigand. It lies beside thee, king,
upon thy bed.
Edward. Sign, sign at once—take,
sign it, Stigand, Aldred!
Sign it, my good son Harold, Gurth,
and Leofwin!
Sign it, my queen!
All.   We have sign'd it.
Edward.   It is finish'd!
The kingliest abbey in all Christian
lands,
The lordliest, loftiest minster ever
built
To Holy Peter in our English isle!
Let me be buried there, and all our
kings,
And all our just and wise and holy
men
That shall be born hereafter. It is fin-
ish'd!
Hast thou had absolution for thine
oath?   [*To* Harold.
Harold. Stigand hath given me ab-
solution for it.
Edward. Stigand is not canonical
enough
To save thee from the wrath of Nor-
man Saints.
Stigand. Norman enough! Be there
no Saints of England
To help us from their brethren yon-
der?
Edward. Prelate,
The Saints are one, but those of Nor-
manland
Are mightier than our own.—Ask it
of Aldred.   [*To* Harold.
Aldred. It shall be granted him, my
king; for he
Who vows a vow to strangle his own
mother

Is guiltier keeping this than breaking
it.
Edward. O friends, I shall not over-
live the day!
Stigand. Why, then the throne is
empty. Who inherits?
For tho' we be not bound by the king's
voice
In making of a king, yet the king's
voice
Is much toward his making. Who in-
herits?
Edgar the Atheling?
Edward. No, no, but Harold.
I love him; he hath served me; none
but he
Can rule all England. Yet the curse is
on him
For swearing falsely by those blessed
bones;
He did not mean to keep his vow.
Harold.   Not mean
To make our England Norman.
Edward.   There spake Godwin,
Who hated all the Normans; but their
Saints
Have heard thee, Harold.
Edith.   O, my lord, my King!
He knew not whom he sware by.
Edward.   Yea, I know
He knew not, but those heavenly ears
have heard,
Their curse is on him; wilt thou bring
another,
Edith, upon his head?
Edith.   No, no, not I!
Edward Why, then thou must not
wed him.
Harold. Wherefore, wherefore?
Edward. O son, when thou didst
tell me of thine oath,
I sorrow'd for my random promise
given
To yon fox-lion. I did not dream then
I should be king.—My son, the Saints
are virgins;
They love the white rose of virginity,
The cold, white lily blowing in her
cell.
I have been myself a virgin; and I
sware
To consecrate my virgin here to
Heaven—

The silent, cloister'd, solitary life,
A life of lifelong prayer against the curse
That lies on thee and England.

Harold.   No, no, no!

Edward. Treble denial of the tongue of flesh,
Like Peter's when he fell, and thou wilt have
To wail for it like Peter. O my son!
Are all oaths to be broken then, all promises
Made in our agony for help from Heaven?
Son, there is one who loves thee; and a wife,
What matters who, so she be serviceable
In all obedience, as mine own hath been?
God bless thee, wedded daughter!
    [*Laying his hand on the* Queen's head.

Queen.   Bless thou too
That brother whom I love beyond the rest,
My banish'd Tostig.

Edward. All the sweet Saints bless him!
Spare and forbear him, Harold, if he comes!
And let him pass unscathed; he loves me, Harold!
Be kindly to the Normans left among us,
Who follow'd me for love! and dear son, swear
When thou art king, to see my solemn vow
Accomplish'd.

Harold. Nay, dear lord, for I have sworn
Not to swear falsely twice.

Edward.   Thou wilt not swear?

Harold. I cannot.

Edward. Then on thee remains the curse,
Harold, if thou embrace her; and on thee,
Edith, if thou abide it,—
    [*The* King *swoons;* Edith *falls and kneels by the couch.*

Stigand.   He hath swoon'd.

Death?—no, as yet a breath.

Harold.   Look up! look up!
Edith!

Aldred. Confuse her not; she hath begun
Her lifelong prayer for thee.

Aldwyth.   O noble Harold,
I would thou couldst have sworn.

Harold.   For thine own pleasure?

Aldwyth. No, but to please our dying King, and those
Who make thy good their own—all England, earl.

Aldred. I would thou couldst have sworn. Our holy King
Hath given his virgin lamb to Holy Church
To save thee from the curse.

Harold.   Alas! poor man,
His promise brought it on me.

Aldred.   O good son!
That knowledge made him all the carefuller
To find a means whereby the curse might glance
From thee and England.

Harold.   Father, we so loved—

Aldred. The more the love, the mightier is the prayer;
The more the love, the more acceptable
The sacrifice of both your loves to Heaven.
No sacrifice to Heaven, no help from Heaven;
That runs thro' all the faiths of all the world.
And sacrifice there must be, for the King
Is holy, and hath talk'd with God, and seen
A shadowing horror; there are signs in heaven—

Harold. Your comet came and went.

Aldred. And signs on earth!
Knowest thou Senlac hill?

Harold.   I know all Sussex;
A good entrenchment for a perilous hour!

Aldred. Pray God that come not suddenly! There is one

Who passing by that hill three nights
    ago—
He shook so that he scarce could out
    with it—
Heard, heard—
    Harold.   The wind in his hair?
    Aldred.   A ghostly horn
Blowing continually, and faint battle-
    hymns,
And cries, and clashes, and the groans
    of men;
And dreadful shadows strove upon
    the hill,
And dreadful lights crept up from out
    the marsh—
Corpse-candles gliding over nameless
    graves—
    Harold. At Senlac?
    Aldred.   Senlac.
    Edward (waking). Senlac! Sangue-
    lac, The Lake of Blood!
    Stigand.   This lightning before
    death
Plays on the word,—and Normanizes
    too!
    Harold. Hush, father, hush!
    Edward. Thou uncanonical fool,
Wilt *thou* play with the thunder?
    North and South
Thunder together, showers of blood
    are blown
Before a never-ending blast, and hiss
Against the blaze they cannot quench
    —a lake,
A sea of blood—we are drown'd in
    blood—for God
Has fill'd the quiver, and Death has
    drawn the bow—
Sanguelac! Sanguelac! the arrow! the
    arrow!   [*Dies.*
    Stigand. It is the arrow of death in
    his own heart—
And our great Council wait to crown
    thee King.

SCENE II

IN THE GARDEN. THE KING'S HOUSE
NEAR LONDON

    Edith. Crown'd, crown'd and lost,
    crown'd King—and lost to
    me!

(*Singing.*)

Two young lovers in winter weather
    None to guide them,
Walk'd at night on the misty heather;
Night, as black as a raven's feather;
Both were lost and found together,
    None beside them.

That is the burthen of it—lost and
    found
Together in the cruel river Swale
A hundred years ago; and there 's
    another,

Lost, lost, the light of day,

To which the lover answers lovingly:

    'I am beside thee.'
Lost, lost, we have lost the way.
    'Love, I will guide thee.'
Whither, O whither? into the river,
Where we two may be lost together,
And lost for ever? 'O, never! O, never!
Tho' we be lost and be found together.'

Some think they loved within the
    pale forbidden
By Holy Church; but who shall say?
    the truth
Was lost in that fierce North, where
    they were lost,
Where all good things are lost, where
    Tostig lost
The good hearts of his people. It is
    Harold!

Enter HAROLD.

Harold the King!
    Harold.   Call me not King, but
    Harold.
    Edith. Nay, thou art King!
    Harold. Thine, thine, or King or
    churl!
My girl, thou hast been weeping; turn
    not thou
Thy face away, but rather let me be
King of the moment to thee, and
    command
That kiss my due when subject, which
    will make
My kingship kinglier to me than to
    reign

King of the world without it.

Edith.   Ask me not,
Lest I should yield it, and the second
     curse
Descend upon thine head, and thou be
     only
King of the moment over England.

Harold.   Edith,
Tho' somewhat less a king to my true
     self
Than ere they crown'd me one, for I
     have lost
Somewhat of upright stature thro'
     mine oath,
Yet thee I would not lose, and sell not
     thou
Our living passion for a dead man's
     dream;
Stigand believed he knew not what
     he spake.
O God! I cannot help it, but at times
They seem to me too narrow, all the
     faiths
Of this grown world of ours, whose
     baby eye
Saw them sufficient. Fool and wise, I
     fear
This curse, and scorn it. But a little
     light!—
And on it falls the shadow of the
     priest;
Heaven yield us more! for better,
     Woden, all
Our cancell'd warrior-gods, our grim
     Walhalla,
Eternal war, than that the Saints at
     peace,
The Holiest of our Holiest One, should
     be
This William's fellow-tricksters;—
     better die
Than credit this, for death is death,
     or else
Lifts us beyond the lie. Kiss me—
     thou art not
A holy sister yet, my girl, to fear
There might be more than brother in
     my kiss,
And more than sister in thine own.

Edith.   I dare not.
Harold. Scared by the church—
     'Love for a whole life long.'
When was that sung?

Edith.   Here to the nightingales.
Harold. Their anthems of no
     church, how sweet they are!
Nor kingly priest, nor priestly king to
     cross
Their billings ere they nest.

Edith.   They are but of spring,
They fly the winter change—not so
     with us—
No wings to come and go.

Harold.   But wing'd souls flying
Beyond all change and in the eternal
     distance
To settle on the Truth.

Edith.   They are not so true,
They change their mates.

Harold. Do they? I did not know it.
Edith. They say thou art to wed the
     Lady Aldwyth.
Harold. They say, they say!

Edith.   If this be politic,
And well for thee and England—and
     for her—
Care not for me who love thee.

     Gurth (calling). Harold, Harold!
Harold. The voice of Gurth! (*Enter
     Gurth.*) Good even, my good
     brother!
Gurth. Good even, gentle Edith.
Edith.   Good even, Gurth.
Gurth. Ill news hath come! Our
     hapless brother, Tostig—
He, and the giant King of Norway,
     Harold
Hardrada—Scotland, Ireland, Ice-
     land, Orkney,
Are landed north of Humber, and in
     a field
So packt with carnage that the dykes
     and brooks
Were bridged and damm'd with dead,
     have overthrown
Morcar and Edwin.
Harold. Well then, we must fight.
How blows the wind?

Gurth.   Against Saint Valery
And William.
Harold. Well then, we will to the
     North.
Gurth. Ay, but worse news: this
     William sent to Rome,
Swearing thou swarest falsely by his
     Saints.

The Pope and that Archdeacon Hilde-
    brand,
His master, heard him, and have sent
    him back
A holy gonfanon, and a blessed hair
Of Peter, and all France, all Bur-
    gundy,
Poitou, all Christendom is raised
    against thee.
He hath cursed thee, and all those who
    fight for thee,
And given thy realm of England to
    the bastard.

   Harold. Ha! ha!
   Edith. Oh, laugh not!—Strange and
    ghastly in the gloom
And shadowing of this double thun-
    der-cloud
That lours on England—laughter!
   Harold.   No, not strange!
This was old human laughter in old
    Rome
Before a Pope was born, when that
    which reign'd
Call'd itself God.—A kindly render-
    ing
Of 'Render unto Cæsar.'—The Good
    Shepherd!
Take this, and render that.
   Gurth.   They have taken York.
   Harold. The Lord was God and
    came as man—the Pope
Is man and comes as God.—York
    taken?
   Gurth.   Yea,
Tostig hath taken York!
   Harold.   To York then, Edith,
Hadst thou been braver, I had better
    braved
All—but I love thee and thou me—
    and that
Remains beyond all chances and all
    churches,
And that thou knowest.
   Edith.   Ay, but take back thy
    ring.
It burns my hand—a curse to thee
    and me.
I dare not wear it.
   [*Proffers* Harold *the ring, which he
    takes.*
   Harold.   But I dare. God with
    thee!

    [*Exeunt* Harold *and* Gurth.
   Edith. The King hath cursed him,
    if he marry me;
The Pope hath cursed him, marry me
    or no!
God help me! I know nothing—can
    but pray
For Harold—pray, pray, pray—no
    help but prayer,
A breath that fleets beyond this iron
    world,
And touches Him that made it.

ACT IV

SCENE I.—IN NORTHUMBRIA

ARCHBISHOP ALDRED, MORCAR, EDWIN,
    and FORCES. *Enter* HAROLD, *the
    standard of the golden Dragon of
    Wessex preceding him.*

   Harold. What! are thy people sul-
    len from defeat?
Our Wessex dragon flies beyond the
    Humber,
No voice to greet it.
   Edwin.   Let not our great King
Believe us sullen—only shamed to
    the quick
Before the King—as having been so
    bruised
By Harold, King of Norway; but our
    help
Is Harold, King of England. Pardon
    us, thou!
Our silence is our reverence for the
    King!
   Harold. Earl of the Mercians! if
    the truth be gall,
Cram me not thou with honey, when
    our good hive
Needs every sting to save it.
   Voices.   Aldwyth! Aldwyth!
   Harold. Why cry thy people on thy
    sister's name?
   Morcar. She hath won upon our
    people thro' her beauty
And pleasantness among them.
   Voices.   Aldwyth, Aldwyth!

Harold. They shout as they would
   have her for a queen.
Morcar. She hath follow'd with our
   host, and suffer'd all.
Harold. What would ye, men?
Voice.   Our old Northumbrian
   crown,
And kings of our own choosing.
Harold.   Your old crown
Were little help without our Saxon
   carles
Against Hardrada.
Voice.   Little! we are Danes,
Who conquer'd what we walk on, our
   own field.
Harold. They have been plotting
   here!   [*Aside.*
Voice.   He calls us little!
Harold. The kingdoms of this world
   began with little,
A hill, a fort, a city—that reach'd a
   hand
Down to the field beneath it, 'Be thou
   mine,'
When to the next, 'Thou also!' If the
   field
Cried out, 'I am mine own,' another
   hill,
Or fort, or city, took it, and the first
Fell, and the next became an empire.
Voice.   Yet
Thou art but a West Saxon; *we* are
   Danes!
Harold. My mother is a Dane, and
   I am English;
There is a pleasant fable in old books,
Ye take a stick, and break it; bind a
   score
All in one faggot, snap it over knee,
Ye cannot.
Voice. Hear King Harold! he says
   true!
Harold. Would ye be Norsemen?
Voices.   No!
Harold.   Or Norman?
Voices.   No!
Harold. Snap not the faggot-band
   then.
Voice.   That is true!
Voice. Ay, but thou art not kingly,
   only grandson
To Wulfnoth, a poor cowherd.
Harold.   This old Wulfnoth

Would take me on his knees and tell
   me tales
Of Alfred and of Athelstan the Great
Who drove you Danes; and yet he
   held that Dane,
Jute, Angle, Saxon, were or should be
   all
One England; for this cowherd, like
   my father,
Who shook the Norman scoundrels off
   the throne,
Had in him kingly thoughts—a king of
   men,
Not made but born, like the great
   King of all,
A light among the oxen.
Voice.   That is true!
Voice. Ay, and I love him now, for
   mine own father
Was great, and cobbled.
Voice.   Thou art Tostig's brother,
Who wastes the land.
Harold.   This brother comes to
   save
Your land from waste; I saved it
   once before,
For when your people banish'd Tos-
   tig hence,
And Edward would have sent a host
   against you,
Then I, who loved my brother, bade
   the King,
Who doted on him, sanction your de-
   cree
Of Tostig's banishment, and choice of
   Morcar,
To help the realm from scattering.
Voice.   King! thy brother,
If one may dare to speak the truth,
   was wrong'd.
Wild was he, born so; but the plots
   against him
Had madden'd tamer men.
Morcar.   Thou art one of those
Who brake into Lord Tostig's treas-
   ure-house
And slew two hundred of his follow-
   ing,
And now, when Tostig hath come back
   with power,
Are frighten'd back to Tostig.
Old Thane. Ugh! Plots and feuds!

This is my ninetieth birthday. Can ye not
Be brethren? Godwin still at feud with Alfgar,
And Alfgar hates King Harold. Plots and feuds!
This is my ninetieth birthday!

Harold. Old man, Harold
Hates nothing; not *his* fault, if our two houses
Be less than brothers.

Voices. Aldwyth, Harold, Aldwyth,

Harold. Again! Morcar! Edwin! What do they mean?

Edwin. So the good King would deign to lend an ear
Not overscornful, we might chance —perchance—
To guess their meaning.

Morcar. Thine own meaning, Harold,
To make all England one, to close all feuds,
Mixing our bloods, that thence a king may rise
Half-Godwin and half-Alfgar, one to rule
All England beyond question, beyond quarrel.

Harold. Who sow'd this fancy here among the people?

Morcar. Who knows what sows it-self among the people?
A goodly flower at times.

Harold. The Queen of Wales?
Why, Morcar, it is all but duty in her
To hate me; I have heard she hates me.

Morcar. No!
For I can swear to that, but cannot swear
That these will follow thee against the Norsemen,
If thou deny them this.

Harold. Morcar and Edwin,
When will ye cease to plot against my house?

Edwin. The King can scarcely dream that we, who know
His prowess in the mountains of the West,
Should care to plot against him in the North.

Morcar. Who dares arraign us, King, of such a plot?

Harold. Ye heard one witness even now.

Morcar. The craven!
There is a faction risen again for Tostig,
Since Tostig came with Norway— fright, not love.

Harold. Morcar and Edwin, will ye, if I yield,
Follow against the Norseman?

Morcar. Surely, surely!

Harold. Morcar and Edwin, will ye upon oath
Help us against the Norman?

Morcar. With good will;
Yea, take the sacrament upon it, King.

Harold. Where is thy sister?

Morcar. Somewhere hard at hand.
Call and she comes.

[*One goes out, then ent*er Aldwyth.

Harold. I doubt not but thou knowest
Why thou art summon'd.

Aldwyth. Why?—I stay with these,
Lest thy fierce Tostig spy me out alone,
And flay me all alive.

Harold. Canst thou love one
Who did discrown thine husband, un-queen thee?
Didst thou not love thine husband?

Aldwyth. O! my lord,
The nimble, wild, red, wiry,, savage king—
That was, my lord, a match of policy.

Harold. Was it?
I knew him brave; he loved his land; he fain
Had made her great; his finger on her harp—
I heard him more than once—had in it Wales,
Her floods, her woods, her hills. Had I been his,
I had been all Welsh.

Aldwyth. O, ay!—all Welsh—and yet
I saw thee drive him up his hills— and women

Cling to the conquer'd, if they love,
  the more;
If not, they cannot hate the con-
  queror.
We never—O good Morcar, speak for
  us,
His conqueror conquer'd Aldwyth.
  Harold.   Goodly news!
  Morcar. Doubt it not thou! Since
    Griffyth's head was sent
To Edward, she hath said it.
  Harold.   I had rather
She would have loved her husband.
    Aldwyth, Aldwyth,
Canst thou love me, thou knowing
  where I love?
  Aldwyth. I can, my lord, for mine
    own sake, for thine,
For England, for thy poor white dove,
  who flutters
Between thee and the porch, but then
  would find
Her nest within the cloister and be
  still.
  Harold. Canst thou love one who
    cannot love again?
  Aldwyth. Full hope have I that love
    will answer love.
  Harold. Then in the name of the
    great God, so be it!
Come, Aldred, join our hands before
  the hosts,
That all may see.
    [Aldred *joins the hands of* Har-
    old *and* Aldwyth, *and blesses
    them.*
  Voices. Harold, Harold and Al-
    dwyth!
  Harold. Set forth our golden
    Dragon, let him flap
The wings that beat down Wales!
Advance our Standard of the Warrior,
Dark among gems and gold; and thou,
  brave banner,
Blaze like a night of fatal stars on
  those
Who read their doom and die.
Where lie the Norsemen? on the Der-
  went? ay,
At Stamford-Bridge.
Morcar, collect thy men; Edwin, my
  friend—
Thou lingerest.—Gurth,—

Last night King Edward came to me
  in dreams—
The rosy face and long down-silver-
  ing beard—
He told me I should conquer.—
I am no woman to put faith in dreams.
    (*To his army.*)
Last night King Edward came to me
  in dreams,
And told me we should conquer.
  Voices.   Forward! Forward!
Harold and Holy Cross!
  Aldwyth.   The day is won!

SCENE II

A PLAIN. BEFORE THE BATTLE OF
STAMFORD-BRIDGE

HAROLD *and his* GUARD.

Harold. Who is it comes this way?
  Tostig? (*Enter* TOSTIG *with a
  small force.*) O brother,
What art thou doing here?
  Tostig.   I am foraging
For Norway's army.
  Harold. I could take and slay thee.
Thou art in arms against us.
  Tostig.   Take and slay me,
For Edward loved me.
  Harold.   Edward bade me spare
    thee.
  Tostig. I hate King Edward, for he
    join'd with thee
To drive me outlaw'd. Take and slay
  me, I say,
Or I shall count thee fool.
  Harold.   Take thee, or free thee,
Free thee or slay thee, Norway will
  have war;
No man would strike with Tostig,
  save for Norway.
Thou art nothing in thine England,
  save for Norway,
Who loves not thee, but war. What
  dost thou here,
Trampling thy mother's bosom into
  blood?
  Tostig. She hath wean'd me from it
  with such bitterness.

I come for mine own earldom, my
    Northumbria;
Thou hast given it to the enemy of
    our house.
    Harold. Northumbria threw thee
    off, she will not have thee.
Thou hast misused her; and, O
    crowning crime!
Hast murder'd thine own guest, the
    son of Orm,
Gamel, at thine own hearth.
    Tostig.   The slow, fat fool!
He drawl'd and prated so, I smote
    him suddenly;
I knew not what I did. He held with
    Morcar.—
I hate myself for all things that I do.
    Harold. And Morcar holds with us.
    Come back with him.
Know what thou dost; and we may
    find for thee,
So thou be chasten'd by thy banish-
    ment,
Some easier earldom.
    Tostig.   What for Norway then?
He looks for land among us, he and
    his.
    Harold. Seven feet of English
    land, or something more,
Seeing he is a giant.
    Tostig.   That is noble!
That sounds of Godwin.
    Harold.   Come thou back, and be
Once more a son of Godwin.
    Tostig (*turns away*). O brother,
    brother, O Harold—
    Harold (*laying his hand on* Tostig's
    shoulder). Nay then, come
    thou back to us!
    Tostig (*after a pause turning to*
    him). Never shall any man
    say that I, that Tostig
Conjured the mightier Harold from
    his North
To do the battle for me here in Eng-
    land,
Then left him for the meaner! thee!—
Thou hast no passion for the house of
    Godwin—
Thou hast but cared to make thyself
    a king—
Thou hast sold me for a cry.—

Thou gavest thy voice against me in
    the Council—
I hate thee, and despise thee, and defy
    thee.
Farewell for ever.   [*Exit.*
    Harold.   On to Stamford-Bridge!

SCENE III

AFTER THE BATTLE OF STAMFORD-
BRIDGE. BANQUET

HAROLD *and* ALDWYTH. GURTH, LEOF-
WIN, MORCAR, EDWIN, *and other*
EARLS *and* THANES.

    Voices. Hail! Harold! Aldwyth!
    hail, bridegroom and bride!
    Aldwyth (*talking with* Harold).
    Answer them thou!
Is this our marriage-banquet? Would
    the wines
Of wedding had been dash'd into the
    cups
Of victory, and our marriage and thy
    glory
Been drunk together! these poor
    hands but sew,
Spin, broider—would that they were
    man's to have held
The battle-axe by thee!
    Harold.   There *was* a moment
When, being forced aloof from all
    my guard,
And striking at Hardrada and his
    madmen,
I had wish'd for any weapon.
    Aldwyth.   Why art thou sad?
    Harold. I have lost the boy who
    play'd at ball with me,
With whom I fought another fight
    than this
Of Stamford-Bridge.
    Aldwyth.   Ay! ay! thy victories
Over our own poor Wales, when at
    thy side
He conquer'd with thee.
    Harold.   No—the childish fist
That cannot strike again.
    Aldwyth.   Thou art too kindly.
Why didst thou let so many Norsemen
    hence?

Thy fierce forekings had clench'd
their pirate hides
To the bleak church doors, like kites
upon a barn.
    Harold. Is there so great a need to
tell thee why?
    Aldwyth. Yea, am I not thy wife?
    Voices.   Hail, Harold, Aldwyth!
Bridegroom and bride!
    Aldwyth.   Answer them!
                    [To Harold.
    Harold (to all).   Earls and thanes!
Full thanks for your fair greeting of
my bride!
Earls, thanes, and all our country-
men! the day,
Our day beside the Derwent, will not
shine
Less than a star among the goldenest
hours
Of Alfred, or of Edward his great son,
Or Athelstan, or English Ironside
Who fought with Knut, or Knut who
coming Dane
Died English. Every man about his
King
Fought like a king; the King like his
own man,
No better; one for all, and all for one,
One soul! and therefore have we shat-
ter'd back
The hugest wave from Norseland ever
yet
Surged on us, and our battle-axes
broken
The Raven's wing, and dumb'd his
carrion croak
From the gray sea for ever. Many
are gone—
Drink to the dead who died for us,
the living
Who fought and would have died, but
happier lived,
If happier be to live; they both have
life
In the large mouth of England, till
her voice
Die with the world. Hail—hail!
    Morcar. May all invaders perish
like Hardrada!
All traitors fail like Tostig!
               [All drink but Harold.
    Aldwyth.   Thy cup's full!

    Harold. I saw the hand of Tostig
cover it.
Our dear, dead traitor-brother, Tostig,
him
Reverently we buried. Friends, had I
been here,
Without too large self-lauding I must
hold
The sequel had been other than his
league
With Norway, and this battle. Peace
be with him!
He was not of the worst. If there be
those
At banquet in this hall, and hearing
me—
For there be those, I fear, who prick'd
the lion
To make him spring, that sight of
Danish blood
Might serve an end not English—
peace with them
Likewise, if *they* can be a peace with
what
God gave us to divide us from the
wolf!
    Aldwyth (aside to Harold). Make
not our Morcar sullen; it is
not wise.
    Harold. Hail to the living who
fought, the dead who fell!
    Voices. Hail, hail!
    First Thane. How ran that answer
which King Harold gave
To his dead namesake, when he ask'd
for England?
    Leofwin. 'Seven feet of English
earth, or something more,
Seeing he is a giant!'
    First Thane.   Then for the bas-
tard
Six feet and nothing more!
    Leofwin.   Ay, but belike
Thou hast not learnt his measure.
    First Thane.   By Saint Edmund
I over-measure him. Sound sleep to
the man
Here by dead Norway without dream
or dawn!
    Second Thane. What, is he brag-
ging still that he will come,
To thrust our Harold's throne from
under him?

My nurse would tell me of a molehill crying
To a mountain, 'Stand aside and room for me!'
First Thane. Let him come! let him come! Here 's to him, sink or swim!   [*Drinks.*
Second Thane. God sink him!
First Thane. Cannot hands which had the strength
To shove that stranded iceberg off our shores,
And send the shatter'd North again to sea,
Scuttle his cockle-shell? What's Brunanburg
To Stamford-Bridge? a war-crash, and so hard,
So loud, that, by Saint Dunstan, old Saint Thor—
By God, we thought him dead—but our old Thor
Heard his own thunder again, and woke and came
Among us again, and mark'd the sons of those
Who made this Britain England, break the North—

Mark'd how the war-axe swung,
Heard how the war-horn sang,
Mark'd how the spear-head sprang,
Heard how the shield-wall rang,
Iron on iron clang,
Anvil on hammer bang—

Second Thane. Hammer on anvil, hammer on anvil. Old dog,
Thou art drunk, old dog!
First Thane. Too drunk to fight with thee!
Second Thane. Fight thou with thine own double, not with me,
Keep that for Norman William!
First Thane.   Down with William!
Third Thane. The washerwoman's brat!
Fourth Thane. The tanner's bastard!
Fifth Thane. The Falaise byblow!

Enter a THANE, *from Pevensey, spattered with mud.*

Harold. Ay, but what late guest,
As haggard as a fast of forty days,
And caked and plaster'd with a hundred mires,
Hath stumbled on our cups?
Thane from Pevensey. My lord the King!
William the Norman, for the wind had changed—
Harold. I felt it in the middle of that fierce fight
At Stamford-Bridge. William hath landed, ha?
Thane from Pevensey. Landed at Pevensey—I am from Pevensey—
Hath wasted all the land at Pevensey—
Hath harried mine own cattle—God confound him!
I have ridden night and day from Pevensey—
A thousand ships—a hundred thousand men—
Thousands of horses, like as many lions
Neighing and roaring as they leapt to land—
Harold. How oft in coming hast thou broken bread?
Thane from Pevensey. Some thrice or so.
Harold. Bring not thy hollowness
On our full feast. Famine is fear, were it but
Of being starved. Sit down, sit down, and eat,
And, when again red-blooded, speak again.
(*Aside.*) The men that guarded England to the South
Were scatter'd to the harvest.—No power mine
To hold their force together.—Many are fallen
At Stamford-Bridge—the people stupid-sure
Sleep like their swine—in South and North at once

I could not be.
(*Aloud.*) Gurth, Leofwin, Morcar,
    Edwin!
(*Pointing to the revellers.*) The curse
    of England! these are drown'd
    in wassail,
And cannot see the world but thro'
    their wines!
Leave them! and thee too, Aldwyth,
    must I leave—
Harsh is the news! hard is our honey-
    moon!
Thy pardon. (*Turning round to his
    attendants.*) Break the ban-
    quet up—Ye four!
And thou, my carrier-pigeon of black
    news,
Cram thy crop full, but come when
    thou art call'd. [*Exit* Harold.

ACT V

SCENE I.—A TENT ON A MOUND, FROM
WHICH CAN BE SEEN THE FIELD OF
SENLAC.

HAROLD, *sitting; by him standing*
HUGH MARGOT *the* MONK, GURTH,
LEOFWIN.

Harold. Refer my cause, my crown
    to Rome!—The wolf
Mudded the brook and predetermined
    all.
Monk,
Thou hast said thy say, and had my
    constant 'No'
For all but instant battle. I hear no
    more.
    Margot. Hear me again—for the
    last time. Arise,
Scatter thy people home, descend the
    hill,
Lay hands of full allegiance in thy
    Lord's
And crave his mercy, for the Holy
    Father
Hath given this realm of England to
    the Norman.
    Harold. Then for the last time,
    monk, I ask again

When had the Lateran and the Holy
    Father
To do with England's choice of her
    own king?
    Margot. Earl, the first Christian
    Cæsar drew to the East
To leave the Pope dominion in the
    West.
He gave him all the kingdoms of the
    West.
    Harold. So!—did he?—Earl—I
    have a mind to play
The William with thine eyesight and
    thy tongue.
Earl—ay—thou art but a messenger
    of William.
I am weary—go; make me not wroth
    with thee!
    Margot. Mock-king, I am the mes-
    senger of God,
His Norman Daniel! Mene, Mene,
    Tekel!
Is thy wrath hell, that I should spare
    to cry,
Yon Heaven is wroth with *thee?* Hear
    me again!
Our Saints have moved the Church
    that moves the world,
And all the Heavens and very God;
    they heard—
They know King Edward's promise
    and thine—thine.
    Harold. Should they not know free
    England crowns herself?
Not know that he nor I had power to
    promise?
Not know that Edward cancell'd his
    own promise?
And for *my* part therein—Back to
    that juggler, [*Rising.*
Tell him the Saints are nobler than
    he dreams,
Tell him that God is nobler than the
    Saints,
And tell him we stand arm'd on Sen-
    lac Hill,
And bide the doom of God.
    Margot.   Hear it thro' me.
The realm for which thou art for-
    sworn is cursed,
The babe enwomb'd and at the breast
    is cursed,

The corpse thou whelmest with thine
    earth is cursed,
The soul who fighteth on thy side is
    cursed,
The seed thou sowest in thy field is
    cursed,
The steer wherewith thou plowest thy
    field is cursed,
The fowl that fleeth o'er thy field is
    cursed,
And thou, usurper, liar—
    Harold.   Out, beast monk!
    [*Lifting his hand to strike him.*
    Gurth *stops the blow.*
I ever hated monks.
    Margot.   I am but a voice
Among you; murder, martyr me if
    ye will—
    Harold. Thanks, Gurth! The sim-
    ple, silent, selfless man
Is worth a world of tonguesters. (*To*
    Margot.) Get thee gone!
He means the thing he says. See him
    out safe!
    Leofwin. He hath blown himself as
    red as fire with curses.
An honest fool! Follow me, honest
    fool,
But if thou blurt thy curse among our
    folk,
I know not—I may give that egg-bald
    head
The tap that silences.
    Harold.   See him out safe.
    [*Exeunt* Leofwin *and* Margot.
    Gurth. Thou hast lost thine even
    temper, brother Harold!
    Harold. Gurth, when I past by Wal-
    tham, my foundation
For men who serve the neighbor, not
    themselves,
I cast me down prone, praying; and,
    when I rose,
They told me that the Holy Rood had
    lean'd
And bow'd above me; whether that
    which held it
Had weaken'd, and the Rood itself
    were bound
To that necessity which binds us
    down;
Whether it bow'd at all but in their
    fancy;

Or if it bow'd, whether it symboll'd
    ruin
Or glory, who shall tell? but they were
    sad,
And somewhat sadden'd me.
    Gurth.   Yet if a fear,
Or shadow of a fear, lest the strange
    Saints
By whom thou swarest should have
    power to balk
Thy puissance in this fight with him
    who made
And heard thee swear—brother—*I*
    have not sworn—
If the King fall, may not the kingdom
    fall?
But if I fall, I fall, and thou art King;
And if I win, I win, and thou art
    King;
Draw thou to London, there make
    strength to breast
Whatever chance, but leave this day
    to me.
    Leofwin (*entering*). And waste the
    land about thee as thou goest,
And be thy hand as winter on the
    field,
To leave the foe no forage.
    Harold.   Noble Gurth!
Best son of Godwin! If I fall, I fall—
The doom of God! How should the
    people fight
When the King flies? And, Leofwin,
    art thou mad?
How should the King of England
    waste the fields
Of England, his own people?—No
    glance yet
Of the Northumbrian helmet on the
    heath?
    Leofwin. No, but a shoal of wives
    upon the heath,
And some one saw thy willy-nilly nun
Vying a tress against our golden fern.
    Harold. Vying a tear with our cold
    dews, a sigh
With these low-moaning heavens. Let
    her be fetch'd.
We have parted from our wife with-
    out reproach,
Tho' we have pierced thro' all her
    practices;
And that is well.

Leofwin.   I saw her even now;
She hath not left us.

Harold. Nought of Morcar then?

Gurth. Nor seen, nor heard; thine,
    William's, or his own
As wind blows, or tide flows. Belike
    he watches
If this war-storm in one of its rough
    rolls
Wash up that old crown of Northum-
    berland.

Harold. I married her for Morcar
    —a sin against
The truth of love. Evil for good, it
    seems,
Is oft as childless of the good as
    evil
For evil.

Leofwin. Good for good hath borne
    at times
A bastard false as William.

Harold.   Ay, if Wisdom
Pair'd not with Good. But I am some-
    what worn,
A snatch of sleep were like the peace
    of God.
Gurth, Leofwin, go once more about
    the hill—
What did the dead man call it—San-
    guelac,
The lake of blood;

Leofwin. A lake that dips in Wil-
    liam
As well as Harold.

Harold.   Like enough. I have seen
The trenches dug, the palisades up-
    rear'd
And wattled thick with ash and wil-
    low-wands,
Yea, wrought at them myself. Go
    round once more;
See all be sound and whole. No Nor-
    man horse
Can shatter England, standing shield
    by shield;
Tell that again to all.

Gurth.   I will, good brother.

Harold. Our guardsman hath but
    toil'd his hand and foot,
I hand, foot, heart and head. Some
    wine! (*One pours wine into a
    goblet which he hands to* Har-
    old.)   Too much!

What? we must use our battle-axe to-
    day.
Our guardsmen have slept well, since
    we came in?

Leofwin. Ay, slept and snored.
    Your second-sighted man
That scared the dying conscience of
    the king
Misheard their snores for groans.
    They are up again
And chanting that old song of Brun-
    anburg
Where England conquer'd.

Harold. That is well. The Norman,
What is he doing?

Leofwin. Praying for Normandy;
Our scouts have heard the tinkle of
    their bells.

Harold. And our old songs are
    prayers for England too!
But by all Saints—

Leofwin.   Barring the Norman!

Harold.   Nay,
Were the great trumpet blowing
    dooms-day dawn,
I needs must rest. Call when the Nor-
    man moves—
                [*Exeunt all but* Harold.
No horse—thousands of horses—our
    shield wall—
Wall—break it not—break not—
    break—   [*Sleeps*

Vision of Edward. Son Harold, I
    thy king, who came before
To tell thee thou shouldst win at
    Stamford-Bridge,
Come yet once more, from where I
    am at peace,
Because I loved thee in my mortal
    day,
To tell thee thou shalt die on Senlac
    Hill—
Sanguelac!

Vision of Wulfnoth. O brother,
    from my ghastly oubliette
I send my voice across the narrow
    seas—
No more, no more, dear brother,
    nevermore—
Sanguelac!

Vision of Tostig. O brother, most
    unbrotherlike to me,

Thou gavest thy voice against me in
 my life,
I give my voice against thee from the
 grave—
Sanguelac!
 Vision of Norman Saints. O hapless
  Harold! King but for an hour!
Thou swarest falsely by our blessed
 bones,
We give our voice against thee out of
 heaven!
Sanguelac! Sanguelac! The arrow!
 the arrow!
 *Harold (starting up, battle-axe in
  hand).* Away!
My battle-axe against your voices.
 Peace!
The King's last word—'the arrow!' I
 shall die—
I die for England then, who lived for
 England—
What nobler? men must die.
I cannot fall into a falser world—
I have done no man wrong. Tostig,
 poor brother,
Art *thou* so anger'd?
Fain had I kept thine earldom in thy
 hands
Save for thy wild and violent will that
 wrench'd
All hearts of freemen from thee. I
 could do
No other than this way advise the
 king
Against the race of Godwin. Is it pos-
 sible
That mortal men should bear their
 earthly heats
Into yon bloodless world, and threaten
 us thence
Unschool'd of Death? Thus then thou
 art revenged—
I left our England naked to the South
To meet thee in the North. The
 Norseman's raid
Hath helpt the Norman, and the race
 of Godwin
Hath ruin'd Godwin. No—our wak-
 ing thoughts
Suffer a stormless shipwreck in the
 pools
Of sullen slumber, and arise again

Disjointed; only dreams—where mine
 own self
Takes part against myself! Why? for
 a spark
Of self-disdain born in me when I
 sware
Falsely to him, the falser Norman,
 over
His gilded ark of mummy-saints, by
 whom
I knew not that I sware,—not for myself—
For England—yet not wholly—

 Enter EDITH.

       Edith, Edith,
Get thou into thy cloister as the King
Will'd it; be safe, the perjury-monger-
 ing Count
Hath made too good an use of Holy
 Church
To break her close! There the great
 God of truth
Fill all thine hours with peace!—A
 lying devil
Hath haunted me—mine oath—my
 wife—I fain
Had made my marriage not a lie; I
 could not.
Thou art my bride! and thou in after
 years
Praying perchance for this poor soul
 of mine
In cold, white cells beneath an icy
 moon—
This memory to thee!—and this to
 England,
My legacy of war against the Pope
From child to child; from Pope to
 Pope, from age to age,
Till the sea wash her level with her
 shores,
Or till the Pope be Christ's.

 Enter ALDWYTH.

 Aldwyth (to Edith*).* Away from
  him!
 Edith. I will.—I have not spoken
  to the king
One word; and one I must. Farewell!
        [*Going.*

Harold.   Not yet.
Stay.

   Edith. To what use?

   Harold. The King commands thee,
woman!

   (*To* ALDWYTH.)

Have thy two brethren sent their
   forces in?

   Aldwyth. Nay, I fear not.

   Harold. Then there 's no force in
   thee!

Thou didst possess thyself of Edward's ear

To part me from the woman that I
   loved!

Thou didst arouse the fierce North-
   umbrians!

Thou hast been false to England and
   to me!—

As—in some sort—I have been false
   to thee.

Leave me. No more—Pardon on both
   sides—Go!

   Aldwyth. Alas, my lord, I loved
   thee.

   Harold (*bitterly*).   With a love
Passing thy love for Griffyth! wherefore now

Obey my first and last commandment. Go!

   Aldwyth. O Harold! husband!
   Shall we meet again?

   Harold. After the battle—after the
   battle. Go.

   Aldwyth. I go. (*Aside.*) That I
   could stab her standing there!
             [*Exit* Aldwyth.

   Edith. Alas, my lord, she loved
   thee.

   Harold. Never! never!

   Edith. I saw it in her eyes!

   Harold.   I see it in thine.
And not on thee—nor England—fall
   God's doom!

   Edith. On *thee?* on me! And thou
   art England! Alfred

Was England. Ethelred was nothing.
   England

Is but her king, and thou art Harold!

   Harold.   Edith,

The sign in heaven—the sudden blast
   at sea—

My fatal oath—the dead Saints—the
   dark dreams—

The Pope's anathema—the Holy
   Rood

That bow'd to me at Waltham—
   Edith, if

I, the last English King of England—

   Edith.   No,
First of a line that coming from the
   people,

And chosen by the people—

   Harold.   And fighting for
And dying for the people—

   Edith.   Living! living!

   Harold. Yea so, good cheer! thou
   art Harold, I am Edith!

Look not thus wan!

   Edith.   What matters how I look?
Have we not broken Wales and Norseland? slain,

Whose life was all one battle, incar-
   nate war,

Their giant-king, a mightier man-in-
   arms

Than William.

   Harold. Ay, my girl, no tricks in
   him—

No bastard he! when all was lost, he
   yell'd,

And bit his shield, and dash'd it on
   the ground,

And swaying his two-handed sword
   about him,

Two deaths at every swing, ran in
   upon us

And died so, and I loved him as I hate
This liar who made me liar. If Hate
   can kill,

And Loathing wield a Saxon battle-
   axe—

   Edith. Waste not thy might before
   the battle!

   Harold.   No,
And thou must hence. Stigand will
   see thee safe,

And so—Farewell.

       [*He is going, but turns back.*
The ring thou darest not wear,
I have had it fashion'd, see, to meet
   my hand.

[*Harold shows the ring which is on his finger.*

Farewell!

[*He is going, but turns back again.*

I am dead as Death this day to aught
of earth's
Save William's death or mine.

Edith. Thy death!—to-day!
Is it not thy birthday?

Harold. Ay, that happy day!
A birthday welcome! happy days and
many!
One—this! [*They embrace.*
Look, I will bear thy blessing into
the battle
And front the doom of God.

Norman Cries (*heard in the distance*). Ha Rou! Ha Rou!

Enter GURTH.

Gurth. The Norman moves!
Harold. Harold and Holy Cross!

[*Exeunt Harold and Gurth.*

Enter STIGAND.

Stigand. Our Church in arms—the
lamb the lion—not
Spear into pruning-hook—the counter
way—
Cowl, helm; and crozier, battle-axe.
Abbot Alfwig,
Leofric, and all the monks of Peter-
boro'
Strike for the king; but I, old wretch,
old Stigand,
With hands too limp to brandish iron
—and yet
I have a power—would Harold ask
me for it—
I have a power.

Edith. What power, holy father?
Stigand. Power now from Harold
to command thee hence
And see thee safe from Senlac.

Edith. I remain!
Stigand. Yea, so will I, daughter,
until I find
Which way the battle balance. I can
see it
From where we stand; and, live or
die, I would
I were among them!

CANONS *from Waltham* (*singing without*).

Salva patriam,
Sancte Pater,
Salva, Fili,
Salva, Spiritus,
Salva patriam,
Sancta Mater.[1]

Edith. Are those the blessed angels
quiring, father?
Stigand. No, daughter, but the can-
ons out of Waltham,
The king's foundation, that have fol-
low'd him.
Edith. O God of battles, make their
wall of shields
Firm as thy cliffs, strengthen their
palisades!
What is that whirring sound?
Stigand. The Norman arrow!
Edith. Look out upon the battle—
is he safe?
Stigand. The King of England
stands between his banners.
He glitters on the crowning of the
hill.
God save King Harold!
Edith. —chosen by his people
And fighting for his people!
Stigand. There is one
Come as Goliath came of yore—he
flings
His brand in air and catches it
again,
He is chanting some old war-song.
Edith. And no David
To meet him?
Stigand. Ay, there springs a Saxon
on him,
Falls—and another falls.
Edith. Have mercy on us!
Stigand. Lo! our good Gurth hath
smitten him to the death.
Edith. So perish all the enemies of
Harold!

CANONS (*singing*).

Hostis in Angliam
Ruit prædator;

[1] The *a* throughout these Latin hymns
should be sounded broad, as in 'father.'

Illorum, Domine,
    Scutum scindatur!
Hostis per Angliæ
    Plagas bacchatur;
    Casa crematur,
    Pastor fugatur,
    Grex trucidatur—

Stigand. Illos trucida, Domine.
Edith.   Ay, good father.

CANONS (*singing*).

Illorum scelera
    Pœna sequatur!

English Cries. Harold and Holy
    Cross! Out! out!
Stigand.   Our javelins
Answer their arrows. All the Norman
    foot
Are storming up the hill. The range
    of knights
Sit, each a statue on his horse, and
    wait.
English Cries. Harold and God Al-
    mighty!
Norman Cries. Ha Rou! Ha Rou!

CANONS (*singing*).

Eques cum pedite
    Præpediatur!
Illorum in lacrymas
    Cruor fundatur!
Pereant, pereant,
    Anglia precatur.

Stigand. Look, daughter, look.
Edith. Nay, father, look for *me!*
Stigand. Our axes lighten with a
    single flash
About the summit of the hill, and
    heads
And arms are sliver'd off and splin-
    ter'd by
Their lightning—and they fly—the
    Norman flies.
Edith. Stigand, O father, have we
    won the day?
Stigand. No, daughter, no—they
    fall behind the horse—
Their horse are thronging to the barri-
    cades;
I see the gonfanon of Holy Peter

Floating above their helmets—ha! he
    is down!
Edith. He down! Who down?
Stigand. The Norman Count is
    down.
Edith. So perish all the enemies of
    England!
Stigand. No, no, he hath risen again
    —he bares his face—
Shouts something—he points onward
    —all their horse
Swallow the hill locust-like, swarming
    up.
Edith. O God of battles, make his
    battle-axe keen
As thine own sharp-dividing justice,
    heavy
As thine own bolts that fall on crime-
    ful heads
Charged with the weight of heaven
    wherefrom they fall!

CANONS (*singing*).

Jacta tonitrua,
    Deus bellator!
Surgas e tenebris,
    Sis vindicatur!
Fulmina, fulmina,
    Deus vastator!

Edith. O God of battles, they are
    three to one,
Make thou one man as three to roll
    them down!

CANONS (*singing*).

Equus cum equite
    Dejiciatur!
Acies, acies
    Prona sternatur!
Illorum lanceas
    Frange, Creator!

Stigand. Yea, yea, for how their
    lances snap and shiver
Against the shifting blaze of Harold's
    axe!
War-woodman of old Woden, how he
    fells
The mortal copse of faces! There!
    And there!
The horse and horsemen cannot meet
    the shield,

The blow that brains the horseman
    cleaves the horse,
The horse and horseman roll along
    the hill,
They fly once more, they fly, the Nor-
    man flies!

Equus cum equite
Præcipitatur.

Edith. O God, the God of truth
    hath heard my cry!
Follow them, follow them, drive them
    to the sea!

Illorum scelera
Pœna sequatur!

Stigand. Truth! no; a lie; a trick, a
    Norman trick!
They turn on the pursuer, horse
    against foot,
They murder all that follow.
    Edith.   Have mercy on us!
    Stigand.   Hot-headed   fools—to
    burst the wall of shields!
They have broken the commandment
    of the king!
    Edith. His oath was broken—O
    holy Norman Saints,
Ye that are now of heaven, and see
    beyond
Your Norman shrines, pardon it, par-
    don it,
That he forsware himself for all he
    loved,
Me, me and all! Look out upon the
    battle!
    Stigand. They thunder again upon
    the barricades.
My sight is eagle, but the strife so
    thick—
This is the hottest of it; hold, ash!
    hold, willow!
English Cries. Out, out!
Norman Cries. Ha Rou!
    Stigand. Ha! Gurth had leapt upon
    him
And slain him; he hath fallen.
    Edith.   And I am heard.
Glory to God in the Highest! fallen,
    fallen!
    Stigand. No, no, his horse—he
    mounts another—wields

His war-club, dashes it on Gurth, and
    Gurth,
Our noble Gurth, is down!
    Edith.   Have mercy on us!
    Stigand. And Leofwin is down!
    Edith.   Have mercy on us!
O Thou that knowest, let not my
    strong prayer
Be weaken'd in thy sight, because I
    love
The husband of another!
    Norman Cries. Ha Rou! Ha Rou!
    Edith. I do not hear our English
    war-cry.
    Stigand. No.
    Edith. Look out upon the battle—
    is he safe?
    Stigand. He stands between the
    banners with the dead
So piled about him he can hardly
    move.
    Edith (takes up the war-cry). Out!
    out!
Norman Cries. Ha Rou!
    Edith (cries out). Harold and Holy
    Cross!
Norman Cries. Ha Rou! Ha Rou!
    Edith. What is that whirring sound?
    Stigand. The Norman sends his
    arrows up to heaven,
They fall on those within the pali-
    sade!
    Edith. Look out upon the hill—is
    Harold there?
    Stigand. Sanguelac—Sanguelac—
    the arrow—the arrow!—away!

SCENE II

FIELD OF THE DEAD. NIGHT

ALDWYTH *and* EDITH.

Aldwyth. O Edith, art thou here? O
    Harold, Harold—
Our Harold—we shall never see him
    more.
    Edith. For there was more than
    sister in my kiss,
And so the Saints were wroth. I can
    not love them,

For they are Norman Saints—and yet
    I should—
They are so much holier than their
    harlot's son
With whom they play'd their game
    against the King!
    Aldwyth. The King is slain, the
        kingdom overthrown!
    Edith. No matter!
    Aldwyth. How no matter. Harold
        slain?—
I cannot find his body. O, help me
    thou!
O Edith, if I ever wrought against
    thee,
Forgive me thou, and help me here!
    Edith.   No matter!
    Aldwyth. Not help me, nor forgive
        me?
    Edith.   So thou saidest.
    Aldwyth. I say it now, forgive me!
    Edith.   Cross me not!
I am seeking one who wedded me in
    secret.
Whisper! God's angels only know it.
    Ha!
What art *thou* doing here among the
    dead?
They are stripping the dead bodies
    naked yonder,
And thou art come to rob them of
    their rings!
    Aldwyth. O Edith, Edith, I have
        lost both crown
And husband.
    Edith.   So have I.
    Aldwyth.   I tell thee, girl,
I am seeking my dead Harold.
    Edith.   And I mine!
The Holy Father strangled him with
    a hair
Of Peter, and his brother Tostig
    helpt;
The wicked sister clapt her hands and
    laugh'd;
Then all the dead fell on him.
    Aldwyth.   Edith, Edith—
    Edith. What was he like, this hus-
        band? like to thee?
Call not for help from me. I knew
    him not.
He lies not here; not close beside the
    standard.

Here fell the truest, manliest hearts
    of England.
Go further hence and find him.
    Aldwyth.   She is crazed!
    Edith. That doth not matter either.
        Lower the light.
He must be here.

Enter two CANONS, OSGOD *and* ATHEL-
RIC, *with torches. They turn over the
dead bodies and examine them as they
        pass.*

    Osgod. I think that this is Thurkill.
    Athelric. More likely Godric.
    Osgod.   I am sure this body
Is Alfwig, the king's uncle.
    Athelric.   So it is!
No, no,—brave Gurth, one gash from
        brow to knee!
    Osgod. And here is Leofwin.
    Edith.   And here is *he!*
    Aldwyth. Harold? O, no—nay, if it
        were—my God,
They have so maim'd and murder'd
    all his face
There is no man can swear to him!
    Edith.   But one woman!
Look you, we never mean to part
    again.
I have found him, I am happy.
Was there not some one ask'd me for
        forgiveness?
I yield it freely, being the true wife
Of this dead King, who never bore re-
    venge.

Enter COUNT WILLIAM *and* WILLIAM
            MALET.

    William. Who be these women?
        And what body is this?
    Edith. Harold, thy better!
    William.   Ay, and what art thou?
    Edith. His wife!
    Malet. Not true, my girl, here is
        the Queen!
            [*Pointing out* Aldwyth.
    William (*to* Aldwyth). Wast thou
        his Queen?
    Aldwyth. I was the Queen of Wales.
    William. Why, then of England.
        Madam, fear us not.

(*To* Malet.) Knowest thou this
    other?
Malet.   When I visited England,
Some held she was his wife in secret
    —some—
Well—some believed she was his
    paramour.
    Edith. Norman, thou liest! liars all
        of you,
Your Saints and all! *I* am his wife!
    and she—
For look, our marriage ring!
            [*She draws it off the finger
                of* Harold.
            I lost it somehow—
I lost it, playing with it when I was
    wild.
That bred the doubt! but I am wiser
    now—
I am too wise—Will none among you
    all
Bear me true witness—only for this
    once—
That I have found it here again?
            [*She puts it on.*
            And thou,
Thy wife am I for ever and evermore.
            [*Falls on the body and dies.*
William. Death!—and enough of
    death for this one day,
The day of Saint Calixtus, and the
    day,
My day when I was born.
    Malet.   And this dead King's,
Who, king or not, hath kinglike fought
    and fallen,
His birthday, too. It seems but yes-
    ter-even
I held it with him in his English halls,
His day, with all his roof-tree ringing
    'Harold,'
Before he fell into the snare of
    Guy;
When all men counted Harold would
    be King,
And Harold was most happy.
    William.   Thou art half English.
Take them away!
Malet, I vow to build a church to
    God
Here on the hill of battle; let our
    high altar

Stand where their standard fell—
    where these two lie.
Take them away, I do not love to see
    them.
Pluck the dead woman off the dead
    man, Malet!
    Malet. Faster than ivy! Must I
        hack her arms off?
How shall I part them?
    William. Leave them. Let them be!
Bury him and his paramour together.
He that was false in oath to me, it
    seems
Was false to his own wife. We will
    not give him
A Christian burial; yet he was a war-
    rior,
And wise, yea truthful, till that
    blighted vow
Which God avenged to-day.
Wrap them together in a purple cloak,
And lay them both upon the waste
    seashore
At Hastings, there to guard the land
    for which
He did forswear himself—a warrior—
    ay,
And but that Holy Peter fought for
    us,
And that the false Northumbrian held
    aloof,
And save for that chance arrow which
    the Saints
Sharpen'd and sent against him—who
    can tell?—
Three horses had I slain beneath me;
    twice
I thought that all was lost. Since I
    knew battle,
And that was from my boyhood, never
    yet—
No, by the splendor of God—have I
    fought men
Like Harold and his brethren, and his
    guard
Of English. Every man about his
    king
Fell where he stood. They loved him;
    and, pray God
My Normans may but move as true
    with me
To the door of death! Of one self-
    stock at first,

Make them again one people—Nor-
    man, English,
And English, Norman; we should
    have a hand
To grasp the world with, and a foot
    to stamp it—
Flat. Praise the Saints! It is over. No
    more blood!

I am King of England, so they thwart
    me not,
And I will rule according to their
    laws.
(*To Aldwyth.*) Madam, we will en-
    treat thee with all honor.
    Aldwyth. My punishment is more
    than I can bear.

BECKET

TO THE LORD CHANCELLOR,

THE RIGHT HONORABLE EARL OF SELBORNE.

My dear Selborne,—To you, the honored Chancellor of our own day, I dedicate this dramatic memorial of your great predecessor;—which, altho' not intended in its present form to meet the exigencies of our modern theatre, has nevertheless—for so you have assured me—won your approbation.   Ever yours,

TENNYSON

DRAMATIS PERSONÆ

HENRY II, (son of the Earl of Anjou).
THOMAS BECKET, Chancellor of England, afterwards Archbishop of Canterbury.
GILBERT FOLIOT, Bishop of London.
ROGER, Archbishop of York.
Bishop of Hereford.
HILARY, Bishop of Chichester.
JOCELYN, Bishop of Salisbury.
JOHN OF SALISBURY } friends of Becket.
HERBERT OF BOSHAM }
WALTER MAP, reputed author of 'Golias,' Latin poems against the priesthood.
KING LOUIS OF FRANCE.
GEOFFREY, son of Rosamund and Henry.
GRIM, a monk of Cambridge.
SIR REGINALD FITZURSE ⎫
SIR RICHARD DE BRITO ⎪ the four knights of the king's household, enemies of
SIR WILLIAM DE TRACY ⎬ Becket.
SIR HUGH DE MORVILLE ⎭
DE BROC OF SALTWOOD CASTLE.
LORD LEICESTER.
PHILIP DE ELEEMOSYNA.
TWO KNIGHT TEMPLARS.
JOHN OF OXFORD (called the Swearer).
ELEANOR OF AQUITAINE, Queen of England (divorced from Louis of France).
ROSAMUND DE CLIFFORD.
MARGERY.

Knights, Monks, Beggars, etc.

BECKET

PROLOGUE

A CASTLE IN NORMANDY. INTERIOR OF
THE HALL. ROOFS OF A CITY SEEN
THRO' WINDOWS

HENRY *and* BECKET *at chess.*

Henry. So then our good Arch-
bishop Theobald
Lies dying.
   Becket. I am grieved to know as
much
Henry. But we must have a
mightier man than he
For his successor.
   Becket. Have you thought of one?
Henry. A cleric lately poison'd his
own mother,
And being brought before the courts
of the Church,
They but degraded him. I hope they
whipt him.
I would have hang'd him.
   Becket.   It is your move.
   Henry.   Well—there. [*Moves.*
The Church in the pell-mell of
Stephen's time
Hath climb'd the throne and almost
clutch'd the crown;
But by the royal customs of our realm
The Church should hold her baronies
of me
Like other lords amenable to law.
I 'll have them written down and
made the law.
   Becket. My liege, I move my
bishop.
   Henry.   And if I live,
No man without my leave shall ex-
communicate
My tenants or my household.
   Becket.   Look to your king.
Henry. No man without my leave
shall cross the seas

To set the Pope against me—I pray
your pardon.
   Becket. Well—will you move?
   Henry.   There. [*Moves.*
   Becket. Check—you move so
wildly.
   Henry. There then!   [*Moves.*
   Becket. Why—there then, for you
see my bishop
Hath brought your king to a stand-
still. You are beaten.
   Henry (kicks over the board).
Why, there then—down go
bishop and king together.
I loathe being beaten; had I fixt my
fancy
Upon the game I should have beaten
thee,
But that was vagabond.
   Becket. Where, my liege? With
Phryne,
Or Lais, or thy Rosamund, or an-
other?
   Henry. My Rosamund is no Lais,
Thomas Becket;
And yet she plagues me too—no fault
in her—
But that I fear the Queen would have
her life.
   Becket. Put her away, put her
away, my liege!
Put her away into a nunnery!
Safe enough there from her to whom
thou art bound
By Holy Church. And wherefore
should she seek
The life of Rosamund de Clifford
more
Than that of other paramours of
thine?
   Henry. How dost thou know I am
not wedded to her?
   Becket. How should I know?
   Henry. That is my secret, Thomas.

Becket. State secrets should be patent to the statesman

Who serves and loves his king, and whom the king

Loves not as statesman, but true lover and friend.

Henry. Come, come, thou art but deacon, not yet bishop,

No, nor archbishop, nor my confessor, yet.

I would to God thou wert, for I should find

An easy father confessor in thee.

Becket. Saint Denis, that thou shouldst not. I should beat

Thy kingship as my bishop hath beaten it.

Henry. Hell take thy bishop then, and my kingship too!

Come, come, I love thee and I know thee, I know thee,

A doter on white pheasant-flesh at feasts,

A sauce-deviser for thy days of fish,

A dish-designer, and most amorous

Of good old red sound liberal Gascon wine.

Will not thy body rebel, man, if thou flatter it?

Becket. That palate is insane which cannot tell

A good dish from a bad, new wine from old.

Henry. Well, who loves wine loves woman.

Becket. So I do.

Men are God's trees, and women are God's flowers;

And when the Gascon wine mounts to my head,

The trees are all the statelier, and the flowers

Are all the fairer.

Henry. And thy thoughts, thy fancies?

Becket. Good dogs, my liege, well train'd, and easily call'd

Off from the game.

Henry. Save for some once or twice,

When they ran down the game and worried it.

Becket. No, my liege, no!—not once—in God's name, no!

Henry. Nay, then, I take thee at thy word—believe thee

The veriest Galahad of old Arthur's hall.

And so this Rosamund, my true heart-wife,

Not Eleanor—she whom I love indeed

As a woman should be loved—Why dost thou smile

So dolorously?

Becket. My good liege, if a man

Wastes himself among women, how should he love

A woman as a woman should be loved?

Henry. How shouldst thou know that never hast loved one?

Come, I would give her to thy care in England

When I am out in Normandy or Anjou.

Becket. My lord, I am your subject, not your—

Henry. Pander.

God's eyes! I know all that—not my purveyor

Of pleasures, but to save a life—her life;

Ay, and the soul of Eleanor from hell-fire;

I have built a secret bower in England, Thomas,

A nest in a bush.

Becket. And where, my liege?

Henry (whispers). Thine ear.

Becket. That 's lone enough.

Henry (laying paper on table). This chart here mark'd 'Her Bower,'

Take, keep it, friend. See, first, a circling wood,

A hundred pathways running everyway,

And then a brook, a bridge; and after that

This labyrinthine brickwork maze in maze,

And then another wood, and in the midst

A garden and my Rosamund. Look,
    this line—
The rest you see is color'd green—
    but this
Draws thro' the chart to her.
    Becket.   This blood-red line?
    Henry. Ay! blood, perchance, ex-
    cept thou see to her.
    Becket. And where is she? There
    in her English nest?
    Henry. Would God she were!—no,
    here within the city.
We take her from her secret bower in
    Anjou
And pass her to her secret bower in
    England.
She is ignorant of all but that I love
    her.
    Becket. My liege, I pray thee let
    me hence; a widow
And orphan child, whom one of thy
    wild barons—
    Henry. Ay, ay, but swear to see to
    her in England.
    Becket. Well, well, I swear, but not
    to please myself.
    Henry. Whatever come between
    us?
    Becket. What should come
Between us, Henry?
    Henry. Nay—I know not, Thomas.
    Becket. What need then? Well—
    whatever come between us.
                    [*Going.*
    Henry. A moment! thou didst help
    me to my throne
In Theobald's time, and after by thy
    wisdom
Hast kept it firm from shaking; but
    now I,
For my realm's sake, myself must be
    the wizard
To raise that tempest which will set
    it trembling
Only to base it deeper. I, true son
Of Holy Church—no croucher to the
    Gregories
That tread the kings their children
    under-heel—
Must curb her; and the Holy Father,
    while
This Barbarossa butts him from his
    chair,

Will need my help—be facile to my
    hands.
Now is my time. Yet—lest there
    should be flashes
And fulminations from the side of
    Rome,
An interdict on England—I will have
My young son Henry crown'd the
    King of England,
That so the Papal bolt may pass by
    England,
As seeming his, not mine, and fall
    abroad.
I 'll have it done—and now.
    Becket.   Surely too young
Even for this shadow of a crown; and
    tho'
I love him heartily, I can spy already
A strain of hard and headstrong in
    him. Say,
The Queen should play his kingship
    against thine!
    Henry. I will not think so, Thomas.
    Who shall crown him?
Canterbury is dying.
    Becket.   The next Canterbury.
    Henry. And who shall he be, my
    friend Thomas? Who?
    Becket. Name him; the Holy
    Father will confirm him.
    Henry (*lays his hand on* Becket's
    shoulder). Here!
    Becket. Mock me not. I am not
    even a monk.
Thy jest—no more. Why—look—is
    this a sleeve
.For an archbishop?
    Henry.   But the arm within
Is Becket's, who hath beaten down
    my foes.
    Becket. A soldier's, not a spiritual
    arm.
    Henry. I lack a spiritual soldier,
    Thomas—
A man of this world and the next to
    boot.
    Becket. There 's Gilbert Foliot.
    Henry.   He! too thin, too thin.
Thou art the man to fill out the
    Church robe;
Your Foliot fasts and fawns too much
    for me.
    Becket. Roger of York.

Henry. Roger is Roger of York;
King, Church, and State to him but
  foils wherein
To set that precious jewel, Roger of
  York.
No.

Becket. Henry of Winchester?

Henry. Him who crown'd Stephen—
King Stephen's brother! No; too
  royal for me.
And I 'll have no more Anselms.

Becket.   Sire, the business
Of thy whole kingdom waits me; let
  me go.

Henry. Answer me first.

Becket.   Then for thy barren jest
Take thou mine answer in bare com-
  mon-place—
Nolo episcopari.

Henry.   Ay, but *Nolo
Archiepiscopari,* my good friend,
Is quite another matter.

Becket.   A more awful one.
Make *me* archbishop! Why, my liege,
  I know
Some three or four poor priests a
  thousand times
Fitter for this grand function. *Me*
  archbishop!
God's favor and king's favor might so
  clash
That thou and I— That were a jest
  indeed!

Henry. Thou angerest me, man; I
  do not jest.

Enter ELEANOR *and* SIR REGINALD
         FITZURSE.

ELEANOR (*singing*).

Over! the sweet summer closes,
  The reign of the roses is done—

Henry (*to* Becket, *who is going*).
  Thou shalt not go. I have not
  ended with thee.

Eleanor (*seeing chart on table*).
This chart with the red line! her
bower! whose bower?

Henry. The chart is not mine, but
Becket's; take it, Thomas.

Eleanor. Becket! O,—ay—and
these chessmen on the floor—the
king's crown broken! Becket hath
beaten thee again—and thou hast
kicked down the board. I know thee
of old.

Henry. True enough, my mind was
set upon other matters.

Eleanor. What matters? State matters? love matters?

Henry. My love for thee, and thine
for me.

ELEANOR.

Over! the sweet summer closes,
  The reign of the roses is done;
Over and gone with the roses,
  And over and gone with the sun.

Here; but our sun in Aquitaine
lasts longer. I would I were in Aquitaine again—your North chills me.

Over! the sweet summer closes,
  And never a flower at the close;
Over and gone with the roses,
  And winter again and the snows.

That was not the way I ended it first
—but unsymmetrically, preposter-
ously, illogically, out of passion, without art—like a song of the people.
Will you have it? The last Parthian
shaft of a forlorn Cupid at the King's
left breast, and all left-handedness
and under-handedness.

And never a flower at the close;
Over and gone with the roses,
  Not over and gone with the rose.

True, one rose will outblossom the
rest, one rose in a bower. I speak after
my fancies, for I am a Troubadour,
you know, and won the violet at Toulouse; but my voice is harsh here, not
in tune, a nightingale out of season;
for marriage, rose or no rose, has
killed the golden violet.

Becket. Madam, you do ill to scorn
wedded love.

Eleanor. So I do. Louis of France
loved me, and I dreamed that I loved
Louis of France: and I loved Henry
of England, and Henry of England
dreamed that he loved me; but the
marriage-garland withers even with

the putting on, the bright link rusts with the breath of the first after-marriage kiss, the harvest moon is the ripening of the harvest, and the honeymoon is the gall of Love; he dies of his honey-moon. I could pity this poor world myself that it is no better ordered.

Henry. Dead is he, my Queen? What, altogether? Let me swear nay to that by this cross on thy neck. God's eyes! what a lovely cross! what jewels!

Eleanor. Doth it please you? Take it and wear it on that hard heart of yours—there.   [*Gives it to him.*

Henry (*puts it on*). On this left breast before so hard a heart, To hide the scar left by thy Parthian dart.

Eleanor. Has my simple song set you jingling? Nay, if I took and translated that hard heart into our Provençal facilities, I could so play about it with the rhyme—

Henry. That the heart were lost in the rhyme, and the matter in the metre. May we not pray you, madam, to spare us the hardness of your facility?

Eleanor. The wells of Castaly are not wasted upon the desert. We did but jest.

Henry. There's no jest on the brows of Herbert there. What is it, Herbert?

Enter HERBERT OF BOSHAM.

Herbert. My liege, the good archbishop is no more.

Henry. Peace to his soul!

Herbert. I left him with peace on his face,—that sweet other-world smile, which will be reflected in the spiritual body among the angels. But he longed much to see your Grace and the Chancellor ere he past, and his last words were a commendation of Thomas Becket to your Grace as his successor in the archbishopric.

Henry. Ha, Becket! thou rememberest our talk!

Becket. My heart is full of tears— I have no answer.

Henry. Well, well, old men must die, or the world would grow mouldy, would only breed the past again. Come to me to-morrow. Thou hast but to hold out thy hand. Meanwhile the revenues are mine. A-hawking, a-hawking! If I sit, I grow fat.
     [*Leaps over the table, and exit.*

Becket. He did prefer me to the chancellorship,
Believing I should ever aid the Church—
But have I done it? He commends me now
From out his grave to this archbishopric.

Herbert. A dead man's dying wish should be of weight.

Becket. His should. Come with me. Let me learn at full
The manner of his death, and all he said.
     [*Exeunt* Herbert *and* Becket.

Eleanor. Fitzurse, that chart with the red line—thou sawest it—her bower.

Fitzurse. Rosamund's?

Eleanor. Ay—there lies the secret of her whereabouts, and the King gave it to his Chancellor.

Fitzurse. To this son of a London merchant—how your Grace must hate him!

Eleanor. Hate him? as brave a soldier as Henry and a goodlier man: but thou—dost thou love this Chancellor, that thou hast sworn a voluntary allegiance to him?

Fitzurse. Not for my love toward him, but because he had the love of the King. How should a baron love a beggar on horseback, with the retinue of three kings behind him, out-royalling royalty? Besides, he holp the King to break down our castles, for the which I hate him.

Eleanor. For the which I honor him. Statesman, not Churchman, he. A great and sound policy that; I could embrace him for it: you could not see the King for the kinglings.

Fitzurse. Ay, but he speaks to a noble as tho' he were a churl, and to a churl as if he were a noble.

Eleanor. Pride of the plebeian!

Fitzurse. And this plebeian like to be Archbishop!

Eleanor. True, and I have an inherited loathing of these black sheep of the Papacy. Archbishop? I can see further into a man than our hotheaded Henry, and if there ever come feud between Church and Crown, and I do not then charm this secret out of our loyal Thomas, I am not Eleanor.

Fitzurse. Last night I followed a woman in the city here. Her face was veiled, but the back methought was Rosamund—his paramour, thy rival. I can feel for thee.

Eleanor. Thou feel for me!—paramour—rival! King Louis had no paramours, and I loved him none the more. Henry had many, and I loved him none the less—now neither more nor less—not at all; the cup's empty. I would she were but his paramour, for men tire of their fancies; but I fear this one fancy hath taken root, and borne blossom too, and she, whom the King loves indeed, is a power in the State. Rival!—ay, and when the King passes, there may come a crash and embroilment as in Stephen's time; and her children—canst thou not—that secret matter which would heat the King against thee (*whispers him and he starts*). Nay, that is safe with me as with thyself; but canst thou not—thou art drowned in debt—thou shalt have our love, our silence, and our gold—canst thou not—if thou light upon her—free me from her?

Fitzurse. Well, Madam, I have loved her in my time.

Eleanor. No, my bear, thou hast not. My Courts of Love would have held thee guiltless of love—the fine attractions and repulses, the delicacies, the subtleties.

Fitzurse. Madam, I loved according to the main purpose and intent of nature.

Eleanor. I warrant thee! thou wouldst hug thy Cupid till his ribs cracked—enough of this. Follow me this Rosamund day and night, whithersoever she goes; track her, if thou canst, even into the King's lodging, that I may (*clenches her fist*)—may at least have my cry against him and her,—and thou in thy way shouldst be jealous of the King, for thou in thy way didst once, what shall I call it, affect her thine own self.

Fitzurse. Ay, but the young colt winced and whinnied and flung up her heels; and then the King came honeying about her, and this Becket, her father's friend, like enough staved us from her.

Eleanor. Us!

Fitzurse. Yea, by the Blessed Virgin! There were more than I buzzing round the blossom—De Tracy—even that flint De Brito.

Eleanor. Carry her off among you; run in upon her and devour her, one and all of you; make her as hateful to herself and to the King as she is to me.

Fitzurse. I and all would be glad to wreak our spite on the rose-faced minion of the King, and bring her to the level of the dust, so that the King—

Eleanor. Let her eat it like the serpent, and be driven out of her paradise.

ACT I

SCENE I.—BECKET'S HOUSE IN LONDON

Chamber barely furnished. BECKET *unrobing.* HERBERT OF BOSHAM *and* SERVANT.

Servant. Shall I not help your lordship to your rest?

Becket. Friend, am I so much better than thyself
That thou shouldst help me? Thou art wearied out
With this day's work; get thee to thine own bed.

Leave me with Herbert, friend.
                    [*Exit* Servant.
Help me off, Herbert, with this—and
    this.
  Herbert. Was not the people's bless-
    ing as we passed
Heart-comfort and a balsam to thy
    blood?
  Becket. The people know their
    Church a tower of strength,
A bulwark against Throne and Bar-
    onage.
Too heavy for me, this; off with it,
    Herbert!
  Herbert. Is it so much heavier than
    thy Chancellor's robe?
  Becket. No; but the Chancellor's
    and the Archbishop's
Together more than mortal man can
    bear.
  Herbert. Not heavier than thine
    armor at Toulouse?
  Becket. O Herbert, Herbert, in my
    chancellorship
I more than once have gone against
    the Church.
  Herbert. To please the King?
  Becket.   Ay, and the King of
    kings,
Or justice; for it seem'd to me but
    just
The Church should pay her scutage
    like the lords.
But hast thou heard this cry of Gil-
    bert Foliot
That I am not the man to be your
    primate,
For Henry could not work a miracle—
Make an archbishop of a soldier?
  Herbert.   Ay,
For Gilbert Foliot held himself the
    man.
  Becket. Am I the man? My mother,
    ere she bore me,
Dream'd that twelve stars fell glitter-
    ing out of heaven
Into her bosom.
  Herbert.   Ay, the fire, the light,
The spirit of the twelve Apostles en-
    ter'd
Into thy making.
  Becket.   And when I was a child,
The Virgin, in a vision of my sleep,

Gave me the golden keys of Paradise.
    Dream,
Or prophecy, that?
  Herbert. Well, dream and prophecy
    both.
  Becket. And when I was of Theo-
    bald's household, once—
The good old man would sometimes
    have his jest—
He took his mitre off, and set it on
    me,
And said, 'My young archbishop—
    thou wouldst make
A stately archbishop!' Jest or proph-
    ecy there?
  Herbert. Both, Thomas, both.
  Becket.   Am I the man? That
    rang
Within my head last night, and when
    I slept
Methought I stood in Canterbury
    Minster,
And spake to the Lord God, and said,
    'O Lord,
I have been a lover of wines, and
    delicate meats,
And secular splendors, and a favorer
Of players, and a courtier, and a
    feeder
Of dogs and hawks, and apes, and
    lions, and lynxes.
Am *I* the man?' And the Lord an-
    swer'd me,
'Thou art the man, and all the more
    the man.'
And then I asked again, 'O Lord my
    God,
Henry the King hath been my friend,
    my brother,
And mine uplifter in this world, and
    chosen me
For this thy great archbishopric, be-
    lieving
That I should go against the Church
    with him,
And I shall go against him with the
    Church,
And I have said no word of this to
    him.
Am *I* the man? And the Lord an-
    swer'd me,
'Thou art the man, and all the more
    the man.'

And thereupon, methought, He drew
    toward me,
And smote me down upon the minster
    floor.
I fell.
    Herbert. God make not thee, but
        thy foes, fall!
    Becket. I fell. Why fall? Why did
        He smite me? What?
Shall I fall off—to please the King
    once more?
Not fight—tho' somehow traitor to
    the King—
My truest and mine utmost for the
    Church?
    Herbert. Thou canst not fall that
        way. Let traitor be;
For how have fought thine utmost for
    the Church,
Save from the throne of thine arch-
    bishopric?
And how been made archbishop hadst
    thou told him,
'I mean to fight mine utmost for the
    Church,
Against the King'?
    Becket.   But dost thou think the
        King
Forced mine election?
    Herbert.   I do think the King
Was potent in the election, and why
    not?
Why should not Heaven have so in-
    spired the King?
Be comforted. Thou art the man—be
    thou
A mightier Anselm.
    Becket. I do believe thee, then. I
        am the man.
And yet I seem appall'd—on such a
    sudden
At such an eagle-height I stand and see
The rift that runs between me and
    the King.
I served our Theobald well when I
    was with him;
I served King Henry well as Chan-
    cellor;
I am his no more, and I must serve
    the Church.
This Canterbury is only less than
    Rome,

And all my doubts I fling from me
    like dust,
Winnow and scatter all scruples to
    the wind,
And all the puissance of the warrior,
And all the wisdom of the Chancellor,
And all the heap'd experiences of life,
I cast upon the side of Canterbury—
Our holy mother Canterbury, who sits
With tatter'd robes. Laics and barons,
    thro'
The random gifts of careless kings,
    have graspt
Her livings, her advowsons, granges,
    farms,
And goodly acres—we will make her
    whole;
Not one rood lost. And for these
    Royal customs,
These ancient Royal customs—they
    are Royal,
Not of the Church—and let them be
    anathema.
And all that speak for them anathema.
    Herbert. Thomas, thou art moved
        too much.
    Becket.   O Herbert, here
I gash myself asunder from the King,
Tho' leaving each, a wound; mine
    own, a grief
To show the scar for ever—his, a hate
Not ever to be heal'd.

Enter ROSAMUND DE CLIFFORD, *flying
    from* SIR REGINALD FITZURSE.
    Drops her veil.

    Becket.   Rosamund de Clifford!
    Rosamund. Save me, father, hide
me—they follow me—and I must not
be known.
    Becket. Pass in with Herbert there.
    [*Exeunt* Rosamund *and* Herbert
        by side door.

Enter FITZURSE.

    Fitzurse. The archbishop!
    Becket. Ay! what wouldst thou,
        Reginald?
    Fitzurse. Why—why, my lord, I
follow'd—follow'd one—

Becket. And then what follows?
    Let me follow thee.
Fitzurse. It much imports me I
    should know her name.
Becket. What her?
Fitzurse. The woman that I fol-
    low'd hither.
Becket. Perhaps it may import her
    all as much
Not to be known.
Fitzurse.   And what care I for
    that?
Come, come, my lord archbishop; I
    saw that door
Close even now upon the woman.
Becket.   Well?
Fitzurse (making for the door).
    Nay, let me pass, my lord, for
    I must know.
Becket. Back, man!
Fitzurse. Then tell me who and
    what she is.
Becket. Art thou so sure thou fol-
    lowedest anything?
Go home, and sleep thy wine off, for
    thine eyes
Glare stupid-wild with wine.
Fitzurse (making to the door). I
    must and will.
ᚦ care not for thy new archbishopric.
Becket. Back, man, I tell thee!
    What!
Shall I forget my new archbishopric
And smite thee with my crozier on
    the skull?
'Fore God, I am a mightier man than
    thou.
Fitzurse. It well befits thy new
    archbishopric
To take the vagabond woman of the
    street
Into thine arms!
Becket.   O drunken ribaldry!
    Out, beast! out, bear!
Fitzurse.   I shall remember this.
Becket. Do, and begone!
                        [*Exit* Fitzurse.
[*Going to the door, sees* De Tracy.
    Tracy, what dost thou here?
De Tracy. My lord, I follow'd Reg-
    inald Fitzurse.
Becket. Follow him out!

De Tracy.   I shall remember this
Discourtesy.   [*Exit.*
Becket. Do. These be those baron-
    brutes
That havock'd all the land in
    Stephen's day.
Rosamund de Clifford!

Re-enter ROSAMUND *and* HERBERT.

Rosamund.   Here am I.
Becket.   Why here?
We gave thee to the charge of John of
    Salisbury,
To pass thee to thy secret bower to-
    morrow.
Wast thou not told to keep thyself
    from sight?
Rosamund. Poor bird of passage!
    so I was; but, father,
They say that you are wise in winged
    things,
And know the ways of Nature. Bar
    the bird
From following the fled summer—a
    chink—he's out,
Gone! And there stole into the city a
    breath
Full of the meadows, and it minded
    me
Of the sweet woods of Clifford, and
    the walks
Where I could move at pleasure, and
    I thought
'Lo! I must out or die.'
Becket.   Or out *and* die.
And what hast thou to do with this
    Fitzurse?
Rosamund. Nothing. He sued my
    hand. I shook at him.
He found me once alone. Nay—nay
    —I cannot
Tell you. My father drove him and
    his friends,
De Tracy and De Brito, from our
    castle.
I was but fourteen and an April then.
I heard him swear revenge.
Becket.   Why will you court it
By self-exposure? flutter out at night?
Make it so hard to save a moth from
    the fire?

Rosamund. I have saved many of
'em. You catch 'em, so,
Softly, and fling them out to the free
air.
They burn themselves *within*-door.
Becket. Our good John
Must speed you to your bower at
once. The child
Is there already.
Rosamund. Yes—the child—the
child—
O, rare, a whole long day of open
field!
Becket. Ay, but you go disguised.
Rosamund. O, rare again!
We'll baffle them, I warrant. What
shall it be?
I'll go as a nun.
Becket. No.
Rosamund. What, not good enough
Even to play at nun?
Becket. Dan John with a nun,
That Map and these new railers at the
Church
May plaister his clean name with
scurrilous rhymes!
No!
Go like a monk, cowling and clouding
up
That fatal star, thy beauty, from the
squint
Of lust and glare of malice. Good-
night! good-night!
Rosamund. Father, I am so tender
to all hardness!
Nay, father, first thy blessing.
Becket. Wedded?
Rosamund. Father!
Becket. Well, well! I ask no more.
Heaven bless thee! hence!
Rosamund. O holy father, when
thou seest him next,
Commend me to thy friend.
Becket. What friend?
Rosamund. The King.
Becket. Herbert, take out a score
of armed men
To guard this bird of passage to her
cage;
And watch Fitzurse, and if he follow
thee,
Make him thy prisoner. I am Chan-
cellor yet.

[*Exeunt* Herbert *and* Rosamund.
Poor soul! poor soul!
My friend, the King!—O thou Great
Seal of England,
Given me by my dear friend, the King
of England—
We long have wrought together, thou
and I—
Now must I send thee as a common
friend
To tell the King, my friend, I am
against him.
We are friends no more; he will say
that, not I.
The worldly bond between us is dis-
solved,
Not yet the love. Can I be under him
As Chancellor? as Archbishop over
him?
Go therefore like a friend slighted by
one
That hath climb'd up to nobler com-
pany.
Not slighted—all but moan'd for.
Thou must go.
I have not dishonor'd thee—I trust I
have not—
Not mangled justice. May the hand
that next
Inherits thee be but as true to thee
As mine hath been! O, my dear friend,
the King!
O brother!—I may come to martyr-
dom.
I am martyr in myself already.—Her-
bert!
Herbert (*re-entering*). My lord, the
town is quiet, and the moon
Divides the whole long street with
light and shade.
No footfall—no Fitzurse. We have
seen her home.
Becket. The hog hath tumbled him-
self into some corner,
Some ditch, to snore away his drunk-
enness
Into the sober headache,—Nature's
moral
Against excess. Let the Great Seal be
sent
Back to the King to-morrow.
Herbert. Must that be?

The King may rend the bearer limb
    from limb.
Think on it again.
Becket.   Against the moral excess
No physical ache, but failure it may
    be
Of all we aim'd at. John of Salisbury
Hath often laid a cold hand on my
    heats,
And Herbert hath rebuked me even
    now.
I will be wise and wary, not the soldier
As Foliot swears it.—John, and out
    of breath!

Enter JOHN OF SALISBURY.

John of Salisbury. Thomas, thou
    wast not happy taking charge
Of this wild Rosamund to please the
    King,
Nor am I happy having charge of
    her—
The included Danaë has escaped again
Her tower and her Acrisius—where to
    seek?
I have been about the city.
Becket.   Thou wilt find her
Back in her lodging. Go with her—at
    once—
To-night—my men will guard you to
    the gates,
Be sweet to her, she has many ene-
    mies.
Send the Great Seal by daybreak.
    Both, good-night!

SCENE II

STREET IN NORTHAMPTON LEADING TO
THE CASTLE

ELEANOR'S RETAINERS *and* BECKET'S
RETAINERS *fighting. Enter* ELEANOR
and BECKET *from opposite streets.*

Eleanor. Peace, fools!
Becket. Peace, friends! what idle
    brawl is this?
Retainer of Becket. They said—
    her Grace's people—thou wast
    found—

Liars! I shame to quote 'em—caught,
    my lord,
With a wanton in thy lodging—Hell
    requite 'em!
Retainer of Eleanor. My liege, the
    Lord Fitzurse reported this
In passing to the Castle even now.
Retainer of Becket. And then they
    mock'd us and we fell upon
    'em,
For we would live and die for thee,
    my lord,
However kings and queens may frown
    on thee.
Becket to his Retainers. Go, go—
    no more of this!
Eleanor to her Retainers. Away!—
    (*Exeunt Retainers.*) Fitz-
    urse—
Becket. Nay, let him be.
Eleanor.   No, no, my lord arch-
    bishop,
'T is known you are midwinter to all
    women,
But often in your chancellorship you
    served
The follies of the King.
Becket.   No, not these follies!
Eleanor. My lord, Fitzurse beheld
    her in your lodging.
Becket. Whom?
Eleanor. Well—you know—the
    minion, Rosamund.
Becket. He had good eyes!
Eleanor. Then hidden in the street
He watch'd her pass with John of
    Salisbury,
And heard her cry, 'Where is this
    bower of mine?'
Becket. Good ears too!
Eleanor.   You are going to the
    Castle,
Will you subscribe the customs?
Becket.   I leave that,
Knowing how much you reverence
    Holy Church,
My liege, to your conjecture.
Eleanor.   I and mine—
And many a baron holds along with
    me—
Are not so much at feud with Holy
    Church

But we might take your side against
the customs—
So that you grant me one slight favor.
  Becket.   What?
  Eleanor. A sight of that same chart
    which Henry gave you
With the red line—'her bower.'
  Becket.   And to what end?
  Eleanor. That Church must scorn
    herself whose fearful priest
Sits winking at the license of a king,
Altho' we grant when kings are dan-
    gerous
The Church must play into the hands
    of kings;
Look! I would move this wanton
    from his sight
And take the Church's danger on my-
    self.
  Becket. For which she should be
    duly grateful.
  Eleanor.   True!
Tho' she that binds the bond, herself
    should see
That kings are faithful to their mar-
    riage vow.
  Becket. Ay, madam, and queens
    also.
  Eleanor.   And queens also!
What is your drift?
  Becket.   My drift is to the Castle,
Where I shall meet the barons and
    my King.   [*Exit.*

DE BROC, DE TRACY, DE BRITO, DE
MORVILLE (*passing*).

  Eleanor. To the Castle?
  De Broc.   Ay!
  Eleanor. Stir up the King, the
    lords!
Set all on fire against him!
  De Brito.   Ay, good madam!
                    [*Exeunt.*
  Eleanor. Fool! I will make thee
    hateful to thy King.
Churl! I will have thee frighted into
    France,
And I shall live to trample on thy
    grave.

SCENE III

THE HALL IN NORTHAMPTON CASTLE

*On one side of the stage the doors of
an inner Council-chamber, half-
open. At the bottom, the great
doors of the Hall.* ROGER ARCH-
BISHOP OF YORK, FOLIOT BISHOP OF
LONDON, HILARY OF CHICHESTER,
BISHOP OF HEREFORD, RICHARD DE
HASTINGS (*Grand Prior of Tem-
plars*), PHILIP DE ELEEMOSYNA (*the
Pope's Almoner*), *and others.* DE
BROC, FITZURSE, DE BRITO, DE MOR-
VILLE, DE TRACY, *and other* BARONS
assembled—a table before them.
JOHN OF OXFORD, *President of the
Council.*

Enter BECKET *and* HERBERT OF
BOSHAM.

  Becket. Where is the King?
  Roger of York. Gone hawking on
    the Nene,
His heart so gall'd with thine ingrati-
    tude,
He will not see thy face till thou hast
    sign'd
These ancient laws and customs of
    the realm.
Thy sending back the Great Seal
    madden'd him;
He all but pluck'd the bearer's eyes
    away.
Take heed lest he destroy thee ut-
    terly.
  Becket. Then shalt thou step into
    my place and sign.
  Roger of York. Didst thou not
    promise Henry to obey
These ancient laws and customs of
    the realm?
  Becket. Saving the honor of my
    order—ay.
Customs, traditions,—clouds that
    come and go;
The customs of the Church are
    Peter's rock.
  Roger of York. Saving thine order!
    But King Henry sware

That, saving his King's kingship, he would grant thee
The crown itself. Saving thine order, Thomas,
Is black and white at once, and comes to nought.
O bolster'd up with stubbornness and pride,
Wilt thou destroy the Church in fighting for it,
And bring us all to shame?
    Becket.   Roger of York,
When I and thou were youths in Theobald's house,
Twice did thy malice and thy calumnies
Exile me from the face of Theobald.
Now I am Canterbury, and thou art York.
    Roger of York. And is not York the peer of Canterbury?
Did not Great Gregory bid Saint Austin here
Found two archbishoprics, London and York?
    Becket. What came of that? The first archbishop fled,
And York lay barren for a hundred years.
Why, by this rule, Foliot may claim the pall
For London too.
    Foliot. And with good reason too,
For London had a temple and a priest
When Canterbury hardly bore a name.
    Becket. The pagan temple of a pagan Rome!
The heathen priesthood of a heathen creed!
Thou goest beyond thyself in petulancy!
Who made thee London? Who, but Canterbury?
    John of Oxford. Peace, peace, my lords! these customs are no longer
As Canterbury calls them, wandering clouds,
But by the King's command are written down,
And by the King's command I, John of Oxford,

The President of this Council, read them.
    Becket.   Read!
    John of Oxford (reads). 'All causes of advowsons and presentations, whether between laymen or clerics, shall be tried in the King's court.'
    Becket. But that I cannot sign; for that would drag
The cleric before the civil judgment-seat,
And on a matter wholly spiritual.
    John of Oxford. 'If any cleric be accused of felony, the Church shall not protect him; but he shall answer to the summons of the King's court to be tried therein.'
    Becket. And that I cannot sign.
Is not the Church the visible Lord on earth?
Shall hands that do create the Lord be bound
Behind the back like laymen-criminals?
The Lord be judged again by Pilate? No!
    John of Oxford. 'When a bishopric falls vacant, the King, till another be appointed, shall receive the revenues thereof.'
    Becket. And that I cannot sign. Is the King's treasury
A fit place for the moneys of the Church,
That be the patrimony of the poor?
    John of Oxford. 'And when the vacancy is to be filled up, the King shall summon the chapter of that church to court, and the election shall be made in the Chapel Royal, with the consent of our lord the King, and by the advice of his Government.'
    Becket. And that I cannot sign; for that would make
Our island-Church a schism from Christendom,
And weight down all free choice beneath the throne.
    Foliot. And was thine own election so canonical,
Good father?
    Becket.   If it were not, Gilbert Foliot,

I mean to cross the sea to France, and
    lay
My crozier in the Holy Father's
    hands,
And bid him re-create me, Gilbert
    Foliot.
    Foliot. Nay; by another of these
    customs thou
Wilt not be suffer'd so to cross the
    seas
Without the license of our lord the
    King.
    Becket. That, too, I cannot sign.

DE BROC, DE BRITO, DE TRACY, FITZ-
URSE, DE MORVILLE, *start up—a
clash of swords.*

                Sign and obey!
    Becket. My lords, is this a combat
    or a council?
Are ye my masters, or my lord the
    King?
Ye make this clashing for no love o'
    the customs
Or constitutions, or whate'er ye call
    them,
But that there be among you those
    that hold
Lands reft from Canterbury.
    De Broc. And mean to keep them,
In spite of thee!
    Lords (shouting). Sign, and obey
    the crown!
    Becket. The crown? Shall I do less
    for Canterbury
Than Henry for the crown? King Ste-
    phen gave
Many of the crown lands to those
    that helpt him;
So did Matilda, the King's mother.
    Mark,
When Henry came into his own again,
Then he took back not only Stephen's
    gifts,
But his own mother's, lest the crown
    should be
Shorn of ancestral splendor. This did
    Henry.
Shall I do less for mine own Canter-
    bury?
And thou, De Broc, that holdest Salt-
    wood Castle—

    De Broc. And mean to hold it, or—
    Becket.   To have my life.
    De Broc. The King is quick to an-
    ger; if thou anger him,
We wait but the King's word to strike
    thee dead.
    Becket. Strike, and I die the death
    of martyrdom;
Strike, and ye set these customs by
    my death
Ringing their own death-knell thro
    all the realm.
    Herbert. And I can tell you, lords,
    ye are all as like
To lodge a fear in Thomas Becket's
    heart
As find a hare's form in a lion's cave.
    John of Oxford. Ay, sheathe your
    swords, ye will displease the
    King.
    De Broc. Why, down then thou!
    but an he come to Saltwood,
By God's death, thou shalt stick him
    like a calf!
                [Sheathing his sword.
    Hilary. O my good lord, I do en-
    treat thee—sign.
Save the King's honor here before his
    barons.
He hath sworn that thou shouldst
    sign, and now but shuns
The semblance of defeat; I have
    heard him say
He means no more; so if thou sign,
    my lord,
That were but as the shadow of an
    assent.
    Becket. 'T would seem too like the
    substance, if I sign'd.
    Philip de Eleemosyna. My lord,
    thine ear! I have the ear of
    the Pope.
As thou hast honor for the Pope our
    master,
Have pity on him, sorely prest upon
By the fierce Emperor and his Anti-
    pope.
Thou knowest he was forced to fly to
    France;
He pray'd me to pray thee to pacify
Thy King; for if thou go against thy
    King,

Then must he likewise go against thy
    King,
And then thy King might join the
    Antipope,
And that would shake the Papacy as
    it stands.
Besides, thy King swore to our car-
    dinals
He meant no harm nor damage to the
    Church.
Smoothe thou his pride—thy signing
    is but form;
Nay, and should harm come of it, it is
    the Pope
Will be to blame—not thou. Over and
    over
He told me thou shouldst pacify the
    King,
Lest there be battle between Heaven
    and Earth,
And Earth should get the better—for
    the time.
Cannot the Pope absolve thee if thou
    sign?
    Becket. Have I the orders of the
        Holy Father?
    Philip de Eleemosyna. Orders, my
        lord—why, no; for what am
        I?
The secret whisper of the Holy
    Father.
Thou, that hast been a statesman,
    couldst thou always
Blurt thy free mind to the air?
    Becket. If Rome be feeble, then
        should I be firm.
    Philip. Take it not that way—balk
        not the Pope's will.
When he hath shaken off the Emperor,
He heads the Church against the King
    with thee.
    Richard de Hastings (*kneeling*).
        Becket, I am the oldest of the
        Templars;
I knew thy father; he would be mine
    age
Had he lived now; think of me as thy
    father!
Behold thy father kneeling to thee,
    Becket.
Submit; I promise thee on my salva-
    tion

That thou wilt hear no more o' the
    customs.
    Becket.   What!
Hath Henry told thee? hast thou
    talk'd with him?
    Another   Templar   (kneeling).
        Father, I am the youngest of
        the Templars,
Look on me as I were thy bodily son,
For, like a son, I lift my hands to thee.
    Philip. Wilt thou hold out for ever,
        Thomas Becket?
Dost thou not hear?
    Becket (*signs*). Why—there then—
        there—I sign,
And swear to obey the customs.
    Foliot.   Is it thy will,
My lord archbishop, that we too
    should sign?
    Becket. O, ay, by that canonical
        obedience
Thou still hast owed thy father, Gil-
    bert Foliot.
    Foliot. Loyally and with good faith,
        my lord archbishop?
    Becket. O, ay, with all that loyalty
        and good faith
Thou still hast shown thy primate,
    Gilbert Foliot.
    [*Becket draws apart with* Herbert.
Herbert, Herbert, have I betray'd the
    Church?
I'll have the paper back—blot out my
    name.
    Herbert. Too late, my lord: you
        see they are signing there.
    Becket. False to myself—it is the
        will of God
To break me, prove me nothing of
    myself!
This almoner hath tasted Henry's
    gold.
The cardinals have finger'd Henry's
    gold.
And Rome is venal even to rottenness.
I see it, I see it.
I am no soldier, as he said—at least
No leader. Herbert, till I hear from
    the Pope
I will suspend myself from all my
    functions.
If fast and prayer, the lacerating
    scourge—

Foliot (from the table). My lord archbishop, thou hast yet to seal.

Becket. First, Foliot, let me see what I have sign'd.
                    [*Goes to the table.*
What, this! and this!—what! new and old together!
Seal? If a seraph shouted from the sun,
And bade me seal against the rights of the Church,
I would anathematize him. I will not seal.   [*Exit with* Herbert.

Enter KING HENRY.

Henry. Where's Thomas? hath he signed? show me the papers!
Sign'd and not seal'd! How's that?

John of Oxford. He would not seal.
And when he sign'd, his face was stormy-red—
Shame, wrath, I know not what. He sat down there
And dropt it in his hands, and then a paleness,
Like the wan twilight after sunset, crept
Up even to the tonsure, and he groan'd,
'False to myself! It is the will of God!'

Henry. God's will be what it will, the man shall seal,
Or I will seal his doom. My burgher's son—
Nay, if I cannot break him as the prelate,
I'll crush him as the subject. Send for him back.
                    [*Sits on his throne.*
Barons and bishops of our realm of England,
After the nineteen winters of King Stephen—
A reign which was no reign, when none could sit
By his own hearth in peace; when murder common
As nature's death, like Egypt's plague, had fill'd
All things with blood; when every doorway blush'd,
Dash'd red with that unhallow'd passover;
When every baron ground his blade in blood;
The household dough was kneaded up with blood;
The mill-wheel turn'd in blood; the wholesome plow
Lay rusting in the furrow's yellow weeds,
Till famine dwarft the race—I came, your King!
Nor dwelt alone, like a soft lord of the East,
In mine own hall, and sucking thro' fools' ears
The flatteries of corruption—went abroad
Thro' all my counties, spied my people's ways;
Yea, heard the churl against the baron —yea,
And did him justice; sat in mine own courts
Judging my judges, that had found a King
Who ranged confusions, made the twilight day,
And struck a shape from out the vague, and law
From madness. And the event—our fallows till'd,
Much corn, repeopled towns, a realm again.
So far my course, albeit not glassy-smooth,
Had prosper'd in the main, but suddenly
Jarr'd on this rock. A cleric violated
The daughter of his host, and murder'd him.
Bishops—York, London, Chichester, Westminster—
Ye haled this tonsured devil into your courts;
But since your canon will not let you take
Life for a life, ye but degraded him
Where I had hang'd him. What doth hard murder care

For degradation? and that made me
 muse,
Being bounden by my coronation
 oath
To do men justice. Look to it, your
 own selves!
Say that a cleric murder'd an arch-
 bishop,
What could ye do? Degrade, imprison
 him—
Not death for death.
 John of Oxford. But I, my liege,
  could swear,
To death for death.
 Henry. And, looking thro' my
  reign,
I found a hundred ghastly murders
 done
By men, the scum and offal of the
 Church;
Then, glancing thro' the story of this
 realm,
I came on certain wholesome usages,
Lost in desuetude, of my grandsire's
 day,
Good royal customs—had them writ-
 ten fair
For John of Oxford here to read to
 you.
 John of Oxford. And I can easily
  swear to these as being
The King's will and God's will and
 justice; yet
I could but read a part to-day, be-
 cause—
 Fitzurse. Because my lord of Can-
  terbury—
 De Tracy. Ay,
This lord of Canterbury—
 De Brito.   As is his wont
Too much of late whene'er your royal
 rights
Are mooted in our councils—
 Fitzurse. —made an uproar.
 Henry. And Becket had my bosom
  on all this;
If ever man by bonds of grateful-
 ness—
I raised him from the puddle of the
 gutter,
I made him porcelain from the clay of
 the city—

Thought that I knew him, err'd thro'
 love of him,
Hoped, were he chosen archbishop,
 Church and Crown,
Two sisters gliding in an equal dance,
Two rivers gently flowing side by
 side—
But no!
The bird that moults sings the same
 song again,
The snake that sloughs comes out a
 snake again.
Snake—ay, but he that lookt a fang-
 less one
Issues a venomous adder.
For he, when having dofft the Chan-
 cellor's robe—
Flung the Great Seal of England in
 my face—
Claim'd some of our crown lands for
 Canterbury—
My comrade, boon companion, my
 co-reveller,
The master of his master, the King's
 king.—
God's eyes! I had meant to make him
 all but king.
Chancellor-Archbishop, he might well
 have sway'd
All England under Henry, the young
 King,
When I was hence. What did the
 traitor say?
False to himself, but ten-fold false to
 me!
The will of God—why, then it is my
 will—
Is he coming?
 Messenger (*entering*). With a
  crowd of worshippers,
And holds his cross before him thro'
 the crowd,
As one that puts himself in sanctuary.
 Henry. His cross!
 Roger of York. His cross! I'll front
  him, cross to cross.
     [*Exit* Roger of York.
 Henry. His cross! it is the traitor
  that imputes
Treachery to his King!
It is not safe for me to look upon him.
Away—with me!
    [*Goes in with his* Barons *to the*

*Council-Chamber, the door of
which is left open.*

Enter BECKET, *holding his cross of
silver before him. The* BISHOPS
come round him.

Hereford. The King will not abide
thee with thy cross.
Permit me, my good lord, to bear it
for thee,
Being thy chaplain.
Becket. No; it must protect me.
Herbert. As once he bore the stand-
ard of the Angles,
So now he bears the standard of the
angels.
Foliot. I am the dean of the prov-
ince; let me bear it.
Make not thy King a traitorous mur-
derer.
Becket. Did not your barons draw
their swords against me?

Enter ROGER OF YORK, *with his cross,
advancing to* BECKET.

Becket. Wherefore dost thou pre-
sume to bear thy cross,
Against the solemn ordinance from
Rome,
Out of thy province?
Roger of York. Why dost thou pre-
sume,
Arm'd with thy cross, to come before
the King?
If Canterbury bring his cross to
court,
Let York bear his to mate with Can-
terbury.
Foliot (seizing hold of Becket's
cross). Nay, nay, my lord, thou
must not brave the King.
Nay, let me have it. I will have it!
Becket.   Away!
                    [*Flinging him off.*
Foliot. He fasts, they say, this
mitred Hercules!
He fast! is that an arm of fast? My
lord,
Hadst thou not sign'd, I had gone
along with thee;

But thou the shepherd hast betray'd
the sheep,
And thou art perjured, and thou wilt
not seal.
As Chancellor thou wast against the
Church,
Now as archbishop goest against the
King;
For, like a fool, thou know'st no mid-
dle way.
Ay, ay! but art thou stronger than
the King?
Becket. Strong—not in mine own
self, but Heaven; true
To either function, holding it; and
thou
Fast, scourge thyself, and mortify thy
flesh,
Not spirit—thou remainest Gilbert
Foliot,
A worldly follower of the worldly
strong.
I, bearing this great ensign, make it
clear
Under what prince I fight.
Foliot.   My lord of York,
Let us go in to the Council, where our
bishops
And our great lords will sit in judg-
ment on him.
Becket. Sons sit in judgment on
their father!—then
The spire of Holy Church may prick
the graves—
Her crypt among the stars. Sign? seal?
I promised
The King to obey these customs, not
yet written,
Saving mine order; true, too, that
when written
I sign'd them—being a fool, as Foliot
call'd me.
I hold not by my signing. Get ye
hence,
Tell what I say to the King.
              [*Exeunt* Hereford, Foliot, *and
              other* Bishops.
Roger of York. The Church will
hate thee.   [*Exit.*
Becket. Serve my best friend and
make him my worst foe;
Fight for the Church, and set the
Church against me!

Herbert. To be honest is to set all
    knaves against thee.
Ah, Thomas, excommunicate them
    all!
Hereford (re-entering). I cannot
    brook the turmoil thou hast
    raised.
I would, my lord Thomas of Canter-
    bury,
Thou wert plain Thomas and not Can-
    terbury,
Or that thou wouldst deliver Canter-
    bury
To our King's hands again, and be at
    peace.
Hilary (re-entering). For hath not
    thine ambition set the Church
This day between the hammer and the
    anvil—
Fealty to the King, obedience to thy-
    self?
Herbert. What say the bishops?
Hilary.   Some have pleaded for
    him,
But the King rages—most are with
    the King;
And some are reeds, that one time
    sway to the current,
And to the wind another. But we hold
Thou art forsworn; and no forsworn
    archbishop
Shall helm the Church. We therefore
    place ourselves
Under the shield and safeguard of the
    Pope,
And cite thee to appear before the
    Pope,
And answer thine accusers.—Art
    thou deaf?
Becket. I hear you. [*Clash of arms.*
Hilary. Dost thou hear those
    others?
Becket.   Ay!
Roger of York (re-entering). The
    King's 'God's eyes!' come now
    so thick and fast
We fear that he may reave thee of
    thine own.
Come on, come on! it is not fit for us
To see the proud archbishop muti-
    lated.
Say that he blind thee and tear out
    thy tongue.

Becket. So be it. He begins at top
    with me;
They crucified Saint Peter downward.
Roger of York.   Nay,
But for their sake who stagger be-
    twixt thine
Appeal and Henry's anger, yield.
Becket.   Hence, Satan!
        [*Exit* Roger of York.
Fitzurse (re-entering). My lord,
    the King demands three hun-
    dred marks,
Due from his castles of Berkhamstead
    and Eye
When thou thereof wast warden.
Becket.   Tell the King
I spent thrice that in fortifying his
    castles.
De Tracy (re-entering). My lord,
    the King demands seven hun-
    dred marks,
Lent at the siege of Toulouse by the
    King.
Becket. I led seven hundred knights
    and fought his wars.
De Brito (re-entering). My lord,
    the King demands five hundred
    marks,
Advanced thee at his instance by the
    Jews,
For which the King was bound se-
    curity.
Becket. I thought it was a gift; I
    thought it was a gift.

Enter LORD LEICESTER (*followed by*
    BARONS *and* BISHOPS).

Leicester. My lord, I come unwill-
    ingly. The King
Demands a strict account of all those
    revenues
From all the vacant sees and abbacies,
Which came into thy hands when
    Chancellor.
Becket. How much might that
    amount to, my lord Leicester?
Leicester. Some thirty—forty thou-
    sand silver marks.
Becket. Are these your customs? O
    my good lord Leicester,
The King and I were brothers. All I
    had

I lavish'd for the glory of the King;
I shone from him, for him, his glory, his
Reflection. Now the glory of the Church
Hath swallow'd up the glory of the King;
I am his no more, but hers. Grant me one day
To ponder these demands.

Leicester. Hear first thy sentence!
The King and all his lords—

Becket. Son, first hear *me!*

Leicester. Nay, nay, canst thou, that holdest thine estates
In fee and barony of the King, decline
The judgment of the King?

Becket. The King! I hold
Nothing in fee and barony of the King.
Whatever the Church owns—she holds it in
Free and perpetual alms, unsubject to
One earthly sceptre.

Leicester. Nay, but hear thy judgment.
The King and all his barons—

Becket. Judgment! Barons!
Who but the bridegroom dares to judge the bride,
Or he the bridegroom may appoint? Not he
That is not of the house, but from the street
Stain'd with the mire thereof.
                          I had been so true
To Henry and mine office that the King
Would throne me in the great archbishopric;
And I, that knew mine own infirmity,
For the King's pleasure rather than God's cause
Took it upon me—err'd thro' love of him.
Now therefore God from me withdraws Himself,
And the King too.
              What! forty thousand marks!
Why, thou, the King, the Pope, the Saints, the world,

Know that when made archbishop I was freed,
Before the Prince and chief justiciary,
From every bond and debt and obligation
Incurr'd as Chancellor.
                      Hear me, son. As gold
Outvalues dross, light darkness, Abel Cain,
The soul the body, and the Church the Throne,
I charge thee, upon pain of mine anathema,
That thou obey, not me, but God in me,
Rather than Henry. I refuse to stand
By the King's censure, make my cry to the Pope,
By whom I will be judged; refer myself,
The King, these customs, all the Church, to him,
And under his authority—I depart.
                                [Going.
[*Leicester looks at him doubtingly.*
Am I a prisoner?

Leicester. By Saint Lazarus, no!
I am confounded by thee. Go in peace.

De Broc. In peace now—but after. Take that for earnest.
[*Flings a bone at him from the rushes.*
De Brito, Fitzurse, De Tracy, and Others (*flinging wisps of rushes*). Ay, go in peace, caitiff, caitiff! And that too, perjured prelate—and that, turncoat shaveling! There, there, there! traitor, traitor, traitor!

Becket. Mannerless wolves!
            [*Turning and facing them.*
Herbert. Enough, my lord, enough!

Becket. Barons of England and of Normandy,
When what ye shake at doth but seem to fly,
True test of coward, ye follow with a yell.
But I that threw the mightiest knight of France,
Sir Engelram de Trie,—

Herbert. Enough, my lord.

Becket. More than enough. I play
the fool again.

Enter HERALD.

Herald. The King commands you,
upon pain of death,
That none should wrong or injure
your archbishop.
Foliot. Deal gently with the young
man Absalom.
[*Great doors of the Hall at the
back open, and discover a
crowd. They shout:*
Blessed is he that cometh in the name
of the Lord!

SCENE IV

REFECTORY OF THE MONASTERY AT
NORTHAMPTON

A Banquet on the Tables.

Enter BECKET. BECKET'S RETAINERS.

First Retainer. Do thou speak first.
Second Retainer. Nay, thou! Nay,
thou!
Hast not thou drawn the short straw?
First Retainer. My lord archbishop,
wilt thou permit us—
Becket. To speak without stam-
mering and like a free man? Ay.
First Retainer. My lord, permit us
then to leave thy service.
Becket. When?
First Retainer. Now.
Becket. To-night?
First Retainer. To-night, my lord.
Becket. And why?
First Retainer. My lord, we leave
thee not without tears.
Becket. Tears? Why not stay with
me then?
First Retainer. My lord, we cannot
yield thee an answer altogether to thy
satisfaction.
Becket. I warrant you, or your own
either. Shall I find you one? The King
hath frowned upon me.

First Retainer. That is not altogether our answer, my lord.
Becket. No; yet all but all. Go, go!
Ye have eaten of my dish and drunken
of my cup for a dozen years.
First Retainer. And so we have.
We mean thee no wrong. Wilt thou
not say, 'God bless you,' ere we go?
Becket. God bless you all! God
redden your pale blood! But mine is
human-red; and when ye shall hear it
is poured out upon earth, and see it
mounting to heaven, my 'God bless
you,' that seems sweet to you now,
will blast and blind you like a curse.
First Retainer. We hope not, my
lord. Our humblest thanks for your
blessing. Farewell!
[*Exeunt* Retainers.
Becket. Farewell, friends! farewell,
swallows! I wrong the bird; she leaves
only the nest she built, they leave the
builder. Why? Am I to be murdered
to-night?
[*Knocking at the door.*
Attendant. Here is a missive left at
the gate by one from the castle.
Becket. Cornwall's hand or Leicester's; they write marvellously alike.
[*Reading.*
'Fly at once to France, to King
Louis of France; there be those about
our King who would have thy blood.'

Was not my lord of Leicester bidden to our supper?
Attendant. Ay, my lord, and divers
other earls and barons. But the hour
is past, and our brother, Master Cook,
he makes moan that all be a-getting
cold.
Becket. And I make my moan along
with him. Cold after warm, winter
after summer, and the golden leaves,
these earls and barons, that clung to
me, frosted off me by the first cold
frown of the King. Cold, but look how
the table steams, like a heathen altar;
nay, like the altar at Jerusalem. Shall
God's good gifts be wasted? None of
them here! Call in the poor from the
streets, and let them feast.

Herbert. That is the parable of our blessed Lord.

Becket. And why should not the parable of our blessed Lord be acted again? Call in the poor! The Church is ever at variance with the kings, and ever at one with the poor. I marked a group of lazars in the marketplace —half-rag, half-sore—beggars, poor rogues (Heaven bless 'em!) who never saw nor dreamed of such a banquet. I will amaze them. Call them in, I say. They shall henceforward be my earls and barons—our lords and masters in Christ Jesus.   [*Exit* Herbert.

If the King hold his purpose, I am myself a beggar. Forty thousand marks! forty thousand devils—and these craven bishops.

A Poor Man (entering) with his dog. My lord archbishop, may I come in with my poor friend, my dog? The King's verdurer caught him a-hunting in the forest, and cut off his paws. The dog followed his calling, my lord. I ha' carried him ever so many miles in my arms, and he licks my face and moans and cries out against the King.

Becket. Better thy dog than thee. The King's courts would use thee worse than thy dog—they are too bloody. Were the Church king, it would be otherwise. Poor beast! poor beast! set him down. I will bind up his wounds with my napkin. Give him a bone, give him a bone! Who misuses a dog would misuse a child—they cannot speak for themselves. Past help! his paws are past help. God help him!

Enter the BEGGARS *(and seat themselves at the Tables)*. BECKET *and* HERBERT *wait upon them*.

First Beggar. Swine, sheep, ox— here's a French supper! When thieves fall out, honest men—

Second Beggar. Is the archbishop a thief who gives thee thy supper?

First Beggar. Well, then, how does it go? When honest men fall out, thieves—no, it can't be that.

Second Beggar. Who stole the wid-ow's one sitting hen o' Sunday, when she was at mass?

First Beggar. Come, come! thou hadst thy share on her. Sitting hen! Our Lord Becket's our great sitting-hen cock, and we should n't ha' been sitting here if the barons and bishops had n't been a-sitting on the arch-bishop.

Becket. Ay, the princes sat in judgment against me, and the Lord hath prepared your table—*Sederunt principes, ederunt pauperes*.

A Voice. Becket, beware of the knife!

Becket. Who spoke?

Third Beggar. Nobody, my lord. What's that, my lord?

Becket. Venison.

Third Beggar. Venison?

Becket. Buck—deer, as you call it.

Third Beggar. King's meat! By the Lord, won't we pray for your lord-ship!

Becket. And, my children, your prayers will do more for me in the day of peril that dawns darkly and drearily over the house of God—yea, and in the day of judgment also, than the swords of the craven sycophants would have done had they remained true to me whose bread they have par-taken. I must leave you to your ban-quet. Feed, feast, and be merry. Her-bert, for the sake of the Church itself, if not for my own, I must fly to France to-night. Come with me.

[*Exit with* Herbert.

Third Beggar. Here—all of you— my lord's health! (*they drink*). Well —if that isn't goodly wine—

First Beggar. Then there isn't a goodly wench to serve him with it; they were fighting for her to-day in the street.

Third Beggar. Peace!

FIRST BEGGAR

The black sheep baaed to the miller's
    ewe-lamb,
  'The miller's away for to-night.'
'Black sheep,' quoth she, 'too black a sin
    for me.'

And what said the black sheep, my
   masters?

'We can make a black sin white.'

Third Beggar. Peace!

'Ewe-lamb, ewe-lamb, I am here by the
   dam.
But the miller came home that night,
And so dusted his back with the meal in
   his sack,
That he made the black sheep white.

Third Beggar. Be we not of the
family? be we not a-supping with the
head of the family? be we not in my
lord's own refectory? Out from among
us; thou art our black sheep.

Enter the four KNIGHTS.

Fitzurse. Sheep, said he? And sheep
without the shepherd, too. Where is
my lord archbishop? Thou the lustiest
and lousiest of this Cain's brotherhood, answer.
Third Beggar. With Cain's answer,
my lord. Am I his keeper? Thou
shouldst call him Cain, not me.
Fitzurse. So I do, for he would murder his brother the State.
*Third Beggar (rising and advanc-
ing).* No, my lord; but because the
Lord hath set his mark upon him that
no man should murder him.
Fitzurse. Where is he? where is he?
Third Beggar. With Cain belike, in
the land of Nod, or in the land of
France for aught I know.
Fitzurse. France! Ha! De Mor-
ville, Tracy, Brito—fled is he? Cross
swords, all of you! swear to follow
him! Remember the Queen!
[*The four* Knights *cross their swords.*
De Brito. They mock us; he is here.
   [*All the* Beggars *rise and ad-
     vance upon them.*
Fitzurse. Come, you filthy knaves,
let us pass.
Third Beggar. Nay, my lord, let *us*
pass. We be a-going home after our

supper in all humbleness, my lord; for
the archbishop loves humbleness, my
lord, and though we be fifty to four,
we daren't fight you with our crutches,
my lord. There now, if thou hast not
laid hands upon me! and my fellows
know that I am all one scale like a
fish. I pray God I haven't given thee
my leprosy, my lord.
   [*Fitzurse shrinks from him, and
     another presses upon* De Brito.
De Brito. Away, dog!
Fourth Beggar. And I was bit by a
mad dog o' Friday, an' I be half dog
already by this token, that tho' I can
drink wine I cannot bide water, my
lord; and I want to bite, I want to
bite, and they do say the very breath
catches.
De Brito. Insolent clown! Shall I
smite him with the edge of the sword?
De Morville. No, nor with the flat
of it either. Smite the shepherd, and
the sheep are scattered. Smite the
sheep, and the shepherd will excommunicate thee.
De Brito. Yet my fingers itch to
beat him into nothing.
Fifth Beggar. So do mine, my lord.
I was born with it, and sulphur won't
bring it out o' me. But for all that the
archbishop washed my feet o' Tuesday. He likes it, my lord.
Sixth Beggar. And see here, my
lord, this rag fro' the grangrene i' my
leg. It's humbling—it smells o' human
natur'. Wilt thou smell it, my lord?
for the archbishop likes the smell on
it, my lord; for I be his lord and master i' Christ, my lord.
De Morville. Faugh! we shall all be
poisoned. Let us go.
   [*They draw back,* Beggars *fol-
     lowing.*
Seventh Beggar. My lord, I ha'
three sisters a-dying at home o' the
sweating sickness. They be dead while
I be a-supping.
Eighth Beggar. And I ha' nine darters i' the spital that be dead ten
times o'er i' one day wi' the putrid
fever; and I bring the taint on it

along wi' me, for the archbishop likes
it, my lord.

[*Pressing upon the* Knights *till
they disappear thro' the door.*

Third Beggar. Crutches, and itches,
and leprosies, and ulcers, and gan-
grenes, and running sores, praise ye
the Lord, for to-night ye have saved
our archbishop!

First Beggar. I'll go back again. I
hain't half done yet.

Herbert of Bosham (entering). My
friends, the archbishop bids you good-
night. He hath retired to rest, and being in great jeopardy of his life, he
hath made his bed between the altars,
from whence he sends me to bid you
this night pray for him who hath fed
you in the wilderness.

Third Beggar. So we will—so we
will, I warrant thee. Becket shall be
king, and the Holy Father shall be
king, and the world shall live by the
King's venison and the bread o' the
Lord, and there shall be no more poor
for ever. Hurrah! Vive le Roy! That's
the English of it.

ACT II

SCENE I.—ROSAMUND'S BOWER

*A Garden of Flowers. In the midst a
bank of wild-flowers with a bench
before it.*

Voices *heard singing among the trees.*

DUET

1. Is it the wind of the dawn that I hear
   in the pine overhead?
2. No; but the voice of the deep as it
   hollows the cliffs of the land.
1. Is there a voice coming up with the
   voice of the deep from the strand,
   One coming up with a song in the
   flush of the glimmering red?
2. Love that is born of the deep coming
   up with the sun from the sea.
1. Love that can shape or can shatter a
   life till the life shall have fled?
2. Nay, let us welcome him, Love that
   can lift up a life from the dead.

1. Keep him away from the lone little
   isle. Let us be, let us be.
2. Nay, let him make it his own, let him
   reign in it—he, it is he,
   Love that is born of the deep coming
   up with the sun from the sea.

Enter HENRY *and* ROSAMUND.

Rosamund. Be friends with him
     again—I do beseech thee.
Henry. With Becket? I have but
one hour with thee—
Sceptre and crozier clashing, and the
     mitre
Grappling the crown—and when I flee
     from this
For a gasp of freer air, a breathing-
     while
To rest upon thy bosom and forget
     him—
Why thou, my bird, thou pipest
     'Becket, Becket'—
Yea, thou my golden dream of Love's
     own bower,
Must be the nightmare breaking on
     my peace
With 'Becket.'
   Rosamund. O my life's life, not to
     smile
Is all but death to me. My sun, no
     cloud!
Let there not be one frown in this
     one hour.
Out of the many thine, let this be
     mine!
Look rather thou all-royal as when
     first
I met thee.
   Henry.   Where was that?
   Rosamund.   Forgetting that
Forgets me too.
   Henry.   Nay, I remember it well.
There on the moors.
   Rosamund.   And in a narrow path.
A plover flew before thee. Then I saw
Thy high black steed among the flam-
     ing furze,
Like sudden night in the main glare
     of day.
And from that height something was
     said to me,
I knew not what.
   Henry.   I ask'd the way.

Rosamund.   I think so.
So I lost mine.

Henry. Thou wast too shamed to
    answer.

Rosamund. Too scared—so young!

Henry.   The rosebud of my rose!—
Well, well, no more of *him*—I have
    sent his folk,
His kin, all his belongings, over-seas;
Age, orphans—and babe-breasting
    mothers—all
By hundreds to him—there to beg,
    starve, die—
So that the fool King Louis feed them
    not.
The man shall feel that I can strike
    him yet.

Rosamund. Babes, orphans, moth-
    ers! is that royal, sire?

Henry. And I have been as royal
    with the Church.
He shelter'd in the Abbey of Pon-
    tigny,
There wore his time studying the
    canon law
To work it against me. But since he
    cursed
My friends at Veselay, I have let
    them know
That if they keep him longer as their
    guest,
I scatter all their cowls to all the hells.

Rosamund. And is that altogether
    royal?

Henry.   Traitress!

Rosamund. A faithful traitress to
    thy royal fame.

Henry. Fame! what care I for
    fame? Spite, ignorance, envy,
Yea, honesty too, paint her what way
    they will,
Fame of to-day is infamy to-morrow;
Infamy of to-day is fame to-morrow;
And round and round again. What
    matters? Royal—
I mean to leave the royalty of my
    crown
Unlessen'd to mine heirs.

Rosamund.   Still—thy fame too;
I say that should be royal.

Henry.   And I say,
I care not for thy saying.

Rosamund.   And I say,

I care not for *thy* saying. A greater
    King
Than thou art, Love, who cares not
    for the word,
Makes 'care not'—care. There have I
    spoken true?

Henry. Care dwell with me for ever
    when I cease
To care for thee as ever!

Rosamund. No need! no need! ...
There is a bench. Come, wilt thou
    sit?—My bank
Of wild-flowers [*he sits*]. At thy feet!
                    [*She sits at his feet.*

Henry.   I bade them clear
A royal pleasaunce for thee, in the
    wood,
Not leave these country-folk at court.

Rosamund.   I brought them
In from the wood, and set them here.
    I love them
More than the garden flowers, that
    seem at most
Sweet guests, or foreign cousins, not
    half speaking
The language of the land. I love *them*
    too,
Yes. But, my liege, I am sure, of all
    the roses—
Shame fall on those who gave it a
    dog's name!—
This wild one (*picking a briar-rose*)—
    nay, I shall not prick myself—
Is sweetest. Do but smell!

Henry.   Thou rose of the world!
Thou rose of all the roses!
                        [*Muttering.*
I am not worthy of her—this beast-
    body
That God has plunged my soul in—I,
    that taking
The Fiend's advantage of a throne,
    so long
Have wander'd among women,—a
    foul stream
Thro' fever-breeding levels—at her
    side,
Among these happy dales, run clearer,
    drop
The mud I carried, like yon brook,
    and glass
The faithful face of heaven—

[*Looking at her, and unconsciously aloud,*
     —thine! thine!
Rosamund.   I know it.
Henry (*muttering*). Not hers. We
 have but one bond, her hate
 of Becket.
Rosamund (*half hearing*). Nay!
 nay! what art thou muttering?
 I hate Becket?
Henry (*muttering*). A sane and
 natural loathing for a soul
Purer, and truer and nobler than her-
 self;
And mine a bitterer illegitimate hate,
A bastard hate born of a former
 love.
 Rosamund. My fault to name him!
 O, let the hand of· one
To whom thy voice is all her music
 stay it
But for a breath!
 [*Puts her hand before his lips.*
    Speak only of thy love.
Why, there—like some loud beggar
 at thy gate—
The happy boldness of this hand hath
 won it.
Love's alms, thy kiss (*looking at her
 hand*)—Sacred! I'll kiss it
 too.   [*Kissing it.*
There! wherefore dost thou so pe-
 ruse it? Nay,
There may be crosses in my line of
 life.
 Henry. Not half *her* hand—no hand
 to mate with *her*,
If it should come to that.
 Rosamund. With her? with
 whom?
 Henry. Life on the hand is naked
 gipsy-stuff;
Life on the face, the brows—clear
 innocence!
Vein'd marble—not a furrow yet—
 and hers [*Muttering.*
Crost and recrost, a venomous spider's web—
 Rosamund (*springing up*). Out of
 the cloud, my Sun—out of the
 eclipse
Narrowing my golden hour!
 Henry.   O Rosamund,

I would be true—would tell thee all
 —and something
I had to say—I love thee none the
 less—
Which will so vex thee.
 Rosamund. Something against *me*?
 Henry. No, no, against myself.
 Rosamund. I will not hear it.
Come, come, mine hour! I bargain
 for mine hour.
I'll call thee little Geoffrey.
 Henry.   Call him!
 Rosamund.   Geoffrey!

    Enter GEOFFREY.

 Henry. How the boy grows!
 Rosamund. Ay, and his brows are
 thine;
The mouth is only Clifford, my dear
 father.
 Geoffrey. My liege, what has thou
 brought me?
 Henry.   Venal imp!
What say'st thou to the Chancellorship of England?
 Geoffrey. O, yes, my liege.
 Henry. 'O, yes, my liege!' He
 speaks
As if it were a cake of gingerbread.
 Dost thou know, my boy, what it is
to be Chancellor of England?
 Geoffrey. Something good, or thou
wouldst not give it me.
 Henry. It is, my boy, to side with
the King when Chancellor, and then
to be made archbishop and go against
the King who made him, and turn the
world upside down.
 Geoffrey. I won't have it then. Nay,
but give it me, and I promise thee not
to turn the world upside down.
 Henry (*giving him a ball*). Here is
a ball, my boy, thy world, to turn any
way and play with as thou wilt—which
is more than I can do with mine. Go
try it, play. [*Exit* Geoffrey.
A pretty lusty boy.
 Rosamund. So like to thee;
Like to be liker.
 Henry. Not in my chin, I hope!
That threatens double.

Rosamund. Thou art manlike perfect.

Henry. Ay, ay, no doubt; and were I humpt behind,
Thou 'dst say as much—the goodly way of women
Who love, for which I love them. May God grant
No ill befall or him or thee when I Am gone!

Rosamund. Is *he* thy enemy?

Henry.   He? who? ay!

Rosamund. Thine enemy knows the secret of my bower.

Henry. And I could tear him asunder with wild horses
Before he would betray it. Nay—no fear!
More like is he to excommunicate me.

Rosamund. And I would creep, crawl over knife-edge flint
Barefoot, a hundred leagues, to stay his hand
Before he flash'd the bolt.

Henry.   And when he flash'd it
Shrink from me, like a daughter of the Church.

Rosamund. Ay, but he will not.

Henry.   Ay! but if he did?

Rosamund. O, then! O, then! I almost fear to say
That my poor heretic heart would excommunicate
His excommunication, clinging to thee
Closer than ever.

Henry (*raising* Rosamund *and kissing her*). My brave-hearted Rose!
Hath he ever been to see thee?

Rosamund.   Here? not he.
And it is so lonely here—no confessor.

Henry. Thou shalt confess all thy sweet sins to me.

Rosamund. Besides, we came away in such a heat,
I brought not even my crucifix.

Henry.   Take this.
[*Giving her the Crucifix which* Eleanor *gave him.*

Rosamund. O, beautiful! May I have it as mine, till mine
Be mine again?

Henry (*throwing it round her neck*). Thine—as I am—till death!

Rosamund. Death? no! I'll have it with me in my shroud,
And wake with it, and show it to all the Saints.

Henry. Nay—I must go; but when thou layest thy lip
To this, remembering One who died for thee,
Remember also one who lives for thee
Out there in France; for I must hence to brave
The Pope, King Louis, and this turbulent priest.

Rosamund (*kneeling*). O, by thy love for me, all mine for thee,
Fling not thy soul into the flames of hell!
I kneel to thee—be friends with him again.

Henry. Look, look! if little Geoffrey have not tost
His ball into the brook! makes after it too
To find it. Why, the child will drown himself.

Rosamund. Geoffrey! Geoffrey!
[*Exeunt.*

SCENE II

MONTMIRAIL

'*The Meeting of the Kings.*' JOHN OF OXFORD *and* HENRY. *Crowd in the distance.*

John of Oxford. You have not crown'd young Henry yet, my liege?

Henry. Crown'd! by God's eyes, we will not have him crown'd.
I spoke of late to the boy, he answer'd me,
As if he wore the crown already—No,
We will not have him crown'd.
'T is true what Becket told me, that the mother

Would make him play his kingship
    against mine.
    John of Oxford. Not have him
    crown'd?
    Henry. Not now—not yet! and
    Becket—
Becket should crown him were he
    crown'd at all;
But, since we would be lord of our
    own manor,
This Canterbury, like a wounded deer,
Has fled our presence and our feeding-
    grounds.
    John of Oxford. Cannot a smooth
    tongue lick him whole again
To serve your will?
    Henry. He hates my will, not me.
    John of Oxford. There's York, my
    liege.
    Henry. But England scarce would
    hold
Young Henry king, if only crown'd
    by York,
And that would stilt up York to twice
    himself.
There is a movement yonder in the
    crowd—
See if our pious—what shall I call
    him, John?—
Husband-in-law, our smooth-shorn
    suzerain,
Be yet within the field.
    John of Oxford. I will. [*Exit*.
    Henry. Ay! Ay!
Mince and go back! his politic Holi-
    ness
Hath all but climb'd the Roman perch
    again,
And we shall hear him presently with
    clapt wing
Crow over Barbarossa—at last
    tongue-free
To blast my realms with excommuni-
    cation
And interdict. I must patch up a
    peace—
A peace in this long-tugged-at, thread-
    bare-worn
Quarrel of Crown and Church—to
    rend again.
His Holiness cannot steer straight
    thro' shoals,

Nor I. The citizen's heir hath con-
    quer'd me
For the moment. So we make our
    peace with him.

Enter LOUIS

Brother of France, what shall be done
    with Becket?
    Louis. The holy Thomas! Brother,
    you have traffick'd
Between the Emperor and the Pope,
    between
The Pope and Antipope—a perilous
    game
For men to play with God.
    Henry. Ay, ay, good brother,
They call you the Monk-King.
    Louis. Who calls me? she
That was my wife, now yours? You
    have her Duchy,
The point you aim'd at, and pray God
    she prove
True wife to you. You have the better
    of us
In secular matters.
    Henry. Come, confess, good
    brother,
You did your best or worst to keep her
    Duchy.
Only the golden Leopard printed in it
Such hold-fast claws that you perforce
    again
Shrank into France. Tut, tut! did we
    convene
This conference but to babble of our
    wives?
They are plagues enough in-door.
    Louis. We fought in the East,
And felt the sun of Antioch scald our
    mail,
And push'd our lances into Saracen
    hearts.
We never hounded on the State at
    home
To spoil the Church.
    Henry. How should you see this
    rightly?
    Louis. Well, well, no more! I am
    proud of my 'Monk-King,'
Whoever named me; and, brother,
    Holy Church

May rock, but will not wreck, nor our
    archbishop
Stagger on the slope decks for any
    rough sea
Blown by the breath of kings. We do
    forgive you
For aught you wrought against us.
            [Henry *holds up his hand.*
            Nay, I pray you,
Do not defend yourself. You will do
    much
To rake out all old dying heats if
    you,
At my requesting, will but look into
The wrongs you did him, and restore
    his kin,
Reseat him on his throne of Canter-
    bury,
Be, both, the friends you were.
    Henry.   The friends we were!
Co-mates we were, and had our sport
    together.
Co-kings we were, and made the laws
    together.
The world had never seen the like be-
    fore.
You are too cold to know the fashion
    of it.
Well, well, we will be gentle with him,
    gracious—
Most gracious.

Enter BECKET, *after him,* JOHN OF
OXFORD, ROGER OF YORK, GILBERT
FOLIOT, DE BROC, FITZURSE, *etc.*

          Only that the rift he made
May close between us, here I am
    wholly king,
The word should come from him.
    Becket (*kneeling*). Then, my dear
    liege,
I here deliver all this controversy
Into your royal hands.
    Henry.   Ah, Thomas, Thomas,
Thou art thyself again, Thomas again.
    Becket (*rising*). Saving God's
    honor!
    Henry.   Out upon thee, man!
Saving the devil's honor, his yes and
    no.
Knights, bishops, earls, this London
    spawn—by Mahound,

I had sooner have been born a Mus-
    sulman—
Less clashing with their priests—
I am half-way down the slope—will
    no man stay me?
I dash myself to pieces—I stay my-
    self—
Puff—it is gone. You, Master Becket,
    you
That owe to me your power over me—
Nay, nay—
Brother of France, you have taken,
    cherish'd him
Who thief-like fled from his own
    church by night,
No man pursuing. I would have had
    him back.
Take heed he do not turn and rend
    you too:
For whatsoever may displease him—
    that
Is clean against God's honor—a shift,
    a trick
Whereby to challenge, face me out
    of all
My regal rights. Yet, yet—that none
    may dream
I go against God's honor—ay, or him-
    self
In any reason, choose
A hundred of the wisest heads from
    England,
A hundred, too, from Normandy and
    Anjou;
Let these dceide on what was custom-
    ary
In olden days, and all the Church of
    France
Decide on their decision, I am con-
    tent.
More, what the mightiest and the
    holiest
Of all his predecessors may have done
Even to the least and meanest of my
    own,
Let him do the same to me—I am
    content.
    Louis. Ay, ay! the King humbles
    himself enough.
    Becket (*aside*). Words! he will
    wriggle out of them like an eel
When the time serves. (*Aloud.*) My
    lieges and my lords,

The thanks of Holy Church are due
to those
That went before us for their work,
which we
Inheriting reap an easier harvest.
Yet—

Louis. My lord, will you be greater
than the Saints,
More than Saint Peter? whom—what
is it you doubt?
Behold your peace at hand.

Becket.   I say that those
Who went before us did not wholly
clear
The deadly growths of earth, which
hell's own heat
So dwelt on that they rose and dark-
en'd heaven.
Yet they did much. Would God they
had torn up all
By the hard root, which shoots again;
our trial
Had so been less; but, seeing they
were men
Defective or excessive, must we fol-
low
All that they overdid or underdid?
Nay, if they were defective as Saint
Peter
Denying Christ, who yet defied the
tyrant,
We hold by his defiance, not his de-
fect.
O good son Louis, do not counsel me,
No, to suppress God's honor for the
sake
Of any king that breathes. No, God
forbid!

Henry. No! God forbid! and turn
me Mussulman!
No God but one, and Mahound is his
prophet.
But for your Christian, look you, you
shall have
None other God but me—me, Thomas,
son
Of Gilbert Becket, London merchant.
Out!
I hear no more.   [*Exit.*

Louis. Our brother's anger puts him,
Poor man, beside himself—not wise.
My lord,

We have claspt your cause, believing
that our brother
Had wrong'd you; but this day he
proffer'd peace.
You will have war; and tho' we grant
the Church
King over this world's kings, yet, my
good lord,
We that are kings are something in
this world,
And so we pray you, draw yourself
from under
The wings of France. We shelter you
no more.   [*Exit.*

John of Oxford. I am glad that
France hath scouted him at
last.
I told the Pope what manner of man
he was.   [*Exit.*

Roger of York. Yea, since he flouts
the will of either realm,
Let either cast him away like a dead
dog!   [*Exit.*

Foliot. Yea, let a stranger spoil his
heritage,
And let another take his bishopric!
            [*Exit.*

De Broc. Our castle, my lord, belongs to Canterbury.
I pray you come and take it. [*Exit.*

Fitzurse.   When you will.
            [*Exit.*

Becket. Cursed be John of Oxford,
Roger of York,
And Gilbert Foliot! cursed those De
Brocs
That hold our Saltwood Castle from
our see!
Cursed Fitzurse, and all the rest of
them
That sow this hate between my lord
and me!

Voices from the Crowd. Blessed be
the lord archbishop, who hath withstood two kings to their faces for the
honor of God.

Becket. Out of the mouths of babes
and sucklings, praise!
I thank you, sons; when kings but
hold by crowns,
The crowd that hungers for a crown
in heaven
Is my true king.

Herbert. Thy true King bade thee be
A fisher of men; thou hast them in thy net.
  Becket. I am too like the King here; both of us
Too headlong for our office. Better have been
A fisherman at Bosham, my good Herbert,
Thy birthplace—the sea-creek—the petty rill
That falls into it—the green field—the gray church—
The simple lobster-basket, and the mesh—
The more or less of daily labor done—
The pretty gaping bills in the home-nest
Piping for bread—the daily want supplied—
The daily pleasure to supply it.
  Herbert. Ah, Thomas,
You had not borne it, no, not for a day.
  Becket. Well, maybe, no.
  Herbert. But bear with Walter Map,
For here he comes to comment on the time.

Enter WALTER MAP.

Walter Map. Pity, my lord, that you have quenched the warmth of France toward you, tho' His Holiness, after much smouldering and smoking, be kindled again upon your quarter.
  Becket. Ay, if he do not end in smoke again.
  Walter Map. My lord, the fire, when first kindled, said to the smoke, 'Go up, my son, straight to heaven.' And the smoke said, 'I go;' but anon the Northeast took and turned him Southwest, then the Southwest turned him Northeast, and so of the other winds; but it was in him to go up straight if the time had been quieter. Your lordship affects the unwavering perpendicular; but His Holiness, pushed one way by the Empire and

another by England, if he move at all —Heaven stay him!—is fain to diagonalize.
  Herbert. Diagonalize! thou art a word-monger.
Our Thomas never will diagonalize.
Thou art a jester and a verse-maker.
Diagonalize!
  Walter Map. Is the world any the worse for my verses if the Latin rhymes be rolled out from a full mouth? or any harm done to the people if my jest be in defence of the Truth?
  Becket. Ay, if the jest be so done that the people
Delight to wallow in the grossness of it,
Till Truth herself be shamed of her defender.
Non defensoribus istis, Walter Map!
  Walter Map. Is that my case? so if the city be sick, and I cannot call the kennel sweet, your lordship would suspend me from verse-writing, as you suspended yourself after sub-writing to the customs.
  Becket. I pray God pardon mine infirmity!
  Walter Map. Nay, my lord, take heart; for tho' you suspended yourself, the Pope let you down again; and tho' you suspend Foliot or another, the Pope will not leave them in suspense, for the Pope himself is always in suspense, like Mahound's coffin hung between heaven and earth—always in suspense, like the scales, till the weight of Germany or the gold of England brings one of them down to the dust—always in suspense, like the tail of the horologe—to and fro—tick-tack—we make the time, we keep the time, ay, and we serve the time; for I have heard say that if you boxed the Pope's ears with a purse, you might stagger him, but he would pocket the purse. No saying of mine—Jocelyn of Salisbury. But the King hath bought half the College of Red-hats. He warmed to you to-day, and you have chilled him again. Yet you both love God. Agree with him quickly

again, even for the sake of the Church.
My one grain of good counsel which
you will not swallow. I hate a split between old friendships as I hate the
dirty gap in the face of a Cistercian
monk, that will swallow anything.
Farewell. [*Exit.*

Becket. Map scoffs at Rome. I all
    but hold with Map.
Save for myself no Rome were left in
    England,
All had been his. Why should this
    Rome, this Rome,
Still choose Barabbas rather than the
    Christ,
Absolve the left-hand thief and damn
    the right?
Take fees of tyranny, wink at sacri-
    lege,
Which even Peter had not dared?
    condemn
The blameless exile?—

Herbert. Thee, thou holy Thomas!
I would that thou hadst been the Holy
    Father.

Becket. I would have done my most
    to keep Rome holy,
I would have made Rome know she
    still is Rome—
Who stands aghast at her eternal self
And shakes at mortal kings—her
    vacillation,
Avarice, craft—O God, how many an
    innocent
Has left his bones upon the way to
    Rome
Unwept, uncared for! Yea—on mine
    own self
The King had had no power except for
    Rome.
'T is not the King who is guilty of
    mine exile,
But Rome, Rome, Rome!

Herbert. My lord, I see this Louis
Returning, ah! to drive thee from his
    realm.

Becket. He said as much before.
    Thou art no prophet,
Nor yet a prophet's son.

Herbert. Whatever he say,
Deny not thou God's honor for a king
The King looks troubled.

Re-enter KING LOUIS.

Louis. My dear lord archbishop,
I learn but now that those poor Poite-
    vins
That in thy cause were stirr'd against
    King Henry
Have been, despite his kingly promise
    given
To our own self of pardon, evilly used
And put to pain. I have lost all trust
    in him.
The Church alone hath eyes—and now
    I see
That I was blind—suffer the phrase—
    surrendering
God's honor to the pleasure of a man.
Forgive me and absolve me, holy
    father. [*Kneels.*

Becket. Son, I absolve thee in the
    name of God.

Louis (*rising*). Return to Sens,
    where we will care for you.
The wine and wealth of all our France
    are yours;
Rest in our realm, and be at peace
    with all. [*Exeunt.*

Voices from the Crowd. Long live
the good King Louis! God bless the
great archbishop!

Re-enter HENRY *and* JOHN OF
OXFORD.

Henry (*looking after* King Louis
    and Becket). Ay, there they go
    —both backs are turn'd to
    me—
Why, then I strike into my former
    path
For England, crown young Henry
    there, and make
Our waning Eleanor all but love me!
               John,
Thou hast served me heretofore with
    Rome—and well.
They call thee John the Swearer.

John of Oxford. For this reason,
That, being ever duteous to the King,
I evermore have sworn upon his
    side,
And ever mean to do it.

Henry (claps him on the shoulder).
Honest John!
To Rome again! the storm begins
   again.
Spare not thy tongue! be lavish with
   our coins,
Threaten our junction with the Em-
   peror—flatter
And fright the Pope—bribe all the
   cardinals—leave
Lateran and Vatican in one dust of
   gold—
Swear and unswear, state and misstate
   thy best!
I go to have young Henry crown'd by
   York.

ACT III

SCENE I.—THE BOWER

HENRY *and* ROSAMUND.

Henry. All that you say is just. I
   cannot answer it
Till better times, when I shall put
   away—
Rosamund. What will you put
   away?
Henry.   That which you ask me
Till better times. Let it content you
   now
There is no woman that I love so
   well.
Rosamund. No woman but should
   be content with that—
Henry. And one fair child to fondle!
Rosamund.   O, yes, the child
We waited for so long—Heaven's gift
   at last—
And how you doted on him then! To-
   day
I almost fear'd your kiss was colder—
   yes—
But then the child *is* such a child!
   What chance
That he should ever spread into the
   man
Here in our silence? I have done my
   best.
I am not learn'd.
   Henry.   I am the King, his father,

And I will look to it. Is our secret
   ours?
Have you had any alarm? no stranger?
   Rosamund.   No.
The warder of the bower hath given
   himself
Of late to wine. I sometimes think he
   sleeps
When he should watch; and yet what
   fear? the people
Believe the wood enchanted. No one
   comes,
Nor foe nor friend; his fond excess of
   wine
Springs from the loneliness of my poor
   bower,
Which weighs even on me.
   Henry.   Yet these tree-towers,
Their long bird-echoing minster-aisles,
   —the voice
Of the perpetual brook, these golden
   slopes
Of Solomon-shaming flowers—that
   was your saying,
All pleased you so at first.
   Rosamund.   Not now so much.
My Anjou bower was scarce as beau-
   tiful.
But you were oftener there. I have
   none but you.
The brook's voice is not yours, and no
   flower, not
The sun himself, should he be changed
   to one,
Could shine away the darkness of that
   gap
Left by the lack of love.
   Henry.   The lack of love!
Rosamund. Of one we love. Nay, I
   would not be bold,
Yet hoped ere this you might—
         [*Looks earnestly at him.*
Henry.   Anything further?
Rosamund. Only my best bower-
   maiden died of late,
And that old priest whom John of
   Salisbury trusted
Hath sent another.
   Henry.   Secret?
   Rosamund.   I but ask'd her
One question, and she primm'd her
   mouth and put

Her hands together—thus—and said,
   God help her,
That she was sworn to silence.
   Henry.   What did you ask her?
   Rosamund. Some daily something-
   nothing.
   Henry.   Secret, then?
   Rosamund. I do not love her. Must
   you go, my liege,
So suddenly?
   Henry. I came to England sud-
   denly,
And on a great occasion sure to wake
As great a wrath in Becket—
   Rosamund.   Always Becket!
He always comes between us.
   Henry.   And to meet it
I needs must leave as suddenly. It is
   raining,
Put on your hood and see me to the
   bounds.

MARGERY (*singing behind scene*).

   Babble in bower
     Under the rose!
   Bee must n't buzz,
     Whoop—but he knows.

   Kiss me, little one,
     Nobody near!
   Grasshopper, grasshopper,
     Whoop—you can hear.

   Kiss in the bower,
     Tit on the tree!
   Bird must n't tell,
     Whoop—he can see.

Enter MARGERY.

I ha' been but a week here and I ha'
seen what I ha' seen, for to be sure it
's no more than a week since our old
Father Philip that has confessed our
mother for twenty years, and she was
hard put to it, and to speak truth, nigh
at the end of our last crust, and that
mouldy, and she cried out on him to
put me forth in the world and to make
me a woman of the world, and to win
my own bread, whereupon he asked
our mother if I could keep a quiet
tongue i' my head, and not speak till
I was spoke to, and I answered for myself that I never spoke more than was
needed, and he told me he would advance me to the service of a great
lady, and took me ever so far away,
and gave me a great pat o' the cheek
for a pretty wench, and said it was a
pity to blindfold such eyes as mine,
and such to be sure they be, but he
blinded 'em for all that, and so
brought me no-hows as I may say, and
the more shame to him after his
promise, into a garden and not into the
world, and bade me whatever I saw
not to speak one word, an' it 'ud be
well for me in the end, for there were
great ones who would look after me,
and to be sure I ha' seen great ones to-
day—and then not to speak one word,
for that 's the rule o' the garden, tho'
to be sure if I had been Eve i' the
garden I should n't ha' minded the
apple, for what 's an apple, you know,
save to a child, and I 'm no child,
but more a woman o' the world than
my lady here, and I ha' seen that I ha'
seen—tho' to be sure if I had n't
minded it we should all on us ha' had
to go, bless the Saints, wi' bare backs,
but the backs 'ud ha' countenanced
one another, and belike it 'ud ha' been
always summer, and anyhow I am as
well-shaped as my lady here, and I ha'
seen what I ha' seen, and what 's the
good of my talking to myself, for here
comes my lady (*enter* Rosamund),
and, my lady, tho' I should n't speak
one word, I wish you joy o' the King's
brother.
   Rosamund. What is it you
   mean?
   Margery. I mean your goodman,
your husband, my lady, for I saw your
ladyship a-parting wi' him even now
i' the coppice, when I was a-getting o'
bluebells for your ladyship's nose to
smell on—and I ha' seen the King
once at Oxford, and he 's as like the
King as fingernail to fingernail, and I
thought at first it was the King, only
you know the King 's married, for
King Louis—
   Rosamund. Married!

Margery. Years and years, my lady, for her husband, King Louis—

Rosamund. Hush!

Margery. And I thought if it were the King's brother he had a better bride than the King, for the people do say that his is bad beyond all reckoning, and—

Rosamund. The people lie.

Margery. Very like, my lady, but most on 'em know an honest woman and a lady when they see her, and besides they say she makes songs, and that 's against her, for I never knew an honest woman that could make songs, tho' to be sure our mother 'ill sing me old songs by the hour, but then, God help her, she had 'em from her mother, and her mother from her mother back and back for ever so long, but none on 'em ever made songs, and they were all honest.

Rosamund. Go, you shall tell me of her some other time.

Margery. There 's none so much to tell on her, my lady, only she kept the seventh commandment better than some I know on, or I could n't look your ladyship i' the face, and she brew'd the best ale in all Glo'ster, that is to say in her time when she had the 'Crown.'

Rosamund. The crown who?

Margery. Mother.

Rosamund. I mean her whom you call—fancy—my husband's brother's wife.

Margery. O, Queen Eleanor. Yes, my lady; and tho' I be sworn not to speak a word, I can tell you all about her, if—

Rosamund. No word now. I am faint and sleepy. Leave me. Nay—go. What! will you anger me?

[*Exit* Margery.

He charged me not to question any
       of those
About me. Have I? no! she question'd *me.*
Did she not slander *him?* Should she
       stay here?
May she not tempt me, being at my
       side,

To question *her?* Nay, can I send her
       hence
Without his kingly leave? I am in the
       dark
I have lived, poor bird, from cage to
       cage, and known
Nothing but him—happy to know no
       more,
So that he loved me—and he loves me
       —yes,
And bound me by his love to secrecy
Till his own time.
              Eleanor, Eleanor, have I
Not heard ill things of her in France?
       O, she 's
The Queen of France. I see it—some
       confusion,
Some strange mistake. I did not hear
       aright,
Myself confused with parting from
       the King.

MARGERY (*behind scene*).

Bee must n't buzz,
Whoop—but he knows.

Rosamund. Yet her—what her? he
       hinted of some her—
When he was here before—
Something that would displease me.
       Hath he stray'd
From love's clear path into the common bush,
And, being scratch'd, returns to his
       true rose,
Who hath not thorn enough to prick
       him for it,
Even with a word?

MARGERY (*behind scene*).

Bird must n't tell,
Whoop—he can see.

Rosamund. I would not hear him.
       Nay — there 's more — he frown'd
'No mate for her, if it should come to
       that'—
To that—to what?

MARGERY (*behind scene*).

Whoop—but he knows,
Whoop—but he knows.

Rosamund. O God! some dreadful
truth is breaking on me—
Some dreadful thing is coming on me.

Enter GEOFFREY.

Geoffrey!
Geoffrey. What are you crying for,
when the sun shines?
Rosamund. Hath not thy father left
us to ourselves?
Geoffrey. Ay, but he 's taken the
rain with him. I hear Margery: I 'll go
play with her.   [*Exit* Geoffrey.

ROSAMUND.

Rainbow, stay,
Gleam upon gloom,
Bright as my dream,
Rainbow, stay!

But it passes away,
Gloom upon gleam,
Dark as my doom—
O rainbow, stay!

SCENE II

OUTSIDE THE WOODS NEAR ROSA-
MUND'S BOWER

ELEANOR. FITZURSE.

Eleanor. Up from the salt lips of
the land we two
Have track'd the King to this dark in-
land wood;
And somewhere hereabouts he van-
ish'd. Here
His turtle builds; his exit is our adit.
Watch! he will out again, and pres-
ently,
Seeing he must to Westminster and
crown
Young Henry there to-morrow.
Fitzurse.   We have watch'd
So long in vain, he hath pass'd out
again,
And on the other side.
          [*A great horn winded.*
Hark! Madam!

Eleanor.   Ay,
How ghostly sounds that horn in the
black wood!
          [*A countryman flying.*
Whither away, man? what are you
flying from?
Countryman. The witch! the witch!
she sits naked by a great heap of gold
in the middle of the wood, and when
the horn sounds she comes out as a
wolf. Get you hence! a man passed in
there to-day. I holla'd to him, but he
did n't hear me; he'll never out again,
the witch has got him. I dare n't stay
—I dare n't stay!
Eleanor. Kind of the witch to give
thee warning, tho'.
          [*Man flies.*
Is not this wood-witch of the rustic's
fear
Our woodland Circe that hath witch'd
the King?
          [*Horn sounded. Another flying.*
Fitzurse. Again! stay, fool, and tell
me why thou fliest.
Countryman. Fly thou too. The
King keeps his forest head of game
here, and when that horn sounds a
score of wolf-dogs are let loose that
will tear thee piecemeal. Linger not
till the third horn. Fly!   [*Exit.*
Eleanor. This is the likelier tale.
We have hit the place.
Now let the King's fine game look to
itself.   [*Horn.*
Fitzurse. Again!—
And far on in the dark heart of the
wood
I hear the yelping of the hounds of
hell.
Eleanor. I have my dagger here to
still their throats.
Fitzurse. Nay, madam, not to-
night—the night is falling.
What can be done to-night?
Eleanor.   Well—well—away.

SCENE III

TRAITOR'S MEADOW AT FRÉTEVAL. PAVILIONS AND TENTS OF THE ENGLISH AND FRENCH BARONAGE

BECKET *and* HERBERT OF BOSHAM.

Becket. See here!
Herbert. What's here?
Becket. A notice from the priest
To whom our John of Salisbury committed
The secret of the bower, that our wolf-Queen
Is prowling round the fold. I should be back
In England even for this.
Herbert. These are by-things
In the great cause.
Becket. The by-things of the Lord
Are the wrong'd innocences that will cry
From all the hidden by-ways of the world
In the great day against the wronger. I know
Thy meaning. Perish she, I, all before
The Church should suffer wrong!
Herbert. Do you see, my lord,
There is the King talking with Walter Map?
Becket. He hath the Pope's last letters, and they threaten
The immediate thunder-blast of interdict;
Yet he can scarce be touching upon those,
Or scarce would smile that fashion.
Herbert. Winter sunshine!
Beware of opening out thy bosom to it,
Lest thou, myself, and all thy flock should catch
An after ague-fit of trembling. Look!
He bows, he bares his head, he is coming hither.
Still with a smile.

Enter KING HENRY *and* WALTER MAP.

Henry. We have had so many hours together, Thomas,
So many happy hours alone together,
That I would speak with you once more alone.
Becket. My liege, your will and happiness are mine.
[*Exeunt* King *and* Becket.
Herbert. The same smile still.
Walter Map. Do you see that great black cloud that hath come over the sun and cast us all into shadow?
Herbert. And feel it too.
Walter Map. And see you yon side-beam that is forced from under it, and sets the church-tower over there all a-hell-fire as it were?
Herbert. Ay.
Walter Map. It is this black, bell-silencing, anti-marrying, burial-hindering interdict that hath squeezed out this side-smile upon Canterbury, whereof may come conflagration. Were I Thomas, I would n't trust it. Sudden change is a house on sand; and tho' I count Henry honest enough, yet when fear creeps in at the front, honesty steals out at the back, and the King at last is fairly scared by, this cloud—this interdict. I have been more for the King than the Church in this matter—yea, even for the sake of the Church; for, truly, as the case stood, you had safelier have slain an archbishop than a she-goat. But our recoverer and upholder of customs hath in this crowning of young Henry by York and London so violated the immemorial usage of the Church, that, like the grave-digger's child I have heard of, trying to ring the bell, he hath half-hanged himself in the rope of the Church, or rather pulled all the Church with the Holy Father astride of it down upon his own head.
Herbert. Were you there?
Walter Map. In the church rope?—no. I was at the crowning, for I have pleasure in the pleasure of crowds, and to read the faces of men at a great show.
Herbert. And how did Roger of York comport himself?
Walter Map. As magnificently and archiepiscopally as our Thomas would

have done: only there was a dare-devil in his eye—I should say a dare-Becket. He thought less of two kings than of one Roger, the king of the occasion. Foliot is the holier man, perhaps the better. Once or twice there ran a twitch across his face, as who should say 'what's to follow?' but Salisbury was a calf cowed by Mother Church, and every now and then glancing about him like a thief at night when he hears a door open in the house and thinks 'the master.'

Herbert. And the father-king?

Walter Map. The father's eye was so tender it would have called a goose off the green, and once he strove to hide his face, like the Greek king when his daughter was sacrificed, but he thought better of it. It was but the sacrifice of a kingdom to his son, a smaller matter; but as to the young crownling himself, he looked so malapert in the eyes, that had I fathered him I had given him more of the rod than the sceptre. Then followed the thunder of the captains and the shouting, and so we came on to the banquet, from whence there puffed out such an incense of unctuosity into the nostrils of our Gods of Church and State, that Lucullus or Apicius might have sniffed it in their Hades of heathenism, so that the smell of their own roast had not come across it—

Herbert. Map, tho' you make your butt too big, you overshoot it.

Walter Map. For as to the fish, they de-miracled the miraculous draught, and might have sunk a navy—

Herbert. There again, Goliasing and Goliathizing!

Walter Map. And as for the flesh at table, a whole Peter's sheet, with all manner of game, and four-footed things, and fowls—

Herbert. And all manner of creeping things too?

Walter Map. Well, there were abbots—but they did not bring their women; and so we were dull enough at first, but in the end we floursheid out into a merriment; for the old King would act servitor and hand a dish to his son; whereupon my Lord of York—his fine-cut face bowing and beaming with all that courtesy which hath less loyalty in it than the backward scrape of the clown's heel— 'great honor,' says he, 'from the King's self to the King's son.' Did you hear the young King's quip?

Herbert. No, what was it?

Walter Map. Glancing at the days when his father was only Earl of Anjou, he answered, 'Should not an earl's son wait on a king's son?' And when the cold corners of the King's mouth began to thaw, there was a great motion of laughter among us, part real, part childlike, to be freed from the dulness—part royal, for King and kingling both laughed, and so we could not but laugh, as by a royal necessity—part childlike again—when we felt we had laughed too long and could not stay ourselves—many midriff-shaken even to tears, as springs gush out after earthquakes—but from those, as I said before, there may come a conflagration—tho', to keep the figure moist and make it hold water, I should say rather, the lacrymation of a lamentation; but look if Thomas have not flung himself at the King's feet. They have made it up again—for the moment.

Herbert. Thanks to the blessed Magdalen, whose day it is!

Re-enter HENRY *and* BECKETT. (*During their conference the* BARONS *and* BISHOPS OF FRANCE *and* ENGLAND *come in at back of stage.*)

Becket. Ay, King! for in thy king-
    dom as thou knowest,
The spouse of the Great King, thy
    King, hath fallen—
The daughter of Zion lies beside the
    way—
The priests of Baal tread her under-
    foot—
The golden ornaments are stolen from
    her—

Henry. Have I not promised to restore her, Thomas,
And send thee back again to Canterbury?

Becket. Send back again those exiles of my kin
Who wander famine-wasted thro' the
world.

Henry. Have I not promised, man,
to send them back?

Becket. Yet one thing more. Thou
hast broken thro' the pales
Or privilege, crowning thy young son
by York,
London, and Salisbury—not Canterbury.

Henry. York crown'd the Conqueror—not Canterbury.

Becket. There was no Canterbury
in William's time.

Henry. But Hereford, you know,
crown'd the first Henry.

Becket. But Anselm crown'd this
Henry o'er again.

Henry. And thou shalt crown my
Henry o'er again.

Becket. And is it then with thy
goodwill that I
Proceed against thine evil councillors,
And hurl the dread ban of the Church
on those
Who made the second mitre play the
first,
And acted me?

Henry. Well, well, then—have thy
way!
It may be they were evil councillors.
What more, my lord archbishop?
What more, Thomas?
I make thee full amends. Say all thy
say,
But blaze not out before the French-
men here.

Becket. More? Nothing, so thy
promise be thy deed.

Henry (*holding out his hand*). Give
me thy hand. My Lords of
France and England.
My friend of Canterbury and myself
Are now once more at perfect amity.
Unkingly should I be, and most un-
knightly,

Not striving still, however much in
vain,
To rival him in Christian charity.

Herbert. All praise to Heaven, and
sweet Saint Magdalen!

Henry. And so farewell until we
meet in England.

Becket. I fear, my liege, we may
not meet in England.

Henry. How, do you make me a
traitor?

Becket. No indeed,
That be far from thee.

Henry. Come, stay with us, then,
Before you part for England.

Becket. I am bound
For that one hour to stay with good
King Louis,
Who helpt me when none else.

Herbert. He said thy life
Was not one hour's worth in England
save
King Henry gave thee first the kiss of
peace.

Henry. He said so? Louis, did he?
look you, Herbert,
When I was in mine anger with King
Louis,
I sware I would not give the kiss of
peace,
Not on French ground, nor any
ground but English,
Where his cathedral stands. Mine old
friend, Thomas,
I would there were that perfect trust
between us,
That health of heart, once ours, ere
Pope or King
Had come between us! Even now—
who knows?—
I might deliver all things to thy
hand—
If—but I say no more—farewell, my
lord.

Becket. Farewell, my liege!
  [*Exit* Henry, *then the* Barons
  and Bishops.

Walter Map. There again! when
the full fruit of the royal promise
might have dropt into thy mouth
hadst thou but opened it to thank
him.

Becket. He fenced his royal promise with an *if*.

Walter Map. And is the King's *if*
too high a stile for your lordship to
overstep and come at all things in the
next field?

Becket. Ay, if this *if* be like the
devil's *'if*
Thou wilt fall down and worship me.'

Herbert. O, Thomas,
I could fall down and worship thee,
my Thomas,
For thou hast trodden this wine-press
alone.

Becket. Nay, of the people there
are many with me.

Walter Map. I am not altogether
with you, my lord, tho' I am none of
those that would raise a storm between you, lest ye should draw together like two ships in a calm. You
wrong the King: he meant what he
said to-day. Who shall vouch for his
to-morrows? One word further. Doth
not the *fewness* of anything make the
fulness of it in estimation? Is not virtue prized mainly for its rarity and
great baseness loathed as an exception: for were all, my lord, as noble
as yourself, who would look up to
you? and were all as base as—who
shall I say?—Fitzurse and his following—who would look down upon
them? My lord, you have put so
many of the King's household out of
communion, that they begin to smile
at it.

Becket. At their peril, at their
peril—

Walter Map. For tho' the drop may
hollow out the dead stone, doth not
the living skin thicken against perpetual whippings? This is the second
grain of good counsel I ever proffered
thee, and so cannot suffer by the rule
of frequency. Have I sown it in salt?
I trust not, for before God I promise
you the King hath many more wolves
than he can tame in his woods of
England, and if it suit their purpose
to howl for the King, and you still
move against him, you may have no
less than to die for it; but God and his

free wind grant your lordship a
happy home-return and the King's
kiss of peace in Kent. Farewell! I
must follow the King.   [*Exit.*

Herbert. Ay, and I warrant the customs. Did the King
Speak of the customs?

Becket.   No!—To die for it—
I live to die for it, I die to live for it.
The State will die, the Church can
never die.
The King's not like to die for that
which dies;
But I must die for that which never
dies.
It will be so—my visions in the
Lord—
It must be so, my friend! the wolves
of England
Must murder her one shepherd, that
the sheep
May feed in peace. False figure, Map
would say.
Earth's falses are heaven's truths.
And when my voice
Is martyr'd mute, and this man dis-
appears,
That perfect trust may come again
between us,
And there, there, there, not here I
shall rejoice
To find my stray sheep back within
the fold.
The crowd are scattering, let us move
away!
And thence to England.   [*Exeunt.*

ACT IV

SCENE I.—THE OUTSKIRTS OF THE
BOWER

Geoffrey (*coming out of the wood*).
Light again! light again! Margery?
no, that's a finer thing there. How it
glitters!

Eleanor (*entering*). Come to me,
little one. How camest thou hither?

Geoffrey. On my legs.

Eleanor. And mighty pretty legs
too. Thou art the prettiest child I
ever saw. Wilt thou love me?

Geoffrey. No; I only love mother.

Eleanor. Ay; and who is thy mother?

Geoffrey. They call her— But she lives secret, you see.

Eleanor. Why?

Geoffrey. Don't know why.

Eleanor. Ay, but some one comes to see her now and then. Who is he?

Geoffrey. Can't tell.

Eleanor. What does she call him?

Geoffrey. My liege.

Eleanor. Pretty one, how camest thou?

Geoffrey. There was a bit of yellow silk here and there, and it looked pretty like a glowworm, and I thought if I followed it I should find the fairies.

Eleanor. I am the fairy, pretty one, a good fairy to thy mother. Take me to her.

Geoffrey. There are good fairies and bad fairies, and sometimes she cries, and can't sleep sound o' nights because of the bad fairies.

Eleanor. She shall cry no more; she shall sleep sound enough if thou wilt take me to her. I am her good fairy.

Geoffrey. But you don't look like a good fairy. Mother does. You are not pretty, like mother.

Eleanor. We can't all of us be as pretty as thou art—(*aside*) little bastard! Come, here is a golden chain I will give thee if thou wilt lead me to thy mother.

Geoffrey. No—no gold. Mother says gold spoils all. Love is the only gold.

Eleanor. I love thy mother, my pretty boy. Show me where thou camest out of the wood.

Geoffrey. By this tree; but I don't know if I can find the way back again.

Eleanor. Where's the warder?

Geoffrey. Very bad. Somebody struck him.

Eleanor. Ay? who was that?

Geoffrey. Can't tell. But I heard say he had had a stroke, or you'd have heard his horn before now. Come along, then; we shall see the silk here and there, and I want my supper.

[*Exeunt.*

SCENE II

ROSAMUND'S BOWER

Rosamund. The boy so late; pray
    God, he be not lost;
I sent this Margery, and she comes
    not back;
I sent another, and she comes not
    back.
I go myself—so many alleys, cross-
    ings,
Paths, avenues—nay, if I lost him,
    now
The folds have fallen from the mys-
    tery
And left all naked, I were lost indeed.

Enter GEOFFREY *and* ELEANOR.

Geoffrey, the pain thou hast put me
    to!   [*Seeing* Eleanor.
                Ha, you!
How came you hither?

Eleanor. Your own child brought
    me hither!

Geoffrey. You said you could n't trust Margery, and I watched her and followed her into the woods, and I lost her and went on and on till I found the light and the lady, and she says she can make you sleep o' nights.

Rosamund. How dared you? Know you not this bower is secret,
Of and belonging to the King of Eng-
    land,
More sacred than his forests for the
    chase?
Nay, nay, Heaven help you; get you
    hence in haste
Lest worse befall you.

Eleanor. Child, I am mine own self
Of and belonging to the King. The
    King
Hath divers ofs and ons, ofs and be-
    longings,
Almost as many as your true Mussul-
    man—

Belongings, paramours, whom it
    pleases him
To call his wives; but so it chances,
    child,
That I am his main paramour, his sul-
    tana.
But since the fondest pair of doves
    will jar,
Even in a cage of gold, we had words
    of late,
And thereupon he call'd my children
    bastards.
Do you believe that you are married
    to him?

Rosamund. I *should* believe it.

Eleanor. You must not believe it,
Because I have a wholesome medicine
    here
Puts that belief asleep. Your answer,
    beauty!
Do you believe that you are married
    to him?

Rosamund. Geoffrey, my boy, I
saw the ball you lost in the fork of
the great willow over the brook. Go.
See that you do not fall in. Go.

Geoffrey. And leave you alone with
the good fairy. She calls you beauty,
but I don't like her looks. Well, you
bid me go, and I'll have my ball anyhow. Shall I find you asleep when I
come back?

Rosamund. Go.

                  [*Exit* Geoffrey.

Eleanor. He is easily found again.
    Do you believe it?
I pray you then to take my sleeping-
    draught;
But if you should not care to take it
    —see!   [*Draws a dagger.*
What! have I scared the red rose
    from your face
Into your heart? But this will find it
    there,
And dig it from the root for ever.

Rosamund.   Help! help!

Eleanor. They say that walls have
    ears; but these, it seems,
Have none! and I have none—to pity
    thee.

Rosamund. I do beseech you—my
    child is so young,

So backward too; I cannot leave him
    yet.
I am not so happy I could not die my-
    self,
But the child is so young. You have
    children—his;
And mine is the King's child; so, if
    you love him—
Nay, if you love him, there is great
    wrong done
Somehow; but if you do not—there
    are those
Who say you do not love him—let me
    go
With my young boy, and I will hide
    my face,
Blacken and gipsyfy it; none shall
    know me;
The King shall never hear of me
    again,
But I will beg my bread along the
    world
With my young boy, and God will be
    our guide.
I never meant you harm in any way.
See, I can say no more.

Eleanor. Will you not say you are
    not married to him?

Rosamund. Ay, madam, I can *say*
    it, if you will.

Eleanor. Then is thy pretty boy a
    bastard?

Rosamund. No.

Eleanor. And thou thyself a proven
    wanton?

Rosamund.   No.
I am none such. I never loved but one.
I have heard of such that range from
    love to love,
Like the wild beast—if you can call it
    love.
I have heard of such—yea, even
    among those
Who sit on thrones—I never saw any
    such,
Never knew any such, and howsoever
You do misname me, match'd with
    any such,
I am snow to mud.

Eleanor.   The more the pity then
That thy true home—the heavens—
    cry out for thee
Who art too pure for earth.

Enter FITZURSE.

Fitzurse.   Give her to me.
Eleanor. The Judas-lover of our
     passion-play
Hath track'd us hither.
     Fitzurse. Well, why not? I follow'd
You and the child: he babbled all the
     way.
Give her to me to make my honey-
     moon.
     Eleanor. Ay, as the bears love
          honey. Could you keep her
Indungeon'd from one whisper of the
     wind,
Dark even from a side glance of the
     moon,
And oublietted in the centre—No!
I follow out my hate and thy revenge.
     Fitzurse. You bade me take re-
          venge another way—
To bring her to the dust.—Come with
     me, love,
And I will love thee.—Madam, let her
     live.
I have a far-off burrow where the
     King
Would miss her and for ever.
     Eleanor. How sayst thou, sweet-
          heart
Wilt thou go with him? he will marry
     thee.
     Rosamund. Give me the poison; set
          me free of him!
               [*Eleanor offers the vial.*
No., no! I will not have it.
     Eleanor.   Then this other,
The wiser choice, because my sleep-
     ing-draught
May bloat thy beauty out of shape,
     and make
Thy body loathsome even to thy
     child;
While this but leaves thee with a
     broken heart,
A doll-face blanch'd and bloodless,
     over which
If pretty Geoffrey do not break his
     own,
It must be broken for him.
     Rosamund.   O, I see now

Your purpose is to fright me—a trou-
     badour,
You play with words. You had **never**
     used so many,
Not if you meant it, I am sure. The
     child—
No—mercy! No! (*Kneels.*)
     Eleanor. Play!—that bosom **never**
Heaved under the King's hand with
     such true passion
As at this loveless knife that stirs the
     riot,
Which it will quench in blood! Slave,
     if he love thee,
Thy life is worth the wrestle for it.
     Arise,
And dash thyself against me that I
     may slay thee!
The worm! shall I let her go? But ha!
     what's here?
By very God, the cross I gave the
     King!
His village darling in some lewd ca-
     ress
Has wheedled it off the King's neck
     to her own.
By thy leave, beauty. Ay, the same! I
     warrant
Thou hast sworn on this my cross a
     hundred times
Never to leave him—and that merits
     death,
False oath on holy cross—for thou
     must leave him
To-day, but not quite yet. My good
     Fitzurse,
The running down the chase is kind-
     lier sport
Even than the death. Who knows but
     that thy lover
May plead so pitifully, that I may
     spare thee
Come hither, man; stand there. (*To*
     Rosamund.) Take thy one
     chance;
Catch at the last straw. Kneel to thy
     lord Fitzurse;
Crouch even because thou hatest him;
     fawn upon him
For thy life and thy son's.
     Rosamund (*rising*).   I am a
          Clifford,
My son a Clifford and Plantagenet.

I am to die then, tho' there stand be-
    side thee
One who might grapple with thy dag-
    ger, if he
Had aught of man, or thou of woman;
    or I
Would bow to such a baseness as
    would make me
Most worthy of it. Both of us will
    die,
And I will fly with my sweet boy to
    heaven,
And shriek to all the saints among the
    stars:
'Eleanor of Aquitaine, Eleanor of
    England!
Murder'd by that adulteress Eleanor,
Whose doings are a horror to the east,
A hissing in the west!' Have we not
    heard
Raymond of Poitou, thine own uncle
    —nay,
Geoffrey Plantagenet, thine own hus-
    band's father—
Nay, even the accursed heathen Sal-
    addeen—
Strike!
I challenge thee to meet me before
    God.
Answer me there.
    Eleanor (raising the dagger). This
        in thy bosom, fool,
And after in thy bastard's!

Enter BECKETT *from behind. Catches
    hold of her arm.*

    Becket.   Murderess!
    [*The dagger falls; they stare at
        one another. After a pause.*
    Eleanor. My lord, we know you
        proud of your fine hand,
But having now admired it long
    enough,
We find that it is mightier than it
    seems—
At least mine own is frailer; you are
    laming it.
    Becket. And lamed and maim'd to
        dislocation, better
Than raised to take a life which
    Henry bade me

Guard from the stroke that dooms
    thee after death
To wail in deathless flame.
    Eleanor.   Nor you nor I
Have now to learn, my lord, that our
    good Henry
Says many a thing in sudden heats
    which he
Gainsays by next sunrising—often
    ready
To tear himself for having said as
    much.
My lord, Fitzurse—
    Becket. He too! what dost thou
        here?
Dares the bear slouch into the lion's
    den?
One downward plunge of his paw
    would rend away
Eyesight and manhood, life itself,
    from thee.
Go, lest I blast thee with anathema,
And make thee a world's horror.
    Fitzurse.   My lord, I shall
        Remember this.
    Becket.   I *do* remember thee;
Lest I remember thee to the lion, go.
                    [*Exit* Fitzurse.
Take up your dagger; put it in the
    sheath.
    Eleanor. Might not your courtesy
        stoop to hand it me?
But crowns must bow when mitres sit
    so high.
Well—well—too costly to be left or
    lost.   [*Picks up the dagger.*
I had it from an Arab soldan, who,
When I was there in Antioch, mar-
    vell'd at
Our unfamiliar beauties of the west;
But wonder'd more at my much con-
    stancy
To the monk-king, Louis, our former
    burthen,
From whom, as being too kin, you
    know, my lord,
God's grace and Holy Church deliv-
    er'd us.
I think, time given, I could have
    talk'd him out of
His ten wives into one. Look at the
    hilt.

What excellent workmanship! In our
   poor west
We cannot do it so well.
   Becket.   We can do worse.
Madam, I saw your dagger at her
   throat;
I heard your savage cry.
   Eleanor.   Well acted, was it?
A comedy meant to seem a tragedy—
A feint, a farce. My honest lord, you
   are known
Thro' all the courts of Christendom
   as one
That mars a cause with over vio-
   lence.
You have wrong'd Fitzurse. I speak
   not of myself.
We thought to scare this minion of
   the King
Back from her churchless commerce
   with the King
To the fond arms of her first love,
   Fitzurse,
Who swore to marry her. You have
   spoilt the farce.
My savage cry? Why, she—she—
   when I strove
To work against her license for her
   good,
Bark'd out at me such monstrous
   charges that
The King himself, for love of his own
   sons,
If hearing, would have spurn'd her;
   whereupon
I menaced her with this, as when we
   threaten
A yelper with a stick. Nay, I deny not
That I was somewhat anger'd. Do
   you hear me?
Believe or no, I care not. You have
   lost
The ear of the King. I have it.—My
   lord paramount,
Our great High-priest, will not your
   Holiness
Vouchsafe a gracious answer to your
   Queen?
   Becket. Rosamund hath not an-
   swer'd you one word;
Madam, I will not answer you one
   word.

Daughter, the world hath trickd' thee.
   Leave it, daughter;
Come thou with me to Godstow nun-
   nery,
And live what may be left thee of a
   life
Saved as by miracle alone with Him
Who gave it.

Re-enter GEOFFREY.

   Geoffrey. Mother, you told me a
   great fib; it was n't in the willow.
   Becket. Follow us, my son, and we
   will find it for thee—
Or something manlier.
      [*Exeunt* Becket, Rosamund, *and*
         Geoffrey.
   Eleanor. The world hath trick'd her
      —that's the King; if so,
There was the farce, the feint—not
   mine. And yet
I am all but sure my dagger was a
   feint
Till the worm turn'd—not life shot
   up in blood,
But death drawn in;—(*looking at the
   vial*) *this* was no feint, then?
   no.
But can I swear to that, had she but
   given
Plain answer to plain query? nay, me-
   thinks
Had she but bowed herself to meet
   the wave
Of humiliation, worshipt whom she
   loathed,
I should have let her be, scorn'd her
   too much
To harm her. Henry—Becket tells
   him this—
To take my life might lose him Aquitaine.
Too politic for that. Imprison me?
No, for it came to nothing—only a
   feint.
Did she not tell me I was playing on
   her?
I'll swear to mine own self it was a
   feint.
Why should I swear, Eleanor, who
   am, or was,

A sovereign power? The King plucks
    out their eyes
Who anger him, and shall not I, the
    Queen,
Tear out her heart—kill, kill with
    knife or venom
One of his slanderous harlots? 'None
    of such?'
I love her none the more. Tut, the
    chance gone,
She lives—but not for him; one point
    is gain'd.
O, I that thro' the Pope divorced
    King Louis,
Scorning his monkery,—I that
    wedded Henry,
Honoring his manhood—will he not
    mock at me,
The jealous fool balk'd of her will—
    with *him?*
But he and he must never meet again.
Reginald Fitzurse!

Re-enter FITZURSE.

Fitzurse.   Here, Madam, at your
    pleasure.
Eleanor. My pleasure is to have a
    man about me.
Why did you slink away so like a cur?
Fitzurse. Madam, I am as much
    man as the King.
Madam, I fear Church-censures like
    your King.
Eleanor. He grovels to the Church
    when he 's black-blooded,
But kinglike fought the proud arch-
    bishop,—kinglike
Defied the Pope, and, like his kingly
    sires,
The Normans, striving still to break
    or bind
The spiritual giant with our island
    laws
And customs, made me for the mo-
    ment proud
Even of that stale Church-bond which
    link'd me with him
To bear him kingly sons. I am not so
    sure
But that I love him still. Thou as
    much man!

No more of that; we will to France
    and be
Beforehand with the King, and brew
    from out
This Godstow-Becket intermeddling
    such
A strong hate-philtre as may madden
    him—madden
Against his priest beyond all helle-
    bore.

ACT V

SCENE I.—CASTLE IN NORMANDY.
KING'S CHAMBER

HENRY, ROGER OF YORK, FOLIOT, JOCE-
LYN OF SALISBURY.

Roger of York. Nay, nay, my liege,
He rides abroad with armed follow-
    ers,
Hath broken all his promises to thy-
    self,
Cursed and anathematized us right
    and left,
Stirr'd up a party there against your
    son—
Henry. Roger of York, you always
    hated him,
Even when you both were boys at
    Theobald's.
Roger of York. I always hated
    boundless arrogance.
In mine own cause I strove against
    him there,
And in thy cause I strive against him
    now.
Henry. I cannot think he moves
    against my son,
Knowing right well with what a ten-
    derness
He loved my son.
Roger of York.   Before you made
    him king.
But Becket ever moves against a king.
The Church is all—the crime to be a
    king.
We trust your Royal Grace, lord of
    more land
Than any crown in Europe, will not
    yield

To lay your neck beneath your citizen's heel.

Henry. Not to a Gregory of my throning! No.

Foliot. My royal liege, in aiming at your love,

It may be sometimes I have overshot
My duties to our Holy Mother Church,
Tho' all the world allows I fall no inch
Behind this Becket, rather go beyond
In scourgings, macerations, mortifyings,
Fasts, disciplines that clear the spiritual eye,
And break the soul from earth. Let all that be.
I boast not; but you know thro' all this quarrel
I still have cleaved to the crown, in hope the crown
Would cleave to me that but obey'd the crown,
Crowning your son; for which our loyal service,
And since we likewise swore to obey the customs,
York and myself, and our good Salisbury here,
Are push'd from out communion of the Church.

Jocelyn of Salisbury. Becket hath trodden on us like worms, my liege,

Trodden one half dead; one half, but half-alive,
Cries to the King.

Henry (aside). Take care o' thyself, O King!

Joselyn of Salisbury. Being so crush'd and so humiliated

We scarcely dare to bless the food we eat
Because of Becket.

Henry.   What would ye have me do?

Roger of York. Summon your barons; take their counsel; yet

I know—could swear—as long as Becket breathes,
Your Grace will never have one quiet hour.

Henry. What?—Ay—but pray you do not work upon me.

I see your drift—it may be so—and yet
You know me easily anger'd. Will you hence?
He shall absolve you—you shall have redress.
I have a dizzying headache. Let me rest.
I'll call you by and by.

[*Exeunt* Roger of York, Foliot, *and* Jocelyn of Salisbury.

Would he were dead! I have lost all love for him.
If God would take him in some sudden way—
Would he were dead!   [*Lies down.*

Page (entering). My liege, the Queen of England.

Henry. God's eyes!   [*Starting up.*

Enter ELEANOR.

Eleanor.   Of England? Say of Aquitaine.

I am no Queen of England. I had dream'd
I was the bride of England, and a queen.

Henry. And,—while you dream'd you were the bride of England,—

Stirring her baby-king against me? ha!

Eleanor. The brideless Becket is thy king and mine;

I will go live and die in Aquitaine.

Henry. Except I clap thee into prison here,

Lest thou shouldst play the wanton there again.
Ha, you of Aquitaine! O you of Aquitaine!
You were but Aquitaine to Louis—no wife;
You are only Aquitaine to me—no wife.

Eleanor. And why, my lord, should I be wife to one

That only wedded me for Aquitaine?
Yet this no-wife—her six and thirty sail

Of Provence blew you to your Eng-
    lish throne;
And this no-wife has borne you four
    brave sons,
And one of them at least is like to
    prove
Bigger in our small world than thou
    art.
Henry.   Ay—
Richard, if he *be* mine—I hope him
    mine.
But thou art like enough to make him
    thine.
    Eleanor. Becket is like enough to
    make all his.
Henry. Methought I had recover'd
    of the Becket,
That all was planed and bevell'd
    smooth again,
Save from some hateful cantrip of
    thine own.
    Eleanor. I will go live and die in
    Aquitaine.
I dream'd I was the consort of a
    king,
Not one whose back his priest has
    broken.
    Henry.   What!
Is the end come? You, will you crown
    my foe
My victor in mid-battle? I will be
Sole master of my house. The end is
    mine.
What game, what juggle, what devilry
    are you playing?
Why do you thrust this Becket on me
    again?
    Eleanor. Why? for I *am* true wife,
    and have my fears
Lest Becket thrust you even from
    your throne.
Do you know this cross, my liege?
    Henry (*turning his head*). Away!
    Not I.
    Eleanor. Not even the central dia-
    mond, worth, I think,
Half of the Antioch whence I had it.
    Henry.   That?
    Eleanor. I gave it you, and you
    your paramour;
She sends it back, as being dead to
    earth,
So dead henceforth to you.

    Henry. Dead! you have murder'd
    her.
Found out her secret bower and mur-
    der'd her.
    Eleanor. Your Becket knew the se-
    cret of your bower.
    Henry (*calling out*). Ho there!
    thy rest of life is hopeless
    prison.
    Eleanor. And what would my own
    Aquitaine say to that?
First, free thy captive from *her* hope-
    less prison.
    Henry. O devil, can I free her from
    the grave?
    Eleanor. You are too tragic; both
    of us are players
In such a comedy as our court of
    Provence
Had laugh'd 'at. That's a delicate
    Latin lay
Of Walter Map: the lady holds the
    cleric
Lovelier than any soldier, his poor
    tonsure
A crown of Empire. Will you have it
    again?
    (*Offering the cross. He dashes it
    down.*)
Saint Cupid, that is too irreverent.
Then mine once more. (*Puts it on.*)
        Your cleric hath your lady.
Nay, what uncomely faces, could he
    see you!
Foam at the mouth because King
    Thomas, lord
Not only of your vassals but amours,
Thro' chastest honor of the Deca-
    logue
Hath used the full authority of his
    Church
To put her into Godstow nunnery.
    Henry. To put her into Godstow
    nunnery!
He dared not—liar! yet, I remem-
    ber—
I do remember.
He bade me put her into a nunnery—
Into Godstow, into Hellstow, Devil-
    stow!
The Church! the Church!

God's eyes! I would the Church were
    down in hell!   [*Exit.*
Eleanor. Aha!

Enter the four KNIGHTS.

Fitzurse. What made the King cry
    out so furiously?
Eleanor. Our Becket, who will not
    absolve the bishops.
I think ye four have cause to love this
    Becket.
Fitzurse. I hate him for his inso-
    lence to all.
De Tracy. And I for all his inso-
    lence to thee.
De Brito. I hate him for I hate him
    is my reason.
And yet I hate him for a hypocrite.
De Morville. I do not love him, for
    he did his best
To break the barons, and now braves
    the King.
Eleanor. Strike, then, at once, the
    King would have him—See!

Re-enter HENRY.

Henry. No man to love me, honor
    me, obey me!
Sluggards and fools!
The slave that eat my bread has kick'd
    his King!
The dog I cramm'd with dainties wor-
    ried me!
The fellow that on a lame jade came
    to court,
A ragged cloak for saddle—he, he, he,
To shake my throne, to push into my
    chamber—
My bed, where even the slave is pri-
    vate—he—
I'll have her out again, he shall ab-
    solve
The bishops—they but did my will—
    not you—
Sluggards and fools, why do you
    stand and stare?
You are no King's men—you—you—
    you are Becket's men.
Down with King Henry! up with the
    Archbishop!
Will no man free me from this pesti-
    lent priest?   [*Exit.*

[*The* Knights *draw their swords.*
Eleanor. Are ye King's men? I am
    King's woman, I.
The Knights. King's men! King's
    men!

SCENE II

A ROOM IN CANTERBURY MONASTERY

BECKET *and* JOHN OF SALISBURY.

Becket. York said so?
John of Salisbury. Yes: a man may
    take good counsel
Even from his foe.
Becket.   York, will say anything.
What is he saying now? gone to the
    King
And taken our anathema with him.
    York!
Can the King de-anathematize this
    York?
John of Salisbury. Thomas, I would
    thou hadst return'd to Eng-
    land
Like some wise prince of this world
    from his wars,
With more of olive-branch and am-
    nesty
For foes at home—thou hast raised
    the world against thee.
Becket. Why, John, my kingdom is
    not of this world.
John of Salisbury. If it were more
    of this world it might be
More of the next. A policy of wise
    pardon
Wins here as well as there. To bless
    thine enemies—
Becket. Ay, mine, not Heaven's.
John of Salisbury. And may there
    not be something
Of this world's leaven in thee too,
    when crying
On Holy Church to thunder out her
    rights
And thine own wrong so pitilessly?
    Ah, Thomas,
The lightnings that we think are only
    Heaven's

Flash sometimes out of earth against
   the heavens.
The soldier, when he lets his whole
   self go
Lost in the common good, the com-
   mon wrong,
Strikes truest even for his own self.
   I crave
Thy pardon—I have still leave to
   speak.
Thou hast waged God's war against
   the King; and yet
We are self-uncertain creatures, and
   we may,
Yea, even when we know not, mix our
   spites
And private hates with our defense of
   Heaven.

Enter EDWARD GRIM

  Becket. Thou art but yesterday
   from Cambridge, Grim;
What say ye there of Becket?
  Grim.   I believe him
The bravest in our roll of primates
   down
From Austin—there are some—for
   there are men
Of canker'd judgment everywhere—
  Becket.   Who hold
With York, with York against me.
  Grim.   Well, my lord,
A stranger monk desires access to you.
  Becket. York against Canterbury,
   York against God!
I am open to him.   [*Exit* Grim.

Enter ROSAMUND *as a Monk.*

  Rosamund.   Can I speak with you
Alone, my father?
  Becket.   Come you to confess?
  Rosamund. Not now.
  Becket. Then speak; this is my
   other self,
Who, like my conscience, never lets
   me be.
  Rosamund (*throwing back the
   cowl*). I know him, our good
   John of Salisbury.
  Becket. Breaking already from thy
   novitiate

To plunge into this bitter world
   again—
These wells of Marah! I am grieved,
   my daughter.
I thought that I had made a peace
   for thee.
  Rosamund. Small peace was mine
   in my novitiate, father.
Thro' all closed doors a dreadful
   whisper crept
That thou wouldst excommunicate the
   King.
I could not eat, sleep, pray. I had
   with me
The monk's disguise thou gavest me
   for my bower;
I think our abbess knew it and al-
   low'd it.
I fled, and found thy name a charm
   to get me
Food, roof, and rest. I met a robber
   once;
I told him I was bound to see the
   archbishop:
'Pass on,' he said, and in thy name I
   pass'd
From house to house. In one a son
   stone-blind
Sat by his mother's hearth. He had
   gone too far
Into the King's own woods; and the
   poor mother,
Soon as she learnt I was a friend of
   thine,
Cried out against the cruelty of the
   King.
I said it was the King's courts, not
   the King,
But she would not believe me, and
   she wish'd
The Church were king; she had seen
   the archbishop once,
So mild, so kind. The people love thee,
   father.
  Becket. Alas! when I was Chan-
   cellor to the King,
I fear I was as cruel as the King.
  Rosamund. Cruel? O, no—it is the
   law, not he;
The customs of the realm.
  Becket.   The customs! customs!
  Rosamund. My lord, you have not
   excommunicated him?

O, if you have, absolve him!

Becket. Daughter, daughter,
Deal not with things you know not.

Rosamund. I know *him.*
Then you have done it, and I call *you*
cruel.

John of Salisbury. No, daughter,
you mistake our good arch-
bishop;
For once in France the King had been
so harsh,
He thought to excommunicate him—
Thomas,
You could not—old affection master'd
you,
You falter'd into tears.

Rosamund. God bless him for it!

Becket. Nay, make me not a
woman, John of Salisbury.
Nor make me traitor to my holy office.
Did not a man's voice ring along the
aisle,
'The King is sick and almost unto
death.'
How could I excommunicate him
then?

Rosamund. And wilt thou excommunicate him now?

Becket. Daughter, my time is short,
I shall not do it.
And were it longer—well—I should
not do it.

Rosamund. Thanks in this life, and
in the life to come!

Becket. Get thee back to thy nun-
nery with all haste;
Let this be thy last trespass. But one
question—
How fares thy pretty boy, the little
Geoffrey?
No fever, cough, croup, sickness?

Rosamund. No, but saved
From all that by our solitude.
The plagues
That smite the city spare the soli-
tudes.

Becket. God save him from the
sickness of the soul!
Thee too, thy solitude among thy
nuns,
May that save thee! Doth he remember me?

Rosamund. I warrant him.

Becket. He is marvellously like
thee.

Rosamund. Liker the King.

Becket. No, daughter.

Rosamund. Ay, but wait
Till his nose rises; he will be very
king.

Becket. Even so; but think not of
the King. Farewell.

Rosamund. My lord, the city is full
of armed men.

Becket. Even so. Farewell!

Rosamund. I will but pass to
vespers,
And breathe one prayer for my liege-
lord the King,
His child and mine own soul, and so
return.

Becket. Pray for me too; much
need of prayer have I.

[*Rosamund kneels and goes.*

Dan John, how much we lose, we celi-
bates,
Lacking the love of woman and of
child!

John of Salisbury. More gain than
loss; for of your wives you
shall
Find one a slut whose fairest linen
seems
Foul as her dust-cloth, if she used it
—one
So charged with tongue that every
thread of thought
Is broken ere it joins—a shrew to
boot,
Whose evil song far on into the night
Thrills to the topmost tile—no hope
but death;
One slow, fat, white, a burthen of the
hearth;
And one that being thwarted ever
swoons
And weeps herself into the place of
power,
And one an *uxor pauperis Ibyci.*
So rare the household honey-making
bee,
Man's help! but we, we have the
Blessed Virgin
For worship, and our Mother Church
for bride;

And all the souls we saved and father'd here
Will greet us as our babes in Paradise.
What noise was that? she told us of
arm'd men
Here in the city. Will you not withdraw?
    Becket. I once was out with Henry
in the days
When Henry loved me, and we came
upon
A wild-fowl sitting on her nest, so
still
I reach'd my hand and touch'd; she
did not stir;
The snow had frozen round her, and
she sat
Stone-dead upon a heap of ice-cold
eggs.
Look! how this love, this mother,
runs thro' all
The world God made—even the beast
—the bird!
    John of Salisbury. Ay, still a lover
of the beast and bird?
But these arm'd men—will you not
hide yourself?
Perchance the fierce De Brocs from
Saltwood Castle,
To assail our Holy Mother lest she
brood
Too long o'er this hard egg, the world,
and send
Her whole heart's heat into it, till it
break
Into young angels. Pray you, hide
yourself.
    Becket. There was a little fair-
hair'd Norman maid
Lived in my mother's house; if Rosamund is
The world's rose, as her name imports
her—she
Was the world's lily.
    John of Salisbury. Ay, and what of
her?
    Becket. She died of leprosy
    John of Salisbury   I know not
why
You call these old things back again,
my lord.
    Becket. The drowning man, they
say, remembers all

The chances of his life, just ere he
dies.
    John of Salisbury. Ay—but these
arm'd men—will *you* drown
yourself?
He loses half the meed of martyrdom
Who will be martyr when he might
escape.
    Becket. What day of the week?
Tuesday?
    John of Salisbury.   Tuesday, my
lord.
    Becket. On a Tuesday was I born,
and on a Tuesday
Baptized; and on a Tuesday did I fly
Forth from Northampton; on a Tuesday pass'd
From England into bitter banishment;
On a Tuesday at Pontigny came to me
The ghostly warning of my martyrdom;
On a Tuesday from mine exile I return'd,
And on a Tuesday—

TRACY *enters, then* FITZURSE, DE BRITO,
and DE MORVILLE. MONKS *following.*

    —on a Tuesday—Tracy!
(*A long silence, broken by* Fitzurse
saying, contemptuously,)
God help thee!
    John of Salisbury (*aside*). How the
good archbishop reddens!
He never yet could brook the note of
scorn.
    Fitzurse. My lord, we bring a mes-
sage from the King
Beyond the water; will you have it
alone,
Or with these listeners near you?
    Becket.   As you will.
    Fitzurse. Nay, as *you* will.
    Becket.   Nay, as *you* will.
    John of Salisbury.   Why, then
Better perhaps to speak with them
apart.
Let us withdraw.
    [*All go out except the four*
Knights *and* Becket.

Fitzurse.   We are all alone with
    him.
Shall I not smite him with his own
    cross-staff?
De Morville. No, look! the door is
    open: let him be.
Fitzurse. The King condemns your
    excommunicating—
Becket. This is no secret, but a pub-
    lic matter.
In here again!

JOHN OF SALISBURY *and* MONKS *re-
    turn.*

    Now, sirs, the King's commands!
Fitzurse. The King beyond the wa-
    ter, thro' our voices,
Commands you to be dutiful and leal
To your young King on this side of
    the water,
Not scorn him for the foibles of his
    youth.
What! you would make his coronation
    void
By cursing those who crown'd him.
    Out upon you!
Becket. Reginald, all men know I
    loved the prince.
His father gave him to my care, and I
Became his second father. He had his
    faults,
For which I would have laid mine
    own life down
To help him from them, since indeed
    I loved him,
And love him next after my lord his
    father.
Rather than dim the splendor of his
    crown
I fain would treble and quadruple it
With revenues, realms, and golden
    provinces
So that were done in equity.
Fitzurse.   You have broken
Your bond of peace, your treaty with
    the King—
Wakening such brawls and loud dis-
    turbances
In England, that he calls you over-
    sea
To answer for it in his Norman courts.

Becket. Prate not of bonds, for
    never, O, never again
Shall the waste voice of the bond-
    breaking sea
Divide me from the mother church
    of England,
My Canterbury. Loud disturbances!
O, ay— the bells rang out even to
    deafening,
Organ and pipe, and dulcimer, chants
    and hymns
In all the churches, trumpets in the
    halls,
Sobs, laughter, cries; they spread their
    raiment down
Before me—would have made my
    pathway flowers,
Save that it was midwinter in the
    street,
But full midsummer in those honest
    hearts.
Fitzurse. The King commands you
    to absolve the bishops
Whom you have excommunicated.
Becket.   I?
Not I, the Pope. Ask *him* for absolu-
    tion.
Fitzurse. But you advised the Pope.
Becket.   And so I did.
They have but to submit.
The Four Knights. The King com-
    mands you.
We are all King's men.
Becket. King's men at least should
    know
That their own King closed with me
    last July
That I should pass the censures of
    the Church
On those that crown'd young Henry
    in this realm,
And trampled on the rights of Canter-
    bury.
Fitzurse. What! dare you charge
    the King with treachery?
He sanction thee to excommunicate
The prelates whom he chose to crown
    his son!
Becket. I spake no word of treach-
    ery, Reginald.
But for the truth of this I make ap-
    peal

To all the archbishops, bishops, prel-
    ates, barons,
Monks, knights, five hundred, that
    were there and heard
Nay, you yourself were there; you
    heard yourself.
    Fitzurse. I was not there.
    Becket.   I saw you there.
    Fitzurse.   I was not.
    Becket. You were. I never forget
    anything.
    Fitzurse. He makes the King a
    traitor, me a liar.
How long shall we forbear him?
    John of Salisbury (*drawing* Becket
    aside). O my good lord,
Speak with them privately on this
    hereafter.
You see they have been revelling, and
    I fear
Are braced and brazen'd up with
    Christmas wines
For any murderous brawl.
    Becket.   And yet they prate
Of mine, my brawls, when those that
    name themselves
Of the King's part have broken down
    our barns,
Wasted our diocese, outraged our ten-
    ants,
Lifted our produce, driven our clerics
    out—
Why they, your friends, those ruffians,
    the De Brocs,
They stood on Dover beach to murder
    me,
They slew my stags in mine own
    manor here,
Mutilated, poor brute, my sumpter-
    mule,
Plunder'd the vessel full of Gascon
    wine,
The old King's present, carried off the
    casks,
Kill'd half the crew, dungeon'd the
    other half
In Pevensey Castle—
    De Morville.   Why not rather
    then,
If this be so, complain to your young
    King,
Not punish of your own authority?

    Becket. Mine enemies barr'd all
    access to the boy.
They knew he loved me.
Hugh, Hugh, how proudly you exalt
    your head!
Nay, when they seek to overturn our
    rights,
I ask no leave of king, or mortal man,
To set them straight again. Alone I do
    it.
Give to the King the things that are
    the King's,
And those of God to God.
    Fitzurse. Threats! threats! ye hear
    him.
What! will he excommunicate all the
    world?
    [*The* Knights *come round* Becket.
    De Tracy. He shall not.
    De Brito.   Well, as yet—I should
    be grateful—
He hath not excommunicated *me*.
    Becket. Because thou wast *born*
    excommunicate.
I never spied in thee one gleam of
    grace.
    De Brito. Your Christian's Chris-
    tian charity!
    Becket.   By Saint Denis—
    De Brito. Ay, by Saint Denis, now
    will he flame out,
And lose his head as old Saint Deni
    did.
    Becket. Ye think to scare me from
    my loyalty
To God and to the Holy Father. No!
Tho' all the swords in England flash'd
    above me
Ready to fall at Henry's word or
    yours—
Tho' all the loud-lung'd trumpets
    upon earth
Blared from the heights of all the
    thrones of her kings,
Blowing the world against me, I would
    stand
Clothed with the full authority of
    Rome,
Mail'd in the perfect panoply of faith,
First of the foremost of their files
    who die
For God, to people heaven in the great
    day

When God makes up his jewels. Once
    I fled—
Never again, and you—I marvel at
    you—
Ye know what is between us. Ye have
    sworn
Yourselves my men when I was
    Chancellor—
My vassals—and yet threaten your
    archbishop
In his own house.

    Knights.   Nothing can be between
    us
That goes against our fealty to the
    King.

    Fitzurse. And in his name we charge
you that ye keep
This traitor from escaping.

    Becket.   Rest you easy,
For I am easy to keep. I shall not
    fly.
Here, here, here will you find me.

    De Morville.   Know you not
You have spoken to the peril of your
    life?

    Becket. As I shall speak again.

    Fitzurse, De Tracy, and De Brito.
    To arms!
      [*They rush out,* De Morville
      lingers.

    Becket.   De Morville,
I had thought so well of you; and
    even now
You seem the least assassin of the
    four.
O, do not damn yourself for company!
Is it too late for me to save your
    soul?
I pray you for one moment stay and
    speak.

    De Morville. Becket, it *is* too late.
                    [*Exit.*

    Becket.   Is it too late?
Too late on earth may be too soon in
    hell.

    Knights (*in the distance*). Close the
    great gate—ho, there—upon
    the town!

    Becket's Retainers. Shut the hall-
    doors!   [*A pause.*

    Becket.   You hear them, brother
    John;

Why do you stand so silent, brother
    John?

    John of Salisbury. For I was mus-
    ing on an ancient saw,
Suaviter in modo, fortiter in re;
Is strength less strong when hand-in-
    hand with grace?
Gratior in pulchro corpore virtus.
    Thomas,
Why should you heat yourself for such
    as these?

    Becket.   Methought I answer'd
    moderately enough.

    John of Salisbury. As one that
    blows the coal to cool the fire.
My lord, I marvel why you never
    lean
On any man's advising but your own.

    Becket. Is it so, Dan John? well,
    what should I have done?

    John of Salisbury. You should have
    taken counsel with your friends
Before these bandits brake into your
    presence.
They seek—you make—occasion for
    your death.

    Becket. My counsel is already
    taken, John.
I am prepared to die.

    John of Salisbury. We are sin-
    ners all,
The best of all not all-prepared to
    die.

    Becket. God's will be done!

    John of Salisbury. Ay, well. God's
    will be done!

    Grim (*re-entering*). My lord, the
    knights are arming in the gar-
    den
Beneath the sycamore.

    Becket.   Good! let them arm.

    Grim. And one of the De Brocs is
    with them, Robert,
The apostate monk that was with
    Randulf here.
He knows the twists and turnings of
    the place.

    Becket. No fear!

    Grim.   No fear, my lord.
      [*Crashes on the hall-doors. The
      Monks flee.*

    Becket (*rising*).   Our dovecote
    flown!

I cannot tell why monks should all be cowards.

John of Salisbury. Take refuge in your own cathedral, Thomas.

Becket. Do they not fight the Great Fiend day by day?

Valor and holy life should go together.

Why should all monks be cowards?

John of Salisbury. Are they so?

I say, take refuge in your own cathedral.

Becket. Ay, but I told them I would wait them here.

Grim. May they not say you dared not show yourself

In your old place?, and vespers are beginning.

[*Bells rings for vespers till end of scene.*

You should attend the office, give them heart.

They fear you slain; they dread they know not what.

Becket. Ay, monks, not men.

Grim. I am a monk my lord.

Perhaps, my lord, you wrong us.

Some would stand by you to the death.

Becket. Your pardon.

John of Salisbury. He said, 'Attend the office.'

Becket. Attend the office?

Why then—the Cross!—who bears my Cross before me?

Methought they would have brain'd me with it, John.

[*Grim takes it.*

Grim. I! Would that I could bear thy cross indeed!

Becket. The mitre!

John of Salisbury. Will you wear it?—there!

[*Becket puts on the mitre.*

Becket. The pall!

I go to meet my King!

[*Puts on the pall.*

Grim. To meet the King?

[*Crashes on the doors as they go out.*

John of Salisbury. Why do you move with such a stateliness?

Can you not hear them yonder like a storm,

Battering the doors, and breaking thro' the walls?

Becket. Why do the heathen rage? My two good friends,

What matters murder'd here, or murder'd there?

And yet my dream foretold my martyrdom

In mine own church. It is God's will. Go on.

Nay, drag me not. We must not seem to fly.

SCENE III

NORTH TRANSEPT OF CANTERBURY CATHEDRAL

On the right hand a flight of steps leading to the Choir, another flight on the left, leading to the North Aisle. Winter afternoon slowly darkening. Low thunder now and then of an approaching storm. MONKS *heard chanting the service* ROSAMUND *kneeling.*

Rosamund. O blessed saint, O glorious Benedict,—

These arm'd men in the city, these fierce faces—

Thy holy follower founded Canterbury—

Save that dear head which now is Canterbury,

Save him, he saved my life, he saved my child,

Save him, his blood would darken Henry's name;

Save him till all as saintly as thyself

He miss the searching flame of purgatory,

And pass at once perfect to Paradise.

[*Noise of steps and voices in the cloisters.*

Hark! Is it they? Coming! He is not here—

Not yet, thank heaven. O, save him!

[*Goes up steps leading to choir.*

Becket (*entering, forced along by* John of Salisbury *and* Grim).
No, I tell you!
I cannot bear a hand upon my person;
Why do you force me thus against my will?

Grim. My lord, we force you from your enemies.

Becket. As you would force a king from being crown'd.

John of Salisbury. We must not force the crown of martyrdom.
[*Service stops. Monks come down from the stairs that lead to the choir.*

Monks. Here is the great archbishop! He lives! he lives!
Die with him, and be glorified together.

Becket. Together?—get you back! go on with the office.

Monks. Come, then, with us to vespers.

Becket. How can I come
When you so block the entry? Back, I say!
Go on with the office. Shall not Heaven be served
Tho' earth's last earthquake clash'd the minster-bells,
And the great deeps were broken up again,
And hiss'd against the sun?
[*Noise in the cloisters.*

Monks. The murderers, hark!
Let us hide! let us hide!

Becket. What do these people fear?

Monks. Those arm'd men in the cloister.

Becket. Be not such cravens!
I will go out and meet them.

Grim and Others. Shut the doors!
We will not have him slain before our face.
[*They close the doors of the transept. Knocking.*
Fly, fly, my lord, before they burst the doors! [*Knocking.*

Becket. Why, these are our own monks who follow'd us!
And will you bolt them out, and have *them* slain?

Undo the doors; the church is not a castle.
Knock, and it shall be open'd. Are you deaf?
What, have I lost authority among you?
Stand by, make way!
[*Opens the doors. Enter* Monks *from cloister.*
Come in, my friends, come in!
Nay, faster, faster!

Monks. O, my lord archbishop,
A score of knights all arm'd with swords and axes—
To the choir, to the choir!
[*Monks* divide, *part flying by the stairs on the right, part by those on the left. The rush of these last bears* Becket *along with them some way up the steps, where he is left standing alone.*

Becket. Shall I too pass to the choir,
And die upon the patriarchal throne
Of all my predecessors?

John of Salisbury. No, to the crypt!
Twenty steps down. Stumble not in the darkness,
Lest they should seize thee.

Grim. To the crypt? no—no,
To the chapel of Saint Blaise beneath the roof!

John of Salisbury (*pointing upward and downward*). That way or this! Save thyself either way.

Becket. O, no, not either way, nor any way
Save by that way which leads thro' night to light.
Not twenty steps, but one.
And fear not I should stumble in the darkness,
Not tho' it be their hour, the power of darkness,
But my hour too, the power of light in darkness!
I am not in the darkness but the light,
Seen by the Church in heaven, the Church on earth—

The power of life in death to make
    her free!

Enter the four KNIGHTS. JOHN OF
    SALISBURY *flies to the altar of
    Saint Benedict.*

Fitzurse. Here, here, King's men!
    [*Catches hold of the last flying
        Monk.
            Where is the traitor Becket?
Monk. I am not he! I am not he,
    my lord.
I am not he indeed!
    Fitzurse.   Hence to the fiend!
Where is this treble traitor to the
    King?
De Tracy. Where is the archbishop,
    Thomas Becket?
Becket.   Here.
No traitor to the King, but Priest of
    God,
Primate of England.
    [*Descending into the transept.*
            I am he ye seek.
What would ye have of me?
    Fitzurse.   Your life.
    De Tracy.   Your life.
    De Morville. Save that you will ab-
        solve the bishops.
Becket.   Never,—
Except they make submission to the
    Church.
You had my answer to that cry be-
    fore.
    De Morville. Why, then you are a
        dead man; flee!
Becket.   I will not.
I am readier to be slain than thou to
    slay.
Hugh, I know well thou hast but half
    a heart
To bathe this sacred pavement with
    my blood.
God pardon thee and these, but God's
    full curse
Shatter you all to pieces if ye harm
One of my flock!
    Fitzurse. Was not the great gate
        shut?
They are thronging in to vespers—
    half the town.

We shall be overwhelm'd. Seize him
    and carry him!
Come with us—nay—thou art our
    prisoner—come!
    De Morville. Ay, make him pris-
        oner, do not harm the man.
    [*Fitzurse lays hold of the* Arch-
        bishop's pall.
Becket. Touch me not!
De Brito. How the good priest gods
    himself!
He is not yet ascended to the Father.
    Fitzurse. I will not only touch, but
        drag thee hence.
Becket. Thou art my man, thou
    art my vassal. Away!
    [*Flings him off till he reels, al-
        most to falling.*
De Tracy (*lays hold of the pall*).
    Come; as he said, thou art our
    prisoner.
Becket.   Down!
    [*Throws him headlong.*
Fitzurse (*advances with drawn
    sword*). I told thee that I
    should remember thee!
Becket. Profligate pander!
Fitzurse. Do you hear that? strike,
    strike.
    [*Strikes off the* Archbishop's
        *mitre, and wounds him in the
        forehead.*
Becket (*covers his eyes with his
    hand*). I do commend my
    cause to God, the Virgin,
Saint Denis of France and Saint
    Alphege of England,
And all the tutelar Saints of Canter-
    bury.
    [*Grim wraps his arms about the*
        Archbishop.
Spare this defence, dear brother.
    [*Tracy has arisen, and ap-
        proaches, hesitatingly, with his
        sword raised.*
    Fitzurse.   Strike him, Tracy!
Rosamund (*rushing down steps
    from the choir*). No, no, no,
    no!
Fitzurse. This wanton here. De
    Morville,
Hold her away.
    De Morville. I hold her.

Rosamund (*held back by* De Mor-
ville, *and stretching out her
arms*).   Mercy, mercy,
As you would hope for mercy!
Fitzurse.   Strike, I say!
Grim. O God, O noble knights, O
     sacrilege!
Strike our archbishop in his own
     cathedral!
The Pope, the King, will curse you—
     the whole world
Abhor you; ye will die the death of
     dogs!
Nay, nay, good Tracy.
                     [*Lifts his arm.*
Fitzurse. Answer not, but strike.
De Tracy. There is my answer
     then.
     [*Sword falls on* Grim's *arm, and
     glances from it, wounding*
     Becket.
Grim.   Mine arm is sever'd.
I can no more—fight out the good
     fight—die
Conqueror.
     [*Staggers into the chapel of
     Saint Benedict.*
Becket (*falling on his knees*). At
the right hand of Power—

Power and great glory—for thy
     Church, O Lord—
Into thy hands, O Lord—into thy
     hands!—   [*Sinks prone.*
De Brito. This last to rid thee of a
     world of brawls! (*Kills him.*)
The traitor's dead, and will arise no
     more.
Fitzurse. Nay, have we still'd him?
     What! the great archbishop!
Does he breathe? No?
De Tracy. No, Reginald, he is dead.
                     [*Storm bursts.*[1]
De Morville. Will the earth gape
     and swallow us?
De Brito.   The deed's done—
Away!
     [*De Brito, De Tracy, Fitzurse,
     rush out, crying 'King's men!'*
     De Morville *follows slowly.
     Flashes of lightning thro' the
     Cathedral.* Rosamund *seen
     kneeling by the body of*
     Becket.

[1] A tremendous thunderstorm actually
broke over the Cathedral as the murderers were leaving it.

THE FALCON

DRAMATIS PERSONÆ

The Count Federigo degli Alberighi.
Filippo, *the Count's foster-brother.*
The Lady Giovanna.
Elisabetta, *the Count's nurse.*

THE FALCON

ELISABETTA *discovered seated on stool
in window, darning. The Count
with Falcon on his hand comes
down through the door at back. A
withered wreath on the wall.*

Elisabetta. So, my lord, the Lady
Giovanna, who hath been away so
long, came back last night with her
son to the castle.

Count. Hear that, my bird! Art
thou not jealous of her?
My princess of the cloud, my plumed
purveyor,
My far-eyed queen of the winds—
thou that canst soar
Beyond the morning lark, and, how-
soe'er
Thy quarry wind and wheel, swoop
down upon him
Eagle-like, lightning-like — strike,
make his feathers
Glance in mid heaven.
            [*Crosses to chair.*
        I would thou hadst a mate!
Thy breed will die with thee, and
mine with me;
I am as lone and loveless as thyself.
            [*Sits in chair.*
Giovanna here! Ay, ruffle thyself—*be*
jealous!
Thou shouldst be jealous of her.
Tho' bred thee
The full-train'd marvel of all fal-
conry,
And love thee and thou me, yet if
Giovanna
Be here again—No, no! Buss me, my
bird!
The stately widow has no heart for
me.

Thou art the last friend left me upon
earth—
No, no again to that!
            [*Rises and turns.*
        My good old nurse,
I had forgotten thou wast sitting
there.
    Elisabetta. Ay, and forgotten thy
    foster-brother too.
    Count. Bird-babble for my falcon!
    Let it pass.
What art thou doing there?
    Elisabetta. Darning, your lordship.
We cannot flaunt it in new feathers
now.
Nay, if we *will* buy diamond neck-
laces
To please our lady, we must darn, my
lord.
This old thing here (*points to necklace round her neck*), they are
but blue beads—my Piero,
God rest his honest soul, he bought
'em for me,
Ay, but he knew I meant to marry
him.
How couldst thou do it, my son? How
couldst thou do it?
    Count. She saw it at a dance, upon
    a neck
Less lovely than her own, and long'd
for it.
    Elisabetta. She told thee as much?
    Count. No, no—a friend of hers.
    Elisabetta. Shame on her that she
    took it at thy hands,
She rich enough to have bought it for
herself!
    Count. She would have robb'd me
    then of a great pleasure.
    Elisabetta. But hath she yet re-
    turn'd thy love?
    Count.   Not yet!
    Elisabetta. She should return thy
    necklace then.

1066

Count.   Ay, if
She knew the giver; but I bound the
    seller
To silence, and I left it privily
At Florence, in her palace.
Elisabetta.   And sold thine own
To buy it for her. She not know? She
    knows
There 's none such other—
Count.   Madman anywhere.
Speak freely, tho' to call a madman
    mad
Will hardly help to make him sane
    again.

Enter FILIPPO.

Filippo. Ah, the women, the
women! Ah, Monna Giovanna, you
here again! you that have the face of
an angel and the heart of a—that 's
too positive! You that have a score of
lovers and have not a heart for any
of them—that 's positive-negative:
you that have *not* the head of a toad,
and *not* a heart like the jewel in it—
that 's too negative; you that have a
cheek like a peach and a heart like the
stone in it—that 's positive again—
that 's better!

Elisabetta. Sh—sh—Filippo!
Filippo (turns half round). Here
has our master been a-glorifying and
a-velveting and a-silking himself, and
a-peacocking and a-spreading to catch
her eye for a dozen year, till he has
n't an eye left in his own tail to flourish among the peahens, and all along
o' you, Monna Giovanna, all along o'
you!

Elisabetta. Sh—sh—Filippo! Can't
you hear that you are saying behind
his back what you see you are saying
afore his face?

Count. Let him—he never spares
me to my face!

Filippo. No, my lord, I never spare
your lordship to your lordship's face,
nor behind your lordship's back, nor
to right, nor to left, nor to round
about and back to your lordship's face
again, for I 'm honest, your lordship.

Count. Come, come, Filippo what
is there in the larder?

[Elisabetta *crosses to fireplace
and puts on wood.*
Filippo. Shelves and hooks, shelves
and hooks, and when I see the shelves
I am like to hang myself on the hooks.
Count. No bread?
Filippo. Half a breakfast for a rat!
Count. Milk?
Filippo. Three laps for a cat!
Count. Cheese?
Filippo. A supper for twelve mites.
Count. Eggs?
Filippo. One, but addled.
Count. No bird?
Filippo. Half a tit and a hern's bill.
Count. Let be thy jokes and thy
jerks, man! Anything or nothing?
Filippo. Well, my lord, if all-but-
nothing be anything, and one plate of
dried prunes be all-but-nothing, then
there is anything in your lordship's
larder at your lordship's service, if
your lordship care to call for it.
Count. Good mother, happy was
    the prodigal son,
For he return'd to the rich father; I
But add my poverty to thine. And all
Thro' following of my fancy. Pray
    thee make
Thy slender meal out of those scraps
    and shreds
Filippo spoke of. As for him and me,
There sprouts a salad in the garden
    still.
(To the Falcon.) Why didst thou miss
    thy quarry yester-even?
To-day, my beauty, thou must dash
    us down
Our dinner from the skies. Away,
    Filippo!
          [*Exit, followed by* Filippo.
Elisabetta. I knew it would come to
this. She has beggard him. I always
knew it would come to this! *(Goes up
to table as if to resume darning, and
looks out of window.)* Why, as I live,
there is Monna Giovanna coming
down the hill from the castle. Stops
and stares at our cottage. Ay, ay!
stare at it: it 's all you have left us.
Shame on you! *She* beautiful! sleek
as a miller's mouse! Meal enough,
meat enough, well fed; but beautiful

—bah! Nay, see, why she turns down the path through our little vineyard, and I sneezed three times this morning. Coming to visit my lord, for the first time in her life too! Why, bless the saints! I 'll be bound to confess her love to him at last. I forgive her, I forgive her! I knew it would come to this—I always knew it must come to this! (*Goes up to door during latter part of speech, and opens it.*) Come in, madonna, come in. (*Retires to front of table and curtseys as the* LADY GIOVANNA *enters, then moves chair towards the hearth.*) Nay, let me place this chair for your ladyship.

[Lady Giovanna *moves slowly down stage, then crosses to chair, looking about her, bows as she sees the Madonna over fireplace, then sits in chair.*

Lady Giovanna. Can I speak with the Count?

Elisabetta. Ay, my lady, but won't you speak with the old woman first, and tell her all about it and make her happy? for I 've been on my knees every day for these half-dozen years in hope that the saints would send us this blessed morning; and he always took you so kindly, he always took the world so kindly. When he was a little one, and I put the bitters on my breast to wean him, he made a wry mouth at it, but he took it so kindly, and your ladyship has given him bitters enough in this world, and he never made a wry mouth at you, he always took you so kindly—which is more than I did, my lady, more than I did—and he so handsome—and bless your sweet face, you look as beautiful this morning as the very Madonna her own self—and better late than never—but come when they will—then or now—it 's all for the best, come when they will—they are made by the blessed saints—these marriages.   [*Raises her hands.*

Lady Giovanna. Marriages? I shall never marry again!

Elisabetta (*rises and turns*). Shame on her then!

Lady Giovanna. Where is the Count?

Elisabetta. Just gone To fly his falcon.

Lady Giovanna. Call him back and say I come to breakfast with him.

Elisabetta.   Holy mother! To breakfast! O sweet saints! one plate of prunes!

Well, madam, I will give your message to him.   [*Exit.*

Lady Giovanna. His falcon, and I come to ask for his falcon,
The pleasure of his eyes—boast of his hand—
Pride of his heart—the solace of his hours—
His one companion here—nay, I have heard
That, thro' his late magnificence of living
And this last costly gift to mine own self,
                [*Shows diamond necklace*
He hath become so beggar'd that his falcon
Even wins his dinner for him in the field.
That must be talk, not truth, but, truth or talk,
How can I ask for his falcon?
                [*Rises and moves as she speaks.*
                O my sick boy!
My daily fading Florio, it is thou
Hath set me this hard task, for when I say,
What can I do—what can I get for thee?
He answers, 'Get the Count to give me his falcon,
And that will make me well.' Yet if I ask,
He loves me, and he knows I know he loves me!
Will he not pray me to return his love—
To marry him?—(*pause*)—I can never marry him.
His grandsire struck my grandsire in a brawl

At Florence, and my grandsire
    stabb'd him there.
The feud between our houses is the
    bar
I cannot cross; I dare not brave my
    brother.
Break with my kin. My brother hates
    him, scorns
The noblest-natured man alive, and
    I—
Who have that reverence for him that
    I scarce
Dare beg him to receive his diamonds
    back—
How can I, dare I, ask him for his
    falcon?
    [*Puts diamonds in her casket.*

Re-enter COUNT *and* FILIPPO. COUNT
    turns to FILIPPO.

Count. Do what I said; I cannot do
    it myself.
Filippo. Why then, my lord, we are
    pauper'd out and out.
Count. Do what I said!
    [*Advances and bows low.*
Welcome to this poor cottage, my
    dear lady.
Lady Giovanna. And welcome turns
    a cottage to a palace.
Count. 'T is long since we have
    met!
Lady Giovanna. To make amends
I come this day to break my fast with
    you.
Count. I am much honor'd—yes—
    [*Turns to* Filippo.
Do what I told thee. Must I do it my-
    self?
Filippo. I will, I will. (*Sighs.*) Poor
    fellow!   [*Exit.*
Count. Lady, you bring your light
    into my cottage
Who never deign'd to shine into my
    palace.
My palace wanting you was but a
    cottage;
My cottage, while you grace it, is a
    palace.
Lady Giovanna. In cottage or in
    palace, being still
Beyond your fortunes, you are still
    the king

Of courtesy and liberality.
Count. I trust I still maintain my
    courtesy;
My liberality perforce is dead
Thro' lack of means of giving.
Lady Giovanna.   Yet I come
To ask a gift.
    [*Moves toward him a little.*
Count.   It will be hard, I fear,
To find one shock upon the field when
    all
The harvest has been carried.
Lady Giovanna.   But my boy—
(*Aside.*) No, no! not yet—I cannot!
Count.   Ay, how is he,
That bright inheritor of your eyes—
    your boy?
Lady Giovanna. Alas, my Lord
    Federigo, he hath fallen
Into a sickness, and it troubles me.
Count. Sick! is it so? why, when
    he came last year
To see me hawking, he was well
    enough;
And then I taught him all our hawk-
    ing-phrases.
Lady Giovanna. O yes, and once
    you let him fly your falcon.
Count. How charm'd he was! what
    wonder?—A gallant boy,
A noble bird, each perfect of the
    breed.
Lady Giovanna (*sinks in chair*).
    What do you rate her at?
Count.   My bird? a hundred
Gold pieces once were offer'd by the
    Duke.
I had no heart to part with her for
    money.
Lady Giovanna. No, not for money.
    [*Count turns away and sighs.*
    Wherefore do you sigh?
Count. I have lost a friend of late.
Lady Giovanna. I could sigh with
    you
For fear of losing more than friend, a
    son;
And if he leave me—all the rest of
    life—
That wither'd wreath were of more
    worth to me.
    [*Looking at wreath on wall.*

Count. That wither'd wreath is of more worth to me

Than all the blossom, all the leaf of this

New-wakening year.

[*Goes and takes down wreath.*

Lady Giovanna. And yet I never saw

The land so rich in blossom as this year.

Count (*holding wreath toward her*). Was not the year when this was gather'd richer?

Lady Giovanna. How long ago was that?

Count.   Alas, ten summers!

A lady that was beautiful as day

Sat by me at a rustic festival

With other beauties on a mountain meadow,

And she was the most beautiful of all;

Then but fifteen, and still as beautiful.

The mountain flowers grew thickly round about.

I made a wreath with some of these; I ask'd

A ribbon from her hair to bind it with;

I whisper'd, Let me crown you Queen of Beauty,

And softly placed the chaplet on her head.

A color, which has color'd all my life,

Flush'd in her face; then I was call'd away;

And presently all rose, and so departed.

Ah! she had thrown my chaplet on the grass,

And there I found it.

[*Lets his hands fall, holding wreath despondingly.*

Lady Giovanna (*after pause*). How long since do you say?

Count. That was the very year before you married.

Lady Giovanna. When I was married you were at the wars.

Count. Had she not thrown my chaplet on the grass,

It may be I had never seen the wars.

[*Replaces wreath whence he had taken it.*

Lady Giovanna. Ah, but, my lord, there ran a rumor then

That you were kill'd in battle. I can tell you

True tears that year were shed for you in Florence.

Count. It might have been as well for me. Unhappily

I was but wounded by the enemy there

And then imprison'd.

Lady Giovanna. Happily, however,

I see you quite recover'd of your wound.

Count. No, no, not quite, madonna, not yet, not yet.

Re-enter FILIPPO.

Filippo. My lord, a word with you.

Count.   Pray, pardon me!

[*Lady Giovanna crosses, and passes behind chair and takes down wreath; then goes to chair by table.*

Count (*to* Filippo). What is it, Filippo?

Filippo. Spoons, your lordship.

Count.   Spoons!

Filippo. Yes, my lord, for was n't my lady born with a golden spoon in her ladyship's mouth, and we have n't never so much as a silver one for the golden lips of her ladyship.

Count. Have we not half a score of silver spoons?

Filippo. Half o' one, my lord!

Count. How half of one?

Filippo. I trod upon him even now, my lord, in my hurry, and broke him.

Count. And the other nine?

Filippo. Sold! but shall I not mount with your lordship's leave to her ladyship's castle, in your lordship's and her ladyship's name, and confer with her ladyship's seneschal, and so descend again with some of her ladyship's own appurtenances?

Count. Why—no man. Only see your cloth be clean.

[*Exit* Filippo.

Lady Giovanna. Ay, ay, this faded ribbon was the mode
In Florence ten years back. What 's here? a scroll
Pinned to the wreath.
　　My lord, you have said so much
Of this poor wreath that I was bold enough
To take it down, if but to guess what flowers
Had made it; and I find a written scroll
That seems to run in rhymings. Might I read?
　　Count. Ay, if you will.
　　Lady Giovanna. It should be if you can.
(*Reads.*) 'Dead mountain.' Nay, for who could trace a hand
So wild and staggering?
　　Count. This was penn'd, madonna,
Close to the grating on a winter morn
In the perpetual twilight of a prison,
When he that made it, having his right hand
Lamed in the battle, wrote it with his left.
　　Lady Giovanna. O heavens! the very letters seem to shake
With cold, with pain perhaps, poor prisoner! Well,
Tell me the words—or better—for I see
There goes a musical score along with them,
Repeat them to their music.
　　Count. 　　　　You can touch
No chord in me that would not answer you
In music.
　　Lady Giovanna. That is musically said.
　　[*Count takes guitar. Lady Giovanna sits listening with wreath in her hand, and quietly removes scroll and places it on table at the end of the song.*
　　Count (*sings, playing guitar*).
　　'Dead mountain flowers, dead mountain-meadow flowers,
Dearer than when you made your mountain gay,
Sweeter than any violet of to-day,

Richer than all the wide world-wealth of May,
To me, tho' all your bloom has died away,
You bloom again, dead mountain-meadow flowers.'

　　Enter ELISABETTA *with cloth.*

　　Elisabetta. A word with you, my lord!
　　Count (*singing*). 'O mountain flowers!'
　　Elisabetta (*louder*). A word, my lord!
　　Count (*sings*). 'Dead flowers!'
　　Elisabetta (*louder*). A word, my lord!
　　Count. I pray you pardon me again!
　　[*Lady Giovanna looking at wreath.*
　　Count (*to Elisabetta*). What is it?
　　Elisabetta. My lord, we have but one piece of earthen-ware to serve the salad in to my lady, and that cracked!
　　Count. Why then, that flower'd bowl my ancestor
Fetch'd from the farthest east—we never use it
For fear of breakage—but this day has brought
A great occasion. You can take it, nurse!
　　Elisabetta. I did take it, my lord, but what with my lady's coming that had so flurried me, and what with the fear of breaking it, I did break it, my lord; it is broken!
　　Count. My one thing left of value in the world!
No matter! see your cloth be white as snow!
　　Elisabetta (*pointing thro' window*). White? I warrant thee, my son, as the snow yonder on the very tip-top o' the mountain.
　　Count. And yet, to speak white truth, my good old mother,
I have seen it like the snow on the moraine.

Elisabetta. How can your lordship
    say so? There, my lord!
                    [*Lays cloth.*
O my dear son, be not unkind to
    me.
And one word more.
                    [*Going—returns.*
    Count (*touching guitar*). Good! let
        it be but one.
    Elisabetta. Hath she return'd thy
        love?
    Count.   Not yet!
    Elisabetta.   And will she?
    Count (*looking at* Lady Giovanna).
        I scarce believe it!
    Elisabetta. Shame upon her then!
                    [*Exit.*
    Count (*sings*). 'Dead mountain
        flowers'—
        Ah, well my nurse has broken
The thread of my dead flowers, as she
    has broken
My china bowl. My memory is as
    dead.
                    [*Goes and replaces guitar.*
Strange that the words at home with
    me so long
Should fly like bosom friends when
    needed most.
So by your leave, if you would hear
    the rest,
The writing.
    Lady Giovanna (*holding wreath
        toward him*). There! my lord,
        you are a poet,
And can you not imagine that the
    wreath,
Set, as you say, so lightly on her head,
Fell with her motion as she rose, and
    she,
A girl, a child, then but fifteen, how-
    ever
Flutter'd or flatter'd by your notice
    of her,
Was yet too bashful to return for it!
    Count. Was it so indeed? was it
        so? was it so?
    [*Leans forward to take wreath,
        and touches* Lady Giovanna's
        *hand, which she withdraws
        hastily; he places wreath on
        corner of chair.*
Lady Giovanna (*with dignity*). I

did not say, my lord, that it
    was so;
I said you might imagine it was so.

Enter FILIPPO *with bowl of salad,
    which he places on table.*

Filippo. Here's a fine salad for my
lady, for tho' we have been a soldier,
and ridden by his lordship's side, and
seen the red of the battle-field, yet
are we now drill-sergeant to his lordship's lettuces, and profess to be great
in green things and in garden-stuff.
    Lady Giovanna. I thank thee, good
        Filippo.   [*Exit Filippo.*

Enter ELISABETTA *with bird on a dish
    which she places on table.*

    Elisabetta (*close to table*). Here's
a fine fowl for my lady; I had scant
time to do him in. I hope he be not
underdone, for we be undone in the
doing of him.
    Lady Giovanna. I thank you, my
good nurse.
    Filippo (*re-entering with plate of
prunes*). And here are fine fruits for
my lady—prunes, my lady, from the
tree that my lord himself planted here
in the blossom of his boyhood—and
so I, Filippo, being, with your ladyship's pardon, and as your ladyship
knows, his lordship's own foster-
brother, would commend them to
your ladyship's most peculiar appre-
ciation.
                    [*Puts plate on table.*
    Elisabetta. Filippo!
    Lady Giovanna (Count *leads her to
        table*). Will you not eat with
        me, my lord?
    Count.   I cannot;
Not a morsel, not one morsel. I have
    broken
My fast already. I will pledge you.
    Wine!
Filippo, wine!
    [*Sits near table; Filippo brings
        flask, fills the* Count's *goblet,
        then* Lady Giovanna's; *Elisa-
        betta stands at the back of*
        Lady Giovanna's *chair.*

Count. It is but thin and cold,
Not like the vintage blowing round
    your castle.
We lie too deep down in the shadow
    here,
Your ladyship lives higher in the sun.
    [*They pledge each other and
    drink.*
Lady Giovanna. If I might send
    you down a flask or two
Of that same vintage? There is iron
    in it.
It has been much commended as a
    medicine.
I give it my sick son, and if you be
Not quite recover'd of your wound,
    the wine
Might help you. None has ever told
    me yet
The story of your battle and your
    wound.
Filippo (*coming forward*). I can
tell you, my lady, I can tell you.
Elisabetta. Filippo! will you take
the word out of your master's own
mouth?
Filippo. Was it there to take? Put
it there, my lord.
Count. Giovanna, my dear lady, in
    this same battle
We had been beaten—they were ten
    to one.
The trumpets of the fight had echo'd
    down,
I and Filippo here had done our best,
And, having passed unwounded from
    the field,
Were seated sadly at a fountain side,
Our horses grazing by us, when a
    troop,
Laden with booty and with a flag of
    ours
Ta'en in the fight—
    Filippo. Ay, but we fought for it
back,
And kill'd—
    Elisabetta. Filippo!
    Count.   A troop of horse—
    Filippo.   Five hundred!
    Count. Say fifty!
    Filippo. And we kill'd 'em by the
        score!
    Elisabetta. Filippo!

Filippo. Well, well, well! I bite my
    tongue.
Count. We may have left their fifty
    less by five.
However, staying not to count how
    many,
But anger'd at their flaunting of our
    flag,
We mounted, and we dash'd into the
    heart of 'em.
I wore the lady's chaplet round my
    neck;
It served me for a blessed rosary.
I am sure that more than one brave
    fellow owed
His death to the charm in it.
    Elisabetta. Hear that, my lady!
    Count. I cannot tell how long we
        strove before
Our horses fell beneath us; down we
    went
Crush'd, hack'd at, trampled under-
    foot. The night,
As some cold-manner'd friend may
    strangely do us
The truest service, had a touch of
    frost
That help'd to check the flowing of
    the blood.
My last sight ere I swoon'd was one
    sweet face
Crown'd with the wreath. *That*
    seem'd to come and go.
They left us there for dead!
    Elisabetta. Hear that, my lady!
    Filippo. Ay, and I left two fingers
there for dead. See, my lady! (*Show-
ing his hand.*)
    Lady Giovanna. I see, Filippo!
    Filippo. And I have small hope of
the gentleman gout in my great toe.
    Lady Giovanna. And why, Filippo?
        [*Smiling absently.*
    Filippo. I left him there for dead
too.
    Elisabetta. She smiles at him—how
        hard the woman is!
My lady, if your ladyship were not
Too proud to look upon the garland,
    you
Would find it stain'd—
    Count (*rising*). Silence, Elisabetta.

Elisabetta. Stain'd with the blood of the best heart that ever
Beat for one woman.
    [*Points to wreath on chair.*
Lady Giovanna (rising slowly). I can eat no more!
Count. You have but trifled with our homely salad,
But dallied with a single lettuce-leaf;
Not eaten anything.
Lady Giovanna. Nay, nay, I can not.
You know, my lord, I told you I was troubled.
My one child Florio lying still so sick,
I bound myself, and by a solemn vow,
That I would touch no flesh till he were well
Here, or else well in heaven, where all is well.
    [Elisabetta *clears table of bird and salad:* Filippo *snatches up the plate of prunes and holds them to* Lady Giovanna.
Filippo. But the prunes, my lady, from the tree that his lordship—
Lady Giovanna. Not now, Filippo.
My lord Federigo,
Can I not speak with you once more alone?
Count. You hear, Filippo? My good fellow, go.
Filippo. But the prunes that your lordship—
Elisabetta. Filippo!
Count. Ay, prune our company of thine own, and go!
Elisabetta. Filippo.
Filippo (turning). Well, well! the women!   [*Exit.*
Count. And thou too leave us, my dear nurse, alone.
Elisabetta (folding up cloth and going). And me too! Ay, the dear nurse will leave you alone, but, for all that, she that has eaten the yolk is scarce like to swallow the shell.
    [*Turns and curtseys stiffly to* Lady Giovanna, *then exit.* Lady Giovanna *takes out diamond necklace from casket.*

Lady Giovanna. I have anger'd your good nurse; these old-world servants
Are all but flesh and blood with those they serve.
My lord, I have a present to return you,
And afterwards a boon to crave of you.
Count. No, my most honor'd and long-worshipt lady,
Poor Federigo degli Alberighi
Takes nothing in return from you except
Return of his affection—can deny
Nothing to you that you require of him.
Lady Giovanna. Then I require you to take back your diamonds—
    [*Offering necklace.*
I doubt not they are yours. No other heart
Of such magnificence in courtesy
Beats—out of heaven. They seem'd too rich a prize
To trust with any messenger. I came
In person to return them.
    [Count *draws back.*
    If the phrase
'Return' displease you, we will say—exchange them.
For your—for your—
Count (takes a step toward her and then back). For mine—and what of mine?
Lady Giovanna. Well, shall we say this wreath and your sweet rhymes?
Count. But have you ever worn my diamonds?
Lady Giovanna. No!
For that would seem accepting of your love.
I cannot brave my brother—but be sure
That I shall never marry again, my lord!
Count. Sure?
Lady Giovanna. Yes!
Count. Is this your brother's order?
Lady Giovanna.   No!

For he would marry me to the richest man
In Florence; but I think you know the saying—
'Better a man without riches, than riches without a man.'
    Count. A noble saying—and acted on would yield
A nobler breed of men and women. Lady,
I find you a shrewd bargainer. The wreath
That once you wore outvalues twenty-fold
The diamonds that you never deign'd to wear.
But lay them there for a moment!
    [*Points to table.* Lady Giovanna *places necklace on table.*
              And be you
Gracious enough to let me know the boon
By granting which, if aught be mine to grant,
I should be made more happy than I hoped
Ever to be again.
    Lady Giovanna. Then keep your wreath,
But you will find me a shrewd bargainer still.
I cannot keep your diamonds, for the gift
I ask for, to *my* mind and at this present
Outvalues all the jewels upon earth.
    Count. It should be love that thus outvalues all.
You speak like love, and yet you love me not.
I have nothing in this world but love for you.
    Lady Giovanna. Love? it *is* love, love for my dying boy,
Moves me to ask it of you.
    Count.   What? my time?
Is it my time? Well, I can give my time
To him that is a part of you, your son.
Shall I return to the castle with you? Shall I

Sit by him, read to him, tell him my tales,
Sing him my songs? You know that I can touch
The gittern to some purpose.
    Lady Giovanna.   No, not that!
I thank you heartily for that—and you,
I doubt not from your nobleness of nature,
Will pardon me for asking what I ask.
    Count. Giovanna, dear Giovanna, I that once
The wildest of the random youth of Florence
Before I saw you—all my nobleness
Of nature, as you deign to call it, draws
From you, and from my constancy to you.
No more, but speak.
    Lady Giovanna.   I will. You know sick people,
More specially sick children, have strange fancies,
Strange longings; and to thwart them in their mood
May work them grievous harm at times, may even
Hasten their end. I would you had a son!
It might be easier then for you to make
Allowance for a mother—her—who comes
To rob you of your one delight on earth.
How often has my sick boy yearn'd for this!
I have put him off as often; but to-day
I dared not—so much weaker, so much worse
For last day's journey. I was weeping for him;
He gave me his hand: 'I should be well again
If the good Count would give me—'
    Count.   Give me—
    Lady Giovanna.   'His falcon.'
    Count (*starts back*). My falcon!
    Lady Giovanna. Yes, your falcon, Federigo!

Count. Alas, I cannot!

Lady Giovanna. Cannot? Even so!
I fear'd as much. O this unhappy
  world!
How shall I break it to him? how
  shall I tell him?
The boy may die; more blessed were
  the rags
Of some pale beggar-woman seeking
  alms
For her sick son, if he were like to
  live,
Than all my childless wealth, if mine
  must die.
I was to blame—the love you said
  you bore me—
My lord, we thank you for your entertainment,
          [*With a stately curtsey.*
And so return—Heaven help him!—
  to our son.   [*Turns.*

Count (rushes forward). Stay,
  stay, I am most unlucky, most
  unhappy!
You never had look'd in on me before,
And when you came and dipt your
  sovereign head
Thro' these low doors, you ask'd to
  eat with me.
I had but emptiness to set before you,
No, not a draught of milk, no, not an
  egg,
Nothing but my brave bird, my noble
  falcon,
My comrade of the house, and of the
  field.
She had to die for it—she died for
  you.
Perhaps I thought with those of old,
  the nobler
The victim was, the more acceptable
Might be the sacrifice. I fear you
  scarce
Will thank me for your entertain-
  ment now.

Lady Giovanna (returning). I bear
  with him no longer.

Count.   No, madonna!
And he will have to bear with it as he
  may.

Lady Giovanna. I break with him
  for ever!

Count.   Yes, Giovanna,
But he will keep his love to you for
  ever!

Lady Giovanna. You? you? not
  you! My brother! my hard
  brother!
O Federigo, Federigo, I love you!
Spite of ten thousand brothers, Federigo!   [*Falls at his feet.*

Count (impetuously). Why, then
  the dying of my noble bird
Hath served me better than her liv-
  ing—then
          [*Takes diamonds from table.*
These diamonds are both yours and
  mine—have won
Their value again—beyond all mar-
  kets—there,
I lay them for the first time round
  your neck.
          [*Lays necklace round her neck.*
And then this chaplet—No more
  feuds but peace,
Peace and conciliation! I will make
Your brother love me. See, I tear
  away
The leaves were darken'd by the bat-
  tle—
          [*Pulls leaves off and throws them
          down.*
          —crown you
Again with the same crown my Queen
  of Beauty.
          [*Places wreath on her head.*
Rise—I could almost think that the
  dead garland
Will break once more into the living
  blossom.
Nay, nay, I pray you rise.
          [*Raises her with both hands.*
          We two together
Will help to heal your son—your son
  and mine—
We shall do it—we shall do it!
          [*Embraces her.*
The purpose of my being is accom-
  plish'd,
And I am happy!

Lady Giovanna. And I too, Federigo.

THE CUP

A TRAGEDY

DRAMATIS PERSONÆ

GALATIANS

{ SYNORIX, *an ex-Tetrarch.*
SINNATUS, *a Tetrarch.*
Attendant.
Boy.

PHŒBE.
CAMMA, *wife of Sinnatus, afterwards Priestess in the Temple of Artemis.*
Maid.

ROMANS

{ ANTONIUS, *a Roman General.*
PUBLIUS.

Nobleman.
Messenger.

THE CUP

ACT I

SCENE I.—DISTANT VIEW OF A CITY OF
GALATIA

*As the curtain rises, Priestesses are
heard singing in the Temple. Boy
discovered on a pathway among
Rocks, picking grapes. A party of
Roman Soldiers, guarding a prisoner in chains, come down the pathway and exeunt.*

Enter SYNORIX (*looking round*). *Singing ceases.*

Synorix. Pine, beech and plane, oak,
    walnut, apricot,
Vine, cypress, poplar, myrtle, bower-
    ing-in
The city where she dwells. She past
    me here
Three years ago when I was flying
    from
My tetrarchy to Rome. I almost
    touch'd her—
A maiden slowly moving on to music
Among her maidens to this temple—
    O Gods!
She is my fate—else wherefore has
    my fate
Brought me again to her own city?—
    married
Since—married Sinnatus, the tetrarch
    here—
But if he be conspirator, Rome will
    chain
Or slay him. I may trust to gain her
    then
When I shall have my tetrarchy re-
    stored
By Rome, our mistress, grateful that
    I show'd her
The weakness and the dissonance of
    our clans,

And how to crush them easily.
    Wretched race!
And once I wish'd to scourge them to
    the bones.
But in this narrow breathing-time of
    life
Is vengeance for its own sake worth
    the while,
If once our ends are gain'd? and now
    this cup—
I never felt such passion for a woman.
    [*Brings out a cup and scroll from
    under his cloak.*
What have I written to her?
        [*Reading the scroll.*
'To the admired Camma, wife of
Sinnatus the Tetrarch, one who years
ago, himself an adorer of our great
goddess Artemis, beheld you afar off
worshipping in her temple, and loved
you for it, sends you this cup rescued
from the burning of one of her shrines
in a city thro' which he past with the
Roman army: it is the cup we use in
our marriages. Receive it from one
who cannot at present write himself
other than
'A GALATIAN SERVING BY FORCE IN
    THE ROMAN LEGION.'
    [*Turns and looks up to Boy.*
Boy, dost thou know the house of Sin-
    natus?
  Boy. These grapes are for the house
    of Sinnatus—
Close to the temple.
  Synorix.   Yonder?
  Boy.   Yes.
  Synorix (*aside*).   That I
With all my range of women should
    yet shun
To meet her face to face at once! My
    boy,
    [*Boy comes down rocks to him.*
Take thou this letter and this cup to
    Camma,

The wife of Sinnatus.
 Boy.   Going or gone to-day
To hunt with Sinnatus.
 Synorix.   That matters not.
Take thou this cup and leave it at her
  doors.
  [*Gives the cup and scroll to the
   Boy.*
 Boy. I will, my lord.
  [*Takes his basket of grapes and
   exit.*

   Enter ANTONIUS.

 *Antonius (meeting the Boy as he
  goes out).*
   Why, whither runs the boy?
Is that the cup you rescued from the
  fire?
 Synorix. I send it to the wife of
  Sinnatus,
One half besotted in religious rites.
You come here with your soldiers to
  enforce
The long-withholden tribute; you sus-
  pect
This Sinnatus of playing patriotism,
Which in your sense is treason. You
  have yet
No proof against him. Now this pious
  cup
Is passport to their house, and open
  arms
To him who gave it; and once there I
  warrant
I worm thro' all their windings.
 Antonius.   If you prosper,
Our Senate, wearied of their tetrarch-
  ies,
Their quarrels with themselves, their
  spites at Rome,
Is like enough to cancel them, and
  throne
One king above them all, who shall be
  true
To the Roman; and from what I
  heard in Rome,
This tributary crown may fall to you.
 Synorix. The king, the crown! their
  talk in Rome? is it so?
      [*Antonius nods.*
Well—I shall serve Galatia taking it,

And save her from herself, and be to
  Rome
More faithful than a Roman.
  [*Turns and sees* Camma *coming.*
       Stand aside,
Stand aside; here she comes!
  [*Watching* Camma *as she enters
   with her Maid.*
 Camma (to Maid). Where is he,
  girl?
 Maid. You know the waterfall
That in the summer keeps the moun-
  tain side,
But after rain o'erleaps a jutting rock
And shoots three hundred feet.
 Camma.   The stag is there?
 Maid. Seen in the thicket at the
  bottom there
But yester-even.
 Camma. Good then, we will climb
The mountain opposite and watch the
  chase.
  [*They descend the rocks and
   exeunt.*
 Synorix (watching her). (Aside.)
  The bust of Juno, and the
  brows and eyes
Of Venus; face and form unmatch-
  able!
 Antonius. Why do you look at her
  so lingeringly?
 Synorix. To see if years have
  changed her.
 Antonius (sarcastically). Love her,
  do you?
 Synorix. I envied Sinnatus when he
  married her.
 Antonius. She knows it? Ha!
 Synorix. She—no, nor even my
  face.
 Antonius. Nor Sinnatus either?
 Synorix.   No, nor Sinnatus.
 Antonius. Hot-blooded! I have
  heard them say in Rome,
That your own people cast you from
  their bounds
For some unprincely violence to a
  woman,
As Rome did Tarquin.
 Synorix.   Well, if this were so
I here return like Tarquin—for a
  crown.

Antonius. And may be foil'd like
  Tarquin, if you follow
Not the dry light of Rome's straight-
  going policy,
But the fool-fire of love or lust, which
  well
May make you lose yourself, may
  even drown you
In the good regard of Rome.
  Synorix.   Tut—fear me not;
I ever had my victories among
  women.
I am most true to Rome.
  Antonius (*aside*). I hate the man!
What filthy tools our Senate works
  with! Still
I must obey them. (*Aloud.*) Fare you
  well.   [*Going.*
  Synorix.   Farewell!
  Antonius (*stopping*). A moment!
If you track this Sinnatus
In any treason, I give you here an
  order   [*Produces a paper.*
To seize upon him. Let me sign it.
  (*Signs it.*) There—
'Antonius, leader of the Roman Le-
  gion.'
    [*Hands the paper to* Synorix.
    Goes up pathway and exit.
  Synorix. Woman again!—but I am
  wiser now.
No rushing on the game—the net,—
  the net.
    [*Shouts of* 'Sinnatus! Sinnatus!'
    Then horn.
Looking off stage.] He comes, a rough,
  bluff, simple-looking fellow.
If we may judge the kernel by the
  husk,
Not one to keep a woman's fealty
  when
Assailed by Craft and Love. I'll join
  with him;
I may reap something from him—
  come upon *her*
Again, perhaps, to-day—*her*. Who are
  with him?
I see no face that knows me. Shall I
  risk it?
I am a Roman now, they dare not
  touch me.
I will.

Enter SINNATUS, HUNTSMEN *and
  hounds.*

Fair sir, a happy day to you!
You reck but little of the Roman
  here,
While you can take your pastime in
  the woods.
  Sinnatus. Ay, ay, why not? What
  would you with me, man?
  Synorix. I am a lifelong lover of
  the chase,
And tho' a stranger fain would be al-
  low'd
To join the hunt.
  Sinnatus.   Your name?
  Synorix.   Strato, my name
  Sinnatus. No Roman name?
  Synorix.   A Greek, my lord; you
  know
That we Galatians are both Greek and
  Gaul.
    [*Shouts and horns in the dis-
    tance.*
  Sinnatus. Hillo, the stag! (*To* Sy-
    norix.) What, you are all un-
    furnish'd?
Give him a bow and arrows—follow
  —follow.
    [*Exit, followed by Huntsmen.*
  Synorix. Slowly but surely—till I
  see my way.
It is the one step in the dark beyond
Our expectation, that amazes us.
    [*Distant shouts and horns.*
Hillo! Hillo!
    [*Exit Synorix. Shouts and horns.*

SCENE II

A ROOM IN THE TETRARCH'S HOUSE

*Frescoed figures on the walls. Eve-
  ning. Moonlight outside. A couch
  with cushions on it. A small table
  with a flagon of wine, cups, plate of
  grapes, etc., also the cup of Scene
  I. A chair with drapery on it.*

CAMMA *enters, and opens curtains of
  window.*

  Camma. No Sinnatus yet—and
  there the rising moon.

[Takes up a cithern and sits on couch. Plays and sings.

Moon on the field and the foam,
  Moon on the waste and the wold,
Moon bring him home, bring him home,
  Safe from the dark and the cold,
Home, sweet moon, bring him home,
  Home with the flock to the fold—
Safe from the wolf—

(*Listening.*) Is he coming? I thought I heard
A footstep. No, not yet. They say that Rome
Sprang from a wolf. I fear my dear lord mixt
With some conspiracy against the wolf.
This mountain shepherd never dream'd of Rome.   [*Sings.*

Safe from the wolf to the fold—

And that great break of precipice that runs
Thro' all the wood, where twenty years ago
Huntsman and hound and deer were all neck-broken!
Nay, here he comes.

Enter SINNATUS *followed by* SYNORIX.

Sinnatus (*angrily*). I tell thee, my good fellow,
My arrow struck the stag.
  Synorix.   But was it so?
Nay, you were further off; besides the wind
Went with *my* arrow.
  Sinnatus I am sure *I* struck him.
  Synorix. And I am just as sure, my lord, *I* struck him.
(*Aside.*) And I may strike your game when you are gone.
  Camma. Come, come, we will not quarrel about the stag.
I have had a weary day in watching you.
Yours must have been a wearier. Sit and eat,
And take a hunter's vengeance on the meats.

Sinnatus. No, no—we have eaten—we are heated. Wine!
Camma. Who is our guest?
Sinnatus.   Strato he calls himself.
  [*Camma offers wine to* Synorix, *while* Sinnatus *helps himself.*
Sinnatus. I pledge you, Strato.
                                  [*Drinks.*
Synorix.   And I you, my lord.
                                  [*Drinks.*
Sinnatus (*seeing the cup sent to* Camma). What's here?
Camma. A strange gift sent to me today.
A sacred cup saved from a blazing shrine
Of our great Goddess, in some city where
Antonius past. I had believed that Rome
Made war upon the peoples, not the Gods.
  Synorix. Most like the city rose against Antonius,
Whereon he fired it, and the sacred shrine
By chance was burnt along with it.
  Sinnatus.   Had you then
No message with the cup?
  Camma.   Why, yes, see here.
                          [*Gives him the scroll.*
Sinnatus (*reads*). 'To the admired Camma,—beheld you afar off—loved you—sends you this cup—the cup we use in our marriages—cannot at present write himself other than
'A GALATIAN SERVING BY FORCE IN THE ROMAN LEGION.'
Serving by force! Were there no boughs to hang on,
Rivers to drown in? Serve by force? No force
Could make me serve by force.
  Synorix.   How then, my lord?
The Roman is encampt without your city—
The force of Rome a thousand-fold our own.
Must all Galatia hang or drown herself?
And you a prince and tetrarch in this province—
  Sinnatus. Province!

Synorix. Well, well, they call it so in Rome.

Sinnatus (*angrily.*) Province!

Synorix. A noble anger! but Antonius

To-morrow will demand your tribute
    —you,

Can you make war? Have you alliances?

Bithynia, Pontus, Paphlagonia?

We have had our leagues of old with
    Eastern kings.

There is my hand—if such a league
    there be.

What will you do?

    Sinnatus. Not set myself abroach

And run my mind out to a random
    guest

Who join'd me in the hunt. You saw
    my hounds

True to the scent; and we have two-
    legg'd dogs

Among us who can smell a true occasion,

And when to bark and how.

    Synorix. My good Lord Sinnatus,

I once was at the hunting of a lion.

Roused by the clamor of the chase he
    woke,

Came to the front of the wood—his
    monarch mane

Bristled about his quick ears—he
    stood there

Staring upon the hunter. A score of
    dogs

Gnaw'd at his ankles; at the last he
    felt

The trouble of his feet, put forth one
    paw,

Slew four, and knew it not, and so
    remain'd

Staring upon the hunter. And this
    Rome

Will crush you if you wrestle with
    her; then,

Save for some slight report in her own
    Senate,

Scarce know what she has done.

    (*Aside.*) Would I could move
    him,

Provoke him any way! (*Aloud.*) The
    Lady Camma,

Wise I am sure as she is beautiful,

Will close with me that to submit at
    once

Is better than a wholly hopeless war,

Our gallant citizens murder'd all in
    vain,

Son, husband, brother gash'd to death
    in vain,

And the small state more cruelly
    trampled on

Than had she never moved.

    Camma. Sir, I had once

A boy who died a babe; but were he
    living

And grown to man and Sinnatus will'd
    it, I

Would set him in the front rank of the
    fight

With scarce a pang. (*Rises.*) Sir, if
    a state submit

At once, she may be blotted out at
    once

And swallow'd in the conqueror's
    chronicle.

Whereas in wars of freedom and defence

The glory and grief of battle won or
    lost

Solders a race together—yea—tho'
    they fail,

The names of those who fought and
    fell are like

A bank'd-up fire that flashes out again

From century to century, and at last

May lead them on to victory—I hope
    so—

Like phantoms of the Gods.

    Sinnatus. Well spoken, wife.

    Synorix (*bowing*). Madam, so well
    I yield.

    Sinnatus. I should not wonder

If Synorix, who has dwelt three years
    in Rome

And wrought his worst against his
    native land,

Returns with this Antonius.

    Synorix. What is Synorix?

    Sinnatus. Galatian, and not know?
    This Synorix

Was tetrarch here, and tyrant also—
    did

Dishonor to our wives.

    Synorix. Perhaps you judge him

With feeble charity; being as you tell
    me
Tetrarch, there might be willing wives
    enough
To feel dishonor honor.
    Camma.   Do not say so.
I know of no such wives in all Ga-
    latia.
There may be courtesans for aught I
    know
Whose life is one dishonor.

          Enter ATTENDANT.

Attendant (*aside*).   My lord, the
    men!
Sinnatus (*aside*). Our anti-Roman
    faction?
Attendant (*aside*). Ay, my lord.
Synorix (*overhearing*). (*Aside.*)
    I have enough—their anti-
    Roman faction.
Sinnatus (*aloud*). Some friends of
    mine would speak with me
    without.
You, Strato, make good cheer till I
    return.   [*Exit.*
Synorix. I have much to say, no
    time to say it in.
First, lady, know myself am that
    Galatian
Who sent the cup.
    Camma.   I thank you from my
    heart.
Synorix. Then that I serve with
    Rome to serve Galatia.
That is my secret; keep it, or you sell
    me
To torment and to death.
            [*Coming closer.*
    For your ear only—
I love you—for your love to the great
    Goddess.
The Romans sent me here a spy upon
    you,
To draw you and your husband to
    your doom.
I'd sooner die than do it.
    [*Takes out paper given him by*
    Antonius.
            This paper sign'd
Antonius—will you take it, read it?
    there!

Camma (*reads*). 'You are to seize
    on Sinnatus,—if—'
Synorix (*snatches paper*). No more.
What follows is for no wife's eyes. O
    Camma,
Rome has a glimpse of this conspir-
    acy;
Rome never yet hath spar'd conspira-
    tor.
Horrible! flaying, scourging, crucify-
    ing—
    Camma. I am tender enough. Why
    do you practise on me?
    Synorix. Why should I practise on
    you? How you wrong me!
I am sure of being every way ma-
    lign'd.
And if you should betray me to your
    husband—
    Camma. Will *you* betray him by
    this order?
    Synorix.   See,
I tear it all to pieces, never dream'd
Of acting on it.   [*Tears the paper.*
    Camma.   I owe you thanks for
    ever.
    Synorix. Hath Sinnatus never told
    you of this plot?
    Camma. What plot?
    Synorix. A child's sand-castle on
    the beach
For the next wave,—all seen,—all
    calculated,
All known by Rome. No chance for
    Sinnatus.
    Camma. Why said you not as much
    to my brave Sinnatus?
    Synorix. Brave—ay—too brave, too
    over-confident,
Too like to ruin himself, and you, and
    me!
Who else, with this black thunderbolt
    of Rome
Above him, would have chased the
    stag to-day
In the full face of all the Roman
    camp?
A miracle that they let him home
    again,
Not caught, maim'd, blinded him.
            [*Camma shudders.*
    (*Aside.*) I have made her
    tremble.

(*Aloud.*) I know they mean to tor-
    ture him to death.
I dare not tell him how I came to
    know it;
I durst not trust him with—my serv-
    ing Rome
To serve Galatia; you heard him on
    the letter.
Not say as much? I all but said as
    much.
I am sure I told him that his plot was
    folly.
I say it to you—you are wiser—Rome
    knows all,
But you know not the savagery of
    Rome.
    Camma. O!—have you power with
    Rome? use it for him!
    Synorix. Alas! I have no such
    power with Rome. All that
Lies with Antonius.
    [*As if struck by a sudden
    thought. Comes over to her.*
            He will pass to-morrow
In the gray dawn before the Temple
    doors.
You have beauty,—O, great beauty,
    —and Antonius,
So gracious toward women, never yet
Flung back a woman's prayer. Plead
    to him,
I am sure you will prevail.
    Camma.   Still—I should tell
My husband.
    Synorix. Will he let you plead for
    him
To a Roman?
    Camma. I fear not.
    Synorix.   Then do not tell him.
Or tell him, if you will, when you re-
    turn,
When you have charm'd our general
    into mercy,
And all is safe again. O dearest lady,
    [*Murmurs of* 'Synorix! Synorix!'
    heard outside.
Think,—torture,—death,—and come.
    Camma.   I will, I will.
And I will not betray you.
    Synorix (*aside, as* Sinnatus *enters*).
                 Stand apart.

Enter SINNATUS *and* ATTENDANT.

    Sinnatus. Thou art that Synorix!
    One whom thou hast wrong'd
Without there knew thee with An-
    tonius.
They howl for thee, to rend thee head
    from limb.
    Synorix. I am much malign'd. I
    thought to serve Galatia.
    Sinnatus. Serve thyself first, vil-
    lain! They shall not harm
My guest within my house. There!
    (*points to door*) there! this
    door
Opens upon the forest! Out, begone!
Henceforth I am thy mortal enemy.
    Synorix. However, I thank thee
    (*draws his sword*); thou hast
    saved my life.   [*Exit.*
    Sinnatus (*to* Attendant). Return
    and tell them Synorix is not
    here.   [*Exit* Attendant.
What did that villain Synorix say to
    you?
    Camma. Is *he*—that—Synorix?
    Sinnatus. Wherefore should you
    doubt it?
One of the men there knew him.
    Camma.   Only one,
And he perhaps mistaken in the face.
    Sinnatus. Come, come, could he
    deny it? What did he say?
    Camma. What *should* he say?
    Sinnatus. What *should* he say, my
    wife!
He should say this, that being tet-
    rarch once
His own true people cast him from
    their doors
Like a base coin.
    Camma.   Not kindly to them?
    Sinnatus.   Kindly?
O, the most kindly prince in all the
    world!
Would clap his honest citizens on the
    back,
Bandy their own rude jests with them,
    be curious
About the welfare of their babes,
    their wives,

O, ay—their wives—their wives!
  What should he say?
He should say nothing to my wife
  if I
Were by to throttle him! He steep'd
  himself
In all the lust of Rome. How should
  you guess
What manner of beast it is?
  Camma.   Yet he seem'd kindly,
And said he loathed the cruelties that
  Rome
Wrought on her vassals.
  Sinnatus.   Did he, *honest* man?
  Camma. And you, that seldom
    brook the stranger here,
Have let him hunt the stag with you
  to-day.
  Sinnatus. I warrant you now, he
    said *he* struck the stag.
  Camma. Why, no, he never touch'd
    upon the stag.
  Sinnatus. Why, so I said, *my* ar-
    row. Well, to sleep.
      [*Goes to close door.*
  Camma. Nay, close not yet the
    door upon a night
That looks half day.
  Sinnatus. True; and my friends
    may spy him
And slay him as he runs.
  Camma.   He is gone already.
O, look,—yon grove upon the moun-
  tain,—white
In the sweet moon as with a lovelier
  snow!
But what a blotch of blackness under-
  neath!
Sinnatus, you remember—yea, you
  must,
That there three years ago—the vast
  vine-bowers
Ran to the summit of the trees, and
  dropt
Their streamers earthward, with a
  breeze of May
Took ever and anon, and open'd out
The purple zone of hill and heaven.
  There
You told your love; and like the sway-
  ing vines—
Yea,—with our eyes,—our hearts,
  our prophet hopes

Let in the happy distance, and that all
But cloudless heaven which we have
  found together
In our three married years! You
  kiss'd me there
For the first time. Sinnatus, kiss me
  now.
  Sinnatus. First kiss. (*Kisses her.*)
    There, then. You talk almost
    as if it
Might be the last.
  Camma.   Will you not eat a
    little?
  Sinnatus. No, no, we found a goat-
    herd's hut, and shared
His fruits and milk. Liar! You will
  believe
Now that he never struck the stag—
  a brave one
Which you shall see to-morrow.
  Camma.   I rise to-morrow
In the gray dawn, and take this holy
  cup
To lodge it in the shrine of Artemis.
  Sinnatus. Good!
  Camma. If I be not back in half an
    hour,
Come after me.
  Sinnatus. What! is there danger?
  Camma.   Nay,
None that I know; 't is but a step
  from here
To the Temple.
  Sinnatus. All my brain is full of
    sleep.
Wake me before you go, I'll after
  you—
After *me* now! [*Closes door and exit.*
  Camma (*drawing curtains*). Your
    shadow. Synorix—
His face was not malignant, and he
  said
That men malign'd him. Shall I go?
  Shall I go?
Death, torture—
'He never yet flung back a woman's
  prayer'—
I go, but I will have my dagger with
  me.   [*Exit.*

SCENE III

SAME AS SCENE I. DAWN

Music and Singing in the Temple.

Enter SYNORIX *watchfully, after him*
PUBLIUS *and* SOLDIERS.

Synorix. Publius!
Publius.   Here!
Synorix.   Do you remember
    what
I told you?
    Publius. When you cry, 'Rome,
    Rome,' to seize
On whomsoever may be talking with
    you,
Or man, or woman, as traitors unto
    Rome.
    Synorix. Right. Back again. How
    many of you are there?
    Publius. Some half a score.
    [*Exeunt* Soldiers and Publius.
    Synorix.   I have my guard about
    me.
I need not fear the crowd that hunted
    me
Across the woods, last night. I hardly
    gain'd
The camp at midnight. Will she come
    to me
Now that she knows me Synorix? Not
    if Sinnatus
Has told her all the truth about me.
    Well,
I cannot help the mould that I was
    cast in.
I fling all that upon my fate, my star.
I know that I am genial, I would be
Happy, and make all others happy, so
They did not thwart me. Nay, she will
    not come.
Yet if she be a true and loving wife
She may, perchance, to save this hus-
    band. Ay!
See, see, my white bird stepping to-
    ward the snare.
Why, now I count it all but miracle,
That this brave heart of mine should
    shake me so,
As helplessly as some unbearded boy's

When first he meets his maiden in a
    bower.

Enter CAMMA (*with cup*)

The lark first takes the sunlight on
    his wing,
But you, twin sister of the morning
    star,
Forelead the sun.
    Camma.   Where is Antonius?
    Synorix. Not here as yet. You are
    too early for him.
    [*She crosses towards Temple.*
    Synorix. Nay, whither go you now?
    Camma.   To lodge this cup
Within the holy shrine of Artemis,
And so return.
    Synorix.   To find Antonius here.
    [*She goes into the Temple, he
    looks after her.*
The loveliest life that ever drew the
    light
From heaven to brood upon her, and
    enrich
Earth with her shadow! I trust she
    will return.
These Romans dare not violate the
    Temple.
No, I must lure my game into the
    camp.
A woman I could live and die for.
    What!
Die for a woman, what new faith is
    this?
I am not mad, not sick, not old enough
To dote on one alone. Yes, mad for
    her,
Camma the stately, Camma the great-
    hearted,
So mad, I fear some strange and evil
    chance
Coming upon me, for, by the Gods I
    seem
Strange to myself!

Re-enter CAMMA.

Camma.   Where is Antonius?
Synorix. Where? As I said before,
    you are still too early.
Camma. Too early to be here alone
    with thee;

For whether men malign thy name,
      or no,
It bears an evil savor among women.
Where is Antonius? (*Loud.*)
      Synorix.   Madam, as you know
The camp is half a league without the
      city;
If you will walk with me we needs
      must meet
Antonius coming, or at least shall find
      him
There in the camp.
      Camma.   No, not one step with
      thee.
Where is Antonius? (*Louder.*)
      Synorix (*advancing towards her*).
      Then for your own sake,
Lady, I say it with all gentleness,
And for the sake of Sinnatus your
      husband,
I must compel you.
      Camma (*drawing her dagger*).
      Stay!—too near is death.
      Synorix (*disarming her*). Is it not
      easy to disarm a woman?

Enter SINNATUS (*seizes him from be-
      hind by the throat*).

      Synorix (*throttled and scarce au-
      dible*).
Rome! Rome!
      Sinnatus.   Adulterous dog!
      Synorix (*stabbing him with* Cam-
      ma's *dagger*). What! will you
      have it?
      [Camma *utters a cry and runs to*
      Sinnatus.
      Sinnatus (*falls backward*). I have
      it in my heart—to the Temple
      —fly—
For *my* sake—or they seize on thee.
      Remember!
Away—farewell!   [*Dies.*
      Camma (*runs up the steps into the
      Temple, looking back*). Fare-
      well!
      Synorix (*seeing her escape*). The
      women of the Temple drag her
      in.
Publius! Publius! No,
Antonius would not suffer me to
      break

Into the sanctuary. She hath escaped.
      [*Looking down at* Sinnatus.
'Adulterous dog!' that red-faced rage
      at me!
Then with one quick short stab—eter-
      nal peace.
So end all passions. Then what use in
      passions?
To warm the cold bonds of our dying
      life
And, lest we freeze in mortal ap-
      athy,
Employ us, heat us, quicken us, help
      us, keep us
From seeing all too near that urn,
      those ashes
Which all must be. Well used, they
      serve us well.
I heard a saying in Egypt, that ambi-
      tion
Is like the sea wave, which the more
      you drink
The more you thirst—yea—drink too
      much, as men
Have done on rafts of wreck—it
      drives you mad.
I will be not such wreck, am no such
      gamester
As, having won the stake, would dare
      the chance
Of double, or losing all. The Roman
      Senate,
For I have always play'd into their
      hands,
Means me the crown. And Camma
      for my bride—
The people love her—if I win her
      love,
They too will cleave to me, as one
      with her.
There then I rest, Rome's tributary
      king.
      [*Looking down on* Sinnatus.
Why did I strike him?—having proof
      enough
Against the man, I surely should have
      left
That stroke to Rome. He saved my
      life too. Did he?
It seem'd so. I have play'd the sud-
      den fool.
And that sets her against me—for the
      moment.

Camma—well, well, I never found
   the woman
I could not force or wheedle to my
   will.
She will be glad at last to wear my
   crown.
And I will make Galatia prosperous
   too,
And we will chirp among our vines,
   and smile
At bygone things till that (*pointing to*
   Sinnatus) eternal peace.
Rome! Rome!

Enter PUBLIUS *and* SOLDIERS.

Twice I cried Rome. Why came ye
   not before?
   Publius. Why come we now? Whom
   shall we seize upon?
   Synorix (*pointing to the body of*
   Sinnatus). The body of that
   dead traitor Sinnatus.
Bear him away.
   Music and Singing in Temple.

ACT II

SCENE.—INTERIOR OF THE TEMPLE OF ARTEMIS

*Small gold gates on platform in front
of the veil before the colossal statue
of the Goddess, and in the centre
of the Temple a tripod altar, on
which is a lighted lamp. Lamps
(lighted) suspended between the
pillars. Tripods, vases, garlands of
flowers, etc., about stage. Altar at
back close to Goddess, with two
cups. Solemn music. Priestesses
decorating the Temple.*

(*The Chorus of* PRIESTESSES *sing as
they enter.*)

Artemis, Artemis, hear us, O Mother,
   hear us, and bless us!
Artemis, thou that art life to the wind,
   to the wave, to the glebe, to the
   fire!

Hear thy people who praise thee! O, help
   us from all that oppress us!
Hear thy priestesses hymn thy glory! O,
   yield them all their desire!

   Priestess. Phœbe, that man from
   Synorix, who has been
So oft to see the priestess, waits once
   more
Before the Temple.
   Phœbe.   We will let her know.
   [*Signs to one of the Priestesses,
   who goes out.*
Since Camma fled from Synorix to
   our Temple,
And for her beauty, stateliness, and
   power,
Was chosen priestess here, have you
   not mark'd
Her eyes were ever on the marble
   floor?
To-day they are fixt and bright—they
   look straight out.
Hath she made up her mind to marry
   him?
   Priestess. To marry him who
   stabb'd her Sinnatus?
You will not easily make me credit
   that.
   Phœbe. Ask her.

Enter CAMMA *as Priestess* (*in front
of the curtains*).

   Priestess.   You will not marry
   Synorix?
   Camma. My girl, I am the bride of
   Death, and only
Marry the dead.
   Priestess. Not Synorix then?
   Camma.   My girl,
At times this oracle of great Artemis
Has no more power than other or-
   acles
To speak directly.
   Phœbe.   Will you speak to him,
The messenger from Synorix who
   waits
Before the Temple?
   Camma.   Why not? Let him
   enter.
   [*Comes forward on to step by
   tripod.*

Enter a MESSENGER.

Messenger (*kneels*). Greeting and
   health from Synorix! More
   than once
You have refused his hand. When last
   I saw you,
You all but yielded. He entreats you
   now
For your last answer. When he struck
   at Sinnatus—
As I have many a time declared to
   you—
He knew not at the moment who had
   fasten'd
About his throat—he begs you to for-
   get it
As scarce his act—a random stroke.
   All else
Was love for you; he prays you to be-
   lieve him.
   Camma. I pray him to believe—
      that I believe him.
   Messenger. Why, that is well. You
      mean to marry him.
   Camma. I mean to marry him—if
      that be well.
   Messenger. This very day the Ro-
      mans crown him king
For all his faithful services to Rome.
He wills you then this day to marry
   him,
And so be throned together in the
   sight
Of all the people, that the world may
   know
You twain are reconciled, and no more
   feuds
Disturb our peaceful vassalage to
   Rome.
   Camma. To-day? Too sudden. I
      will brood upon it.
When do they crown him?
   Messenger.   Even now.
   Camma.   And where?
   Messenger. Here by your temple.
   Camma.   Come once more to me
Before the crowning,—I will answer
   you.   [*Exit* Messenger.
   Phœbe. Great Artemis! O Camma,
      can it be well,

Or good, or wise, that you should
   clasp a hand
Red with the sacred blood of Sin-
   natus?
   Camma. Good! mine own dagger
      driven by Synorix found
All good in the true heart of Sinnatus,
And quench'd it there for ever. Wise!
Life yields to Death, and Wisdom
   bows to Fate,
Is wisest doing so. Did not this man
Speak well? We cannot fight imperial
   Rome,
But he and I are both Galatian-born;
And tributary sovereigns, he and I
Might teach this Rome—from knowl-
   edge of our people—
Where to lay on her tribute—heavily
   here
And lightly there. Might I not live
   for that,
And drown all poor self-passion in the
   sense
Of public good?
   Phœbe. I am sure you will not
      marry him.
   Camma. Are you so sure? I pray
      you wait and see.
   [*Shouts* (*from the distance*)
      'Synorix! Synorix!'
   Camma. Synorix, Synorix! So they
      cried Sinnatus
Not so long since—they sicken me.
   The One
Who shifts his policy suffers some-
   thing, must
Accuse himself, excuse himself; the
   Many
Will feel no shame to give themselves
   the lie.
   Phœbe. Most like it was the Roman
      soldiers shouted.
   Camma. Their shield-borne patriot
      of the morning star
Hang'd at midday, their traitor of the
   dawn
The clamor'd darling of their after-
   noon!
And that same head they would have
   play'd at ball with
And kick'd it featureless—they now
   would crown!
               [*Flourish of trumpets.*

Enter a Galatian NOBLEMAN *with crown on a cushion.*

Noble (*kneels*). Greeting and
   health from Synorix. He sends
   you
This diadem of the first Galatian
   Queen,
That you may feed your fancy on the
   glory of it,
And join your life this day with his,
   and wear it
Beside him on his throne. He waits
   your answer.
   Camma. Tell him there is one
   shadow among the shadows,
One ghost of all the ghosts—as yet so
   new,
So strange among them—such an alien
   there,
So much of husband in it still—that if
The shout of Synorix and Camma sit-
   ting
Upon one throne, should reach it, *it*
   would rise—
HE!—HE, with that red star between
   the ribs,
And my knife there—and blast the
   king and me,
And blanch the crowd with horror. I
   dare not, sir!
Throne him—and then the marriage
   —ay, and tell him
That I accept the diadem of Galatia—
                [*All are amazed.*
Yea, that ye saw me crown myself
   withal.
                [*Puts on the crown.*
I wait him his crown'd queen.
   Noble. So will I tell him. [*Exit.*

*Music. Two Priestesses go up the
steps before the shrine, draw the
curtains on either side (discovering
the Goddess), then open the gates
and remain on steps, one on either
side, and kneel. A priestess goes off
and returns with a veil of marriage,
then assists* PHŒBE *to veil* CAMMA.
*At the same time Priestesses enter
and stand on either side of the
Temple.* CAMMA *and all the Priest-*
*esses kneel, raise their hands to the
Goddess, and bow down.*
   [*Shouts,* 'Synorix! Synorix!' *All
   rise.*
   Camma. Fling wide the doors, and
   let the new-made children
Of our imperial mother see the show.
   [*Sunlight pours through the
   doors.*
I have not heart to do it. (*To* Phœbe.)
   Look for me!
   [*Crouches.* Phœbe *looks out.*
   [*Shouts,* 'Synorix! Synorix!'
   Phœbe. He climbs the throne. Hot
   blood, ambition, pride
So bloat and redden his face—O,
   would it were
His third last apoplexy! O, bestial!
O, how unlike our goodly Sinnatus!
   Camma (*on the ground*). You
   wrong him surely; far as the
   face goes
A goodlier-looking man than Sinnatus.
   Phœbe (*aside*). How dare she say
   it? I could hate her for it
But that she is distracted.
             [*A flourish of trumpets.*
   Camma.   Is he crown'd?
   Phœbe. Ay, there they crown him.
   [*Crowd without shout,* 'Synorix!
   Synorix!'
A Priestess brings a box of spices to
   Camma, *who throws them on
   the altar-flame.*
   Camma. Rouse the dead altar-
   flame, fling in the spices,
Nard, cinnamon, amomum, benzoin.
Let all the air reel into a mist of odor,
As in the midmost heart of Para-
   dise.
Lay down the Lydian carpets for the
   King.
The King should pace on purple to
   his bride,
And music there to greet my lord the
   King.   [*Music.*
(*To* Phœbe.) Dost thou remember
   when I wedded Sinnatus?
Ay, thou wast there—whether from
   maiden fears
Or reverential love for him I loved,
Or some strange second-sight, the
   marriage-cup

Wherefrom we make libation to the
    Goddess
So shook within my hand that the red
    wine
Ran down the marble and lookt like
    blood, like blood.
    Phœbe. I do remember your first-
      marriage fears.
    Camma. I have no fears at this my
      second marriage.
See here—I stretch my hand out—
    hold it there.
How steady it is!
    Phœbe. Steady enough to stab him!
    Camma. O, hush! O, peace! This
      violence ill becomes
The silence of our Temple. Gentle-
    ness,
Low words best chime with this so-
    lemnity.

*Enter a procession of Priestesses and
Children bearing garlands and
golden goblets, and strewing flowers.*

Enter SYNORIX (*as King, with gold
laurel-wreath crown and purple
robes*), *followed by* ANTONIUS,
PUBLIUS, *Noblemen, Guards, and
the Populace.*

    Camma. Hail, King!
    Synorix.   Hail, Queen!
The wheel of Fate has roll'd me to
    the top.
I would that happiness were gold,
    that I
Might cast my largess of it to the
    crowd!
I would that every man made feast
    to-day,
Beneath the shadow of our pines and
    planes!
For all my truer life begins to-day.
The past is like a travell'd land now
    sunk
Below the horizon—like a barren
    shore
That grew salt weeds, but now all
    drown'd in love
And glittering at full tide—the bon-
    teous bays

And havens filling with a blissful sea.
Nor speak I now too mightily, being
    King
And happy! happiest, lady, in my
    power
To make you happy.
    Camma.   Yes, sir.
    Synorix.   Our Antonius,
Our faithful friend of Rome, tho'
    Rome may set
A free foot where she will, yet of his
    courtesy
Entreats he may be present at our
    marriage.
    Camma. Let him come—a legion
    with him, if he will.
(*To* Antonius.) Welcome, my lord
    Antonius, to our Temple.
(*To* Synorix.) You on this side the
    altar. (*To* Antonius.) You on
    that.
Call first upon the Goddess, Synorix.
    [*All face the Goddess. Priest-
    esses, Children, Populace, and
    Guards kneel—the others re-
    main standing.*
    Synorix. O thou that dost inspire
    the germ with life,
The child, a thread within the house
    of birth,
And give him limbs, then air, and send
    him forth
The glory of his father—thou whose
    breath
Is balmy wind to robe our hills with
    grass,
And kindle all our vales with myrtle-
    blossom,
And roll the golden oceans of our
    grain,
And sway the long grape-bunches of
    our vines,
And fill all hearts with fatness and the
    lust
Of plenty—make me happy in my
    marriage!
    Chorus (*chanting*). Artemis, Arte-
    mis, hear him, Ionian Artemis!
    Camma. O thou that slayest the
    babe within the womb
Or in the being born, or after slayest
    him

As boy or man, great Goddess, whose
    storm-voice
Unsockets the strong oak, and rears
    his root
Beyond his head, and strows our
    fruits, and lays
Our golden grain, and runs to sea and
    makes it
Foam over all the fleeted wealth of
    kings
And peoples, hear!
Whose arrow is the plague—whose
    quick flash splits
The mid-sea mast, and rifts the tower
    to the rock,
And hurls the victor's column down
    with him
That crowns it, hear!
Who causest the safe earth to shud-
    der and gape,
And gulf and flatten in her closing
    chasm
Domed cities, hear!
Whose lava-torrents blast and blacken
    a province
To a cinder, hear!
Whose winter-cataracts find a realm
    and leave it
A waste of rock and ruin, hear! I call
    thee
To make my marriage prosper to my
    wish!
    Chorus. Artemis, Artemis, hear her,
    Ephesian Artemis!
    Camma. Artemis, Artemis, hear
    me, Galatian Artemis!
I call on our own Goddess in our own
    Temple.
    Chorus. Artemis, Artemis, hear her,
    Galatian Artemis!
            [*Thunder. All rise.*
    Synorix (*aside*). Thunder! Ay, ay,
    the storm was drawing hither
Across the hills when I was being
    crown'd.
I wonder if I look as pale as she?
    Camma. Art thou—still bent—on
    marrying?
    Synorix.   Surely—yet
These are strange words to speak to
    Artemis.
    Camma. Words are not always
    what they seem, my King.

I will be faithful to thee till thou die.
    Synorix. I thank thee, Camma,—I
    thank thee.
    Camma (*turning to* Antonius). An-
    tonius,
Much graced are we that our Queen
    Rome in you
Deigns to look in upon our barba-
    risms.
    [*Turns, goes up steps to altar be-
    fore the Goddess. Takes a cup
    from off the altar. Holds it
    towards* Antonius. Antonius
    *goes up to the foot of the steps
    opposite to* Synorix.
You see this cup, my lord.
            [*Gives it to him.*
    Antonius.   Most curious!
The many-breasted mother Artemis
Emboss'd upon it.
    Camma.   It is old, I know not
How many hundred years. Give it me
    again.
It is the cup belonging our own Tem-
    ple.
    [*Puts it back on altar, and takes
    up the cup of Act I. Showing it
    to* Antonius.
Here is another sacred to the Goddess,
The gift of Synorix; and the Goddess,
    being
For this most grateful, wills, thro' me
    her priestess,
In honor of his gift and of our mar-
    riage,
That Synorix should drink from his
    own cup.
    Synorix. I thank thee, Camma,—I
    thank thee.
    Camma.   For—my lord—
It is our ancient custom in Galatia
That ere two souls be knit for life and
    death,
They two should drink together from
    one cup,
In symbol of their married unity,
Making libation to the Goddess.
    Bring me
The costly wines we use in marriages.
    [*They bring in a large jar of
    wine.* Camma *pours wine into
    cup.*

(*To* Synorix.) See here, I fill it. (*To* Antonius.) Will you drink, my lord?

Antonius. I? Why should I? I am not to be married.

Camma. But that might bring a Roman blessing on us.

Antonius (*refusing cup*). Thy pardon, priestess!

Camma. Thou art in the right. This blessing is for Synorix and for me,
See, first I make libation to the Goddess,   [*Makes libation.*
And now I drink.
          [*Drinks and fills the cup again.*
Thy turn, Galatian King.
Drink and drink deep—our marriage will be fruitful.
Drink and drink deep, and thou wilt make me happy.
          [*Synorix goes up to her. She hands him the cup. He drinks.*

Synorix. There, Camma! I have almost drain'd the cup—
A few drops left.

Camma. Libation to the Goddess.
          [*He throws the remaining drops on the altar and gives* Camma *the cup.*

Camma (*placing the cup on the altar*). Why, then the Goddess hears.
          [*Comes down and forward to tripod.* Antonius *follows.*
                              Antonius,
Where wast thou on that morning when I came
To plead to thee for Sinnatus's life,
Beside this temple half a year ago?

Antonius. I never heard of this request of thine.

Synorix (*coming forward hastily to foot of tripod steps*). I sought him, and I could not find him. Pray you,
Go on with the marriage rites.

Camma.   Antonius—
'Camma!' Who spake?

Antonius.   Not I.

Phœbe.   Nor any here.

Camma. I am all but sure that some one spake. Antonius,

If you had found him plotting against Rome,
Would you have tortured Sinnatus to death?

Antonius. No thought was mine of torture or of death,
But had I found him plotting, I had counsell'd him
To rest from vain resistance. Rome is fated
To rule the world. Then, if he had not listen'd,
I might have sent him prisoner to Rome.

Synorix. Why do you palter with the ceremony?
Go on with the marriage rites.

Camma.   They are finish'd.

Synorix.   How!

Camma. Thou hast drunk deep enough to make me happy.
Dost thou not feel the love I bear to thee
Glow thro' thy veins?

Synorix.   The love I bear to thee
Glows thro' my veins since first I look'd on thee.
But wherefore slur the perfect ceremony?
The sovereign of Galatia weds his Queen.
Let all be done to the fullest in the sight
Of all the Gods.
                    Nay, rather than so clip
The flowery robe of Hymen, we would add
Some golden fringe of gorgeousness beyond
Old use, to make the day memorial, when
Synorix, first King, Camma, first Queen o' the Realm,
Drew here the richest lot from Fate, to live
And die together.
                    This pain—what is it?—again?
I had a touch of this last year—in—Rome.
Yes, yes. (*To* Antonius.) Your arm—a moment—it will pass.
I reel beneath the weight of utter joy—

This all too happy day, crown—queen
at once.   *[Staggers.*
O all ye Gods—Jupiter!—Jupiter!
     [Falls backward.

Camma. Dost thou cry out upon
the Gods of Rome?
Thou art Galatian-born. Our Artemis
Has vanquish'd their Diana.

Synorix (on the ground). I am poison'd.
She—close the Temple door. Let her
not fly.

Camma (leaning on tripod). Have
I not drunk of the same cup
with thee?

Synorix. Ay, by the Gods of Rome
and all the world,
She too—she too—the bride! the
Queen! and I—
Monstrous! I that loved her.

Camma.   I loved *him,*

Synorix. O murderous mad-
woman! I pray you lift me
And make me walk awhile. I have
heard these poisons
May be walk'd down.
     *[Antonius and Publius raise him
up.*
     My feet are tons of lead,
They will break in the earth—I am
sinking—hold me—
Let me alone.
     *[They leave him; he sinks down
on ground.*
Too late—thought myself wise—
A woman's dupe! Antonius, tell the
Senate
I have been most true to Rome—
would have been true
To *her*—if—if— *[Falls as if dead.*

*Camma (coming and leaning over
him).* So falls the throne of an
hour.

Synorix (half rising). Throne? is it
thou? the Fates are throned,
not we—
Not guilty of ourselves—thy doom
and mine—
Thou—coming my way too—Camma
—good-night.   *[Dies.*

*Camma (upheld by weeping Priest-
esses).* Thy way? poor worm,

crawl down thine own black
hole
To the lowest hell. Antonius, is *he*
there?
I meant thee to have follow'd—better
thus.
Nay, if my people must be thralls of
Rome,
He is gentle, tho' a Roman.
     *[Sinks back into the arms of the
Priestesses.*

Antonius.   Thou art one
With thine own people, and though a
Roman I
Forgive thee, Camma.

Camma (raising herself). 'Cam-
ma!' why, there again
I am most sure that some one call'd.
O women,
Ye will have Roman masters. I am
glad
I shall not see it. Did not some old
Greek
Say death was the chief good? He had
my fate for it,
Poison'd. *(Sinks back again.)* Have I
the crown on? I will go
To meet him, crown'd! crown'd vic-
tor of my will—
On my last voyage—but the wind has
fail'd—
Growing dark too—but light enough
to row.
Row to the Blessed Isles! the Blessed
Isles!—
Sinnatus!
Why comes he not to meet me? It is
the crown
Offends him—and my hands are too
sleepy
To lift it off *(Phœbe takes the crown
off).* Who touched me then? I
thank you.
     [Rises, with outspread arms.
There—league on league of ever-
shining shore
Beneath an ever-rising sun—I see
him—
'Camma, Camma!' Sinnatus, Sinna-
tus!   *[Dies.*

THE PROMISE OF MAY

'A surface man of theories, true to none.'

This play was produced at the Globe Theatre in London in November 1882; and though generally condemned by the critics, it had a run of five weeks. This was partially due to an incident of a somewhat sensational character which occurred at one of the earlier representations. At the beginning of the opening scene the Marquis of Queensberry rose from his seat in the stalls, and loudly protested against what he regarded as Tennyson's attack upon freethinkers in the character of Edgar. After some delay the performance was allowed to proceed, but at its close the Marquis rose again, declaring himself a freethinker and denouncing the play as a travesty of the sect. The next day he explained in a morning paper that his indignation had been particularly excited by Edgar's comments on marriage. He added:—

'I am a secularist and a freethinker, and, though I repudiate it a so-called atheist, and, as President of the British Secular Union, I protest against Mr. Tennyson's abominable caricature of an individual whom [sic], I presume, he would have us believe represents some body of people which, thanks for the good of humanity, most certainly does not exist among freethinkers.'

DRAMATIS PERSONÆ

FARMER DOBSON.
MR. PHILIP EDGAR (*afterwards* MR. HAROLD).
FARMER STEER (DORA *and* EVA'S *Father*).
MR. WILSON (*a Schoolmaster*).
HIGGINS
JAMES
DAN SMITH ⎬ *Farm Laborers.*
JACKSON
ALLEN
DORA STEER.
EVA STEER.
SALLY ALLEN ⎬ *Farm Servants.*
MILLY
Farm Servants, Laborers, etc.

THE PROMISE OF MAY

ACT I

SCENE.—BEFORE FARMHOUSE

Farming Men and Women. Farming Men carrying forms, etc., Women carrying baskets of knives and forks, etc.

First Farming Man. Be thou a-gawin' to the long barn?

Second Farming Man. Ay, to be sewer! Be thou?

First Farming Man. Why, o' coorse, fur it be the owd man's birthdaäy. He be heighty this very daäy, and 'e telled all on us to be i' the long barn by one o'clock, fur he 'll gie us a big dinner, and haäfe th' parish 'll be theer, an' Miss Dora, an' Miss Eva, an' all!

Second Farming Man. Miss Dora be coomed back, then?

First Farming Man. Ay, haäfe an hour ago. She be in theer now. (*Pointing to house.*) Owd Steer wur afeärd she would n't be back i' time to keep his birthdaäy, and he wur in a tew about it all the murnin'; and he sent me wi' the gig to Littlechester to fetch 'er; and 'er an' the owd man they fell a kissin' o' one another like two sweet-'arts i' the poorch as soon as he clapt eyes of 'er.

Second Farming Man. Foälks says he likes Miss Eva the best.

First Farming Man. Naäy, I knaws nowt o' what foälks says, an' I caäres nowt neither. Foälks does n't hallus knaw thessens; but sewer I be, they be two o' the purtiest gels ye can see of a summer murnin'.

Second Farming Man. Beänt Miss Eva gone off a bit of 'er good looks o' laäte?

First Farming Man. Noä, not a bit.

Second Farming Man. Why, coöm awaäy, then, to the long barn.

[*Exeunt.*

DORA *looks out of window. Enter* DOBSON.

DORA (*singing*).

The town lay still in the low sunlight,
The hen cluckt late by the white farm gate,
The maid to her dairy came in from the cow,
The stock-dove coo'd at the fall of night,
The blossom had open'd on every bough;
O, joy for the promise of May, of May,
O, joy for the promise of May!

(*Nodding at Dobson.*) I'm coming down, Mr. Dobson. I haven't seen Eva yet. Is she anywhere in the garden?

Dobson. Noä, Miss. I ha'n't seed 'er neither.

DORA (*enters singing*).

But a red fire woke in the heart of the town,
And a fox from the glen ran away with the hen,
And a cat to the cream, and a rat to the cheese;
And the stock-dove coo'd, till a kite dropt down,
And a salt wind burnt the blossoming trees;
O, grief for the promise of May, of May,
O, grief for the promise of May!

I don't know why I sing that song; I don't love it.

Dobson. Blessings on your pretty voice, Miss Dora! Wheer did they larn ye that?

Dora. In Cumberland, Mr. Dobson.

Dobson. An' how did ye leäve the owd uncle i' Coomberland?

Dora. Getting better, Mr. Dobson. But he 'll never be the same man again.

Dobson. An' how d' ye find the owd man 'ere?

Dora. As well as ever. I came back to keep his birthday.

Dobson. Well, I be coomed to keep his birthdaäy an' all. The owd man be heighty to-daäy, beänt he?

Dora. Yes, Mr. Dobson. And the day's bright like a friend, but the wind east like an enemy. Help me to move this bench for him into the sun. (*They move bench.*) No, not that way—here, under the apple-tree. Thank you. Look how full of rosy blossom it is. [*Pointing to apple-tree.*

Dobson. Theer be redder blossoms nor them, Miss Dora.

Dora. Where do they blow, Mr. Dobson?

Dobson. Under your eyes, Miss Dora.

Dora. Do they?

Dobson. And your eyes be as blue as—

Dora. What, Mr. Dobson? A butcher's frock?

Dobson. Noä, Miss Dora; as blue as—

Dora. Bluebell, harebell, speedwell, bluebottle, succory, forget-me-not?

Dobson. Noä, Miss Dora; as blue as—

Dora. The sky? or the sea on a blue day?

Dobson. Naäy then. I meän'd they be as blue as violets.

Dora. Are they?

Dobson. Theer ye goäs ageän, Miss, niver believing owt I says to ye—hallus a-fobbing ma off, tho' ye knaws I love ye. I warrants ye 'll think moor o' this young Squire Edgar as ha' coomed among us—the Lord knaws how—ye 'll think more on 'is little finger than hall my hand at the haltar.

Dora. Perhaps, Master Dobson. I can't tell, for I have never seen him. But my sister wrote that he was mighty pleasant, and had no pride in him.

Dobson. He 'll be arter you now, Miss Dora.

Dora. Will he? How can I tell?

Dobson. He's been arter Miss Eva, haän't he?

Dora. Not that I know.

Dobson. Did n't I spy 'em a-sitting i' the woodbine harbor togither?

Dora. What of that? Eva told me that he was taking her likeness. He 's an artist.

Dobson. What 's a hartist? I doänt believe he 's iver a 'eart under his waistcoat. And I tells ye what, Miss Dora: he's no respect for the Queen, or the parson, or the justice o' peace, or owt. I ha' heärd 'im a-gawin' on 'ud make your 'air—God bless it!—stan' on end. And wuss nor that. When theer wur a meeting o' farmers at Littlechester t' other daäy, and they was all a-crying out at the bad times, he cooms up, and he calls out among our oän men, 'The land belongs to the people!'

Dora. And what did *you* say to that?

Dobson. Well, I says, s'pose my pig 's the land, and you says it belongs to the parish, and theer be a thousand i' the parish, taäkin' in the women and childer; and s'pose I kills my pig, and gi'es it among 'em, why there wud n't be a dinner for nawbody, and I should ha' lost the pig.

Dora. And what did he say to that?

Dobson. Nowt—what could he saäy? But I taäkes 'im fur a bad lot and a burn fool, and I haätes the very sight on him.

Dora (*looking at* Dobson). Master Dobson, you are a comely man to look at.

Dobson. I thank you for that, Miss Dora, onyhow.

Dora. Ay, but you turn right ugly when you 're in an ill temper; and I promise you that if you forget your-

self in your behavior to this gentleman, my father's friend, I will never
change word with you again.

Enter FARMING MAN *from barn.*

Farming Man. Miss, the farming
men 'ull hev their dinner i' the long
barn, and the master 'ud be straänge
an' pleased if you 'd step in fust, and
see that all be right and reg'lar fur
'em afoor he coöm.   [*Exit.*
Dora. I go. Master Dobson, did you
hear what I said?
Dobson. Yeäs, yeäs! I 'll not meddle wi' 'im if he doänt meddle wi' meä.
(*Exit* Dora.) 'Coomly,' says she. I
niver thowt o' mysen i' that waäy;
but if she 'd taäke to ma i' that waäy,
or ony waäy, I 'd slaäve out my life
fur 'er. 'Coomly to look at,' says she
—but she said it spiteful-like. To look
at—yeäs, 'coomly;' and she may n't
be so fur out theer. But if that be
nowt to she, then it be nowt to me.
(*Looking off stage.*) Schoolmaster!
Why if Steer han't haxed schoolmaster to dinner, thaw 'e knaws I was
hallus ageän heving schoolmaster i'
the parish! fur him as be handy wi' a
boöök beänt but haäfe a hand at a
pitchfork.

Enter WILSON.

Well, Wilson. I seed that one cow
o' thine i' the pinfold ageän as I wur
a-coomin' 'ere.
Wilson. Very likely, Mr. Dobson.
She *will* break fence. I can't keep her
in order.
Dobson. An' if tha can't keep thy
one cow i' horder, how can tha keep
all thy scholards i' horder? But let
that goä by. What dost a knaw o' this
Mr. Hedgar as be a-lodgin' wi' ye? I
coom'd upon 'im t' other daäy lookin'
at the coontry, then a-scrattin' upon a
bit o' paäper, then a-lookin' ageän;
and I taäked 'im fur soom sort of a
land-surveyor—but a beänt.
Wilson. He 's a Somersetshire man,
and a very civil-spoken gentleman.

Dobson. Gentleman! What be he
a-doing here ten mile an' moor fro' a
raäil? We laäys out o' the waäy
fur gentlefoälk altogither—leästwaäys
they niver cooms 'ere but fur the trout
i' our beck, fur they be knaw'd as far
as Littlechester. But 'e doänt fish
neither.
Wilson. Well, it 's no sin in a gentleman not to fish.
Dobson. Noä, but I haätes 'im.
Wilson. Better step out of his road,
then, for he 's walking to us, and with
a hook in his hand.
Dobson. An' I haätes boööks an' all,
fur they puts foälk off the owd
waäys.

Enter EDGAR, *reading—not seeing*
DOBSON *and* WILSON.

Edgar. This author, with his charm
          of simple style
And close dialectic, all but proving
          man
An automatic series of sensations,
Has often numb'd me into apathy
Against the unpleasant jolts of this
          rough road
That breaks off short into the abysses
          —made me
A quietist taking all things easily.
Dobson (*aside*). There mun be
summut wrong theer, Wilson, fur I
doänt understan' it.
Wilson (*aside*). Nor I either, Mr.
Dobson.
Dobson (*scornfully*). An' thou
doänt understan' it neither—and thou
schoolmaster an' all!
Edgar. What can a man, then, live
          for but sensations,
Pleasant ones? men of old would un-
          dergo
Unpleasant for the sake of pleasant
          ones
Hereafter, like the Moslem beauties
          waiting
To clasp their lovers by the golden
          gates.
For me, whose cheerless Houris after
          death

Are Night and Silence, pleasant ones
—the while—
If possible, here! to crop the flower
and pass.

Dobson. Well, I never 'eärd the
likes o' that afoor.

Wilson (*aside*). But I have, Mr.
Dobson. It 's the old Scripture text,
'Let us eat and drink, for to-morrow
we die.' I 'm sorry for it, for, tho' he
never comes to church, I thought better of him.

Edgar. 'What are we,' says the
blind old man in Lear?
'As flies to the gods; they kill us for
their sport.'

Dobson (*aside*). Then the owd man
i' Lear should be shaämed of hissen,
but noän o' the parishes goäs by that
naäme 'ereabouts.

Edgar. The gods! but they, the
shadows of ourselves,
Have past for ever. It is Nature kills,
And not for *her* sport either. She
knows nothing.
Man only knows, the worse for him!
for why
Cannot *he* take his pastime like the
flies?
And if my pleasure breed another's
pain,
Well—is not that the course of Na-
ture too,
From the dim dawn of being—her
main law
Whereby she grows in beauty—that
her flies
Must massacre each other? this poor
Nature!

Dobson. Natur! Natur! Well, it be
i' *my* natur to knock 'im o' the 'eäd
now; but I weänt.

Edgar. A quietist taking all things
easily—why—
Have I been dipping into this again
To steel myself against the leaving
her?
[*Closes book, seeing* Wilson.
Good day!

Wilson. Good day, sir.
[Dobson *looks hard at* Edgar.

Edgar (*to Dobson*). Have I the
pleasure, friend, of knowing
you?

Dobson. Dobson.

Edgar. Good day, then, Dobson.
[*Exit.*

Dobson. 'Good daäy then, Dobson!'
Civil-spoken i'deed! Why, Wilson,
tha 'eärd 'im thysen—the feller could
n't find a Mister in his mouth fur me,
as farms five hoonderd haäcre.

Wilson. You never find one for me,
Mr. Dobson.

Dobson. Noä, fur thou be nobbut
schoolmaster; but I taäkes 'im for a
Lunnun swindler, and a burn fool.

Wilson. He can hardly be both, and
he pays me regular every Saturday.

Dobson. Yeäs; but I haätes 'im.

Enter STEER, FARM MEN *and* WOMEN.

Steer (*goes and sits under apple-
tree*). Hev' ony o' ye seen Eva?

Dobson. Noä, Mr. Steer.

Steer. Well, I reckons they 'll hev'
a fine cider-crop to-year if the blossom 'owds. Good murnin', neighbors,
and the saäme to you, my men. I
taäkes it kindly of all o' you that you
be coomed—what 's the newspaäper
word, Wilson?—celebrate—to celebrate my birthdaäy i' this fashion.
Niver man 'ed better friends, and I
will saäy niver master 'ed better men;
fur thaw I may ha' fallen out wi' ye
sometimes, the fault, mebbe, wur as
much mine as yours; and, thaw I says
it mysen, niver men 'ed a better master—and I knaws what men be, and
what masters be, fur I wur nobbut a
laäborer, and now I be a landlord—
burn a plowman, and now, as far as
money goäs, I be a gentleman, thaw
I beänt naw scholard, fur I 'ednt naw
time to maäke mysen a scholard while
I wur maäkin mysen a gentleman, but
I ha' taäen good care to turn out boäth
my darters right down fine laädies.

Dobson. An' soä they be.

First Farming Man. Soä they be!
soä they be!

Second Farming Man. The Lord
bless boäth on 'em!

Third Farming Man. An' the saäme to you, master!

Fourth Farming Man. And long life to boäth on 'em. An' the saäme to you, Master Steer, likewise!

Steer. Thank ye!

Enter EVA.

Wheer 'asta been?

Eva (*timidly*). Many happy returns of the day, father.

Steer. They can't be many, my dear, but I 'oäpes they 'll be 'appy.

Dobson. Why, tha looks haäle anew to last to a hoonderd.

Steer. An' why should n't I last to a hoonderd? Haäle! why should n't I be haäle? fur thaw I be heighty this very daäy, I niver 'es sa much as one pin's prick of paäin; an' I can taäke my glass along wi' the youngest, fur I niver touched a drop of owt till my oän wedding-daäy, an' then I wur turned huppads o' sixty. Why should n't I be haäle? I ha' plowed the ten-aäcre—it be mine now—afoor ony o' ye wur burn—ye all knaws the ten-aäcre—I mun ha' plowed it moor nor a hoonderd times; hallus hup at sunrise, and I 'd drive the plow straäit as a line right i' the faäce o' the sun, then back ageän, a-follering my oän shadder—then hup ageän i' the faäce o' the sun. Eh! how the sun 'ud shine, and the larks 'ud sing i' them daäys, and the smell o' the mou'd an' all. Eh! if I could ha' gone on wi' the plowin' nobbut the smell o' the mou'd 'ud ha' maäde ma live as long as Jerusalem.

Eva. Methuselah, father.

Steer. Ay, lass, but when thou be as owd as me thou 'll put one word fur another as I does.

Dobson. But, Steer, thaw thou be haäle anew I seed tha a-limpin' up just now wi' the roomatics i' the knee.

Steer. Roomatics! Noä, I laäme't my knee last night running arter a thief. Beänt there house-breäkers down i' Littlechester, Dobson—doänt ye hear of ony?

Dobson. Ay, that there be. Immanuel Goldsmith's was broke into o' Monday night, and ower a hoonderd pounds worth o' rings stolen.

Steer. So I thowt, and I heärd the winder—that's the winder at the end o' the passage, that goäs by thy chamber. (*Turning to* Eva.) Why, lass, what makes tha sa red? Did 'e git into thy chamber?

Eva. Father!

Steer. Well, I runned arter thief i' the dark, and fell ageän coalscuttle and my kneeä gev waäy or I 'd ha' cotched 'im, but afoor I coomed up he got thruff the winder ageän.

Eva. Got thro' the window again?

Steer. Ay, but he left the mark of 'is foot i' the flower-bed; now theer be noän o' my men, thinks I to mysen, 'ud ha' done it 'cep' it were Dan Smith, fur I cotched 'im once a-stealin' coäls, an' I sent fur 'im, an' I measured his foot wi' the mark i' the bed, but it would n't fit—seeäms to me the mark wur maäde by a Lunnun boot. (*Looks at* Eva.) Why, now, what maäkes tha sa white?

Eva. Fright, father!

Steer. Maäke thysen eäsy. I 'll hev the winder naäiled up, and put Towser under it.

Eva (*clasping her hands*). No, no, father! Towser 'll tear him all to pieces.

Steer. Let him keep awaäy, then; but coom, coom! let's be gawin'. They ha' broached a barrel of aäle i' the long barn, and the fiddler be theer, and the lads and lassies 'ull hev a dance.

Eva (*aside*). Dance! small heart have I to dance. I should seem to be dancing upon a grave.

Steer. Wheer be Mr. Edgar? about the premises?

Dobson. Hallus about the premises!

Steer. So much the better, so much the better. I likes 'im, and Eva likes 'im. Eva can do owt wi' 'im; look for 'im, Eva, and bring 'im to the barn. He 'ant naw pride in 'im, and we 'll git 'im to speechify for us arter dinner.

Eva. Yes, father! [*Exit.*

afoor to him, and it seems to me nob-but t'other day. Hes n't he left ye nowt?

Dora. No, Mr. Dobson.

Dobson. But he were mighty fond o' ye, warn't he?

Dora. Fonder of poor Eva—like everybody else.

Dobson (handing Dora *basket of roses).* Not like me, Miss Dora; and I ha' browt these roses to ye—I for-gits what they calls 'em, but I hallus gi'ed soom on 'em to Miss Eva at this time o' year. Will ya taäke 'em? fur Miss Eva, she set the bush by my dairy winder afoor she went to school at Littlechester—so I allus browt soom on 'em to her; and now she be gone, will ye taäke 'em, Miss Dora?

Dora. I thank you. They tell me that yesterday you mentioned her name too suddenly before my father. See that you do not do so again!

Dobson. Noä; I knaws a deäl bet-ter now. I seed how the owd man wur vext.

Dora. I take them, then, for Eva's sake.

[*Takes basket, places some in her dress.*

Dobson. Eva's saäke. Yeäs. Poor gell, poor gell! I can't abeär to think on 'er now, fur I 'd ha' done owt fur 'er mysen; an' ony o' Steer's men, an' ony o' my men 'ud ha' done owt fur 'er, an' all the parish 'ud ha' done owt fur 'er, fur we was all on us proud on 'er, an' them theer be soom of her oän roses, an' she wur as sweet as ony on 'em—the Lord bless 'er—'er oän sen; an' weänt ye taäke 'em now, Miss Dora, fur 'er saäke an' fur my saäke an' all?

Dora. Do you want them back again?

Dobson. Noä, noä! Keep em. But I hed a word to saäy to ye.

Dora. Why, Farmer, you should be in the hay-field looking after your men; you could n't have more splen-did weather.

Dobson. I be a going theer; but I thowt I 'd bring tha them roses fust.

The weather's well anew, but the glass be a bit shaäky. S'iver we 've led moäst on it.

Dora. Ay! but you must not be too sudden with it either, as you were last year, when you put it in green, and your stack caught fire.

Dobson. I were insured, Miss, an' I lost nowt by it. But I weänt be too sudden wi' it; and I feel sewer, Miss Dora, that I ha' been noän too sudden wi' you, fur I ha' sarved fer ye well nigh as long as the man sarved for 'is sweet'art i' Scriptur'. Weänt ye gi'e me a kind answer at last?

Dora. I have no thought of mar-riage, my friend. We have been in such grief these five years, not only on my sister's account, but the ill suc-cess of the farm, and the debts, and my father's breaking down, and his blindness. How could I think of leav-ing him?

Dobson. Eh, but I be well to do; and if ye would nobbut hev me, I would taäke the owd blind man to my oän fireside. You should hev him al-lus wi' ye.

Dora. You are generous, but it can-not be. I cannot love you; nay, I think I never can be brought to love any man. It seems to me that I hate men, ever since my sister left us. O, see here. (*Pulls out a letter.*) I wear it next my heart. Poor sister, I had it five years ago. 'Dearest Dora,—I have lost myself, and am lost for ever to you and my poor father. I thought Mr. Edgar the best of men, and he has proved himself the worst. Seek not for me, or you may find me at the bottom of the river.—Eva.'

Dobson. Be that my fault?

Dora. No; but how should I, with this grief still at my heart, take to the milking of your cows, the fatting of your calves, the making of your but-ter, and the managing of your poul-try?

Dobson. Naäy, but I hev an owd woman as 'ud see to all that; and you should sit i' your oän parlor quite like a laädy, ye should!

Dora. It cannot be.

Dobson. And plaäy the pianner, if ye liked, all daäy long, like a laädy, ye should an' all.

Dora. It cannot be.

Dobson. And I would loove tha moor nor ony gentleman 'ud loove tha.

Dora. No, no; it cannot be.

Dobson. And p'raps ye hears 'at I soomtimes taäkes a drop too much; but that be all along o' you, Miss, because ye weänt hev me; but, if ye would, I could put all that o' one side eäsy anew.

Dora. Cannot you understand plain words, Mr. Dobson? I tell you, it cannot be.

Dobson. Eh, lass! Thy feyther, eddicated his darters to marry gentlefoälk, and see what's coomed on it.

Dora. That is enough, Farmer Dobson. You have shown me that, though fortune had born *you* into the estate of a gentleman, you would still have been Farmer Dobson. You had better attend to your hay-field. Good afternoon.   [*Exit.*

Dobson. 'Farmer Dobson!' Well, I be Farmer Dobson; but I thinks Farmer Dobson's dog 'ud ha' knaw'd better nor to cast her sister's misfortin inter 'er teeth arter she 'd been a-reädin' me the letter wi' 'er voice a-shaäkin', and the drop in 'er eye. Theer she goäs! Shall I foller 'er and ax 'er to maäke it up? Noä, not yet. Let 'er cool upon it; I likes 'er all the better fur taäken' me down, like a laädy, as she be. Farmer Dobson! I be Farmer Dobson, sewer anew; but if iver I cooms upo' Gentleman Hedgar ageän, and doänt laäy my cartwhip athurt 'is shou'ders, why then I beänt Farmer Dobson, but summun else— blaäme't if I beänt!

Enter HAYMAKERS *with a load of hay.*

The last on it, eh?

First Haymaker. Yeäs.

Dobson. Hoäm wi' it, then.
                                        [*Exit surlily.*

First Haymaker. Well, it be the last loäd hoäm.

Second Haymaker. Yeäs, an' owd Dobson should be glad on it. What maäkes 'im allus sa glum?

Sally Allen. Glum! he be wuss nor glum. He coom'd up to me yisterdaäy i' the haäy-field, when meä and my sweet'art was a-workin' along o' one side wi' one another, and he sent 'im awaäy to t' other end o' the field; and when I axed 'im why, he telled me 'at sweet'arts niver worked well togither; and telled *'im* 'at sweet'arts allus worked best togither; and then he called me a rude naäme, and I can't abide 'im.

James. Why, lass, doänt that knaw he be sweet upo' Dora Steer, and she weänt sa much as look at 'im? And wheniver 'e sees two sweet'arts togither like thou and me, Sally, he be fit to bust hissen wi' spites and jalousies.

Sally. Let 'im bust hissen, then, for owt *I* cares.

First Haymaker. Well, but, as I said afoor, it be the last loäd hoäm; do thou and thy sweet'art sing us hoäm to supper—'The Last Loäd Hoäm.'

All. Ay! 'The Last Loäd Hoäm.'

SONG

What did ye do, and what did ye saäy,
Wi' the wild white rose, an' the wood-
    bine sa gaäy,
An' the midders all mow'd, an' the sky
    sa blue—
What did ye saäy, and what did ye do,
When ye thowt there were nawbody
    watchin' o' you,
And you an' your Sally was forkin' the
    haäy,
        At the end of the daäy,
        For the last loäd hoäm?

What did we do, and what did we saäy,
Wi' the briar sa green, an' the willer sa
    graäy,
An' the midders all mow'd, an' the sky
    sa blue—
Do ye think I be gawin' to tell it to
    you,

What we mowt saäy, and what we mowt
　　do,
When me an' my Sally was forkin' the
　　haäy,
　　　At the end of the daäy,
　　　For the last loäd hoäm?

But what did ye saäy, and what did ye
　　do,
Wi' the butterflies out, and the swallers
　　at plaäy,
An' the midders all mow'd, an' the sky
　　sa blue?
Why, coom then, owd feller, I 'll tell it
　　to you;
For me an' my Sally we sweär'd to be
　　true,
To be true to each other, let 'appen
　　what maäy,
　　　Till the end of the daäy,
　　　And the last loäd hoäm.

All. Well sung!
James. Fanny be the naäme i' the
song, but I swopt it fur *she.*
　　　　　　　　[*Pointing to* Sally.
Sally. Let ma aloän afoor foälk, wilt
tha?
First Haymaker. Ye shall sing that
ageän to-night, fur owd Dobson 'll
gi'e us a bit o' supper.
Sally. I weänt goä to owd Dobson;
he wur rude to me i' tha haäy-field,
and he 'll be rude to me ageän to-
night. Owd Steer's gotten all his grass
down and wants a hand, and I 'll goä
to him.
First Haymaker. Owd Steer gi'es
nubbut cowd tea to *'is* men, and owd
Dobson gi'es beer.
Sally. But I 'd like owd Steer's cowd
tea better nor Dobson's beer. Good-
bye.　　　　　　　　[*Going.*
James. Gi'e us a buss fust, lass. [211]
Sally. I tell'd tha to let ma aloän!
James. Why, was n't thou and me
a-bussin' o' one another t' other side
o' the haäycock, when owd Dobson
coom'd upo' us? I can't let tha aloän
if I would, Sally
　　　　　　　[*Offering to kiss her.*
Sally. Git along wi' ye, do! [*Exit.*
　　[*All laugh; exeunt singing.*

To be true to each other, let 'appen
　　what maäy,
　　　Till the end o' the daäy,
　　　An' the last loäd hoäm.

Enter HAROLD.

Harold. Not Harold! 'Philip Edgar,
　　Philip Edgar!'
Her phantom call'd me by the name
　　she loved.
I told her I should hear her from the
　　grave.
Ay! yonder is her casement. I remem-
　　ber
Her bright face beaming starlike down
　　upon me
Thro' that rich cloud of blossom. Since
　　I left her
Here weeping, I have ranged the
　　world, and sat
Thro' every sensual course of that
　　full feast
That leaves but emptiness.

SONG.

To be true to each other, let 'appen
　　what maäy
　　　To the end o' the daäy,
　　　An' the last loäd hoäm.

Harold. Poor Eva! O my God, if
　　man be only
A willy-nilly current of sensations—
Reaction needs must follow revel—
　　yet—
Why feel remorse, he, knowing that
　　he *must* have
Moved in the iron grooves of Des-
　　tiny?
Remorse then is a part of Destiny,
Nature a liar, making us feel guilty
Of her own faults.
　　　　　My grandfather—of him
They say, that women—
　　　　　O, this mortal house,
Which we are born into, is haunted
　　by
The ghosts of the dead passions of
　　dead men;
And these take flesh again with our
　　own flesh,

And bring us to confusion.
                    He was only
A poor philosopher who call'd the
    mind
Of children a blank page, a *tabula
    rasa*.
There, there, is written in invisible
    inks
'Lust, Prodigality, Covetousness,
    Craft,
Cowardice, Murder'—and the heat
    and fire
Of life will bring them, out, and black
    enough,
So the child grow to manhood. Bet-
    ter death
With our first wail than life—

SONG (*further off*).

Till the end o' the daäy,
An' the last loäd hoäm,
    Loäd hoäm.

This bridge again!
            (*Steps on the bridge.*)
            How often have I stood
With Eva here! The brook among its
    flowers!
Forget-me-not, meadow-sweet, wil-
    low-herb.
I had some smattering of science
    then,
Taught her the learned names, anat-
    omized
The flowers for her—and now I only
    wish
This pool were deep enough, that I
    might plunge
And lose myself for ever.

Enter DAN SMITH (*singing*).

Gee oop! whoä! Gee oop! whoä!
Scizzars an' Pumpy was good uns to goä
    Thruf slush an' squad
        When roäds was bad,
But hallus 'ud stop at the Vine-an'-the-
    Hop,
    Fur boäth on 'em knawed as well as
        mysen
    That beer be as good fur 'erses as
        men.
Gee oop! whoä! Gee oop! whoä!
Scizzars an' Pumpy was good uns to goä.

The beer 's gotten oop into my 'eäd.
S'iver I mun git along back to the
farm, fur she tell'd me to taäke the
cart to Littlechester.

Enter DORA.

Dora. Half an hour late! why are
you loitering here? Away with you
at once.   [*Exit* Dan Smith.
    (*Seeing* Harold *on bridge.*)
Some madman, is it,
Gesticulating there upon the bridge?
I am half afraid to pass.
    Harold.   Sometimes I wonder,
When man has surely learnt at last
    that all
His old-world faith, the blossom of
    his youth,
Has faded, falling fruitless—whether
    then
All of us, all at once, may not be
    seized
With some fierce passion, not so much
    for Death
As against Life! all, all, into the
    dark—
No more!—and science now could
    drug and balm us
Back into nescience with as little pain
As it is to fall asleep.
                This beggarly life,
This poor, flat, hedged-in field—no
    distance—this
Hollow Pandora-box,
With all the pleasures flown, not even
    Hope
Left at the bottom!
                Superstitious fool,
What brought me here? To see her
    grave? her ghost?
Her ghost is everyway about me here.
    Dora (*coming forward*). Allow me,
    sir, to pass you.
    Harold.   Eva!
    Dora.   Eva!
    Harold. What are you? Where do
    you come from?
    Dora.   From the farm
Here, close at hand.
    Harold. Are you—you are—that
    Dora,

The sister. I have heard of you. The likeness
Is very striking.

Dora.   You knew Eva, then?

Harold. Yes—I was thinking of her when— O, yes,
Many years back, and never since have met
Her equal for pure innocence of nature,
And loveliness of feature.

Dora.   No, nor I.

Harold. Except, indeed, I have found it once again
In your own self.

Dora.   You flatter me. Dear Eva
Was always thought the prettier.

Harold.   And *her* charm
Of voice is also yours; and I was brooding
Upon a great unhappiness when you spoke.

Dora. Indeed, you seemed in trouble, sir.

Harold.   And you
Seem my good angel who may help me from it.

Dora (*aside*). How worn he looks, poor man! who is it, I wonder.
How can I help him? (*Aloud.*) Might I ask your name?

Harold. Harold.

Dora. I never heard her mention you.

Harold. I met her first at a farm in Cumberland—
Her uncle's.

Dora. She was there six years ago.

Harold. And if she never mention'd me, perhaps
The painful circumstances which I heard—
I will not vex you by repeating them—
Only last week at Littlechester, drove me
From out her memory. She has disappear'd,
They told me, from the farm—and darker news.

Dora. She has disappear'd, poor darling, from the world—
Left but one dreadful line to say, that we

Should find her in the river; and we dragg'd
The Littlechester river all in vain,
Have sorrow'd for her all these years in vain.
And my poor father, utterly broken down
By losing her—she was his favorite child—
Has let his farm, all his affairs, I fear,
But for the slender help that I can give,
Fall into ruin. Ah! that villain, Edgar,
If he should ever show his face among us,
Our men and boys would hoot him, stone him, hunt him
With pitchforks off the farm, for all of them
Loved her, and she was worthy of all love.

Harold. They say, we should forgive our enemies.

Dora. Ay, if the wretch were dead I might forgive him;
We know not whether he be dead or living.

Harold. What Edgar?

Dora.   Philip Edgar of Toft Hall
In Somerset. Perhaps you know him?

Harold.   Slightly.
(*Aside.*) Ay, for how slightly have I known myself!

Dora. This Edgar, then, is living?

Harold.   Living? well—
One Philip Edgar of Toft Hall in Somerset
Is lately dead.

Dora. Dead!—is there more than one?

Harold. Nay—now—not one, (*aside*) for I am Philip Harold.

Dora. That one, is he then—dead!

Harold (*aside*). My father's death,
Let her believe it mine; this, for the moment,
Will leave me a free field.

Dora.   Dead! and this world
Is brighter for his absence, as that other
Is darker for his presence.

Harold.   Is not this

To speak too pitilessly of the dead?

Dora. My five-years' anger cannot
    die at once,
Not all at once with death and him. I
    trust
I shall forgive him—by and by—not
    now.
O sir, you seem to have a heart; if you
Had seen us that wild morning when
    we found
Her bed unslept in, storm and shower
    lashing
Her casement, her poor spaniel wail-
    ing for her,
That desolate letter, blotted with her
    tears,
Which told us we should never see her
    more—
Our old nurse crying as if for her own
    child,
My father stricken with his first
    paralysis,
And then with blindness—had you
    been one of us
And seen all this, then you would
    know it is not
So easy to forgive—even the dead.

Harold. But sure am I that of your
    gentleness
You will forgive him. She you mourn
    for seem'd
A miracle of gentleness—would not
    blur
A moth's wing by the touching; would
    not crush
The fly that drew her blood; and, were
    she living,
Would not—if penitent—have denied
    him *her*
Forgiveness. And perhaps the man
    himself,
When hearing of that piteous death,
    has suffer'd
More than we know. But wherefore
    waste your heart
In looking on a chill and changeless
    past?
Iron will fuse, and marble melt; the
    past
Remains the past. But you are young,
    and—pardon me—
As lovely as your sister. Who can tell

What golden hours, with what full
    hands, may be
Waiting you in the distance? Might I
    call
Upon your father—I have seen the
    world—
And cheer his blindness with a travel-
    ler's tales?

Dora. Call if you will, and when
    you will. I cannot
Well answer for my father; but if you
Can tell me anything of our sweet Eva
When in her brighter girlhood, I at
    least
Will bid you welcome, and will listen
    to you.
Now I must go.

Harold.   But give me first your
    hand;
I do not dare, like an old friend, to
    shake it.
I kiss it as a prelude to that privilege
When you shall know me better.

Dora (*aside*).   How beautiful
His manners are, and how unlike the
    farmer's!
You are staying here?

Harold.   Yes, at the wayside inn
Close by that alder-island in your
    brook,
'The Angler's Home.'

Dora.   Are *you* one?

Harold.   No, but I
Take some delight in sketching, and
    the country
Has many charms, altho' the inhabit-
    ants
Seem semi-barbarous.

Dora.   I am glad it pleases you;
Yet I, born here, not only love the
    country,
But its inhabitants too; and you, I
    doubt not,
Would take to them as kindly, if you
    cared
To live some time among them.

Harold.   If I did,
Then one at least of its inhabitants
Might have more charm for me than
    all the country.

Dora. That one, then, should be
    grateful for your preference.

Harold. I cannot tell, tho' standing
 in her presence.
(*Aside.*) She colors!
Dora.   Sir!
Harold.   Be not afraid of me,
For these are no conventional flour-
 ishes.
I do most earnestly assure you that
Your likeness—   [*Shouts and cries
                            without.*
Dora. What was that? my poor
 blind father—

Enter FARMING MAN.

Farming Man. Miss Dora, Dan
Smith's cart hes runned ower a laädy
i' the holler laäne, and they ha' ta'en
the body up inter your chaumber, and
they be all a-callin' for ye.
Dora. The body!—Heavens! I
 come!
Harold.   But you are trembling.
Allow me to go with you to the farm.
                            [*Exeunt.*

Enter DOBSON.

Dobson. What feller wur it as 'a'
been a-talkin' fur haäfe an hour wi'
my Dora? (*Looking after him.*)
Seeäms I ommost knaws the back on
'im—drest like a gentleman, too.
Damn all gentlemen, says I! I should
ha' thowt they 'd hed anew o' gentlefoälk, as I telled 'er to-daäy when she
fell foul upo' me.
 Minds ma o' summun. I could sweär
to that; but that be all one, fur I
haätes 'im afoor I knaws what 'e be.
Theer! he turns round. Philip Hedgar
o' Soomerset! Philip Hedgar o' Soomerset!—Noä—yeäs—thaw the feller 's
gone and maäde such a litter of his
faäce.
 Eh lad, if it be thou, I'll Philip tha!
a-plaäyin' the saäme gaäme wi' my
Dora—I'll Soomerset tha!
 I'd like to drag 'im thruff the herse-
pond, and see how he to be a-lookin' at it.
I'd like to leather 'im black and blue,
and she to be a-laughin' at it. I'd like
to fell 'im as deäd as a bullock!
                    (*Clenching his fists.*)

But what 'ud she saäy to that? She
telled me once not to meddle wi' 'im,
and now she be fallen out wi' ma, and
I can't coom at 'er.
 It mun be *him*. Noä! Fur she 'd
niver 'a' been talkin' haäfe an hour wi'
the divil 'at killed her oän sister, or
she beänt Dora Steer.
 Yeäs! Fur she niver knawed 'is
faäce when 'e wur 'ere afoor; but I 'll
maäke 'er knaw! I 'll maäke 'er knaw!

Enter HAROLD.

 Naäy, but I mun git out on 'is waäy
now, or I shall be the death on 'im.
                            [*Exit.*
Harold. How the clown glared at
 me! that Dobbins, is it,
With whom I used to jar? but can he
 trace me
Thro' five years' absence, and my
 change of name,
The tan of Southern summers and the
 beard?
I may as well avoid him.
                            Lady like!
Lilylike in her stateliness and sweet-
 ness!
How came she by it?—a daughter of
 the fields,
This Dora!
She gave her hand, unask'd, at the
 farm-gate;
I almost think she half return'd the
 pressure
Of mine. What, I that held the orange
 blossom
Dark as the yew? but may not those,
 who march
Before their age, turn back at times,
 and make
Courtesy to custom? and now the
 stronger motive,
Misnamed free-will—the crowd would
 call it conscience—
Moves me—to what? I am dreaming;
 for the past
Look'd thro' the present, Eva's eyes
 thro' hers—
A spell upon me! Surely I loved Eva
More than I knew! or is it but the
 past

That brightens in retiring? O, last
    night
Tired, pacing my new lands at Little-
    chester,
I dozed upon the bridge, and the black
    river
Flow'd thro' my dreams—if dreams
    they were. She rose
From the foul flood and pointed
    toward the farm,
And her cry rang to me across the
    years,
'I call you, Philip Edgar, Philip Ed-
    gar!
Come, you will set all right again, and
    father
Will not die miserable.' I could make
    his age
A comfort to him—so be more at
    peace
With mine own self. Some of my
    former friends
Would find my logic faulty; let them.
    Color
Flows thro' my life again, and I have
    lighted
On a new pleasure. Anyhow we must
Move in the line of least resistance
    when
The stronger motive rules.
                But she hates Edgar.
May not this Dobbins, or some other,
    spy
Edgar in Harold? Well then, I must
    make her
Love Harold first, and then she will
    forgive
Edgar for Harold's sake. She said her-
    self
She would forgive him, by and by, not
    now—
For her own sake *then,* if not for mine
    —not now—
But by and by.

Enter DOBSON *behind.*

Dobson. By and by—eh, lad, dosta
knaw this paäper? Ye dropt it upo'
the road. 'Philip Edgar, Esq.' Ay, you
be a pretty squire. I ha' fun' ye out,
I hev. Eh, lad, dosta knaw what tha
meäns wi' by and by? Fur if ye be
goin' to sarve our Dora as ye sarved
our Eva—then, by and by, if she
weänt listen to me when I be a-tryin'
to saäve 'er—if she weänt—look to
thysen, for, by the Lord, I'd think na
moor o' maäkin' an end o' tha nor a
carrion craw—noä—thaw they hanged
ma at 'Size fur it.

Harold. Dobbins, I think!

Dobson. I beänt Dobbins.

Harold. Nor am I Edgar, my good
fellow.

Dobson. Tha lies! What hasta been
saäyin' to *my* Dora?

Harold. I have been telling her of
the death of one Philip Edgar of Toft
Hall, Somerset.

Dobson. Tha lies!

Harold (*pulling out a newspaper.*)
Well, my man, it seems that you can
read. Look there—under the deaths.

Dobson. 'O' the 17th, Philip Edgar,
o' Toft Hall, Soomerset.' How coom
thou to be sa like 'im, then?

Harold. Naturally enough; for I am
closely related to the dead man's family.

Dobson. An' 'ow coom thou by the
letter to 'im?

Harold. Naturally again; for, as I
used to transact all his business for
him, I had to look over his letters.
Now then, see these (*takes out letters*). Half a score of them, all di-
rected to me—Harold.

Dobson. 'Arold! 'Arold! 'Arold, so
they be.

Harold. My name is Harold! Good
day, Dobbins!   [*Exit.*

Dobson. 'Arold! The feller's cleän
daäzed, an' maäzed, an' maäted, an'
muddled ma. Deäd! It mun be true,
fur it wur i' print as black as owt.
Naäy, but 'Good daäy, Dobbins.'
Why, that wur the very twang on 'im.
Eh, lad, but whether thou be Hedgar,
or Hedgar's business man, thou hes n't
naw business 'ere wi' *my* Dora, as I
knaws on, an' whether thou calls thysen Hedgar or Harold, if thou stick to
she I'll stick to thee—stick to tha like
a weasel to a rabbit, I will. Ay! and
I'd like to shoot tha like a rabbit an'

all. 'Good daäy, Dobbins.' Dang
tha!

ACT III

SCENE.—A ROOM IN STEER'S HOUSE.
DOOR LEADING INTO BEDROOM AT
THE BACK.

Dora (*ringing a handbell*). Milly!

Enter MILLY.

Milly. The little 'ymn? Yeäs, Miss;
but I wur so ta'en up wi' leädin' the
owd man about all the blessed murnin'
'at I ha' nobbut larned mysen haäfe
on it.

O man, forgive thy mortal foe,
Nor ever strike him blow for blow;
For all the souls on earth that live
To be forgiven must forgive.
Forgive him seventy times and seven;
For all the blessed souls in heaven
Are both forgivers and forgiven.

But I 'll git the book ageän, and
larn mysen the rest, and saäy it to ye
afoor dark; ye ringed fur that, Miss,
did n't ye?
Dora. No, Milly; but if the farming men be come for their wages, to
send them up to me.
Milly. Yeäs, Miss. [*Exit.*
Dora (*sitting at desk counting
money*). Enough at any rate for the
present. (*Enter* Farming Men.) Good
afternoon, my friends. I am sorry Mr.
Steer still continues too unwell to attend to you, but the schoolmaster
looked to the paying you your wages
when I was away, did n't he?
Men. Yeäs; and thanks to ye.
Dora. Some of our workmen have
left us, but he sent me an alphabetical
list of those that remain, so, Allen, I
may as well begin with you.
Allen (*with his hand to his ear*).
Halfabitical! Taäke one o' the young
uns fust, Miss, fur I be a bit deaf, and
I wur hallus scaäred by a big word;
leästwaäys, I should be wi' a lawyer.

Dora. I spoke of your names, Allen,
as they are arranged here (*shows
book*)—according to their first letters.
Allen. Letters! Yeäs, I sees now.
Them be what they larns the childer'
at school, but I were burn afoor
schoolin'-timė.
Dora. But, Allen, tho' you can't
read, you could whitewash that cottage of yours where your grandson
had the fever.
Allen. I'll hev it done o' Monday.
Dora. Else if the fever spread, the
parish will have to thank you for it.
Allen. Meä? why, it be the Lord's
doin', noän o' mine; d' ye think *I'd*
gi'e 'em the fever? But I thanks ye all
the saäme, Miss. (*Takes money.*)
Dora (*calling out names*). Higgins,
Jackson, Luscombe, Nokes, Oldham,
Skipworth! (*All take money.*) Did
you find that you worked at all the
worse upon the cold tea than you
would have done upon the beer?
Higgins. Noä, Miss; we worked naw
wuss upo' the cowd tea; but we 'd ha'
worked better upo' the beer.
Dora. Come, come, you worked
well enough, and I am much obliged
to all of you. There 's for you, and
you, and you. Count the money and
see if it 's all right.
Men. All right, Miss; and thank ye
kindly.
[*Exeunt* Luscombe, Nokes, Oldham, Skipworth.
Dora. Dan Smith, my father and I
forgave you stealing our coals.
[Dan Smith *advances to* Dora.
Dan Smith (*bellowing*). Whoy, O
lor, Miss! that wur sa long back, and
the walls sa thin, and the winders
brokken, and the weather sa cowd,
and my missus a-gittin' ower 'er lyin'-
in.
Dora. Did n't I say that we had forgiven you? But, Dan Smith, they tell
me that you—and you have six children—spent all your last Saturday's
wages at the ale-house; that you were
stupid drunk all Sunday, and so ill in
consequence all Monday that you did

not come into the hay-field. Why should I pay you your full wages?

Dan Smith. I be ready to taäke the pledge.

Dora. And as ready to break it again Besides, it was you that were driving the cart—and I fear you were tipsy then, too—when you lamed the lady in the hollow lane.

Dan Smith (bellowing). O lor, Miss! noä, noä, noä! Ye sees the holler laäne be hallus sa dark i' the arternoon, and wheere the big esh-tree cuts athurt it, it gi'es a turn like, and 'ow should I see to laäme the laädy, and meä coomin' along pretty sharp an' all?

Dora. Well, there are your wages; the next time you waste them at a pot-house you get no more from me. (*Exit* Dan Smith.) Sally Allen, you worked for Mr. Dobson, did n't you?

Sally (advancing). Yeäs, Miss; but he wur so rough wi' ma, I could n't abide 'im.

Dora. Why should he be rough with you? You are as good as a man in the hay-field. What 's become of your brother?

Sally. 'Listed for a soädger, Miss, i' the Queen's Real Hard Tillery.

Dora. And your sweetheart—when are you and he to be married?

Sally. At Michaelmas, Miss, please God.

Dora. You are an honest pair. I will come to your wedding.

Sally. An' I thanks ye fur that, Miss, moor nor fur the waäge.

(*Going—returns.*) 'A cotched ma about the waäist, Miss, when 'e wur 'ere afoor, an' axed ma to be 'is little sweet'art, an' soä I knaw'd 'im when I seed 'im ageän an' I telled feyther on 'im.

Dora. What is all this, Allen?

Allen. Why, Miss Dora, meä and my maätes, us three, we wants to hev three words wi' ye.

Higgins. That be 'im, and meä, Miss.

Jackson. An' meä, Miss.

Allen. An' we weänt mention naw

naämes, we 'd as lief talk o' the divil afoor ye as 'im, fur they says the master goäs cleän off his 'eäd when he 'eärs the naäme on 'im; but us three, arter Sally 'd telled us on 'im, we fun' 'im out a-walkin' i' West Field wi' a white 'at, nine o'clock, upo' Tuesday murnin', and all on us, wi' your leave, we wants to leather 'im.

Dora. Who?

Allen. Him as did the mischief here, five year' sin'.

Dora. Mr. Edgar?

Allen. Theer, Miss! You ha' naämed 'im—not me.

Dora. He 's dead, man—dead; gone to his account—dead and buried.

Allen. I beänt sa sewer o' that, fur Sally knaw'd 'im. Now then?

Dora. Yes; it was in the Somersetshire papers.

Allen. Then yon mun be his brother, an' we 'll leather *'im.*

Dora. I never heard that he had a brother. Some foolish mistake of Sally's; but what! would you beat a man for his brother's fault? That were a wild justice indeed. Let bygones be bygones. Go home! Good-night! (*All exeunt.*) I have once more paid them all. The work of the farm will go on still, but for how long? We are almost at the bottom of the well: little more to be drawn from it—and what then? Encumbered as we are, who would lend us anything? We shall have to sell all the land, which father, for a whole life, has been getting together, again, and that, I am sure, would be the death of him. What am I to do? Farmer Dobson, were I to marry him, has promised to keep our heads above water; and the man has doubtless a good heart, and a true and lasting love for me; yet—though I can be sorry for him—as the good Sally says, 'I can't abide him'—almost brutal, and matched with my Harold is like a hedge thistle by a garden rose. But then, he, too—will he ever be of one faith with his wife? which is my dream of a true marriage. Can I fancy him kneeling with me, and uttering the same prayer; standing up side by side with me, and singing the same hymn? I fear not. Have I done wisely, then, in accepting him? But may not a girl's love-dream have too much romance in it to be realized all at once, or altogether, or anywhere but in heaven? And yet I had once a vision of a pure and perfect marriage, where the man and the woman, only differing as the stronger and the weaker, should walk hand in hand together down this valley of tears, as they call it so truly, to the grave at the bottom, and lie down there together in the darkness which would seem but for a moment, to be wakened again together by the light of the resurrection, and no more partings for ever and for ever. (*Walks up and down. She sings.*)

O happy lark, that warblest high
    Above thy lowly nest,
O brook, that brawlest merrily by
    Thro' fields that once were blest,
O tower spiring to the sky,
    O graves in daisies drest,
O Love and Life, how weary am I,
    And how I long for rest!

There, there, I am a fool! Tears! I have sometimes been moved to tears by a chapter of fine writing in a novel; but what have I to do with tears now? All depends on me—father, this poor girl, the farm, everything; and they both love me—I am all in all to both; and he loves me too, I am quite sure of that. Courage, courage! and all will go well. (*Goes to bedroom door; opens it.*) How dark your room is! Let me bring you in here where there is still full daylight. (*Brings EVA forward.*) Why, you look better.

Eva. And I feel so much better that I trust I may be able by and by to help you in the business of the farm; but I must not be known yet. Has any one found me out, Dora?

Dora. O, no; you kept your veil too close for that when they carried you in; since then, no one has seen you but myself.

Eva. Yes—this Milly.

Dora. Poor blind father's little guide, Milly, who came to us three years after you were gone, how should she know you? But now that you have been brought to us as it were from the grave, dearest Eva, and have been here so long, will you not speak with father to-day?

Eva. Do you think that I may? No, not yet. I am not equal to it yet.

Dora. Why? Do you still suffer from your fall in the hollow lane?

Eva. Bruised; but no bones broken.

Dora. I have always told father that the huge old ash-tree there would cause an accident some day; but he would never cut it down, because one of the Steers had planted it there in former times.

Eva. If it had killed one of the Steers there the other day, it might have been better for her, for him, and for you.

Dora. Come, come, keep a good heart! Better for me! That's good. How better for me?

Eva. You tell me you have a lover. Will he not fly from you if he learn the story of my shame and that I am still living?

Dora. No; I am sure that when we are married he will be willing that you and father should live with us; for, indeed, he tells me that he met you once in the old times, and was much taken with you, my dear.

Eva. Taken with me; who was he? Have you told him I am here?

Dora. No; do you wish it?

Eva. See, Dora; you yourself are ashamed of me (*weeps*), and I do not wonder at it.

Dora. But I should wonder at myself if it were so. Have we not been all in all to one another from the time when we first peeped into the bird's nest, waded in the brook, ran after the butterflies, and prattled to each other that we would marry fine gentlemen, and played at being fine ladies?

Eva. That last was my father's fault, poor man. And this lover of yours—this Mr. Harold—is a gentle-man?

Dora. That he is, from head to foot. I do believe I lost my heart to him the very first time we met, and I love him so much—

Eva. Poor Dora!

Dora. That I dare not tell him how much I love him.

Eva. Better not. Has he offered you marriage, this gentleman?

Dora. Could I love him else?

Eva. And are you quite sure that after marriage this gentleman will not be shamed of his poor farmer's daughter among the ladies in his draw-ing-room?

Dora. Shamed of me in a drawing-room! Was n't Miss Vavasour, our schoolmistress at Littlechester, a lady born? Were not our fellow-pupils all ladies? Was n't dear mother herself at least by one side a lady? Can't I speak like a lady; pen a letter like a lady; talk a little French like a lady; play a little like a lady? Can't a girl when she loves her husband, and he her, make herself anything he wishes her to be? Shamed of me in a draw-ing-room, indeed! See here! 'I hope your lordship is quite recovered of your gout?' (*Curtsies.*) 'Will your ladyship ride to cover to-day? (*Curt-sies.*) I can recommend our Voltigeur.' 'I am sorry that we could not attend your grace's party on the 10th!' (*Curtsies.*) There, I am glad my non-sense has made you smile!

Eva. I have heard that 'your lord-ship,' and 'your ladyship,' and 'your grace' are all growing old-fashioned!

Dora. But the love of sister for sis-ter can never be old-fashioned. I have been unwilling to trouble you with questions, but you seem somewhat better to-day. We found a letter in your bedroom torn into bits. I could n't make it out. What was it?

Eva. From him! from him! He said we had been most happy together, and he trusted that some time we should meet again, for he had not forgotten his promise to come when I called

him. But that was a mockery, you know, for he gave me no address, and there was no word of marriage; and, O Dora, he signed himself 'Yours gratefully'—fancy, Dora, 'gratefully'! 'Yours gratefully'!

Dora. Infamous wretch! (*Aside.*) Shall I tell her he is dead? No; she is still too feeble.

Eva. Hark! Dora, some one is com-ing. I cannot and I will not see any-body.

Dora. It is only Milly.

Enter MILLY, *with basket of roses.*

Well, Milly, why do you come in so roughly? The sick lady here might have been asleep.

Milly. Pleäse, Miss, Mr. Dobson told me to saäy he's browt some of Miss Eva's roses for the sick laädy to smell on.

Dora. Take them, dear. Say that the sick lady thanks him! Is he here?

Milly. Yeäs, Miss; and he wants to speak to ye partic'lar.

Dora. Tell him I cannot leave the sick lady just yet.

Milly. Yeäs, Miss; but he says he wants to tell ye summut very par-tic'lar.

Dora. Not to-day. What are you staying for?

Milly. Why, Miss, I be afeared I shall set him a-sweäring like onythink.

Dora. And what harm will that do you, so that you do not copy his bad manners? Go, child. (*Exit* Milly.) But, Eva, why did you write 'Seek me at the bottom of the river.'?

Eva. Why? because I meant it!—that dreadful night! that lonely walk to Littlechester, the rain beating in my face all the way, dead midnight when I came upon the bridge; the river, black, slimy, swirling under me in the lamplight, by the rotten wharfs —but I was so mad that I mounted upon the parapet—

Dora. You make me shudder!

Eva. To fling myself over, when I heard a voice, 'Girl, what are you doing there?' It was a Sister of Mercy, come from the death-bed of a pauper, who had died in his misery blessing God, and the Sister took me to her house, and bit by bit—for she promised secrecy—I told her all.

Dora. And what then?

Eva. She would have persuaded me to come back here, but I could n't. Then she got me a place as nursery governess, and when the children grew too old for me, and I asked her once more to help me, once more she said, 'Go home;' but I had n't the heart or face to do it. And then—what would father say?—I sank so low that I went into service—the drudge of a lodging-house—and when the mistress died, and I appealed to the Sister again, her answer—I think I have it about me—yes, there it is!

Dora (*reads*). 'My dear Child,—I can do no more for you. I have done wrong in keeping your secret; your father must be now in extreme old age. Go back to him and ask his forgiveness before he dies.—SISTER AGATHA.' Sister Agatha is right. Don't you long for father's forgiveness?

Eva. I would almost die to have it!

Dora. And he may die before he gives it; may drop off any day, any hour. You must see him at once. (*Rings bell. Enter* Milly.) Milly, my dear, how did you leave Mr. Steer?

Milly. He 's been a-moänin' and a-groänin' in 'is sleep, but I thinks he be wakkenin' oop.

Dora. Tell him that I and the lady here wish to see him. You see she is lamed, and cannot go down to him.

Milly. Yeäs, Miss, I will.

[*Exit* Milly.

Dora. I ought to prepare you. You must not expect to find our father as he was five years ago. He is much altered; but I trust that your return —for you know, my dear, you were always his favorite—will give him, as they say, a new lease of life.

Eva (*clinging to* Dora). O, Dora, Dora!

Enter STEER *led by* MILLY.

Steer. Hes the cow cawved?

Dora. No, father.

Steer. Be the colt deäd?

Dora. No, father.

Steer. He wur sa bellows'd out wi' the wind this murnin', 'at I tell'd 'em to gallop 'im. Be he deäd?

Dora. Not that I know.

Steer. What hasta sent fur me, then, fur?

Dora (*taking* Steer's *arm*). Well, father, I have a surprise for you.

Steer. I ha' niver been surprised but once i' my life, and I went blind upon it.

Dora. Eva has come home.

Steer. Hoäm? fro' the bottom o' the river?

Dora. No, father, that was a mistake. She 's here again.

Steer. The Steers was all gentle-foälks i' the owd times, an' I worked early an' laäte to maäke 'em all gentlefoälks ageän. The land belonged to the Steers i' the owd times, an' it belongs to the Steers ageän: I bowt it back ageän; but I could n't buy my darter back ageän when she lost hersen, could I? I eddicated boäth on 'em to marry gentlemen, an' one on 'em went an' lost hersen i' the river.

Dora. No, father, she's here.

Steer. Here! she moänt coom here. What would her mother saäy? If it be her ghoäst, we mun abide it. We can't keep a ghoäst out.

Eva (*falling at his feet*). O, forgive me! forgive me!

Steer. Who said that? Taäke me awaäy, little gell. It be one o' my bad daäys.

[*Exit* Steer *led by* Milly.

Dora (*smoothing* Eva's *forehead*). Be not so cast down, my sweet Eva. You heard him say it was one of his bad days. He will be sure to know you to-morrow.

Eva. It is almost the last of my bad days, I think. I am very faint. I must

lie down. Give me your arm. Lead
me back again.

[*Dora takes* Eva *into inner room.*

Enter MILLY.

Milly. Miss Dora! Miss Dora!
Dora (*returning and leaving the
bedroom door ajar*). Quiet! Quiet!
What is it?
Milly. Mr. 'Arold, Miss.
Dora. Below?
Milly. Yeäs, Miss. He be saäyin' a
word to the owd man, but he 'll coom
up if ye lets 'im.
Dora. Tell him, then, that I'm wait-
ing for him.
Milly. Yeäs, Miss.

[*Exit.* Dora *sits pensively and
waits.*

Enter HAROLD.

Harold. You are pale, my Dora!
but the ruddiest cheek
That ever charm'd the plowman of
your wolds
Might wish its rose a lily, could it look
But half as lovely. I was speaking with
Your father, asking his consent—you
wish'd me—
That we should marry. He would an-
swer nothing,
I could make nothing of him; but, my
flower,
You look so weary and so worn! What
is it
Has put you out of heart?
Dora.   It puts me in heart
Again to see you; but indeed the state
Of my poor father puts me out of
heart.
Is yours yet living?
Harold.   No—I told you.
Dora.   When?
Harold. Confusion!—Ah well, well!
the state we all
Must come to in our spring-and-win-
ter world
If we live long enough! and poor Steer
looks
The very type of Age in a picture,
bow'd

To the earth he came from, to the
grave he goes to,
Beneath the burthen of years.
Dora.   More like the picture
Of Christian in my 'Pilgrim's Prog-
ress' here,
Bow'd to the dust beneath the burthen
of sin.
Harold. Sin! What sin?
Dora.   Not his own.
Harold.   That nursery-tale
Still read, then?
Dora. Yes; our carters and our
shepherds
Still find a comfort there.
Harold.   Carters and shepherds!
Dora. Scorn! I hate scorn. A soul
with no religion—
My mother used to say that such a one
Was without rudder, anchor, compass
—might be
Blown every way with every gust and
wreck
On any rock; and tho' you are good
and gentle,
Yet if thro' any want—
Harold.   Of this religion?
Child, read a little history, you will
find
The common brotherhood of man has
been
Wrong'd by the cruelties of his reli-
gions
More than could ever have happen'd
thro' the want
Of any or all of them.
Dora.   But, O dear friend,
If thro' the want of any—I mean the
true one—
And pardon me for saying it—you
should ever
Be tempted into doing what might
seem
Not altogether worthy of you, I think
That I should break my heart, for you
have taught me
To love you.
Harold. What is this? some one
been stirring
Against me? he, your rustic amorist,
The polish'd Damon of your pastoral
here,
This Dobson of your idyll?

Dora.   No, sir, no!
Did you not tell me he was crazed
    with jealousy,
Had threaten'd even your life, and
    would say anything?
Did *I* not promise not to listen to
    him,
Nor even to see the man?
    Harold.   Good; then what is it
That makes you talk so dolefully?
    Dora.   I told you—
My father. Well, indeed, a friend just
    now,
One that has been much wrong'd,
    whose griefs are mine,
Was warning me that if a gentleman
Should wed a farmer's daughter, he
    would be
Sooner or later shamed of her among
The ladies, born his equals.
    Harold.   More fool he!
What, I that have been call'd a So-
    cialist,
A Communist, a Nihilist—what you
    will!—
    Dora. What are all these?
    Harold.   Utopian idiotcies.
They did not last three Junes. Such
    rampant weeds
Strangle each other, die, and make
    the soil
For Cæsars, Cromwells, and Napo-
    leons
To root their power in. I have freed
    myself
From all such dreams, and some will
    say because
I have inherited my uncle. Let them.
But—shamed of you, my empress! I
    should prize
The pearl of beauty, even if I found it
Dark with the soot of slums.
    Dora.   But I can tell you,
We Steers are of old blood, tho' we be
    fallen.
See there our shield. (*Pointing to arms
    on mantelpiece.*)
            For I have heard the Steers
Had land in Saxon times; and your
    own name
Of Harold sounds so English and so
    old
I am sure you must be proud of it.

Harold.   Not I!
As yet I scarcely feel it mine. I took
    it
For some three thousand acres. I have
    land now
And wealth, and lay both at your feet.
    Dora.   And *what* was
Your name before?
    Harold.   Come, come, my girl,
    enough
Of this strange talk. I love you, and
    you me.
True, I have held opinions, hold some
    still,
Which you would scarce approve of;
    for all that,
I am a man not prone to jealousies,
Caprices, humors, moods, but very
    ready
To make allowances, and mighty slow
To feel offences. Nay, I do believe
I could forgive—well, almost any-
    thing—
And that more freely than your formal
    priest,
Because I know more fully than *he*
    can
What poor earthworms are all and
    each of us,
Here crawling in this boundless Na-
    ture, Dora,
If marriage ever brought a woman
    happiness
I doubt not I can make you happy.
    Dora.   You make me
Happy already.
    Harold.   And I never said
As much before to any woman living.
    Dora. No?
    Harold. No! by this true kiss, *you*
    are the first
I ever have loved truly.
            [*They kiss each other.*
Eva (*with a wild cry*). Philip Ed-
    gar!
Harold. The phantom cry! *You*—
    did *you* hear a cry?
Dora. She must be crying out 'Ed-
    gar' in her sleep?
Harold. Who must be crying out
    'Edgar' in her sleep?
Dora. Your pardon for a minute.
    She must be waked.

Harold. Who must be waked?
Dora.   I am not deaf; you fright
    me.
What ails you?
Harold.   Speak.
Dora.   You know her, Eva.
Harold.   Eva!
    [*Eva opens the door and stands
        in the entry.*
She!
Eva. Make her happy, then, and I
    forgive you.   [*Falls dead.*
Dora. Happy! What? Edgar? Is it
    so? Can it be?
They told me so. Yes, yes! I see it all
    now.
O, she has fainted! Sister, Eva, sister!
He is yours again—he will love *you*
    again;
I give him back to you again. Look up!
One word, or do but smile! Sweet, do
    you hear me?
    [*Puts her hand on Eva's heart.*
There, there—the heart, O God!—the
    poor young heart
Broken at last—all still—and nothing
    left
To live for.
    [*Falls on body of her sister.*
Harold. Living—dead—She said
    'all still.
Nothing to live for.'
        She—she knows me—now—
            (*A pause.*)
She knew me from the first, she
    juggled with me,
She hid this sister, told me she was
    dead—
I have wasted pity on her—not dead
    now—
No! acting, playing on me, both of
    them.
They drag the river for her! no, not
    they!
Playing on me—not dead now—a
    swoon—a scene—
Yet—how she made her wail as for
    the dead!

Enter MILLY.

Milly. Pleäse, Mister 'Arold.
Harold (*roughly*).   Well?

Milly. The owd man's coom'd ageän
    to 'issen, an' wants
To hev a word wi' ye about the mar-
    riage.
Harold. The what?
Milly.   The marriage.
Harold.   The marriage?
Milly.   Yeäs the marriage.
Granny says marriages are maäde i'
    'eaven.

Harold. She lies! They are made in
    hell. Child, can't you see?
Tell them to fly for a doctor.
Milly.   O, law—yeäs, Sir.
I'll run fur 'im mysen.   [*Exit.*
Harold.   All silent there,
Yes, deathlike! Dead? I dare not look.
    If dead,
Were it best to steal away, to spare
    myself,
And her too, pain, pain, pain?
                My curse on all
This world of mud, on all its idiot
    gleams
Of pleasure, all the foul fatalities
That blast our natural passions into
    pains!

Enter DOBSON.

Dobson. You, Master Hedgar, Har-
    old, or whativer
They calls ye, for I warrants that ye
    goäs
By haäfe a scoor o' naämes—out o'
    the chaumber!
    [*Dragging him past the body.*
Harold. Not that way, man! Curse
    on your brutal strength!
I cannot pass that way.
Dobson.   Out o' the chaumber!
I'll mash tha into nowt.
Harold.   The mere wild-beast!
Dobson. Out o' the chaumber, dang
    tha!
Harold.   Lout, churl, clown!
    [*While they are shouting and
        struggling* Dora *rises and
        comes between them.*
Dora (*to* Dobson). Peace, let him
    be; it is the chamber of Death!
Sir, you are tenfold more a gentleman,

A hundred times more worth a
woman's love,
Than this, this—but I waste no words
upon him:
His wickedness is like my wretched-
ness—
Beyond all language.
(*To* Harold.) You—you see her
there!
Only fifteen when first you came on
her,
And then the sweetest flower of all
the wolds,
So lovely in the promise of her May,
So winsome in her grace and gaiety,
So loved by all the village people here,
So happy in herself and in her home—
    Dobson (*agitated*). Theer, theer!
    ha' done. I can't abeär to see
    her.   [*Exit.*
Dora. A child, and all as trustful as
a child!
Five years of shame and suffering
broke the heart
That only beat for you; and he, the
father,
Thro' that dishonor which you
brought upon us,
Has lost his health, his eyesight, even
his mind.
    Harold (*covering his face*).
    Enough!
Dora. It seem'd so; only there was
left
A second daughter, and to her you
came
Veiling one sin to act another.
    Harold.   No!
You wrong me there! hear, hear me!
    I wish'd, if you—   [*Pauses.*
Dora. If I—

Harold. Could love me, could be
brought to love me
As I loved you—
    Dora.   What then?
    Harold.   I wish'd, I hoped
To make, to make—
    Dora. What did you hope to make?
    Harold. 'T were best to make an
    end of my lost life.
O Dora, Dora!
    Dora. What did you hope to make?
    Harold. Make, make! I cannot find
    the word—forgive it—
Amends.
    Dora. For what? to whom?
    Harold.   To him, to you!
        [*Falling at her feet.*
    Dora. To *him!* to *me!*
        No, not with all your wealth,
Your land, your life! Out in the fierc-
est storm
That ever made earth tremble—he,
nor I—
The shelter of *your* roof—not for one
moment—
Nothing from *you!*
Sunk in the deepest pit of pauper-
ism,
Push'd from all doors as if we bore the
plague,
Smitten with fever in the open field,
Laid famine-stricken at the gates of
Death—
Nothing from you!
        But she there—her last word
Forgave—and I forgive you. If you
ever
Forgive yourself, you are even lower
and baser
Than even I can well believe you. Go!
    [*He lies at her feet. Curtain falls.*

CROSSING THE BAR

Although written in 1889, this poem is used to close all editions of the poet's works, according to his own request.

SUNSET and evening star,
  And one clear call for me!
And may there be no moaning of the bar,
  When I put out to sea,

But such a tide as moving seems asleep,
  Too full for sound and foam,
When that which drew from out the boundless deep
  Turns again home.

Twilight and evening bell,
  And after that the dark!
And may there be no sadness of farewell,
  When I embark;

For tho' from out our bourne of Time and Place
  The flood may bear me far,
I hope to see my Pilot face to face
  When I have crost the bar.